W9-AXY-441

1001 CHILDREN'S BOOKS

YOU MUST READ BEFORE YOU GROW UP

1001 CHILDREN'S BOOKS
YOU MUST READ BEFORE YOU GROW UP

GENERAL EDITOR JULIA ECCLESHARE

PREFACE BY QUENTIN BLAKE

UNIVERSE

A Quint**essence** Book

First published in the United States of America in 2009 by
UNIVERSE PUBLISHING
A Division of Rizzoli International Publications, Inc.
300 Park Avenue South
New York, NY 10010
www.rizzoliusa.com

Copyright © 2009 Quint**essence**

All rights reserved. No part of this publication may be reproduced, stored in a retrieval system or transmitted in any form or by any means, electronic, mechanical, photocopying, recording, or otherwise, without the permission of the copyright holder.

ISBN-13: 978-0-7893-1876-3
QSS.CBOO

Library of Congress Control Number: 2009922846

Second printing, 2010
2010 2011 2012 2013 / 10 9 8 7 6 5 4 3 2

This book was designed and produced by
Quint**essence**
226 City Road
London EC1V 2TT
www.1001beforeyoudie.com

Senior Editor	Jodie Gaudet
Editors	Rebecca Gee, Fiona Plowman
Editorial Assistant	Philip Contos
Designer	Nicole Kuderer
Picture Researcher	Jo Walton
Editorial Director	Jane Laing
Publisher	Tristan de Lancey

Color reproduction by Pica Digital Pte Ltd., Singapore.
Printed in China by Toppan Leefung Printing Ltd.

Contents

Preface

By Quentin Blake

As it happens, it's almost exactly fifty years ago that I embarked for the first time on producing a set of illustrations for a children's book. I think I can remember pretty well what my thoughts were then: I wanted to take drawing beyond the world of jokes in which I had started professional life and into that other world where you could embrace narrative and organize the sequence and placing of drawings through pages from the front cover to the back. The fact that I had been trained as a teacher (of English) meant that even then I could begin to see some parallels between the way that a good lesson might work and a book might involve to stimulate a young person by its words and its pictures.

I don't suppose that I ever thought (just to stick to the illustration aspect for the moment) that my job was simply to draw the people and things mentioned in the text; but even so I had to get used, over time, to the realization that when you were at work on a set of illustrations, or a whole picture book, there were quite a number of activities going on in your head—in parallel, as it were—at the same time. They included identifying with the characters, and conceiving what they looked like and their expressions and gestures: from the infant mewling and puking in its nurse's arms through to the lean and slippered commedia dell'arte pantaloon. And then also taking in assorted crocodiles, dogs, mice, monkeys, goats, elephants and insects. Then there's identifying with the reader to envisage his or her reactions to certain promptings disposed in the pictures: Does she really look sad? Where are those cockatoos? And of course: How many pictures? Of which moments (the author's best moments may not be your best moments)? Where do they fall in the text? When does the page turn? What is the appropriate implement to draw with (there are lots to choose from)? If there's colour, what part does it have to play and how does it contribute to the atmosphere of the book? And so on and so forth.

At the same time, simply from having to write a few short texts of my own, I became aware that the authors of children's books had a similar gamut of professional concerns—of imaginative creation, of moral discrimination, of voice, drama, structure, rhythm, pace—and often more complicated than any I was likely to encounter. So that by the time I was appointed the first Children's Laureate in 1999, I was determined that this was one of the aspects of children's literature that I wanted to place emphasis on. In consequence, in my short speech of acceptance I said, referring to the authors present on that occasion, "I believe . . . people like us take writing children's books seriously, because we take writing seriously, in the same way those of us who draw take drawing seriously." I went on to add ". . . these books, at their best, are primers in the development of the emotional, the moral, the imaginative life. And they can be a celebration of what it is like to be a human being. That is why they are important."

I seem to remember that on some other occasion I made the observation that for me getting involved in children's books was like going through a gate into an enchanted grove—which was perhaps a rather exaggeratedly poetical way of saying that I was having a nice time; but also, of course, more than that. I might also have said that for the reader it was like going through a gate into a rich and varied landscape. It is indeed a landscape so varied that one can be at a loss about which of many paths to take. That is what I find so valuable about this book. It's a guidebook, full of maps and hints and local information and suggestions about where to go next. And its huge virtue in my eyes is that it doesn't restrict itself to the well-trodden paths. Its remit relates to quality and interest; there are books from many countries and earlier times. Clarice Bean from England is on the same page as the dog with the yellow heart from Germany; Thursday's child from Australia faces Opal and her dog Winn-Dixie from Florida, USA. If you don't know the Little Engine That Could she comes puffing in here, and you can say Goodnight Moon with Margaret Wise Brown and Clement Hurd. And you won't miss Ernest and Celestine in the beautiful drawings of Gabrielle Vincent. Every now and then a golden age of children's books is announced, but there are glitterings of gold all through their history, and Julia Eccleshare's book sifts out a thousand and one for us.

Quentin Blake

London, United Kingdom

Introduction

By Julia Eccleshare

There is little that is more influential than the stories we read in childhood. From their meaning and their language come a welter of emotional experiences—and the words with which to express them—that cannot easily be reached in any other way. Stories are places of enchantment, mystery, surprise, dread, and—above all—consolation, and nowhere can they be found in richer abundance than in children's books. Delving into *1001 Children's Books You Must Read Before You Grow Up,* readers will find all of the above in the most memorable stories written for children across the world.

Yet this fascinating collection offers more than just a reminder of the enduring pleasure that is to be found in children's books. Grouped into broad age bands to provide simple guidance as to who the books are primarily for, it is an invaluable guide for any adult who wants to give an informed answer to the conundrum children so often pose—"What shall I read next?" From wordless picture books to novels that are as happily read by adults as they are by children, there is something here for all kinds of readers. International in its scope and wide-ranging in its choices, it will remind adults of the books they loved as children as well as introducing them to some of the best contemporary authors and illustrators writing today.

The books selected for this volume offer a history of the perception of childhood in different countries and at different times in history. They show how sometimes childhood is idolized, sometimes it is demonized, and how stories chart the social changes that affect children so profoundly. This is achieved through a chronological layout that shapes the book into an intriguing study of how expectations and opportunities for children have changed over time and how stories function as education, entertainment, or just plain escapism.

The shifting nature of children's literature as an art form is another feature that is easy to trace through the pages of this book. The entries, which have been illustrated wherever possible with their first edition covers in their original language, show how dramatically children's books have changed both in what they are saying and in how they attract their readers. Some changes are quite obvious; images that have long been abandoned on the grounds of political incorrectness reveal much about the prevailing attitudes of an era. However, there are other changes in the illustration of children's books that are subtler but also

Key to symbols in the book

Author

Illustrator

informative. The muted, dreamy colors used in picture books in the pre-digital age have gradually been replaced by bright colors and hard-edged lines that compete with the other visual references surrounding children. Some changes in book illustration have sprung from technical innovation, but others come from the recognition that while picture books were once the only visual stimulus for the young, they are now just one among many.

Among the selection are personal favorites chosen by some of the world's best-known contemporary writers. Philip Pullman celebrates the subversive nature of Geoffrey Willans's *Down with Skool!*, relishing Ronald Searle's illustrations in particular. Margaret Atwood remembers the classic tale of Canadian girlhood, *Anne of Green Gables*; Eric Carle loves *Der Struwwelpeter* while realizing, even as a boy, that the cruelty is exaggerated and not to be taken literally; and Judy Blume cherishes Ludwig Bemelman's *Madeline,* who can easily be seen as an inspiration for some of Blume's own characters. *Sans Famille* inspired Marie-Aude Murail when she was young and Gustavo Martín Garzo enjoyed *El Capitan Tormenta.* As might be expected the strongest influence on these children's writers generally came from their own culture but, while some have logical connections, others are unexpected. Whichever, all the choices offer insight into the connection between the reader as a child and the writer they eventually became.

Any grouping of children's books inevitably raises as many questions as it answers. What are books for children? Simply, they are stories that children enjoy and typically they have a child or a childlike character, often an animal, at their heart. Loosely, that definition works up to a certain age, but there are also adult books that children read and children's books that adults enjoy reading. Perhaps a better definition comes from the poet and Children's Laureate Michael Rosen: "I think of children's books as not so much for children, but as the filling that goes between the child world and the adult world. One way or another, all children's books have to negotiate that space."

This is a useful definition, particularly as it acknowledges that the precise borders of those worlds may slip and be redrawn as notions of what is suitable for children shift. Content thought too explicit in one decade may be regarded as completely acceptable decades later, thus leading to books written for adults being reclassified for teenagers. Or,

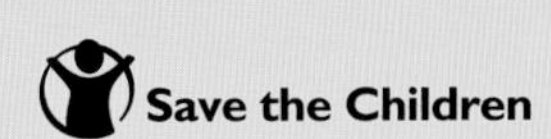

Save the Children would like to extend their thanks for the donations to the Rewrite the Future campaign by some of the contributors to this book. Save the Children's Rewrite the Future campaign is helping to provide quality education for millions of children out of school due to war and armed conflict.

For more information visit **www.savethechildren.org.uk**

more alarmingly, some children's fiction, despite the freedoms is has enjoyed, can become restricted or censored in a different time or place. Rosen's definition also partly explains why children's books remain so popular among adults: the "filling" between the two worlds is a place that adults enjoy revisiting for many reasons, not least because it presents a way of stepping back into a seemingly unchanging aspect of childhood.

Putting together an international selection such as this one underlines both the particularity and the universality of children's books. It shows the way in which children's books are eternal and how they emerge from the society in which they are conceived; they reflect the actual world that children inhabit but also act as a vehicle to show how different childhood might be. Children's books carry the twin ambitions of providing entertainment while also offering educational or cultural improvement. The balance between these two sometimes complementary and sometimes conflicting intentions, varies according to the prevailing attitudes to children, but their existence seems to be universal. Some stories can cross cultures and time periods and be easily understood by all. This has been demonstrated across the centuries by the oral tradition and over the last decade by J. K. Rowling's phenomenally successful Harry Potter series. Children's stories can be great ambassadors; the cross-cultural bonds that develop as a result of children from around the world knowing variations of the same stories provides an invaluable shared experience for children whose lives, in reality, would share nothing.

Learning to enjoy reading in childhood paves the way for adult reading. While the impetus to "get children reading" often begins within education, it can soon develop into a lifetime pleasure. Children, when happily introduced to the words and pictures created for them especially in the early stages of being read to, embrace them eagerly. The route into these diverse story worlds is usually character led. Children's imaginations make it seemingly easy for them to identify with animals, dolls, teddies, trains, cars, and so on. Children's books have a directness and honesty that adults often find alarming, but that children adore. To be frightened within the safety of a story can be a delicious experience. There is nowhere better than in fiction for children to take the risks that may be denied them in real life and to live out other lives and experiences.

In children's literature, examples of children managing to live in an adult world without adults on hand to help are ubiquitous. Indeed, getting rid of the adults and striking out on one's own is a near prerequisite of all great children's books so that children can take on adult roles, sometimes successfully, sometimes not (and often adults come to the rescue just in time).

While adult fiction is often concerned with form and structure, children's books are identified as "the home of the story." Because children love surprise and excitement, they demand from fiction a narrative that offers both in an engaging and wholly engrossing way. Even before the rise of other leisure media, many of the most successful children's books have been driven by adventure.

Selecting the 1001 entries that make up this book was the greatest pleasure. Foraying into the past to revisit national and international classics is a lesson in history and cultural change as much as it is a journey of literary discovery. Snapshots of attitudes to children, expectations of them, and messages thought suitable for them are all held within the pages of these stories. This volume also reminds us of the stories through which children may have formed their first and often most important views of another country or way of life.

On revisiting, many of these turn out to be even better than remembered. It is often the illustrations, absorbed in early childhood, that will rekindle the strongest and warmest memories. Stories and the images that accompany them have a rare capacity for taking even the oldest reader straight back into the essence of their own childhood. Much of the pleasure of choosing these books, however, has been to bring them to the attention of a new generation of readers. Alongside enduring classics, there has also been the enjoyment of highlighting some of the most successful, contemporary illustration and writing taking place throughout the world. Where once upon a time children's books took their time to travel, publishing is now almost instantly global.

For the contributors, too, there has been a delight (possibly even childish delight) in championing old and new personal favorites. They have relished the opportunity to revisit old friends and to praise their many qualities. The result is a unique guide to some of the greatest and most imaginative journeys into fantasy, mystery, adventure, history, real life, and more. Whether told in words or pictures or both, these books are the perfect introduction to the imagination of childhood and the storytelling that fuels it.

Index of Titles

0-3

Rosie's Walk, written and illustrated by Pat Huchins.

THE LITTLE ENGINE THAT COULD

The Little Engine That Could 1930

Watty Piper Lois Lenski

Nationality | Pseudonym used by the publisher (Watty Piper); American, born 1893 (illustrator)
Publisher | Platt and Munk, USA
Theme | Classics, Favorite characters

A trainload of toys and presents, destined for the children's Christmas trees over the steep mountain, is stranded when the locomotive breaks down. A clown, the leader of the toys, asks several locomotive engines for help but is rebuffed by all, including the pompous passenger engine who is too snobbish for the task, the powerful freight engine who is otherwise engaged, and the elderly engine without stamina. Finally, the clown asks the little blue engine who lives in the railway yard. At first, the little blue engine is not sure she is up to the task, but she whistles and puffs her catchy mantra up the hill: "I-think-I-can, I-think-I-can." Ultimately, she rounds the summit to pull the train triumphantly down the other side, puffing out jubilantly, "I-thought-I-could! I-thought-I-could!"

The Little Engine That Could is a version of a Sunday-school story called "Thinking One Can" (1906). Mary C. Jacobs (1877–1970) rewrote it as *The Pony Engine*, published 1910. Other versions appeared, but the one attributed to "Watty Piper" by its publishers came to be the accepted text. The Little Engine is an exemplar of the American credo that hard work will succeed. "Remember the little engine that could!" is the kind of injunction that all moral educators issue from time to time. Young children enjoy the catchy refrains and the anthropomorphic engines, whose characters predate even the British Thomas the Tank Engine. Interestingly, the Little Engine may be the only anthropomorphic locomotive that is female. **VN**

Pat the Bunny 1940

Dorothy Kunhardt

Nationality | American, born 1901
Publisher | Golden Books, USA
Theme | Animal stories, Favorite characters, Classics, Family

One of the very first "touch and feel" books, *Pat the Bunny* is often chosen as a baby's first book. It remains a staple present at baby showers and a stalwart of family nursery bookshelves everywhere, with more than seven million copies in print. There are many reasons that this book has become and remained a classic for nearly seventy years.

In the late 1930s, Dorothy Kunhardt, an established children's author, was trying to find ways to build interactivity into a book she was creating for her infant daughter Edith. The end result proved to be a huge leap forward in books for the very young—the addition of simple "touch and feel" and "scratch and sniff" elements.

You would be hard pressed to find a child today who does not have some memory of this classic title, from stroking the bunny's soft fur, to looking in the mirror, to feeling Daddy's scratchy beard, to playing peek-a-boo, or to trying on Mommy's ring.

As an extra bonus, and something Kunhardt had not foreseen, it was discovered that the book also gave the opportunity for parents of visually impaired children to use books that offered tactile learning instead of purely visual learning.

Several decades later, Edith Kunhardt, Dorothy's daughter for whom the book was written, responded to the enduring success of the original book by writing her own. She published *Pat the Cat* in 1984, *Pat the Puppy* in 1991, and *Pat the Pony* in 1997. **KD**

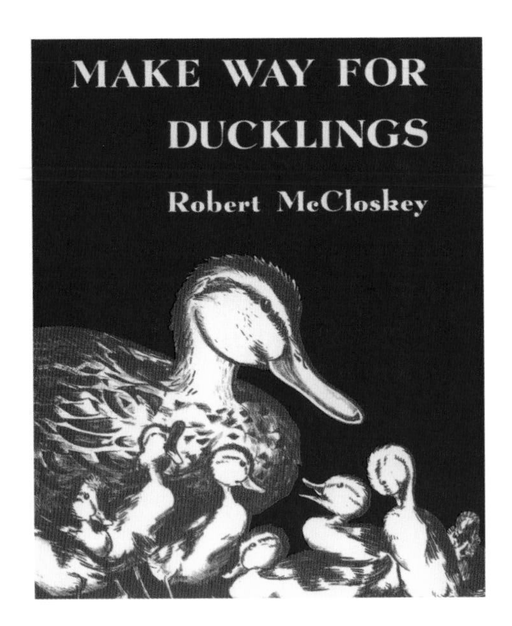

Make Way for Ducklings 1941

Robert McCloskey

Nationality | American, born 1915
Publisher | Viking Press, USA
Award | Caldecott Medal
Theme | Animal stories, Classics, Family

Make Way for Ducklings was Robert McCloskey's second picture book. It brought him immediate acclaim and assured him, and the delightful duck family he created, a permanent place in the hearts of the people of Boston in the United States.

Mr. and Mrs. Mallard come to Boston looking for a place to raise a family, away from the danger of turtles and foxes. They investigate the pond in the Public Garden, see the famous Swan Boats, narrowly escape being run over by boys on bicycles, nest on an island near the St. Charles Bridge, and eventually make their home in the Public Garden.

The ducks never look or act other than as real birds, but they have engaging personalities: persnickety Mrs. Mallard and proud and responsible Mr. Mallard, who, once the ducklings start growing, is happy to go off alone exploring. The bouncy ducklings—Jack, Kack, Lack, Mack, Nack, Ouack, Pack, and Quack—are as noisy and unruly as their names suggest.

Boston and its inhabitants are the other heroes of McCloskey's bold and detailed charcoal drawings. Nearly every double-page spread lovingly depicts a landmark of the city. At the end, the redoubtable Mrs. Mallard leads all her ducklings through the heart of Boston and its traffic to a rendezvous with their father, their way cleared by the Boston Police Department.

In 1987, Mrs. Mallard and her ducklings were immortalized in bronze statues in the Boston Public Garden, where children can meet them today, still on their unstoppable way to the pond. **CB**

The Runaway Bunny 1942

Margaret Wise Brown Clement Hurd

Nationality | American, born 1910 (author); American, born 1908 (illustrator)
Publisher | Harper and Row, USA
Theme | Animal stories, Family

The Runaway Bunny has never been out of print since it was first published and it remains a classic read today. For many families this companion to *Goodnight Moon* has become essential bedtime reading.

The Runaway Bunny was published first, and if you look closely at the illustrations in *Goodnight Moon* you will find that a copy of *The Runaway Bunny* appears in the book. Little bunny is determined to run away from his mother in order to have an adventure of his own. Readers love the way that mother bunny listens to her son and then alway finds a way to be there for him whatever he decides to do.

As the little bunny suggests becoming a fish, or a bird, or a rock, among other things, mother bunny counters each idea: "I will become a fisherman and I will fish for you," or "I will be a tree that you come home to," so that she can always watch over her little bunny. Eventually, of course, the little bunny concedes defeat, "'Shucks,' said the bunny. 'I might just as well stay where I am and be your little bunny.'" "Have a carrot," the mother bunny says to her little one, and brings the book to a comforting close. Parents should prepare for not only nightly readings of this title, but also to hear the words "again, please" at the end of every reading. Very young children never tire of this bedtime tale and always enjoy the charming illustrations, too.

Margaret Wise Brown's other classic tales include *Goodnight Moon* (1947), *My World* (1949), and *Little Fur Family* (1946). **KD**

The Three Railway Engines 1945

Reverend W. Awdry William Middleton

Nationality | English, born 1911 (author); English, birth date unknown (illustrator)
Publisher | Edmund Ward, UK
Theme | Favorite characters, Classics

When his three-year-old son Christopher was ill, the Reverend Wilbert Awdry made up a story to soothe him. It was about three railway engines on a scenic railway on Sodor, a fictional island in the Irish Sea.

The engines were anthropomorphized and given easily identifiable characters: Gordon the big, self-important engine, Henry the green engine who got scared, and Edward the blue engine who had adventures. Christopher Awdry loved the story and pestered his father to tell it to him again and again. It might have remained a private family tale had Awdry's wife not recognized its potential and persuaded her husband to send his ideas to a publisher. The result was *The Three Railway Engines*, a collection of four stories about Edward, Gordon, and Henry. It was not guaranteed to be a success—being published at the end of World War II, when paper prices were high and books consequently expensive—yet it caught the public's imagination and sold more than 22,000 copies.

William Middleton illustrated *The Three Railway Engines*, but Awdry was not pleased with his work and the publishers commissioned Reginald Payne to illustrate his next title, *Thomas the Tank Engine*. He was followed by C. Reginald Dalby. (Many years and many books later, he was replaced by John T. Kenney.) Dalby closely observed the E2 Class 0-6-0T locomotives built for the London, Brighton, and South Coast Railway between 1913 and 1916 before illustrating his first book, *James the Red Engine*. He also made changes to later editions of *The Three Railway Engines*. **VN**

C. Reginald Dalby's later endpapers for *The Three Railway Engines*.

Thomas the Tank Engine 1946

Reverend W. Awdry Reginald Payne

Nationality | English, born 1911 (author); English, birth date unknown (illustrator)
Publisher | Edmund Ward, UK
Theme | Favorite characters, Classics

The character of Thomas the Tank Engine was born when Reverend Awdry carved a wooden tank engine for his son. Reputedly, it was young Christopher, not his father, who chose the name of Thomas.

Thomas the Tank Engine was a collection of four stories: "Thomas and Gordon," "Thomas's Trains," "Thomas and the Trucks," and "Thomas and the Breakdown Train." Throughout them all, the blue-painted Thomas, with his distinctive cheeky smile, had adventures and riled the Fat Controller, who owned the railway, but always ended up doing the right thing, becoming a Really Useful Engine.

Most people believe this to be the first book in the series, but it actually came second, after *The Three Railway Engines*. The series, which has been adapted for television and the stage, remains a firm favorite, with railway buffs, children, and adults, for such characters as the coaches Annie and Clarabel, Bertie the Bus, and the argumentative Toby the Tram Engine.

The illustrations for this book are often erroneously attributed to C. Reginald Dalby, but they were actually the work of Reginald Payne. It was Payne who created the much-loved iconic images we know today, which Dalby then used as the basis for his works (from the third book onward). Payne's life remains frustratingly shadowy, despite the best attempts of researchers.

Reverend Wilbert Awdry wrote twenty-six books. Since the reverend's death in 1997, Christopher Awdry has continued his father's work, writing more adventures for Thomas and his friends. **LH**

Goodnight Moon 1947

Margaret Wise Brown   Clement Hurd

Nationality | American, born 1910 (author); American, born 1908 (illustrator)
Publisher | Harper and Row, USA
Theme | Animal stories, Family, Rhyming stories

Goodnight Moon is a much-loved bedtime picture book. Margaret Wise Brown's story has stood the test of time. It was published in the late 1940s, and has since earned its rightful place in the canon of classic American children's literature.

Illustrated with a simple color scheme, the book's soothing, rhyming poem is set in a familiar, family house where a bunny rabbit wearing blue-and-white striped pajamas is saying good night to everything he can possibly see in his room.

The entire story takes place in just this one room, but such are the skills of both author and illustrator that the words and pictures, along with careful details, reveal some very subtle touches. For example, the lighting in the room grows slowly darker as each page is turned, and the moon can be seen rising throughout the duration of the story, gradually appearing and expanding in the left-hand window.

In addition to the little rabbit, other characters include a small cat and mouse, who provide ample visual narratives along the way. They also add other possible stories to this heartwarming and cozy book.

Parents will be all too familiar with the little bunny's continual attempts to postpone the time he has to go to sleep, and much fun can be had when looking in detail at all the other characters in the pictures.

This is an ideal first book for any child, with its strong rhymes and reassuring drawings. Parents should make sure they have an interesting explanation ready for the inevitable question, "What is mush?" **NH**

"In the great green room there was a telephone. . . ."

BUNNY

Lavender's Blue 1954

Kathleen Lines Harold Jones

Nationality | English, born 1902 (author); English, born 1904 (illustrator)
Publisher | Oxford University Press, UK
Theme | Nursery rhymes, Poetry

OTHER GREAT COLLECTIONS OF VERSE

The Book of Nonsense by Edward Lear, 1846
House That Jack Built by Randolph Caldecott, 1878
Mother Goose by Kate Greenaway, 1881
Marigold Garden by Kate Greenway, 1885
Poems for the Very Young by Michael Rosen, 1993

Every small child needs a book of nursery rhymes. These traditional little poems have lasted for centuries and yet still have resonance and meaning for today's children. There are learned books of annotated nursery rhymes, explaining every quirky word, but small children respond to the rhythm and zany surrealism of "Sing a Song of Sixpence," "Humpty Dumpty," and "Hey Diddle Diddle." Nursery rhymes can be spoken or sung or acted out with gestures—but they only truly come alive when they are appropriately illustrated.

Kathleen Lines was a children's book specialist who gathered together this comprehensive collection of nursery rhymes, but the distinctive, limpid, delicately detailed illustrations of award-wining artist Harold

> *"Lavender's blue, dilly, dilly, lavender's green; when I am king . . . you shall be queen."*

Jones make *Lavender's Blue* a book that should be on every nursery shelf. He adds an extra dimension to each rhyme—when the cradle falls in "Hush-a-bye, Baby," four angels catch it by each rocker while the baby peers out with interest. When Daddy goes off hunting in "Bye, baby Bunting," Mother and baby are there on the doorstep to see him trudge off while two rabbits scamper undetected in the foreground. "Oranges and Lemons" (the original version) is illustrated with a magnificent double-spread of all the church spires of London Town, with two little bell ringers clanging their bells with gusto.

There is such an abundant variety of gorgeous color spreads that any child exposed to this book will have an art education in itself. This magical world is safe, soothing, and endlessly stimulating. It is a book to last a lifetime.

Jones's image of "There was an old woman who lived in a shoe." ➔

Bedtime for Frances 1960

Nationality | American, born 1925 (author); American, born 1912 (illustrator)
Publisher | Harper and Row, USA
Theme | Animal stories, Family

Frances may happen to look like a badger, but she is a gloriously real "child": self-centered, naughty, imaginative, and playful. This is the debut book in Hoban's series and in it Frances is not at all sleepy at bedtime. At first, she makes up excuses to stay up later—a glass of milk, more bedtime kisses—and once in bed, the "giants and tigers and scary and exciting things" she imagines send her creeping out of bed for parental assistance. Eventually, exhausted with her antics, Frances manages to fall asleep.

The book has been criticized for mentioning spanking, and although Frances is not actually spanked, it is the threat of spanking that finally keeps her in bed. However, most children will not find this troubling, and parents who feel strongly about it can always use it to explain their own attitudes to corporal punishment.

The real joy of this book is in the language. The first sentences have a staccato rhythm, reminiscent of an early reading book: "The big hand of the clock is at 12. The little hand is at 7. It is seven o'clock." The rhythm changes, with the sentences lengthening as Frances's imagination gets the better of her when she is alone: "'I do not like the way those curtains are moving,' said Frances. 'Maybe there is something waiting, very soft and quiet.'" Watch out for the first of Frances's songs, which are a prominent feature of later books and were collected in a book of their own: "*A* is for apple pie, *B* is for bear, *C* is for crocodile, combing his hair . . ." so like the type of nonsense songs that children make up. No other picture book child ever seemed so real. **CW**

Miffy 1963

Dick Bruna

Original Title | Nijntje
Nationality | Dutch, born 1927
Publisher | A. W. Bruna and Zoon, Netherlands
Theme | Animal stories, Favorite characters

As Dick Bruna himself said, in his work a house is always a house and Miffy is always Miffy. Only the smallest variation in a character's face or clothing express emotions or a special event. Bruna explains that he has created an alphabet of pictures, so that every story unfolds unambiguously and that children happily recognize what each story is about. Nothing is realistic, but it is familiar. Miffy always looks the same: a rabbit in a dress.

Once other characters, including Boris, Barbara Bear, Poppy Pig, or Grandma and Grandpa, appear in the series, they continute to look the same, too. Bruna takes great care with the palette for his minimalist pictures, using bold colors with simple black outlines and eschewing gloomy or unusual shades. "I looked at Matisse and I saw Miffy," explained Bruna.

With almost thirty titles in the Miffy series (and more than one hundred books altogether), Bruna has sold more than eighty million books worldwide. Each of the original titles is a storybook across sixteen pages, in small format—Bruna is insistent that small children prefer this—with an illustration and a rhyming quatrain. They are clearly written to the rhythms of a small child's life, covering such daily events as a trip to the playground, going to school, a birthday party, camping, even crying or dancing. Some are a little more serious, focusing on going to the hospital or Grandma Bunny's death, but a single tear is enough to signify sorrow in Bruna's world and every book ends happily. **VN**

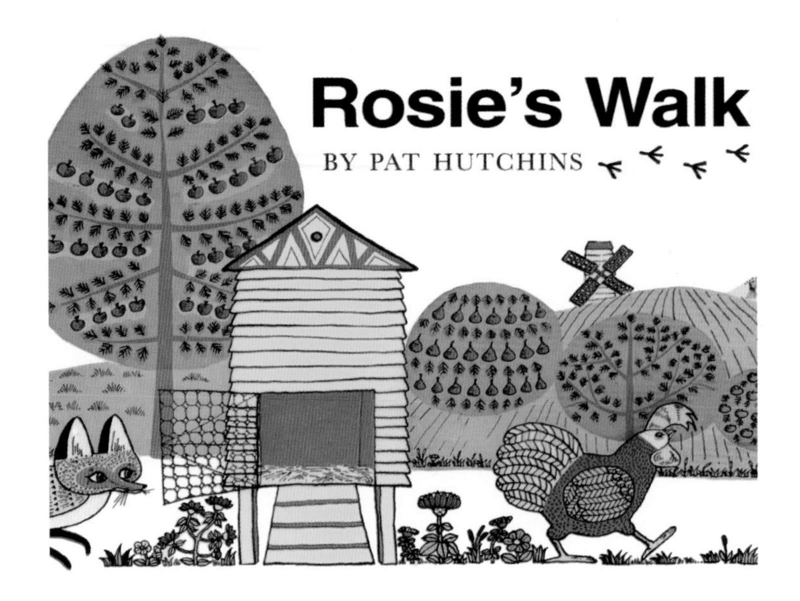

Rosie's Walk 1968

Pat Hutchins

Nationality | English, born 1942
Publisher | Bodley Head, UK; Macmillan, USA
Award | A.L.A. Notable Children's Book
Theme | Animal stories, Friendship, Classics

Rosie's Walk remains fresh and delightful for every new generation of children who discover it. This book contains every single element that goes into making a perfect picture book.

This delightful story is simple enough for the youngest child to enjoy, making it an ideal book to share with a baby, particularly because it allows plenty of room for improvisation on the part of the adult reader. Best of all, it teaches young readers the skill of picture book interpretation, because what is going on in the illustrations is, in effect, a very clever and quite sophisticated joke at the expense of the villain of the piece. The story begins when Rosie the hen goes for a walk. She is oblivious to the fox chasing her, but the reader is not. We see how the fox gets one comeuppance after another in a deliciously satisfying way, and he ends up being chased out of the farmyard by a swarm of angry bees. Unaware of the chaos going on around her, Rosie gets home in time for dinner, leaving hilarious mayhem in her wake.

The text contains only thirty-one words, but adults can point things out to children, discuss the suspense and wonder: will Rosie turn around and see the fox? The three colors in which the whole tale unfolds, orange, yellow, and olive green, are calming. The title page lays out the farmyard in one spread, so that readers are familiar with Rosie's landscape before the story even begins. The book is a model of economy, simplicity, and beauty: a wonderful book to help a child embark on a lifetime of happy reading. **AG**

The Elephant and the Bad Baby 1969

Elfrida Vipont Raymond Briggs

Nationality | English, born 1902 (author); English, born 1934 (illustrator)
Publisher | Hamish Hamilton, UK
Theme | Animal stories, Family

The Elephant and the Bad Baby, with energetic and detailed illustrations by Raymond Briggs, is one of those cumulative tales, like the classic, *The Great Big Enormous Turnip*. First one character then another start chasing the eponymous Bad Baby as she runs away on a huge Elephant. Eventually there is a long line of irate shopkeepers, all racing after the naughty infant and her big, gray companion.

The contrast between the matter-of-fact words and the outlandishness of the giant beast going "rumpeta rumpeta rumpeta all down the road" through a very recognizable urban landscape is both funny and surreal. The major point of the story is that the Bad Baby never says "please." All that the shopkeepers require is simple politeness.

In the end, the Bad Baby says the magic word, "please," and the Elephant takes everyone back to the Bad Baby's house to have pancakes cooked by an understanding mother, with all the shopkeepers saying: PLEASE very loudly.

It is a book to join in with—you can almost sing the cumulative "refrain." You can point out small details, like the array of items the shopkeepers manage to drop during their chase. Best of all, the Bad Baby can be either a boy or a girl, so that every child reading the book can completely identify. Vipont and Briggs manage to make the spectacle of an Elephant rampaging through shops, markets, and everyday streets all entirely believable. This is a classic picture book that can be enjoyed over and over again. **AG**

The Very Hungry Caterpillar 1969

Eric Carle

Nationality | American, born 1929
Publisher | World Publishing, USA
Award | American Institute of Graphic Arts, 1970
Theme | Animal stories, Classics

A little egg hatches on a leaf and becomes a small caterpillar. It is very, very hungry. Readers put their fingers through the holes on the pages and follow a ravenous caterpillar's path over the course of a week. On Monday he eats an apple; on Tuesday, two pears; on Wednesday, three plums; and so on through cherry pie and sausage until he has eaten ten pieces of food, gets really fat, and has a stomachache. Unsurprisingly, it is then time to curl up into a cocoon until he emerges as a beautiful butterfly.

Eric Carle's jewel-colored illustrations and simple repetitive text have enthralled generations of children, who love to put their hands through the enlarging holes left by the caterpillar—an idea stimulated, according to the author, by time he spent idly playing with a hole punch.

The pictures, constructed by collage on white backgrounds, are inspiring, while the text is as rhythmic as a nursery rhyme. Like many of Carle's picture books, *The Very Hungry Caterpillar* is used in nursery classes as a reader, a science information book, and an inspiration for art activities.

A perfect book for adult and child to read together, children love to chant along with the text's refrain ("He was still hungry"), shout out the days of the week, and guess what the caterpillar will eat next. The fun and nonsense blend in with the caterpillar's life cycle in a short book that has won numerous awards, sold more than twenty-five million copies worldwide, and has been translated into more than thirty languages. **VN**

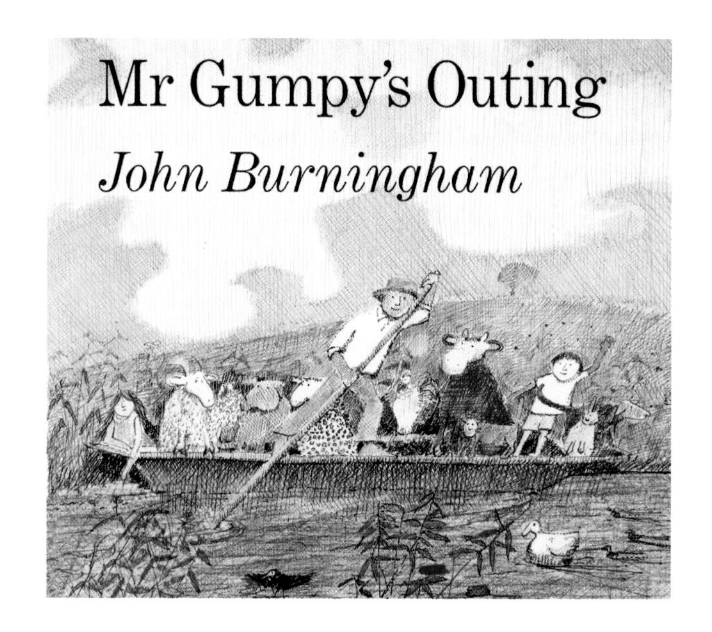

Mr. Gumpy's Outing 1970

John Burningham

Nationality | English, born 1936
Publisher | Jonathan Cape, UK
Award | Kate Greenaway Medal
Theme | Friendship

The opening page of *Mr. Gumpy's Outing* offers a scene of British rural idyll: Mr. Gumpy stands smiling in the foreground, watering can in hand; behind him a path leads to an archetypal English, double-fronted home. The colors, crosshatched in inks, are those of a bright summer morning.

One by one, a succession of children and animals ask to accompany Mr. Gumpy on his punting trip, and Mr. Gumpy, though clearly aware of the possible consequences, nevertheless cheerfully agrees, "Yes, if you don't squabble. / Yes, but don't hop about." While the right-hand side of each spread shows an ink and color-washed picture of the pleading animal, on the left a sepia sketch of the boat hints at the drama to come. When it inevitably does, a change in the layout creates a tumultuous double-page spread in which the boat tips and everyone tumbles into the water, while behind them the sun shines a vivid ball of yellow as it drops toward the horizon.

Order and harmony are quickly restored, with Mr. Gumpy leading everyone, now in an orderly line, back home to tea—a scene of domestic comfort, complete with teapot and cake. The final page brings the story satisfyingly full circle. This time we see the back view of the house crosshatched in black against a cloudy night sky, a trace of green still visible in the trees as Mr. Gumpy waves his guests off from a doorway whose bright light shines out. His final invitation "Come for a ride another day" is taken up in a sequel, *Mr. Gumpy's Motor Car* (1973). **KA**

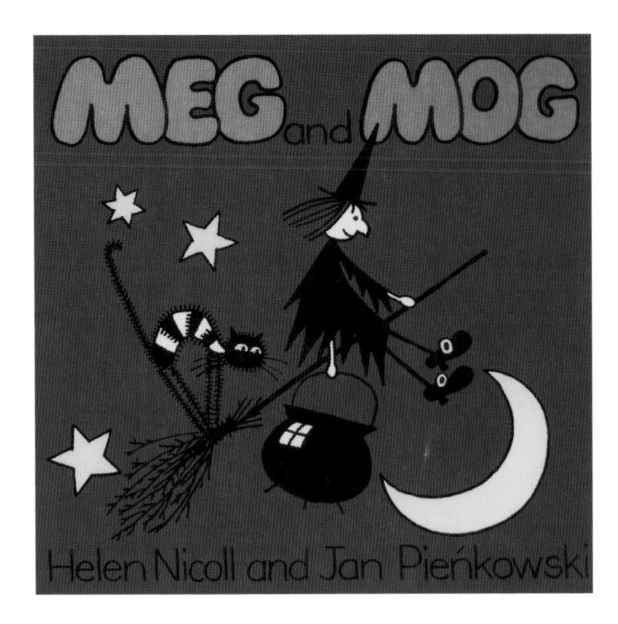

Meg and Mog 1972

Helen Nicoll Jan Pieńkowski

Nationality | English, born 1937 (author); English, born 1936 (illustrator)
Publisher | Heinemann, UK
Theme | Magical stories, Favorite characters

The Meg and Mog books chart the adventures of hapless but goodhearted witch Meg, whose spells rarely turn out as they are supposed to, her long-suffering striped cat Mog, and their wise friend Owl. This is the first in the series.

At the stroke of midnight, Owl hoots three times to wake Meg up to go to a Halloween party; poor Mog has a ruder awakening when Meg accidentally steps on his tail. In the kitchen, Meg stirs an unappetizing breakfast in her large cauldron, then chooses what to wear—black, of course. After checking they have all the essentials (broomstick, cauldron, spider), Meg and Mog leave via the chimney and fly through the night to the hill on which the spell-casting party is taking place. With a cry of "Abracadabra!" Meg unintentionally turns all her friends into mice. She decides to wait until next Halloween to restore them to their true form; in the meantime Mog has fun chasing the squealing rodents.

Meg and Mog's style is original and immediately distinctive, with skinny, elongated black-and-white characters on bright, bold backgrounds. The limited palette, including a rich turquoise and a striking red, is inspired by traditional Polish embroidery. Each page is carefully constructed, making powerful use of minimal words and unfussy drawings. The vocabulary used is more educational than creative, but wildly imaginative storylines and an inherent sense of fun make a dramatic impression. The books have been adapted for the stage and television. **MK**

Meg flies up the chimney with Mog in tow in her cauldron. 

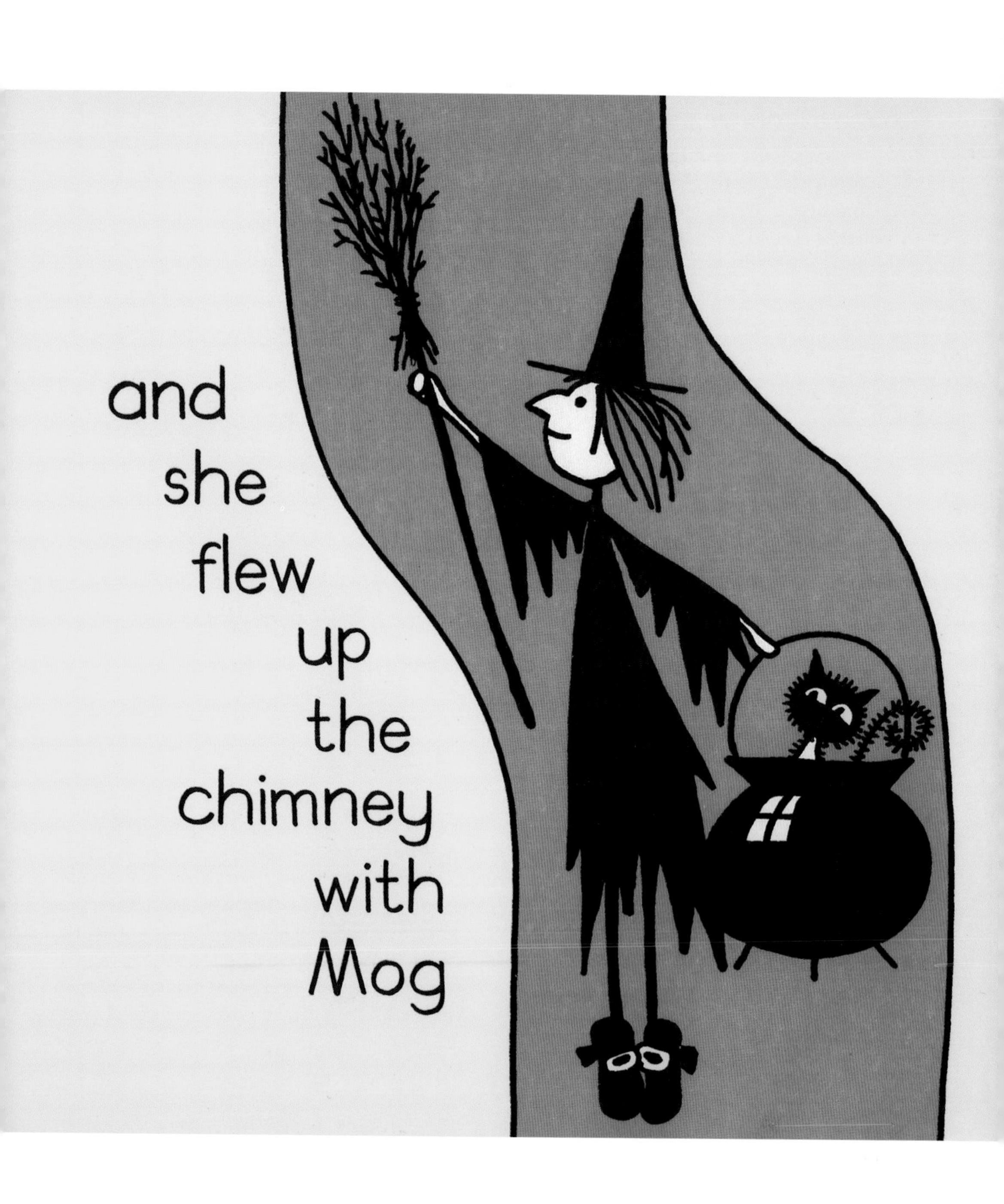
and
she
flew
up
the
chimney
with
Mog

Good Night, Alfie Atkins 1972

Gunilla Bergström

Original Title | God natt Alfons Åberg
Nationality | Swedish, born 1942
Publisher | Rabén and Sjögren, Sweden
Theme | Favorite characters, Family

Cranky four-year-old Alfie Atkins does not feel like going to bed at all: "Alfie doesn't want to sleep tight. He doesn't want to sleep at all." There are just so many other things that he wants to do before falling asleep. First, Dad must read him a long good-night story; then Alfie remembers he has not brushed his teeth yet. Oh, and suddenly he is feeling thirsty. Whoops, he has spilled the drink! Now he needs to go to the bathroom—and then he realizes that Teddy is missing. All this to-ing and fro-ing exhausts his patient father, who falls asleep on the floor, long before Alfie is ready to sleep.

This is Gunilla Bergström's first book about Alfie Atkins, a little boy who has become one of the most beloved and popular characters in Swedish children's literature. The books were groundbreaking when first published because they featured a single-parent family—just Alfie and his dad.

"Alfie Atkins is sometimes cranky, and sometimes nice. Tonight he is cranky. . . ."

Bergström has an easy ability to write about everyday themes that children from countries all over the world can relate to. Her beautiful illustrations entice children to turn the pages: clean, cartoonlike drawings mixed with a collage technique that uses fabric, yarn, lace, and cut paper. Bergström also uses color to illustrate movement and manages to get her characters, although simply drawn, to register a wide range of feelings through their facial expressions. There is always an underlying tone of humor in Bergström's books as well as some sort of twist to the story. The Alfie books have been translated into twenty-nine languages. **CC**

OTHER GREAT ALFIE ATKINS STORIES

Hurry Up, Alfie Atkins! (Raska på, Alfons Åberg), 1975
Are You a Coward, Alfie Atkins? (Är du feg, Alfons Åberg?), 1981
Who's Scaring Alfie Atkins? (Vem räddar Alfons Åberg), 1983

Little Brown Bear 1975

Claude Lebrun Daniele Bour

Little Brown Bear is the hero of a highly popular series of fifty-two stories first published in French as *Petit ours brun*. Created by Claude Lebrun and taken up by the editorial team of the children's magazines *Popi* and *Pomme d'Api*, Little Brown Bear is also the central character of a cartoon series that has been translated into several languages.

Little Brown Bear tells the story of the special moments in the everyday life of a young bear. Living with Mother Bear and Father Bear, he has many exciting adventures, similar to those that mark the life of any toddler. His incessant curiosity mirrors the first surprising experiences of childhood. Children will observe him eating an egg on his own for the first time, fiddling with the telephone, or simply playing with a ball. They will share his fear when he gets lost in the market and his amazement when he looks at the stars for the first time. Every moment in a small child's life can be precious and amazing, as they discover the world, the importance of friends, and the love of their family. Young children can easily identify with Little Brown Bear, for he is very like them—mischievous and innocent at the same time—and through him they can even get to know themselves better.

"Little Brown Bear loves being little. But sometimes he would like to be big immediately!"

The short, simple stories are illustrated in Danielle Bour's distinctive naive style. Her lively, colorful drawings depict a wealth of detail for children to explore. *Little Brown Bear* is a cheerful, affectionate journey to the heart of childhood—older children end up knowing the stories by heart—and an ideal companion for children and their parents to share. **SL**

Nationality | French, born 1937 (author); French, born 1939 (illustrator)
Publisher | Bayard Jeunesse, France
Theme | Favorite characters, Animal stories

OTHER LITTLE BROWN BEAR BOOKS

Little Brown Bear and the Potty (Petit ours brun et le pot), 1997
Little Brown Bear and the Baby (Petit ours brun et le bébé), 1998
Little Brown Bear Says No (Petit ours brun dit non), 1998

Little Spook's Baby Sister 1977

Inger Sandberg Lasse Sandberg

Inger och Lasse Sandberg
Lilla spöket Laban får en lillasyster

Nationality | Swedish, born 1930 (author); Swedish, born 1924 (illustrator)
Publisher | Rabén and Sjögren, Sweden
Theme | Family, Ghost stories

"Little Spook's baby sister makes more noise than all of us put together."

When Inger and Lasse Sandberg's son was young, he was scared of ghosts. "Well, we'll have to vaccinate you against ghosts then," Inger Sandberg told him. That simple conversation led to the first book (*Lilla spöket Laban får en lillasyster*) about the adorable child-ghost Little Spook.

Little Spook is a kind and playful ghost who comes with a nonscary guarantee. Even children who are frightened of ghosts will not be able to resist him. Lasse Sandberg's illustrations are ingenious in their simplicity. His line-drawn characters are uncomplicated yet full of charm and expression. The backgrounds are a mix of different media, including India ink, collage, and crayon. Though from the 1970s, the Sandbergs' style still manages to feel very modern.

Little Spook lives with his nonscary mom and dad in the Morning Sun Castle. Little Prince and his royal family also live in the castle. Little Prince and Spook are playmates and the best of friends. Spook's parents prefer to stay in the cellar during the daytime and come out at night. One day Spook and Little Prince hear strange noises coming from the cellar. They go down to investigate and discover that Little Spook now has a baby sister who "makes more noise than all of us put together."

The Little Spook books are great for reading to children who are going through a phase when they are afraid of ghosts and monsters. They make something that could be scary, funny and cute. **CC**

OTHER BOOKS BY THE SANDBERGS

Little Ghost Godfrey (*Lilla spöket Laban*), 1965
Little Anna's Mother Has a Birthday (*Lilla Annas mamma fyller år*), 1966
Little Spook's Grubby Day (*Labolinas snubbeldag*), 1977

Fly, Little Bird 1977

Francesco Tullio Altan

Original Title | Vola, uccellino!
Nationality | Italian, born 1942
Publisher | Edizioni E. L., Italy
Theme | Animal stories

Francesco Tullio Altan (known simply as Altan) originally worked as a set designer and scriptwriter in cinema and television, a background that was to strongly influence his later illustrative style. After moving from Italy to Brazil in 1970, he successfully broke into the world of comics and cartoons. The first character he invented was named for his daughter Kika, and the stories were first published in the newspaper *Jornal de Brasil*.

The little bird Kika inspired a whole series of books (*Il primo libro di Kika*) suitable for children who are just beginning to match words with pictures and who are starting to read. Altan litters his narrative with simple objects—a ball that rolls, a fish that swims, a little bird that flies—that gradually change shapes. For example, the little rolling ball transforms into a face, then into a boy who runs through the grass. A white elephant morphs into a small child playing in the mud, who then cleans himself up before eating his dinner and taking a nap in his hammock.

In addition to his popular Kika series, Altan is also the creator of Pimpa the puppy, another iconic character in Italian children's literature. Other characters to emerge from his pen include Nino the penguin and Pippo the woodpecker. His distinctive style combines a strong graphic design sensibility and bright colors with comedy and plenty of action. The small format picture books with their easy-to-turn pages are ideal for tiny hands. **SMT**

Each Peach Pear Plum 1978

Allan Ahlberg Janet Ahlberg

Nationality | English, born 1938 (author); English, born 1944 (illustrator)
Publisher | Kestrel Books, UK
Theme | Nursery rhymes, Poetry

This I-spy game in verse introduces little ones to the pleasures of rhyming text and to the characters they will meet in nursery rhymes and fairy tales, such as Tom Thumb, the Three Bears, and Old Mother Hubbard. Each line of verse, short enough to hold a young child's attention, prompts the reader to find a familiar character on the facing illustrated page. The rich detail of the written and visual text offers plenty to intrigue and excite older children, who become adept at spotting the references and predicting the storyline as each character picks up the thread—Cinderella with a duster, Bo-Peep with a crook, and so on. The game is so much fun that you might miss the most accomplished aspect of the book, the illustrations (for which Janet won the Kate Greenaway Medal).

Compositional delights help adults survive repeat readings. The landscape that opens the book marks out the territory to be explored: hills, two houses, a stream, a field, an orchard. Subsequent right-hand pages, introducing one character's immediate world at a time, show scenes as they appear within the bigger landscape, with a vignette from the scene on the left-hand page. The landscape contains the whole world of the story, within which all the characters can be found. Each scene has a different viewpoint, from which you can see exactly what you would expect from the rest of the landscape. The worlds of the tales seem separate, but the story brings them together, just as in the child's imagination they are one. **GB**

Where's Spot? 1980

 Eric Hill

Nationality | English, born 1927
Publisher | Heinemann, UK
Theme | Classics, Animal stories, Favorite characters, Family

Spot, the friendly yellow puppy with his distinctive brown spots, is a classic and much-loved picture book character. *Where's Spot?* was the first title in what became a charming series of books filled with bright, colorful illustrations.

Spot was originally created for Hill's son Christopher. The response he gave to flaps that could be opened inspired the innovative design of *Where's Spot?*, a book that launched a new trend in interactive storybooks.

Hill shies away from depicting the obvious: "I thought it would be fun to draw a chair in a period style rather than a straightforward type. A grand piano instead of an upright—pink rather than brown," he explains. "All to broaden the visual scope that a book can bring to a young mind."

In *Where's Spot?*, Sally, Spot's mother, is exploring the house, looking for her errant pup. Large, bold captions ask where Spot could be hiding. Is he in the chest? No! Behind the door? No! The story is short and simple, but a flap must be lifted to reveal the answer to each of the eight questions, adding a fun and engaging element. This charming book also helps preschool children develop basic literacy and numeracy in an entertaining manner.

The Spot books have been translated into sixty languages and their canine hero is recognized throughout the world. He is an inquisitive puppy and always on a voyage of discovery, similar to a child's burgeoning experience of his or her surroundings. This, perhaps, is the great secret to Spot's success. **MK**

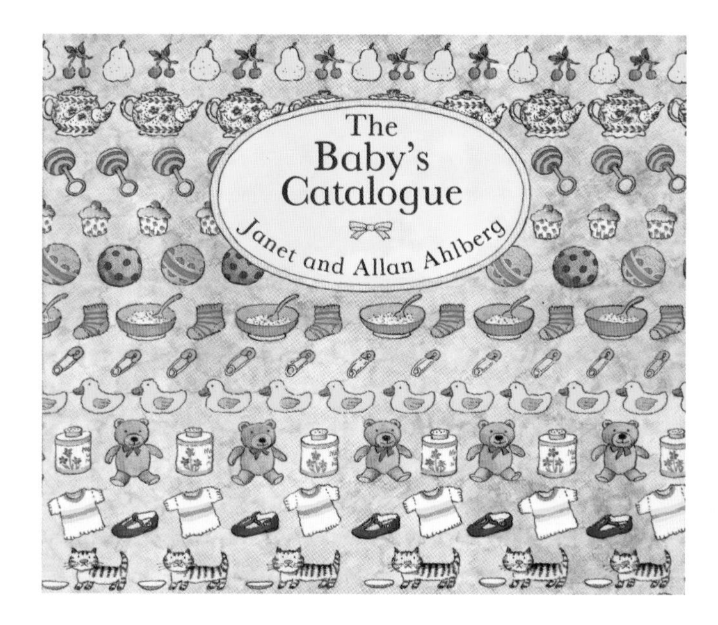

The Baby's Catalogue 1982

Allan Ahlberg Janet Ahlberg

Nationality | English, born 1938 (author); English, born 1944 (illustrator)
Publisher | Kestrel Books, UK
Theme | Family, Classics

In our era of online shopping, there are probably fewer children than before cutting up mail order catalogs to construct the ideal home and family. The Ahlbergs tapped into this pleasure when they put together their self-assembly kit for family life, beautifully illustrated with soft, watercolor drawings. The first section of the catalog introduces six babies to be followed through a typical day. The term "baby" covers the newborn-to-toddler range. One strapping child is already climbing out of his cot.

The introduction of moms and dads hints at the pleasures to come in poring over the catalog to build up a picture of each family, note what is special about them, and embellish their stories. The mom who goes out to work (only one of those) is from the family of redheads, who have the puppy and the patterned ball. The father of the very small baby is a painter and decorator, and always looks tired. The father of the twins has a beard and glasses, and they have a very fancy stroller. The mother of the big fair-haired boy is expecting a fourth child. The elephant and the yellow duck belong to the black boy in the wicker cot. The details are of the kind children notice but adults would not find obvious. Adults are more likely to appreciate the accidents—heads stuck in buckets and between railings, a mom's handbag emptied.

There is something very British about this book, such as the teatime selection of watercress, radishes, and Battenberg cake. However, it has been translated happily into many languages, its appeal universal. **GB**

Dear Zoo 1982

Rod Campbell

Nationality | Scottish, born 1945
Publisher | Abelard-Schuman, UK
Theme | Classics, Animal stories, Family, Rhyming stories

Dear Zoo kick-started the revolution in innovative British children's books with its sturdy lift-the-flap format. Seemingly simple, it has proved a classic literary design and has spawned hundreds of imitators. The book is constructed so that young audiences engage on a physical level as well as an imaginative one. The text is repetitive yet varied with humor. It uses literary devices such as alliteration, repeating phrases, and rhymes.

Although Campbell's stories are simple and clearly plotted, they do not talk down to even the youngest reader. Instead, they smile along with him or her. Children can enjoy *Dear Zoo* throughout their early years, its simple and friendly denouement being greeted with cries of joy and satisfaction every time.

The story is quickly told. A child writes to the zoo for a pet. The zoo sends a series of unsuitable animals, each of whom is revealed behind sturdily constructed paper flaps in the form of crates and packing cases. They are drawn with bold black outlines and bright colors on white backgrounds.

All the animals have to be sent back for different reasons: too scary, too heavy, too fierce. Happily, the last one is perfect, so it can be kept. In mixing the everyday with fantasy, Campbell speaks to children as if he were in the room with them. How many children must have asked for an elephant of their own after returning from a visit to the zoo? And what excuses have adults given? Here is that experience, distilled into a classic, lift-the-flap book. **VN**

Good Dog, Carl 1985

Alexandra Day

Nationality | American, born Sandra Louise Woodward Darling 1941
Publisher | Green Tiger Press, USA
Theme | Animal stories, Family

There are more words in this sentence than there are in the entire book *Good Dog, Carl*. Using merely twelve words, Day's wonderful illustrations are able to relate a nearly silent story with an eloquence only a master illustrator can accomplish.

To appreciate the book, parents must suspend all previous notions about babysitting and Rottweilers. Very young children, having no preconceived notions in these areas, will have no such dilemmas. The fun begins when the mother goes shopping and leaves her baby in the care of Carl, the Rottweiler, with the words, "Look after the baby, Carl. I'll be back shortly."

Carl is no ordinary dog, and once the baby's mother is gone, the fun starts in earnest. Carl looks out of the window to make sure no adults are around—once the coast is clear, the baby crawls out of the crib and onto Carl's back.

First, they go for a bounce on the mother's bed; next, they move on to the top of the dresser where powder puffs are worn as hats. The infant—now in Carl's capable paws—slides down the laundry chute, swims in the fish tank, dances, raids the refrigerator, and makes a huge mess. Carl then dutifully bathes the baby, cleans up, puts his charge back in the crib, and plays innocent when his owner comes home. She is very pleased and says "Good dog, Carl!"

Even the littlest child will enjoy telling the story through the pictures over and over again. They will also love the sequels: *Carl Goes Shopping* (1992), *Carl goes to Daycare* (1993), and *Carl's Birthday* (1995). **KD**

Bathwater's Hot 1985

Shirley Hughes

Nationality | English, born 1927
Publisher | Walker Books, UK
Series | The Nursery Collection
Theme | Favorite characters, Rhyming stories

This is one of those classic books that makes adults misty-eyed about their early childhood. Multiple award-winning writer and illustrator Hughes—who has been described as the "doyenne of the picture book world"—excites such loyalty because she creates believable characters in everyday situations, and has a canny ability to capture what her changing readership wants (over a very long career).

This book's principal players are the curious and bubbly toddler, Katie, and her baby brother. Hughes brings together several winning elements. The simple, rhyming text is perfect for reading aloud over and over, and the singsong rhythms engage listeners with the cadence of words. The tale shows Katie exploring very ordinary activities in a way that effortlessly introduces ideas such as colors, shapes, numbers, sounds, and opposites. These concepts are re-created beautifully by Hughes's pictures: bold outline, strong color, and decisive poses that capture the energy, joy, and vulnerability of children. These images will draw in youngsters with very different reading abilities.

Hughes started her career as a freelance illustrator for other writers, including Noel Streatfeild and Dorothy Edwards's legendary My Naughty Little Sister books. Like many successful children's authors, Hughes began making picture books when her own children were very young—spotting an important gap in children's literature of books that depicted everyday life. Her close, loving observation of small people is what makes books like this speak to so many. **AK**

Tickle, Tickle 1987

Helen Oxenbury

Nationality | English, born 1938
Publisher | Walker Books, UK
Theme | Family, Friendship, Rhyming stories

Tickle Tickle is a delightful book that adults, babies and young children love. In it a happy, fun-loving group of multiracial babies are all shown playing together and enjoying the simplest aspects of everyday life. Alongside the warm, friendly text, it features a minimalist illustrative style—simple faces and shapes created by a strong outline filled in with bold color—that Oxenbury developed and for which she has become known worldwide.

Helen Oxenbury has been described as the "grande dame" of babies' picture books. A prolific children's illustrator and writer, she is perhaps best known as a leading pioneer of the board book in the 1980s, an interest that was jump-started by having to entertain one of her young children when they were ill. Oxenbury's intuitive understanding of babies and children helped her gravitate toward picture books, further encouraged by being married to successful children's author and illustrator, John Burningham.

In *Tickle, Tickle,* the images of the toddlers loom large on the uncluttered pages, placing them right at the heart of the action and further underlining Oxenbury's fascination with every detail of their behavior. The few words take a rhyming form that works superbly with the images.

Oxenbury has been much-praised for having an illustrative style that aims to talk directly to—and never down to—babies and toddlers, and for its subtle comedy that engages adults just as much as it does children. **AK**

Elmer 1989

 David McKee

Nationality | English, born David McKee Owns 1935
Publisher | Andersen Press, UK
Theme | Animal stories, Friendship

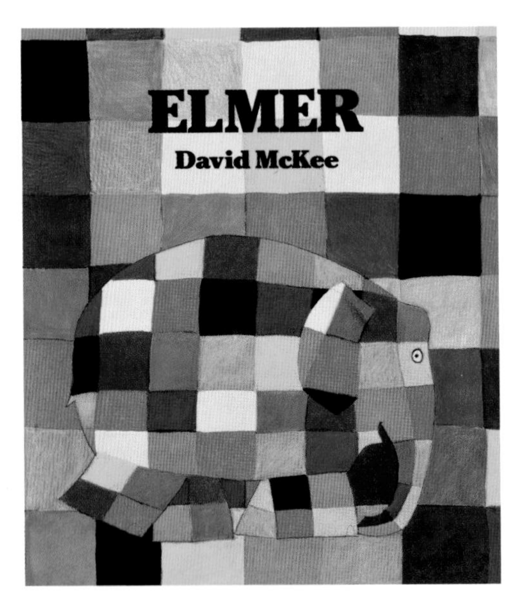

"Elmer was different. Elmer was patchwork. . . . Elmer was not *elephant color."*

RECOMMENDED DAVID McKEE TITLES

King Rollo's Playroom, 1983
Not Now, Bernard, 1983
Two Monsters, 1987
Elmer Again, 1991
Mr. Benn, Gladiator, 2001

Elmer the patchwork elephant decides that the reason the other elephants laugh at him is because he is different. As David McKee tells us: "Elmer was yellow and orange and red and pink and purple and blue and green and black and white. Elmer was not elephant color." So one morning, before anyone awakes, Elmer sneaks away and paints himself gray. Pleased with his disguise, he goes back to stand among the herd—but without Elmer to make them laugh, the elephants just stand there, still and serious.

Elmer cannot pretend to be the same as the rest of the herd for very long, however. He just can't help being a joker. When he yells "Boo!" all the elephants tumble over with surprise. "It must be Elmer," they declare, and sure enough, the rain washes off Elmer's disguise. The elephants declare that this is Elmer's best trick ever, and decide to celebrate Elmer's Day every year by painting themselves in bright colors, while Elmer paints himself ordinary elephant gray.

Like many of McKee's picture books, *Elmer* is a moral tale, dealing warmly and gently with issues of diversity and tolerance. Elmer worries that his unusualness makes the other elephants treat him differently from the way they treat one another, but he discovers that his difference is not only tolerated by the others, but relished.

This is a stunning picture book, drawn with simple, cartoon-style lines (McKee is also an animator) and vivid use of color. The flat slabs of colors making Elmer's patchwork and the shaded gray elephants are set against a weird landscape of strange spiky plants. There are subtle atmospheric changes of color, too: the yellow dawn as Elmer sneaks off; the blues and purples as a black rain cloud covers the sky; the dark early morning sky as the other animals greet Elmer in the dense jungle, which becomes paler later in the day when he comes back, elephant color. **CW**

Elmer smothers himself in berries to cover up his patchwork. 

We're Going on a Bear Hunt 1989

Michael Rosen   Helen Oxenbury

Nationality | English, born 1946 (author); English, born 1938 (illustrator)
Publisher | Walker Books, UK
Theme | Rhyming stories, Classics, Family

Children, parents, and teachers all adore this book. It is based on an American nursery rhyme, and here it is retold by poet Michael Rosen, British Children's Laureate from 2007 to 2009. There is not much story: it is about a family going for a walk, crossing a series of obstacles, such as mud and long grass, encountering a bear, and then running away home. Yet, the enticing language and rhythm make it something special. The words are a perfect chant for a walk, with repetition to keep up the pace and changing rhythms to keep it interesting. Children love the sound of the words used for the obstacles encountered on the way ("swishy swashy," "squelch, squerch," "stumble trip"), and they love to act out the actions suggested by them.

Oxenbury's pictures weave a deeper story around the rhyme. We see a father and three children starting out on an ordinary walk, happy and carefree. Black-and-white drawings that show the family standing and considering each hazard alternate with watercolor scenes as they cross the obstacles. As the hazards become more and more threatening, the family's smiles disappear; they huddle together when they come to a snowstorm. They peer with disbelief into the gloomy cave, see the bear, and then run. Here the action, along with the rhythm, speeds up in a spread where they are seen running back through all the obstacles, with the bear in pursuit. We see them at home huddled up safe in bed, while the endpapers show the bear wandering back to his cave, looking rather sad. Perhaps he was not fierce, after all. **CW**

Bunny Bath 1990

Lena Anderson

Original Title | Kanin-bad
Nationality | Swedish, born 1939
Publisher | Rabén and Sjögren, Sweden
Theme | Friendship

With just two characters, a child and a rabbit, Lena Anderson tells a wordless story about getting undressed to have a bath. The child comes in from the cold and hands over garment after garment as he undresses. The rabbit helps in the pictures on the left-hand page while the right-hand side features the different items of clothing: wet gloves, thick cap, tricky boots, long trousers, polka-dot underpants, jacket, and sweater. The rabbit takes care of all the clothes—until the rubber duckie unexpectedly turns up and indicates a scene change. On the last spread, the child and rabbit relax in the bathtub, much satisfied.

Anderson's work has been likened to the soft naturalism of fellow Swede Elsa Beskow. Anderson combines Beskow's style of decorative watercolors and dark ink outlines with a freshness that belongs to a more modern time. The rabbit is big, soft, and welcoming and plays the role of patient and secure parent. It folds and hangs up the clothes like a responsible adult, but shows itself fully ready to play as well. The understanding between the two is charming, and they both seem to expect the shared bath at the end of the book.

Anderson is one of several Swedish authors whose work is refreshing the otherwise rather static picture book genre. Her *Rabbit* series combines the classic word-picture combination with lively, theatrical narratives. In that way it inspires discussion that goes beyond just naming words and concepts and involves the playful element of learning that is so important to children. **UR**

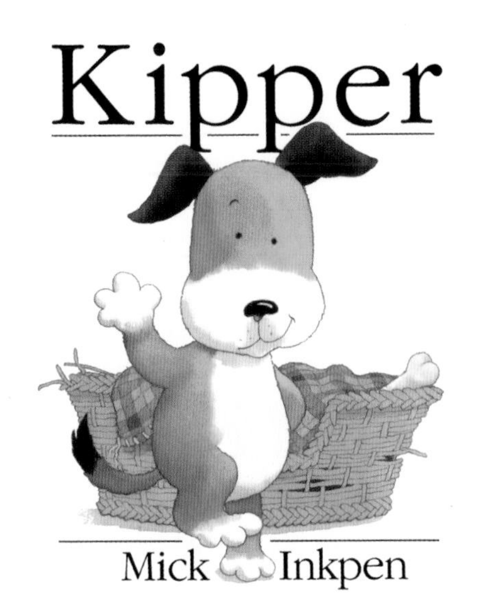

Kipper 1991

 Mick Inkpen

Nationality | English, born 1952
Publisher | Hodder and Stoughton, UK
Theme | Favorite characters, Classics, Animal stories, Friendship

Kipper the dog, with book sales now totaling more than five million worldwide, started his career in *The Blue Balloon* (1989), in which he featured as the companion to a small boy, the proud owner of a possibly magical balloon. *Kipper* later became the first in a series featuring the appealing character in his own right. A small brown-and-white dog drawn with clear black outlines against a predominantly white background, he has an oversized head, perky black ears, and an enthusiastically optimistic outlook. His endearing naivety frequently lands him in comic misunderstandings whereas his well-intentioned attempts to solve life's difficulties often lead to a series of gently amusing scrapes that have earned him enduring family-wide appeal.

In this first book, he is in the mood for tidying his basket: Out go the much-loved soft toy, ball, chewed-up bone, and smelly old comforter—to Kipper's relief. However, when he tries to sleep, Kipper's basket is no longer comfortable, wriggle as he may. He decides to go and discover how other animals get to sleep. A series of comical illustrations picture him upside down and looking perplexed as he tries to fit into a flowerpot like the wrens, tickled by long grass like the sheep, and standing soggily in the pond after an attempt to sleep on a lily pad like a frog.

Young readers will anticipate the ending long before it has been reached, waiting expectantly for Kipper to restore his basket to all its former shabby glory and at last gain a good night's sleep. **KA**

Kipper sorts through the old toys in his basket

Maisy Goes to Playschool 1992

Lucy Cousins

Nationality | English, born 1964
Publisher | Walker Books, UK
Theme | Favorite characters, Friendship, Animal stories, School

Maisy began life as a doodle on a piece of paper but is now one of the world's most familiar picture book characters. She is a friendly white mouse who explores the world around her and enjoys the same small everyday adventures that all young children share. Although she has mouse ears and a tail, she has hands and feet and acts like a human toddler.

This is a simple story about Maisy's first day at nursery school. She paints pictures, frolics in the playhouse, dresses up, dances, and feeds the fish before going home again. These are all reassuring activities that small children can relate to, and many of the Maisy books feature new experiences, such as visiting the dentist or a trip to the museum. Maisy and her friends Cyril the Squirrel, Charley the Crocodile, Eddie the Elephant, Tallulah the Chick, and her favorite panda toy are stylized characters illustrated in primary colors. They feature in an ever-growing series of books in which they have a number of mini-adventures involving swimming, playing in the garden, visiting a farm, riding tricycles, and making friends.

More than twelve million Maisy books have been sold worldwide, and the series is popular with parents, preschools, and librarians because it introduces basic concepts such as colors, numbers, and opposites as well as reinforces the values of sharing and helping one another. The books are available in a number of formats, including cloth books, pull-the-tab, and three-dimensional play sets, which allow children to explore different textures and shapes. **HJ**

Owl Babies 1992

Martin Waddell Patrick Benson

Nationality | Irish, born 1941 (author); English, born 1956 (illustrator)
Publisher | Walker Books, UK
Theme | Family, Animal stories

In the middle of the night, in a small corner of a dark wood, three baby owls sit in a tree, waiting for their mother to come home—Sarah on a big branch, Percy on a small one, and Bill, the youngest, perched on an old bit of ivy. As they watch and wait, the story explores their growing anxiety. Older sister Sarah, bringing her younger siblings close together on her branch, provides some comfort as reader and owls alike grow increasingly apprehensive. At last, and with a memorably triumphant page turn, their mother returns. Enormously popular with both children and adults, the book's great strength lies in its subtle interplay between text and illustration. The former—strongly patterned, repetitive, and predominantly monosyllabic—appears superficially simple, but at crucial moments the use of stylized alliteration and telling changes to established patterns give great pleasure to both reader and listener. The latter contrasts the rich blackness of nighttime with the almost luminous whites of the baby owls and the deep, dark colors of the surrounding wood. Though the setting never changes, the pictures offer variety through their skilled use of viewpoint, panning out from a close-up scene in which the baby owls are drawn comfortingly together on their branch, to distant perspectives that hint at their vulnerability in the vast wood. By exploring childhood anxieties through characters whose interactions firmly establish them in the domestic sphere so familiar to small children, it has become an established favorite. **KA**

Handa's Surprise 1994

Eileen Browne

Nationality | English, birth date unknown
Publisher | Walker Books, UK
Theme | Favorite characters, Friendship, Classics

Handa's Surprise has become a firm favorite with young children, parents, and teachers. Eileen Browne had worked as a teacher and wanted to write books for children featuring strong female characters and different cultural backgrounds because there was little that was available at the time.

Set in Africa, it is about a small girl who decides to take her friend Akeyo a basket of fruit as a surprise. As she thinks about each piece of delicious fruit she is carrying in a basket on her head—an avocado, a guava, an orange, a mango, a passion fruit, and a pineapple—a different animal reaches down from the trees and takes it. But all is not lost. As Handa approaches the village, a goat charges at a tree and shakes tangerines into her basket. Handa has not noticed what the mischievous animals have been up to, and it is she that gets the real surprise when she finds her fruit has been replaced. Happily, Akeyo tells Handa that tangerines are her favorite fruit.

It is a simple tale, simply told, but young readers will enjoy the joke, and the warm and vibrant illustrations. They will get a great deal from the story—the names of various exotic fruits and animals, as well as counting skills. They will also enjoy hunting for the animals who are partly hidden in the trees and in the long grass.

The story has been published in more than twenty languages, and was adapted as a successful stage play. Browne wrote a sequel, *Handa's Hen*, in which Handa and Akeyo search for Handa's grandmother's hen. **HJ**

Alvin Says Good Night 1996

Ulf Löfgren

Original Title | Albin säger godnatt
Nationality | Swedish, born 1931
Publisher | Almqvist and Wiksell, Sweden
Theme | Favorite characters, Animal stories

Alvin goes out to say good night to all the animals on the farm. But where are they? The horse is gone and so is the cow. The rooster, the pig, and the sheep are also hiding. Alvin looks for the goose, the cat, and the goat, but without luck—they are nowhere to be found. The animals are playing tricks on him.

Alvin Says Good Night is a simple but clever story for the younger reader. The colorful illustrations, uncomplicated language, and short sentences make the book ideal for reading aloud to infants, or as a first book for the slightly older child learning to read on his or her own. (Indeed, the Alvin series was initially intended to be used in schools to teach children to read, although children enjoy reading it for leisure just as much.)

The young Alvin is a boy who finds himself in all kinds of adventurous situations. He is never afraid, always hopeful, and has a vivid imagination. At times he pretends to be a Viking, at others a knight, and his adventures continue in books such as *Alvin the Pirate* and *Alvin and his Friend Ali Baba*.

The role of imagination in everyday life is the theme that Ulf Löfgren most commonly works with, and his ability to capture a child's emotional life is key to his success as a children's author. Löfgren's watercolor illustrations are uncomplicated, friendly, humorous, and charming. The hide-and-seek theme and funny ending in *Alvin Says Good Night* are sure to amuse even the smallest child. **CC**

The Bear Went Over the Mountain 1999

 John Prater

Nationality | English, born 1947
Publisher | Bodley Head, UK; Barron's, USA
Theme | Animal stories, Family, Rhyming stories, Adventure

British writer and illustrator John Prater has been much praised by picture book reviewers for bringing the everyday realities of early life alive in a fresh way—both for children and their parents. He has said that his picture books were initially sparked by watching his own two mischievous daughters. Prater's main trademarks are minimal text (he says he finds writing very difficult); simple, bold but expressive pencil and watercolor illustrations; and a warm, humorous take on the joys and misadventures of childhood.

The Bear Went Over the Mountain is the perfect example of all of these elements. This is one of his Baby Bear Books series, inspired by becoming a grandfather. The low-key story simply depicts a baby bear playing affectionately with "Grandbear," but in a way that turns into something of an adventure for the baby—showing Prater's keen observation about early experience. As in other Prater books, the very brief text takes the form of a singsong rhyme that also perfectly matches the amusing and affectionate actions he depicts. This makes his words ideal to say or sing with a baby or young child over and over again, as a great way to learn basic sounds, words, and concepts. He also gives his bears' faces lively expressions that instantly appeal and engage.

Prater worked as an illustrator and a teacher; these skills blended well to bring him great success in children's books, kick-started in 1982 by his first picture book, *On Friday Something Funny Happened.* **AK**

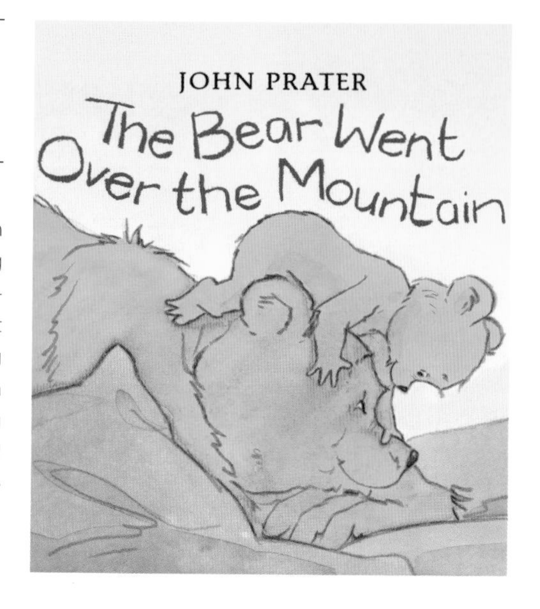

"The bear went over the mountain, the bear went over the mountain, the bear went over the mountain . . . to see what he could see."

OTHER GREAT BOOKS ABOUT BEARS

Little Brown Bear by Claud LeBrun, 1975
Old Bear by Jane Hissey, 1986
Can't You Sleep Little Bear? by Martin Waddell, 1988
Where's My Teddy? by Jez Alborough, 1992
Sleep Well Little Bear by Quint Buchholz, 1993

Humphrey's Corner

Sally Hunter

Humphrey's Corner 1999

Sally Hunter

Nationality | English, born 1965
Publisher | Viking Children's Books, UK
Theme | Favorite characters, Family, Friendship, Animal stories

Hugely endearing without being sickly sweet, this picture book tells a simple tale, but is also subtly packed with learning opportunities. Humphrey is a small, lovable elephant on a mission. Having rescued his faithful toy friend, Mop, from being squashed down the side of his bed, the two set off in search of the perfect place to play. This quest takes them all around Humphrey's house, in and out of rooms and cupboards. Each place in turn is not quite right, and so they move on. Hunter's text is simple, affectionate, and well integrated with her images. The plot is an inspired one as it allows small children to explore and discuss the different rooms in a typical house. At each location, Humphrey collects a new object, which offers opportunities for fun memory games. We read on because we are intrigued by where he will go next and whether he will ever find that special place.

Every room is lovingly illustrated with Hunter's evocative images: spare, soft pencil outlines washed with delicate, warm color. This is very much the safe, sunny childhood of happy nostalgia, and Hunter has said that she has been heavily influenced by the family life she knew as a child and by the characters of her relatives and her own three children. Humphrey is based on Hunter's son Ralph, when he was age three, and other Humphrey family members—featured in subsequent books—include Lottie (inspired by her daughter Georgie, age five) and Baby Jack (Hunter's baby boy, Kim). **AK**

Julian the Rabbit 2001

Nicoletta Costa

Original Title | Giulio coniglio: storie per un anno
Nationality | Italian, born 1953
Publisher | Franco Cosimo Panini, Italy
Theme | Animal stories, Favorite characters

Julian the Rabbit is the creation of one of Italy's best-known illustrators of children's books. Her trademark visual style is instantly recognizable—fluid lines, geometric shapes, and soft pastel colors blended together, even in one small butterfly, bring a host of captivating characters to life. Lighthearted and tongue-in-cheek, her creations are variously happy, decisive, sheepish, or ingenuous, and are pictured in warm, reassuringly safe surroundings. For example, the round face of a maternal-looking, warm-hearted moon looks down from a dusty blue sky in one bedtime scene.

This is the first in the series featuring Julian, a timid, loyal rabbit with a great passion for carrots, one of Costa's most successful picture book figures. In the book she guides young readers through the changing seasons of a year. Whether in spring, summer, fall, or winter, Julian the Rabbit is seen marveling at some small though significant transformation of nature, and delighting in the fun that each season brings. He is joined in his discoveries by his engaging friends: Caterina the Goose, Tommaso the Mouse, Walter the Fox, Laura the Snail, and Ignazio the Porcupine.

Nicoletta Costa published her first book at the age of twelve. She has won several awards, including the Grinzane Junior Award (2002) and Premio Andersen Best Author of the Year (1989 and 1994). Other memorable characters to spring from her imagination include Olga the Cloud and Teodora the Witch. **SMT**

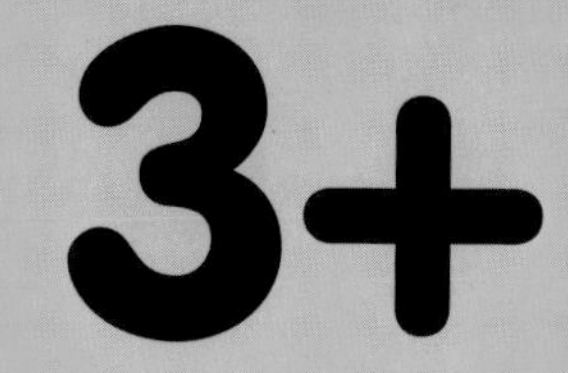

3+

Gorilla, written and illustrated by Anthony Browne.

The Quangle Wangle's Hat 1876

Edward Lear

Nationality | English, born 1812
Publisher | Thomas McLean, UK; originally published in *Laughable Lyrics*
Theme | Poetry, Classics

The English artist, illustrator, and author Edward Lear became famous in the nineteenth century for his limericks, a form he helped popularize, and nonsense poems. He is perhaps best known for "The Owl and the Pussycat." Children today still revel in Lear's absurd, witty, and irreverent take on the world.

The Quangle Wangle's Hat is a story about a strange creature, the Quangle Wangle, who sits all alone at the top of a Crumpetty Tree. He wears a magnificent hat, which hides his face; it is 102 feet wide and decorated with "ribbons and bibbons on every side / and bells, and buttons, and loops, and lace."

The Quangle Wangle loves his tree because it provides him with "jam; and jelly; and bread," but he feels sad because no one ever visits him at the top of his solitary tree. When Mr. and Mrs. Canary request permission to build a nest on his hat, the Quangle Wangle agrees. Soon other creatures come: the stork, the duck, the owl, the snail, the bumblebee, and the frog, as well as the weird and wonderful "Fimble Fowl with a corkscrew leg." They are joined by a whole host of characters who sprang from Lear's amazing imagination, such as the "Attery Squash," a "small Olympian Bear," a flute-playing baboon, the "Bisky Bat," and "the Orient Calf from the Land of Lute." Lear also brings in characters from his other poems, such as the "Pobble who has no toes" and "the Dong with the luminous nose." All the creatures become friends and the Quangle Wangle is no longer lonely. **LH**

Mother Goose 1881

Kate Greenaway

Subtitle | The Old Nursery Rhymes
Nationality | English, born 1846
Publisher | Routledge, UK
Theme | Nursery rhymes, Classics

Kate Greenaway's third book, *Mother Goose or The Old Nursery Rhymes*, contains forty-two traditional nursery rhymes: some well known, such as "Jack and Jill" and "Tom, Tom, the Piper's Son," and others less familiar, such as "Pippin Hill." She changed the rhymes when she felt it was necessary. The illustrations present an idealized view of childhood lived out in a pretty rural setting. Brought up in the East End of London, Greenaway's own experience of the countryside was obtained on visits to her relatives in Nottinghamshire.

The costumes in Greenaway's illustrations are drawn from the Regency period and inspired a return to those fashions. The Victorians were enamored with such a charming representation of the innocence of childhood, perhaps as an antidote to the realism of Charles Dickens. Greenaway studied at the Slade School of Art, London, which was a fairly liberal institution at the time in that it allowed women to study from the figure. She was taught the process of wood-block printing from her father, and her style was perfectly suited to this medium. *Mother Goose* is a fine example of Greenaway at the peak of her creativity.

After the success of her first book, *Under the Window* (1879), she was under considerable pressure to provide another best seller, and although it did not achieve the same commercial success, *Mother Goose* gained the admiration of many critics, including the artist Walter Crane, who included it in his 1897 book, *Of the Decorative Illustration of Books*. **WO**

Marigold Garden 1885

Kate Greenaway

Nationality | English, born Catherine Greenaway 1846
Publisher | Routledge, UK
Theme | Nursery rhymes, Poetry, Classics

3+

Kate Greenaway began her career designing greeting cards and calendars for Marcus Ward. After an initially successful collaboration, she left the partnership after a dispute concerning ownership. Through her father's connections, she began to work for the engraver, Edmund Evans. Her first illustrated book for Evans, *Under the Window* (1879), was a resounding success, both financially and creatively.

After the success of her anthology *Mother Goose*, Greenaway wanted to continue to illustrate nursery rhymes. *Marigold Garden* is a collection of fifty-one rhymes, which, it must be said, are considered poor in terms of literary style. The book is dedicated to its readers: the little girls and boys "with wondering eyes."

Although the verses may not excite in terms of content, the accompanying illustrations are crisp and beautiful. In "First Arrivals," three children—a boy and two girls—are painted sitting demurely on a red sofa in their best silk clothes and sashes, clearly influenced by the portraits of Reynolds and Gainsborough. Greenaway often uses the page in an imaginative way. For example, in "The Wedding Bells," in which six young girls climb up and down stairs surrounding the verse, and the child at the end of the line peeks out at the viewer. In "The Cats Have Come to Tea," thirteen cats appear from all directions, as decorative elements regardless of perspective, and the little girl wonders what she will feed them, "Dear me—oh, dear me / All the cats had come to tea." **WO**

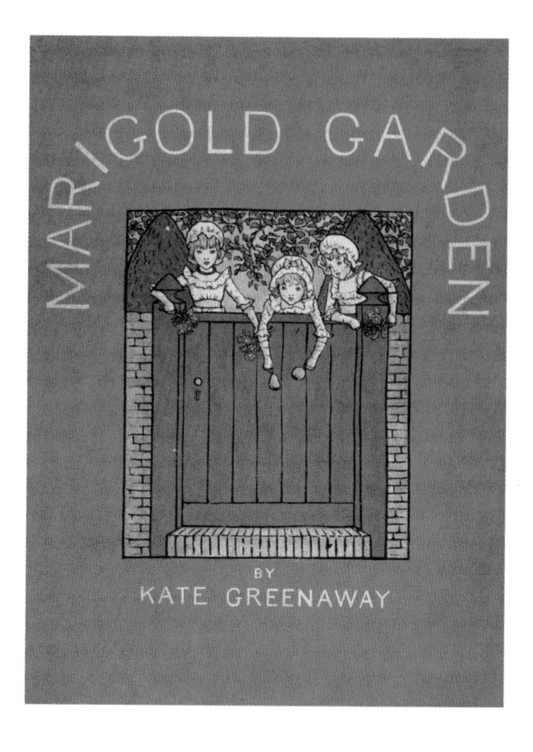

"Dancing and prancing to town we go, On the top of the wall of the town we go."

OTHER GREAT KATE GREENAWAY READS

***Under the Window*, 1879**
***Mother Goose or The Old Nursery Rhymes*, 1881**
***The Language of the Flowers*, 1884**
***A Day in a Child's Life*, 1881**

Die lustige Tante.
Ein komisches
Verwandlungsbilderbuch
von
L. Meggendorfer.

The Jolly Aunt 1891

Lothar Meggendorfer

Original Title | Die Lustige Tante
Nationality | German, born 1847
Publisher | Schreiber, Germany
Theme | Design classics

German-born Lothar Meggendorfer was a well-known illustrator and painter at the turn of the nineteenth century. He is often considered to be the inventor of pop-up books, even though examples of this popular book design had been around since the mid-nineteenth century. Nevertheless, he played a significant role in the history of "movable" books and developed increasingly elaborate techniques, using levers, rivets, and wires, to make the pop-ups more appealing. Many modern creators of pop-up books (paper engineers) think of Meggendorfer as the founder of their art, and his sophisticated works fetch very high prices in the antiquarian book trade.

However, the appeal of Meggendorfer's books does not merely lie in their detailed pop-ups—he is also renowned for his witty text and humorous drawings, which add an entirely new dimension to his charming characters. Unlike the works of numerous paper engineers, his pop-up scenes depict diverse and quite complex settings, such as circuses, parks, and dollhouses.

Meggendorfer's unique approach to book design even survives in the new edition of *The Jolly Aunt* (2007). Although his complex technique is simplified nowadays—each page split into three interchangeably movable pieces—the new edition still exudes Meggendorfer's exceptional wit and keen eye for detail, making this an entertaining, wordless picture book for the whole family. **GS**

Peter in Blueberry Land 1901

Elsa Beskow

Original Title | Puttes äventyr i blåbärsskogen
Nationality | Swedish, born 1874
Publisher | Bonnier Carlsen, Sweden
Theme | Magical stories, Fantasy

Elsa Beskow is recognized as the first author to have successfully introduced Swedish children's books to the rest of the world. *Peter in Blueberry Land* was one of her most popular early books. It tells the story of a little boy called Peter, who goes to the forest to pick berries as a gift for his mother on her name day (a European and Latin American tradition in which each day of the year is associated with certain first names). Unfortunately Peter is unable to find any berries, so he sits down on a stump and starts to cry.

Suddenly, a strange figure appears in front of the crying child. It is the king of Blueberry Land who proclaims, "I'm the king of Blueberry Land and I'll show you where they grow." The king takes Peter—and the reader—on a wonderful adventure through his beautiful kingdom. Peter gets to meet all the berry children and, with their help, he manages to harvest blueberries and lingonberries as big as apples. When little Peter wakes to find himself sitting on the stump again, he thinks it must have been a dream—until he sees his basket full to the brim with berries.

Beskow's books are characterized by their distinctive illustrations and rhyming text. Although more than a century old, the story is far from stuffy and dull, evidenced by the fact that *Peter in Blueberry Land* has been translated into fourteen languages and is available in new mini-editions. Beskow's creativity seems endless when it comes to exploring a fantasy world set in familiar natural surroundings. **CC**

The Tale of Peter Rabbit 1902

Beatrix Potter

3+

Nationality | English, born 1866
Publisher | Frederick Warne, UK
Theme | Favorite characters, Classics, Animal stories

Forget cute cartoons and furry bunnies. Eccentrically charming as her drawings of frogs in galoshes and hedgehog washerwomen are, Beatrix Potter's tales of the English countryside are full of dark doings and acidic comments. Potter, a keen botanist and mycologist, who made important contributions to the natural sciences of her day, drew all her animal characters and their country settings from life—although she did add clothes. She was also an unsentimental chronicler of nature "red in tooth and claw." The foolish Jemima Puddleduck lured by the "foxy gentleman," the devil-may-care Tom Kitten rolled up in a roly-poly pudding by the ever-hungry rat Samuel Whiskers and his wife Anna Maria, the unpleasant fight between Brock the badger and Tod the fox—these events are no less savage for being expressed in impeccably polite and precise prose.

The Tale of Peter Rabbit is her first book and one of her best. Peter is a mischievous rabbit in a blue coat with bright brass buttons. He does not heed his mother's injunction to stay away from the McGregor garden ("Your father had an accident there; he was put in a pie by Mrs. McGregor.") The produce is just too tempting. When Peter sneezes, Mr. McGregor is after him in a flash. There is an exciting chase from the watering can through the potting shed and along the onions, avoiding a cat and being misdirected by a mouse. Peter gets tired and cries, before finally making a dash for freedom. At home under the tree, old Mrs. Rabbit puts Peter to bed with camomile tea, but his sisters Flopsy, Mopsy, and Cottontail have bread, milk, and blackberries for supper. A keen gardener, Potter's feelings for rabbits may have been ambiguous. The book, however, is suffused with delight in nature and a humorous appreciation of its constant conflicts, exquisitely illustrated in watercolors. **VN**

OTHER CLASSIC BEATRIX POTTER TALES

***The Tale of Squirrel Nutkin*, 1903**
***The Tailor of Gloucester*, 1903**
***The Tale of Benjamin Bunny*, 1904**
***The Tale of Mrs. Tiggy-Winkle*, 1905**
***The Tale of Jemima Puddle-Duck*, 1908**

The Tale of Mr. Jeremy Fisher 1906

Beatrix Potter

Jeremy Fisher is a brown frog who lives in "a little damp house amongst the buttercups at the edge of a pond." Deciding one rainy day to go on a fishing trip to stock up on minnows for that night's dinner, he dons galoshes and a mackintosh, and sets sail on a large lily leaf.

His only catch after a long, wet wait is a stickleback, covered with dangerously sharp spines. Worse is to come when Jeremy is suddenly gobbled up by an enormous trout, who only spits him out because it dislikes the taste of Jeremy's fawn-colored mackintosh. Losing his rod, basket, and one of his galoshes, Jeremy makes his escape. He soon recovers his contented nature and goes ahead that evening

"Mr. Jeremy liked getting his feet wet; nobody ever scolded him, and he never caught a cold!"

with entertaining his old friends, the lizard Sir Isaac Newton and Mr. Alderman Ptolemy Tortoise. That night for dinner, "instead of a nice dish of minnows—they had a roasted grasshopper with lady-bird sauce; which frogs consider a beautiful treat; but I think it must have been nasty!"

Beatrix Potter loved frogs, often including them in the picture-letters she sent to young friends and producing a series of black-and-white frog drawings published in a children's annual in 1902. *The Tale of Mr. Jeremy Fisher* was written and illustrated the year after the sudden death of Potter's much-loved fiancé, Norman Warne, a member of the publishing firm that produced her books. Containing some of her most beautiful and closely detailed paintings, this book is clearly a labor of love, both for the natural world and possibly for the memory of the man she lost. **NT**

Nationality | English, born 1866
Publisher | Frederick Warne, UK
Theme | Favorite characters, Classics, Animal stories

3+

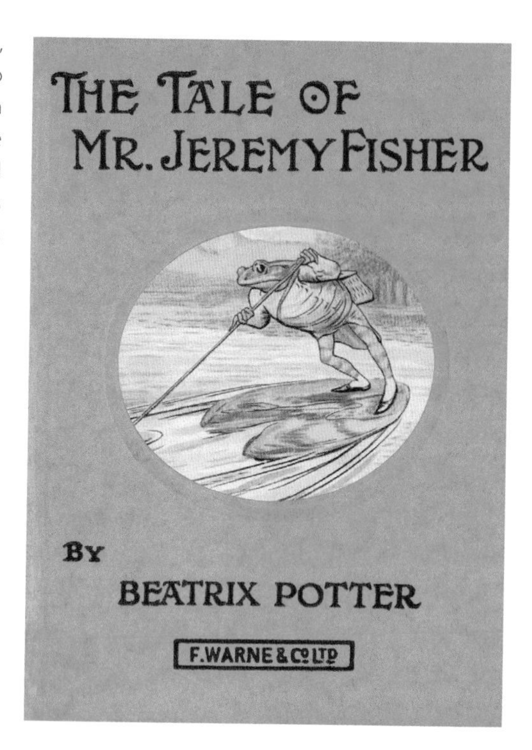

OTHER CLASSIC BEATRIX POTTER TALES

***The Tale of Two Bad Mice*, 1904**
***The Tale of Tom Kitten*, 1907**
***The Tale of Samuel Whiskers*, 1908**
***The Tale of Mr. Tod*, 1912**
***The Tale of Pigling Bland*, 1913**

The Story of the Root Children 1906

Sibylle von Olfers

3+

"Now go to bed, my little dear, and stay asleep until next year."

OTHER GREAT SIBYLLE VON OLFERS READS

What Marilenchen Saw, 1905
Mother Earth and Her Children: A Quilted Fairy Tale, 1906
The Princess in the Forest, 1909
The Story of the Wind Children, 1910

Original Title | Etwas von den Wurzelkindern
Nationality | German, born 1881
Publisher | Schreiber, Germany
Theme | Fantasy, Adventure

The Root Children are humanoid weeds and flowers who sprout and bloom in springtime and live in close proximity to beetles and insects. The dwarf- and elflike creatures, with their round baby faces and brown-hooded coats, are depicted in elegant, romantic full-page illustrations as the different seasons unfold and affect the Root Children's hidden microcosm.

The story starts in spring, when the sleeping plants are roused by Mother Earth, and the girls sort out their wardrobes while the boys paint the beetles in the workshop. Summer arrives and they all penetrate the Earth's surface as the shoots grow upward. They play in the green landscape, of which they are, in fact, a part, swim in the clear water, and cavort under the blue skies. In the autumn, they happily return home to Mother Earth, who puts them to bed during winter. The Root Children are characterized by their cheery eagerness to do whatever nature requires of them, thus conveying a reassuring sense of life's simplicity.

Like her predecessors, Swiss illustrator Ernst Kreidolf and Swedish author and illustrator Elsa Beskow, Sibylle von Olfers uses anthropomorphic characters, although hers are more simplistic. In older editions of this book, the images are framed, in keeping with the art nouveau design fashionable during the author's lifetime. The recent revival of this style, as well as the colorful, naturelike depictions of the world and the short verses accompanying them, may account for the book's enduring appeal. **CS**

The Tale of Jemima Puddle-Duck 1908

Beatrix Potter

Nationality | English, born 1866
Publisher | Frederick Warne, UK
Theme | Favorite characters, Classics, Animal stories

Putting on her best poke bonnet and shawl, Jemima Puddle-duck decides to quit the farm where she lives in order to find a safe nesting place for her batch of eggs, which are due at any moment. A smooth-tongued fox who she meets on the way directs her to a dismal-looking but comfortable shed, where she can lay her eggs in peace. Once the eggs are laid, Jemima tells him that she will start to sit on them, but the fox suggests that they first have a dinner party and directs her to bring back some sage and onions. Little realizing that she is to be the main course, Jemima is rescued at the last minute by Kep, the farm dog, accompanied by his puppies who gobble up the precious eggs in all the excitement. Jemima is escorted home in tears, but she does eventually manage to hatch four more eggs that same summer.

Beatrix Potter was well versed in fairy tales, and there are touches of "Little Red Riding Hood" in this story of innocence in which the protagonist is at risk from an unscrupulous predator. But the tale Potter tells here is affectionate rather than moralistic and firmly rooted in her own experience. Kep is taken from her favorite sheepdog, and she also included her farm manager's wife, seen here feeding the poultry. Jemima herself was copied from one of the author's own ducks, popular with everyone for her naive sense of self-importance. This story also contains many delightful views of the Lake District village of Sawrey, Beatrix Potter's home for thirty years. **NT**

The Children of the Forest 1910

Elsa Beskow

Original Title | Tomtebobarnen
Nationality | Swedish, born 1874
Publisher | Albert Bonniers, Sweden
Theme | Fantasy, Science and nature

Nature always plays an integral and dominating part in Elsa Beskow's books. In these tales, set deep in a forest, the acorns, wild mushrooms, flowers, and blueberries all spring to life. The children in the story find Beskow's forests inhabited by insects and animals, elves, gnomes, and not-so-scary trolls. In this skillfully and beautifully illustrated work, the reader finds very realistic detail combined with freely flowing imagination. Beskow said of children finding familiarity in her motifs: "There is something blessed about children, and that is that they always come to meet you half way. If one didn't know that, one wouldn't dare to present what one's got."

In *The Children of the Forest* we meet the small family of forest people. It is made up of mother gnome, father gnome, and their four children—Tom, Harriet, Sam, and Daisy—who live in the roots of a gnarled old pine tree. We join the little family in their joys and challenges in the forest through the different seasons of the year. We are invited to share in their adventures that take place among all the creatures of Beskow's soul-filled natural world.

Beskow is one of Sweden's best-known children's authors and illustrators, and comparisons have been drawn with Beatrix Potter. The original Beskow story was written in rhyme, whereas the English translation has not kept faithful to the original text. Seek out the earlier bigger format, because the later smaller edition does not do this beautiful book justice. **CC**

Clever Bill 1926

William Nicholson

Nationality | English, born 1872
Publisher | Heinemann, UK
Award | Olympic Gold, Graphic Art, 1928
Theme | Friendship

Young Mary, packing her suitcase for a visit to her aunt in Dover, forgets at the last moment to include her beloved toy bandsman Bill Davis. However, after a brief bout of tears, this resourceful cymbal-playing guardsman is determined not to be left behind. He runs after Mary's train and continues to run so fast that he finally gets to Dover at the same time as Mary. Overjoyed to see him, Mary reaches down from the train window to retrieve her prized possession. Clever Bill, indeed.

Sir William Nicholson was an influential artist of his time who brought a fresh look to illustration. This famous picture book has all the appearance of spontaneous work done for fun but in fact shows complete artistic mastery throughout. Heavy black lines frame each picture, with captions in thick handwriting running along the bottom of every page. Illustrations of old-fashioned toys, children's clothes, steam trains, dolls, musical instruments, and hats all give a powerful impression of a world long gone but still fascinating to revisit.

The front- and endpapers show a horse first resting in a field and then pulling a mail cart bearing the artist's initials "W. N." By its side are two parcels, each addressed to one of the artist's own children by way of a joint dedication. Such details give this charming book a genuinely personal feeling, as if readers are dropping in on a family game. The back cover shows Mary heartily embracing her temporarily lost toy; young readers may well feel like doing the same thing at the end of this delightful story. **NT**

Winnie-the-Pooh 1926

A. A. Milne E. H. Shepard

Nationality | English, born 1882 (author); English, born 1879 (illustrator)
Publisher | Methuen, UK
Theme | Favorite characters

Is there anyone who does not know *Winnie-the-Pooh*? The adventures of a small round teddy bear and his friends have long been standard fare for young children. Pooh, as he is known for short, is a benign bumbler, loved by his owner Christopher Robin and his friends: the toy pig Piglet and toy donkey Eeyore. Pooh's mild adventures include trips to the honey bees, getting stuck in a hole, trying to catch the legendary Heffalump or Woozle, and mounting an abortive expedition ("expotition") to the Hundred-Acre Wood. Piglet tries desperately hard, Eeyore gloomily gives up, ponderous Owl and bossy Rabbit, who has so many friends and relations, play supporting parts, later joined by motherly Kanga and her squeaky son Roo, the stuffed kangaroos. The sequel, *The House at Pooh Corner,* introduces Tigger, an insufferably bouncy stuffed tiger.

Milne's continued and overwhelming popularity rests on his merry humor and witty turns of phrase, exemplified in Pooh's summary of Rabbit. "'Rabbit's clever. And he has Brain.' 'Yes,' said Piglet, 'Rabbit has Brain.' There was a long silence. 'I suppose,' said Pooh, 'that that's why he never understands anything.'"

The cast of furry characters, originally invented by Milne's wife, pokes gentle fun at human attributes. Pessimist Eeyore, for example, on his birthday gloomily remarks, "'One can't complain. I have my friends. Someone spoke to me only yesterday.'" Yet the fun always leaves readers with a warm cozy feeling, even those who, like nervous Piglet, think of themselves as a Very Small Animal. **VN**

Pooh and Piglet go hunting and nearly catch a Woozle, by E. H. Shepard.

The Story of Babar 1931

Jean de Brunhoff

Original Title | Histoire de Babar le petit éléphant
Nationality | French, born 1899
Publisher | Le Jardin des Modes, France
Theme | Favorite characters, Classics

The Story of Babar the Little Elephant begins with Babar's childhood in the forest. When his mother is killed, Babar runs away to the city. There he is befriended by an old lady, who clothes and educates him. Babar is beginning to miss the forest when his cousins, Arthur and Celeste, turn up. Babar introduces them to the wonders of city life, buying them clothes and taking them out for cakes before their mothers turn up to scold them for running off. All the elephants return to the forest, where Babar marries Celeste and becomes king.

When Babar first appeared in 1931, no picture book like this had ever been seen before. The first edition was larger than most picture books, with hand-lettered text in varying sizes winding around lithographed pictures. The layout varies from spread to spread—some spreads feature lots of small pictures that move the action on, whereas others are filled with detailed scenes that children can pore over. Other pages have a single arresting image that stops the action altogether, such as the sepia photograph of Babar and the marvelous black-and-white wedding night scene. Occasionally there are sequences, such as the scene of Babar traveling up and down in the elevator, which even now take a degree of visual sophistication for a child to understand, and in 1931 must have seemed quite radical. Why are there three Babars? Is he in two different elevators?

The author died of tuberculosis at the age of thirty-seven, having written seven Babar books. His son, Laurent de Brunhoff (born 1925), continued the series; however, these books fail to live up to his father's. Since its first publication, Babar has been regarded as a picture book masterpiece. It prompted A. A. Milne to exclaim: "I salute M. de Brunhoff. I am at his feet." Today Babar remains an inspiration to creators of picture books around the world. **CW**

OTHER GREAT BABAR BOOKS

***Babar's Voyage (Le voyage de Babar),* 1932**
***Babar the King (Le Roi Babar),* 1933**
***Babar's ABC (L'ABC de Babar),* 1933**

The animals of the forest all attend Babar and Celeste's wedding.

The Story About Ping 1933

Marjorie Flack   Kurt Wiese

3+

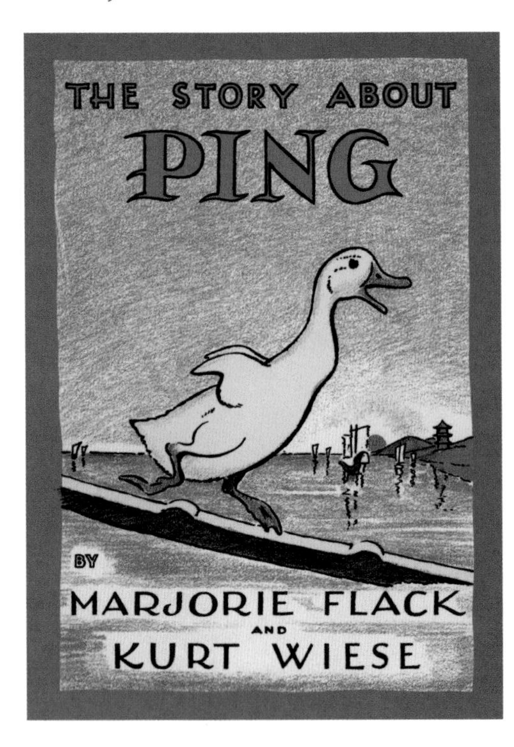

"Ping did not hear the call because Ping was wrong side up trying to catch a little fish."

OTHER GREAT MARJORIE FLACK READS

***Angus and the Ducks*, 1930**
***Angus and the Cat*, 1931**
***Angus Lost*, 1932**

Nationality | American, born 1897 (author); German, born 1887 (illustrator)
Publisher | Viking Press, USA
Theme | Adventure, Family, Animal stories

The Story About Ping focuses on the reassuring warmth of family life and the lonely excitement of adventuring outside it. Ping is a beautiful yellow duck who lives with "his mother and his father and two sisters and three brothers and eleven aunts and seven uncles and forty-two cousins" on "a boat with two wise eyes on the Yangtze river." Every day the ducks go fishing, and at the end of the day they are counted back onto the boat. "Ping was always careful, very very careful not to be last, because the last duck to cross the bridge always got a spank on the back." The story tells of how Ping becomes separated from his family when he chooses to hide on the riverbank rather than suffer a spank for being last on the boat. In his search for his family the next day, Ping watches various people going about their daily business on the river, and eventually, through the kindness of a little boy, he narrowly escapes becoming dinner for the boy's family and finds his way back to his own family.

Marjorie Flack's story is satisfying to read aloud, full of rhythm and repetition, and the sights and sounds of the Yangtze. Kurt Wiese was a prolific illustrator and spent time in China as a young man. Winning critical recognition at the time, his depiction of Chinese life has since been criticized for racial stereotyping. However, he tells *The Story About Ping* with affection and gentle humor. His pictures use the newly available lithographic techniques to bring to life the colors of the ducks, people, river, and riverbank. **CB**

Blinky Bill 1933

Dorothy Wall

Full Title | Blinky Bill: The Quaint Little Australian
Nationality | New Zealander, born 1894
Publisher | Angus and Robertson, Australia
Theme | Adventure, Animal stories

Do not be fooled by Blinky Bill's innocent appearance—this furry marsupial gets himself into a lot of trouble. He first appeared in 1933 in a work subtitled *The Quaint Little Australian*, which together with *Blinky Bill Grows Up* and *Blinky Bill and Nutsy* make up the *Complete Adventures of Blinky Bill*.

The inspiration for the stories came from the escapades of the author's son, to whom the book is dedicated. Dorothy Wall was a great lover of bush creatures, graphically arguing for their protection in her books. Set in the bush and populated with native animals, these works echo the spirit of nationalism prevalent in Australia between the wars. Mischievous Blinky himself could be said to personify qualities associated with the Aussie "digger": irrepressible, with a certain reckless indifference to danger and authority. Nevertheless, the bear is endearingly cute, and Blinky's exploits have struck a chord with children and parents over many years.

The collection follows Blinky Bill's boyhood, his age amusingly reflected by the length of his pants: first shorts, then knickerbockers, and finally full-length dungarees. The black-and-white illustrations of the original books have been supplemented with full-page color illustrations, and in the last book a girl koala named Nutsy and a kangaroo called Splodge make an appearance. With the same unquenchable spirit as her character, Dorothy Wall made her living as an artist and illustrator. **SM**

The Story of Ferdinand 1936

Munro Leaf Robert Lawson

Nationality | American, born 1905 (author); American, born 1892 (illustrator)
Publisher | Viking Press, USA
Theme | Adventure, Animal stories

Ferdinand the Bull is funny and thought provoking. Ferdinand ignores the rough butting and kicking of the other young bulls and likes nothing better than to laze under a cork tree, smelling the flowers. When some men from Madrid come looking for fierce bulls to fight in the bullring, however, Ferdinand is stung by a bee, and his antics convince the men that he is the fiercest bull of all. Once in the bullring, though, Ferdinand settles down comfortably and drifts off on the scent of the flowers on the ladies' hats. He refuses to be provoked into a fight, which drives the matador to tears and tantrums, and so is sent back home where he is happy once more beneath his tree.

The illustrations are on single pages and in black and white. The images, the use of space, and the relationship between the words and pictures are clever and immensely satisfying. The cork tree has bunches of wine corks hanging from its branches, for example, and the bullfighters are hilariously preening and shambolic. The Banderilleros enter bumping into each other and arguing, and the proud Picadores have broken lances and exhausted horses.

Amid the fun, the book implicitly poses questions about the way humans use animals, and about the way men and boys (and bulls) are expected to behave. It is perhaps no accident that the book appeared at the same time as Ernest Hemingway's adult novels were extolling the bullfight as the epitome of male adventure and courage. **CB**

Orlando 1938

Kathleen Hale

Series Title | Orlando the Marmalade Cat
Nationality | English, born 1898
Publisher | Country Life, UK
Theme | Animal stories

Orlando, the masterful marmalade cat (later described by his creator as "unbearably smug") first stalked onto the page in 1938 and continued to make new appearances until 1972. Each of the stories has just enough edge to entertain the adult reader while being friendly enough to amuse a small child. The graphics owe their wonderful use of comic detail and bold color to Kathleen Hale's training as an artist and her skill with lithographs. She made the 128 plates for every Orlando book herself. The character of Orlando was based on Hale's husband, whom she loved but found boring, whereas she saw herself as the naughty kitten Tinkle, who aspired to be like the long-suffering but gracious tabby cat Grace. The incidents in the books are based on the author's life: a seaside holiday in Suffolk and summers spent outside drawing wildlife.

Verbal jokes abound: Tinkle wonders if a pair of antlers are the horns of the dilemma about which he has heard grown-ups speak; Orlando says that the language sheepdogs understand best is "doggerel," so Tinkle writes a couple of verses. The cats enjoy home life like the middle classes of the 1930s: celebrating silver weddings and taking trips abroad.

The illustrations are the true glory of the series, packed with details such as frogs and newts crawling in the margins or a horse leaving his four horseshoes outside to be cleaned. A world full of the innocent ploys of domestic animals is very comforting: strange that Hale's own life was full of intrigue and drama. Perhaps that is why Orlando is so compelling, with his "eyes like electric green gooseberries." **VN**

Little Toot 1939

Hardie Gramatky

Nationality | American, born 1907
Publisher | G. P. Putnam's Sons, USA
Award | Lewis Carroll Shelf Award, 1969
Theme | Favorite characters, Adventure

One of the most common themes in all literature, from myths and legends to contemporary novels, is that of the unlikely hero who unexpectedly performs a heroic act. Their actions take center stage, and they finally get the respect that they deserved all along. This theme is also very popular in children's literature, and millions of children have cheered on the perky little tugboat, Little Toot, as he learns to conquer his fears and save the day.

Little Toot is a sturdy tugboat who loves chugging up and down the river. His toot may be tiny and insignificant, but he can blow out enormous clouds of steamy smoke. Toot has a secret however: He is afraid to leave the relatively calm river to work with his fellow boats on the rough ocean waters. The other tugboats do not think that this is fair and complain that Little Toot is always in their way when they are trying to work. Worse still, they tease him and call him a sissy.

One stormy day, when a steamship is stuck in the harbor, Little Toot summons together all his courage to venture where he fears most because only his huge smoke clouds can help in this particular rescue. Little Toot overcomes his fears and childish ways and becomes the hero of the day. Hardie Gramatky was inspired to write this story when he saw a tugboat that was in difficulties in New York's East River. He painted several watercolors of the incident and then wrote the story of *Little Toot* to accompany the illustrations. This timeless tale is sure to remain a family favorite for many more generations. **KD**

LITTLE TOOT

HARDIE GRAMATKY

Madeline 1939

Ludwig Bemelmans

Nationality | Austrian/American, born 1898
Publisher | Simon and Schuster, USA
Award | Caldecott Honor Book, 1940
Theme | Favorite characters, Classics, School

OTHER GREAT MADELINE TITLES

***Madeline's Rescue*, 1953**
***Madeline and the Bad Hat*, 1956**
***Madeline and the Gypsies*, 1959**
***Madeline in London*, 1961**
***Madeline's Christmas*, 1985**

When I was small my mother took me to the public library in Elizabeth, New Jersey, where I would sit on the floor and browse among the books. I not only liked the pictures and the stories but the feel and the smell of the books themselves. It was here that I discovered *Madeline* by Ludwig Bemelmans. I loved that book! I loved it so much that I hid it in my kitchen toy drawer so my mother would not be able to return it to the library. Even after several overdue notices came, I didn't tell my mother where the book was. If only I had asked, I am sure she would have bought me my own copy but I didn't know that was a possibility then. I thought the copy I had hidden was the only copy in the whole world. I knew it was wrong to hide the book but there was no way I was going to part with Madeline.

"'Good night, little girls! Thank the lord you are well! And now go to sleep!' said Miss Clavel."

Bemelmans used the same lines to open each of the Madeline books: "In an old house in Paris, that was covered with vines, lived twelve little girls in two straight lines." Madeline may be the smallest of the girls, but she is also the bravest. Like Madeline, I was the smallest in my class. But Madeline was not afraid of anything and I was afraid of everything! Oh, how I wished I could be as brave as my literary heroine. I memorized the words in the book and although I couldn't really read I pretended that I could.

Many years have passed since I hid that copy of *Madeline* but I can still recite the story by heart. And when my daughter was born *Madeline* was the first book I bought for her. Some books you never forget. Some characters become your friends for life.

The girls brushed their teeth and went to bed.

3+

Mike Mulligan 1939

Virginia Lee Burton

Full Title | Mike Mulligan and His Steam Shovel
Nationality | American, born 1909
Publisher | Houghton Mifflin, USA
Theme | Friendship, Adventure

Mike Mulligan and His Steam Shovel is as beloved today as it was when it was first published. It is Virginia Lee Burton's best-known work, and she wrote the book for her two young sons who, like children everywhere, then and now, were fascinated by machines and mechanical transportation. Burton's books are known for their determined characters, happy endings, and wonderful illustrations.

The story deals with the concept of whether or not progress creates obsolescence; but in simple terms that a child can understand. Construction worker Mike and his reliable steam shovel, Mary Anne, work together on important building jobs. They dig deep canals for boats to travel along, they cut vast tunnels through mountains for trains, and they hollow out foundations for huge city skyscrapers. But with industrial progress comes new machinery—gasoline, diesel, and electric shovels—and soon the partners are out of work. Mike sets out to prove that he and Mary Anne can outperform the new machines. This story of friendship, working together for a common goal, and the belief that together Mike and Mary Anne can do anything reinforces the concepts of loyalty, determination, and not giving up on what you believe in.

The illustrations are remarkable, all the more so because they were created with the same sort of wax crayons that children find in their crayon boxes today. However, it is the ingenious plot and clever ending that holds the reader's attention and keeps children coming back for more. **KD**

Curious George 1941

Margret Rey H. A. Rey

Nationality | German, born 1906 (author); German, born 1898 (illustrator)
Publisher | Houghton Mifflin, USA
Theme | Favorite characters, Adventure

H. A. Rey and his wife Margret were born in Hamburg and left Europe to escape Nazi persecution in 1940. They eventually reached the United States, with the manuscript of *Curious George*. The little monkey was an instant hit, appearing in a series of books.

George (originally known as Zozo in the United Kingdom) does not intend to be mischievous; but, like a lively child, his curiosity and his eagerness to imitate get him into scrape after scrape. In this first book, his fascination with a big yellow hat leads to him being captured by the man who wears it and taken to "a big zoo in a big city." A series of misadventures follows. George, trying to fly high in the sky like a seagull, falls into the sea and has to be rescued. In the city, he randomly dials on the telephone and calls up the emergency services and, as a consequence of his hoax, is thrown into jail. During his escape, he is carried over the city by a bunch of balloons, causing traffic chaos, only to be rescued by his original captor, "the man with the big yellow hat," who sees him safely to the zoo.

H. A. Rey's colorful cartoon-style illustrations make the most of the excitement, knockabout humor, and occasional pathos in Margret's story, with clever little touches: George using a pile of books on his chair to be able to sit at the table and George helpless and clumsy in a pair of oversize pajamas. Even at the worst moments, George's eyes are wide with wonder and his mouth open in amazement, and in this and every subsequent book, the man with the big yellow hat is there to look after him. **CB**

Curious George flies high above the city with a bunch of balloons. 

Rey
5

3+

The Little House 1942

Virginia Lee Burton

Nationality | American, born 1909
Publisher | Houghton Mifflin, USA
Award | Caldecott Medal, 1943
Theme | Family

This magical picture book shows what happens to a small house originally built by nineteenth-century settlers in the American countryside. To start with, the Little House simply watches the seasons change while its owners' children variously play in the brook, swim in the pool, and skate during the winter. But eventually things change, with the children growing up and moving to the nearby city. After that, new roads are built, suburbs encroach and finally the Little House is surrounded by buildings, with an elevated train running above it and a subway going back and forth underneath. Neglected and deserted, it is finally rescued by the great-great granddaughter of the man who originally built it. It is towed back to the countryside by a truck and can now make a new start on top of a pretty hill, watching the seasons changing once again in peace and quiet.

Virginia Lee Burton had a genius for endowing inanimate objects with human thoughts and feelings. She was also thoroughly at home with modern machinery and all the urban details of life in the big city. In this book, children can see historical change happening in front of them as rural landmarks gradually merge into new roads and railways, all teeming with people hurrying to their next appointment. Generously illustrated with glowing watercolors facing each page of text, this is a book to pore over long after its simple but touching story about the importance of preserving countryside values has been read and digested. **NT**

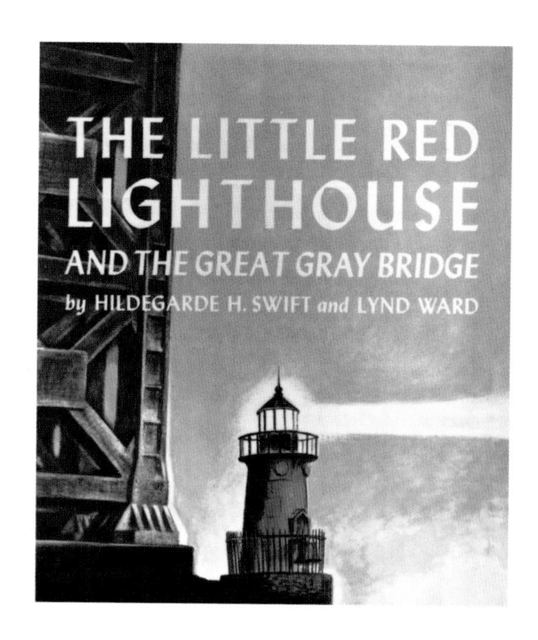

3+

The Little Red Lighthouse 1942

Hildegarde H. Swift Lynd Ward

Nationality | American, born 1890 (author); American, born 1905 (illustrator)
Publisher | Harcourt Brace, USA
Theme | Friendship

At the base of the great George Washington Bridge in New York City stands the little red lighthouse that was immortalized in Hildegard H. Swift's classic story, *The Little Red Lighthouse and the Great Gray Bridge*. Built as a navigational aid for sailors on the Hudson River, the lighthouse proudly guided boats of all types into the port of New York. In this delightful story, the Little Red Lighthouse is concerned that its important job might be redundant once the Great Gray Bridge is built above it.

The lighthouse feels small and insignificant and fears that it has outlived its usefulness; the bridge is so big and its flashing lights so bright that there no longer seems any need for an old-fashioned lighthouse. The bridge, however, knows better and kindly reassures the red lighthouse—"I call to the airplanes," cried the bridge, "I flash to the ships of the air. But you are still master of the river. Quick, let your light shine again. Each to his own place little brother."

Through a magical collaboration of imaginative storytelling and brilliant pictures, the author and illustrator aim to teach young children the timeless lesson that all things big or small have their rightful place in the world. The lesson is one that children need to learn over and over again, because they too sometimes feel small and unimportant. This touching story celebrates the close friendship and teamwork between the bridge and the lighthouse. Although no longer in operation, the red lighthouse can still be seen in New York City today. **KD**

TOVE JANSSON

boken om Mymlan, Mumintrollet och lilla My

HUR GICK DET SEN?

Moomin, Mymble and Little My 1952

Tove Jansson

Original Title | Hur gick det sen?
Nationality | Finnish, born 1914
Publisher | Gebers, Sweden
Theme | Favorite characters, Adventure

Ever since the Moomin family came into being in 1945, the adorable family of white trolls has fascinated people the world over. The round white faces and large noses make the characters appear like a friendly family of hippopotamuses. They live in a place called Moominland, where together they experience a whole series of captivating adventures, thanks to Tove Jansson's expansive imagination, which are brought to life by her charming illustrations.

This picture book is one of the most popular from the Moomin series, and it opens with Moomintroll taking milk back home to his mother, Moominmamma. On the way, he meets Mymble, who is searching for her missing sister, Little My. Together they decide to go looking for her. The story takes the form of rhyming poetry, and there are holes cut into the pages so that readers can get a sneak preview of what is to come on the next page. This also allows the author to play with the idea of the different characters asking if they can take the place of others in the story. Despite the bizarre and fantastic landscapes and situations (in this story there is a vacuum cleaner that swallows people), the Moomin adventures have many parallels that can be drawn with families in the real world, and their ups and downs are well observed by Jansson.

Ultimately all the Moomin stories are about love—love from family, friends, and the community that surrounds you. **NH**

My Naughty Little Sister 1952

Dorothy Edwards H. Garland

Nationality | English, born 1914 (author); details unknown (illustrator)
Publisher | Methuen, UK
Theme | Family, Favorite characters

There can be no more perfect rendering of the way a grown-up relates stories of childhood to a very young audience than those told in *My Naughty Little Sister*. You can almost hear the listener saying, "Tell me a story about when you were little" before the narrator begins: "When I was a little girl, and my naughty little sister was a very little girl . . ." The narrator draws the listener into the stories with questions and comments—"There, wasn't that bad of her? I'm glad you're not like that"—and the first-person narrative and the two sisters' lack of names give the stories a semblance of authenticity, as if the reader were really the older sister of the tales.

Originally written for the BBC radio program *Listen with Mother*, the stories are set in the 1930s, but nothing in them is very far from the experience of a small child today. No big events take place, just ordinary things that occur in every small child's life, such as amusement parks, wobbly teeth, and birthday parties. And the naughty little sister is not really so bad, just disobedient and thoughtless and stubborn, like many small children.

Although originally illustrated by Henrietta Garland, Shirley Hughes reillustrated the book, and her expressive drawings from the 1960s have become inseparable from *My Naughty Little Sister*. These are comfortable, funny stories to read aloud to very young children, possibly the first stories that are not picture books that will hold a toddler's attention. **CW**

Martine 1954

Gilbert Delahaye Marcel Marlier

Nationality | Belgian, born 1923 (author); Belgian, born 1930 (illustrator)
Publisher | Casterman, Belgium
Theme | Favorite characters, Adventure

Ever since poet Gilbert Delahaye first created *Martine à la Ferme* (*Martine at the Farm*) in 1954, the Martine books have been remembered by countless women as a key part of their childhood, and the series promises to be every bit as important for little girls who are discovering her now.

Martine is a perfect child: she is pretty, wise, humorous (her cat Minet and her dog Patapouf are the mischievous ones), and adventurous. Everybody loves her, and she loves everybody. Some critics found the character of Martine from the early albums to be too conservative and were reluctant to pass the books on to their little girls. However, the series has evolved over the years, adapting itself to new audiences. Children love Martine's moralistic adventures, which mirror the events of their everyday lives: whether learning to ride, experiencing the first day at school, running away from home, babysitting, losing the family cat, or moving homes. Little girls can easily identify with the character as well as enjoy her fantastic, magical escapades. The illustrations by Marcel Marlier are also fascinating and memorable, and no doubt readers will recall vividly some of the beautiful pictures, even once the plot of the story has been long forgotten.

Martine's fifty-one adventures have been translated into numerous languages: she has become Debbie in the United States, Martita in Spain, and Mimmi in Sweden. More than fifty million books about this popular heroine have been sold in France since her first appearance in 1954. **MGR**

Eloise 1955

Kay Thompson 

Nationality | American, born 1908 (author); American, born 1926 (illustrator)
Publisher | Simon and Schuster, USA
Theme | Adventure, Friendship

Author Kay Thompson was a singer, actress, and resident of the famous Plaza Hotel in New York City when she collaborated with a young, up-and-coming illustrator Hilary Knight to create the book *Eloise: A Book for Precocious Grown-ups*. It was published in 1955 and thus one of U.S. literature's most unique—or more appropriately legendary—heroines was born.

Six-year-old Eloise lives in the Plaza with her "rawther" British nanny, her dog Weenie who looks like a cat, and a turtle named Skiperdee who eats raisins and wears sneakers. Eloise has the run of the hotel, but she does not just run—she "skibbles, skitters, slomps, scampers, and sklonks" as well. Reading *Eloise* is not an adventure for the fainthearted; our heroine is indefatigable, breathless, and prone to repeating things three times for emphasis. The book is written with absolutely no punctuation, so remember to take a breath every now and then. The delightful story chronicles Eloise's adventures in the hotel, the people she meets, the things she does to amuse herself, and what life is like when you are just six years old.

This timeless classic is a riot of words, images, and verbal and visual jokes. The pages that fold out and open up help to perfectly encompass what it would be like for a very precocious child living in a very stuffy hotel. Every reader will want to be Eloise, or at least will think that they do, and for that matter so too will every one of those "Precocious Grown-ups" referred to in the full title. It is unlikely that anyone who reads *Eloise* will ever forget the character. **KD**

KAY
THOMPSON'S
ELOISE
DRAWINGS BY HILARY KNIGHT

Harry the Dirty Dog 1956

Gene Zion Margaret Bloy Graham

3+

Nationality | American, born 1913 (author); Canadian, born 1920 (illustrator)
Publisher | Harper and Brothers, USA
Theme | Favorite characters, Adventure

Gene Zion and his first wife, Caldecott Honor winner Margaret Bloy Graham, collaborated on many books, including the popular Harry the Dog books. Zion's stories and characters deal with some of the "universal" problems children encounter, while Graham's chalky sketches, re-released recently with more color, mesh perfectly. Young readers will identify with the characters' plights, as well as their zany humor.

As the book begins, Harry, a white dog with black spots, realizes that he is about to be given a bath. Harry likes just about everything, but he does not like baths at all. So he quickly steals the scrub brush, buries it in the backyard, and runs away from home before his owners can catch him and put him into the dreaded tub. Harry then proceeds to get really dirty, playing in the street and at the railroad, and dirtier still during a game of tag with the other dogs. Eventually he even slides down a coal chute, which changes him from a white dog with black spots to a black dog with white spots! After his wild adventures Harry returns home, but no one in the family recognizes him—not even when he does all his clever flip-flopping tricks. But clever Harry digs up the brush he buried, begs for a bath, and is restored to the white dog with black spots who his family knows and loves.

"Harry was a white dog with black spots who liked everything . . . except baths."

This is a perfect story for children who resist the necessity of bath time, especially after a day of playing outside. The antics of this wacky canine character will make children laugh and cheer, and maybe even make it easier to convince them to take a dip in the tub before bedtime. **KD**

OTHER GREAT HARRY BOOKS

Hide and Seek, 1954
Dear Garbage Man, 1957
No Roses for Harry, 1958
Harry and the Lady Next Door, 1960
Harry by the Sea, 1965

The Cat in the Hat 1957

 Dr. Seuss

3+

With just 223 rhyming words, Dr. Seuss cemented his enduring impact on early reading books in this tale of anarchy and order on a rainy afternoon. The eponymous Cat, behatted and bewhiskered, visits a boy slumped lonely and bored with his sister, Sally. The Cat does most of what the children are not allowed to do, with his sidekicks, Thing One and Thing Two. The family pet, a sensible and articulate goldfish, objects but to no avail, and is mocked by the Cat. Although the Cat is a kind of Lord of Misrule turning the children's dull, predictable lives upside down, he magically vacuums up all the mess just before Mom returns home.

Seuss was concerned at reports that children were not learning to read and figured that the stereotypical early reading books that were routinely inflicted on them in school were to blame. No one could ever call Seuss's work insipid and although adults can be reduced to distraction by the relentless rhyming, children seem never to tire of it. Nonetheless, Seuss has sold tens of millions of books in the English-speaking world and has convinced generations of young readers that books can be fun.

"The sun did not shine. It was too wet to play. So we sat in the house, all that cold wet day."

Some moralistic readers have seen the Cat as a force of evil. Seuss himself addresses this possibility with a final question: Should the children tell their mother what has been going on? If any reader does find the gleeful chaos disturbing, this is a perfect peg for a discussion on the rights and wrongs of respecting property. And there is always a mystery to ponder: How exactly does the Cat remove all evidence of his misdemeanors? **VN**

Nationality | American, born Theodor Seuss Geisel 1904
Publisher | Random House, USA
Theme | Favorite characters, Fantasy, Classics

OTHER GREAT DR. SEUSS STORIES

***Horton Hears a Who!*, 1954**
***How the Grinch Stole Christmas*, 1957**
***The Cat in the Hat Comes Back*, 1958**
***The Lorax*, 1971**
***Fox in Socks*, 1975**

The Cow Who Fell in the Canal 1957

Phyllis Krasilovsky Peter Spier

Nationality | American, born 1926 (author); American, born 1927 (illustrator)
Publisher | Doubleday, USA
Theme | Animal stories, Adventure

Krasilovsky and Spier conjure up a world of windmills, canals, horse-drawn carts, and cheese markets—a world that was fading away in the Netherlands even as they were re-creating it in this delightful book.

Hendrika the cow, tired of her life on Mr. Hofstra's farm, enjoys an accidental adventure. Grown fat on boredom, she falls into the canal, struggles into a convenient raft, and floats off to the big city, where she creates havoc by charging down the cobbled streets and through the cheese market, pursued by a cheering crowd. Luckily, Mr. Hofstra is there too, selling his cheeses, and he takes Hendrika home, where she quickly settles back into her quiet life, content now that she has seen something of the world.

This is a placid tale, with its pace set by the slow currents of the canal. Readers glide with Hendrika through the Dutch countryside: "Past the barn, the house and the windmill. Past the tulips." Then on through the city, with time to study the shops and houses with their distinctive "stair-cased roofs." Spier realizes these typical Dutch scenes in double-page spreads in pen and bright watercolor and alternates them with black-and-white drawings. There is detail and atmosphere in both the open spaces of the countryside and the hectic life of the city. Hendrika herself is at turns shy and boisterous; sometimes overawed by her adventure, sometimes reveling in the attention it brings her, seizing a cheese seller's green straw hat that "tasted just as good as she thought it would." **CB**

Hendrika the cow floats down the canal past the windmill. 

A Bear Called Paddington 1958

Michael Bond Peggy Fortnum

Nationality | English, born 1926 (author); English, born 1919 (illustrator)
Publisher | William Collins, UK
Theme | Favorite characters, Classics

The label read, "Please Look After This Bear. Thank You." Luckily, Mr. and Mrs. Brown found the stowaway bear at London's Paddington railway station and gave him not just a home but the name of the station. From there, it was a short step to the hearts of thirty-five million readers, who found his predilection for marmalade sandwiches and cocoa—coupled with a propensity for getting into scrapes—truly endearing.

Paddington, clad in Wellingtons and duffle coat, has stomped his way through numerous adventures and editions, and is memorialized in countless toys, not forgetting a bronze statue at Paddington station itself. Originally from Darkest Peru, Paddington finds gentle mischief in simple adventures, such as having a bath, going shopping, or making a trip to the theater or seaside. He is extremely polite and friendly, although if people get on the wrong side of him, he will give them his famous "hard stare," taught to him by his aunt Lucy before she entered the Home for Retired Bears in Lima. He does not mean to do wrong, as his friend Mr. Gruber understands, but mean neighbor Mr. Curry is less forgiving. Many of his mishaps involve food or showing off: stuffing bacon sandwiches in his suitcase and attracting dogs; getting sticky with cream buns; inadvertently becoming the star of a store window or a play. It is all quite familiar, cozy, and comical.

Paddington's enduring popularity is perhaps due to his resemblance to a human toddler. He messes up, but who could be angry with such a sweet bear? **VN**

3+

Little Blue and Little Yellow 1959

 Leo Lionni

Nationality | Dutch/American/Italian, born 1910
Publisher | Astor-Honor, USA
Theme | Friendship

In his first published book, Leo Lionni introduces the concept of color to his young audience through his characters, Little Blue and Little Yellow, so named for the colors they represent. These little blobs are best friends who live across the street from one another, sit next to each other in school, and love to play games. One day, after a long search for his friend, Little Blue finds Little Yellow and, overjoyed, they hug each other until their embrace merges them into one green blob. As a single blob, they enjoy a day of adventure, but when it is time to go home, their parents, not recognizing their children, turn them away. Luckily, Little Blue and Little Yellow manage to separate back into their original colors, and the whole situation is resolved.

This book is illustrated using Lionni's innovative use of torn-paper collage, an idea he came upon while entertaining his grandchildren on a long train ride. The artwork is deceptively simple, featuring vibrantly colored blobs on plain backgrounds, yet children are able to understand what is happening simply by looking at where the torn-paper protagonists are distributed on the page.

Lionni, whose father was Jewish, has denied that he created *Little Blue and Little Yellow* as a plea for racial integration. Yet, as well as educating young children about colors, the book does also teach children that it is unfair to judge others on their appearance, and that color proves to be no boundary. **CVB**

Green Eggs and Ham 1960

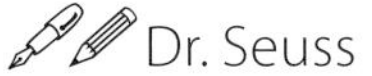 Dr. Seuss

Nationality | American, born Theodor Seuss Geisel 1904
Publisher | Random House, USA
Theme | Classics, Favorite characters

In this much-loved classic a grouchy, flop-eared, not-quite-human personage in a big hat, consistently rejects the attempts of a certain Sam-I-am to get him to try a dish of "green eggs and ham." Despite Sam-I-am coaxing him to try it out in a house, with a mouse, in a box, with a fox, with a goat, or on a boat, the grumpy one still refuses to taste this repellent-sounding meal. Sam-I-am triumphs when the narrator, standing in shallow water after a boat sinks, surrounded by various people and beasts, finally agrees to try the delicacy and satisfyingly enjoys it.

People have interpreted Seuss's bouncing rhyming tale as a fable to encourage children to try new things so that they can learn and develop. Certainly, there is room for discussion as to why the narrator refuses so often and so firmly: Could it be fear, pride, or a feeling of superiority? However, the delight of the book lies in Seuss's facility with rhyme and rhythm, his infectious enjoyment of the flexibility of the English language, and his bold sorties into nonsense situations and illustrations, which capture beginning readers.

Seuss figured that the sentimental books routinely inflicted on children failed to instill a love of reading. His own works attempt to branch out from the everyday See Spot Run variety—children seem never to tire of them. Whether this book will ever get anyone to try broccoli before they are ready is debatable, although true Seuss fans, of whom there are many, claim wisdom as well as whimsy for the author. **VN**

Green Eggs and Ham

By Dr. Seuss

Go, Dog. Go! 1961

P. D. Eastman

Nationality | American, born Philip Dey Eastman 1909
Publisher | Random House, USA
Theme | Classics, Rhyming stories

How many of you learned to read your first sight words with this charming, and now classic, beginner book? Eastman's brilliant use of simple one-syllable words—in rhythmic repetition and rhyme—along with the introduction of prepositions and colors, will put children confidently on the road to reading all by themselves.

The text may be simple, but the rhythm of the language when spoken by a child or read by a parent can in itself be endlessly entertaining. Add in the quirky illustrations of dogs in every size, shape, and color (even polka dots) in cars, on skis, on roller skates, on foot, wearing hats, and going in and out, and many a giggle is produced—all the while teaching children how to recognize and read simple words by sight. A disagreement about hats runs throughout, but is resolved at the end of this delightfully goofy book. It has been said that this book can be viewed as a microcosm of life: you have a diversity of dogs of every shape and color, and even a little romance between a big yellow dog and a preening pink poodle. That may be so, however, the real gift of the book is the simple ease that marries the pictures and words. With enough sounding out of words and reading them together with adults, children will be successfully reading in no time.

"Dog. Big dog. Little dog. . . .
Look at those dogs go.
Go, dogs. Go!"

A protegé of Dr. Seuss, P. D. Eastman worked as a screenwriter for Walt Disney and Warner Brothers Cartoons, as well as writing for the series *Mr. Magoo* before he turned his hand to creating his playful and distinctive books for children. **KD**

Go, Dog. Go!
I CAN READ IT ALL BY MYSELF
Beginner Books
by P.D.Eastman

OTHER GREAT P. D. EASTMAN READS

***Are You My Mother?*, 1960**
***Sam and the Firefly*, 1958**
***The Best Nest*, 1968**
***Big Dog, Little Dog*, 1969**

The Berenstain Bears 1962

Stan and Jan Berenstain

Original Title | The Big Honey Hunt
Nationality | American, born 1923 (both)
Publisher | Random House, USA
Theme | Favorite characters, Family, Classics

Stan and Jan Berenstain met at art school in 1941 and went on to write more than fifty books together. Their now-famous family of bears first appeared in *The Big Honey Hunt*, and the characters from this story are now known as the Berenstain Bears. In this book we meet Papa Bear, Mama Bear, and Small Bear (who, in the later books, becomes known as Brother Bear, after the birth of Sister Bear). They live in Bear County.

The story begins with an empty honey pot. Mama Bear asks Papa Bear and Small Bear to buy some honey at the honey store, which is opposite their house, but Papa Bear has another idea: "If a bear is smart, if a bear knows how, he goes on a honey hunt." He takes Small Bear with him and teaches him all about honey: what it looks like, tastes like, smells like, feels like, and where it comes from. Unfortunately Papa Bear's plan goes very wrong when they upset a swarm of bees and end up having to jump into a pond to escape them. In the end, Papa Bear has to swallow his pride and buy some honey from the store, as Mama Bear looks on with a smile.

"We ate our honey. We ate a lot. Now we have no honey. In our honey pot."

Today, parents love the Berenstain Bears' books for their help with practical problem-solving, such as children's fears of visiting the doctor. However, *The Big Honey Hunt* was a more simple story, part morality tale, part fun rhyme. The early illustrations are slightly different bears from those in the later books. Since Stan's death, Jan has written and illustrated the books with their son, Mike, which is appropriate as the authors were originally inspired to create their first book for their own children. **LH**

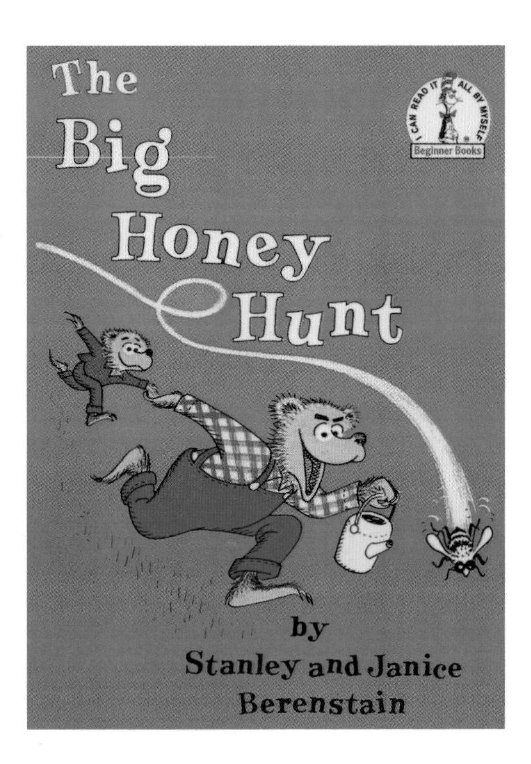

OTHER GREAT BERENSTAIN BEAR TITLES

The Berenstain Bears Go To School, 1978
The Berenstain Bears Go To the Doctor, 1981
The Berenstain Bears and Too Much TV, 1984
The Berenstain Bears on the Moon, 1985
The Berenstain Bears and the Bully, 1993

BY OLIVER POSTGATE

PICTURES BY PETER FIRMIN

Ivor the Engine 1962

Oliver Postgate Peter Firmin

Nationality | English, born 1925 (author); English, born 1928 (illustrator)
Publisher | Abelard-Schumann, UK
Theme | Favorite characters, Classics

This is the first in a series of children's picture books about Ivor, an idiosyncratic little green steam engine with a mind of his own. Ivor first appeared in 1959 on British television in ten-minute slots preceding the news. The popular series was written and narrated by Oliver Postgate (who also performed rudimentary sound effects such as Ivor's puffing) and Peter Firmin did the animations.

Ivor belongs to the fictitious Merioneth and Llantisilly Rail Traction Company Ltd., in "the top left-hand corner of Wales." In this story Ivor is unhappy although he has enough coal and enough water in his boiler, and it is up to his driver, Jones the Steam, and the stationmaster, Dai Station, to discover the problem. When they learn that Ivor wants to sing in the choir they take him to Evans the Song (the choirmaster) who is not impressed with Ivor's minor half-tone whistle. Mr. Jenkins the Builder takes them to see Mr. Morgan of Morgan's Amusements, who just happens to have an old steam organ that is surplus to requirements. Once Mog the Plumber has fixed the pipes, Ivor is accepted into the Grumbley and District Choral Society as a bass, and all is well with the world.

Oliver Postgate was strongly influenced by the Welsh poet Dylan Thomas (of *A Child's Christmas in Wales* fame), and his whimsical text is a joy to read and to hear. Peter Firmin's illustrations have a simple, timeless appeal. **WO**

Clifford the Big Red Dog 1963

Norman Bridwell

Nationality | American, born 1928
Publisher | Scholastic, USA
Theme | Favorite characters, Classics, Animal stories, Family, Friendship

The inhabitants of Birdwell Island find themselves having to quickly make room—a great deal of room—when eight-year-old Emily Elizabeth Howard and her gigantic puppy, Clifford, arrive at their new home on the island. Emily Elizabeth's love and dedication have transformed her pup from the forlorn runt of the litter into a gigantic, bounding, and happy member of the Howard family. Although Clifford's large size and zealous desire to do the right thing often get him into tricky situations, he usually manages to untangle himself, and in the process always learns something about sharing, cooperation, kindness, or respect.

Clifford was born when author Norman Bridwell decided to earn some extra income when his own daughter—Emily Elizabeth—was born. (The books include the dedication "For the real Emily Elizabeth.") He turned to his childhood love of drawing and, after suffering repeated rejections, landed on the winning combination of Emily and Clifford. The modest 1963 publication of *Clifford the Big Red Dog* has spawned a thriving industry of spin-offs, including the PBS television series, a movie, and Internet sites.

Mirroring Emily Elizabeth's disbelief as she watches her dog grow to more than 25 feet (7 m) tall, Clifford's enormous commercial success was crucial to the establishment of Scholastic Books as a top publishing company. The series teaches us one lesson above all—to never give up. **JSD**

Where the Wild Things Are 1963

Maurice Sendak

Nationality | American, born 1928
Publisher | Harper and Row, USA
Awards | Caldecott Medal, 1964
Theme | Classics, Fantasy

One of the truly great children's books, *Where the Wild Things Are* is instantly readable as well as profound. The story it tells is of an angry boy, Max, so angry that he says that he'll eat up his mother. For this, he is sent to his room with no supper. In his room a forest grows; Max gets himself a boat and sails away to a strange place "where the wild things are." These creatures—human, reptilian, dinosauroid—are both funny and horrific. Max can do three things with the wild things: tame them, have a wild "rumpus" with them, and leave them behind. On returning to his room, he finds that someone has left a meal for him, and it is still hot.

At one level this is a fable about anger and the struggle to control our demons. Lying at the heart of this, is a deep ambivalence about the person who loves you the most. What is staggering and beautiful about the book is that Sendak doesn't say that this is what it is about. Instead, he takes us on Max's journey of discovery. When Max is far away in the land of the wild things, he suddenly wants to be where he is loved the most. After about the fifteenth reading of the book to my then three-year-old son, his response to that phrase was "Mummy!" Nowhere in the book do we see "Mummy." We know that Max was horrible to his mother earlier in the book, but that is all.

Sendak has created a story that can draw out of a three-year-old an interpretation and a discovery. It is also a story that a child will learn and an adult can ponder alongside, letting us wonder about how we live and how best to love our children.

A costumed Max on his way to visit where the wild things are. ➔

Lyle, Lyle, Crocodile 1965

Bernard Waber

3+

Nationality | American, born 1924
Publisher | Houghton Mifflin, USA
Award | Lewis Carroll Shelf Award, 1979
Theme | Favorite characters, Animal stories

Under the heading of "the most unlikely things do actually happen in children's books," meet Lyle, a crocodile who lives in a town house (in the bathtub, of course) on East 88th Street in New York City. Bernard Waber's whimsical illustrations bring this large reptile lovingly, and not at all scarily, to life. Moreover, as is often the case in children's books, his living in a brownstone in New York City seems perfectly logical.

Lyle loves where he lives and the family he lives with: the Primms. Who wouldn't love having Lyle around? After all he helps Joshua with his homework, is willing to jump rope with the neighborhood kids, and even shops with Mrs. Primm; in other words, he is great company. However, sweet and harmless as Lyle is, he still manages to drive his neighbor's cat, Loretta, nuts, which in turn makes Mr. Grumps, Loretta's owner, even grumpier than usual.

"Mr. and Mrs. Primm and their son Joshua live in the house on East 88th Street. So does Lyle."

One day, when Mrs. Primm and Lyle are shopping, a customer rush to a sale in the pajama department causes Lyle to get separated from Mrs. Primm. The store manager is none other than Mr. Grumps, who—never having liked Lyle in the first place—has the lovable Lyle put in Central Park Zoo where he fights back his crocodile tears. After a few twists and turns of the plot, Lyle ends up back home. Waber's lively illustrations and witty text turn most readers into Lyle fans. This book in the Lyle Crocodile series is often the favorite, but once children have learned to love Lyle, they will be anxious to read all the books. **KD**

OTHER GREAT BOOKS ABOUT LYLE

The House on East 88th Street, 1962
Lovable Lyle, 1969
Nobody Is Perfick, 1971
Funny Funny Lyle, 1987

Brown Bear, Brown Bear, What Do You See? 1967

Bill Martin, Jr. Eric Carle

3+

When Bill Martin, Jr., the creator of the Instant Readers series, asked Eric Carle to illustrate his new book, children's books changed forever—for the better. *Brown Bear, Brown Bear, What Do You See?* has sold more than six million copies as a board book alone.

Martin has explained his love of rhyming language: "Reading was hard for me growing up and I didn't like it. But I had a teacher that read to my class every day and I loved stories. Then another teacher many years later introduced me to poetry and that changed everything." Eric Carle creates bright, colorful illustrations from a combination of collage, paint, textures, and tissue paper. As he once said, "Many children have done collages at home or in their classrooms. In fact, some children have said to me, 'Oh, I can do that.' I consider that the highest compliment."

"Purple Cat, Purple Cat, What do you see? I see a White Dog looking at me."

This book is a simple as can be. An animal sees another animal looking at him; turn the page and the next animal does exactly the same. Yet it is the rhythmic language and the incredibly vibrant art that catches the attention of preschoolers. "Brown Bear, Brown Bear, What do you see? I see a Red Bird looking at me." Young children love to anticipate the wonderful menagerie of animals as the pages turn, and quickly have them committed to memory. For toddlers and preschoolers, blue horses and purple cats only add to the fun—but fair warning to parents—the word you will most likely hear when you reach the end will be "Again!" **KD**

Nationality | American, born 1916 (author); American, born 1929 (illustrator)
Publisher | Holt, Rinehart and Winston, USA
Theme | Animal stories, Classics, Rhyming stories

Pictures by Eric Carle
Brown Bear, Brown Bear, What Do You See?
by Bill Martin, Jr.

OTHER GREAT READS IN THIS SERIES

***Polar Bear, Polar Bear, What Do You Hear?*, 1991**
***Panda Bear, Panda Bear, What Do You See?*, 2003**
***Baby Bear, Baby Bear, What Do You See?*, 2007**

What Does the Mouse Think on Thursday? 1967

Josef Guggenmos Günther Stiller

3+

Nationality | German, born 1922 (author); German, birth date unknown (illustrator)
Publisher | Georg Bitter, Germany
Theme | Poetry, Classics

OTHER GREAT GUGGENMOS RHYMES

Funny Verses for Little People (Lustige Verse für kleine Leute), 1956
Sun, Moon, and the Balloon (Sonne, Mond und Luftballoon), 1984

This collection of 121 poems for children (originally published as *Was denkt die Maus am Donnerstag?*) ensured Josef Guggenmos's popularity with both his young readership and the German critics. Today, along with Erich Kästner, he is one of Germany's most important children's authors.

His poems are characterized by his startling wit. What the mouse thinks about on Thursday turns out to be exactly the same as what he ponders on any other day of the week—sausage- and ham- sandwiches. This is vintage Guggenmos: His poems portray lively and charming characters and often end in surprising twists and turns. Most importantly, however, Guggenmos encourages his readers to think, raising surprising questions such as the relationship between a needle and thread. Not many children's poets manage to find the right balance between beautiful verse and meaningful content. Guggenmos, however, presents weighty subjects, such as accepting one's identity, in an engaging and thought-provoking way, with the mouse contemplating what life would be like if it was a different kind of animal, perhaps a bigger one, such as an ox.

"I wrote a letter to Amsterdam, which had a weight of twenty grams."

Guggenmos always stressed that he tried to convey the real world to his young readers, and that those writers who did not had no profound understanding of children. In fact, the very reason for the success of his work may be that Guggenmos managed to preserve something of the child in himself. **GS**

What Do People Do All Day? 1968

 Richard Scarry

3+

Even though this book was published back in 1968, most people born many years since will know it from their own childhood. Richard Scarry has influenced the learning of countless children all around the world. The characters in his Busytown are anthropomorphic animals who somehow manage to look human, while still looking like the pigs, cats, dogs, rabbits, mice (even owls, beavers, raccoons, hyenas, and crocodiles), and so on that they are. Recurring characters in Scarry's Busytown include Father Cat the grocer, his son Huckle Cat, Sergeant Murphy a cocker spaniel police motorcyclist, and Farmer Fox.

Young children are fascinated by the many different things that people do every day, and Scarry's

"Mommy took Abby to visit Dr. Lion. He looked at her tonsils. 'Hmmmm. Very bad tonsils.'"

signature, detail-packed illustrations of daily activities will have children poring over the pages for hours on end. (Look out for Lowly Worm on every page.) Whether the figures are driving a taxi or a bus, flying a plane, selling groceries, going to school or the post office, building houses, or growing food, the book is guaranteed to teach children new vocabulary along with object identification, and reveal things both familiar and totally new with each reading.

In the 1990s Nickelodeon produced the animation *The Busy World of Richard Scarry*. This prolific author and illustrator wrote more than three hundred books—including *Best Word Book Ever* and *Cars and Trucks and Things That Go*—and his Busytown books have sold a staggering 100 million copies worldwide. **KD**

Nationality | American, born 1919
Publisher | Random House, USA
Theme | Favorite characters, Classics, Family, Friendship

OTHER GREAT RICHARD SCARRY BOOKS

***Best Word Book Ever*, 1963**
***Busy, Busy World*, 1965**
***Best Storybook Ever*, 1970**
***Cars and Trucks and Things that Go*, 1974**

Corduroy 1968

Don Freeman

Nationality | American, born 1908
Publisher | Viking Penguin, USA
Theme | Classics, Favorite characters, Friendship

Corduroy the teddy bear sits on the shelf of the toy department, waiting anxiously for someone to take him home. Who could not fail to warm to him, with his lost look and loose shoulder strap? He plainly needs looking after. No, says the girl's mother, we have spent enough already and, anyway, he has a button missing. As soon as the store closes, Corduroy is off to find the button. He makes his way to the furniture department and, trying to pull a button off a mattress, knocks over a lamp, and is returned to his shelf by a bemused night watchman. The next day, the girl, Lisa, returns with her own money to buy Corduroy.

This simple story of kindness and friendship is in some ways old-fashioned—it was even when it was first created. Yet, in its own quiet way, it is also revolutionary. Not just because it was one of the first picture books to feature an African-American family, but because it sees the world so resolutely through a child's eyes. Corduroy's adventures at night are exactly as Lisa might have imagined them—his anxiety about the button, his perception of the escalator as a mountain—so that somehow we are not as surprised as Corduroy by Lisa's return. And how significant it is that she buys him with her own money, affirming her right to make her own choices.

The depth of feeling in the words and pictures speaks eloquently of the author's empathy. As Lisa sews on the button, she says tells Corduroy, "I like you the way you are . . . but you will be more comfortable with your shoulder strap fastened." Heartwarming. **CB**

Det underbara trädet
Text och bild: Ulf Löfgren
AWE/GEBERS

The Wonderful Tree 1969

Ulf Löfgren

Original Title | Det underbara trädet
Nationality | Swedish, born 1931
Publisher | Almqvist and Wiksell, Sweden
Theme | Fantasy, Magical stories

The Wonderful Tree is a somewhat surreal story about a little boy called Edward. He is a rather ordinary boy, who goes on what he thinks will be a quiet walk on a rather ordinary day.

Suddenly, he sees a seed flying through the air; it lands near him, and he decides to plant it. After digging a little hole, Edward plants the seed and waters it carefully. In just a short while he starts to see a tree sprouting up through the ground.

The tree grows extremely fast, its branches reaching high up toward the sky. It grows and grows and grows until it turns into the biggest tree Edward has ever seen, and he is determined to explore it. When he eventually climbs up into the tree, he finds a little home, perfect for him to live in. Being inside the tree is like being inside another world. A green, a blue, a red, and a yellow day pass; he also goes through four consecutive days of fall, winter, spring, and summer. It is a wonderful, mysterious tree.

This slightly psychedelic story, which many readers see as representing a little boy's dream, is as imaginatively illustrated as it is written. Ulf Löfgren's unique style means that his skillful illustrations are full of authentic detail. Each picture tells the story as effectively as the text does, and allows younger viewers to understand the story vividly. In his native Sweden, as well as overseas, Löfgren has become renowned as an accomplished storyteller who glides between fantasy and reality, a reputation that can be seen to perfection in *The Wonderful Tree*. **CC**

In the Night Kitchen 1970

Maurice Sendak

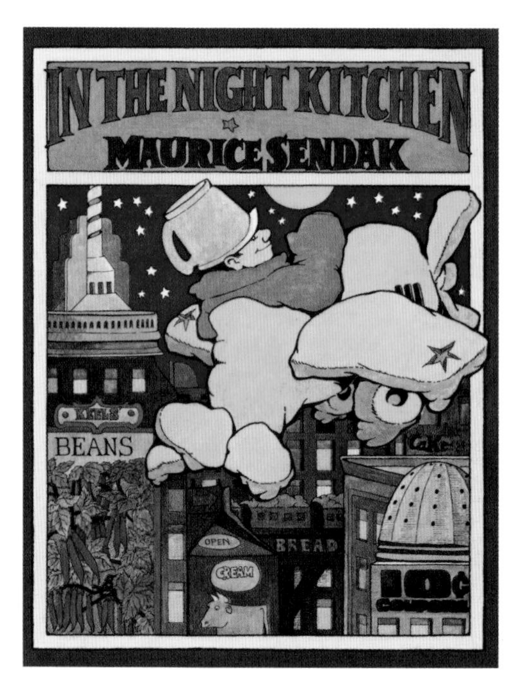

Nationality | American, born 1928
Publisher | Harper and Row, USA
Award | Caldecott Honor Book, 1971
Theme | Magical stories, Rhyming stories

After young boy Mickey falls asleep one night he hears alarming noises. Dreaming, he slowly floats out of his clothes and down to the night kitchen. Drawn out of scale, it is strangely populated with three bakers, all with round shiny faces and big white hats. Mickey falls into a giant mixing bowl containing batter for the morning cake.

The bakers start mixing up their cake, seemingly unaware of the little boy inside. Just as they are going to put the mixture into the "Mickey oven," Mickey pops out, protesting. Encased in a bodysuit of batter from the neck down, Mickey constructs a working airplane out of bread dough to reach the mouth of a gigantic milk bottle, into which he dives. Frolicking in the milk as his covering of batter disintegrates, he pours it in a stream, down to the bakers who joyfully finish their cake. As dawn breaks, the naked Mickey crows like a rooster and slides down the bottle, returning to bed.

Loved by children for its comic-book style and its zany, anarchic narrative, this book has nevertheless aroused controversy among some adults. There are those who claim the book has too much sexual symbolism—the phallic milk bottles, fecund batter, and sloshing liquids—perhaps this was prompted by knowledge of Sendak's deep interest in Freudian psychoanalysis. Others have slammed the nakedness of such a very young boy as obscene. Sendak is a revolutionary children's writer, unafraid to tackle the deep levels of human experience, and this book deserves its place in readers' hearts and minds. **VN**

"Milk in the batter! Milk in the batter! Stir it! Scrape it! Make it! Bake it! And they put that batter up to bake a delicious Mickey-cake."

OTHER GREAT MAURICE SENDAK BOOKS

***The Sign on Rosie's Door*, 1960**
***Where the Wild Things Are*, 1963**
***Higglety Pigglety Pop!, Or: There Must be More to Life*, 1967**
***Outside Over There*, 1985**

Barbapapa 1970

Annette Tison and Talus Taylor

Nationality | French, born 1942 (Tison); American, born 1933 (Taylor)
Publisher | L'Ecole des Loisirs, France
Theme | Magical stories, Friendship

When young François's watering can nurtured to life a pink vegetable-animal called Barbapapa, it also spawned a long-running, popular series of books and animated cartoons.

In the first book, François's parents decide that this newly grown creature—a flexible blob with wide, endearing eyes—is too big for the house, so Barbapapa ends up in a Paris zoo. Here, his ability to change shape and to squeeze himself into seemingly impossible places means that he is able to leave his cage—much to the displeasure of his keepers. On entering the big busy city, however, Barbapapa discovers that being so large makes it very difficult for him to fit in. Barbapapa likes to make people happy, but the Parisians are frightened of him, and he soon finds himself alone amid the hustle and bustle. It is when he is able to use his unique ability to change shape to help people that they stop being frightened of him and he gets the friendship he's been craving.

This is an understated but affecting story about being different and about the search for acceptance. *Barbapapa* is also a wonderful portrait of Paris itself. Tison and Taylor's subtle line-drawings capture the aging splendor of the city's houses and streets, while their use of snaking, curling forms and bright but earthy colors evokes the art nouveau style still familiar in the town's Metro awnings and Morris columns. *Barbapapa* is an optimistic but unsentimental tale of Paris past and present that is beautiful in its simplicity. Young readers will love guessing the shapes he will transform into from page to page. **NA**

Mr. Tickle 1971

Roger Hargreaves

Nationality | English, born 1935
Publisher | Fabbri, UK
Theme | Favorite characters, Classics, Quirky, Fantasy

In 1971, Roger Hargreaves was asked by his son, Adam, "What does a tickle look like?" That question led to the creation of *Mr. Tickle*, the first in what would become a much-loved series of *Mr. Men* books. He later also created the *Little Miss* series.

"Tickles are small and round and they have arms that stretch and stretch," the book explains to its young readers. Mr. Tickle himself is orange-colored; he wears a blue fedora; has a big, broad smile; short legs; and very, very long arms. There is nothing he likes more than to tickle people, especially people who cannot see him. Mr. Tickle's "extraordinarily long" arms also have lots of other uses, such as stretching all the way out of the bedroom and down the stairs, allowing him to get cookies from the kitchen without needing to get out of bed.

One morning Mr. Tickle wakes up and decides it is a "tickling day," so he sets off to see whom he can tickle. He causes all sorts of chaos. He tickles a policeman on traffic duty, causing mayhem at the crossroads, and a teacher in class, whose pupils cannot stop laughing at the sight of his hysterical giggles. Mr. Tickle also tickles a doctor, a butcher, a guard at the train station—making a train ten minutes late—a shopkeeper who drops apples all over the road, and Mr. Stamp, the elderly postman, who drops his mailbag full of letters into a puddle.

After all his exertions, Mr. Tickle goes home to laugh about all the people he has tickled. At the end of the story, the author warns the reader to watch out—Mr. Tickle might just be waiting to tickle them too. **LH**

Visst kan Lotta cykla
av Astrid Lindgren
och Ilon Wikland

Lotta's Bike 1971

Astrid Lindgren   Ilon Wikland

Nationality | Swedish, born 1907 (author); Estonian, born 1930 (illustrator)
Publisher | Rabén and Sjögren, Sweden
Theme | Favorite characters

Lotta is one of the most popular characters in Swedish children's literature, and she has attracted an audience of young readers from around the world. Lotta is a small girl who is never far from trouble. She often gets into scrapes with her older siblings, Jonas and Maria. The trio fall out of windows, learn bad language, put meatballs down the chimney, and generally irritate their long-suffering father. Lotta is also extremely inquisitive and is constantly asking questions—the source of much of the humor in the books.

In *Lotta's Bike* (originally published as *Visst kan Lotta cykla*), Lotta is hoping to get a bike for her birthday, but when her parents buy her something else, she decides to "borrow" her neighbors' bike and take her toy pig Barnsie for a ride. Unfortunately the bike is too big for Lotta and the hill she attempts to cycle down is much too steep. There are inevitable consequences, involving a rose bush and the owner of the bike.

The Lotta stories focus on everyday events that small children will instantly empathize with. In *Lotta Leaves Home*, Lotta is cross with her whole family, so she decides to run away. She soon realizes, however, that there is no place quite like home. Each story in the series is told with gentle humor, and there is often an underlying moral. The books are ideal for sharing and for children who have begun reading alone.

Lotta is younger than Astrid Lindgren's most famous creation, Pippi Longstocking, but like Pippi, Lotta is highly independent and unconventional and—like all Lindgren's characters—she is extremely mischievous and engaging. **NH**

Little I Am I 1972

Mira Lobe   Susi Weigel

Nationality | Austrian, born Hilde Rosenthal, 1913 (author); Austrian, born 1914 (illustrator)
Publisher | Jungbrunnen, Austria
Theme | Animal stories, Friendship

Little I Am I (or *Das kleine Ich bin Ich* in the original title) charmingly discusses the problem of finding one's identity and the need to accept one's peculiarities. This beautifully illustrated book, with its delightful rhymes, follows a little animal with pink-and-white checks, whose purpose is determined after being asked by a frog what it is. Realizing it cannot give a satisfying answer, the little animal decides to find out which species it belongs to.

On its journey it makes comparisons with all the animals it encounters and always discovers certain similarities, yet, none of the animals match it completely, and so the search continues. The little hero is greeted with mixed reactions. By some, such as the parrot, it is treated with contempt and hostility, but others treat it kindly and are willing to help. Eventually, the little animal is on the verge of giving up, questioning whether it is anything significant at all. At this low point it suddenly recognizes the essence of its nature, exclaiming, "I am I!" Having finally found its identity, it retraces its journey to tell all the other animals, "I am I."

Susi Weigel's illustrations complement Mira Lobe's engaging narrative, alternating between color and black-and-white images as well as highly realistic and fantastical ones in order to emphasize the complexity of I am I's character. The images and Lobe's funny and delightful rhymes present the difficult and at times even distressing subject matter in a lighthearted and optimistic way, guaranteeing that both children and adults enjoy the book. **GS**

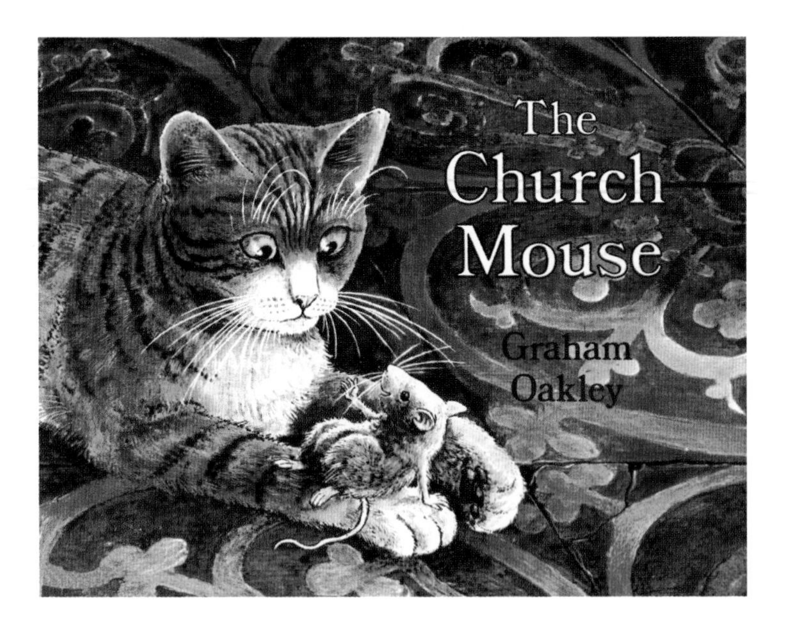

The Church Mouse 1972

Graham Oakley

Nationality | English, born 1929
Publisher | Atheneum Books, UK
Theme | Favorite characters, Animal stories, Friendship

Originally intended to be the first in a series set in various buildings in the fictional town of Wortlethorpe, Graham Oakley's church setting in *The Church Mouse* was so successful that he never moved his characters elsewhere. With its gentle humor, parochial backdrop, and detailed artwork, the book remains a firm favorite with young children and parents alike.

After graduating from art school, Oakley had various design jobs, including working on the sets of several BBC TV programs, before becoming an author and illustrator. *The Church Mouse* is the simple story of Arthur, a mouse who lives in the town church in the reasonably friendly company of Sampson the cat. Arthur's main mission is to gather other mice to live in the church with him, not only to keep them safe from the town's unfriendly cats, but to bring him some much-needed companionship. However, it is not the story's plot but the detailed illustrations that form the main attraction of the book. The drawings are almost Victorian in their highly traditional style, and feature little pockets of action in every corner. Oakley's tale maintains a fairly moral slant, with its church setting and benevolent ethics, and despite several jokes aimed at older children and adults, the story will still entertain the youngest of readers.

The Church Mouse is a perfect bedtime book for preschool and early-age school children. It is followed by a whole series of beautifully illustrated mouse adventures that still appeal to today's generation of children as much as they did in the 1970s. **LK**

3+

The Sea-Thing Child 1972

Russell Hoban Abrom Hoban

Nationality | American, born 1925 (author); American, birth date unknown (illustrator)
Publisher | Harper and Row, USA; Gollancz, UK
Theme | Fantasy, Rhyming stories

This extraordinarily vivid picture book opens dramatically—with a strange bird-child being washed onto a wide, empty shore one dark, storm-tossed night. From the very first, the ideas and language reflect Russell Hoban's unique style, which is often described as a very personal take on "magic realism."

An American writer who settled in London, Hoban writes for adults and children—novels, short stories, poetry, and picture books—including more than fifty picture books for children. His children's books often embrace complex underlying themes that appeal equally to adults as well as their intended audience.

The Sea-Thing Child is the tale of a child-creature who resembles a cross between a small dodo and a puffin. His three fellow travelers are an adventurous eel, a highly emotional crab, pining for a bow so he can play the fiddle, and a pipe-smoking albatross.

The characterization and symbolic surrealism owe more than a little to Lewis Carroll, yet Hoban's style remains unique. His lyrical language, in what is essentially a fable about facing life's challenges, is advanced for young children, but its poetic qualities are unusual and stimulating. The themes may need teasing out for children by adult readers.

The Sea-Thing Child was reillustrated in 1999 by Patrick Benson (born 1956), and children will love his beautiful, large illustrations, which are relaxed yet expressive. Hoban often deals with nature in his work, and Benson perfectly captures the wide, elemental open seas and skies of this moving story. **AK**

Father Christmas 1973

Raymond Briggs

Nationality | English, born 1934
Publisher | Hamish Hamilton, UK
Award | Kate Greenaway Medal
Theme | Favorite characters, Classics

This comic strip was one of the first successful attempts to give Santa Claus a personality, drawing on logic to answer children's questions, including some they may not have thought of.

Raymond Briggs's Father Christmas is a hard-working man who many readers will recognize from their families and communities; he could be their dad or their grandpa. Like Raymond Briggs's own father, a milkman, Father Christmas has to be out in all weathers to get the job done (the milkman who Father Christmas meets on his way home at dawn is a tribute to Briggs's father), and he does it all by himself with no attendant elves. So he is allowed to be grumpy sometimes. To let off steam, he directs his grumbles and curses into thin air and is never grumpy with his reindeer, whom he lovingly calls "silly deers."

Briggs confirms children's expectations but with a twist: Father Christmas lives in the Arctic, but in an ordinary, cozy, slightly shabby house rather than an ice palace or igloo (we even see him sitting on the toilet). He has a cat, a dog, and hens, as well as reindeer.

Father Christmas hates stairs, soot, and chimneys that end in wood-burning stoves. Worse are deliveries to people with no chimneys or who live in caravans or lighthouses. On the bright side, he enjoys the mince pies and sherry left out for him. He delivers to everyone, even the Queen. He hates the cold, dreams of lying on a beach, pins posters of Mallorca and Capri on the walls—and fully appreciates the holiday Raymond Briggs sends him on in the sequel. **GB**

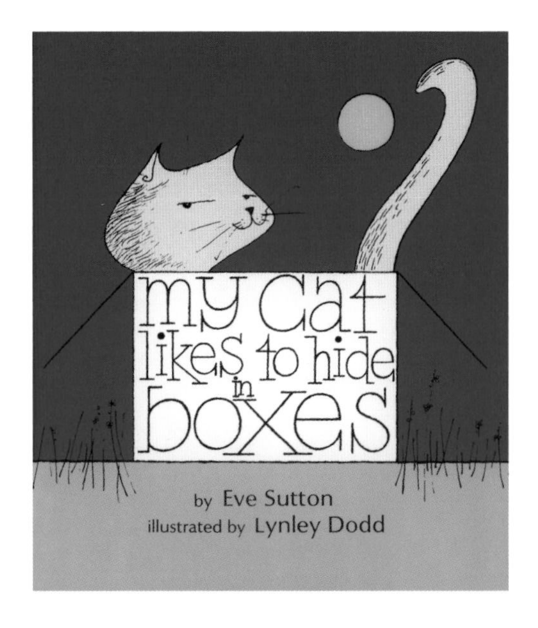

3+

My Cat Likes to Hide in Boxes 1973

Eve Sutton Lynley Dodd

Nationality | English, born 1906 (author); New Zealander, born 1941 (illustrator)
Publisher | Hamish Hamilton, UK
Theme | Animal stories, Rhyming stories

For those people who have ever had a cat who spends his days hiding away, the central character of this book will be immediately familiar. While some more energetic cats are flying airplanes or joining the police, this cat simply hides in boxes.

Eve Sutton based the story on a family cat called Wooskit, who liked to hide in boxes, supermarket bags, cupboards, and all kinds of hidey-holes. Sutton asked her cousin Lynley Dodd, a freelance illustrator, to provide some artwork for the story. It was Dodd's first book, and she went on to become an acclaimed author and illustrator, most notably of the much-loved Hairy Maclary series, about a scruffy dog and his doggy companions, as well as the Slinky Malinki series about a cat who is always in trouble.

My Cat Likes to Hide in Boxes is a favorite with children who love its repetitive rhyming scheme, such as "The cat from France liked to sing and dance. But my cat likes to hide in boxes."

The quirky illustrations rarely show the hero in his entirety, only a tail, paws, or eyes poking out of a box. Each page features a clever and exotic cat with a special talent—the cat from Berlin, for example, plays the violin, and the cat from Japan has a big, blue fan—and each is dressed in appropriate national costume. Our hero, however, does not appear to possess any particular skills, but likes to stay at home in a succession of different boxes, ranging from a hatbox to a crate before we finally see him curled up asleep in a toy box. **HJ**

3+

Who's Seen the Scissors? 1975

Fernando Krahn

Original Title | ¿Quién ha visto las tijeras?
Nationality | Chilean, born 1935
Publisher | Dutton, USA
Theme | Magical stories, Quirky, Adventure

Unlike most children's stories, the protagonist in *Who's Seen the Scissors?* (published in Spanish as *¿Quién ha visto las tijeras?*) is neither a person nor an animal but an adventurous pair of scissors. The pair of scissors belongs to a busy elderly tailor, Don Hipólito, and after many years of repetitive work, it has grown weary of always cutting the same thing—cloth. One day, the pair of scissors decides to escape so that it can fulfill its dreams and experience new things in the outside world. The pair of scissors leaves the tailor's house and sets off on a rampage around the town. In its excitement, the scissors cuts anything it encounters, including the wind, the clouds, the hair of passersby, and even the flowers of a young man in love.

Fernando Krahn's illustrations, which are executed with gentle humor and a light artistic touch, are the essence of the book. The title was originally published without any words; it was only in later editions that Spanish text, written by María Luz Uribe, appeared to accompany the pictures. Krahn's drawings are colorful, marvelously imaginative, and surprising. They are humorous masterpieces of illustration, and they fully deserve the praise they—and the book—received. *Who's Seen the Scissors?* is an enchanting and enchanted tribute to freedom and diversity, and encourages young readers to use their imagination. Krahn won several awards, including the Premio Apel Les Mestres (1982) and the Premio Austral de la Literatura Infantil (1986). **LB**

Morris's Disappearing Bag 1975

Rosemary Wells

Nationality | American, born 1943
Publisher | Dial Press, USA
Award | A.L.A. Notable Children's Book
Theme | Animal stories, Family

Rosemary Wells is a versatile author and illustrator whose books for younger readers are about the ups and downs of family life. The narratives are humorous and lighthearted.

Morris's Disappearing Bag is about a rabbit family at Christmastime. In the opening illustration, four children eagerly bounce down the stairs to look for their presents. Victor gets a hockey outfit; Rose gets a beauty kit; Betty gets a chemistry set; and Morris, the youngest, gets a bear. Morris discovers that his bear does not have the same scope for active enjoyment as the presents his brother and sisters have received, nor is he invited to take part in the other children's games. Morris decides to sulk under the Christmas tree. There he discovers an overlooked package that contains a magic bag. The bag cannot be seen and nor can anyone who climbs inside it. It allows Morris to hide and later becomes a means of getting the children out of the way so that he can play with their presents.

The illustrations and text explore the dynamics of family life, encouraging children to take a humorous and detached view of the conflicts and frustrations in their lives. The disappearing bag itself is an inspired creation, providing the opportunity for amusing illustrations of the children disappearing and re-emerging, and an invitation for the reader to take part in the hide-and-seek with the children in the story, for the ears and tail of the "invisible" Morris are always visible to readers who look carefully. **CB**

Uppo the Bear 1977

Elina Karjalainen Hannu Taina

3+

Nationality | Finnish, born 1927 (author); Finnish, born 1941 (illustrator)
Publisher | WSOY, Finland
Theme | Animal stories, Friendship

Uppo the Bear (whose original title is *Uppo-Nalle,* meaning "sunken bear") has delighted young readers since it was first published in 1977. It tells the story of a very courageous little bear, who has sailed the seven seas and experienced many exciting adventures. He has been floating in the sea for a long time, waiting for any creature to come along and befriend him.

When he finally reaches the shore of a white sandy beach, he is greeted by a kind little girl, Reeta, who is also in need of a special friend. This is the beginning of a great friendship, and *Uppo the Bear* is the first in a much-loved series of picture books. Reeta takes Uppo to live with her parents and their dog, the Singing Bird-Dog. The bear tells Reeta and her family about his many wonderful and often dangerous adventures, and they all share their dreams and fears. The bear's biggest dream is to write a collection of poetry. He creates poems from his everyday life and recites them to his new friends. However, Uppo is afraid of birds, particularly finches. Reeta is determined to rid Uppo of his strange fear, and together they embark upon new adventures to help Uppo overcome his phobia. Along the way, Reeta and Uppo find in each other the close friend they have both always craved.

Elina Karjalainen's narrative style is brilliant and fun; the book is filled with poems, wordplay, and rhymes that will make readers laugh out loud. Karjalainen's witty use of language is beautifully complemented by Hannu Taina's charming illustrations. **LKK**

"There was white sand and someone, some kind creature, to meet him."

OTHER GREAT UPPO THE BEAR READS

***Uppo the Bear's Winter Coat (Uppo-Nallen talviturkki),* 1978**
***Uppo the Bear and Uncle Tonton (Uppo-Nalle ja setä Tonton),* 1981**

Burglar Bill 1977

Allan Ahlberg Janet Ahlberg

3+

Nationality | English, born 1938 (author); English, born 1944 (illustrator)
Publisher | Heinemann, UK
Theme | Quirky, Rhyming stories, Family

"It is a noise that Burglar Bill has heard before . . . 'Blow me down . . . I'm being burgled!'"

OTHER GREAT BOOKS BY THE AHLBERGS

Each Peach Pear Plum, 1978
Mrs. Wobble the Waitress, 1980
The Jolly Postman, 1986
The Bear Nobody Wanted, 1992
Janet's Last Book, 1996

Burglar Bill is a perfect story to read to small children who are old enough to appreciate the alliterative humor of bad Bill the burglar and equally bad Burglar Betty, whose baby Bill finds in a box that he has stolen.

Allan and Janet Ahlberg present an untroubled world in which Bill's thieving is not malicious and is not even done for a purpose: Although everything in Bill's life is stolen, he does not need or want most of the things he steals. There is no clash with the police in the story, and perhaps this is just as well because it is inferred that the "Old Bill" is no match for Burglar Bill, who not only brazenly burgles a house in a little street behind the police station, but also steals a policeman's helmet. It is the power of love rather than law enforcement that helps Bill and Betty to see the error of their ways.

There is great potential for discussions with younger children about the subject matter of the text. These need not be directly about whether or not Bill should have stolen things, but can be centered around all the items Bill has stolen: those that he uses (the House of Lords jug and the potty from HMS *Eagle*), those that he most certainly cannot have needed (half a gross of hairnets), and the belongings that he returns to their owners, such as a fox fur, the policeman's helmet, a pub piano, and a stuffed fish in a glass case. Children reading the book by themselves will enjoy spotting all these things and will find the restoration program, outlined in pictures, as entertaining as the imagined burglaries. The drama lies in the fact that Bill and Betty need all their burgling skills to give the stolen goods back without being caught.

The illustrations subvert Bill and Betty's antisocial image. Although they have the requisite burglar masks and striped sweaters (and a striped cat), Bill also has a cozy dressing gown and slippers, and Betty has a white wedding dress. **GB**

Burglar Bill helps himself to loot, including a can of beans and a hat.

Beans

Dogger 1977

Shirley Hughes

3+

Nationality | English, born 1927
Publisher | Bodley Head, UK
Award | Eleanor Farjeon Award, 1984
Theme | Family, School

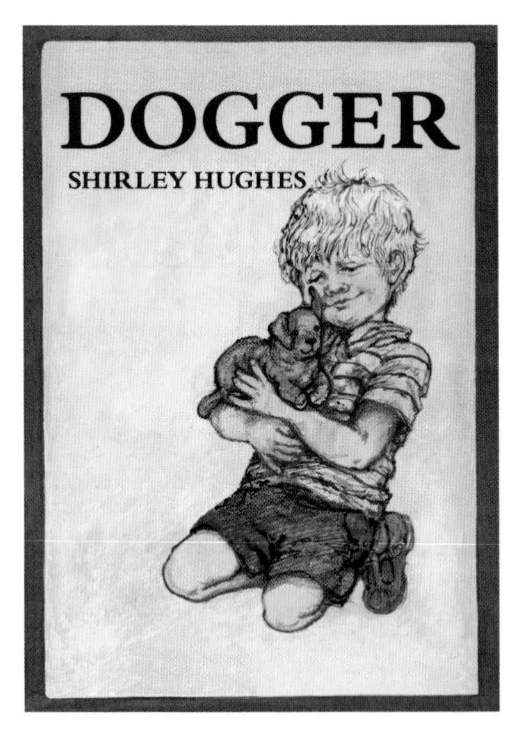

One day Dave loses his beloved, battered toy dog somewhere between getting an ice cream and fetching his older sister Bella from school. Dave is very upset and becomes very quiet. When the dog turns up unexpectedly for sale at the school fair, Dave has no money to buy it. By the time he finds his older sister, disaster has struck: his toy has been sold to a little girl. Fortunately, Bella manages to save the day, and Dave and his toy dog are reunited in a way that is highly satisfactory for both sleepy young children and adults reading bedtime stories.

Dogger is rendered by one of England's most skillful and successful children's authors and illustrators. Shirley Hughes explores the world of small children in quintessentially English settings with a kindly eye and an affectionate ear. Her distinctive graphic style is achieved using pen and ink, watercolor, and gouache. Her sketchbook drawings are done very quickly, "almost at the speed of seeing," as she says herself; she then uses the sketches as visual and memory references for storyboards and finished illustrations. Her tone of voice is tinged sometimes with the rueful exasperation of the adult, and then with the naive surprise of the child.

"Mum looked everywhere. Dave waited anxiously but Dogger could not be found."

Hughes was awarded the Kate Greenaway Medal for *Dogger* in 1977. Her picture books celebrate the minute details of children's lives, including simple pleasures from puddles to ice creams, and capture the warmest moments of childhood. Reading them is like being with an ideal grandmother. **VN**

OTHER GREAT SHIRLEY HUGHES BOOKS

***Lucy and Tom*, 1960**
***Alfie Gets In First*, 1981**
***Chips and Jessie*, 1986**
***The Big Concrete Lorry*, 1989**
***Ella's Big Chance*, 2003**

Up in the Tree 1978

Margaret Atwood

3+

This is an odd little picture book, reminiscent of Dr. Seuss in looks and tone, but more gentle and whimsical. Renowned author Margaret Atwood wrote, illustrated, and hand-lettered this book in 1978, at a time when most publishers thought it was too much of a financial risk.

To save on printing costs, only two colors were used, so the pictures and text are all shades of red and blue and a brownish color that is created by mixing the two. All this gives the book a primitive look, like an old-fashioned, hand-printed poster. Atwood's beautiful hand-lettering dances across the page, with words picked out expressively in different colors and sizes for emphasis.

"How will we get down, down, down to the ground? Are we stuck here FOREVER. . . ?"

Two children live up in a tree, where they can swing and crawl and dance, through changes of weather and season. They are very happy there, free to do as they please, until a pair of hungry beavers come along and reduce their ladder to woodchips. Suddenly they are stuck in the tree, and now that their freedom to get down has been taken away, the tree no longer seems such a good place to be: "Oh moan! Oh groan! There's no telephone!" they wail and query, "Are we stuck here FOREVER in this horrible tree?" After a whole night in the tree, an enormous masked bird comes to rescue them. The two children rejoice momentarily; then, of course, they just want to climb back up. So they nail planks on to the tree to make stairs, giving them the freedom to go up and down as they please, then happily go to sleep up there, in the company of a friendly owl. **CW**

Nationality | Canadian, born 1939
Publisher | McClelland and Stewart, Canada
Honor | Order of Ontario, 1990
Theme | Rhyming stories, Animal stories

MARGARET ATWOOD'S BOOKS FOR KIDS

***Anna's Pet*, 1980**
***For the Birds*, 1990**
***Princess Prunella and the Purple Peanut*, 1995**
***Rude Ramsay and the Roaring Radishes*, 2003**
***Bashful Bob and the Doleful Dorinda*, 2004**

The Snowman 1978

Raymond Briggs

Nationality | English, born 1934
Publisher | Hamish Hamilton, UK
Award | Dutch Silver Pen Award, 1979
Theme | Friendship, Magical stories

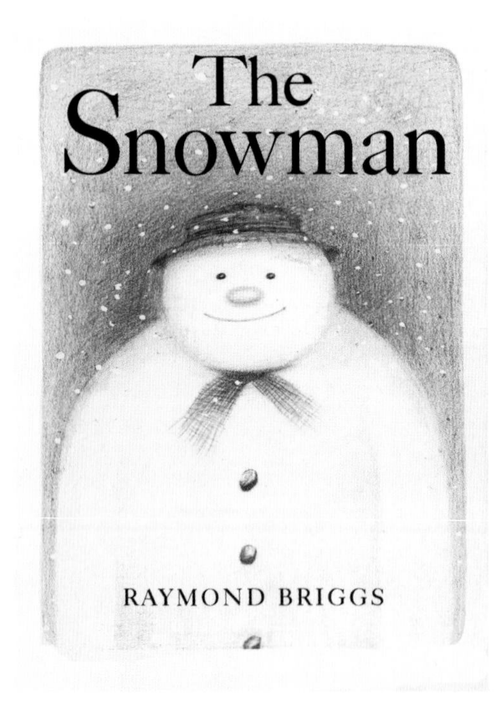

OTHER CLASSICS BY RAYMOND BRIGGS

Father Christmas, 1973
Fungus the Bogeyman, 1977
Unlucky Wally, 1987
The Bear, 1994
Ethel & Ernest, 1998

The pencil-and-crayoned—and wordless—world of *The Snowman* begins on a snowy day when a small boy builds a friend in his garden. The story does not necessarily happen at Christmas. It was when the book was turned into a film that the Christmas trimmings were added, turning the story into what has become for many a seasonal institution.

At midnight, the snowman comes to life. The little boy has already gone to bed, but he gets up and, in his pajamas and dressing gown, goes out to play with his new friend. The snowman is an ideal companion: he is big and cuddly and, unlike usual snow, he is warm to the touch. The snowman is like a child himself, playful and exploratory, eager to try out everything in the boy's world.

As in Briggs's *Father Christmas*, the reader has the pleasure of placing an often-imagined figure into their everyday life and of establishing how he acts and behaves. Children will enjoy confirming that the snowman is afraid of the fire and can only eat cold food. They will also enjoy the snowman's fascination with the television and with playing with the lights.

The climax of this wordless tale comes when the snowman, who can fly just like the snowflakes he is made of, takes the boy on a magical journey through the sky. The landscape they fly through is Briggs's home territory of England's South Downs and the seaside town of Brighton, where they land on its famous pier. They stay there until the first sign of sunrise sends them home.

The little boy goes to bed at dawn. When he wakes up, his friend has melted in the morning sun. This reminder that some pleasures and friendships are transitory need not constitute a downbeat ending to the story. The boy (or any child) has the possibility of repeating the experience next time it snows, and meanwhile he has been given a joyful memory. **GB**

The little boy is whisked off on a magical flight with his new friend.

Freight Train 1978

Donald Crews

Nationality | American, born 1938
Publisher | Greenwillow Books, USA
Award | Caldecott Honor Book, 1979
Theme | Classics

Donald Crews is an African-American author and illustrator whose books feature a strong, bold look and many familiar urban inspirations but very few actual people. The powerful, bright graphic design and his ability to tell a story visually, with few words, make Crews's work perfect for infants and preschool children.

Transportation, especially trains, is a strong theme in Crews's books. His father worked on the railroad, and as a child, Crews often took the train to spend the summer with his grandparents in Florida. *Freight Train* is a very simple book with no real plot as such. It sets out to do only two things, both of which it does brilliantly: it begins to teach children to recognize primary colors and gives them a sense of what motion looks like, which is no easy task on a flat white page. Crews uses brightly colored, static pictures of train cars to introduce the concept of different colors. He then photographically blurs the images to simulate motion, with little shading and no shadows. This flat visual graphic technique was innovative for children's books, and won him many awards. He shows the progression from day to night, and as readers move through the pages, they follow the "motion" of the train through the landscape until it disappears from the page and the book comes to an end.

All children love "things that go," and this book is the ideal introduction to the concepts of motion and colors for readers who are so young that they can only look at, not read, a book. **KD**

Speed, motion, and color are all emphasized in *Freight Train*. 

3+

Is That a Monster, Alfie Atkins? 1978

Gunilla Bergström

Original Title | Alfons och odjuret
Nationality | Swedish, born 1942
Publisher | Rabén and Sjögren, Sweden
Theme | Favorite characters

Poor Alfie cannot sleep. He has a monster under his bed. He also has a gnawing feeling: "Alfie thinks serious thoughts in the dark. He punched the little boy." He is thinking of what happened today when he was playing soccer. He hit somebody. He hit a boy who is smaller than him. Alfie has been mean, and he is painfully aware of it. The next day at school, the small boy is not in the playground, and he is not there the following week either. Where could he be? Is it Alfie's fault that he has disappeared? Every night when Alfie goes to sleep, there is a monster growling in the dark. Alfie's conscience is not giving him any rest. The coming week is spent making things good again, and then—would you believe it?—the monster under Alfie's bed disappears.

Is That a Monster, Alfie Atkins? is one of the books in Gunilla Bergström's popular Alfie series. Although humorous and heartwarming, these books do not hesitate to bring up uncomfortable themes, such as fear, jealousy, and selfishness. Bergström investigates the child psyche and manages to inspire courage and goodness in her readers. She has called her books "mini-dramas on a psychological level," and she works with subjects that all children can relate to. Bergström manages to find something funny and unexpected in everyday situations, and her deft illustrations bring her stories to life, in particular through the facial expressions of her characters. Children have an ability to find magic in their lives, and Bergström manages to capture that uniqueness of children. **CC**

3+

Ox-Cart Man 1979

Donald Hall Barbara Cooney

Nationality | American, born 1928 (author); American, born 1917 (illustrator)
Publisher | Viking Press, USA
Theme | Family

The lyrical rhythms of rural life underlie this engaging tale. It takes us through the seasons of the year in the life of an isolated nineteenth-century family. The book has all the qualities of a bedtime favorite—lines with a welcome familiarity and illustrations you want to walk directly into.

The father, mother, daughter, and son all work together in harmony to make everything they need to survive. In October the father packs into the oxcart the excess produce that the family has grown over the year. He takes it to sell in the faraway town, a few days' journey away, and ends up selling more than just the produce, "Then he sold his ox, and kissed him goodbye on his nose." With his profits, he buys things to take home for his family, and so the cycle begins again.

Donald Hall, a U.S. Poet Laureate, created the story by revising one of his original poems. He uses simple words and poetic echoes to convey a comforting, ordinary serenity in his description of the rural year. The oxcart man is a kind of everyman, and this is an "every family."

Younger children will love the predictability of the recurring words that match the year's activities, whereas older children will appreciate the layers of information about life, work, togetherness, and the family's seasonal tasks. Barbara Cooney's naive-style illustrations have meaning and attraction for all ages, with each page revealing aspects of the season, the town and the country, and the relationships between people, animals, and the earth. "I will never talk down to—or draw down to—children," says Cooney. **CER**

Mister Magnolia 1980

Quentin Blake

Nationality | English, born 1932
Publisher | Cape, UK
Award | Kate Greenaway Medal
Theme | Rhyming stories, Fantasy

This effervescent story in nonsense rhyme is about Mr. Magnolia, who has only one boot. It is a fine example of words and pictures working successfully together. Mr. Magnolia's supporting cast, as he capers around with only one boot, includes dancing mice, a purple fruit-eating dinosaur, green cloth-eating parakeets, and owls who sleep above his bed. He attracts an audience, too, including rabbits, cows, and a market stallholder and her children. As well as a highly memorable rhyme, *Mister Magnolia* also gives us a counting book, as Mr. Magnolia encounters two flute-playing sisters, three pond creatures, four parakeets, five owls, and so on. Sometimes the numbers are in the text; sometimes the reader has to count the marching mice or the pieces of fruit on the page.

The line "Mr. Magnolia has only one boot" anchors the alternate three- and four-line stanzas of the jaunty text, which makes it clear that our protagonist does not allow his lack of footwear to stop him from enjoying himself. The spreads introduce new adventures in the pond, at the swimming pool, on a scooter, and at a fruit stall, where he juggles with the goods for sale. Like many Quentin Blake heroes, Mr. Magnolia has an air of energy that is captured on the page by Blake's decisive lines, accentuated by his costume: flowing scarf, flapping tailcoat, and a shock of flyaway hair. Finally, a package arrives, and Mr. Magnolia eagerly puts on his new boot: it does not match, but he does not give a hoot. Nonsense generates more nonsense, and it is fun to wonder about what happened to his other boot. **GB**

Peace at Last 1980

 Jill Murphy

Nationality | English, born 1949
Publisher | Macmillan, UK
Award | Shortlisted for Kate Greenaway Medal
Theme | Family, Animal stories

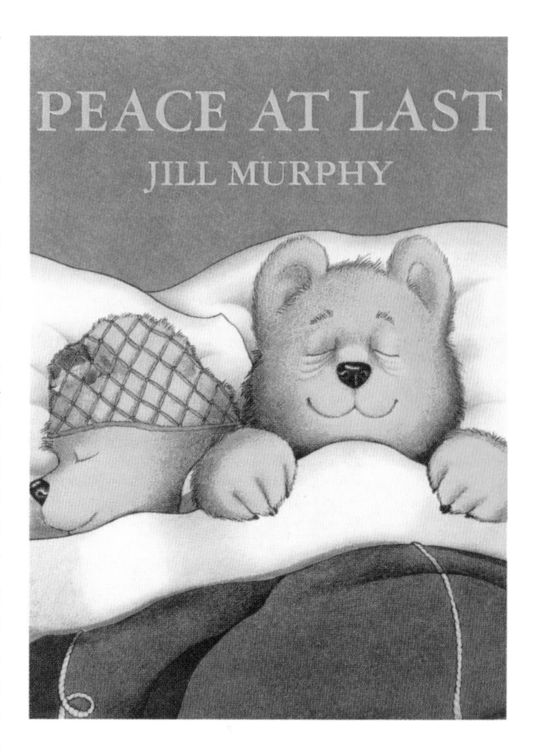

"The hour was late. Mr. Bear was tired, Mrs. Bear was tired and baby Bear was tired . . . so they all went to bed." So begins this much-loved bedtime story, which was commended for the Kate Greenaway Medal.

The opening pages, with their predominantly monosyllabic language in which the rhythms of everyday speech dominate, and the clever use of page turns give momentum to a commonplace scene and set the style for the story to follow. With the household settled into its nighttime routine and the moon shining in a dark world outside, Mr. Bear cannot get to sleep. He wanders from room to room, in each one disturbed by a different noise. "'Oh NO!' says Mr. Bear in every room, 'I can't stand THIS!'" and he goes off to try elsewhere. The repeated pattern of language invites children to join in with the story, until eventually poor Mr. Bear collapses into his car where, just as the sun is rising, he finally nods off, only to be roused by the dawn chorus. Driven back to his bedroom, he at last falls asleep in his own bed where he is woken, immediately it seems, by the alarm clock. Mrs. Bear's waking ignorance of his plight adds a final delightful touch, and parents everywhere will empathize with the closing scene, in which baby Bear bounds over the bed where his father slumps bleary-eyed.

The illustrations show cheerful domestic scenes, gingham curtains at the windows, and baby Bear's bib hanging expectantly on the back of a chair. Mr. Bear's growing desperation is evident to even the youngest reader in the half-turning of an eye and his heavy posture as he climbs wearily upstairs. **KA**

"Mrs. Bear fell asleep. Mr. Bear didn't. Mrs. Bear began to snore. 'SNORE,' went Mrs. Bear, 'SNORE, SNORE, SNORE.'"

OTHER BEDTIME READS BY JILL MURPHY

***The Worst Witch*, 1974**
***A Bad Spell for the Worst Witch*, 1982**
***Five Minute's Peace*, 1986**
***A Piece of Cake*, 1989**
***A Quiet Night In*, 1993**

Mr. Archimedes' Bath 1980

Pamela Allen

Nationality | New Zealander, born 1934
Publisher | William Collins, Australia
Award | Ashton Scholastic Award
Theme | Science and nature

Mr. Archimedes is having a bath with his friends Kangaroo, Wombat, and Goat. The problem starts when they all jump into the filled bath at the same time. The bathwater overflows, and it seems as though somebody is adding more water into the bath. Mr. Archimedes gets tired of mopping up the water on the floor. Who could be the culprit?

Mr. Archimedes and his friends all take turns jumping in and out of the bath in order to find out who is guilty of spilling the water. Finally, Mr. Archimedes has a eureka moment and realizes why the bathwater is overflowing onto the floor.

Mr. Archimedes' Bath is a clever children's book that makes science fun and understandable for small children. It is loosely based on the story about the ancient Greek scholar Archimedes, who reputedly first understood, while having a bath, that the volume of water displaced must be equal to the volume of his submerged body. In Pamela Allen's popular version, Archimedes is accompanied by his marsupial friends (and a goat). With short lines of cumulative, repetitive, and simple text, together with humorous and expressive illustrations on each side, this picture book will not only teach children something scientific, but also keep them entertained. *Mr. Archimedes' Bath* confirms Allen's reputation as a fine creator of children's books that capture attention, engage the imagination, and teach, as well as excite, small children. Other recommended works include *Who Sank the Boat?* and *Bertie and the Bear*. **CC**

3+

Léo and Popi 1980

Marie-Agnes Gaudrat Helen Oxenbury

Nationality | French, birth date unknown (author); English, born 1938 (illustrator)
Publisher | Bayard Jeunesse, France
Theme | Animal stories, Friendship

Popi is a stuffed monkey, brought to life by the imagination of Léo, his little owner. The characters feature in a popular series of books, Les histoires de Léo et Popi, which includes topics such as bedtime and bathtime. Always with his Popi alongside, Léo discovers the world. We follow them at the beach, at Christmas, and at a party, and every story brings some learning and experience for the reader.

Helen Oxenbury's illustrations are made in pastel colors and are very soft and very round. There is no background to the artwork: The drawings are simple so that a *Léo and Popi* book can be enjoyed as a picture book, each page focusing on one or two details of the tale: a toy, person, mood, fruit, or animal, for example.

Léo and Popi have been famous characters for decades now: The series has been praised by parents and specialists for its educational purpose and the sweetness of the plots, which are beautifully caught in between reality and the imaginary world of a two-year-old boy. Léo takes his Popi everywhere, shares everything with him, talks to him, and respects his answers. The indirect speech conveys the manner of speaking and vocabulary of a young boy, and participates in the innocent point of view of the series, making the identification with Léo even more accessible for children.

The series has now been adapted into short animation cartoons. They capture the style of the books by using a voiceover to narrate the stories to the viewers as the characters move on screen. **MGR**

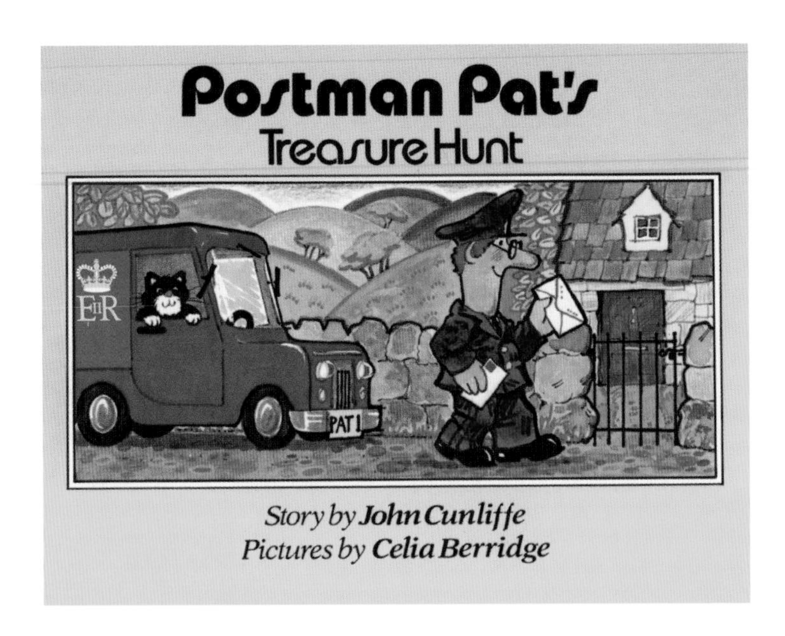

3+

Postman Pat's Treasure Hunt 1981

John A. Cunliffe Celia Berridge

Nationality | English, born 1933 (author); English, birth date unknown (illustrator)
Publisher | André Deutsch, UK
Theme | Favorite characters

In 1981 animator Ivor Wood took a character called Postman Pat and turned his adventures into an immensely popular children's series for BBC television in the United Kingdom, which was later broadcast in more than fifty countries. John Cunliffe wrote the scripts, but his books were not published until after the television series. The books quickly became a best-selling series, and over twelve million copies have been sold throughout the world.

The stories follow Postman Pat as he drives his post office delivery van around the hills and villages of Greendale (inspired by the valleys of Cumbria in the north of England) accompanied by Jess, his black-and-white cat. His friends include the Reverend Timms, Mrs. Goggins the postmistress, farmer Alf Thompson, handyman Ted Glen, and busybody and flower arranger Miss Hubbard, who is usually encountered on her bicycle. New episodes were made in 1991 that introduced Postman Pat's wife, Sara, and his son, Julian. More recently, a bigger school, an Indian family running the railway, and pastimes like ten-pin bowling have been included in the storylines.

All the adventures center around Pat's postal delivery round, in which small frustrations and inconveniences—such as laundry blowing away or blocked roads—coincide improbably with bigger dramas—a circus, a spy, a runaway train. Pat takes everything in stride and all is eventually resolved. Phlegmatic, kind, and reliable, family man Pat is a low-key, likable hero in an age of inflated superheroes. **VN**

3+

Ernest and Celestine Have Lost Simon 1981

Gabrielle Vincent

Full Title | Ernest et Célestine ont perdu Siméon
Nationality | Belgian, born 1928
Publisher | Casterman, Belgium
Theme | Friendship

You do not even have to open this book to know you will be touched by the story and its characters. Gabrielle Vincent's drawings of Ernest and Celestine convey, from the front cover, all the tenderness and poetry with which she has infused her texts.

Ernest is a poor bear who has sheltered and fathered Celestine ever since he discovered the mischievous baby mouse in the garbage when he was cleaning the streets. Together they live poorly but happily. Each book in the Ernest and Celestine series brings forth key values such as love, generosity, and the power of imagination, most strikingly in the Christmas episode in which Ernest and Celestine are too poor to afford a Christmas tree but nevertheless manage to delight all their friends with thoughtful, small presents.

Ernest and Celestine is a series of a rare perfection. Its illustrations, reminiscent of Beatrix Potter's humanlike animals, focus on emotions more than actions. In *Ernest and Celestine Have Lost Simon*, the first book in the series, Celestine has lost her stuffed penguin. We see Ernest's relentless efforts to soothe his foster child as he brings her dozens of other stuffed animals and dolls. His efforts are in vain, so to divert her from her pain, he decides to throw a big party. The simple story deals tactfully with poignant matters, such as loss, mourning, and, above all, attachment in a manner that young children can relate to. The books are charming, and it is easy to see why Gabrielle Vincent gained worldwide recognition. **MGR**

3+

Alfie Gets In First 1981

Shirley Hughes

Nationality | English, born 1927
Publisher | Bodley Head, UK
Honor | O.B.E. for Children's Literature, 1999
Theme | Favorite character, Adventure

Alfie Gets In First introduces the young hero as he runs determinedly home along the pavement ahead of his mother and baby Annie Rose. The scene is a street of brick row houses in England. The events that follow are those everyday occurrences that, when imbued with all the emotional significance of early childhood, carry the weight of whole worlds condensed into small familiar spaces. Desperate to get into the house first, Alfie slams the door shut behind him, locking his mother out and himself in the house alone.

The tension derives from the split narrative: Alfie, on the right-hand side of the double-page spreads, stands forlornly isolated, his tensely stretched fingers and anguished posture conveying his utter misery to even the youngest child. Meanwhile, on the left-hand side, in a nod to the traditional cumulative tale, a succession of friends arrives offering helpful but unsuccessful suggestions. The growing size of the group outside makes Alfie's isolation painfully evident; the divide between them is indicated in the white space between the two pages and made explicit in the black vertical line of the door that separates them, its latch high above Alfie's head. By the time the group comes up with a solution, young listeners are already happily conscious that Alfie is working on a plan of his own, one unvoiced in the text but manifested in the illustrations. Their delight is mirrored in Alfie's own pleasure as he holds the door open, standing back "grandly" to let everyone in. **KA**

One Woolly Wombat 1982

Rod Trinca Kerry Argent

Nationality | Australian, born 1954 (author); Australian, born 1960 (illustrator)
Publisher | Omnibus Books, Australia
Theme | Animal stories, Rhyming stories

One Woolly Wombat contains many iconic Australian animals, including koalas, kangaroos, echidnas, and the duck-billed platypus. They are beautifully depicted doing typically Aussie things—sunbathing, partying, and splashing in the water. Each animal is accompanied by engaging text that uses rhyme, rhythm, and alliteration and is a joy to read aloud. Kerry Argent's stunning, highly detailed pencil-and-watercolor illustrations make this a book to treasure.

It is not easy to convincingly portray animals doing things that do not come naturally, and yet Argent's animals look comfortable and "normal" engaging in distinctly nonanimal activities. Her kangaroos dance, wear bow ties and pearls, and look like they are having loads of fun. The goanna, wearing a chef's hat and apron and wondering what to cook for dinner, is inspired. The wombat reclining in a deck chair in his shorts, hat, and sunglasses is simply adorable. These illustrations work well because Argent matches each animal as closely as possible to their human activity: the koalas, which in the wild have a penchant for leaves, are drinking tea; the possums, notorious for their appetites, are searching for treats; and the kookaburras, also known as laughing jackasses, are aptly shown writing riddle books.

The design of the book also adds to its excellence. The appropriate numeral is ghosted under the text, and this informative book is perfect for introducing children to numbers and Australian animals. **SOR**

Avocado Baby 1982

John Burningham

Nationality | English, born 1936
Publisher | Jonathan Cape, UK
Theme | Family, Quirky, Classics, Adventure

3+

With its vivid illustrations and ironic text, *Avocado Baby* has delighted young readers and their parents since it was first published in 1982. The award-winning author and illustrator explores the problems of children who are picky eaters and just what a superhuman baby might get up to.

Mr. and Mrs. Hargreaves and their children are a kind but scrawny family. When a new baby is born, they fear that he will be just as scrawny as they are. They want him to grow up to be big and strong, but the baby refuses to eat any of the food that is put in front of him. In desperation, Mrs. Hargreaves gives him an avocado that she has found in the fruit bowl, and strange things begin to happen. The baby develops superhuman strength and breaks out of the straps of his high chair. Still wearing his blue pajamas, he accomplishes feats of amazing strength and bravery: He scares off a burglar, pushes the car when it will not start, and moves the grand piano. His father is then forced to put a "Beware of the Baby" sign on the garden gate. In the final sequence, the baby takes decisive action when his older siblings are being threatened in the park. He jumps out of his stroller and throws the bothersome bullies into the pond.

In fewer than 350 words, John Burningham weaves a tale of hilarious derring-do that will have young children in fits of giggles. Burningham has said that he does not just write for children, he writes for people; this story bears reading again and again. **HJ**

"Nobody knew how it had got there because the Hargreaves never bought avocados."

OTHER JOHN BURNINGHAM TITLES

***Mr. Gumpy's Outing,* 1970**
***Come Away from the Water, Shirley,* 1977**
***Would You Rather?,* 1978**
***Granpa,* 1984**
***Oi! Get Off Our Train,* 1989**

Gorilla 1983

Anthony Browne

Nationality | English, born 1946
Publisher | Julia MacRae Books, UK
Award | Kate Greenaway Medal
Theme | Fantasy, Friendship

Gorilla was Anthony Browne's breakthrough book, winning both the Kate Greenaway Medal and the Kurt Maschler Award in 1983. As well as being a classic of anthropomorphism, it is a story about the power of imagination and dreams that console a lonely little girl who lives with her depressed father.

Hannah's father buries himself in work, and the only sign of her absent mother is a blank picture frame. Hannah is sustained by her love of art and her obsession with gorillas—she has drawn and painted so many gorillas that one has somehow entered her psyche and shown itself as her shadow. When she has a silent breakfast with her father, images of gorillas can be seen in the cereal box and on her father's newspaper. Hannah's wild and adventurous gorilla world appears after dark, encroaching on the wall as she watches television.

When she is disappointed by her father's gift of a small toy gorilla, tame in every sense, the vertical bars of Hannah's iron bed frame suggest the bars of a cage at the zoo, where she longs to go. The gorilla grows in the night, fills her father's clothes, and takes her on her dream outing. She is happy that her loneliness is over, but saddened by the plight of the primates behind bars. She prefers the celluloid primate in *Supergorilla*, one of many witty visual references, and the topiary primates that join her and her father-gorilla in a dance. When she wakes up, she finds life imitating art: Her father has come out of his depression sufficiently to begin to notice her. **GB**

Angelina Ballerina 1983

Katharine Holabird Helen Craig

Author | American, born 1948 (author); English, born 1934 (illustrator)
Publisher | Aurum Press, UK
Theme | Favorite characters

Angelina Ballerina is a little mouse who dreams of being a ballet dancer. Her real name is Angelina Mouseling, she lives in Chipping Cheddar with her parents, and she spends every waking moment dancing. She dances when she is supposed to be doing her homework, cleaning her bedroom, or helping to lay the table. She makes herself late for school because she cannot stop dancing.

For a while Angelina's parents are cross about her constant dancing, but then they realize that she should be encouraged and they come up with a wonderful idea: They give Angelina a tutu and tell her that they have decided she should start ballet lessons. Angelina is enrolled at Miss Lilly's School for Girls, where she makes new friends—and rivals—and where she becomes one of Miss Lilly's star pupils. Her parents are much happier because now that Angelina is dancing at school she is much more focused at home and always helps her parents when they ask her. Angelina grows to idolize Miss Lilly and wants to be as good at dancing as her teacher.

Angelina Ballerina shows that no matter what shape or size you are, it is always possible to dance and follow your dreams. Since the publication of this, the very first Angelina book, the little mouse who longed to dance has become a phenomenon, appearing in a series of books dealing with subjects that include learning how to ice-skate, having a new baby sister, discovering the thrill of performing onstage, and coping with jealousy. **LH**

Dusty Wants to Help 1983

Inger Sandberg Lasse Sandberg

3+

Nationality | Swedish, born 1930 (author); Swedish, born 1924 (illustrator)
Publisher | Rabén and Sjögren, Sweden
Theme | Family

Dusty, the title character in the Swedish best-seller *Hjälpa till, sa Pulvret,* is a charming and energetic two-year-old boy. His mother has to leave him while she goes out to do the shopping, and Grandpa, who has promised to stay and babysit, decides it would be a good idea to make pancakes. To Grandpa's distress, Dusty wishes to get involved, too, in his own special way: "'I want to help,' says Dusty, swishing his hands in the egg mixture." The determined little boy manages to create quite a mess. When his mother returns in time for the pancakes, she finds an exhausted Grandpa, and Dusty has his own little surprise for them both.

Married couple Inger and Lasse Sandberg worked together as author and illustrator for more than half a century (Lasse died in November 2008), becoming one of the biggest successes in Swedish children's literature, as well as popular figures internationally. Their mission was to write for the most important people—the little ones. They have produced more than one hundred books, including *Little Spook's Baby Sister* and *The Little Ghost Godfrey.*

"'I want to help,' says Dusty, swishing his hands in the egg mixture . . ."

The right of children to play is a common theme throughout their work, and *Dusty Wants to Help* is no exception. The beauty with this award-winning book lies in the balance between the action-filled, well-adapted text and the funny, clever illustrations. The charming figures are simple yet full of expression. *Dusty Wants to Help* is a vivid picture book, full of character, that will appeal to young children and their parents. **CC**

OTHER WORKS BY THE SANDBERGS

***Little Ghost Godfrey* (*Lilla spöket Laban*), 1965**
***Little Spook's Grubby Day* (*Labolinas snubbeldag*), 1977**
***Dusty Wants to Borrow Everything* (*Låna den, sa Pulvret*), 1984**

We Are the Triplets 1983

Roser Capdevila

Original Title | Som les tres bessones
Nationality | Spanish, born 1939
Publisher | Arin, Spain
Theme | Family, Friendship

3+

The triplets in these stories—Ana, Teresa, and Elena (Anna, Teresa, and Helena in the English version)—are distinguished only by the color of their hair ribbons (pink for Ana, blue for Teresa, and green for Elena). However, these bonds are far from being a symbol of coquetry or recklessness, as can be the case with other female characters in children's literature. These three sisters are an inquisitive, intelligent, and self-sufficient trio of girls.

The author, Roser Capdevila, created these characters in 1983; they were based on her triplet daughters. Capdevila was an enthusiastic admirer of the drawings of Jean-Jacques Sempé and studied fine arts in Barcelona. The first book, entitled *We Are the Triplets* (*Som les tres bessones*) was published in Catalan, and it is based on the three girls' first year. This book was followed by eight more, including *We Go to School* (*Ya vamos a la escuela*), *We Are Making Music* (*Hacemos musica*), and *We Build a City* (*Construimos una ciudad*).

Two years later, in 1985, the series The Triplets and . . . (*Las Tres mellizas y . . .*) appeared, later reissued under the title *The Triplets and Classic Tales* (*Las Tres mellizas y los cuentos clásicos*). Over the course of more than one hundred books, the triplets get into scrapes and binds. Their misbehavior is "punished" by the Bored Witch, who magically inserts them into traditional stories and fairy tales—from fables such as Cinderella, Little Red Riding Hood, and Hansel and Gretel, to universal fictional favorites such as Oliver Twist, Romeo and Juliet, and Don Quixote. The plots of each story are altered and some of its values are modified to fit the whims of the three little girls. Each book ends with a series of games and puzzles. The Triplets books were so popular that a television series was made, which was translated into more than thirty languages and appeared in 158 countries. **EB**

LAS TRES MELLIZAS,
HANSEL Y GRETEL
M. Company ⋆ R. Capdevila
Planeta

MORE BOOKS IN THE TRIPLETS SERIES

The Triplets and Gaudi (Las Tres mellizas y Gaudi), 2002
The Triplets and Moby Dick (Las Tres mellizas y Moby Dick), 2002
The Secret Diary of the Bored Witch (El diario secreto de la bruja Aburrida), 2007

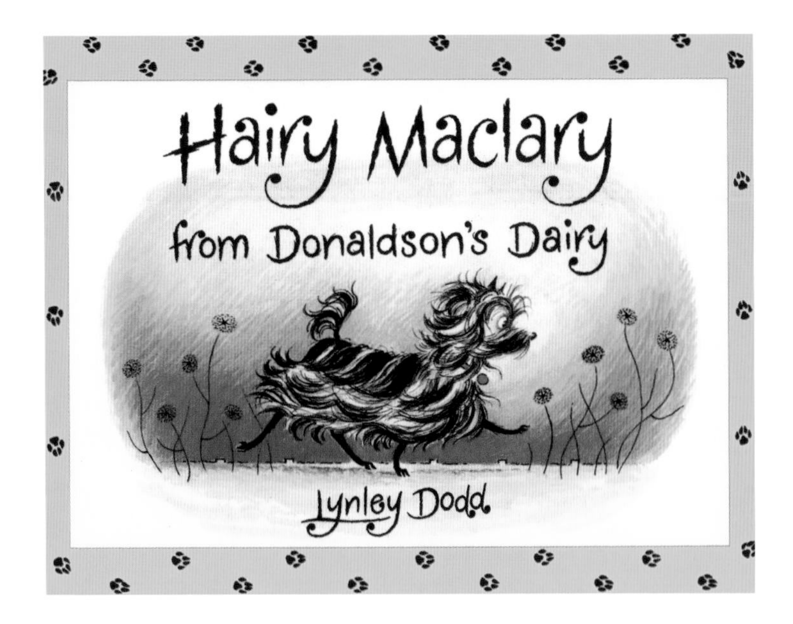

Hairy Maclary from Donaldson's Dairy 1983

Lynley Dodd

Nationality | New Zealander, born 1941 (author); English, born 1934 (illustrator)
Publisher | Mallinson Rendel, New Zealand
Theme | Favorite characters, Adventure

Dogs, says Lynley Dodd, are universal. Although the lively canines that scamper across the pages of the sixteen Hairy Maclary books are loved the world over, their setting is distinctively that of Dodd's native New Zealand, where a "dairy" is a corner store and has nothing to do with milk. As much as the drawings zing with the flair of a trained artist, it is their partnership with the snazzy, repetitive rhymes that has made Dodd's picture books favorites with young children and nursery teachers. All the characters have rhyming characteristics: Bottomley Potts, covered in spots; Hercules Morse, big as a horse; Schnitzel von Krumm, with the very low tum. Their adventures are unashamedly doggy—stealing a bone, upsetting the veterinarian's waiting room, or chasing the terrifying cat, Scarface Claw.

Like all great fictional characters, Hairy Maclary has taken on a life of his own. "I was only going to write one Hairy book," Dodd reminisces, "but one day I saw a small dog come out of the butcher's with a large amount of meat hanging from its jaws and trot away down the street, and I thought, 'That's Hairy number two: What does he do when he gets home? Does he ever get to eat it?'" Hairy Maclary books show, as Dodd has said, "a world of chaos and anarchy, but not bleak. I tell a story to entertain. I don't know if bleak is good for children." The cozy, dog-friendly resolution of another Dodd favorite, *Dragon in a Wagon,* puts it well: "No sharks, no bats, no hairy yaks, no dragons in a jam. Just the face, the friendly face, the DOGGY face of Sam." **VN**

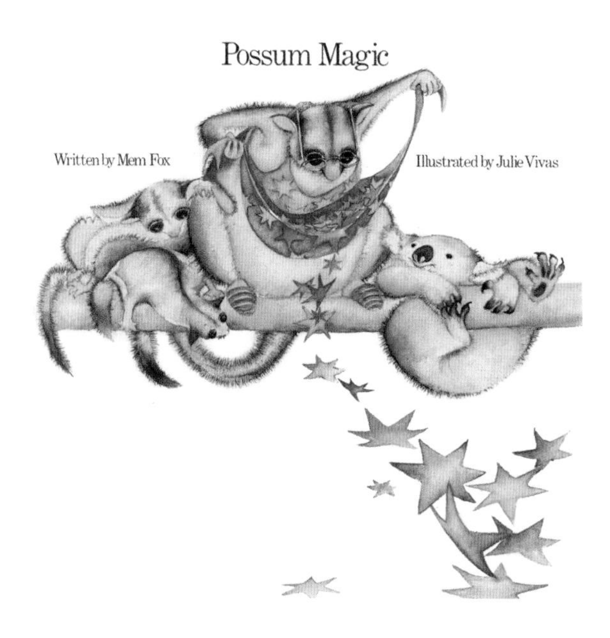

Possum Magic
Written by Mem Fox
Illustrated by Julie Vivas

3+

Possum Magic 1983

Mem Fox Julie Vivas

Nationality | Australian, born 1946 (author); Australian, born 1947 (illustrator)
Publisher | Omnibus Books, Australia
Theme | Magical stories, Animal stories

Deep in the Australian bush, Grandma Poss makes bush magic, and her best trick is making her granddaughter Hush invisible. The young possum has lots of fun sliding down kangaroos' tails and staying safe from snakes, but when she wants to rejoin the world of the visible, Grandma Poss cannot remember how to reverse the spell. She rereads all her books before she remembers something about "people food." The two of them set off on a trip around Australia, looking for the dish that will make Hush reappear. Many of the foods of Australia make an appearance—from Anzac biscuits and pumpkin scones to pavlova, lamingtons, and Vegemite sandwiches—and bit by bit, Hush rematerializes. Now, every year, Grandma and Hush eat a feast of these foods, just to make sure that Hush never disappears again.

Mem Fox's original story featured a mouse, but her publisher wanted more Australian content, so the book was rewritten and reillustrated, and *Possum Magic* quickly became the best-known picture book in Australia. Its jaunty rhythms, with dashes of rhyme and alliteration, make it fun to read aloud. Julie Vivas's vibrant watercolor illustrations are humorous and quirky. Grandma Poss's sneakers and eyeglasses make her a lovable eccentric, and the sparkles and stars that indicate the presence of magic will delight readers.

Parents and children can also learn a lot about Australia. On the last page is a glossary that describes the dishes for non-Australians and a map that traces the pair's journey around the country. **CQ**

Felix & Alexander

Terry Denton

Felix and Alexander 1985

Terry Denton

Nationality | Australian, born 1950
Publisher | Oxford University Press, Australia
Award | C.B.C.A. Picture Book of the Year
Theme | Friendship

Fear of the dark can be very real when you are a child. *Felix and Alexander* explores this fear in an ultimately reassuring way. Felix, a toy dog, is the loving companion of Alexander who, although he is small, goes for a walk near his apartment block every afternoon. One evening Alexander does not come home at the usual time and, as darkness descends, a very worried Felix makes a daring escape down a drainpipe and goes out into the unfamiliar city streets to find his friend.

Although the tale is simply and engagingly told, Terry Denton's haunting illustrations bring it to life. As night closes in, the houses on the streets have an anthropomorphic look, looking down on the tiny figure of the dog like disapproving maiden aunts. As Felix ventures deeper into the city, the threatening mauves and purples of night dominate the pictures. A double-page spread shows a clearly terrified Felix scampering past a row of houses, whose darkened doorways look like the mouths of ravening monsters.

There is little sign here of the quirky style that has since become Denton's trademark. His illustrations are detailed and architectural, and the design adds to the impact of the book because each page of text is colored to match the emotions expressed in the accompanying illustrations. Once the brave little dog has rescued his friend from the "terrors" of the night, they find their way home by following a trail made by the stuffing that has leaked out from a tear in Felix's side. The ending is suitably warm and reassuring. **SOR**

Pancakes for Findus 1985

Sven Nordqvist

Original Title | Pannkakstårten
Nationality | Swedish, born 1946
Publisher | Bokförlaget Opal, Sweden
Theme | Friendship, Quirky

Has Farmer Pettson gone nuts? Granted, he is scatterbrained and nothing short of original, and yes, he is constantly talking to his cat, but why is he climbing all over the house, tying a red curtain to his cat's tail? And what is the plan with the giant bucket full of pancake batter?

All these strange things take place on Pettson's cat's birthday. His cat, Findus, celebrates his birthday three times a year because the inseparable duo find it much more fun to celebrate often. Every time it is the cat's birthday, Pettson thoughtfully makes him a cake. It is in the making of the cake that all the confusion takes place, much to the amusement of his watchful neighbor, Gustavsson: "'Hello, Pettson. Working hard as usual, I see,' said Gustavsson, peering curiously at the eggy mess." But the farmer is far from nuts. Pettson manages to make his stack of pancakes and clear up the chaos, and he and his cat enjoy yet another lovely birthday together.

Sven Nordqvist's pictures are both colorful and full of detail. A lot of action takes place in each and every illustration. Throughout the series of nine books, the observant reader is rewarded with many discoveries alongside the main story. There are little mice taking baths under the drainpipe, a miniature bicycle leaning against the mixing bowl, and little green figures laughing at one of the crazy events. Nordqvist admits to being inspired by the illustration style of *MAD* magazine. **CC**

Love You Forever 1986

Robert Munsch Sheila McGraw

Nationality | Canadian, born 1945 (author); Canadian, birth date unknown (illustrator)
Publisher | Firefly Books, Canada
Theme | Family, Illness and death

There is no denying the fact that parents either love or hate this book. But when a book has sold more than twenty million copies, large numbers of people are enjoying it somewhere. And make no mistake: *Love You Forever* is written as much for parents as it is for children. Robert Munsch wrote the book when he and his wife were suffering from the loss of two stillborn children. Be warned, the storyline pulls firmly on the heartstrings as the loving mother in the book eventually grows old and dies. If your children are sensitive, you should read the book yourself before you read it to them.

This is a sentimental story of a mother who rocks her newborn baby to sleep each night while singing these words: "I'll love you forever / I'll like you for always / As long as you're living / My baby you'll be." She continues to sing the words to her son throughout his life–during the difficult "terrible twos" period, when he is an active nine-year-old, and through his teenage years. She even sneaks into his house by climbing up a ladder to sing to him when he is an adult. Eventually the mother ages, and the son sings the song to her as she dies, and then to his own infant son back at home.

Popular with mothers of sons, *Love You Forever* is guaranteed to bring tears from some readers, both young and old. The simple pastel palette of the artwork suits the emotional storyline, but the subject matter of this book is not for everyone, and probably not for any preschool children who are prone to getting easily upset. **KD**

This Is the Bear 1986

Sarah Hayes Helen Craig

Nationality | English, born 1945 (author); English, born 1934 (illustrator)
Publisher | Walker Books, UK
Theme | Adventure, Friendship, Animal stories

This Is the Bear is the story of a boy, a dog, and a much-loved teddy bear called Fred. When the dog pushes Fred into the garbage and he is carted off to the dump, his young owner bravely sets out to find him. He encounters grumpy garbage men who reluctantly search through piles of trash without success. The day is eventually saved by the dog who sniffs out Fred, "all cold and cross," and the trio returns home, thanks to a ride in the garbage man's van. Fred refuses to tell the other toys where he has been, and then to add a happy twist, asks his young owner if they can have another day out.

With its reassuringly happy ending, young children will delight in this simple tale, and it has become a firm favorite among young readers and their parents. Sarah Hayes's rhyming couplets ("This is the bear who fell in the bin. This is the dog who pushed him in,") and repetitive structure mean that readers can quickly learn the words by heart and anticipate what comes next. Helen Craig—who has subsequently enjoyed great success with the Angelina Ballerina series about the adventures of a ballet-dancing mouse—provides warm, thoughtful, and funny illustrations. These come complete with speech bubbles showing what all the characters are thinking—from the dog who thinks he is a champion for finding Fred to the trash man who thinks he must be mad to drive them all home, for example.

Their adventures continue in a number of books, including *This Is the Bear and the Scary Night* in which Fred is accidentally left on a bench in the park. **HJ**

Old Bear 1986

Jane Hissey

Nationality | English, born 1952
Publisher | Hutchinson, UK
Theme | Favorite characters, Animal stories, Friendship

Old Bear is a worn and frayed teddy bear who was put in the attic by his owners for safekeeping and has long been forgotten. The other toys in the nursery, which include Little Bear, a giraffe called Jolly Tall, Hoot the owl, and Ruff the dog, set about rescuing him. It is no easy feat, but with the help of a toy airplane, they eventually bring him down to the nursery where he then continues to live with his new friends.

Old Bear and his friends went on to feature in a number of stories created by author and illustrator Jane Hissey. Their adventures involve the sort of activities that small children love: helping each other, playing games, celebrating birthdays, putting on plays, and making camps.

These are gentle and funny stories that will delight younger readers. In *Little Bear's Trousers*, for example, Little Bear wakes up one morning to find his trousers missing. He asks his friends if they have seen them, and it soon becomes clear that they have all used them for various purposes—Rabbit has used them as a skiing hat and Duck as a flag for his sand castle. In *Little Bear Lost*, Little Bear manages to hide himself so well during a game of hide-and-seek that he completely disappears. Soon, a frantic bear hunt is underway, but as in all the books in the Old Bear series, there is a happy ending with some surprises along the way.

Hissey slowly and carefully creates her illustrations using pencil and crayons and chooses her characters based on their texture. She uses real toys—some of which she had as a child—to create an enchanting world for the under five age group. **HJ**

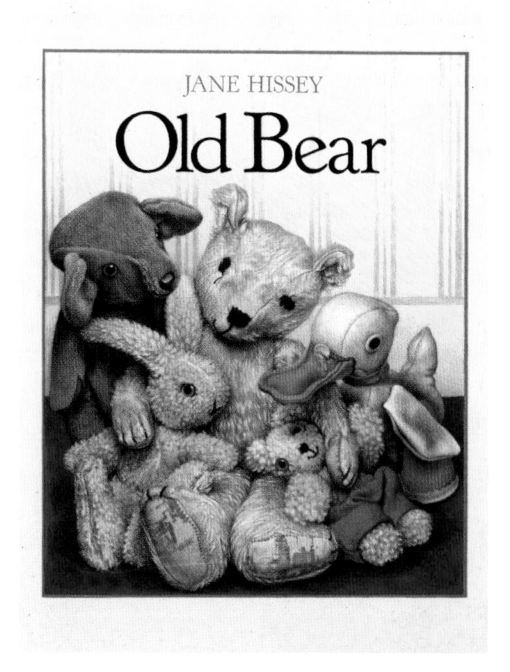

"One day the toys were sitting by the window when they remembered their friend Old Bear."

OTHER CUTE TEDDY BEAR BOOKS

Corduroy by Don Freeman, 1968
Little Bear's Trousers by Jane Hissey, 1987
Where's My Teddy by Jez Alborough, 1992
Good Night, Little Bear (Schlaf gut, kleiner Bär) by Quint Buchholz, 1997

Owl Moon 1987

Jane Yolen John Schoenherr

3+

Nationality | American, born 1939 (author); American, born 1935 (illustrator)
Publisher | Philomel Books, USA
Theme | Science and nature, Family

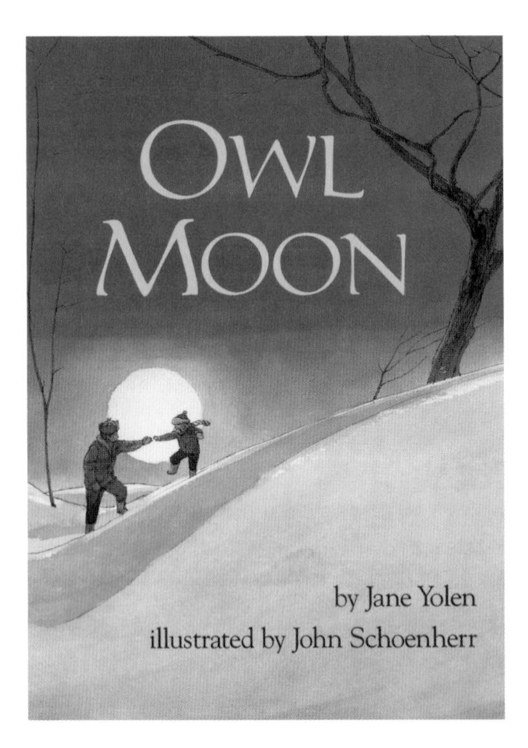

This poetic narrative clearly presents a meditative account of a child experiencing the beauty of the natural world. One snowy winter's night, a father takes his young daughter on a special expedition to see a great horned owl for the first time. The storyline is simple and the pace, slow: *Owl Moon* is a sensitive tale of hope and discovery that encourages young children to observe wildlife respectfully and to feel reverence for the wonder of nature. The daughter is taught that she must be aware of her environment and be patient and quiet if she wants to see an owl. When the owl finally arrives, the relief of the daughter is clear—not only has she seen an owl, but she can now break her silence.

"An owl shadow, / part of the big tree shadow, / lifted off and flew right over us."

John Schoenherr's icy illustrations are a striking accompaniment to Jane Yolen's evocative text, which, according to the author, is a biographical amalgam of the many nighttime owling trips her husband David and daughter Heidi were so fond of making together. *Owl Moon* is one of Yolen's best-known works and was awarded the 1988 Caldecott Medal for Schoenherr's delicate and picturesque watercolors, based on the winter wonderland setting of his own family farm in New Jersey. The story has been translated into many languages, including French, German, Chinese, and Korean, and has even inspired a song by the musician Bruce O'Brian. It is an enduring tale that captures the tender relationship between a father and a daughter, as well as that between human beings and the environment, instilling in children an interest in the beauty and fragility of the natural world. **ML**

OTHER BEAUTIFUL JANE YOLEN READS

***Dragon's Blood*, 1982**
***Heart's Blood*, 1984**
***A Sending of Dragons*, 1987**
***Sister Light, Sister Dark*, 1988**
***Wizard's Hall*, 1991**

Winnie the Witch 1987

Valerie Thomas Korky Paul

Winnie is daffy, ditzy, and desperately disorganized. As she drifts around on her disobedient broom, her cat, Wilbur, keeps a sardonic eye on her. Since her first appearance in 1987, Winnie has won a special place in the hearts of young children. In each of the nine books so far published, she struggles with such everyday tasks as redecorating, having a birthday, or going on holiday. She is even less adept at magical tasks such as buying a new wand, adopting a baby dragon, or breaking in a magic carpet. Her forgetfulness is compounded by short-sightedness, to hilarious effect. The comedy, and much of the series' success, is largely due to the skill of illustrator Korky Paul, who has realized Valerie Thomas's idea

"Winnie lived . . . with her cat, Wilbur. He was black. And that is how the trouble began."

in incident-filled illustrations in which spidery pen-and-ink drawings dance over delicate watercolors.

Parents who recognize their own unimportant inadequacies, as well as teachers wanting to reinforce lessons about learning from mistakes, enjoy these books on a deeper level than the slapstick fun that children love. This first in the series has fun with the idea of a witch, traditionally clad in black with a black cat, planning to redecorate her black castle so that she can find her cat instead of walking all over him by mistake. She changes Wilbur's color to green, only to find she cannot find him outside. She tries waving her wand over him five times and turns him into a five-color cat. With a strong sense of his own dignity, Wilbur does not enjoy looking ridiculous. Tender-hearted Winnie finally hits on an obvious solution: Turn the cat back to black and paint the house in bright colors. **VN**

Nationality | Australian, birth date unknown (author); English, born 1951 (illustrator)
Publisher | Oxford University Press, UK
Theme | Magical stories, Favorite characters

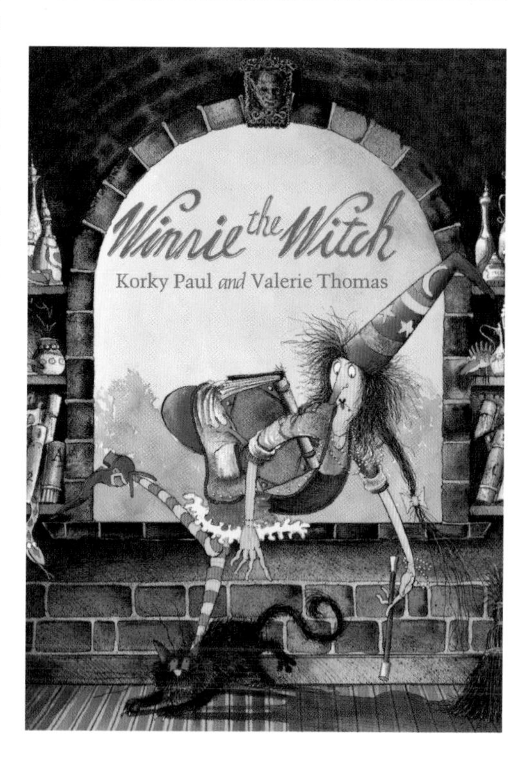

OTHER BOOKS STARRING WINNIE

***Winnie in Winter*, 1996**
***Winnie Flies Again*, 1999**
***Winnie's New Computer*, 2003**
***Happy Birthday Winnie*, 2007**

3+

Martin Waddell **Barbara Firth**

Can't You Sleep, Little Bear? 1988

Martin Waddell Barbara Firth

Nationality | Irish, born 1941 (author); English, born 1928 (illustrator)
Publisher | Walker Books, UK
Theme | Favorite characters

In the award-winning first book of Martin Waddell and Barbara Firth's Little Bear series, Little Bear cannot sleep because he is scared of the dark. Big Bear brings a series of progressively bigger lanterns to stop Little Bear from being scared, but still Little Bear does not go to sleep. Although Big Bear really wants to finish reading his book, which is just getting to the interesting part, he remains calm and reasonable with Little Bear. But even when Big Bear has brought the "Biggest Lantern of Them All," Little Bear still fears the dark outside. Big Bear is stumped for a moment, but then he leads Little Bear out of the cave into the night. Here two fabulous contrasting spreads show first the bears stepping from the brightly lit cave into the dark, and then outside in the dark night, with the light issuing from the cave. Big Bear has come up with an answer: "I brought you the moon, Little Bear. The bright yellow moon and all the twinkly stars." He has brought the moon to light up the dark. It is a beautiful and touching expression of the trust small children invest in their parents. Problem solved, Little Bear falls asleep, and at last Big Bear gets to finish his book.

This is a book that is great for reading aloud. With each reading, there is more to spot in Firth's charmingly believable illustrations. She spent hours watching bears at a zoo before drawing *Little Bear*, and as a result the two bears have a genuine "bearishness," which is often absent in children's books. *You and Me, Little Bear* and *Let's Go Home, Little Bear* are equally delightful. **CW**

Crocodile Beat 1988

Gail Jorgensen Patricia Mullins

Nationality | Australian, born 1951 (author); Australian, born 1952 (illustrator)
Publisher | Omnibus Books, Australia
Theme | Rhyming stories, Animal stories

Crocodile Beat is a perfect read-aloud, all-join-in picture book for babies and toddlers. Gail Jorgensen cleverly combines rhyming couplets with animal sounds, actions, and an element of surprise.

First comes Crocodile who is feeling rather hungry, "Down by the river in the heat of the day / the crocodile sleeps and awaits his prey / *Zzzzzz Zzzzzz Zzzzzz Zzzzzz*." He dozes as he waits for his dinner to come along. A colorful cast of noisy animals is then introduced to the reader: quacking, splashing ducks; thumping, booming elephants; chattering monkeys; swooping birds; a lion king who wants to sing; brown bears dancing; and a long snake hissing. They join into a long, riotous procession that stretches colorfully across a double-page spread. The parade of animals dances together to the rhythm of the jungle beat. As Crocodile begins to wake up, King Lion is feeling very brave and is determined to protect his friends from the jaws of Crocodile.

The illustrations are memorable. Patricia Mullins is famous for her paper collage technique. She skillfully captures each animal's shape and gestures perfectly, using only layers of torn tissue paper. Tiny details, such as eyes and whiskers, are drawn later with a pen. Fake crocodile skin gives the crocodile his handsome hide, and scrunched paper creates the elephants' wrinkled skin. The white space behind all the colorful creatures highlights the movement and shapes of the animals in this fresh and original picture book. **AJ**

Stina 1988

Lena Anderson

3+

Original Title | Storm-Stina
Nationality | Swedish, born 1939
Publisher | Rabén and Sjögren, Sweden
Theme | Family

OTHER GREAT LENA ANDERSON TITLES

Linnea in Monet's Garden **by Christina Björk, illustrated by Lena Anderson, 1985**
***Stina's Visit*, 1991**
***Tea for Ten*, 1998**
***Hedgehog's Secret*, 2000**

Stina is a little girl who spends the long summer vacations with her grandfather on a small Swedish island. The days are filled with simple pleasures, such as fishing trips, walking, and playing on the sand. One night Stina decides to sneak out from her grandfather's little gray cottage and have an adventure of her own—but a huge storm is about to break, and Stina soon learns that the best way to watch it is with her grandfather.

Lena Anderson writes simple, funny, and engaging picture books for younger readers. Although there is not much action in the narrative, the stories all reflect a world that young children will instantly recognize. In this sense, her work has been compared with that of the highly successful British children's writer, Shirley Hughes. Anderson's beautiful watercolor illustrations convey a real sense of atmosphere and, in this book, conjure up a nostalgic world of seaside childhood vacations.

Stina was the first of two books, and in its sequel, *Stina's Visit*, our heroine is once again spending time with her grandfather. They decide to pay a birthday visit to Axel (whose nickname is "Stretchit"), an old friend of her grandfather who is feeling down in the dumps. The pair take along a special birthday meal and listen to Stretchit's tall tales of life at sea. It is a warm description of friendship, and even though Grandfather knows that Stretchit's stories are an exaggeration, he sits and listens to make his friend happy. Stina is very pleased to receive an old bathtub from Stretchit, which she can use as a boat for her toy hippo. Anderson has enjoyed international success with her books about Stina, although she is best known outside her native Sweden for *Linnea in Monet's Garden*, a gentle introduction to art history that was illustrated by Anderson and written by Christina Björk. **HJ**

Fire-Engine Lil 1989

Janet McLean Andrew McLean

Fire-Engine Lil is a great story to share with young children. Lil, an old pumper fire engine, still feels as young and as strong as the day she was built. She and her firefighter friends, Bob and Bill, have extinguished hundreds of fires over the years. Sadly, Lil has not been used to put out a fire for a very long time.

One hot summer morning, when all the flashy new fire engines are out at work, news comes in that a big grass fire is threatening to destroy Brown's farm. "My turn at last," Lil hums, and Bill, Bob, a cat, and a dog all clamber aboard the engine and away they go, her siren blaring. The evocative illustrations have readers experiencing all the feelings of Lil and her crew as they rush off to the fire: exasperation at being caught in a flock of sheep; exhilaration as they streak down the grassy hillsides; and caution as Lil, up to her mudguards in water, crosses a river. Finally they arrive at the scene of the fire, and soon Lil's hoses are sucking water from the dam and spraying the flames. Children will love the excitement and well-observed details in the firefighting scenes. The fire is almost out when a strong wind whips it up again to threaten the farmhouse. Hot and exhausted Lil pants, "I can't stop now . . . I was built to fight fires." She keeps on pumping the water for hours, and in the end, of course, Lil and her helpers save the day.

"She careered down the track, dodging stumps and rabbit holes as well as she could."

Andrew and Janet McLean's charming book features strong characters, a sense of drama, and a realistic backdrop to the narrative. The McLeans brilliantly capture gesture, expression, and place as only true storytellers can. **AJ**

Nationality | Australian, born 1946 (author); Australian, born 1946 (illustrator)
Publisher | Allen and Unwin, Australia
Theme | Adventure

OTHER TRANSPORTATION CLASSICS

***The Little Engine That Could* by Watty Piper, 1930**
***Little Toot* by Hardie Gramatky, 1939**
***Ivor the Engine* by Oliver Postgate, 1962**
***The Riverboat Crew* by Janet and Andrew Maclean, 1978**

3+

One Snowy Night 1989

Nick Butterworth

Nationality | English, born 1946
Publisher | William Collins, UK
Theme | Favorite characters, Animal stories, Friendship, Adventure

Percy the Park Keeper stories have been delighting young children since 1989 when the first, *One Snowy Night*, was published. The series has sold millions of copies worldwide and has been adapted into a popular television program. The stories featuring Percy and his friends have become children's classics thanks to the warmth and humor of the magical tales and the delightful illustrations.

Percy tends to the park by day with his green wheelbarrow before retiring each night to his hut with some cocoa, gingerbread cookies, and his old radio. He may live alone, but Percy is by no means lonely. As well as caring for the park, he is also a friend and a father figure to the animals, who are often getting themselves into scrapes. Although Percy is busy with his work, he is always on hand and happy to help. Whether he is surrounded by ice-dancing ducks, rabbits having snowball fights and falling down wells, an upset hedgehog who cannot hold a balloon without popping it, or a badger in need of a bath, Percy always knows what to do. Even when faced with freezing conditions, a storm toppling the animal's treetop home, or food going missing, he has a solution for his friends.

The animals get their opportunity to show their gratitude when Percy falls ill and they have to take control of the park, with typically surprising consequences. Percy's adventures are sure to enchant young children and feed their curiosity about what happens in the park when they are not looking. **SR**

3+

Mousehole Cat 1990

Antonia Barber Nicola Bayley

Nationality | English, born 1932 (author); English, born 1949 (illustrator)
Publisher | Walker Books, UK
Theme | Adventure

This is a traditional Cornish story about a brave fisherman who went to sea despite the storm that was keeping the tiny port of Mousehole under siege conditions. It is told through the eyes of his cat, Mowser.

In this dramatic and moving tale, the sprightly black-and-white Mowser accompanies Tom Bawcock into battle with the Great Storm-Cat (a towering tabby whose markings are echoed in the sea and the visible sound waves of the howling wind). The Storm-Cat has stopped fishing boats from getting past the tiny harbor-mouth. When Tom's craft slips into the open sea, a deadly game of cat and mouse begins, until Mowser soothes the Storm-Cat with purrs and meows. Tom catches enough fish to feed the village and brings his catch home on the night before Christmas Eve, welcomed by lights from the village.

The first section of the story, which sets up Tom and Mowser's adventure, is rich with wit and charm as it visits key village scenes (the pub, the shop, and Tom's cottage) from the point of view of comfort-seeking. The fine pointillist-style artwork has an enameled quality in the intricate interiors. The weave of a rope, the cable stitch on Tom's Aran sweater, and the embossed decoration on the iron stove are captured in great detail, with the overall glow to the pictures adding to the sense of a community battening down the hatches for winter. In contrast, the storm scenes are flooded with light and dynamism, suggesting a parallel fantasy world beyond the harbor wall that offers excitement as well as danger. **GB**

Amazing Grace 1991

Mary Hoffman   Caroline Binch

3+

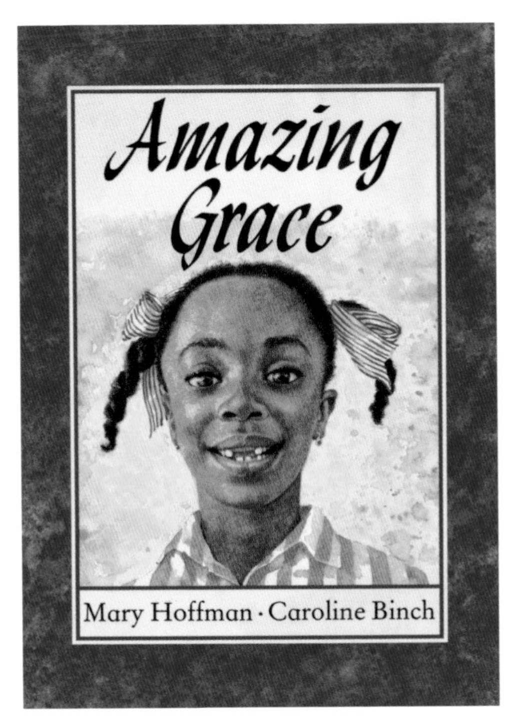

Nationality | English, born 1945 (author); English, born 1947 (illustrator)
Publisher | Frances Lincoln, UK; Dial Books, USA
Theme | School, Family, Friendship

The first sentence, "Once upon a time there was a little girl called Grace who loved stories," captures the energy of this profound picture book. Absorbing the wisdom of her grandmother, along with Nana's font of stories, Grace learns to let nothing stand in the way of the stories she wants to share with the world.

Acting out her favorite stories with her toys and her cat Paw-Paw, Grace is her own cast of thousands. She loves to fill the roles of Anansi, Hiawatha, Dick Whittington, and Mowgli, as well as to play pirates and doctors. Nonetheless, her confidence is shaken when classmates say she cannot be Peter Pan in the school play because she is a girl and she is black. Although Grace's mother is angry, her grandmother insists: "You can be anything you want to be, if you put your mind to it." Grace shines in the auditions and finally plays her dream role before an enchanted audience.

Caroline Binch's watercolors present affirming glimpses of real family life, including an exhausted working mother and Nana, who is playful as well as wise and dignified. The iconic images of Grace, Ma, and Nana are based on photographs of a real family. The illustrations extend the text in portraying Grace's multicultural classroom, and there is an enjoyable supplementary storyline in Paw-Paw's varying levels of willingness to join in Grace's shows.

Amazing Grace provides an opening for talking about race, gender, and self-esteem with young children. It has been used extensively through the early school years to generate activities and discussion on respect for difference and equal opportunities. **GB**

"Grace crossed the Alps with Hannibal and a hundred elephants, and she sailed the seven seas with a peg-leg . . ."

OTHER AMAZING BOOKS ABOUT GRACE

***Grace and Family,* 1995**
***Starring Grace,* 2000**
***Encore, Grace!,* 2003**
***Bravo, Grace!,* 2005**
***Princess Grace,* 2007**

Window 1991

Jeannie Baker

Nationality | English/Australian, born 1950
Publisher | Julia MacRae Books, UK; Greenwillow Books, USA
Theme | Science and nature

As with her earlier book *Where the Forest Meets the Sea*, Jeannie Baker once more chooses as her subject the impact that humans have on the natural world. Her picture book tells its story via painstakingly produced collages that hover somewhere between beautiful decoration and hyperrealism. This somehow makes us look more closely and contemplate her message all the more deeply. The major difference with this book, however, is that there are no words at all.

The book, quite literally, gives us a window into a world where nature is rapidly losing the race against creeping urbanization. Baker's pictures consist of a series of views out of windows to a changing vista outside. A mother and her baby son, Sam, look out of their window onto unspoiled landscape, but as Sam gets older, the view gradually changes. A farm appears, then more housing, and finally, by the time Sam has turned twenty, a sprawling, dirty city. Sam marries and settles in the country. He holds his own baby and gazes out of a window onto empty wilderness. Outside, however, some trees have been cleared and an ominous sign erected: "House Blocks For Sale." This echoes the ghostly boat bobbing in the waters at the end of *Where the Forest Meets the Sea*, which bears the words "Paradise Real Estate."

Younger children will love the textures of the wilderness and spotting the animals living in it. Older ones will appreciate some of the smaller visual details and connect with Baker's brief parting message: "By understanding and changing the way we personally affect the environment, we can make a difference." **AK**

Slinky Malinki 1991

Lynley Dodd

Nationality | New Zealander, born 1941
Publisher | Mallinson Rendel, New Zealand
Theme | Animal stories, Adventure, Rhyming stories

By day, Slinky Malinki is a well-behaved and innocent-looking pussycat. At night, however, he becomes an unscrupulous thief who steals anything that he fancies: a clothes peg, a slipper, a string of sausages, a clock. Slinky Malinki lopes across the page in a perfect marriage of words and pictures, all bristling black fur, sinuous limbs, and glinting green eyes. Lynley Dodd, who also created the popular character Hairy Maclary, is well acquainted with cats of all kinds. She grew up with hordes of cats in the countryside and owns a "very badly behaved Burmese" cat herself.

As with the Hairy Maclary books, Slinky Malinki's adventures are described with repetitive, enjoyable rhymes and a vocabulary that relishes the sounds of words as well as their meaning: "Slinky Malinki was blacker than black, . . . a stalking and lurking adventurous cat." However, this is no anthropomorphic puss dressed up like Beatrix Potter's Tom Kitten; this is the kind of mischievous cat at whom people readily shoot water pistols.

In *Open the Door*, for example, Slinky Malinki teams up with Stickybeak Syd, the rainbow lorikeet, to wreak havoc in the house. In *Catflaps*, he sneaks out to confront his savage enemy, Scarface Claw, but loses courage—despite the help of his accomplices such as Greywacke Jones, Butterball Brown, and the Poppadum Kittens—and flees home to his comfortable cushion by the fire. The consequences, as in all Dodd's work, are "anarchy and chaos." Dodd has said that she writes what she liked to read as a child. Millions of young children and teachers like it, too. **VN**

T'choupi 1992

Thierry Courtin

Nationality | French, born 1954
Publisher | Nathan, France
Theme | Animal stories, Adventure, Favorite characters

The character of T'choupi, who is a funny and endearing penguin, was created by Thierry Courtin when his son was born. Since the publication of the first book, the antics of the cute little penguin have been narrated in a series of popular picture books. The modern design of *T'choupi* catches the eye: It is all round, simple, and vividly colored, and appeals to very young children and adults alike.

The main reason *T'choupi* has become so popular among young readers is that the little penguin is childlike himself; he lives at home with his parents, often spends time with his grandparents, and soon has a new addition to his family when his little sister is born. He has a favorite toy, Doudou, who is a stuffed bear that he takes everywhere. For T'choupi, Doudou is not merely a soft toy: he is a real friend, or even a brother, and T'choupi feels that he can share everything with him.

The different stories in the series mirror a child's everyday progress, misdeeds, and learning: T'choupi learns to use his potty (a most effective book according to parents), he does not want to go to bed, he does not like to lend his toys, and he is afraid of storms. All the books deal with events that are very familiar to children, including *T'choupi Is Too Greedy* in which T'choupi gets a stomachache after eating too much (the tragedy of this episode is that he is not hungry enough at dinner to eat his French fries). Parents have grown fond of the little penguin's adventures, too, and its success was such that in 2004, *T'choupi* was made into a movie. **MGR**

Frog in Winter 1992

Max Velthuijs

Nationality | Dutch, born 1923
Publisher | Andersen Press, UK
Theme | Friendship, Adventure, Animal stories, Science and nature

One morning Frog wakes up and discovers, to his surprise, that a new season has arrived. Like most frogs at this time of year, he is completely ill equipped to deal with the cold, wintry conditions. He cannot understand why everything is blanketed in white, and he slides and slips as he makes his way across the icy pond. Frog is not enjoying himself one bit and is far too cold to take part in any of the fun that Duck is having, skating around on the ice, or that Hare is having, throwing snowballs with his friends. All is not lost, however, because the other animals decide to come together to help Frog enjoy his winter; they build him a fire, give him hot soup, and fetch a cozy scarf in an attempt to warm him up. Even in the coldest of climes the animals are prepared to help their friend, although Frog will only be truly happy when spring arrives.

With his neat and simple lines and powerful, bold colors, Max Velthuijs tells his story just as it is, leaving interpretations of what lies behind this tale of friendship for the reader to decide. Despite his Dutch origins, Velthuijs's Frog character books were first published in English. The bright green character has all the traits of a wide-eyed child with the accompanying aspirations and thoughts. Each of the adventures in the series deals with its topics in a straightforward way, including books in which Frog has to cope with fear (*Frog Is Frightened*), falling in love (*Frog in Love*), and strangers (*Frog and the Stranger*), for example. In an ever-complicated world, Frog is a character to which young children can easily relate. **NH**

Max Velthuijs

Frog in Winter

WHERE'S MY TEDDY?
Jez Alborough

Where's My Teddy? 1992

Jez Alborough

Nationality | English, born 1959
Publisher | Walker Books, UK
Theme | Friendship, Adventure, Animal stories, Rhyming stories

Little Eddy sets off into a dark wood in search of his missing teddy. Surrounded by tall trees, he looks increasingly small. He suddenly comes across a giant stuffed teddy that is many times his own size, and then hears in the distance the sound of sobbing. This sad noise comes from a gigantic bear, who is holding Eddy's own tiny toy in the crook of its arm. The big bear is loudly grieving the loss of the huge toy bear that Eddy has just found. Having met face to face, each party makes off with the right teddy back to their own houses, where boy and bear snuggle down in their own beds, reunited with their favorite toy.

Told in rhyme, this clever picture book also deals with a whole host of interesting topics that are relevant to the very young. There is the issue of relative size: The teddy bear that looks huge to Eddy looks tiny to the giant bear. Infants are often accustomed to being the smallest person in the room and may not have thought, up to this moment, that they must also appear very big to anything that is smaller than they are. Then there is the whole question of who is frightened of whom. Eddy is naturally scared of a bear that is much bigger than he is, but then the bear is frightened, too, of someone who looks so very different from himself. Young readers may possibly be a little apprehensive about Eddy's journey into such a lonely and densely wooded forest and may, therefore, take heart from the idea that there could often be something else around the corner that is more scared than they are. Full of humor as well as insight, this delightful book is a real winner. **NT**

Okilélé 1993

Claude Ponti

Nationality | French, born 1948
Publisher | L'Ecole des Loisirs, France
Theme | Fairy tales, Family, Friendship, Fantasy, Controversial

Claude Ponti's stories are fairy tales that are aimed at children of all ages. With their rich graphics and colors, the illustrations immediately attract the attention of younger children; the many cultural references and the profusion of details appeal to older children.

Okilélé tells the story of a small creature in search of recognition. Okilélé was so named by his family because of his repulsive appearance: *"Oh, qu'il est laid!"* ("Oh, how ugly he is!") Aware of his ugliness, the little creature will do everything in his power to be accepted by his family. But his attempts exasperate his parents, who accuse him of being intrusive. The lonely child finds refuge under the kitchen sink, among the old bottles and garbage. There he meets Martin Réveil, who teaches him to read and write. With the help of his friend, Okilélé builds an underground house and invents a giant "parlophone," a device that enables him to communicate with the stars. Because his parents feel they can no longer put up with him, they decide to abandon their son and wall him up alive. But the parlophone has spoken: Okilélé is expected on a planet by someone who needs him! So begins a healing quest in which he will be metamorphosed and find answers to his existential questions.

Okilélé is a rich and dense story in which dreams and imagination play key roles. It deals with the themes of difference and happiness, using means of expression that are never menacing to the young reader but always funny and ingenious. It is a long story and a very beautiful journey that you will never want to end. **SL**

Sleep Well, Little Bear 1993

Quint Buchholz

3+

Original Title | Schlaf gut, kleiner Bär
Nationality | German, born 1957
Publisher | Sauerländer, Germany
Theme | Animal stories, Rhyming stories

OTHER GREAT QUINT BUCHHOLZ READS

The Collector of Moments, 1997
Nero Corleone: A Cat's Story, 1997
Some Folk Say the South Pole's Hot: The Three Tenors Play the Antarctic, 2001
Summer of the Pike, 2006

Quint Buchholz is known in Germany first and foremost as an illustrator. In *Sleep Well, Little Bear,* he brings together enchanting rhythmic prose and his trademark illustrations. The language captures a sleepy rhythm, and this picture book is the perfect bedtime read for a tired, wound-up child.

The narrative follows the thoughts of a little bear who does not feel tired at bedtime. He scrambles to the window and looks out at the meadows and the moon. Little Bear remembers all the adventures he had during the day: playing with the children in the river, pretending to be a pirate searching the high seas for gold, and digging in the garden with Mrs. Rose. He thinks of all the adventures he will have in the morning—in the meadow in the sun, or if it is raining, he will snuggle in the barn loft, looking out at the wet world.

"In the evening quiet, the clown is playing a sleep song on his violin for the baby elephant."

Finally, the little bear falls asleep. The language has such a dreamy quality that it is sure to lull readers to sleep, too. Inside the back cover of *Sleep Well, Little Bear* is an envelope attached to an illustration of a red balloon, which contains a letter. This mysterious red balloon floats through the narrative and provides a delightful surprise at the close of the story.

The illustrations also have a sleepy nighttime quality. Buchholz's delicate pencil drawings, which reflect the use of pointillism, capture scenes of the landscape as if they have been stopped in time. Moonlight reflects on the river, on the windows of the bedroom, on magical musicians playing softly from somewhere in the night. **RA**

Little bear stares at the moon shining through his window. 

Poems for the Very Young 1993

Michael Rosen Bob Graham

Nationality | English, born 1946 (editor); Australian, born 1942 (illustrator)
Publisher | Kingfisher, UK
Theme | Poetry

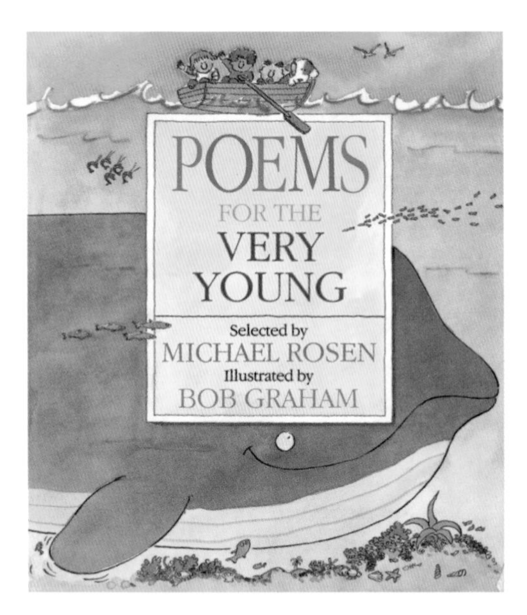

"Spaghetti! Spaghetti! / You're wonderful stuff / I love you spaghetti / I can't get enough."

OTHER CLASSIC MICHAEL ROSEN TITLES

***We're Going on a Bear Hunt*, 1989**
***Snore*, 1998**
***Oww*, 2003**
***The Bear in the Cave*, 2007**

As a poet, educator, and broadcaster, Michael Rosen understands that small children like the sounds that words make and appreciate patterns such as repetition, alliteration, and rhyming. It is, as he says, a physical experience.

In this anthology for very young children, Rosen (as the editor) has chosen more than one hundred short poems, with this experience in mind. The poems are from different periods of time and from a variety of cultures; they are grouped together thematically with several poems dotted about each page. Rosen has even included some rhymes that are written by children. All of the poems are delicious to roll around on the tongue and tickle the funny bone, even for older readers and adults. Willard R. Espy's poem, for example, opens with, "Whipper–snapper, rooty–tooty / Helter–skelter, tutti–frutti / Have a wing-ding, silly Billy / Lickety-split, don't shally-shilly." Apart from such delightful nonsense rhymes, there are also thought-provoking poems, such as John Cunliffe's "Snow Thoughts," a meditation in four lines on the life of a snowman. It is good to see the inclusion in the anthology of a few older rhymes, such as "Little Jumping Joan" and "Up and Down," as well as poems by illustrious authors such as A. A. Milne ("The more it snows / (Tiddely pom)"), Robert Louis Stevenson ("We built a ship upon the stairs / All made of the back-bedroom chairs"), and Eve Merriam ("Chitchat, wigwag, rickrack, zigzag / knickknack, gewgaw, riffraff, seesaw).

Artist Bob Graham provides small self-contained illustrations, comic strips, and double-page spreads to complement the text, including a large horizontal man who has squashed his hat and a convergence of penguins. All his drawings are full of absorbing details. It would be difficult, if not impossible, to find a better book of poems for small children to enjoy. **WO**

Guess How Much I Love You 1994

Sam McBratney   Anita Jeram

This tender picture book has become a modern classic for millions of children and their families at bedtimes and it was shortlisted for the prestigious Kurt Maschler Award. With its warm and simple narrative on the depth of the love between a mother hare and her baby hare, Sam McBratney's moving dialogue is perfectly matched by Anita Jeram's realistic ink-and-watercolor illustrations that move the young reader's eyes literally up and down the pages. The sensitive drawings and soothing text take the reader through the book at an easy pace, with a lullaby-like quality.

As Little Nutbrown Hare prepares to go to bed for the night, he wants to make sure that Big Nutbrown Hare is listening to him. He gets his mother's attention by asking the question, "Guess how much I love you?" And so begins the fun with the comparative sizes of the two hares and the love they have for each other. The dialogue raises all sorts of questions about how we show our emotions to our nearest and dearest and how good it can make us feel. The delicate, rural backdrop and humanized hare expressions bring the characters close to everybody's hearts.

As their prolonged bedtime game progresses and the night draws in, their comparisons grow ever larger: "'I love you across the river and over the hills,' said Big Nutbrown Hare." Eventually both their gazes reach the night sky and the inevitable moon. With sleep all but overcoming the little hare, he fixes his gaze on the expansive sky and glowing moon and declares that his love for his mother will reach as far as the moon. Finally, as his little bed of leaves is made for him and he is gently settled into bed, Little Nutbrown Hare is given the softest of good-night kisses and told that the love Big Nutbrown Hare has for the little one reaches all the way to the moon and back. **NH**

Nationality | Irish, born 1943 (author); English, born 1965 (illustrator)
Publisher | Walker Books, UK
Theme | Classics, Family, Animal stories

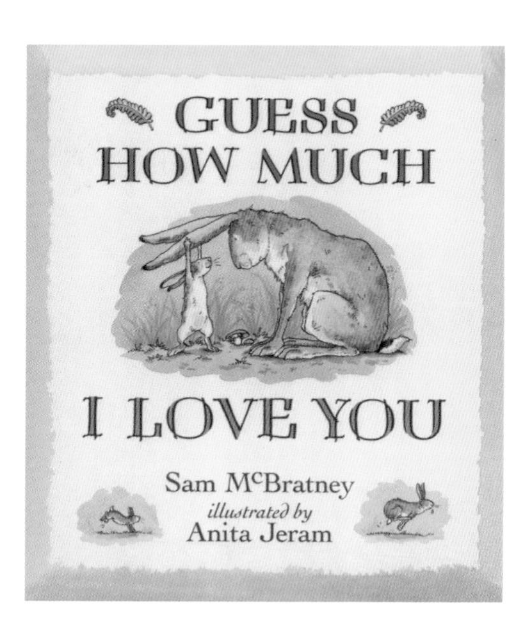

"'I love you all the way down the lane as far as the river,' cried Little Nut Brown Hare."

OTHER GREAT SAM McBRATNEY READS

The Chieftain's Daughter, 1993
The Dark at the Top of the Stairs, 1995
Just You and Me, 1998
You're All My Favourites, 2004

The Story of the Little Mole 1994

Werner Holzwarth Wolf Erlbruch

Nationality | German, born 1947 (author); German, born 1948 (illustrator)
Publisher | David Bennett Books, UK
Theme | Animal stories, Controversial, Classic

When a little mole pokes his head out from his mole hill one morning, a great big poo lands on his head. The little mole is very upset and wants to know who has done this to him. "How mean! . . . Who had done this on my head?" He sets out to investigate. The first creature he meets is a dove. When he asks the dove if he did it, the answer is "no." To prove it, the dove shows the little mole just what his poo looks like. The same thing happens with each creature that the mole encounters, including a horse, a hare, a goat, a cow (the mole is very relieved it was not the cow), and a pig. The only thing the animals are able to tell the little mole is that it was not them. Eventually, little mole meets two flies, who test the poo and tell him exactly who made it: "It is clear to us that it was A DOG."

Now the little mole knows for sure who the culprit is: Basil, the butcher's great big dog. He goes to Basil's dog house and finds the dog fast asleep, so the little mole climbs up to the roof of the dog house and does a little poo that plops down onto the dog's head.

This is a hilarious book about a controversial topic, and the text contains witty asides, such as the description of the hare's poo: "Plippety plop—a pile of toffee-colored little balls tumbled on the grass. The little mole found them almost appealing." The amusing illustrations and text help children laugh about a subject they sometimes find embarrassing. Originally published in German as *Vom kleinen Maulwurf, der wissen wollte, wer ihm auf den Kopf gemacht hat*, it has been hailed as a modern children's classic. **LH**

3+

Garden of Little Creatures 1994

Antoon Krings

Original Title | Droles de petites betes
Nationality | French, born 1962
Publisher | Gallimard Jeunesse, France
Theme | Animal stories

This is a charming collection of stories about little animals—their houses, their unusual life, and their unexpected adventures. The series begins with the story of Mireille l'Abeille, a sweet little bee who works day and night to make lovely honey and golden sweets. One day her honey pots disappear. After having looked for them in the garden, the flowers, the trees, and every other place she can possibly think of, she decides to go home, sad and puzzled. When she opens the door, however, she discovers a sleeping dwarf in her bed who helps her solve the mystery of the vanished pots.

Another story is about Adèle la Sauterelle, a cicada, who is not very bright. She has two very important letters from Léon le Bourdon to deliver: one, of praise, for the queen of bees; the other, of reproach, for Mireille l'Abeille. After spending hours wondering what the content of the letters might possibly be, Adèle gives in to temptation and opens the envelopes. However, when she has finished reading the letters, she replaces them in the wrong envelopes by mistake.

Then there is the tale of Adrien le Lapin, a hare who rejoices at the return of spring. Mireille l'Abeille is surprised to find him hidden among the flowers, because Adrien is an Easter hare made of chocolate. Antoon Krings's imaginative stories are filled with a host of animal characters—including bats, dogs, cats, and many others—which he weaves into mysteries and adventures that will intrigue young children. **LB**

Clown

QUENTIN BLAKE

Clown 1995

Quentin Blake

Nationality | English, born 1932
Publisher | Jonathan Cape, UK
Honor | Hans Christian Andersen Award, 2002
Theme | Friendship, Adventure

This wordless picture book tells a profound story about loyalty to friends and perseverance in the face of setbacks. It helps children draw meaning out of pictures by speculating about the clown's thoughts, feelings, and intentions.

One day Clown finds himself among an armful of shabby toys that are thrown out into the garbage. He manages to escape because, unlike Teddy, Blue Elephant, and the rest of the toys, he has human powers. Realizing that the other toys are still in the garbage, he sets off to get help. What follows echoes Hans Christian Andersen's "Constant Tin Soldier," as Clown is buffeted by fate and survives encounters with traffic, dogs, and humans. In the adult world, he is as powerless and frustrated as a small child. One advantage of this is that he can communicate with children when he fails to reach grown-ups. While children can connect with the human aspect of his clown nature and understand his rescue mission, adults see only a grubby toy and hurl him into space. Similarly, as soon as he has told his story to a small girl, her mother whisks her away out of reach. By helping a young girl in a messy apartment soothe her crying brother and tidy up in time for her mother's return, he finds a new home where shabby toys are welcome.

Quentin Blake's artwork is masterly, with glowing skies brightening gray cityscapes, a clearly realized sense of traffic noise and speed, the claustrophobia of a rich girl's mother's boudoir, and the desolation of the poor family's high-rise apartment before Clown lets the joy flood in. **GB**

Runaway Train 1995

Benedict Blathwayt

Nationality | English, born 1951
Publisher | Julia MacRae Books, UK
Theme | Adventure, Friendship
Favorite characters

Duffy Driver oversleeps one day, and in his hurry to start up his red steam engine, he accidentally leaves off the brake. The result is a runaway train! Duffy follows in hot pursuit, first on a truck and then on a boat, bicycle, pony, tractor, and finally in a helicopter, from which he makes a daringly successful landing back at last into the engine cab. He can now relax and enjoy a lazy afternoon at the beach before driving his train back to town in the evening.

This book is a great read and also a work of art. On one striking double-page spread, Benedict Blathwayt provides a bird's-eye view of miles of idyllic countryside, showing the roads, railway lines, and rivers, all leading to a small town in the distance that is preparing itself for the night. Details elsewhere include horses being led to stables while the hay is being gathered. Two young lovers lie basking in the setting sun, while in the corner, visitors are preparing to leave a ruined abbey. Small children love this sort of detail; they also relish cumulative stories where different characters end up seeking the same outcome, just as the owners of the various means of transport borrowed by Duffy do here.

Steam engines remain perennially popular with young children, and few look more generally inviting and fun to drive than the one illustrated in these pages. Three final wordless pictures, showing the train arriving home safely, bring this story to a suitably elegiac end. There are several other books in the popular Little Red Train series by the same author, including *Race to the Finish* and *Faster, Faster.* **NT**

Bad Habits! 1998

Babette Cole

Subtitle | Or the Taming of Lucretzia Crum
Nationality | English, born 1949
Publisher | Hamish Hamilton, UK
Theme | Family, Controversial

What do you do when your child is an "uncivilized little monster"? Introduce him or her to some real monsters. Lucretzia Crum is a vile child—her habits include spitting, screaming, kicking, stealing from babies, and pulling other people's hair. Her father, a mad scientist, invents remedies, such as antifoulmouth soap, in an attempt to control his daughter, but without much success. When Lucretzia's friends begin to mimic her appalling behavior, thinking it is "dead cool," the parents decide to adopt shock tactics. They gatecrash Lucretzia's birthday party dressed as monsters, and shock the guests by behaving even more appallingly than Lucretzia and her friends. In a frenzy of bad manners, the grown-ups scoff all the food and open the birthday presents. Perhaps stretching credulity a little far, Lucretzia instantly reforms into "a civilized little angel."

There is no doubt that children love all matters that pertain to bodily functions: the grosser the better. Although one or two adult reviewers have balked at the references to burping and flatulence, Babette Cole tells it how it is.

Cole acknowledges John Tenniel, Edward Lear, and Quentin Blake as having been influential in her career, as well as her parents: "My father was a painter with a wonderful sense of humor and my mum was a very good liar! I suppose that qualifies me as an artist and a writer." Her work with Oliver Postgate and Peter Firmin for BBC television has also contributed to her unique and riveting graphic style. **WO**

Pumpkin Soup 1998

Helen Cooper

Nationality | English, born 1963
Publisher | Doubleday, UK
Award | Kate Greenaway Medal
Theme | Animal stories, Friendship

This is a delightful story about friendship and loyalty, and about compromise and overcoming differences. Cat plays the bagpipes, Squirrel plays the banjo, and Duck sings. When they are not playing music, they make pumpkin soup, and each animal has a specific role: Cat does the slicing of the vegetables, Squirrel is in charge of stirring in the water, and Duck adds the salt. This perfect arrangement leads to a contented domestic life until Duck becomes uppity and insists on a more elevated position. After a monumental fight, beautifully illustrated with broken text and flying wooden spoons, Duck leaves home.

When he does not return after quite some time, the other two animals become anxious and set off to look for him. They clearly fear the worst. When they eventually give up the search and go back to the cabin, Duck is already there, safe and sound. The animals celebrate by making pumpkin soup, which Duck is allowed to stir. Just when you think everything is back to normal, the anarchic Duck decides that he wants to play the bagpipes.

Helen Cooper is a self-taught artist who originally trained at the Royal Academy of Music, and her interest in music is evident. She says: "Children's perception of the world fascinates me. . . . Books are a way of finding solutions." Her writing has a lyrical quality, and the text and pictures together result in the best kind of storytelling. *Pumpkin Soup* won the Kate Greenaway Medal in 1998 and was shortlisted for the Kurt Maschler Award. **WO**

Molly Goes Shopping 1998

3+

Eva Eriksson

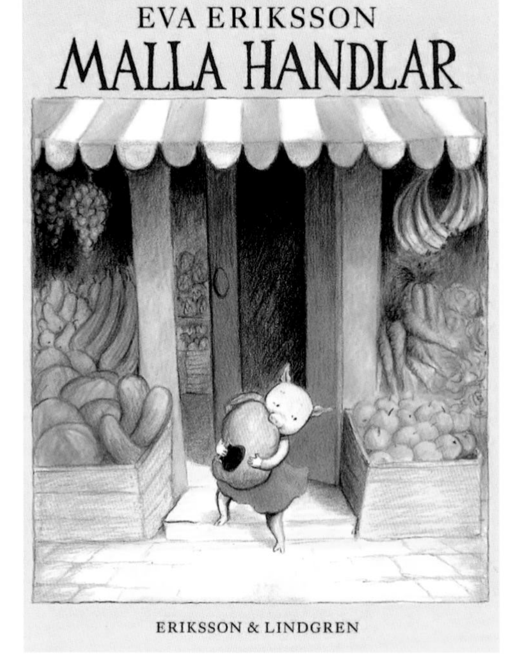

Original Title | Malla handlar
Nationality | Swedish, born 1949
Publisher | Eriksson and Lindgren, Sweden
Theme | Adventure, Family

This is an adorable picture book about the yearning most children have to grow big enough and mature enough to be trusted with responsibility. It also deals with what might happen if you are not big enough for the entrusted task and the feeling of inadequacy in failure. The tale deals with trust and the consequences of telling (or not telling) the truth.

Little Molly is staying with her grandmother and has been asked to go shopping, "Molly has gotten so smart lately." Proud as can be, she goes to the shops on her own to buy a bag of beans. She stands patiently in line, and when it is finally Molly's turn to be served in the shop, she cannot for the life of her remember what it was Grandma had told her to buy. Eventually she comes back with a sack of potatoes. There are more tasks and more to-ing and fro-ing to the shops to come, which lead to even more misunderstandings and the embarrassment of a lost wallet. However, with an understanding and patient Grandma to help her with her tasks, Molly manages to get it right in the end.

Eva Eriksson's illustrations are sensitively and beautifully drawn in earthy, mild colors. The characters are all different toy pets. For example, little Molly is a toy piglet and Grandma is a big polar bear; they are both full of expression and warmth. *Molly Goes Shopping* is a charming everyday story that is told in a touching and humorous manner and easily engages the young reader. **CC**

"Now [Molly's] going to the store to shop. Can she really go that far all by herself?"

MORE BOOKS ILLUSTRATED BY ERIKSSON

The Wild Baby (Den vilda bebin) **by Barbro Lindgren, 1979**
Sam's Car (Max bil) **by Barbro Lindgren, 1981**
Alone in the World (När vi var ensamma i världen) **by Ulf Nilsson, 2009**

The Magic Pocket 1998

Michio Mado, Mitsumasa Anno

Nationality | Japanese, born 1909 (author); Japanese, born 1926 (illustrator)
Publisher | Suemori Books, Japan
Theme | Poetry

This delightful selection of poems is from the much-loved Japanese author and winner of the Hans Christian Andersen Illustration Award, Michio Mado. The poems appear in their original language with English translations on the facing page. The translations retain all their Japanese charm, both in content—references to plum cherries, slices of pickle, and bread with sweet soybeans—and in the meter: "Fingers / Fingers / Fingers / All in a row. No quarrels."

The poems engage playful and childlike imagery, and several are written in the voice of a child. "Let's Play Together" reads like the request of a child for an elephant and then a bear to come and play at the child's house. The subtly humorous "The Goats and the Letters" is written as a conversation between two goats, one white and one black, who eat the letters they are attempting to converse with. The poems are deceptively simple; what at first seems fun and funny is actually thought provoking.

The poems are complemented by the artwork of Mitsumasa Anno. The subtle, one-color, collage-style illustration allows space for contemplating the poems while still retaining a sense of humor. The poem "Hail" is surrounded by little hailstones with legs, arms, and faces that show varying degrees of happiness. In another work, an excited rabbit hops across the page. *The Magic Pocket* is the companion to an earlier, equally enchanting collaboration between Mado and Anno: *The Animals: Selected Poems*, of 1992. **RA**

Rosa Goes To Daycare 1999

Barbro Lindgren, Eva Eriksson

Nationality | Swedish, born 1937 (author); Swedish, born 1949 (illustrator)
Publisher | Groundwood Books, USA
Theme | Animal stories, School

Barbro Lindgren's books about the black-and-white puppy Rosa have become perennial favorites. *Rosa Goes to Daycare* is aimed at helping young readers to understand what life will be like once they start at a new daycare center, with a childminder, or at nursery school. Rosa is furious when she is sent to doggie daycare, but the main reason for her anger is because she is nervous about what to expect. She is worried that she will not understand what she is supposed to do and that she will not like the daycare rules.

Once she gets there, Rosa meets lots of other pups that she can become friends with, but there is also a routine to get used to, such as the daily nap time, as well as a number of trials and worries for her to overcome, mirroring those that children have to deal with. Rosa becomes ill with "doggy cough," and her friend Jock suffers the embarrassment of being sent home with fleas. Rosa also has to decide which of her new friends will be her best friend, which her second best, and so on. However, the most frightening experience is when she fails to listen to the leader and runs around excitedly: She falls into a freezing, icy river and has to be rescued.

The Rosa series has been lauded for the way its plots help children to cope with the anxieties of facing their first days away from home and their usual routine. The books are made up almost entirely of canine characters, with barely any humans mentioned, despite most of the dogs having owners. **LH**

Jamela's Dress 1999

Niki Daly

3+

Alternative Title | Jamela's Red Dress
Nationality | South African, born 1946
Publisher | Frances Lincoln, UK
Theme | Family, Adventure

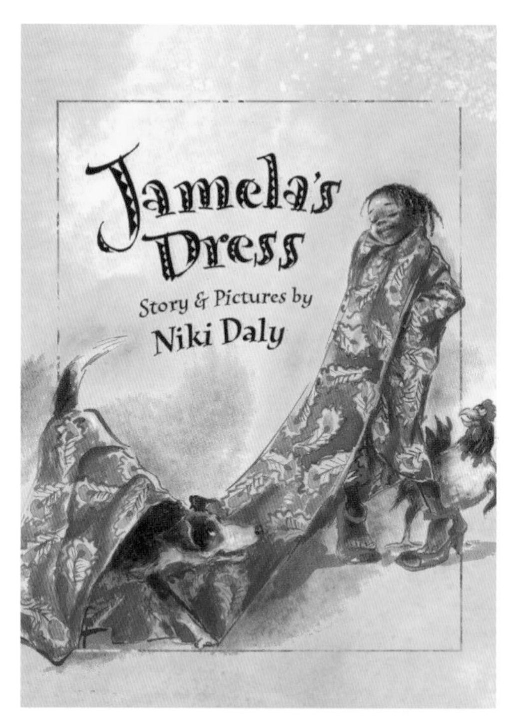

OTHER GREAT NIKI DALY READS

***The Little Girl Who Lived Down the Road*, 1978**
***Not So Fast Songololo*, 1985**
***Why the Sun and Moon Live in the Sky*, 1994**
***Bravo, Zan Angelo!*, 1996**
***Ruby Sings the Blues*, 2005**

In this busy and engaging tale, Niki Daly has captured a reflection of multicultural, modern South Africa. Told through the perspective of a child, Jamela's joyous dance through the streets tells a larger story of acceptance and change.

Jamela is a mischievous character who surfaces in a series of Daly's books. In this story, her mother buys a length of gorgeous red, feathery fabric. Jamela helps Mama wash and hang the fabric in the sun. It is her job to look after it until it dries. But Jamela is caught in a dream by the soft folds of fabric as it flaps and wraps around her. She parades through the neighborhood with the red material flying like a flag behind her. Jamela, in her red dress, is an African Queen! But

"Children sang, 'Kwela Jamela African Queen!' Taxi barked. Mrs. Zibi's chicken went wild."

barking dogs rip at the fabric, chickens scratch at it, and it drags in the dirt in the street. Jamela actions land her in big trouble. Disaster is averted when a local photographer wins a prize for a picture he has taken of Jamela as the African Queen, and he purchases new fabric for Mama's dress. There is even enough fabric for Jamela to have a red dress of her own. Daly captures the movement and excitement of the story through frenetic brushstrokes in his signature watercolors.

Daly's passion for change is evident in his commitment to creative books for South African children. From 1989 to 1992 he developed Songololo Books, a children's book division of David Philip Publishers. As a writer, editor, and provider of writing workshops, Daly has furthered South African children's literature that is inclusive of all races. **RA**

Harry and the Bucketful of Dinosaurs 1999

Ian Whybrow Adrian Reynolds

Nationality | English, birth date unknown (author); Welsh, born 1963 (illustrator)
Publisher | David & Charles Children's Books, UK
Theme | Friendship, Adventure

Everyone knows how attached small children get to their favorite toys, and this story about dinosaurs really captures the imagination of young readers. Our hero is a small boy called Harry, who is helping his grandmother clear out her attic when he stumbles upon a box full of dusty toy dinosaurs. Harry is thrilled and he begins to lovingly clean and fix each dinosaur. He then carries them around with him in a large bucket wherever he goes. So serious is Harry about his task that he even goes to the library to research each dinosaur's name. The creatures become his firm friends. One day, disaster strikes when Harry accidentally leaves his bucket on the train. Happily, it turns up in the lost property office where, in a humorous twist,

"He found out all the names . . . and told them to the dinosaurs. He spoke softly to each one."

Harry is able to prove his identity to the lost property man by reciting all of the names of the dinosaurs.

Ian Whybrow's text has a gentle, charming quality, and Adrian Reynolds's bold illustrations echo this with their clear, bright colors. The expressive faces of the dinosaurs underline the fact that only Harry can see each dinosaur's individual personality. This detail has instant appeal to small children who feel that they alone can communicate with special toys. Having established this direct link with his readers, Whybrow injects some solid information in the form of the dinosaurs' names, which also provides wordplay opportunities, as well as subtle propaganda for the value of books and libraries.

This is the first of an enormously successful series of Harry adventures. Whybrow has also written the best-selling Little Wolf series. **AK**

OTHER GREAT READS IN THIS SERIES

***Harry and the Dinosaurs Romp in the Swamp*, 2002**
***Harry and the Dinosaurs Go Wild*, 2005**
***Harry and the Dinosaurs Make a Christmas Wish*, 2005**

THE GRUFFALO

Julia Donaldson Axel Scheffler

The Gruffalo 1999

Julia Donaldson Axel Scheffler

Nationality | English, born 1948 (author); German, born 1957 (illustrator)
Publisher | Macmillan, UK
Theme | Fantasy, Rhyming stories

A mouse manages to scare off three creatures that are planning to make a meal of him by telling them that he is going to meet a scary "gruffalo." Little do these creatures know that there is really no such thing as a gruffalo. To the mouse's horror, he comes across a real gruffalo, looking exactly as he has described him. The gradual description of all the scary parts of the Gruffalo, orange eyes, purple prickles, poisonous wart, and so on, cranks up the suspense, but the big revelation—when we finally get to see the Gruffalo—would have had more impact if the Gruffalo were not pictured on the front cover.

Having said that, Axel Scheffler's Gruffalo is spot-on, rather like one of Maurice Sendak's wild things: scary in a cuddly sort of way. The clever little mouse gets the Gruffalo to walk behind him through the wood, and the Gruffalo becomes convinced that the mouse is, as he claims, the scariest creature in the wood because all the creatures run off in terror. When the mouse then turns on the Gruffalo: "Now my tummy's beginning to rumble. My favorite food is—gruffalo crumble!" the Gruffalo flees in fear of his life.

Julia Donaldson was inspired by a Chinese folktale about a fox who borrows the fear of a tiger, but she invented the word "gruffalo" because she could not think of a rhyme for "tiger." Like most of her picture books, *The Gruffalo* is written in rhyming couplets with repeating phrases and rhythms. The words trip off the tongue and bounce through your brain so that, after a few readings, the text will stick in your head as if it had always been there. **CW**

Crispin 2000

Ted Dewan

Nationality | American, born 1961
Publisher | Doubleday, UK
Theme | Friendship, Adventure, Family, Animal stories

It is a perpetual dilemma: What do you buy for someone who has it all? But the question can also be asked differently: Can anyone really have it all?

In *Crispin: The Pig Who Had It All*, Crispin Tamworth pig has all the latest and most expensive toys in the world. Yet when you peek into his room, you see all his pricey toys—the SpeedPony, Zybox teddy bear, and Giga-Pigstation—broken and forgotten, and Crispin bored and dejected. One Christmas, the spoiled Crispin receives a huge box containing "the very best thing in the whole wide world." However, on unwrapping it, Crispin discovers that the box is empty. Gloomily he puts it out in the yard. The next day the rejected box attracts Nick and Penny, his neighbors. They use it for a spirited game of "Space Base" and ask Crispin to join in. The three become completely engrossed in the game until sunset. Very quickly the empty box becomes a great tool for the children's resourceful imagination. They reinvent it over and over again for their many games, and play: Store, Pirates, Castle, and, of course, their favorite, Space Base. Most importantly, the gift of an empty box teaches Crispin the value of friendship. He discovers that the true value of a toy is not in its cost but in the opportunities it offers to forge new relationships with others.

This engaging story is written in flowing and plain language, which is easily accessible to a young audience. Ted Dewan's meticulous and accurate illustrations make the reading a pleasurable and memorable experience. **IW**

Max 2000

Bob Graham

Nationality | Australian, born 1942
Publisher | Walker Books, UK
Award | Nestlé Children's Book Prize
Theme | Adventure, Family, Quirky

"Let's call him a small hero; a small hero doing quiet deeds. The world needs more of those."

OTHER GREAT BOB GRAHAM READS

***Greetings from Sandy Beach*, 1990**
***Rose Meets Mr. Wintergarten*, 1992**
***Queenie the Bantam*, 1997**
***Jethro Byrde: Fairy Child*, 2002**
***The Trouble with Dogs!*, 2007**

All children—and quite a few adults—love a superhero, and highly popular writer and illustrator Bob Graham has created a particularly fine one in this amusing, entertaining, and wise picture book.

Max is "a superbaby—son of superheroes, Captain Lightning and Madam Thunderbolt." He is a lively little boy who was born in a yellow house "the color of the sun and the shape of a lightning bolt." His parents, like his grandparents before them, are daredevil superheroes who can soar high in the sky and are famed for their high-profile brave deeds. However, Max's path in life does not appear to be starting out in quite the way he expected. He does not seem to be able to master the art of flying: somewhat essential if he is to follow in his parents' footsteps. Happily our small superboy soon finds his own way of being a hero, and in the process his story lightheartedly explores some important lessons about finding your place in the world and being true to yourself. These can be quite difficult themes to explore in children's literature without appearing to preach to the reader or to be trite, and Graham, who is known for his optimism and his promotion of the differences between people, succeeds completely with his picture book *Max*.

Not surprisingly Graham's major childhood influences were the superheroes of American comics, and his illustration credits include regular comic-strip work for a French magazine. Comic-strip elements play a strong role in *Max*, and Graham's characteristic loose, amusing, and colorful style, filled with movement, owes much to animation. The text is simple and direct, but it has some nicely poetic moments and does not resort to slang. This combination has brought Graham great success in the picture-book field worldwide, but especially in his homeland, Australia. **AK**

Olivia 2000

Ian Falconer

This sweet and funny story introduces us to Olivia, a pig who is so strong-willed and exuberant that she wears everyone out, including herself. She sings, dances, builds incredibly ambitious sandcastles, and tries on every piece of clothing she owns. Like Eloise, the children's book character with whom Olivia is most often compared, Olivia takes herself very seriously—and adults will enjoy the cultural references that make up Olivia's Big City world. She constructs the Empire State Building at the beach and reads a bedtime story about Maria Callas; at the museum she admires details from real paintings by Degas and Jackson Pollock (the latter of which she claims she could do herself in five minutes). Olivia in the bathtub even has shades of Jacques-Louis David's famous painting *The Death of Marat*.

The drawings, like the story, are spare and witty, and made in black and white with bright red accents. Ian Falconer thinks that much of their appeal is because "pigs are shaped like little kids." It is true that the drawings really capture the essence of a precocious and proud little girl, while lovingly poking fun at her. With her nose upturned and her winglike ears askew, Olivia looks more than a little ridiculous in her tutu and dress-up finery. But even more hilarious is a small, easy-to-miss drawing of Olivia up to the neck in one leg of a pair of pantyhose, the other leg trailing limply to the ground.

Olivia is so true to life that it will come as no surprise that she is based on a real person. A stage designer and illustrator for the *New Yorker*, Falconer initially wrote the book as a gift for his niece, Olivia. Apparently, the real Olivia takes all this success in her stride, and once at a reading when she was five years old, she took a chair beside her uncle when book-signing began, carefully writing out O-L-I-V-I-A on each copy of the book that she inspired. **CQ**

Nationality | American, born 1959
Publisher | Simon and Schuster, UK
Award | Caldecott Honor Book
Theme | Animal stories, Adventure

OLIVIA

"Every day Olivia is supposed to take a nap. 'It's time for your you-know-what,' her mother says."

OTHER BOOKS STARRING OLIVIA

***Olivia Saves the Circus*, 2001**
***Olivia and the Missing Toy*, 2003**
***Olivia Forms a Band*, 2006**
***Olivia Helps with Christmas*, 2007**

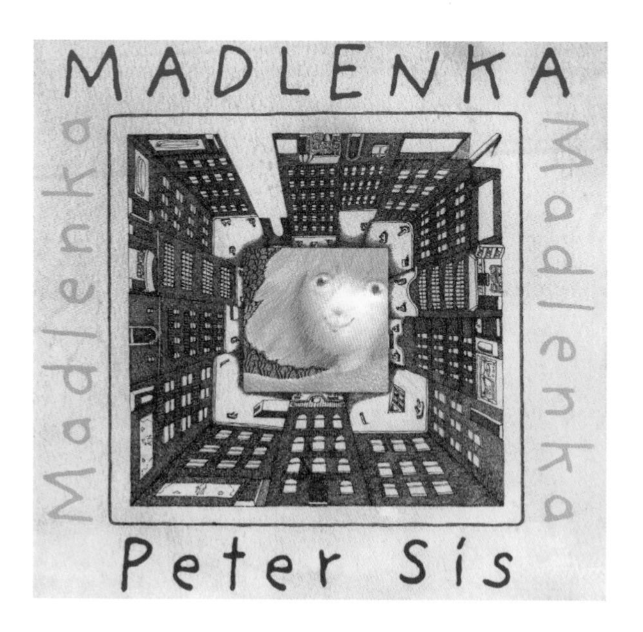

Madlenka 2000

Peter Sis

Nationality | Czech, born 1949
Publisher | Farrar, Straus and Giroux, USA
Award | Children's Book of the Year, *New York Times*
Theme | Friendship, Adventure

When you first open one of Peter Sis's books, the strong visual narratives are as striking as they are deep. This book's end papers open with a red dot on the planet Earth, zoom into Manhattan island, and then end finally on Madlenka sitting in her apartment window on the Lower East Side.

Madlenka invites you into her world where there are many surprises in store. With news of a loose tooth the premise for her wanderings, Madlenka goes to see her neighbors: a French baker, an Indian news vendor, an Italian ice-cream seller, a Latin American grocer, a retired opera singer from Germany, an African-American school friend, and an Asian shopkeeper. Through these encounters and the memories these characters have brought from old country to new, readers experience the rich diversity of the inhabitants of Madlenka's block.

Sis was granted asylum in the United States in 1984, and his insights into where people in a great metropolis come from (he lives in New York City) are very well observed. His ink-pen sketch style has great detail, intricacy, and subtle colors as Sis takes readers on a tour of the world through Madlenka's eyes. The character of Madlenka is based on Sis's daughter, and the book will appeal to all wide-eyed young children whose whole reason to be in the world is to soak up experience, learn all things new, and tell everyone all about it. Whether you live in a city or a small town, you will definitely want to explore Madlenka's fascinating world. **NH**

Marc Just Couldn't Sleep 2001

Gabriela Keselman Noemí Villamuza

Nationality | Argentinean, born 1953 (author); Spanish, born 1971 (illustrator)
Publisher | Kókinos, Spain
Theme | Family, Fantasy

Gabriela Keselman, who writes for older as well as younger children, takes an everyday situation and transforms it into a surprising and magical story. *Marc Just Couldn't Sleep* (originally published as *De verdad que no podía*) is a seemingly simple story about a little boy who is frightened to fall asleep. His mother reassures him, "Don't worry my darling, I shall find the solution . . . and you will sleep like a dormouse."

Marc calls his mother five times so that he can explain what he is afraid of this time and why he cannot sleep. The comic nature of the book lies in the crazy, over-the-top solutions of the mother and in the expressiveness of Noemí Villamuza's illustrations. Keselman shows her mastery of simple language by writing an entertaining story that works well through the use of wordplay.

Marc's mother comes up with amusing and creative ideas to help banish her son's fears. When he is scared of being terrorized by bugs, she makes anti-mosquito pajamas and produces a teddy bear that repels "buzzes." She attempts to combat other fears by sending a card to the moon and inventing an invisible trap to catch ghosts. In the end, she discovers the best thing she can do is to sit with Marc while he tells her about the things that scare him. He is soon fast asleep.

This book is a delight for both parents and children, helping parents discover with real pleasure that patience and imagination can help solve difficult situations and fun for children because of the author's exciting imagination. **EB**

The Widemouthed Frog 2001

Francine Vidal Elodie Nouhen

Nationality | French, born 1974 (author); French, born 1970 (illustrator)
Publisher | Didier Jeunesse, France
Theme | Animal stories, Adventure

The Widemouthed Frog (*La grenouille à grande bouche*) is the story of a very green frog with a large red mouth who lives quietly in a hot country on a water lily. One evening, the frog can no longer bear to swallow flies for every meal so he decides to go off in search of adventure, and a more varied diet. First he meets an anteater who tells the frog that it eats ants. Disgusted by what he has heard, the frog continues his journey. During his travels he crosses forests and climbs mountains. Every time he meets someone, the frog asks the same question and then goes on his way, astonished at the strange eating habits of other animals. Weary of this long expedition, the frog finally decides to go back to his own pond, but there finds himself face to face with a large crocodile who has very sharp teeth.

The story told by Francine Vidal was inspired by a tale often heard in playgrounds. Aimed at younger readers, the text works because of its simplicity and the effect of the repetition that punctuates the travels of the little frog. Children also love the comic effect of the final scene. The little frog is just like them, always asking questions. Elodie Nouhen's collages illustrate the journey beautifully and feature the colors of a wild land with juxtaposed shades of red, ocher, and green; little details are emphasized by materials such as canvas or wire.

Children will love to identify with this strange frog who invites them on an adventure but who also warns them to be careful! **SL**

3+

Tatu and Patu in Helsinki 2003

Aino Havukainen and Sami Toivonen

Nationality | Finnish, born 1968 (Havukainen); Finnish, born 1971 (Toivonen)
Publisher | Otava, Finland
Theme | Adventure

In *Tatu and Patu in Helsinki* (originally published as *Tatu ja Patu Helsingissä*), brothers Tatu and Patu arrive in the capital of Finland, Helsinki, for a fast-paced adventure. Used to doing things a little differently to city people, the boys sometimes seem a little bit strange. They visit their cousin Jori, who has promised to show them around the city. Unfortunately, he seems to be very busy, and the brothers have a hard time keeping up with their cousin. The boys get whisked away by the hectic life of the capital. Having never been to Helsinki before, there is lots to see and capture on film. The boys cause havoc wherever they go, visiting the National Museum, the Olympic Stadium, and other popular sights in Helsinki.

When they accidentally lose track of their cousin, the resourceful brothers find their own method of transport to travel around the city, such as borrowing bumper cars from the amusement park. When they catch sight of their cousin heading for the ferry to take him to the zoo, Tatu and Patu miss the boat but, as usual, this does not stop them from getting where they want to be. They buy two huge watermelons and paddle their way across the river in man-made rafts.

This fun children's book shows readers what the capital has to offer young travelers like Tatu and Patu who have never been there. Collaborators Aino Havukainen's and Sami Toivonen's humorous text and innovative illustrations really bring the book to life. The brightly colored pictures convey the fast life of the city perfectly. **LKK**

Don't Let the Pigeon Drive the Bus! 2003

Mo Willems

Nationality | American, born 1968
Publisher | Hyperion, USA
Award | Caldecott Honor Book, 2004
Theme | Quirky, Adventure

After spending many years as an award-winning animator, Mo Willems burst onto the children's book scene in 2003 and introduced young readers to his irresistible pigeon character. The eponymous pigeon is the reincarnation of every stubborn three-year-old child, complete with all too familiar episodes of wheedling and begging, attempts at negotiation, hysterical tantrums, and a short attention span. The simple, retro, animation-inspired art is immediately compelling to both parents and young readers.

This clever story involves the reader at the start as an active participant in the book. The bus driver steps out of his vehicle for a short break, asking that the reader keep an eye on things while he is gone. However, before he leaves the scene, the driver makes a request of the reader: "Don't let the pigeon drive the bus." A big-eyed pigeon soon appears and tries to negotiate a spot behind the wheel, at various points telling the reader, "I'll be your best friend," and "I'll bet your mom would let me," and "How 'bout I give you five bucks?" Finally, the pigeon throws a huge, highly entertaining but futile tantrum when the driver returns, kindly thanks the reader, and pulls away at the wheel of the bus. The pigeon's disappointment is expressed, of course, in the perfect preschooler sulk, but it is only temporary because he spots a big red tractor-trailer truck coming up the road. This book will have toddlers screaming out the pigeon's lines in no time at all, whereas older readers will be amused by the pigeon's negotiations to drive the bus. **KD**

3+

Knuffle Bunny: A Cautionary Tale 2004

Mo Willems

Nationality | American, born 1968
Publisher | Hyperion, USA
Award | Caldecott Honor Book, 2005
Theme | Adventure, Family

Mo Willems's early career as an animator shines through in this award-winning picture book. His illustrations are drawn against a backdrop of sepia-toned photographs, with the text in an olive-colored band surrounding the artwork itself. This style makes the characters in the book, especially Dad and Trixie—based on Mo and his daughter of the same name—jump into life from the pages.

The story begins with toddler Trixie happily carrying her favorite toy, a stuffed bunny, while going on errands with her Dad—down the street, through the park, past the school, and eventually to the Laundromat. Trixie is pleased to help with the laundry by putting the money into the machines herself. On the walk home, Trixie realizes that she has left her stuffed bunny behind. Not yet able to talk, she tries every sort of gibberish to tell her Dad what has happened, but he just does not understand. In frustration Trixie starts to wail and goes "boneless," a scenario to which most parents will relate. When they get home, Mom immediately sees the problem—Knuffle Bunny is missing—and so they head back to the Laundromat to look for him. Eventually Dad finds Knuffle Bunny, and Trixie joyously squeals "Knuffle Bunny!" The tale ends with the line: "And those were the first words Trixie ever said."

Young kids will love the story and the artwork, and every parent who has ever had a child who had a public meltdown will laugh and celebrate along with Trixie as she utters her first words. **KD**

Unknown or Forgotten Princesses 2004

Philippe Lechermeier Rébecca Dautremer

Nationality | French, born 1968 (author); French, born 1971 (illustrator)
Publisher | Gautier-Languereau, France
Theme | Fantasy, Rhyming stories

Originally published as *Les Princesses oubliées ou inconnues*, this album is an alternative encyclopedia featuring forty forgotten and unknown princesses. Each one is introduced over the course of two pages, in which the author presents the princesses' family, her tastes, and her moods against the background of secrets, palace rumors, and enchanted forests.

Among the most charming princesses are Princess Esperluette, who has a passion for reading and words ending in "–ette"; Princess Fatrasie, a chatterbox with an extraordinary talent for boring people and a penchant for difficult words; Princess Poupoupidou, tiny and sweet, who falls asleep at the sound of a lullaby; Princess Cappriciosa, a fussy young girl who is never satisfied and is known for her extravagant requests; and Princess Amnésie, who forgets her engagements, always arrives late, and misses trains because in lieu of a good memory there is only a big black hole in her head. The last few pages contain practical guides to distinguish real princesses from fake ones and a quiz to find out to which type of princess every young female reader corresponds.

These lighthearted stories are written in rhyme, each portrait being built around specific rhyming patterns that are a delight for the ear and a constant surprise because of their humor, their impeccable structure, and the vivacity of their inventiveness. Rébecca Dautremer's illustrations are the perfect visual counterpart, thanks to the rich colors and mixed techniques of collage and watercolor. **LB**

Lost and Found 2005

Oliver Jeffers

Nationality | Irish, born 1977
Publisher | HarperCollins, UK
Award | Nestlé Children's Book Prize
Theme | Friendship, Adventure

This lovable story features the same charming boy character as Oliver Jeffers's first book *How To Catch a Star*. This time the boy finds a solitary penguin at his door looking sad and lost. He decides to take the little penguin back home on his own, having first asked a bird and a bath duck for help. After a sleepless night, he finds out where the penguin comes from and, with more trials and tribulations, ends up rowing him there in a little boat: "They floated through good weather and bad, when the waves were as big as mountains." On reaching the welcome sign to the South Pole, the boy is surprised that the penguin is still sad. He says goodbye and then realizes that the penguin was not lost at all, just lonely. He immediately rows back but does not see (as the reader and child do) that the penguin has already left to look for the boy at the same time. Fearing that he has lost his friend for good, the boy thinks it best to head for his own home.

Jeffers's simplistic touch always means that the plot's meandering ways are never too mysterious, and finally the boy spots his long-lost penguin rowing an umbrella in the sea. The friends are reunited and decide to share their stories of adventure all the way back home. Jeffers is one of a handful of British contemporary illustrators whose books mark a shift in the usual visual styles on the UK picture-book market. With Jeffers's unique watercolor wash and well-referenced visual tones and styles, his fresh and mixed pallet styles offer interesting landscapes for both children and adults to enjoy. **NH**

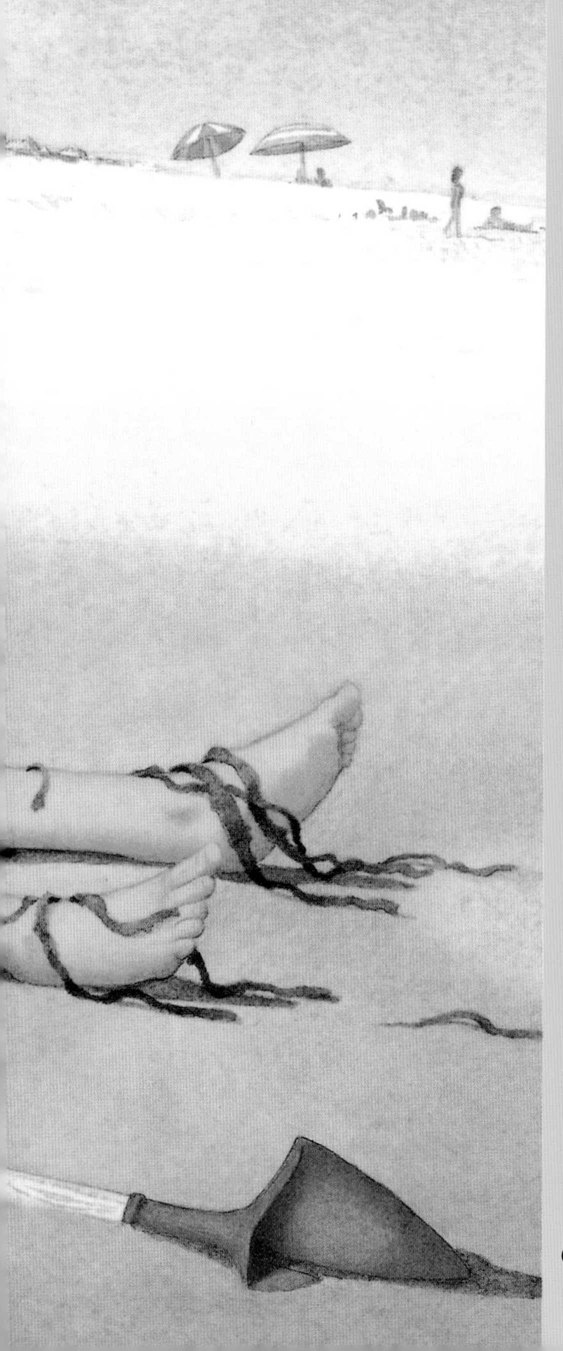

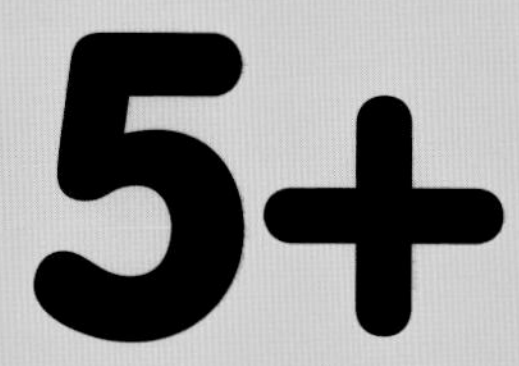

Flotsam, written and illustrated by David Wiesner.

Traditional Chinese Folktales 221–206 B.C.E.

 Unknown

Original Title | Shan Hai Jing
Country of Origin | China, Qin Dynasty 221–206 B.C.E.
Theme | Folktales

China is renowned for the importance of its poetry, literature, and philosophy, but not many books were written specifically for children until more recent years. However, some of the earliest Chinese folktales on record date to the Qin dynasty (221–206 B.C.E.).

Shan Hai Jing (now known as *Traditional Chinese Folktales*) is a collection of the oral folklores told to children, and is considered the earliest children's book on record. One classic Chinese folktale is "The Lost Horse" ("Sài Wēng Shī Mă"). It recalls a wise man in northern China who takes things as they happen. Sài Wēng lives on the outskirts of his village. One day, he finds that his horse has gone missing. When the neighbors come to console him, he says that it might not be a bad thing after all. Some time passes and his lost horse returns, bringing with it a pedigree stallion. Everyone in the village is happy for the old man and congratulates him on his good fortune. He replies that it may not necessarily be a good thing. Soon after, his son takes the stallion out for a ride; he falls and breaks his leg. The old man remarks that it might actually be a good thing. War breaks out and all young men are called to join the army but the old man's son is exempt because of his disability, proving the old man right.

Other tales teach children about the benefits of hard work or study. In "The Scroll that Never Leaves Your Hand" ("Shŏu bú shì juàn"), a young man is only ever seen engrossed in his reading materials. His inability to be distracted and his complete concentration are praised as worthy and admirable traits. **HL**

A young man reads his scrolls, undeterred by all distractions. 

Tales of Otogizōshi 1392

Unknown

Original Title | Urashima Tarō
Country of Origin | Japan, Muromachi Period 1392–1573
Theme | Folktales, Classics

The *Tales of Otogizōshi* is a collection of illustrated medieval Japanese folktales. The tales address themes ranging from family and marriage through fantasy and martial adventures to spiritual enlightenment. One of the most famous, "Urashima Tarō," is retold in many versions throughout Oceania. A young fisherman, Urashima Tarō, rescues a baby sea turtle from the clutches of some sadistic youths who plan to kill it. As he releases the turtle into the ocean, he ponders on the paradox of the life of a creature, whose longevity is renowned in the animal world, being squandered at the hands of humans whose life span is infinitely smaller in comparison.

Time passes, and one day Urashima is invited by a sea turtle to visit the underwater kingdom of the Dragon King. The three days he spends there are filled with marvel until the memory of his aging parents and the duty he has toward them awakens him from his enchantment. Upon leaving, he is presented with a Pandora-type box that, according to some versions, he is told never to open. However, when he returns to his village and realizes that 300 years have lapsed, he opens the box, which contains the accumulation of time and age, and is instantly transformed into an old man. This tale alludes to Eastern and Buddhist concepts of time as opposed to the linearity of Western thought. Rather than seeing Urashima's aging as his punishment for opening the box, it can represent the reconciliation between being and time. **AR**

The Adventures of Peach Boy 1603

Unknown

Original Title | Momotarō
Country of Origin | Japan, Edo Period 1603–1868
Theme | Folktales, Classics

The Japanese folktale *Momotarō* is thought to date to the Edo Period (beginning in1603). The present form of the tale, however, has undergone considerable changes, especially since the nineteenth century, when it was used as a text to promote virtue and filial piety.

The story begins when an old woman fishes a huge peach out of the stream where she washes clothes. When her husband cuts it open, a boy appears, whom the childless couple name Momotarō. They decide to raise Momotarō, and he grows up to be a fearless and exceptionally strong boy, who lovingly cares for his aging foster parents. When terror is wrought by ferocious demons all over the land, young Momotarō sets out to fight them. On his way to Demons' Isle, he befriends a spotted dog, a monkey, and a pheasant. When they reach the island, the four of them bravely battle the demons. Eventually victorious, Momotarō returns home, laden with treasures the demons present to him as a tribute.

Momotarō lives on in Japan through various media. Ralph McCarthy's rendering of the story is a tribute to the original storyteller form, reminding today's readers that Momotarō was once a popular folk hero. Ioe Saito's colorful illustrations from a half century ago, while capturing the spirit of traditional Japanese rural culture and religious beliefs, also anticipate the stylized aesthetics of postwar manga artists who themselves often turn to traditional Japanese folktales for their popular comics. **MKG/FHG**

Urashima Tarō, riding on the back of his sea turtle.

Fairy Tales from the Past 1696

Charles Perrault

Original Title | Histoires ou contes du temps passé
Nationality | French, born 1628
Theme | Fairy tales, Classics

5+

Fairy tales are as old as time, but in Europe, it was Charles Perrault who first published a collection in a form that is still recognizable today. Perrault's fairy tales broke new ground. The refined stories of most Parisian salon writers at the time owed more to Ovid than folktales, but Perrault's plots were faithful to the original oral tales, and his crisp style set the tone for traditional fairy tales as we now know them. The subtle stories of his contemporaries have sunk into obscurity, but Perrault's versions will be familiar to anybody who grew up with European fairy tales.

His book was a collection of eight stories, including "Cinderella," "Sleeping Beauty," and "Puss in Boots," all engagingly written and—with the exception of "Little Red Riding Hood," who has no huntsman to save her here—they are happier and of a lighter tone than the more famous versions by the Brothers Grimm. While the Grimms' tales take joy in describing gruesome punishments for the wicked, Perrault focuses more on the happy endings. Like all authentic fairy tales, however, these have their share of horrors, such as the murdered wives in Bluebeard's closet. Parents should bear in mind that these are not sanitized stories.

Perrault was born into an upper-class bourgeois family. He published poetry, and became a member of the Academie Française in 1671, but it was his collection of fairy tales that earned him the greatest popularity. He also published two fairy tales in verse and a separate prose version of "Sleeping Beauty." **JM**

Grimms' Fairy Tales 1812

Jacob and Wilhelm Grimm

Original Title | Kinder- und Hausmärchen
Nationality | German, born 1785 (Jacob); German, born 1786 (Wilhelm)
Theme | Fairy tales, Classics

Jacob and Wilhelm Grimms' collected tales have become recognized as veritable cultural assets. In 1805 the brothers began to record German as well as Celtic and Romance-language tales, legends, myths, riddles, songs, and sayings. Along with many other oral and written accounts, the stories narrated by the famous storyteller Dorothea Viehmann were their main sources. Over the years, numerous editions have been translated into more than 160 languages.

The tradition of telling stories at home was still very much alive at the time of publication, so with each new edition, the content and the narrative of the tales changed. Initially, many readers were unhappy with the lack of Christian values in the tales, so a great deal of contemporary Christian thinking began to influence and, therefore, alter the stories. In addition, some myths and legends were added to the collection at a later stage.

At first, the tales were not intended as stories for children—they were only considered children's literature when illustrations were added to later editions. An ongoing debate about whether Grimms' fairy tales are suitable for children continues today. Some stories describe murder, parents abandoning their children, wizards casting evil spells, and other cruelties. All fairy tales can be disturbing for young children and often require adults to interpret them. Yet when fairy tales are understood properly, they can contribute significantly to a child's development. **CS**

Deutsche Märchen in Wort und Bild.
2
Schneeweißchen.
Widmung.
Was wärst du schöne Jugendzeit
Denn ohne Märchenblüthen?
Wenn sie nicht goldnen Sternen gleich
An deinem Himmel glühten.
Ein Jugendmorgen ohne sie
Er wäre halbes Leben;
Du glücklich Kind, dem sie den Lenz
Der Jugend hold umschweben.
Gewiß man sagt es unbewußt:
„Das Märchen sei nur Lüge;"
Es ist des Kindes reinste Lust,
Des Kindergeistes Wiege.
Gedeih'! du ewig grüner Baum
Streu deinen Blüthensegen
Der goldnen Jugend in den Schooß
Wie einen Zauberregen.
Frankfurt am Main
Verlag von
E. G. May Söhne.

A Visit from St. Nicholas 1822

Clement Clarke Moore

5+

"A broad face and a little round belly, / That shook when he laughed like a bowlful of jelly."

OTHER FESTIVE WORKS

A Christmas Carol by Charles Dickens, 1843
Father Christmas by Raymond Briggs, 1973
The Jolly Christmas Postman by Janet Ahlberg, 1991
Mr. Christmas by Roger Hargreaves, 2002

Later Title | 'Twas the Night Before Christmas
Nationality | American, born 1779
Publisher | *Troy Sentinel* magazine, USA
Theme | Rhyming stories, Classics

"'Twas the night before Christmas, when all through the house / Not a creature was stirring / Not even a mouse" are some of the most famous opening lines ever published. *A Visit from St. Nicholas* was written by Moore as a Christmas present for his children. The poem was first published, anonymously, in *Troy Sentinel* magazine. Perhaps because the author originally chose to remain anonymous, today there is some scholarly dispute about the poem's authorship. Although most sources attribute it to Moore, some query whether it could have been written by someone else, and at least two other names have been put forward.

The story is a narrative poem about the arrival of St. Nicholas at a family's home in North America on Christmas Eve. The children are in bed, dreaming; the stockings are hung up by the chimney; and the parents have just settled down to sleep, when the father hears a noise. He rushes to the window and looks out to see "a miniature sleigh and eight tiny reindeer" driven by a jolly, old gentleman. They swoop up to the sky and then the father hears the sound of hooves landing on the roof. Then St. Nicholas appears in the fireplace, covered with soot. St. Nicholas sees the dad, gives a wink to let him know all is fine, and then goes about his silent work of filling the stockings. He disappears back up the chimney as quickly as he appeared. As St. Nicholas flies away he calls out, "Merry Christmas to all, and to all a good-night." **LH**

Fifty Fables for Children 1833

Wilhelm Hey   Otto Speckter

Nationality | German, born 1789 (author); German, born 1807 (illustrator)
Publisher | Friedrich Perthes, Germany
Theme | Fairy tales, Poetry

Fifty Fables for Children (originally published as *Fünfzig Fabeln für Kinder*) is a magnificent collection of stories written by the theologian and priest Wilhelm Hey. The stories and their narrative bring the world of the nineteenth century to life. Beautifully illustrated by Otto Speckter, the work includes fifty poems by Hey, each one consisting of two stanzas that mostly talk about animals and children. The book was clearly created to serve an educational purpose, which is still relevant today.

In "The Swan," the eponymous protagonist admonishes a boy for throwing things at it and its fledglings. "Bat and Birds" is about discrimination, with a bat being singled out by the birds because of its appearance. Hey also included comedy in his poems in order to render the serious subtexts more palatable. For instance, in "Rocking Horse and Hobby Horse," a boy reminds a snooty rocking horse that it is merely made of wood.

In Germany, Hey is most famous for his song lyrics. His Christmas carol "Alle Jahre wieder" remains one of the most popular German Christmas songs. Both his songs and his poems display a deep understanding of human emotions, and despite the fact that a long time has passed since he composed his work, his collection still captures the moods and actions of children. Reading his fables is therefore a journey into a distant past, but also a lesson about the world that surrounds us today. **GS**

The Emperor's New Clothes 1837

Hans Christian Andersen

Original Title | Keiserens nye Klæder
Nationality | Danish, born 1805
Publisher | C. A. Reitzel, Denmark
Theme | Fairy tales

5+

The originality of Andersen's fairy tales lies less in the plots—*The Emperor's New Clothes*, for instance, was adapted from a medieval Spanish translation of a Jewish or Arabic parable—than in their distinctive narrative tone of detached melancholy. So many of his characters display unusually outlandish magical habits. Tiny Thumbelina, who lives with the swallows, is no less human than Gerda, who is kidnapped by the Snow Queen; the shallow emperor who prefers a metal nightingale to the drab real bird is no less human than the poor tin soldier who loves the fairy on top of the Christmas tree so much that he gladly lets himself be burned up.

The story of the vain ruler in *The Emperor's New Clothes* has a more obvious moral than many of Andersen's tales. When two swindlers come to court, the emperor is taken in by their promise to tailor for him the finest suit of clothes from the most beautiful cloth. It is a cloth, they say, invisible to anyone either stupid or unfit for his position. Naturally the emperor cannot see the cloth, since it does not exist, but he pretends to do so for fear of seeming stupid or incompetent; his toadying ministers follow suit. The day comes when the swindlers report that the suit is finished and "dress" the naked emperor. They are miming, but the emperor goes along with the charade and proceeds through the streets, showing off his new "clothes." A stunned populace also pretends to see the clothes until a small child blurts out the truth. **VN**

Jamila Gavin reviews:

The Little Mermaid 1837

Hans Christian Andersen

Original Collection | Eventyr, fortalte for Børn
Nationality | Danish, born 1805
Publisher | C. A. Reitzel, Denmark
Theme | Fairy tales

5+

The Fairy Tales of Hans Christian Andersen was the book whose stories and pictures most fired my imagination. Andersen introduced me to a world where the characters were not just either good or bad, but often both or in between; where all didn't end happily ever after, and where people were prepared to suffer and make sacrifices—people who had unfulfilled desires, aspirations and sadness, who searched for happiness, and who were victims of fortune and misfortune.

And how beautifully did William Heath Robinson illustrate them in my treasured edition—the largest book on my shelf. How mysterious and otherworldly his pictures seemed, the magical color plates lying under tissue paper, as well as the exquisite black-and-white drawings, with wonderful captions underneath that lured you to read the stories, captions such as: "the Nile flood had retired" or "up flew the trunk" or "she understood the speech of birds." I was inspired to draw my own pictures for nonexistent stories.

"Once more she looked at the prince, with her eyes already dimmed by death."

FAIRY TALES BY HANS CHRISTIAN ANDERSEN
ILLUSTRATED BY HARRY CLARKE

I especially grieved for the Little Mermaid and wanted to plunge into the book to tell the prince that he should marry her. In Andersen's world, there were robber barons and marsh kings, wistful soldiers, childless women, and lost boys. Storks, swallows, dormice, and cockchafers interacted with fairies and magicians, and babies were cradled in walnut shells. Although many of his stories are about moral dilemmas and transgressions, about people's weaknesses and failures, they are always told with compassion. Andersen seems to say that redemption is always possible—a lesson I have carried with me to this day.

MORE GREAT ANDERSEN FAIRY TALES

The Princess and the Pea, **1835**
The Tinder Box, **1835**
Thumbelina, **1835**
The Red Shoes, **1845**
The Little Match Girl, **1848**

Illustration of the Little Mermaid and the Sea Witch by Munro S. Orr. 

5+

The Ugly Duckling 1843

Hans Christian Andersen

Original Title | Den grimme Ælling
Nationality | Danish, born 1805
Publisher | C. A. Reitzel, Denmark
Theme | Fairy tales, Friendship

This is one of Hans Christian Andersen's best-loved tales, published in a small collection of stories six years after the publication of *The Little Mermaid*. The story is a simple and affecting one about being—and, particularly, about looking—different. It begins with a mother duck sitting on her clutch of eggs. She is tired and bored, longing to take her ducklings out and show them off to the world. The largest egg of all takes a long time to hatch, and when it does, everyone is shocked by the duckling's ugliness.

The duckling's life is very hard. He is aware of how ugly he is, and it makes him shy and sad. His mother tries to make the best of it by telling the other ducks he is the best swimmer of them all, but she confesses to a friend, "I hope his looks will improve with age." He is bullied by the other animals as well as by the girl who feeds them. Even his own siblings are cruel to him, telling him they wish the cat would get him. The ugly duckling's life becomes so unbearable that he runs away. He makes friends with a gaggle of geese, but when they are shot by hunters, he is left alone.

One evening he sees a flock of white swans flying overhead. He thinks they are the most beautiful birds he has ever seen, and envies them. He cannot forget the swans, and dreams of them all through the long winter. In the spring the swans return and fly down to where he is swimming. Certain they are going to kill him, he bows his head and waits for the attack, but nothing happens. Suddenly he catches sight of his reflection in the water. He is no longer an ugly duckling—he has grown into a beautiful swan. **LH**

Book of Nonsense 1846

Edward Lear

Nationality | English, born 1812
Publisher | Thomas McLean, UK
Theme | Favorite characters, Classics, Poetry, Quirky

Edward Lear was a painter and poet who enjoyed combining his nonsensical, fantastic rhymes with his own illustrations. He started working as an artist at the age of fourteen, when his father could no longer earn enough money to support his enormous family—there were twenty children in the Lear household.

Lear began writing at a time when literature written especially for children was coming to the fore. He traveled widely, which helped his vivid imagination to flourish and brought new sounds into his vocabulary, and he delighted in making up unusual words for his poems, many of which he wrote for the children of his friends and acquaintances.

The Book of Nonsense is a collection of limericks (poems made up of five rhyming lines) about a cast of characters from all over the world. They include the "Old Man with a Beard," whose facial hair is so long, he discovers several species of birds have built their nests in it, and a young lady "whose chin / Resembled the point of a pin"; she makes the best of her unusual appearance by learning to play the harp with her pointy chin. There is also the "Old Lady of Chertsey," who makes "such a remarkable curtsey" that she cannot stop spinning until she has twirled so deep into the ground that she gets stuck, and an "Old Man of Kilkenny," who "never had more than a penny" and spends all that he has on onions and honey.

Lear's limericks have become famous, and continue to be loved by generations of children for their general silliness, their easy rhymes, and for how much fun they are to read aloud. **LH**

Lear's images of "Old Persons" who eat root vegetables and rabbits. 

Max and Moritz 1865

Heinrich Christian Wilhelm Busch

Nationality | German, born 1832
Publisher | Braun and Schneider, Germany
Theme | Favorite characters, Rhyming stories, Classics, Controversial

5+

Max and Moritz (first published as *Max und Moritz—eine Bubengeschichte in sieben Streichen*) was Wilhelm Busch's first children's book. Before its publication, he had worked as a caricaturist and a poet.

Critics are divided as to the controversial nature of the book—some believe it is possible to interpret the children's pranks as misguided, childish attempts to break free rather than as acts of genuine malice. Others find the book full of horrors. The two protagonists gain strength from each other and together they take on a world full of old-fashioned adults who reject and suppress any new ideas. Unfortunately their attempts to free themselves from the shackles of society go beyond what is acceptable.

> *"Max and Moritz (naught could awe them!) / Took a saw when no one saw them."*

The boys steal and kill chickens, force an old man to fall into the river, and fill their teacher's pipe with dynamite. They put cockroaches in their uncle's bed and try to steal a baker's pretzels—almost being baked in his dough as a consequence (they escape by eating their way free). The end finally comes after the children cut holes into a farmer's crop bags. In revenge, the farmer puts them inside the bags and shreds them to pieces in his mill. The remains of the two naughty children are then eaten by his poultry.

Max and Moritz was not very popular when first published, yet these two juvenile offenders have become Busch's most famous characters, and passages from the book have entered common German speech. Busch's fantastic illustrations and superb rhymes are now considered to be an ancestor of modern comics. **CS**

MORE STORIES OF MISCHIEVOUS KIDS

Der Struwwelpeter **by Heinrich Hoffmann, 1845**
Just William **by Richmal Crompton, 1922**
Pippi Longstocking **by Astrid Lindgren, 1945**
Ramona the Pest **by Beverley Cleary, 1968**
Horrid Henry **by Francesca Simon, 1993**

Max and Moritz get up to one of their typical boyish pranks. 

The Magic Fishbone 1868

Charles Dickens John Gilbert

Nationality | English, born 1812 (author); American, birth date unknown (illustrator)
Publisher | *All the Year Round* magazine, UK
Theme | Magical stories, Family

5+

"It instantly flashed upon the King that she must be a Fairy, or how could she know that?"

OTHER GREAT DICKENS READS

***Oliver Twist*, 1838**
***The Old Curiosity Shop*, 1840**
***A Christmas Carol*, 1843**
***A Child's History of England*, 1851**
***The Life of Our Lord*, 1934, posthumous**

This is one of Charles Dickens's few stories that is written specifically for children. Its subtitle was *A Holiday Romance from the Pen of Miss Alice Rainbird, Age Seven*, and Dickens wrote it in a style suggestive of a child's vocabulary. The story's first publication was not in book form. It was published simultaneously in two magazines: *All the Year Round*, which Dickens edited, in England, and *Our Young Folks* in the United States. The English version did not have illustrations; the U.S. version was illustrated by John Gilbert.

Princess Alicia is the eldest of nineteen children born to an impoverished king and queen. Her father, King Watkins I, is out shopping one day, buying an economical cut of fish, when a mysterious old woman appears. Although the king does not know it, she is the Fairy Grandmarina. She tells him to give some of the fish to Princess Alicia and to give her a message. Princess Alicia must take the fish bone left on her plate, dry it, rub it, and polish it until "it shines like mother-of-pearl," then keep it safe until it is needed to grant her a wish. It is a magic fish bone that can only be used once—and then only "at the right time."

The next day, the queen becomes very ill. Princess Alicia nurses her, takes care of the other children, does the mending and housework, and, when the cook runs away with a "very tall but very tipsy soldier," all the cooking, too. The king wants Alicia to use the magic fish bone, but she knows the time is not yet right. Eventually, when her father tells her that his finances are depleted, she wishes for it to be his "quarter day" (payday). The timing is perfect because she waited until they had tried everything else that could be done before making the wish. Fairy Grandmarina arrives, cures the queen, and magically dresses all the children in fine new clothes, and Princess Alicia as a bride. They are all taken to meet Prince Certainpersonio who is to be Princess Alicia's husband. **LH**

The House that Jack Built 1878

Unknown Randolph Caldecott

Many people will have undoubtedly seen the work of Randolph Caldecott without actually knowing who he was. His beautifully depicted illustrations are instantly recognizable and set the tone for many Victorian childhoods.

The House that Jack Built is, in fact, an old nursery rhyme, although it is unclear who the original author was. Through Caldecott's visualization, the story has become a timeless classic. On the very first page we see a beautifully concise and colorful illustration of a picturesque Victorian house in its prime. From the birds dancing in the sky to the two dogs playfully rolling in the garden, the reader feels an immediate sense of well-being. The same can be said for the picture of the majestic figure proudly showing off "the house that Jack built" to three contented onlookers surrounded by pastel-colored flowers. The rhyme itself builds and grows across the pages, and the story unfolds through a mixture of simple line drawings and vivid color prints.

This is one of the first books that Caldecott illustrated. He was given the commission by engraver Edmund Evans to produce two books for Christmas, after another illustrator serendipitously pulled out. Evans's commission resulted in *The House that Jack Built* and *The Diverting History of John Gilpin*, both of which were both published in 1878 and were instant successes. They were so successful, in fact, that Caldecott was commissioned to produce two books every year until he died.

Although he was predominantly an illustrator of novels and picture books, Caldecott was also a keen artist, and his sculptures and paintings can be found in several art galleries. To further cement his name in history, the Caldecott Medal, awarded to the artist of the most distinguished American picture book of the year, is named after him. **RS**

Nationality | English, born 1846
Publisher | George Routledge and Sons, UK
Theme | Nursery rhymes, Classics, Magical stories

5+

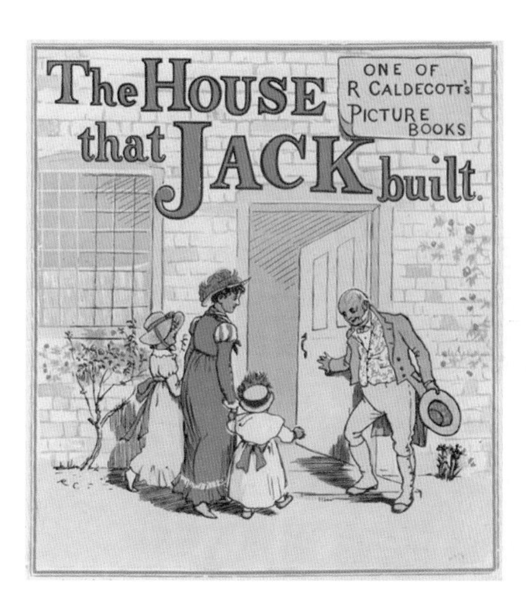

"This is the Cat / That killed the Rat / That ate the Malt / That lay in the House that Jack built."

OTHER CLASSIC CALDECOTT WORKS

The Babes in the Wood, 1879
Sing a Song for Sixpence, 1880
The Farmer's Boy, 1881
A Frog He Would A-Wooing Go, 1883
Jackanapes, 1883

Cole's Funny Picture Book 1879

Edward William Cole

Nationality | English, born 1832
Publisher | E. W. Cole and Co., Australia
Theme | Classics, Design classics, Comics

When *Cole's Funny Picture Book* or *Family Amuser and Instructor to Delight the Whole Family and Make Home Happier* was published in 1879, it was an instant success. Its author and publisher, E. W. Cole offered £100 to anyone who could prove it was not the funniest picture book in the world. No one could. With each new edition, the book grew in size as William Cole added to it. I was four years old in 1950 when I was given a copy from the sixty-eighth edition.

Edward William Cole was born in Kent, England, in 1832. At sixteen he left England and eventually arrived in South Australia. After a variety of careers he established the first of his famous stores, Cole's Book Arcade, in Melbourne in 1873. His other books include *Cole's First Book for Little Australians*, *Cole's Comic Animal Story Book*, and *Cole's Peep Show Story Book*.

In essence, *Cole's Funny Picture Book* is a scrapbook of stories, pictures, riddles, and puzzles that were clipped without concern for copyright from books and Victorian periodicals, such as *Punch*, and arranged into chapters called "Lands." There is "Boy Land," "Girl Land," "Dolly Land," and "Play Land," to mention a few. I spent hours poring over the pictures, some of which today might be regarded by some as cruel and frightening. But "Cole's Machine for Scolding Naughty Girls" and his "Whipping Machine for Naughty Boys" were cleverly barbed jokes: Cole was lampooning the education system of the time. He abhorred the violence in nineteenth-century schools, and had his own children privately tutored.

Cole's Funny Picture Book is really like a "big dipper," similar to the omnibus annuals for boys and girls published in the 1950s. It could be opened at any page to entertain you with a story, a funny picture, or some puzzles. During my childhood it was always kicking around somewhere in my bedroom, usually within reach for a quick dip.

BOOKS WITH INNOVATIVE ARTWORK

***The Jolly Aunt* by Lothar Meggendorfer, 1891**
***The Little Pot Boiler* by Spike Milligan, 1963**
***Haunted House* by Jan Pieńkowski, 1979**
***Jolly Postman* by Allan Ahlberg, 1986**
***Tar Beach* by Faith Ringgold, 1991**

Cole's clever artwork made the book a design classic.

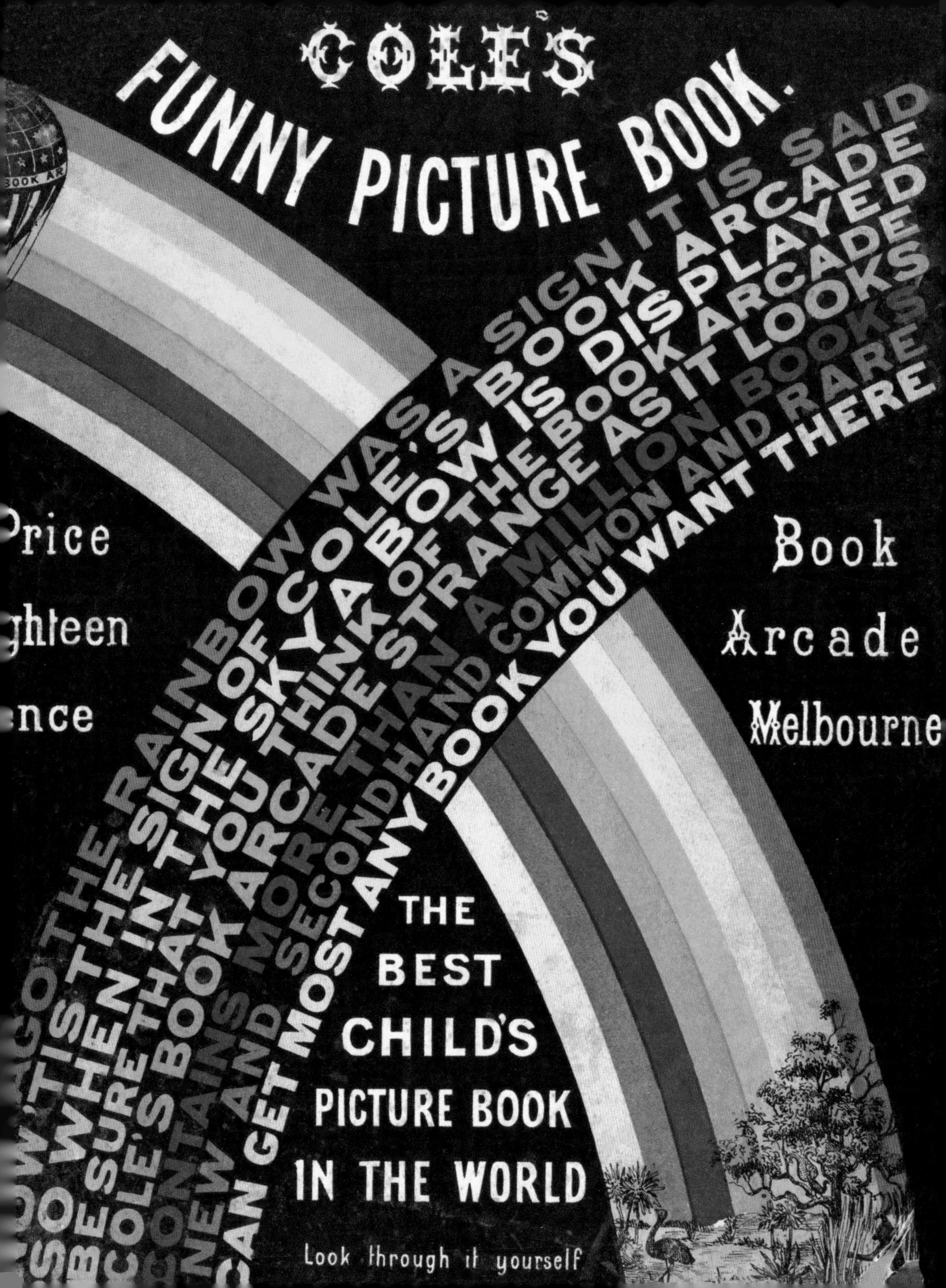

COLE'S FUNNY PICTURE BOOK.

...AGO THE RAINBOW WAS A SIGN IT IS SAID
SO NOW 'TIS THE SIGN OF COLE'S BOOK ARCADE
BE SURE WHEN IN THE SKY A BOW IS DISPLAYED
COLE'S SURE THAT YOU THINK OF THE BOOK ARCADE
CONTAINS BOOK ARCADE IS STRANGE AS IT LOOKS
NEW AND MORE THAN A MILLION BOOKS
CAN GET SECONDHAND COMMON AND RARE
MOST ANY BOOK YOU WANT THERE

Price
ghteen
nce

Book
Arcade
Melbourne

THE
BEST
CHILD'S
PICTURE BOOK
IN THE WORLD

Look through it yourself

Tessa Duder reviews:

A Child's Garden of Verses 1885

Robert Louis Stevenson Charles Robinson

Nationality | Scottish, born 1850 (author); English, born 1870 (illustrator)
Publisher | Longmans, Green and Co., UK
Theme | Poetry

5+

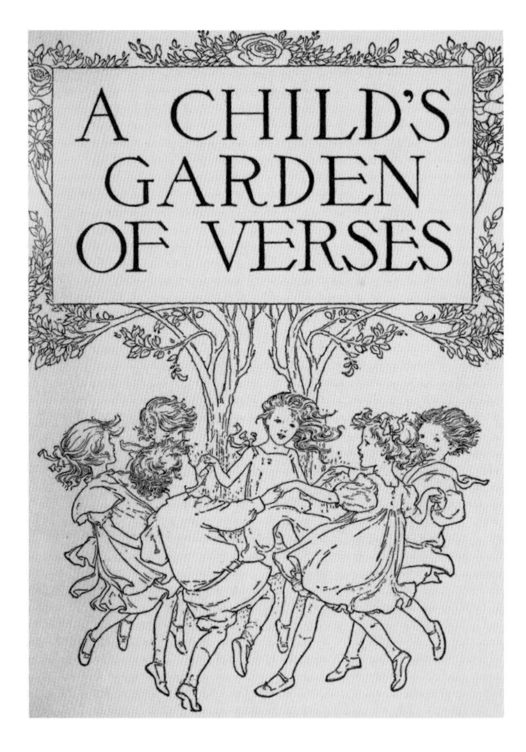

I was just three years old, and my father was far away patching up soldiers in a New Zealand army field ambulance somewhere in a North African desert. My childhood in a small New Zealand market town could hardly have been further from the late Victorian world of R. L. Stevenson's *A Child's Garden of Verses*—and yet it was here in the musicality of those short poems, even more than A. A. Milne or *Milly-Molly-Mandy*, that I believe my love of language, books, and travel began.

I still have two childhood editions: one a small leather-bound edition from Collins Library of Classics, the other a big American hardback in full color. The cozy illustrations by Clara M. Burd show children in pantaloons and bonnets playing by rivers, sick in bed,

"Oh wind, a-blowing all day long! / Oh wind, that sings so loud a song!"

flying kites, and dressing by candlelight; few writers have come close to Stevenson's gentle yet astute evocation of childhood. Any wonder that when I visited England aged five, again at seventeen, and later as an adult, I felt a sense of homecoming.

Until the 1980s, New Zealand children had little of their own lives reflected in books. My generation read about English or American children. *Ballet Shoes* stoked an unrealistic ambition for a career in ballet; *The Water-Babies* opened my young eyes to the horrors of child labor and inclined me permanently toward socialism. Only a 1944 publication, *Richard Bird in the Bush* by Mollie Miller Atkinson, indicated to this New Zealand child that we could have stories and handsomely illustrated books of our own; an odd sort of influence, maybe, but it is why I felt compelled to write stories set in the city—Auckland—and country I call home.

OTHER RECOMMENDED BOOKS OF VERSE

Marigold Garden **by Kate Greenaway, 1885**
Songs of Travel and Other Verses **by Robert Louis Stevenson, 1896**
Figgie Hobbin **by Charles Causley, 1970**
Where the Sidewalk Ends **by Shel Silverstein, 1974**

One of the elegant pen and ink drawings from the first edition.

The Blue Fairy Book 1889

Nationality | Scottish, born 1844 (editor); English, born 1860 (illustrator)
Publisher | Longmans, Green and Co., UK
Theme | Fairy tales, Myths and legends

THE

BLUE FAIRY BOOK

EDITED BY

ANDREW LANG

WITH NUMEROUS ILLUSTRATIONS BY H. J. FORD
AND G. P. JACOMB HOOD

LONDON
LONGMANS, GREEN, AND CO.
AND NEW YORK: 15 EAST 16th STREET
1889

All rights reserved

Andrew Lang was educated at the Edinburgh Academy and later became a fellow of Merton College, Oxford, where he studied myth, ritual, and totenism. He moved to London in 1875 and became one of the most famous writers of the day. He specialized in mythology and always maintained that folktales were the foundation of literary mythology. He amassed a vast collection of folktales from all over the world, blatantly plundering the collections of the Brothers Grimm, Charles Perrault, Hans Christian Andersen, and others (although he was always careful to credit them).

Together with his wife, Leonora Alleyne, Lang began to compile a series of fairy-tale books for children. The first was *The Blue Fairy Book*; eleven

"It was even whispered about the Court that she had Ogreish inclinations. . . ."

more followed, each one a different color. Beneath the fantastic element of the fairy tales, there are some brutal truths. Luckily most children will listen to the stories with an adult who can reassure them should the story become too frightening. Once the child is familiar with the tales and is happy to wander through the pages alone, what a feast these stories provide: giants and ogres, changelings and trolls, magic rings and poisoned apples. It is no wonder that so many writers acknowledge the power of these magical tales.

All fiction helps us to escape the troubles of the world, but fairy tales do more than that. They arouse our imagination and lead us into places where we are free to do battle with our demons and eventually win the day. If I had to single out one book in the series, it would be *The Blue Fairy Book*, because it contains my favorite tale: "Beauty and the Beast."

OTHER MAGICAL FAIRY TALES

Cinderella by Jacob and Wilhelm Grimm, 1812
The Little Mermaid by Hans Christian Andersen, 1837
Rumpelstiltskin and other Grimm Tales by Carol Ann Duffy, 1999

A gold-leaf witch soars across the original edition hardcover.

The Jungle Book 1894

✎ Rudyard Kipling ✎ John L. Kipling

Nationality | English, born 1865
Publisher | Macmillan, UK
Theme | Animal stories, Classics, Friendship, Favorite characters

Mowgli, the "man cub" brought up by wolves in the Seownee forest, somewhere in India during the British Empire, is the hero of just eight short stories. Three are in *The Jungle Book* and five more in *The Second Jungle Book*. Mowgli has become world famous, and Kipling's creations—such as the Law of the Jungle, the Lone Wolf, the cowardly man-eating tiger, the Tribe's Hunting Grounds, the dance of the hunting snake, and many more—are deeply woven through popular imagery and thought. Kipling's genius as a storyteller and poet has not always been recognized, but his superb imagination and the characters he created have become part of a general consciousness (helped by Disney film versions of his works).

Many readers see the stories as allegories or fables. They certainly have a moral code, clearly seen in the tales of Rikki-Tikki-Tavi the heroic mongoose, Toomai of the Elephants, and Kotick the white seal, yet Kipling's characters are subtle, multilayered, and eloquent. Who does not believe in Akela as he grimly submits to his redundancy as leader of the pack or Baloo as he admits how much he loves Mowgli? These are not simply anthropomorphized fauna but aspects of humanity. Kipling was a great writer.

Kipling said that he put into the stories everything that he "heard or dreamed about the Indian jungle." Although he was born in India and spent the first years of his working life there, he was not in reality an outdoors sort of person. The jungle in his stories was an entirely invented jungle, just as the animals' behavior was invented. **VN**

Perez the Mouse 1894

✎✎ Luis Coloma

Original Title | El Ratón Pérez
Nationality | Spanish, born 1851
Publisher | Corazón de Jesús, Spain
Theme | Folktales

Perez the Mouse is responsible for leaving children a little gift under their pillow when they lose a milk tooth. Inspired by this ancient popular tradition, the writer and Jesuit priest Luis Coloma wrote *Perez the Mouse*, a story that he dedicated to the young King Alfonso XIII, then eight years old.

When King Buby loses a tooth at the age of six, he is told to put it under his pillow with a letter to Perez the Mouse. That night, Perez the Mouse visits King Buby and turns him into a mouse so that the boy-king can accompany Perez on a journey—a journey that begins in a palace and ends in a little loft. On the way, King Buby learns something that he did not know: there are poor children in his kingdom.

Coloma wrote many stories based on folktales and traditions, using a lively, casual style that helps to make the overtly moralistic and educational intention more effective. The story of Perez the Mouse highlights the belief that everyone, rich or poor, is a child of God, and it encourages the boy-king to be as fair and courageous as possible with his fellow brothers and sisters.

True to its period, the story includes information about local customs and manners, as well as places and people that actually existed. Coloma wrote several short stories and novels, some of which, such as *Pequeñeces* (*Little Things*), were remarkably successful. This work is the first known literary re-creation of this popular children's tradition, which has various references in other cultures, such as the Anglo-Saxon tooth fairy. **EB**

Baloo, Kaa, Bagheera, and the elephants from the 1894 edition.

Just So Stories 1902

Rudyard Kipling

Nationality | English, born 1865
Publisher | Macmillan, UK
Theme | Animal stories, Classics, Friendship, Favorite characters

Great stories can change lives. I know, because "The Elephant's Child," one of the *Just So Stories* by Rudyard Kipling, changed mine. My mother used to read this to us—to me and to my brother, Pieter—when we were little, sitting on the bed, just her and us and the story. She loved it—we could tell that by how she read it. So we loved it, too. It is the tale of a little elephant "full of satiable curtiosity," who will ask awkward questions. For his pains his various relations spank him, but he keeps asking. He is told to go to "the great grey green greasy Limpopo river," and ask the crocodile. The crocodile grabs him by his snout—up to that moment, you understand, an elephant had a only stubby-looking snout, not a trunk—and after the

"He asked questions about everything he saw, or heard, or felt, or smelt, or touched . . ."

crocodile grabs it, he pulls and pulls so that his snout becomes a trunk. Whereupon he goes home and spanks all his relatives with it—sweet revenge!

Of course, like all the best stories about animals, this one is about us as much as it is about a little elephant. It is about a child growing up and finding out how the world is, how grown-ups do not have all the answers, and how children can sometimes get even with them. It is a thoroughly empowering story for a child to hear—a lot of wish fulfillment! What also makes the story so special for me is the way Kipling tells it. He talks to us, calls us his "best beloved," and then when we are sitting comfortably, he tells us the story in a language so lyrical and musical, so suited to the story that we are at once entranced. I was entranced when I was three. Now I'm sixty-five and I'm still entranced.

MORE POPULAR TITLES FROM KIPLING

***The Jungle Book*, 1894**
***Kim*, 1901**
***Puck of Pook's Hill*, 1906**
***Rewards and Fairies*, 1910**
***Thy Servant a Dog*, 1930**

Kipling's original drawing of the Elephant's Child reaching for bananas.

The Dutch Twins 1911

Lucy Fitch Perkins

"'Keep still, can't you?' said Kit crossly. 'You'll scare the fish. Girls don't know how to fish . . .'"

OTHER BOOKS IN THE TWINS SERIES

The Cave Twins, 1915
The Belgian Twins, 1917
The Spartan Twins, 1918
The Filipino Twins, 1923
The Indian Twins, 1938

Nationality | American, born 1865
Publisher | Houghton Mifflin, USA
Theme | Family, Friendship, Adventure, Love, Quirky

Kit and Kat are five-year-old boy and girl twins. They are the children of Dutch farmers, and their participation in the daily household chores and the activities on the farm form the basis for their various adventures and misadventures. These six short narratives are accessible to early readers and introduce young children to a rural lifestyle, in which Kit and Kat go fishing with Grandfather, take the farm produce to market on a boat with Father, and dress up in their best clothes to deliver the milk.

One of twenty-six books in the popular series of Twins books, *The Dutch Twins* might seem a little old-fashioned to some readers, such as the refrainlike argument that takes place between Kit and Kat about girls not being as capable as boys. "Boys can do a great many things that girls can't do," says Kit. Further into the story, however, Kat triumphs in a skating race, and Kit is suitably put in his place. Any issues that are potentially disruptive to the equilibrium of the twins' relationship are cast swiftly aside by common sense. A fitting metaphor for this is to be found in the majestic windmills that pump the excess water from the fields, allowing them to become arable and a source of livelihood for the proud Dutch farmers.

There is a constant stream of jobs to be done. The work ethic of the family across three generations dominates the story and informs the reader about the traditional rural Dutch lifestyle that, against all odds, led to the nation's continued survival. **AR**

The Adventures of Maya the Bee 1912

Waldemar Bonsels

Original Title | Die Biene Maja und ihre Abenteuer
Nationality | German, born 1880
Publisher | Deutsche Verlags-Anstalt, Germany
Theme | Animal stories, Science and nature

The Adventures of Maya the Bee became a best seller around the world when it was first published in 1912. Since then, it has been translated into more than forty languages. The novel tells its readers about the adventures of an individualistic bee who abandons her hive to explore the world. Today, many more children have come to know Maya and her insect friends through the anime television series.

On her journey, Maya makes the acquaintance of a number of fellow insects, including Peter the rose-beetle, the dragonfly Loveydear, Puck the housefly, the daddy longlegs Hannibal, Fred the butterfly, the poet-ladybug Alois, and Thomas the millipede. The chapter "Wonders of the Night," in which Maya experiences the singing of a tree cricket during a starlit night and makes friends with an elf, is particularly lyrical and beautiful. When Maya becomes a prisoner of the hornets, she learns of their plan to attack her old hive. Maya manages to escape, and by returning to her hive and warning her queen of the impending attack, she saves the hive from annihilation by the predatory yet nevertheless courageous hornets.

Bonsels's work is charming and educational in that all the creatures and their habitats are described with great biological accuracy, except, of course, for their ability to speak. Through her often witty conversations with them, Maya not only learns many of nature's secrets, but also some profound truths about the meaning of life and death. **FHG**

Josephine and Her Dolls 1916

H. C. Cradock Honor C. Appleton

Nationality | English, born 1863 (author); English, born 1879 (illustrator)
Publisher | Blackie and Son, UK
Theme | Friendship

Josephine and Her Dolls is the first in a series of short picture books written by Mrs. Henry Cowper Cradock during World War I. Mrs. Cradock was a vicar's wife who initially wrote the stories for her own daughter before finding a wider public.

Josephine is eight years old and an only child. She is rather bossy and spends her days creating adventures for her family of sixteen dolls. These include two Korean dolls; Quacky Jack, a yellow duck in a sailor suit; assorted teddy bears; and a soldier doll, Sunny Jim, who goes off to fight in the war. In all the books, Josephine is the narrator and plays an adult role; whereas her dolls are her "children" and they are taught various valuable lessons. The toys enact a series of everyday events, such as going to school, shopping, and playing house, as well as enjoying adventures, such as watching a pantomime.

This is the only book in the series that focuses on the events taking place when the book was written. It reflects the sense of patriotism and self-sacrifice of World War I as the toys wave Sunny Jim off to the front. At the end of the book, the dolls enact a peace scene between the King and the Kaiser. Although the books no longer attract many young readers, they are very popular with adult collectors who appreciate the quality of the printing and production and above all, the charming illustrations by Honor Appleton. These delicate watercolors depict the imaginative world of childhood in all its innocence. **HJ**

The Magic Pudding 1918

Norman Lindsay

5+

"Eat away, chew away, munch and bolt and guzzle
Never leave the table till you're full up to the muzzle."

OTHER BOOKS ABOUT PUDDINGS

***The Tale of Samuel Whiskers, or the Roly-Poly Pudding* by Beatrix Potter, 1908**
***Pudding* by Pippa Goodheart, 2003**
***Invasion of the Christmas Puddings* by Jeremy Strong, 2008**

Nationality | Australian, born 1879
Publisher | Angus and Robertson, Australia
Theme | Magical stories, Friendship, Quirky, Animal stories

When artist Norman Lindsay decided to write a book about an enchanted pudding called Albert, he created a magical group of friends—Bill Barnacle, a sailor; Sam Sawnoff, a penguin; and Bunyip Bluegum, a koala—to protect the bad-tempered pudding from thieves. Albert is a very special pudding: He can walk, talk, change flavor at will, and can be eaten continually without ever disappearing.

The story, which is told in slices not chapters, begins when Bunyip leaves home to escape his Uncle Wattleberry's offensive whiskers. He meets Sam and Bill, who are enjoying Albert as a steak and kidney pudding, and is offered a slice to eat. When the pudding thieves—a possum and a wombat—try to steal Albert, Bunyip helps fight them off. He, Bill, and Sam then pledge to devote themselves to Albert's safety and form the Society of Puddin' Owners. The book relates the friends' adventures and the varied characters they meet along the way, including a kookaburra who constantly insults Bill but gets away with it because Bill has vowed he will never fight anyone with a beak. When the pudding thieves eventually manage to steal Albert, the three friends have to fight a legal battle to be declared his rightful owners.

Lindsay wrote *The Magic Pudding* while mourning the death of his brother and the horrors of World War I. Despite his great sadness, the book—which is superbly illustrated—is full of humor and continues to enchant children and adults. Philip Pullman described it as "the funniest children's book ever written." **LH**

Tales of Snugglepot and Cuddlepie 1918

May Gibbs

Nationality | Australian, born 1877 (in England)
Publisher | Angus and Robertson, Australia
Theme | Family, Animal stories, Fantasy, Favorite characters

5+

Two cherubic half brothers named Snugglepot and Cuddlepie, clad only in gum-nut caps, are the unlikely heroes of this classic Australian children's series. The two nut babies were first seen peeping from behind a gumleaf in *Tales of Snugglepot and Cuddlepie*; their further adventures introduced other characters such as Little Ragged Blossom and Little Obelia, a sea sprite met during an undersea adventure. The stories have retained iconic status in Australian children's literature.

The nut and flower babies dwell in gum-leaf nests, deep in the bush where they have many encounters with creatures, both friendly and dangerous. The contrast between the tender, pink bodies of the babies and the prickly, somewhat threatening world of the bush they inhabit hints at a certain European ambivalence toward the antipodean environment. May Gibbs's stories are populated with threatening ants and beetles, sharp-beaked birds, lizards, and snakes, not to mention the archetypal baddies of the series, the "ugly, wicked" Banksia men. Their huge, bristly faces, inspired by the large, hairy seed heads of the Banksia bush, must have haunted many a childhood imagination over the years.

Gibbs's artistic training is evident in her naturalistic rendering of Australia native plants and animals. Tapping into a wave of national pride in the wake of World War I, her illustrations show a conscious attempt to embrace the flora and fauna of her adopted homeland. A genuine love for the creatures of the bush inspired her work, and her message to children is to be kind to all bush creatures—except perhaps snakes. **SM**

"'These Humans,' said Mr. Kookaburra, 'are as bad as bad, but there must be bad things in this world as well as good.'"

MORE CUTE TALES FROM MAY GIBBS

***The Gumnut Babies*, 1916**
***Wattle Babies*, 1922**
***Nuttybub and Nittersing*, 1923**
***Chucklebud and Wunkydoo*, 1929**

AMELIAR ANNE AND
THE GREEN UMBRELLA

Ameliaranne and the Green Umbrella 1920

Constance Heward   Susan Pearse

Nationality | English, born 1884 (author); English, born 1878 (illustrator)
Publisher | Harrap, UK
Theme | Friendship

Ameliaranne and the Green Umbrella is the first in a series of picture books about the life of a resourceful little girl. Other books in the series had different authors, but most were illustrated by Susan Pearse. The pictures set the story from the frontispiece (in which Ameliaranne Stiggins, with her characteristic look of baggy stockings and long knickers hanging beneath her hem, is surrounded by her adoring siblings) through the first few pages where Ameliaranne is shown carrying shopping and her hardworking mother appears, sleeves rolled up and her skirt hitched up, carrying a huge basket of washing. Ameliaranne is going to the Squire's tea party, but "the five little Stigginses" cannot go because they have colds. Rather mysteriously Ameliaranne takes an umbrella to the party with her.

The illustrations flesh out the simple text, showing the Squire, "a jolly old man . . . like Father Christmas," at the gate of his house, while his sister, Miss Josephine, "a cross old maid," lurks reluctantly at the top of the stairs. When the party is over, Miss Josephine impatiently tries to open the umbrella for Ameliaranne. After a struggle, it flies open and cakes and biscuits come tumbling out. Ameliaranne bursts into tears as Miss Josephine chastises her, but the kind Squire comes to her rescue. It turns out that Ameliaranne has eaten nothing herself, but hidden the food to share with her brothers and sisters. Ameliaranne triumphs in the end, as the Squire sends her home with "cakes enough for six and Mrs. Stiggins as well." **CW**

Rupert the Bear 1921

Mary Tourtel

Full Title | Adventures of Rupert the Little Lost Bear
Nationality | English, born 1874
Publisher | Thomas Nelson and Sons, UK
Theme | Favorite characters, Adventure

5+

Rupert Bear began his literary life as a cartoon in a British newspaper, the *Daily Express*. "Little Bear Lost," about a nameless brown bear, began on November 20, 1920. The *Daily Express* has kept the bear on its pages ever since (taken off for urgent news only three times). Throughout World War II, Rupert was seen as a symbol of an unscarred, peaceful England where bad things could not happen. Rupert and his friends, who include Podgy Pig, Bill Badger, Raggety, Bingo, and Ping-Pong, live in Nutwood. Nothing is ever too surreal for Rupert, whether it be the arrival of a hot-air balloon, a flying carpet, or a trip to see his uncle at the North Pole.

In 1921, the Rupert cartoon was put into a book, *The Adventures of Rupert the Little Lost Bear*. Rupert has had his own TV series, been on postage stamps, and even appeared in a pop video with Sir Paul McCartney. There is a gallery dedicated to Rupert at the museum of Canterbury, England, the city where Mary Tourtel grew up. Tourtel had an adventurous lifestyle, and her enthusiasm for life went into her cartoons, making the characters funny, endearing, and somehow never out-of-date. Her Rupert wore a blue sweater and gray trousers, but after she retired in 1935, illustrator Alfred Bestall gave Rupert his signature clothing of bright red sweater, yellow scarf, and yellow trousers. Rupert has had several illustrators, but he remains the same lovable bear that generations of British children grew up with—and about whom they still become nostalgic well into old age. **LH**

Velveteen Rabbit 1922

Margery Williams William Nicholson

Nationality | English, born 1881 (author); English, born 1872 (illustrator);
Publisher | Heinemann, UK
Theme | Animal stories, Friendship

Some call it overly sentimental, but *The Velveteen Rabbit*, or *How Toys Become Real*, has a touch of magic about it. Since its publication, Margery Williams's first U.S. work has been widely read and adapted for television, film, radio, and the stage. Influenced by the wistful whimsy of Walter de la Mare (whom she called her mentor) and by the loss of her father in childhood, Williams explores deep feelings of attachment and loss in a tender, simply expressed narrative.

A small Boy (unnamed) gets a nice, fat velveteen rabbit for Christmas, but he soon bores with it in the excitement of other fancier presents, especially the mechanical ones. For a long time, Rabbit is shunned by these toys and his owner until Skin Horse tells him that in the end they will break, but that he is one of those toys that can become Real. How do you become Real? By being loved, of course, although it does take a long time. One night, when Boy cannot find his china dog, his Nana gives him the Rabbit. Boy and Rabbit have a long honeymoon, playing at night and outdoors, where one day the Rabbit sees other real rabbits. He is certainly loved and feels Real, despite becoming shabby. When Boy gets scarlet fever, Rabbit comforts him with thoughts of the seaside. When Boy recovers, however, the doctor decrees that the old Rabbit must be burned to prevent infection. Awaiting his fate, Rabbit cries a real tear, from which a fairy emerges. She tells him that he had become Real to the boy because he loved him, but now he shall be Real to everyone. A story guaranteed to make anyone rush and hug their old teddy bear. **VN**

Come Hither 1923

Walter de la Mare Alec Buckels

Nationality | English, born 1873 (editor); details unknown (illustrator)
Publisher | Constable, UK
Theme | Poetry, Nursery rhymes

Described by no less than W. H. Auden as "the best possible introduction to poetry," this anthology of well-loved rhymes and poems for children deserves to be on every bookshelf. Walter de la Mare takes his audience and his mission seriously. Although the story that opens the book is a whimsical account of poetic inspiration and somewhat faded by time, the poems themselves are among the very best that England has produced. Proving that "like a carpenter who makes a table, a man who has written a poem has written it like that on purpose," de la Mare gleans lyrics from fourteenth-century Chaucer through to the early twentieth-century Georgian poets, such as Edmund Blunden and Harold Monro.

The anthology is organized thematically, under such headings as "Morning and May," "Elphin, Ouph, Fay," "Far," and "Old Tales and Balladry," outlandish titles that give a fair indication of de la Mare's poetic interests. As a poet, he loved the uncanny and the eerie; as a reader, he wished to be rapt away. Funnily enough, he was wiser as an anthologist than as a reader. Although ostensibly for children, this is a more mature, challenging, and far lovelier set of poems than Palgrave's Victorian *Golden Treasury*. Hardy, Coleridge, Shakespeare, Blake, and Clare are not soft, wispy poetic options, even though some of the notes with which the book ends under the heading "About and Roundabout" may seem to wander deeply into some misty faerie reverie. Yet poetry is an enchanted wood after all: put yourself and your children under its spell. **VN**

The adorable rabbit that cast its spell over generations of readers.

When We Were Very Young 1924

A. A. Milne   E. H. Shepard

Nationality | English, born 1882 (author); English, born 1879 (illustrator)
Publisher | Methuen, UK
Theme | Poetry, Favorite characters

In this collection of poems, A. A. Milne turned the playful notions and random sillinesses of small children into accomplished and popular verses. Whether the subject is watching out for predatory bears while playing on flagstones on the street or has a very young child's intense desire for looking after his mother, Milne strings words on skipping wheels of rhyme to evoke an innocent view of the world. The nursery cast of characters includes Milne's own son, Christopher Robin, later immortalized as the owner of Winnie-the-Pooh, as well as the bear himself. The real-life Christopher Robin found these poems less affecting than adults might imagine and once flung his teddy bear behind the sofa saying, "He does not like *When We Were Very Young*." For decades, these poems have been memorized, anthologized, recorded, and loved for their childish preoccupations and quirky worries. Yet Milne believed that, "A children's book must be written, not for children, but for the author himself."

Paradoxically, Milne was "not inordinately fond" of children, and his son later wrote a book excoriating his loveless childhood. He particularly hated the poem "Vespers," with its pious refrain, "Hush, Hush, whisper who dares, Christopher Robin is saying his prayers," commenting that most three-year-old children do not pray in any meaningful sense of the word. Surely it was from domestic dramas such as these that Milne drew inspiration for his gentle satires. **VN**

"Halfway down the stairs / Is a stair / Where I sit."

Now We Are Six 1927

A. A. Milne   E. H. Shepard

Nationality | English, born 1882 (author); English, born 1879 (illustrator)
Publisher | Methuen, UK
Theme | Poetry, Friendship

This collection of poems is the companion to *When We Were Very Young*. The verses in *Now We Are Six* are highly enjoyable to read aloud. From short simple rhymes, like "Solitude," to longer poems, such as "The Knight Whose Armor Didn't Squeak," there is a poem to suit any occasion. For example, E. H. Shepard's original color illustrations add zany energy to such merry skipping rhymes as "Sneezles," and some of the poems feature Winnie-the-Pooh, in tearjerkers such as "Us Two" and "Forgotten," or saccharine-sweet paeans to friendship in "The Friend" and "Twice Times."

Gentle satire animates some of the best-known poems, such as "King John's Christmas," which parodies the child in all of us, even the most grown-up and unpleasant of men. For sheer silliness, "Waiting at the Window," which races two raindrops down a windowpane, is hard to beat. "Binker," which charts a child's imaginary friend—always there, kindly, and interested—is a keen favorite with children who love to recognize Binker's secret. Sometimes Milne tips into sentimentality, as in "Pinkle Purr," but at times he also reaches greater heights, as in the mysterious "Wind on the Hill" ("where it comes from, nobody knows").

Milne's affinity for the gentle, easy pleasures of childhood was probably a reaction to the horrors he had seen in World War I. While contemporaries sought to dissipate themselves as "Bright Young Things," Milne constructed a retreat into an idyll where bad things could not threaten him. **VN**

Milly-Molly-Mandy Stories 1928

Joyce Lankester Brisley

Nationality | English, born 1896
Publisher | Harrap, UK
Theme | Family, Classics, Friendship, Adventure

5+

Millicent Margaret Amanda wears a pink-striped frock and lives in a "nice white cottage with a thatched roof" with her mother, father, grandma, grandpa, uncle, auntie, and dog. As Milly-Molly-Mandy, the character has been delighting generations of children (usually girls) since her first appearance in the 1920s. A cheerful, resourceful little girl who has never gotten any older than seven, she and her pals, Little-friend Susan and Billy Blunt, putter about the small world of her village, helping to thatch a roof, making a garden, going to the seaside, and having a tea party. The tone is kindly, the exclamations frequent ("and what do you think?" the author asks), and the endings happy.

For modern children, these gentle stories may need some explanation: The rural 1920s are a long way from the Internet and convenience foods. For example, women make all their food from scratch; they sew all the clothes and occasionally go to a tiny village store. The social circle is small and family based; outings are rare and hence deeply exciting; the cycle of life is close to the cycle of nature.

Picturesque drawings by the author reinforce the idyllic aspects of a world that in real life entailed a great deal of backbreaking work. But no one is impatient or unpleasant, and the only mishaps involve looking after a fretful baby, getting pricked when picking blackberries, or getting errands mixed up. Nostalgia for parents and a safe space for imagination for young readers keep these stories popular. **VN**

Millions of Cats 1929

Wanda Gág

Nationality | American, born 1893
Publisher | Faber and Faber, UK
Award | Newbery Honor Book
Theme | Animal stories, Family, Friendship

Wanda Gág's enchanting tale begins with a very old man and his very old wife who are very lonely. The old man goes in search of the prettiest white cat in the world for his wife, but he finds he cannot make a decision, so he returns instead with an extraordinary problem. He has brought home every cat he could find for his wife to choose from.

There are "Cats here, cats there, / Cats and kittens everywhere, / Hundreds of cats, Thousands of cats, / Millions and billions and trillions of cats. . . ." When his wife points out that they cannot support so many cats, it is left to the cats themselves to decide who among them is the prettiest. Of course, the cats get into a fight over who gets to stay, and in the end the very old couple is left with just one scrawny little kitten, who is not particularly beautiful. Yet with love, that scrawny little kitten grows up to become the most beautiful cat in the world.

Millions of Cats has become regarded as one of the first modern picture books. A wonderful tale of vanity versus humility, it remains as popular today as it was when it was first published. Gág's charming, folk-art style, simple black-and-white illustrations, lyrical language, and catchy refrain that children will happily repeat with each reading, make this a family favorite. At the age of seventeen, Gág wrote in her diary, "My Own Motto—Draw to Live and Live to Draw," and for all the years since, children everywhere have been grateful that she grew up to do just that. **KD**

The Squirrel, the Hare and the Little Grey Rabbit 1929

Alison Uttley Margaret Tempest

Nationality | English, born 1884 (author); English, born 1892 (illustrator);
Publisher | Heinemann, UK
Theme | Animal stories, Friendship

The iconic small-format books, which chronicle the simple lives of sweet Little Grey Rabbit, silly Squirrel, and vainglorious Hare, have delighted millions of children since they first appeared in print. In this, the first book in the series, Little Grey Rabbit's common sense enables the friends to escape predatory Weasel.

Alison Uttley's plots are simple and often gently moralistic, such as Squirrel taking her friends skating although the ice is thin, or Hare getting confused over his role as the Easter Bunny. Tender depictions of nature, friendship, and early social experiences are what make the series so endearing and enduring. Baby hedgehog Fuzzypeg is just starting school: Will it be scary? Moldy Warp, the knowledgeable mole, helps the others to learn new things. Sam Pig gets lost and loses his money, but still manages to get home safe and sound. Little Grey Rabbit plants birdseed and is disappointed not to grow canaries. Here are very small children being affectionately taught about life.

Uttley was no sweet little rabbit. She was fiercely intelligent (the second woman ever to take a physics degree at Manchester University), a passionately possessive wife and mother, and a combative author who quarreled long and hard with her illustrator over who should take the credit for creating Little Grey Rabbit. A countrywoman from England's Derbyshire dale region, Uttley liked to write about animals because she "thought they had a raw deal." That intelligence underpins these charming stories. **VN**

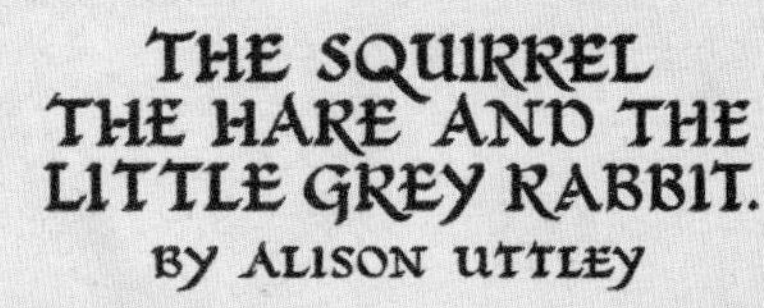

PICTURES BY MARGARET TEMPEST
LONDON: WILLIAM HEINEMANN LTD.

"Little Grey Rabbit's . . . candles were made from pith of rushes dipped in wax."

OTHER ANIMAL STORIES BY UTTLEY

How Little Grey Rabbit Got Back Her Tail, 1930
The Story of Fuzzypeg the Hedgehog, 1932
Moldy Warp the Mole, 1940
Sam Pig Goes to Market, 1941
The Cobbler's Shop and Other Stories, 1950

All About Doggie and Pussycat 1929

Josef Čapek

Original Title | Povidani o pejskovi a kocicce
Nationality | Czech, born 1887
Publisher | Aventinum, Czechoslovakia
Theme | Animal stories

"They love each other like a cat and a dog" is a Czech proverb, ironically referring to animosity between people. Josef Čapek took the proverb literally and put together a charming collection of stories about Doggie and Pussycat, who like each other, live together, and—to use the book's subtitle—"keep house and all sorts of things as well."

The relationship between Doggie and Pussycat is meant to be a humorous take on the complex one between a man and a woman. Čapek's eleven stories are quirky and full of nonsense. Doggie and Pussycat help the Proud Nightgown, who must undress before going to bed; they find a doll that weeps real tears; and they create their own theatrical play. One of the stories—about Independence Day, and in which Doggie makes comments about the revolutionary politician Tomas Masaryk—was left out of editions printed during communist rule. Their adventures are illustrated by black-and-white line drawings specked with color that reflect the author's childlike playfulness and creativity. In fact, the illustrations play a crucial role: Not only do they contribute to the book's easy, relaxed tone, but they also become a part of the narrative, commenting upon key moments in the stories, adding to their poignancy and humor.

Josef Čapek was a preeminent Czech author and artist, and was the brother of the more famous writer Karel Čapek. Josef also invented the word "robot," though his brother introduced the term to literature. **PO**

The Wonderful Farm 1934

Marcel Aymé Natalie Parain

Nationality | French, born 1902 (author); Russian, born 1897 (illustrator)
Publisher | Gallimard, France
Theme | Animal stories, Family

The Wonderful Farm (originally published as *Les Contes du Chat Perché*) consists of two anthologies, "The Red Stories" and "The Blue Stories." In his preface, Marcel Aymé tells us that his musing tales are intended for children aged from four to seventy-seven years old.

The stories take place in the heart of rural France where two sisters, Delphine and Marinette, live with their parents on a farm. The family farm is also home to a strange little world of animals who can think for themselves and who express their thoughts elegantly, without anyone being surprised. All the animals in the farmyard have their own distinctive personalities, such as the white ox who wants to devote his time to study and the pleasures of the mind; the pig who thinks that he is a peacock; the duck who decides to travel around the world to escape from the terrible fate he knows awaits him; and the wolf who promises faithfully never to eat little girls again. As for the cat—he rules the roost.

Faced with parents who are not very understanding and who often treat their daughters harshly, the two little girls can only rely on the friendship of the animals to help them get out of dangerous situations. Aymé chose to tell the stories from the point of view of the two little girls in order to introduce his readers to a world where reality, fantasy, and imagination exist side by side. *The Wonderful Farm* has been adapted for television and film. The stories are short and instructive but always funny. **SL**

Doggie and Pussycat found lots of toys for "little doll" to play with.

Little Tim and the Brave Sea Captain 1936

Edward Ardizzone

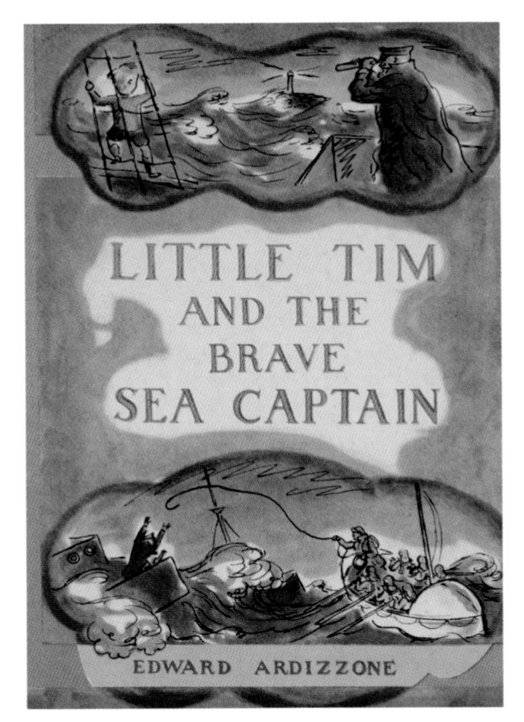

"He was so sad that he resolved, at the first opportunity, to run away to sea."

OTHER LITTLE TIM BOOKS

***Tim and Lucy Go to Sea*, 1938**
***Tim to the Lighthouse*, 1949**
***Tim to the Rescue*, 1949**
***Tim All Alone*, 1956**
***Tim's Last Voyage*, 1972**

Nationality | English, born 1900
Publisher | Oxford University Press, UK
Theme | Adventure, Classics, Favorite characters, Friendship

Edward Ardizzone's Tim has the sort of adventures that every child needs, unshakably rooted in the real world, but unhampered by interference from anxious adults. His stirring but comforting maritime experiences are those a child might dream of—full of storms, shipwrecks, and fascinating knots. He deals doggedly with dangers, never stints on chores below deck, and always gets home after the voyage.

His adventures begin as he walks along the shore in the posture of an old seadog, inspired by his neighbor and friend Captain McFee. When McFee takes Tim out in his launch, *Saucy Sue*, to visit an old friend who is about to sail on a steamer, Tim is so excited that he stows away. He is made to scrub decks by the irritable steamer captain and is rewarded with a mug of cocoa and tidbits from the cook.

As in all the Tim books, the images of life aboard ship are both homely and wonderfully detailed, and most of the characterization of Tim's shipmates is achieved through illustration as the sparing words drive the story forward. The sea is a character in its own right, constantly shifting color and mood, present in sight, smell, and taste. The romantic appeal of a sailor's life is never in doubt even when the perils of the deep are revealed. After a storm, Tim is rescued by a handy lifeboat crew and returned home to his parents, who are not only unperturbed by his absence but willing to let him embark on a career at sea. Which, thanks to Ardizzone, he does. **GB**

Elsie Piddock Skips in Her Sleep 1937

Eleanor Farjeon

Anthology Title | Martin Pippin in the Daisy Field
Nationality | English, born 1881
Publisher | Michael Joseph, UK
Theme | Fantasy, Friendship

This is one of Eleanor Farjeon's best-known stories. Three-year-old Elsie Piddock asks her parents for a skipping rope. When they tell her she is too young, she skips using her father's suspenders; her parents are so impressed that they buy her a rope. By the time she is six years old, "her name and fame were known to all the villages in the county."

One night the fairies take Elsie to skip with them, and their skipping teacher, Andy-Spandy, promises to make her the best skipper in the world. Once a month, always in her sleep, Elsie skips with the fairies, and after a year Andy gives her a magic skipping rope. As Elsie gets older, she outgrows the magic rope and skips less and less. By the time she is an old woman, the name Elsie Piddock is a legend—but no one knows who she actually is.

One day a new lord arrives and treats the people badly. He decides to build factories on the park, which is common land and is the ancient skipping ground of fairies. A mysterious old woman talks to a little girl who is crying in the park and tells her to tell the lord he should let everyone skip there one last time. When the last skipper stops, then he can build his factory. Just as the last skipper is about to tire, "a tiny, tiny woman, so very old, so very bent and fragile" appears. It is Elsie Piddock. She is 109 years old, and has shrunk back to the size of a child, allowing her to use her magic skipping rope again. She is sound asleep and skips without stopping. The lord is defeated. **LH**

Mr. Popper's Penguins 1938

Richard Atwater Robert Lawson

Nationality | American, born 1892 (author), American, born 1892 (illustrator)
Publisher | Little, Brown, USA
Theme | Animal stories

Mr. Popper, a poor house painter, lives with his family in a modest house in the town of Stillwater. He dreams of traveling the world and especially of visiting Arctic regions. His predictable life and its dulling routine, however, is turned into chaos when a penguin arrives in the mail from Antarctica. It is not long before Mr. Popper has twelve penguins living in his house, which has become an icy refuge (Mr. Popper even builds them an ice rink in the cellar). The Poppers, facing financial ruin by the arrival of the penguins and their expensive taste for fresh fish, create Popper's Performing Penguins, a penguin troop that travels the country performing mischief on and off the stage.

The penguins are beautifully illustrated by Robert Lawson as they sleep in the refrigerator, march in unison, bite buttons off a bellboy's coat, and get into trouble. The arrival of spring spells new troubles for the cold weather-loving penguins, but Admiral Drake, an Arctic explorer, averts disaster. The penguins wave their flippers good-bye and journey to the North Pole alongside the explorer—and Mr. Popper, whose dreams of Arctic travel have finally come true.

Richard Atwater began writing *Mr. Popper's Penguins* after watching a documentary about Richard E. Byrd's Antarctic expedition. Forced to abandon the project after suffering a stroke in 1934, his book was revised and completed by his wife, Florence. Charming and hilarious, *Mr. Popper's Penguins* will have children and adults laughing out loud. **RA**

The Little Wooden Horse 1938

Ursula M. Williams Joyce L. Brisley

Nationality | English, born 1911 (author); English, born 1896 (illustrator)
Publisher | Harrap, UK
Theme | Friendship, Fantasy

Few books for this age group contain as much heartache as the poignant epic of the little wooden horse. When his master, Uncle Peder, falls on hard times, the little wooden horse goes out into the world to seek his fortune. He goes from one crisis to the next—making and losing fortunes, getting farther and farther away from his master, trapped, injured, and facing certain death. It is the kind of book that has the reader begging for the next chapter, desperate to know if the little wooden horse will survive

For a small wooden toy fixed on a wheeled wooden platform, he performs extraordinary feats: pulling a canal barge, walking a tightrope in the circus, and running in a horse race (on one wheel!). He can unscrew his own head and at one point loses it and then has to look for it.

Williams's skillful storytelling makes such absurdities seem utterly credible. The little wooden horse is brave, resourceful, determined, and kind. Although his humility and self-pity can be a little irritating, they serve as a constant reminder that he is the little guy battling against the big, scary world on his own. He makes many friends—an elephant, princes and princesses, the father of some very rowdy children—and plenty of enemies, although he did manage to turn more than one enemy into friends. Finally, he returns to Uncle Peder, stuffed full of pirates' treasure, and with enough orders for wooden horses to keep Uncle Peder busy for many years to come. **CW**

Caps for Sale 1938

Esphyr Slobodkina

Nationality | Russian, born 1908
Publisher | William R. Scott, USA
Theme | Animal stories, Folktales, Traditional, Quirky

Esphyr Slobodkina was born in Siberia, grew up in Manchuria (China), and emigrated to the United States, where she became an American citizen. Slobodkina, an artist and sculptor, took her work as a children's author and illustrator equally seriously, and in her memoir she wrote, "The verbal patterns and the patterns of behavior we present to children in these lighthearted confections are likely to influence them for the rest of their lives." *Caps for Sale: A Tale of a Peddler, Some Monkeys and Their Monkey Business*, her second and perhaps best-loved book, has sold more than two million copies and been translated into more than a dozen languages.

The story is delightfully simple and features a peddler who sells caps from village to village. Rather than carry his caps, he wears them all in a tall stack on top of his head. Unable to make any sales, one day, he decides to take a nap in the shade of a tree. Generations of children have loved following the peddler's efforts to outwit the naughty monkeys who steal his hats as he sleeps. When the peddler wakes, he finds a group of monkeys up the tree, and they are all wearing his caps. No matter what the peddler does as he tries to get his caps back, the monkeys only imitate him. Finally, the peddler is so enraged that he throws his own cap on the ground in a fit of temper and, of course, all the monkeys follow suit! This quirky story, based on an old folktale, will enchant children as much today as it did when it was first published. **KD**

CAPS FOR SALE
A Tale of a Peddler, Some Monkeys and Their Monkey Business
TOLD & ILLUSTRATED BY
Esphyr Slobodkina

5+

Michka 1941

Marie Colmont Feodor Rojankovsky

Nationality | French, born 1895 (author); Russian, born 1891 (illustrator)
Publisher | Flammarion, France
Theme | Adventure

Michka tells the story of a little teddy bear and how he discovers freedom, nature, and the world around him, then experiences self-sacrifice. As early as 1954, the book was available with a recording of the story being read by Paul Fauchet, the founder of Père Castor. Together with *Marlaguette* and *Perlette the Rain Drop* (*Perlette goutte d'eau*), *Michka* is one of Marie Colmont's best-known tales. French by birth, she also lived in the United States and London.

Michka is tired of being a toy and can no longer put up with the whims of his mistress, Elizabeth, a spoiled little girl who mistreats him. One day he leaves the warm bedroom and finds that everything is covered with a white blanket of snow. In the forest he takes advantage of his newfound freedom, eating, sleeping, and promising himself that he will never be a toy again. Thanks to two wild geese who are passing by, he discovers that it is Christmas Eve and that it is the perfect day to do a good deed. He goes off to find an opportunity to do good and meets the Christmas reindeer, pulling his sled of presents. Michka helps distribute the presents and has great fun in the process, but when they get to the last house, a miserable hut in which a sick little boy lives, there are no toys left. Michka offers himself as a gift, giving up his freedom so that the boy will have a present when he awakes.

With its ingenuous approach to the subject, the text relates a sense of justice and benevolence. This little adventure story, between dreams and reality, advocates generosity. **CD**

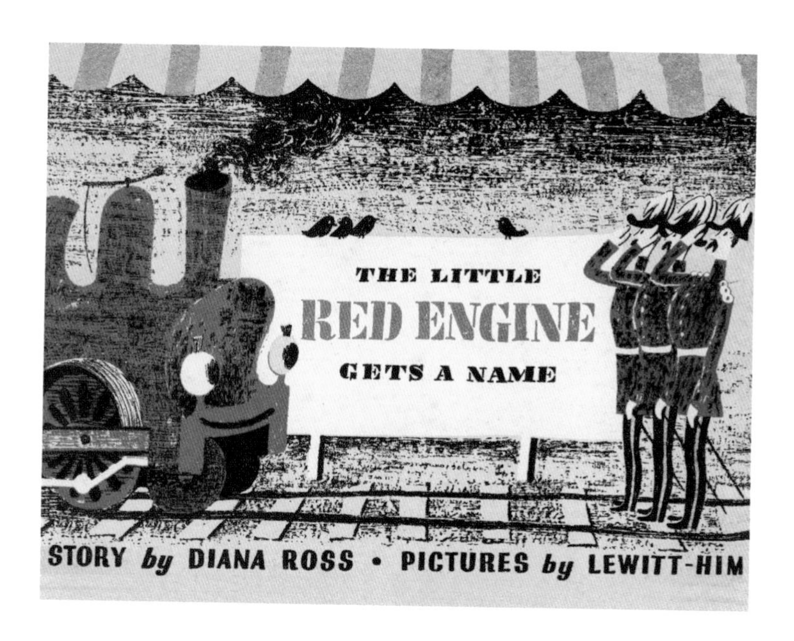

The Little Red Engine Gets a Name 1942

Diana Ross Jan Lewitt and George Him

Nationality | Maltese/British, born 1910 (author); Polish, born 1907 (Lewitt) and 1900 (Him)
Publisher | Faber and Faber, UK
Theme | Adventure

Although author Diana Ross was an illustrator as well as a writer, her first book in the Little Red Engine series (*The Little Red Engine Gets a Name*) was actually illustrated by the Lewitt-Him partnership, who were well-known Polish graphic designers in exile in Britain during World War II. The story displays the wartime spirit that characterized Britain in World War II.

The Little Red Engine is disrespected for its diminutive size by the bigger, main-line engines, and regarded as a country bumpkin because it works on the countryside routes. So inconsequential is the locomotive that it does not even have a name, and is known merely as "Engine 394." It yearns to have a name and travel beyond the confines of its home at Taddlecombe junction. One day, however, the Little Red Engine gets the chance to reveal its worth when the Big Black Engine—the "Pride of the North"—runs into a snowdrift, and the Big Green Engine—the "Beauty of the South"—is derailed after running into a tree. The Little Red Engine comes to the rescue of the King, who is stranded, by taking him home. The grateful King promotes the train to the main line and christens it the "Royal Red."

The story captures the wartime atmosphere of bulldoggish bravura, and the fact that everyone can help in the smallest way in the war effort, but it is also a book that stands the test of time. *The Little Red Engine* shows that one can stand up to bullies, however important or small one feels, and will amuse, comfort, and inspire the book's young readers. **CK**

Tweet Tweet 1943

Ľudmila Podjavorinská

Original Title | Čin-Čin
Nationality | Slovakian, born 1872
Publisher | Ikar, Slovakia
Theme | Family, Animal stories

Tweet Tweet (originally published as *Čin-Čin*) is one of Ľudmila Podjavorinská's most popular stories. The main character is a sparrow, Čimo Čimčarara, who has a very colorful and varied personality. He is confident, brave, and enterprising, as well as being lazy and egotistical, with a tendency to brag. The author wisely and with great humor captures the whole life of the main characters—Čimo and his wife—and the transformation in their personalities. Through their childhood, courting, wedding, and difficult times in their marriage, the two sparrows learn valuable lessons about home and family, and are allowed a happy ending.

Ľudmila Podjavorinská, the first women in Slovak history to publish a book of poems, was loved by generations of readers, who affectionately called her "Auntie Ľudmila." Yet the author's life was one of sadness and poor health, and she claimed she had never experienced real love. She was the daughter of a poor teacher, and had a very basic education, and low self confidence. It was her natural intelligence and self-taught writing skills that led to her becoming such an important figure of Slovakian literature. Podjavorinská created the foundation for modern Slovakian children's literature, introducing a new writing style that avoided being too didactic, or "preachy." Instead she created her own emotional, aesthetic style that spoke directly to children.

Podjavorinská used simple and clear language. In 1947, she was awarded the Národná umelkiňa (the highest artistic recognition in Slovakia). **JR**

Tales and Legends 1945

Javier Villafañe Tabaré

Nationality | Argentinian, born 1909 (author); details unknown (illustrator)
Publisher | La Plata University Press, Argentina
Theme | Myths and legends, Adventure

Javier Villafañe was a successful poet, playwright, and puppeteer, and also one of the greatest collectors of stories and legends from Argentine folklore. He retold many of these stories as texts for his popular puppet theater performances.

Some of the best tales are gathered in this collection (originally published as *Cuentos y Leyendas*), which includes such timeless classics as "The Magic Pot," "The Fortune Tree," "The Man Who Had to Guess the Devil's Age," and many others. Best known perhaps is "The Horse Who Lost its Tail," which tells the story of a beautiful white horse that inexplicably loses its tail and the various adventures that ensue in its search to retrieve it. In this story, the narrator involves the readers by speaking directly to them about the story's development, just as a puppeteer or an actor might when performing onstage: "Ladies, gentlemen, and children: I must give this story a proper ending. I have paper, a pen and I can write—this is my job."

Villafañe merges folk stories, legends, puppet theater, and poetry in this superbly written collection of stories by one of the most influential Argentine authors of children's literature. Tabaré's artistic, subtle caricatures are a humorous accompaniment to each story. The illustrations are at their most powerful and successful in the stories about the popular rogue Pedro Urdemales, who is featured in "The Magic Pot" and "The Fortune Tree." Other books by Villafañe include *Stories of Birds* (*Historias de pájaros*) and *The Dreams of the Toad* (*Los sueños del sapo*). **LB**

Pippi Longstocking 1945

Astrid Lindgren

Original Title | Pippi Långstrump
Nationality | Swedish, born 1907
Publisher | Rabén and Sjögren, Sweden
Theme | Fantasy, Favorite characters

5+

Despite initial fears that Pippi Longstocking was too independent a character to become truly popular, Astrid Lindgren's story about a wild, funny, and unusually strong nine year old, who lives alone—except for her horse and monkey—in a little house called Villekulla Cottage was an instant hit when it was first published. Since then, Pippi Longstocking has gained worldwide popularity, and the books have been translated into numerous languages.

This, the first story about Pippi, was dreamed up by Lindgren when her own daughter was ill with pneumonia. The author's spirited story of hijinks and fun creates a unique and mesmerizing world of adventure that has no time for cynicism or downbeat moments. Despite the surprise deaths of both her parents, Pippi lives life to the fullest, enjoying dancing, making pancakes, and playing games.

Much to the delight of her neighbor's children, Tommi and Annika, the red-headed Pippi, her hair always in unruly pigtails, never attends school. Instead she seems to spend her time chatting with her neighbors over coffee and facing any challenge, be it bully boys or condescending old ladies.

With a new translation published in 2007, Pippi Longstocking has been reenergized by the brilliant illustrations of author and artist Lauren Child. Her characteristically vivid artwork brings Lindgren's text about Pippi's madcap escapades up-to-date and has helped to attract a whole new generation of children—and adults—to enter with delight into the topsy-turvy, higgledy-piggledy world of Pippi. **NH**

"There was no one to tell her to go to bed just when she was having the most fun . . . or make her take cod liver oil."

MORE GREAT ASTRID LINDGREN TITLES

The Six Bullerby Children, 1947
Mio, My Son, 1954
Emil in the Soup Tureen, 1963
The Brothers Lionheart, 1973
Ronia, the Robber's Daughter, 1981

Stone Soup 1947

Marcia Brown

Nationality | American, born 1918
Publisher | Charles Scribner's Sons, USA
Award | Caldecott Honor Book, 1948
Theme | Folktales

5+

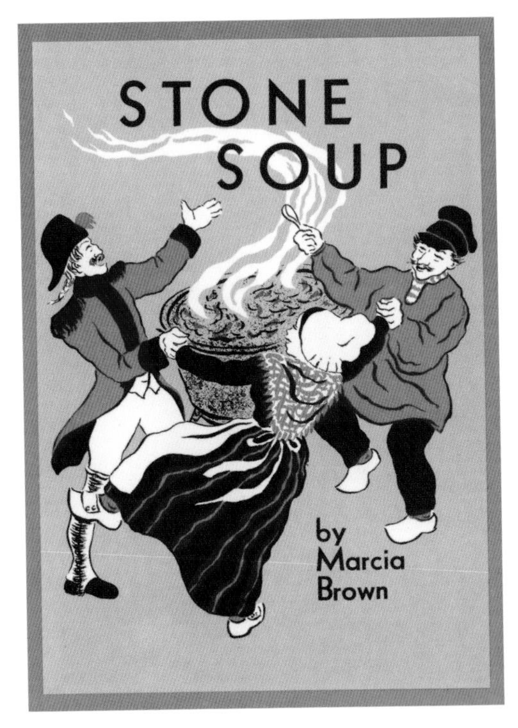

Marcia Brown's popular and enduring retelling of this folktale is a classic. Three hungry soldiers come to a village and ask for food, but the villagers have hidden all the provisions away. The soldiers need to eat and so they decide to make themselves a soup out of stones—all they need is a big pot. The villagers are so curious that they oblige, saying, "Stone soup? Now that would be something to know about."

When the soldiers comment that the soup would be much improved if only they had some carrots, the subtle hint seems such a small thing that one of the villagers rushes off to find some. If cabbage would help, they will bring that too—and so it continues until between them the villagers have contributed

"Never had there been such a feast! Never had the local peasants tasted such soup."

potatoes, beef, barley, and milk. There is enough stone soup to share, and the villagers lay a grand table in the square and light torches. But what is soup without bread and a roast and cider? They all eat and drink and dance together, and when it is all done the villagers give the soldiers the best beds in the village to sleep in. This story is originally an old French tale; the Brothers Grimm also had a version, and northern European accounts tell of nail or ax soup.

In Brown's version, bright red, double-page pictures bring the scene to life, as the lively and idiosyncratic peasants learn how to share and celebrate their bounties. Children will pick up on the subtle ironies and the gentle trickery of the soldiers. The ending is quirky and witty, too, as the villagers watch wistfully when the soldiers go on their way, thinking, "Such men don't grow on every bush." **CQ**

OTHER GREAT FOLKTALES AND FABLES

Uncle Remus Stories by Joel Chandler Harris, 1881
Perez the Mouse by Luis Coloma, 1894
Caps for Sale by Esphyr Slobodkina, 1938
The Loon's Necklace by Elizabeth Cleaver, 1970
The Little Bird by Paro Anand, 1993

The Dolls' House 1947

Rumer Godden

Tottie is a little Dutch doll with a kind heart. Handed down through the generations, she arrives at the home of Charlotte and Emily, where she lives with her adoptive doll parents, Mr. and Mrs. Plantaganet; her brother, Apple; and their darning-needle dog. Although the sensible Tottie is fashioned from good strong wood, Mrs. Plantaganet, known as Birdie, is made of celluloid, making her light-headed and ominously flammable. The make-believe family is a loving and cheerful one, but their home is a drafty shoebox. Tottie tells them stories of a beautiful doll's house where she lived long ago with Marchpane, a cruel china doll.

When their great aunt dies, Charlotte and Emily inherit her Victorian doll's house—complete with Marchpane, who has grown more vain and mean. Emily, taken in by Marchpane's beautiful appearance, permits her to treat the Plantaganets as servants and Apple as her plaything. When Marchpane smilingly allows Apple to play near a lit candle, a terrible tragedy happens. The ending of the story, however, offers hope for the reader through a final scene in which the surviving dolls come to see their places in the world as part of the great passage of time; bad may happen, but good will eventually return.

"It is an anxious, sometimes a dangerous thing to be a doll. Dolls cannot choose."

Published not long after World War II, the book's themes of change and mortality, morality, and an emphasis on making do and mending all reflect its era. Yet the recognizable dilemmas faced by the dolls, coupled with their plausible characterizations, ensure the book's continuing appeal. **KA**

Nationality | English, born Margaret Rumer Foster 1907
Publisher | Michael Joseph, UK
Theme | Family, Fantasy, Illness and death

5+

OTHER NOTABLE WORKS BY GODDEN

***The Mousewife*, 1951**
***The Greengage Summer*, 1958**
***Miss Happiness and Miss Flower*, 1961**
***The Diddakoi*, 1972**
***The Rocking Horse Secret*, 1977**

MY FATHER'S DRAGON

YEARLING

My Father's Dragon 1948

Ruth S. Gannett Ruth C. Gannett

Nationality | American, born 1923 (author); American, born 1896 (illustrator)
Publisher | Random House, USA
Theme | Magical stories, Fantasy, Animal stories

Young children will love having this story read aloud to them. It is told in short chapters, full of magic and adventure, and makes a perfect bedtime read. The stylized black-and-white illustrations, which help bring the dramatic story to life, were the work of the author's stepmother; a successful collaboration that saw the two women working together regularly.

The story begins when Elmer Elevator finds a stray cat and gives her food and milk. The cat turns out to be a magical cat and tells Elmer about the plight of a baby dragon. The dragon has fallen accidentally from a low-flying cloud onto a magic place called Wild Island. In the fall he bruised his wing, so he is unable to fly back home. Now he is being held captive on the island and is forced to ferry passengers across the river. Determined to rescue the dragon, Elmer runs away from his mother (who was rude to the cat) and travels to Wild Island.

The story is told by a narrator who we learn is the son of Elmer Elevator. This magical yarn is full of imagination, adventure, and humor. Elmer stows away on a ship, is nearly eaten by several different animals, befriends others, lives off a diet of tangerines, and uses a variety of everyday objects—including lollipops, rubber bands, chewing gum, hair ribbons, and magnifying glasses—to keep himself safe and to help the dragon escape. The book won a Newbery Honor award and was an A.L.A. Notable Book. Gannett went on to write two popular sequels as well. **KD/LH**

Blueberries for Sal 1948

Robert McCloskey

Nationality | American, born 1914
Publisher | Viking Press, USA
Awards | Caldecott Honor Book, 1949
Theme | Family

When little Sal and her mother decide to spend a day picking blueberries, Sal manages to eat the berries as fast as she can pick them. Sal's mother explains that she wants to can the blueberries when they get home so that they can enjoy them all through the winter. At the same time, a mother bear and her cub are also out blueberry picking, hoping to eat as much as possible before hibernating for the winter.

Both Sal and her mother are enjoying their day out; they are so engrossed in their blueberry picking that they slowly wander away from each other. Eventually, Sal's mother discovers that she is picking berries with the bear cub instead of with her daughter, and the mother bear discovers she is eating berries alongside Sal. The theme of mistaken identity is a common one in children's books, but nobody has done it better than McCloskey in this story.

This classic book, by the author of *Make Way for Ducklings*, turns what could be a scary situation into a funny one. Both mothers are finally reunited with their own children. On their way home, they discover new wonders of the natural world, and Sal's blueberry-picking bucket is still empty because she has eaten them all. Aided by charming illustrations that look quite "retro" today, the story moves along beautifully and keeps kids interested in how the families will be reunited. McCloskey is believed to have based the characters of Sal and her mother on his own young daughter and wife. **KD**

Apoutsiak 1948

Paul-Emile Victor

Nationality | French, born 1907
Publisher | Flammarion, France
Award | Prix d'Académie Française, 1973
Theme | Family, Science and nature

The story recounts the birth, life, and death of Apoutsiak in a land white with snow. As soon as he can walk, Apoutsiak ("little snowflake") learns to hunt, to train the dogs, and to drive a sled. He plays with his brothers and sisters in the igloo, and when the good weather arrives, he sets off with his family in their big *umiak*.

Having read and reread the book, I know this story by heart. Apoutsiak has almond-shaped eyes and high, red cheekbones. The dogs have bushy tails that curl back on themselves, and their eyes are surrounded with white, like an owl's "glasses." It all seemed so different: the half-moon knife used to cut up animals; the pieces of sealmeat put out to dry; the incredible chaos of the family home, arms and legs all tangled up. The people are always smiling, and the kids play with the pups—it is bliss. I envied Apoutsiak's freedom when he used a kayak for the first time. And, naturally, I was bothered by the fact that Apoutsiak grows old.

With each new reading, I seize on details that I had previously overlooked: the dogs' demeanor, the mother's odd dress (she wears shorts and fur boots that leave a strip of flesh showing above the knee), her method of carrying the baby in her hood, her bun, and the same apple-red cheekbones under the curve of mischievous, slanting eyes. The real life, for me, happened in the pictures. What remains of this world so simply described disturbs me: I do not know how to distinguish what captured my imagination more: my love of the drawings or the strangeness of the remote life in the cold and snow.

Apoutsiak feeding seal meat to his husky dogs. ➔

5+

Foxie 1949

Ingri and Edgar Parin D'Aulaire

Nationality | Norwegian/American, born 1904 (Ingri); Swiss/German born 1898 (Edgar)
Publisher | Doubleday, USA
Theme | Animal stories, Friendship

Whether bringing to life the legends of the mighty Greek and Norse gods in their widely beloved collections of myths, or retelling Russian folklore, the d'Aulaires always excelled at the arts of storytelling and illustration, charming children of all ages.

This beautifully illustrated retelling of a story by the famous Russian writer Anton Chekhov centers on an adorable red-haired dog called Foxie who, we are told, "had a head like a fox and her tail was like a cinnamon roll." Foxie lives with her master, who spends most of his time teasing her and is not good at remembering mealtimes. One day a prank goes too far when he lures Foxie out onto the busy city streets with a tasty bone—and then loses her among a marching band.

Foxie wanders alone, fearing she might end up becoming a stray dog, until she is fortunate enough to meet a circus animal trainer. He spots her singing skills, and she joins his troupe of performing animals, including a piano-playing cat and a strutting rooster. When the night of her debut onstage arrives, something unexpected happens. In the audience, Foxie hears a familiar voice calling out her name. Foxie rejoices at the sight of her long-lost master in a classic happy ending.

Ingri and Edgar Parin D'Aulaire first met while studying in Paris in the 1920s; they moved to the United States in 1929, where they remained. They collaborated on a number of successful children's books and were awarded the prestigious Caldecott Medal, jointly, in 1940. **LB**

5+

Peanuts 1950

Charles M. Schulz

Nationality | American, born 1922
Publisher | Fantagraphics Books, USA
Award | Reuben Award, 1955 and 1964
Theme | Friendship, Animal stories, Quirky

Charles M. Schulz's *Peanuts* comic strip is a phenomenon. Published in newspapers worldwide, the life of its hero, Charlie Brown, and the musings of his beagle dog, Snoopy, have been read by more than 355 million people in 75 countries and in 21 different languages. The cartoons spawned a television series, oodles of memorabilia, and a series of books. *The Complete Peanuts* is an ongoing project to compile Schulz's work into one magnum opus.

Young Charlie Brown is something of a loser, particularly at baseball. The charm of the character lies in his musings, his daydreams and his interactions with his pals, from know-it-all bossy-boots Lucy van Pelt, to his admirer, the lovable tomboy Peppermint Patty.

Yet, the real star of the comic strip is Snoopy, a black-eared canine who is much savvier about the world than his owner. Schulz anthropomorphizes the dog, whose take on the world as he lies back on the roof of his doghouse ranges from social commentary to philosophy, as he chats to his friend, the tiny yellow bird Woodstock, who speaks in a language only Snoopy can understand. Snoopy is also given a fertile imagination and ambition. He frequently dons goggles and a hat to live out his fantasy life as an ace World War I pilot, or sits typing a novel that is never finished. Occasionally Snoopy dons sunglasses to become Joe Cool, as cool a dude as Charlie Brown is a fumbling but ever hopeful dreamer. These classic stories are loved for their pithy aphorisms, smart observations, practical jokes, and hope. **CK**

Roule Galette 1950

Natha Caputo Pierre Belvès

Nationality | French, born 1904 (author); French, born 1917 (illustrator)
Publisher | Flammarion, France
Theme | Animal stories, Fairy tales, Folktales

Roule Galette, a rewriting of the Russian tale *Kolobok*, is one of the most famous stories in the Père Castor collection of children's books. Written in 1950, it is still widely read, admired for Belvès's Slavic-looking illustrations, and has been adapted for television.

A man asks his wife to cook him a special cake (a *galette*, or *kolobok*). She leaves it to cool on the windowsill. Roule Galette is a cake with a fidgety temperament. She rolls from the window, down onto the grass, and starts her journey through the country. She encounters many sweet teeth during her little odyssey, including those of a rabbit and a wolf. She always manages to escape, rolling away with a scoffing song. That is until she encounters a fox who does not bluntly state that he wants to eat her. He uses flattery and feigns admiration at how gold her crust is, how delicious she smells. Lulled by his praises, Roule Galette does not flee and gets devoured.

As in a classic fairy tale or fable, the same motif is repeated many times before a variant occurs, triggering the denouement that gives the story a moralistic ending. Readers are shown how perilous sweet talk can be. Natha Caputo's story can be read as a distant version of the fable of the crow and the fox. Both stories star a dangerously seductive fox, a traditionally wicked figure in French literature. Yet, the cathartic morality at the end of the tale is not the only reason for its popularity in the education of young children—all the animals the cake encounters prove useful in the learning of animal names. **MGR**

The fox's patience is rewarded when he devours the cake.

One Morning in Maine 1952

Robert McCloskey

Nationality | American, born 1914
Publisher | Viking Penguin, USA
Award | Caldecott Honor Book, 1953
Theme | Family

5+

One Morning in Maine revisits the characters of Sal and her family who were first encountered in Robert McCloskey's highly acclaimed picture book *Blueberries for Sal*. This time the focus of the story is on the emotions that Sal experiences when she discovers her first loose tooth. In many ways, Sal is having a typical Maine day—from enjoying a clamming trip with her father to going by boat across to Buck's Harbor to get supplies—but in other ways nothing about the day is like any other day because one of her teeth is wobbly. She is keen to share her exciting news: "'I have a loose tooth!' Sal called up to the fish hawk. The fish hawk flew straight to her nest on top of a tree without answering."

"... Sal woke up. She peeked over the top of the covers. The bright sun made her blink ..."

When her tooth unexpectedly pops out and falls into the clam-filled mud, Sal is absolutely devastated. She fears that a clam will get to make her wish with the tooth fairy. "I guess some clam will find my tooth and get what I wished for. ... If we come back here tomorrow and find a clam eating a chocolate ice-cream cone, why, we'll have to take it away from him and make him give my tooth back."

Robert McCloskey's story and art capture the natural beauty and spirit of Maine, where he and his young family settled after World War II. The book has a sweet and nostalgic style. For young children, losing their first tooth is a sign of growing up and is both scary and exciting at the same time. This book explores these emotions with a great deal of humor and in a way that children can relate to and understand. **KD**

OTHER NOTABLE McCLOSKEY TITLES

***Make Way for Ducklings,* 1941**
***Homer Price,* 1943**
***Blueberries for Sal,* 1948**
***Centerburg Tales,* 1951**
***Time of Wonder,* 1957**

The Bears on Hemlock Mountain 1952

Alice Dalgliesh   Helen Sewell

Young Jonathan is convinced that there are bears living on Hemlock Mountain, but all the grown-ups disagree with him and say that there are not. As Jonathan soon discovers in *The Bears on Hemlock Mountain*, grown-ups are not always right.

Jonathan is sent over Hemlock Mountain on an important errand to fetch an enormous iron pot from his aunt. Hemlock Mountain is not really a mountain; it is more of a hill, but to Jonathan, on a snowy winter's day, it seems very large, indeed. On the journey, Jonathan makes friends with the squirrels and birds, but he cannot stop thinking about bears. As he tramps up the mountain, to keep up his courage, he repeats a refrain about how there are no bears on Hemlock Mountain. This gives the story great pace, making it pleasurable to read aloud. When Jonathan finally tramps back over the hill with the pot, it gets rapidly dark and he finds that there are bears on Hemlock Mountain. He cleverly escapes by hiding under the enormous iron pot, and the grown-ups finally admit that there are bears on Hemlock Mountain. Children will enjoy the delightful tension between the adults' and the child's viewpoints.

"It was the year when Jonathan was eight that he went over Hemlock Mountain."

Alice Dalgliesh was a pioneer in the field of children's literature. Her historical fiction, combined with its believable characters and dramatic plots, is renowned for its accuracy and detail. *The Bears on Hemlock Mountain* is a perfect example of Dalgliesh getting this delicate balance right. According to the author, the story is based on an old Pennsylvania tall tale, to which Dalgliesh has given great detail and form. **RA**

Nationality | Trinidadian, born 1893 (author); American, born 1896 (illustrator)
Publisher | Charles Scribner's Sons, USA
Theme | Adventure

5+

OTHER GREAT BEAR ADVENTURES

***The Bear's Famous Invasion of Sicily* by Dino Buzzati, 1943**
***The Biggest Bear* by Lynd Ward, 1952**
***A Bear Called Paddington* by Michael Bond, 1958**
***Two Little Bears* by Hanna Muschg, 1983**

The Biggest Bear 1952

Lynd Ward

Nationality | American, born 1905
Publisher | Houghton Mifflin, USA
Award | Caldecott Medal, 1953
Theme | Adventure, Controversial

5+

A fierce tale of courage, rivalry, and determination, *The Biggest Bear* tells the moving story of Johnny Orchard, a young boy who feels inadequate because his neighbors all boast huge bear pelts hanging from their barns, while his father is yet to bring home the bounty. Taking matters into his own hands, Johnny goes hunting in the woods to trap a bear whose hide he can proudly display for all to see. Ironically, the bear that Johnny finds is a tiny cub, which he decides to adopt as a companion.

As the anarchic bear matures, he unfortunately wreaks havoc in the neighborhood. Although Johnny tries to return him to his natural habitat in the woods, his father decides that the only solution is for the bear to be killed. As Johnny pauses to load his rifle and commit the odious task, the bear bounds off toward a baited trap that has been set by some rangers from a zoo. They are extremely pleased with their catch and thank Johnny, assuring him that he can visit his bear there as often as he likes.

"The other barns in the valley usually had a bearskin nailed up to dry, but never Johnny's barn."

Outstanding illustrations are provided by Lynd Ward's detailed wood engravings, which won him the 1953 Caldecott Medal. Ward, predominantly an artist, had also published several successful wordless books, such as *The Silver Pony* and *God's Man*, which are told entirely in lithographs. Freudian analysts, such as Ernest Becker, have interpreted *The Biggest Bear* as a darker allegory about the human fear of sexual violence. Nonetheless, generations of children have enjoyed the book simply for its lively illustrations and captivating tale, and it remains popular today. **ML**

OTHER BOOKS ILLUSTRATED BY WARD

The Little Red Lighthouse and the Great Gray Bridge by Hildegarde Swift, 1942
Johnny Tremain by Esther Forbes, 1943
The Silver Pony by Lynd Ward, 1973

The Little Horse Bus 1952

Graham Greene Dorothy Craigie

"There is always one moment in childhood when the door opens and lets the future in," we are told by Graham Greene, one of the twentieth century's most eminent writers of adult fiction and author of this wonderful book. *The Little Horse Bus* is one of his four books for children, based on the actions of an heroic vehicle. Young readers are engaged and encouraged to turn the pages to see what is happening, as well as offered picture puzzles to solve.

Mr. Potter owns a corner shop; he is kind to children and always listens to his customers' problems. When a large store, the Hygienic Emporium, opens across the road, Mr. Potter cannot compete with their hansom cab delivery service and is worried that he will lose his livelihood. He starts his own delivery service, with an old horse bus pulled by Brandy, a rescued pony, but it is not a great success. One day Brandy and the bus see some robbers escaping with their loot in the hansom cab. A comic-strip sequence depicts the chase, and Brandy and the horse bus charge at the robbers, who soon give themselves up. Mr. Potter receives a large cash reward, his customers flock back, and the Hygienic Emporium goes out of business.

The illustrations, which are lively, colorful, and full of detail, were created by Dorothy Glover, a theatrical costume designer, who published under the pen name Dorothy Craigie. The text, which is as relevant today as it was in the 1950s, is littered with advertisements for familiar contemporary products, such as Bird's custard. Craigie (who had a relationship with Greene) illustrated all four books that he wrote for children, which also include *The Little Train* (1946), *The Little Fire Engine* (1950), and *The Little Steamroller* (1955). In the 1970s, Greene's friend Edward Ardizzone reillustrated the books. Ardizzone's illustrations are beautiful and painterly, but they do not have the directness of the original Craigie pictures. **WO**

Nationality | English, born 1904 (author); English, born 1908 (illustrator)
Publisher | Max Parrish, UK
Theme | Animal stories, Friendship

5+

MORE TRAINS, BOATS, AND ENGINES

***Little Toot* by Hardie Gramatky, 1939**
***The Ship that Flew* by Hilda Lewis, 1939**
***Ivor the Engine* by Oliver Postgate, 1962**
***The Polar Express* by Chris Van Allsburg, 1981**
***Fire-Engine Lil* by Janet McLean, 1989**

Charlotte's Web 1952

E. B. White Garth Williams

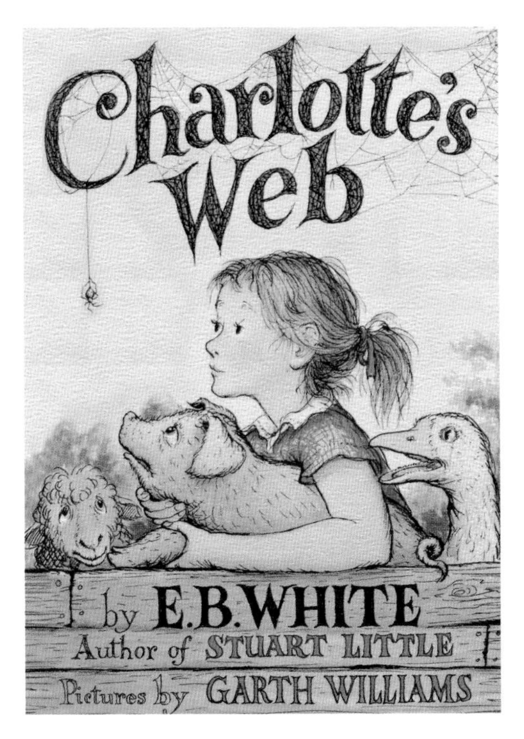

"I will bring the runt when I come in. I'll let you start it on a bottle like a baby. Then you'll see what trouble a pig can be."

OTHER ZOO AND FARM FAVORITES

***The Sheep-Pig* by Dick King-Smith, 1984**
***Curious George Visits the Zoo* by Margret Rey, 1988**
***The Great Escape from the City Zoo* by Tohby Riddle, 1997**

Nationality | American, born 1899 (author); American, born 1912 (illustrator)
Publisher | HarperCollins, USA
Theme | Animal stories, Adventure, Classics

"Don't kill Wilbur!" begs eight-year-old Fern. As the runt of the litter, Wilbur is a piglet of immense curiosity. Instead of being killed, he is sold to Fern's uncle, Homer Zuckerman, on whose farm he gets very lonely. One day he hears a warm voice telling him that she is going to be his friend. Who can it be?

Charlotte A. Cavatica is a beautiful gray spider and the presiding genius of the animals in Zuckerman's barn, and she weaves Wilbur into their community. But according to the testy old sheep, Wilbur is to be killed at Christmas. Charlotte comes to the rescue by writing messages in her web in praise of Wilbur's virtues: The words "SOME PIG," "TERRIFIC," and "RADIANT" all appear. But although Charlotte can affect Wilbur's future, she cannot change her own. She must die, leaving her egg sac behind and her offspring to keep Wilbur company.

Charlotte's Web captivates young readers with the originality of its story and the precision of its dialogue. White was a notable critic of literary style, and his own is full of piquant detail without sentimentality. The character of the sneaky rat Templeton, for instance, adds a sour touch of realism to the caring atmosphere in the barn: he would rather eat Charlotte's egg sac than preserve her offspring. This is not a cute cartoon: Wilbur gobbles down scraps like any pig; Charlotte is a big hairy spider who follows the normal arachnic life cycle; and animals do get the chop so that we can get our chops. Nonetheless, it is a life-enhancing and touching story that does not shy away from big emotions. **VN**

Marlaguette 1952

Marie Colmont Gerda Muller

Nationality | French, born 1895 (author); Dutch, born 1926 (illustrator)
Publisher | Flammarion, France
Theme | Animal stories, Friendship

Marlaguette is one of Marie Colmont's best-known tales, together with *Michka* and *Perlette the Rain Drop* (*Perlette goutte d'eau*). French by birth, she also lived in the United States and London and played a pivotal role in the revival of the Youth Hostel movement.

Marlaguette is a fable of the beautiful friendship that develops between a little girl and a wolf. One day Marlaguette goes to the woods and is attacked by a wolf. There is a fight, and it is the wolf who is hurt. The little girl takes pity on him and dresses the wound, protects him, and brings him herbal tea. For the first time in his life, he allows himself to be pampered. Little by little, the wolf recovers his strength. But during one of their walks together, the wolf eats a jay, which makes the little girl furious. The wolf then promises that he will give up meat, and Marlaguette gives him berries, leaves, and other vegetables. But a wolf is a carnivore. He is literally dying of hunger to please Marlaguette. Then, seeing him so weakened, the girl understands that she must respect his nature. She releases him from his promise, and each returns to the life they had before—without ever forgetting the other.

The text and illustrations may appear a little simple and outdated, but they are also moving and instructive. The story introduces the concept of life in the wild, the idea that there are limits to domestication, and that diets vary. And with friendship, there are always concessions to be made. This is a short tale in which we learn that the greatest proof of friendship is respect for one another's differences, accepting the other as he or she is. **CD**

Jip and Janneke 1953

Annie M. G. Schmidt

Original Title | Jip en Janneke
Nationality | Dutch, born 1911
Publisher | De Arbeiderspers, the Netherlands
Theme | Family, Friendship

Jip and Janneke are the most famous infants in the Netherlands, and it can safely be said that every child there is brought up on these "children next door." The stories are quotidian but topical to children—going shopping with their mother, playing with the dog, or going to the post office.

The stories are based on a simple narrative tradition whereby one character completes the other. Each one of Jip's actions produces a reaction on the part of Janneke, and naturally the other way around. The interest of each story lies in this clash between the two children. In his games Jip pretends he is a pilot while Janneke is allowed onboard as a lady passenger. The division of roles in their everyday life is based on the customs of the 1950s; modern feminist critics, however, may take umbrage with this old-fashioned view of life.

All of Jip's and Janneke's adventures were written by Annie M. G. Schmidt for the children's page of the daily paper *Het Parool*. Every week for five years, she wrote a new, engaging story about Jip and Janneke. The stories are told in a flowing style, with short sentences that rarely exceed seven words.

Jip and Janneke are inquisitive and sometimes make life very difficult for the grown-ups with their constant questioning. Schmidt creates a realistic, recognizable children's world, but one that at the same time remains relatively idyllic and insular. Parents never remain angry for long—they always know how to solve little catastrophes, and injustice is quickly removed from the world. **AD**

5+

Teddy Robinson Stories 1953

Joan G. Robinson

Nationality | English, born 1910
Publisher | Harrap, UK
Theme | Adventure, Family, Friendship, Favorite characters

Teddy Robinson lives with Deborah, his "favorite little girl," and her parents. Deborah and Teddy Robinson go almost everywhere together—except on the rare occasions when Deborah forgets or loses him, and then Teddy Robinson has adventures on his own. All through the book, Teddy Robinson makes up little rhymes that he sings to Deborah or to anyone else who happens to be around, such as the kitten from next door, the tortoise in the garden, or the toy dog, Cloppety, who belongs to their new friend, Tommy.

In *About Teddy Robinson*, Deborah and her bear go to a fairground, spend a few days in the hospital, and have a birthday party for Teddy Robinson (who has never had one before because he arrived at Christmas). Teddy Robinson also spends a night outside all by himself, gets lost in a shop, and finds out what it is like to be part of a display in a shop window. He meets a dog called Toby and stays awake to see Father Christmas. That night, after he has finished filling Deborah's Christmas stocking, Father Christmas tells Teddy Robinson the story of the night he first brought him, in his sleigh, to live with Deborah.

Throughout these stories, Teddy Robinson has little side adventures, such as unwittingly winning a game at a birthday party and having to wear a ballet dress, even though he thinks it is "soppy." *About Teddy Robinson* was the first book in what became a very popular series. The stories were written about the author's daughter, Deborah, and her favorite bear. **LH**

Detectives in Togas 1953

Henry Winterfeld Charlotte Kleinert

Nationality | American/German, born 1901 (author); details unknown (illustrator)
Publisher | Blanvalet, Germany
Theme | Adventure, School, Friendship

Originally published as *Caius ist ein Dummkopf,* this mystery story is set in ancient Rome and was inspired by graffiti found on a wall excavated at Pompeii. Fascinated by the fact that youngsters in ancient times apparently also disfigured walls, Henry Winterfeld wrote this book about a prank that ends up having far-reaching political consequences.

Caius is not the brightest boy in Rome. Rufus, one of his fellow students at their exclusive school, has gathered as much and has written "Caius is a dumbbell" on his wax tablet, before hanging it up for all to see. Furious, the teacher sends Rufus home and threatens to tell his mother about the incident. The next day, all the boys wait in vain for the teacher to appear at school. After a while they go to the teacher's house and discover that someone has broken in and locked him in a wardrobe. They free their teacher, who tells them that he overreacted the previous day and that Rufus will not be punished. Overjoyed, the boys set off to Rufus's house to bring him the good news, but as they walk past the holy temple of Minerva, they see that it has been desecrated: on its walls are the words, "Caius is a dumbbell." The whole of Rome is outraged, and although Rufus fiercely denies any wrongdoing, he is jailed anyway. The other boys launch their own investigation and bring the true culprit to justice.

A gripping mystery story with young heroes who children can relate to, the book also serves as a lively introduction to life in ancient Rome. **DaH**

Harold and the Purple Crayon 1955

 Crockett Johnson

Nationality | American, born David Johnson Leisk 1906
Publisher | HarperCollins, USA
Theme | Adventure, Fantasy

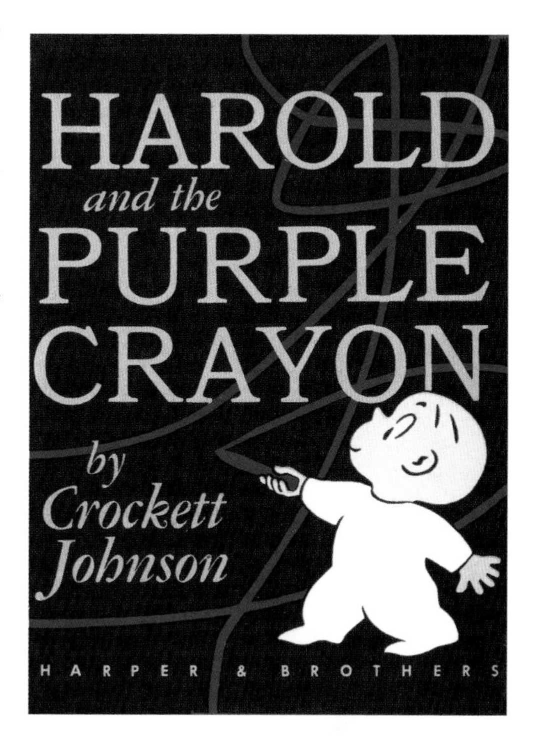

5+

Harold is a dreamy little boy who goes for a walk one night with his trusty purple crayon. It is a magic crayon, and he uses it to draw himself into and out of trouble. He draws the path as he goes, always accompanied by a nice purple moon. Leaving the path, he draws himself into a forest, an ocean (watch those sharks!), and a balloon. He tires and gets lost—or was he always lost? How can he find his house and bedroom window? He tries to draw them but draws a whole city full of windows, towering high and bleak. In the end, he recalls how his window is always right around the moon, that trusty purple moon. So he draws his window properly, goes back home through it, makes his bed, and goes safely to sleep.

The power of this charming book lies in its simplicity of expression. Although the ideas are quite complex, the thick purple line drawings and straightforward sentences carry young readers along. Harold, at the same time brave and scared, is a character with whom children readily identify. His vivid imagination is both outlandish and homespun. He eats a simple pie, rows a simple boat, pulls up simple bedcovers. Yet these are a self-created pie, boat, and covers. How much of what we experience do we imagine for ourselves? Many parents and teachers have found Harold's adventures to be an invaluable trigger for discussions of children's hopes and fears. The book, which has never been out of print since its publication, was the precursor to a series but remains the best. **VN**

"One evening, after thinking it over for some time, Harold decided to go for a walk. . . ."

OTHER BOOKS IN THE HAROLD SERIES

Harold's Fairy Tale, 1956
Harold's Trip to the Sky, 1957
Harold at the North Pole, 1958
Harold's Circus, 1959
A Picture for Harold's Room, 1960

Clever Polly and the Stupid Wolf 1955

Catherine Storr Marjorie-Ann Watts

Catherine Storr
CLEVER POLLY
AND THE
STUPID WOLF
INTRODUCTION BY BABETTE COLE

"'Oh my poor Wolf,' Polly exclaimed. 'You have made a fool of yourself.'"

MORE TALES FROM CATHERINE STORR

Marianne Dreams, 1968
Polly and the Wolf Again, 1970
Cold Marble and Other Ghost Stories, 1985
Last Stories of Polly and the Wolf, 1990

Nationality | English, born 1913 (author); English, birth date unknown (illustrator)
Publisher | Faber and Faber, UK
Theme | Traditional, Adventure

First published more than fifty years ago, these delightful stories in which a quick-thinking young girl consistently outwits a lugubrious wolf who longs to eat her have been popular with generations of children. While the hapless wolf makes plans based on half-remembered versions of traditional tales (in which his lupine hero generally ends up with a good dinner), Polly, ever the pragmatist, frequently reminds him that wolves are rather more prone to meet disastrous fates than to find themselves making tasty meals of little girls.

Polly is an able and resourceful child, mature and wise beyond her years. She is also very much a product of her time: often on her own at home, her domestic skills in particular are well honed and put to good use in outmaneuvering the wolf. Despite the wolf's threats, the relationship remains predominantly that of amicable sparring partners. When the wolf gets locked in a zoo, Polly helps him to escape. In the background, Polly's parents are aware of the wolf, but remain laconically untroubled by him, apparently confident of Polly's ability to take care of herself. "'Good heavens!' says Polly's father on hearing of the wolf's plans to eat up Polly and her grandmother. 'What a horrible idea! We certainly shan't give you a lift if that is what you are planning to do.'"

Three further books followed; the last, published in 1990, shows Polly in a contemporary setting in which she faces, for a time at least, very real danger. **KA**

A Toad Who Wanted to Be a Star 1955

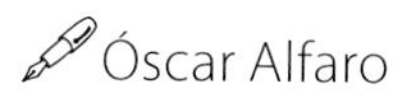 Óscar Alfaro

Original Title | El sapo que quería ser estrella
Nationality | Bolivian, born 1921
Publisher | Plus Ultra, Argentina
Theme | Classics, Animal stories

Óscar Alfaro was one of the most important poets in the Spanish-speaking world who wrote mainly for children. This beautiful moral fable about vanity is written in simple but evocative language.

One evening a toad sees a glowing snake creep past his pond, and is amazed at its beauty: It looks like a necklace made of shining stars. After realizing that the snake's glow is due to its having eaten a number of fireflies, the toad decides to do the same. He swallows as many fireflies as he can until he shines like crystal. When he jumps back into the water, the stunned fish think that a star has fallen into their pond.

The toad enjoys his new status, calling the other creatures his satellites. The fish beg him to stay and be the light of their dark world. However, the toad knows that his true identity will become known at dawn. He ceremoniously leaves, with the excuse that he has to go back to the sky and join the other stars. Unfortunately, the hens, who have woken and realized that the alleged morning star is, in fact, a toad who has swallowed fireflies, attack him to avenge the murder of the innocent fireflies. The fireflies, however, are not dead: they are still in the toad's stomach and, as soon as they feel the blows from outside, they fly away, carrying the toad with them. Seeing that he can fly, the toad believes himself to be a real star, and begins to sing to get the attention of the other stars. But when he opens his mouth, the fireflies fly out from his belly, and the toad falls from the sky, and dies. **LB**

Italian Folktales 1956

 Italo Calvino

Original Title | Fiabe Italiane
Nationality | Italian, born 1923
Publisher | Einaudi, Italy
Theme | Folktales, Fairy tales

This is a collection of 200 Italian folktales assembled by fabulist writer Italo Calvino. He was influenced by the Brothers Grimm and took two years putting together what was the first collection of Italian fairy tales. He occasionally altered the stories to enable readability and to create a logical sequence. The collection draws on stories from regions across the country, and he credits sources when available.

Many of the stories will have a familiar feel because European fairy tales gained national characteristics as they made their way from one country to another. For example, "Beautiful Venice" is an Italian version of "Snow White." The stories are traditional fare, with titles such as "The Prince Who Married a Frog" and "Sleeping Beauty and Her Children," and include tales of monstrous transformations and fortunate metamorphoses; the innocent maiden who marries a prince; the trickery and spells of witches; woodlands and paths strewn with life-threatening obstacles; dragons, enchanted castles, and pacts made with the devil.

As one might expect from a nation obsessed with all matters culinary, the Italian variants of familiar fairy tales pay more attention to food than the gore prevalent in the tales of the Brothers Grimm, and the collection is rich in the sensual experience of eating. The stories have their roots in Christian medieval Italy and have a strong moral slant in which evildoers are punished. They have stood the test of time and offer a unique Italian twist on the world of fairy tales. **CK**

5+

A Tree Is Nice 1956

Janice May Udry   Marc Simont

Nationality | American, born 1928 (author); American, born 1915 (illustrator)
Publisher | HarperCollins, USA
Theme | Science and nature

Janice May Udry once noted that the test of a good children's book is that it "will not bore an adult." This delightfully simple (and environmentally friendly) tale about the love of nature—trees in particular—is suitable for even the youngest child and will entertain readers of all ages.

The story is all about what trees are for, how important they are in so many ways, and the pleasure that they bring: "Trees are beautiful. They fill up the sky. If you have a tree, you can climb up its trunk, roll in its leaves, or hang a swing from one of its limbs. Cows and babies can nap in the shade of a tree. Birds can make nests in the branches. A tree is good to have around. A tree is nice." Some parts of the book will make readers giggle as the story explores humorous uses for trees and how much fun can be had; other pages seek to impart facts about trees. The end of the book describes how to plant a tree and the pride that is felt as you watch it grow. "Even if you have just one tree, it is nice, too."

In *A Tree Is Nice*, the text and concept are clear and easy to understand. However, the elegant illustrations by Marc Simont are what set the picture book apart: Half in color and half in black and white, they manage to be sweet, simple, and thoroughly expressive all at the same time. The book was awarded the Caldecott Medal in 1957. The simple poetry of the language and the accessibility of the words and artwork will make this a great experience for both the very young and the parent reading the story. No one will get bored even after numerous retellings. **KD**

Captain Pugwash 1957

John Ryan

Full Title | Captain Pugwash: A Pirate Story
Nationality | Scottish, born 1921
Publisher | Bodley Head, UK
Theme | Adventure, Favorite characters

In those terrible times when Blackbeard the Pirate terrorized the Seven Seas, a jovial and innocent pirate captain, Horatio Pugwash, commanded the ship, the *Black Pig*. His motley crew comprised the lackadaisical Master Mate, simple Pirate Willy, grumpy Pirate Barnabas, and Tom the Cabin Boy, the only intelligent member of the pirate's crew. In their search for hidden treasure, they are hindered as much by their captain's cowardly and stupid decisions, as by Pugwash's evil enemy, Cut-Throat Jake, captain of the *Flying Dustman*. John Ryan's rich, inventive language (expressions such as "Lolloping landlubbers!," "Suffering seagulls!," and "Blistering barnacles!") has thrilled young children for generations.

Captain Pugwash's sea-faring adventures first appeared in *The Eagle* magazine in 1950. In 1957 the pirate swashed his buckle on BBC television for the first time in an animated series for children. Ryan devised his own real-time method of animation, using cut-out puppets against painted backgrounds and props with cardboard levers to make the boats rock and to move the eyes, mouths, and limbs of the characters. Since then, many television series and books (the best of which are *Pugwash and the Sea Monster* and *Captain Pugwash and the Mutiny*) have kept the sea crew alive and in perpetual fear of attack: "Help! It's Cut-Throat Jake! Avast, me hearties!" However, Pugwash's crew is as endearing as they are inept: about as far from the real pirates of the eighteenth century as a stuffed tiger is from the real thing. Captain Pugwash is good clean fun. **VN**

Things never quite seem to go as planned for Captain Pugwash. 

Crictor 1958

Tomi Ungerer

Nationality | French, born 1931
Publisher | Harper Trophy, USA
Award | A.L.A. Notable Children's Book
Theme | Animal stories, Quirky

5+

Crictor is a charming tale that tells of the affection of a boa constrictor for the inhabitants of a small French town. One day an old lady, Louise Bodot, receives a birthday present from her son that is as unusual as it is terrifying: a snake. Having overcome her initial fear, Madame Bodot decides to bring up the young snake as well as she can. She helps him get used to his new environment, she feeds him, and she takes him on outings. Being a very civilized snake, Crictor follows his mistress to the classroom, where he learns the alphabet and how to do math, snake style. As he grows up, he becomes more and more helpful; he is a popular playmate for the children and, in the end, is hailed as a hero by the little community.

"Well fed, Crictor became longer and longer, and stronger and stronger."

To enhance this quirky text, Tomi Ungerer has accompanied it with illustrations drawn with India ink in light strokes, shaded with pastel colors. The lines are fine and delicate and, for instance, the miniscule details that fill the rooms in Madame Bodot's home are absolutely delightful.

Crictor is the first of a series of short and surprising stories by Tomi Ungerer making heroes of animals that were often ignored in illustrated books of the time: Adelaide the winged kangaroo, Emile the octopus, Rufus the bat, and Orlando the vulture. These frightening, unloved creatures always manage to win the hearts of readers with their wit, courage, and imagination. *Crictor* and *Emile* are two stories that teach children not to judge others too hastily. This recurring theme offers a view of humanity that is both kind and critical at the same time. **SL**

OTHER GREAT TOMI UNGERER TITLES

***The Mellops Go Flying*, 1957**
***Adelaide*, 1959**
***Emile*, 1960**
***The Three Robbers*, 1961**
***Orlando, the Brave Vulture*, 1966**

Madame Bodot knits a long woolen sweater for Crictor. 

Chanticleer and the Fox 1958

Barbara Cooney

Nationality | American, born 1917
Publisher | Crowell Jr. Books, USA
Award | Caldecott Medal, 1959
Theme | Classics, Traditional

"Once upon a time a poor widow, getting on in years, lived in a small cottage beside a grove . . ."

OTHER RECOMMENDED COONEY TITLES

***Ox-Cart Man,* 1979**
***Island Boy,* 1988**
***Hattie and the Wild Waves,* 1990**
***Emily,* 1992**
***Basket Moon,* 1999**

Barbara Cooney's output was prolific and saw her turn her hand to writing her own stories and adapting others. She first came to widespread attention for her adaptation of Geoffrey Chaucer's "Nun's Priest's Tale" from *The Canterbury Tales—Chanticleer and the Fox.* She reworked the tale of a rooster into a picture book format. The beautiful colors of Cooney's drawings were created using a scratchboard technique, and her painstaking attention to detail re-creates what life may have looked like in a medieval village. The result is Chaucer's classic story retold in a form that children can enjoy, without the vagaries of Middle English yet still with its fablelike cautionary note and sense of fun.

The story features a poor widow with two daughters who all live together in a small cottage. She keeps several farmyard animals, including cows, sows, sheep, and chickens. The story's hero is one of the chickens: the handsome, boisterous, crowing rooster Chanticleer, who is adored by the hens around him and everyone else in his farmyard kingdom. Yet Chanticleer has met his match in his female companion, the beautiful hen Pertelote. Chanticleer struts around the yard, lapping up the adoration, but his arrogance is to prove his downfall. He is deceived by the flattery of a wily fox, who carries the cockerel away. All comes to an eventual happy ending as Chanticleer manages to escape and return home, learning a valuable lesson about life along the way: never trust a flatterer. **CK**

Little Old Mrs. Pepperpot 1958

Alf Prøysen Björn Berg

Nationality | Norwegian, born 1914 (author); Swedish, born 1923 (illustrator)
Publisher | Hutchinson, UK
Theme | Adventure, Quirky

Mrs. Pepperpot is an elderly lady who lives with her husband in a country cottage. Life seems normal enough, but Mrs. Pepperpot has a secret: From time to time she shrinks to the size of a pepperpot. It is something she has no control over nor knowledge of when it will happen. It just takes her by surprise. Occasionally her husband is on hand to pop her in his pocket and smooth over the situation, but most of the time Mrs. Pepperpot is on her own and has to deal with the consequences herself, using her intellect and cunning to get herself out of potentially dangerous or embarrassing situations. Whether dealing with a wily animal, such as a moose on the loose, or trying to make her way out of a drawer full of macaroni, Mrs. Pepperpot always manages to come up with a trick or a clever solution to save her skin.

Of course, shrinking to the size of a pepperpot makes it very difficult to do everyday things, too, such as housework, and she is always worrying about what her husband will think if she has not had time to do the cleaning or make his favorite bilberry jam (not that the mild Mr. Pepperpot would notice). So bossy Mrs. Pepperpot persuades, or coerces, others to help her. She gets the cat to wash the dishes, the dog to make her bed, and she even gets a mouse to clean her house. Just as suddenly as she shrinks, Mrs. Pepperpot grows back to normal size, and it is usually just at the time when the reader is worrying that Mrs. Pepperpot's secret is about to be found out. **LH**

Little Nicholas 1959

René Goscinny Jacques Sempé

Nationality | French/Polish, born 1926 (author); French, born 1932 (illustrator)
Publisher | Denoël, France
Theme | School, Adventure, Family

Nicholas is a little boy whose adventures were first published in 1959 in the newspaper *Dimanche Sud Ouest* and in the strip-cartoon magazine *Pilote*. The *Petit Nicholas* stories have survived for half a century, enjoyed by generations of readers, without ever losing any of their humor or freshness.

Nicholas is between six and ten years old and is the narrator of his adventures. An only son, he is rather average at school, but he is surrounded by a happy gang of friends at a time when French schoolboys still wear short trousers and write with penholders and ink pots. His best friend is Alceste, who eats all the time and whose hands are always sticky. In the playground the atmosphere is often quite lively because the friends all have big personalities. Eudes is the strong, strapping boy who punches other boys; Rufus is always ready for a scrap, too; Geoffroy is the one who has brilliant ideas; Clotaire is bottom of the class and is often sent to stand in the corner; and Agnan is very serious, but he is the only one who wears glasses so no one fights with him. Other characters in Nicholas's world include his parents, his granny who makes him laugh a lot, the schoolteacher, who is "cool," the headmaster, and a general supervisor nicknamed Bouillon.

The highly detailed black-and-white illustrations are full of finesse and wit, affectionately reflecting the candor and mischievousness of children. A refreshing read with the prospect of a good laugh as well! **SL**

Are You My Mother? 1960

P. D. Eastman

Nationality | American, born 1909
Publisher | Random House, USA
Theme | Classics, Family, Animal stories

Contrary to popular belief, "P. D. Eastman" is not a pseudonym for Dr. Seuss. Philip Dey Eastman did work closely with Dr. Seuss (born Theodor Seuss Geisel) not only during their military service, where they collaborated on the Private Snafu training films, but also throughout their individual writing careers. At the time, the children's literature market was crying out for innovative books that would engage early readers, and the works of Eastman and Seuss more than filled that niche. Although not a particularly high-profile author, Eastman was responsible for many of the books in the Beginner Books series, including *Go, Dog. Go!*, *Sam the Firefly*, and others.

Many of the people who learned to read from the Beginner Books have fond memories of *Are You My Mother*? It follows a confused baby bird who hatched from his egg while his mother is away from the nest and promptly falls out of it. It is a simple story of a baby bird's search for his mother, yet there is plenty going on to captivate young readers. The sweet little bird is curious about everyone and everything he encounters, and asks them all the same Big Question: "Are you my mother?"

Children will chuckle at the visual jokes as the bird asks his question of dogs, cows, airplanes, and steam shovels, to name but a few. Readers will also rejoice with the little bird when, in the end, he is blissfully reunited with his mother in a wonderful moment of recognition. **KD**

The Orange Cow 1961

Nathan Hale Lucile Butel

Nationality | American, born 1930 (author); French, born 1929 (illustrator)
Publisher | Flammarion, France
Theme | Classics, Animal stories

First published in France as *La vache orange, The Orange Cow* is one of the great classics of children's literature. Remarkably, the story is the invention of a seven-year-old American boy whose father sent the manuscript to the publisher, Paul Fauchet, in 1939.

This unusual tale tells the story of an orange cow who is sick and is looked after by a gentle gray fox. Monsieur Leblanc's Orange Cow has run away from the farm, and is going on a spree. She meets a kind fox, but as she seems rather weak and says she is sick, the fox takes her back to his house and puts her to bed. He studies the cow's symptoms with great seriousness and takes good care of her, although she does not always behave well. The Orange Cow enjoys all this pampering and takes advantage of it. Like children, the cow eats bread and butter for breakfast, brushes her teeth, and hides under her bed when she has nightmares. The kind fox is as patient as a nurse. One morning, the cow, full of energy, meets up with her friend, the fox, who has just discovered an advertisement in the paper: Monsieur Leblanc is offering a handsome reward to anyone who brings back his Orange Cow. The fox takes her to the farm, where Monsieur Leblanc is delighted to have his cow back and rewards the fox as promised.

This original tale makes gentle fun of our weaknesses through a story about animals who can think and speak. Butel's delicate, pastel drawings bring to life this strange, engaging character. **CD**

S
ETITS
ÈRE
ASTOR"

la vache orange

12

LAMMARION

Grégoire Solotareff reviews:

The Three Robbers 1961

Tomi Ungerer

Original Title | Die Drei Räuber
Nationality | French, born 1931
Publisher | Diogenes Verlag, Switzerland
Theme | Adventure

5+

The Three Robbers was published in France in 1968 by l'Ecole des Loisirs. I was fifteen at the time, and it had been a long time since I had read any illustrated books. I was too busy getting myself kicked out of high school on account of my unruliness. I didn't discover Tomi Ungerer until 1984, when I was looking for something that might inspire me in children's books. Some years previously I had stumbled across the work of André François, the freedom of whose line seemed dazzling in this sober era, and a bit earlier still I had seen books by Saul Steinberg on my parents' bookshelves. These were two major discoveries.

When I found *The Three Robbers*, it was a shock: pleasure and jealousy at the same time. I turned the book over and over in my hands: what a free style of drawing, how stripped down, how energetic! No extraneous details, just the essentials. I said to myself, "Here is a master." This is what I have to do, absolutely, books for children that are strong, funny, and lighthearted. If my drawing style is different—very different—from Tomi's, I might be able to create books that are as lighthearted as those of Tomi, less dark, but just as strong. And if I replaced the darkness in his work with color, then that is not plagiarism! I love using strong colors, colors that are alive. Some of my books are timid, wan, and blurred, and sometimes it seems a miracle that they were published.

"When Tiffany woke up she saw chests full of treasure. 'What are you doing with all that?'"

When I was little, I had a puppet of a wolf. It was funny and I loved it. A wolf! Ungerer didn't do wolves! I had found my inspiration. I wrote *Loulou* and I illustrated it in a single night.

OTHER GREAT ROBBER ADVENTURES

The Little Horse Bus by Graham Greene, 1950
Der Räuber Hotzenplotz by Otfried Preußler, 1962
The Real Thief by William Steig, 1973
Burglar Bill by Allan Ahlberg, 1977
Ronia the Robber's Daughter by Astrid Lindgren, 1981

One of the robbers carefully carries the little girl to the cave. 

Old Master Q 1962

Wong Chak

Original Title | Lao Fu Zi
Nationality | Chinese, born Wong Kar Hei, 1924
Publisher | Various newspapers, Hong Kong
Theme | Adventure, Quirky

These humorous stories were written by Alfonso Wong under the pen name Wong Chak. The various tales center around the life of Lao Fu Zi (Old Master Q), a mature man of uncertain age, and his close friends: Mr. Big Sweet Potato, Mr. Chin, Miss Chan (a love interest), and Mr. Chiu, Lao's rival. Many of the storylines are outrageous and unpredictable, yet the nature of the stories is always comedic and the narrative well told. The stories are simply illustrated, often without the need for any dialogue, which means that they can be easily understood. Wong effortlessly turns art, fashion, music, and modern-day life into hilarious episodes and adventures that are enjoyed by readers of all ages.

Many of the comic strips have an appropriate Chinese idiom (Chengyu) as a title. The strips express a satirical view of events in Hong Kong that was contemporary at the time they were written. Wong liberally makes fun of human weaknesses, such as greediness, pettiness, and the decline of moral values. Although short, the stories are succinct and to the point. The reader is less judgmental of Lao's foibles than if he were a younger character.

Since 1965, numerous films have been made based on the characters in *Old Master Q*. A cartoon series appeared in the 1980s, followed by two television series. Between 2001 and 2002, *Lao Fu Zi* was printed in color and in English in *Tai Wan News*. The comic is enjoyed by all ages and has a global following. **HL**

The Robber Hotzenplotz 1962

Otfried Preußler   Franz Josef Tripp

Nationality | German, born 1923 (author); German, born 1915 (illustrator)
Publisher | Thienemann Verlag, Germany
Theme | Magical stories, Fantasy

The Robber Hotzenplotz (or *Der Räuber Hotzenplotz*) was the first in what became a three-volume series featuring traditional German puppet characters, such as the good-humored boy Kasperl, his friend Sepperl, a policeman, a magician, and the crook himself. In the first book, the protagonist steals Kasperl's grandmother's coffee grinder, which the boys built for her and which plays her favorite tune. The policeman, Dimpfelmoser, seems unable to catch Hotzenplotz, so Kasperl and Sepperl go into the forest to find him. They devise a shrewd plan to catch him but end up as his prisoners.

Hotzenplotz sells Kasperl to evil magician Petrosilius Zwackelmann. In the magician's castle, Kasperl discovers the good fairy Amaryllis locked in a dungeon. He leaves the castle in search of herbs that can help free her. The story continues in a whirl of magic, mistaken identity, and twists and turns, one of which brings Sepperl face-to-face with Zwackelmann. The magician ends up being furious with Hotzenplotz and casts a spell on him. After Kasperl rescues Amaryllis, Zwackelmann winds up in his own dungeon. Amaryllis grants the boys a wish, and the coffee grinder is returned to Kasperl's grandmother.

This very successful book has been translated into around thirty languages. Thousands of children inundated Otfried Preußler with letters demanding further installments. Despite his initial reluctance, he indulged them twice, and he made sure the third volume had no unresolved storylines. **DaH**

Otfried Preußler
Der Räuber
Hotzenplotz
TR

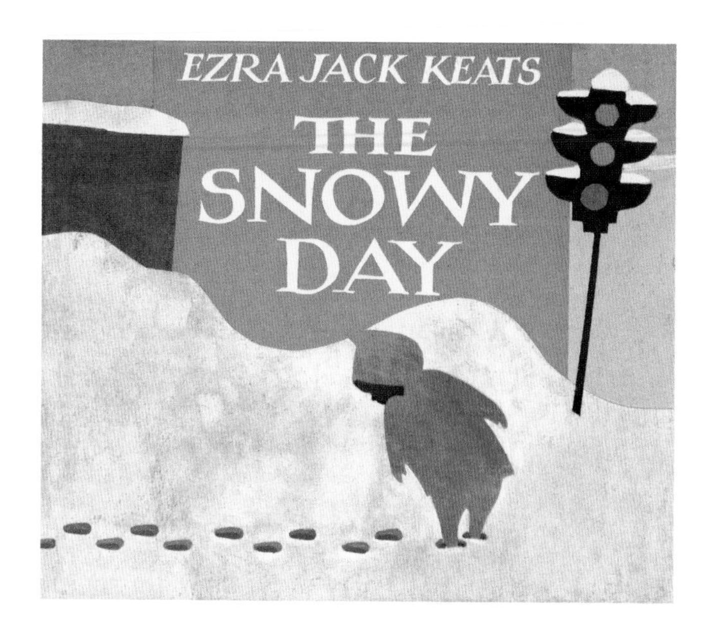

The Snowy Day 1962

Ezra Jack Keats

Nationality | American, born Jacob Ezra Katz, 1916
Publisher | Viking Press, USA
Award | Caldecott Medal, 1963
Theme | Family, Science and nature

Jacob Ezra Katz was the child of impoverished Polish–Jewish immigrants who lived in Brooklyn, New York. As an adult, in reaction to the anti-Semitic prejudices of the time, he changed his name to Ezra Jack Keats. His memories of being a target of discrimination created a sympathy and understanding that is evident in his books and their characters, which are all drawn from the community in which he grew up.

Ezra Jack Keats wrote *The Snowy Day* long before multicultural characters and themes came to the forefront in children's literature. The book tells the story of Peter, a young African–American boy (although he could be any boy, his race is incidental to the story) waking up to discover that it has snowed during the night. "One winter morning Peter woke up and looked out the window. Snow had fallen during the night. It covered everything as far as he could see." He goes outside and enjoys the magical pleasures of a snow day: laying down in the snow to make snow angels, experimenting with footprints, knocking the clumps of snow off trees—all the things little boys and girls have been doing in the snow since time began. Adding to the charm of the story are Keats's illustrations, which use cut-outs, watercolors, and collage in his signature style and result in strikingly beautiful art.

This is a simple timeless tale that children will remember for a lifetime. A series of books follows Peter's growth to adolescence, including *Peter's Chair*, *A Letter to Amy*, and *Goggles!* **KD**

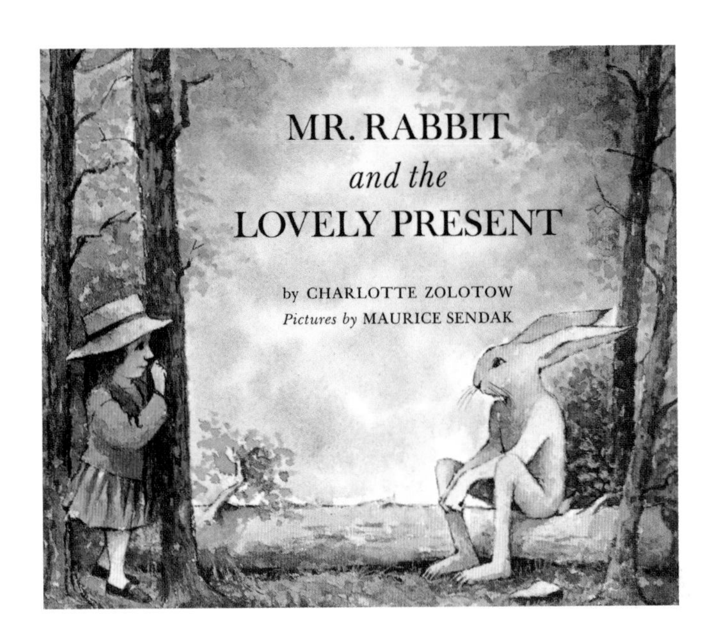

5+

Mr. Rabbit and the Lovely Present 1962

Charlotte Zolotow Maurice Sendak

Nationality | American, born 1915 (author); American, born 1928 (illustrator)
Publisher | Harper and Row, USA
Theme | Magical stories, Friendship, Family

A little girl wants to give her mother a really good birthday present but needs help in making the right choice. Fortunately for her, Mr. Rabbit is on hand to provide advice. All the little girl can think of are the colors her mother particularly likes: red, yellow, green, and blue. Quickly rejecting Mr. Rabbit's initial, unrealistic suggestions—stretching from fire engines to emeralds—the girl finally decides on a basket of green pears, yellow bananas, red apples, and blue grapes. A lovely present, indeed.

The story mixes repetition with novelty in just the right balance, presenting young readers with a tale that they can soon come to anticipate as well as enjoy. Maurice Sendak's accompanying illustrations also explore a wide range of emotions. The girl, (whose name the reader never learns), sometimes beams with pleasure, but at other moments she looks pensive, even a little distressed. Mr. Rabbit, meanwhile, mixes human and animal characteristics, walking unclothed on his hind legs and never being short of fatherly encouragement mixed with wild imaginings all of his own. Continually pictured against a rustic background of fields, apple trees, woods, and rivers, the two characters occupy a half-real, half-magical existence, made all the more mysterious by the girl's exceedingly formal attire: straw hat, brown jacket, white socks, and fancy shoes. Gentle, humorous, unpredictable, and seemingly with a logic all of its own, this is one of those picture books that once experienced proves impossible to forget, whatever your age. **NT**

Borka 1963

John Burningham

Nationality | English, born 1936
Publisher | Jonathan Cape, UK
Award | Kate Greenaway Medal
Theme | Adventure, Animal stories

5+

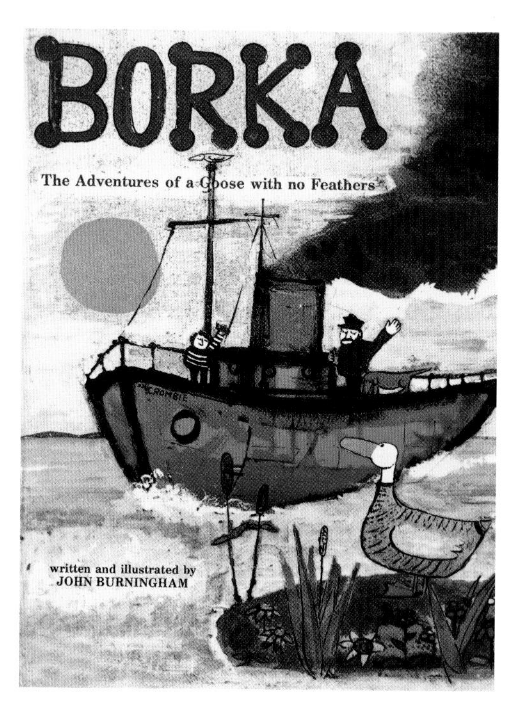

Borka: The Adventures of a Goose with No Feathers is the story of a goose who lives on the east coast of England. Borka is an ordinary enough young goose except for one vital difference: she was born with no feathers. Although her mother knits her a gray woolen jersey, the other geese still tease her and laugh at her. Discouraged, Borka feels isolated and never learns to swim; she is finally left behind on her own when every other goose in the family flies off to a warmer climate. Borka, taking refuge in a fishing boat, is fortunate enough to find herself a member of the crew sailing to London. She makes herself as useful as possible and is finally deposited in Kew Gardens, where there are already so many strange-looking geese that she can now get by without any more cruel and upsetting comments.

"A goose on board! She'll have to work her passage if she's coming with us to London."

John Burningham's atmospheric illustrations for this charming story fill each page with a near riot of color, form, and texture. Using heavy black lines to pick out humans and animal characters from their densely illustrated backgrounds, he is a master at conveying thoughts and feelings with minimal effects. His geese are affectionate caricatures of the real thing: all beak and feet, and given to standing up straight; sometimes wearing glasses or drying their tears with a pocket handkerchief. Children love Cinderella-style stories, and this one owes something to Hans Christian Andersen's *The Ugly Duckling*. *Borka* is never condescending to the reader. It is quietly humorous and beautifully illustrated throughout, and is a true classic for all time. **NT**

OTHER NOTABLE BURNINGHAM TITLES

Mr. Gumpy's Outing, 1970
Mr. Gumpy's Motor Car, 1973
Granpa, 1984
Oi! Get Off the Train, 1989
Husherbye, 2000

Swimmy 1963

Leo Lionni

Nationality | Dutch/American/Italian, born 1910
Publisher | Pantheon Books, USA
Theme | Friendship, Adventure, Animal stories

5+

Leo Lionni was born in Holland, moved to Milan after his marriage, and eventually lived and worked in the United States, where he wrote and illustrated more than forty acclaimed children's books.

The picture book *Swimmy* starts out as a rather sad and intrepid tale of survival, but ends up being a moving story of friendship and teamwork. After a big tuna fish gulps up a school of little red fish who are Swimmy's friends and family, the tiny black fish escapes alone, swimming bravely through the ocean. On his journey, he discovers many marvelous sea creatures, such as the "eel whose tail was almost too far away to remember" and a "lobster who walked about like a water-moving machine." Unfortunately

"One bad day a tuna fish, swift, fierce and very hungry, came darting through the waves . . . "

some of these creatures are dangerous to Swimmy and want to eat him. Eventually he meets up with another school of tiny red fish. These fish are very frightened because they are so small, and Swimmy uses his creativity and kindness (and experience) to show them how to swim together as a group to outsmart the big fish and protect themselves from their natural enemies in the sea.

Told with minimal text, the real star of the story is the artwork, which received a Caldecott Honor award in 1964. Lionni creates his delightful underwater world with a combination of collage and paint, which results in pages with all the luminosity of the ocean. Young children will love finding the tiny black fish (and he is tiny) within the illustrations on every page and will cheer Swimmy on as he teaches the other fish the value of teamwork. **KD**

MORE BOOKS ABOUT FRIENDSHIP

The Squirrel, the Hare and the Little Grey Rabbit **by Alison Uttley, 1929**
The Giving Tree **by Shel Silverstein, 1964**
Amos & Boris **by William Steig, 1971**
Friends from the Other Side **by Gloria Anzaldúa, 1997**

Amelia Bedelia 1963

Peggy Parish   Fritz Siebel

5+

"Amelia Bedelia got some scissors. She snipped a little here and she snipped a little there."

MORE QUIRKY CHARACTER BOOKS

Bécassine **by Jacqueline Rivière, 1905**
Mary Poppins **by P. L. Travers, 1934**
Little Old Mrs. Pepperpot **by Alf Prøysen, 1958**
Winnie the Witch **by Valerie Thomas, 1987**
Amelia Bedelia Helps Out **by Peggy Parish, 1994**

Nationality | American, born 1927 (author); Austrian/American, birth date unknown (illustrator)
Publisher | Greenwillow Books, USA
Theme | Adventure, Favorite characters

The idea for the Amelia Bedelia series came to Peggy Parish from the years she spent teaching young children. Sometimes, as a joke, her students would respond literally to things she said, and they thought it was hilarious. If she said, "Let's call roll," they would respond by saying "Hey, Roll!" And so she created Amelia Bedelia, the housemaid who takes everything literally, with amusing results. Parish had strong feelings about teaching children to read, and was involved in schools and education throughout her life: "What I try to show teachers is that all the skills needed to read can be taught outside of textbooks. Today's children are not going to read what they are not interested in."

Amelia Bedelia is a very literal-minded housemaid with good intentions. She does everything she is asked to do—just not exactly in the way you would expect it to be done. Want the curtains drawn? Amelia happily gets out her sketch pad and draws them. Need the chicken dressed? Well, she first has to decide whether to dress it as a boy or a girl. Change the towels? Scissors will do the trick. Of course this behavior leaves her employers fuming and exasperated, but Amelia is also a great cook, and her delicious lemon meringue pie saves the day!

The first of a series, *Amelia Bedelia* is perfect for early readers with a sense of humor, and subtly teaches children a number of verbal idioms that they may never have thought about quite so literally. **KD**

The Dreams of the Toad 1963

Javier Villafañe Tabaré

Nationality | Argentinian, born 1909 (author); details unknown (illustrator)
Publisher | Editorial Hachette, Argentina
Theme | Folktales, Animal stories

The simple opening phrase: "One afternoon, a toad said, 'Tonight, I am going to dream that I am a tree,'" immediately sets the scene for the story of a toad who dreams of becoming a tree, a river, the wind, and many other objects and animals before discovering that nothing is as beautiful as being a toad. It is the title story of this collection of short stories, which was first published as *Los sueños del sapo*. The protagonists of the various stories are animals, circus artists, children, scissors, and, most importantly, the old *titiritero*, or puppeteer, of Argentine folklore who acts as the author's alter ego. Rather like a storyteller in a puppet theater, the narrator introduces the individual characters before leaving the floor to them. The narrative is deliberately simple and colloquial, and the stories are full of idiosyncratic dialogue.

Villafañe's narratives owe much to the Argentine oral tradition from which they originate. One of the best-known stories of the collection, "The Scissors That Cut the Earth," is intriguing for its poetic title: in this mythical tale a simple pair of scissors, in the hands of a beautiful woman, create a whole new world. In "Maese Trotamundos," a simple negligent episode about a handful of puppets forgotten in the rain becomes a moving story about friendship, betrayal, death, and guilt. *Los sueños del sapo* is one of Villafañe's most successful collections of stories and a classic of Argentine children's literature. Other collections of stories include *Historia de pájaros* (*History of Birds*). **LB**

The Black Smurfs 1963

Peyo

Original Title | Le Schtroumpfs Noirs
Nationality | Belgian, born Pierre Culliford, 1928
Publisher | Dupuis, Belgium
Theme | Comics, Friendship, Quirky

The very first Smurfs appeared in the comic *Le Journal de Spirou* in October 1958. They proved so popular that they were given their own series. *The Black Smurfs* was the first comic book to be published. It contained three stories (the other two were "The Flying Smurf" and "The Smurfnapper"). Since then the original comics have been collected into anthologies.

In *The Black Smurfs*, the Smurfs are fixing a bridge, but Lazy Smurf has fallen asleep. When a strange insect bites him, he turns from blue to black and starts leaping around wildly, unable to say anything but "Gnap," and biting the other Smurfs. Every Smurf who gets bitten turns black and runs into the forest; they begin terrorizing the peaceful Smurf village.

The blue Smurfs catch the insect that began all the fuss, and Papa Smurf examines it. He comes to realize that the afflicted Smurfs could be saved by a certain type of pollen, but the black Smurfs are very angry and do not want to be helped. They just want to bite as many Smurfs as they can. Eventually, Papa Smurf is the only blue Smurf left. The Smurfs are saved after an explosion occurs in the factory set up to make the special pollen. Clouds of pollen burst into the air, turning all the black Smurfs back to blue. The story has often been criticized for racist overtones, and for many years it was not translated into English and was banned in the United States. Although Peyo died in 1992, the Smurfs still live on through the books produced by Peyo's son, Thierry Culliford. **LH**

Flat Stanley 1964

Jeff Brown Tomi Ungerer

Nationality | American, born 1925 (author); French, born 1931 (illustrator)
Publisher | Harper and Row, USA
Theme | Adventure, Favorite characters

5+

Meet Stanley Lambchop, an ordinary boy with an extraordinary problem. He is four feet tall, about a foot wide, and half an inch thick. The original idea for the book and resulting series came from the author Jeff Brown while reading to his son at bedtime. Stalling for time, his son declared a fear that his big bulletin board might fall on him during the night, to which his father replied, "Well, then I guess you'd be flat." And so a classic children's book character was born.

Stanley Lambchop is a normal, young boy who finds himself flattened by a bulletin board, "'Gosh,' said Arthur [his brother], 'Stanley's flat!' 'As a pancake,' said Mr. Lambchop, 'darndest thing I've ever seen.'" Stanley's misfortune is soon turned into an advantage when he is sent through the mail to different places all around the world. His friends and family take him on trips sightseeing in famous cities and far-flung places, thus increasing Stanley's and the reader's knowledge of the world.

The phenomenon of *Flat Stanley* began when a teacher in Canada saw the educational potential of using the book as a way to teach children about the world around them and about current events. Today young students the world over make their own Flat Stanleys and then mail them to friends and families abroad. The people who receive their new flat friend take him on all sorts of adventures—to work, to the zoo, on plane and boat trips, and to historic locations. They photograph Flat Stanley and send back the pictures. The range of Stanley's destinations is limited only by the creativity of the people he visits. **KD**

The Giving Tree 1964

Shel Silverstein

Nationality | American, born 1930
Publisher | HarperCollins, USA
Theme | Family, Friendship, Classics, Science and nature, Controversial

Shel Silverstein enjoyed a long and successful career as a writer, cartoonist, and songwriter for adults before writing his first book for children. *The Giving Tree* was initially rejected by his publisher as too maudlin. In fact, many adults still find the moral lesson of this story to be a controversial one—the story of a tree who gives and gives to the boy she loves until she has nothing left to give him. This story of a tree that would do anything for the boy she loves has become a classic, and has never been out of print since its initial publication in 1964.

Unlike Silverstein's other classic stories, this one is not a collection of poetry, but takes a more traditional story format. The story begins with a boy and a tree. Every day the boy comes to the tree to eat the tree's apples, swing from her branches, or slide down her trunk, and this makes the tree happy. However, as the boy grows older, he begins to want more from the tree. When he asks for money, the tree replies that she has none but suggests that he pick her apples and sell them. When he asks for a house for his family, she offers him her branches to build one. The tree gives and gives to the boy—her leaves, her limbs, her trunk—until all that is left is a stump for the boy, now a man, to sit on.

No matter how you feel about the story itself—whether you find it sad and disturbing, or see it as a beautiful story of the self-sacrificing love that a parent feels for their child—there is no arguing with the millions of copies that have been sold of this simple yet powerful fable about giving. **KD**

The Giving Tree
by
Shel Silverstein

Dailan Kifki 1966

María Elena Walsh S. Lavandeira

Nationality | Argentinian, born 1930 (author); details unknown (illustrator)
Publisher | Alfaguara, Spain
Theme | Family, Adventure, Animal stories

5+

A classic of Argentine children's literature, *Dailan Kifki* is María Elena Walsh's most famous and beautiful creation. One morning the narrator finds her hall blocked by something resembling a huge gray mountain. She pushes it out on the street and realizes that the mountain is, in fact, an elephant. Surprised and frightened, she is about to scream for help when she notices that this huge animal has a letter hanging from its ear and that her name is written on the envelope. The letter reads: "'Dear Lady, my name is Dailan Kifki and I beg you not to be frightened because I am an elephant. My owner has abandoned me because he cannot feed me anymore. He trusts that you will take care of me. I am very diligent and affectionate, and I love cartoons.'" The woman takes him to the backyard, trying not to wake up anyone, although Dailan Kifki's steps resound like thunder. Soon the whole family appears at the window and sees the elephant: "My mother fainted, my dad got hiccups, and my brother Roberto said: 'We are fried.'"

This is only the beginning of the troubles that are in store in this hilarious and tender tale. Raising an elephant is not easy in any circumstances. It is even harder if he falls asleep on a sapling that grows as fast as Jack's beanstalk until it reaches the sky, leaving poor Dailan Kifki trapped in its branches until a fireman climbs up and fastens wings to the elephant's back so that he can fly away. Unfortunately, Dailan Kifki flies too far, and the narrator has to track him down, which requires the support of the entire diplomatic network of South America. **LB**

Gumdrop 1966

Val Biro

Original Title | The Adventures of a Vintage Car
Nationality | Hungarian, born 1921
Publisher | Hodder and Stoughton, UK
Theme | Favorite characters, Adventure

Gumdrop is a vintage car—a beautiful blue Austin Clifton—and the star of thirty-seven picture books. Young readers first meet him in *The Adventures of a Vintage Car* when, having been neglected by his owners, Gumdrop is discovered in a scrap yard by Mr. Oldcastle, who takes him home and lovingly restores him. Mr. Oldcastle gives the car his name because of the "Guuuuum "Drrrropopopop" noise he makes, and the pair, accompanied by a dog called Horace, begin a series of adventures.

Hungarian Val Biro emigrated to England at the outbreak of World War II. He went to art school in London, and throughout the 1950s he was a much-sought-after graphic artist who created memorable book jackets for many best-selling authors. In the early 1960s he wrote and illustrated his first children's book, *Bumpy's Holiday*. However, when Biro bought a vintage Austin Clifton car in the mid-1960s, he was inspired to create a new central character whose adventures he would continue to write about for almost forty years.

Gumdrop, Mr. Oldcastle, and Horace's escapades involve a wide range of mishaps. They meet pirates, chase burglars, get mistaken for smugglers, save an elephant at the zoo, and encounter ghosts, Martians, and monsters. They get into heaps of trouble, rescue people and animals, and usually manage to save the day. These charming tales have an enduring popularity and have been successfully translated into a number of languages, including French, German, Japanese, and Swedish. **HJ**

Gumdrop

THE ADVENTURES OF A VINTAGE CAR

Frederick 1967

Leo Lionni

Nationality | Dutch/American/Italian, born 1905
Publisher | Pantheon Books, USA
Theme | Animal stories

Frederick is a field mouse quite unlike any other. During the last few days of autumn, while his whole family labors industriously to collect supplies of corn, nuts, wheat, and straw to last them through the long and snowy winter, Frederick does not help. Instead he sits in the meadow looking dreamy. He tells his reproachful family that he is busy gathering sun rays, colors, and words. The true significance of Frederick's efforts eventually becomes clear in the heart of winter, when the family is cold and hungry in its hideout. Frederick conjures up words to color the gray days, to evoke the warm glow of the sun, and to stir his family's heart. To his bewitched family, Frederick's powers are those of a magician. At first misjudged for his apparent "laziness," Frederick is ultimately elevated to the position of poet: "'But Frederick, you are a poet!' Frederick blushed, took a bow, and said shyly, 'I know it.'" It is the triumph of the emotional imagination over logical reason.

Frederick's touching story represents an interesting twist on Jean de la Fontaine's famous fable about the grasshopper and the ant. In winter, the grasshopper, who had spent the long summer days dancing in the meadows, comes begging at the ant's door for "some grain to keep herself alive." However, the industrious ant, who has wisely collected plentiful supplies of grain, sends her away, cynically suggesting it is now time "to dance."

The story is told in short, succinct sentences, and Leo Lionni's flowing style and beautiful illustrations make this a little gem of a book. **IW**

Cion Cion Blue 1968

Pinin Carpi Iris de Paoli

Nationality | Italian, born 1920 (author); Italian, birth date unknown (illustrator)
Publisher | Vallardi, Italy
Theme | Adventure

In *Cion Cion Blue*, color is very important. Cion Cion Blue has very dark blue hair; he wears blue pants, blue slippers, and has a blue pipe. His top and socks, however, are orange, as is the handkerchief in his pocket. Cion Cion Blue's dog is orange, but his name is Blue, whereas his cat is blue and is called Orange; furthermore the blue fish swims in orange water.

Cion Cion Blue is a Chinese farmer who grows oranges and lives a simple life. "Cion Cion Blue was a good farmer, he was in his fields day and night. Since it was always warm where he lived he could stay outdoors even at night. And anyway, he was so poor that he did not have a house, just a big orange umbrella; under the umbrella were his bed with blue blankets and orange sheets, the pillow was blue, and a cooking stove with a nice orange flame." When it snows for the first time, Cion Cion Blue thinks that the snow is sugar. He mixes it with freshly squeezed orange juice in an attempt to make a cake and instead discovers a delicious flavor of ice cream.

Cion Cion Blue decides to go to the imperial city to sell the newly discovered ice cream but encounters some formidable characters and challenges on the way: bad bandits, wicked witches, and a lovestruck emperor, for example. How can a farmer help the emperor find his lost love? How can he convince the fairy Biancaciccia to become his wife? Cion Cion Blue, being a good man, struggles to help all the people he meets and learns that things are not always as they seem. Eventually he retires to a humble home by the water, tired yet happy. **SMT**

The Tiger Who Came to Tea 1968

Judith Kerr

Nationality | German/British, born 1923
Publisher | Collins, UK
Theme | Family, Adventure, Quirky, Animal stories, Classics

Sophie and her mother are sitting down to tea one day when the doorbell rings. When Mom answers the door, there is a furry, striped tiger on the step. He is invited to sit down at the table and then proceeds to eat these accommodating humans out of house and home. He eats all the food available; he drinks all the tea, then Daddy's supply of beer, and even all the water in the faucet. Then he leaves. When Daddy comes home, he takes the family to a restaurant because there is absolutely nothing left to eat.

The story's appeal is twofold. Initially, there is the intrusion of the exotic tiger into a completely ordinary domestic house where, because no one is alarmed or surprised to see him, he suddenly becomes almost ordinary and domestic himself. The other part of the magical appeal is that there is an ever-present edge of danger: a possibility of things changing and becoming really worrying, even though Sophie and her mother are never fearful of the tiger. However much young readers love the tiger, there is a sigh of relief when the door closes behind the visitor with the bottomless stomach, and preparing for his next visit by buying tiger food becomes a sensible precaution.

This is a reassuring, unpretentious, and humorous story, with simple yet interesting illustrations. It has remained popular for so long, because of its threat of imminent peril. The tale would not work as well if it were a giraffe who came to tea. A tiger has connotations already attached to it, and these spread wonderfully into the story. It is a triumph. **AG**

"Suddenly there was a ring at the door. Sophie's mom said, 'I wonder who that can be? It can't be the milkman . . .'"

OTHER GREAT JUDITH KERR STORIES

Mog the Forgetful Cat, 1970
When Hitler Stole Pink Rabbit, 1971
Mog and the Baby, 1980
How Mrs. Monkey Missed the Ark, 1992

The Best Nest 1968

P. D. Eastman

Nationality | American, born 1909
Publisher | Random House, USA
Theme | Rhyming stories, Classics, Animal stories

5+

P. D. Eastman is responsible for writing and illustrating several of the well-known books in the famous Beginner Books series, including *Are You My Mother?* and others. Later in his career he collaborated with Dr. Seuss on *The Cat in the Hat Dictionary*.

The Best Nest is an excellent picture book for young children who are beginning to learn to read independently. It could be said that it is one of the best of its genre, but *The Best Nest* also has a bit more to teach children about life. Mr. Bird is very satisfied with his comfortable life, and he loves the nest that he shares with his wife. As for Mrs. Bird, well, unfortunately the same cannot be said for her. Unlike Mr. Bird, she is positive that there is a better nest out

"Then Mrs. Bird came out of the house. 'It is NOT the best nest,' she said."

there somewhere, and all they have to do is find it. Being a good husband, Mr. Bird agrees to go out and search for a better nest for her. Each time Mr. and Mrs. Bird think that they have found the perfect new home—the very best nest—something happens to make them realize that it is far from ideal, whether it be atop a bell tower (too loud), in an old shoe (here comes the foot), or in a chimney (warm but too smoky). They end up trying out new homes in some pretty peculiar spots.

Young children will quickly learn to sing along with Mr. Bird as he crows his famous refrain each time he builds a new nest: "'I love my house. I love my nest. In all the world my nest is best!'" By the end of the book, of course, it becomes clear to all that it is not where you build your nest but who lives in it that makes it the best nest. **KD**

OTHER FAVORITE EASTMAN BOOKS

***Sam and the Firefly*, 1958**
***Are You My Mother?*, 1960**
***Go, Dog. Go!*, 1961**
***Big Dog, Little Dog*, 1969**

Kangaroo for All 1968

Gloria Fuertes

Original Title | Cangura para todo
Nationality | Spanish, born 1917
Publisher | Lumen, Spain
Theme | Poetry, Animal stories

There is probably no more popular representative of Spanish children's literature than Gloria Fuertes. She also won the title of "children's poet," despite the fact that in her vast poetic oeuvre, she deals mainly with universal and "serious" themes—love, solitude, and death—without abandoning irony, her antiwar stance, or her commitment to social issues.

Her voice and her particular way of rhyming are unmistakable. She writes simple rhymes, so easy and plain that they sound comic, like jokes; poems full of tenderness and humor. Her poems for children and children's stories, as well as her theater production, both reflect a very particular way of seeing the world as well as explaining it, one of extraordinary liveliness and musicality.

Cangura para todo is a compilation of sixteen stories, written in the 1950s. The main characters are mostly animals: a kangaroo, a monkey, a flea, cats, and camels, but also an ogre who does not like to frighten children but prefers to make them laugh, and a Chinese man who manages to completely outwit a prince and marry his princess.

Fuertes's writing did not need magic or fairies or spells. Instead, she used innocence and the fact that everything is possible to lead her stories. A perfect example is Timotea the cat, who, after coughing for a while and acting like a chicken, lays five eggs, and although at first she is embarrassed, she later incubates them because "she believed in imaginary and magical things and what had happened to her immediately seemed wonderful." **EB**

Ramona the Pest 1968

Beverly Cleary Louis Darling

Nationality | American, born Beverly Atlee Bunn, 1916 (author); American, born 1916 (illustrator)
Publisher | Harper Collins, USA
Theme | School, Family

This is a story about an ordinary, if imperfect, American girl. However, if you asked her sister, Beatrice (or "Beezus," as she is known to Ramona), she would say that this is a book about a very pesty little girl. Ramona Geraldine Quimby—expert fusser—has just begun kindergarten at Glenwood School, and is doing her very best to grow up as quickly as possible so she can finally catch up to Beezus.

Ramona mostly loves school, and we follow her as she moans about wearing hand-me-down boots, fights the temptation of pulling a bossy schoolmate's "boing-boing" curls, disrupts the class during rest time, chases Davy for kisses in the schoolyard, learns about sharing, and falls desperately in love with her teacher Miss Binny. However, Ramona does not always feel that she belongs at school, and sometimes finds herself hiding from schoolyard games and being told off by her beloved teacher as a result. Feeling ostracized, the drama of the book culminates in Ramona's outright refusal to go back to school.

Beverly Cleary wrote the Ramona series to address the lack of U.S. children's literature available in the United States (at a time when British children's literature dominated), a complaint that she herself recorded while working in a children's library in Washington in the early 1940s. It is greatly significant that today the Ramona series still sells in many languages and countries across the globe—reaching out to ordinary kids (and their annoying little sisters)—and their extraordinary common misunderstandings about the world—everywhere. **JSD**

A Necklace of Raindrops 1968

Joan Aiken Jan Pieńkowski

Nationality | English, born 1924 (author); Polish, born 1936 (illustrator)
Publisher | Jonathan Cape, UK
Theme | Fantasy, Adventure

A baker's cat growing to an enormous size after eating some yeast? A house laying an egg? A huge apple pie with a piece of sky baked into it? These and several other outlandish fantasies can be found in this collection of eight stories by one of the most imaginative authors who has ever written for children. *A Necklace of Raindrops* is perfect for reading aloud. The storytelling techniques are kept simple, and some of the tales also involve rhyme as well as the type of repetition that can be so popular with young children. Although they read like a collection of folktales, each story is, in fact, totally original.

The title story is typically ingenious, all about a gift of a necklace made of magical raindrops from the North Wind to baby Laura. Accumulating one more raindrop on each birthday, she eventually has the power to start and then stop any rain shower in its tracks. But when the necklace is stolen, Laura has to travel all the way to Arabia to get it back.

These charming stories are illustrated by Jan Pieńkowski, best known for his Meg and Mog series. Mostly using black silhouettes but occasionally breaking into full color, he brings exactly the right mixture of the homey and the exotic to each tale, whether he is illustrating magic carpets, flying tigers, air-borne camels, or old-fashioned steam trains. Utterly in sympathy with each other, author and illustrator make an ideal match in this perfect little book for young readers. **NT**

The Duck in the Gun 1969

Joy Cowley Edward Sorel

Nationality | New Zealander, born 1936 (author); American, born 1929 (illustrator)
Publisher | Doubleday, USA
Theme | War

Effectively ridiculing the notion of war, *The Duck in the Gun* is about a mother duck who builds her nest in a cannon, just as the General of a small army decides that he wants to fire at the nearby town. With his men refusing to move the duck, who is sitting on some eggs, the General elects to visit the small town to ask if he can borrow their gun. The Prime Minister of the town only has one gun and sensibly turns down any suggestion of sharing it, so they decide to compromise on a three-week break from war: "That's fair enough. . . . We'll forget about the war for three weeks." After a week the General asks the Prime Minister for some money, because his men still expect to be paid even though they are doing nothing. The Prime Minister offers to let the soldiers repaint the town for a fee. When the eggs hatch and the ducklings are safely out of the cannon, the General suggests that they start the war again, but his men do not want to ruin their hard work, and the war is put off for good.

Joy Cowley's antiwar parody was first illustrated by Edward Sorel in 1969, and then later reillustrated by Robyn Belton in 1984, with the book's reissue. Belton's revised drawings for the book resulted in it winning the Russell Clark Award in 1985, with her neutrally toned pictures bringing a rustic charm to this internationally loved classic. With Cowley using a common duck as the basis of a ceasefire, she is able to highlight the absurdity of war and provide a powerful message of peace for all children. **CVB**

Jan Pieńkowski's unique silhouettes for *A Necklace of Raindrops*.

Sylvester and the Magic Pebble 1969

William Steig

Nationality | American, born 1907
Publisher | Windmill Books, USA
Award | Caldecott Medal, 1970
Theme | Magical stories, Family

5+

William Steig was best known as a cartoonist and cover artist for the *New Yorker* and other publications. At the age of sixty-one, after a long and successful career, Steig wrote his first children's book. More than thirty books for children followed, including classics like *Dr. De Soto*, *Pete's a Pizza*, *The Real Thief*, and the now infamous *Shrek*.

Sylvester and the Magic Pebble is the story of a young donkey who collects pebbles of unusual shape and color for a hobby. On his travels one day, he finds a magic red pebble that allows him to make wishes. Delighted with his extraordinary discovery, Sylvester hurries home to show the pebble to his parents. However, on the way, he finds himself face to face with a lion, and without thinking wishes he were a rock so that the lion cannot hurt him. He gets his wish and is trapped as a stone, leaving his parents to worry and wonder what has become of him. Eventually his parents go on a picnic and sit on the rock that was once Sylvester. They find the pebble and, without knowing that it is magic, wish that Sylvester was with them, thereby returning their son to his true form.

Although *Sylvester and the Magic Pebble* has been interpreted as both a metaphor for death and for childish helplessness, children will only see a classic story of an unfortunate, lost child who is found by the parents who never stopped loving him. The simple yet evocative art and the timeless story will resonate with all families. **KD**

A Lion in the Meadow 1969

Margaret Mahy Jenny Williams

Nationality | New Zealander, born 1936 (author); English, born 1939 (illustrator)
Publisher | Franklin Watts, USA; Dent, UK
Theme | Animal stories, Friendship

Margaret Mahy's fairy-tale writer's life began with this book. Her work was spotted by a New York editor in an exhibition, and a year later Mahy had five of her picture books published simultaneously in New York and London. The most acclaimed and enduring of them is *A Lion in the Meadow*. This elegant book is about the power of the imagination to alter reality.

A little boy in New Zealand is afraid that a lion (not a native species to the plains of New Zealand) is awaiting him in the meadow. To ease his fears, the boy's mother gives him a matchbox, which she says contains a baby dragon that will scare away any lions. When the boy opens the matchbox, however, there really is a dragon inside, which is even scarier than the lion. The boy and the lion together hide from the dragon, and in so doing become friends. Mahy blurs the lines between fear and friendship, as well as fact and illusion, in this enchanting tale.

There is a considerable difference between Jenny Williams's strong 1969 illustrations and those of the cozier 1986 version. Also, the 1986 ending requested by the publisher is much softer, verging on the sentimental. Mahy herself rather regrets the change, "feeling the ruthlessness of the first ending still lurking under the second kinder one, and believing it to be the true ending." However, the book established Mahy as a gifted writer. Her story lines are inventive, her characters true, and her language is filled with energy, music, and often outrageous wit. **TD**

Joseph's Yard 1969

Charles Keeping

Nationality | English, born 1924
Publisher | Oxford University Press, UK
Award | Kate Greenaway Honor's List
Theme | Science and nature

5+

Young Joseph lives in a city and has a yard rather than a garden. It is a barren yard, where nothing grows until one day when Joseph pulls up a piece of stone and plants a rose. A beautiful flower eventually grows, only to wither and die once Joseph has picked it. Annoyed with himself, Joseph lets the plant grow freely the following year, but this time he becomes overprotective and smothers it with his coat in a futile attempt to protect the rose from visiting insects and marauding cats. Finally Joseph realizes that he should just let nature take its course; his story ends with the rose growing into a large shrub that fills the whole yard, with birds happily perched in its branches and cats lying underneath its shady limbs.

Charles Keeping was a London boy and Joseph—with his red hair and glasses—could easily pass for the artist when he was young. Each glorious page captures the wonder of nature as seen in the early days of childhood. Objects that adults take for granted glow here with all the freshness of things seen for the first time. The sun seems brighter, insects look more colorful, and even the tradesman calling out for "any old iron" becomes a creature of wonder. With each picture painted against dramatically different full-color backgrounds, this truly is a book to linger over long after its simple but poignant story has come to an end. Keeping is an illustrator who is capable of making readers see the world around them in quite different ways, and never more so than here. **NT**

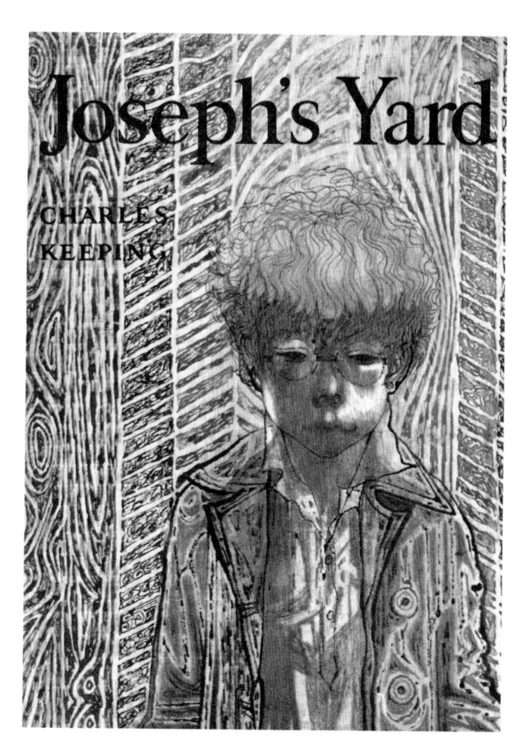

"... a wooden fence, stone paving and rusty old iron—that's all there was in this yard."

OTHER GREAT CHARLES KEEPING READS

Shaun and the Cart-Horse, 1966
Charley, Charlotte and the Golden Canary, 1967
Alfie and the Ferryboat, 1968
Through the Window, 1970

Frog and Toad Are Friends 1970

Arnold Lobel

Nationality | American, born 1933
Publisher | HarperCollins, USA
Award | Caldecott Honor Book, 1971
Theme | Friendship

5+

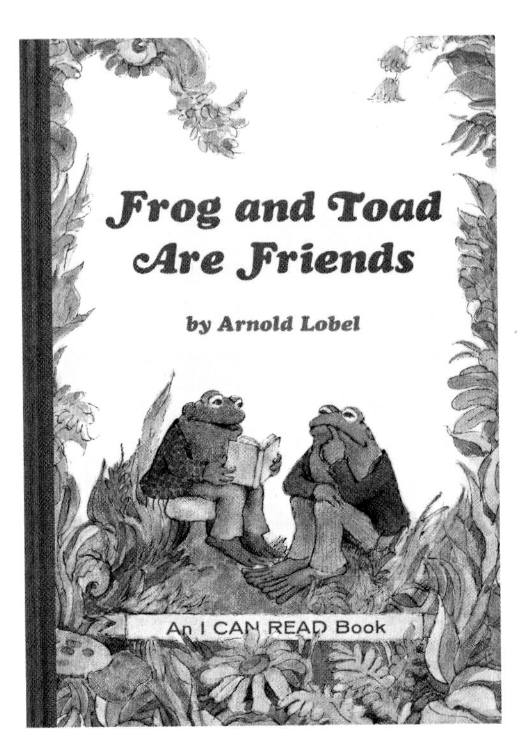

MORE BOOKS ABOUT BEST FRIENDS

Amos & Boris by William Steig, 1971
John Brown, Rose and the Midnight Cat by Jenny Wagner, 1977
Hey, Al by Arthur Yorinks, 1986
Henry and Mudge by Cynthia Rylant, 1987

Arnold Lobel wrote and illustrated more than seventy books for children. He won many awards along the way, including a Caldecott Honor and a Newbery Honor Award, but more importantly, his well-known Frog and Toad series has given millions of children a love of reading. The books have helped to teach young children to read on their own and taught them the importance of best friends.

Each book consists of five short stories written in an easy-to-read format that will help to boost the confidence of children who are beginning to read independently. *Frog and Toad Are Friends* is the first book in the series, and readers are introduced to the characters of Frog and Toad, who are quite different from each other yet the best of friends. The illustrations, although somber in tone, help children to figure out the words as they follow the adventures of these charming amphibians. Whether Frog and Toad are looking for lost buttons, welcoming the season of spring, going for a swim, or waiting for their mail to arrive, the sweet and caring relationship that exists between them is a delight. Young readers will laugh with easy-going Frog as he watches Toad try to make up a story, and they will cheer on Frog when he finally wakes up the irritable Toad who has been hibernating all winter. "'You have been asleep since November.' said Frog. 'Well then,' said Toad, 'A little more sleep will not hurt me.'"

"Toad said, 'Frog you are looking quite green.' 'But I always look green,' said Frog. 'I am a frog.'"

This book, the first of four, will warm the hearts of any would-be pen pal or anyone who has ever known what it is like to have a true best friend. **KD**

Mog the Forgetful Cat 1970

 Judith Kerr

Mog is "a very forgetful cat," who lives with Mr. and Mrs. Thomas and their children Debbie and Nicky. We learn that "Mog was nice but not very clever. She didn't understand a lot of things," and her forgetfulness gets her into a lot of trouble; there is a constant refrain of "Bother that cat!" from the succession of people that Mog manages to annoy.

Mog forgets all sorts of things, such as how to use her cat flap, which results in her sitting on—and crushing—the flowers in the window box. She eats Nicky's breakfast, sleeps on Mrs. Thomas's hat, creeps into Debbie's bedroom at night and licks her (which gives Debbie a nightmare about being eaten by a tiger), falls asleep on the television when Mr. Thomas

"She wanted to go back into the house but she couldn't remember how."

is trying to watch it, her tail obscuring the screen, and generally makes a nuisance of herself. The only person who always loves her is Debbie.

Thinking that she is not loved by anyone but Debbie makes Mog very sad so she runs away, although she does not get very far. She sits in the garden until she becomes scared of the dark and wants to get back inside. It is the middle of the night and when Mog sees a man in the kitchen she starts meowing to be let in. He is a burglar and Mog scares him so much that he drops his bulging bag of stolen goods, making a huge clattering noise and waking everyone up.

Caught in the act, it is the burglar's turn to say "Bother that cat!" but this time everyone in the family disagrees and hugs Mog. The policeman comments "What a remarkable cat." Mog gets a medal and is given an egg for breakfast every day. **LH**

Nationality | German/British, born 1923
Publisher | Collins, UK
Theme | Family, Adventure, Quirky, Animal stories

5+

Mog
the forgetful cat
Written and illustrated by Judith Kerr

OTHER WELL-LOVED CAT BOOKS

***Millions of Cats* by Wanda Gág, 1928**
***Cat That Lived a Million Times* by Yoko Sano, 1977**
***Mog and the Baby* by Judith Kerr, 1980**
***Slinky Malinki* by Lynley Dodd, 1992**
***Old Tom* by Leigh Hobbs, 1994**

Figgie Hobbin 1970

Charles Causley Pat Marriott

Nationality | English, born 1917 (author); English, born 1920 (illustrator)
Publisher | Macmillan, UK
Theme | Poetry

Charles Causley claimed that he never knew whether his poems were aimed at children or adults because they have different layers of meaning. Nonetheless, his clear and direct use of language and his sense of rhythm appeal to readers of all ages. Poems such as "I Saw a Jolly Hunter," which is in his poetry collection *Figgie Hobbin*, were influenced by the ballads and popular songs of Causley's youth when he played piano in a dance band. He is perhaps best known for his poem "Timothy Winters" ("Timothy Winters comes to school, with eyes as wide as a football pool"), which is much anthologized and is used extensively in schools. Causley, himself a former teacher, said that he could have lived comfortably off the reproduction fees alone.

The title poem reflects Causley's ties to Cornwall. It is the story of an old king of Cornwall who is offered an increasingly exotic selection of dishes but tells his servants that all he wants is Figgie Hobbin, a Cornish dish of sweet pastry, raisins, and currants. This collection has a real breadth of tone: Some poems are funny, such as "Colonel Fazackerley," which tells the tale of a soldier who buys an old castle complete with a ghost but believes that the specter is just a man on his way to a costume party; others are more introspective. "My Mother Saw a Dancing Bear" is deeply sad with its final lines: "They paid a penny for the dance, but what they saw was not the show; only in Bruin's aching eyes, far distant forest and the snow." The poems in *Figgie Hobbin* will make young readers laugh, but also pause for thought. **HJ**

"Hunter jolly eager—
Sight of jolly prey.
Forgot gun pointing
Wrong jolly way."

OTHER NOTABLE POETRY COLLECTIONS

The Book of Nonsense by Edward Lear, 1846
Cautionary Tales for Children by Hilaire Belloc, 1907
Old Possum's Book of Practical Cats by T.S. Eliot, 1939
Where the Sidewalk Ends by Shel Silverstein, 1974

5+

Hodja from Pjort 1970

Ole Lund Kirkegaard

Original Title | Hodja fra Pjort
Nationality | Danish, born 1940
Publisher | Gyldendal, Denmark
Theme | Adventure, Fantasy

Ole Lund Kirkegaard is one of Denmark's most celebrated children's authors, and *Hodja from Pjort* is among his most successful books.

Hodja is a small and very curious nine-year-old boy. He lives in the idyllic town of Pjort, in an imaginary country called Bulgislav. There the men wear red fezzes and colorful shoes, and the women have long flowing veils. Hodja's father is a tailor and he is also the most cross-eyed man in Pjort. He hopes that Hodja will one day take over his business; Hodja meanwhile has other plans. Only a child, but full of imagination, his main wish is to leave Pjort and discover a completely different world. As the locals come to know about the little boy's audacious dreams, they start to make fun of him. Luckily, Hodja meets the old man el-Faza, who listens to him and fulfills his dreams. He trusts Hodja with a flying red carpet with which he leaves Pjort to go to the capital Petto. After the boy arrives at a local inn and falls asleep, a villain rat steals the carpet and brings it to the sultan. Hodja is determined to get it back, however, and showing intelligence and courage he succeeds. On returning to Pjort, he feels safe from the thieves and, more importantly, is now full of new experiences.

Kirkegaard illustrated Hodja's tale with quirky little drawings that capture a faraway world. The reader learns about the differences between cultures and customs, and about the relationships and distinctions between grown-ups and children. Kirkegaard gives a voice to all sorts of children, whether naughty, well-behaved, or just a little bit out of the ordinary. **SML**

"East of the sun and west of the moon, seven wild winds shall carry you, east of the sun and west of the moon."

RECOMMENDED KIRKEGAARD READS

Little Virgil (Lille Virgil), 1967
Otto Is a Rhinoceros (Otto is een neushoorn), 1972
Rubber Tarzan (Pudding Tarzan), 1975

Tow Truck Pluk 1971

Annie M. G. Schmidt Fiep Westendorp

Nationality | Dutch, born 1911 (author); Dutch born 1916 (illustrator)
Publisher | Em Querido's Uitgeverij, Netherlands
Theme | Friendship, Animal stories

5+

Annie M.G. Schmidt
Pluk van de Petteflet
Met illustraties van Fiep Westendorp

Pluk always rides in a red pick-up truck and lives entirely on his own in the small turret room of the Petteflet, which he has moved into because he has no parents. But he does have many friends. Pluk is a clever little boy—he is friendly and always prepared to help people and animals. Zaza, a cockroach, also lives in his room, along with his best friend, the pigeon Dolly, who conveys messages whenever necessary.

In this book, Schmidt gives her views on topical themes—such as the housing shortage, ecological woes, and even city-planning measures—but from the point of view of the child. She believes that young readers should know what happens in the world. By starting from the child's point of view she

"'I have a house and a roof over my head,' he thought. 'And I have two friends. No, three!'"

can introduce all kinds of strange characters into the book, such as the park janitor who finds concrete and gravel much more convenient than plants and animals, or the "*krullevaar*" ("curlicue"), a cranelike bird in danger of extinction. No situation is ever too scary or difficult for Pluk, who always finds a solution.

Tow Truck Pluk (*Pluk van de Petteflet*) is a quest for a safe world and at the same time it is a struggle against injustice, all expressed in a flowing narrative. Pluk's views as a defender of freedom reflects those of the late 1960s. Children's books critics were very enthusiastic about the book when it was published and praised it for its combination of elements of fantasy, clear language, humor, and contemporary themes. Meanwhile, Pluk has grown into a children's hero, and his picture often adorns garments and posters throughout the Netherlands. **AD**

OTHER TALES BY ANNIE M. G. SCHMIDT

This is Sebastian the Spider (Dit is de spin Sebastiaan), 1951
Jip and Janneke (Jip en Janneke), 1953
A for Abel (De A van Abeltje), 1955
Wiplala, 1957

Leo the Late Bloomer 1971

Robert Kraus Jose Aruego

This story addresses a common parental anxiety: that their children are not keeping up with their peers. Unlike his friends, Leo cannot read, write, or draw. He is also "a sloppy eater" and "he never said a word." Robert Kraus's minimal text unerringly picks up the kind of remarks that children might overhear from adults. In this case, it is Leo's father who is the worrier. Leo's mother is confident that Leo is "a late bloomer" and counsels patience: "A watched bloomer doesn't bloom."

Kraus's text lightheartedly picks on those areas that are commonly regarded as milestones in development and provides reassurance to parents and particularly children. The story lampoons Leo's father's fears, vindicates Leo's mother's faith, and, when Leo blooms,

"[Leo] also spoke. . . . It was a whole sentence. And that sentence was . . . 'I made it!'"

properly gives credit to Leo for his achievement. Aruego's illustrations create a wacky technicolor animal world around Kraus's words. Leo and his precocious friends—an owl, an elephant, a snake, a plover, and a crocodile—are vibrant and cuddly, at home in a landscape where it snows in winter and the spring blooms with eye-bogglingly bright tulips and daffodils. Leo is depicted with great empathy, and all the fun that Kraus and Aruego conjure around him serves to underline the foolishness of measuring one child's progress against another's. Leo's friends can read, write, and draw; but when asked to speak they can only hoot, thrump, hiss, pip, and crunch.

Leo the Late Bloomer was the first of a successful series of animal picture books about family life that was written by Kraus and illustrated by Aruego and Ariane Dewy. **CB**

Nationality | American, born 1925 (author); Filipino, born 1932 (illustrator)
Publisher | Windmill Books, USA
Theme | Family, Animal stories

5+

OTHER GREAT ANIMAL FABLES

The Jungle Book **by Rudyard Kipling, 1894**
Why Mosquitoes Buzz in People's Ears **by Verna Aardema, 1975**
The Enormous Crocodile **by Roald Dahl, 1978**
The Widemouthed Frog **by Francine Vidal, 2001**

5+

Amos & Boris 1971

William Steig

Nationality | American, born 1907
Publisher | Farrar, Straus and Giroux, USA
Award | A.L.A. Notable Children's Book
Theme | Friendship

Before William Steig started writing children's books, he was a respected cartoonist at the *New Yorker*. In 1968, at the age of sixty-one, when most people are contemplating retirement, Steig wrote his first children's book. From that point on—while he continued his work for the *New Yorker* and other adult publications—he never stopped creating brilliant books for children.

Amos & Boris tells the story of a most unlikely friendship between Amos the mouse and Boris the whale. Unlikely it may be, yet it is one of the most charming tales of friendship in children's literature. It describes the devotion of true friends, who on the surface have nothing at all in common, except good hearts and a desire to help their fellow mammal. Amos sets out to sea in his homemade boat, the *Rodent*, and soon finds himself in need of rescue. Boris sees Amos's plight and offers to help him get back to his home on dry land. When they discover that they are both mammals, even though one lives on land and the other in the sea, a close bond is formed. Mouse and whale learn to respect and admire each other's differences, and they wonder in awe at the different worlds they inhabit.

And there will come a day, long after Boris has gone back to his life in the sea, and Amos has gone back to his life on land, when the tiny mouse will have a chance to repay the favor and rescue the great whale. This is a timeless story of the true nature of friendship, brought to life by a master author and illustrator. **KD**

5+

Balloon Cat 1972

Keiko Sena

Nationality | Japanese, born 1932
Publisher | Fukuinkan Shoten, Japan
Translator | Richard McNamara, Peter Howlett
Theme | Family

Balloon Cat is part of Keiko Sena's Crying and Blubbering series. The picture book tells the story of an angry little boy cat who gets extremely annoyed very easily. He becomes so angry that his head inflates and he floats off into the sky like a balloon.

Sena was a pioneer of Japanese children's literature. She completed an apprenticeship with the acclaimed artist Takeo Takei and since then has written more than thirty-five books; her most popular work is the I Won't Do It series. This series, like the Crying and Blubbering books, always includes a narrative that gives a touch of the surreal to an everyday situation.

In *Balloon Cat*, the young cat is always angry, huffing and puffing, and pouting. The cat is so upset and frustrated that he does not want to share anything with his sister, he only wants to eat lollipops for dinner, and he does not want to put his belongings away. His face starts to swell and swell until it gets so big that he floats away: "Huff! Puff! So puffed up with anger that he inflated!"

The moral of the story, hidden within this hilarious pretext, is that there are consequences to every action, especially if one refuses to do what one is told. Perhaps surprisingly, Sena does not provide a happy ending to her didactic tale; instead, the balloon cat is left to float off alone into the unknown, leaving the mother cat yowling below. The illustrations are unique, colored paper cutouts. This gives the pictures a textured, furry look that invites young readers to reach out and touch. **RA**

5+

Alexander and the Terrible, Horrible, No Good, Very Bad Day 1972

Judith Viorst Ray Cruz

Nationality | American, born 1931 (author); American, born 1933 (illustrator)
Publisher | Simon and Schuster, USA
Theme | Family, School

We have all had one of those days when absolutely everything goes wrong. Children have those days, too, although they do not always understand the feelings of frustration that result from a really bad day. This classic title from acclaimed children's author Judith Viorst has sold more than two million copies and helps explain the feelings that are experienced when you have had a truly terrible day. Young children will easily understand and relate to this story in which everything goes wrong for Alexander.

When Alexander realizes that he fell asleep with gum in his mouth and now it is in his hair, readers know that they are in for a wild ride. Things go quickly from bad to worse: "When I got out of bed this morning I tripped on the skateboard and by mistake I dropped my sweater in the sink while the water was running. . . ." On the way to school, he has to sit in the middle seat; his teacher likes a classmate's art better than his; Mom forgot to put dessert in his lunch bag; a family trip to the dentist finds "a cavity only in me"; there are lima beans for dinner and kissing on the television; and he has to wear his railroad pajamas at bedtime.

The repetition of Alexander's laments will have children chanting along and laughing as they think of their own "very bad days." **KD**

The Giant Jam Sandwich
Story and pictures by John Vernon Lord
with verses by Janet Burroway

5+

The Giant Jam Sandwich 1972

Janet Burroway John Vernon Lord

Nationality | American, born 1936 (author); English, born 1939 (illustrator)
Publisher | Jonathan Cape, UK
Theme | Rhyming stories

The little village of Itching Down is in crisis after being invaded by wasps. At a hurriedly convened meeting in the local hall, Bap the Baker comes up with the notion of trapping all the troublesome wasps in a giant jam sandwich.

A loaf of bread the size of a small hill is towed to Farmer Seed's field, where it is cut in two by six strong men using a huge saw. Pulled by eight horses over to a massive tablecloth in an adjoining field, one half of the sandwich is then spread thickly with truckloads of butter and strawberry jam. Easily tempted but then hopelessly stuck, the wasps are doubly trapped when the other slice of bread is lowered onto them by four helicopters plus one flying tractor. The village duly celebrates the insect's demise with a dance.

Told in verse, this widely translated picture book has always had universal appeal. John Vernon Lord's illustrations are a particular delight. Drawing on memories of his own father, who was a baker, Lord re-creates a gentle rural atmosphere in meticulous detail. Various village dignitaries, each drawn with distinctive personalities of their own, stand outside beautifully drawn little shops. Hills and a windmill form the background to Farmer Seed's field, where there is enough going on to keep young readers entertained long after the story comes to its end. **NT**

Dinosaurs and All That Rubbish 1972

Michael Foreman

"At last the rocket was ready but there was nowhere for it to be launched. Everywhere was piled high with heaps of waste."

Nationality | English, born 1938
Publisher | Hamish Hamilton, UK
Theme | Science and nature, Fantasy, Animal stories

Dinosaurs have taken over the Earth and they are stamping and stomping all over the place. They are dancing merrily on the roads to break them up and they are clearing up all the piles of trash that careless humans have left behind. Michael Foreman's thought-provoking environmental tale is perhaps even more relevant today than when it was first published in 1972, and his watercolor illustrations add a real sense of magic to the book.

When the dinosaurs have finished cleaning up, a person returns in a rocket from a far distant star. He sees that the Earth is a beautiful place now, full of flowers and animals. He asks for a small part of it back, and the dinosaurs respond that he is free to take some land but that it also belongs to everyone and we must all take care of it.

Dinosaurs and all that Rubbish is widely used by teachers as a way of talking about environmental issues because, instead of preaching, Foreman uses gentle humor to get his message across. The book has also been adapted as a stage play for use in schools. Foreman says of his work: "I'm always conscious of putting in things a child hasn't yet understood or experienced. That way, they ask questions of adults and then it becomes a shared experience."

Foreman's early work, which includes *War and Peas*, often tackles political issues such as pacifism and inequality but he has also illustrated more than fifty books by classic writers such as Charles Dickens and Rudyard Kipling, and contemporary writers such as Terry Jones and Michael Morpurgo. **HJ**

MORE ECO-FRIENDLY STORIES

A Tree Is Nice **by Janice May Udry, 1956**
Where the Forest Meets the Sea **by Jeannie Baker, 1988**
Oi! Get Off Our Train **by John Burningham, 1989**
Song of the Earth **by Mary Hoffman, 1995**

5+

The Companions 1972

Lygia Bojunga Nunes

Original Title | Os colegas
Nationality | Brazilian, born 1932
Publisher | Sabia, Brazil
Theme | Animal stories, Friendship

In *The Companions* (first published as *Os colegas*), a young rabbit is abandoned by his family and left to fend for himself. He soon meets and befriends two other animals with whom he embarks on adventures: a bear who has escaped from the zoo and a pampered dog who has run away from home to be free.

When the dog and the bear are captured, the usually frightened rabbit unexpectedly finds the courage to rescue the dog, who eventually joins him to rescue their mutual friend from captivity: "Who would have thought that he, a rabbit, would find the courage for such a daring enterprise?"

Lygia Bojunga Nunes has been widely praised (she won the prestigious Astrid Lindgren Memorial Award in 2004) for contrasting oppression and freedom at a level that young readers can understand. The author dissolves the boundaries between fantasy and reality with all the exhilarating ease of a child at play. In her dramatic and word-of-mouth-style narratives, where animals are endowed with human characteristics, the reader can directly relate to the dreams and fantasies of her characters. In a deeply original way she fuses playfulness, poetic beauty, and absurd humor with social critique, a love of freedom, and a strong empathy with the vulnerable.

The Companions was Lygia Bojunga's (the addition of Nunes is her pen name) first children's book, and she has since won many awards. Bojunga's style enables the young reader to enter directly into the dreams of her principal characters and to share in their experiences. **LB**

The Real Thief 1973

William Steig

Nationality | American, born 1907
Publisher | Farrar, Straus and Giroux, USA
Award | A.L.A. Notable Children's Book
Theme | Friendship, Animal stories

The Real Thief is a meditation on greed, guilt, and the importance of friendship. William Steig's tale of a mysterious theft in an otherwise happy and peaceful animal kingdom explores the feelings of loneliness and injustice that come from being falsely accused and shows that a solid reputation and good standing in the community are not always defense enough against rumor.

Gawain is the goose who guards the treasure of King Basil the Bear. He is meticulous in carrying out his duty, and yet one day he notices that the pile of rubies seems smaller than usual. Indeed, there are twenty-nine missing. In the following days more and more treasure goes missing until finally the famous Kalikak diamond is stolen. Despite his honest reputation, Gawain is put on trial for the thefts. His friends, at first supportive, desert him as the seemingly irrefutable evidence is laid before them. Unable to face the betrayal of his beloved king and friends, Gawain denounces them, proclaims his innocence, and escapes from the courtroom, flying out of the window. Meanwhile, the real thief has been observing the proceedings. What begins as some innocent "borrowing" on the part of Derek the mouse grows into the crime spree that lands Gawain in exile. Derek is tormented by his conscience when he sees the consequences of his actions, but can he find the courage to admit his crimes and clear Gawain's name?

Steig writes calmly, clearly, and compassionately about how actions can have far-reaching consequences, accompanied by his own delightful illustrations. **PC**

5+

Mind Your Own Business 1974

Michael Rosen Quentin Blake

Nationality | English, born 1946 (author); English, born 1932 (illustrator)
Publisher | André Deutsch, UK
Theme | Poetry

It has often been said that *Mind Your Own Business* opened the door to a new kind of poetry for children. The content is about the real experiences of real children expressed in the sounds and forms of common speech: "Late last night / I lay in bed / driving buses / in my head." This style of poetry became known as "urchin verse," and, although there were critics who lamented the loss of tradition, Michael Rosen's work very quickly became popular with children, teachers, and parents for its immediacy. The poems are accessible and shot through with humor, but they are by no means lightweight. They deal with subjects such as loneliness, fear, siblings, parental authority, and physical changes. They also speak about the child's place in the natural world of fields and woods, rain and wind, birds, spiders, dogs, and the unforgettable cats in the snow dunes.

The collection of poems was originally intended for adult readers as an exploration of Rosen's own childhood. It is this authenticity along with a sense of honesty that sets the works apart from lesser imitators. It can be argued that, twenty-five years on, children experience the world in a very different way, but the poems still speak to a contemporary audience in a vivid manner.

The illustrations are by Rosen's favorite illustrator and the first British Children's Laureate, Quentin Blake, whose compulsive movement of line perfectly matches Rosen's breathing, living poetry. **WO**

Where the Sidewalk Ends 1974

Shel Silverstein

Nationality | American, born 1930
Publisher | HarperCollins, USA
Award | A.L.A. Notable Children's Book
Theme | Poetry

Shel Silverstein is often considered to be the "bad boy" of children's literature. His slightly menacing picture on the book jacket is often enough to send softhearted children running from the room in fear. It is difficult to categorize Silverstein's poems, or to which age group they are aimed. As he noted, "I would hope that people, no matter what age, would find something to identify with in my books, pick up one and experience a personal sense of discovery."

The poems range from the sublime to the ridiculous: "Teddy said it was a hat, / So I put it on / Now Dad is saying, 'Where the heck's the toilet plunger gone?'" With subjects that are ordinary and extraordinary, such as nose-picking, nail-biting, being eaten by snakes, and decapitation, these poems are by turns tender, romantic, funny, gross, unsavory, and sweet. In other words they are just like children, and that is what makes them perfect reading material for children.

Where the Sidewalk Ends provides great fun for families who enjoy reading poems together. Silverstein's poems take readers to a world where you might get eaten by a boa constrictor or write a poem from inside a lion; you could be one inch tall and ride a worm to school; or your belly button may cave in or your head might fall off. You could meet a boy who turns into a television set or a girl who eats a whale. Whatever else might happen (and plenty does), you and your children will laugh together while reading these poems and you will never ever be bored. **KD**

"He opened his jaws so wide / That the dentist climbed inside."

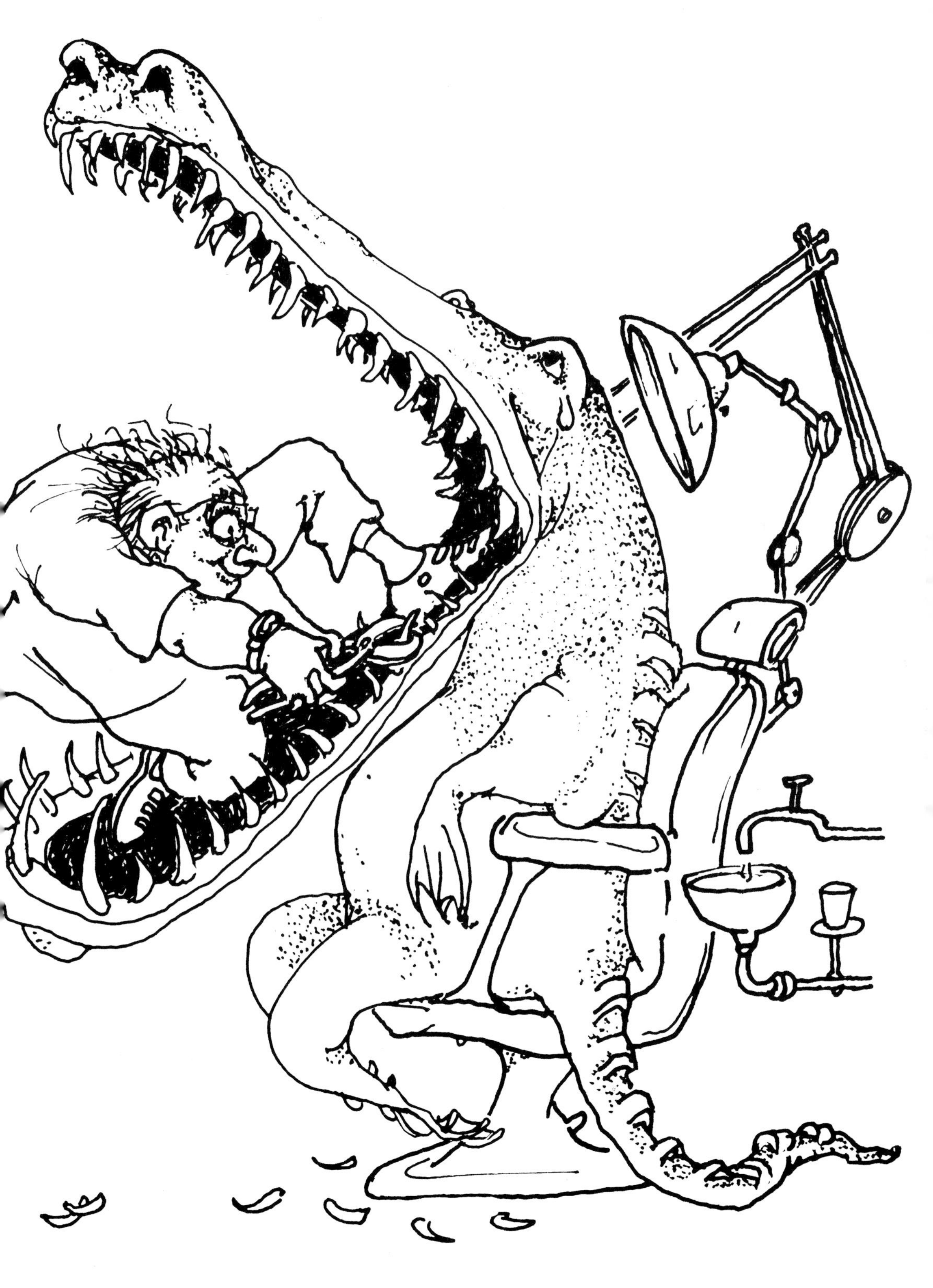

The Worst Witch 1974

Jill Murphy

Nationality | English, born 1949
Publisher | Puffin, UK
Theme | Magical stories, School, Favorite characters, Friendship

5+

Mildred Hubble is the worst witch in the whole of Miss Cackle's Academy: Her broomstick—smashed in half after only two days at the school—is now rather difficult to control; her cat is not black but tabby; and her spells have a nasty habit of going horribly wrong, which is amusing for readers but troublesome for Mildred. On top of all this, Mildred has made an enemy of Ethel, the spiteful teacher's pet whom she turned into a pig after a sparring match. Matters are even worse because the teacher in question is the humorless Miss Hardbroom, pictured with long thin face and hair drawn back into an unforgiving bun.

When Miss Hardbroom's class has to perform a flying display at Halloween, all begins well, but readers, aware that Ethel has already laid a spell on the unfortunate Mildred's broom, wait expectantly for the inevitable disaster to unfold. When it does, the chagrined Mildred runs away in the middle of the night only to encounter a group of evil witches who are plotting to overthrow the school. Armed with her spell book, she saves the day and thereby earns her peers a welcome half-day holiday.

The story offers an appealing blend of the much-loved staples of witchcraft stories (long black cloaks and pointed hats, cauldrons and invisibility potions) with the high jinks, stern teachers, and strong friendships of school stories. These elements have served to make this story enormously popular since its publication more than twenty years before *Harry Potter* brought boarding schools and witchcraft into the limelight. **KA**

Strega Nona 1975

Tomie DePaola

Nationality | American, born 1934
Publisher | Prentice Hall, USA
Award | Caldecott Honor Book, 1976
Theme | Magical stories, Fairy tales

Strega Nona tells a story that appears in many different guises in many cultures. It is about the perils of imperfectly understood knowledge and of getting above oneself.

Strega Nona is an old wise woman who takes on an apprentice, Big Anthony. A condition of the job is that Big Anthony must never touch Strega Nona's pasta pot. But, having overheard Strega Nona singing to her pot and seeing the pot magically produce limitless amounts of pasta, Big Anthony is tempted to try it for himself. His opportunity comes when Strega Nona goes off on a visit; the result is both predictable and catastrophic. The town is flooded with pasta, and when Strega Nona returns to put things right, Big Anthony must eat the surplus as his penance.

The story is set in Renaissance Italy, in a town with a *piazza*, red-tiled roofs, and the townspeople dressed according to the period with some strikingly unusual hats. The intriguing illustrations are a series of framed pictures blending comic-strip art with the techniques of early Renaissance artists such as Giotto. The story's characters are simply and clearly shown either in profile or facing the reader with little use of naturalism or perspective. It is like watching a play, acted out against a backdrop, with the text as a voiceover narrative. The result is dramatic: humorous in its understanding of human foibles and distinctive in its mix of modern and traditional. It is perhaps this ability to present traditional stories in a way that is new that has made Tomie DePaola's retellings of folk tales the best known of his many picture books. **CB**

The townspeople fight against a flood of pasta. 

Why Mosquitoes Buzz in People's Ears 1975

Verna Aardema D. and L. Dillon

Nationality | American, born 1911 (author); American, born 1933 (both illustrators)
Publisher | Dial Press, USA
Theme | Myths and legends

In Verna Aardema's retelling of this ancient African myth, she explains the importance of telling the truth by illustrating the consequences of telling lies. The story is cumulative—each action by an animal affects the action of the next animal, with the ultimate result that the sun does not rise in the morning. The tale is entrancing, and the illustrations by Diane and Leo Dillon help to guide young readers through the story.

Mosquito triggers the disaster by telling Iguana a silly fib. Distressed by what he has heard, Iguana puts sticks in his ears to plug them, which inadvertently begins a series of misunderstandings. Later, when Python says good morning, Iguana does not hear him and thus appears to ignore him. Python then assumes that Iguana is plotting against him, so he hides in a rabbit hole, which obviously scares Rabbit. And so this African legend continues, until finally the chain of mishaps ends in the death of a baby owlet. Mother Owl is so sorrowful at the loss of her child as a result of the mayhem that she refuses to hoot and wake up the sun, and so it does not rise.

The animals realize that Mosquito is to blame. Eventually all is resolved, and jungle life returns to normal. Mosquito learns her lesson and recognizes the importance of the truth. Repentant, she gives up telling lies, but instead she adopts a worse habit. According to the legend, this is why mosquitoes buzz in people's ears: they are simply asking if everyone is still angry with them. **KD**

Mr. and Mrs. Pig's Evening Out 1976

Mary Rayner

Nationality | English, born 1933
Publisher | Macmillan, UK; Atheneum Books, USA
Theme | Folktales, Family, Animal stories

As the parents of ten lively piglets who are all the same age, it is hardly surprising that Mr. and Mrs. Pig occasionally want to enjoy a night on their own. When they finally get the chance for an evening out, they are in such a hurry to leave that they do not notice anything strange about the babysitter sent by the agency. Even the fact that she is named Mrs. Wolf and has a pointy nose, furry tail, and dark hairy legs fails to ring any warning bells with Mrs. Pig.

Once she is left on her own, Mrs. Wolf wastes no time before switching on the oven and snatching a little piglet for her supper. But the high-pitched squeals arouse the piglet's brothers and sisters, who together trap the snarling Mrs. Wolf under a heavy blanket. Tied up and left on the kitchen floor, the big, bad wolf is finally thrown into the river when Mr. Pig returns home.

Mary Rayner's witty illustrations bring this ostensibly alarming but in fact highly entertaining traditional story up to date. All the activities that the excited little pigs get up to—from jumping on the bed to fighting with wooden swords—are exactly the sort of thing small children will know from their own lives. Mrs. Wolf is so obviously not the respectable babysitter she is taken for that all young readers will be well prepared for her sudden change of behavior once the coast is clear. As with all the best folktales, there is also a sensible warning (about not trusting strangers) amid all the fun. **NT**

Mr. and Mrs. Pig dressed up for a night on the town.

BP

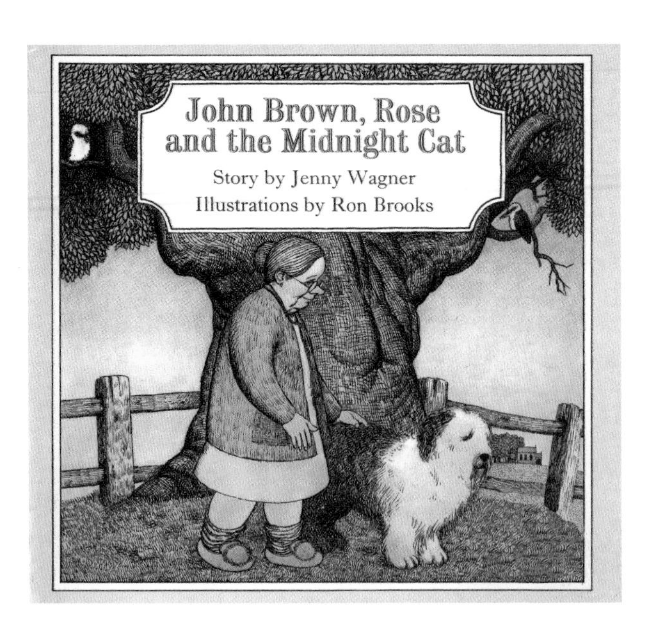

5+

John Brown, Rose and the Midnight Cat 1977

Jenny Wagner Ron Brooks

Nationality | Australian, born 1939 (author); Australian, born 1948 (illustrator)
Publisher | Kestrel Books, UK
Theme | Friendship, Illness and death

This Australian classic is guaranteed to give you a warm inner glow. Like all good picture books, it is multilayered. On one level, it is a simple story about an old lady, her dog, and a stray cat; on another, it imparts a philosophical message about learning to let go and accepting the inevitability of the death of loved ones.

Widow Rose and her dog John Brown live together in an old farmhouse in the countryside. They lead a companionable existence, pottering around the farm and dozing in front of the fire. One night a black cat appears in the garden, and their relationship is never the same again. Rose wants to let the Midnight Cat in, but John Brown is content to let things stay as they are. Eventually, John Brown accepts that change—and all that it implies—is an inevitable part of life.

Jenny Wagner writes with the lyrical simplicity of a poet. Each word of the text is carefully chosen and perfectly pitched. Her beautifully nuanced sentences are short and to the point, and yet a wider world is implied in every phrase. Ron Brooks visually re-creates this world. His setting is a delightfully old-fashioned home, with its own history. Rose is a cuddly grandmotherly figure, John Brown is a large and fluffy sheepdog, and the Midnight Cat is suitably sleek, with an edge of menace. The interweaving of Wagner's concise text and Brooks's gentle but compelling watercolor illustrations, with their carefully crosshatched details, strikes just the right note, drawing the reader into this poignant tale of love, companionship, and loss. **SOR**

Come Away from the Water, Shirley 1977

John Burningham

Nationality | English, born 1936
Publisher | Jonathan Cape, UK
Award | *Horn Book* Fanfare
Theme | Family, Adventure

It is too cold to go swimming, so Shirley's parents get comfortable in their deck chairs on the beach and tell their little daughter to go and play. Although Shirley's mother cannot stop fussing ("Don't stroke that dog, Shirley, you don't know where he's been,") her daughter is soon miles away in her own imaginary world, all wordlessly pictured here by the brilliant John Burningham.

Readers follow the story with delight as Shirley enjoys an adventure with her new dog friend in which she is captured by pirates who try to force her to walk the plank. She then imagines herself fighting back and after that rowing away in her own boat in order to find some buried treasure. When it is time for her to stop daydreaming and return home with her rather ordinary parents, Shirley also brings her own private story to an end. She imagines herself dressed up in all the jewels she has found as she sails away with the dog into the night.

Children know how powerful the imagination can be at a young age, and the contrast between Shirley's wild fantasies and the prosaic concerns of her parents will be one that they may often have experienced themselves. They will also enjoy Burningham's over-the-top pirates, all so fierce and fearless until Shirley stands up to them, after which they tumble over in comic despair. Children who have already discussed their fantasies with others will surely love this book; those who have kept such imaginings a secret may enjoy a delicious sense of recognition. **NT**

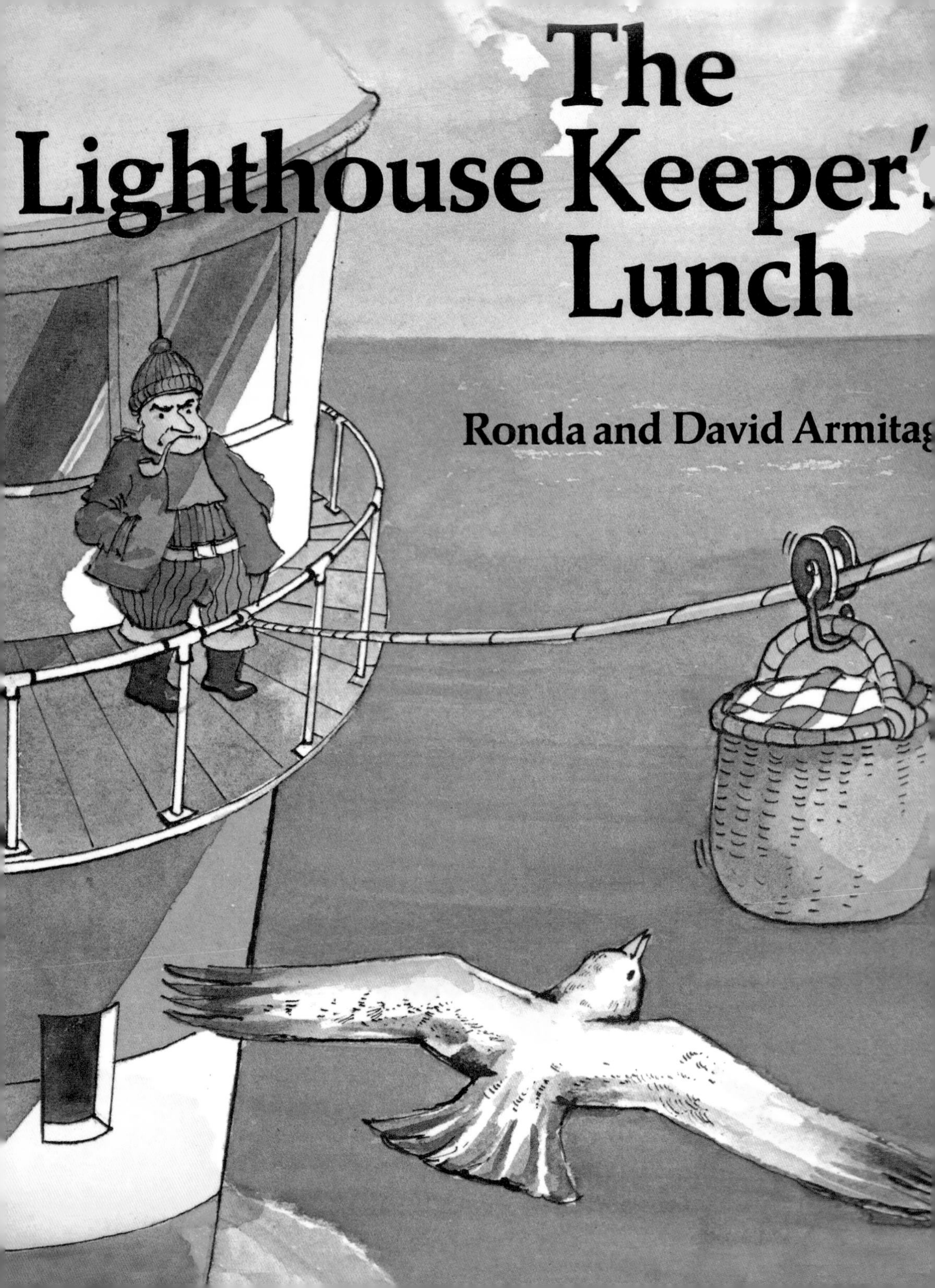
The
Lighthouse Keeper'
Lunch
Ronda and David Armitag

The Lighthouse Keeper's Lunch 1977

Ronda Armitage   David Armitage

Nationality | New Zealander, born 1943 (author); Australian, born 1943 (illustrator)
Publisher | André Deutsch, UK
Theme | Family, Quirky

Usually Mrs. Grinling packs her husband's lunch every morning in a strong shopping basket. She then winds it along a wire extending from the couple's clifftop cottage to the lighthouse out at sea where he works. But one day three scavenging seagulls descend on this comfortable arrangement, eating all Mrs. Grinling's delicious food before it has a chance to arrive.

A napkin spread over the lunch next time still does not deter these greedy birds, nor does the unwilling presence of the family cat in an accompanying basket the time after that. But when Mrs. Grinling substitutes extra strong mustard sandwiches for her normal ones, the birds have had enough and decide to prey on a local fisherman's picnic instead.

Most young readers like reading about food and may have some sneaking sympathy for the hungry birds that descend on the mixed seafood salad, frosted cookies, peach surprise, and other delicacies with which Mrs. Grinling delights her husband. These meals are then splendidly brought to life by David Armitage, splashing paint around with the same generosity that the lighthouse keeper's wife brings to her own cooking. Small children also tend to be fascinated by lighthouses, so elegant by day and so bright and focused by night. Ending with the contented couple back to their normal routine, this affectionately told and illustrated story has remained a favorite for more than thirty years. **NT**

Teo Discovers the World 1977

Violeta Denou

Nationality | Pseudonym for a Spanish collective established in 1968
Publisher | Timun Mas, Spain
Theme | Favorite characters, Friendship

Teo is a character with reddish hair, overalls, and a striped jersey, who was created in 1977 by three designers: Asunción Esteban, Carlota Goyta, and Ana Vidal. In spite of the popularity of their creation, they have managed to preserve their anonymity and have continued the Teo books for more than thirty years. The first collection, *Teo Discovers the World (Teo descubre el mundo)*, contained three titles: *Teo by Train*, *Teo by Boat*, and *Teo by Plane*. This was followed by other collections created in response to the interests of young readers, such as *I am Teo!* (*¡Soy Teo!*), which featured calligraphic lettering, and *My First Teo Books* (*Mis primeros libros de Teo*), books without text intended to initiate a child into the habit of reading.

Teo is a good-natured, inquisitive child who is curious about the environment around him. The stories about him attract early readers with their simple, everyday content and their very detailed illustrations of situations that children feel close to and can readily identify with.

Even without the support of major advertising campaigns, decades later Teo has become a phenomenon, with a total of 150 volumes published and six million copies sold, in addition to television series, board games, and all kinds of merchandise. After all this time, Teo is still wearing the same overalls and sailor shirt, he does not need the latest video games to amuse himself, and he is still living in the idyllic world of a perfect childhood. **EB**

On the Antilles Sea in a Paper Boat 1977

Nicolás Guillén Rapi Diego

Nationality | Cuban, born 1902 (author); details unknown (illustrator)
Publisher | Lóguez Ediciones, Spain
Theme | Poetry

This book (*Por el mar de las Antillas anda un barco de papel* in Spanish) is an exceptional collection of poems for children, which takes its title from the first lines of the first poem: "Through the West Indian Sea / Sails a little paper boat / It sails and sails / Without a rudder." It was written by one of the greatest Cuban poets of the twentieth century, Nicolás Guillén, known as the country's national poet. The highly poetic use of language in the book is all the more amazing because it remains simple and intelligible to very young readers.

The most famous poems include the eponymous "*Por el mar de las Antillas*," about a paper boat containing two sailors, a black woman, and a Spaniard that travels from island to island in the Caribbean Sea, shooting sugar balls against the enemy's chocolate cannons. "*Que te corta corta*" is a humorous tongue-twister for Spanish speakers and a hilarious challenge for foreigners. Another poem tells the story of two boys, Sapito and Sapón, who try to attract their parents' attention by pretending to be ill. The poems are simple and very short and are enhanced by illustrations reflecting the colors and vitality of the Caribbean world, something that Guillén was keen to celebrate. The extraordinary charm of the book lies in the playful innocence of the world it evokes, its poetic language, and its musical rhymes, which together make the poems so memorable and enjoyable. **LB**

Fungus the Bogeyman 1977

Raymond Briggs

Nationality | English, born 1934
Publisher | Hamish Hamilton, UK
Theme | Fantasy, Adventure, Quirky, Favorite characters

Five years after *Father Christmas*, Raymond Briggs created another outsider, but a much more outrageous one. Like Father Christmas, Fungus is a hardworking man with an important mission to carry out (and is rather more good-humored about it than Father Christmas). But the presents Fungus distributes are not the kind that anyone wants. He is a Bogeyman, who comes by night from a nether world to bring to the "Surface" all the inexplicable stains, smells, slime, muck, and rot that apparently appears from nowhere.

Every aspect of Fungus's life is an offence to Surface people. The Bogey world turns Surface preoccupations upside down: A Bogey family calls for help to block a working lavatory. Bogeys prefer their food to be rotten, they marinate their clothes overnight to make sure they are nicely damp and smelly for morning, and they are revolted by the Surface preference for cleanliness and dryness. Fungus confounds expectations; like all Bogeys, he is an intellectual who waits patiently at the "liberality" for "*Lady Chatterley's Bogey*" and "*A Room with a Bogey*." He thinks poetic thoughts as he rides to work on his Bogeybike; he adores his wife Mildew and son Mould.

Fungus became a cult hero for students who enjoyed the mixture of the squalid and the cerebral. His world is so finely detailed and the obsessive wordplay so richly composted that readers will never grow out of Bogeyphilia, but younger children can start by enjoying the grossness for its own sake. **GB**

Fungus the Bogeyman
RAYMOND BRIGGS

Loon's Necklace 1977

William Toye   Elizabeth Cleaver

Nationality | Canadian, born 1926 (author); Canadian, born 1939 (illustrator)
Publisher | Oxford University Press, Canada
Theme | Myths and legends, Fairy tales

According to native Canadian Indian legend, loons (known as divers in Europe) can cure blindness. The story goes that an old man gave the loon his precious shell necklace out of gratitude when he regained his sight. The necklace landed around the bird's neck and some loose shells sprinkled onto its back, and that is why the bird now has a white collar and speckled body. *The Loon's Necklace* pairs this native story of natural justice with vivid and faux-naive pictures. Award-winning illustrator Elizabeth Cleaver uses collage techniques such as torn paper, paper cutouts, and lino cuts to bring the Canadian landscape to life.

In the story, an old man is struggling to find food to feed his family because he is blind. The witch tricks a young boy into sharing the food that he has caught but then refuses to share it with the old man. As she denies a stranger food, the wind eventually brings her house down. In contrast, the honest loon helps the man get his sight back, and at the end of the story is shown soaring free across a wild plain. "When loon called to them from far away, his cry was no longer always sad and lonely. Often it was a long, joyful trill. 'Loon is laughing!' the old man would say. 'How proud he is of my necklace!'"

Cleaver was one of the first authors and illustrators to use stories that had previously been passed on primarily by word of mouth, and she repeatedly wrote about Canada's folklore history. The book's simplistic language and magic landscapes aim to balance entertainment with educating children about the heritage of their land. **SD**

A Walk in the Park 1977

Anthony Browne

Nationality | English, born 1946
Publisher | Hamish Hamilton, UK
Award | Kurt Maschler Emil Award
Theme | Fantasy

Anthony Browne's second picture book set out themes that he returned to years later in *Voices in the Park*. In the later book he cast primates as the four humans who each experience a day in a park differently. Here we encounter the original human characters. A girl called Smudge and her shabbily dressed father (Mr. Smith) meet a well-heeled, tight-lipped woman (Mrs. Smythe) and her timid son, Charles, in the park. Albert, the Smiths' boisterous mongrel, meets Victoria, the Smythes' pedigree Labrador. The dogs quickly bridge the social gulf and, a little later, so do the children. The adults, however, continue to inhabit separate universes.

Using many references to Surrealist paintings, Browne shows how the park visitors are transformed by their experience. When they enter the park it is winter, but the trees pass through the four seasons, and it is summer in the flower bed. The children climb a tree where night has fallen in the upper branches. A man walks an apple on a leash; a woman pushes a dog in a stroller; Santa Claus kicks an apple.

Compared to the toothbrush sticking out of the Smiths' chimney, the eye in the middle of the Smythes' front door looks almost normal, as does the topiary figure of Mrs. Smythe in her fancy coat, hat, and fox fur. When Smudge and her father get home, the stuffed dog and gramophone in the junk pile outside their house mimic the His Master's Voice advertisement. The longer you look at the pages, the more there is to see in this unusual and absorbing picture book that satirizes social class. **GB**

Miss Nelson Is Missing! 1977

Harry Allard   James Marshall

Nationality | American, born 1928 (author); American, born 1942 (illustrator)
Publisher | Houghton Mifflin, USA
Theme | School

The team of Harry Allard and James Marshall is responsible for many classic children's titles—produced both together and individually. The highly acclaimed *Miss Nelson* series is perfect for preschoolers and young children who might be worried about going to school: what their teacher will be like, how to behave, how to make friends, and all the other attendant school-age issues. Allard's ability to see the humor in any situation and to see it from the perspective of a child, coupled with Marshall's amusing illustrations, makes this laugh-out-loud story one that children will never forget.

Everybody agrees that Miss Nelson is the nicest teacher in the school. Even so, the children in Miss Nelson's class misbehave all the time. Miss Nelson has had enough, so she decides that there will be no more "nice" Miss Nelson. She hatches a brilliant plan, which parents will figure out pretty quickly but children will be left wondering about even at the end. When Miss Nelson cannot take any more poor behavior, a strange thing happens: she goes missing, and the class has a substitute teacher—the ugly, nasty, and mean Miss Viola Swamp. She pours on the homework, never has a story hour, and is generally a tyrant. Eventually Miss Nelson returns, and the children are so thrilled that they behave like angels. But now Miss Swamp is missing. Of course, parents will realize that Miss Nelson and Miss Swamp are one and the same, but the lesson about appreciating what you have is a good one, delivered with much humor along the way. **KD**

"A woman in an ugly black dress stood before them. I am your new teacher, Miss Viola Swamp."

OTHER INTRIGUING SCHOOL STORIES

Detectives in Togas by Henry Winterfeld, 1953
The Worst Witch by Jill Murphy, 1974
Miss Nelson Is Back by Harry Allard, 1982
Mister Majeika by Humphrey Carpenter, 1984
I Hate School by Jeanne Willis, 2003

5+

Anno's Journey 1977

Mitsumasa Anno

Original Title | Tabi no Ehon
Nationality | Japanese, born 1926
Publisher | Fukuinkan Shoten, Japan
Theme | Adventure

The opening page of *Anno's Journey* shows a bird's-eye view of a solitary boatman plying his way toward a verdant coastline. This is a picture book without words, but full of stories. The traveler takes his boat ashore and begins to explore this new land on horseback. We follow his progress through a country of medieval villages, gardens, towns, and cities, in which small figures carry out everyday activities: chopping wood, harvesting, gardening, and playing. Each group of figures represents a story full of detail and interest.

Mitsumasa Anno left his native Japan to explore Europe, and in this book he recorded the enchantingly different world he discovered there. Anno's drawings are meticulously detailed yet never overcrowded or confusing. Readers can find various optical tricks and a number of miniature thematic vignettes that unfold over several pages. Figures borrowed from Impressionist paintings lend an air of familiarity as Anno pays homage to European culture.

Anno's Journey is not simply a "find the man" puzzle book. In a landscape that could be French or English, there are ancient-looking buildings that form the background for the activities of the tiny people who could be medieval or modern. Adults and children will enjoy the clever detail and touches of humor on each page, and educational discussions about nature, architecture, history, agriculture, and art are likely to naturally take place. There is also something intrinsically sweet about this simple image of life in which humans, forests, and buildings exist in harmony. **SM**

100万回生きたねこ
佐野洋子 作・絵

5+

The Cat That Lived a Million Times 1977

Yoko Sano

Original Title | Hyakuman kai ikita neko
Nationality | Japanese, born 1938
Publisher | Kodansha, Japan
Theme | Adventure, Illness and death

Ever since its publication, Yoko Sano's book about a capricious cat with a million lives has moved children and adults alike with its subtle exploration of love, death, and the meaning of life.

A tomcat is owned by a king who the cat despises. When the cat dies, he is reborn to another owner who he also despises, this time a sailor. This process continues a million times; the sailor is followed by a magician, then a thief, an old woman, and a little girl. Every time the cat dies, his owner sheds tears for him, but the cat never once cries in his million lives because he never loves anyone. Finally, the cat is reborn without an owner and rejoices in his freedom. He narcissistically brags about his experiences of a million lifetimes, and is admired by all the female cats. But he falls in love with a beautiful white cat who is not taken in by his boasting. For the first time, the tomcat loves someone other than himself. The white cat bears him many kittens, and he realizes that she and their offspring are more important to him than anything. The two grow old together, until one day the white cat dies. Heartbroken, the tomcat cries a million tears and dies next to his mate, never to be reborn again.

With its plain prose and profound meaning, *The Cat That Lived a Million Times* has found countless readers in Japan and also abroad, thanks to Judith and James Huffman's masterful translation. Sano's own illustrations are true marvels—colorful and impressionistic, they complement the narrative in a captivating way. **MKG/FHG**

The Battle of Bubble and Squeak 1978

Philippa Pearce   Alan Baker

Nationality | English, born 1920 (author); English, birth date unknown (illustrator)
Publisher | André Deutsch, UK
Theme | Family, Animal stories

Philippa Pearce writes as Vermeer paints. She illuminates everyday domestic dramas with her calm, compassionate gaze, allowing deep emotions to reveal themselves without exploiting them for melodrama. In this tale, a young boy, Sid, wants to keep the two gerbils that his friend has given him, against the wishes of his house-proud mother. Pearce mingles the mundane comedy of rodent behavior with the deep tangle of family emotions. Sid is willing to suffer for his gerbils: protecting them is integral to his sense of self and his sense of right and wrong. Not that Pearce ever spells this out: She is a writer in whom emotional honesty is matched with delicacy of touch, even in narratives of the smallest scale like this.

Sid and his two sisters live with their mother and Bill, their stepfather. Bill is a nice man, but mother, for whatever reason, is fierce. She wants the family to conform to her ideas of what is right. "Expert at preventing mess," she does not want the gerbils in her house. The reader is on the side of the gerbils, who are closely modeled on and named after those belonging to Pearce's daughter. They gnaw the best curtains, scurry up and down Sid's trouser legs, and sit at the table like pompous public speakers. They are unshakably cute, with their little feet and twitching whiskers. But it is only when Bubble, the quiet gerbil, is attacked by the cat that Sid's mother gives in. In so doing, she mends the relationship with her son so that the family is able to laugh together. **VN**

Cloudy with a Chance of Meatballs 1978

Judi Barrett   Ron Barrett

Nationality | American, birth date unknown (author); American, birth date unknown (illustrator)
Publisher | Atheneum Books, USA
Theme | Magical stories, Family

Cloudy with a Chance of Meatballs is framed as a tall tale told by a grandfather to his grandchildren about the land of Chewandswallow—and what a tale it is. Imagine a town where you never have to buy or cook food, where three times a day (at breakfast, lunch, and dinner, of course) the skies open up and down comes your meal. Whatever the weather served the people ate, and they always carried their plates, bowls, and silverware with them. Would tomorrow bring a soup storm, might a breeze blow in with some hamburgers, or could there be a slight chance of pie? Watching the weather report provided the people of Chewandswallow with the next day's menu: "After a brief shower of orange juice, low clouds of sunny-side up eggs moved in, followed by pieces of toast."

But the weather in Chewandswallow suddenly takes a turn for the worse, and it starts to rain really BIG food with dangerous tomato tornados, a nasty salt and pepper wind, and a pea soup fog. The residents realize what they have to do. They glue together boats made of stale bread and peanut butter, with Swiss cheese sails, and sail off in search of a new land—a land as it turns out, where they actually have to buy and cook their own food.

Judi and Ron Barrett concoct a delectably tasty story with hilarious illustrations that will keep families reading and laughing together night after night. Kids will love finding the visual jokes within the illustrations that bring this imaginative story to life. **KD**

The Girl Who Loved Wild Horses 1978

 Paul Goble

Nationality | English, born 1933
Publisher | Bradbury, USA
Award | Caldecott Medal, 1979
Theme | Myths and legends, Fairy tales

5+

Paul Goble's interest in the lifestyle of the Native Americans began as a child. Inspired as a young man by the contemporary American Indian Movement for Civil Rights, his first three picture books were accounts of Plains Indian history. *The Girl Who Loved Wild Horses* is the story of a girl who has a deep sympathy with the horses who roam the plains just as her people do. Carried off with the herd in the midst of a wild storm, she lives with the horses and their charismatic stallion until she is rescued. She soon becomes lonely, and each evening the stallion calls to her from a nearby hilltop. Her people reluctantly accept that she must return to the herd. Eventually, she is seen no more, but a beautiful mare now runs beside the stallion.

This story, with its feminist implications, is strikingly different from Goble's earlier books, which celebrated the more familiar figure of the Native American male warrior. Not only does its connection with Plains mythology seem more profound, but pictorially it is wonderfully exciting, creating scenes that draw on Plains Indian story painting and the vibrant colors and geometric designs of Native American crafts. Goble's style here moves between storytelling and symbolic, almost abstract, expressions of the relationship of Native Americans with nature, for example in the striking final page, which shows the necks and heads of the two horses within the circle of the red evening sun. He developed this style for many more retellings of Native American myths. **CB**

"She spoke softly and they followed. People noticed that she understood horses."

OTHER NATIVE AMERICAN ACCOUNTS

Red Hawk's Account of Custer's Last Battle, 1969
Star Boy, 1983
Iktomi and the Boulder, 1988
Return of the Buffaloes, 1996
Mystic Horse, 2003

A Pocket for Corduroy 1978

Don Freeman

Nationality | American, born 1908
Publisher | Viking Press, USA
Theme | Adventure, Classics, Favorite characters, Friendship

In this sequel to the much-loved story *Corduroy* about a little stuffed bear who finds a loving home, we go on yet another adventure with Corduroy, Lisa the little Hispanic girl who owns him, and Lisa's mother—this time to the Laundromat.

Ever observant, Corduroy notices Lisa looking through her pockets to see if she has left anything in them before her clothes are put in the washing machine. Corduroy checks his overalls and realizes that he does not have any pockets; he goes off in search of something with which he can make a pocket of his own. His adventure results in him getting lost and being left behind in the Laundromat overnight, in a bag of someone else's wet laundry: "'How in thunder did that bear ever get mixed up with all my things?' the artist wondered." Corduroy is, of course, found safe and well the next day by the man who owns the Laundromat, and when Lisa returns looking for her lost bear, they are happily reunited. Lisa then promptly takes Corduroy home and sews a colorful pocket onto his overalls. Corduroy can now carry a name card with him in his pocket—and never be lost again.

The author Don Freeman was himself an orphan, and it is probably no accident that his most famous books deal with beloved toys being abandoned and happily rescued. The ending of this story, with the bear getting his wish for a pocket and Lisa putting a name card in it, brings to the forefront the issue of children and safety. **KD**

The Quinkins 1978

Percy Trezise and Dick Roughsey

Nationality | Australian, born 1923 (Trezise); Australian, born 1924 (Roughsey)
Publisher | Collins, Australia
Theme | Myths and legends, Fairy tales

When writer and painter Percy Trezise collaborated with Australian Aboriginal artist Dick Roughsey to produce a series of children's picture books based on Aboriginal myths, they had two clear aims: to help preserve Aboriginal culture by making it a part of national folklore and to improve the quality of Australian picture books.

The Quinkins is the third book in their series. It recounts the tale of two young children, Moonbi and Leealin, who live with their tribe in the shelter of a rock cave in the stunning Cape York area of northern Australia. One day, the children are lured away from the safety of their family campsite by an evil spirit called Imjin Quinkin. Luckily, in this cautionary tale, the evil Quinkin is matched by the good Timara Quinkin. Thanks to Timara's quick thinking the children are released from the Imjin's spell and escape an untimely death. This precipitates a great battle between the good and bad Quinkins that neither ultimately wins—and so the balance of life continues.

Roughsey and Trezise's text employs the formal cadences and carefully chosen wording of a traditional tale. Interestingly, the illustrations were produced by Trezise painting the landscapes and Roughsey peopling them with characters. Trezise's luminous double-page spreads beautifully capture the rich ocher soils, gray-green foliage, azure skies, and glowing sunsets of northern Australia, whereas Roughsey sensitively portrays the traditional way of life of his people. **SOR**

The Enormous Crocodile 1978

Roald Dahl Quentin Blake

Author | Welsh, born 1916 (author); English, born 1932 (illustrator)
Publisher | Jonathan Cape, UK
Theme | Animal stories, Adventure

5+

ROALD DAHL
The Enormous Crocodile
with pictures by Quentin Blake

MORE ROALD DAHL CLASSICS

***James and the Giant Peach,* 1961**
***Charlie and the Chocolate Factory,* 1964**
***The Twits,* 1980**
***The Giraffe, the Pelly and Me,* 1985**
***Matilda,* 1988**

The Enormous Crocodile tells the Notsobig One that he is going to have a yummy, juicy child for dinner instead of boring old fish. But the Notsobig One is not so sure: Aren't children nasty and bitter, and didn't the Enormous Crocodile try this before, without success? However, the Enormous Crocodile is quite determined and sets off through the jungle, astounding the animals he meets with his dastardliness and raising squeals of horrified delight from children listening: "One child isn't going to be nearly enough for me today. I won't be full up until I've eaten at least three juicy little children." When he reaches the village, the Enormous Crocodile's "secret plans and clever tricks" turn out to be rather inspired as he disguises himself in all sorts of unlikely ways: as a tree, a seesaw, part of a fairground ride, and a bench.

"It's the Enormous Crocodile and he wants to eat you up!"

But the other animals arrive in the nick of time to warn the children to run away, and the Enormous Crocodile gets his comeuppance when Trunky the elephant grabs him with his trunk and sends him whizzing into space until he is sizzled up like a sausage in the sun.

This is Roald Dahl at his witty best, full of the wonderful turns of phrase that make his books such fun to read aloud: "Oh you foul and filthy fiend! I hope you get squashed and squished and turned into crocodile stew." Quentin Blake manages with just a few lines to draw a wonderfully expressive crocodile, mouth upturned with glee as he considers his coming dinner: sneakily peeking through one eye when pretending to be a seesaw, angry when Trunky picks him up, and finally fearful as he flies off into space. **CW**

Haunted House 1979

Jan Pieńkowski

Its cover shaped and painted like an old front door, with the words "Let yourself in" written on a note stuck over the handle, this picture book offers young readers an intoxicating mixture of fear and excitement that is more often associated with a spooky ride at an amusement park than with a book.

Something evil is clearly going on, with one sinister green tentacle poking through the door's letter box. "Come in, Doctor. Yes, it is a quaint old place—chilly, though." Once inside the haunted house, an old staircase rises from the page in the first of a series of brilliant paper-engineering feats. Open a paper cupboard door under the stairs, and a ghost moves into view. Pull a tab, and in a portrait of a dark-haired lady and her cat, two sets of eyes move from side to side. Watch out for the skeleton in the closet.

"Do you think it's all imagination? Doctor . . . ? DOCTOR, WHERE ARE YOU . . . ?"

There is so much happening visually on the page that there is no need, or indeed room, for many words.

The narrative serves mainly as a vehicle for even more astonishing pop-ups and pull-outs. Jan Pieńkowski is a witty and marvelously inventive artist, who has since devised and illustrated many other fine picture books. *Haunted House* brought new standards of artistic excellence to what was then a rather limited world of pop-up books. A few younger children may dislike some of the skeletons and vampires on view, but most will relish the sheer exuberance of these brightly colored pages, each one packed with an astonishing amount of detail. Look out for the cat that appears in every double-page spread, eyes flashing and clearly having a good time. **NT**

Nationality | English, born 1936
Publisher | Heinemann, UK
Award | Kate Greenaway Medal
Theme | Design classics

5+

OTHER GREAT JAN PIEŃKOWSKI BOOKS

***Meg and Mog*, 1972**
***Meg's Eggs*, 1972**
***Meg on the Moon*, 1973**
***Owl at School*, 1984**
***Pizza!*, 2000**

The Prince of Motordu 1980

Pef

Original Title | Le belle lisse poire du prince de Motordu
Nationality | French, born Pierre Elie Ferrier 1939
Theme | Fantasy, Adventure

The Prince of Motordu is the eponymous hero of an immensely successful series of books created by Pef in 1980. This novel tells of the life of the bizarre little prince—his games, hobbies, and jokes—up to his marriage to the princess Dézécolles, and of the adventures of the growing Motordu family thereafter.

Motordu's defining characteristic is his affinity for hilarious malapropisms (his name comes from the French *mots tordus*, meaning "deformed words"). His manner of speaking becomes the language in which all the stories are written. It creates a universe that comes from the imagination of young children, with its mixture of surreal and irresistible humor. In this world (which even has its own dictionary written by Pef—the *Dictionnaire des mots tordus*), Father Christmas is actually Brother Christmas; a stomachache (*mâle au ventre*) surreally becomes "belly pallor" (*pâle au ventre*), and an Olympic champion becomes a mushroom (*champignon* instead of "champion"). Even the castle in which Motordu lives—haunted by ghosts, of course—looks like a hat, because Motordu calls it a *chapeau* (hat) instead of a *château* (castle). The bizarre language is made real by the accompanying illustrations; the prince wears a hat in the shape of a castle.

Pef's stories display a rare linguistic beauty in their simplicity, authenticity, and immediacy. Brilliant though his work is, and as successful as it is in French-speaking countries, it proves a great challenge for translators, which explains his belated success abroad. **LB**

5+

Not Now, Bernard 1980

 David McKee

Nationality | English, born David McKee Owns 1935
Publisher | Andersen Press, UK
Theme | Classics, Family, Fantasy

Besides the droll, deadpan humor and the bitter logic, in *Not Now, Bernard*, David McKee shows compassion for children who feel as bored and lonely as Bernard. He makes a little dig at self-absorbed parents and suggests that in neglecting their children, they are the real monsters.

Bernard's parents are too busy to talk to, listen to, or even to look at their son. When he tries to tell them that there is a monster in the garden, their reaction is the same. After the purple monster has eaten Bernard, his mother goes through the motions of caring for the monster in his place, not noticing that her son has vanished. She puts his dinner in front of the television but does not stay to watch him eat it, she takes his milk to his bedroom without looking at him, and switches the light off without saying good night. When he roars at Mom and bites Dad's foot, the parents give their standard response.

The story can be seen as a warning for parents who persistently ignore their children or never spend any time with them. Children, however, enjoy being part of a secret that adults are not privy to, and watching adults get their comeuppance. They will recognize the power balance portrayed in the book from both perspectives. Both adults and children will enjoy the images of the monster trying to fit into Bernard's world, pouring food into his mouth from a plate, and watching TV from above the set. The repeated refrain of "Not now, Bernard!" draws children into the story, and there is plenty for older readers to talk about. **GB**

The Paper Bag Princess

by Robert N. Munsch
illustrated by Michael Martchenko

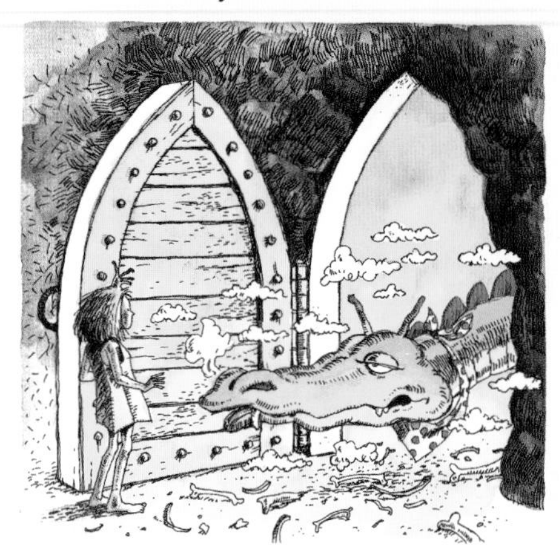

5+

The Paper Bag Princess 1980

Robert Munsch   Michael Martchenko

Nationality | Canadian, born 1945 (author); Canadian, born 1942 (illustrator)
Publisher | Annick Press, Canada
Theme | Classics, Fairy tales

In this funny and quirky story, Robert Munsch, much to the delight of his readers, reverses the usual expected story in which a prince saves a princess from a dragon. In the 1970s Munsch was making up dragon stories while reading to children at the daycare center where he worked, and this twist in tradition came at his wife's suggestion.

The story is simple, and Michael Martchenko's distinctive illustrations are filled with humor. Beautiful Princess Elizabeth loves Prince Ronald. When he is captured by a dragon that burns down her castle, leaving her singed and wearing only a paper bag, Elizabeth sets off to rescue her prince. She uses her wits to outsmart the dragon and rescues her prince, only to be told: "Elizabeth you are a mess! You smell like ashes, your hair is all tangled and you are wearing a dirty old paper bag. Come back when you are dressed like a real princess."

Needless to say, the young royals do *not* live happily ever after. The princess retorts: "Your clothes are really pretty and your hair is very neat. You look like a prince, but you are a bum." For subsequent editions published in England, New Zealand, and Australia, the word "bum" was changed to "toad;" however, the author maintains that he prefers his original choice.

The heroine of *The Paper Bag Princess* is named for a girl Munsch taught at preschool, who on her first day dropped her coat and waited for Munsch to pick it up. This Canadian classic will have readers, young and old, laughing all the way through. **KD**

5+

Jumanji 1981

Chris Van Allsburg

Nationality | American, born 1949
Publisher | Houghton Mifflin, USA
Award | Caldecott Medal, 1982
Theme | Classics, Fantasy

Jumanji is a classic book, although perhaps not for children who are easily frightened or who cannot appreciate the difference between fantasy and reality. Indeed, as it says on the game of the same name that the children discover under a tree: "Free game, fun for some, but not for all." There is a postscript: "Read instructions carefully." Chris Van Allsburg's detailed black-and-white illustrations make what is a compelling story even more magical.

Peter and Judy's parents are out for the afternoon, and the children are bored. Having emptied their toy box and made a mess of the house, they decide to go for a walk. They find a mysterious game under a tree, which they bring home. This is no ordinary game, however, and as they begin to play, they suddenly have to deal with very real lions, monkeys, rhinoceroses, a volcano, and much more. Just as they seem to have completely lost control of the situation (a recurring theme in Van Allsburg's fiction), they manage to speak the one word—"Jumanji"—that brings their life back to normal, just before their parents return home. Of course, no one believes the children when they tell about their adventures, but the reader knows the truth and wonders about the next unsuspecting child to play the bizarre game.

As in all Van Allsburg's books, Fritz the bull-terrier, who is based on his brother-in-law's dog, puts in an appearance, making it fun for readers to spot him. This inventive author and illustrator also created the award-winning classic *The Polar Express* in 1985. **KD**

5+

Mr. Fox 1982

Gavin Bishop

Nationality | New Zealander, born 1946
Publisher | Oxford University Press, New Zealand
Award | New Zealand Picture Book of the Year, 1983
Theme | Animal stories, Folktales

Mr. Fox, based on an old Massachusetts folktale, tells the story of another foxy character who is both greedy and impolite, qualities that lead to his ultimate undoing. However, Mr. Fox does not start the story as an ill-mannered and loutish figure. He is courteous and polite when he asks the little white woman to look after his bag, which holds a fat, juicy bumblebee that he has just caught. On his return, he discovers that the little white woman ignored his request and let the fat, juicy bumblebee get eaten by her plump, red rooster, so he takes her plump red rooster as a replacement and continues on his journey. Along the way, he comes across an assortment of different-colored little women, all of whom let the creature in Mr. Fox's bag escape. As a punishment to them, he takes something of theirs to replace his missing loot, getting progressively more cranky and rude to each new woman he meets. It is not until he approaches the little golden woman that Mr. Fox finally gets what he deserves for his cantankerous attitude, with the story ending in a suitably traditional way.

Gavin Bishop, whose illustrations have been compared with those of Maurice Sendak, has won many awards for his books, which use bright colors and feature New Zealand scenery. Each illustration continues to the next page, and children will delight in trying to guess what happens next. *Mr. Fox* appeals on all fronts, with its distinctive illustrations, engaging storyline, and important message that being greedy and impolite will get you nowhere. **CVB**

A Chair for My Mother 1982

Vera B. Williams

Nationality | American, born 1927
Publisher | Greenwillow Books, USA
Award | Caldecott Honor Book, 1983
Theme | Family, Friendship

The story of this book is deceptively simple. Three generations of African-American women are trying to recover from a disastrous fire in which all of their furniture and possessions have been lost. The women have learned the hard way that material possessions do not make a family.

Fortunately they have a place to live, and furniture is donated by family and friends, but it includes only hard, straight-backed chairs. They all long for one thing—a soft, cozy armchair that's big enough for them to all fit into together. In their home is a big glass jar, slowly filling with coins. The daughter narrates the story. Her mother works as a waitress at the Blue Tile Diner, and her tips go into the jar after each shift. Grandma shops for bargains at the store, and she puts the money she saves into the same jar: "When we can't get a single other coin into the jar, we are going to take out all the money and go and buy a chair." One day the jar is full, and off the family goes to shop for the longed-for piece of furniture. The final scene, where the women shop for the chair, memorably has Grandma, feeling like Goldilocks, trying out all the different chairs.

With vibrant colorful artwork and a sweet and tender story of familial love that's strong enough to survive disaster, award-winning author and illustrator Vera B. Williams tells a heartwarming story that begins with tragedy but ends with a strong family cuddled up snugly in a big warm chair, putting the past behind them and looking with hope toward the future. **KD**

Doctor De Soto 1982

William Steig

Nationality | American, born 1907
Publisher | Farrar, Straus and Giroux, USA
Award | Newbery Honor Book
Theme | Animal stories

In 2007, William Steig's art was the subject of a popular retrospective exhibition in New York City's Jewish Museum. After a long and successful career as an illustrator and cartoonist, notably on the *New Yorker*, Steig wrote his first children's book at the age of sixty-one. From that point on, he did not stop creating brilliant books for children, winning multiple awards as well as the hearts of children the world over. Steig's most famous creation was the lovable ogre Shrek.

In the award-winning *Doctor De Soto*, a mouse-dentist and his able assistant, Mrs. De Soto, deal with the toothaches of animals large and small. His expertise is so great that his patients never feel any pain; he treats all animals except for "cats and other dangerous animals," as stated clearly on the sign outside his office door.

One day a large fox shows up in great pain and begs Doctor De Soto to help him with a very painful tooth. The kind De Sotos cannot turn away an animal in pain, and so with trepidation they agree to treat the fox, who has "a rotten bicuspid and unusually bad breath." The fox does in fact behave himself, but when he returns the next day to get his gold tooth, he has mouse-flavored thoughts on his mind. The De Sotos of course manage to outfox the wily fox. In addition to being a wonderful story well told, this may also serve as a reassuring read for young children who are frightened of going to the dentist.

Steig's other children's books include *Sylvester and the Magic Pebble*, *Amos & Boris*, *Gorky Rises*, *Brave Irene*, and the superb *When Everybody Wore a Hat*. **KD**

Two Little Bears 1983

Hanna Muschg Käthi Bhend

Nationality | Swiss, born Hanna Johansen, 1939 (author); Swiss, born 1942 (illustrator)
Publisher | Bradbury Press, USA
Theme | Family, Animal stories

Two bear cubs, Brother Bear and Sister Bear, have spent the whole winter in a cozy subterranean den with their mother, mostly sleeping and sometimes drinking, playing, and arguing. However, a new and unexpected chapter of their lives begins when their mother walks off one day, leaving them behind. What is happening?

"'Maybe she's hungry,' says Sister Bear. 'Why?' her brother asks, pointing out that she's already grown up. 'That's right, she doesn't need to grow any more,' Sister Bear confirms. 'It's strange that she should be hungry all of a sudden.'" This innocent childlike dialogue shows the author's detailed knowledge of animal behavior (animals are always the protagonists of her books), as well as her ability to poetically ascribe human attributes to them. The young bears, who are waiting in vain for their mother's return, decide to leave the vicinity of the den on their own, to search for food. However, not knowing which of nature's offerings are edible and which are not, and unable to distinguish their mother's footsteps from those of the gigantic bear living close by, the two cubs encounter several problems as they struggle to cope alone.

Originally published with the title *Bruder Bär und Schwester Bär*, this was Hanna Muschg's first children's book. Käthi Bhend, who has worked often with the author, supplied the expressive pen-and-ink drawings that bring the bears—sometimes playful, sometimes serious—to life. No child who has read this book and identified with the heroes of this short, poetic story will ever forget it. **CS**

The compassionate De Sotos relieve the fox of his rotten tooth.

The Big Sister 1984

Siv Widerberg Cecilia Torudd

Nationality | Swedish, born 1931 (author); Swedish, born 1942 (illustrator)
Publisher | Rabén and Sjögren, Sweden
Theme | Family, Controversial

The Big Sister (Den stora systern) discusses the issue of sibling rivalry. Siv Widerberg captures the theme brilliantly in a very short text, using uncomplicated language. She writes convincingly about children's thoughts and has described her writing as "one-third imagination and two-thirds reality."

The story is told in the third person, from the older sibling's perspective: "Once there was a big sister who was always biggest and oldest and tallest and strongest. She was Mommy's big girl," the book begins. As the bigger sister's list of excellence grows longer and longer, so does the younger sister's jealousy and resentment grow deeper. Yet who is the lucky one, really? Sometimes the big sister longs to be the littlest person in the family.

Cecilia Torudd's humorous and recognizable illustrations depict the everyday world of children and are also lively and action filled. They complement the narrative and carry the story forward eloquently. Every picture covers a whole page and has a single, short line of text above it, making the book suitable for young children. Although, the philosophical subject makes it equally relevant for older children and grown-ups. This is not a book that all parents will necessarily approve of, as at times the sisters are very nasty to each other and some incidents may seem disturbingly too true. This book about family roles and relationships is one to reflect on, discuss with your children, and return to. It is a thought-provoking book about a topic that concerns many of us. It will have particular resonance for sisters everywhere. **CC**

Dragon Ball 1984

Akira Toriyama

Nationality | Japanese, born 1955
Publisher | Shueisha, Japan
Theme | Comics, Favorite characters, Fantasy, Adventure

In the great Chinese sixteenth-century novel *Journey to the West*, Son Goku was the name of the fine monkey king whose power was so great that he challenged the celestial authority of Buddha himself. From this character, Akira Toriyama created *Dragon Ball*, a manga (Japanese comic book) about an improbably strong and naively innocent boy with a monkey's tail (Goku). He is on a special quest to find seven magical spheres that, when assembled, will allow any wish to be granted.

Dragon Ball begins as a comedy, with frequent visual gags and scandalous dialogue (the obvious puns on the titular "balls" are also possible in Japanese). In the course of its 519 chapters and decades-long storyline, however, the style shifts toward martial arts action, as the adult Goku, his sons, Gohan and Goten, and their companions are forced to defend Earth against increasingly powerful villains. Energy attacks capable of destroying entire planets are exchanged, and Goku twice dies and is resurrected.

The protracted battles that characterize *Dragon Ball Z* (the second phase of the series) are worlds apart from the early lighthearted adventures. In these later chapters, the influence of Hong Kong action cinema and Western sources, such as Superman and the *Terminator* films, are evident. Yet what makes Toriyama's work unique and so influential is the sense of fun its characters maintain in challenging and surpassing their limits. *Dragon Ball* is violent, but at its heart is the pure thrill of accomplishment that we find in and share with our heroes. **CR**

Mr. Majeika 1984

Humphrey Carpenter   Frank Rodgers

Nationality | English, born 1946 (author); Scottish, born 1944 (illustrator)
Publisher | Kestrel Books, UK
Theme | School, Magical stories

The first in a much-loved series, *Mr. Majeika* introduces its readers to the inept but amiable wizard who enlivens the educational experience of Class Three at St. Barty's Primary School, after becoming their teacher. St. Barty's is the epitome of a provincial English school, but the headmaster, Mr. Potter, is too distracted to notice anything unusual about his new member of staff. After witnessing his dramatic arrival on a magic carpet, the pupils, however, recognize at once that Mr. Majeika is no ordinary teacher and are entranced by his unorthodox methods. Obnoxious Hamish Bigmore learns how to behave himself after being turned into a frog, and for a while—to his long-suffering classmates' delight—it seems he will have to remain that way because Mr. Majeika has forgotten how to undo the spell. Melanie Brace-Girdle, class crybaby, overcomes her horror of an unkempt stranger who flew in through the window to enjoy a thrilling magic carpet ride to Buckingham Palace, and everyone digs into a feast that the wizard conjures up to replace the abysmal school lunch.

It is clear that with Mr. Majeika in charge, there is no chance of being bored on a drizzly Monday morning ever again. Aware that the Worshipful Wizard of Walpurgis is keeping a close eye on him, Mr. Majeika does his best to carry out his teaching duties without using magic, but sometimes a little enchantment is the only way to get things done. This funny, affectionate portrait of school days is endlessly appealing, and the mischievous Mr. Majeika is the teacher everyone wishes they had. **MK**

"People don't believe in wizards nowadays, so naturally they don't often pay them to do some work."

OTHER MARVELOUS MAGICAL TITLES

The Magic Fishbone by Charles Dickens, 1868
The Magic Pudding by Norman Lindsay, 1918
Little Old Mrs. Pepperpot by Alf Prøysen, 1958
The Worst Witch by Jill Murphy, 1974
Jumanji by Chris Van Allsburg, 1981

The New Kid on the Bloc
poems by JACK PRELUTSKY
drawings by JAMES STEVENSON

The New Kid on the Block 1984

Jack Prelutsky James Stevenson

Nationality | American, born 1940 (author); American, born 1929 (illustrator)
Publisher | Greenwillow Books, USA
Theme | Poetry, Quirky

Jack Prelutsky—the first recipient of the Children's Poet Laureate award in the United States—is often credited with bringing children's poetry back to life. In this much-loved collection, more than one hundred poems feature all manner of fantastic creatures from Prelutsky's inventive and often surreal imagination.

Meet the "Flotz," who gobbles up dots and apostrophes; the shy and somewhat dim "Flimsy Fleek"; and the "Underwater Wibbles" who "dine exclusively on cheese / they keep it in containers / which they bind about their knees." Strange humans also abound: the inept juggler Clara Cleech; Euphonica Jarre ("has a voice that's bizarre"); and Dainty Dottie Dee, so house-proud that she launders lightbulbs. There are performing bananas, mice on tricycles, and earth-shattering questions, such as "Do oysters sneeze?"

This sheer silliness and love of words are Prelutsky trademarks; in many ways his work is a modern version of nonsense rhymes, such as Lewis Carroll's "Jabberwocky." The poems often have one foot in reality but build up to wild improbability, gaining an irresistibly funny momentum as they go. This is liberating writing that encourages a freethinking delight in language and the imagination. The poems are perfectly partnered by James Stevenson's spare, energetic, and comical cartoons. Stevenson is a prolific writer, illustrator, and cartoonist who has produced many children's books himself, and is famed for his *New Yorker* cartoons. **AK**

Katie Morag Delivers the Mail 1984

Mairi Hedderwick

Nationality | Scottish, born 1939
Publisher | Bodley Head, UK
Theme | Favorite characters, Family, Friendship

Katie Morag Delivers the Mail is the first in a much-loved series exploring the ups and occasional downs of life on the fictional island of Struay (based on the real Hebridean Isle of Coll). Life is seen through the eyes of Katie Morag, a young redheaded girl dressed invariably in a kilt and Wellington boots. She is a cheerful, independent heroine, somewhat prone to mishaps, whose parents run the island shop and post office, which sells everything from cans of beans to beach balls. Wednesdays are especially busy, as the boat brings the mail and provisions from the mainland. This particular Wednesday is more chaotic than usual because baby Liam is cutting his first tooth. Katie Morag is asked to deliver the packages to the far side of the bay but she stops for a paddle en route, getting the packages soaked and everything in a muddle. Luckily, resourceful Grannie Island is on hand to help sort things out and give Katie Morag a lift home in her tractor at the end of an exhausting day.

Lively text and absorbingly detailed illustrations work together to set the themes developed in later books—the cheerful chaos and everyday worries of family life, the nature and character of island ways, and the search for a balance between inevitable change and reassuring stability. Unusually for a picture book series, later titles see Katie Morag and Liam growing older while the island itself is subject to irrevocable change when a new pier is built, enabling the boat to come from the mainland three times a week. **KA**

If You Give a Mouse a Cookie 1985

Laura Joffe Numeroff / Felicia Bond

Nationality | American, born 1953 (author); American, born 1955 (illustrator)
Publisher | HarperCollins, USA
Theme | Animal stories, Classics

This brilliantly written and charmingly illustrated story is all about "go togethers"—how one thing or action relates to another—that is, actions and consequences. *If You Give a Mouse a Cookie* has sold millions of copies in dozens of languages purely because it is fun to read, and young children love the rhythm of the language, the logic of the story, and the beauty of the illustrations. An added and important benefit is that parents love to read it as well. In fact, the expression "If you give a mouse a cookie" has become so much part of American popular culture that it was quoted in the 1997 movie *Air Force One*.

So what happens if you give a mouse a cookie? Why, he will ask for a glass of milk, of course. And then he will need a straw and a napkin. . . . As the mouse in the story wears out the young boy who is doing his best to get the mouse everything he asks for, children will be laughing along knowingly and trying to figure out what the mouse will ask for next. In the end, the story returns to the mouse wanting another cookie, which starts the cycle all over again, setting the stage for many enjoyable future readings. This is one of those books that young children memorize quickly and will want to hear again and again.

Laura Joffe Numeroff's endearing mouse launched the If You Give a . . . series, which introduced other animal characters, such as a moose, a pig, and a cat. The author was an avid reader as a child, and says that E. B. White's *Stuart Little* was an important inspiration. **KD**

The People Could Fly 1985

Virginia Hamilton / Diane & Leo Dillon

Nationality | American, born 1936 (author); American, born 1933 (illustrators)
Publisher | Alfred A. Knopf, USA
Theme | Myths and legends, Magical stories

"The words of ancient Africa once heard are never remembered completely. The young man forgot them as soon as he heard them. They went way inside him. He got up and rolled over on the air. He rode it awhile, and he flew away." Thus opens the title story from Virginia Hamilton's poetic retelling of an African-American folktale. This truly timeless picture book version, illustrated by the award-winning Dillons, is a book that should be included in every family library. It tells how some Africans flew on shiny black wings before they were captured and forced into slavery. Although they shed their beautiful wings when forced onto crowded slave ships, those who possessed the flying magic still retained the ability to fly. When the story moves to America, slave Sarah and her baby are shown working the cotton fields, being whipped by the overseer. Elderly Toby, remembering the words that allowed him to fly, helps them to escape.

The Dillons' illustrations are magical stunning images yet they depict cruelty close up. Whether depicting richly robed men in traditional African attire or the slaves in the fields, the artwork is as compelling as it is beautiful. People are shown flying to freedom, joining their hands together in the sky as an inspiration to those left behind, who "had only their imaginations to set them free." Discussing the history of slavery with children can be difficult. Although this tale does not minimize the horrors of "The Middle Passage," it is also an uplifting tale of survival. **KD**

In need of a nap, the little rodent revels in his new luxurious bed.

Not So Fast Songololo 1985

Niki Daly

Nationality | South African, born 1946
Publisher | Gollancz, UK
Award | *Horn Book*, Fanfare, 1987
Theme | Family

5+

Songololo is the pet name given to young South African boy Malusi by his aging grandmother Gogo. She visits his family one morning with the request that one of her grandchildren help her with the shopping in the city. Malusi happily agrees, even though his hand-me-down "tackies"—the local name for sneakers—are now battered and full of holes. Getting on and off the bus together, the two push their way through crowds of shoppers as Gogo stocks up on groceries. Malusi looks longingly in shop windows at new sneakers but does not ask his grandmother to buy him some. However, the final thing she buys is a special gift for the boy—a pair of brand-new red tackies—and he is naturally overjoyed.

"Gogo is old, but her face shines like new shoes. Her hands were huge and used to hard work."

This charming picture book, set in postapartheid South Africa, vividly evokes the atmosphere, color, and bustle of a fast-developing country. Although young Malusi and his grandmother are now free to shop wherever they choose, despite their skin color, they are still very poor, which is why the purchase of a new pair of tackies means so much to both of them. The proud little boy strides ahead at such a pace in his new sneakers that Gogo is forced to call out after him, "Not so fast Songololo!"

Niki Daly's expressive watercolors highlight all the points that his text merely hints at: from the elderly Gogo's smiling love for her grandson to the boy's touching care and concern for someone so much older than he is. This picture book is a simple story about a universally shared experience and has already become a classic in its own time. **NT**

OTHER NOTABLE NIKI DALY WORKS

***The Little Girl Who Lived Down the Road*, 1978**
***Why the Sun and Moon Live in the Sky*, 1994**
***Jamela's Dress*, 1999**
***Once Upon a Time*, 2003**
***Where's Jamela?*, 2004**

Linnea in Monet's Garden 1985

Christina Björk Lena Anderson

This wonderful tale, originally published as *Linnea i Målarens Trädgård*, is about the friendship between a little Swedish girl, Linnea, and a retired gardener called Mr. Bloom. To learn more about the French artist Claude Monet and his incredible impressions of light and nature, the friends travel to Paris to see his works of art, and to Giverny to visit his home and garden. Linnea takes her camera and sketchbook, and through her vibrant descriptions and images young children are introduced to a variety of information on French culture, geography, art, and nature. In this way, the reader learns of Paris, Monet, Impressionism, and of the botanical world that means so much to both Linnea and Mr. Bloom.

"I love flowers . . . and I'm interested in everything that grows. That's just the way I am!"

Linnea enthusiastically presents a host of interesting trees, plants, and flowers: a robinia, now thought to be the oldest tree in Paris, and poplars and weeping willows seen from the train to Giverny. In Monet's garden, standing on the Japanese bridge, we admire the real white water lilies in the pond, and in the museums we can enjoy the painted lilies on the canvases. Through the lens of Linnea's camera, the reader observes close-ups of purple and blue hibiscuses, pink roses, red poppies, and white and violet hydrangeas. Appropriately, the little girl is named for the national flower of Sweden.

Thanks to Christina Björk's lively language and Lena Anderson's beautiful drawings, the reader is quickly engaged in a synthesis of learning. The words interact with the pictures perfectly in this interesting eye-opener to French culture and art. **SML**

Nationality | Swedish, born 1938 (author); Swedish, born 1939 (illustrator)
Publisher | Rabén and Sjögren, Sweden
Theme | Friendship, Science and nature

5+

OTHER BOOKS ABOUT ART AND NATURE

A Tree Is Nice by Janice Udry, 1956
My Place by Nadia Wheatley, 1987
Where the Forest Meets the Sea by Jeannie Baker, 1988
Flotsam by David Wiesner, 2006

The Polar Express 1985

Chris Van Allsburg

Nationality | American, born 1949
Publisher | Houghton Mifflin, USA
Award | Caldecott Medal, 1986
Theme | Classics, Magical stories

This award-winning story has become a family read-aloud classic in homes the world over at Christmas time. The softly luminous paintings, the tender story of a boy's magical Christmas "dream," and the sound of a single bell will ring in children's imaginations at the holidays for years to come.

Late one Christmas Eve, after the town has gone to sleep, a young boy—who is becoming skeptical about the magic of Christmas—reluctantly boards a mysterious train that waits for him—the *Polar Express*—bound for the North Pole. The train is full of other children from all different walks of life, also dressed in their pajamas. When the boy arrives, Santa Claus offers him any gift he desires. However, unlike the other children, the boy is not interested in all the toys in Santa's sack and modestly asks for a sleigh bell from the harness of the reindeer. The gift is granted, but on the way home, the precious bell is lost.

Is it a dream or did it really happen? On Christmas morning, the boy finds the bell under the tree, with a note signed "S. C." The mother of the boy admires the bell but laments that it is broken, although the boy and his sister can, in fact, hear it loud and clear. At the end, the boy-narrator-turned-adult tells readers: "Though I've grown old, the bell still rings for me, as it does for all who truly believe." This first-person story makes it all the more earnest and believable for children, and the atmospheric illustrations of the night scenes at the North Pole will mesmerize them as they learn, once again, to believe in magic. **KD**

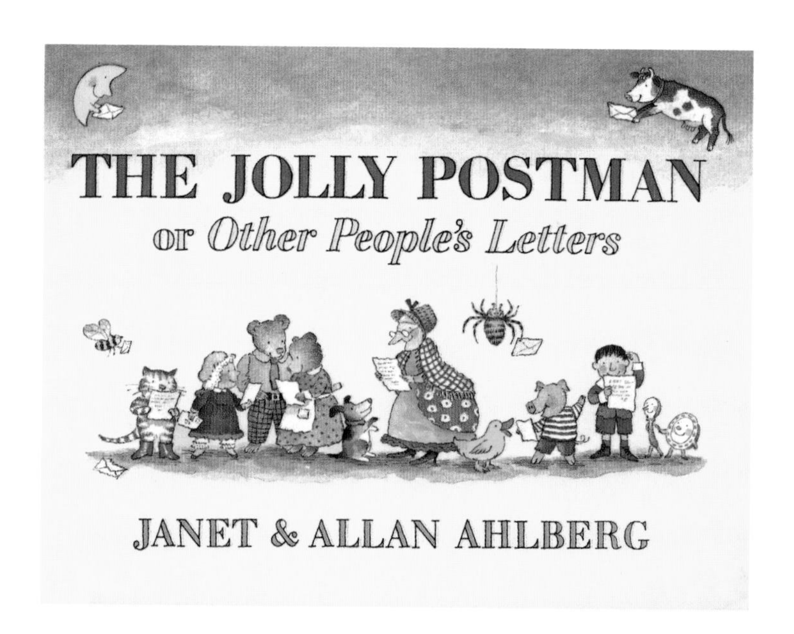

5+

The Jolly Postman 1986

Allan Ahlberg Janet Ahlberg

Nationality | English, born 1938 (author); English, born 1944 (illustrator)
Publisher | Heinemann, UK
Theme | Nursery rhymes, Fairy tales

This book takes the intertextual concept of *Each Peach Pear Plum* further for older children, linking events and characters from classic fairy tales and nursery rhymes through the device of a new character who cannot only travel between all their worlds, but also show that their worlds are, in fact, part of the same bigger fairy-tale universe. As in *Each Peach Pear Plum*, the characters are united in a final celebration, this time at Goldilocks's birthday party. The Ahlbergs were trailblazers in devising high-quality supporting materials to extend the text of a book. *The Jolly Postman* delivers a range of goodies for children to unfold and enjoy with various levels of sophistication. Children up to the age of eight, the birthday that Goldilocks celebrates, will be able to read the story of Cinderella in a mini-edition (in which the Ahlbergs make the story their own by having sausages on sticks at the Prince's ball). Others will cackle with the Witch over Hobgoblin Supplies' ghoulish catalogue (Deadly Lampshades and nonstick cauldrons) and enjoy the smug postcard Jack sends the Giant as he takes the Golden Goose on a tour of nursery rhyme land.

The Ahlbergs' trademark attention to detail means the delights of this book never run out, from Goldilocks's first letter to the Three Bears, a misspelled apology postmarked Banbury Cross, and the stamp carrying a picture of Old King Cole. In another favorite scene, inside the Witch's cottage, the Postman reads the fairy-tale community's top newspaper, *Mirror Mirror*, while the Witch's cat washes up. **GB**

Animalia 1986

Graeme Base

Nationality | English/Australian, born 1958
Publisher | Penguin, Australia
Award | Dromkeen Medal, 1998
Theme | Classics

5+

Graeme Base's spectacular *Animalia* proves that alphabet books are not just for the very young. While showcasing his extraordinary artistic talent, Base challenges readers of all ages to identify a cornucopia of items, ranging from the domestic and ordinary to the exotic and extraordinary.

Each spread teems with images, all presented in Base's colorful style, with its strong decorative elements, draftsmanlike precision, and predilection for classical perspective. He combines his realistic portrayals of animals with flights of the imagination, as horrible, hairy hogs ride horses, iguanas improvise on fantastic musical instruments, and majestic lions laze around a well-stocked library. The variety of images shown ensures that the visual sense of young and old alike is frequently challenged. Even letters that are traditionally difficult to illustrate, such as "Q," contain a variety of items, ranging from the obvious queens and quails, to the more obscure quadratic equations and Don Quixote. There are references to popular culture and a passing parade of familiar characters. As well as the obvious, ghosted images are hidden in things, such as a butterfly's wings or on wallpaper. And, just to add to the challenge, a small boy dressed in jeans and a yellow-and-orange-striped shirt is hidden on every page.

Each highly entertaining puzzlelike illustration is matched with beautifully crafted text, full of alliterative flourishes that roll off the tongue: "Eight enormous elephants expertly eating Easter eggs." Base is the master of visual engagement. **SOR**

Hey, Al 1986

Arthur Yorinks   Richard Egielski

Nationality | American, born 1953 (author); American, born 1952 (illustrator)
Publisher | Farrar, Straus and Giroux, USA
Theme | Friendship

The stories that have the simplest messages are often the ones that ring most true, and this is certainly the case with Arthur Yorinks's *Hey, Al*.

Al is a janitor and he lives a simple life in a single room on the West Side of New York with his faithful dog, Eddie. They eat together, work together, and, in fact, they do everything together. However, their room is rather crowded and cramped, and they complain to one other that their life is an endless struggle. Al and Eddie begin to bicker constantly until, one day, a large and mysterious bird offers them a new life in paradise, where there are "no worries" and "no cares." After some discussion, they accept the offer and set off on an adventure. At first paradise is everything they expect it to be—beautiful, filled with color, flowers, birds, and more—but they soon discover that this ideal world is not quite as perfect as they thought. Al and Eddie soon begin to miss their old life at home and decide to return. Catastrophe strikes on the journey home when the two become separated. In the end, of course, the friends are reunited and they are both happy to be home, proving the old adage of "home is where the heart is."

The muted colors of Richard Egielski's art at the beginning of the book contrast with the brilliant colors of paradise and, along with the humor of the tale itself, help make the moral of the story evident to young readers. The happy acceptance of a life at home will be a comfort to anyone who has ever wondered about what it might be like where "the grass is greener." This is a classic family favorite. **KD**

Al's life is about to change, as the bird appears at the window. 

The Hound of the Mound and the Frog of the Bog 1986

Ana María Machado Irene Savino

Nationality | Brazilian, born 1941 (author); Brazilian, birth date unknown (illustrator)
Publisher | Ediciones Ekaré, Venezuela
Theme | Rhyming stories, Animal stories

In this funny rhyming story (original title *El Perro del Cerro y la Rana de la Sabana*), a dog and a frog start out as enemies and end up as friends. The hound from the mound and the frog from the bog engage in a heated discussion. Each animal is convinced that he is braver than the other. They decide to prove their bravery by pitting themselves against savage beasts. Curious as to what all the fuss is about, other animals approach to watch. The frog and the dog first confront creatures that are small rather than savage, such as an innocent, harmless butterfly. The farcical competition continues until a ferocious lion's roar is heard. Now the frog and the dog must cooperate with each other, as well as all the other animals, in order to face the mighty animal. They finally realize the value of working together and that there is more strength in numbers.

Ana María Machado is a prominent Brazilian children's writer whose trademark is her playful and lively language. She always makes her messages more attractive to young readers by embedding them within humorous and enjoyable narratives. Her rhymes are almost musical, perfect for reading aloud, and perhaps the best part of the book is precisely the sound of the words as they "rrrrroll" out of your mouth. Captivating, colorful illustrations are the finishing touch on every page of this beautiful book. **LB**

Lend Me Your Wings
Words by John Agard
Pictures by Adrienne Kennaway

5+

Lend Me Your Wings 1987

John Agard Adrienne Kennaway

Nationality | Guyanan, born 1949 (author); New Zealander, born 1945 (illustrator)
Publisher | Hodder and Stoughton, UK
Theme | Myths and legends, Animal stories

In *Lend Me Your Wings*, Guyanese poet and writer John Agard tells the story of Sister Fish and Brother Bird, two creatures who decide to swap places in order to see the world from a different point of view. After Brother Bird offers to lend Sister Fish his wings in return for her fins, both take the opportunity to explore. Brother Bird dives into the ocean and plays hide-and-seek with the crabs and the shrimps, while Sister Fish sees her first mango tree and flies alongside a child's kite. However, they discover that with their newfound abilities come problems. As a strong wind blows in, Sister Fish finds herself falling from the sky, landing back in the river. Sister Fish and Brother Bird decide that it is time for the experiment to end.

This folktalelike story is illustrated using bright watercolors that cheerfully complement Agard's adoption of native-style Guyanese language. The vividly drawn characters appeal to children while the backgrounds convey a level of depth through Adrienne Kennaway's ability to create shadows and distance, so that the character is always the main focus.

Although Agard is well regarded as a performance poet in England, most of his published works are for children and they include *Laughter Is an Egg*. They are infused with aspects of the Caribbean and help to provide a renewed appreciation for folktales. **CVB**

Henry and Mudge 1987

Cynthia Rylant Suçie Stevenson

Nationality | American, born 1954 (author); American, born 1956 (illustrator)
Publisher | Bradbury Press, USA
Theme | Family, Friendship

5+

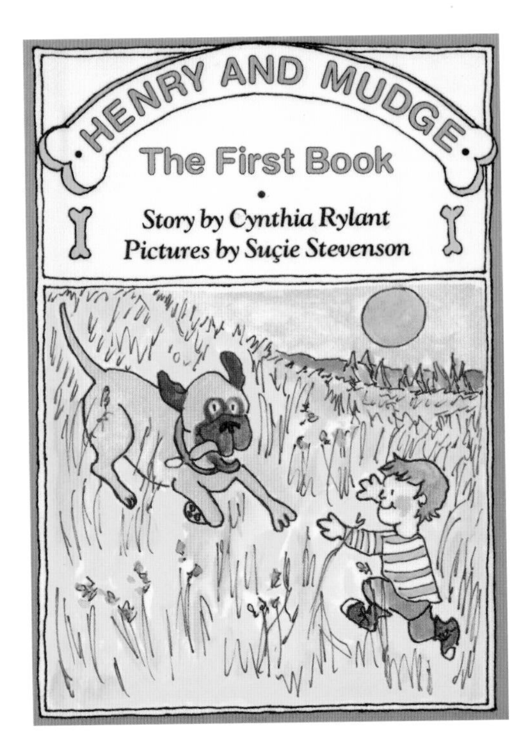

Henry is a small boy who feels rather alone. He has no brothers or sisters nor does he have any friends to play with on his street. His parents are not amenable to the idea of producing siblings for him or moving house, so when Henry decides he wants a dog, he gets his way. Here begins a wonderful friendship between a boy of seven years and a dog of seven weeks who grows up to be Henry's huge canine best friend, Mudge. Here also begins a long-lasting, much-loved series of books detailing the pair's adventures together. In this first book calamity strikes when Mudge goes missing and Henry realizes the real value of their friendship. When and how will they find each other again?

"Henry had no pets at home. 'I want to have a dog,' he told his parents. . . ."

Cynthia Rylant's words are simple but subtly smart and amusing, and she genuinely understands the feelings of loss and of being an "outsider," born partly from her own childhood experiences of divorce and the loss of her father. She has found her ideal illustrator in Suçie Stevenson, whose bright, exuberant, cartoonlike images have the same energy as those of her father—famous writer and illustrator James Stevenson—plus an affectionate warmth that is perfect for this age group. Stevenson's inspiration for Mudge was her brother's Great Dane, Jake. The straightforward, but not overly simple, text and colorful illustrations of the Henry and Mudge books provide an ideal link between picture books and more advanced books. Parents who have struggled to engage their children with reading have found these titles really helpful. **AK**

MORE IN THE HENRY AND MUDGE SERIES

Henry and Mudge in Puddle Trouble, 1987
Henry and Mudge in the Sparkle Days, 1988
Henry and Mudge and the Bedtime Thumps, 1991
Henry and Mudge and the Starry Night, 1999
Henry and Mudge and the Funny Lunch, 2005

My Place 1987

Nadia Wheatley Donna Rawlins

Nationality | Australian, born 1949 (author); Australian, born 1956 (illustrator)
Publisher | Collins Dove, Australia
Theme | Family, Historical fiction

The publication of *My Place* coincided with the Australian bicentennial, acknowledging 200 years of European settlement. Nadia Wheatley and Donna Rawlins celebrate a much longer history, however, in this creative picture book, where time goes backward in decades from 1988 to 1788. It recognizes that children have always been capable of deep thoughts and profound ideas about their world, as well as being playful and observant of their surroundings.

My Place is one story made up of many stories—twenty-one in fact, each told by a different child about "my place." This place, we discover, is one that they have all shared but in different moments of time. Their stories are told in words and pictures, and illustrated with hand-drawn maps, always marking the places that are important to each individual child. Along the way we encounter the introduction of electricity and television, the Great Depression, World War II, the Beatles, the Vietnam War, McDonald's, and so on. The book is playfully child-centered and told in the first person and allows the reader to get right inside each story of "my place." It will very likely arouse questions about their own place in the world—the past, and the future: Have other children lived here before? Did they play here, too? Did my dad climb trees when he was little?

The story of *My Place* ends with Barangaroo, an Aboriginal girl living in 1788. She has a different way to describe her place in Australia: "My name's Barangaroo. I belong to this place." This is a wonderful, thought-provoking book. **AJ**

The Hodgeheg 1987

Dick King-Smith Ann Kronheimer

Nationality | English, born 1922 (author); English, birth date unknown (illustrator)
Publisher | Hamish Hamilton, UK
Theme | Animal stories

The Hodgeheg is the charming story of a family of hedgehogs who live in a comfortable suburban flowerbed but dream of finding a safe passage across a busy road to the wonderful hunting ground of the park, where succulent delicacies such as mice, garden snakes, and frogs are to be found. The youngest and smallest member of the family, Max (christened Victor Maximilian St. George by his father) decides to live up to his noble-sounding name and solve the problem. Unfortunately, his first attempt to negotiate the traffic results in a nasty bump on the head that leaves him confusing the order of his words when he speaks; he has become a "hodgeheg." Luckily, Max's eyes, ears, and wits remain as sharp as his spines, and he eventually finds a way to cross the road safely.

King-Smith's lighthearted sense of humor is apparent throughout the story, which, like all his children's tales, successfully avoids being fluffy or sentimental. An ex-farmer with a fondness for pigs, he writes mostly about animals, from the perspective of animals—a genre he terms "farmyard fantasy." His farms are realistic places where creatures are subject to the usual predators and laws of nature. King-Smith says that, "Much as I like *The Wind in the Willows* and the work of Beatrix Potter . . . I never dress my animals in clothes. . . . They behave as animals should behave, with the exception that they open their mouths and speak the Queen's English." A recurring feature in his stories is the triumph of the underdog, the smallest or weakest of the group, which could explain part of their popularity with young children. **MK**

A Balloon for Grandad 1988

Nigel Gray Jane Ray

"'If I know that Grandad's happy,' said Sam's father, 'then I feel happy too. . . .'"

MORE GREAT BOOKS ABOUT GRANDADS

***Charlie and the Chocolate Factory* by Roald Dahl, 1964**
***Granpa* by John Burningham, 1985**
***Matthew and Grandpa* by Roberto Piumini, 1997**
***Little Bear's Grandad* by Nigel Gray, 2000**

Nationality | Irish/Australian, born 1941 (author); English, born 1960 (illustrator)
Publisher | Orchard Books, UK
Theme | Family

This colorfully illustrated and lyrical work tells the story of a young boy named Sam who is comforted by his father following the loss of a balloon that escapes from the open door of their home.

Sam is reassured by an uplifting tale in which his father suggests that the balloon has gone on a joyful adventure to visit Sam's grandfather Abdulla who lives far away in North Africa. Rather than mourning the loss, Sam becomes proud that his red-and-silver balloon has embarked on a journey to let his grandfather know that he is thinking of him. His father's explanation thus turns the loss of the balloon into a gentle but cheerful story about maintaining familial connections.

Nigel Gray is a prolific author of children's stories, who began writing when incarcerated in a Thai prison. His tragic and unconventional upbringing saw him separated from his parents and siblings during World War II, after which he was raised in foster homes before settling in Australia with his Sudanese wife. *A Balloon for Grandad* revisits themes of diaspora and bereavement from Gray's own life, sensitively exploring the ideas of loss and displacement in a way that is accessible to a young audience. Not only does Gray address childhood experiences of disappointment and separation with an inspirational approach, but the story also depicts a multicultural family life and the emotions that inevitably arise when generations are distanced by geography. **ML**

Anancy Spiderman 1988

James Berry / Joseph Oiobu

Nationality | Jamaican, born 1924 (author); Jamaican, birth date unknown (illustrator)
Publisher | Walker Books, UK
Theme | Myths and legends, Fairy tales

James Berry is perhaps best known for his poetry, in which he blends his Jamaican oral and English literary heritages to dazzling effect. In *Anancy Spiderman* he offers Caribbean versions of the familiar spider trickster tales, partly remembered from the stories his parents told and partly taken from folklore collections.

The tales center on the cunning and ingratiating Anancy, and his friends and adversaries: Bro Nancy, Bro Puss, Bro Goat, Bro Tiger, and others. Berry cleverly re-creates the atmosphere in which he remembers hearing the stories as a child, "out in moonlight or in dim paraffin lamplight" in a Jamaican village. His language has the immediacy and abruptness of the spoken word, and, spiced with chants and refrains, it has the sound of the Caribbean. His characters, while sometimes retaining their animal characteristics, grow crops, cook, tend their gardens, go hunting, and enjoy music and dancing, like any Jamaican villagers.

Berry keeps the magic of the original stories and while he admits to fleshing out the characterization, he does not try to create any more explanation for these tales other than that they all involve Bro Nancy. Some stories feature exotic creatures—such as tigers and monkeys, others talking flames and skulls, and witches and chiefs—recalling the African origins of the tales and carrying with them the flavor of forgotten fables. This makes for a volume that is both down to earth and mysterious, as well as fascinating in its exploration of human nature. **CB**

Drac and the Gremlin 1988

Allan Baillie / Jane Tanner

Nationality | Australian, born 1943 (author); Australian, born 1946 (illustrator)
Publisher | Penguin, Australia
Theme | Magical stories, Family

Drac and the Gremlin is a magical tale that takes two seemingly different paths—one in the illustrations and one in the text—and through their interweaving, creates an enchanting story that is far more than the sum of its parts. Jane Tanner's photorealistic illustrations sing with energy, color, and texture. She achieves such visual clarity that you feel you can smell the flowers in the garden, pat the dog, and caress the girl's long silken hair, as she shows two exuberant children enjoying a game of imaginative play. A girl and her brother, dressed in homemade costumes made from a garbage sack and a tablecloth, chase each other through their lushly overgrown garden. Aided by a white butterfly and a green parrot, they evade the "dangers" posed by the garden sprinkler; the clothes hanging on the line; their cat, Minnie; and her kittens; and their overly enthusiastic sheepdog.

The text, however, makes it clear that something much more intriguing is going on. Allan Baillie's imagination soars as he recounts how Drac, the brave Warrior Queen of Tirnoil Two, helped by the wise White Wizard, battles the dangerous Gremlin of the Groaning Grotto. Yet when they are beset by General Min, her Hissing Horde, and the Terrible Tongued Dragon, Drac and the Gremlin join forces to defeat their foes and finally prevail. This stunning celebration of childhood and the delights of imaginative play is a great way to encourage children to get out in the open air where anything is possible. **SOR**

Matilda 1988

Roald Dahl Quentin Blake

"She felt as though she had touched something that was not quite of this world, the highest point of the heavens."

DON'T MISS THESE ROALD DAHL BOOKS

James and the Giant Peach, 1961
Charlie and the Chocolate Factory, 1964
The Twits, 1980
The BFG, 1982
Esio Trot, 1990

Nationality | Welsh, born 1916 (author); English, born 1932 (illustrator)
Publisher | Jonathan Cape, UK
Theme | Classics, Family, Quirky

Matilda Wormwood, age five, is a genius, but her crooked car salesman father and bingo- and TV-obsessed mother refuse to accept that there is anything special about her and regard her constant reading as a rather unsavory habit. Fed up with being constantly told that she is stupid, Matilda proves more than a match for her parents when she decides to get her revenge on them. Matilda finds an ally in her teacher, Miss Honey, who recognizes her brilliance. At school she also comes across a very scary bully, the terrifying head teacher, Miss Trunchbull. The entire school lives in terror of Miss Trunchbull, who rules with such outrageous violence that children complain "no parent is going to believe [it], not in a million years." When Miss Trunchbull picks on her, Matilda discovers that she possesses an extraordinary power—a power she can use to get the better of Miss Trunchbull and help the lovely Miss Honey.

In *Matilda*, there is plenty of Dahl's slapstick violence—sticking hats on with superglue, hurling small girls by their pigtails—which makes children roll about laughing and squeamish parents, teachers, and librarians shudder. Most adults, however, will love Dahl's lobbying for the joy and empowerment of reading: "All the reading she had done had given her a view of the world that [her parents] had never seen." A wildly fluctuating plot, which lurches hilariously between home and school, reality and fantasy, this is an entertaining book to read aloud, and its simplicity and swift turnover of events will capture the attention of a child beginning to read alone. **CW**

The Keeping Quilt 1988

Patricia Polacco

Nationality | American, born 1944
Publisher | Simon and Schuster, USA
Award | Carnegie Honor Book
Theme | Family

This moving story centers around a traditional handmade quilt that was created by a Russian Jewish immigrant. It also tells the true story of nearly a century of the author's own family history.

When Patricia Polacco's great-great-grandmother came to the United States, she made a quilt from old clothes brought from Russia for her daughter, Anna—"Anna's old dress and babushka, Uncle Vladimir's shirt, Aunt Havalah's nightdress, an apron of Aunt Natasha's. We will make a quilt to help us remember home." The story plots the many important family events in the years that follow, all of which involve the quilt in one way or another.

Young Anna goes on a picnic with her eventual husband on the quilt; when they are married, the quilt is used as a huppah (canopy); it is used as a Sabbath tablecloth; and it warms and welcome generations of new babies. The quilt covers the legs of Gramma Anna as she grows old, and she passes away under the same quilt. The author herself was wrapped in the quilt at birth, got married under it, and brought home her children in it as well. The keeping quilt still exists: Polacco takes it along to all her signings and events, and her own daughter will pass it on to yet another generation of the family.

Polacco's charcoal drawings are a striking feature of this heartwarming story. This wonderfully illustrated tale of the constancy of family, with its customs and celebrations, will appeal to people of all faiths and generations, and it may even start new traditions for readers within their own families. **KD**

Lon Po Po 1989

Ed Young

Nationality | Chinese, born 1931
Publisher | Philomel Books, USA
Award | Caldecott Medal, 1990
Theme | Myths and legends, Classics

The tale of Little Red Riding Hood is given an Asian twist in Ed Young's adaptation. Shang, Tao, and Paotze live with their mother in the Chinese countryside. One day, their mother goes to visit Granny (Po Po), and she warns her three daughters not to let anyone in while she is out. Not long after her departure, there is a knock at the door. When the girls ask who it is, they are told that the visitor is their po po.

The girls reluctantly let in their po po, who really is a wolf disguised as the old woman. As soon as it enters, the wolf blows out the candle the children are holding and suggests that they all go to bed. A wary Shang questions the wolf on its hairy tail and sharp claws, but the wolf's answers do not ease her suspicions. Shang lights her candle, immediately seeing the wolf's hairy face and realizing what has happened. The clever girl pretends to be concerned that her po po has not eaten and suggests that they get some ginkgo nuts, which grow at the top of the tree just outside the house. The girls rush out to the tree, climb to the top, and hatch a plan to trick the wolf, telling it to climb into a basket so they can haul it up. Feigning weakness, the girls let the basket drop to the ground, instantly killing the wolf.

Young's adaptation comes from an ancient oral tradition that is similar to the European version that was popularized by Charles Perrault and the Brothers Grimm. Young captures the feel of Chinese art in his watercolor and pastel illustrations, using traditional panel art to create an intense portrait of the girls' fear as they confront the big bad wolf. **CVB**

Loulou 1989

Grégoire Solotareff

Nationality | French, born 1953
Publisher | L'Ecole des Loisirs, France
Theme | Friendship, Animal stories, Quirky, Illness and death

5+

"Would you by any chance be a rabbit?" the wolf asked.

OTHER GREAT SOLOTAREFF BOOKS

Don't Call Me Little Bunny (Ne m'appelez plus jamais "mon petit lapin"), 1988
Mathieu, 1990
Three Witches (3 sorcières), 2001
Titi in Paris (Titi à Paris), 2008

With its bright, bold colors and striking, playful illustrations, this picture book was an instant hit with young children. Its delightful story of a meeting between a wolf and a rabbit that grows into an unlikely friendship as the two rather different characters get to know each other and themselves has inspired children for two decades. Both rhythmic and simple to understand, *Loulou* is a lively story that is often used in schools to teach children to read and was recently made into a film.

We first meet Loulou (a play on *loup*, the French word for "wolf") when he is being taken out by his uncle on his first hunt. Our hero still has a lot to learn—for one thing, he's never even seen a rabbit before! Unfortunately, the hunt doesn't last very long, however, because in his haste the wolf's uncle runs straight into a rock and dies instantly.

The young orphan then has an unusual encounter: he meets a rabbit named Tom who has never seen a wolf before. Despite the inherent opposition in their natures, Tom and Loulou become the best of friends; after all, a rabbit can learn a lot from a wolf, and a wolf can learn a lot from a rabbit. Fear of wolves, though, is instinctive to all rabbits, and when Loulou and Tom take turns trying to frighten each other, Tom is truly terrified. One night, Tom has a terrible nightmare that Loulou is eating him; it is no longer possible for their friendship to continue as before, and Loulou must leave his newfound friend.

Solotareff explores the themes of friendship, solitude, and the ability to understand fundamental differences in another person by employing the archetypal figure of the wolf and the primal fear that it inspires. The story is amusing and lighthearted at times, but the issue of fear demands to be taken seriously. Loulou and Tom are intrinsically different: can a wolf and a rabbit ever be friends? **SL**

The True Story of the Three Little Pigs 1989

Jon Scieszka Lane Smith

When Jon Scieszka's wife introduced him to Lane Smith, the husband of one of her coworkers, a fruitful collaboration began. Scieszka was already an accomplished children's writer and he and Smith soon produced their first work, *The True Story of the Three Little Pigs*. It was a groundbreaking idea and when they tried to get the book published, it was initially rejected for being "too dark and too sophisticated." Eventually, however, the merit of this amusing parody of a familiar fairy tale was recognized and it was published to great acclaim.

The story is basically an inversion of the traditional children's story *The Three Little Pigs*, as told by A. Wolf (short for Alexander T. Wolf). The wolf claims that he was framed and that the whole story is one big misunderstanding. In this version, all the wolf was trying to do was to bake a cake for his dear granny's birthday. He ran out of sugar and, by the way, he had a terrible sneezing cold that day. When he went to the first little pig's house to borrow some sugar, he happened to sneeze and the house blew down, and because the little pig was already dead, he ate him. The story continues in this vein until the wolf is caught by the police who inevitably see events differently. At the end, it is revealed that the wolf has been telling his story from prison. Children will enjoy being able to make up their own minds about what to believe, now they have heard the "whole story."

In 2008, Scieszka, a former schoolteacher, was made National Ambassador for Young People's Literature to promote reading in the United States. He says that he writes to make children laugh and his stories, which are a riot of irreverent language—such as the pig is "a rude little porker"—will have kids howling with laughter. Lane Smith's art style is original and quirky and is also a perfect complement for this nontraditional version of a classic tale. **KD**

Nationality | American, born 1954 (author); American, born 1959 (illustrator)
Publisher | Penguin, USA
Theme | Myths and legends, Fairy tales

5+

"Hey, it's not my fault wolves eat cute little animals . . . like pigs."

OTHER CRAZY BOOKS BY JON SCIESZKA

The Stinky Cheese Man and Other Fairly Stupid Tales, 1992
Math Curse, 1995
Squids Will Be Squids, 1998
Science Verse, 2004

Oh, the Places You'll Go! 1990

Dr. Seuss

Nationality | American, born Theodor Seuss Geisel, 1904
Publisher | Random House, USA
Theme | Classics, Rhyming stories

5+

Dr. Seuss's final book marked a departure for the grand master of children's rhyming readers. *Oh, the Places You'll Go* tackles independent life and its challenges. Written and designed in a similar style to classics such as *Green Eggs and Ham* and *The Cat In the Hat*, this book is more complex in structure. It starts by asking children to use their imagination to figure out what the real world might be like, and then asks parents to help their children by teaching them about that world. This sets up possible discussions between parent and child as they follow a young boy's journey out of the safety of home and on into the future. The illustrations are delightful, portraying scenes of brightly colored balloons and vivid checkerboard landscapes. This world is not simply seen through rose-colored spectacles. The boy, whose journey represents the reader's life choices, faces lonely slumps as well as intoxicating highs; dark moments in times of solitude as well as fun with friends.

"Will you succeed?
Yes, you will indeed.
(98 ¾ percent guaranteed)."

The words in this gentle rite-of-passage book are well chosen, they are infused with subtle humor and calm kindness. In the United States, the book is often given to students graduating from high school and college. Even non-Seuss fans enjoy its gentler rhythms, although the rhymes still scamper along well enough for Seuss lovers. After all, who would not like to be reassured that their head is full of brains and their shoes full of feet that are too smart to go down any not-so-good street? Some readers claim it is a Christian book, whereas others disagree; but undoubtedly its tone is positive and encouraging. **VN**

OTHER DR. SEUSS BOOKS YOU'LL LOVE

***Horton Hears a Who!*, 1954**
***How the Grinch Stole Christmas*, 1957**
***The Cat In the Hat*, 1957**
***Green Eggs and Ham*, 1960**

"But on you will go / though the weather be foul . . ."

Else-Marie and Her Seven Little Daddies 1990

Pija Lindenbaum

Original Title | Else-Marie och småpapporna
Nationality | Swedish, born 1955
Publisher | Bonniers Juniorförlag, Sweden
Theme | Family, Quirky, Controversial

5+

Else-Marie is, in most respects, a very normal six-year-old girl, not unlike other children her age. However, there is one thing that certainly sets her apart—she has seven daddies. They are all diminutive and look exactly the same. Her seven daddies work as commercial travelers and are away most of the week.

Usually Else-Marie's mother takes her to preschool and picks her up. However, one ordinary afternoon, her mother says in passing that she is going to a meeting and that the daddies are to fetch Else-Marie after school. This spells disaster for Else-Marie. What are the other children going to say? Else-Marie is fine with having seven tiny daddies, in fact, it can be quite practical and fun, but she is not sure that the other children at school will understand. Will they not find them—and therefore Else-Marie, too—terribly strange?

"All my friends at playgroup have just one daddy. One big one."

Else-Marie and Her Seven Little Daddies is a very original book, but despite the zany story line, the theme is common, universal, and timeless—the fear of standing out, being different, and not belonging. How comforting for our heroine when all the worrying and angst proves to be in vain. Nobody takes particular notice of Else-Marie's knee-high fathers. In fact, some of the children find them really entertaining. This is a delightfully quirky book that deals with a serious subject in a seriously funny way. Pija Lindenbaum is an award-winning author and illustrator whose success partly lies in presenting the world from a child's perspective. The story can also be seen as a plea for tolerance for children whose families do not conform to popular convention. **CC**

OTHER BOOKS ABOUT BEING DIFFERENT

Leo the Late Bloomer by Robert Kraus, 1971
A Bad Case of Stripes by David Shannon, 1998
That Pesky Rat by Lauren Child, 2002
Beegu by Alexis Deacon, 2003
Skippyjon Jones by Judith Byron Schachner, 2003

My Friend Percy's Magical Gym Shoes 1991

Ulf Stark Olof Landström

Ulf lacks confidence. He is slightly chubby, so has become the butt of everyone else's joke in gym class. *My Friend Percy's Magical Gym Shoes* (originally *Min vän Percys magiska gymnastikskor*) tells of the day a new boy starts at school. His name is Percy and he is everything Ulf wants to be—strong, brave, and cocky.

One day after gym class, Percy confides to Ulf that he is the way he is because of his magic gym shoes. Ulf finds it hard to believe that a pair of dirty, stinky, and seriously worn-out shoes could be enchanted. Then again, they do seem to work. Percy, who is, in fact, very much in need of some new gym shoes, promises Ulf he can buy the magic shoes. Obviously, they come at a high price but Ulf is prepared to pay whatever they cost. Ulf gives Percy his most beloved belongings, as well as some of his brother's and his father's favorite magazines and records.

"'You see,' whispered Percy. 'These are not just any old treads. . . .'"

Ulf is finally rewarded with the much sought-after shoes. When he puts them on, he experiences a wonderful and extraordinary feeling. He can feel the magic spread all over his body. From that moment on, Ulf's life—and Ulf himself—changes. He is now strong, brave, confident, and cocky, everything he wanted to be and everything he admired so much in Percy. The reader, though, is led to question whether, just maybe, Ulf has changed too much?

My Friend Percy's Magical Gym Shoes is the first of three books about Ulf, Percy, and their unlikely friendship. It is a wonderful, funny, and touching story based on the author's childhood in suburban Stockholm during the 1950s. **CC**

Nationality | Swedish, born 1944 (author); Finland, born 1943 (illustrator)
Publisher | Bonnier Carlsen, Sweden
Theme | Friendship, Magical stories, School

5+

MORE MAGICAL STORIES

My Father's Dragon **by Ruth S. Gannett, 1948**
The Robber Hotzenplotz **by Otfried Preußler, 1962**
Sylvester and the Magic Pebble **by William Steig, 1969**
George's Marvelous Medicine **by Roald Dahl, 1981**
Drac and the Gremlin **by Allan Baillie, 1988**

Tar Beach 1991

 Faith Ringgold

Nationality | American, born 1930
Publisher | Crown, USA
Award | Caldecott Honor Book, 1992
Theme | Magical stories

5+

"I will always remember when the stars fell down around me."

MORE STORIES ABOUT CASSIE

***Aunt Harriet's Underground Railroad in the Sky*, 1992**
***Cassie's Colorful Day*, 1999**
***Counting to Tar Beach*, 1999**
***Cassie's Word Quilt*, 2002**

Award-winning artist Faith Ringgold is best known for her imaginative painted "story quilts"—works of art that combine techniques of painting, quilting fabric, and storytelling. *Tar Beach* has been described as a work of modern art translated into a children's picture book. Ringgold's original painting of the same name hangs at the Solomon R. Guggenheim Museum in New York City.

Based on a story quilt created by the author, this "quilt painting" tells the moving story of eight-year-old Cassie Louise Lightfoot, who, in 1939, desperately longs to be free to go wherever she wants for the rest of her life. One warm summer night, when she is enjoying a family picnic on the "tar beach"—slang for the black, flat rooftops of apartment buildings—her dream comes true. "All you need is somewhere to go you can't get to any other way. The next thing you know, you're flying above the stars." The stars gently lift Cassie up from her blanket and she finds herself flying among them all over the city. Swooping high over the city lights and looking down at where she lives, Cassie dreams of wearing the George Washington Bridge as a necklace, and she imagines giving her father the union building that he is not allowed to join because of his half-black, half-Indian heritage. Her ambitions are limitless and wonderfully unrestrained.

The sequel to *Tar Beach* is *Aunt Harriet's Underground Railroad in the Sky* in which young Cassie goes on a magical voyage back through time with her little brother, Be Be. They meet famous people from U.S. history, including the slave-turned-freedom-activist Harriet Tubman. Cassie's dreams give her hope and help her survive the real everyday hardships of living through the Great Depression era. Part story, part autobiography, part social history, this brilliantly illustrated book is accessible to young children of any heritage who can still imagine being able to fly. **KD**

The Stinky Cheese Man 1992

Jon Scieszka   Lane Smith

Following the runaway success of their first collaboration—a parody of the three little pigs and the big, bad wolf tale—Jon Scieszka and Lane Smith here take the concept of fractured fairy tales to another level. Their efforts were rewarded with a Caldecott Honor and numerous other accolades, and in 2008 Scieszka was named the United States first National Ambassador for Young People's Literature by the Librarian of Congress.

Forget everything you know and love about fairy tales—the traditional happy endings, the moral lessons about truth and justice, good versus evil—because none of these characteristics come into play here. *The Stinky Cheese Man and Other Fairly Stupid Tales* has readers asking all sorts of previously inconceivable questions: What if kissing the frog prince does not turn him into a real prince, but just leaves the princess with frog slime all over her mouth? What if the tortoise was not racing with a hare, but a rabbit who was growing his hair? And as for the ugly duckling. . . . "Well, as it turned out, he was just a really ugly duckling. And he grew up to be just a really ugly duck. The end." Other familiar tales given a humorous twist include "Little Red Riding Hood," which becomes Little Red Running Shorts, and "The Gingerbread Man," is the Stinky Cheese Man of the title, who does not realize that everyone is trying to get away from his terrible smell.

Reading these tales may not yield familiar or predictable endings but it will leave children and adults helplessly laughing together. If you have had enough of traditional fairy tales, these "fairly stupid tales," coupled with brilliant illustrations and radical typeface and font changes that seem to leap off the pages, are guaranteed to entertain. Fairy tales will never be the same again, thanks to this subversive award-winning duo. **KD**

Nationality | American, born 1954 (author); American, born 1959 (illustrator)
Publisher | Viking Penguin, USA
Theme | Myths and legends, Fairy tales

5+

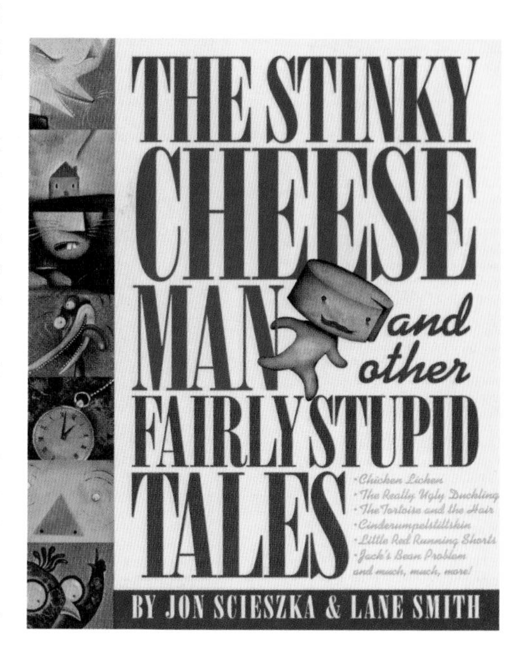

"[Chicken Licken] wasn't the brightest thing on two legs . . . "

OTHER VERY SILLY BOOKS TO ENJOY

The Book of Nonsense **by Edward Lear, 1846**
Fungus the Bogeyman **by Raymond Briggs, 1977**
The Twits **by Roald Dahl, 1980**
The Paper Bag Princess **by Robert Munsch, 1980**
Math Curse **by Jon Scieszka, 1995**

The Little Bird 1993

Paro Anand

Original Title | The Little Bird: A Modern Fable
Nationality | Indian, born 1957
Publisher | HarperCollins, India
Theme | Fantasy, Animal stories

5+

Paro Anand is one of India's foremost children's writers. She says: "Somebody once described my writing as 'the voice of the underdog'—I've never thought about it, but perhaps that's what it is." Anand has written eighteen books for young children and teenagers, and is passionate about children's literature and theater. She also works as a performance storyteller, and has traveled around India, the United Kingdom, France, and Switzerland, reading her stories. She has headed the National Center for Children's Literature—India's national organization for children's books—and has promoted the setting up of libraries in underprivileged areas of India. Anand writes stories about animals told from their perspectives, as well as contemporary stories about multicultural issues. One of her best-known works is *No Guns at My Son's Funeral*, a novel written for teenagers set against the ongoing conflict in Kashmir.

The Little Bird is a modern fantasy-fable that deals with current environmental issues. The creatures of an Indian forest are living in dread because the floods that have devastated their home in the past are threatening to rise again. What is to become of them and who will save them? The unlikely heroine turns out to be Piddi, a courageous little bird who bravely holds the sky up with her feet and eventually sacrifices her life for the other animals. This simple but affecting tale is about the hidden strengths of the underdog and is intended to encourage self-confidence in its readers. It also explores how the other birds of the forest honor Piddi's memory.

Young children who enjoyed reading this moving tale about Piddi may also like to try *Pepper the Capuchin Monkey* and *Elephants Don't Diet*. Slightly older children will enjoy *School Ahead*, which explores the ups and downs of school life with great sensitivity and humor. **HJ**

MORE CHARMING TALES ABOUT BIRDS

***The Ugly Duckling* by Hans Christian Andersen, 1843**
***The Story about Ping* by Marjorie Flack, 1933**
***The Loon's Necklace* by Elizabeth Cleaver, 1977**
***Owl Moon* by Jane Yolen, 1987**
***Lend Me Your Wings* by John Agard, 1987**

Friends from the Other Side 1993

Gloria Anzaldúa   Consuelo Méndez

When a young Mexican-American girl called Prietita meets the cheerful Joaquin, she knows she has found a reliable and affectionate friend. However, she soon has to face up to the bleak social reality that her new friend represents. For Joaquin is a "wetback" or "mojado" in Spanish, the derogatory expression commonly used at the time for those who had crossed the river from Mexico to begin a new life in the United States.

Prietita courageously defends Joaquin from the jibes and attacks of the local children, including her own cousin. She also plans to take him to a herbalist to treat the sores he hides under long sleeves. Finally, she finds herself having to hide him from the border patrol, who are searching for illegal immigrants. Thanks to her resourcefulness, Prietita manages to help hide Joaquin and they escape discovery.

"We had to cross the river because the situation on the other side was very bad."

In this narrative, Gloria Anzaldúa skillfully mingles a faithful portrait of the hard reality of life on the Mexican-American border with an insightful description of the bonds of friendship and love that unite Mexican-Americans and Mexican immigrants. Consuelo Mendez's illustrations are powerful; freely drawn graphite lines define the strong faces and the poverty of the surroundings. The pervasive bleakness is only occasionally tempered by the hot, bright colors of Latino clothing and the desert. The book, written in Spanish (*Amigos del otro lado*) and English, allows young readers to compare the two languages, providing them with the opportunity to learn some basic vocabulary as well, as about both cultures. **LB**

Nationality | Mexican, born 1942 (author); American, birth date unknown (illustrator)
Publisher | Children's Book Press, USA
Theme | Friendship, Controversial

5+

FRIENDS
from the
OTHER SIDE
AMIGOS DEL OTRO LADO
Story by/Escrito por
GLORIA ANZALDÚA
Pictures by/Ilustrado por
CONSUELO MÉNDEZ

TALES ABOUT CROSS-CULTURAL FRIENDS

The Secret Garden by Frances Hodgson Burnett, 1911
Chicken Sunday by Patricia Polacco, 1992
Yo! Yes? by Chris Raschka, 1993

Stellaluna 1993

Janell Cannon

Nationality | American, born 1957
Publisher | Harcourt, USA
Award | ABBY Award, 1994
Theme | Animal stories

5+

Janell Cannon has established a brilliant career by writing stories about animals that children might ordinarily find strange, frightening, or ugly. In Cannon's capable hands, as both an author and gifted illustrator, these otherwise scary animals become adorable and teach a few lessons to readers along the way. The stunning illustrations, which are both zoologically accurate and still remarkably beautiful, will fascinate young readers and make them rethink everything they ever believed about bats.

Stellaluna is a baby fruit bat who, during a sudden attack by an owl, is knocked out of her mother's grasp. Luckily she lands in a nest of baby birds. This event literally turns her world upside down. Stellaluna's adopted bird mother accepts her into the nest on the condition that she acts like a bird, not a bat. Desperately wanting to fit in, Stellaluna stops hanging by her feet and starts to eat bugs.

Eventually, she has the chance to show her bird siblings what life as a bat is like, and together they learn that it is possible to be alike and different at the same time, and more important, that being friends means overlooking those differences: "'How can we be so different and feel so much alike?' one asks. 'And how can we feel so different and be so much alike?'" This delightful story, about a traditionally unlovely creature, offers a great lesson in understanding and tolerance for any child who has ever felt different or has had trouble "fitting in." The book ends with Stellaluna being happily reunited with her mother, followed by two useful pages of facts about bats. **KD**

Horrid Henry 1994

Francesca Simon Tony Ross

Nationality | American, born 1955 (author); English, born 1938 (illustrator)
Publisher | Orion Children's Books, UK
Theme | Favorite characters, Family

When this first *Horrid Henry* book was published, Francesca Simon could hardly have foreseen that every new title in the series would be a best seller in her adopted country and that Henry would have his own television show and website. This first title sets the pattern for all those that followed. Each of the four short chapters follows an incident in the life of Horrid Henry, his younger brother, Perfect Peter, and their long-suffering parents. Illustrator Tony Ross's quickfire cartoons and affectionate caricatures are the perfect complement to Simon's stories.

The character of the badly behaved boy has many antecedents in British children's literature and popular culture, perhaps the most well-known being Richmal Crompton's William and the *Beano* comic's Dennis the Menace, although few of these forerunners are as young as Henry himself. Horrid Henry and all his friends with alliterative names, including the overbearing Moody Margaret, are drawn larger than life, as are the comic catastrophes that they suffer or provoke. The frustrations of family life will, however, be recognized by every child and parent—whether it is behavior at the dinner table, playing with the bossy girl next door, or having the kind of holiday your parents like rather than the one you would prefer.

The extremes of behavior displayed by Perfect Peter and Horrid Henry are reactions to the perennial power struggle between adults and children. Child readers will laugh out loud and be secretly delighted at Henry's outrageous behavior and his ability to generally come out on top. **CB**

Old Tom 1994

Leigh Hobbs

Nationality | Australian, born 1953
Publisher | Puffin, Australia
Award | S. A. Kanga Award, 2004
Theme | Favorite characters, Family

One day Angela Throgmorton answers a knock at her door to find "a baby monster" tucked up in a basket. She calls him Old Tom and decides to raise him. So begins the first in the *Old Tom* series. Even as a baby, Old Tom is a rare character. With no more than three lines of text per page, most of the narrative is visual, each page filled with the chaotic detail of Angela's efforts and Old Tom's antics, drawn in spirited and cartoonlike pen and ink.

Angela, a fastidious, house-proud woman, has landed herself with a slovenly, mischievous, wayward creature. Old Tom seems impossible, but Angela struggles on, trying to teach him to be tidy and to have good manners. Eventually, she gets so fed up that she kicks him out of the house. At this point, they both revel in their freedom: Angela gets stuck into her dusting, and Old Tom gets out and about. He has a wonderful time, but then he falls on hard times, is captured, and put into the pound. Angela, meanwhile, is missing her "baby" dreadfully. She sets out to look for him, finds him and, happily reunited, they walk home together hand in hand.

Although he looks vaguely catlike, Hobbs has described Old Tom as "more of a Tasmanian Devil mixed with a Blue Heeler dog than a cat." The Old Tom books appeal to readers of many ages, including adults who share Hobbs's sense of humor. The series can be read aloud to children younger than five and is suitable for emerging readers to tackle independently. The brilliant Old Tom has also been the star of his own animated television show. **AJ**

"He's more like a cheeky seven-year-old boy. He's scruffy and war-torn, and carries a fish skeleton, his dolly."

OTHER AMUSING LEIGH HOBBS BOOKS

Old Tom at the Beach, 1995
Horrible Harriet, 2002
Fiona the Pig, 2004
Old Tom, Man of Mystery, 2005

5+

Jennifer Jones Won't Leave Me Alone 1995

Frieda Wishinsky Linda Hendry

5+

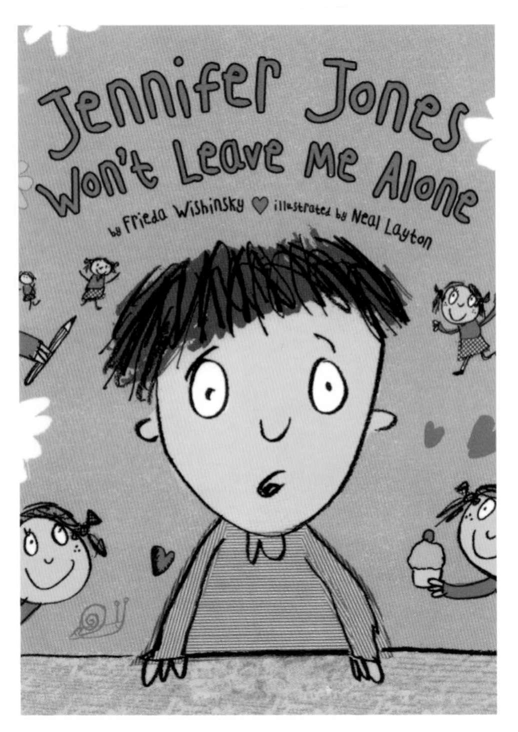

"She writes me love poems
Full of words like adore,
Then she sticks on red hearts
That she bought at the store."

OTHER PESKY KID STORIES

Pippi Longstocking by Astrid Lindgren, 1945
My Naughty Little Sister by Dorothy Edwards, 1952
Naughty Children, edited by Christianna Brand, 1962
Ramona the Brave by Beverley Cleary, 1975
Horrid Henry by Francesca Simon, 1993

Nationality | German/Canadian, born 1948 (author); Canadian, born 1961 (illustrator)
Publisher | HarperCollins, Canada
Theme | Love, School, Poetry

Jennifer Jones has a huge crush on the boy who sits next to her. She shouts in his ear, professes her love, and writes him amorous poems decorated with red hearts. The poor boy is mortified by her attention, a sentiment exacerbated by the jokes and sniggers of his friends. Vehemently, he wishes Jennifer gone, imagining her moving to the jungle and transferring her affection to the monkeys, to the Arctic where she can bother the bears, or stranded on the moon, anywhere but near him!

Yet when Jennifer leaves to go and live in Europe, the narrator feels her absence more keenly than he could have possibly anticipated. Immersing himself in schoolwork does not help him forget his pesky companion: "It's boring! It's lonely! I miss her a lot. I wish she'd come back to her usual spot." Absence does indeed make the heart grow fonder. On hearing that Jennifer is due to return, the newly enamored boy rushes out to buy a bundle of red hearts.

This tale in verse has universal appeal: everyone can identify with a first crush. Neal Layton reillustrated the book in 2003, and his cute, colorful drawings bring the story to giddy life, with dozens of shrieking Jennifers on a spread helping to illustrate the extent of her unwavering ardor. The perplexed expression and uncomfortable wriggling of the narrator perfectly capture his gruff embarrassment. Jennifer's travels around Europe are depicted as photo-collages of the capital cities, adding an appealing visual depth. Frieda Wishinsky's amusing rhymes and canny awareness of human foibles make it a hilarious book. **MK**

Math Curse 1995

Jon Scieszka Lane Smith

Nationality | American, born 1954 (author); American, born 1959 (illustrator)
Publisher | Viking Press, USA
Theme | Fantasy

Award-winning duo Jon Scieszka and Lane Smith are at it again this time in a hilarious romp through the most anxiety-inducing math question on every test—the word problem. Just reading the author's dedication to *Math Curse* will let children know exactly what they are in for: "If the sum of my nieces and nephews equals 15, and their product equals 54, and I have more nephews than nieces, how many nephews and how many nieces is this book dedicated to?"

It starts out simply enough. During a math lesson, a teacher tells her class, "You know, you can think of almost everything as a math problem." Suddenly, our narrator is suffering from a serious "Math Curse" that causes her entire world to become a math problem: "Does tunafish + tunafish = fournafish?" She reaches into the refrigerator for the milk to put on her cereal and finds herself wondering, "1. How many quarts in a gallon? 2. How many pints in a quart? 3. How many inches in a foot? 4. How many feet in a yard? 5. How many yards in a neighborhood? How many inches in a pint? How many feet in my shoes?"

The stories by Scieszka, a former teacher, have been described as "fractured fairy tales," where the story is told from a different point of view. Our narrator's frustration and panic leads to eventual elation when she has a dream that shows her the way out of her Math Curse. Once again, Lane Smith's bold paintings use collage, paint, and typefaces to create the bizarre and entertaining world in which a Math Curse is credible. For every child (or adult) who has ever had a case of math anxiety, this book could be the cure. **KD**

Moka the Cow 1995

Agostino Traini

Original Title | La mucca Moka
Nationality | Italian, born 1961
Publisher | Emme Edizioni, Italy
Theme | Favorite characters, Animal Stories

Full of captivating, colorful pictures, this is a delightful series for children who are just starting to read. The energetic and inventive Moka is a charming cow character, a friend to her companions in the story, as well as to young readers.

When Moka finds a coin in the sweet-smelling grass of her mountain pastures, she decides to venture to the city. There, she attends a school where she learns the art of making hot chocolate. Moka makes her way back to the mountains, where her delicious hot chocolate proves enormously popular with everyone. She makes enough money to open a hotel, which has its own patisserie on the ground floor. Using her hard-earned coins, the generous Moka decides to purchase a train ticket for each of her friends. The train will take them to the city, where they too can attend the hot chocolate-making school, just as she did.

Agostino Traini's illustrations are light and full of expression. They sensitively depict the emotions of Moka and her friends. Each picture uses lively colors and is framed with a photographer's sense of composition. At the end of this charming yet simple story, in a particularly memorable illustration, Moka personally delivers hot chocolate from her hotel to the skiers on the slopes. This fun-filled book finishes with several extra pages dedicated to games. The munificent and gentle cow, Moka, went on to feature in a whole series of books set in the scenic mountain valley. Traini has created other popular figures featuring the same distinctive illustrative style including Leo Leopardo. **SMT**

David Almond reviews:

Lilly's Purple Plastic Purse 1996

Kevin Henkes

Nationality | American, born 1960
Publisher | Greenwillow Books, USA
Award | A.L.A. Notable Children's Book
Theme | Animal stories, School, Friendship

LILLY'S PURPLE PLASTIC PURSE

BY KEVIN HENKES

The first time I read *Lilly's Purple Plastic Purse* with my daughter, she said, "Let's read it again." So we turned straight back to the first page, started again, and we enjoyed it even more. We must have read it twenty times when she was growing up, and it continued to be funny, touching, and true.

Lilly might look like a mouse, but she perfectly embodies the passions, joys, shames, delights, and despairs of childhood. Her relationships—with her family and schoolmates, and especially with her artistic and eccentric teacher, Mr. Slinger—are lightly sketched and totally convincing. The devastating impact of the plastic purse—with its jaunty tune that Lilly just has to let everyone hear and its contents that she just has to let everyone see—is absolutely believable. We are given Lilly's whole world—with its pointy chalk, film star sunglasses, jingly coins, lightbulb lab, lurching stomach, uncooperative chair, interpretive dance, and Mr. Slinger's ties—and the whole thing is a delight.

"'Let's be considerate . . .' [said Mr. Slinger.] Lilly had a hard time being considerate."

The writing is lovely and rhythmical. The illustrations are sharp and affecting. The book even contains a wonderful, illustrated book-within-a-book written by Lilly herself in which "the sun shined its smiley face down on everyone and everything. Even the beetles and the worms." The story takes us on a beautiful exuberant journey: Lilly dances with joy at the start, slumps with dejection in the middle, and skips with irrepressible optimism at the end. *Lilly's Purple Plastic Purse* is truly a little masterpiece: read it, and like Lilly and Mr. Slinger, you will say, "Wow."

OTHER ADORABLE MOUSE BOOKS

Perez the Mouse **by Luis Coloma, 1894**
The Mouse and His Child **by Russell Hoban, 1967**
Doctor De Soto **by William Steig, 1982**
Angelina Ballerina **by Katherine Holabird, 1983**
Lilly's Chocolate Heart **by Kevin Henkes, 2003**

Lilly did an "interpretive dance" with her purple plastic purse. 

The Sea at the End of the Forest 1997

Pinin Carpi

Original Title | Il mare in fondo al bosco
Nationality | Italian, born 1920
Publisher | Einaudi Ragazzi, Italy
Theme | Fantasy, Adventure

Every page of Pinin Carpi's *The Sea at the End of the Forest* (originally published as *Il mare in fondo al bosco*) is like an exquisite painting—rich in detail, with as much attention paid to the figures in the foreground as there is to the surrounding landscape. In this title, Carpi has created a magical forest that is guaranteed to capture the imagination of young readers.

The fast-paced story follows its young protagonist, a boy who finds himself transported into the tropical forests of India. The little boy was based on none other than the author's son, Paolo. In the forest he encounters pirates, wild beasts, mysterious-looking alleyways, astronauts, slave-traders, thieves, pirates, monkeys, goblins, crocodiles, and scary monsters, all of which lead to many adventures.

The plot is full of suspense—it is wonderfully easy to get lost in *The Sea at the End of the Forest*—yet Carpi never lets go of the reins of the story. A hugely talented and award-winning writer and illustrator, Carpi always makes sure his young reader is eventually lulled to sleep.

Pinin Carpi was born into a family of artists, and painted for many years before he began writing. Most of his books are illustrated with watercolor drawings. His other works include a series in which the paintings of famous artists, including Van Gogh, Matisse, Klee, Canaletto, and Goya, served as inspiration for remarkable stories. Most of Carpi's books came out of stories he invented for his own children. **SMT**

My Kingdom for a Horse 1997

Ana M. Machado   Elisabeth Teixeira

Nationality | Brazilian, born 1941 (author); Brazilian, birth date unknown (illustrator)
Publisher | Salamandra, Brazil
Theme | Family, Animal stories

Parents who wonder what makes a boy happy know full well that the answer varies from individual to individual. In the case of Prince Richard, the protagonist of Ana María Machado's *My Kingdom for a Horse* (originally published as *Meu Reino por um Cavalo*), the answer is, quite simply, a horse. For Prince Richard already has many clothes and innumerable toys; as a prince, he already owns a castle, and he is, of course, heir to a vast kingdom. In short, he has almost everything he might wish for. Everything, that is, except a horse.

Richard wants a horse because he knows that it is an indispensable requirement for a brave knight. He wants it so badly that he would swap his entire future kingdom for a horse. And not a toy horse—a real one.

Richard speaks the words "My kingdom for a horse!" and Machado tells her readers, "These words sounded harmless but left a strange echo in the air." The words turn out to be some kind of magic formula and a number of horses of all different types start to appear. These include wooden horses, racing horses, carthorses, even chess pieces in the shape of a horse. After finally choosing the right horse, Richard embarks on a series of adventures that give him the opportunity to realize his dreams of rescuing people in trouble. This brings him respect, fame, and prestige. Above all, it brings Richard the esteem of his father, who recognizes his young boy's courage and decides to give him a special prize—a proper horse. **LB**

The Great Escape from City Zoo 1997

Tohby Riddle

Nationality | Australian, born 1965
Publisher | HarperCollins, Australia
Theme | Animal stories, Adventure, Fantasy, Friendship

5+

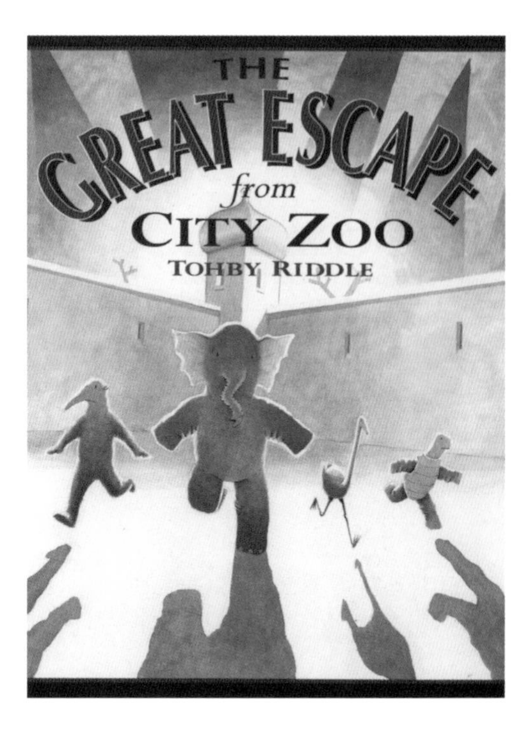

This universal picture story already has the feel of a classic, partly because the cleverly constructed tale has so many familiar icons woven into its fabric. Tohby Riddle's architect training and cartoon work have provided him with a wealth of twentieth-century visual references. *The Great Escape from City Zoo* is equally engaging for adults and children. Readers will chuckle as they spot famous paintings, people, films, photographs, and buildings. Although adults might regard it as a satire, a parable, or a spoof, children will enjoy it as a daring tale of escape and adventure.

One night, by the light of a full moon, an anteater, an elephant, a turtle, and a flamingo escape from the city zoo. Disguised as a chef, a businessman, a sailor, and a postman, they discover the big city. They walk the streets, see a film, and go to an art exhibition. In danger of being caught, they hatch a plan and hitch a freight train out of town—except the anteater who decides to try his luck in the big city. Just as things seem to be working out, they blow their cover. One by one the animals are recaptured, returning to the zoo as heroes—except for the flamingo who, we are told, may still be out there.

Riddle sets his story in the past, written in a deadpan tone reminiscent of 1930s detective stories, which is perfectly in tune with what appear as slightly overexposed black-and-white illustrations. Reading it is a quietly hilarious experience that reminds one of watching a silent movie. **AJ**

"There had been some strange goings-on at City Zoo for some time. Something was brewing."

OTHER ENTERTAINING ANIMAL TALES

Just So Stories by Rudyard Kipling, 1902
The Wonderful Farm by Marcel Ayme, 1934
Mr. Popper's Penguins by Richard Atwater, 1938
Foxie by Ingri and Edgar Parin D'Aulaire, 1949
Dodo Gets Married by Petra Mathers, 2001

Henry and Amy 1998

Stephen Michael King

"Henry and Amy are the very, very best of friends . . . right-way-round and upside down. . . ."

MORE FROM STEPHEN MICHAEL KING

***The Man Who Loved Boxes,* 1995**
***Emily Loves to Bounce,* 2000**
***Pocket Dogs,* with Margaret Wild, 2000**
***Where Does Thursday Go?,* with Janeen Brian, 2001**
***Milli, Jack and the Dancing Cat,* 2003**

Nationality | Australian, birth date unknown
Publisher | Scholastic Press, Australia
Award | C.B.C.A. Book of the Year (shortlist), 1999
Theme | Friendship, Quirky

This is a cheerful picture book about two very different young children who become best friends. Henry is playful and eccentric, but often finds that his life is a bit out of his control. He is the sort of person who, when he plans a sunny picnic, ends up under a tablecloth in the rain (with his dog and his toys).

One morning when he's out walking backward (even though he is trying very hard to walk forward), he bumps into Amy. Amy who is quite the opposite to Henry, is neat, sweet, and very capable—but deep down, she would like to be a little bit less perfect. Henry shows her back-to-front while Amy shows him his right from his left. When they build a treehouse, Amy works on the plan so it will sit in the tree just right, and Henry adds the wiggly bits that make it beautiful. They discover that together they make a great team.

This is a quirky, sweet title about what it is like to feel, and to be, different and not to have to conform. It is a celebration of individuality and a funny, sometimes charmingly silly, look at children's friendships and the minutiae of their lives. Stephen Michael King is a writer and illustrator—who sometimes illustrates for other authors—and has worked for a children's library and as a children's book designer. His thorough knowledge of all aspects of children's literature shines forth in *Henry and Amy*. His lively drawings, with their happy splashes of color, capture the spontaneity of the two children's play and are full of whimsical detail. His popular books have been shortlisted for a number of awards and translated into several languages. **AJ**

A Bad Case of Stripes 1998

David Shannon

Nationality | American, born 1960
Publisher | Scholastic, USA
Theme | Friendship, Quirky, School, Fantasy, Controversial

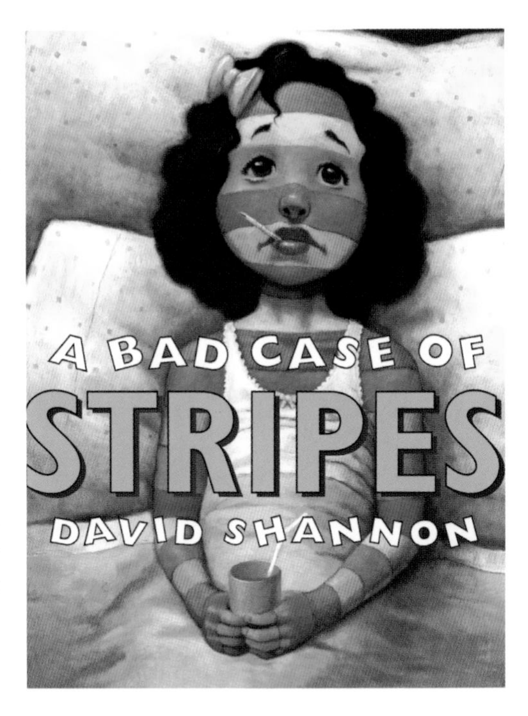

One of the trickiest things parents have to teach their children is how to "fit in." Parents want their children to be well liked and to get along with others, but it is often a struggle for young children to learn how to be part of a group and still maintain their sense of individuality. Although children themselves do not use these words, they still know what it feels like to be ostracized.

David Shannon is an award-winning author and illustrator who tackles the issue of being true to one's self in this story of a young girl who tries so hard to fit in that she breaks out in a very bad case of stripes, not to mention at various times, stars and stripes, roots, crystals, feathers, and a long furry tail.

The story of Camilla Cream is an allegory of a young girl who "changes her stripes" at anybody's suggestion, and can only be cured of this terrible malady when she finally embraces nonconformity and admits her terrible secret—she loves lima beans, a vegetable loathed by children everywhere, even though all her friends hate them! "Camilla was always worried about what other people thought of her" we are told.

There is a great deal of dark humor in this book, as well as a strong message about not giving in to peer pressure. While some children may find a few of the images disturbing as Camilla's skin physically shows the price of trying to fit in, many others will find them hysterically funny. The message for young children, which Shannon delivers with great humor and understanding, is a good one—be true to your self. **KD**

"Camilla Cream loved lima beans. But she never ate them. All of her friends hated lima beans and she wanted to fit in."

OTHER GREAT SCHOOL BOOKS

Miss Nelson Is Missing by Harry Allard, 1977
Else-Marie and her Seven Little Daddies by Pija Lindenbaum, 1990
David Goes to School by David Shannon, 1999
I Hate School by Jeanne Willis, 2003

Rumpelstiltskin and Other Grimm Tales 1999

Carol Ann Duffy Markéta Prachatická

Nationality | Scottish, born 1955 (author); Czech, birth date unknown (illustrator)
Publisher | Faber and Faber, UK
Theme | Fairy tales

These sixteen stories from the collection of the Brothers Grimm were developed from Carol Ann Duffy's 1997 play, produced for the Young Vic Theatre in London. Her rewriting of the tales returns them to their original state—dark, wicked, capricious, and funny, where nature is untamed and can wreak havoc on human beings. Humans, on the other hand, almost always precipitate the events of the story through their greed, stupidity, or cruelty. As Duffy herself writes, "No matter how grand someone might be they should not poke fun at anyone beneath themselves—not even a hedgehog."

Duffy is one of Britain's most highly regarded poets and her skill with rhythm and sound is evident throughout the text and elevates it from mere storytelling. "Clever Hans," for example, is largely in direct speech and in a poetic form that uses repetition. Poetry turns up in other stories, such as "Ashputtel," a far more satisfying version of the Cinderella story than the one people are familiar with. Ashputtel is helped by nature rather than a fairy godmother, and the ugly sisters get their just rewards—they are blinded. In "Snow White," Duffy does not flinch from making the wicked queen dance to her death in red-hot iron shoes.

Duffy is always concerned with the authentic flavor of the originals, not about producing toothless, sanitized versions. She embraces street language where appropriate and frequently adds her own observations. The text is beautifully illustrated with forty black-and-white line drawings by celebrated artist, Markéta Prachatická. **WO**

"The witch's dreadful, gluttonous plan was to shut the oven door once Gretel was inside, so she could roast her."

MORE FAIRY TALES TO READ ALOUD

The Ugly Duckling by Hans Christian Andersen, 1843
The Blue Fairy Book by Andrew Lang, 1891
Italian Folktales by Italo Calvino, 1956
Lon Po Po by Ed Young, 1989
The Three Pigs by David Wiesner, 2001

The Death Book 1999

Pernilla Stalfelt

Original Title | Dödenboken
Nationality | Swedish, born 1962
Publisher | Eriksson and Lindgren, Sweden
Theme | Illness and death, Controversial

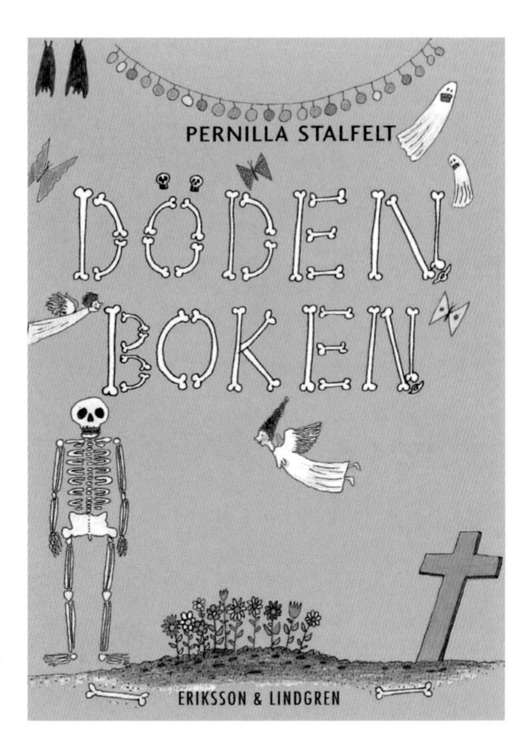

The Death Book is exactly what it says it is. But, how do you write about death without making it scary, sad, or gloomy? Well, if you are Pernilla Stalfelt, author and illustrator of a long list of popular and critically acclaimed books, you make it funny. Stalfelt's approach is to try to explain death in a very matter-of-fact way. Typically, she begins with a quote from an encyclopedia. She then goes through all aspects of death in her characteristic way, always with a big portion of humor. How do people, animals, and plants look when they are dead? She continues with death caused by age, accidents, and sickness.

It might all sound rather morbid (in the very real sense of the word), but Stalfelt deals with the subject in a disarming, warm, and, believe it or not, charming way. She points out the difficulty of understanding death for young and old alike through cartoonlike drawings; a child and an adult are pictured pondering the theme with "think" bubbles above their heads. She then comments that "It can be hard even if you're really big," and an elephant is shown with its own thoughts on the subject. The book takes up the sadness experienced by those left behind, as well as different beliefs around ideas of the afterlife: "Some think you become a star in the sky."

The Death Book benefits from Stalfelt's trademark whimsical illustrations and from the short lines of text intertwined between the pictures. It is a great starting point for reflection and conversation with children about a troubling subject, as well as being informative and thought-provoking for grown-ups, too. **CC**

"It's hard to understand what death is . . . not only when you're little, but when you're big, too. . . ."

OTHER ACCLAIMED BOOKS BY STALFELT

***The Hair Book (Hårboken),* 1996**
***The Poo Book (Bajsboken),* 1997**
***The Love Book (Kårlekboken),* 2001**

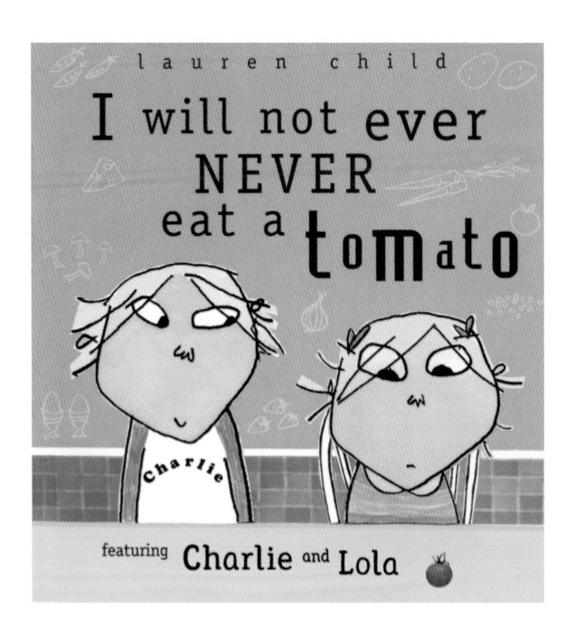

I Will Not Ever Never Eat a Tomato 2000

Lauren Child

Nationality | English, born 1967
Publisher | Orchard Books, UK
Award | Kate Greenaway Medal, 2001
Theme | Family, Quirky

Getting his little sister, Lola, to eat her dinner "is a hard job because she is a very fussy eater," Charlie tells us. So Charlie decides to appeal to her imagination. When he tells her carrots are orange twiglets from Jupiter, Lola has her doubts—"They look just like carrots to me"—but she allows herself to be convinced by the explanation that carrots don't grow on Jupiter.

Charlie persuades Lola to eat peas (green drops from Greenland) by trying to keep these "incredibly rare" delicacies for himself, and by the time he gets to the mashed potatoes (cloud fluff from Mount Fuji) and fish sticks (ocean nibbles from a supermarket under the sea), no persuasion is necessary—Lola is gobbling and asking for more. Before Charlie can congratulate himself on the success of his deception, Lola turns the tables, asking for a tomato, the one thing she has assured him she will "not ever never" eat. "Moonsquirters are my favorites," she says triumphantly, showing she understood the game all along.

The charmingly witty lives of Charlie and Lola are juxtaposed with glorious fantasy scenes in a collage of photographs, cartoon drawings, and retro fabrics. The type bounds and weaves across the page, in a variety of sizes and fonts, heaped up to imitate Mount Fuji or set in ripples under the sea. There is a thrill at every page turn, as each spread contrasts with the last in perspective, background, or setting. In *I Will Not Ever Never Eat a Tomato*, Child has captured the essence of a great picture book, with text and illustration perfectly balanced and in tune with one another. **CW**

5+

Fox 2000

Margaret Wild Ron Brooks

Nationality | Australian, born 1948 (author); Australian, born 1948 (illustrator)
Publisher | Allen and Unwin, Australia
Theme | Friendship, Illness and death

In this powerful story about friendship, betrayal, and courage, the language is beautifully spare and the illustrations are vibrant and haunting. The text, written with scratchy pen, creates an edgy atmosphere.

A powerful bond grows between Dog, who is partly blind, and Magpie, who cannot fly. Dog invites Magpie to climb on his back, and together they gallop through the bush. One day Fox comes looking for shelter. Magpie is distrustful, but Dog welcomes Fox in. While Dog sleeps, Fox asks Magpie to go with him and "fly faster than the wind," but she is loyal to Dog. Yet when Fox tempts her a third time, she goes.

"Magpie and Fox streak past coolibah trees, rip through long grass, pelt over rocks." In the illustration, Fox stretches, red orange across a double page, with Magpie seemingly standing on the sky. Below them are thick, streaky-painted rocks, trees scraped through the olive browns of a low horizon, and behind, a heavy blue sky. Then Fox stops, shakes Magpie off, and pads away. Looking back he says, "Now you and Dog will know what it is like to be truly alone." Magpie, left in the heat to die, thinks of Dog alone, and courageously begins her long trek home.

Brooks's images grow out of Wild's careful language, and are perfectly in tune. The position of the spidery text sets the pace and tone of the story, and there is a strong sense of place, with rich, vegetable-like colors. The paper's surface is streaked and gouged with brush lines, scratches, and finely etched drawings. The animals, though stylized, are also thoroughly real. **AJ**

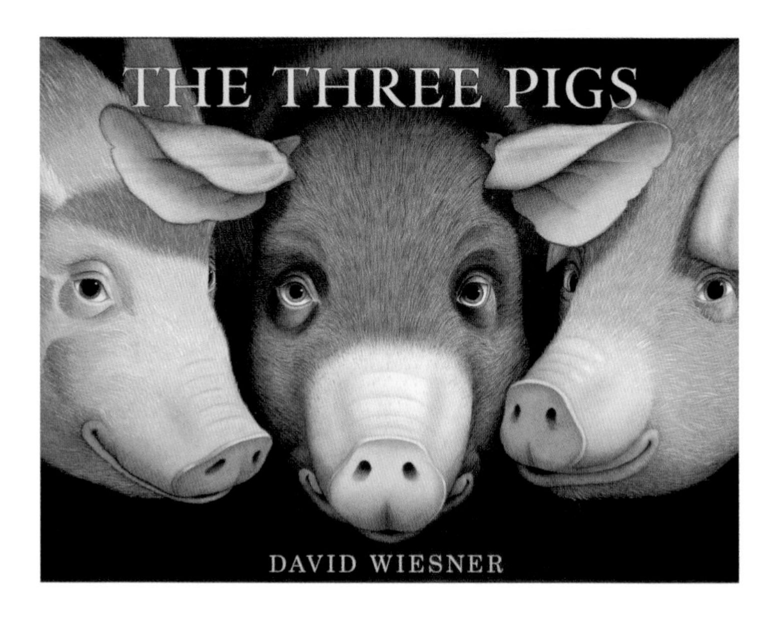

5+

The Three Pigs 2001

David Wiesner

Nationality | American, born 1956
Publisher | Clarion Books, USA
Award | Caldecott Medal, 2002
Theme | Fairy tales, Animal stories

The original story of *The Three Little Pigs* is a familiar one. The pigs are tracked down by a wolf who attempts to destroy their homes and eat the pigs in turn. In David Wiesner's adaptation, however, the reader sees an unconventional shift in the telling. The idea of the characters disappearing off into blank, unorthodox space is explored, and an invitation to other well-known characters to join the tale is given.

Wiesner uses the universally familiar beginnings of the story as a departure point before sending the audience into a wilderness of narrative offshoots. Tradition flies out of the window when the pigs are blown right off the page by the huffing and puffing of the wolf. The pigs thus embark on a surreal adventure outside the traditional format, complemented by Wiesner's simple and soft-hued illustrations. Differing illustrative techniques are used to great effect, for example, a more traditional style of drawing is used in the initial frames, whereas a sharper set of images accompanies the unorthodox splitting of the plot.

Wiesner's playful deconstruction takes a classic story and leads it away from the confines of its own narrative, making this reworking of *The Three Little Pigs* a fresh and enjoyable read for young children. Adults will also appreciate the change from the version they heard in their own childhoods. As the plot takes off in unexpected directions, children will become aware of the myriad possibilities within a story and will be exposed to an element of freedom that cannot be found in many other books. **LK**

5+

Dodo Gets Married 2001

Petra Mathers

Nationality | German, born 1945
Publisher | Atheneum Books, USA
Theme | Friendship, Family, Animal stories, Quirky

Despite growing up in Germany, Petra Mathers is much better known in her adopted home, the United States, where she moved at the age of twenty-three. She is best known as the author and illustrator of the popular Lottie's World series.

Dodo Gets Married is the fourth book in the series about Lottie the chicken, Herbie the duck, and their flamboyant and peculiar friend, the pink German bird Dodo. In this book Dodo first befriends and then falls in love with the seabird and former helicopter pilot Captain Vince. An unlikely couple, the two nevertheless connect on an emotional level as Dodo manages to penetrate the barrier Vince has put up between himself and the world because of the physical and emotional wounds he has suffered.

Vince, having lost a leg in a rescue mission, has become grumpy and miserable, although deep inside he is kind and giving. He will not admit he suffers from loneliness, but Dodo's charming company lightens his mood and eventually leads him to pop the question. He does so by inscribing his proposal on a ring before flying over to Dodo's house in a helicopter and dropping the ring in her garden. In reply, she takes the clothes hanging outside to dry and puts them on the floor to spell out her reply, thus paving the way for a wonderful wedding: "The sun set, the moon rose. It was a glorious day on Crook Road."

With its funny, lovable characters, as well as Mather's magnificent watercolors, the book has a great charm that will leave young readers enthralled. **DaH**

Ug: Boy Genius of the Stone Age 2001

Raymond Briggs

Nationality | English, born 1934
Publisher | Jonathan Cape, UK
Award | Nestlé Children's Book Prize (shortlist)
Theme | Friendship, Family

5+

Readers moving on from Raymond Briggs's *The Snowman* and *The Bear* (not that anyone ever really moves on from *The Snowman* or *The Bear*) will empathize with Ug, who represents the universal inquisitive and creative child, systematically squashed by adults. *Ug: Boy Genius of the Stone Age*, as well as being a story about children and parents, is a series of philosophical reflections that will absorb older children and adults. It explores how people with big ideas inevitably suffer from the insecurity they induce in others, looking at how much of the progress of civilizations may have been held back as a result and how little we understand about our place in history while we are living in it.

Ug is a forward-thinking inventor who can see beyond the limited technology of his times (a Flintstones-type Stone Age), but is ridiculed by his community for his outlandish ideas, such as cooking dead animals on the fire or skinning them to make soft trousers. His father (Dug), his mother (Dugs), and his friend (Ag) cannot keep up with Ug's energy and questioning spirit. Like Briggs's much-loved characters Gentleman Jim and Fungus the Bogeyman, Ug is a doomed hero. His attempts to improve his condition by inventing irrigation, enclosures, boat building, and the wheel (although he's not sure what the wheel is for) come to nothing, simply because the world is not ready for him.

The final page reveals a grown-up Ug who is still firmly living in the Stone Age—his mother, whose grasp of history is poor, had assured him that the Ice Age would be there before he knew it—and frustrated at the lack of progress in his lifetime. On a positive note, Ug is still striving to improve his environment by creating the cave paintings of Lascaux, his mother having predicted he would "end up painting animals on the walls." **GB**

MORE FROM RAYMOND BRIGGS

***Fungus the Bogeyman,* 1977**
***Gentleman Jim,* 1980**
***The Man,* 1992**
***The Bear,* 1994**
***The Puddleman,* 2004**

The Love Book 2001

 Pernilla Stalfelt

Original Title | Kärlekboken
Nationality | Swedish, born 1962
Publisher | Eriksson and Lindgren, Sweden
Theme | Love, Controversial

5+

Love, the greatest thing of all, the driving force in life, and a subject that truly is inexhaustible. To try to explain love in twenty-five pages—and to children of all ages—takes real courage. This funny and slightly crazy book bravely attempts to do exactly that.

In *The Love Book*, Stalfelt uses a straightforward, matter-of-fact manner to thoroughly investigate love. The approach is at times almost clinical and scientific, although also humorous and heart-warming. We get served a long list of what love can be and how love feels—love for a person, love for a flower, love for a pet, love for God. She also goes through the darker side of love, including jealousy and unrequited love, all exemplified with funny "case studies." The reader is

"Love is like a gift. You get it for free if someone wants to give it away."

given practical information, for example, on how to flirt, how to write a love letter, and what gift to give to one's beloved, as well as more general knowledge, such as the fact that there is a God called Amor and that his sole concern is love. "Love can be the easiest thing," Stalfelt tells us, "or the hardest thing ever," she adds sagely.

The smart and humorous text is complemented with Stalfelt's hilarious illustrations. The pictures are integral to the book and are probably best described as rather ugly but full of humor, detail, and color. There is also a section about marriage and how children are created, with rather explicit yet clear scientific drawings. As an extra bonus, Stalfelt generously shares a secret recipe of a love potion at the end of the book. *The Love Book* has deservedly received attention from readers and critics alike. **CC**

MORE GREAT BOOKS ABOUT LOVE

Love You Forever by Robert Munsch, 1986
Jennifer Jones Won't Leave Me Alone by Frieda Wishinsky, 2003
The Biggest Kiss in the World by Ricardo Chávez Castañeda, 2003

That Pesky Rat 2002

Lauren Child

Nationality | English, born 1967
Publisher | Orchard Books, UK
Award | Nestlé Children's Book Prize
Theme | Friendship, Animal stories

This stunning children's book tells the story of a street rat who is itching to be loved. With no owner and no name—simply referred to as "that pesky rat"—he feels as if he does not belong. The reader is taken on a journey by this strangely likable and—in his own words "cutesy"—rat during which he encounters many different pets. From the lop-eared rabbit, Nibbles, who performs in a circus but craves a quiet life, to Pierre, the chinchilla who lives a life of luxury but has to be shampooed frequently. This is a lovely tale that children will enjoy, but the main theme of the need to be loved will also resonate with adults.

Lauren Child uses her distinctive illustrative style to make the book a design classic. The words sprawl randomly across the page and the collagelike illustrations give the book a vibrant style and charm. "Sometimes when I am tucked up in my crisp packet," the rat tells us, "I . . . wonder what it would be like to live with creature comforts. To belong to somebody. To be an actual pet."

Child's work came to prominence through the bestselling Charlie and Lola series, which have been adapted into a popular TV show. With the creation of her Clarice Bean character, Child seems to go from strength to strength. *That Pesky Rat* was adapted into a highly acclaimed stage show in 2006. The fact that all the profits from the sale of this book go to UNESCO's program for the Education of Children in Need is just one more reason to come away from reading this book with a big smile on your face. **RS**

5+

Beegu 2003

Alexis Deacon

Nationality | English, born 1979
Publisher | Hutchinson, UK
Theme | Friendship, Family, Quirky, Fantasy, Controversial

Beegu is different. She is from another planet, and she accidentally crashes her spaceship on Earth and finds herself all alone. Author and illustrator Alexis Deacon says the book is based on his own experience after he graduated from art school, moved to London, "and was inspired to write about loneliness."

"Beegu was not supposed to be here. She was lost." She is a yellow, rabbitlike creature with three eyes and long floppy ears. All she wants is a friend, but nobody speaks her language, which is a strange mix of symbols and hieroglyphics. Grown-up humans just ignore her or send her on her way. Deacon's illustrations show what it is like to be small in an adult world. Things change for the better when she meets a group of children who accept her for who she is and include her in their games. The story ends happily when she is reunited with her parents.

Beegu is funny, touching, and hopeful. It is about loneliness, rejection, and the joy of friendship, and a whole range of emotions are explored in a few short pages. Deacon's simple and gently paced text is beautifully illustrated, and he has been described by critics as one of the most exciting new talents in children's books. He uses an unusual technique, photocopying and enlarging his original drawings to create a very distinctive style. The backgrounds are stark and Beegu stands out luminously.

Beegu was Deacon's second book, and fans of this heartwarming tale will also take pleasure in his *Slow Loris* and *While You Are Sleeping*. **HJ**

Bridget and the Moose Brothers 2003

Pija Lindenbaum

5+

"[Bridget] wants a brother or a sister, a small, thin one that will fit in her doll's bed."

Original Title | Gittan och älgbrorsorna
Nationality | Swedish, born 1955
Publisher | Rabén and Sjögren, Sweden
Theme | Family, Animal stories

Bridget is an only child. She is curious, ingenious, and sometimes rather lonely: "Bridget's room is too quiet, and she's tired of it," reveals the author. Bridget wishes she had a brother; a funny, playful, noisy brother who would listen to loud rock music at full blast. How lucky then, that her friend Nicky comes to visit so that they can play together.

Nicky wants to go snow sledding. On the way back home from their sledding trip, Bridget sees three giant moose sitting by the entrance to her house. They have been sledding, too and are having a rest because they are tired. Bridget invites the three moose into her house to play at being her "brothers." What seemed a great idea at the time, however, soon turns into a complete nightmare. The moose brothers are loud, rude, and messy. They turn the place upside down and inside out. The moose brothers think it is all "great" fun but Bridget does not—and she needs to use all her wits to get rid of them.

Bridget and the Moose Brothers is the third of three books about Bridget and her encounters with wild animals, and the series is very familiar to young readers from northern Scandinavia. Lindenbaum has said that the character of Bridget is similar to how she herself was as a child and also shares similarities with her daughter. Bridget is a funny, original child, and has traits that all parents will recognize. Lindenbaum is a very successful author and illustrator whose works are highly prized in her native Sweden. **CC**

MORE PICTURE BOOKS BY LINDENBAUM

***Else-Marie and Her Seven Little Daddies,* 1990**
***Bodil, My Dog,* 1991**
***Britt and Prince Benny,* 1996**
***Bridget and the Gray Wolves,* 2000**
***Bridget and the Numbskulls,* 2001**

The Day the Babies Crawled Away 2003

Peggy Rathmann

Nationality | American, born 1953
Publisher | G. P. Putnam's Sons, USA
Award | *Horn Book*, Fanfare
Theme | Family, Rhyming stories

Sometimes it is the simplest concept executed in a unique way that makes a children's book an instant classic. That is certainly the case with *The Day the Babies Crawled Away*. Told in rollicking rhyme, with short, easy to understand phrases, the story begins as several families are gathering at a fair. While the adults get caught up in a pie-eating contest, a group of five babies begins to crawl away into the woods. They are followed by a brave five year old in a fireman's hat who hollers, "HEY! You babies, STAY!"

Rathmann depicts the characters and the landscape in black silhouette throughout the book, with an infusion of airbrushed color on each page for the sky, which changes subtly throughout the book to show the change in the time of day. We see the outlines of the babies, each with a distinctive feature—a curl, a bonnet, or a specific hairdo—and our plucky hero in his fireman's hat, along with the trees, butterflies, and bats, in incredible detail.

Even very young children will follow the story easily. It is a tale filled with adventure, near misses, and, of course, a hero and a happy ending. The illustrations are filled with subtle humor that children will be able to pick up on, such as the baby found in the bat cave, who on the last page is seen back at home, hanging upside down. While some adults may shudder at unattended babies let loose, little ones will cheer their wild bravery and spirit, knowing that all will come out right in the end. **KD**

The Biggest Kiss in the World 2003

R. Chávez Castañeda M. Rodríguez

Nationality | Mexican, born 1961 (author); Mexican, birth date unknown (illustrator)
Publisher | Libresa, Ecuador
Theme | Friendship, Love

The Biggest Kiss in the World (originally titled *El beso más largo del mundo*) presents four short stories about the emotions that revolve around everyday adventures. All four narratives, however, are actually four different versions of the same story. This one story, from which all the others have grown, is about the longest kiss in the world, and each version of the story is addressed to readers of different ages (six, seven, eight, and nine, respectively). In what is possibly Castañeda's best book, the importance of the kiss develops in connection with the age of the reader involved.

In the last story, the kiss reflects the complex emotional world of adults, with its contradictions, longing, and doubts; whereas in the first narrative, aimed at younger readers, Castañeda tells the story of how an accidental kiss, given under rather tragicomic circumstances, paves the way for powerful feelings that the protagonist has never experienced before.

The story begins when Emiliano sets out to make his first snowman, but ends up making a snowgirl. As he is about to finish his snow sculpture, he accidentally kisses the snowgirl in what turns out to be the longest kiss in the world—because his lips get painfully stuck on the icy surface. Castañeda demonstrates great humor, a clear style that always keeps the reader interested, and an insightful depiction of the characters, highlighting the importance of emotions, especially love, as essential elements of human existence. **LB**

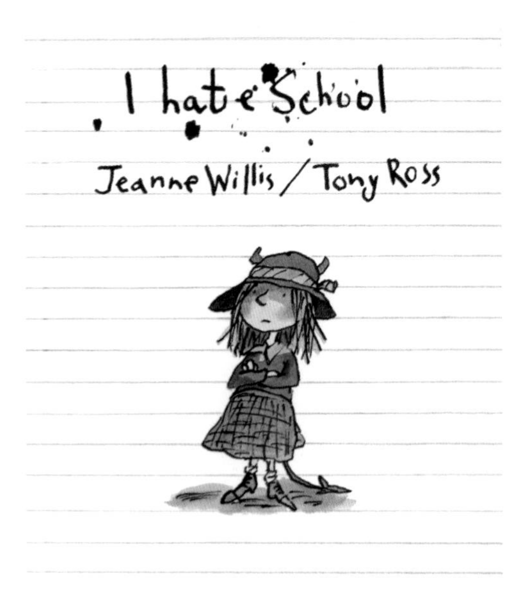

I Hate School 2003

Jeanne Willis Tony Ross

Nationality | English, born 1959 (author); English, born 1938 (illustrator)
Publisher | Andersen Press, UK
Theme | School, Friendship

The reverse psychology at play in this highly amusing story makes it the perfect book to share with a child facing his or her first day at school. Honor Brown's school is a pretty dreadful and terrifying place—according to her—and she clings to her mother's leg, crying and screaming that she doesn't want to go.

Apparently her teacher is a "warty toad"; lunch consists of worms, rabbit poop, and coal; anyone who talks in class has her head chopped off; Honor has been fired into space as a human rocket by demented classmates; and there are killer sharks in the water—and that's just for starters. It is strange, then, that Honor has something of a change of heart when it comes to her last day at school.

Willis is a highly successful author and shows her usual brand of down-to-earth humor in easy, rhyming text. Some critics find her a little too frank, but others love this aspect of her. Few could find anything offensive in this book, apart from a certain boisterousness.

Many of Willis's ideas come to her in dreams, and a taste for slightly surreal fantasy is clear in *I Hate School*. A good half of the book's delight, however, comes from Tony Ross's illustrations. An incredibly popular and prolific author and illustrator, his highly charged style, full of movement and with fluid, energetic black outlines that are filled with washes of color, perfectly partners Honor's entertainingly crazy view of school life. Willis and Ross have produced several best-selling collaborations, including *Dr. Xargle's Book of Earthlets* (1990) and *Tadpole's Promise* (2003). **AK**

5+

Skippyjon Jones 2003

Judy Schachner

Nationality | American, born 1951
Publisher | Dutton Books, USA
Award | E. B. White Read Aloud Award, 2004
Theme | Animal stories

Skippyjon Jones is a Siamese kitten with an identity problem. His head and ears seem much too big for his body, so Skippyjon starts to think that he must be a Chihuahua—not to mention being a Spanish-speaking, sword-fighting superhero intent on securing Mexican independence.

His wild imagination annoys his mother, who sends Skippyjon to his room to think about what it means to be a Siamese cat. Our very imaginative friend then decides he must be a bird—after all, his best friends are the birds he plays with every morning—until he finds his true alter ego, Skippito Friskito.

As Skippito, he goes off in search of imaginary adventures; in this case, to save a group of dogs called the Chimichangos from an enormous bumblebee named Alfredo Buzzito (who is actually a piñata at a birthday party). The resulting adventure is both disastrous and hilarious.

The author took her inspiration from her own Siamese cat, whose antics one day as he swiped at a bumblebee reminded her of the film *Zorro*. At that moment Skippito Friskito was born. Schachner's superb illustrations are engagingly full of humor. Her text is filled with Spanish references, slang, and Spanish sounding made-up words, so Spanish-speaking families will enjoy it and non-Spanish speakers will pick up a few key phrases. This is a great read-aloud book for anyone with a sense of humor (and the ability to assume an authentic-sounding Mexican accent will not hurt either!) **KD**

Constable Sniffler 2003

Asko Sirkiä Pirjo Lipponen

Nationality | Finnish, born 1957 (author); Finnish, born 1953 (illustrator)
Publisher | WSOY, Finland
Theme | Animal stories, Detective stories

5+

This exciting detective story (whose full title is *Komisario Nuusku ja makkaratehtaan arvoitus* or *Constable Sniffler and the Sausage Factory Mystery*) follows canine Constable Sniffler and his loyal partner, Detective Scentington, in the fight against crime. This easy-to-read novel is full of clever humor and plenty of action.

One day, as Constable Sniffler and Detective Scentington are enjoying their morning coffee, someone calls to tell them that the local sausage factory has been robbed. Not a single sausage, bratwurst, or any other meaty treat has been left behind. It is up to the canine duo to solve this heinous crime so the citizens of Dog Town can enjoy sausages once more. Sniffler and Scentington immediately start investigating leads and interviewing employees, but what they do not know is that the culprit may be closer than they realize. The evidence suggests it might have been an inside job. It is time for Sniffler and Scentington to put their snouts to good use. The criminal cannot have gone far, but will the canine police be quick enough for this sneaky crook?

This witty detective novel offers children the chance of solving the case themselves, even before the main characters manage to do it. Smart readers will find the clues Sirkiä has cleverly hidden in the story. Children will love these canine characters as they help protect Dog Town in their fight against crime, and Sirkiä's engaging use of language draws children into the fast-paced story. **LKK**

The Girl and the Jackdaw Tree 2004

Riitta Jalonen Kristiina Louhi

Nationality | Finnish, born 1954 (author); Finnish, born 1950 (illustrator)
Publisher | Tammi, Finland
Theme | Illness and death, Family

The Girl and the Jackdaw Tree (originally entitled *Tyttö ja naakkapuu*) is a highly sensitive portrayal of how a young girl's world is changed by the death of her father. Riitta Jalonen does not shy away from sensitive issues such as grief or death, and writes about these themes in a beautiful and touching way.

As the girl tries to figure out what it means now that her father is dead, the world around her inevitably changes. She realizes that her father has gone somewhere she cannot see and that her mother wants to move somewhere new. This realization takes place as the little girl waits at the train station while her mother is buying train tickets. Standing outside, she watches jackdaws in a nearby tree. She is fascinated by the birds as she watches them fly away.

The memory of her father suddenly comes to her mind. She remembers the things they used to do together; her father singing and the piggyback rides he gave her. She wonders if he can see her from heaven. Although she feels she can still see her father, she knows that her life will never be the same again, and we go through the experience with her. As the author tells us simply, "A memory never ends."

Jalonen's words and Louhi's illustrations work seamlessly together to make a genuine and intense story. The pictures bring to life even the saddest of images. The girl's inner monologue gives the story great honesty and takes the reader inside a child's mind, where sorrow and joy exist side by side. **LKK**

Tyttö ja naakkapuu

Riitta Jalonen · Kristiina Louhi

Tammi

5+

You're All My Favourites
Sam McBratney ILLUSTRATED BY Anita Jeram

You're All My Favourites 2004

Sam McBratney Anita Jeram

Nationality | Irish, born 1943 (author); English, born 1965 (illustrator)
Publisher | Candlewick Press, UK
Theme | Family

In *You're All My Favourites*, the creators of *Guess How Much I Love You*—one of the best-selling children's books in recent years—produced another reassuring tale for the very young, this time dealing with the issue of sibling rivalry.

The little bear cubs in this book are not fighting with one another—that is not the issue. They all love one another and their parents, but they begin to question how their parents could love them all equally, because they are so different.

Every night at bedtime their parents tuck in their three beloved cubs with the same phrase, "You are the most wonderful baby bears in the whole wide world!" but the little cubs begin to doubt those words. How can they all be equally wonderful? What if one is more beautiful? What about one being a girl or one being the littlest? Can they then all still be the most wonderful? So they ask their father one night, "Which one of us do you like the most? Who is your favourite? We can't all be the best."

Birth order and favoritism are issues that are eventually dealt with in every family with more than one child. Jeram's soft and sweet illustrations of a truly loving family of bears helps make this calm and reassuring book one that will help both parents and children deal with this age-old question in a positive, nonthreatening way. This charming book goes a long way toward reassuring young children that they are loved for exactly who they are, and not for whom they are compared to. **KD**

Are We There Yet? 2004

Alison Lester

Nationality | Australia, born 1952
Publisher | Viking Books, Australia
Award | C.B.C.A. Picture Book of the Year, 2005
Theme | Family

Are We There Yet? perfectly captures the highs and lows of long-distance travel with children as a family of five travels around the vast reaches of Australia. The ennui of endless miles stuck in a car is contrasted with the excitement of visiting new places, meeting different people, and experiencing the unexpected.

Based on Lester's own family trip, it documents the journey of the narrator, eight-year-old Grace, her parents, and her two brothers, Luke and Billy. They embark on the vacation of a lifetime in a four-by-four car, towing their grandparents' old camper. The family travels around the coastal fringes of Australia, with detours into the Red Center to witness the stunning Uluru at sunset; to the beautiful capital city of Canberra, and across the Bass Strait to the amazing wilderness areas of Tasmania.

Before arriving back home, the family have discovered deserts, beaches, rainforests, monoliths, whales, and bottle-shaped trees, and they have experienced rain, heat, snow, and ice—and all in just three months on one continent! They also encounter the animals, plants, human inhabitants, and natural and man-made attractions of this huge, varied land.

Lester's wonderfully evocative watercolor illustrations are full of humorous details and insights. She perfectly captures the landscape and its exotic attractions. However, it is her depiction of the family—their interactions, foibles, and affection for one another—that lingers in the mind. There is humor, wonder, and adventure in this entertaining tale. **SOR**

5+

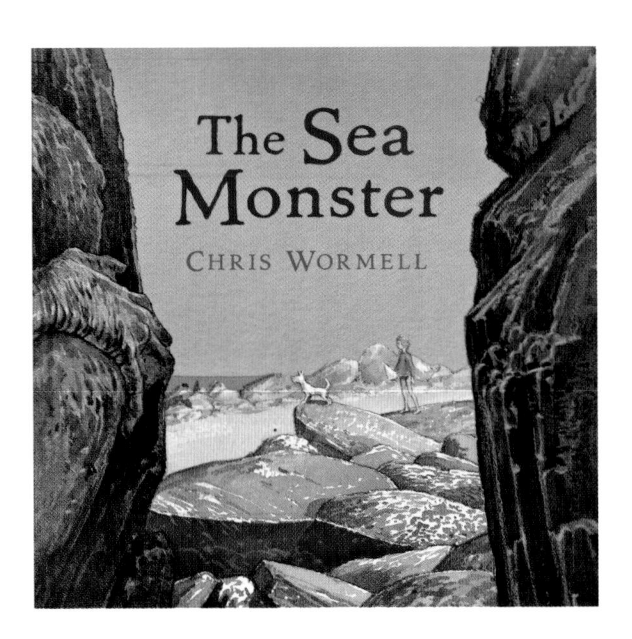

5+

The Sea Monster 2005

Christopher Wormell

Nationality | English, born 1955
Publisher | Jonathan Cape, UK
Theme | Fantasy, Friendship, Magical stories, Adventure

There is a huge monster with vivid green eyes, living at the bottom of the ocean. Every so often he rises from the water and sits among rocks at the edge of the beach, keeping very still and covering his giveaway eyes with seaweed: "Barnacles and limpets clung to his scaly skin and seaweed grew from every wrinkle." Here, camouflaged against discovery, the monster watches the beach world go by.

One day a little boy and his dog come into the monster's vision. The boy is playing among the rock pools, sailing his toy boat and watching sea anemones and crabs. Suddenly the boat is swept out to sea and the boy dives into the waves in pursuit. Soon he is caught in fast-moving currents. Meanwhile, an old man in his cliff-top cottage hears the distressed barking of a dog far below. The adventure gathers pace as man and dog set out to save the boy. The monster, too, has his special part to play.

The Sea Monster's text is simple but also lyrical, and has a quality that makes it especially good to read aloud. Perhaps the main stars of the show, though, are Wormell's atmospheric illustrations. With his rich coloration, light effects, and fluid painting style, Wormell's art really captures the wide expanses of sea, sky, and beach, as well as the dizzying cliff heights and the monster's bulk. He also uses interesting viewpoints in his pictures to draw readers in. The pictures' calmness is echoed by the tone of the text. Wormell's other notable works include *Two Frogs* (2002) and *George and the Dragon* (2003). **AK**

5+

Zen Shorts 2005

Jon J Muth

Nationality | American, born 1960
Publisher | Scholastic Press, USA
Award | Caldecott Honor Book, 2006
Theme | Fairy tales

Stillwater, the giant panda, first became acquainted with Michael, Addy, and Karl when his umbrella—and he himself holding it—was blown by the wind into the children's backyard.

On the following days each of the siblings went to visit Stillwater, and each was told a Zen story. Addy heard about Uncle Ry, who never let a visitor leave his home empty-handed. One night he gave his old tattered robe to a robber he surprised, regretful for being unable to offer him the beautiful silvery moon. Michael was told the story about the old farmer's son who broke his leg falling off a horse, which ultimately saved the boy's life as he was not drafted into the army to fight a war in which all the youth perished. Karl was treated to the story about two monks, one young and one old. One day, while traveling the road, the old monk volunteered to carry a woman across the river. When she safely reached the opposite shore, she left without thanking the monk. Hours later the young monk was still angry about it, to which the older monk says: "I set the woman down hours ago, why are you still carrying her?"

Muth has commented: "I like my stories to offer the possibility to consider something, but I don't want to teach a specific lesson." His Zen stories describe familiar situations and suggest surprising and fresh resolutions to them. They appeal to a childlike mind by promoting an instinctive and spontaneous understanding of the world. Muth's splendid illustrations beautifully complement his words. **IW**

Leonardo, the Terrible Monster 2005

Mo Willems

Nationality | American, born 1968
Publisher | Hyperion, USA
Award | A.L.A. Notable Children's Book, 2006
Theme | Fantasy

Leonardo is a terrible monster—that is to say, he is terrible at being a monster. No matter what he does, he just cannot seem to do what he wants to do most, which is to scare someone—anyone for that matter.

Mo Willems's career as an animator is evident on every page of this book. His soft pastel backgrounds are the perfect base for his lively characters, and the typeface is used as effectively as the illustrations. In some cases, blank or nearly blank pages are used to express isolation, relative size, or simply to give the reader space for thought. The story is a simple but funny one, with the title itself being a play on words.

Leonardo's trouble is that children realize the moment they see him that, even though he is a monster, he does not look scary; in fact, he is really rather adorable. Leonardo laments that he does not have lots of big teeth, he is not huge, or even weird like his other monster friends. So he decides to do some research. He is determined to learn everything there is to know about being scary and to find the perfect candidate to scare—who turns out to be a bespectacled little boy named Sam. It is not very difficult to make Sam cry, as there are so many little things that are already making him feel sad.

Leonardo gives it his all and succeeds in making Sam cry, but what he learns in the process is that although, if he worked hard enough, he might one day manage to be a terrible, scary monster, perhaps what he would really rather be is Sam's friend. **KD/LH**

Llama, Llama, Red Pajama 2005

Anna Dewdney

Nationality | American, birth date unknown
Publisher | Viking, USA
Theme | Family, Animal stories, Rhyming stories

Every parent will empathize with the delaying antics that the adorable baby llama enacts at bedtime. The trials of bedtime and separation anxiety are familiar territories for parents and toddlers—as is the desire for children to stay up later than their parents would like. This book will help ease children's nighttime fears, and it does so in a genuine and humorous way that will be appreciated by both parents and children.

There are many books on the subject of going to bed and all its attendant rituals, but this book uses both the illustrations and the short rhyming couplets to bring out the emotions of a llama baby who needs comforting. Children will enjoy seeing his worried expressions reflected on the face of his llama stuffed toy as the story progresses from getting tucked in, to the anxiety of being left alone in the dark.

After being put into bed, read his story, and kissed good night, baby llama watches his mother leave the room with a worried expression on his face. When he calls out to her, and she does not come back immediately, things escalate into a panicky bedtime drama. Of course, Mrs. Llama returns in the nick of time (she was on the phone), to reassure her baby with a cuddle and the words, "Mama is always near, even if she's not right here," resulting in her baby finally settling down and drifting off to sleep. A wonderful book to read aloud, the infectious rhyme of the text and the boldly painted illustrations will soothe even the most fearful toddler to a peaceful sleep. **KD**

"Eyes wide open, covers drawn . . . What if Mama Llama's GONE?"

Wolves 2005

Emily Gravett

Nationality | English, born 1972
Publisher | Macmillan, UK
Award | Kate Greenaway Medal
Theme | Animal stories, Quirky

5+

WOLVES

Emily Gravett

This sharp, funny tale is laden with visual jokes and wordplay. *Wolves* is also the title of the book within the book, a much-handled work about lupine predators with a shabby red cloth jacket, a removable library ticket, and an overdue notice: it is the property of West Bucks Public Burrowing Library.

The gullible rabbit who has "burrowed" this book is destined never to return it. The safe world of the library is no protection when the creatures in the book he has borrowed come to life. As Rabbit is drawn into the text (failing to notice he is being followed home as he reads), the illustrations he is viewing become larger until the brutish, thickly pencilled wolf is ready to devour his dainty figure. While we are informing ourselves along with Rabbit about the terrifying creatures, we are also watching his experiences.

"Luckily this wolf was a vegetarian, so they shared a jam sandwich."

There are two endings to choose from: children of a nervous disposition can enjoy the wolf eating a jam sandwich while those who relish a more grisly outcome will draw their own conclusions from the scratched and gnawed cover of the book. Either way, Emily Gravett's debut is reminiscent of some of Janet and Allan Ahlberg's collaborations in its inclusion of well-crafted texts within a text, from the library ticket to the mail that has accumulated on Rabbit's doormat, pictured on the endpapers. Yet it is also a truly original and multiaward-winning work. Children are encouraged to share Gravett's delight in wordplay. The title page lists "Emily Grrrabbit" as the author, and the pseudo quotes on the back cover come from *The Daily Carrot*, *The Hareold*, and *Rabbit Review*. **GB**

MORE AMUSING WOLF STORIES

Clever Polly and the Stupid Wolf by Catherine Storr, 1955
Lon Po Po by Ed Young, 1989
The True Story of the Three Little Pigs by Jon Scieszka, 1989

The Boy Who Grew Flowers 2005

Jen Wojtowicz Steve Adams

Nationality | American, birth date unknown (author); Canadian, birth date unknown (illustrator)
Publisher | Barefoot Books, UK
Theme | Magical stories, Friendship, Quirky

5+

High up at the very top of Lonesome Mountain, past Black Bear Creek and overlooking a wild forest, a house stands all on its own. Inside lives the Bowagon family, known for being out of the ordinary, to say the least. Some of the Bowagons are shapeshifters and one of them tames rattlesnakes as a hobby. Rink Bowagon, a quiet, unusual boy, has an extraordinary secret—when there is a full moon he sprouts lovely flowers all over his body, which his mother clips off before school. Rink's classmates tell wild tales about his strange family, and his teachers ignore him.

One day, a new pupil, Angelina, arrives. She always wears a flower behind her right ear. Everyone likes her, especially Rink, who admires her honesty and kindness from afar. She, too, is curious about the withdrawn boy sitting at the back of the class. When a school dance comes up and Angelina refuses invitations, because her dancing skills are hampered by having one leg shorter than the other, Rink is inspired. He rushes home and fashions a pair of beautiful dancing shoes from the "shucked-off" skin of Uncle Dud's pet rattlesnake. One shoe has a thicker sole than the other, to even up Angelina's legs. He then delivers the shoes to her door.

"She had an easy manner, a luminous smile, and her right leg was shorter than her left."

An artist and writer who teaches artists with disabilities, Wojtowicz was inspired to write this tale by her autistic brother, Wally, and by observing the power of kindness and acceptance. In *The Boy Who Grew Flowers*, Wojtowicz creates a celebration of difference through a story that has a timeless quality, perfectly blending folktale, fairy tale, and reality. **AK**

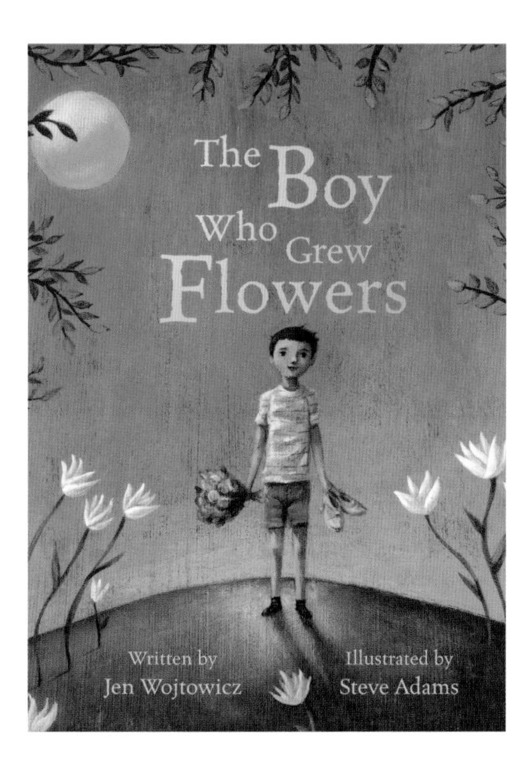

MORE BOOKS ABOUT SPECIAL NEEDS

Tobin Learns to Make Friends by Diane Murrell, 2001
My Friend Isabelle by Eliza Woolson and Bryan Gough, 2003
Looking After Louis by Lesley Ely and Polly Dunbar, 2004

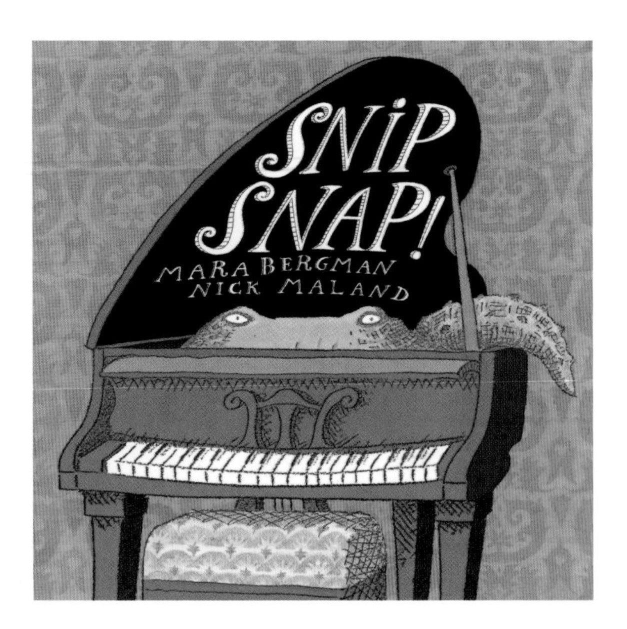

Snip Snap 2005

Mara Bergman Nick Maland

Nationality | American, born 1956 (author); English, born 1959 (illustrator)
Publisher | Hodder Children's Books, UK
Theme | Animal stories, Rhyming stories

Snip snap goes the alligator's jaws. It creeps up the stairs and into the children's apartment, biting the door; gnashing the tables, the chairs, and the piano; and ripping the sofa and curtains. Readers will be deliciously scared, as they relish the alligator's every wicked move: the swishing and swooshing of its tremendous tail, "which was shiny and spiked and full of scales," and the mouth that "opened up v-e-r-y wide ... as if to invite the children inside."

Bergman's rhyming tale winds up the suspense, beguiles its readers with the fascinating pleasure of the terrible alligator—its flashing eyes, its flicking tongue, its kicking feet—and invites them to join in with the refrain that punctuates the reptile's progress: "Were the children scared? YOU BET THEY WERE."

Maland's illustrations cleverly balance fun and thrills and introduce the beast a little at a time. There is the tip of its tail disappearing, its feet climbing the stairs, the shadow of its head on the wall, its eyes through the letter box, and its body slithering past the hidden children. Finally, when we, and the children, meet its huge grinning head, which fills a double-page spread, it is a heart-stopping moment. Of course, that is not the end of the tale. The children at last screw up their courage and send the alligator home in no uncertain terms: "Was the alligator scared. YOU BET IT WAS!"

Maland was already an award-winning illustrator when he teamed up with Bergman. Their partnership was so successful that they have since produced two more picture books, about a boy called Oliver. **CB**

The Night Pirates 2005

Peter Harris Deborah Allwright

Nationality | English, born 1933 (author); English, birth date unknown (illustrator)
Publisher | Egmont, UK
Theme | Adventure, Rhyming stories

The Night Pirates is a refreshing take on traditional pirate stories and is aimed as much at girls as boys. It features Tom, who is a "nice little boy" and "a brave little boy" who is about to have a very big adventure.

In the dead of night, while everyone else is sleeping, through the "dark, dark streets" comes something strange. At first Tom thinks it may be trolls or monsters but it turns out to be a band of rough, tough girl pirates who steal the front of Tom's house and sail it away in search of treasure. Tom joins the voyage across the ocean and does battle with a bunch of lazy and cowardly grown-up pirates. They are terrified that their island has been invaded by girl pirates and issue the worst pirate curse in the world: "If you don't give my treasure back, I'll tell my mum."

Tom and the girl pirates steal the treasure before sailing home and restoring the front of Tom's house. He climbs wearily back into bed knowing that in the morning his adventures will remain a secret. There is a twist in the tale, however. As the postman attempts to deliver his letters we discover that Tom's house is now upside down.

Peter Harris's story uses rhyme and repetition to great effect, adding a sense of pace and magic to the story and making it excellent for reading aloud. *The Night Pirates* is witty, surprising, and beautifully illustrated by Deborah Allwright. By using a range of styles and multimedia techniques, she allows her detailed, surreal illustrations to add a dreamlike quality to the book. **HJ**

5+

Flotsam 2006

David Wiesner

Nationality | American, born 1956
Publisher | Clarion Books, USA
Award | Caldecott Medal, 2007
Theme | Fantasy, Science and nature

Pictures really do tell thousands of words when it comes to *Flotsam*. As is usual for David Wiesner's books, there is no conventional text. The dreamlike story unfolds entirely through his stunning illustrations.

The book opens with a typical lazy family day on the beach. A young boy is engrossed in studying the small creatures he finds around him in the sand. When his observations take him to the shoreline, he does not see a big breaker creeping toward him and is suddenly upended in the crashing water. As he rights himself on the sand and the spuming water retreats, he sees that a very old-fashioned camera has been washed ashore along with scraps of seaweed. Not only has the boy been turned upside down, but so has his day. The camera turns out to be a very unusual kind of flotsam, revealing to the boy how it links places and children that are far away from one another—in distance and in time—as it drifts from shore to shore.

Wiesner's detailed but soft watercolors capture the hazy bright light along the beach as well as fantastical underwater worlds, encouraging children to enter into the mesmerizing pictures.

Wiesner uses a variety of framing devices and shifting viewing angles to involve readers and indulge his fascination with the process of capturing images. The lack of words gives free rein to the imagination, and the book creates countless opportunities for creative spin-off activities for children of all ages. Wiesner still vacations at the New Jersey shore, which so inspired him for this book. **AK**

A wind-up fish swims in the underwater fantasy seascape. 

5+

In Mr. Thunder's House 2006

Guido Quarzo Fabrizio Monetti

Nationality | Italian, born 1948 (author); Italian, birth date unknown (illustrator)
Publisher | Edizioni Lapis, Italy
Theme | Animal stories, Magical stories

In Mr. Thunder's House (originally published as *Nella casa del signor Tuono*) is an outstanding collaboration between one of Italy's most popular children's authors and one of Italy's most popular illustrators. Fabrizio Monetti's illustrations seem to change font, size, and color specifically to fit in with the text, perhaps even helping to inspire Guido Quarzo's words.

Blue is a shy little bird whose name is very apt because he manages to create the blue of the sky when he flaps his wings. This timid little bird discovers that he is also able to produce a myriad of other colors when he moves across the landscape, when he flies over cities, and when he approaches children. When Blue flies above the rooftops of the town, he becomes red; when he sees a laughing boy at a windowsill, "The laughter of the boy and the somersault of the bird were of the same color, a color that nobody had ever seen, and so it had no name. They called it *oplà*."

Then Mr. Thunder comes into the story's frame. Mr. Thunder is colorless. He has no empathy for the bird, and puts him in a cage. Monetti skillfully personifies the abstract—thunder, color, sky—while Quarzo sets about freeing little Blue from the house of Mr. Thunder.

Liberating the bird brings forth a whole palette of colors—yellow, violet, orange. Mr. Thunder realizes the error of his ways, asks forgiveness, and thanks the little bird for the blue that he leaves in his mirror. Words, colors, and shapes literally dance on each page of this wonderful book. **SMT**

The Adventures of the Dish and the Spoon 2006

Mini Grey

Nationality | Welsh, birth date unknown
Publisher | Jonathan Cape, UK
Award | Kate Greenaway Medal, 2007
Theme | Friendship, Nursery rhymes

A cameo role expands into a rags-to-riches-to-rags saga for these nursery-rhyme characters turned vaudeville act. The runaway Dish and Spoon (who are drawn as fully believable romantic leads) pull the crowds in Depression-era America and blow their earnings on high living. They turn into Bonnie and Clyde to appease the loan sharks of the Knife Gang, and are captured in a Keystone Cops sequence. With Dish broken and Spoon imprisoned in Alcatraz, they look despair in the face.

Spoon, released decades later and deported back to Britain, finds a scarily bright new world of color television and miniskirts (with a fresh, airy, almost acid palette to contrast with the richer but more muted shades of the seedily glamorous 1930s). In a junk shop, he finds the couple's past laid out on the shelves. The shop can fix anything, including broken bits of ceramic, and the pair are reunited.

Spoon and Dish's early obsession, money, is the ever-present villain of the piece, and the source of all their problems. Currency appears on almost every spread, from a dollar doubling as the moon to a broken cup begging for pennies. There is a moral and when Dish and Spoon take their show on the road again, they have learned that money does not buy happiness, so all their performances are done for free.

This tender, witty story is delivered with rich technical accomplishment, in a feast of collage, watercolor, and computer artistry, and has a stirring sense of performance about it. **GB**

"'Stop! Untie the Dish! I've got a plan!' screamed the Spoon."

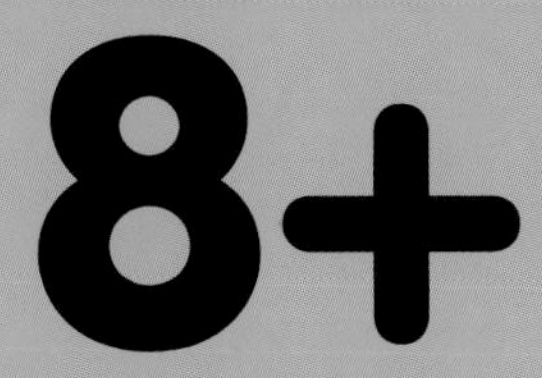

8+

Peter Pan in Kensington Gardens, written by J. M. Barrie, this illustration by Arthur Rackham.

Aesop's Fables *c.* 550 B.C.E.

 Aesop

Nationality | Greek, born *c.* 620 B.C.E.
Publisher | Unknown; first English translation 1484 by Caxton, UK
Theme | Classics, Folktales

There are more than 600 fables attributed to the ancient Greek writer, Aesop. Fables are morality tales or stories told to help teach or amuse the reader (or listener). Little is known about Aesop himself. Some sources claim he was a slave who told stories as part of his enforced labor, although this is not known for certain. It cannot even be verified exactly which stories he composed. It is likely Aesop was not the actual author, at least not of all his fables, but that he was the first person to write down stories that had been passed orally through many generations.

Almost all the fables attributed to Aesop are about animals with human characteristics, a device by which the storyteller imparted his wisdom to his readers. Many of his phrases, or phrases inspired by his works, have passed into common usage, such as "sour grapes" (from "The Fox and the Grapes") and "more haste, less speed" (which derives from "The Hare and the Tortoise"). Many of Aesop's fables contain social commentary such as in "The Ant and the Grasshopper," which tells of the flamboyant grasshopper who spends his summer happily singing, not caring about the future and laughing at the boringly industrious ant, who never has time to enjoy himself but works all through the warm weather. When winter arrives, the ant is well fed because of his earlier hard work, whereas the grasshopper is starving.

Aesop's Fables has become such a part of the literary fabric that children all over the world still read his works, without necessarily knowing Aesop's name. His classic stories are often retold by modern writers. **LH**

Arabian Nights *c.* 1400

 Unknown

Alternative Title | One Thousand and One Nights
Publisher | Unknown; existing copy is a Syrian version of earlier Sanskrit and Persian manuscripts
Theme | Classics, Myths and legends, Fairy tales

Also known as *One Thousand and One Nights*, *Arabian Nights* is a collection of traditional stories. Some of them are thought to date back to the early ninth century, although generally it is believed that the stories were first collected together in the first part of the fifteenth century. Many of the stories were handed down orally, and popular translations include those by the famous English explorer Richard Burton (1821–1890) and the Scottish author Andrew Lang (1844–1912).

Many of the earliest stories originate from Persia (modern-day Iran) and India. Later, more Arabic, Syrian, and Egyptian stories were added. The framework holding all the stories together is the narrator Scheherazade who, according to Persian legend, tells a different story to her husband every night for 1,001 nights. The legend has it that the king was convinced no woman was capable of being faithful, so he decided that every time he got married, he would kill his wife the day after their wedding night to ensure she would never be unfaithful. When Scheherazade is chosen to be the king's wife, she hatches a plan to keep herself alive by promising to tell her husband a new story every night, but not tell him the ending until the following morning.

The tales from *Arabian Nights* first gained popularity outside the Middle East in the nineteenth century, when they were translated into French. Many stories that are popular in the West as traditional folk tales actually originated in *Arabian Nights*; these include the tales of Aladdin, Ali Baba and the forty thieves, and the voyage of Sinbad the sailor. **LH**

Adolescents Bathing (1895)—a color engraving from *Arabian Nights*. 

Fairy Tales 1697

Marie Catherine Baronne D'Aulnoy

Original Title | Les Contes de Fées
Nationality | French, born *c.* 1650
Publisher | Unknown, France
Theme | Fairy tales, Fantasy

8+

These fairy tales, first written for adults, became popular as soon as they were published and were widely available during the eighteenth century. At the start of the nineteenth century, they waned in popularity, but were brought back to public attention by reinterpretations of the stories, retold and published by Scottish writer Andrew Lang (in the late-nineteenth and early twentieth centuries), and by a translation of Countess D'Aulnoy's original tales by Annie Macdonell and Miss Lee in 1892. In these retellings, the tales were often sanitized to make them "suitable" for children. Many critics felt this spoiled them, something that has only been fully regained through the studies of Jack Zipes and other scholars.

D'Aulnoy's incredible life involved incarceration in a nunnery, abduction and forced marriage, overseas travel, and exile after possible involvement in murder and spying. She later became a famous salon hostess.

Although the tales draw on the oral tradition of peasant folklore, D'Aulnoy retold them in a complex literary form for educated readers; they are stories within stories. Her extraordinary biography explains an obsession with themes such as the child-bride and beasts in, for example, "The Ram" and "The Green Serpent," and variations on "Beauty and the Beast." She also presents strong, independent heroines, such as Finette-Cendron, who saves her ungrateful sisters and forgives the parents who abandoned her. They are simply wonderful stories. **WO**

Robinson the Younger 1779

Johann Heinrich Campe

Original Title | Robinson der Jüngere
Nationality | German, born 1746
Publisher | Unknown, Germany
Theme | Favorite characters, Adventure

Clearly borrowing from Daniel Defoe's *Robinson Crusoe*, Campe's captivating book tells the story of Robinson from Hamburg, a spoiled and lazy child who is nicknamed Krusoe by his parents. One day he is persuaded by a friend to set out to sea together. Without bidding his parents good bye, Robinson and his friend board a ship and leave their hometown. When they are shipwrecked, Robinson—who is the only survivor—is stranded on a deserted island.

Left to his own devices, Robinson realizes that he has never learned to do anything properly, and he starts to blame himself for his laziness and his lack of respect for his parents. Nevertheless, he discovers ways to find food, as well as to build a house and to light a fire. He even becomes friendly with a native he calls Friday. After a series of adventures—all of them important learning experiences—an English ship appears and takes Robinson and Friday back to Hamburg, where they start working as carpenters.

Even though Campe adopted large parts of Defoe's work, his book is still considered groundbreaking for German children's literature. It is full of philanthropic principles, and the author showed how individuals can change for the better. By choosing a young boy as the protagonist, Campe used Defoe's famous story as a means to educate children, emphasizing both the need to learn and to obey one's parents. Although Campe wrote his book more than two hundred years ago, it has a timeless quality. **GS**

The title page of Johann Heinrich Campe's *Robinson the Younger.*

ROBINSON

Tales from Shakespeare 1807

Adapted by Charles and Mary Lamb

Nationality | English, born 1764 (Mary); English, born 1775 (Charles)
Publisher | Thomas Hodgkins, UK
Theme | Classics

Fourteen of the stories from *Tales from Shakespeare: Designed for the Use of Young Persons* (to give the book its full title), were adapted by Mary Lamb, her brother Charles took on the remaining six tragedies. When the book was first published in 1807, however, Charles was listed as the sole author and Mary's name was not included on the cover. It was well known that Mary suffered from periods of insanity. In 1796 she had murdered their mother—although she was kept from prison and her brother appointed her legal guardian —and this may have been why her name was concealed until a new edition was published in 1838.

The book contains twenty stories in a prose style that is suitable for children. The preface states, however, that the book was written mainly for girls because boys tended to have access to the original plays at an earlier age. Boys are asked to explain the difficult passages and select suitable sections from the originals for their sisters to read.

The Lambs were conscientious in including Shakespeare's own words whenever possible, and attempted to avoid words that were not in use during the Elizabethan period. Although the authors removed some plot elements for the sake of decency or simplicity, the writing is lively and certainly preserves something of the beauty of Shakespeare's text. Generations of children have enjoyed the stories as an introduction to the plays, and the book has never been out of print. **WO**

The Swiss Family Robinson 1812

Johann D. Wyss Johann E. Wyss

Nationality | Swiss, born 1743 (author); Swiss, born *c.*1781 (illustrator)
Publisher | Johann Rudolph Wyss, Switzerland
Theme | Classics

Johann David Wyss, a Swiss pastor, was inspired to write *The Swiss Family Robinson* (originally entitled *Der Schweizerische Robinson*) to entertain his four sons, who loved Daniel Defoe's *Robinson Crusoe* (1719). One of Wyss's sons, Johann Emmanuel, then illustrated the book, and another son, Johann Rudolph, published it.

The story of a Swiss family shipwrecked on a desert island became enormously popular around the globe. In the original version, the story is told from the father's perspective. It is written as a journal that recounts the lives of himself, his wife, and their four sons—Jack, Ernest, Fritz, and Franz over the ten years the family spend on the island they come to name New Switzerland.

It is a tale of survival, but with a moralizing Christian tone, as one might expect given its author. The picture Wyss paints is of a family who colonizes an Edenesque environment and learns to live in harmony with nature—although they eventually control the environment. Father Robinson is ever knowledgeable about the birds, plants, mammals, and fish the family encounter as they explore the island's terrain and many riches. Such know-how helps the family to eat well and learn what to cultivate. However, much of the father's knowledge is inaccurate, and the number of species encountered on the tiny island would not be found living in one place. Yet such flaws add to the charm of the story, which, although old-fashioned, is still an entertaining read. **CK**

Sprite and Monster (1909) by Arthur Rackham illustrates *The Tempest*.

The Nutcracker and Other Tales *c.* 1816

E. T. A. Hoffmann

Nationality | Prussian, born 1776
Publisher | Verlag der Realschulbuchhandlung, Prussia
Theme | Magical stories, Classics

This collection of highly imaginative short stories epitomizes E. T. A. Hoffmann's unconventional spirit and his belief in the supernatural. His often surreal tales frequently veer into horror, as paranormal characters reveal peoples' secret thoughts. The exact date that these stories were first published is unknown, but "The Nutcracker and the Mouse King" (probably Hoffman's most famous story) first appeared circa 1816 in the collection *Kindermärchen von E. W. Contessa, Briedrich Baron de la Motte Fouque und E. T. A. Hoffmann*.

The first tale is an account of the narrator's random encounters with a strange musician in Berlin in 1809, who turns out to be the ghost of composer Christoph Willibald Gluck. "Mademoiselle de Scuderi" (the first German crime novella) is about a well-respected author who tries to solve a series of murders in seventeenth-century Paris. Another acclaimed story in the collection is "The Golden Pot," a frantic account of a young student whose bourgeois existence is jeopardized when he is sucked into a magical world of serpent women.

Hoffmann's stories always tread a fine line between fantasy and madness, and they depict the difficulties people experience in the face of unforeseen events. Despite a sinister side, the tales are characterized by a great sense of humor and offer children a view of the world that is very different from the messages conveyed in many children's stories. **DaH**

The Pied Piper of Hamelin 1842

Robert Browning

Nationality | English, born 1812
Publisher | First published in *Dramatic Lyrics*, UK
Later Illustrated By | Kate Greenaway
Theme | Magical stories, Classics, Poetry

This gripping and melancholy narrative poem was first written for Willie Macready, the young son of Browning's friend and colleague, the great tragic actor and theater manager William Charles Macready.

Willie was ill and had asked for a poem he could illustrate to amuse himself. Browning wrote the piece to be read aloud and liked to perform it at children's parties. Its structure, pace, wit, rhythm, and intensity are all calculated to hold an audience. The characters of the piper and of the mayor and corporation, who try to cheat him out of his fee for ridding their town of rats, are as real as those in a contemporary soap opera. The accounts of the single surviving rat and the lame boy who is left behind when the children are piped away in retribution are successful dramatic monologues. There is great entertainment value in the depiction of the vermin, their "shrieking and squeaking / in fifty different sharps and flats" and the visions of a banquet that the Piper lays before them.

Based on a tale in a seventeenth-century collection, *The Wonders of the Little World* by Nathaniel Wanley, the poem has a clear moral and prompts many questions. Who is most at fault—the piper for exacting such terrible revenge, or the mayor and corporation for forcing him to drastic means by their dishonesty? Has the piper really led the children to "a joyous land"? The piper's garments suggest he is a court jester or a fool showing the city fathers the error of their ways. The origin of the legend continues to be debated. **GB**

A caricature by Rainer Ehrt of E. T. A. Hoffmann surrounded by his creations.

A Christmas Carol 1843

Charles Dickens John Leech

Nationality | English, born 1812 (author); English, born 1817 (illustrator)
Publisher | Chapman and Hall, UK
Theme | Classics, Ghost stories

8+

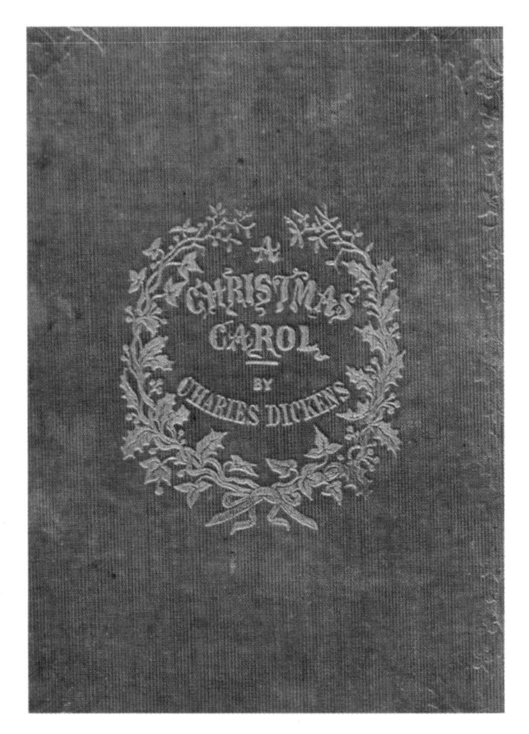

This story is so well known it has become part of the cultural bloodstream. The miserly Ebenezer Scrooge refuses to celebrate Christmas and begrudges his wretched clerk, Bob Cratchit, any paid leave. On this particular Christmas, seven years after the death of his business partner, Jacob Marley, Scrooge receives a series of supernatural warnings to mend his ways. First comes the ghost of Marley, then the Ghost of Christmas Past, showing Scrooge where his life has gone wrong. The Ghost of Christmas Present takes him to see how the Cratchit family, including disabled son Tiny Tim, defy their poverty to enjoy family life. He also lets Scrooge see the jolly family party to which he had been invited by his nephew Fred (and refused),

"Scrooge, a squeezing, wrenching, grasping, scraping, clutching, covetous old sinner!"

and then reveals the twin waifs and strays of Ignorance and Want (poverty) haunting the world. Finally, the Ghost of Christmas Yet to Come shows him the Cratchit family bereft of Tiny Tim and Scrooge's own body lying unmourned in a looted house. When Scrooge awakes, however, it is still only Christmas morning. Time to rise, repent, and spread rejoicing, with gifts to the Cratchits and fun with Fred.

Written early in Dickens's career, this was the first of five Christmas books and an instant best seller. Films, plays, and cartoons of the book have since been made. Dickens's masterly control of language, inventiveness of plot and character, innovation of form, and shrewd yet sentimental eye for human nature have seldom been matched. Few writers are so enjoyable to read, even for the young. This book played a major part in the Victorian revival of Christmas. **VN**

OTHER CLASSIC DICKENS NOVELS

Oliver Twist, 1838
The Chimes, 1844
The Battle of Life, 1846
David Copperfield, 1850
Great Expectations, 1861

The ghost of Jacob Marley appears before Scrooge.

Der Struwwelpeter 1845

Heinrich Hoffmann

Alternative Title | Shock-headed Peter
Nationality | German, born 1809
Publisher | Ruetten and Loening, Germany
Theme | Classics

I didn't have many books as a child. I don't remember anyone reading to me except for my father reading aloud from the Sunday funny pages. For some time, I almost felt bad about that. Then it dawned on me: I grew up in a large extended family in a four-family house. We sat together and my aunts and uncles and parents and grandparents talked and argued, the whole time telling stories. They loved each other and got mad at each other, but their voices and stories made up a kind of oral tradition. It was almost like ancient times when cave people sat around the fire telling stories. At some point I realized this is where my ability as a storyteller came from.

In Syracuse, where I was born, I had Mickey Mouse and Flash Gordon comic books. In Germany, I read *Der Struwwelpeter*. It contains ten short poems, some instructive, some gruesome. Shock-headed Peter describes a boy bullied for his shaggy locks; Cruel Frederick who terrorizes people and animals is given a taste of his own medicine when he is bitten by a dog; Harriet learns her lesson about playing with matches; and Little Suck-a-Thumb has his thumb cut off by a man with giant scissors. I loved this book—despite its cruel content. I don't think *Struwwelpeter* would be popular nowadays but the stories were so exaggerated, I understood it wasn't true.

Books are wonderful and we should read to our children, but there are many ways to tell stories. You can pick up the phone book, find a listing for a plumber, ask "What does a plumber do?" and then tell a story about a plumber. Whether it's the yellow pages or a well-known book, I think it is important to tell stories to our children. Take your child into your lap; physical contact is so valuable. By taking this time to tell a story or read a book, and by making this physical contact with your child, you are saying: "I have time for you. I respect you and love you."

OTHER GRUESOME RHYMES

Max and Moritz by Wilhelm Busch, 1865
Cautionary Tales for Children by Hilaire Belloc, 1907
Mind Your Own Business by Michael Rosen, 1974
Grizzly Tales for Gruesome Kids by Jamie Rix, 1990

St. Nicholas dips the three naughty boys in a pot of black ink. 

Morality Tales 1854

Rafael Pombo

Nationality | Colombian, born 1833
Publisher | Unknown, Colombia
Later Illustrated By | Lorenzo Jaramillo
Theme | Fairy tales, Poetry

Colombian poet Rafael Pombo was originally an engineer and a mathematician. He spent many years living in the United States, initially as a diplomat and later as a translator. It was while translating nursery rhymes into Spanish that he developed a love for children's stories. After seventeen years in the United States, Pombo returned to Colombia, having already published there his *Morality Tales* (or *Cuentos morales para niños formales*), a celebrated collection of children's poems with one clear aim: to teach children to behave morally.

Two of the more famous poems are "*La Pobre Viejecita*" ("The Poor Old Lady") and "*El Renacuajo Paseador*" ("The Tripping Tadpole"). In "The Poor Old Lady," Pombo presents the children with an old lady who seems to think she possesses nothing, although she has everything. Despite her abundance of food, clothes, luxury living conditions, and friends, she still believes she is poor, never feeling full, always thirsty, walking around barefoot, and in constant search for companionship. Forever unsatisfied, the old lady dies after years of unhappiness. Through Pombo's verses, consisting of double meanings that give the poem humor, his message is clear: be grateful for what you have. In "The Tripping Tadpole" the reader learns what happens when a child does not listen to his parent.

Pombo constructs his poems with a careful use of rhythmic language, one that is almost musical, using words and expressions that children are encouraged to memorize. He also uses dark humor and irony to good effect. **SML**

The Water-Babies 1863

Charles L. Kingsley J. Noel Paton

Nationality | English, born 1819 (author); Scottish, born 1821 (illustrator)
Publisher | Macmillan, UK
Theme | Fantasy, Friendship

Chimney sweep Tom—orphaned, ignorant, and unloved—falls into a river after encountering pretty upper-class Ellie and being chased out of her house. He dies (although readers do not suspect this for a while), which is rather to his pleasure, since this means he can escape his brutal master Grimes. Tom is transformed into a "water baby," as he is told by a caddis fly, and begins his underwater education, which is carried out under the guidance of fairies: stern Mrs. Doasyouwouldbedoneby, Mother Carey, and gentle Mrs. Bedonebyasyoudid.

Through a series of comic adventures and lessons, Tom learns that the duty of life is to help others, and that Doasyouwouldbedoneby is the twin sister of Bedonebyasyoudid. He is then allowed to make friends with other water babies and once a week he can meet Ellie, who fell into the river shortly after he did. Finally, he goes on a terrifying journey to the end of the world to try and help Grimes, now being punished for his evil deeds. Having overcome his reluctance to help his enemy, Tom earns a return to human form and becomes a successful scientist and inventor, reunited with Ellie (though not in marriage).

The Water-Babies outlines Kingsley's own doctrine of muscular Christianity, which fought the evils of child labor, poor wages, and prostitution. J. Noel Paton illustrated the first edition, but cartoonist Linley Sambourne's remarkable illustrations, from the 1886 edition, have become the most famous. Despite Victorian preachiness, the book remains a compelling, powerful read. **VN**

Sophie's Misfortunes 1864

Sophie Rostopchine, Countess of Ségur Horace Castelli

Nationality | French, born 1799 (author); French, born 1825 (illustrator)
Publisher | Hachette, France
Theme | Family

Certainly the most popular of the works of the Countess de Ségur, *Sophie's Misfortunes* (originally published as *Les Malheurs de Sophie*) is the first in a trilogy that describes a family life very close to that enjoyed by the author. For more than a century, generations of young (and older) children have delighted in these tales with their old-world charm.

The scene is the château of Fleurville, in the French countryside of the second empire (when France was ruled by Prince Louis-Napoléon Bonaparte). Sophie de Réan is a mischievous girl, well acquainted with misfortune. Curious and impatient, she is never short of ideas when it comes to doing something silly. Madame de Réan, her mother, knows how to forgive her tantrums, but Sophie's naughtiness reminds her every time that children who disobey and lie will always be punished.

Sophie can count on Paul, her cousin and playmate, who is always ready to console her. He is the one who generously stands up for Sophie when she clumsily puts herself in danger from wolves, or when he wants to avoid getting her punished after she nastily scratches his face. Sophie acknowledges Paul's patience and goodness and is often filled with a sense of guilt toward her cousin. She also tries, with difficulty, to imitate the sweetness and gentleness of Camille and Madeleine, two wise young girls whose discretion also often protects their friend. The heroine of our story must patiently learn from her disappointments that it is in everyone's interest to be good, kind, and guileless. **SL**

"Sophie told Paul how she had eaten the whole box of candied fruits."

MORE TITLES BY THE COUNTESS

New Fairy Tales (*Nouvée contes de fées*), 1857
Model Little Girls (*Les petites filles modèles*), 1859
Vacation (*Les Vacances*), 1859

8+

Alice's Adventures in Wonderland 1865

Lewis Carroll Sir John Tenniel

Nationality | Both English, born Charles Lutwidge Dodgson 1832 (author); born 1820 (illustrator)
Publisher | Macmillan, UK
Theme | Fantasy, Classics

The world of a middle-class, mid-Victorian child, full of stuffy adult rules, rigid etiquette, and rote learning, is remote from the experience of children reading about Alice's adventures today. Yet such is the author's ability to communicate directly with children for the sole purpose of inspiring and entertaining them (this was revolutionary at the time of publication) that the story transcends the occasional points at which Carroll's wordplay is hard for a contemporary child to appreciate. Children need not be concerned with whether the text is Freudian, Jungian, or psychedelic—the story still speaks directly to them, although young readers may be scared by the nightmarish growing-and-shrinking scenes and the persecution of Bill the Lizard.

Beneath her veneer of good manners, Alice is outspoken and forthright in challenging authority in a way that would not have been possible in real life. She meets the "curiouser and curiouser" events of her dream with an open-mind, and copes courageously with the more distressing episodes. Used to life being governed by rules, she only becomes frustrated when the rules do not work, as in the Mad Hatter's Tea Party, or are clearly being made up on the spot, as in the courtroom. Even when the rules are crazy, as in the croquet game, Alice does her best to apply them, extending the comic potential of the logically ludicrous dream sequences. Helen Oxenbury's illustrated edition of the unabridged text is the most child-friendly of the many editions available. **GB**

Through the Looking Glass 1871

Lewis Carroll Sir John Tenniel

Nationality | Both English, born Charles Lutwidge Dodgson 1832 (author); born 1820 (illustrator)
Publisher | Macmillan, UK
Theme | Fantasy, Classics

As in *Alice's Adventures in Wonderland*, the apparently random world of a dream sequence is given order—that of a living game of chess—but order that is always vulnerable to collapse. Looking-Glass Land seems a more structured world than Wonderland (although the structure is back to front) and a less challenging environment for Alice, although she has to work her way up from mere pawndom in a universe governed by a formidable queen. When she decides to leave her dream, it is because of frustration at the breakdown of order (and lack of food) at the banquet.

The second story is set six months after the first, opening by a winter fireside rather than on a sunny riverbank. Hardly any "real world" time passes in Alice's second dream (Dinah the cat is still washing her white kitten when her mistress wakes), yet the events of Looking-Glass Land could absorb years of Alice's dreamlife. When she runs with the Red Queen, she covers no distance: in Looking-Glass Land, the queen explains, people run to stand still.

Some episodes may be disturbing for sensitive children, such as Alice's search for her name in the dark wood and the claim by Tweedledum and Tweedledee that she is not real. Carroll provides the antidote to their concerns in a heroine who is as firmly real as ever, constantly talking to herself to bolster her own courage. Children who enjoy chess, mathematical problems, and codes will enjoy this book, but it also offers the same eternal pleasures as Wonderland. **GB**

At the Back of the North Wind 1871

Nationality | Scottish, born 1824 (author); English, born 1832 (illustrator)
Publisher | Strahan and Co., UK
Theme | Family, Fantasy

This story of inherent goodness—a classic Victorian theme—tells the haunting tale of a young boy named Diamond, who travels with the North Wind. The author, and Christian minister, George MacDonald was perhaps memorializing his own son who had died young. He was certainly trying to portray goodness in a troubled world. He was criticized for this, accused of making Diamond somewhat Christlike.

Diamond, the son of a coachman, lives in a hayloft. It is chilly at night, with the wind blowing through the loft. When the North Wind blows, she appears to him as a beautiful lady who takes him to countries where pain and death do not exist. Afterward, Diamond becomes ill (but recovers); he drives his father's cab while he is unwell, saves an orphan from the streets, and soothes his neighbor's baby. He spreads goodness around him. He is so good that a rich man gives his father a house and a job in the countryside. Perhaps Diamond is too good to live, because the next time he goes away, Diamond does not return from that special country at the back of the North Wind.

Poems and songs break up the narrative; reflections on existence are interspersed with descriptions of London or of fantasy flights with the North Wind. MacDonald succeeds in exploring children's fear of death in a way that has never been matched. His idiosyncratic imagination influenced Dickens, Lewis Carroll, C. S. Lewis, and Tolkien, and this book was illustrated by pre-Raphaelite artist Arthur Hughes. **VN**

The Adventures of Tom Sawyer 1876

Nationality | American, born Samuel Langhorne Clemens 1835
Publisher | Chatto and Windus, UK
Theme | Favorite characters, Classics, Friendship

Tom Sawyer is always getting into scrapes. He lives in a small town by the Mississippi River with his stern but loving Aunt Polly and his half-brother. Even when Tom tries to make good, his imagination leads him astray, but his heart is warm and his loyalties sound.

Tom good-humoredly tricks his friends, gets himself into awkward situations, and forfeits the love of pretty Becky Thatcher by lying. Worst of all, while out with scallywag Huckleberry Finn, Tom witnesses the murder of Dr. Robinson by scary Injun Joe. Joe's mate, Muff Potter, is arrested for the crime, but Tom's conscience nags him until he bravely gives evidence to acquit Muff. When Tom, Huck, and another friend run away from home to become pirates, they are unaware of the worry this will cause. Eventually the boys realize the trouble that their disappearance has caused and they stage a surprise return at their own funerals. A far-fetched plot revolving around Injun Joe's revenge and ill-gotten gold occupies much of the novel, but what really sings in the memory and has burnished Mark Twain's reputation is his ability to get under the skin of the delightful, truculent Tom.

As an unromantic celebration of boyhood and with a deal of knockabout humor, *The Adventures of Tom Sawyer* takes some beating. The book was slow to gain popularity but has become a literary gem. Twain was a genial anatomist of human nature, who turned his acute comic sense to recording the small changes of everyday life in the American South. **VN**

"Her hair was flying about her head, and the wind was blowing a breeze . . ."

Black Beauty 1877

Anna Sewell

"There were six young colts in the meadow besides me; they were older than I was."

RECOMMENDED BOOKS ABOUT HORSES

A Pony for Jean by Joanna Cannan, 1936
Black Stallion by Walter Farley, 1941
My Friend Flicka by Mary O'Hara, 1941
Misty of Chincoteague by Marguerite Henry, 1947
War Horse by Michael Morpurgo, 1982

Nationality | English, born 1820
Publisher | Jarrold and Sons, UK
Later Illustrated By | Charlotte Hough
Theme | Animal stories, Classics, Friendship

The narrator of this timeless story is a horse named Black Beauty who thinks and feels like a human being but cannot speak. He was born a handsome foal ideal for riding, until some careless handling sees him reduced to much tougher work. Black Beauty ends up pulling a horse-drawn carriage around London in the days before motor cars.

There, Black Beauty meets Ginger, an old friend who has fallen on even harder times, overworked and continually whipped. The description of Ginger's subsequent death is unforgettably moving. Black Beauty himself is finally recognized by his former groom, who sees that this noble animal, who has experienced so much suffering, ends his days happily.

After an accident at the age of fourteen, Anna Sewell became so lame that she could no longer walk. Utterly dependent on horses for travel, she came to feel strongly about the common misuse of these hardworking animals. One of her reasons for writing *Black Beauty* was an attempt to change attitudes. She particularly hated the "bearing-rein," which was used to keep horses' heads unnaturally and painfully high. She condemned it frequently in her pages, and the device was eventually banned by law. She also spoke out against the poverty that sometimes led owners to treat their animals badly, yet Sewell always ensured that the beautifully written story she was telling always came first. Its impassioned message continues to grip readers just as it did upon first publication. **NT**

The Cuckoo Clock 1877

Mrs. Molesworth Walter Crane

Nationality | Scottish, born Mary Louisa Stewart, 1839 (author); English, born 1845 (illustrator)
Publisher | Macmillan, UK
Theme | Friendship

When Griselda goes to stay with her aunts, Grizzel and Tabitha, there are an awful lot of household tasks and lessons, and no one at all to play with. The aunts (who are nice enough in themselves) and the oppressive atmosphere of the Victorian house just weigh heavily on a little girl who is forever being told to be good.

Furious that even the cuckoo clock's song is telling her to do her duty, Griselda flings a book at the clock, which, to her aunts' dismay, stops working. Happily, in the stifling atmosphere of sorrow and repentance that ensues, the cuckoo who lives in the clock turns out to be a godsend. A kind of fairy, the cuckoo is not only able to get the clock working again, but when he sees that Griselda is genuinely sorry, he also guides her on a series of magical adventures. These are just the kind of adventures that a child marooned in a house full of old ladies might imagine: Griselda visits the inhabitants of the carved Chinese ornaments from the cabinet, the country of the people in the astronomical clock, the land of the fairies and butterflies, and the sea by moonlight. Finally, the cuckoo brings Griselda the company of Phil, a real little boy with dirt on his clothes and fun in his heart. And that is much better than fantasy.

Mrs. Molesworth has been called the "Jane Austen of the nursery," with a crisp, assured prose style, but her overt preaching of self-sacrifice and duty is less likely to sit well with modern children. The cuckoo's adventures better withstand the test of time. **VN**

The Princess and the Goblin 1878

George MacDonald Arthur Hughes

Nationality | Scottish, born 1824 (author); English, born 1832 (illustrator)
Publisher | Strahan and Co., UK
Theme | Fantasy, Magical stories

George MacDonald created fantasy worlds for children that remain fresh more than a century later. "I write, not for children but for the child-like, whether they be of five, or fifty, or seventy-five," he commented. *The Princess and the Goblin*, like its sequel, *The Princess and Curdie*, is a wild, strange tale of two children pitted against wicked goblins. The fairy story provides a structure on which MacDonald hangs a series of bewitching, otherworldly scenes.

Little Princess Irene lives with her nursemaid, Lootie, in a castle in the mountains. One day she discovers a steep and winding stairway to a bewildering labyrinth of unused passages and closed doors—and a further stairway. There she finds her secret great-grandmother, a kind of fairy of the conscience. At the same time, young miner Curdie is captured by goblins and overhears their fiendish plot to capture Irene and make her marry their idiotic prince. The two meet one night when Irene and Lootie are nearly caught by a goblin. Curdie rescues them and realizes Irene's danger. The two need all their resourcefulness—and Irene's magic ring—to foil the goblins.

Anything seems possible in MacDonald's lyrical prose—people and shadows, flowers and flames, mountains and houses, could all morph into one other. It would be hard to find a better antidote to computer games than Curdie's slowly realized sense of love and responsibility, yet there is still plenty of battle action with the grim underground goblins. **VN**

Nobody's Boy 1878

Hector Malot Emile Bayard

Nationality | French, born 1830 (author); French, born 1837 (illustrator)
Publisher | Hetzel, France
Theme | Family, Friendship, Adventure

8+

The initial misfortune of Remi—the "nobody's boy" of Hector Malot's book, *Sans famille*—the misfortune from which all the others follow, always seemed to me to be the fact that the crepes that mother Barberin promised him are in the end turned into a late supper for father Barberin. Let me explain. Remi is a foundling, what George Sand would have called a "waif," but at the beginning of his long story he believes himself to be the child of his wet nurse. He learns the truth when it is brought to light by the terrible father Barberin, a laborer who leaves for Paris to earn his living and who returns destitute and disabled.

I was eight then, I was Remi, and I was sorry about the crepes. Compared to this frustration, the rest was

"Will it always be like this? Will I never find anyone to love for ever?"

rather cheerful. I took to the roads with Master Vitalis, he with such a promising name, surrounded by three performing dogs and a capricious monkey, I earned some pennies performing in the village squares, I slept under the stars, and I got myself taken onto a houseboat and won the affections of a young girl who was mute.

Telling how things are on rereading the book forty years later, *Nobody's Boy* is a harsh melodrama where the dogs get eaten by wolves, Vitalis dies of cold out in the snow, the children, reduced to begging, are beaten by a sadist, the miners are crushed, the good are sent to prison, and the villains are often triumphant. *Nearly*, because this is Malot and not Zola. One day, I guessed it from the very first lines, one day I would eat crepes with my family, the (of course) rich family that is the due of poor orphans.

OTHER GREAT FRENCH CLASSICS

Sophie's Misfortunes (Les Malheurs de Sophie) by Sophie Rostopchine, Countess of Ségur, 1864
20,000 Leagues Under the Sea (Vingt mille lieues sous les mers) by Jules Verne, 1870
Carrot Top (Poil de carotte) by Jules Renard, 1894

Families of the miners gather after the disaster in the mine shaft. 

Simple National Slovak Tales 1880

Pavol Dobšinský

Original Title | Prostonárodné slovenské povesti
Nationality | Slovakian, born 1828
Publisher | Self-published
Theme | Folktales, Fairy tales, Traditional

MORE TRADITIONAL DOBŠINSKÝ TALES

Slovak Tales (Slovenské povesti), 1858
Simple National Slovak Customs, Superstitions, and Plays (Prostonárodné obyčaje, povery a hry slovenské), 1880

8+

This exceptional collection of folk and fairy tales is one of the most popular Slovak books ever written. Folktales, fairy tales, legends, riddles, proverbs, sayings, customs, and superstitions have been an extremely important part of Slovak culture for centuries. Some critics have argued that there have been times when these folktales and traditional stories have served as the only witnesses of the Slovak national identity and existence.

This was especially important during the difficult years of Hungarian persecution and the suppression of Slovaks within the Austro-Hungarian Empire, which existed up to 1918, when an independent Czech-Slovak Republic was established.

"'And you my daughter, tell me how much you love me.' 'Father, I love you like salt . . .'"

Often referred to as a "Slovakian Hans Christian Andersen," Pavol Dobšinský succeeded not only in creating the largest and most complete collection of Slovak folktales, but he also published them, in a series of eight books, at his own expense between 1880 and 1883. The colorful, rich, and often humorous collection of ancient tales and folklore includes stories about magic, animals, and traditional legends.

The folk and fairy tales were originally intended for an adult audience, so before publishing them, Dobšinský had to edit out a great deal of explicit eroticism, brutality, and juicy humor. This made them suitable for children, helping to make them extremely popular. The original eight volumes have been rewritten a number of times since the 1880s, and this national cultural treasure has now been published in more than twenty-one countries. **JR**

"Popolvár" the "boy Cinderella" traveling to the kingdom of gold. 

Uncle Remus Stories 1881

Joel Chandler Harris

Nationality | American, born 1848
Publisher | Appleton, USA
Later Illustrated By | Milo Winter
Theme | Animal stories, Classics

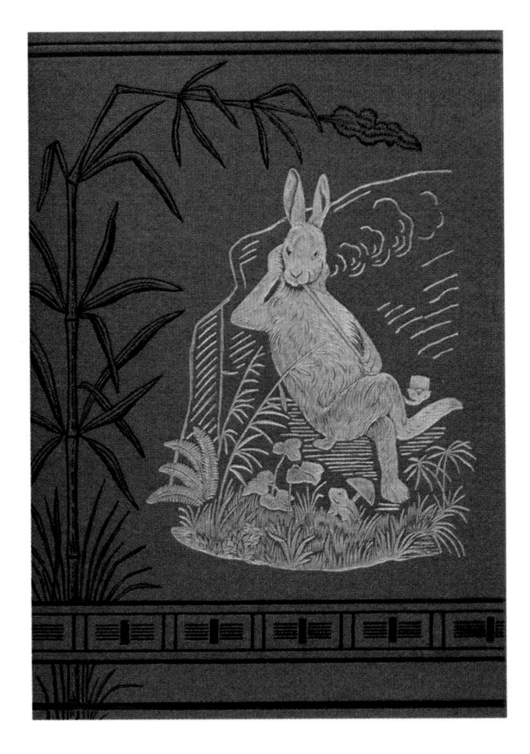

In Joel Chandler Harris's book, the character of Uncle Remus is an elderly black man, an ex-slave. A young white boy visits the old man's cabin every night to hear Uncle Remus relate his wonderful stories. Harris is not the original author of most of these stories, but he is the first person who is known to have written them down. By the nineteenth century, the stories of Brer Rabbit and his friends had been passed down orally through generations of African–Americans. Harris, a white journalist, first heard the stories when he was traveling around the southern states of the United States. An abolitionist, Harris had long used his writing to communicate his antiracism beliefs. He wanted to keep these oral stories alive.

Some scholars claim that the Brer Rabbit stories originated in Africa; others claim they are Native American, but no one knows for certain. In the twentieth century the stories were revived again, in the United Kingdom, by the author Enid Blyton.

The stories center on the wily Brer Rabbit, who is always getting into scrapes but who nearly always manages to get out of them and get the better of the other animals. One of his sworn enemies is Brer Fox, and many stories involve the two characters absorbed in some kind of conflict: "Brer Rabbit and Brer Fox . . . were always trying to trick one another," we are told. Other characters include Brer Terrapin, Brer Wolf, Brer Bear, Brer Buzzard, Brer Raccoon, Mr. Benjamin Ram, Mr. Wildcat, Brer Gibbley Gobbler, Mr. Dog, Mammy-Bammy Big-Money (a witch rabbit), Brer Mink, Sister Cow, and the infamous Mr. Man.

The main theme of the stories is little Brer Rabbit managing to defeat animals who are much bigger or stronger than him. For Harris, this was representative of the downtrodden people he had met in the South, who hoped to finally overcome the social and political situations that kept them oppressed. **LH**

OTHER COLLECTIONS OF FABLES

Aesop's Fables by Aesop, *c.* 550 B.C.E.
Fables by Jean de la Fontaine, 1668
Kinder- und Hausmärchen by Brothers Grimm, 1812
Nights with Uncle Remus by Joel Chandler Harris, 1882

The Prince and the Pauper 1881

Mark Twain Frank Merrill, John Harley, and L. S. Ipsen

Nationality | American, born Samuel Langhorne Clemens, 1835
Publisher | Dawson Brothers, Canada
Theme | Classics, Historical fiction

It is the Tudor era and pauper Tom Canty lives in squalor in London with his difficult father. In the meantime, the future Edward VI lives in splendor in London with his difficult royal relations. One day the two meet and strike up a friendship, based partly on their uncanny resemblance. They decide to swap places.

Tom is a level-headed boy who quickly learns to cope with the demands of royalty, including sitting in on legal judgments. Although quite ignorant of court customs, he can read and write (unusual for the time), although he has nothing of the immense learning for which the real Edward VI was renowned. At first the courtiers think their prince has gone mad, but he not only carries off his imposture but grows to like it. Edward does not have such a happy experience. He is bullied by Tom's drunken father, has little to eat and less to do. He sees the wretched poverty and harsh justice meted out to the poor and, fired up by his subjects' miseries, he unwisely reveals his identity to a gang of thieves, who mock him and declare him king of the insane.

Luckily, Miles Hendon, a soldier returning from the wars, takes Edward under his wing. He knows that King Henry VIII has died and Edward is now the rightful king. How can Edward regain the throne before Tom is crowned in his place? It all hinges on the Great Seal of England, which Edward had squirreled away before swapping places. In the end, the natural order is restored and all live happily ever after (although in reality, Edward VI died at fifteen).

Written in a style more akin to Dickens than to Twain's usual dry humor, the story is animated by the same anger at injustice and enjoyment of boyish high spirits as *Tom Sawyer* and *Huckleberry Finn*. Twain's commitment to the value of literacy as a civilizing force is woven through the nail-biting ups and down of the plot. **VN**

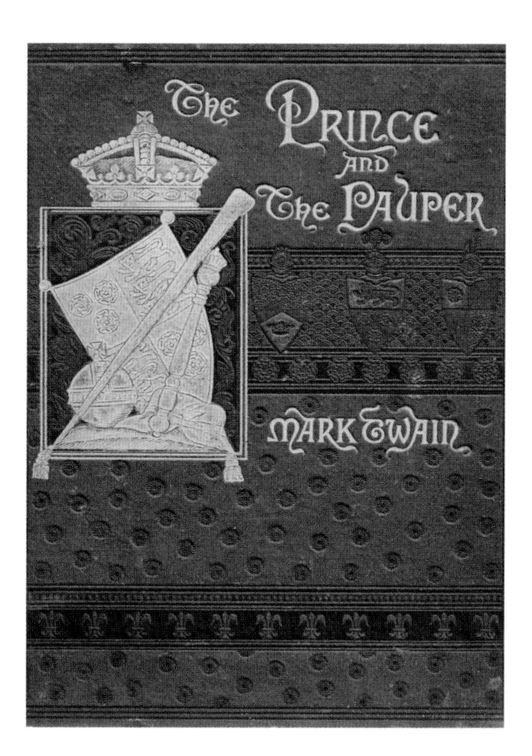

OTHER GREAT MARK TWAIN TITLES

The Adventures of Tom Sawyer, 1876
Adventures of Huckleberry Finn, 1885
A Connecticut Yankee in King Arthur's Court, 1889
Pudd'nhead Wilson, 1895

8+

8+

Bevis 1882

Richard Jefferies

Nationality | English, born 1848
Publisher | Sampson Low, UK
Later Illustrated By | E. H. Shepard
Theme | Adventure, Friendship

This "boy's own" adventure by Victorian author and naturalist Richard Jefferies, tells the tale of best friends Bevis and Mark who find a previously undiscovered lake. They set out to explore the island at its center using a raft that they have built themselves. They imagine the island is home to wild animals and savages so they equip themselves with a homemade gun and enough supplies to keep them going.

The story, based on Jefferies's own childhood adventures on his father's farm, is an idealized vision of an endless summer, free of any adult influence. It was originally intended for adults but soon became popular among boys and has a very masculine tone—there are no female characters at all. Bevis and Mark spend eleven days on the island, where they build a shelter and shoot game to eat. The book is a real celebration of childhood freedom and is reminiscent of Arthur Ransome's *Swallows and Amazons*, which depicts the adventures of children having fun in the English countryside without parental interference. Bevis and Mark get into all sorts of scrapes and stage a large Roman battle against local boys. Jefferies explains to readers how to build a raft and sail it, how to use a sundial, how to build a homemade musket, and how to survive in the great outdoors. Bevis's and Mark's experiences also help the boys to learn more about themselves.

At more than 500 pages, *Bevis* is a lengthy but absorbing novel that will appeal to readers interested in nature and learning practical skills. There are lots of lyrical descriptions but also plenty of action. **HJ**

Pinocchio 1883

Carlo Collodi Enrico Mazzanti

Nationality | Italian, born Carlo Lorenzini 1826 (author); Italian, born 1852 (illustrator)
Publisher | *Il Giornale dei Bambini*, Italy
Theme | Adventure, Favorite characters, Fantasy

The Adventures of Pinocchio (originally entitled *Le avventure di Pinocchio*) is the story of a wooden puppet carved by a man called Geppetto, in a small Tuscan village in Italy. It was written as a magazine story for children in 1883 and has proved immensely popular ever since. The story's animation by Walt Disney in 1940 turned it into a classic.

What sets Pinocchio apart from any other marionette is his desire to be a real boy. The story tells how the puppet acquires sufficient wisdom, through a series of adventures, to become a living boy. The relationship between the poor woodcarver, Geppetto, and his creation is that of a father and son. It is touching to see the pair develop love and respect for each other through sacrifice and understanding. Pinocchio is often naughty—made apparent by his nose, which grows if he lies or does something wrong. Collodi's story is rich in morals, with frequent allusions to the Bible and classical literature (less obvious in the movie adaptation).

The original story is well worth reading, especially for its characters, including a talking cricket; a fairy with turquoise hair; a green fisherman; and the terrible dogfish who have lessons, good and bad, to teach the wooden puppet. Pinocchio's thirst for adventure leads to him being swallowed by a dogfish, sold to a circus, and even changed into a donkey as he visits strange places such as the city of Catchfools and the Field of Miracles. Amusing and poignant, *The Adventures of Pinocchio* is a cautionary tale rich in allegory that seeks to teach children what is important in life. **CK**

Early twentieth-century cover illustration by Eugenio Cherubini. 

Treasure Island 1883

Robert Louis Stevenson

Nationality | Scottish, born 1850
Publisher | Cassell, UK; previously serialized in *Young Folks* between 1881 and 1882
Theme | Adventure

8+

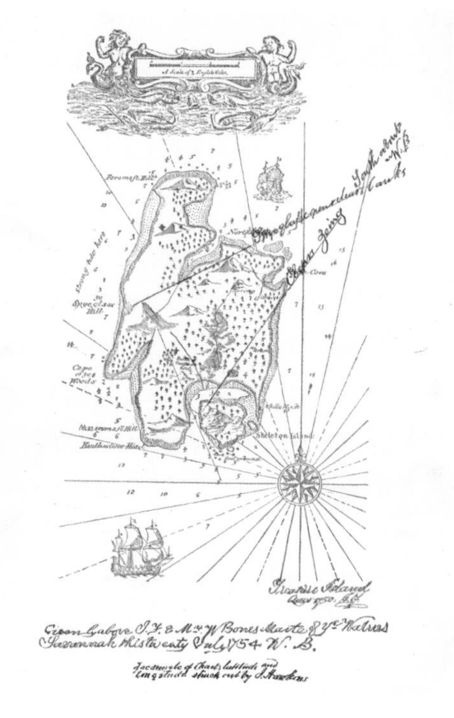

Treasure Island deserves its reputation as a classic work of children's literature. The tale is told by Jim Hawkins, a young boy whose ordinary life at the Admiral Bembo Inn will never be the same again following his extraordinary encounters with the unsavory shipmates of the feared, but now dead, Captain Flint. Billy Bones has a map that reveals the whereabouts of Flint's treasure hoard. Others mean to get their share, including the most famous of all pirates, the treacherous Long John Silver. With the sudden death of Billy Bones, the map is passed by Jim Hawkins to the trusted Squire Trelawney and Doctor Livesey. They decide to make an expedition to the Caribbean themselves and claim the treasure as their own. The devious Silver, however, subtly gains their confidence so that a band of pirates is unwittingly enlisted to crew the ship.

The gripping story of skulduggery and good-hearted courage is permeated with a continuously menacing air. The original serial form shapes the book's style. Every chapter sees events unfolding dramatically, moving the story on at pace and always finishing on a cliff-hanger. The language, formal by today's standards, permits a richness of expression that fires the imagination. On a cold and foggy moonlit night, a petrified Jim Hawkins hides in a ditch from the murderous pirates: "I was scarcely in position ere my enemies began to arrive, seven or eight of them, running hard, their feet beating out of time along the road . . ."

Treasure Island has been called a coming-of-age adventure story. When I was eleven years old, no book I had read before so wonderfully transported me to another time and place. When I had finished reading the book, I almost felt as though I had sailed on the *Hispaniola* with Jim Hawkins. Like him, on his return, I too felt I had grown up a little.

OTHER GREAT STORIES OF THE SEA

Robinson Crusoe **by Daniel Defoe, 1719**
Twenty Thousand Leagues Under the Sea **(*Vingt mille lieues sous les mers*) by Jules Verne, 1870**
Kidnapped **by Robert Louis Stevenson, 1886**
Moonfleet **by J. Meade Falkner, 1898**

Illustration of John Silver by Sir William Nicholson (1900).

Adventures of Huckleberry Finn 1884

Mark Twain Edward W. Kemble

Nationality | American, born Samuel Clemens, 1835 (author); American, born 1861 (illustrator)
Publisher | Chatto and Windus, UK
Theme | Adventure, Friendship, Classics

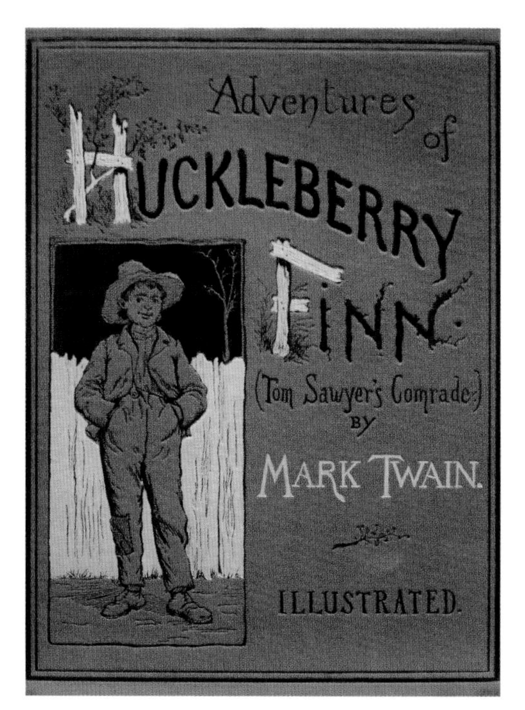

On my first reading of *Adventures of Huckleberry Finn* at about the age of ten, I was inspired to climb down the rainspouts to avoid taking an afternoon nap. On subsequent readings I was motivated to canoe up the Yellow Breeches Creek to find adventure, then when older, to become politically aware. For readers at all ages, Mark Twain's humor is tremendous—"feels as good as church letting out." Later, as a writer, Huckleberry Finn taught me to observe people, places, plants, and animals, and to write only about that which I knew. I don't know any novel that has influenced more writers than *Adventures of Huckleberry Finn*. It is a masterpiece that every young writer should read.

"I listened to a faint droning of flies and bugs in the air that makes it seem so lonesome . . ."

Written in three different dialects, Huck Finn's adventures begin when he runs away from his drunken father and finds his friend, the runaway slave Jim, on an island trying to escape as well. They find a raft and head for the free city of Cairo, pass it in the night, and continue on down the Mississippi. Through the eyes of Huck, Twain satirizes and condemns injustices and racial prejudices. Although written after the Civil War, the book is set beforehand. Ever since its publication, some critics have panned the book as coarse or, in more recent times, racist, for its use of contemporary words such as "nigger."

Hysterical adventures overtake the friends, especially when they take aboard the two rapscallions "duke" and "king." The trip culminates in Huck meeting his friend, Tom Sawyer, and their joy when they learn that Jim has been free all along.

MORE TALES OF MISCHIEF

***The Adventures of Tom Sawyer* by Mark Twain, 1876**
***The Paul Street Boys* by Ferenc Molnár, 1906**
***Just William* by Richmal Crompton, 1922**
***Jennings and Darbishire* by Anthony Buckeridge, 1952**

The original frontispiece by Edward Windsor Kemble. 

E·W·Kemble

Little Lord Fauntleroy 1886

Frances Hodgson Burnett Reginald Birch

Nationality | English, born 1849 (author); English, born 1856 (illustrator)
Publisher | Charles Scribner's Sons, USA
Theme | Family

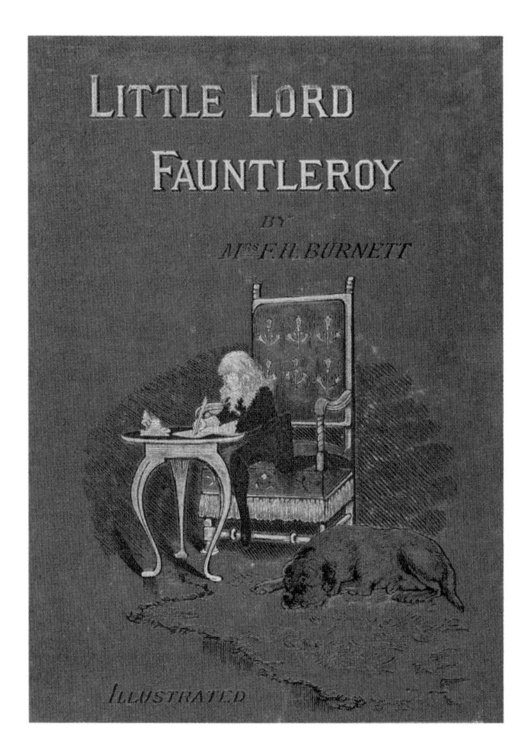

8+

OTHER HODGSON BURNETT TITLES

A Little Princess, 1905
The Secret Garden, 1911
The Lost Prince, 1915

In popular parlance, "Little Lord Fauntleroy" has come to mean a spoiled, precocious child, given to airs and graces. Yet the young Lord Fauntleroy of Frances Hodgson Burnett's charming novel is anything but. Born in England, Burnett moved to the United States as a child. *Little Lord Fauntleroy* draws on her own experience on both sides of the Atlantic and examines the prejudices of both the English and the Americans toward each other, and the concepts of class, nobility, and filial love, with the sometimes brash spirit of the U.S.-born young lord winning the day over the rigid ways of the English aristocracy.

Cedric Errol is the young lord, the son of an English aristocratic father, who dies young, and an American mother. He is set to inherit the properties of Dorincourt Castle, Wyndham Towers, and Chorlworth from his grandfather, the grumpy John Arthur Molyneux Errol, Earl of Dorincourt. Errol's father was the youngest of the earl's three sons, and his father's favorite. Yet when he went to the United States and married a local commoner, he became estranged from his father, who is staunchly anti-American. After the death of the earl's two eldest sons, Errol is set to become Lord Fauntleroy, and is summoned to England to be educated in the ways of the aristocracy by his grandfather. The pair have a strange relationship, as the young lord's common touch and affectionate ways are alien to his grandfather, who had a distant relationship with all his own sons. The story is as much about how the earl learns to be more sympathetic and compassionate in his old age, as it is about what it takes to be a noble.

The novel was a huge success when it was published, first in serial and then in book form, and the illustrations of the young lord with his curly hair, lacy collar, and velvet suit spawned a fashion craze that embarrassed many a young boy. **CK**

"Dick boards the steamer to bid good-bye to Lord Fauntleroy." 

Isabel Allende reviews:

The Canterville Ghost 1887

Oscar Wilde Frederick Henry Townsend

Nationality | Irish, born 1854 (author); English, born 1861 (illustrator)
Publisher | *Court and Society Review*, UK
Theme | Classics, Love, Ghost stories

MORE GREAT WORKS BY OSCAR WILDE

The Happy Prince, 1888
The Selfish Giant, 1888
The Nightingale and the Rose, 1888
The Remarkable Rocket, 1888
The Devoted Friend, 1888

8+

One of my favorite tales is *The Canterville Ghost* by Oscar Wilde, with its mixture of humor and drama, horror and comedy, love and death. When I was a little girl I read it many times and I always laughed out loud at the misadventures of the ghost and wept at the unexpected end.

The Otises are an American family—father, mother, older son, mischievous twins, and a girl of fifteen, Virginia—who go to live in an old mansion in England. It is an enormous, sinister house with sliding panels, secret passages, hidden objects, spiral staircases, attics, and so on. The owner warns them that it is haunted by the ghost of an ancestor, Sir Simon, but the Otises do not believe in the supernatural and move in. Meanwhile Sir Simon prepares to frighten them to death with his squeaking chains, wailing moans, discordant laughs, bloodstains, and apparitions from beyond the grave. All are in vain; his efforts only meet with the overwhelmingly practical mind of the Otis family.

The contrast between English tradition and American pragmatism is delightfully ironic: Mrs. Otis produces lubricating oil for the ghostly Sir Simon's rusty chains or wipes the blood off the carpet with stain remover. The twins make death unbearable for Sir Simon with their traps and jokes, even giving him a terrible fright by disguising themselves with a sheet. The only one who does not make fun of him is Virginia, who guesses the suffering of this lost soul.

Finally Sir Simon, defeated by the Otises, confides in Virginia, telling her about the crime he committed for which he must atone over centuries. He asks her to cry and pray for him because he has neither tears nor faith left, and only she can help to free him. The hilarious tone of the story changes when Virginia accompanies Sir Simon to the Kingdom of Death. The end is magical and moving, but it would be unforgivable to ruin the suspense by telling it here . . .

"'Quick, quick,' cried the Ghost, 'or it will be too late.'"

The Happy Prince 1888

Oscar Wilde Walter Crane and George Percy Jacomb Hood

8+

THE HAPPY PRINCE
AND OTHER TALES BY
OSCAR WILDE
ILLUSTRATED BY
WALTER CRANE
& JACOMB
HOOD
1888

Nationality | Irish, born 1854 (author); English, born 1845 and 1857 (illustrators)
Publisher | David Nutt, UK
Theme | Friendship, Love

The statue of the Happy Prince stands on a high column. He is made of lead, covered with gold leaf; his eyes are sapphires, and in the hilt of his sword is a ruby. When the prince was alive he was always happy, but now from his elevated position, he can see all the poor, hungry, cold, and unhappy people in his city.

Migrating birds have flown south for the winter, but one little swallow stayed behind because he was in love with a beautiful reed. After six weeks, he decides they are incompatible and determines to fly to Egypt. On his first night he stops to rest on the statue, but keeps getting wet. The Happy Prince is crying. The prince asks the swallow to take the ruby to a poor seamstress whose child is ill. The following night, the swallow reluctantly agrees to take one of the sapphires to a poor poet. The next night the prince tells him to take the other sapphire to a match girl. Knowing the Happy Prince is now blind, the swallow decides to stay with him and be his eyes.

By day, the swallow flies around, returning to tell the statue all he has seen. Every night he picks off pieces of the gold leaf and takes it to the poor. Soon the people are well fed and happy, but the cold winter takes its toll on the swallow and he dies at the statue's feet. The Happy Prince's leaden heart cracks in two. The statue now looks shabby, so the mayor orders it to be taken down and melted, but the broken heart refuses to melt. It is thrown on the rubbish heap, next to the body of the swallow. When God sends an angel to find the two most precious things in the city, he chooses the broken heart and the dead bird. **LH**

"High above the city . . . stood the statue of the Happy Prince. He was gilded all over with thin leaves of fine gold."

OTHER NOTABLE TALES OF PRINCES

The Wicked Prince **by Hans Christian Andersen, 1840**
The Prince and the Pauper **by Mark Twain, 1881**
The Little Prince **by Antoine de Saint-Exupéry, 1943**
Prince Caspian **by C. S. Lewis, 1951**
The Prince of Motordu **by Pef, 1980**

Carrot Top 1894

Jules Renard Félix Vallotton

Nationality | French, born 1864 (author); Swiss, born 1865 (illustrator)
Publisher | Flammarion, France
Theme | Family, Controversial

Carrot Top (originally entitled *Poil de Carotte*) is an semi-autobiographical novel, in which a child must learn to survive in a cruel and indifferent world.

Madame Lepic really dislikes her red-haired youngest child. She finds pleasure in intimidating and humiliating him and always punishes him harshly. Carrot Top is always given the hardest chores and punishments. His family find him secretive, uncommunicative, and heartless. His father is often too busy with work or out shooting to pay any attention to his son. His older brother, Felix, always takes advantage of the situation and his sister Ernestine is a little pest most of the time. Carrot Top suffers a great deal from his misfortune and his clumsiness, but through his adventures he learns to become tougher, more cunning, to make sure he does not get caught, and to be an excellent observer.

Childhood is far from an ideal world for Jules Renard; Carrot Top is lonely and sad but he is not an innocent child. He can be hypocritical, sly, and heartless when he applies his violence to animals or when he hides stones in snowballs. The ordeals he undergoes are terrible but his strength of character transforms this poignant story into an amusing and delightful read. It is impossible to forget this young hero and not to be moved by his deep desire to be noticed and loved by his family.

Carrot Top was adapted for the theater in 1900 and is still performed regularly today. It was made into a film in 1926, 1952, and 1972 and was adapted for television in 2003. **SL**

Moonfleet 1898

J. Meade Falkner

Nationality | English, born 1858
Reillustrated By | Robert Tilleard
Publisher | Edward Arnold, UK
Theme | Adventure, Classics

Moonfleet tracks an eighteenth-century maritime adventure story through the eyes of its protagonist, fifteen-year-old orphan John Trenchard. The plot moves briskly through the villages and coastline of Dorset, England, where Falkner spent his youth, across the sea to Holland, and back to Moonfleet bay. It includes a boy trapped in a cold crypt, his friendships with two father figures of ambiguous moral authority—one a pub landlord, one the smugglers leader—shipwreck, hidden gems, coded parchments, a hard spell in a prison camp, and an unexpected happy ending tinged with mystery: Falkner clearly owes a debt to Robert Louis Stevenson's *Treasure Island*. Although less wildly poetic, *Moonfleet* still makes its readers hold their breath in anguished tension.

Of course, smuggling is a violent criminal activity that needs no glamorizing. It is a topsy-turvy kind of moral universe in *Moonfleet*, where enforcing the law seems the most wicked of actions and evading tax on spirits the most heroic. The story is interwoven with games of backgammon, played by the regulars of the Why Not? public house where John lives with foster father, Elzevir Block, who took him in when his own son was killed by the coastguard. Rakish backgammon seems to operate in the book as a vector for Victorian virtues of individual resourcefulness and the ability to take advantage of fate, which reinforces the amorality of adventure. Readers can vicariously enjoy living by their wits, through the motto on the pub's backgammon board, "As in life, so in a game of hazard, skill will make something of the worst of throws." **VN**

The Black Corsair 1898

Emilio Salgari   Pipein Gamba

Nationality | Italian, born 1862 (author); Italian, born Giuseppe Garuti birth date unknown (illustrator)
Publisher | Donath, Italy
Theme | Adventure

The Black Corsair (*Il Corsaro Nero*) was the first title in a series of adventure books written by Emilio Salgari, about noblemen who have forsaken their castles and lands to take to the sea. The Black Corsair is more usually known as the Lord of Ventimiglia and Roccabruna. Ventimiglia is a Ligurian city situated near the French border on the northwest coast of Italy, which was at one time part of the kingdom of Piedmont. He is a pirate intent on avenging the killing of his brothers, the Red Corsair and the Green Corsair, by the Duke of Van Guld. Together with his band of pirates, the Black Corsair travels the Caribbean Seas. Some of the book's action takes place on the lake of the city of Maracaibo, in Venezuela.

"Large tracts of sea, which seconds before were as black as ink, suddenly lit up. . . ."

The plot centers on the brave and determined character of Lord Ventimiglia. After he falls in love with Honorata, he is devastated to discover that she is the daughter of his archenemy, Van Guld. True to his principles, the Black Corsair, in front of his astounded men, banishes Honorata into a stormy sea on a dinghy. He does not hide his despair at having to carry out this painful act of revenge.

Salgari, who was born in Verona but lived in Turin, wrote prolifically and created some of the most iconic figures of Italian literature. He set his stories in what represented for him distant and exotic locations, and embellished his plots with historical details of real places, battles, and people. In reality, Salgari himself never ventured farther than the Ligurian Riviera. It is a tribute to his vast imagination that he managed to describe so vividly his far-off locations. **SMT**

OTHER CLOAK AND DAGGER CLASSICS

Treasure Island by Robert Louis Stevenson, 1833
The Three Musketeers by Alexandre Dumas, 1844
Queen of the Caribbean by Emilio Salgari, 1901
Peter Pan by J. M. Barrie, 1906
Jack Holborn by Leon Garfield, 1964

The Story of the Treasure Seekers 1899

E. Nesbit Gordon Browne and Lewis Baumer

Nationality | English, born 1858 (author); English, born 1858 and 1870 (illustrators)
Publisher | Fisher Unwin, UK
Theme | Family, Adventure

Although *The Story of the Treasure Seekers* was first published more than a century ago and has, therefore, become somewhat dated, its characters have retained their freshness. Its theme—how to make money quickly, more-or-less honorably, and without adult assistance—has become an enduring motif in children's literature.

The story is set in south London toward the end of the nineteenth century, and tells of the successes and failures of the six Bastable children, who attempt to "restore the fallen fortunes" of their home. With their widowed father weighed down by the anxieties of his failing business, the children are largely left to their own devices and, in their quest for treasure, they try their hand at everything from digging and divining through to kidnapping and ransom. Nothing goes according to plan, but the difficulties encountered by the children along the way add to the sense of adventure, while the ongoing petty rivalries and minor misdemeanors of large family life remain engagingly plausible to contemporary readers.

With the timely help of Albert-next-door's sympathetic uncle, they occasionally come into some money, but it never amounts to enough to restore their status. It does, however, yield enough for a small feast and, when they invite their supposedly poverty-stricken uncle to share in their celebrations, their magnanimous jollity brings a far greater reward. Told in the first person by one of the Bastable children (he likes to keep his identity secret but readers soon recognize eldest brother Oswald), the cheerful narrative is imbued with a strong, though never didactic, moral sense, a love of adventure, and an appealingly robust resilience in the face of adversity. Cecil Leslie illustrated the 1958 Puffin edition. Further Bastable adventures take place in *The Wouldbegoods* (1901) and *New Treasure Seekers* (1904). **KA**

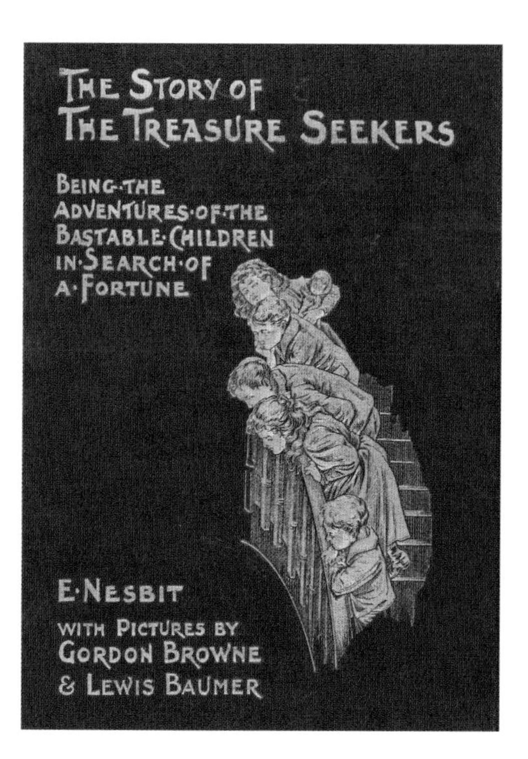

MORE GREAT TITLES FROM E. NESBIT

The Wouldbegoods, 1901
Five Children and It, 1902
The Phoenix and the Carpet, 1904
New Treasure Seekers, 1904
The Railway Children, 1906

8+

The Wonderful Wizard of Oz 1900

Lyman Frank Baum   William Wallace Denslow

Nationality | American, born 1856 (author); American, born 1856 (illustrator)
Publisher | George M. Hill, USA
Theme | Classics, Magical stories, Fantasy

MORE BOOKS ABOUT WIZARDS

The Hobbit by J. R. R. Tolkien, 1937
The Sword in the Stone by T. H. White, 1938
The Wizard of Earthsea by Ursula K. Le Guin, 1968
Harry Potter and the Philosopher's Stone by J. K. Rowling, 1997

In the English-speaking world, almost everyone is familiar with "Over the Rainbow," Judy Garland's signature song. The tune comes from the classic movie *The Wizard of Oz* (1939), which has entertained generations of children. Far fewer people today are likely to have read the book on which the film is based, L. Frank Baum's *The Wonderful Wizard of Oz*, which is a shame because the novel is just as endearing and uplifting as its successor. Much of the novel has become part of popular culture, from phrases such as "There's no place like home" to the image of the yellow-brick road. Such was the story's success when it was first published that Baum went on to write thirteen sequels.

Baum's tale of a young girl from Kansas, Dorothy, and her dog, Toto, sees the pair plucked from daily life by a tornado and transported to the land of Oz. In this magical place Dorothy befriends memorable characters such as the Scarecrow, the Tin Woodman, and the Cowardly Lion, who all join her in her quest to reach the Emerald City and find the Wizard of Oz, who can help her to return home. Their journey involves great risk as they face down the Wicked Witch of the West and her troop of fearsome flying monkeys.

The motley trio who accompany Dorothy are on their own mission—the Scarecrow to find a brain, the Tin Woodman a heart, and the Cowardly Lion, courage. Yet this is a story where nothing is as it seems. Baum's real purpose is to show how people have different fears and anxieties, and yet, with time and the support and encouragement of friends, they are able to overcome them—and perhaps even have some fun along the way as they do so.

The book has been widely interpreted as having a plethora of hidden references to the contemporary U.S. cultural landscape, but above all it is a fantastical and inspiring story of friendship in adversity. **CK**

W. W. Denslow's image of Scarecrow being lifted away by a stork.

E. SALGARI
LA REGINA DEI CARAIB
ILLUSTRATA DA DISEGNI A COLORI DI P. GAMBA

Queen of the Caribbean 1901

Emilio Salgari, Pipein Gamba

Nationality | Italian, born 1862 (author); Italian, born G. Garuti birth date unknown (illustrator)
Publisher | Donath, Italy
Theme | Adventure, Favorite characters

This second book in the Black Corsair series (*La regina dei Caraibi*) is set in and around the region of the Gulf of Mexico, in countries such as Panama, Venezuela, and Colombia. Lord Ventimiglia (the Black Corsair) is among the most feared pirates who sack and plunder the Spanish settlements in the New World. Ventimiglia, however, has one thing in mind: to destroy the Duke of Van Guld and thereby avenge his brothers.

In this story, the Black Corsair enlists the help of Yara, a young Indian princess whose family and village were destroyed by Van Guld. The Black Corsair is flanked by his men—Carmaux, Morgan, Wan Stiller, and Moko—together with three intrepid pirates: Grammont, Laurent, and Wan Horn. The three pirates plan to conquer the city of Veracruz in Mexico, and the Black Corsair joins them. In Veracruz the Black Corsair finds Van Guld in the company of the Marchioness of Bermejo. A duel ensues but Van Guld escapes. The Marchioness tells the Black Corsair how to find information about the whereabouts of Honorata, the woman Lord Ventimiglia banished to sea on a dinghy.

Rich in action and dialogue, the narrative speeds along in typical Salgari style. Many battles and sword fights ensue, as well as escapes. After a battle between the ships *La Folgore* and *L'Alambra*, Van Guld dies, but the Black Corsair and his men are left stranded in open seas. Once ashore, they are captured by the same Indians who had befriended Honorata. Reunited, the couple return to Piedmont to settle down. **SMT**

Sussi and Biribissi 1902

Collodi Nipote

Original Title | Sussi e Biribissi
Nationality | Italian, born Paolo Lorenzini 1876
Publisher | R. Bemporad and Figlio, Italy
Theme | Adventure, Friendship

Sussi and Biribissi are two friends living in Florence, Italy, at the start of the twentieth century. Physically they are quite different from each other: "Sussi is blonde, a yellow blonde color like that of freshly cooked cornmeal porridge. He is chubby and round like a butter roll . . . "; his best friend Biribissi is tall, dark, and thin. They have both read Jules Verne's novel *A Journey to the Center of the Earth,* and are inspired to set off on an adventure of their own. They decide that they will travel in the footsteps of their literary heroes and so begin their journey by descending into the sewers of the city of Florence. Along the way, Sussi and Biribissi encounter the talking Gatto Buricchio and Talpa Sforacchiona, a charming cat and a mole, respectively. Together they discover the hidden underground tunnels. Instead of going deeper toward the center, however, Sussi and Biribissi emerge from the tunnels of the sewer at different points. In so doing, they discover parts of Florence that they had never before imagined. They enter secret places such as the wine cellar of a monastery.

Author Paolo Lorenzini was the nephew of Carlo Collodi who wrote *The Adventures of Pinocchio.* Trading on his famous uncle's name, Lorenzini signed his name as Collodi. Like his uncle, Lorenzini captures the imagination of his readers and guides them, not to the center of the Earth, but to the mystery at the heart of Florence. Lorenzini deftly contrasts the very socially different Florentine worlds. **SMT**

Five Children and It 1902

E. Nesbit H. R. Millar

Nationality | English, born Edith Nesbit 1858 (author); Scottish, born 1869 (illustrator)
Publisher | Fisher Unwin, UK
Theme | Fantasy

Five Children and It is the first of seven comic fantasy novels that turned E. Nesbit from a prolific hack into one of the most celebrated of children's writers.

"It" is the Psammead, a grumpy sand fairy with a hairy body and eyes on stalks. When Robert, Anthea, Cyril, Jane, and their baby brother, the Lamb, dig the Psammead up in a gravel pit, it agrees to grant them a wish a day. The children soon discover that fairy-tale magic in the real world brings a whole heap of problems and almost always leaves them without their dinner. Badly thought-out wishes bring disappointment: no one accepts their money when they wish to be "rich beyond the dreams of avarice," and no one recognizes them when they are "beautiful as the day." Accidental wishes backfire: wishing that everyone wanted the Lamb leads to him being kidnapped, and wishing to be bigger than the baker's boy turns Robert into a giant. It is a considerable relief that each wish only lasts until sunset, although this too brings its problems, stranding the children on the top of a tower when their wished-for wings disappear.

"Why, almost everyone had Pterodactyl for breakfast in my time!"

Eventually the children create such trouble for everyone around them that they have to beg the Psammead to undo their last wish, promising in return never to ask for another. Much relieved, the Psammead makes them swear to secrecy, because it fears that if grown-ups discovered its powers they would wish for "graduated income-tax, and old-age pensions and manhood suffrage, and free secondary education" (all issues of which the fervently socialist Nesbit approved). **CW**

OTHER CLASSIC E. NESBIT TITLES

***The Story of the Treasure Seekers,* 1899**
***The Phoenix and the Carpet,* 1904**
***The Railway Children,* 1906**
***The Story of the Amulet,* 1906**
***The Enchanted Castle,* 1907**

Rebecca of Sunnybrook Farm 1903

✎ Kate Douglas Wiggin ✎ Helen Mason Grose

Rebecca of Sunnybrook Farm has become a classic tale about the pain of growing up. Beautifully written with a humorous touch, Kate Douglas Wiggin opens the novel by describing the journey of the ten-year-old Rebecca Rowena Randall as she leaves the life she has shared on Sunnybrook Farm with her widowed mother, brothers, and sisters. It is the turn of the nineteenth century, and Rebecca is traveling to stay with her two elderly aunts, Jane and Miranda, who need help with the daily chores.

Rebecca is intermittently nervous and excited as she goes off on her adventure into an unknown world. The aunts live in Riverboro, Maine, and the book follows Rebecca's life with them for the next seven years as she learns how to cook, sew, and keep house. Rebecca gets on well with sweet Aunt Jane, but falls foul of her strict Aunt Miranda's quick temper and sharp tongue. This is often because of Rebecca's own indomitable spirit that leads her into a series of amusing escapades. Nevertheless, Rebecca's brains and charm eventually win over Miranda, and her guile and savvy prove to be her aunts' saving grace when Rebecca rescues them from losing all their money. Yet it is also Aunt Miranda's firm, guiding hand that proves to be the making of the rebellious Rebecca.

"Rebecca was a thing of fire and spirit . . . [she] was plucky at two and dauntless at five."

This story may, at times, seem saccharine to modern tastes. However, its theme of a clever but willful young girl who has to say good bye to her daydreams in order to face the harsh realities of life, and realizes that there are compensations to be found in the mundane, is one that stands the test of time. **CK**

Nationality | American, born 1856 (author); American, born 1880 (illustrator)
Publisher | Houghton Mifflin, USA
Theme | Adventure, Classics, Family

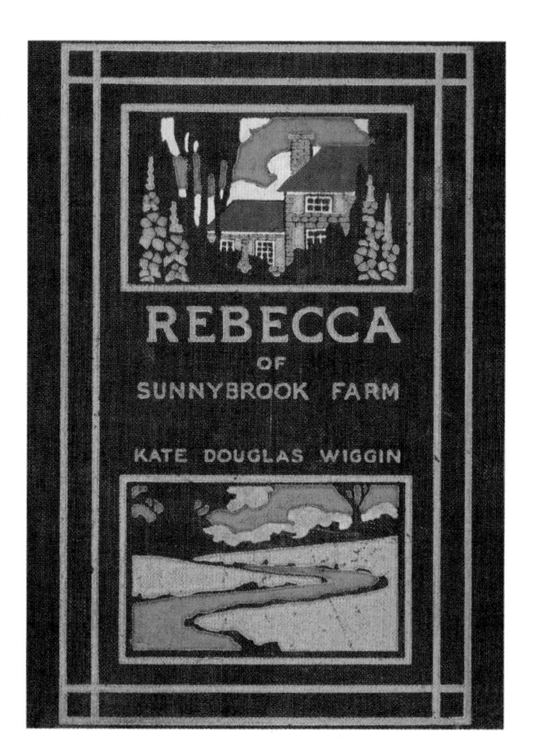

OTHER BOOKS ABOUT GROWING UP

***Les Malheurs de Sophie* by Comtesse de Ségur, 1864**
***Anne of Green Gables* by L. M. Montgomery, 1908**
***Betsy-Tacy* series by Maud Hart Lovelace, 1940**
***The Warden's Niece* by Gillian Avery, 1957**
***Anastasia Krupnik* by Lois Lowry, 1979**

8+

The Bobbsey Twins 1904

Laura Lee Hope Martha E. Miller

Nationality | American, born Edward Stratemeyer 1862 (author); details unknown (illustrator)
Publisher | Mershon, USA
Theme | Adventure, Detective stories

This book is part of a classic series that lasted for seventy-five years. It is thought Edward Stratemeyer, who wrote under the pseudonym "Laura Lee Hope," penned only this, the first book (also titled *Merry Days, Indoors and Out)*, then commissioned the subsequent editions via a succession of ghostwriters. Despite spin-offs and multiple revisions, the two pairs of Bobbsey twins have stayed much the same.

Twelve-year-olds Nan and Bert are responsible enough to take their younger siblings camping and to rescue grown men from drowning. Six-year-olds Freddie and Flossie are blond, chubby, and impetuous. The foursome attract unsolved mysteries, which they tackle with intelligence, resourcefulness, and luck. Adults seem to respect their detecting abilities, too—so much so that the police will even share their leads.

In this first in the series, the Bobbseys decide to help Mrs. Marden, an elderly neighbor who has just moved into a retirement home. Her old house is soon to be demolished, and Mrs. Marden cannot remember where she hid her valuables. The twins volunteer to help find them before the wrecking machines arrive, but their search is complicated by Danny Rugg, the school bully, a missing pet, and by the possibility that the house itself is haunted.

Although adults might find the characterizations somewhat dated and the plots a little far-fetched, the reading level is pitched for children who are ready for their first novels. The twins' lives are full of adventure, but their playful exuberance and conspiratorial plans are the real charm of the books. **CQ**

A Little Princess 1905

Frances H. Burnett Harold Piffard

Nationality | English, born 1849 (author); British, born 1867 (illustrator)
Publisher | Frederick Warne, UK
Theme | Adventure, Friendship, School

Like *Little Lord Fauntleroy*, Frances Hodgson Burnett's first successful novel for children, *A Little Princess* is the story of a reversal of fortune, but this time in reverse. Cedric in *Fauntleroy* escapes straitened circumstances for the life of an heir to an English earldom; in *A Little Princess*, Sara Crewe starts her school career as an heiress but is turned into a maid-of-all-work and is outcast after her bankrupt father's death.

The story of Sara's banishment to the attic of Miss Minchin's Select Seminary for Young Ladies and of the mysterious benefactor who sends the desolate child comforts via his Indian servant depends heavily on coincidence. However, Sara is a strong enough character to make suspension of disbelief possible. Even while still in Miss Minchin's favor, Sara is intelligent enough to assess the woman's true nature. She loses fair-weather friends but is sustained by others, such as the maid Becky and the despised schoolgirl Ermengarde, who both remember her kindness in happier times. Above all, the courage and imagination that helped Sara cope with separation from her father give her the strength to survive her decline in fortunes. If Sara can be shown to imagine that her chilly attic is a cell in the Bastille and Becky is the prisoner next door, the reader can believe it, too.

Contemporary children may find some of Sara's fancies a little sentimental but will cheer her on through her trials and relish her eventual triumph and Miss Minchin's downfall. Along the way, they will learn the importance of being kind to those you pass on the way up life's ladder. **GB**

A LITTLE PRINCESS

Gustavo Martín Garzo reviews:

Captain Storm 1905

Emilio Salgari   Alberto della Valle

Nationality | Italian, born 1862 (author); Italian, born 1851 (illustrator)
Publisher | Donath, Italy
Theme | Adventure, Historical fiction

8+

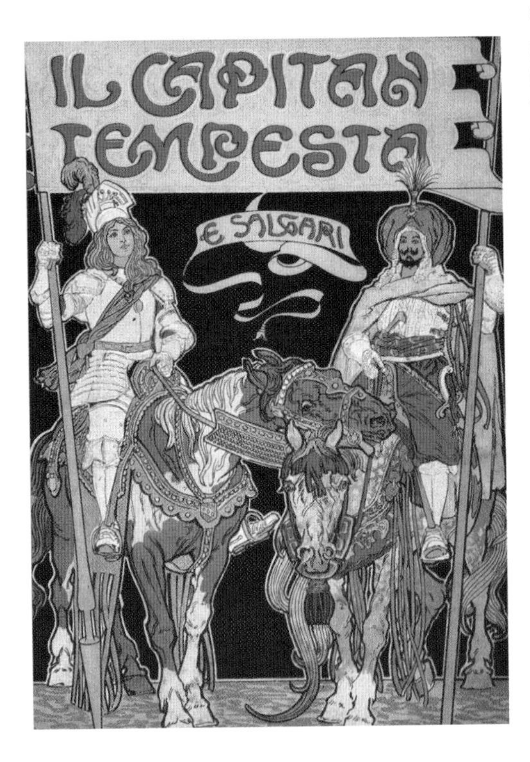

OTHER GREAT SALGARI ADVENTURES

The Pirates of Malaysia (I Pirati della Malesia), 1896
The Black Corsair (Il Corsaro Nero), 1898
Queen of the Caribbean (La regina dei Caraibi), 1901
The Two Tigers (Le due Tigri), 1904
Son of the Red Corsair (Il figlio del Corsaro Rosso), 1908

Captain Storm (Il Capitan Tempesta) was not the first book I ever read but it was the one that made me discover the true power of reading. I had read other novels by Emilio Salgari, in particular The Black Corsair adventures and those of The Pirates of Malaysia. I was thirteen or fourteen years old then and I was particularly interested in the heroines who appeared in these adventures. I shall never forget Honorata De Van Guld on the deck of a ship during a stormy night, or the moment when Sandokan, who had been wounded, suddenly woke up and discovered The Pearl of Labuan at his side. Salgari's heroines were always very brave and free; capable, as Isak Dinesen would have put it, of risking their soul to satisfy a desire. And this mixture of romanticism, generosity, and absence of fear drove my adolescent heart wild.

The hero of *Captain Storm* is a brave Christian captain, in the time of the Crusades. The novel deals with the ancient conflicts between Christians and Muslims for control of the Holy Land and is full of action and color. But there is a surprise that is only revealed later on in the book. The brave captain is in fact a girl—a girl who has disguised herself as a man to join a world full of danger and anxiety, where she hopes to be reunited with the man she loves. Everything changes with this revelation because it is no longer a matter of following her military adventures; there are other considerations that are much more intimate and indefinable: the adventures of her heart.

This book taught me that in literature there should always be a secret story behind the more obvious one, and that as you read, the other story unravels. This is why we read: to overhear the delicate course of the characters' thoughts and desires. Honorata De Van Guld, the girl who hid herself in mannish clothes in those first chapters, became this secret story. Since then, I have never stopped searching for it in reading.

The "captain" fights to protect her identity in this original illustration.

Bécassine 1905

Jacqueline Rivière   Joseph Pinchon

Nationality | French, born 1885 (author); French, born 1871 (illustrator)
Publisher | La Semaine de Suzette, France
Theme | Favorite characters, Adventure

8+

Bécassine, more correctly known as Annaik Labornez, is a farmer's daughter from a remote corner of Brittany, in France. One day she decides to leave her native Finistère to go to the grand city of Paris and become a housemaid in the household of the wealthy, cultivated, and arrogant Marquise de Grand'Air. In the twenty-three adventures that follow, readers join the naive Breton servant girl as she is faced with the terrifying novelty, flamboyant attractions, and class distinctions of the unfamiliar big city.

Bécassine was the first female comic-strip character in France (on a par with Astérix and Obélix) and one of the first female protagonists in the history of comics worldwide. Depicted in traditional Breton costume, with simple features and without a mouth, Bécassine is the typical provincial girl as seen by the refined inhabitants of the grande ville of Paris at the beginning of the twentieth century: "This Bécassine! No brains but a great heart!" However, over the course of the adventures—ranging from her job-hunting escapades in the French capital, her experiences during World War I, and even her encounters with foreigners—and coupled with her great popularity—the character of Bécassine came to be depicted more favorably than as a simple stereotype.

Today, her hilarious adventures are still extremely popular with French children, as well as being an insight for young readers into the France of yesterday. Some favorite titles of the series include *Bécassine During the War* (1916), *Bécassine Travels* (1921), and *Bécassine Looks for a Job* (1937). **LB**

Paul Street Boys 1906

Ferenc Molnár

Original Title | A Pál-utcai fiúk
Nationality | Hungarian, born 1878
Translation Published | 1927, Macy-Masius, USA
Theme | Adventure, Illness and death

The backdrop of this novel is Budapest in 1885, however, the story it tells is both timeless and universal, and has the power to move and inspire.

Two groups of adolescents, the Paul Street Boys, led by Boka, and the Botanical Gardenites, led by Terrible Feri Áts, get into a fierce fight over the control of the grund, a vacant lot in the back of a lumberyard. Until now, the grund has been the playground of the Paul Street Boys, but the Botanical Gardenites (a.k.a. the Red Shirts) want the grund for their football field.

The first act of hostility occurs when Áts sneaks into the grund and captures the Paul Street Boys' banner. He is discovered by Nemecsek, a blond and frail youngster to whom most people pay little attention. The encounter with Áts propels Nemecsek to the forefront of the unfolding events, enabling him to show courage and integrity and win everybody's respect. Nemecsek twice infiltrates the Red Shirts' camp—once in the company of Boka, to drop the provocative note "The Paul Street Boys Were Here!" and once alone, to spy on the Red Shirts.

When the war breaks out, the superior strength of the Red Shirts is countered by the superior strategy of the Paul Street Boys. When the situation starts to turn, however, victory is finally achieved by Nemecsek, who arrives feverish from his sick bed to help. There is no happy ending to this story. Nemecsek dies of consumption, and his heroism proves ultimately pointless when the construction of a tenement house on the grund commences and the territory is lost to both gangs forever. **IW**

Peter Pan in Kensington Gardens 1906

J. M. Barrie Arthur Rackham

Nationality | Scottish, born 1860 (author); English, born 1867 (illustrator)
Publisher | Hodder and Stoughton, UK
Theme | Classics, Fantasy

For James Barrie, who never quite grew up himself, Peter Pan was an image of boyhood: "gay and innocent and heartless." For generations of readers and theater lovers, *Peter Pan* has been a magic harbinger of adventure.

The Darlings—glamorous mother, grumpy father, pretty Wendy, and little brothers John and Michael—are watched over by their faithful nurse: the dog Nana. Even Nana, however, cannot prevent the children being enticed away by naughty Peter, who has been listening to their bedtime stories at the window. The children fly away to Neverland, where their many adventures include brushes with the Lost Boys and the Red Indians. While there they lead a generally cozy existence with Wendy in her little house sewing on buttons and failing to sew on a shadow to Peter. Sadly, Peter's mischievous fairy, Tinker Bell, is jealous of Wendy; she tries to poison her and nearly kills Peter instead. Tinker Bell is not, however, as much of a threat as the evil Captain Hook, leader of the pirates and enemy of the Red Indians. The fearless Peter defeats Hook, who is tracked down by a fearsome crocodile. In the end, the children go home to grow up. Peter refuses to join them, afraid they will "catch him and make him a man."

Although the story rollicks along, full of invention, comedy, and nail-biting climaxes, it is the way it embodies deep anxieties about maturity and mortality, shared by us all, that has led to its enduring popularity, whereas Barrie's many other works, highly successful at the time, have faded into history. **VN**

"Wendy knew that she must grow up. You always know after you are two. Two is the beginning of the end."

MORE CLASSIC FANTASY STORIES

The Water-Babies by Charles Kingsley, 1863
Alice's Adventures in Wonderland by Lewis Carroll, 1865
The Wonderful Wizard of Oz by L. Frank Baum, 1900
Mary Poppins by P. L. Travers, 1934

8+

Cautionary Tales for Children 1907

Hilaire Belloc B. T. B.

"Matilda told such dreadful lies, it made one gasp and stretch one's eyes."

MORE AMUSING POETRY BY BELLOC

The Bad Child's Book of Beasts, 1896
More Beasts for Worse Children, 1897
A Moral Alphabet, 1899
New Cautionary Tales, 1930

Nationality | English, born 1870 (author); American, born Basil Blackwood 1870 (illustrator)
Publisher | Eveleigh Nash, UK
Theme | Poetry

More than one hundred years after they were first published, Hilaire Belloc's hair-raising rhymes can still make families gasp and stretch their eyes in amusement and horror. Having ignored the sound advice of their doting parents, the unfortunate boys and girls in the book come to various gory and extreme ends, yet the reading of their adventures aloud is good simple fun. Amid compulsive rhyme schemes and rollicking rhythms, Jim gets eaten by the lion Ponto, Henry King knots his stomach up with little bits of string, and Rebecca slams doors and is felled by a marble bust. These naughty children are, on the whole, so hapless and so unpleasant that even the most tenderhearted soul will not shed a tear at their demise.

This is not really an anthology of moral fables like the lurid *Der Struwwelpeter*, however. Although violent death figures often, the events are as unrealistic as some of the drawings that illustrate the poems: George's balloon, for instance, brings the house down when it bursts. Some of the misdemeanors, such as Franklin Hyde's playing with mud, do not seem so very terrible in these days of washing machines. Ironically, perhaps, the least sympathetic character in this gallery of misdeeds is the good boy, Charles Augustus Fortescue, who becomes rich by doing right. Belloc was not short on irony. An old favorite in the book is the tale of Algernon, "Who played with a Loaded Gun, and, on missing his Sister, was reprimanded by his Father." Such a light touch is typical of the author. **VN**

Arsène Lupin, Gentleman-Burglar 1907

Maurice Leblanc

Original Title | Arsène Lupin, gentleman-cambrioleur
Nationality | French, born 1864
Publisher | Lafitte, France
Theme | Detective stories

The character of Arsène Lupin was first introduced in stories serialized in French magazine *Je Sais Tout* in 1905, and its success led author Maurice Leblanc to write some twenty volumes about the professional burglar and charmer. Lupin appeared on the scene in response to Sir Arthur Conan Doyle's famous English detective Sherlock Holmes, and Leblanc even included Holmes in some of his works. When Conan Doyle made legal objections to Leblanc's pastiche, a Holmeslike character—"Herlock Sholmès"—began to appear instead.

Despite being a thief, Lupin is known for his gentlemanly charm and sense of fair play, and he often defeats those who are more villainous than himself. Leblanc's first short-story collection sees the aristocratic Lupin make his debut as a lovable rogue battling it out with his foe, the detective Ganimard. The story begins with the stylish Lupin aboard the transatlantic steamship *La Provence*. Despite the obvious confines of the ship, the Gallic daredevil and master of disguise manages to evade capture through his guile, cunning, and sweet-talking way with the fairer sex. What makes these stories so readable is the characterization of the romantic hero, the suave and irresistible Lupin. His daring and panache are appealing, his adventures always take place in the most exotic and salubrious of settings, and Leblanc's tongue-in-cheek tone must have been a welcome addition to the canon of detective fiction. **CK**

". . . the man of a thousand disguises: in turn a . . . robust youth or decrepit old man."

OTHER MAURICE LEBLANC TITLES

Arsène Lupin vs. Herlock Sholmes (Arsène Lupin contre Herlock Sholmès), 1908
The Golden Triangle (Le Triangle d'or), 1918
The Damsel with Green Eyes (La Demoiselle aux yeux verts), 1927

8+

The Wonderful Adventures of Nils 1907

Selma Lagerlöf

Nationality | Swedish, born 1858
Publisher | Details unknown, Sweden
Honor | Nobel Prize for Literature, 1909
Theme | Science and nature, Adventure

8+

NILS HOLGERSSONS UNDERBARA RESA GENOM SVERIGE AV SELMA LAGERLÖF

OTHER NOTABLE LAGERLÖF WORKS

Gösta Berling's Saga (*Gösta Berlings saga*), 1891
Further Adventures of Nils (*Nils Holgerssons underbara resa genom Sverige 2*), 1911
The Emperor of Portugalia (*Kejsam av Portugalien*), 1914

Originally trained as a teacher, Selma Lagerlöf spent many years researching the environment before writing *The Wonderful Adventures of Nils* (*Nils Holgerssons underbara resa genom Sverige*.) The story is conveyed through a captivating combination of geographical facts and natural phenomena with a child's point of view.

Nils Holgersson is a naughty boy who lives on a farm. He does not get up to very much other than sleeping, eating, and making mischief by annoying the farm animals. One day, when his parents are at church, Nils finds an elf whom he captures and teases. The elf promises Nils a gold coin if he sets him free. Nils refuses and, after a battle, he wakes up to find that he has become an elf himself. As Nils sits wondering what will happen to him, a flock of wild geese passes by. One of the domestic farm geese tries to join them. Nils reaches out for its neck and before he knows it he is flying with the goose on its back.

"The . . . wild geese flocked around him and stroked him with their beaks."

Nils journeys across the entire country, where the geese introduce him to another world, giving him an entirely different point of view than he ever thought possible. As Nils learns more and more about the natural world, and the mutual esteem between humans and animals, he regains his normal size but has a new, changed outlook on life.

Selma Lagerlöf was the first female writer to win the Nobel Prize for Literature, a reflection of the impact this book made. Her expression, language, and moral storytelling have often been compared with Rudyard Kipling. **SML**

The Wind in the Willows 1908

Kenneth Grahame

The Wind in the Willows began as a series of stories told to Kenneth Grahame's four-year-old son, and there is a sense of a particular expectant listener in the author's mind as we read the adventures of animals who dress like humans while mostly retaining their animal characteristics. It seems natural to see Ratty the water rat in a rowing boat, and homebody Mole needs the privacy and warmth of his mole hole.

Bad Mr. Toad, the most entertaining character, is the exception: He does not behave like a toad and his character is modeled on the grotesque image that toads present to the world. Toad is greedy, bumptious, and irresponsible, but passionate about his interests and a great source of comedy. Readers can laugh with him, even if they are more often laughing at him. His riotous exploits in a stolen motorcar, his resulting imprisonment, and his battle with the Wild Wood hoodlums (the stoats and weasels) who have squatted Toad Hall are the most memorable chapters.

"I would have you to know that I am a Toad, a very well-known, respected, distinguished Toad!"

The story is also admired for Mole and Ratty's more low-key escapades as they picnic on the Thames and get lost in the Wild Wood, and for the gentler, more philosophical passages celebrating the beauty of the English countryside. The creatures inhabit a blissful state: they are free from childhood constraints on one hand and adult responsibilities on the other. They work hard at making their homes secure and feeding themselves but no one tells them what to do.

Although the book was not initially illustrated, subsequent editions of this children's classic included the work of Arthur Rackham and E. H. Shepard. **GB**

Nationality | Scottish, born 1859
Publisher | Methuen, UK
Theme | Classics, Adventure, Animal stories, Friendship

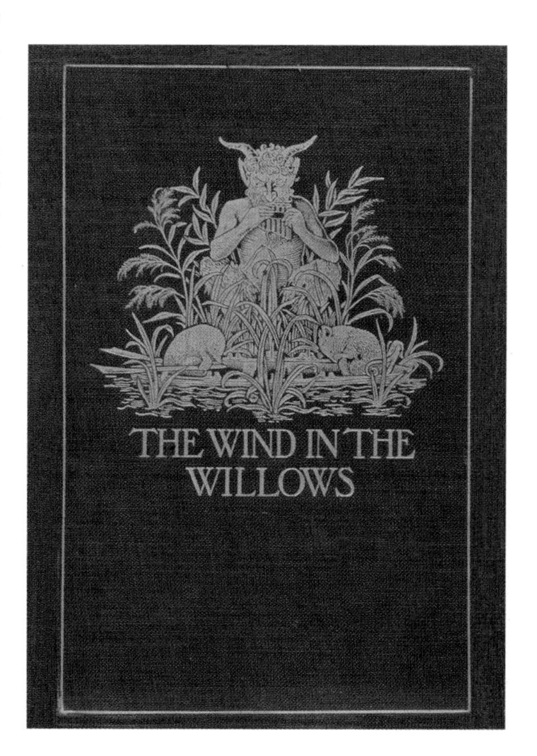

8+

MORE ANIMAL ADVENTURES

The Jungle Book by Rudyard Kipling, 1894
The Story of Doctor Dolittle by Hugh Lofting, 1920
Mrs. Frisby and the Rats of NIMH by Robert C. O'Brien, 1971
The Tale of Despereaux by Kate DiCamillo, 2003

Margaret Atwood reviews:

Anne of Green Gables 1908

Lucy Maud Montgomery   May and William Claus

8+

Nationality | Canadian, born 1874 (author); American, born 1882; German, born 1862 (illustrators)
Publisher | L. C. Page and Co., USA
Theme | Family, Friendship, Classics

For any of you who did not read this book as a child, *Anne of Green Gables* is the story of a spunky, strange, but endearing orphan, Anne Shirley, who hits Prince Edward Island's Green Gables farmhouse in a splatter of exclamation marks, apple blossoms, freckles, and embarrassing faux pas.

Marilla and Matthew Cuthbert, the elderly brother and sister who own Green Gables, want a boy orphan to help with the chores, but drama-queen Anne is sent to them by mistake. She makes such an impression on shy old bachelor Matthew that he wants her to stay, and tart, stern Marilla comes around to his way of thinking. As talkative, redheaded Anne grows from ugly-duckling waif to beautiful swan, having famously dyed her hair temporarily green in the meantime, ultimately she wins the admiration not only of Marilla, but of just about everyone in Avonlea. There is a bittersweet ending, too, wherein the wonderful Matthew dies and scholarship-winning Anne renounces her college ambitions to stay with Marilla. This is the part where you really cry a lot.

Millions of young girls, myself included, have been amused, shocked, and touched by Anne's escapades. I liked the parts in which Anne breaks the taboo forbidding outbursts of temper on the part of young people. She acts out spectacularly, stamping her feet and hurling insults, "I hate you—I hate you—I hate you! You are a rude, unfeeling woman!" and even resorting to physical violence, "You mean, hateful boy! How dare you!" followed by the sharp crack of a slate being broken over a thick skull.

What distinguishes *Anne* from so many "girls' books" is a dark underside that gives the story its frenetic energy and makes its heroine's idealism poignantly convincing. Author L. M. Montgomery was an orphan who was sent to live with two old people, but, unlike Anne, she never won them over.

MORE BOOKS WITH ENDEARING ORPHANS

***Oliver Twist* by Charles Dickens, 1838**
***Heidi* by Johanna Spyri, 1880**
***The Little Princess* by Frances Hodgson Burnett, 1905**
***Anne of Avonlea* by L. M. Montgomery, 1909**
***Pollyanna* by Eleanor H. Porter, 1913**

"Oh, how pretty.... But the sleeves—they were the crowning glory!" 

The Extraordinary Adventures of Massagran 1910

Josep Maria Folch i Torres   Joan García Junceda i Supervia

"Nothing was safe. . . . They ate a human leg with the same ease that we eat a fried egg."

RECOMMENDED FOLCH I TORRES WORKS

White Spirits (Ànimes blanques), 1904
The Shepherds (Els pastorets), 1916
Cinderella (Ventafocs), 1920
Children's Library (Biblioteca Gentil), 1924–1928
The King Who Did Not Laugh (El rey que no ríe), 1931

Nationality | Spanish, born 1880 (author); Spanish, born 1881 (illustrator)
Publisher | Casals, Spain
Theme | Adventure

The book of the adventures of Massagran was first published as *Las aventuras extraordinarias de Massagran* in the collection *Biblioteca Patufet*. Massagran is the son of a customs officer; he has been obsessed with ships ever since he was a little boy and cannot rest until he embarks on a schooner. Always accompanied by Pom, his dog, Massagran clashes with a hippo, lions, and whales; he also has great adventures that take him to an unknown place in Africa where he teaches the Kukamusques of Penkamuska to read and write. Through his ingenuity and some luck, he emerges triumphant from all his adventures.

Published at a time of colonial euphoria in Europe, the book reflects the historic circumstances and Catalan views of the author without affecting the relationship with readers of different generations. The book is popular because it has a humorous vein. The play upon words and the absurdity of the situations form the basis of the comedy. Folch i Torres uses language to convey a surreal everyday life in a natural, expressive style, bursting with irony and linguistic expedients, such as the language that he invents for the Africans.

This book represents the author's definitive move into children's literature: adventure stories for boys and romantic novels for girls (*Biblioteca Gentil*), published in Catalan and translated, mostly after the war, into Castilian. His body of work meant that he could live off his writing until the end of the Spanish Civil War, thus becoming the Catalan writer for the masses. **EB**

The Secret Garden 1911

F. Hodgson Burnett C. Robinson

Nationality | English, born 1849 (author); English, born 1870 (illustrator)
Publisher | Heinemann, UK
Theme | Classics, Friendship

The two unlikable children at the heart of *The Secret Garden* play a key part in its enduring charm as they become transformed alongside the dormant garden at Misselthwaite Manor. Sour-tempered orphan Mary, whose parents have spoiled but neglected her, is an unlikely ally for her fretful, sickly cousin Colin. Like the neglected garden, the children need a little coaxing to flourish. And like the garden, they have to do the most important work themselves.

With help from down-to-earth Martha and her brother Dickon, the children's transformation is convincing because it comes from within, rather than being imposed by others. The adults in Colin and Mary's lives have either died or failed them, so the children have to be self-reliant and brave, and care for each other. This starts when they stop thinking only of themselves. The "magic" that Dickon promises will heal Colin is a combination of the children's own imagination and self-belief. These truths about human behavior are not delivered in a moralizing way but as common sense, and the story always comes first. The children's rebirth follows the seasons, from Mary's arrival in winter through a spring of hard labor in the garden to the regeneration of summer.

Children will be lured through the hidden door into the overgrown garden because the mystery has been so well built up and the isolated setting of the manor is so intriguing. When Mary sets foot in the garden, the reader shares the gift she has been given. **GB**

The Adventures of Gian Burrasca 1911

Vamba

Original Title | Il giornalino di Gian Burrasca
Nationality | Italian, born Luigi Bertelli, 1858
Publisher | Bemporad and Figlio, Italy
Theme | Family, Adventure

Luigi Bertelli was a Florentine, born just before the unification of Italy (1861). His pseudonym, Vamba, was in honor of a character in Walter Scott's novel *Ivanhoe*.

Vamba was a journalist of satire, and this story, in the form of a diary, began as a contribution to *Il giornalino della domenica*, a weekly journal that was edited by Vamba and dedicated to children. The story is set at the beginning of the twentieth century in an upper-class household. Gian Burrasca is the nickname that Giannino Stoppani is given by his parents and three sisters, Ada, Luisa, and Virginia. "Gian" is short for "Giannino" and "*burrasca*" means "storm."

Gian is delighted when his mother gives him a diary so that he can recount the difficulties of being a young boy and the many disastrous but hilarious incidents of which he is inadvertently the cause. To start off his new diary, he copies some pages from his older sister's diary. However, he is found out when the diary is read aloud during a visit by Mr. Capitani, who reads about Ada's dislike of him. Gian Burrasca then decides to fill the pages of his diary with his own thoughts. He is a witty boy who does as he pleases and often creates chaos. As the youngest child and the only boy in a well-to-do family, Gian feels a certain amount of pressure, which leads him to rebel. He makes up songs that reflect his mischievous view on things, such as "*Viva la pappa al pomodoro*" ("Hooray for tomato soup"). The book was made into a television series in 1964. **SMT**

Nesthäkchen im Kinderheim

von

Else Ury

Nesthäkchen 1913

Else Ury

Original Title | Nesthäkchen und ihre Puppen
Nationality | German, born 1877
Publisher | Meidingers Jugendschriften, Germany
Theme | Family, Adventure

Else Ury's Nesthäckchen series provides a fascinating insight into German life at the beginning of the twentieth century. *Nesthäkchen and Her Dolls*, the first of ten books, introduces Annemarie as the well-to-do Braun family's six-year-old *"Nesthäkchen,"* a German term describing the youngest person in a family.

Annemarie is a curious and lively character. Although she is well educated and generally well behaved, her inquisitive mind tends to get her into trouble. For example when she swaps her expensive shoes for the clogs of a Dutch girl she meets, despite not being allowed to mingle with other children in the street. However, she always makes up for any misdeeds by being kind and honest. Ury not only relates bright and strong-minded Annemarie's many adventures, but also describes the atmosphere during the German Empire and the Weimar Republic. Even though those days are long gone, their values are still universally important. In each book, Annemarie becomes more mature and learns about fundamental issues such as social behavior, responsibility, and tolerance toward others, thus educating the reader as the story unfolds.

Ury died at the Auschwitz-Birkenau concentration camp in January 1943. It is noteworthy that one of her most interesting works, *Nesthäkchen and the World War*, was banned in Germany after 1945 because of its nationalistic take on World War I. However, the Nesthäkchen series as a whole, with its endearing characters, is a fascinating and engaging vehicle to learn about both history and life in general. **GS**

Pollyanna 1913

Eleanor H. Porter

Nationality | American, born 1868
Publisher | L. C. Page and Co., USA
Theme | Classics, Family, Friendship, Illness and death

When rich and emotionally cold Polly Harrington is forced to take in her orphaned niece, Pollyanna Whittier, her life changes irrevocably. With both her parents dead, Pollyanna arrives to stay with her only living blood relative and is convinced that her aunt will be as kind and loving as her parents were. These expectations of Aunt Polly astonish the local community, but thanks to Pollyanna's perseverance, they are eventually proved true. The young girl's presence affects the whole community, turning even the grumpy local miser, John Pendleton, into a friend. By playing a game that her father taught her—"the glad game"—Pollyanna encourages everyone to count their blessings and tries to persuade the people she meets to turn their misfortunes into something positive. She also endeavors, together with Aunt Polly's maid, Nancy, to discover the secret behind Aunt Polly's mysterious lost love.

Although Pollyanna is very good at inspiring hope in others and cheering up those in need, when she herself is in need of hope, she finds she has lost her way. When an accident leaves her without the use of her legs, Pollyanna is unable to play "the glad game" anymore and begins to despair. All her friends rally around, trying to do for her what she did for them. At the close of the story, Pollyanna is in a specialist hospital and writes home to her newly married aunt that she has finally taken her first tentative steps.

Seemingly a type of Jane Austen novel for children, *Pollyanna* is a story that continues to be loved by new generations of young readers. **LH**

Platero and I 1914

Juan Ramón Jiménez

Original Title | Platero y yo
Nationality | Spanish, 1881
Publisher | La Lectura, Spain
Theme | Animal stories, Poetry

Platero is a little silver-colored donkey with a friendly, cheerful nature. He is one of those fictional animals that has become part of the collective imagination, making us believe that he really existed once upon a time. And, indeed, in a sense, this donkey did exist because Platero is an abstraction of all the donkeys that the author knew as a child; the character is at the same time a poetic re-creation of an ideal of aesthetic purity and a pretext to tell us about intimate emotions.

This collection of prose poems describes the life of Platero, from his childhood to his death. Platero appears as the inseparable companion of the poet; he is the mute witness of the thoughts and anxieties of his master. And we see him walking with the children, cheerful, innocent, and as stubborn as they are; enjoying the relaxation of the siesta; and braying in pain when he treads on a thorn or is kicked by a horse.

But *Platero and I* is also an anthology of scenes, characters, and events extracted from the reality of the author's native town. They express the poet's obsession with beauty, nature, and simple things as well as his dislike of injustice, cruelty, and the consequences of ignorance. Juan Ramón Jiménez transforms reality into something lyrical through the use of metaphors and comparisons, incorporating into his language poetic phrases from Ultraism and other artistic movements such as Impressionism. His name has become indissolubly linked to *Platero and I*, a book that has transcended the boundaries of time to become a key work in contemporary literature. **EB**

The Young Visiters 1919

Daisy Ashford

Alternative Title | Mr. Salteena's Plan
Nationality | English, born 1881
Publisher | Chatto and Windus, UK
Theme | Friendship

Daisy Ashford was just nine years old when she wrote this social comedy about a young lady called Ethel Monticue. Her mother kept the manuscript, and the adult Daisy published it in her late thirties. She wrote novels and plays into her teens, but did not pursue a literary career in adult life. She worked as a secretary, ran a canteen during World War I, and, shortly after the publication of *The Young Visiters* [*sic*], got married and settled in Norfolk, where she ran a hotel.

The wit and charm of a young girl's observations of high society ensure that readers are laughing with her rather than at her, and her idiosyncratic spelling is part of the appeal. Her accounts of the aristocracy's daily doings are likely to have been overheard from her mother's visitors (the family lived in wealthy Sussex at the time of writing). There is a clear sense of a child fascinated by the freedom of adults to do as they liked: have tea in bed, paint their faces with "ruge," and eat unlimited "merangs."

The story is short and bittersweet: Mr. Salteena wants to marry Ethel, but makes the mistake of introducing her to his better-looking and richer acquaintance, Bernard Clark. Mr. Salteena, a butcher's son, wants to better himself in order to be worthy of Ethel and takes lessons in etiquette from the Earl of Clincham, who claims to be "rarther intimate" with the Prince of Wales. They visit court while the Queen (Victoria) is "not her usual self . . . she feels the heat poor soul." There is a wedding when we would expect one, and a nine year old's dream wedding banquet—"ices jelly merangs jam tarts with plenty of jam in each." **GB**

The Story of Doctor Dolittle 1920

Hugh Lofting

Nationality | American, born 1886
Publisher | Stokes, USA
Theme | Classics, Adventure
Animal stories

Doctor Dolittle lives in the country town of Puddleby-on-the-Marsh. Having decided to treat animals rather than humans, he travels out to Africa to cure thousands of sick apes. Doctor Dolittle has been taught how to communicate with animals by his parrot Polynesia, so the creatures are able to tell him exactly what is wrong with them. Once cured, the grateful patients present the doctor with a "pushmi-pullyu," a creature with a head at each end. He joins the doctor's other animal friends: Chee-Chee the monkey, Too-Too the owl, Dab-Dab the duck, and Gub-Gub, a very greedy pig. Returning home, Doctor Dolittle makes his fortune showing off the pushmi-pullyu at local fairs. He then goes back to Puddleby with his animal friends to live a quiet life, little knowing that more adventures await him in subsequent books.

This classic story started life as letters sent home by the author to his children while he was a soldier in France during World War I. Intent on making them laugh, he included many comic drawings of the amiable, balding, top-hatted doctor, whose habitual vagueness coexists with a will of iron when he comes across examples of animal suffering. Hopeless with money, Doctor Dolittle only gets by thanks to the care and ingenuity of Tommy Stubbins, a ten-year-old cobbler's son who becomes his assistant. With animals and humans in constant conversation with each other, there is always plenty of room for humor in these gentle stories, whose overall message about trying to better understand animals has proved popular with generations of children. **NT**

"Having thanked the sharks for their kindness, the Doctor and his pets set off once more. . . ."

OTHER GREAT DOLITTLE TITLES

***The Voyages of Doctor Dolittle*, 1922**
***Doctor Dolittle's Zoo*, 1925**
***Doctor Dolittle's Caravan*, 1926**
***Doctor Dolittle in the Moon*, 1928**
***Doctor Dolittle's Return*, 1933**

JUST—
WILLIAM

RICHMAL
CROMPTON

The first *EVER* William book!

Just William 1922

Richmal Crompton Thomas Henry

Nationality | English, born 1890 (author); English, born 1879 (illustrator)
Publisher | Newnes, UK
Theme | Adventure, Favorite characters, Family

William Brown is the arch-enemy within a typical middle-class household in an English village, in which Mr. and Mrs. Brown and their grown-up children, Ethel and Robert, are foils for the younger boy's anarchy and subversion. The setting for this gently satirical domestic comedy may be dated, with its parlor maids, gardeners, and drawing-room teas, but the character of William certainly is not. Adventurous, unbookish but imaginative, greedy, lazy, loyal to his dog and his gang, and motivated only by mischief, he thunders through thirty-eight different collections of stories pursued by outraged citizens and leaving a stream of chaos in his wake.

The first story in this first collection, "William Goes to the Pictures," sets the tone. William cannot separate the narratives he sees on the cinema screen from real life, and drags along his family as unwilling players in his drama. The formula of the stories seems set in stone: William encounters pompous adults, the adults come off worse, William is unscathed by any retribution, and he survives to cause havoc another day. He challenges, provokes, and overturns grown-up reasoning, revealing much of it as self-serving.

The Brown family and the relatives, neighbors, and visitors who encounter William are a stereotypical bunch, especially the female characters. William tends to find his allies among the more colorful lower classes—kitchen maids, burglars, and tramps—who conform to their own set of stereotypes. In allowing the Browns to parody their own world, Crompton gives the stories enduring appeal. **GB**

The Boxcar Children 1924

Gertrude Chandler Warner

Nationality | American, born 1890
Publisher | Scott Foresman and Co., USA
Theme | Family, Adventure, Friendship

The Boxcar Children tells the story of four orphaned brothers and sisters, Benny, Violet, Jessie, and Henry Alden, ranging in age from five to fourteen years old, who have lost their parents. They have run away from their cruel grandfather because they are afraid he will bully them and make them do chores. The story opens with the hungry children buying some bread from a bakery, but they go on the run again because the baker's wife thinks she can get the three oldest children to work for her, and give the youngest, Benny, to a children's home.

Seeking shelter from a storm they come across an abandoned red railway boxcar. It becomes their home and they furnish it with items scavenged from the dump. The children live on thrown-away food, bathe in a nearby pond, and the eldest, Henry, does odd jobs for Dr. Moore in the nearby town, which provides them with some money on which to survive. Then Violet becomes ill, and the children realize that they need adult help. They befriend an old man, who is not what he seems, and the children learn not to judge everyone by their appearance.

The charm of this book comes from the camaraderie and affection between the children, who form their own nuclear family. Ultimately the message of the book is that although it can be fun for children to strike out on their own, a life away from the protection of adults is harsh, and they are reunited with their grandfather, whom they have misjudged. The author went on to write a series charting the children's adventures as they solve a number of mysteries. **CK**

The School at the Châlet 1925

Elinor M. Brent-Dyer Nina K. Brisley

Nationality | English, born 1894 (author); English, born 1898 (illustrator)
Publisher | Chambers, UK
Theme | School, Friendship, Adventure

8+

OTHER GREAT SCHOOLGIRL STORIES

The Fortunes of Philippa by Angela Brazil, 1906
Jo of the Châlet School by Elinor M. Brent-Dyer, 1926
Autumn Term by Antonia Forest, 1948
Hurrah for St. Trinians by Ronald Searle, 1948
Charlotte Sometimes by Penelope Farmer, 1969

This is the first of fifty-eight books about the trilingual school where the mountain scenery is only eclipsed by the allure of the "Continental" food (whipped cream, Apfeltorte, and black cherry preserve). Most semesters at the Châlet School feature big drama—a natural disaster, kidnapping, or an accident-prone Alpine excursion, for example. Once smitten with the unique, sometimes irritating but addictive institution, fans will want to read all the books.

This first one introduces Joey Bettany, the only character who sustains interest throughout the series. Intrepid and gutsy, Joey is a pillar of the school community, from junior pupil to head girl and beyond. She grows up to be a prolific children's author and equally prolific parent; her eleven children include triplet girls.

"We are proud, proud, *PROUD of belonging to such a school—the Châlet School!"*

At thirteen, Joey is in frail health, so her sister Madge opens a school in the Austrian Tirol to make treatment easier. The Châlet School site is at Briesau am Tiernsee (near a sanatorium where Madge and Joey later find doctors to marry) until 1938, when external events bring about a move. Brent-Dyer relocated the school first to Guernsey, then swiftly to Herefordshire after publication of *The Châlet School in Exile* (one of the most dramatic titles in the series) coincided with the German invasion of the Channel Islands. In the 1950s the school moved back to the mountains: Switzerland this time, where more than half the books are set. The forty-five-year parade of Châlet girls, mainly from the moneyed classes of Europe, mostly live up to Joey's reputation for mischief, adventure, and chutzpah. **GB**

The Hardy Boys 1: The Tower Treasure 1927

Franklin W. Dixon

Nationality | Canadian, born Leslie McFarlane 1902
Publisher | Grosset and Dunlap, USA
Theme | Adventure, Detective stories

The Hardy Boys are teenage brothers who are following in the footsteps of their father Fenton, a legendary private investigator formerly of the New York Police Department. Along with fellow Stratemeyer Syndicate titles such as *Nancy Drew*, the *Bobbsey Twins*, and *Tom Swift*, the original Hardy Boys novels are classic preteen fiction and provide their readers not only with excitement and adventure, but also some charming glimpses into teenage life in the 1930s and 1940s.

Frank Hardy and his younger, more impetuous brother Joe live in the fictional town of Bayport with their parents and their spinster aunt, Gertrude, who disapproves of their detective work. The boys are sometimes helped out by their plump school chum Chet Morton, and also by their friends Biff Hooper, Tony Prito, and the police chief, Ezra Collig.

At heart, the Hardy Boys stories are police procedurals that describe in detail how the youthful detectives go undercover, engage in surveillance, interrogate witnesses, search for fingerprints, and escape from dangerous situations. Every chapter ends on a cliff-hanger, and it is rare for the Hardys to take a case where a rock, arrow, or smoke bomb does not find its way into their living room, attached to a note warning them to walk away. The unflappability of the boys in the face of frequently ludicrous criminal behavior makes up a large part of the books' appeal, to both older and younger readers. The Hardy Boys may be only teenagers, but they are more capable and self-sufficient than many adults.

From 1959 onward, the Hardy Boys books were reworked and rewritten. Outdated language and racial stereotypes were removed from the early books to make them more suitable for contemporary audiences. The original books have been adapted into several spin-off series, computer games, and even a television show in the late 1970s. **SY**

MORE IN THE HARDY BOYS SERIES

***The Mystery of Cabin Island*, 1929**
***The Hidden Harbor Mystery*, 1935**
***The Sinister Signpost*, 1936**
***The Secret Panel*, 1946**
***The Haunted Fort*, 1965**

8+

Tintin in the Land of the Soviets 1929

Hergé

Original Title | Tintin au pays des Soviets
Nationality | Belgian, born Georges Remi, 1907
Publisher | Le Vingtième Siècle, Belgium
Theme | Adventure, Favorite characters

8+

LES AVENTURES DE TINTIN REPORTER DU "PETIT VINGTIEME„ AU PAYS DES SOVIETS

-HERGÉ-

This is the first in a series of twenty-four comic-strip stories written and illustrated by Georges Remi under the pen name of Hergé. More than 250 million copies of the Tintin stories have been sold worldwide in more than fifty different languages, and Tintin's image has even appeared on postage stamps and coins. The comic strips continue to be popular, despite the fact that some of the stories now appear dated (and in some cases almost racist) because of the colonial attitudes that were acceptable when they were written. They have attained a cult fan following.

What makes the stories popular is the visual draw of Hergé's stylish images, with their bold outlines and bright colors, the humor and cute appeal of his cast of characters, and the wonderfully blended mix of narratives that combine globe-trotting adventure, science fiction, fantasy, mystery, thriller, and even political and social satire. The hero of the piece is the noble, brave, and intelligent Tintin, a boyish blond reporter with a distinctive haircut, who is aided in his exploits by his white fox terrier, Snowy. The pair are inseparable and frequently get each other out of the various scrapes in which they find themselves.

"I'm innocent! I'm Tintin, reporter for the Petit Vingtieme! *Free me at once!"*

Tintin in the Land of the Soviets sees Tintin battling against the injustices of the Communist Bloc. Successive stories introduced characters such as Tintin's best friend, the cantankerous bearded seafarer, Captain Archibald Haddock; the blundering twin detectives, Thomson and Thompson, who Tintin often finds himself at odds with; and an archetypal mad scientist, Professor Cuthbert Calculus. **CK**

OTHER FAVORITE TINTIN TITLES

The Seven Crystal Balls (Les Sept boules de cristal), 1936
The Secret of the Unicorn *(Le Secret de* La Licorne*)*, 1943
Destination Moon (Objectif Lune), 1953

Emil and the Detectives 1929

Erich Kästner Walter Trier

Emil is traveling on his own by train to Berlin to spend his holidays with relatives. In his pocket is an envelope containing money that he is to give to his grandmother. This is his widowed mother's hard-earned savings, so Emil is worried about losing it. While he is sleeping, one of the other passengers steals the envelope. Emil doubts that the police will be able to help because he cannot prove the money is his, and he also fears he may be in trouble already for drawing a mustache on a statue. Determined not to let his mother down, he sets off to tail the thief. Emil confides in a boy called Gustav, who rounds up a group of boys to help. After a night's stakeout, a crowd of boys surrounds the thief as he leaves his hotel. Emil confronts the thief in a bank and proves that the money is his. When the police reveal that the thief is a wanted bank robber, Emil gets a reward and delights his beloved mother with a trip to Berlin, a new coat, and a hairdryer for her hairdressing business.

"Going after a real thief... would be something! I think I'll help you, if you don't mind."

Emil and the Detectives (*Emil und die Detektive*) was one of the earliest books to feature a juvenile detective. The action is fast and furious, with all the classic elements of a detective story: car chase, stakeout, and vital last-minute clue. Few words are wasted in character description, yet the main characters are fully three-dimensional: Emil, responsible but rather wishing he could just have fun; the thief, teasing and pleased with himself; the irritating, bossy Pony; the intelligent, organizing Professor; and little Tuesday, who wants to be part of the action but is left to answer the telephone. **CW**

Nationality | German, born 1899 (author); Czech, born 1890 (illustrator)
Publisher | Cecilie Dressler Verlag, Germany
Theme | Detective stories

8+

MORE DETECTIVE STORIES TO ENJOY

Arsène Lupin series by Maurice Leblanc, 1907–1939
Hardy Boys series by Stratemeyer Syndicate, 1927–1979
Nancy Drew series by Stratemeyer Syndicate, 1930–1986

What Celia Says 1929

Elena Fortún Molina Gallent

Nationality | Spanish, born 1886 (author); Spanish, born 1911 (illustrator)
Publisher | Aguilar, Spain
Theme | Favorite characters

8+

Celia is a pioneer character among female heroines in children's literature. Like many of her successors, she is rebellious and nonconformist, brimming over with an imagination that leads her to the most absurd pranks. Yet Celia is also full of contradictions: sometimes a saint; at others a real devil. Originally published with the title *Celia lo que dice,* the book is the first in a series of more than twenty titles, the success of which lasted until 1970. It consists of forty-four short stories narrated in the first person that the author originally published in magazines in 1928.

Celia is a good girl, in the old-fashioned sense of the word, who spends most of her time in the sewing room surrounded by servant women whom she is sure she is helping. In spite of her obsession with being a good girl who shares her toys with poor children and who is frightened of going to hell, her soul is that of a freethinker, especially when it comes to drawing conclusions from her ill-fated experiences or to exposing the incongruities and lies of the world of grown-ups.

This combination of rebellion and submission to rules constitutes the literary framework of the Celia books. Both the character and the books in which she is the heroine have passed the test of time. Although nowadays some of the material may be considered politically incorrect, generations of readers enjoy the cheekiness of the dialogues and the mischievousness of this spirited little girl from the last century. **EB**

Swallows and Amazons 1930

Arthur Ransome

Nationality | English, born 1884
Publisher | Jonathan Cape, UK
Theme | Adventure, Classics, Friendship, Science and nature, Family

The first of Arthur Ransome's series of twelve novels introduces the Walker children—John, Susan, Titty, and Roger. Their nickname comes from their boat, *Swallow*. On vacation in the Lake District, in England, their plea to be allowed to camp on Wild Cat Island is answered by a now legendary telegram from their father: "Better Drowned Than Duffers If Not Duffers Won't Drown." It heralds the start of a vacation spent in the company of the Amazons, Nancy and Peggy Blackett, who share the Swallows' love of all things nautical but who are, temporarily, rendered enemies in a fight to determine whose boat is to be flagship.

Their friendly warfare provides the opportunity for Titty in particular to display her courage and ingenuity on a nerve-wracking solitary vigil, during which she consoles herself with thoughts of Robinson Crusoe. Her nocturnal exploits afford her the means to bring to an end the unfounded dispute that has been festering between the Swallows and Captain Flint, the Amazon's uncle, who, as a retired pirate, turns out to be a great asset in their adventures.

The Walker siblings, watched over by the motherly Susan, adhere broadly to a comfortingly firm social and moral code, but the Amazons, constantly late for dinner and repeatedly failing to conform to patterns of ladylike behavior, hint at an enticing degree of anarchy. The story, which draws on Ransome's own childhood vacations, has to this day a devoted following of adults and children. **KA**

SWALLOWS AND
AMAZONS
ARTHUR RANSOME
author of 'Swallowdale'

Nancy Drew Mystery Stories
THE SECRET OF THE OLD CLOCK
By
CAROLYN KEENE

The Secret of the Old Clock 1930

Carolyn Keene

Nationality | American, born Mildred Wirt Benson 1905
Publisher | Grosset and Dunlap, USA
Theme | Detective stories, Favorite characters

This is the first book about the teenage detective Nancy Drew. The ensuing series was written by a group of twenty-eight ghostwriters. Mildred Wirt Benson wrote *The Secret of the Old Clock* to an outline supplied by the head of the Stratemeyer Syndicate, Edward Stratemeyer, and she wrote twenty-three of the first twenty-five mysteries.

The novel comes in two versions: the original, published in 1930, and a revised version updated by Harriet S. Adams published in 1959. In the original, the independent-minded Nancy is sixteen years old and has left high school. Her widowed father, Carson, is a well-known attorney in the fictional town of River Heights, Indiana. The feisty Nancy comes to the aid of the recently bereaved Crowley family when other relatives come forward and say they have Josiah Crowley's will, and that he has left his wealth to them. Nancy attempts to discover an old clock wherein lies information regarding the whereabouts of Josiah's true will. In the later version, Nancy is eighteen years old and a more sophisticated character. There are also some changes to the plot, but Nancy's desire to enable a struggling family to recover their rightful inheritance is still the main theme.

As time has passed, so the sleuth's character has evolved in the way she dresses, the car she drives, and how her friends behave. Yet her enthusiastic talent and intelligence in solving the mysteries she encounters keep the stories alive. **CK**

Kubula and Kuba Kubikula 1931

Vladislav Vančura Ondřej Sekora

Nationality | Czech, born 1891 (author); Czech, born 1899 (illustrator)
Publisher | Adolf Synek, Czechoslovakia
Theme | Fantasy, Friendship

When Vladislav Vančura published his only children's book in 1931, it came as a great surprise to his readers. The high priest of Czech literary modernism transformed his complex, ornamental style into an easy-to-read, tender story that remains popular.

The story of a boy, Kuba Kubikula, and his bear cub Kubula is set in "the times when the world was still young and people readily believed in fairy tales." Kuba and his cantankerous bear wander through the winter countryside, earning their bread by performing tricks and doing odd jobs. One night, while sleeping in a blacksmith's shop, the bear gets mischievous and Kuba makes up a scary story about the bugbear Barbucha. Before long, Barbucha comes to life, scaring the little bear and the blacksmith's children out of their wits. The blacksmith drives the two heroes and their newfound spooky friend out of his house.

In the next village, Barbucha offends the mayor, and they all end up in jail. A public trial is held, but it turns into a farce when the bear starts his show and the bugbear joins him. The scene is crowned by a snowball fight involving all the villagers. At the climax of the fight, the blacksmith's children come to the rescue and persuade the mayor to release the bear and his master, while the bugbear flees on its own. The boy becomes a blacksmith apprentice, the bear joins a local school, and the bugbear is turned into a poodle. Thus, a grotesque story of overcoming fear and finding one's place in the world has a happy ending. **PO**

8+

The Red U: A Story for Lads 1932

Wilhelm Matthiessen

Full Title | Das Rote U: eine Jungensgeschichte
Nationality | German, born 1891
Publisher | Hermann Schaffstein, Germany
Theme | Detective stories

Wilhelm Matthiessen's captivating detective story is often compared with Enid Blyton's *Famous Five* and Astrid Lindgren's Kalle Blomquist stories. His story is as charming, intriguing, and thrilling as the best works of these aforementioned peers.

The Red U's protagonists—nicknamed Mala, Knöres, Döll, Bodda, and Silli—are a gang of children who enjoy playing pranks on the people in their hometown. They are pressured into stopping their shenanigans, however, when they receive a letter from a stranger who calls himself "The Red U" and claims that he knows exactly what they are up to. In this letter and subsequent ones, the mystery person gives the children various tasks that they have to complete in order to ensure that The Red U does not inform their teachers of their misdeeds. Hence, they are forced to free badly kept birds belonging to an alcoholic shoemaker, and they have only one week to find work for someone who is unemployed. When criminals enter the frame and a child is kidnapped, the children manage to solve the case and become heroes.

Like Erich Kästner's *Emil and the Detectives*, from the same era, this mystery story takes the reader back in time. Although written in the 1930s, the world of The Red U is still fascinating for today's readers. Matthiesen writes in a lively and engaging way, ensuring that children continue to learn valuable lessons from reading this enjoyable book. **GS**

Little House in the Big Woods 1932

Laura Ingalls Wilder, Garth Williams

Nationality | American, born 1867
Publisher | Harper and Brothers, USA
Award | A.L.A. Laura Ingalls Wilder Award, 1954
Theme | Family

Five-year-old Laura lives with her parents, older sister Mary, and baby Carrie in a log cabin set in the Wisconsin woods. "There were no houses. There were no roads. There were no people. There were only trees and the wild animals who had their home among them."

The year is 1872, and the cabin has been built by Laura's father, who is always referred to as Pa. Surrounded by woods teeming with deer, squirrels, and wolves, the children have never visited a town but know how to make cheese and butter, how animal skins are turned into leather, and how to clean and load a rifle. In between making pumpkin pies and maple sugar candy, there are also moments of real danger, such as when a wild bear is discovered in the barnyard. Most evenings, however, end up quietly enough, sometimes to the sound of Pa playing his fiddle and everyone singing around the fire.

The author was over sixty years old when she wrote this book. Enormously successful, it was followed by seven more titles taking Laura's story up to the time when she leaves home at the age of fifteen in order to become a teacher. Suffused with a loving nostalgia for the past, these charming stories also pack a powerful punch, at one time describing conditions where Laura could easily have died of starvation. But the prevailing mood is one of warmth and security, as the endlessly self-sufficient family once again manages to get by almost entirely on its own resources, bound together by unwavering feelings of love and loyalty. **NT**

Laura checking the smoker that Pa made out of an old tree. 

Farmer Boy 1933

Laura Ingalls Wilder   G. Williams

Nationality | American, born 1867 (author); American, born 1912 (illustrator)
Publisher | Harper and Brothers, USA
Theme | Historical fiction, Family

This is a story, first and foremost, about a little boy who is desperate to become a farmer, like his father. Nine-year-old Almanzo rises with the sun to shear the sheep, break the colts, feed and clean the other animals, plant and help harvest the crops, haul logs, and fill the ice house—all before he goes to school.

Contemporary readers will be enthralled by Laura Ingalls Wilder's careful chronicling of pioneer family life in early nineteenth-century North America. The historical record featured in the nine books in the Little House series is one of its foremost attractions. *Farmer Boy* is based on the life of the author's husband, Almanzo Wilder, who grew up in the late nineteenth century in upstate New York, and whom we watch grow throughout the series: breaking land, struggling to survive, getting married, and having his own children. In *Farmer Boy,* however, Almanzo is still a child—and one with a huge passion for horses.

The author's own family were descendants of a *Mayflower* passenger. Wilder wrote *Farmer Boy* to preserve the way of life she had experienced as a child, and to encourage readers to understand how America had changed in the previous century. In this she has undoubtedly succeeded, and along the way she reminds us that finding a place in one's family, making a house a home, and striving toward those first dreams we have as children are common to childhoods everywhere—themes that have guaranteed this classic has remained in print. **JSD**

Professor Branestawm 1933

Norman Hunter   W. Heath Robinson

Nationality | English, born 1899 (author); English, born 1872 (illustrator)
Publisher | Bodley Head, UK
Theme | Favorite characters, Science and nature

Professor Theophilus Branestawm is the original batty professor: a lovable genius who wears a white lab coat and five pairs of spectacles and invents the strangest contraptions. These often go wrong, due to his absentmindedness or because the devices take on a life of their own. The machines are wonderfully illustrated by cartoonist William Heath Robinson. Norman Hunter first wrote about the professor for a BBC radio series. It was so popular that he went on to write a series of books cataloguing the professor's wacky inventions. *The Incredible Adventures of Professor Branestawm* (to give the book its full title) was the first in the series.

Branestawm lives in the fictional town of Great Pagwell, a quintessentially English village of the 1930s. Looked after by his long-suffering housekeeper, Mrs. Flittersnoop, the professor is aided in his escapades by his chum, Colonel Dedshott of the Catapult Cavaliers, whose militaristic approach contrasts amusingly with the professor's own almost freefall imagination.

Hunter's inventiveness is hugely appealing, as he describes devices such as burglar catchers, everlasting clocks, and pancake-making machines. His professor is a truly endearing character and an affectionate parody of English inventiveness and eccentricity. Yet he is a positive and inspiring character, too, and the professor's unfailing optimism always enables him to wriggle out of the scrapes in which he finds himself. Funny and action-packed, *The Incredible Adventures of Professor Branestawm* has stood the test of time. **CK**

Night on the Galactic Railroad 1934

Kenji Miyazawa Bryn Barnard

Nationality | Japanese, born 1896 (author); American, born 1956 (illustrator)
Publisher | Bunpodō, Japan
Theme | Fantasy, Science fiction, Friendship

This classic Japanese children's book explores the meaning of friendship, self-sacrifice, death, and the wonders of the galaxy.

Young Giovanni has no friends other than the loyal Campanella. On the night of the Centaurus Festival, when lanterns are lit to show deceased ancestors their way home, he climbs atop a hill and gazes at the stars. All of a sudden, he finds himself aboard a train traveling along the Milky Way, with Campanella in the seat opposite. On the journey, the two experience the wonders that await them: the archaeological excavations on the shore of the translucent river of heaven, the bird catcher who catches herons and cranes and turns them into delicious candy, and the glowing fire of Scorpio that burns for the happiness of all. As they reach the Southern Cross, the other passengers get off to conclude their journey to God. The two friends continue, until Campanella disappears as they pass a beautiful field "that is real heaven." Giovanni awakes, and on his way home learns that Campanella has drowned that night while trying to rescue another boy.

The fusion of Western elements, actual astronomical phenomena, and Japanese-Buddhist beliefs about the universe reflect the spirit of early twentieth-century Japan when the country borrowed much from Western learning, but also institutionalized many of its own traditions. Bryn Barnard's illustrations beautifully capture this cultural hybridity. **FHG**

"I wouldn't mind being like the scorpion and having my body burned a hundred times . . . "

KENJI MIYAZAWA COLLECTIONS

The Restaurant of Many Orders, 1924
Once and Forever: The Tales of Kenji Miyazawa, 1993

Mary Poppins 1934

P. L. Travers Mary Shepard

Nationality | Australian, born Helen Lydon Goff 1899 (author); English, born 1909 (illustrator)
Publisher | Gerald Howe, UK
Theme | Magical stories

In some magical English time when park attendants knew local children by name and children were all in bed by dark, the East Wind blows Mary Poppins to the Banks household at number seventeen Cherry Tree Lane, London. With a parrot-headed umbrella, her hat pinned neatly on shining black hair, and a carpet-bag full of mystery, Mary Poppins sniffs in a superior way and immediately starts setting the nursery to rights. Hip-hop, spit-spot, into the bath at once! She may well know the cockney Wigg family who spend their lives upside down, the ancient Mrs. Corry who sells gingerbread (or is it stars?), and be able to travel around the world with a compass, but lights out is lights out and baths are always needed. For the Banks children, Jane, Michael, and baby twins John and Barbara, she is the best nanny in the world, a "marvel," as the chatty starling on the windowsill calls her. She is formidable, but marvelous and never unkind.

From the moment that, as she claimed, she "saw" Mary Poppins sail past her window, P. L. Travers wrote children's novels that cross the comforts of a nursery world with the thrill of myth. There is a hint of awe around Mary Poppins, an aura of pagan divinity. Who is she, really? Where does she come from, so suddenly, and why? Shifting between that supernatural disquiet and the Banks children's cozy middle-class childhood induces constant little shocks of recognition in the reader and makes the books much funnier, and also much deeper and darker, than the movie. **VN**

Little House on the Prairie 1935

Laura Ingalls Wilder G. Williams

Nationality | American, born 1867 (author); American, born 1912 (illustrator)
Publisher | Harper and Brothers, USA
Theme | Classics, Family

Many readers think of *Little House on the Prairie* as the first in Laura Ingalls Wilder's series of Little House books, but it is actually the second. Wilder was born in the log cabin she described in the first book, *Little House in the Big Woods*. She; her husband, Almanzo; and their daughter, Rose, traveled by covered wagon across the Midwest to Mansfield, Missouri, where Laura began to write her classic series of books.

In *Little House on the Prairie*, the author tells the story of her family's move by covered wagon from Wisconsin to Kansas. Her parents' optimism and courage, along with Laura's independent spirit and curiosity, make the perilous journey seem so real that children will actually feel as if they are riding along with Laura, listening to Pa's fiddle, rocking in Ma's chair, and fearing the Osage Indians themselves.

For contemporary young readers and those who desire political correctness in their children's books, the attitudes to the Native American Osage Indians, while historically accurate, may be problematic. That said, this is not only an engrossing pioneer tale and charming family saga, but also a neat lesson in American history. The stories—some of which were named as Newbery Honor Books—resulted from a collaboration between Wilder and her daughter, who took on the responsibility of editing her mother's words. Wilder lived to the age of ninety, but to her millions of readers, she will always be the little pioneer girl of the books. **KD**

Mary Poppins "floating away over the roofs of the houses."

The Good Master 1935

Kate Seredy

Nationality | Hungarian, born 1899
Publisher | Viking, USA
Award | Newbery Honor Book, 1936
Theme | Family, Adventure

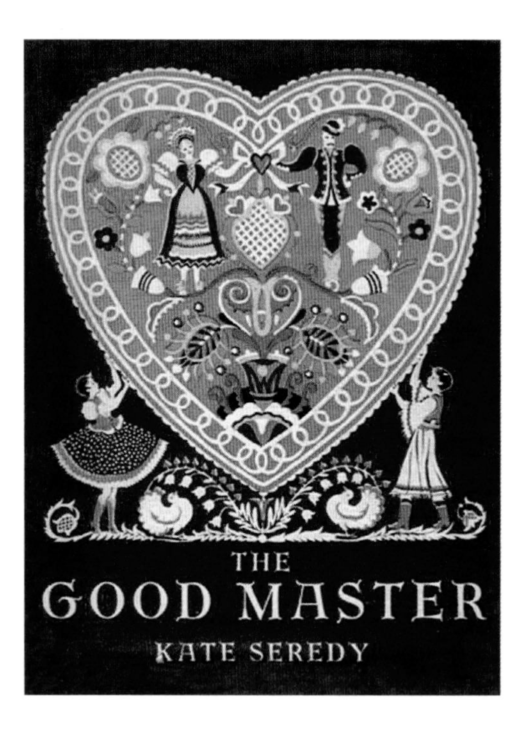

MORE TO ENJOY FROM KATE SEREDY

The White Stag, 1937
The Singing Tree, 1939
A Tree for Peter, 1941
Gypsy, 1951
The Tenement Tree, 1959

I was given *The Good Master* when I was ten. I loved the story so much that I often turned straight back to the beginning when I had finished it. I would study the map on the endpapers showing the farm of the Good Master and the surrounding countryside, local village, woods, and river. On the next pages were two color portraits: on the left Kate, the heroine, and on the right, her cousin, Jancsi, who I thought very handsome.

The story centers around Kate from Budapest who comes to stay with her aunt, Uncle Márton, and Cousin Jancsi on their farm on the Hungarian plains. With her comes a letter from her father, confessing that he has spoiled Kate since her mother died and that she is now completely out of control. Márton is known as the "Good Master," owing to his gift for taming wild horses with kindness and understanding. Kate's father hopes Márton can apply this talent to his daughter. Jancsi is disappointed with his unruly cousin with wild, black hair and long, thin legs. Soon, however, he finds he is intrigued and amused by her pranks, some of which are so fearless and dangerous that he is filled with secret admiration.

Kate responds to the firm hand of the Good Master. Her cousin teaches her to ride, and the Good Master gives her a beautiful white mare. How I envied Kate! Horses were my passion at that age. Another highlight of the book was dressing up in national costume for Easter. Kate wakes to find ten petticoats lying on her bed. They are all to be worn one on top of one another. The Good Master gives her the "prettiest, trimmest pair of little red boots" as a surprise. Oh, how I wanted those ten petticoats and little red boots!

The rest of the story concentrates on the adventures of Jancsi and Kate. They become inseparable with, I hoped, a hint of romance. Although Kate is "tamed," she never loses her wicked streak and remains feisty and great fun, which pleased me.

Kate's wild antics are tempered by Cousin Jancsi.

8+

The Box of Delights 1935

John Masefield

Alternative Title | When the Wolves Were Running
Nationality | English, born 1878
Publisher | Heinemann, UK
Theme | Fantasy

This sequel to *The Midnight Folk* sees innocent Kay Harker once more embroiled in mysterious events in the cathedral town of Condicote. He is coming home for the holidays the week before Christmas and is entrusted with a magical box by an old man who runs a Punch and Judy puppet show and who is shortly thereafter "crobbled" (abducted). Kay discovers that the box can make you either shrink or run swiftly, as well as display beauties and wonders and allow travel into the past. He and his friends, the redoubtable, revolver-toting Maria Jones and her brother, Peter, set out to rescue the old man, Cole Hawlings, who is revealed as a magical being. Cole has been seized by scary wolf figures, minions of the infamous villain Abner Brown. Brown's wickedness grows ever more grandiose, culminating in his kidnapping the entire staff of the cathedral and demanding the box of delights as ransom. Kay, of course, saves the day and the wolves are routed.

Few books are as magical as *The Box of Delights*. Apart from its perfunctory ending, it breathes enchantment on every page. John Masefield, an accomplished poet, conjures up stupendous adventures, from the snowy encampment of Roman legions to the bewildered appearance of medieval mage Arnold of Todi, the inventor of the box. He even evokes a fairy dance without corniness, while the squabbles between pirate rats and house mice are hilarious. Above all, the box serves as a symbol of the imagination, which children must protect from the sinister forces of commercialism, stupidity, and violence. **VN**

A Pony for Jean 1936

Joanna Cannan   Anne Bullen

Nationality | English, born 1896 (author); English, birth date unknown (illustrator)
Publisher | Bodley Head, UK
Theme | Animal stories

Pony books have always been popular with young girls, but it was Joanna Cannan who created the winning formula that still attracts readers today. Her prolific output was necessitated by her role as family breadwinner following her husband's injury during the war. Until Cannan wrote *A Pony for Jean*, pony books were almost always told from the point of view of the pony. Cannan wrote from the point of view of the pony's owner, Jean, and her adventures on horseback.

When Jean moves to the countryside, she has to come to terms with her new environment. She also has to deal with the hostility of her cousins, who laugh at her ignorance about country life. But as she learns to ride, her life changes.

Cannan's work inspired her three daughters, Josephine, Diana, and Christina Pullein-Thompson, to write their own pony stories. They began writing in their teens and produced dozens of books between them. After World War II, Joanna Cannan switched to writing detective novels for adults.

While Cannan's pony books have been eclipsed by those of her daughters, young readers will also take pleasure in *We Met Our Cousins*, which was reprinted in 2008 and focuses on John and Antonia, who are sent from London to spend their vacations with their cousins in the Scottish Highlands. They spend their time riding and sailing, and they solve a mystery concerning some stolen jewels. The Scottish setting was inspired by Cannan's family vacations in the Highlands—a world away from her day-to-day life in Oxford, where her father was a don. **HJ**

Ballet Shoes 1936

Noel Streatfeild Ruth Gervis

Nationality | English, born 1895 (author); English, birth date unknown (illustrator)
Publisher | Dent, UK
Theme | Family, School, Friendship

The early life stories of the three girls collected and adopted as a family of Fossils by their eccentric great-uncle Matthew (or "Gum") are as exciting as anything on the stage: Pauline is the only survivor of a shipwreck; Petrova is the child of destitute Russian émigrés; and Posy arrives at Gum's house on Cromwell Road in a basket, with only her mother's ballet shoes. Later, the girls' experiences at stage school and their early days earning their living in the theater are less starry, emphasizing the routine of daily classes, the rules, the paperwork, and the sheer unfairness of auditions. Their home life with a loving guardian, the fierce Nana, provides heartwarming interludes between the scenes from Madame Fidolia's academy.

In the Fossils, Noel Streatfeild has created engaging portraits of hardworking children who know the value of money, let success go to their heads only briefly, and support one another through the low points that the author knew only too well from her own ten years spent in theater.

Through Posy, tipped for stardom, Streatfeild shows the importance of single-minded perseverance in addition to talent. The most affectionately drawn character is Petrova (like the author, a willful and sometimes misunderstood middle daughter). Petrova is uncomfortable onstage but good with engines, and her destiny as a pilot makes this a satisfactory story about finding one's niche in life. Streatfeild's elder sister, Ruth Gervis, illustrated the book and visualized the characters for generations of readers to come. **GB**

Ballet Shoes
A story of three children
on the stage
Noel Streatfeild

"Really, Sir, I don't know what you'll be bringing to the house next. Who do you suppose has time to look after a baby?"

MORE GREAT BOOKS ABOUT SISTERS

***Little Women* by Louisa May Alcott, 1868**
***Little House on the Prairie* by Laura Ingalls Wilder, 1935**
***Lottie and Lisa* by Erich Kästner, 1949**
***Mufaro's Beautiful Daughters* by John Steptoe, 1987**

Worzel Gummidge 1936

Barbara Euphan Todd E. Alldridge

Nationality | English, born 1890 (author); English, birth date unknown (illustrator)
Publisher | Burns, UK
Theme | Quirky, Favorite characters

If you love the English countryside, you will love *Worzel Gummidge*. The ten books in the series are set in the lush, idyllic Cotswolds, where visiting city children John and Susan meet a lively community of walking, talking scarecrows. The scarecrows, with heads carved out of mangel-wurzels (a kind of beet) and stuffed with straw or sawdust, are personifications of the landscape they tend to. Although the dialect may tax modern children's reading skills, the silly wordplay and zany logic with which the scarecrows express themselves are appealing, as are their gentle pokes at the self-importance and lack of imagination of some adults. The plots are simple and revolve around the clash between the worldviews of the scarecrows and the adults, whether it be solving a crime, finding treasure, or going to the circus.

Barbara Euphan Todd's sympathy for the detail of the natural world extends to sympathy with the child's point of view. The characters may be fictional, but they seem more in touch with real values than the local bigwigs. In this, they are part of a tradition of English literature that views country life as more virtuous than city life, because it is simpler. Yet there is no need to read too much into *Worzel Gummidge*. The scarecrow is a richly humorous figure, both ignorant and oddly wise, who talks in a funny way, gets into ridiculous difficulties, insults people by accident, and does the right thing by mistake—only for everything to end happily as you knew it would. **VN**

Pigeon Post 1936

Arthur Ransome

Nationality | English, born 1884
Publisher | Jonathan Cape, UK
Award | Carnegie Medal
Theme | Adventure, Science and nature

The sixth Swallows and Amazons novel is again set in Ransome's beloved English Lake District where the Swallows and Amazons are joined by the *Ds*—Dick and Dorothea—who were first introduced in *Winter Holiday* (1933). Over a long hot summer, with the threat of forest fires looming, the children prospect for gold from a camp high on the lakeside fells.

This story explores themes of isolation and danger and, despite the overt joviality of the protagonists, their relationships are tenser and more fully psychologically realized than in the earlier books. Camping farther away from home than is normally permitted, and with few adults keeping an eye on them, their camp relies on daily messages sent via homing pigeons. The *Ds*, who begin the novel as comparative outsiders, come into their own with repeated calls on Dick's scientific expertise, leaving Roger, somewhat disgruntled, to head off on his own and make a fortuitous and very welcome discovery.

While the children's main concern is a mysterious figure who appears to be spying on them, they face very real danger; first, when one of the old tunnels in the hillside collapses and later, when a sweeping fire threatens the destruction of the fell. Their quick thinking—and their homing pigeons—save both children and countryside, and the novel ends on a triumphant note when the true nature of their discovery is revealed and the children's determined efforts are satisfyingly vindicated. **KA**

"The large flapping things were scarecrows."

The Adventures of the Wishing Chair 1937

Enid Blyton   Hilda McGavin

Nationality | English, born 1897 (author); details unknown (illustrator)
Publisher | Newnes, UK
Theme | Magical stories, Fantasy

8+

Mollie and Peter can hardly believe their luck when an old chair in an antique shop grows wings and flies them home. The chair, secreted in the playroom at the bottom of the garden, well away from parental view, provides them with wonderful adventures. It also leads them to a new friend, the amiable pixie, Chinky.

In Enid Blyton's *The Adventures of the Wishing Chair*, the first book in the Wishing Chair series, the children travel to magical lands inhabited by elves, gnomes, witches, wizards, and goblins. Chinky and the children often encounter problems on their various missions, but always manage to arrive home safely. As Peter says, "Talk about adventures! Every one seems more exciting than the last! Wherever shall we go next?"

Blyton wrote this book early in her career, and it has a pace and richness of imaginative incident all of its own. Using direct if sometimes repetitive language—the word "horrid" occurs at least fifty times—the children's adventures offer young readers the type of fantasy wish fulfillment found in the most benign traditional fairy tales. A few villainous characters occasionally appear to up the excitement level, but there is never any doubt that Chinky and the ever-resourceful children will succeed in the end, leaving them ready for their next adventure. Many sequels followed, and the stories have remained popular. Adventures in which young children experience vast numbers of magical trips are the stuff of daydreams, as well as the very best imaginary games. **NT**

The Far-Distant Oxus 1937

K. Hull and P. Whitlock   P. Whitlock

Nationality | English, born 1921 (Katharine Hull); English, born 1920 (Pamela Whitlock)
Publisher | Jonathan Cape, UK
Theme | Adventure, Friendship

The Far-Distant Oxus is unusual in that it was written by children for children. Katherine Hull was fourteen years old and Pamela Whitlock fifteen when they met and discovered that they shared a mutual interest in books and ponies. They began to work on their novel, drawing up the plot and characters, then writing alternate chapters. Once they had completed the first draft, they exchanged chapters and revised each other's work. They kept the project a secret from their parents and teachers and sent the completed manuscript to their favorite author, Arthur Ransome. He recommended it to his publisher, saying it was the best children's book of 1937.

Like Ransome's books, this novel describes the adventures of a group of schoolchildren during the summer vacations. The story focuses around ponies, den building, races, sleeping in hammocks, and sailing rafts down the River Oxus. It is a celebration of friendship and the things people can achieve when working together. The characters are well drawn and the Exmoor landscape, with its characteristic moorland, rivers, and forests, is vividly described. This is a world that the pair explored in three further highly successful books. In adulthood Whitlock continued to write, but Hull never published anything else.

The Far-Distant Oxus, after long being out of print, was reissued in 2008, and will appeal to a new generation of readers who may not enjoy the same level of freedom as the authors did in the 1930s. **HJ**

The Family from One End Street 1937

 Eve Garnett

Nationality | English, born 1900
Publisher | Frederick Muller, UK
Award | Carnegie Medal
Theme | Family, Adventure

Eve Garnett's depiction of working-class life in a small town in the 1930s was rejected as unsuitable for children when she first sought a publisher. It was the first book for young readers to move beyond generic descriptions of "the poor." The portraits of the Ruggles family—Josiah the dustman, Rosie the washerwoman, and their seven children—are completely realistic, especially in their dialogue and relationships.

Garnett wanted her observation of people and her flair for comedy to raise awareness about the reality of family life just above the poverty line. There is plenty of discussion of hand-me-down clothes and worn-out boots. The Ruggles children learn early about the value of money and suffer retribution for burning a customer's dress or losing a school hat. Mrs. Ruggles is dictatorial as well as loving, and is an uncompromising enforcer of chores and respectability.

Whatever their place in the complex pecking order, each one of the Ruggles children (except for youngest-but-one Peg) gets a chapter in which to have an adventure. These are especially entertaining when they involve encounters higher up the social scale. Chatty and confident John Ruggles is instantly at home when he gatecrashes a middle-class boy's birthday party, but John's father feels uncomfortable when he encounters genteel poverty in the form of an author whose rubbish he collects. The rich seam of mother Rosie's humor and wisdom runs effortlessly throughout the book. **GB**

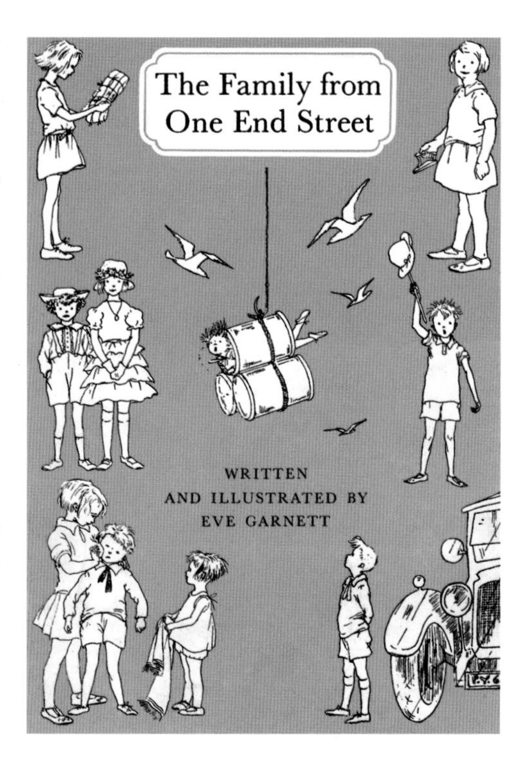

"Nearly every week one of the Ruggles could be seen running with a boot in either hand . . ."

OTHER FAMILY SAGAS TO ENJOY

***The Swiss Family Robinson* by Johann D. Wyss, 1812**
***The Railway Children* by E. Nesbit, 1906**
***Farmer Boy* by Laura Ingalls Wilder, 1933**
***The Fantastic Antoñita* by Borita Casas, 1948**
***The Borrowers* by Mary Norton, 1952**

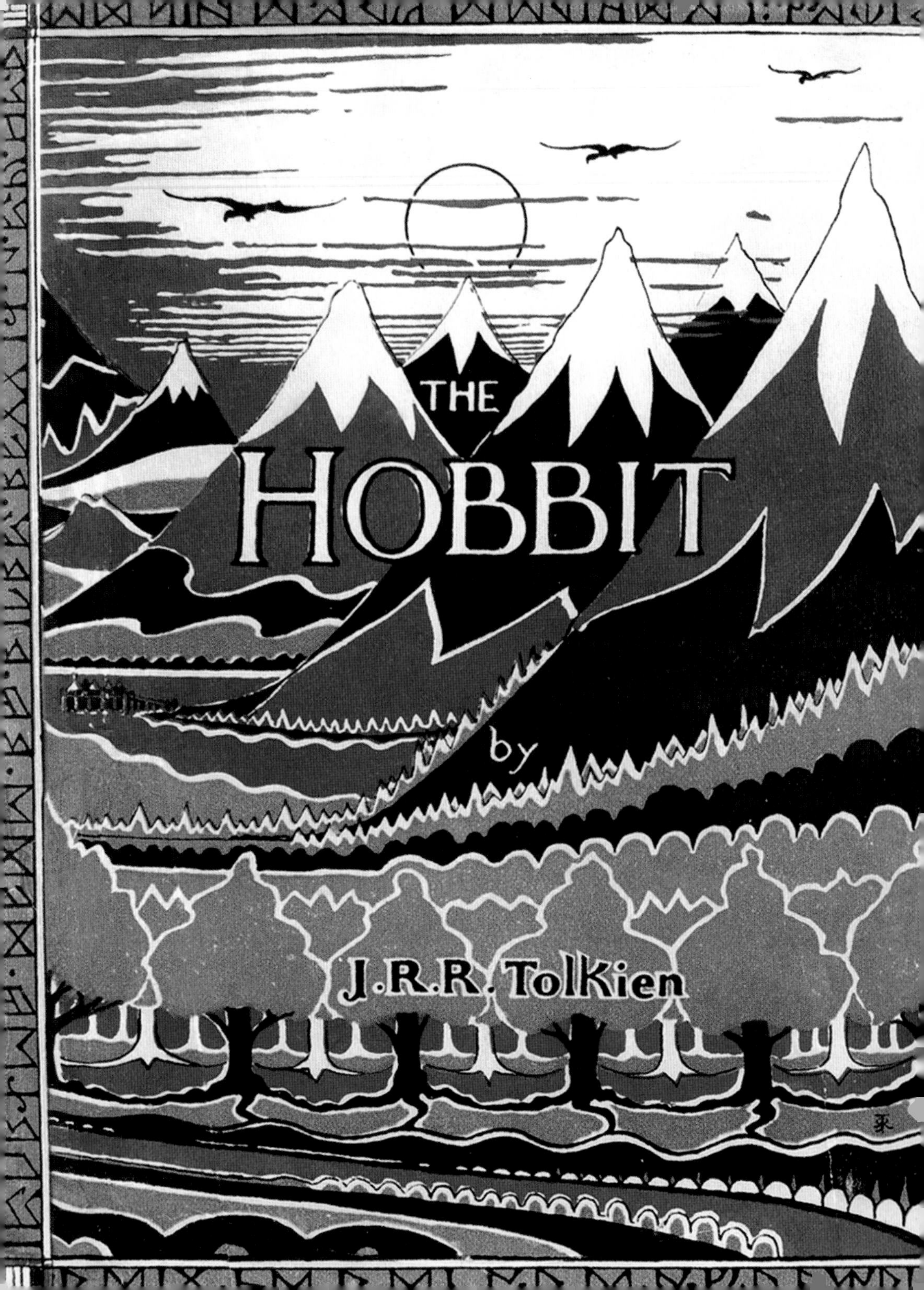
THE
HOBBIT
by
J.R.R. Tolkien

The Hobbit 1937

J. R. R. Tolkien

Alternative Title | There and Back Again
Nationality | English, born in South Africa, 1892
Publisher | Allen and Unwin, UK
Theme | Fantasy, Classics

This story was originally told to the author's own children and describes the fantasy world of Middle-earth, which is inhabited by elves, dwarves, wizards, dragons, and, of course, hobbits. Invented by their author, these good-humored, pleasure-loving, diminutive hobbits live in traditional villages untouched by industrialization. One of them, middle-aged Bilbo Baggins, finds himself, rather to his surprise, on an expedition to raid the treasure of a fire-breathing and dangerously marauding dragon. Trolls, goblins, and giant spiders all conspire to make this journey as difficult as possible before finally coming to its triumphant end.

Maps drawn by the author, fantastical settings, and detailed descriptions of the scenery through which the gallant band of adventurers pass all lend total authenticity to this stirring tale of courage over adversity. More informally written than its successor, *The Lord of the Rings* (1954–1955), *The Hobbit* provides young readers with the perfect start for entering into one of the most convincing imaginative literary worlds ever created.

J. R. R. Tolkien was born in Bloemfontein, in the Orange Free State, where he lived until he was three. He is widely regarded as the father of modern fantasy literature. He was a writer, poet, and philologist, as well as a professor of Anglo-Saxon at Oxford from 1925 until 1945 and a professor of English language and literature from 1945 until 1959. After Tolkien's death in 1973, his son Christopher organized some of his father's previously unpublished material into *The Silmarillion*, which was published in 1977. **NT**

The Red Pony 1937

John Steinbeck

Nationality | American, born 1902
Publisher | Covici Friede, USA
Honor | Nobel Prize for Literature, 1962
Theme | Animal stories, Illness and death

Jody, "a little boy, ten years old, with hair like dusty yellow grass," lives on a ranch with his parents and Billy Buck, the cowhand. Jody is trying to learn everything that his father and Billy know about animals. One day his father takes him to see a young colt, a little red pony, and tells him that the pony is his to look after. The pony is too young to be ridden yet, but in a few months Billy will be able to teach Jody how to break the pony. First they have to get him strong and used to wearing a saddle. Jody's relationship with the pony reveals a tender coming-of-age story. When Jody brings some of his schoolfriends home to see the pony, the boys start to look at Jody with a new respect: "Before today Jody had been a boy . . . now he was different." It is a defining moment between boyhood and manhood.

One day, when Jody is at school, the red pony is caught in a terrible storm. Billy tries to nurse him, but just as Jody is beginning to hope he will get better, the pony dies. As buzzards circle overhead, waiting to begin their feast, Jody tries to beat them away, killing one of them in his fury with his bare arms. The red pony has died before Jody ever got the chance to ride him. At the end of the book, Jody is assisting Billy with a difficult birth, during which the mare, Nellie, dies and Jody is left to raise the colt himself.

John Steinbeck wrote *The Red Pony* as four short stories, and Covici Friede published an edition in 1937 without the fourth story. It was not until 1945 that the four stories were published together in a version illustrated by Wesley Dennis. **LH**

My Friend Mr. Leakey 1937

J. B. S. Haldane

Nationality | English, born 1892
Publisher | Cresset Press, UK
Theme | Magical stories, Adventure, Science and nature

Mr. Leakey is a magician who has his meals grilled by a dragon called Pompey and is served by Oliver the octopus, who lives in a large copper pot. When Mr. Leakey has a party, he transforms his guests into whatever they choose to be—one visiting film star, for example, is changed into a butterfly. He travels via a magic carpet, with longer journeys undertaken by a djinn (genie) who, on one occasion, nips over to New Zealand for some strawberries. Three separate stories at the end of this fun-packed book introduce readers to other characters and situations, but it is the benign Mr. Leakey, with his constant capacity to spring surprises, who dominates the main action, endlessly telling stories about his ever more weird adventures—and always prepared to embark on yet another one.

The author, J. B. S. Haldane, was a famous scientist, geneticist, and evolutionary biologist. He was one of the founders of population genetics and was noted for his restless intelligence. As he himself wrote, "Professor Haldane has been used for experiments ever since he was three . . . some of the things that happened to him are nearly as queer as the things that happen in this book." It is this zest for investigation and invention, linked to a lively curiosity about what would happen if impossible things suddenly became possible, that gives this book its particular energy. Plenty of genuine scientific information is also packed into these stories, in addition to the ongoing fantasy of a magician who can quite literally do whatever he wants. **NT**

The Circus Is Coming 1938

Noel Streatfeild, Stephen Spurrier

Nationality | English, born 1895 (author); English, born 1878 (illustrator)
Publisher | Dent, UK
Theme | Adventure, Friendship

The Circus Is Coming (known as *Circus Shoes* in the United States) has not achieved the enduring status of *Ballet Shoes*, but it attracted critical acclaim on publication and won the Carnegie Medal. Like *Ballet Shoes*, this book shows convincing child characters learning to succeed as professionals in a tough world.

Noel Streatfeild traveled with a circus to research the story of runaway orphans Peter and Santa, who find a new home with their estranged uncle Gus, who is a clown in Cob's Circus, a hardworking, self-reliant community. In order not to be sent off to separate children's homes, the youngsters have to show Gus and the other circus people that they can earn their keep and be competent and useful. Peter and Santa have been brought up to consider themselves rather special, and they suffer as their pretensions and superior airs are exposed. As well as working hard to develop their talents, they have to accept that their former concepts about respectability count for nothing in this new world of committed people with pride in what they do.

During the summer that they spend traveling with the circus, the children find their niches: Peter discovers that he loves horses, whereas Santa finds that she has the potential to be a good acrobat. They also mature and learn through others that Gus has made sacrifices to keep them with him through the season. The question of what will happen to them afterward is resolved in a satisfying conclusion. **GB**

The Sword in the Stone 1938

T. H. White

Nationality | English, born 1906
Publisher | Collins, UK
Theme | Classics, Magical stories, Fantasy, Adventure

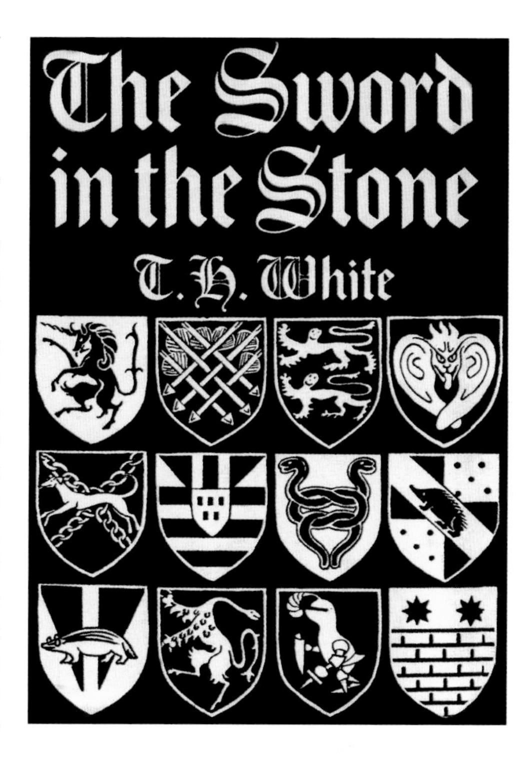

It is medieval England, and in the Forest Sauvage a young Arthur, known as the Wart, encounters Merlyn: a magician who lives with a talking owl and can tell the dishes to wash themselves. The Wart is a bit of a dullard and is bullied by his foster brother, Kay. Merlyn magically changes the Wart into an ant, a fish, a hawk, a snake, and a badger, so that Arthur can experience life from different angles. He is enchanted in and out of various magic scenarios, such as being captured by boy-eating witches and meeting the goddess Athene. The Wart and Kay meet Robin Hood, Maid Marian, and Little John and fight fearsome battles with outlandish enemies, such as the Anthropophagi. On hearing that the king has died and that his heir will be the one who can pull the sword out of the stone, Kay and Arthur go to London, where a chance event reveals Arthur to be the true heir to the throne.

T. H. White knew much about medieval life, from heraldry to falconry, and was well versed in Arthurian legend. *The Sword in the Stone* is often reprinted as part of an Arthurian tetralogy, *The Once and Future King*, but only its plot sits well in that sequence. The other books are fairly serious explorations of power politics and chivalry, whereas *The Sword in the Stone* is a high-spirited romp through stock Merrie England situations. The most lively and original parts, lifted for the Disney film, follow Wart through his animal transformations and suggest what human beings can learn from nature. **VN**

"Who so Pulleth Out This Sword of this Stone and Anvil, is Rightwise King of All England."

OTHER GREAT READS BY T. H. WHITE

England Have My Bones, 1936
The Queen of Air and Darkness, 1939
The Ill-Made Knight, 1940
Mistress Masham's Repose, 1946
The Book of Merlyn, 1977

Old Possum's Book of Practical Cats 1939

T. S. Eliot Nicolas Clerihew Bentley

8+

Nationality | American/English, born 1888 (author); English, born 1907 (illustrator)
Publisher | Faber and Faber, UK
Theme | Poetry, Animal stories

"Skimble where is Skimble for unless he's very nimble / Then the Night Mail just can't go."

Plunge into *Old Possum's Book of Practical Cats*, T. S. Eliot's masterly exploration of rhythm and image, where every poem weaves a different spell. Eliot admired cats for their beauty and grace, but had no illusions about their innate cunning and sensual selfishness. At night, Jennyanydots, the old Gumbie Cat, trains mice and cockroaches in the art of keeping a clean house; Growltiger, the old bravo cat, has "no eye or ear for aught but [the lady] Griddlebone," a fatal weakness that leads to being forced to walk the plank; Rum Tum Tugger, a curious and contrary cat "will do as he do do, and there's no doing anything about it." Macavity the mystery cat, the Napoleon of crime, controls even notorious scoundrels like Mungojerrie. Echoes of Berthold Brecht's *Mac the Knife* in rhyme, meter, name, and character are no accident: Eliot was an obvious literary craftsman whose poetry is shot through with cultural allusions.

There is no need to be pious and reverential about *Old Possum's*, however. These are rollicking poems to read aloud. The short character sketches and narratives are just as much about the sounds of words and phrases as they are accounts of events. This aspect of the collection makes it an excellent introduction for young readers to the pleasures of poetry, pleasures that can, in their way, be as sensual as those of rat-catching or dancing in the moonlight.

The Broadway and West End musical *Cats* was based on this selection of T. S. Eliot's poems. **VN**

OTHER COLLECTIONS OF VERSE

The Book of Nonsense by Edward Lear, 1846
Marigold Garden by Kate Greenaway, 1885
Cautionary Tales for Children by Hilaire Belloc, 1907
Where the Sidewalk Ends by Shel Silverstein, 1974

The Ship That Flew 1939

Hilda Lewis Nora Lavrin

Nationality | English, born 1896 (author); details unknown (illustrator)
Publisher | Oxford University Press, UK
Theme | Magical stories, Historical fiction

When Peter sees an old model Viking ship in a junk shop he so desperately wants it that he is willing to pay the price that the shopkeeper requests: "All the money you have in the world—and a bit over." Peter soon discovers that he has bought a magical ship: a ship with the power to grow to fit whoever wants to travel in it and to carry them to any place they desire.

Peter and his brother and sisters first use the ship to visit their mother, who lives far away recuperating from an illness. The children take a trip to Egypt, and discover that their vessel is the magic ship of the Norse god Frey, which not only can travel through space but also through time. The children then travel back in time to Asgard, home of the Norse gods, where Frey tells them that passing a hand over the ship's boar's head prow will make them speak the language and look like the people of the place and time they are visiting. The children realize then that the possibilities are endless. Further time-travel adventures take them to Norman England, ancient Egypt, and the time of Robin Hood. Eventually Peter decides he has to honor his promise to Frey and give the ship back.

The Ship That Flew is reminiscent of those classic E. Nesbit fantasies, such as *The Phoenix and the Carpet*, in which contemporary children have magical adventures. This was the first children's book written by Hilda Lewis, the author of many historical novels for adults, and it was hugely popular and much admired when it was first published. **CW**

A Traveller in Time 1939

Alison Uttley

Nationality | English, born 1884
Publisher | Faber and Faber, UK
Theme | Adventure, Historical fiction, Fantasy, Family

Wouldn't you love to be able to walk through a door and go back in time? Bookish Penelope, recovering from illness at her great-aunt Tissie's farm, finds, quite by chance, that she can travel in time via the library. Is it a secret passage? Or is it a metaphor for the journeys on which books can take us? Such reflections quickly dissipate in the thrill of the plot, for Penelope is caught up in the life of the Tudor farmhouse and slips between her ordinary nineteenth-century life and the high romance of Elizabethan times. Her own distant ancestor, Aunt Cicely Taberner, is a cook to the Babington family. Penelope—along with the reader—falls in love with the impossibly glamorous Francis Babington, but our infatuation is clouded by the knowledge that the family's plot to free Mary Queen of Scots from her long imprisonment is doomed.

Although readers may find the book a little hard to get into, particularly if they are not versed in the tangled history of Queen Elizabeth I and the Catholic Mary, Queen of Scots, its gentle, unobtrusive elegance of style and unexpected plot twists have much to offer. Derbyshire in northern England was Alison Uttley's native region, and she trained as a natural scientist, so the setting is beautifully evoked with writing that echoes her books of fictionalized reminiscences, beginning with *A Country Child*. The slow pace builds into a convincing picture of a past where country houses were a world all to themselves and politics were about personal allegiance and sworn honor. **VN**

Lassie Come-Home 1940

Eric Knight   Marguerite Kirmse

Nationality | English, born 1897 (author); American, born 1885 (illustrator)
Publisher | John C. Winston, USA
Theme | Classics, Animal stories, Adventure

Lassie Come-Home was written during the Great Depression and is one of the world's best-loved dog stories. Author Eric Knight had a collie dog, Toots, and it is thought that Toots's devotion was the inspiration for the character of Lassie. Knight wrote the story in 1938, and it was first published in the *Saturday Evening Post*, in Yorkshire, England. What made Lassie really famous was the 1944 film directed by Frank Capra, starring Roddy McDowell and Elizabeth Taylor. Later, Lassie also became part of a popular American television series that went on to run for twenty years.

The story is set in Yorkshire in the wake of World War I. Lassie belongs to young Joe Carraclough, and the pair are constant companions. However, when Joe's father, Sam, loses his job at the local mine, the family is unable to care for Lassie and sells her to the wealthy Duke of Rudling. The faithful collie escapes from her new owner three times, each time returning home to her beloved Joe. Lassie is then taken to the duke's estate in a remote part of Scotland, but once again she returns home on an epic journey south that sees her receive help from many kind people, including the poor peddler Rowlie Palmer. She also encounters less kindly humans in the shape of dogcatchers, farmers, and bullying young boys, but always escapes.

The story reaches a happy conclusion when Lassie is eventually reunited with Joe. This is a wonderful story of courage and loyalty that will melt the heart of even the most cynical young reader. **CK**

Betsy-Tacy 1940

Maud Hart Lovelace   Lois Lenski

Nationality | American, born 1892 (author); American, born 1893 (illustrator)
Publisher | HarperCollins, USA
Theme | Friendship, Family

Betsy-Tacy is the first in a series of ten books written by Maud Hart Lovelace between 1940 and 1955. The stories follow the adventures of Betsy Ray, her friends, and her family, from the time that Betsy turns five until she marries in her early twenties. Set in the period from 1897 to 1917, Betsy Ray is loosely based on the author herself. Betsy is an outgoing, imaginative child who loves to tell stories and dreams of being a writer.

In this first book, Betsy and Tacy's experiences are taken from everyday life, such as going to school, making a playhouse, dressing up to "go calling," and playing imaginary games. It also deals with shyness, the birth of new siblings (Betsy is one of eleven children), the creative imagination of a child who dreams of writing stories, and even touches on more sobering subjects, such as a death within the family.

From today's perspective, the stories take place in a much simpler time and place, but that is part of their charm, and the story of a long and abiding friendship formed in early childhood still rings true. As the characters in the series age, the books are aimed at older readers, so that the characters and the readers grow and develop together. Lovelace's stories draw upon her own childhood and family life, and the Tacy of the title is based on her long-standing friend Frances "Nick" Kenney, whom she had known since her fifth birthday. Likewise "Tib" who features in other stories, was based on another childhood friend, Marjorie "Midge" Gerlach. **KD**

The Black Stallion 1941

Walter Farley Keith Ward

Nationality | American, born 1915 (author); American, born 1906 (illustrator)
Publisher | Random House, USA
Theme | Adventure, Animal stories

Readers do not need a passion for horses to be swept up in the pure excitement of this classic novel. The tale is about Alec Ramsay, a boy from New York who, as the story opens, is heading home on the steamer *Drake* after a long stay with relatives in India.

One of his fellow passengers is a wild and beautiful black stallion that fascinates Alec. When the steamer is caught in a violent storm, boy and horse find themselves in the open sea, with Alec tethered to the stallion by a rope. The horse, a miraculously powerful swimmer, drags Alec onto a deserted island where the two survive and form a bond as Alec tries to tame and ride the wild creature. After being rescued, the boy and still-wild horse return to New York where, with the help of former horse trainer Henry Dailey, Alec secretly continues his quest to ride the stallion. Dailey is convinced that the horse and young jockey can achieve great things, and the duo enter as mystery contestants in a major race, which they win.

The story may seem a little old-fashioned and some of its characters two-dimensional, but this is a classic adventure, and its verve and energy are highly infectious. The great race at the end is truly exciting, and Walter Farley is well informed about his subject. It is not hard to see why the book, Farley's first and written while he was still an undergraduate, was an instant success. He went on to write a huge number of books about the black stallion and other horses, spawning movies and a television series. **AK**

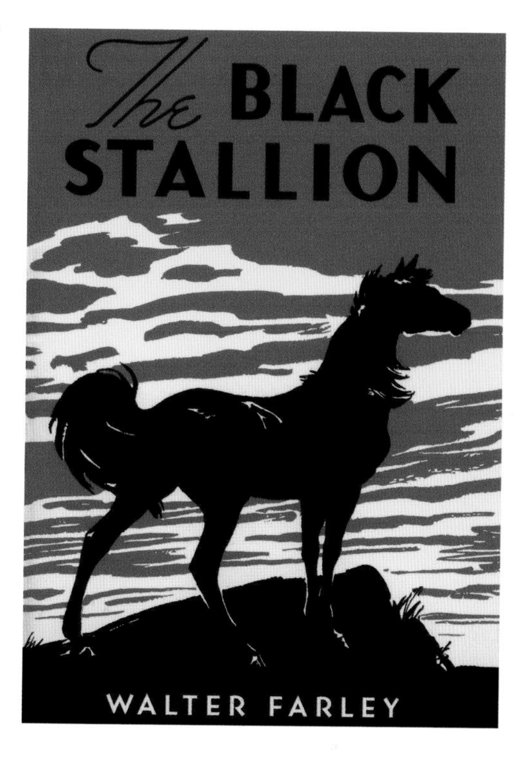

"White lather ran from the horse's body, his mouth was open, his teeth bared."

MORE WILD HORSE STORIES

Black Beauty by Anna Sewell, 1877
National Velvet by Enid Bagnold, 1935
The Red Pony by John Steinbeck, 1937
My Friend Flicka by Mary O'Hara, 1941
Misty of Chincoteague by Marguerite Henry, 1947

8+

The Swish of the Curtain 1941

Pamela Brown

Nationality | English, born 1924
Publisher | Nelson, UK
Theme | Friendship, Adventure, Theater and arts, Classics

8+

This is a book about theater-mad youngsters written by a theater-mad youngster. Pamela Brown was still at school when she began her series about the Blue Door Theater, about passionate and driven young people "following their dream" and overcoming obstacles. The author can be imagined impatiently urging on her peers as they renovate a derelict building and write and produce their first play. The practical obstacles and emotional upheaval as the children grow frustrated with the project and one another are painstakingly documented, but are never allowed to dominate the narrative. The story of goodwill, team spirit, and hard work succeeding in unlikely circumstances must have inspired young readers in 1941, when personal dreams and projects were necessarily on hold.

The players are well characterized, from talented but slightly too self-absorbed Lynette to effervescent Maddy and ever-reliable Sandra. Each child realizes a personal goal: Vicky completes her most difficult acrobatic routine for the first time in front of the drama competition panel, and Bullfrog, star comedian, finally perfects the swish of the curtain. The novel ends with the older children heading for drama school and planning to return to the Blue Door when they have the skills needed to form a repertory company. Pamela Brown, who used the proceeds of this book to fund her own stage training, wrote another four Blue Door stories about how the children fared. **GB**

The Little Grey Men 1942

B. B.

Nationality | English, born Denys Watkins-Pitchford 1905
Publisher | Eyre and Spottiswoode, UK
Theme | Fantasy

This story begins in spring, lasts through a verdant summer, and ends as the first frosts bite. Close by a brook live the last four gnomes in England. One of them, Cloudberry, goes off exploring and does not come back, so Dodder, Baldmoney, and Sneezewort go to find him—but they leave it two years before they set out. They are country folk, not to be hurried.

Although the gnomes are small, they are brave and resourceful. They make new friends, battle formidable enemies, deal with the vagaries of boat and water, survive natural catastrophes, and finally come home to a roaring fire and a fine elderberry wine. They are full of affection and good cheer, despite occasional grumpiness and gloom. Above all, they love the English countryside, as did their creator, "B.B." He spent many years exploring the countryside, usually while wandering away from lessons, and the landscape of the book speaks directly from his childhood vision. B.B. was convinced that he had seen gnomes by the riverbank so, as an adult, he began to ponder on their lives, conjuring up little beings strangely like himself. He was a trained artist and teacher who took his pseudonym from the name of a shotgun pellet and was a countryman through and through. His gnomes enjoy eating, drinking, hunting, fishing, and making clothes out of animal skins. The book is no sentimental version of rural life but a meaty, satisfying evocation of the wonder of the natural world, and the black-and-white illustrations are equally delightful. **VN**

Five on a Treasure Island 1942

Enid Blyton Eileen Soper

Nationality | English, born 1897 (author); English, born 1905 (illustrator)
Publisher | Hodder and Stoughton, UK
Theme | Adventure, Fantasy, Friendship

8+

This is the first story featuring the Famous Five—Julian, Dick, Georgina (always known as George), Anne, and Timothy the dog. Julian, Dick, and Anne are going to stay on the Cornish coast with Uncle Quentin (George's severe scientist father) and initially find their cousin, proud, stubborn George, hard work. Once friendship has been established, however, the adventurers are irresistibly drawn to nearby Kirrin Island, a rough, uninhabited place owned by George herself. They soon stumble across buried treasure, after finding a map in a submerged wreck, but a gang of crooks is after it too and imprisons the children in the castle's ancient dungeons, before Timothy the dog comes to the rescue. The children finish their story snug in their beds after being heaped with praise and can hardly wait until their next adventure. Twenty-four more books followed about the Famous Five.

Although Enid Blyton had a limited vocabulary and often repeated herself, she did have a huge talent for storytelling, constantly leaving readers wanting more at the end of each chapter. She also instinctively understood children's need for fantasy in fiction, of the type where they can happily imagine themselves possessed of adult skills without any accompanying responsibilities. The result in this instance—as with the others in the series—is a splendidly satisfying, if extremely unlikely, story that has been thrilling children ever since it was written more than sixty years ago. **NT**

"She could hardly believe that these strange brick-shaped things were really gold."

MORE CLASSIC ADVENTURE STORIES

Adventures of Tom Sawyer by Mark Twain, 1876
Five Children and It by E. Nesbit, 1902
Swallows and Amazons by Arthur Ransome, 1930
Five Go Off in a Caravan by Enid Blyton, 1946
Amazon Adventure by Willard Price, 1949

ANTOINE DE SAINT-EXUPERY

Le Petit Prince

The Little Prince 1943

Antoine de Saint-Exupéry

Original Title | Le Petit prince
Nationality | French, born 1900
Publisher | Gallimard, France
Theme | Fantasy, Adventure

The Little Prince comes from an asteroid so small that he can watch the sun set forty-four times a day. He visits the narrator, who is trying to repair his plane, which has crashed in the Sahara Desert. The prince asks the pilot to draw him a sheep, and so their dialogue begins—a dialogue full of the unexpected and poetic. The Little Prince has left his own planet, which is plagued by baobab trees but is the home of his true love, a rose who cannot express her affection in return. He recounts his travels on six other planets, each ruled by a prototype of human foolishness. Antoine de Saint-Exupéry describes, with elegantly satirical phrases, a pompous, futile king; a conceited egoist; a shamefaced drinker; a covetous businessman; an overly conscientious lamplighter; and an academic geographer who tells the prince that his rose must one day die. Now on Earth, he has met a snake with the power to send him home and a fox, which he tames. The fox, in contrast to men, knows about love and consoles him that his rose, although ephemeral, is unique. After helping the narrator find water, the prince lets the snake bite him, so that he can go home.

The story, absurd though it is in structure, strikes a chord with readers young and old, even though its subject matter is not particularly childish. *The Little Prince*, illustrated by the author in flowing, colorful sketches, transcends genre to live long in the memory and resonate in the heart. **VN**

The Hundred Dresses 1944

Eleanor Estes  Louis Slobodkin

Nationality | American, born 1906 (author); American, born 1903 (illustrator)
Publisher | Harcourt, USA
Theme | School, Friendship

Bullying, unfortunately, is not a new trend. As this charmingly illustrated novella from 1944 shows, being an immigrant with a "funny" name, or just being different, and not appreciated for who you are, has sadly not changed over the years.

Wanda Petronski is the new girl in school, an immigrant to the United States from Poland—possibly a refugee or Holocaust survivor. She wears shabby clothes, lives on the "wrong side of the tracks," and has a foreign accent. When she boasts of having one hundred dresses in her closet and sixty pairs of shoes, Peggy and Maddie begin to tease her mercilessly. Maddie also comes from a poor background, but is too afraid of being Peggy's next victim to stand up for Wanda. Eventually, on the day that the girls find out the truth about the one hundred dresses—when Wanda wins a dress design contest with meticulous drawings of dresses she has described—they also find out that Wanda and her family have moved away to find a place where they will not be shunned because of their funny last name or their financial burdens.

In a touching reversal, Peggy and Maddie write to Wanda to tell her how beautiful her one hundred dresses are, and Wanda writes back. This is a good tale for sometimes thoughtless young girls, who may not realize the power of words spoken in jealousy. It is a sad but ultimately redeeming story that teaches a difficult lesson about how even words alone can cause hurt to others. **KD**

Brendon Chase 1944

B. B.

Nationality | English, born Denys Watkins-Pitchford 1905
Publisher | Hollis and Carter, UK
Theme | Adventure, Science and nature

MORE GREAT TITLES FROM B. B.

The Little Grey Men, 1942
The Wayfaring Tree, 1945
The Wind in the Wood, 1952
Bill Badger and the Pirates, 1960
A Child Alone, 1978

8+

Three brothers escape from home to avoid returning to boarding school and live in the forest for eight months. Of course, for any child who dreaded returning to school at the end of the summer holidays, the story is bliss. I do not think that I have ever come across a piece of writing that describes with such passion the English countryside.

Here we are discussing not only a writer with immense talent, but also an artist whose drawings are superb. B. B. is a highly skilled draftsman, which can be seen in his ability to tackle extremely difficult compositions, such as the boy climbing the Scots pine tree to get the eggs from the nest of a honey buzzard. It is a long time since I have read this book,

"Nothing has been heard of them, nor has any trace been found of the missing boys."

but that composition still impresses me. B. B. used scraperboard to produce the illustrations, which is hardly ever used these days, and like all engraving techniques, this method means you cannot easily correct your mistakes.

I suppose my affection for this book is because I too spent long periods away from school in the remote countryside. The amount learned by the trio of boys far outweighs, I suspect, the conventional academic slog that we avoided. How does this apply to today's children who by and large have no access to this kind of a countryside experience? It is a beautifully written and structured story, and the repeated quotation in B. B.'s books still applies. "The wonder of the world / The beauty and the power / The shape of things / Their colours, lights, and shades / These I saw / Look ye also while life lasts."

Robin, one of B. B.'s boys, climbs up to a honey buzzard's nest.

Rabbit Hill 1944

Robert Lawson

Nationality | American, born 1892
Publisher | Viking Press, USA
Award | Newbery Medal, 1945
Theme | Animal stories

Robert Lawson wrote and illustrated the children's book *Ben and Me: An Astonishing Life of Benjamin Franklin by His Good Mouse Amos*, which told of the life of the American Founding Father, Benjamin Franklin, through an animal companion. Publishers were initially unconvinced by Lawson's novel idea. Nevertheless, the book was published, and Lawson established a new genre in children's literature.

Rabbit Hill tells the story of an animal community that lives in the Connecticut countryside. The main characters are the young rabbit Little Georgie, his Southern gentleman father, his ever-fretful mother, and the other little animals: Willie Fieldmouse and his large family, the Gray Squirrel, Foxy, Phewie the Skunk, Porkey the Woodchuck, the Red Deer and his Doe and Fawn, and the short-sighted Mole. Nearby is the Big House, whose inhabitants were at one time kind to the local animals. However, when they moved away, the new owners were mean and let the house and grounds fall into bad repair. The lack of cultivated land from which to forage caused the animals to suffer. Another new family arrives, and the animals are concerned by what the "new folks" will be like: Will they be generous, will they hunt down the animals with traps and guns, and, most of all, will they be "planting folks"? As things stand the animals are having to risk encounters with dogs and travel across dangerous terrain of the Black Road to find food. This book is beautifully illustrated, fun, and poignant with an underlying message on the benefits of tolerance and sharing. **CK**

Wind on the Moon 1944

Eric Linklater Nicholas C. Bentley

Nationality | Scottish, born 1899 (author); English, born 1907 (illustrator)
Publisher | Macmillan, UK
Theme | Fantasy, Adventure

This book, written in the last years of World War II, has two main themes, both of which were foremost in people's minds at that time—freedom and food. Today's readers might find the story rambling, but there are many funny and magical moments.

Dorinda and Dinah are compelled to behave badly when the wind blows on the moon. Their father is absent, their mother is weak, and their governess is boring. The girls stuff themselves with food until they are as round as balloons, then weep themselves as thin as matchsticks, in both cases earning the taunts of local children. A very amusing court case follows, reminiscent of *Alice's Adventures in Wonderland*, where half the town, including the jury, is imprisoned.

There are two main adventures in this book. First, the two children, with the help of a witch, turn themselves into kangaroos, end up in a zoo, and try to solve a robbery. A falcon spots the python in the act of stealing an ostrich's egg, and the children organize the capture of the miscreant, who is killed by a *Times*-reading bear. When they are restored to the form of children, Dorinda and Dinah escape with the falcon and a puma.

The second adventure involves rescuing their father from the clutches of Count Hulagu Bloot—a tyrant who loves torturing people—in Bombardy with the help of their dancing master, Casimir Corvo, the falcon, and the puma. Two forgotten old sappers from the Boer War, who have been tunneling across Europe for decades, provide the means of escape, and they return home. **WO**

Stuart Little 1945

E. B. White · Garth Williams

Nationality | American, born 1899 (author); American, born 1912 (illustrator)
Publisher | Harper Trophy, USA
Theme | Animal stories, Family, Adventure

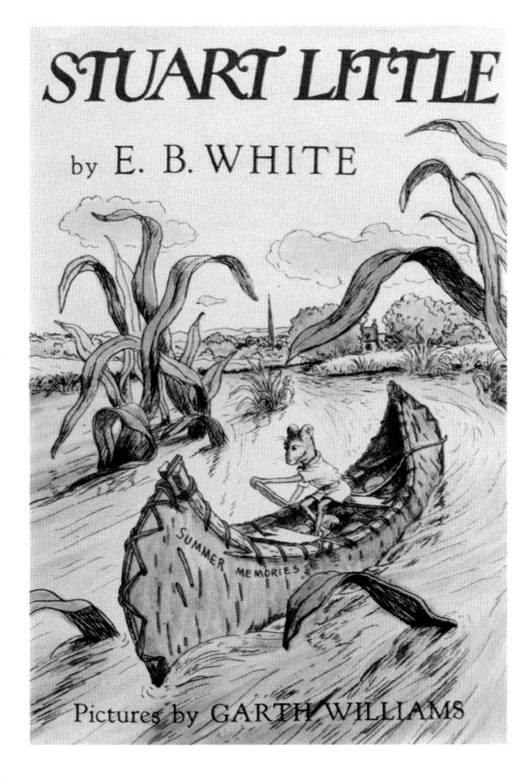

Even in New York City, few families have a mouse as a child. However, the Little family gamely accept their second adopted son, Stuart—with the exception, that is, of Snowbell the cat, who wants to eat him.

Despite his diminutive size, Stuart bravely goes down the drain looking for a ring, sails a boat on a pond in Central Park, and struggles back from being thrown out with the garbage. Even though his parents are loving—Mrs. Little makes the mouse a little suit—Stuart leaves home in search of his friend, the bird Margalo. He never returns, but drives his bright yellow car on a series of adventures, including a ghastly stint as a substitute teacher, that shed a wry light on America.

It is perhaps not too fanciful to suggest that E. B. White casts Stuart's adventures as a hero's quest in the tradition of self-discovery novels. He leaves home for the first time, grows up, and learns to stand on his own two feet, tiny as they are. The book can be read on many levels, of which the small-scale humor of a mouse living as a human in a human world is not the most interesting, although it is probably the most appealing to younger readers. What does it mean to feel very small in a fast-paced, predatory world? How can we learn to draw on our own resources? White was a notable critic of literary style—and coauthor of the writers' style bible, *The Elements of Style*. His own writing is full of piquant detail and without sentimentality; Stuart does not mope about the Littles once he has left. The focus is on living by his wits and confronting new experiences. **VN**

"When [Stuart] arrived, everybody noticed that he was not much bigger than a mouse."

UNMISSABLE ANIMAL CLASSICS

The Jungle Book by Rudyard Kipling, 1894
Wind in the Willows by Kenneth Grahame, 1908
The Story of Doctor Dolittle by Hugh Lofting, 1920
Charlotte's Web by E. B. White, 1952
Watership Down by Richard Adams, 1972

The Bears' Famous Invasion of Sicily 1945

Dino Buzzati

Full Title | La famosa invasione degli orsi in Sicilia
Nationality | Italian, born 1906
Publisher | Rizzoli, Italy
Theme | Fantasy, Animal stories

8+

The Bears' Famous Invasion of Sicily is a charming story set on the island of Sicily in southern Italy. It has all the traits of a superb fantasy: mystery, action, exciting landscapes, moral dilemmas, and battles. The book is filled with fantastic creatures to delight young readers: a troll, Marmoset the Cat, ghosts, the Old Man of the Mountain, and of course the Bears (Bear Salnitro, Bear Babbone, Bear Gelsomino, Bear Frangipane, Bear Smeriglio, and Bear Teofilo).

After one exceptionally cold winter, the bears decide to leave their mountain home. In so doing, they come into contact with human beings and quickly discover just how disagreeable human behavior can be. The grand duke who rules the lowlands soon declares himself an enemy of the Bears, and the magician De Ambrosiis attempts many tricks. When King Leander discovers that his son Tony, who had been kidnapped many years before, is being held in a circus, a plan to free Tony is put into action by the Bears, and a bloody battle ensues. Tony is freed. Unfortunately, the Bears gradually begin to pick up human habits, such as getting drunk. Finally, on the advice of King Leander, they decide to return to the high mountains, disillusioned with human ways.

Dino Buzzati was a journalist, painter, and poet, as well as an author. This book, now considered a classic of children's literature, is imbued with observations on philosophy and nature. Buzzati also wrote a number of short stories featuring animals. **SMT**

Lucky Luke—Arizona 1880 1946

Morris

Nationality | Belgian, born Maurice De Bévère 1923
Publisher | *Le Journal de Spirou*, Belgium
Theme | Adventure

Cartoonist Morris's Lucky Luke is a lonesome cowboy from the American Wild West. Accompanied by his loyal and, at times, know-all horse, Jolly Jumper, he is constantly traveling through the wilds on a simple mission: to fight injustice and crime. Characteristic of Luke is his secluded yet ironic behavior, never seeking public acclaim or attention when combating the criminals. After fighting the lawbreakers, Lucky Luke is often seen riding off into the sunset, playing a tune on his mouth organ, or singing the refrain "I'm a poor lonesome cowboy." As is typical in cowboy movies, Luke will already be on his way to new adventures, forever in quest of justice.

Lucky Luke was created for Belgian comic *Spirou*. *Arizona 1880* was the cowboy champion's first adventure. With humor and satire, the author plays with the reader's preconceptions of how a cowboy should look and act. We are introduced to three bad guys: Big Belly, Pablo, and Cheat, who steal gold from the goldmine workers living in Nugget City. After several shootings, a saloon fight, and horseback chases, Lucky Luke creatively captures and wraps the thieves in barbed wire, bringing back the gold to the sheriff of Nugget City. Lucky Luke draws and shoots his six-gun faster than his own shadow, a life-saving ability that has often rescued him and his fellow citizens of the Wild West. The author keeps the reader's attention on the rapidly moving cowboy world through a blend of comic outbursts. **SML**

The Little White Horse 1946

Elizabeth Goudge C. Walter Hodges

Nationality | English, born 1900 (author); English, born 1909 (illustrator)
Publisher | University of London Press, UK
Theme | Animal stories

In 1842, after the shameful collapse of her family's fortunes, thirteen-year-old Maria Merryweather is journeying to mysterious Moonacre Manor with her governess Miss Heliotrope and dog, Wiggins. There, her cousin, Sir Benjamin Merryweather, lives in a Norman castle in the village of Silverydew at the base of Paradise Hill in the English West Country. Maria enters into a world of gentle gothic romance. Populated by characters with names such as Digweed (a gardener) and Wrolf (a dog), the valley is a magical place, where the Little White Horse of the title—a unicorn—appears at times of need. Maria's imaginary friend, Robin, from her London life, appears in real life with a cozy mother, Loveday Minette.

Maria discovers that there are "sun" and "moon" Merryweathers. Her cousin Benjamin is a sun, and she is a moon. To her dismay, sun and moon are locked in a struggle that resonates from the original founding of the estate. With self-sacrifice, perseverance, and the help of all the wonderful beasts in the valley—not forgetting disdainful and intelligent cat Zachariah and regal and elusive hare Serena—Maria is able to heal the ancient feud and bring peace to Moonacre.

This tale lingers in the mind like a magical tapestry, with a child's view of grotesque yet lovable adults and the glowing benevolence of pet animals. Goudge was writing at a time of austerity, and a delight in sensuous pleasures, of food, and color—and peaceful coexistence—permeates this charming novel. **VN**

"And then the little cavalcade . . . trotted gaily out of the stable-yard."

OTHER ELIZABETH GOUDGE TITLES

Island Magic, 1934
Smoky House, 1940
Henrietta's House, 1942
Green Dolphin Country, 1944
The Scent of Water, 1963

8+

Anne Fine reviews:

Mistress Masham's Repose 1946

T. H. White Fritz Eichenberg

Nationality | English, born 1906 (author); American, born 1901 (illustrator)
Publisher | G. P. Putnam's Sons, USA
Theme | Fantasy

8+

OTHER T. H. WHITE CLASSIC READS

The Sword in the Stone, 1938
The Queen of Air and Darkness, 1939
The Ill-Made Knight, 1940
The Goshawk, 1951
The Candle in the Wind, 1958

Open this book and you step into a magic place: the gloriously shabby, half-forgotten palace of Malplaquet, with corridors so long that Cook needs to use a bicycle and magnificent overgrown gardens that stretch almost forever, rich with vistas and cascades and studded with obelisks and rotundas.

Young orphan Maria wanders away from the great house with its gun rooms and ballrooms, and finds—on a tiny island in the middle of the lake—a hidden world peopled by descendants of the few Lilliputians it seems Gulliver brought back from his travels. So tiny that a frog's leg does them for their Christmas dinner, they are stalked by foxes as large as the National Gallery, and their babies are in constant danger of being snatched from their walnut-shell cradles by magpies. So they are justly proud of their 200 years of secret self-reliance in the old pillared summer temple where Mistress Masham once reposed.

"She looked at the shell—looked with the greatest astonishment. There was a baby in it."

This book has everything an imaginative young reader could want: a hidden will; a sneaky and grasping vicar; a mean-minded, kitten-drowning governess; a bumbling scholar starving gently in his tumbledown cottage in the grounds; and dangers, excitements, chases, imprisonments, and revelations. We love the heroine as much for her weaknesses and wild moods as for her passionately high ideals and boundless generosity. A few passages will test even the most passionate reader, but they will soon learn which parts to skate over until they are old enough to understand them better, and the rest is bliss to read—over and over and over.

Maria must help protect the civilization of tiny people. 

Comet in Moominland 1946

Tove Jansson

Original Title | Kometjakten
Nationality | Finnish, born 1914
Publisher | Söderström, Finland
Theme | Fantasy

This book introduces the Moomins—white, round, furry, musical characters that somewhat resemble hippopotamuses. At the start of the story, Moomintroll and Sniff decide to follow a mysterious path to the sea. They have a wonderful day and also meet some of the characters who appear in other Moomin books, including the cheeky, cackling silk monkey and the philosophical Muskrat. Muskrat tells Moomintroll and Sniff that he feels the doom of approaching comets.

Frightened that the coming comet will mean the end of life in Moominvalley, Moomintroll and Sniff leave their families and embark on an expedition to find an observatory that they have been told is hidden in the Lonely Mountains. On the way they have exciting adventures, including an encounter with a giant spiny lizard who is jealously guarding a hoard of beautiful, shining garnets. Snufkin, "one of the world's wanderers," joins their expedition, and they are all saved from peril by the Hemulen, a gloomy philatelist. They also meet the Snork Maiden and her brother. Moomintroll saves the Snork Maiden's life, when she is threatened by a poisonous bush. This leads to her falling in love with him.

When they fail to find the observatory, Moomintroll and Sniff return to Moominvalley, where everyone takes shelter in the cave. Eventually they emerge to discover, to their amazement, that the comet has passed by safely. Filled with Nordic charm and gloom, the Moomin books ponder life and its meaning. **LH**

The School for Cats 1947

Esther Averill

Nationality | American, born 1902
Publisher | Harper and Brothers, USA
Theme | Animal stories, School, Adventure

Jenny Linsky is a shy black cat living in New York with Captain Tinker. You can recognize Jenny by her red scarf. It is the one that the captain knitted for her himself. It is summer, and Captain Tinker is going to sea, so he sends Jenny to the country to a boarding school for cats. Jenny has never been to any school before and she is scared and homesick.

On the first evening things take a turn for the worse when Pickles, a big spotted cat who lives with the firemen in the engine house, bumps his fire truck into Jenny's bed. Jenny jumps off the bed and escapes into the chimney. The next morning, still fearful, she runs away and gets to the train station just as the train pulls in bringing two more students to the school. Looking at the new arrivals, whom she deems the "most attractive cats she had ever seen," Jenny regrets having run away and decides to return to school.

On the way back, Jenny spends the night in the forest and reaches school just in time for breakfast. There, all the cats are seated around the table and, to her joy, she is seated between Florio and Tiger James, whom she saw the previous day at the train station. Pickles gets into his fire truck and comes honking straight at her, but this time Jenny is not scared. She flies at him with a big shout, knocking the truck over with Pickles beneath it. When he crawls out, Pickles acknowledges defeat and becomes Jenny's best friend. It turns out to be one of the happiest summers Jenny has ever had. **IW**

8+

The Moomins make their way through the Lonely Mountains.

Misty of Chincoteague 1947

Marguerite Henry   Wesley Dennis

"There was no wild sweep to her mane and tail now. The free wild thing was caught . . ."

MARGUERITE HENRY'S HORSE BOOKS

King of the Wind, 1948
Sea Star Orphan of Chincoteague, 1949
Brighty of the Grand Canyon, 1953
Stormy Misty's Foal, 1963
Mustang, Wild Spirit of the West, 1966

Nationality | American, born 1902 (author); American, born 1903 (illustrator)
Publisher | Rand McNally, USA
Theme | Animal stories

Marguerite Henry's wonderful books about horses have delighted generations of readers, both boys and girls. *Misty of Chincoteague* is based on a true story from the author's own experience.

Youngsters Paul and Maureen Beebe who live with their grandparents, desire to own Phantom, one of the wildest mares on the island (off the coast of Maryland and Virginia; home to the famous Chincoteague ponies). The children have worked hard to raise the money to buy her. They are sure that they can tame her and train her, even though it was said that she was like the wind and that the "white map" on her shoulders was her own mark of freedom.

Phantom is the wildest mare on the entire island and has evaded the roundup men who have tried to capture her during the Wild Pony Penning Day for the last two years. When Paul manages to do what no one else has been able to do—capture Phantom, as well as her colt—no one is more surprised than he, but he and Maureen now need to raise the money to buy both horses. As it turns out, Phantom is forever a creature of the wild, but her loyal colt, Misty, is another story. The plot evokes the magical life on the Island of Chincoteague, but it also captures the dilemma of wild animals being brought into captivity and the dichotomy of the human and natural world.

The story of Misty was made into a movie of that name in 1961, which was filmed largely on location on the Virginian island of Chincoteague. **KD**

Billy Bunter of Greyfriars School 1947

Frank Richards

Nationality | English, born Charles Harold St. John Hamilton 1876
Publisher | Charles Skilton, UK
Theme | School, Favorite characters

Stories about life at boarding school are as popular now as when William George "Billy" Bunter, or "the fat Owl of the Remove," was first invented. Bunter and his school chums at Greyfriars School—the "Famous Five" of Harry Wharton, Bob Cherry, Frank Nugent, Johnny Bull, and Hurree Jamset Ram Singh, or "Inky"—were the precursors to such contemporary characters and first appeared in the boys' weekly comic, *The Magnet*. When the comic ceased publication in 1940, writer Charles Hamilton, under the *nom de plume* of Frank Richards, began a series of novels featuring the escapades of Bunter and his friends.

A fat, bespectacled, comic figure, given to eating piles of (often stolen) treats, Bunter is an antihero, whose nemesis is his teacher Henry Samuel Quelch. The character of Bunter has become infamous in popular culture as a signifier of a greedy, fat boy, yet this fails to take into account the affection engendered by the character of Hamilton's stories. It still remains today, although Bunter's gluttony is likely to be less desirable to contemporary parents than in the postwar years of rationing.

Hamilton's books were adapted into a television series that charmed a generation of young British viewers with their tales of crazy capers in the school quad. Although now somewhat dated in their world-view, what continues to makes the Bunter stories appealing is their humor, slapstick comedy, and subversive sense of fun. **CK**

The Twenty-One Balloons 1947

William Pène Du Bois

Nationality | French, born 1916
Publisher | Viking Press, USA
Award | Newbery Medal, 1948
Theme | Fantasy, Adventure

This eccentric, fun tale builds on the traditions of fantasy and science fiction. It tells the story of a retired mathematics teacher, Professor William Waterman Sherman, who decides to spend a year in a hot-air balloon circumnavigating the globe. He sets off in his giant balloon, *The Globe*, in August, 1883. However, while crossing the Pacific Ocean, he has to crash-land on the volcanic island of Krakatoa (the real Krakatoa is in the Indian Ocean). There he discovers its inhabitants share the profits from a secret diamond mine and have created a world of fantastical inventions, such as beds that change their own sheets, which William Pène Du Bois beautifully illustrates.

The twenty families living on the island are referred to only by their initials, Mrs. F, Mr. M, and so on. They appear to live in a state of Utopian peace in what is a close-knit community, dining at one another's houses on a daily basis and each offering their guests a different kind of cuisine according to the dictates of the community's own "gourmet government." The twenty-one balloons featured in the book's title refer to the escape vessel that the professor builds with the islanders when they are forced to flee their island paradise because the volcano is due to erupt.

The Twenty-One Balloons packs elements of fantasy, travel, science fiction, and adventure into its pages, but Du Bois's droll prose also subtly questions what wealth and a lack of worry about money can mean for society. **CK**

SPORTI

Hurrah for St. Trinian's 1948

Ronald Searle

Nationality | English, born 1920
Publisher | Macdonald, UK
Theme | School, Classics, Adventure, Controversial

Cartoonist Ronald Searle's hell-raising St. Trinian's schoolgirls have become some of the most loved antiheroines of children's literature. Their popularity has endured from the 1950s to the present day, where they have been inscribed into popular culture through the medium of film. The concept of the exclusive girls' boarding school, traditionally the kind of institution governed by the strictest of discipline, is blown apart at the shambolic St. Trinian's. Under the vague watch of several disreputable schoolmistresses, the students are a terrifying troupe of smoking, drinking, gambling, scruffily attired young girls with no regard for authority.

Searle's cartoons are unapologetically rough around the edges; the girls are dressed in a school uniform said to be modeled on one worn by his daughter. The figures are all angles, with sharp little expressions knotted into mischief, and not a pretty face in sight. Committing various violent but comical acts on one another, often during alarmingly rough sporting events, the schoolgirls run rampant through the school and its surrounding environment, playing out their various rivalries.

Although Searle's illustrations have often been based on more serious topics, he remains best known for these original naughty schoolgirls. It might be a parent's worst nightmare, but *Hurrah for St. Trinian's* provides the ultimate respite for good little girls in need of some mischief. **LK**

The Fantastic Antoñita 1948

Borita Casas Mariano Zaragüeta

Nationality | Spanish, born Liborio Reguerio Casas 1911 (author); details unknown (illustrator)
Publisher | Gils, Spain
Theme | Adventure, Family

Antoñita was a very popular character during the postwar period—a sentimental girl, playful and with boundless imagination. She always talked more than necessary and was constantly living in a world of fantasy. Initially her stories were broadcast on the radio, and they enlivened many afternoons of chores. Her greatest success, however, was achieved not through the air waves, but through the printed word.

Antoñita la fantástica was created by Liborio Reguerio Casas, who was a writer and broadcaster on Radio Madrid at the end of the war. He started out writing dialogues between a child and an adult, Antoñita and Antonio respectively, and the immense popularity of his radio broadcasts led to the publication of the first Antoñita book in 1948. The series lasted until the late 1950s and comprised twelve books. The various installments are presented as notebooks in which Antoñita gathers together episodes of her life. With her own peculiar point of view, Antoñita recounts amusing stories involving her parents, grandmother, and aunt Carol, as well as other people of her world, such as the family's two maids and Malul, her best friend. Her adventures are filled with imagination and show the dichotomy that exists between the different ways adults and children understand the world.

The series was a best seller in its time. Its value as a classic of Spanish children's literature is that it chronicles everyday life in 1940s and 1950s Madrid from a child's point of view. **EB**

8+

"Hard cheese, Maisie—your horse wasn't placed."

Autumn Term 1948

 Antonia Forest

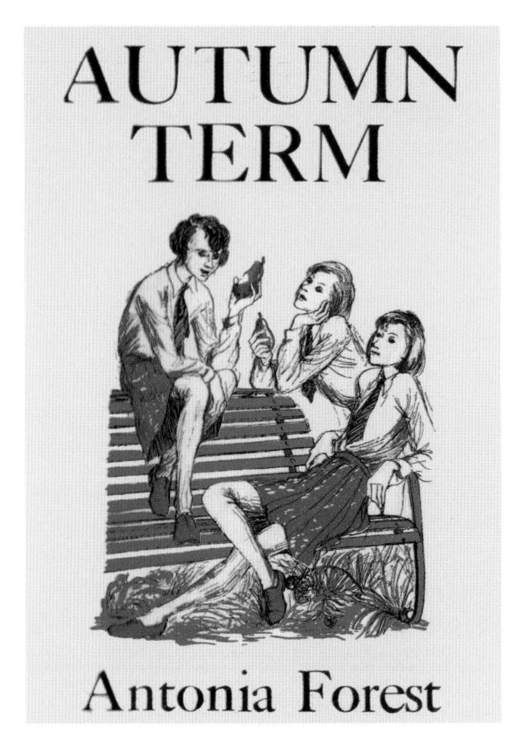

Nationality | English, born Patricia Giulia Caulfield Kate Rubinstein, 1915
Publisher | Faber and Faber, UK
Theme | School

Antonia Forest wrote thirteen books for children. *Autumn Term* was the first of her stories about the Marlow children and their time at Kingscote School. The series was hailed as being unlike any other books in children's fiction. Although firmly set in a conformist middle-class England between the 1940s to 1970s, where children go to boarding school, think about religion and history, farm ancestral land, and strive for sporting glory, the stories are subversive. All the characters have complex inner lives, even the bullies. They fall into rages, are disappointed by unrealistic aspirations, are cut down to size by family and friends, and reflect on books and the oddness of adults. In short, they grow up, little by little, in each volume.

Autumn Term begins with twins Nicola and Lawrie Marlow setting off with high hopes for their first term at Kingscote School. Nicola, one of the most rounded female characters in literature, wants to excel at sports, academic work, popularity, and—life, really. Highly strung Lawrie is unreliable and inattentive, with an exasperating talent for dramatics. Despite their best efforts to not spoil the reputation of their family, they get into scrapes—suspected arson, unauthorized stopping of a train, and demotion to the dunces' class.

Forest's other titles about the school include *End of Term* (1959), *The Cricket Term* (1974), and *The Attic Term* (1976). The author carefully retained a great air of anonymity, requesting that not even her real name be revealed during her lifetime. **VN**

"Nicola knew that the true, keen edge of pleasure was, if ever so little, dulled."

OTHER SCHOOL ADVENTURES

***Hurrah for St. Trinian's* by Ronald Searle, 1948**
***The Turbulent Term of Tyke Tiler* by Gene Kemp, 1977**
***Harry Potter and the Philosopher's Stone* by J. K. Rowling, 1997**

Finn Family Moomintroll 1948

Tove Jansson

Original Title | Trollkarlens hatt
Nationality | Finnish, born 1914
Publisher | Holger Schildts Förlag, Finland
Theme | Fantasy

This is the third book in the Moomin series and one of the best known of Tove Jansson's books. In the first two books, the Moomins have encountered a great flood and a fearful comet. In *Finn Family Moomintroll* they have to contend with a hobgoblin's magic hat.

The adventure starts with a snowy winter in Moominvalley, with everyone preparing for the long winter's sleep. When the first cuckoo announces the arrival of spring, Moomintroll and his friends, Snufkin and Sniff, set out for an adventure. They climb a mountain and find a hat, which they take home. Moominpappa tries it on, but it does not suit him, so he uses it as a wastebasket. Unbeknownst to the Moomins, things thrown into the hat change into other things (for example an eggshell thrown into it becomes five little clouds).

Moomintroll, Snufkin, and Sniff have all been having the same bad dream "about a nasty little man." They do not know it but he is the hobgoblin, the owner of the hat. They realize the hat has strange powers when Moomintroll hides in it during a game and is changed into an animal that none of them recognize; then when they try to throw the hat away in the stream, the water turns into raspberry juice. They decide to put the hat in their cave, but it still manages to cause mischief. Eventually the angry hobgoblin comes to find his hat, but the residents of Moominvalley make friends with him and, at the end of the story, the hobgoblin grants wishes for his new friends. **LH**

Amazon Adventure 1949

Willard Price

Nationality | American, born 1887
Publisher | John Day, USA
Theme | Adventure, Animal stories, Science and nature

Teenagers Hal and Roger Hunt are about to go to the Amazon with their zoologist father in search of specimens for zoos when they receive a threatening anonymous message warning them not to go. Nevertheless, they set off along the river in a large convoy of boats that will house their growing menagerie. News of a disaster at home means the boys' father has to leave, but the brothers continue the expedition without him. Pursued by murderous enemies, the boys and their crew struggle to collect yet larger and more dangerous species. Hal and Roger are shot at, crushed by snakes, and attacked by jaguars. There is real danger here, and both animals and people die. Hal and Roger's situation becomes more and more precarious until they are left without crew, boat, or animals and with angry, bloodthirsty Indians on their tail. By sheer chance, they catch up with their stolen boat and animals, and manage to capture the enemy.

Amazon Adventure is an entertaining story interwoven with an informative portrait of the Amazon and its wildlife, and is filled with fascinating facts about survival in the wild. Some of the information may be a little out-of-date—and certainly the thrill of hunting and the collecting of animals for zoos is not condoned today—but the combination of sheer exuberance for the natural world with edge-of-the-seat excitement is likely to have readers reaching out for the next book in the series. **CW**

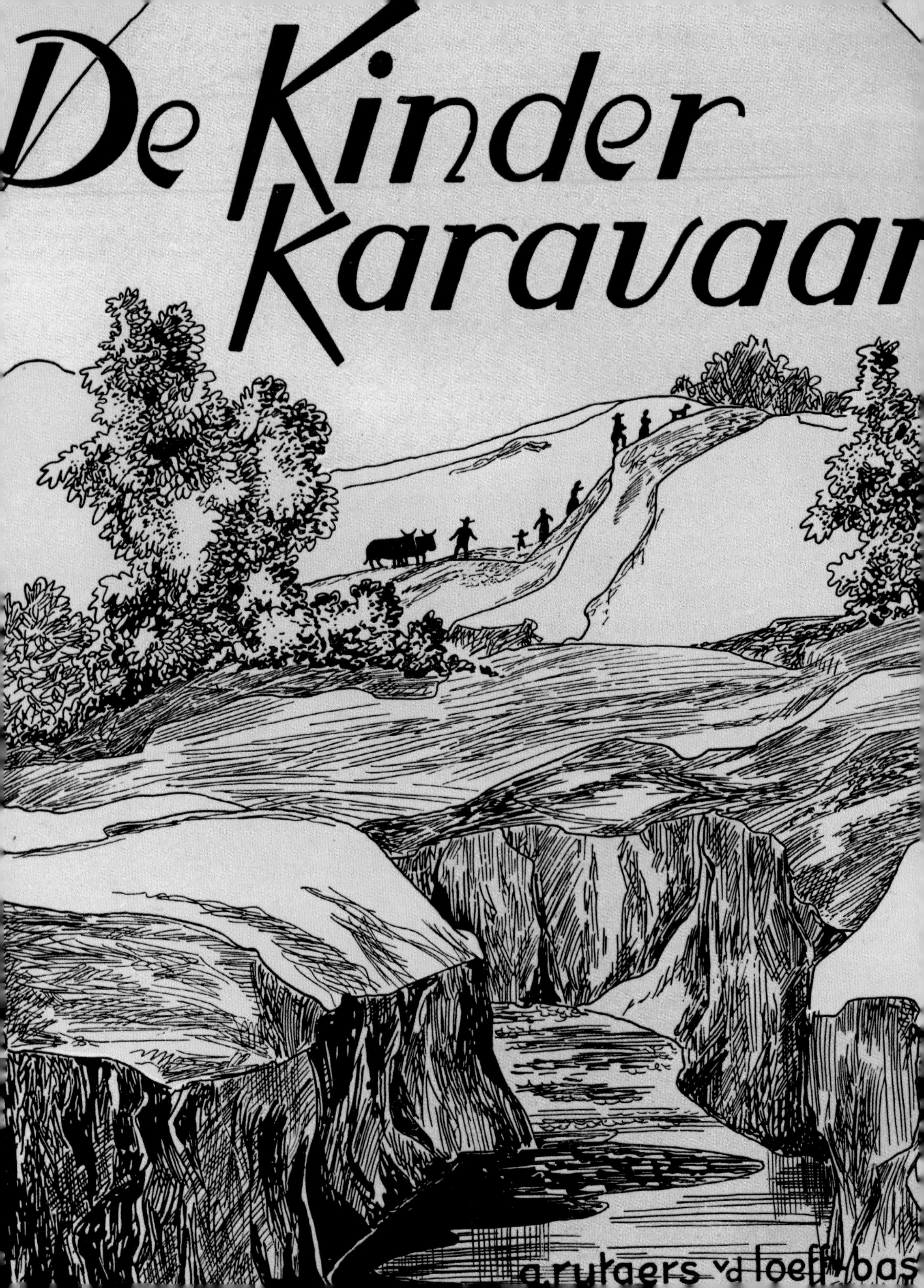
De Kinder
Karavaa
a.rutgers v.d loeff-bas

Children on the Oregon Trail 1949

A. Rutgers van der Loeff C. Hollander

Nationality | Dutch, born 1910 (author); Dutch, born 1934 (illustrator)
Publisher | Ploegsma, the Netherlands
Theme | Adventure, Historical fiction

In 1844, the seven Sager children actually made the difficult journey across hostile territory in the Pacific Northwest to Oregon, as their father had wished, and their story is told in this tale of endurance, hardship, and courage (originally titled *De kinder karavaan*).

Father had a dream to settle in the lush valleys of Oregon with his family, but when he and Mother die during the arduous journey, thirteen-year-old John determines to travel on, even though the rest of the wagon train decides to take the easier route to California. The seven children, including the newborn baby, Independentia, strike out across the mountains together with their animals Oscar the wolf dog, Walter the ox, and Anna the cow, who provides the milk vital to keep the baby alive.

Battling the elements and the harsh countryside, the seven children make it to Fort Boise. From there, they are accompanied on the last leg of their journey by Indian guides. However, the guides force a pace that the youngsters cannot maintain, and in the end they leave, taking everything except the cow. John, through sheer will and sometimes force, makes the children walk on until they arrive at their destination at the mission station.

John's loneliness as the leader forcing the pace and the individual characters of the other children—and even the cow—come alive on the pages and leave readers full of admiration for a truly remarkable adventure story. **JF**

The Thirteen Clocks 1950

James Thurber Marc Simont

Nationality | American, born 1894 (author); French, born 1915 (illustrator)
Publisher | Simon and Schuster, USA
Theme | Fantasy, Myths and legends, Fairy tales

This fantasy tale is a classic story. It tells of a prince in disguise seeking the hand of a beautiful princess who is held captive by the fearsome Duke of Coffin Castle. This book is delightfully embellished by hidden rhymes and all manner of extraordinary words, such as "guggle" and "zatch." As well as James Thurber's wordplay, it features many familiar fairy tale themes.

The duke has thirteen clocks, all of which have stopped at ten to five. Because they cannot be mended, he thinks he is powerful enough to have slain Time. He does not want his captive, Princess Saralinda, to marry, so he has set all sorts of near-impossible tasks for potential suitors—and those who have a name beginning with *X* will be killed. The prince, disguised as a minstrel, has called himself Xingu, but he manages to escape death because it is not his real name. His next task is to find a thousand jewels in ninety-nine hours and to restart all the clocks to strike five on his return. Xingu—now revealed as Prince Zorn—sets off to find Hagga, a woman on whom a spell has been cast so that she cries jewels and not tears. Our hero of course triumphs, and he also makes the clocks strike five, thus winning Saralinda.

Thurber was blind by the time he wrote this and so he could not illustrate it himself. Instead, it was beautifully visualized by his friend, the French artist and cartoonist Marc Simont, who had to describe all his pictures to Thurber in great detail. A later edition is illustrated by Ronald Searle. **JF**

The Lion, the Witch and the Wardrobe 1950

C. S. Lewis Pauline Baynes

Nationality | English, born 1898 (author); English, born 1922 (illustrator)
Publisher | Geoffrey Bles, UK
Theme | Classics, Fantasy

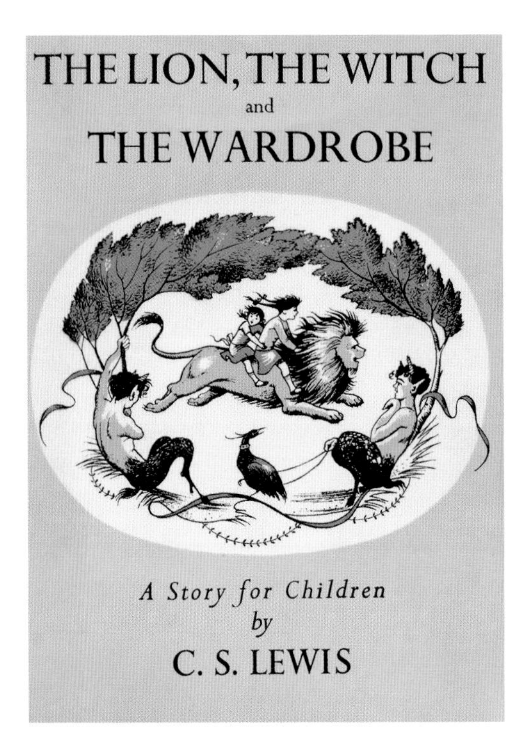

OTHER GREAT FANTASY READS

The Phantom Tollbooth by Norton Juster, 1961
The Carpet People by Terry Pratchett, 1971
The Indian in the Cupboard by Lynne Reid Banks, 1980
The Field Guide by Holly Black, 2003

The first to be published and, according to many, the best of the Narnia books, *The Lion, the Witch and the Wardrobe* is actually the second book in the series. Set during World War II, it follows the adventures of Peter, Susan, Edmund, and Lucy, four middle-class children sent to safety in the English countryside, where they stay with an eccentric professor. Left to their own devices, the children discover an old wardrobe, through which they can enter into the land of Narnia. Populated by talking animals and mythical creatures, such as centaurs and hags, Narnia is under the sway of a wicked White Witch, who has decreed that it be always winter but never Christmas. The only being who can challenge the witch is the mysterious Aslan, a lion of supernatural prowess and benevolence. The children struggle to bring down the White Witch, although they are hampered by Edmund's weakness and treachery.

"Don't you know who is the King of Beasts? Aslan is a lion—the Lion, the great Lion."

C. S. Lewis was a complex man—an academic authority on English literature and a committed Christian and theologian, with a passion for nature and mythology. All these strands find a place here. Aslan, son of the Emperor Overseas, who is resurrected after dying on a great stone table, is a Christlike figure, who gives himself up to atone for Edmund's sin and embodies Christian renunciation and redemption. The concepts of eternal winter and the lion being freed by nibbling mice come from Norse mythology and Aesop, respectively. However, the humor and joy of the endearing characters Mr. and Mrs. Beaver and Tumnus the Faun are all Lewis's own. **VN**

8+

Aslan frolics with Susan and Lucy in the original frontispiece. 

BAYNES

The Princess Who Had Magic Fingers 1950

María Luisa Gefaell Pilarín Ballés

8+

"We must teach children not to let their imagination become dull; to dream, to dare, to rebel."

OTHER FANTASTICAL FAIRY TALES

Grimms' Fairy Tales (Kinder- und Hausmärchen), **1812**
The Magic Finger **by Roald Dahl, 1966**
The Fairies of Villaviciosa de Odón (Las hadas de Villaviciosa de Odón) **by Maria Luisa Gefaell, 1979**

Nationality | Spanish, born 1918 (author); Spanish, birth date unknown (illustrator)
Publisher | José Janés, Spain
Theme | Magical stories

The Princess Who Had Magic Fingers (originally titled *La Princesita que tenía los dedos mágicos*) is about the daughter of a good king. Their neighbor is a bad king in whose kingdom birds do not want to live. Despite the beauty that surrounds her and the fact that she is loved by her father and the whole kingdom, the princess is unhappy. This is because a witch has cursed her eyes so they can only see the bad side of things. Luckily her fairy godmother, the Sun, gives her a magic gift—whatever she touches is transformed into something beautiful and full of goodness. When the princess discovers the power of her magic fingers she becomes happy at last. This is until she meets Peñasco (Rocky), the son of the evil king, who can be even more cruel than his father.

María Luisa Gefaell won the National Literature Prize of Spain in 1952 for this book (which includes a number of other short stories within it). Her book offered a new vision of traditional stories written specifically for children that were praised for their literary quality, their musicality, and their use of Spain's rich tradition of oral literature.

Gefaell began writing by writing down the stories she invented for her own children. She contributed to magazines, wrote historical novels, and translated other people's works under the pseudonym María Campuzano. Although many of her works are difficult to find today, one of her most important books, *Antón Rétaco*, is still in print and is considered a classic. **EB**

Adventurous Tales of Machu Picchu 1950

Ciro Alegría

Original Title | Las aventuras de Machu Picchu
Nationality | Peruvian, born 1909
Publisher | Unknown
Theme | Folktales, Traditional

The Adventurous Tales of Machu Picchu tells the story of a young shepherd who has spent his childhood and adult life in the beautiful Peruvian highlands. The story is a simple one and its protagonist an ordinary, unambitious shepherd who only dreams of having a wife, a cozy house and, above all, an heir to his earthly possessions, so passing on his simple wealth from generation to generation.

Ciro Alegría's real concern when writing this story, however, was much more ambitious. Just like other great writers of his generation concerned with *Indigenismo*—such as José María Sánchez Barra, José Pérez Vargas, César Vega Herrera, and José María Arguedas—his intentions were literary, ethnographic, and patriotic. His goal was to write about the lives of the Peruvian indigenous people of whom he had gained firsthand knowledge when growing up in the province of Huamachuco. Through the life of an ordinary shepherd, he aimed to make his readers familiar with the native clothing, traditions, and legends of the Peruvian region.

In these simple adventures he also retells ancient stories that are rooted in the oral traditions of pre-Columbian civilizations, some dating as far back as the Incas. There are few Peruvian writers specializing in children's literature, so Alegría's work, which skillfully rescues themes, characters, legends, and stories from the Peruvian oral tradition, has ensured these tales' integration into modern Peruvian culture. **LB**

Tales of Uncle Rabbit 1950

Euclides Jaramillo

Original Title | Cuentos del picaro tio conejo
Nationality | Colombian, born 1910
Publisher | Editorial Iquiema, Colombia
Theme | Folktales, Classics

The adventures of Juan el Zorro (John the Fox), as they are usually known in the Spanish-speaking world, have a Colombian equivalent in Euclides Jaramillo's *Tales of Uncle Rabbit*. These picaresque stories form the first of Jaramillo's collections of folktales, a field in which this polymath (lawyer, novelist, politician, and journalist) would become famous for his research, the vastness of his collections, and his prolific writing.

Uncle Rabbit is a cunning, consummate joker who appears as the main character in hundreds of stories, legends, tales, and adventures in the folk tradition. While these stories were normally passed orally from one generation to the next, Jaramillo was one of the first to systematically collect them and write them down. The most famous story in the collection is "*Tío conejo y la zorra muerta*" ("Uncle Rabbit and the Dead Fox"), in which Uncle Wolf and Aunt Fox, who are tired of being constantly harassed by Uncle Rabbit, devise a plan to get rid of him. Aunt Fox will pretend to be dead, and when the curious Uncle Rabbit comes to have a look they will kill him. However, Uncle Rabbit is clever enough to suspect a trap. When he sees Aunt Fox lying on her bed he exclaims, "I know you are not dead, because when a fox dies, she shakes her right leg, and yours lies still," whereupon Aunt Fox frantically shakes her right leg, revealing her deceit. The simple, humorous stories were famously illustrated by two ten-year-old children, simply known as Hernán and Marietta, rather than a professional illustrator. **LB**

Kimba 1950

Osamu Tezuka

Original Title | Jyangeru taitei
Nationality | Japanese, born 1928
Publisher | Kodansha, Japan
Theme | Animal stories

Before becoming a creator of manga comics, Osamu Tezuka studied for a career in medicine. Consequently, a concern for the delicacy of all living creatures informs most of his literary work. *Kimba the White Lion* (known in Japan as *Jungle Emperor*) is the story of a lion who tries to foster understanding between the natural and the human world. It is full of the interconnectedness between living things and the damaging effects of violence upon the natural cycles of life and death.

Kimba (Leo in the original) is born in captivity after his father is killed by a hunter and his mother is captured and placed in a circus. Most of the story concerns Kimba's journey to his parents' home and the relationships he forms with other animals and humans along the way. Kimba assumes his father's role as leader and protector of the jungle and tries to incorporate certain human values into the animal world. An almost messianic figure, Kimba sacrifices his own life to save a human friend, who learns from the lion how to find the path of peaceful coexistence between humans and animals.

This popular manga was made into Japan's first full-color animated TV series in 1965 (later re-dubbed in English-speaking countries as *Kimba*). In 1994, controversy erupted when Disney denied claims that its film *The Lion King* had borrowed heavily from Kimba without permission. Had he been alive, Tezuka, who freely admitted to lifting story elements from films such as *Bambi* and *Pinocchio*, would no doubt have been amused. **CR**

Prince Caspian 1951

C. S. Lewis Pauline Baynes

Nationality | English, born 1898 (author); English, born 1922 (illustrator)
Publisher | Geoffrey Bles, UK
Theme | Classics, Fantasy

This book begins a year after the end of *The Lion, the Witch and the Wardrobe*. The four Pevensey children are whisked back to Narnia, where centuries have passed. Again, the talking animals and mythical creatures need human help, this time to assist the rightful king, Caspian, fight his usurping uncle and the invading Telmarines. It turns out the children have been summoned by a council of war—led by Trumpkin the dwarf, Reepicheep the mouse, Glenstorm the centaur, and Trufflehunter the badger—who are disconcerted that the kings and queens of Narnian legend are a bunch of teenagers. The magic works, however, and soon Aslan reappears. Again, the forces of good have to contend with treachery in their ranks, but they win the battle at the fords of Beruna, partly helped by Lucy's magic cordial. Some of the defeated Telmarines choose to go back through the doorway between worlds, just as the human children must.

This is a simpler book than its predecessor, with more emphasis on the comedy of talking animals and the evocation of mythical characters. Yet it is still full of Lewis's characteristic allusions to Christian morality and the Bible, including possibly the story of Moses. Courage and chivalry are heralded in the context of moral difficulties, such as how to make others do the right thing. Some critics claim that Lewis intended the disbelief in Aslan to be widespread in Narnia at the start of the series, to mirror modern secularism; its rout, then, is a vicarious triumph for faith. Generations of readers have enjoyed the novels, however, simply for their imaginative adventures. **VN**

Little Onion 1951

Gianni Rodari Raul Verdini

Nationality | Italian, born 1920 (author); Italian, birth date unknown (illustrator)
Publisher | Edizioni di Cultura Sociale, Italy
Theme | Classics, Fantasy, Quirky

Gianni Rodari is one of Italy's greatest children's writers and a winner of the Hans Christian Andersen Award (1970). *Little Onion* (published in Italian as *Le avventure di Cipollino*) is one of his early works. It is a tale of magical realism and biting satire. Rodari takes readers into a topsy-turvy world in which the protagonists come from the world of vegetables. There is Prince Lemon (Principe Limone), Knight Tomato (Cavaliere Pomodoro), Craftsman Raisin (Mastro Uvetta), Leek Pirro (Pirro Porro), Sister Pumpkin (Sora Zucca), and, of course, Little Onion (Cipollino).

Rodari once said that when he discovered he could write for children, he took a month's holiday in order to write a novel. He rented a barn on a farm in the Modena countryside and borrowed a typewriter from the local Communist Party. The farmer's children, with whom he was constantly surrounded, would wake him in the morning and remind him that he was there to work. During this time Rodari wrote the adventures of Little Onion.

Little Onion is forced to leave the city because the totalitarian Prince Lemon cannot bear the smell of onion, nor the sight of it. The prince also has Little Onion's father thrown into prison. Little Onion secretly visits his father, taking him some possessions, and then escapes from Prince Lemon's kingdom. Unable to go to school, the world becomes his education. He discovers that many others are also oppressed by Prince Lemon and resolves to work to overthrow the prince and restore a fair and just society, even instituting a republic. **SMT**

"The honest onion family were good people . . . but they didn't have an easy time of it. Where there are onions, there are tears."

OTHER GIANNI RODARI FAVORITES

Nursery Rhymes in the Sky and on Earth (Filastrocche in cielo e in terra), 1960
Telephone Tales (Favole al telefono), 1962
The Book of Errors (Il libro degli errori), 1964
A Pie in the Sky (La Torta in cielo), 1966

8+

The Voyage of the *Dawn Treader* 1952

C. S. Lewis Pauline Baynes

Nationality | English, born 1898 (author); English, born 1922 (illustrator)
Publisher | Geoffrey Bles, UK
Theme | Classics, Fantasy

8+

OTHER BOOKS IN THE NARNIA SERIES

***The Lion, the Witch and the Wardrobe*, 1950**
***Prince Caspian*, 1951**
***The Silver Chair*, 1953**
***The Horse and His Boy*, 1954**
***The Magician's Nephew*, 1955**

The sequel to *Prince Caspian* sees the youngest Pevensey children, Edmund and Lucy, returning to Narnia with their unappealing cousin Eustace Scrubb. Caspian is now a king, voyaging with Reepicheep the mouse to the far edges of the world to find the seven lost lords of Narnia, as he had promised Aslan. Eustace does not pull his weight and on the second port of call he is trapped by his own greed into becoming a dragon, until Aslan helps him repent. They also call at Burnt Island, Deathwater Island (so-called for a pool of water that turns everything immersed in it into gold), Duffers' Island, and the Island Where Dreams Come True (but so do nightmares). Finally they arrive at a huge waterfall that Reepicheep crosses in a coracle.

"So all afternoon with great joy they sailed southeast with a fair wind."

They see him no more, but travel on to a paradisiacal land beyond the edge where they meet Aslan, transmogrified into a lamb.

Non-Christians have sometimes found Lewis's overtly Christian symbolism unsatisfactory. The children ask Aslan if he is not in their world. He replies, "I am . . . but there I have another name. You must learn to know me by that name. This was the very reason why you were brought to Narnia, that by knowing me here for a little, you may know me better there." There are occasional slippages of tone when some of Lewis's interests—in religion, mythology, and nature—collide. However, his inventiveness mostly succeeds in blending allusions to Arthurian quests, Greek myths, Dante, and even, perhaps, the abdication crisis of the British King Edward VIII into a playful and engaging story. **VN**

The Borrowers 1952

Mary Norton Diana Stanley

Nationality | English, born 1903 (author); American, birth date unknown (illustrator)
Publisher | Dent, UK
Theme | Classics, Fantasy

Most children long to grow up and venture into the outside world; it is a rite of passage to want to explore. The adventurous protagonist of the Borrowers series, thirteen-year-old Arrietty Clock, faces particular difficulties in that she is a mere seven inches tall. Arrietty is one of the "borrowers," tiny people who live secretly in houses, making their diminutive homes behind mantelpieces and skirting boards, all the time doing everything they can to avoid being spotted by the big people they call "human beans."

Arrietty lives with her father, Pod, and her mother, Homily, under the floorboards of an English country house. Part of the book's considerable charm is its Lilliputian perspective on the world. What may be ordinary and harmless to human beings can become fascinating or malevolent for this tiny species. It's also fun to see how the family purloin (or in the story's parlance "borrow") everyday items such as buttons that are recycled to become useful pieces of furniture.

"They imagined they had their own names but . . . you could tell they were borrowed."

Pod is ever inventive in finding ways to support his family and navigate his surroundings, such as his daring way of scaling curtains with the aid of a hat pin, but the foraging expeditions that Arrietty and her father go on are often fraught with danger. It is during one of her forays to the outside world that Arrietty is spotted by the Boy, a young lad who has come to stay with his bedridden great aunt. Arrietty befriends the lonely boy, who soon showers her family with gifts of dollhouse furniture. It is the tale of their friendship, and how the Boy comes to the family's rescue, that makes this book a classic. **CK**

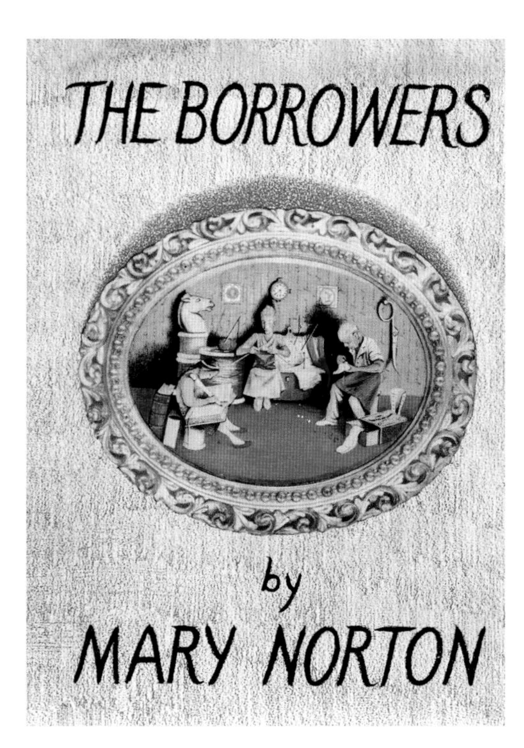

8+

OTHER GREAT MARY NORTON TITLES

The Magic Bed Knob; or, How to Become a Witch in Ten Easy Lessons, 1943
The Borrowers Afield, 1955
The Borrowers Afloat, 1959
The Borrowers Aloft, 1961

Astro Boy (Mighty Atom) 1952

Osamu Tezuka

Original Title | Tetsuwan Atomu
Nationality | Japanese, born 1928
Publisher | Kodansha, Japan
Theme | Fantasy, Classics, Comics

8+

Unquestionably the most widely known Japanese comic character (and one of the world's most recognizable cartoon figures), the diminutive robot Astro Boy was created by Japan's "god of manga," Osamu Tezuka. *Astro Boy* stands at the pinnacle of his oeuvre in terms of popularity, both at home and internationally, largely because of the success of the animated television series broadcast in Japan and abroad in 1963.

In the story, Astro Boy ("Mighty Atom" in Japan) was created by the genius roboticist Dr. Tenma as a replacement for his deceased son, Tobio. After being rejected by his inventor, Astro is discovered in the circus by a kind scientist, who creates a robotic family for him. Although equipped with an atomic engine and an array of devices, such as rockets in his hands and feet, a finger laser and twin machine guns mounted in his posterior, Astro's greatest asset is his ability to feel love and compassion. Thus, he only uses his great powers to protect those in need, uphold justice, and preserve peace between humans and robots, the latter having become a new underclass with limited rights in a futuristic society.

The character of Astro Boy has come to represent the responsible and altruistic use of technology, reflecting Tezuka's ideals of pacifism and tolerance. Much more than a simple adventure series, *Astro Boy* is a touchstone for the technological age, with all its wonders and potential dangers explored. **CR**

Marcelino, Bread and Wine 1952

José María Sánchez Silva L. Goñi

Nationality | Spanish, born 1911 (author); Spanish, born 1911 (illustrator)
Publisher | Editorial Cigüeña, Spain
Theme | Classics, Friendship

In *Marcelino, Bread and Wine* (originally titled *Marcelino, pan y vino)*, the title character is a little boy who was abandoned at the gates of a monastery. By the time the book starts, he has lived for five years in the care of the monks. Marcelino is like any normal child, mischievous and rebellious, but he lives in a sort of earthly paradise, hunting wall lizards and playing in the monastery's fields and orchard. One day, in spite of it being strictly forbidden, he climbs up to the attic. There he meets a very tall man who is the image of the crucified Jesus Christ. Marcelino feels sorry for him and secretly takes food to him each day.

This book can be read as an imaginary work, in which the miracles are an integral part of the plot and do not adversely affect its narrative structure, still less its originality, its simplicity, and the richness of its prose. Similarly, it can be seen as a serious theological work, without sentimentality and far from the clichés of devout literature, in spite of the fact that the tear-jerking movie version of 1955 caused much irritation. Nonetheless, it is also a story written in the style of a wonderful tale, the hero of which is an orphan who must pass a test before ultimately achieving his dream: to be reunited with his mother.

Sánchez Silva was himself orphaned at the age of ten. When he published the three Marcelino stories in one volume, it was an unprecedented success. More than 200 editions were sold and it was translated into more than thirty languages. **EB**

Jennings and Darbishire 1952

Anthony Buckeridge

Nationality | English, born 1912
Publisher | Collins, UK
Theme | School, Favorite characters, Classics, Friendship

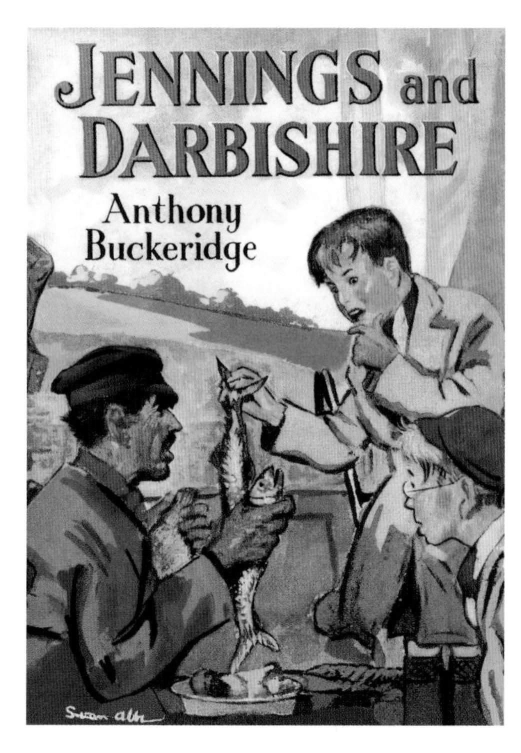

Schoolboy characters Jennings and Darbishire appeared in twenty-five books that spanned more than forty years. Throughout them all, the boys remain ten years old and the community of Linbury Court Preparatory School (influenced by the author's years of teaching in a similar institution) does not change. The housemaster Mr. Carter is forever calm and forbearing; form master (homeroom teacher) Mr. Wilkins is always on the edge of a "supersonic bate" at some "frantic bishes" committed by the boys; and the headmaster, Mr. Pemberton-Oakes, is permanently pompous. *Jennings and Darbishire* is the fourth book in the series. In it, the two friends create all sorts of havoc when they publish *The Form Three Times*.

Anthony Buckeridge, whose first Jennings stories were written for radio, understood the importance of a solid structure and strong characters. Jennings is like William Brown in the Just William books—he does not mean to get into trouble but trouble seems to get into him. Darbishire, a mild-mannered and dreamy son of a clergyman, finds himself carried along in Jennings's wake. Linbury Court offers rules to be broken and a stable environment to be shaken up.

The Jennings books are for literate readers, who will relish the catchphrases ("fossilized fish-hooks!" and "petrified paint-pots!") and get maximum value from the malapropisms and misunderstandings. It is the writing that sets the books apart, keeping them eternally fresh and funny for each new generation. **GB**

"'For goodness' sake,' Jennings protested, 'how can we have a race if you go on sitting there?'"

MORE WACKY JENNINGS STORIES

Jennings Goes to School, 1950
Jennings Follows a Clue, 1951
Jennings's Little Hut, 1951
Jennings's Diary, 1953
Jennings at Large, 1977

8+

Down with Skool! 1953

Geoffrey Willans Ronald Searle

Nationality | English, born 1911 (author); English, born 1920 (illustrator)
Publisher | Max Parrish, UK
Theme | Quirky, School, Classics

Down with Skool! and its successors are set in the world of a richly satirized British preparatory school—in this case, a private boarding school for boys aged nine to thirteen. The hero and narrator Nigel Molesworth ("the goriller of 3b and curse of St. Custard's"), a pupil at one such establishment, provides a guide to the rigors of school life.

What gives the series (which is consistent in quality throughout) its particular and, to its admirers, irresistible flavor is partly Willans's deft way with language: Molesworth's misspellings, schoolboy slang, and inventive phrase-making are enjoyed not only by young readers but by adults as well, and his characterizations of the variously helpless, cynical, decrepit, idle, or comically sadistic "Masters" are still recognizable by anyone who has ever taught, or been taught.

> *"This agane is due to Pythagoras and it formed much of his conversation at brekfast."*

However, a large part of the pleasure that the books provide comes from the drawings by Ronald Searle. Whereas some of Willans's satire might seem a little dated after more than fifty years, these wildly and gothically extravagant masterpieces of comic art remain timeless and pointed: "A Corner of the Playing Fields," for instance, showing a single crow looking down from a dead tree at a bleak rainswept expanse of mud, littered with empty bottles and cans; or "Masters at a Glance," with the various characters caught mercilessly ("You may think I'm soft, but I'm hard, damned hard.") In 1999 the Molesworth books were deservedly published anew in Penguin's Twentieth-Century Classics series.

OTHER QUIRKY BOOKS ABOUT SCHOOL

Hurrah for St. Trinians by Ronald Searle, 1948
Fergus Crane by Paul Stewart and Chris Riddell, 2004
Ottoline Goes to School by Chris Riddell, 2008

The wacky scribbles by Ronald Searle that adorn the book. 

Zoom
OW!!
I dye

A Kid for Two Farthings 1953

Wolf Mankowitz

Nationality | English, born 1924
Publisher | André Deutsch, UK
Theme | Classics, Magical stories, Animal stories, Illness and death

WOLF MANKOWITZ
A Kid
For
Two Farthings
WOLF MANKOWITZ

This touching story is set in a poor Jewish community in the East End of London during the 1950s. Five-year-old Joe is a child in a world filled with adults. The landlord, Mr. Kandinsky, is unhappy because he needs a steam presser for his business, and his assistant, Schmule, is unhappy because his fiancée, Sonia, wants a diamond ring. Sonia is unhappy because she wants to get married, and Joe's mother is unhappy because Joe's father is in Africa.

Joe wanders the streets alone, fearful only of a tramp, who he thinks might be the cannibal king. In the animal market he finds a Billy goat with a single budding horn. Believing that he is a unicorn, and having been told a tale that a captured unicorn will grant any wish, Joe buys the kid with his accumulated pocket money and names him Africana.

"He rode Africana through the jungle where they fought a lion, two tigers . . . They beat them all."

In the backyard Joe invents fantastic games in which he and Africana are great heroes. Later he creates a magical wish-fulfilling ritual for his friends using the magic from Africana's horn. Their desires come true, more or less, but Africana is so ill that a neighbor secretly takes the poor goat to be put down. Mr. Kandinsky pretends that the goat has returned to its parents in Africa, leaving Joe a gold sovereign.

Mankowitz, a writer, playwright, and screenwriter of Russian-Jewish descent, is superb at evoking a sense of place. The descriptions of the area and the inhabitants at this particular time are as magical as the narrative itself. He followed the book with the screenplay for the very successful movie in 1955, which was directed by Carol Reed. **WO**

OTHER SIMILAR WORKS

The Hundred Dresses by Eleanor Estes, 1944
Tar Beach by Faith Ringgold, 1991
Refugee Boy by Benjamin Zephaniah, 2001
The Arrival by Shaun Tan, 2006
How I Learned Geography by Uri Shulevitz, 2008

Half Magic 1954

Edward Eager   N. M. Bodecker

Half Magic seems a universe away from the modern world yet it still charms children today. It is set in Toledo, Ohio, during one long summer in the 1920s. The story centers on four siblings: Jane, Mark, Katharine, and Martha. While their widowed mother works at a newspaper, the children are cared for by the highly strung Miss Bick, who refuses to take them on interesting trips. One day the children discover a glinting object on the sidewalk, which turns out to be a magic charm that makes wishes come true. The catch is, it is rather worn out, so it only grants half of the wish stated. This leads to confusion and many funny episodes, from wreaking havoc in King Arthur's Camelot to being kidnapped in the desert.

"The library was two miles away; walking there was dull but coming home splendid."

This is highly wholesome fare from a simpler era, but there are still timeless episodes, such as when Jane misses her father and is not happy about the small, neatly bearded bookseller, Mr. Smith, encroaching on her mother's life. The idea of a group of children having adventures together is always engaging and finding an everyday kind of magic, as the children ultimately do, is a theme that always appeals.

Eager was a well-known playwright and lyricist in his day, who turned to children's stories when seeking material to read to his own child. Magic is a major preoccupation in his books and he owes a great deal to the creative worlds of children's writer E. Nesbit, whom he greatly admired. Buried in here, too, as in Eager's other children's books, are references to classic children's writing (such as the word "whiffling," which comes from Lewis Carroll's poem "Jabberwocky"). **AK**

Nationality | American, born 1911 (author); Danish/American, born 1922 (illustrator)
Publisher | Harcourt Brace, USA
Theme | Magical stories

MORE MAGICAL EDWARD EAGER READS

Knight's Castle, 1956
Magic by the Lake, 1957
Magic or Not?, 1959
The Well-Wishers, 1960
Seven-Day Magic, 1960

8+

The Children of Green Knowe 1954

Lucy Boston   Peter Boston

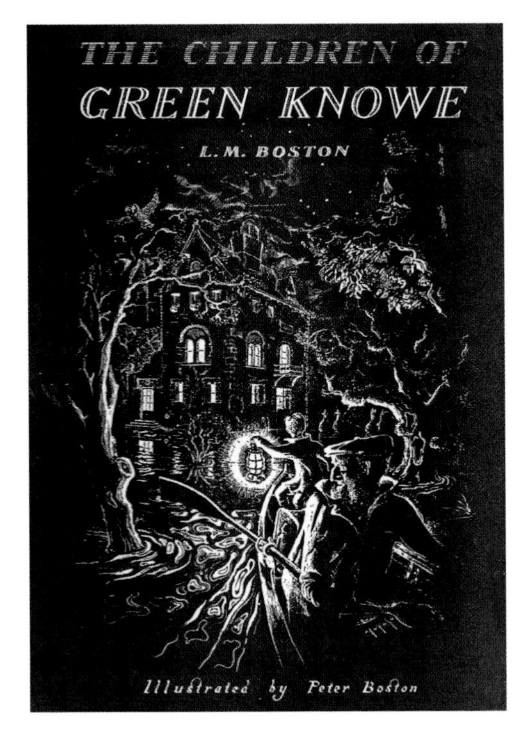

Nationality | English, born 1892 (author); English, born 1918 (illustrator)
Publisher | Faber and Faber, UK
Theme | Adventure

"Once you get [to Green Knowe] you won't be able to get out again till the flood goes down."

Green Knowe, which is based on Lucy Boston's home in Cambridgeshire, England, is an ancient manor house, sometimes called Green Noah after the shape of the ancient yew tree in its garden. The house itself is the unifying character of the six Green Knowe books.

In this first Green Knowe story, a lonely schoolboy called Tolly comes to spend Christmas with his great-grandmother, Mrs. Oldknow, the current owner of the manor. Like Mrs. Oldknow, Tolly can communicate with his forebears, Alexander, Toby, and Linnet, who lived at Green Knowe during the reign of Charles II. The seventeenth-century children are not ghosts, although they are elusive and tantalizing figures. Their connection with Tolly is very human, and he is able to share their world as an equal as well as through Mrs. Oldknow's stories and through caring for their possessions: Linnet's bracelet, Alexander's flute, and Toby's sword, not forgetting the stable still inhabited by Toby's almost magical horse, Feste.

The house, cut off from the world by flood and later snow, is the perfect setting for an adventure with just enough of the unexplained about it to be slightly scary. Tolly is the perfect child to enjoy such an adventure, with his inquisitive energy and delight in the bonds he forms with the children of the past. The presence on the page of the three siblings is immediate and life enhancing, as is Tolly's growing sense of his own worth. A wonderful story to read aloud, especially as Christmas approaches. **GB**

OTHER TALES FROM GREEN KNOWE

The Chimneys of Green Knowe, 1958
The River at Green Knowe, 1959
A Stranger at Green Knowe, 1961
An Enemy at Green Knowe, 1964
The Stones of Green Knowe, 1976

A Child's Christmas in Wales 1954

Dylan Thomas Edward Ardizzone

Nationality | Welsh, born 1914 (author); British, born 1900 (illustrator)
Publisher | Dent, UK
Theme | Classics, Family

First broadcast as a radio feature in 1953, this torrent of words makes for one of the most potent prose poems ever written. Starting with the poet's recollection of throwing snowballs, it passes on to a description of imaginary games played with friends, an affectionate account of Christmas Day itself, and a spooky reminiscence of an episode of carol singing that ends with the young Thomas scurrying home in terror. At times told as if to a small boy, who occasionally interrupts the narrative with his own questions, the story concludes with memories of the poet finally tucked into bed all those years ago from where he could still "see the lights in the windows of all the other houses on our hill and hear the music rising from them up the long, steadily falling night."

Packed with typically arresting images, this loving autobiographical fragment is immeasurably enhanced by Edward Ardizzone's accompanying illustrations. Expertly picturing all the different adults around during Thomas's childhood, which he describes so lyrically, Ardizzone's drawings and watercolors combine cheeky humor with an elegiac sense of nostalgia for a past when so many things seemed that bit brighter and more mysterious. While Thomas's mature poems remain somewhat inaccessible to younger readers, this account of the various events leading up to what is normally still a child's most exciting day of the year is a modern classic for all ages. **NT**

The Wheel on the School 1954

Meindert DeJong Maurice Sendak

Nationality | Dutch/American, born 1906 (author); American, born 1928 (illustrator)
Publisher | Harper, USA
Theme | Friendship

This novel is set in the Friesland region of the Netherlands where Meindert DeJong lived until he was eight years old. *The Wheel on the School* tells the story of six children in the small village of Shora, who are inspired by their teacher to ask why storks do not nest in their village as they do in all the others around. The five boys and one girl, Lina, decide that the ridges of the rooftops are too sharp for the storks to be able to build a nest. The children can solve this problem by placing a wheel on the roof to give the storks a place to nest, but where will they find a wheel? This task proves difficult and the children meet several interesting characters during their search.

Eventually Lina finds a wagon wheel buried beneath a boat. The children are aided by Janus, who has lost his legs in an accident and is much feared. They bring the whole village together to dredge the wheel out of the sand before the tide comes in. A fierce storm hits the village, frustrating the placement of the wheel on the roof of the school. When the winds die down slightly, the children's fathers, led by Janus, manage to place the wheel on the roof just in time for two nearly drowned storks to nest.

In this book, a series of seemingly small yet compelling incidents are written about with warmth and understanding; it teaches that dreams can come true. *The Wheel on the School* is beautifully illustrated by Maurice Sendak, with soft, smudgy pictures that convey the movement of the sea and the wind. **JF**

Hobberdy Dick 1955

Katharine M. Briggs Jane Kingshill

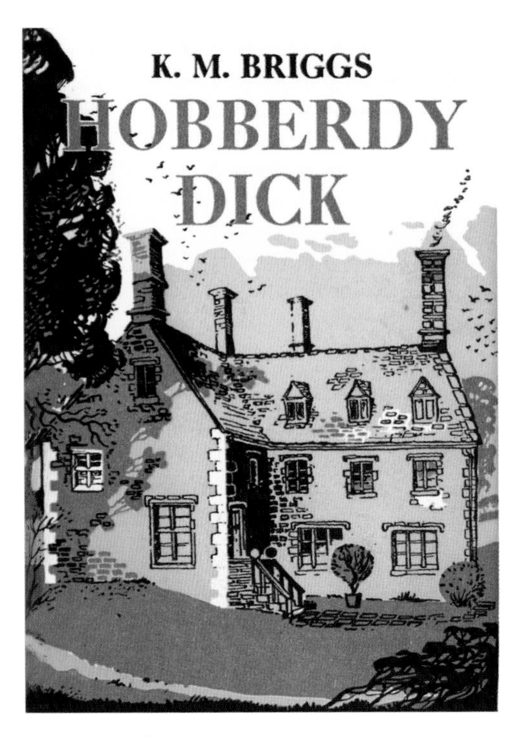

"'I don't know his name,' said Martha. 'He's a little ragged man that does things about the house. I see him sometimes.'"

OTHER GREAT FANTASY READS

Night on the Galactic Railroad **by Kenji Miyazawa, 1934**
The Hobbit **by J. R. R. Tolkien, 1937**
The Thirteen Clocks **by James Thurber, 1950**
Inkheart **by Cornelia Funke, 2003**

Nationality | English, born 1898 (author); details unknown (illustrator)
Publisher | Eyre and Spottiswoode, UK
Theme | Fantasy, Myths and legends

Hobberdy Dick is set during the English Civil War, and although the conflict between the Roundheads and Cavaliers serves as a backdrop, it is not the central focus of the story. The hero is Dick, a "hob," or friendly house fairy, who sweeps floors, churns butter, and generally helps around the house. He remains in the shadows and is only rarely glimpsed out of the corner of an eye by humans. The story begins when the Royalist owners of a large house in the English countryside are forced to leave, and a family of Puritans moves in. The new residents, who do not believe in magic, are at first unaware that they are sharing their home with a spirit. Hobberdy Dick has to learn to live with them, and they with him.

As the story progresses, Hobberdy Dick helps the son of the family pursue his romance with a girl who was a lady's maid to the house's previous owners. The couple, assisted by Dick, overcome a series of obstacles in their relationship, and Dick also prevents the abduction of a daughter of the house by witches. In gratitude Dick is offered freedom from servitude.

Katharine M. Briggs was a folklore scholar, and wrote a number of academic works, but she wears her learning lightly, and the story never becomes bogged down in historic or academic detail. Fantasy and the supernatural have become a staple of twenty-first-century children's literature, and this evocation of English folklore, written more than half a century ago, with its cast of benign spirits, magical creatures, ghosts, and witches, will appeal to a new generation of readers. **HJ**

Little Bookroom 1955

Eleanor Farjeon E. Ardizzone

Nationality | English, born 1881 (author); English, born 1900 (illustrator)
Publisher | Oxford University Press, UK
Theme | Fairy tales

As a child, Eleanor Farjeon spent hours reading in the little bookroom at the top of her house, a tranquil place where "no servant ever came with duster and broom to polish the dim panes through which the sunlight danced." The stories she read there included the mesmerizing poetry of Emily Dickinson, and numerous stories of witches and fairies, which she loved best of all.

This is a collection of Farjeon's own favorite short stories. Described by the author as "a muddle of fiction and fact and fantasy and truth," they recall the happy hours she spent being inspired by reading those authors who came before her. The style of the stories recalls ancient fairy tales—lyrical and gentle with enthralling and amusing plots, peopled by timeless characters, such as Willie the Simpleton, who is not as simple as he seems, or the king's daughter who cries piteously because she wants to own the moon but cannot reach it. There are twenty-seven stories in the collection, and the influences range from pharaonic myths of ancient Egypt to the poetry of John Keats.

Many of the stories are clearly influenced by earlier writers, such as the Brothers Grimm, Hans Christian Andersen, and Oscar Wilde, but all of Farjeon's tales have a modern twist. "The Little Dressmaker" is a story of an overworked and overlooked seamstress whom the reader believes will end up marrying a future king. The young king does not want to get married so he persuades his footman to pretend to be him. It is the footman whom the dressmaker marries and, of course, they live happily ever after. **LH**

Minnow on the Say 1955

Philippa Pearce E. Ardizzone

Nationality | English, born 1920 (author); English, born 1900 (illustrator)
Publisher | Oxford University Press, UK
Theme | Adventure, Friendship, Family

Philippa Pearce based this, her first novel, on her own country childhood near Cambridge, England; she lived next to the river where she and her brothers went canoeing, fishing, swimming, and ice-skating. In the book, the hero, David, meets a boy called Adam Codling. Unless Adam can find the family treasure, hidden in the late sixteenth century, his family estate will be lost and Adam sent away. The boys' only clue is a four-line poem and their only tool is Adam's canoe, named *Minnow*. The search takes them all summer.

Pearce was one of the greatest British children's writers of the twentieth century. In this book she was not content just to draw a conventional treasure hunt. Along the way, the boys encounter deep sorrow, social inequality, and crushing worry, as well as the beauty and fun of life along the riverbank. The scenes where Adam's grandfather mistakes him variously for his long-dead son, the boy's father, or for the gardener's boy are not easily passed over. Philippa Pearce wrote in 1962, "There is very much unpleasantness in childhood that we adults forget—and much that some simply dare not remember. For, let's face it, a good deal of childhood is strong stuff for adults and totally unsuitable for children."

But if there is sadness in *Minnow on the Say*, there is much joy, too. Working together in the canoe, talking about their families, sharing homemade meals—these are real boys with good hearts coming together on a real problem. An innate delicacy and respect colors all of Pearce's writing—you like her characters in the same way that you like people in real life. **VN**

A Hundred Million Francs 1955

Paul Berna · Richard Kennedy

Nationality | French, born Jean Sabran 1908 (author); English, born 1910 (illustrator)
Publisher | Bibliotheque Rouge et Or, France
Theme | Detective stories

8+

Paul Berna was the pseudonym of Jean Sabran when he turned from adult novels to write for children. *A Hundred Million Francs* (also translated as *The Horse Without a Head*, from the French title *Le Cheval sans tête*), brought him international recognition, confirmed by a Disney film of the book in 1963.

The most striking aspect of this tale about a group of children involved in the detection and capture of train robbers, is its celebration of the street life of children in a working-class suburb of Paris following World War II. The gang range freely across railway sidings, bomb sites, and ruined buildings, and camp in an abandoned shed in a saw mill. The horse of the title is a shabby, headless, hollow body fixed on a tricycle that the children take in turns to ride recklessly downhill and across roads, to the alarm of pedestrians and motorists. It is the theft of the horse that sets the adventure in motion.

"And there it was: a horse on three iron wheels that ran like a thorough-bred. . . ."

Inspector Sinet, the world-weary local policeman, provides an understanding, if sometimes exasperated, view of the children's activities. The story has touches of the humorous and fantastic. Marion, the sole girl in the gang, has rescued and found homes for a host of neglected dogs, and, at her whistle, these come from everywhere to the gang's aid.

The final confrontation in a novelty factory is a fitting climax to a thrilling story: as the children battle from behind an avalanche of carnival paraphernalia, to the sound of revolver shots, exploding fireworks, and the barking of Marion's invading dogs, they hold the villains at bay before the police arrive. **CB**

OTHER GREAT PAUL BERNA TITLES

The Clue of the Black Cat (Témoignage du chat noir), 1964
They Didn't Come Back (Un Pays sans légende), 1969
The Myna Bird Mystery (L'opération oiseau-noir), 1970
The Vagabonds Ashore (Le Grand nuit de Mirabel), 1973

Old Yeller 1956

Fred Gipson

Set in the late 1860s, just after the end of the American Civil War, Fred Gipson's classic story tells of the relationship between a fourteen-year-old boy, Travis, and his dog, Old Yeller. Travis Coates lives in Salt Licks, a wild frontier settlement in the Texas hill country. Times are hard, and his father heads off with the other local men on a cattle drive to Abilene in Kansas. With the prospect of being away from his wife, his son, and five-year-old Little Arliss for several months, he leaves Travis in charge of taking care of the family and running the ranch.

An ugly, stray dog arrives and steals the family's meat. However, he goes on to save Little Arliss from the wrath of an angry mother bear, and so Travis adopts the scruffy dog and they become inseparable friends. Travis calls his canine companion Old Yeller: "The name had a sort of double meaning. One part meant that his short hair was a dingy yellow, a color that we called 'yeller' in those days. The other meant that when he opened his head, the sound he let out came closer to being a yell than a bark." Old Yeller proves to be a rascal and a thief, yet he also shows himself to be loyal, courageous, and smart, well able to protect Travis and his family in the wilderness.

"A good dog around the place was sometimes worth more than two or three men. . . ."

The book was highly popular and was also made into a successful Disney movie in 1957. What makes the tale such a classic is not just the story of Old Yeller and Travis's adventures, but Gipson's evocation of life just after the Civil War. However, it is the relationship between the boy and his dog that is touching, and proves to have a heartrending conclusion. **CK**

Nationality | American, born 1908
Publisher | Harper, USA
Award | Newbery Honor Book, 1957
Theme | Animal stories, Friendship

OTHER GREAT READS BY FRED GIPSON

Trail Driving Rooster, 1955
Recollection Creek, 1955
Savage Sam, 1962
Little Arliss, 1978
Curley and the Wild Boar, 1980

8+

The Hundred and One Dalmatians 1956

Dodie Smith Janet and Anne Grahame Johnstone

Nationality | English, born 1896 (author); English, born 1928 (illustrators)
Publisher | Heinemann, UK
Theme | Classics, Animal stories

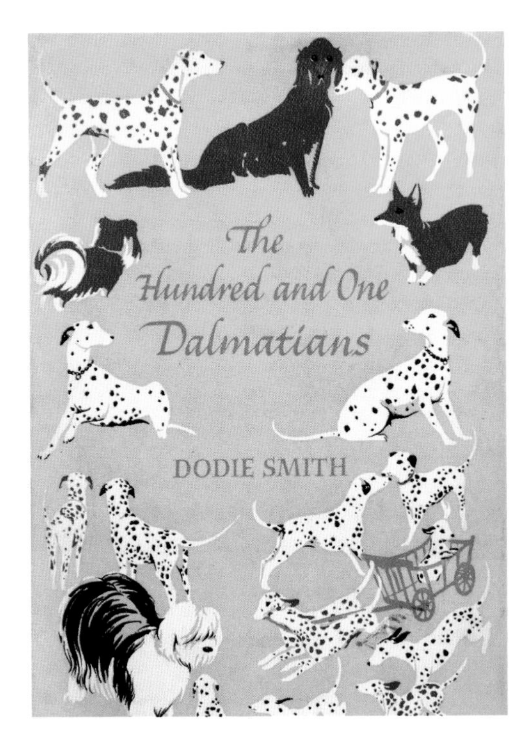

MORE FAVORITE ANIMAL STORIES

Stuart Little by E. B. White, 1945
The Cricket in Times Square by George Selden, 1960
Mrs. Frisby and the Rats of NIMH by Robert C. O'Brien, 1971
The Tale of Despereaux by Kate DeCamillo, 2003

Dodie Smith was already an accomplished playwright and novelist when she got the idea for her first children's book after a friend remarked of her Dalmatians: "Those dogs would make a lovely fur coat!" That is precisely what the scheming Cruella de Vil, a wealthy socialite who lives in a black-and-white color-coordinated house, thinks when she sees the fifteen puppies born to adorable Pongo and Missis Pongo. Pongo and Missis live with the Dearly family, near London's Regent's Park. The Dearlys are loving dog-owners who adopt a wet nurse, Perdita, to help Missis with her litter, which includes the sickly Cadpig. Cruella, on the other hand, is married to a furrier and kicks her own cat. When the puppies disappear, the grieving parents are able to trace them through the dog grapevine, the "Twilight Barking." The story of their rescue—and that of the eighty-two other puppies also facing fate as a fur coat—involves a thrilling cross-country car chase, narrow escapes, clever disguises, and a satisfying revenge on cold-hearted Cruella.

"Mr. and Mrs. Dearly . . . were gentle, obedient, and unusually intelligent—almost canine. . . ."

Smith's book offers many enjoyments that do not appear in the movie. She relishes the absurdity of interactions between dogs and humans: Cadpig watches television; the Dearlys are too poorly trained to be allowed out on their own. Her eye and ear are sharp to the nuances of English life: Cruella is terribly nouveau riche, while the Staffordshire bull terrier who works with some furniture removers is a cockney bad boy. The whole narrative whizzes along with great panache, so that readers accept without question such whimsical ideas as the "Twilight Barking." **VN**

The Warden's Niece 1957

Gillian Avery Dick Hart

Maria is a shy but resolute child who dreams of becoming a professor of Greek, even though at Oxford University in the late 1870s women had only just been allowed to attend university lectures. At her repressive girls' school, however, she is in constant trouble for minor violations of petty rules and, after one particularly disastrous geography lesson, she ends up running away to Oxford.

Her uncle, warden of the fictitious Canterbury College at Oxford, is as sympathetic to her academic aims as he is dismissive of girls' schools. Maria will, he decides, take lessons with the three renegade sons of the professor who lives next door—the insufferably cocky youngest brother, James; the anxious middle son, Joshua; and lofty Thomas, bound shortly for the prestigious Rugby School. They are taught by Mr. Copplestone, a maverick tutor who proves something of a liability. On his first day alone, he manages to fall out of a pear tree and into the professor's henhouse.

Mr. Copplestone's madcap schemes, coupled with the mostly good-natured sparring and occasionally reckless exploits of the three boys, provide a lighthearted backdrop for Maria's serious ambitions. One day, on a trip to a nearby historic house, she uncovers a mystery surrounding an unnamed boy in a portrait and, determined to prove her academic worth, embarks upon some "original research" to establish his identity.

Faced with innumerable obstacles in the path to scholarship and goaded on by her irrepressible companions, she finds herself drawn into a series of entertaining escapades: heart-stopping for Maria, but wittily entertaining for the reader. With a combination of dedication and good luck, she eventually finds answers, and the conclusion brings a satisfying end to a novel that works both as a lively domestic comedy and as an avowal of girls' academic capabilities. **KA**

Nationality | English, born 1926 (author); details unknown (illustrator)
Publisher | Collins, UK
Theme | Adventure, Historical fiction

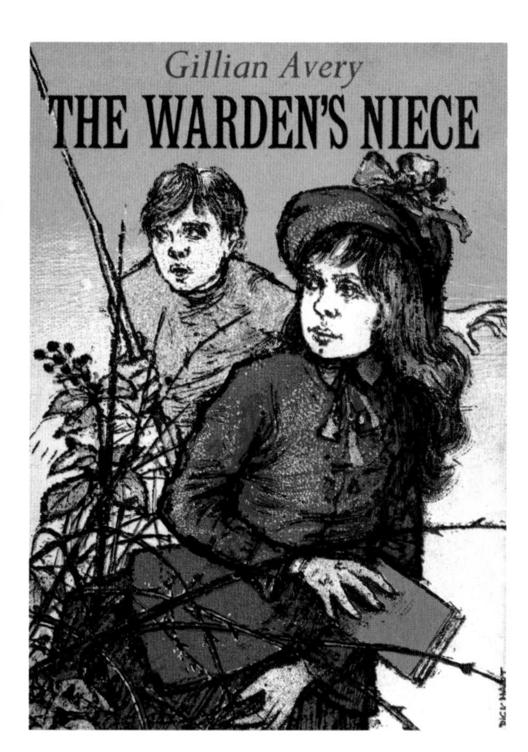

8+

OTHER GREAT READS BY GILLIAN AVERY

The Elephant War, 1960
The Greatest Gresham, 1962
The Italian Spring, 1964
A Likely Lad, 1971
Ellen and the Queen, 1972

Thorn Castle 1957

István Fekete

Nationality | Hungarian, born 1900
Publisher | Móra, Hungary
Award | Best Novel, Hungary's Big Read, 2005
Theme | Friendship, Science and nature

Thorn Castle (originally *Tüskevár*) is one of the most enduringly popular Hungarian children's books. It tells the story of two boys from the city who spend their summer vacation in rural Hungary on the shores of Lake Balaton. They are unused to country ways but are guided by an old, wise man who teaches them about nature, and they gradually come to love their new surroundings.

The boys learn to row on the lake, are scared by grass snakes, set a fire that gets out of hand, and one of them almost loses a finger, but these experiences help them to grow up, to learn how to become more self-sufficient, and to appreciate nature. This lyrical but humorous story provides a real insight into the natural world. Its lasting popularity in Hungary is due in part to the fact that many of the places and animals described by the author are now disappearing. *Thorn Castle* was awarded the Attila Jozsef Literary Prize in 1960 and the book was made into a film in 1967. A sequel, *Winter Grove* (*Téli berek*), was published in 1959. In it, the boys revisit the area in the depths of winter and experience the differences in the landscape, and in themselves.

István Fekete is one of Hungary's most famous and well-loved novelists. The vast majority of his work focuses on nature, animals, and the countryside and includes nonfiction as well as novels. His relationship with the natural world was recognized with the establishment of the István Fekete Educational Center of Nimfea—a conservation center that teaches young people about wildlife and the countryside. **HJ**

Gaston 1957

André Franquin et al.

Nationality | All Belgian, born 1924 (Franquin); born 1928 (Yvan Delporte); born 1935 (Jidéhem)
Publisher | Dupuis, Belgium
Theme | Comics, Favorite characters

Comic-strip character Gaston Lagaffe first stumbled into print in 1957. Initially, he was nothing more than an elaborate joke designed to fill space in the *Journal de Spirou*. However, his numerous antics soon made him one of the paper's most popular and much-loved features. Indeed, when Dupuis tried to ax the character, a campaign by the readers saved him.

Office-boy Gaston Lagaffe (his surname means "blunder" in French) spends his working hours napping and dodging work; unanswered mail piles up on his desk, which is in a constant mess. His energies are always engaged in hare-brained schemes and bizarre machines: a contraption to produce smoke rings; a life-sized latex replica of himself; a monstrous harplike musical instrument; and a remote-controlled iron. None of these inventions land Gaston the fame and fortune of his daydreams. Instead, they unleash mayhem; the newspaper office is flooded or blown up several times, and the all-important business deals his boss tries to negotiate are never signed. This does not dampen Gaston's enthusiasm for gadgetry, and after each disaster he throws himself into the next endeavor. No matter what he does, his colleagues (and employer) always forgive him. For all his gaffes and mishaps, Gaston has some genuine qualities: his love of nature, his deep-felt pacifism, and the dreamy individuality he manages to retain in an otherwise bland corporate world.

Although, Gaston was the creation of cartoonist André Franquin, *Spirou* colleagues Yvan Delporte and Jidéhem also contributed creatively. **CFR**

Tom's Midnight Garden 1958

Philippa Pearce Susan Einzig

Nationality | English, born 1920 (author); German, born 1922 (illustrator)
Publisher | Oxford University Press, UK
Theme | Classics, Fantasy, Friendship

If your children never read another book, they ought to read this one. This is Philippa Pearce's masterpiece. It tells the story of young Tom, sent to stay with his childless aunt and uncle in their apartment in a converted house in England's flat East Anglian countryside. Exiled from home by his brother's measles, Tom is lonely and fed up, until one night he hears the clock strike thirteen and goes down to investigate. He enters a beautiful garden, which seems to have belonged to the house in another era and there befriends Hatty, an orphan girl living on the charity of her late Victorian relations.

Tom and Hatty have much in common and they play together and go on trips, but each time they meet, Hatty gets a little older and Tom seems more ghostly to her eyes. In a wonderful climactic scene, they skate down the frozen river to the cathedral town of Ely, just ahead of the river melting, but then Hatty vanishes and Tom has to return to his real home. Poignantly, the book ends with Hatty revealed as the ancient landlady still living in the upstairs flat in the house of her childhood, the original garden having been built over long since. Old Hatty and Tom recognize each other across the ages and briefly embrace.

Pearce writes lovingly of the walled garden, based on her own childhood play space, but with even greater love of the tenderness between the two protagonists. Pearce always respects her characters: her delicacy of touch and emotional honesty infuse this absorbing story with deep insight into the transience and permanence of affections. **VN**

"Thirteen? Tom's mind gave a jerk. Had it really struck that? Even mad old clocks never struck that."

OTHER TIME-SLIP FANTASIES

Stig of the Dump by Clive King, 1963
Charlotte Sometimes by Penelope Farmer, 1969
The Ghost of Thomas Kempe by Penelope Lively, 1973
A Chance Child by Jill Paton Walsh, 1978
King of Shadows by Susan Cooper, 2008

Warrior Scarlet 1958

Rosemary Sutcliff Charles Keeping

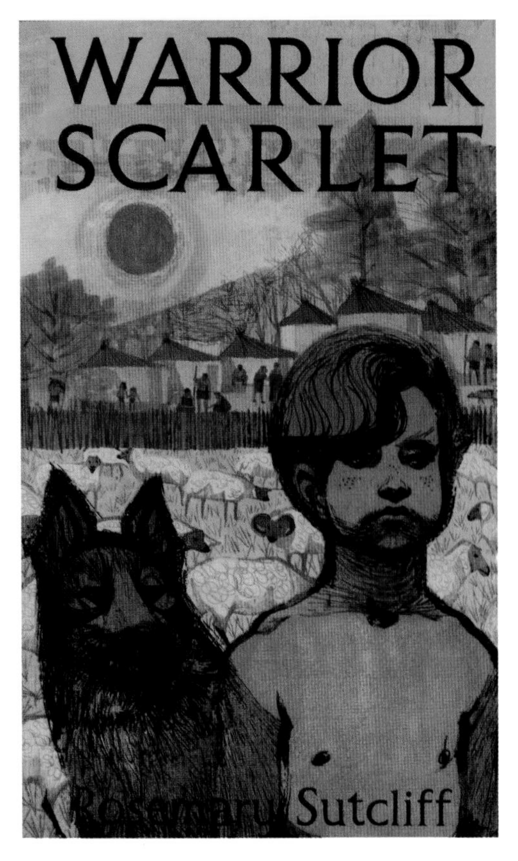

"Our flint spears were but brown-tufted rushes."

MORE NOTABLE HISTORICAL FICTION

***The Once and Future King* by T. H. White, 1958**
***Charlotte Sometimes* by Penelope Farmer, 1969**
***Fire, Bed and Bone* by Henrietta Branford, 1997**
***The Sterkarm Handshake* by Susan Price, 1998**
***Wolf Brother* by Michelle Paver, 2004**

Nationality | English, born 1920 (author); English, born 1924 (illustrator)
Publisher | Oxford University Press, UK
Theme | Historical fiction

Drem, an inquisitive, eager boy in a British tribe during the Bronze Age, is at the end of his adolescence. Now he must kill his wolf in order to become a man in the tribe and wear the Warrior Scarlet. Yet there is a problem. How can he do this when his right arm is crippled? Suddenly, the tribe that has seemed so accepting and safe is harsh and unfriendly. Drem has to prove himself or be outcast. He sets out on a painful journey in which he learns much about himself and makes three great friends: a faithful hound, a blood brother who saves his life, and a loving girl.

As Sutcliff said herself, "I've only got one plot, a boy growing up and finding himself." She wrote novels about the Roman legions in Britain, Arthurian chivalry, and medieval England as well as others about Scottish, English, and Greek legends. Her heroes are mostly athletic youths who overcome wounds and disabilities to battle for social acceptance; it is surely significant that disease confined her to a wheelchair. She trained as an artist, never married, and was writing on the day she died.

Two other elements dominate her books: dogs and the British countryside. Canine companions are constant, their behavior lovingly and humorously described. The landscape is detailed by her artist's eye, whether in summers, where golden harvests gleam along low hills, or winters shrouded in mists rolling over the moors. Sutcliff was widely read in Anglo-Saxon epics and early British history, and she created novels where the plots slowly unfold but where the characters seem to grow organically from their historical roots. **VN**

Mort and Phil 1958

Francisco Ibáñez

Original Title | Mortadelo y Filemón
Nationality | Spanish, born 1936
Publisher | Bruguera, Spain
Theme | Detective stories, Comics

Few comic-strip characters survive more than fifty years and maintain the same freshness and appeal as they had at the beginning. Yet this has been the case with the characters Mortadelo and Filemón (Mort and Phil), two Spanish private detectives. More than 150 million copies of the various Mort and Phil books have been sold. They even won the Goya Prize.

Throughout the first series the personality of the two characters developed and built the foundation for what was to become the sometimes surreal graphic humor of this very popular comic strip. Phil is a grumpy, intransigent boss who wears a checkered jacket and smokes a pipe. Mort, his assistant, wears a frock coat and a bowler hat. He has two very striking character traits: an extraordinary ability to disguise himself and the gift of inopportuneness.

In 1969 the two characters changed their appearance, becoming parodies of secret agents in spy stories. Other characters were added: the Boss, Professor Bacterio and, a couple of decades later, the secretary, Ofelia. In a typical Mort and Phil story there are plenty of misunderstandings, chases, fights, and, since the 1980s, some references to or parodies of political and social situations. Ibáñez now increasingly includes elements of humor in the background of the drawings that have little to do with the subject.

Today all the albums are arranged in different collections, such as *Olé!,* which include some of the best short comic strips, and *Súper humor clasicós* (*Super Humor Classics*) for those who hanker after the early adventures of the series. **EB**

Walkabout 1959

James Vance Marshall

Alternative Title | The Children
Nationality | English, born Donald G. Payne 1924
Publisher | Michael Joseph, UK
Theme | Adventure

"When a boy is only eight, having a big sister of thirteen is wonderfully comforting." The boy in Marshall's novel is Peter, the older sister is Mary, and both are American children from Charleston, South Carolina. Following a plane crash, they find themselves in Australia's Northern Territory, some 1,400 miles from Adelaide, the home of the uncle they had hoped to visit. With neither water nor food—other than the remnants of a stick of barley sugar—they embark on a trek that, they trust, will eventually lead them to their intended destination.

What might have been a straightforward adventure story of childhood survival becomes something quite different when Mary and Peter encounter a teenage aboriginal boy. He is on his "walkabout," a significant tribal rite of passage from childhood to manhood, involving an endurance test in the wilds of the Australian desert. From the moment of their first meeting, the novel becomes an exploration of the two contrasting cultures represented by the American children and the young aboriginal. The former bring to their new experience the racial prejudices of 1950s America: "Darkie" is Peter's recurring mode of address to the aboriginal whereas Mary, through her inherited fear and suspicion of black people, perceives his gestures of friendship as a form of sexual advance. Slightly dated, the book occasionally resorts to superficial stereotypes. However, it remains a powerful story tracing the development of the relationships between the very different children, against a vividly described Australian outback. **RD**

The Boy, the Swallow and the Cat 1959

Miguel Buñuel / Lorenzo Goñi

Nationality | Spanish, born 1924 (author); Spanish, born 1911 (illustrator)
Publisher | Doncel, Spain
Theme | Friendship, Fantasy, Animal stories

Originally entitled *El niño, la golondrina y el gato*, this book was one of the most important Spanish children's books to emerge in the postwar years. A poetic book, full of symbolism, it tells the story of the fantastic voyage of a boy, a bird, and a cat who journey far beyond the boundaries of Earth, "at the very edge of the sky, where the roar of the stars ended and the silence of nothingness began."

The boy is a boy without a name, sensitive and thoughtful, carrying his belongings on his shoulder. He goes into the forest accompanied by a swallow that cannot migrate because of a broken wing, and a white cat. Their adventure is punctuated by crazy stories peopled by characters drawn from nature,

"The stars of the Boy, the Swallow and the Cat sparkle against the . . . lake, like suns."

reminiscent of the dream world of *Alice's Adventures in Wonderland* with its stimulating play of metaphors, or *The Little Prince*, which also deals with a journey of initiation. Like a mirror reflecting representations of the subconscious, Goñi's lively illustrations enhance the novel's poetic tone, conceived like a parable, with its pacifist message and mystical undertones in which death and eternity coexist.

A creative and fantastical novelist, Buñuel has been awarded the Premio Lazarillo and the Diploma de Mérito Andersen for his other children's book: *Narcissus under the Water* (*Narciso bajo las aguas*). Today, it is recognized as a modern classic, a unique, original book, written in an elegant, musical prose, which tells stories that invite the reader to contemplate the stars. Buñuel was also awarded the Premio Nacional de Literatura in 1950. **EB**

OTHER BOOKS BY MIGUEL BUÑUEL

Manuel and the Men (Manuel y los hombres), 1961
The Little Ditch (El aquerralito), 1965
Life in Colors (La vida en colores), 1968

8+

The boy dreams of a fantastical kingdom under the sea. 

My Great-Grandfather and I 1959

James Krüss Jochen Bartsch

8+

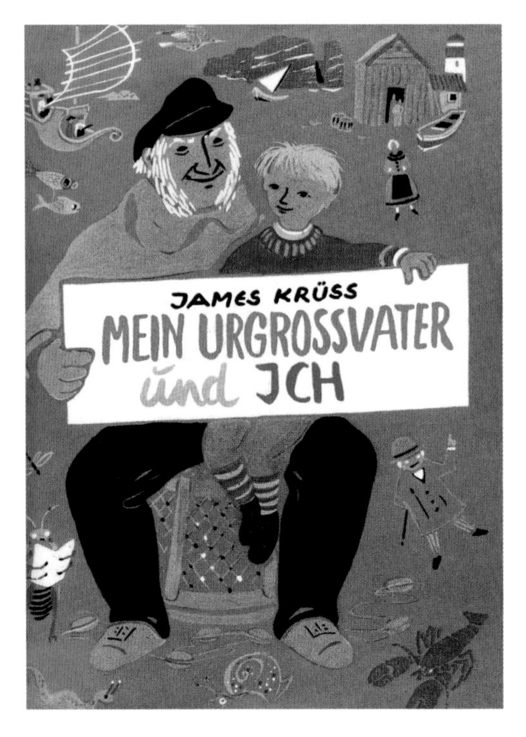

"So that means that words are the clothes to dress the whole world, great granddad!"

OTHER GREAT READS BY JAMES KRÜSS

The Lighthouse on Lobster Island (Der Leuchtturm auf den Hummerklippen), 1956
Ladislaus and Anabella, 1957
Timm Thaler (Timm Thaler oder das verkaufte Lachen), 1962

Nationality | German, born 1926 (author); German, birth date unknown (illustrator)
Publisher | Oetinger, Germany
Theme | Family, Poetry

In *My Great-Grandfather and I* (originally entitled *Mein Urgroßvater und Ich*) ten-year-old "Boy" is elated when he is allowed to stay at his great-grandfather's home for a week. The great-grandfather—also called Boy—was a sailor in his youth. Now eighty-four years old, he does not go to sea anymore. Instead he writes poetry and carves wood, and young Boy becomes his attentive student. Together they retreat to their "workshop" like two conspirators (the female members of the family regard them as weird), where they use thick pencils to write their poems on wooden planks.

Boy learns from his great-grandfather how to use language properly and that you have to stop writing poetry when it stops being fun. He also learns that when a poem is translated into different languages things may be changed, but the content must stay the same. One day they discover that all the planks they have used as notebooks have been used to build a boat. It looks like all their writing has been lost, but to their surprise, Boy's grandmother—the elder Boy's daughter—has, unknown to them, copied out all their poems and even added some of her own. She gives them to her father for his eighty-fifth birthday.

The deserved winner of many literary awards, this book celebrates language and poetry, as well as friendship between people of different generations. James Krüss tells his delightful story about the zest for life humorously and with great affection. **CS**

The Cricket in Times Square 1960

George Selden · Garth Williams

Nationality | American, born 1929 (author); English, born 1912 (illustrator)
Publisher | Farrar, Straus and Giroux, USA
Theme | Animal stories, Classics

"One night I was coming home on the subway, and I did hear a cricket chirp in the Times Square subway station. The story formed in my mind within minutes. An author is very thankful for minutes like those, although they happen all too infrequently." So author George Selden described the inspiration behind the perhaps unlikely event of finding, or indeed hearing, a cricket in Times Square in New York.

Since its publication in 1960, Tucker Mouse, Harry Cat, Chester Cricket, and their special friendship, brought to life by Garth Williams's remarkable pen-and-ink illustrations, have lived in the hearts and minds of many children. The streetwise city mouse and experienced city cat, along with a young boy named Mario, befriend the countryside cricket, and together they have many adventures in the big city, adventures Chester Cricket could never have imagined in his wildest dreams.

Mario's family run a newsstand in Times Square that is slowly going bankrupt. Since Mario rescued him from a pile of dirt in the subway station, the musically gifted Chester wants to help the family out, but he is beginning to think he is bringing them bad luck instead when he accidentally sets fire to the newsstand. When Chester comes up with his plan to help Mario, he shows them all what a little country cricket can do in the big city. A great book for emerging readers and a wonderful read-aloud for younger children. **KD**

The Bonny Pit Laddie 1960

Frederick Grice · Brian Wildsmith

Nationality | American, born 1910 (author); English, born 1930 (illustrator)
Publisher | Oxford University Press, UK
Theme | Historical fiction

Quietly and subtly written, this at first somewhat episodic tale, set in a northern English pit village at the beginning of the twentieth century, gathers pace when the miners go on strike and consequent hardship hits the families.

Young Dick Ullathorne has to follow his brother and father down the mine when his father is blacklisted as a troublemaker on the miners' return to work. A horrifying explosion in the pit, caused by the careless negligence of the mine owner, leaves Dick trapped underground with other pit workers; this would have cost many lives but for Dick's quick thinking and his memory of an alternative escape route out of the mine, discovered accidentally when he and his brother were exploring earlier in the story. Dick is an intelligent boy and, if given the opportunity, he would have stayed on at school to further his education. Ironically, the accident down the mine gives him the chance of a different future with employment outside of the pit village.

The closeness of the pit community and their care and concern for one another contrasts starkly with the thoughtless greed of Mr. Sleath, the mine owner. The harshness of the pit worker's life and total dependence on the mine for work and housing is not hidden from the reader and has all the more impact because of the seeming lack of drama at the start of the story. Grice revisited working-class life in *The Courage of Andy Robson* and *Young Tom Sawbones*. **JF**

Knight's Fee 1960

Rosemary Sutcliff Charles Keeping

Nationality | English, born 1920 (author); English, born 1924 (illustrator)
Publisher | Oxford University Press, UK
Theme | Historical fiction, Friendship

KNIGHT'S FEE
Rosemary Sutcliff

8+

Not long after the Norman invasion of England in 1066, Norman lord Robert de Bellême is taking possession of his lands in England with his younger brother, Hugh Goch, newly made Lord of Arundel. Randal, the half-Saxon, half-Breton, wholly unwanted dog-boy at Arundel Castle, annoys Hugh, who sets out to torment him. Then Herluin, the mysterious minstrel, wagers Hugh a game of chess for the boy. Herluin's elegance defeats Hugh's evil temper and Randal is left in the care of Herluin's old friend, becoming best friend and eventually squire to his grandson, Bevis.

Life in the lower ranks of chivalry is dangerous, however, particularly if you have enemies. The story of the two boys' developing friendship across such a sweeping social divide and its tragic end are poignantly drawn. Sutcliff fills this book—as she does all her absorbing stories—with fascinating historic fact and compelling detail about life in a long-gone era. Equally enjoyable are the careful descriptions of the rituals and rites of passage that marked a medieval boy's progress to the status of knighthood.

"It is too good a hound boy to waste, and we can always thrash it again another day."

As a very ill child, Rosemary Sutcliff spent hours having stories read to her. She grew to love historic stories, ancient legends, and the works of Rudyard Kipling. She also painted, mostly scenes inspired by history. Sutcliff's debilitating illness (a type of early-onset arthritis) also meant a great deal of time spent sitting still, observing the land, animals, and people around her. This close observation stood her in great stead when it came to writing fiction. **VN**

OTHER BOOKS BY ROSEMARY SUTCLIFF

***The Queen Elizabeth Story*, 1950**
***The Armourer's House*, 1951**
***The Eagle of the Ninth*, 1954**
***Warrior Scarlet*, 1958**
***The Lantern Bearers*, 1959**

Jim Button and Luke the Engine Driver 1960

Michael Ende Franz Josef Tripp

Originally published with the title *Jim Knopf und Lukas der Lokomotivführer*, this quirky story is set on the island of Lummerland. The tiny island is no bigger than an average-sized living room and only has space for one mountain with a castle on top, two houses, and one train station. King Alfons lives in the palace, and Luke and his locomotive, Emma, live in the station. In one of the houses there is a shop, which is run by Mrs. Waas.

One day, the inhabitants of the island receive a special delivery. They open the parcel and are surprised to find a little black boy inside. They decide to call him Jim, and Mrs. Waas immediately offers to adopt him. However, as Jim grows taller, the space on the island becomes more restricted so the king orders Luke to get rid of his beloved old locomotive. Not wanting to lose Emma, Luke decides to convert her into a sailing boat and to leave Lummerland with Jim, who does not want to stay behind without his best friend. Thus, their adventures begin.

They set sail and travel to a mysterious nearby island, Mandala, where the ruler asks Luke and Jim to rescue his daughter, who was abducted to Kummerland (German for "Land of Sorrow"), the town of dragons. The children at the local school are horribly mistreated by the headmistress, a "half-dragon," but Jim and Luke manage to free the little girl. Jim and the girl become friends and plan to get married when they are older. Meanwhile, Emma has a baby locomotive she offers to Jim. When a floating island is anchored to Lummerland, there is enough space for everyone to live there again.

Ende's book is full of philosophical metaphors that are intelligible even to small children. This was his first children's book, it was rejected by several publishers before finally being taken on—whereupon it won the German Youth Literature Prize in 1961. **CS**

Nationality | German, born 1929 (author); German, born 1915 (illustrator)
Publisher | Thienemann, Germany
Theme | Quirky, Adventure, Magical stories

8+

OTHER GREAT READS BY MICHAEL ENDE

The Grey Gentleman (Morno), 1973
The Dream Eater (Das Traumfresserchen), 1978
The Neverending Story (Die unendliche Geschichte: von A bis Z), 1979

R. GOSCINNY Astérix A. UDERZO

Texte de
René GOSCINNY

Dessins
d'**Albert UDERZO**

HACHETTE

Astérix the Gaul 1961

René Goscinny Albert Uderzo

Nationality | French, born 1926 (author); French, born 1927 (illustrator)
Publisher | Dargaud, France
Theme | Friendship, War

Astérix first appeared in serial form in the French comic *Pilote* in 1959. It proved so popular that the duo—René Goscinny and Albert Uderzo—were inspired to turn the comic-book strips into full-length books that appeal to both children and adults.

The central character of all the stories is the heroic Astérix, a daredevil warrior whose main purpose is to oust the Romans from Gaul. Astérix is assisted by the sagelike druid, Getafix, who brews magical potions, including one for superhuman strength. Astérix's sidekick and friend is the hefty strong man, Obelix, whose strength is attributed to his falling into a cauldron of Getafix's potion when he was a child. In *Astérix the Gaul*, when the Romans kidnap Getafix and try to make him hand over the potion, Astérix and Obelix have plenty of fun at the Romans' expense.

Uderzo's drawings are bright, lively, and witty, and Goscinny stories are incredibly funny. Both make regular references to contemporary European culture to add to the comic effect. In the original French, Goscinny makes much use of puns and great care has been taken to adapt these into the translations for foreign readers. The Astérix books often contain caricatures of individuals as well as inoffensive cultural stereotypes (such as the British drinking warm beer). Overall, the layering of such detail is fascinating, and the playful references to other animated series—such as iconic events, art, and figures in both historic and popular culture—are a joy. **CK**

The Incredible Journey 1961

Sheila Burnford

Nationality | Scottish, born 1918
Publisher | Hodder and Stoughton, UK
Award | Canadian Children's Book of the Year
Theme | Animal stories

The Incredible Journey was originally written for adults, but it became popular with children and has since been made into two successful Walt Disney films. Author Sheila Burnford was known for her novels about life in the wilderness in her adopted country of Canada. The story, which is set in northwestern Ontario, is about three house pets: a wheat-colored Siamese cat, Tao; an old white English bull terrier, Bodger; and a large, red-gold Labrador retriever, Luath. The pets belong to Jim Hunter, his wife, and their two children, Peter and Elizabeth.

Jim is a professor of English and when he has to travel to give a series of university lectures his family go with him, leaving their pets in the care of John Longridge, Elizabeth's godfather. Longridge is a bachelor who lives in a stone house among the lakes and woods of Ontario, approximately 250 miles away from the Hunters. When Longridge goes off on a hunting trip, the animals miss human company and decide to go in search of their owners. Along the way, as they head west to find the family they love, they face many obstacles, including starvation, exposure, and wild animals in the forests, such as bears.

The pets' story is one of courage and camaraderie, as they encounter both kindness and danger from animals and humans in the form of farmers and Native Americans. The story of their journey is enhanced by Burnford's evocative descriptions of the harsh beauty of the Canadian wilderness. **CK**

James and the Giant Peach 1961

Roald Dahl Nancy Ekholm Burkert

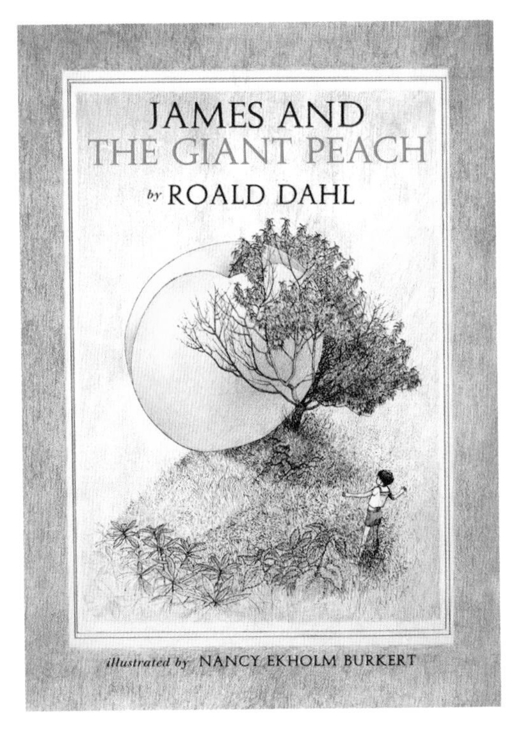

"James was sent away to live with his two aunts . . . who, I am sorry to say, were both really horrible people."

OTHER FANTASTIC ROALD DAHL READS

Charlie and the Chocolate Factory, 1964
The Magic Finger, 1966
The BFG, 1982
The Witches, 1983
Matilda, 1988

Nationality | Welsh, born 1916 (author); American, born 1933 (illustrator)
Publisher | Alfred A. Knopf, USA
Theme | Fantasy, Magical stories

When Roald Dahl's first children's book, *James and the Giant Peach*, appeared, he was already a renowned writer of bizarre and grotesque short stories for adults. This sparkling gem of a tale, with strong characters and a fast-moving plot, is one of his best.

James Henry Trotter suddenly finds himself a Cinderella-style orphan, forced to live with his two very unpleasant aunts and leading a thoroughly unhappy and friendless life. One day, an unknown man offers him a bag of magic beans that will make marvelous things happen to him. So far, so fairy tale; but this is Roald Dahl, so now the craziness starts.

Instead of eating the beans, James drops them and they wriggle down into the roots of a peach tree. Almost at once, a peach begins to grow and grow until it is as big as a house. James finds a tunnel leading into the center of the giant peach, through which he climbs. Once he is inside the peach, he befriends a crowd of bugs who have also grown to enormous size.

Suddenly, the peach begins to roll away down the hill, squashing the two revolting aunts on its way, and falls into the sea. Attacked by sharks, James and his crew harness a flock of seagulls that lift the peach out of the water. The skies are not safe either. Here they are attacked by the terrifying cloud men. At last, they reach the safety of New York, where the vast peach comes to rest, impaled on the Empire State Building. All the creatures find useful jobs to do, and James lives in the peach pit in Central Park where he has plenty of children to play with. **CW**

8+

Fantômette 1961

Georges Chaulet J. Bazin-Hives

Nationality | French, born 1931 (author); French, born 1927 (illustrator)
Publisher | Hachette, France
Theme | Fantasy, Adventure

In 1961, Georges Chaulet created a heroine like no other: a mysterious, masked young girl who fights to restore order and justice. She operates mostly at night and she knows how to thwart the most Machiavellian plans. She fears no danger and can appear from nowhere. Her name is Fantômette. Dressed in a yellow tunic, a black cape lined with red, a black hat, and a mask that conceals her identity, the young righter of wrongs fights evil, armed with a dagger in her belt and a brooch with a blade hidden inside.

In the little town of Framboisy, many young girls dream of meeting Fantômette and becoming like her: notably Ficelle, a tall, skinny girl with blond hair, dreamy and clumsy with a lot of imagination; and Boulotte, her close friend who loves food and sometimes comes very close to discovering the real identity of the heroine. Ficelle and Boulotte often spend time with their best friend, Françoise. She is interested in everything, reads a lot, and is amazingly good at sports, yet Françoise leads a life that is sometimes rather lonely and mysterious. Together the three girls have many adventures and find themselves facing serious dangers. Fortunately Fantômette always intervenes even in the most desperate situations. She has many enemies but the one she has to fight most often is a formidable gangster, nicknamed Le Furet (The Ferret) who tries constantly to eliminate her.

According to the author, *Fantômette* is aimed mainly at young female readers. The forty-nine episodes have captivated a wide public, and the series's success continues unabated. **SL**

Six Companions 1961

Paul-Jacques Bonzon A. Chazelle

Nationality | French, born 1908 (author); details unknown (illustrator)
Publisher | Hachette, France
Theme | Adventure, Friendship

Six Companions (originally titled *Les Six Compagnons*) is a series of forty-nine books, written mainly for children. Their author, Paul-Jacques Bonzon, was a schoolteacher and headmaster, and in his books he describes the solidarity that is found among the lower classes from which he draws his heroes.

The series features a group of six boys, one girl, and a dog (Kafi), who live in the Croix-Rousse district in Lyons, France; they are always looking for exciting adventures to distract them from their everyday lives. The first book in the series, *The Companions of the Croix-Rousse*, tells how the heroes met. Tidou has left his native village to come and live in Lyons. When his dog disappears, the "gones" (the name given to Lyons children) of his school and Mady, a handicapped little girl, help him to find it. The succeeding books are detective stories in which the children solve mysteries, often helping out new or old friends. Each character is inventive, curious, and extremely brave and bold. Tidou Aubanel is the narrator and his dog, Kafi, is completely devoted to the gang. Corget, for his part, is seen as the leader until he leaves for Toulouse. Mady is the only girl and she is often the trigger for the discoveries and travels that start off the adventures.

This series of books differs from most children's literature of the period because of the realistic and sometimes sad nature of some of the situations: The companions are confronted with personal misery, handicap, and abandonment. The stories are thrilling and easy to read, which helps young readers to identify with the plots. **CD**

The Phantom Tollbooth 1961

Norton Juster Jules Feiffer

Nationality | American, born 1929 (author); American, born 1929 (illustrator)
Publisher | Random House, USA
Theme | Fantasy, Magical stories

Milo is very bored, until the day he comes home to a mysterious package. It contains a magic purple tollbooth. When Milo drives through it in his little car, he sets off on a weird and wonderful journey.

He gets stuck in the Doldrums, where no thinking is allowed, and is rescued by the watchdog, Tock (whose body actually *is* a watch). He is then put on the road to the kingdom of Wisdom. In one of the capitals, Dictionopolis, where they grow words in orchards, he meets Faintly Macabre, the not-so-wicked Which (*sic*), who tells him about Wisdom's two rulers, King Azaz and the Mathemagician, and their adopted sisters, Rhyme and Reason. The two princesses could not settle their brothers' debate over the relative importance of letters or numbers and so have been banished to the Castle in the Air, high in the demon-infested Mountains of Ignorance. The story continues, to a surprising and gleeful ending with Juster's delight in his play of words and ideas constantly manifesting itself in jokes such as the Isle of Conclusions.

For Juster, as for his characters, "The universe is full of magical things, patiently waiting for our wits to get sharper." Such cerebral fun appeals to adults as well. Yet interwoven with Juster's literary approach to the magic of concepts is great humor, snappy plotting, and empathy with the difficulty of being a child and having to find out what all this education and reading is meant to be about. Feiffer's illustrations perfectly capture the blend of adult and juvenile. **VN**

Where the Red Fern Grows 1961

Wilson Rawls

Nationality | American, born 1913
Publisher | Doubleday, USA
Theme | Science and nature, Adventure, Animal stories, Family

The story begins with a man telling us about a time he saved a dog from a street fight. The dog had clearly traveled a long way, probably out of loyalty to a lost owner he was trying to find. This makes the man reminisce about his own dogs when he was a child in the Cherokee territory of eastern Oklahoma's Ozarks (where the author, Wilson Rawls, grew up).

The narrator tells us that as a boy he badly wanted two hound puppies, so that he could train them for tracking and hunting raccoons. Because his parents could not afford the dogs, the boy, Billy, saved his nickels and dimes for two years to buy them himself. The novel emphasizes the hard work that went into purchasing and training the dogs. The satisfaction that comes from a job well done is one of the most important messages of the novel. Once the dogs are trained, Billy tells us a series of long, drawn-out hunting stories like the ones men tell one another around the campfire. The novel ends on a melancholy note, as the two dogs sacrifice themselves to protect Billy from a mountain lion.

Billy's parents reveal shortly afterward that they have saved enough money to move into town and send him and his sisters to school. As they leave the family home, the boy looks back to the graves of the two dogs on the side of a hill; the red fern growing between them, sacred in Cherokee legend, symbolizes their sacrifice. This classic story realistically depicts the love children feel for their pets. **SY**

"It seems to me that almost everything is a waste of time."

D'Aulaires' Book of Greek Myths 1962

Ingri and Edgar Parin D'Aulaire

Nationality | Norwegian/American, born 1904 (Ingri); German/American, born 1898 (Edgar)
Publisher | Doubleday, USA
Theme | Myths and legends

8+

Some of the world's finest literature and art has been based on the ancient mythology of the Greeks, including the plays of Sophocles and Aeschylus and the writings of Aristotle. Ingri and Edgar Parin D'Aulaires' *Book of Greek Myths* helps children to appreciate these legends, while providing detailed lithographic illustrations throughout the book.

Covering all of the most important characters, including the king of the gods, Zeus, and his family, as well as more minor gods, such as Prometheus, and mortal descendants of Zeus, such as Heracles (or Hercules) and Helen of Troy, this book is a fantastic reference for children interested in myths and legends of the ancient Greeks. The stories of heroic deeds, bitter quarrels, supernatural actions, and intense rivalries have been compiled from traditional Greek material and told in a series of sections, with the story of each character drawn out figuratively as well as literally on the pages.

The D'Aulaires' illustrations vary from full-page portraits to small and detailed graphics; they use both color and black and white. Unlike some of their previous books, in which they used the traditional method of drawing directly onto lithograph stone, in this book the lithographing process was adapted onto acetate separations. This modernization of the process allowed the D'Aulaires to bring their illustrations to life and to continue to provide a distinctive folktale quality that is so rare in many children's books. **CVB**

The Winged Watchman 1962

Hilda van Stockum

Nationality | Dutch, born 1908
Publisher | Farrar, Straus and Giroux, USA
Award | Brotherhood Award
Theme | War, Family, Historical fiction

Set in occupied Holland during World War II, *The Winged Watchman* tells the story of two young boys, Joris and Dirk Jan, and how the war affects their lives. The boys live in a windmill whose sails are used to send secret signals to the Dutch resistance, right under the noses of the occupying Nazis.

The Winged Watchman is a tale of courage, compassion, and suspense. The boys' adventures include rescuing a downed British airman, disguising him as a woman, and taking him to their uncle, Cor, who is a member of the resistance and therefore able to help the airman escape. The boys are also involved in hiding weapons, and their parents take in a Jewish baby and bring her up as their own when her real parents are rounded up by the Nazis. The tension mounts throughout the story as a local youth who supports the Nazis begins spying on his neighbors and informing on their activities.

Hilda van Stockum based her story on letters received from relatives in her native Holland during the war. Van Stockum was also an accomplished painter and often illustrated her own books as well as those written by other authors. She wrote more than twenty books for children, set in a wide range of locations. *The Winged Watchman* gives a realistic picture of life under Nazi occupation. It does not flinch from describing the daily fear and hunger experienced by the Dutch but also highlights their sense of patriotism. **HJ**

The Winged Watchman

8+

A Dog So Small 1962

Philippa Pearce   Jules Feiffer

Nationality | English, born 1920 (author); English, birth date unknown (illustrator)
Publisher | Constable, UK
Theme | Animal stories

Ben is just an ordinary boy with an ordinary dream—he wants a dog. He wants a dog so badly that he is pretty certain his grandfather will get him one for his birthday. His grandfather lives in the country, so Ben gets to play with his dog when he visits, but he knows that is not the same as having a dog of your own.

As the middle child in a family of seven children, Ben needs someone special all for himself. His hopes are dashed when he receives a picture of a dog instead. Was that what all the hints and winks amounted to? Even if living in the middle of London is unsuitable for a dog, Ben wants one all the more and so retreats into a fantasy in which his need for a dog conjures up the smallest, least noticeable of dogs, the feisty Chihuahua, Chiquitita, "a dog so small that you could only see it with your eyes shut." Ben's obsession with having a dog of his own reaches a climax when he is hit by a car while crossing a road in search of his imaginary companion (although this nasty accident does result in his getting the puppy of his dreams).

As with her more complex works, Philippa Pearce summons up her fictional world with sensitivity and respect, painting a down-to-earth picture of working-class life, where everyone gets along as best they can and there is little room for fancy. No one is unkind, but Ben's problem is that he wants the dog so much that he gives up trying to influence the adults in his family. The reader really feels for Ben and his hectic folly with Chiquitita, an accident waiting to happen that is happily resolved. **VN**

The Garden 1962

Jiří Trnka

Original Title | Zahrada
Nationality | Czech, born 1912
Publisher | Albatros, Czechoslovakia
Theme | Fantasy, Adventure, Animal stories

This timeless story—originally entitled *Zahrada*—by painter, illustrator, filmmaker, and puppeteer Jiří Trnka has become one of the cornerstones of Czech children's literature. Combining masterful illustrations with unusual language and a sense of melancholy, the book looks at how children's adventures are abandoned as childhood becomes young adulthood.

On their way to school, five unnamed boys encounter a rusty gate. After painstakingly opening it, they discover it leads to a mysterious garden: a labyrinth, a jungle, an unmapped land promising countless adventures. They are also confronted by the strange master of the garden, a morose old tomcat who scares them out of the gate.

When the boys overcome their fear and return to the garden, they grow fond of the cat, who hesitantly returns their feelings and introduces them to the garden's mysteries: A stone garden gnome who knows everything but says nothing; a learned whale who lives in the fountain; the neighborhood dogs who hold monthly meetings at full moon; and five kind elephants who are always ready to help.

Knowing that all things must pass, Trnka ends the story on a melancholic, almost heartbreaking note. On a warm spring day the boys find it a little harder to open the garden gate. This is also the time they start to realize that they might have more fun in the school alley, where everyone will admire their new clothes. So they turn around and walk away, never to return, leaving the garden and all its wonders and mysteries behind forever. **PO**

The Wolves of Willoughby Chase 1962

Joan Aiken   Pat Marriott

Nationality | English, born 1924 (author); English, born 1920 (illustrator)
Publisher | Jonathan Cape, UK
Theme | Historical fiction, Adventure

This exciting, compelling novel tells the story of Bonnie and her orphan cousin, Sylvia, who face a succession of appalling obstacles they have to overcome. The girls are living in a chilling version of nineteenth-century Britain, which has become infested with wolves migrating from Russia through a recently constructed tunnel.

Bonnie and Sylvia also have to cope with the evil Miss Slighcarp, a criminal governess-turned-guardian, out for their destruction. Moving at breakneck speed, this enthralling adventure story also takes in a secret passage, a helpful Gypsy boy, and imprisonment for the girls—first in a cupboard and then at a cruel boarding school, run by the dastardly Mrs. Brisket.

In the tradition of great storytelling, everything ends happily—but not before the readers have joined their two heroines on some enjoyably heart-stopping moments, as the two cousins refuse to be intimidated, however great the forces ranged against them.

The Wolves of Willoughby Chase deservedly won the Lewis Carroll Shelf Award in 1963 and was made into a film in the 1980s. It has remained a classic of children's literature ever since it was first published. Joan Aiken was a superb adventure story writer, mixing ripe melodrama with sly jokes and a mastery of spoken dialogue. This was her most famous novel, and she constructed it by mixing genuine historical facts with details forged by her own unpredictable imagination. Never allowing the pace to slacken, Aiken regularly ends chapters on just the type of cliff-hanging note that leaves readers begging for more. **NT**

"Sylvia screamed . . . and a wolf precipitated itself through the aperture. . . . It turned snarling on the sleeping stranger."

OTHER GRIPPING JOAN AIKEN BOOKS

Black Heart in Battersea, 1964
Nightbirds on Nantucket, 1966
The Whispering Mountain, 1968
Midnight Is a Place, 1974
The Stolen Lake, 1981

8+

The Little Pot Boiler 1963

Spike Milligan

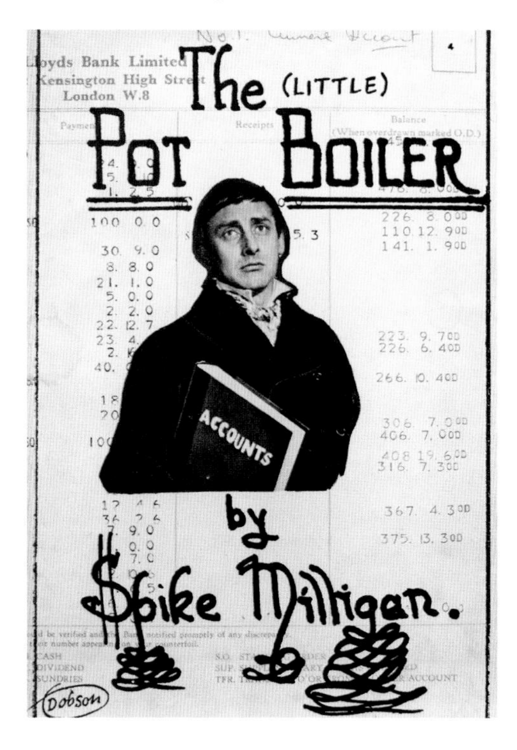

"People who live in glass houses / Should pull the blinds / When removing their trousers."

MORE CLASSIC NONSENSE BOOKS

***Silly Verse for Kids*, 1959**
***A Book of Milliganimals*, 1968**
***Badjelly the Witch*, 1973**
***Sir Nobonk and the Terrible, Awful, Dreadful, Naughty, Nasty Dragon*, 1982**

Nationality | Irish, born in India 1918
Publisher | Dobson Books, UK
Theme | Poetry, Quirky, Rhyming stories, Controversial, Fantasy

Comic, musician, writer, and actor Spike Milligan was synonymous with absurd, nonsensical humor in his heyday—between the 1950s and 1970s, when he appeared regularly on British radio and TV.

This is a scrapbook of his highly original mind and his apparently haphazard skill—of producing seemingly simple comedy that was actually cleverly constructed. An eye for visual humor and the silly, small things in life that make us laugh, plus the use of wonderful made-up words and names, give Milligan a direct way of communicating with young readers. *The Little Pot Boiler* will inspire children to think about combining words, ideas, and images in creative ways.

This book brims over with doggerel-like poetry, photos with strange captions, and longer prose musings on random topics. There are plenty of Milligan's own rapid cartoons, often hand-annotated to provide "helpful" information on strange subjects.

This exuberant wordplay and absurd characters and situations brought Milligan and his colleagues (Peter Sellers and Harry Secombe, who wrote the book's foreword) great success in the adult world with the groundbreaking radio sketch program, *The Goon Show*. Part of the show's success was a black, anti-establishment humor that would inspire the Monty Python team. Milligan often gave the impression that he lived outside the normal, respectable world of grown-ups. Perhaps this book is ample proof of that; it is truly entertaining stuff for any age. **AK**

How the Whale Became 1963

Ted Hughes George Adamson

Nationality | English, born 1930 (author); American, born 1913 (illustrator)
Publisher | Faber and Faber, UK
Theme | Myths and legends, Fantasy

This collection of fables and creation tales introduces young readers to the pleasures of a great poet's prose style and his core material of the natural world and the stories that shape it. The eleven tales, written for Hughes's own children, demonstrate his refusal to compromise on sophistication of language and ideas when writing for children, confident that their minds were ready for his vision. They are ripe for reading aloud, and children will develop storytelling skills as they enjoy the jokes in each story.

Sometimes the creature is in the trickster role, like the Owl who persuades the other birds that night is day by only allowing them outside at night and is punished by being left alone every night. The Whale starts life as a plant called whalewort growing in God's garden, swiftly increasing from the size of a bean to the size of a bus. Worried about the threat to his tender young crops, God sends the whalewort out to sea and tells it to make itself smaller by blowing. It's still out there, blowing and blowing, and as big as ever. Then there's the Hare whose ears never get long enough to hear the Moon say she will marry him, and the Polar Bear who has been sent far north because the other bears are jealous of her beauty. The tales celebrate the uniqueness of each species and give children much to think and talk about as they work out their own how and why of the universe. *How the Whale Became* is a wonderful introduction to the poetic imagination of Ted Hughes. **GB**

The Seasons in the City 1963

Italo Calvino

Original Title | Marcovaldo
Nationality | Italian, born 1923
Publisher | Einaudi, Italy
Theme | Family, Science and nature

This is a collection of twenty short, allegorical stories, many of which were written in the early 1950s. The stories are structured to represent the yearly seasonal cycle. They tell of the life of a poor rural man, Marcovaldo, who is devoted to his wife, Domitilla, and their children. They live in a large industrial city in northern Italy; like many people from the south, they moved from the countryside to urban life in the north in search of work and a better standard of living.

Calvino's theme is how life among nature is preferable to that in the city. His blue-collar worker protagonist longs for and dreams of the beauty of a simple life. Marcovaldo attempts to reconcile his old country ways and habits with his new existence, where he encounters pollution, poverty, and the harsh realities of modern consumerism. Yet along the way, the humble Marcovaldo does see glimpses of nature in the apparently ugly city—the moon shining in the night sky above neon signs, the beauty of fallen snow, an outcrop of mushrooms growing among the concrete jungle, and the expanse of sky from a park bench. The naive Marcovaldo's attempts to deal with the alienation and culture shock he has experienced often have humorous results, as things are not always as they first appear to him.

This is a well-written, witty, and often poetic book that tackles the subject of the country versus the city, and the natural versus the mechanical in a gentle and refreshing way. **CK**

Stig of the Dump 1963

Clive King   Edward Ardizzone

Nationality | English, born 1924 (author); English, born 1900 (illustrator)
Publisher | Penguin, UK
Theme | Friendship, Fantasy

STIG OF THE DUMP
by
Clive King
Illustrated by Edward Ardizzone

8+

Barney, a little boy prone to going off by himself, wanders off one day and, by chance, discovers a hidden cave at the bottom of a local chalk pit. Curious, he enters the cave and meets a Stone Age boy, dressed in rabbit skins.

Although his only form of language is to speak only in grunts, the Stone Age boy soon becomes Barney's firm friend. Barney names his friend Stig, and the two boys go on to have some exciting adventures. These include outwitting burglars who are attempting to raid Barney's house and rescuing an escaped leopard. Stig shows Barney how to hunt and how to make a fire. In quieter moments Barney and Stig busy themselves improving Stig's cave, adding a tin chimney and making makeshift shelves in what passes for his kitchen.

"Now . . . he could see further into the dark part of the cave. There was somebody there!"

Barney chooses never to tell his parents about his strange new friend in case they disbelieve in the existence of someone to whom he has gotten so close. One night, when Barney cannot sleep, he and his sister, Lou, find themselves with Stig, surrounded by other members of his tribe. It is the last time Barney and Stig see each other.

Stig of the Dump is artfully written and beautifully illustrated. It makes real a child's world of fantasy, by turning the sort of invisible companion children sometimes invent for themselves into an actual person. While some readers may decide that Stig only exists in Barney's imagination, the adventures they have together are so convincing that in the end it does not really matter whether Stig is real or not. **NT**

OTHER GREAT CLIVE KING READS

Hamid of Aleppo, 1958
The Twenty-Two Letters, 1966
The Night the Water Came, 1973
My and My Million, 1976
The Devil's Cut, 1978

Uncle 1964

J. P. Martin Quentin Blake

This is grand, crazy British comedy at its best, and it has inspired a cult following all over the world; the more so because its origins are slightly unusual.

The book's creator was a church minister with a lively, surreal sense of humor who told his children wonderfully funny tales that he made up himself, often sparked by dreams. Those children later insisted he write the stories down, and the collection that is *Uncle* was finally published (after lengthy delays because the tales were considered too rowdy), just before his death.

Martin's barmy universe has its own compellingly believable logic, and at the heart of it is a pompous, fabulously wealthy elephant called Uncle. Uncle

> *"You know jolly well that you would be bored stiff if we didn't have a dust-up occasionally."*

sports a purple dressing gown, has a university degree, and is locked into a struggle with the people of Badfort, led by Beaver Hateman. Uncle's home ("Homeward") is a fantastical conglomeration of structures dominated by skyscrapers and including water slides and treacle towers. His life is peopled by characters with wonderful names, such as Butterskin Mute, Old Monkey, Jellytussles, and Hitmouse.

Like all great children's writing, people delight in finding multiple levels of meaning. Uncle's entertaining nonsense makes it perfect for children (and adults), while some readers claim it exposes society's hypocrisies and critiques capitalism.

No better illustrator could have been found for these very tall tales than Quentin Blake, who became Britain's first Children's Laureate in 1999. His boldly eccentric illustrations are fully equal to the task. **AK**

Nationality | English, born 1880 (author); English, born 1932 (illustrator)
Publisher | Jonathan Cape, UK
Theme | Fantasy, Animal stories

8+

UNCLE

J. P. Martin

OTHER COMEDIC UNCLE BOOKS

Uncle Cleans Up, 1965
Uncle and his Detective, 1966
Uncle and the Treacle Trouble, 1967
Uncle and Claudius the Camel, 1969
Uncle and the Battle for Badgetown, 1973

8+

Chitty Chitty Bang Bang 1964

Ian Fleming   John Burningham

Nationality | English, born 1908 (author); English, born 1936 (illustrator)
Publisher | Glidrose Productions, UK
Theme | Fantasy, Adventure

This is the story of the Pott family and their amazing, magical car. Caractacus Pott (the name was changed to Potts for the movie) is an explorer and inventor, who lives with his wife and their twin children. One day he invents a special candy with holes in it that makes a whistling noise as it is being sucked. Lord Skrumshus, who owns a candy factory, loves the idea and buys the invention. Caractacus decides to buy a car with the money, but instead of buying a new one, he falls in love with an old wreck about to be sold for scrap. It is a "Paragon Panther." Only one was ever made and in her heyday she was a champion racing car.

Caractacus works on her for many weeks before she is ready to take the family for a drive. The children are very excited about the number plate, which is GEN II; they think it means that she is a genius car. Caractacus admits that he does not know what all the car's buttons and levers do. The children name the car Chitty Chitty Bang Bang, after the noises she makes when starting up. Chitty Chitty Bang Bang turns out to be a magical car with a mind of her own. She can fly, turn herself into a hovercraft, and think for herself. In the last of the family's adventures she even helps capture the notorious gangster, Joe the Monster.

Chitty Chitty Bang Bang was actually written as three separate adventures. The first two were published in 1964, the last in 1965. In 1971 all three were published together as a complete book. Ian Fleming took his inspiration from "the original Chitty Chitty Bang Bang," a car built in 1920 by his friend Count Zoborowski. **LH**

Chitty Chitty Bang Bang soars above the English Channel.

IAN FLEMING

CHITTY CHITTY BANG BANG

THE MAGICAL CAR

ILLUSTRATED BY
JOHN BURNINGHAM

ADVENTURE NUMBER
1

The White Stone 1964

Gunnel Linde   Eric Palmquist

Nationality | Swedish, born 1924 (author); Swedish, birth date unknown (illustrator)
Publisher | Bonniers Junior Förlag, Sweden
Theme | Friendship, School

8+

OTHER GREAT GUNNEL LINDE READS

I Am a Werewolf Kid (Jag ar en varulvsunge), 1972
Radda Joppe—Dead or Alive (Radda Joppe—död eller levande), 1985
Charlie Karlsson and His Babysitters (Charlie Karlsson och hans barnvakter), 1990

The story in this multi-award-winning novel (originally published under the title *Den vita stenen*) takes place in a Swedish village, sometime in the early twentieth century. Fia, a little girl, lives in the district judge's house with her mother, the piano teacher. Fia is having a difficult time in school because of her mother's profession: "What a useless occupation to play the piano all day," her classmates say. Fia, who has no friends and has been nicknamed Fia-pling-plong, loves her mother dearly, but wishes that she had chosen to become a shop assistant or something more ordinary, like some of the other village mothers.

One day a new boy, Hampus, a shoemaker's son arrives in town. He sees Fia standing by the gate and asks her name; she tells him she is called Fideli. "My name is Prince Perilous," says Hampus, as he sees a gaudy poster on a circus wagon passing by.

"'Now the stone is yours again,' Prince Perilous said as he swiftly handed it back to her."

Fia is holding a treasured possession, her white and smooth "comfort stone" in her hand and Hampus asks, "If I was to paint a face on the church clock, would you give me your stone as a reward?" She agrees. From here on Fia's life changes. She has become Fideli and her life has become an adventure, with constant competition between the two friends revolving around the possession of the mystical white stone. The tasks they set grow increasingly difficult as the story progresses, keeping the reader in suspense.

The White Stone is a captivating story about friendship and challenges, but it is also about poverty and the rigidity of class structure. It is now considered a modern Swedish classic. **CC**

Harriet the Spy 1964

Louise Fitzhugh

Nationality | American, born 1928
Publisher | Harper and Row, USA
Award | Sequoyah Book Award, 1967
Theme | Controversial, School, Family

Harriet the Spy was groundbreaking, pointing the way ahead for a strand of realistic children's fiction tackling the issues of growing up and adolescence. The heroine of Fitzhugh's story is eleven-year-old Harriet Welsch, who starts a journal packed with her thoughts on family, friends, school classmates, and a succession of neighbors who Harriet secretly watches on her "spy route." Harriet's observations are generally entertaining, but not always complimentary.

Apart from her desire to write and become a spy, Harriet also keeps a journal because she is lonely. She lives in New York, in Manhattan's affluent Upper East Side. Her busy parents are rarely around and she is looked after by a nanny, Ole Golly.

"Miss Whitehead has buck teeth, thin hair, feet like skis, and a very long hanging stomach."

Harriet experiences the ultimate disaster feared by all diarists when her notebook is discovered, and her friends read what she has written about them. They establish the Spy Catcher Club and set about exacting revenge on Harriet for her spiteful comments, and Harriet becomes increasingly isolated. Meanwhile, Harriet's parents fire her nanny, so the one stable and positive influence in Harriet's life is no longer there to support her. Her parents become increasingly perturbed by their daughter's need to scribble her thoughts down, and she is sent to a psychologist.

The story ends on an optimistic note: Harriet's talents are recognized and channeled constructively into the school newspaper, and she is reconciled with her friends. This story is packed with humor and observations on life, yet it packs no punches in portraying the imperfections of its protagonist. **CK**

MORE BOOKS ABOUT NONCONFORMISTS

What Celia Says (Celia lo que dice) **by Elena Fortún, 1929**
Secret Diary of Adrian Mole **by Sue Townsend, 1982**
Bill's New Frock **by Anne Fine, 1989**
Clarice Bean: That's Me **by Lauren Child, 1999**

The Adventures of Rupert the Toad 1964

Roy Berocay José Miguel Silva Lara

Nationality | Uruguayan, born 1955 (author); Uruguayan, birth date unknown (illustrator)
Publisher | Editorial Alfaguara, Uruguay
Theme | Animal stories, Friendship, Adventure

The Adventures of Rupert the Toad (originally entitled *Las aventuras del sapo Ruperto*) is part of one of the most successful children's book series in contemporary Latin American literature. This, the first book in the series, introduces its readers to the life and times of a toad who lives in a pond near the banks of the river Solis Chico.

Rupert the toad is not like other toads. He is lively and curious, with a passion for detective stories, an entrepreneurial spirit, and an unquenchable thirst for adventure—in short, "the most famous toad in Solis Chico." His adventures are tragicomic and bizarre, for Rupert not only wants to leave his pond; he also dreams of becoming a rock 'n' roll star and of being the first toad to travel in space as an astronaut.

These are not just stories about adventure, they are also tales of altruism and solidarity, such as the episode in which Ruperto courageously rescues a dolphin, or the one in which he saves a whale in distress. Berocay portrays a world in which it is normal for toads to speak. "What? A speaking toad!" is the first reaction when people meet Rupert in his adventures. "Of course," he always replies, "have you never read a story before? In stories toads always speak!" Berocay's fiction is populated by animals who have strong feelings of kinship and mutual love, a rare ability to interact with humans and, most important, a profoundly moral nature that is an example to many young readers. **LB**

Charlie and the Chocolate Factory 1964

Roald Dahl Joseph Schindelman

Nationality | Welsh, born 1916 (author); American, born 1923 (illustrator)
Publisher | Alfred A. Knopf, USA
Theme | Fantasy, Classics

When impoverished Charlie Bucket finds a Golden Ticket, winning him a trip around Mr. Willy Wonka's Chocolate Factory, his life changes forever. While the four other ticket-winning children all come—quite literally—to sticky ends, through their own bad behavior, Charlie is well-behaved and mesmerized by the eccentric and sometimes macabre Willy Wonka.

As the only child not to disappear in the course of the factory tour, we discover Charlie has passed a series of character tests with flying colors. In return, Willy Wonka, who has no children or heirs, announces he is going to bequeath the whole factory and everything in it to Charlie. The Bucket family—Charlie, his parents, and all four of his grandparents—can leave their tumbledown home to live in the factory for the rest of their lives. Instead of barely surviving on meager helpings of watery cabbage soup they can now eat as much chocolate as they like.

Roald Dahl always loved chocolate, remembering the comfort it had brought him when he was a lonely boy at boarding school. He first read this story to his own children and found they thoroughly enjoyed these references along with every other aspect of its child-centered exuberance, including those moments when Dahl attacks the child characters he particularly dislikes. Sometimes turning to rhyme, and on occasions using the made-up words he was always so good at inventing, this book won Dahl a huge audience he would retain for the rest of his life. **NT**

BY **Roald Dahl**

Illustrated by Joseph Schindelman

Concerning
the adventures
of four nasty children
and Our Hero
with Mr. Willy Wonka and
his famous candy plant

Shy Violet 1964

Giana Anguissola

Original Title | Violetta la timida
Nationality | Italian, born 1906
Publisher | Ugo Mursia Editore, Italy
Theme | School, Friendship

Shy thirteen-year-old Violet Mansueti lives in the city of Milan in Italy. At school she is mercilessly teased by her classmates, who have given her the humiliating nickname "Mammola Mansueta" (which, roughly translated, means "shrinking violet") because of her chronic shyness.

One day Violet is called to the principal's office, where she meets the editor of *Il Corriere dei Piccoli*, the popular Italian weekly newspaper for children that began as a supplement to the national newspaper *Il Corriere della Sera*. (The story is partly autobiographical, as Giana Anguissola herself began to work as a journalist when she was only in her teens.) Casting herself in the role of the editor, Anguissola—Mrs. A. for short—proposes that Violet write a weekly column for the newspaper. In spite of her overwhelming timidity, Violet decides that she would like to write about her own experiences and have them published. She learns, however, that shyness will not just go away by itself. She has to learn to laugh at herself and that she must fight her urge to run away and hide.

Helped by the editor's mentoring and the support of her caring grandfather, Oreste, and friend, Terence, Violet's self-esteem grows through her passion for writing. The pieces she writes for the newspaper are in turn enriched by the honest and often hilarious accounts of her inner emotions as she attempts to overcome the problem. *Shy Violet* is an empowering and helpful story for children who are trying to deal with their own shyness. **SMT**

The Book of Three 1964

Lloyd Alexander

Nationality | American, born 1924
Publisher | Henry Holt, USA
Theme | Fantasy, Adventure, Friendship, Classics

This is the first of The Chronicles of Prydain series, which has become popular on both sides of the Atlantic and inspired Disney's 1985 animation *The Black Cauldron*. In his author's note, Lloyd Alexander commented that the tales are only loosely influenced by Welsh mythology, although some of the characters do actually exist in legends.

The hero, Taran, is an adolescent boy who works quietly as assistant pig-keeper for one of his guardians, Coll the farmer, though he yearns for adventure in the big wide world. The enchanter, Dallben, his other guardian, is instructing him from the book in the title. The Book of Three is said to contain everything worth knowing and Taran is forbidden from even touching it.

Taran eventually does find himself on an adventure when the oracular white pig, Hen Wen, runs away and he follows in pursuit. He meets many different characters: the strange Gollum-type creature, Gurgi—forever hungry for munchings and crunchings; Gwydion, a king in disguise; Doli the dwarf; the terrible and irredeemably evil Horned King; and Queen Achren. Taran finally overcomes his problems with Arawn the Death-Lord and the Horned King, thanks to his loyal companions, and returns home a little wiser, and perhaps slightly in love.

While some of Alexander's characters are familiar stereotypes in fantasy fiction, Achren's spirited, intelligent, and fearless niece, Eilonwy, is a wonderful creation, as is Fflewddur Fflam, an ex-king and compulsive liar who is trying, rather unsuccessfully, to become a bard. **WO**

Nurse Matilda 1964

Christianna Brand Edward Ardizzone

Nationality | English, born 1907 (author); English, born 1900 (illustrator)
Publisher | Brockhampton Press, UK
Theme | Family

The Brown family are in trouble, and it seems only one person can come to their rescue: Nurse Matilda. How the fierce, aging nanny manages to bring a sense of order to the chaos of the Brown household is revealed in this, the first of Brand's trilogy about Matilda.

This is an enchanting story, even more so because of the illustrations by Brand's cousin, the war artist Edward Ardizzone. His exquisite images help create the atmosphere of a sprawling Victorian home inhabited by a very large family, including some highly mischievous children. Brand describes the children as belonging to groups: "There were the Big Ones and the Middling Ones and the Little Ones and the Littlest Ones; and the Baby."

The story opens with Mr. and Mrs. Brown trying to find a nanny for their misbehaving children after the current nanny and nurse maid walk out. It is obvious that the children's often amusing naughtiness and general lack of manners are the result of being pampered. Mrs. Brown refuses to see her offspring as culpable for their actions; to her they are blameless victims, "My poor, dear, darling children!"

The outgoing staff advise the Browns that only Nurse Matilda can help them with their wayward children, and when Matilda magically appears, her no-nonsense approach, stern tactics, and forbidding appearance promise that things are going to change. Yet beneath Matilda's ugly exterior—with her wrinkled brown face, potato-like nose, and protruding tooth—lies a person who not only can discipline children but can also win their hearts, minds, and affection. **CK**

"'Your children are so naughty that we can't stand it one minute longer. . . . What you need . . . is Nurse Matilda.'"

OTHER FICTIONAL NANNIES

Mary Poppins by P. L. Travers, 1934
The Manny Files by Christian Burch, 2006
Emmy and the Incredible Shrinking Rat by Lynne Jonell, 2007
The Willoughbys by Lois Lowry, 2008

8+

Elidor 1965

Alan Garner · Charles Keeping

Nationality | English, born 1934 (author); English, born 1924 (illustrator)
Publisher | William Collins, UK
Theme | Fantasy

Elidor is woven together from the mythologies of England, Ireland, and Wales. As with other Alan Garner books, this mythical place intrudes into the real world, bringing staggeringly huge dangers not present in most children's everyday lives. In it, the characters "drove themselves toward its glass and concrete as if the danger behind, the danger of spear-edge and shield rim, would be powerless in the neon glare."

The hero, Roland, walks through a door in a half-demolished church into the dying world of Elidor to rescue his sister and brothers. They take the treasures of Elidor—a spear, a sword, a cauldron, and a golden stone—back to their own world to keep them safe from the dark forces. In their own world, the treasures take on the appearance of things they might have picked up among the demolition rubble: a piece of railing, two boards nailed together, a broken cup, and a lump of stone. But magic still clings to the treasures, making the television go haywire and powering unplugged electrical devices.

The children bury the treasures in the garden, and for a while everything returns to normal. Then two men from Elidor break through, forcing the children to take the treasures and run. The chase brings them back to the derelict landscape where the adventure started and they meet Findhorn, a unicorn. Findhorn's song is the key to saving Elidor, but the children do not know how to make him sing. At last, fatally wounded and with his head in Helen's lap, Findhorn sings his extraordinary song. This is an absorbing children's fantasy and a tense, atmospheric read. **CW**

The Little Fox 1965

István Fekete

Original Title | Vuk
Nationality | Hungarian, born 1900
Publisher | Móra Publishing, Hungary
Theme | Animal stories

This is one of the most popular children's books ever published in Hungary. It tells the story of Vuk, an adventurous fox cub who returns home one day from exploring the forest to find that a local hunter has destroyed his family. Vuk, frightened and alone, is found by his uncle Karak, who takes him to his cave and begins to teach him the skills that he will need in order to survive.

Soon Vuk becomes one of the cleverest foxes in the forest and plans to take revenge on the hunter who killed his family. When he visits the hunter's house he discovers a female fox trapped in a cage. Karak and Vuk use all their cunning to help her to escape and they all return to the forest.

Following a series of action-packed adventures, Vuk and the other foxes are almost caught by hunters when they are betrayed by the swallows and other birds. Once again demonstrating great craftiness, Vuk formulates a plan to help them escape, but sometimes cunning is not enough. During the hunting season, while the other foxes run and take shelter, old uncle Karak is shot and killed. Vuk returns alone to his cave in the cliffs. As winter draws on, Vuk finds a vixen mate and they then have cubs of their own so that the natural cycle begins again.

Vuk has captivated children's imaginations since it was first published and gained a new international audience when it was made into an animated film in 1981. Regarded as a classic piece of Hungarian film-making, it was marketed in English-speaking countries as *The Little Fox*. **HJ**

FEKETE ISTVÁN
VUK

THE MOUSE AND THE MOTORCYCLE

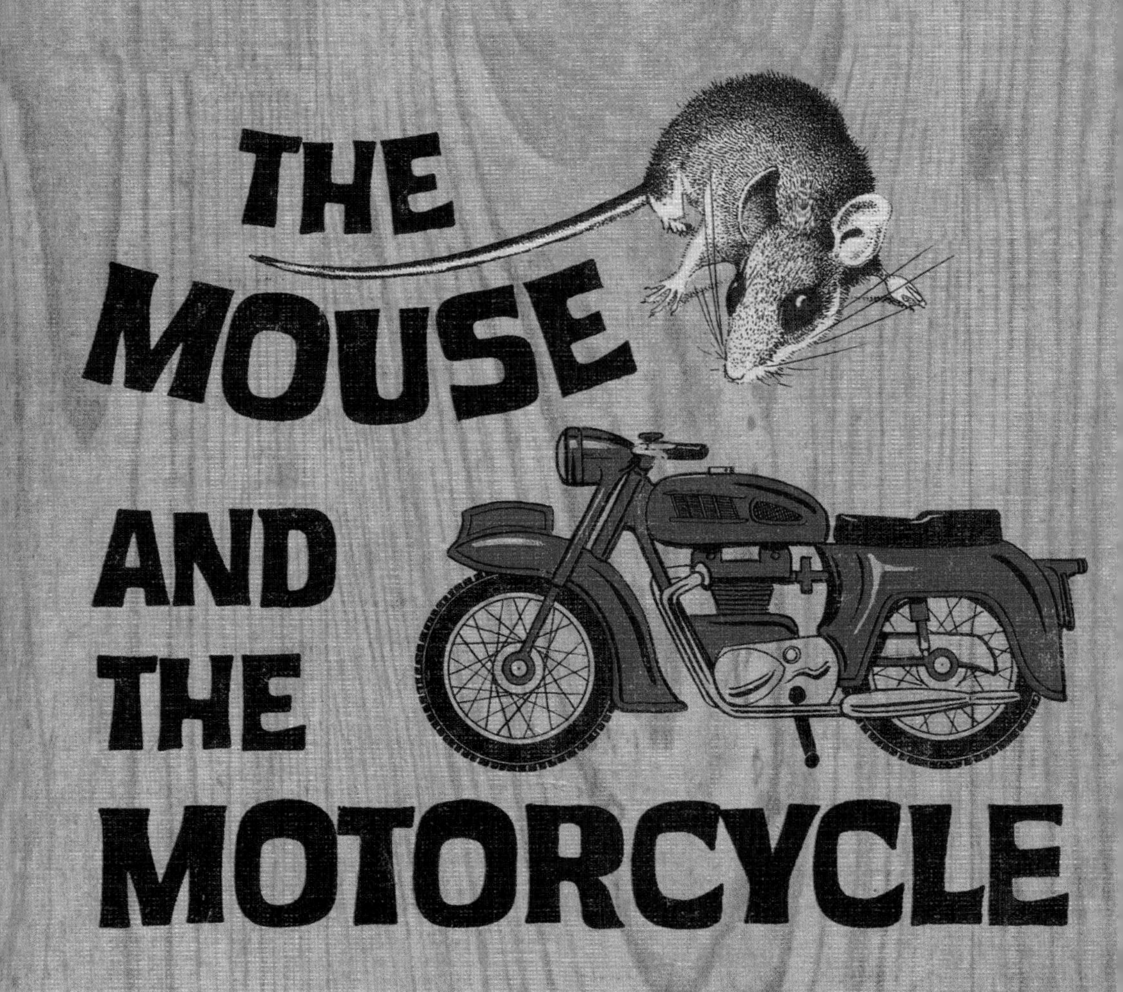

BEVERLY CLEARY

ILLUSTRATED BY LOUIS DARLING

The Mouse and the Motorcycle 1965

Beverly Cleary   Louis Darling

Nationality | American, born 1916 (author); American, birth date unknown (illustrator)
Publisher | HarperCollins, USA
Theme | Animal stories, Friendship

Kicking off Beverly Cleary's most fanciful series, *The Mouse and the Motorcycle* introduces us to Ralph S. Mouse, in a coming-of-age story writ small. Ralph is a young mouse, with a worrisome mother and a large family, who has spent his entire life in Room 215 of the creaky old Mountain View Inn. Ralph's world is changed forever when the room is occupied by a young boy, Keith, who teaches Ralph how to ride his toy motorcycle, even making him a helmet out of half of a ping-pong ball. The motorcycle becomes Ralph's passport to the larger world; of not only the hallway outside the room, but also the ground floor and even outside. Along the way Ralph avoids danger in the form of dogs, owls, vacuum cleaners, and all of the everyday things that make life as a mouse so perilous.

At first, Keith only allows Ralph to ride the motorcycle at night, so that nothing will happen to it. When Ralph ignores this prohibition and loses the motorcycle in the laundry, Keith chides him for his irresponsibility. However, when Keith becomes sick, Ralph manages to redeem himself by defying his mother to search the hotel for the only thing that can make his friend feel better: an aspirin. When the motorcycle is returned by a friendly bellboy, Keith gives it to Ralph as a gift, to ride whenever he wants.

Cleary's prose always sparkles throughout the series, as she perfectly captures that particular joy that young children (and especially young boys) take in their shiny, noisy machines. **SY**

Telephone Tales 1965

Gianni Rodari   Bruno Munari

Original Title | Favole al telefono
Nationality | Italian, born 1920 and 1907
Publisher | Einaudi, Italy
Theme | Fantasy

Italian author Gianni Rodari is a wonderful observer of tiny details, which he cleverly inverts using rhyme, action, and humor. Each of these *Telephone Tales* includes a topsy-turvy situation. Things are difficult or do not go as planned, however, a resolution is always reached and with it a reflection on what really matters in the world of children—the joy of a gift and the delight of the unexpected.

In "*Lo sbaglio delle Befane*," the Befana, pictured by illustrator Bruno Munari as a raggedy old woman on a broomstick who brings presents to children on the night of the Epiphany, has got it all wrong. In fact, all of the bringers of gifts—whether in Rome, Sarajevo, or Freiburg—have picked up the wrong sacks and delivered the wrong presents.

"*La pioggia di Piombino*" is about a day when sugared almonds rain from a cloud in the sky and the children scramble to collect them; the green ones taste of mint and the pink ones of strawberry. In "*Il semaforo blu*," a traffic light flashes only blue. The day the workmen come to mend it, the traffic light sighs mournfully—nobody has understood that blue is the color of the sky: by now everyone should be flying.

Rodari is a master storyteller; he makes it easy for children to suspend their beliefs when reading his enchanting and universal tales. As the Befana from Rome concludes at the close of "*Lo sbaglio delle Befane*": "Now I get it. . . . Children the world over are equal and they like the same toys." **SMT**

The King of Copper Mountains 1965

Paul Biegel

Original Title | Het Sleutelkruid
Nationality | Dutch, born 1925
Publisher | Haarlem, The Netherlands
Theme | Myths and legends

King Mansolain has ruled the Copper Mountains for a thousand years but he is tired and his heart is slowing down. His physician, the Wonder Doctor, goes in search of Golden Speedwell—a rare life-giving plant found only in a distant land. Before setting off on his quest, he instructs the animals of the mountains to tell stories to the king to make his heart beat faster.

Like the *Arabian Nights*, fantastical tales are at the heart of this story. Each night a different creature knocks on the castle door, enters, and constructs a tale powerful enough to keep the king alive. A ferocious wolf, a lovesick donkey, and a three-headed dragon breathing fire are among the storytellers. Some of the tales are funny, some are sad, and some are eerie but they all interconnect and weave in elements of the king's own past to make up a truly magical whole. The final storyteller is a dwarf armed with four ancient books, who prophesizes that the king will reign for a 1,000 years more if the doctor accomplishes his task.

Highly acclaimed across Europe, this book remains one of Beigel's most popular works. He was influenced by the Brothers Grimm, and wrote more than fifty books for children. Most of his stories contain magical elements and feature robbers, princesses, kings, witches, dwarves, myths, and legends, as well as multilayered plots and unexpected endings. With elements of folklore and magic, this enchanting book has recently been reprinted in English due to public demand. **HJ**

Ash Road 1965

Ivan Southall Clem Seale

Nationality | Australian, born 1921 (author); Australian, born 1922 (illustrator)
Publisher | Angus and Robertson, Australia
Theme | Adventure, Friendship

This gripping story begins on a Friday afternoon in January, when three young teenagers—Harry, Graham, and Wallace—embark on a long-anticipated camping expedition to the Australian outback. Initially, they relish their freedom and sense of independence and there is a fair measure of good-natured banter among them. One of their intentions is to make contact with a school friend whose family have a weekend home in the area. However, their plans are dramatically altered when Graham inadvertently spills some camping stove fuel, causing a fire to break out in a locality described as "a fire-trap."

Once lit, the resulting fire threatens the lives of all those who live on the Ash Road of the title. The encroaching ferocity of the fire—its sights, sounds, and smells—are vividly described by Southall, and the chaos that it unleashes among the road's various inhabitants, young and old, is brilliantly portrayed. It soon becomes clear, however, that the real revelation of the story is how, in such a situation, there are deep-seated psychological pressures at play, other than those that are merely physical. This applies to the characters, adults and youths alike, although it is the latter, on their way from early adolescence to adulthood, who seem to benefit most from the experiences. As one of them, Peter, reflects toward the end: "He knew, without being able to frame the words, that he was running into manhood and leaving childhood behind." **RD**

The Magic Finger 1966

Roald Dahl William Pène du Bois

Nationality | Welsh, born 1916 (author); French/American, born 1916 (illustrator)
Publisher | Harper and Row, USA
Theme | Magical stories, Classics

The eight-year-old narrator of this story has a finger with magical abilities, capable of casting a nastily appropriate spell on all those who make her angry. She uses it on her bullying teacher at school, who grows whiskers and a tail. However, what really makes her mad is hunting. The girl lives next door to farmer Gregg, whose favorite activity is hunting for fun with his two boys. One day, when she sees them coming home carrying the dead body of a young deer she turns her magic finger on them.

On waking up next morning, the Greggs discover they are bird-size and that they have all grown wings. They practice flying, which they thoroughly enjoy, and then see from above that their house is being occupied by four enormous wild ducks who are taking possession of the family guns. Even worse, these are now aimed at their former owners who are about to find out what it is like to be on the receiving end of their guns. A last minute promise from the Greggs to never shoot any animals again saves the day. The family returns to their human forms, and rechristen themselves the Eggs in honor of their newly appreciated feathered friends.

Although this little novella—originally entitled *The Almost Ducks*—lacks the verbal fireworks found in other Dahl books, its characteristic dark humor, strong plot, and popular message about respecting wild life—or else—have continued to make it a favorite among children. **NT**

"I can't tell you how I do it . . . But it always happens when I get cross, when I see red."

OTHER FAMOUS ROALD DAHL READS

James and the Giant Peach, 1961
Charlie and the Chocolate Factory, 1964
Fantastic Mr. Fox, 1970
The Twits, 1980
George's Marvelous Medicine, 1981

Graveyard Kitaro 1966

Shigeru Mizuki

Original Title | Hakaba Kitaro
Nationality | Japanese, born 1922
Publisher | Kodansha, Japan
Theme | Fantasy, Horror, Comics

8+

Shigeru Mizuki is an old master of the manga form, best known for the Graveyard Kitaro series, which has spawned many spin-offs: anime, multiple screen adaptations, and video games. It also popularized traditional Japanese folklore, particularly the creatures known as *yōkai*, a class of goblinlike spirit-monster to which the main characters in *Graveyard Kitaro* belong. With the series, Shigeru created a whole genre of "horror manga," but despite the grotesque nature of the genre he still manages to give his characters great charm. Kitaro, with his fringe flung over an empty eye socket, is no exception.

The one-eyed hero was born in a cemetery, and aside from his mostly decomposed father (now a talking eyeball), he is the last living member of a ghost tribe. Kitaro fights for peace between humans and *yōkai*, which usually involves Kitaro protecting the humans from the other spirit-monsters. At this one-eyed boy's disposal is an arsenal of supernatural weapons: spiny hairs that can be shot like arrows; a detachable remote-controlled hand; and hair that can detect spirit activity. The spirit-monsters that Kitaro must battle range from evil ogres, a rat man, and a little girl who turns into a frightening cat-monster, to the mischievous fox, and a snow woman. Most of these possess part-animal, part-human features and have spiritual and supernatural powers. Populated by misshapen creatures, *Graveyard Kitaro* is definitely weird, but wonderful. **RA**

The Hedgehog Tree 1966

Antonio Gramsci

Original Title | L'albero del riccio
Nationality | Italian, born 1891
Publisher | Editori Riuniti, Italy
Theme | Traditional

Antonio Gramsci is best known for his political and philosophical writing. A communist politician, he was arrested when the fascists took power in Italy in 1926. During his time as a political prisoner, Gramsci wrote many letters to his two children, Delio and Giuliano.

In the letters he asks each of them to write to him and talk about their lives, how their studies are going, what interests them, and how they are feeling. In turn, Gramsci writes about his life, especially about his childhood experiences in rural Sardinia. He also retells classic children's stories by Kipling, Pushkin, and Tolstoy. With the letters, Gramsci tried to keep alive his presence for his children and maintain some kind of normality for them even though he was in prison. Although he was never reunited with his children, who remained in Russia with their mother, Giulia Schucht, Gramsci never lost his identity as a father to his children. The letters stand as testimony to the voice of a doting father, and are very touching.

In the story of the title, the young Antonio and his friend come across a family of hedgehogs. They hide behind some bushes and observe the hedgehogs under an apple tree in the orchard, gathering together fallen apples. The mother and father hedgehogs climb the tree and shake it so the apples fall. The hedgehogs then turn into balls and roll over the gathered apples, which remain stuck in their spikes. Happily, they then trot away with the apples on their backs. **SMT**

The Mouse and His Child 1967

Russell Hoban   Lillian Hoban

Nationality | American, born 1925 (both)
Publisher | Harper and Row, USA
Theme | Traditional, Classics, Adventure, Animal stories

A tin clockwork mouse and his child, joined by their hands and designed to dance together under a Christmas tree, are thrown into a garbage can after they are broken by the family cat. Rescued by a tramp, they then search for a magnificent dollhouse, which they have decided will be their new home and where they will be reunited with the other toys they have gotten to know in their former shop window. However, they first have to escape the attentions of Manny the Rat, a thief, gangster, and bully out to ruin their quest at every opportunity.

This haunting story, written in the spirit of Hans Christian Andersen, manages to be both funny and sad at the same time. While their task appears hopeless, father and son mouse never doubt that they are going to succeed. Each chapter introduces new, sometimes bizarre, situations, all argued through by a marvelous cast of toys, animals, and insects. During the course of the story the animals produce an experimental play, paint pictures, fight, and speculate about the meaning of life.

Moving between jokes, contemporary references, and the occasional philosophical conundrum, this poignant, dreamy, and utterly enthralling novel was the last Russell Hoban wrote for children before turning to his equally distinctive adult fiction. Many of his early works were illustrated by his first wife, Lillian. The book, now considered a children's classic, was out of print for a while but was reprinted in 1990. **NT**

"'Where are we?' the mouse child asked his father. His voice was tiny in the stillness of the night."

OTHER GREAT TOY STORIES

The Midnight Folk by John Masefield, 1927
The Miraculous Journey of Edward Tulane by Kate DiCamillo, 2006
Toys Go Out by Emily Jenkins with Paul Zelinsky, 2006

From the Mixed-Up Files of Mrs. Basil E. Frankweiler 1967

E. L. Konigsburg

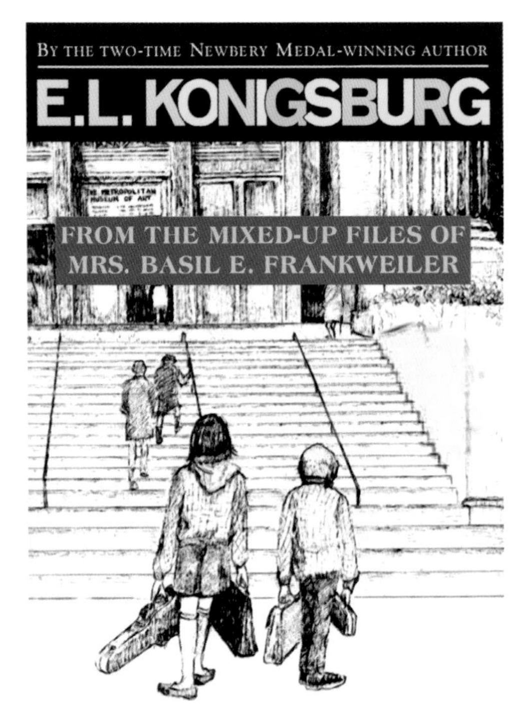

"Claudia knew for sure that she had chosen the most elegant place in the world to hide."

OTHER E. L. KONIGSBURG TITLES

***Jennifer, Hecate, Macbeth, William McKinley, and Me, Elizabeth*, 1967**
***The View from Saturday*, 1996**
***Silent to the Bone*, 2000**
***The Mysterious Edge of the Heroic World*, 2007**

Nationality | American, born 1930
Publisher | Atheneum, USA
Award | Newbery Medal, 1968
Theme | Adventure, Family

Claudia Kinkaid decides to run away just before her twelfth birthday. Bored rather than unhappy at home, she chooses her resourceful young brother, Jamie, as her companion. He, at the age of nine, looks after the couple's meager savings while Claudia makes all the plans. They hide away in the school bus and proceed to New York's Metropolitan Museum of Art—the venue Claudia has chosen for their big adventure.

Once in there they sleep in or sometimes under the antique furniture on display, wash in the museum's fountain, and eat sparingly from whatever they can either buy or find. They also become intrigued by a tiny statue, thought to be by Michelangelo. Claudia feels that if she can only crack this mystery, then she can return home having at last done something truly memorable with her life.

This engaging and eccentric story is told by eighty-two-year-old Mrs. Frankweiler, the former owner of the statue, who knows its secrets but has so far declined to reveal them. When the children finally find their way to her house, where she lives as a recluse, everything is resolved. Packed with incidental knowledge yet never setting out to teach, this good-humored story about two children taking control of their lives in such a matter-of-fact way has proved enduringly popular. In 2001 the Metropolitan Museum of Art devoted an issue of their publication, *MuseumKids*, to answering some of the many questions about the book put by enthusiastic young readers over the years. **NT**

The Goalkeeper's Revenge 1967

Bill Naughton

Nationality | Irish, born 1910
Publisher | Puffin, UK
Theme | Family, School, Friendship, Short stories, Classics

Bill Naughton is best remembered for his adult plays and novels, including *Alfie*. He also wrote books for children, the best loved of which is this collection of warm and moving short stories about childhood in a working-class community in the north of England in the 1930s. The stories focus on the lives of a group of children who spend their days playing soccer in the streets, racing homemade trolley carts, and whiling away the hours on street corners. But there is also the sense that childhood will not last forever as the children grow up and start looking for work.

Although written in the 1960s, the stories still have resonance with young readers. They are lively, and the language is direct and punchy. The characters are engaging and sharply defined, including Sam Dalt the goalkeeper of the title, whose goalkeeping skills keep him one step ahead of his arch enemy. Another favorite character from the collection is Spit Nolan, "a thin lad with a bony face" who cannot go to school because of illness. Spit Nolan is a champion rider of homemade trolleys, but when he takes part in a race with another boy, it has tragic consequences. Other stories include "Seventeen Oranges," about a delivery boy who works at the docks and steals seventeen oranges. He is caught by a policeman, but before he can be charged with theft he eats the evidence.

This witty collection will make readers laugh and groan with recognition at the things that go wrong at school, as well as make them think. **HJ**

D'Aulaires' Norse Gods and Giants 1967

Ingri and Edgar Parin D'Aulaire

Nationality | Norwegian/American, born 1904 (Ingri); German/American, born 1898 (Edgar)
Publisher | Doubleday, USA
Theme | Myths and legends, Folktales

The myths of the Norsemen, as recorded in Iceland's *Poetic and Prose Eddas*, use an unlikely mixture of understatement and hyperbole. The jaws of the monstrous wolf Fenrir, for example, are said to touch both Earth and the vault of heaven when opened, yet when brave Tyr loses his right hand between those jaws, we get the impression that it merely spoils his mood. The fact that the D'Aulaires took on illustrating such descriptions is commendable; the fact that they succeeded so well is extraordinary.

Ingri D'Aulaire was deeply familiar with the myths and tales recounted in the book. The narrative is a straightforward retelling of the mythology of the Norsemen from Creation to Ragnarokk (the death of the gods and destruction of the world). Along the way there are descriptions of each of the main gods and goddesses, along with the nine Norse worlds and the races that inhabited them. Nearly every page is illuminated by the D'Aulaires' signature lithographs, which are sometimes colorful, sometimes spare, yet always capture the essence of the characters and events they detail.

While the sheer bloody-mindedness of the Norsemen may be too much for some concerned parents or sensitive children, the stories and artwork never venture into overtly gruesome territory. The D'Aulaires present us with true myth, which in all cultures speaks to us of both the darkest and most noble aspects of humanity. **CR**

Tales of the Rue Broca 1967

Pierre Gripari Claude Lapointe

Nationality | French, born 1925 (author); French, born 1938 (illustrator)
Publisher | La Table Ronde, France
Theme | Traditional, Fairy tales

Rue Broca, in *Contes de la rue Broca,* is not a street like other streets. In this part of Paris you come across all kinds of people, little children and giants wearing red socks, talking potatoes and fairies who live in faucets; there is also Monsieur Pierre who loves telling stories so much that he ends up inventing them. The children of the neighborhood love them; then they invent extraordinary stories together. One day, Monsieur Pierre finds five francs in his pocket and decides to go to the notary and buy a house. It is rather difficult to find one at this price but in the end he does. This particular house is also home to a terrifying creature: a witch who lives in the broom cupboard and comes out when you sing a strange little song!

The children of Rue Broca inhabit their own stories. Bachir, the grocer's son, relies on his magic doll to persuade his father to buy him a bicycle. The universe that fills this street is very much like ours, but magic and the humdrum business of everyday life exist side by side. *Tales of the Rue Broca* consists of thirteen colorful, imaginative stories of which the most famous is undoubtedly "The Witch of the Rue Mouffetard." The characters who inhabit these tales can be found in all fairy tales (you will find a devil, witches, kings and a giant), but at the same time they are incredibly contemporary. Younger children love to have these amusing and insolent tales read to them before devouring the book themselves when they have learned to read. **SL**

A Wizard of Earthsea 1968

Ursula K. Le Guin

Nationality | American, born 1929
Publisher | Parnassus, USA
Award | *Horn Book* Fanfare, 1968
Theme | Fantasy

This is the first in the Earthsea Quartet, in which Ursula K. Le Guin creates in precise detail the fantasy world of islands and sea that form the background to the story of Ged, a boy with a talent for magic, who saves his village. Tutored by Ogion the mage, Ged is impatient to learn more so he travels to the School of Wizards on Roke. He learns well and quickly, but his instant dislike of fellow student, Jasper, leads him to boast and use a spell that brings from the dead a shadow that will haunt him.

At the cost of Archmage Nemmerle's life, Ged is rescued and nursed back to health by the skill of the other mage at the school. Ged starts to learn again but he knows he cannot escape the shadow except on Roke, where he is protected. When he receives his staff, he leaves the safety of Roke knowing that he will have to keep on the move. Only when Ged is nearly captured by Serret and her husband does he realize that he has to confront the shadow and this quest takes him beyond Earthsea's boundaries, where he is at last able to defeat it and be free.

Le Guin brilliantly envisions an altogether fantastical world with its own map and language, incorporating elements of other mythological tales and legendary creatures, such as dragons, to make a spellbinding experience for the reader. This title, together with *The Tombs of Atuan* (1971), *The Farthest Shore* (1972), and *Tehanu* (1990) make up this award-winning quartet. **JF**

The Iron Man: A Children's Story in Five Nights 1968

Ted Hughes George Adamson

Nationality | English, born 1930 (author); American/English, born 1918 (illustrator)
Publisher | Faber and Faber, UK
Theme | Myths and legends, Classics

This is an exciting and profound story about the power for good and evil that coexists in all of us and the importance of greeting the unknown with courage and imagination. Hughes wrote it to read to his own children, and reading it aloud is an excellent way to introduce children to the energy and power of the late British Poet Laureate's language.

The hulking Iron Man (Iron Giant in the U.S.), who chews barbed wire and devours farm machinery, is one of the most memorable monsters in fiction. His ability to survive any amount of punishment gives him the air of an action hero. He also has a heart, agreeing to protect his former persecutors when needed. The story draws on common themes in myths and traditional tales, such as the figure of the innocent but wise child who befriends the apparent enemy. Here, the farmer's son, Hogarth, builds a relationship with the Iron Man after the farmers have trapped him, and negotiates a way for the creature to live peacefully with the community. The shift in the Iron Man's status from enemy of the people to Earth's defender against destruction by a space-bat-angel-dragon as big as Australia, and the trial of strength between the two adversaries, also have mythological echoes.

The Iron Man is now a mythical figure in his own right, having inspired four decades of writing, drama, and art in schools. Children in Hughes's birthplace, Mytholmroyd in Yorkshire, have illustrated the entire text for display at their local railway station. **GB**

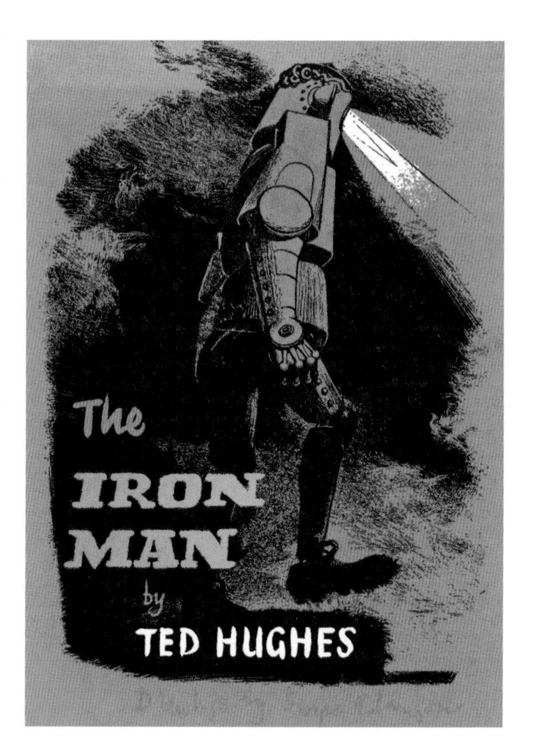

"Where had he come from? Nobody knows. How was he made? Nobody knows."

OTHER UNUSUAL FRIENDSHIPS

Night on the Galactic Railroad by Kenji Miyazawa 1927
Stig of the Dump by Clive King, 1963
My Friend the Painter by Lygia Bojunga Nuñes, 1987
Skellig by David Almond, 1998

8+

My Sweet-Orange Tree 1968

José Mauro de Vasconcelos

Original Title | O meu pé de laranja lima
Nationality | Brazilian, born 1920
Publisher | El Ateneo, Argentina
Theme | Family, Illness and death

This novel, which courageously and tactfully deals with social exclusion, the trauma of extreme poverty in the favelas, and the death of a friend, is one of the most successful novels of contemporary Brazilian literature. Five-year-old Zezé is extraordinarily mature for his age, and has already taught himself how to read. His family, who are very poor, live in the favelas around Rio de Janeiro. His father is unemployed and his mother works in a factory for a very low wage. Zezé spends most of his life on the streets; his many siblings, with the exception of his sister Gloria and brother Luis, beat him. Zezé takes refuge in the world of his imagination, where a small orange tree, which grows with only one branch and without fruit in their backyard, becomes a magical speaking tree.

Despite his initial suspicion and detachment from the real world of adults, Zezé becomes friends with a well-off man called Portugal, who is deeply moved by the child's plight. Friendship grows into affection and profound trust, to the extent that, in what is perhaps the most moving scene in the story, Zezé asks Portugal to adopt him. Portugal refuses, but promises to watch over him. Sadly, Portugal dies in a car accident. Zézé despairs and becomes seriously ill. His family, who are unaware of the friendship, believe that his deterioration is due to the recent road works that have destroyed part of their garden and Zezé's orange tree. The novel ends on an optimistic note when Zezé starts to recover and his father finds a job. **LB**

Doraemon: Gadget Cat from the Future 1968

Fujiko Fujio

Nationality | Pseudonym. Japanese, born Hiroshi Fujimoto 1933; Japanese, born Motoo Abiko 1910
Publisher | Shōgakukan, Japan
Theme | Fantasy, Friendship

Visitors to Japan are often struck by the proliferation of advertising images and merchandise featuring a round-headed, blue-and-white cartoon cat with an enormous smiling mouth. This is Doraemon, a robotic feline from the twenty-second century, who has become a cultural icon in Japan, China, Southeast Asia, and South America. Although the character achieved his popularity largely via the animated films and television series produced since the early 1980s, he made his debut much earlier, in the manga comic book cocreated by Hiroshi Fujimoto and Motoo Abiko under the pen name Fujiko Fujio.

Doraemon's human protagonist is an unlucky and untalented young boy named Nobita. One day, his dresser drawer opens and out pops Doraemon, who has been sent back in time by Nobita's ancestor to help him change the course of his unsuccessful life. The robot has a kangaroo-like pouch from which he extracts such fanciful inventions as an "anywhere door," a beanie with a propeller that allows one to fly, and a time machine. Although these devices should enable Nobita to overcome any dilemma, they almost invariably backfire, with hilarious results.

Doraemon's popularity has been attributed to the wish-fulfillment fantasies it offers to its young readers, who dream of owning such devices themselves. Yet it is the appeal of Doraemon himself that has ensured the series' continued success. He is the ideal companion: steadfast, optimistic, and caring. **CR**

A Pair of Jesus Boots 1969

Sylvia Sherry

Alternative Title | The Liverpool Cats
Nationality | English, born 1932
Publisher | Jonathan Cape, UK
Theme | Friendship, Family

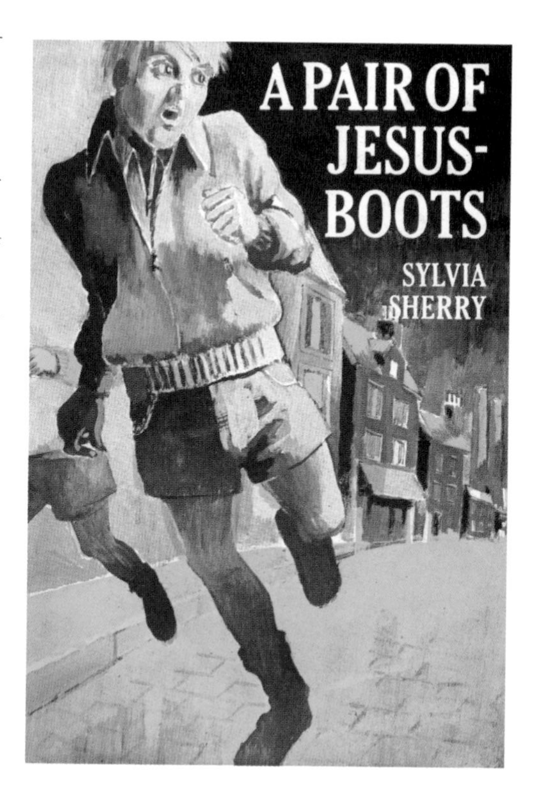

Rocky O'Rourke, growing up in the poorest part of Liverpool with his mother and stepsister, Suzie, aspires to become either a famous soccer player or a crook like his idolized older brother, Joey, who is currently serving time for a crime he says he did not commit. As the leader of the Cats gang, thirteen-year-old Rocky believes he has a point to prove by committing small "jobs" such as stealing cookie packets from the back of trucks, and breaking into empty buildings.

It is not until Joey is set free from prison that Rocky begins to realize that the life of a gangster is more dangerous than he thought. Jim Simpson, the London criminal who "framed" Joey is out to get him and his family, and is determined to see them "disappear."

Rocky, with his trademark "Jesus boots" (British slang for men's sandals) and flaming red hair, is a lovable character, despite his sometimes abrasive attitude toward policemen (who the children call "scuffers") and some of the adult characters. His relationship with his neighbor, old Mrs. Abercrombie, while initially tentative, brings out the softer side in him, as he attempts to look after her during her illness. He also shows considerable care for seven-year-old Suzie, who doesn't fit in with the other girls her age.

Published as *The Liverpool Cats* in the United States, the book charts Rocky's growth to maturity as he realizes that a life of crime is not a good one. His life in postwar Liverpool is well-drawn by Sherry, whose portrait of the city provides a vivid backdrop. **CVB**

"Our Joey'll be out soon . . . he'll be along to see yer—you bet!"

OTHER GREAT READS BY SYLVIA SHERRY

Frog in a Coconut Shell, 1968
A Pair of Desert Wellies, 1985
Rocky and the Ratman, 1988
Rocky and the Black-Eye Mystery, 1992

8+

Charlotte Sometimes 1969

Penelope Farmer

Nationality | English, born 1939
Publisher | Chatto and Windus, UK
Theme | Fantasy, School, Friendship, Historical fiction

After her first night spent at Aviary Hall, an English boarding school, Charlotte wakes to find that she has changed places with Clare, a girl from 1918, more than forty years earlier. Over the semester, Charlotte spends one day in her own time and the next in 1918, struggling to remember schoolwork, teachers' names, and different rules. A day's delay in Clare and her sister Emily's move to new lodgings, strands Charlotte in 1918. After an abortive attempt to get into the school at night to sleep in the bed that is key to the time swap, Charlotte resigns herself to living Clare's life for the time being. When she finally gets back to her own era, Charlotte discovers that one of her fellow pupils is Emily's daughter.

"Charlotte began to dream that she was fighting to stay as Charlotte . . ."

Charlotte Sometimes is more than just a time-slip fantasy—it is a story about identity. Even before Charlotte finds herself in the past, she feels she is losing herself in her new boarding school: "She . . . spent much of her time hunting for her name . . . as if she needed it to prove her own reality." Once she has started to swap places with Clare, Charlotte cannot believe that no one else notices. Emily tells her: "I just expected to see Clare and so I thought it was." But once Charlotte becomes stuck in 1918, she gradually begins to lose herself in Clare's identity, so that when, back in her own time, she learns of Clare's death, she cries as much for herself as for Clare.

This is the third of the Aviary Hall books featuring the Makepeace sisters. A little gem of a story, it inspired English rock band The Cure's haunting song of the same title in 1981. **CW**

OTHER READS BY PENELOPE FARMER

***The Summer Birds*, 1962**
***Emma in Winter*, 1966**
***A Castle of Bone*, 1972**
***Thicker than Water*, 1989**

8+

The Little Captain 1970

Paul Biegel / Carl Hollander

The Little Captain is a story that truly fizzes with adventure. Tony is a timid nine-year-old boy who lives by the sea. One day he discovers a ship—the *Neverleak*—that has been beached on the nearby shore. Tony is somewhat surprised to find that its captain is a small boy who is waiting for a big wave to sweep him back out to sea. When a storm begins, Tony—together with his two friends, Tubby and Marinka—join the Little Captain and sail away to the Island of Great and Growing. Along the way they encounter unusual sights such as a ghost town that is built on stilts and a mountain that spits fire. Like much of Paul Biegel's work for children, this charming story has an underlying message: that it is normal to be scared of adventure.

One of the Netherlands' best-loved writers, Paul Biegel wrote dozens of books over a career spanning forty years, and he won many prestigious awards, as well as a sizable international readership. Although this book is one of his best sellers, *The Little Captain* is not one of his favorite works. He is said to have preferred his stories that were written for older children, such as *The Soldier Maker* and *The Gardens of Orr*, the latter of which is generally considered to be his masterpiece.

Much of Biegel's work is influenced clearly by fairy tales and by the fantasy books of J. R. R. Tolkien; however, the Dutchman's stories are still certainly unique in their own way. Filled with fun, jokes, rhymes, and invented words and phrases, they demonstrate a genuine love of language and a sense of humor to which his young readers can relate. Biegel was never worried about being particularly fashionable and he wrote about the things that he knew children loved—pirates, robbers, witches, princesses, riddles that need solving, and the eternal battle between good and evil. **NH**

Original Title | De kleine kapitein
Nationality | Dutch, born 1925 and 1934
Publisher | Uitgeverij Holland, the Netherlands
Theme | Fantasy

8+

OTHER GREAT PAUL BIEGEL BOOKS

The King of the Copper Mountains (Het Sleutelkruid), 1965
The Gardens of Dorr (De Tuinen van Dorr), 1969
The Elephant Festival (Het olifantenfeest), 1973
The Great Little Master (De grote kleine kapitein), 2007

Are You There God? It's Me, Margaret. 1970

Judy Blume

A NOVEL BY JUDY BLUME
ARE YOU THERE GOD?
IT'S ME, MARGARET.

"Suppose I hate my new school? Suppose everybody there hates me? Please help me God."

OTHER FAMOUS JUDY BLUME BOOKS

***Iggie's House*, 1970**
***Then Again, Maybe I Won't*, 1971**
***It's Not the End of the World*, 1972**
***Blubber*, 1974**
***Forever*, 1975**

Nationality | American, born 1938
Publisher | Bradbury Press, USA
Award | *New York Times* Best Books
Theme | Classics, School, Family, Friendship

This groundbreaking novel by American novelist Judy Blume was one of the first to speak frankly about sex and religion for a young audience without ever seeming to preach or judge. Within it, soon to be twelve-year-old Margaret—faced with having to attend a new school—asks God some serious questions during her prayers every evening, not only about religion but also about her own particular personal uncertainties. With so many of her female friends starting menstruation, when is she going to get her first period? What sort of bra should she buy? With a Jewish mother and a Christian father and both sets of grandparents at war, which church should she join?

In between all these questions, Margaret leads the life of an ordinary American middle-class girl, occupied with various typical mini-dramas revolving around schoolwork, friends of both sexes, and family issues. Other authors since have written equally or even more frankly about approaching puberty, but Judy Blume is still the master at effortlessly re-creating what it is like to be on the verge of entering into new social and physical realities.

This best-selling novel continues to attract readers who are still looking for some of the answers to the questions Margaret poses so effectively. By the end of her story, everything in her life finally starts falling into place, with the last page describing the arrival—at last—of her first menses, something duly celebrated by Margaret and her mother alike. **NT**

When Hitler Stole Pink Rabbit 1971

 Judith Kerr

Nationality | German/British, born 1923
Publisher | Collins, UK
Theme | Historical fiction, War, Family

When Hitler Stole Pink Rabbit combines insight and humor with the honesty of a memoir and the drama of a novel. It is the first book in a trilogy that follows Anna, a child character based on the writer and illustrator Judith Kerr, into adulthood.

Anna grows up in Berlin, the sheltered daughter of a Jewish intellectual. In 1933, the family have to leave, just before Hitler comes to power. The story begins with the cover-up of Anna's father's early departure for Switzerland and her perilous journey with her mother and brother to join him. It balances the subjective response of a ten-year-old to dangerous times (Anna is distressed at leaving behind toys, friends, and the family dog) with later understanding. The family takes three years to reach London via Switzerland and France, by which time Anna's childhood is over.

Contemporary children who are refugees or have been taught in a language other than their mother tongue will identify with many of Anna's experiences at school in Paris: the struggles and delights at starting to think and learn in a new language, and the sadness when too much life experience means old friends have to be left behind. *When Hitler Stole Pink Rabbit* was written partly for Kerr's children and partly as a tribute to her parents, who kept the newly destitute family safely together against the odds. The later novels describe the trials of life as refugees in wartime London, but this one is the most effective introduction for children to a bleak period in history. **GB**

Friday, or The Savage Life 1971

Michel Tournier G. Lemoine

Nationality | French, born 1924 (author); French, born 1935 (illustrator)
Publisher | Gallimard, France
Theme | Classics, Friendship

This is an adaptation for younger readers of Tournier's earlier novel—*Vendredi ou les Limbes du Pacifique* (*Friday, or the Other Island*)—which was inspired by Daniel Defoe's *Robinson Crusoe*. Shipwreck survivor Robinson ends up on a desert island with the dog Tenn as his only companion. To try and cope with loneliness and counteract the dangers of idleness, Robinson invents an organized world; he declares himself governor of the island, which he has called Sperenza, and gradually succeeds in re-creating a civilized environment: a safe home, a herd of goats, fields, and orchards.

That all changes when a group of dangerous Indians land on the island. Condemned to death by his tribe, a young Indian takes refuge with Robinson, who takes him on as his servant, calls him Friday, and teaches him his language. Friday learns to wear trousers, milk animals, harvest crops, and make bread and cheese. One day, while Friday is smoking his master's tobacco he sparks off an explosion, shattering the delicate balance established by the governor. This leads to a complete reversal of everything: Friday manages to free himself from his master and becomes his equal, whereas Robinson discovers a wilder, purer life on the island.

Written in a direct, lively, free style, the story offers readers a philosophical view of the complexity of human relationships and the absolute need to live with other people. **SL**

The Shrinking of Treehorn 1971

Florence Parry Heide Edward Gorey

Nationality | American, born 1919 (author); American, born 1925 (illustrator)
Publisher | Holiday House, USA
Theme | Fantasy, School, Family

I discovered *The Shrinking of Treehorn* late in life; I was already eleven. I feel lucky to have come across it when I did, because it's a book that gets richer with age. I remember my teacher reading it out loud, holding up the pictures for us to see. I attended a tiny village school with just one classroom and she had to find stories suitable for all ages and different levels. This one was perfect—a tale about a boy who shrinks while his parents refuse to notice. "'I'm shrinking. Getting smaller,' said Treehorn. 'If you want to pretend you're shrinking, that's all right,' said Treehorn's mother, 'as long as you don't do it at the table.'"

The language is simply phrased and beautifully paced. It has a subversive subtext that artfully shows the way adults so often don't listen to children. It is a book full of humor and very much on the child's side.

Sadly, we are discouraged from reading books with pictures when we get past seven. I am not sure why; pictures can greatly enhance the experience of reading. The illustrations in *The Shrinking of Treehorn* are by Edward Gorey, a sophisticated and wonderfully surreal artist, who creates witty, elegantly balanced, pen-and-ink compositions. I had never seen his work before reading this book, but he is one of the reasons I wanted to become an illustrator. His pictures are a perfect example of what book illustration should do. They draw on the writer's imagination, expand upon it, and pull the reader into another world. The text and art go hand in hand so perfectly, I could not imagine one without the other.

"Treehorn liked cereal for breakfast. But mostly he liked cereal boxes."

ZIPPY
ZAPPIES
1971

The Carpet People 1971

Terry Pratchett

Nationality | English, born 1948
Publisher | Colin Smythe, UK
Honor | OBE (Knighted for Services to Literature)
Theme | Fantasy

Jokes, morals, wordplay, and a topsy-turvy look at the tangle humans get their lives into suffuse the work of Terry Pratchett, the thinking person's humorist. This early work features tiny people, Munrungs, who live in the world of Carpet. They journey through a landscape of treelike hairs, clambering over large grains of dust. They are searching for a new home because their village has been destroyed by the powerful and mysterious natural force Fray (unidentified but possibly the natural decay of fabric hastened by sweeping). The hero of the story is Snibril, who is able to detect Fray a few minutes before it strikes and is said to have the kind of inquiring mind that is dangerous.

These people are really tiny, yet tiny as they are, they are brave. The Munrungs and neighboring Deftmenes are subject to the Dumii empire, which is benevolent but bureaucratic. The Dumii are menaced by Mouls. Mouls worship Fray and seize advantage of the destruction it leaves behind to attack and enslave the inhabitants of Carpet. An epic battle ends with Snibril setting off for the far reaches of Carpet.

Pratchett wrote (and illustrated) this book when he was very young and has since extensively revised it. There are inconsistencies in its plotting and tone, but Pratchett's trademark inventiveness and wonderful ability to poke fun at pomposity, prejudice, and ignorance is fully fledged. After reading this highly enjoyable romp, you will never get out the vacuum cleaner in quite such a cavalier way again. **VN**

Mrs. Frisby and the Rats of NIMH 1971

Robert C. O'Brien

Nationality | American, born Robert Leslie Conly 1918
Publisher | Atheneum Books, USA
Theme | Animal stories, Adventure

Mrs. Frisby is a field mouse who is faced with terrible danger when the local farmer decides to plow up the field where she lives with her family. Her youngest son, Timothy, is so ill that she does not think he will survive the move. Fortunately, help is at hand from a band of rats who have recently escaped from a research laboratory where they were subject to a series of experiments that rendered them superintelligent. Now living in neatly furnished accommodation lit by electric light, the rats tell their dramatic story in detail to Mrs. Frisby before helping move her house to somewhere safer. However, everything goes wrong when Mrs. Frisby is caught in her attempt to slip a sleeping potion to the cat who otherwise threatened all her plans to relocate. Trapped under a colander, she is rescued once more by the rats before they too move off to start a new life and civilization in the nearby Thorn Valley.

This beautifully written fable puts young readers in the unusual position of seeing the world from the point of view of a species that is usually reviled. It is humans, with their experiments on live animals, who come out of this novel badly, and children may well find themselves thinking about the implications of this particular twist in the plot. They can also enjoy a thoroughly gripping story, where the little people—for that is how the rats and mice come over in these pages—finally get the better of those humans out to get them, whatever the cost in suffering. **NT**

The Cucumber King 1972

Christine Nöstlinger   Werner Maurer

Nationality | Austrian, born 1936 (author); German, birth date unknown (illustrator)
Publisher | Beltz and Gelberg, Germany
Theme | Fantasy, Family

In *The Cucumber King* (*Wir pfeifen auf den Gurkenkönig*), twelve-year-old Wolfgang lives with his family: his grandfather (who has suffered a stroke); his parents; sister Martina (who is not that annoying, compared to her friends at school); and Niki (the youngest). One day a small, cucumber-like creature called Kumi-Ori appears on their doorstep. It is wearing a crown on its head, and its toenails are painted red. It talks in a curious, grammatically incorrect way. Kumi-Ori says that his subjects have thrown him out and he is seeking asylum. The father looks after the creature, and little Niki is also fascinated by the self-proclaimed king. However, the rest of the family is desperate to get rid of the possessive and irritating gnome.

Soon they find out that the "Cucumberer" (as the grandfather calls him) is a liar. He promises to get the father a good job using his extensive connections. In return for his help, the creature asks the father to assist him in annihilating the king's rebellious former subjects. The rest of the family is opposed to these plans, and luckily the father gets a promotion without having to ask the Cucumberer for assistance.

Since the 1970s Christine Nöstlinger has proved to be a refreshing new voice in German children's literature. The heroes of her stories are mostly disadvantaged children and people on the fringes of society. Her impudent sense of humor and sarcastic musings on relationships across the generations reinvigorated the genre. **CS**

"Since my leg is broken and I can't go swimming anyway, I will just start to write . . ."

OTHER GREAT BOOKS BY NÖSTLINGER

Fiery Frederica (Die feuerrote Friederike), 1970
Fly Away Home (Maikäfer flieg), 1973
Conrad: The Factory-Made Boy (Konrad, oder Das Kind aus der Konservenbüchse), 1975

Watership Down 1972

Richard Adams

8+

"'There isn't any danger here at the moment, but it's coming— it's coming. Oh, Hazel, look!'"

Nationality | English, born 1920
Publisher | Rex Collings, UK
Theme | Classics, Adventure, Animal stories

This exciting epic tale of a band of rabbits and their search for a safe warren has echoes of Biggles as well as Homer and Virgil. The young Richard Adams saw active service in Holland during World War II, and leadership, courage, and morale are shown as crucial to the creatures' success. However, there is room in the rabbit kingdom for all kinds of courage. The weak, timid but visionary Fiver spurs the rabbits' exodus when he foresees that their warren is about to be destroyed by developers. Hazel, Fiver's brother, becomes the group's leader through common sense and compassion.

The rabbits' adventures take place over five months, a long time in the two-year lifespan of a wild rabbit. Adams uses various models of rabbit society to reflect on rabbit and human nature and nurture. For example, the wild rabbits are disturbed by the compromises of fellow creatures who live under factory farm conditions. These animals are well fed in return for a shorter life expectancy, and have channeled the energy that they would have used for survival into creative arts. Meanwhile, the charismatic, brutal leader, Woundwort, exploits rabbits' natural fear of predators to ensure order in his military-style warren.

Much of this rabbit lore is true (the females absorb their young if they cannot care for them), some might well be true (they can only count up to four, hence Fiver's name), and some is not true but is a pleasure to imagine, such as their words for things they like (*silflay*, "food") and things they do not like (*hrudru*, "cars"). **GB**

OTHER GREAT RABBIT TALES

Uncle Remus Stories by Joel Chandler Harris, 1881
Rabbit Hill by Robert Lawson, 1945
Bunnicula by James and Deborah Howe, 1979
Rabbit and Coyote: Myths and Legends (Conejo y Coyote: Mitos y Leyendas) by Beatriz Donnet, 2005

Efrem the Knight 1972

Mino Milani

Original Title | Efrem il cavaliere
Nationality | Italian, born 1928
Publisher | Mursia, Italy
Theme | War, Historical fiction

Efrem il cavaliere was first serialized in the newspaper *Corriere dei piccoli*. Set in the Middle Ages against a backdrop of bloody war, the tale presents young readers with the reality of what it means to be a soldier who fights and has to kill others.

Efrem is a peasant who, driven by the demands of a kingdom at war in 1366, reluctantly decides to become a soldier. When he goes into battle with the soldiers in his legion, his whole universe as he knew it is turned upside down. Efrem has joined the legion of the English captain John Hawkwood (1320–1394), who went to Italy as a soldier of fortune (*capitano di ventura*) for the Visconti and Pope Gregory XI among others. (The Santa Maria del Fiore church in Florence has an Uccello fresco in his honor.) Despite Efram's dislike of war, the demands of surviving in a legion of soldiers mean that he soon masters the art of javelin throwing, riding a horse, and standing his ground. Slowly, Efrem transforms from a young boy to one of the most revered soldiers in Hawkwood's legion.

Milani is a sophisticated writer of adventure stories, and his work is much admired by Gianni Rodari, one of Italy's most respected children's authors: "In telling adventure stories, according to me, considering how many have arisen since Emilio Salgari, there is nobody better than Mino Milani." Milani is also well known for the Tommy River stories and for his retelling of many medieval legends including Robin Hood, King Arthur, Tristan and Isolde, and Orpheus and Eurydice. **SMT**

The Ghost of Thomas Kempe 1973

Penelope Lively A. Maitland

Nationality | English, born 1933 (author); English, birth date unknown (illustrator)
Publisher | Heinemann, UK
Theme | Fantasy, Ghost stories

When the Harrison family buys East End Cottage, the attic, closed for years, is made into a bedroom for James. The builders dislodge and smash an old bottle, yet are clueless to what they have unleashed. Inside lies the ghost of Thomas Kempe, a sorcerer from the time of King James I. Determined to take up where he left off, Kempe chooses James as his apprentice and tries to reestablish himself as a physician, alchemist, geomancer, astrologer, and finder of "Goodes Loste."

James's parents are not the kind of people James can confide in about a poltergeist; they are convinced the strange happenings are a result of James playing elaborate jokes. Luckily, James meets Bert Ellison, a builder who believes in ghosts and practices exorcism. James discovers a diary from 1856, belonging to a Miss Fanny Spence, which tells of the visit of her nephew Arnold and the first time Kempe was exorcized. Arnold becomes James's imaginary friend, allowing him to understand the spirit world.

Things get serious when Kempe begins vandalizing homes and businesses. Eventually Kempe cannot cope with modern life and asks James to help him rest. While digging in the garden, James discovers an ancient pair of spectacles and a pipe. The ghost asks James to find his grave and lay his pipe and spectacles on it. There are no graves in the graveyard bearing Kempe's name, but Bert remembers some graves he once spotted in an underground vault at the church, and Thomas Kempe is finally laid to rest. **LH**

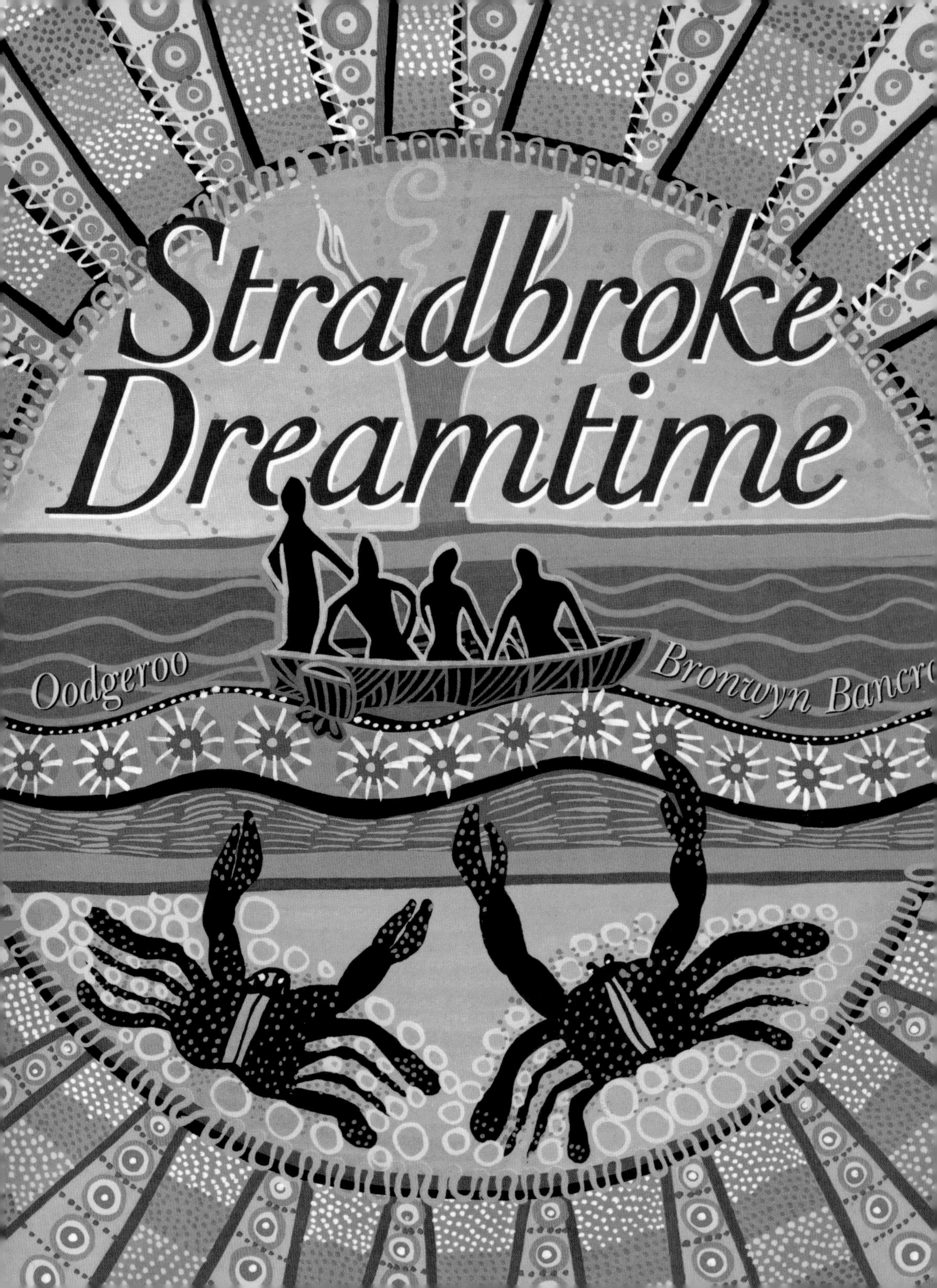
Stradbroke Dreamtime
Oodgeroo
Bronwyn Bancro

Stradbroke Dreamtime 1972

Noonuccal Oodgeroo B. Bancroft

Nationality | Australian, born 1920 (author); Australian, born 1958 (illustrator)
Publisher | Angus and Robertson, Australia
Theme | Folktales, Traditional

This unusual book has two parts. "Stories from Stradbroke" is a collection of stories by Noonuccal Oodgeroo about growing up with her Aboriginal family on Stradbroke Island, off the northeast coast of Australia. "Stories from the Old and New Dreamtime" consists of Aboriginal folklore the author was told as a child and newer stories that she has written in the same style. Oodgeroo narrates in a friendly, conversational way. Told from vivid memories and from a child's perspective, the details are brilliantly clear and the sense of place is strong. When Oodgeroo was little, her father taught his children Aboriginal ethics and hunting skills. They hunted parrots with slingshots and fished for mullet and mud-crabs, but never killed for the sake of killing. It was forbidden to take more than they needed for themselves and others in their tribe. There is a funny story about their black dog dragging home a shark, and a sad one about being left-handed.

The Dreamtime stories also contain strong lessons. One is about a woman who has lost the old stories of her people. She calls for help from Biami the Good Spirit and is given memory of the long-ago stories. She writes them onto paper bark with charred sticks.

Bronwyn Bancroft's illustrations sing with color and pattern. Quite stylized, they combine silhouetted figures and areas of fluid color giving a sense of great depth. They evoke the pristine world of Oodgeroo's childhood and add to the magic of the stories. **AJ**

The Eighteenth Emergency 1973

Betsy Byars

Nationality | American, born 1928
Publisher | Story House Corp, USA
Honor | Regina Medal, Lifetime Achievement
Theme | Friendship

Mouse Fawley is not a brave soul, but somehow he has to learn to be. His mother, occupied with trying to earn enough money to support the family, cannot help him. The Garbage Dog, who befriends Mouse almost by accident, cannot help either, and his friend Ezzie most certainly cannot help. So it is down to Mouse himself to stand up to the fearsome bullies who are out to get him. As anyone who has been in this predicament knows, standing up to bullies is easier said than done. While Mouse is waiting for the worst to happen, his imagination runs wild. He thinks of seventeen other emergencies that could occur, including attack by an unfriendly lion and gruesome strangulation by a boa constrictor, all of which he is sure he can handle. So then, how bad can bully Marv Hammerman be?

Byars combines wry sympathy with a keen eye for knockabout comedy. As befits a woman who lives above an aircraft hangar and shares a plane with her husband, she is not afraid to take an unconventional look at things, and Mouse, like Ezzie, is no plaster saint himself. After all, he only got into trouble with Marv because he wrote Marv's name under a picture of Neanderthal man pinned on the board at school. Mouse is not especially charming, helpful, kind, or even bright but he does discover an ability to say "boo" to a goose. Many of Byars's stories have this structure: moral dilemmas for fragile children with a big helping of frank humor. **VN**

Chlorophyll from the Blue Sky 1973

Bianca Pitzorno G. Santini Valeriani

Nationality | Italian, born 1942 (author); Italian birth date unknown (illustrator)
Publisher | Bietti, Italy
Theme | Science and nature

8+

This book, originally published as *Clorofilla dal cielo blu*, is based on a story written in the 1970s about ecological awareness. Topically relevant, it mentions how chemicals that pollute the sea, air, and ground affect the lives of humans, animals, and vegetation.

This is a story populated by children who seem to have other things on their minds. But these are no ordinary children: They have a shared secret that is powerful enough to change an adult's mindset. Bianca Pitzorno delightfully sides with her young protagonists; she manages to delve into the thoughts of the youthful characters, especially when they are trying to understand the rather incomprehensible behavior of the adults in their lives. The author also manages to empower the children despite their obvious disadvantage in the world of adults.

The secret the children share is the discovery of a young plant called Chlorophyll. She was just a seed when she fell out of her spaceship, delicately moving through the blue sky, and landed on Earth. Two children on their way to their uncle's house in the city of Milan find her. The threesome accidentally end up in the home of famous botanist Erasmus, an adult unamused by children, cats, or dogs. Despite his grumpiness, he is willing to help save Chlorophyll, who is affected adversely by the smog of the city. Will the children, with Erasmus's invention, finally transform Milan into a green city? A thought-provoking tale. **SMT**

The Brothers Lionheart 1973

Astrid Lindgren Ilon Wikland

Nationality | Swedish, born 1907 (author); Estonian/Swedish, born 1930 (illustrator)
Publisher | Rabén and Sjögren, Sweden
Theme | Illness and death

Astrid Lindgren is perhaps best known as the author of the Pippi Longstocking series. However, this story, told in the style of an ancient Norse saga, is a morality tale about being good and kind in order to prosper. An important part of the story centers around a huge, swirling waterfall known as Karma Falls. The narrative is written in the first person, from the point of view of ten-year-old Karl Lion, who lives with his mother and older brother, Jonathan.

Karl, who is disabled, has been ill for six months when one day he overhears his mother and her friends talking about the fact that he is dying. When he questions thirteen-year-old Jonathan about what he has heard, Jonathan tells Karl that only his "shell" will be dead and that the rest of him will embark on a journey to a magical place called Nangiyala, "on the other side of the stars." However, in a tragic twist of fate, this wonderfully kind and brave older brother, who has protected Karl from all the bad things in life, is destined to die first, while saving his brother from a fire. He then becomes Jonathan Lionheart. Within a couple of months, Karl also dies and finds himself reunited with his brother in Nangiyala.

Their new life seems like paradise until Jonathan and his friend, Sofia, the Queen of the Pigeons, reveal to Karl that there is a traitor in their midst working for the evil Tengil. Together, the brothers, helped by their adoptive grandfather, save Nangiyala and become worthy of their name: the Brothers Lionheart. **LH**

Astrid Lindgren
Bröderna
Lejonhjärta
RABÉN & SJÖGREN

Crusade in Jeans 1973

Thea Beckman

"This extraordinary machine that made contact with the past made Dolf feel very small and insignificant."

OTHER BOOKS BY THEA BECKMAN

Give Me Space (Geef me de ruimte), 1976
City in the Storm (Stad in de storm), 1979
The Golden Dagger (De gouden dolk), 1982
The Golden Fleece of Thule (Het Gulden Vlies van Thule), 1989

Original Title | Kruistocht in spijkerbroek
Nationality | Dutch, born Thea Petie 1923
Publisher | Lemniscaat, the Netherlands
Theme | Historical fiction, Adventure

Thea Beckman is rightly regarded as one of the most important Dutch writers for children of the twentieth century. *Crusade in Jeans* was the first historical novel she wrote for children and it is an action-packed, epic adventure story set during the Middle Ages.

Fifteen-year-old Dolf Wega travels back in time to 1212 and finds himself in the middle of the Children's Crusade, when thousands of barefoot children set out to walk from Germany to Jerusalem led by two monks and a shepherd boy. Initially, Dolf is completely bewildered by the situation in which he finds himself. Many of the children are sick and at the point of starvation, however, Dolf uses his modern knowledge to organize the chaos around him and prevent disease spreading, as well as fight evil knights and help the children to walk over the Alps into Italy.

After the publication of *Crusade in Jeans*, Beckman continued to write children's novels that explored historic events, and she spent a great deal of time researching life in different periods throughout history. Among these works are *Give Me Space*, the first in a trilogy about the Hundred Years' War, and *City in the Storm*, which is about the 1672 invasion of the Dutch province of Utrecht and the ensuing panic among the people. However, Beckman also wrote a series of books set in the future. *Children of Mother Earth* is the first in a series of futuristic novels set ten centuries after World War III. Regardless of when her books are set, they are all tales of heroism, courage, and adventure, and peopled by convincing and memorable characters. **HJ**

Grinny 1973

Nicholas Fisk

Nationality | English, born David Higginbottom 1923
Publisher | Heinemann, UK
Theme | Science fiction, Adventure

Eleven-year-old Tim Carpenter and his sister, Beth, who is younger by three years, suspect that there is something not quite right about the elderly lady who unexpectedly turns up where they live claiming to be their Great-Aunt Emma. Although their parents cannot at first recall her, they do so immediately when Grinny (as Tim and Beth come to call her) insists that they really do remember her.

But Grinny remains a mystery to the children, and they are far more inquisitive than their parents. How come she has no smell, does not bleed after receiving a bad gash, and seems to have bones made of steel? After Tim sees an Unidentified Flying Object (UFO) hovering outside his window early one morning, all becomes clear. He and Beth now know for certain that Grinny is actually a visitor from outer space, intent on a mission of total evil. But what can they do about it when no one will believe them?

This sparky science fiction novel is written as if by Tim himself, making a record of these strange events in his diary four years after the fact. This format gives the novel a nicely informal atmosphere as Tim describes how, with Beth and his best friend, Mac, he finally makes sure that Grinny will never return again. A novel for young children that ends with the dismemberment of an old lady might be considered too horrific, but then Grinny is not really human at all; more a "torch thing" able to masquerade as a real person. Exciting, witty, and with a plot that forges ahead at a great pace, this novel has since been adapted for the stage where it was equally successful. **NT**

The Fib 1975

George Layton

Original Title | The Fib and Other Stories
Nationality | English, born 1943
Publisher | Longman, UK
Theme | School, Family, Friendship

This funny, touching, and bittersweet collection of short stories is set in the north of England in the 1950s. Although each story stands alone, together they also form a continuous tale as the same characters reappear throughout the book: the hero, who finds it easier to get into trouble than to get out of it; his best friends, Tony and Barry; and the hapless Norbert Lightowler.

In the title story "The Fib," a boy is so tired of the class bully showing off all the time that he declares that the famous soccer player Bobby Charlton is his uncle: "'Listen Barraclough. My uncle is Bobby Charlton.' 'You're a liar.' I was." When Bobby Charlton is invited to switch on the town's Christmas lights, the schoolboy is terrified that he will be exposed as a liar. Fortunately, Bobby Charlton plays along with the ruse. In "The Balaclava Story," a boy desperately wants a balaclava so that he can join his friends in the balaclava gang who wear their wooly headgear—even during the summer. When his mother refuses to buy him one, he steals another boy's balaclava and puts it down his coat sleeve. Later he is wracked with guilt and is sure he will be found out and ostracized by his friends, but there is an unexpected twist in the tale.

Although set during the 1950s the stories still have relevance to readers today who will identify with the scrapes and moral dilemmas that everyone faces when growing up. The collection also sensitively explores what it is like to be a child in a one-parent family with an overprotective mother and the touching relationship between the boy and his grandfather. **HJ**

Conrad: The Factory-Made Boy 1975

Christine Nöstlinger Franz Wittkamp

8+

Nationality | Austrian, born 1936 (author); details unknown (illustrator)
Publisher | Oetinger, Germany
Theme | Fantasy, Family

Originally published in German with the title *Konrad oder Das Kind aus der Konservenbüchse,* this book is Christine Nöstlinger's most successful and best-known story. In 1984 she won the Hans Christian Andersen Medal for her contribution to children's literature.

In this clever tale, Conrad—an obedient boy with perfect manners who has been made-to-order in a factory—is accidentally delivered to the wrong person. The surprised recipient, Mrs. Bartolotti, is a bohemian woman who eats huge German breakfasts in her rocking chair, never worries about the mess, and then hops around the room to shake off crumbs. Neighbors regard Mrs. Bartolotti as eccentric and they barely speak to her. One day after breakfast, while wondering whether she should do any work at all or go straight back to sleep, she receives a parcel containing an exemplary, ready-made, seven-year-old boy, who she takes in as her child. Mrs. Bartolotti does not expect perfection from Conrad, and he is very happy with his new family. However, when the cold, demanding parents who actually ordered the "perfect child" arrive to regain their lost delivery, Conrad has to quickly "learn" how to be naughty so that he can stay with Mrs. Bartolotti.

The great success of Nöstlinger's fantasy story lies mainly in her closely observed characters who are described with psychological insight. Her plot is imaginative and linguistically playful, and successfully deals with themes such as child rearing, growing up, the danger of uninformed, preconceived values, and the relationship between children and parents. **LB**

"On Mrs. Bartolotti's doorstep stood a rather large parcel, just over a meter long. She was not expecting anything special . . . "

OTHER IMAGINATIVE FANTASY READS

***Stuart Little* by E. B. White, 1945**
***Flat Stanley* by Jeffrey Brown, 1964**
***The Shrinking of Treehorn* by Florence Parry Heide, 1971**
***Coraline* by Neil Gaiman, 2002**

Granny 1975

Peter Härtling Peter Knorr

Nationality | German, born 1933 (author); German, born 1939 (illustrator)
Publisher | Beltz and Gelberg, Germany
Theme | Illness and death, Family

The theme of generational conflict in this highly acclaimed novel (originally titled *Oma*) about the orphan Kalle who moves in with his grandmother is a recurrent one in the works of Peter Härtling. Here, five-year-old Kalle—whose parents have died in a car accident—is forced to bridge the gap between two very different generations, and he and his grandma have to learn to live together and understand, as well as accept, each other's peculiarities.

The elderly lady has to put up with Kalle's rowdy friends and his passion for watching Westerns, whereas the boy has to accept his grandmother's compulsion to wallow in memories of "the olden days" and her tendency to alter the truth ever so slightly in order to spice up her stories. However, they manage to coexist, not least because they openly discuss their conflicting points of view. When the grandmother falls ill and is taken to the hospital, Kalle—then aged ten—has to learn to look after himself. They both realize that there may come a time in the not-too-distant future when Kalle will be left on his own. Terrified as they are by this idea, they are reassured by the way Kalle copes while his grandmother is in the hospital.

Härtling manages to delicately describe serious issues such as the inevitable conflict between generations, the processes of growing up and growing old, as well the presence of death and how to cope with loss. He shows that it is possible to move on and that people can always get along with one another as long as they are willing to understand and love the other person. **GS**

The Stone Book 1976

Alan Garner Michael Foreman

Nationality | English, born 1934 (author); English, born 1938 (illustrator)
Publisher | Collins, UK
Theme | Family, Short stories

Stretching across four generations in the history of one family, each of these stories describes one day as experienced by a child at the time.

The first story, "The Stone Book," is set in the summer of 1864 with young Mary climbing the village church steeple in order to bring her stonemason father his lunch. The next, "Granny Reardun," concentrates on Mary's son, Joseph, who is determined to break away from the family tradition of working with stone by becoming a blacksmith. "The Aimer Gate" takes the family story up to 1916, with Joseph's son Robert now fascinated by early wheeled transport. Lastly, "Tom Fobble's Day" finishes in 1941 with the death of Joseph, who has just made a sledge for his grandson William, using all the different technical skills passed down the family line over the years.

These short but unforgettable stories take their inspiration from the author's own family. Told largely in dialogue drawn from the local Cheshire dialect, each story shows a child trying to come to terms both with family tradition and with their own needs in a swiftly changing world. The book is superbly illustrated by Michael Foreman, whose rough-hewn etchings are totally in sympathy with Alan Garner's descriptions of what it is like to work as a skilled craftsman. Effortlessly covering a wide range of social issues while cleverly planting clues in one story that then reappear in later ones, this quartet celebrates both continuity and change, and is widely considered to be one of the best books produced for children in the last fifty years. **NT**

Ordinary Jack 1977

Helen Cresswell

Title of the Series | The Bagthorpe Saga
Nationality | English, born 1934
Publisher | Faber and Faber, UK
Theme | Family, Adventure

8+

OTHER READS BY HELEN CRESSWELL

Lizzie Dripping, 1973
The Bongleweed, 1973
The Winter of the Birds, 1976
The Piemakers, 1980
The Night-Watchmen, 1983

Helen Cresswell wrote more than a hundred books for children, and this saga is one of the best loved. It is a series of ten books that follows the anarchic adventures of the extremely eccentric Bagthorpe family, which Cresswell based on her own childhood.

The Bagthorpe children are prodigiously talented. William is brilliant at math, tennis, and drumming; his sister, Tess is translating Voltaire from the French and is a black belt at judo; and Rosie's talents include playing the violin and painting. Only Jack, the hero of the tales, is ordinary and has no special abilities. In the first book in the series, *Ordinary Jack*, bumbling Uncle Parker endeavors to help Jack get noticed by his parents and siblings. Jack decides to pose as a prophet and uses crystal balls, tarot cards, and water divining to predict events that he has already planned. Unfortunately his plans go awry with hilarious results.

> *"What I've hatched up for you, young Jack, is going to shake that family of yours to its core."*

Bagthorpe aficionados often rate *Bagthorpes Unlimited* as their favorite in the series. In this book, the wayward Bagthorpe children are visited by their perfectly behaved cousins. They vow to get rid of their unwanted guests, but the cousins are made of strong stuff and are not going to leave easily. The extended Bagthorpe family is made of up of some very odd relatives indeed: Aunt Penelope sterilizes library books before allowing her children to read them, and four-year-old Daisy's hobbies include arson and morbidity. The series is characterized by a cast of eccentrics, madcap adventures, and Cresswell's wry humor. The comedy comes as much from the sharply drawn characters as from the situations in which they find themselves. **HJ**

Bridge to Terabithia 1977

Katherine Paterson   Donna Diamond

It is unusual and possibly controversial to include the death of a child in a story aimed at eight-year-olds. However, the book was inspired after Katherine Paterson's son lost his best friend, who was hit by lightning. It is perhaps the real-life fact of this eight-year-old's death that holds the resolution to the debates that have ensued about whether or not the book is appropriate for its intended market: children encounter all manner of troubles, including death. However, the book not only holds this relevant event at its center, but provides those characters whom it affects with the resources to build the emotional bridges necessary to overcome being different, lonely, and grief stricken.

"He believed her because in the shadowy light of the stronghold everything seemed possible."

First and foremost, this is the story of a friendship between two lonely kids. Jesse Aarons is the only boy in a family of five. He has a largely absent father and a mother who prefers her daughters, and when we meet him, he is pouring his desire for attention into winning the annual race at school and becoming the fastest runner in the fifth grade. Leslie Burke is the new kid at school who beats him to the finish line, winning his admiration and the friendship that helps them both discover who they really are.

The magic of the imaginary kingdom of Terabithia that Jesse and Leslie build together in the forest near their houses will never leave those who encounter it. Nor will the message of the power of friendship in helping one another manage the pressures—and overcome the lowest points—that life throws, when it is inevitably time to leave. **JSD**

Nationality | American, born 1932 (author); American, birth date unknown (illustrator)
Publisher | HarperCollins, USA
Theme | Friendship, Illness and death

MORE BOOKS BY KATHERINE PATERSON

Of Nightingales that Weep, 1974
The Master Puppeteer, 1976
The Great Gilly Hopkins, 1978
Jacob Have I Loved, 1980
Jip, His Story, 1996

The Turbulent Term of Tyke Tiler 1977

Gene Kemp Carolyn Dinan

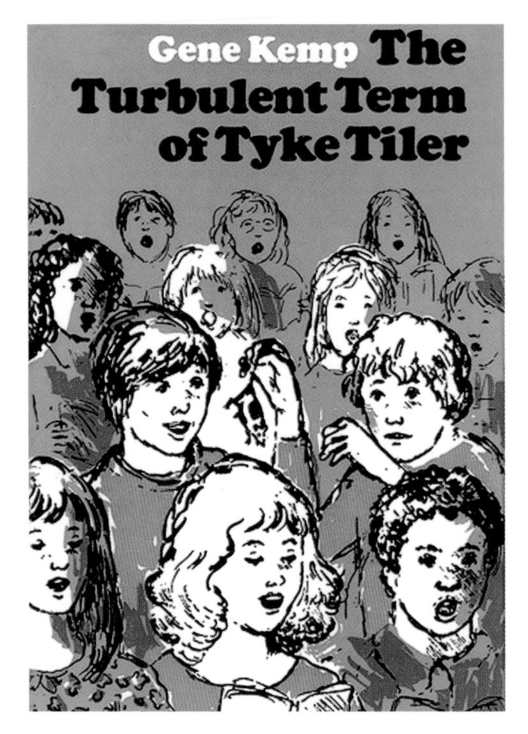

Gene Kemp The Turbulent Term of Tyke Tiler

"'Where didja get that, you nutter?' 'Out of Bonfire's purse. She'd left it open. On the desk. So I took it. No one saw me.'"

MORE GREAT STORIES BY GENE KEMP

Gowie Corby Plays Chicken, 1981
Charlie Lewis Plays for Time, 1984
Juniper, 1986
Just Ferret, 1990
Seriously Weird, 2003

Nationality | English, born 1926 (author); English, born 1942 (illustrator)
Publisher | Faber and Faber, UK
Theme | School, Friendship

Eleven-year-old Tyke Tiler is as bright as they come, but unfortunately his best friend, Danny Price, has problems with all his lessons. Together they make a troublesome pair in the classroom during their last term at Cricklepit Combined School, with Tyke forever trying to extricate Danny from his latest blunders. One thing that is troubling the boys is the fact that they have end-of-year exams coming up. If Danny fails his final academic tests, he may get sent to a special school, unless Tyke can help out here as well (illegally, of course). Yet the biggest surprise comes just before the end; something so extreme that readers may well find themselves wanting to read this gloriously funny and subversive book all over again.

With each chapter headed by a typical playground joke, *The Turbulent Term of Tyke Tiler* is a good, fun read from start to finish. However, the book also carries a serious message about the necessity of accepting differences between people, especially when they are young. This book is not to everyone's taste; the language is slangy and sometimes rude, but the narrative is always utterly engaging. The characters are well drawn, and young readers can relate to the predicaments in which Tyke and Danny find themselves. The story offers children both enjoyment and something to think about afterward.

A former teacher, Gene Kemp never misses a trick, clearly enjoying herself as one absurd school situation follows the next, all patiently tolerated by staff who somehow manage to remain good-humored whatever the provocation. **NT**

Storm Boy 1977

Colin Thiele

Nationality | Australian, born 1920
Publisher | Rigby, Australia
Award | Hans Christian Andersen Award
Theme | Adventure, Family, Animal stories

Colin Thiele is a much-loved writer whose stories are steeped in the Australian landscape, its animals, and its history. *Storm Boy* is the best known of his works and the first to be made into a feature film. The book has a small cast: a hermitlike father and son who live in a "rough little humpy" in the dunes on the South Australian coast; a local Aboriginal, Fingerbone Bill; and, most important of all, three pelicans—Mr. Proud, Mr. Ponder, and Mr. Percival, who are raised by Storm Boy and his father, Hide-Away Tom, after their parents are killed by hunters who have illegally violated the sanctuary in which they live.

The story is told in language that is direct, matter-of-fact, and poetic; unpretentiously conveying the sights and sounds of Storm Boy's world and his feelings of contentment and wonder. His oneness with nature is encapsulated in his relationship with Mr. Percival, the weakest of the three pelicans, who does not return to the wild but follows Storm Boy like a faithful dog and, like a dog, learns to retrieve. This is a skill that he uses, one stormy night, to carry a line to a foundering boat, earning himself and Storm Boy legendary status among the fishermen of the area, and the offer of a place at school in the city for the boy.

Inevitably tragedy happens: Mr. Percival is shot by hunters, and Storm Boy leaves his father to go to school in Adelaide. A male-only family story, an adventure story, and an animal story, the book is also an elegy to a pioneering Australian way of life that has disappeared or perhaps has only ever existed in national memory. **CB**

Charmed Life 1977

Diana Wynne Jones

Nationality | English, born 1934
Publisher | Macmillan, UK
Award | *Guardian* Award for Children's Books
Theme | Fantasy, Adventure, Magical stories

Diana Wynne Jones weaves gripping tales of humorous magical fantasy. *Charmed Life* tells the story of Cat Chant and his older sister, Gwendolen; two orphans who are summoned to live with a distant relative (who also happens to be a powerful enchanter). This wizard holds the title of Chrestomanci, a government-appointed position charged with controlling the misuse of magic. Spoiled Gwendolen, piqued by the lack of pandering to which she is accustomed, plays a series of vicious magical pranks, then absconds to a parallel universe leaving a dumbfounded look-alike in her place. For timid, dependent Cat, this selfish act has far-reaching consequences, as he begins to discover his sister's true nature and the existence of his own, previously undreamed of, magical abilities.

The author's talent lies in mixing everyday domestic scenes with touches of sorcery. Long before Harry Potter was written (Wynne Jones is acknowledged as an influence by J. K. Rowling), Wynne Jones successfully created a credible and familiar world where casting spells is just another lesson alongside history and mathematics. *Charmed Life* is set in an old-fashioned England of horse-drawn carriages. It introduces the recurring character of Christopher Chant as a suave and charming Chrestomanci, usually seen clad in an elegant silk dressing gown, looking deceptively vague, as well as the idea of multiple parallel universes, with a double existing in each one. Funny and moving, bewitching and highly addictive, the story deserves to be read and reread. **MK**

The Little Man Dressed in Gray 1978

Fernando Alonso  Ulises Wensell

Nationality | Spanish, born 1941 (author); Spanish, born 1945 (illustrator)
Publisher | Alfaguara, Spain
Theme | Fantasy, Short stories

In this book (originally titled *El Hombrecito Vestido de Gris*) are eight short tales with just the right balance of sadness and hope. The characters swiftly grab our attention and the plots suggest thousands of other story lines that could have been told. The title story concerns a man of very ordinary appearance who wants to be an opera singer, but who is prevented from singing wherever he goes. The author himself suggests the possibility of a sad or a happy ending, thus inviting us as readers to create countless stories with innumerable endings.

Alonso started writing the book in 1972 and completed it in 1975, but did not publish until the advent of democracy in Spain. Having accepted the compromise of the writer faced with the society in which he lives, the author has created characters loaded with symbolism—a ship made of lead, children who have no trees to play under, or time kept by a clock wanting to be something else—who are subjected to strict rules within a society that restricts and destroys every dream.

An expert in literature for children and adolescents, Alonso has also been a scriptwriter for television. In addition to his great command of the technique of tales of the fantastic, when it comes to creating worlds of fiction, Alonso's writing is marked by a sober style, striving to achieve clarity and simplicity. His work champions freedom and imagination as the only possible ways of overcoming any obstacle. **EB**

The Kaziranga Trail 1978

 Arup Kumar Dutta

Nationality | Indian, born 1946
Publisher | Children's Book Trust, India
Honor | Shankar Prize for Children's Literature, 1979
Theme | Adventure

The Kaziranga Trail is an adventure story set in the Kaziranga Wildlife Sanctuary in Assam, India, and with its strong focus on environmental issues, it was ahead of its time when it was first published.

The story centers on three village boys, Dhanai, Bubul, and Jonti, and their young elephant, Makhoni. During the school vacation the boys find a dead rhinoceros in the wildlife sanctuary. It has been killed for its horn, which is highly prized as a medicine in some parts of Asia. The boys report their discovery to the park ranger, Neog, but while they are looking for clues to the crime, they discover that Neog is the middle man between a gang of poachers and a dealer in horn, who has placed an order for six of them. After a series of escapades the boys manage to outsmart the poachers, assist in their arrest and save the rhinos.

Already an internationally acclaimed writer, Dutta was struck by the shortage of available books in English for Indian children, so set about writing his own. Among his other popular works for children is *Blind Witness*, a mystery story in which the central character, Ramu, a blind child, "witnesses" a murder. It provides a moving and realistic portrayal of blindness and follows Ramu's determination to convince those around him that he is a credible witness.

As well as being packed with action and adventure, Arup Kumar Dutta's award-winning novels for children provide an insight into Indian life, culture, and the country's natural environment. **HJ**

Under the Mountain 1979

 Maurice Gee

Nationality | New Zealander, born 1931
Publisher | Oxford University Press, New Zealand
Theme | Fantasy, Adventure, Magical stories

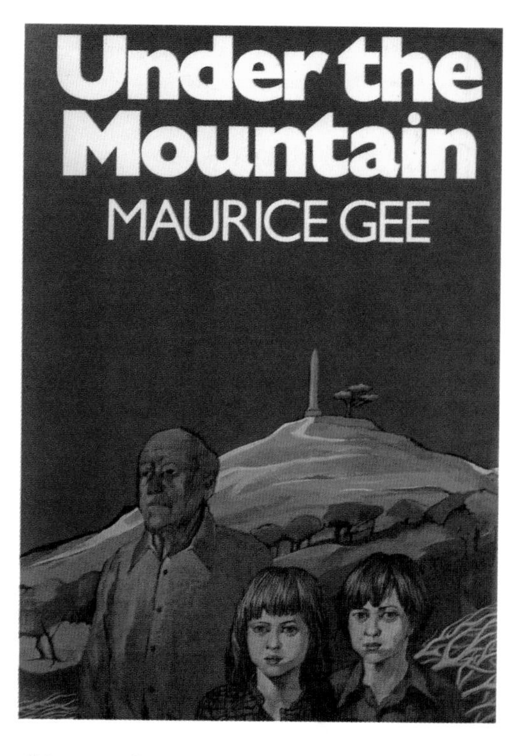

Maurice Gee's *Under the Mountain* heralded a new era of children's books in New Zealand. Until then, local publishing had been limited, the settings usually rural, and the quality uneven. But here was an already acclaimed novelist surprisingly turning his hand to a work for children, supported by a prestigious publisher determined to create a significant list of books for children. The result was spectacular: a fantasy thriller set among the supposedly extinct volcanoes, crater lakes, and harbor waters of the city of Auckland. Gee's protagonists are redheaded twins Rachel and Theo. Mysteriously the possessors of magic stones, they become drawn into the murky underground world of the Wilberforces, sluglike creatures with sinister designs who trigger eruptions in hopes they will ultimately rule the world. Time is running out and only the twins can thwart them.

Gee's novels for children since *Under the Mountain* (produced in between a string of award-winning publications for adults) have included further fantasies, science fiction, and narratives of social realism. All demonstrate his precise, graceful language and evocative sense of place, whether set in New Zealand or fantasy landscapes. The battle between good and evil is a common theme and often harshly played out, with a power and violence that is sometimes disturbing. The bleak ending of *Under the Mountain* provoked controversy at the time of publication, but time has seen it become a modern classic. **TD**

"One afternoon outside a small town . . . two children wandered into the bush and were lost."

MORE GREATS FROM MAURICE GEE

The Halfmen of O, 1982
The Priests of Ferris, 1984
Motherstone, 1985
The Fire-Raiser, 1986
The Champion, 1989

8+

8+

Fray Perico and His Donkey 1979

Juan Muñoz Antonio Tello

Nationality | Spanish, born 1929 (author); details unknown (illustrator)
Publisher | Ediciones SM, Spain
Theme | Humor

The quiet life of the friary, praying and working, is disrupted by the arrival of Fray Perico and his donkey Calcétin ("Sock"), a dying animal that the friar bought from some gypsies and that St. Francis miraculously healed. This nineteenth-century friar is the main character of one of the most successful and widely read children's series of the last thirty years in Spain. The secret is probably that the innocent pranks of Fray Perico are very funny, but it is a comedy full of nuances, not hurtful or absurd or mocking, but based on the contrast between a naive and uninhibited view of the world and a constrictive reality.

Juan Muñoz Martín, a professor of language, won the Doncel Prize for children's literature in 1966. Earlier, he went from one publisher to another with his book under his arm, and it took fifteen years to find one who did not think it was irreverent to have a monk involved in a comic story. After winning the Barco de Vapor (Steam Boat) Prize, *Fray Perico* (*Fray Perico y su borrico* in the Spanish) became a best-seller.

It is said that the author found inspiration in a book he was given in a nativity competition, *The Little Flowers of St. Francis*, and that it was the humor of St. Francis of Assisi that led him to write a story about friars. To achieve the right tone for the story, his students provided invaluable help, reading the chapters as they were written. Anecdotes apart, the book occupies a well-deserved place among the classics of children's literature. **EB**

Anastasia Krupnik 1979

Lois Lowry Diane deGroat

Nationality | American, born 1937 (author); American, born 1947 (illustrator)
Publisher | Houghton Mifflin, USA
Theme | Family, School

This is the first in a popular series featuring the endearing Anastasia Krupnik, a precocious yet naive ten-year-old girl trying to deal with the confusing business of growing up. The reader shares her preoccupations: a fascinating pink wart on her left thumb; a crush on divine sixth-grader, Washburn Cummings; the trials of having to visit a senile grandmother in a nursing home that reeks of medicine and bleach; and how to cope with the impending arrival of an (in her view) entirely unnecessary baby brother.

Anastasia lives with her liberal, middle-class parents in a Boston suburb. Her mother is a bohemian painter, whereas her father is a poet and university professor. The affectionate portrait of a disorganized but loving family rings true on every page. Her parents encourage their daughter to fulfill her ambitions, and after attempting ice-skating and ballet, but failing to coordinate her feet, she decides to become a writer. In her treasured green notebook, she diligently writes down interesting new words, such as "corn pads" and "mutant," as well as hilariously precise lists of likes and dislikes. Trying to analyze why she dislikes her new teacher, Mrs. Vestvessel, and finding herself stumped for reasons, Anastasia crosses out the entry.

Each chapter functions as a mini-episode, with a loose narrative thread driving the plot. In Anastasia, Lois Lowry has created a likable, sassy girl who does her best to understand the world around her. **MK**

Jacob Have I Loved 1980

Katherine Paterson

Nationality | American, born 1932
Publisher | Crowell, USA
Award | Newbery Medal, 1981
Theme | Family, Young adult

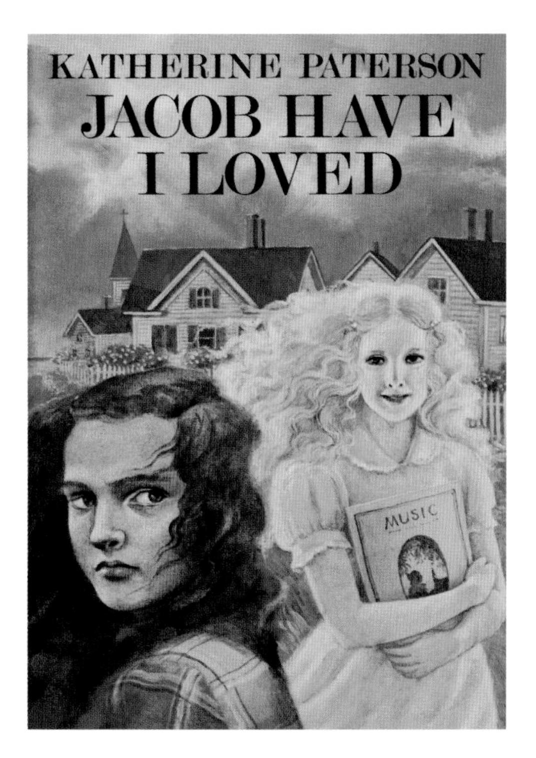

Author Katherine Paterson takes on the theme of sibling rivalry in this award-winning book. Set in the early 1940s on Rass Island in Chesapeake Bay, on the Atlantic coast of the United States, the novel follows the story of the Bradshaws, a family who depend on the father Truitt's crabbing and fishing business. Truitt and his wife Susan's two daughters, Sara Louise and Caroline, are twins. Caroline, although starting life small and sickly, is somehow always ahead of her twin. Sara Louise is prettier, smarter, more talented, and kinder, yet it is frail, artistic Caroline who receives the most attention from her family and the rest of the small community in which she lives.

Even the grandmother favors Caroline; it is she who cruelly whispers to Louise the Bible verse from which the title is taken, where God says: "Jacob have I loved, but Esau have I hated." As the story develops, Louise has to come to understand and value her own sense of self and her place in the world. Slowly, she finds the inner resources to make her life successful and learns to trust in her own gifts and rely on herself, rather than the opinions of others. When she has the chance to go to college, she almost misses it, but for the good advice from a close friend.

Preteens and teenage readers will find much to relate to in this novel and will root for Louise all the way through. The dominant themes are about resolving sibling rivalry and developing self-reliance and a positive sense of self. **KD**

"But what of me? Who took care of me while you were gone?"

OTHER BOOKS ABOUT SIBLINGS

Ballet Shoes by Noel Streatfeild, 1936
Autumn Term by Antonia Forest, 1948
Tales of a Fourth Grade Nothing by Judy Blume, 1972
Mufaro's Beautiful Daughters by John Steptoe, 1987

Night Swimmers 1980

Betsy Byars

Nationality | American, born 1928
Publisher | Delacorte, USA
Theme | Family, Young adult, School, Friendship, Adventure

Roy, Johnny, and Rhetta Anderson's mother has died, and their father works nights singing country and western classics in bars, so Rhetta has to assume a maternal role with her two younger brothers. As the narrator says, it's a "lonely existence." It's a particularly long and hot summer, and the children break into their rich neighbor's yard to swim in the pool. But, as the summer drags on and Johnny falls under the influence of a dangerous new friend, youngest brother Roy tries to break free of his suffocating family. He goes into their neighbor's house, and swims alone. Roy almost drowns, but is saved by their neighbor, who takes him home for a confrontation with the whole family. Byars says the book was inspired by a friend who had a pool, who told her one night: "Every time we go out, kids come over and swim in our pool, and I'm really worried someone is going to get hurt.'"

The Anderson children are among the first wave of latchkey kids: children left home alone by parents forced, by financial necessity, to work. In *The Night Swimmers*, Byars examines parental responsibility and the problems of combining a career and fatherhood. Shorty Anderson is an unsympathetic and absent figure who seems more interested in his velour suits and getting a chart hit than being around for his children. He eventually realizes that he must marry his long-suffering girlfriend to provide a mother figure for his wayward children. This final scene of resolution may seem dated and simplistic, but a return to old-fashioned values has long been trumpeted as a way to solve contemporary problems. **SD**

Superfudge 1980

Judy Blume

Nationality | American, born 1938
Publisher | E. P. Dutton, USA
Award | National Book Foundation Medal
Theme | Family

Farley Drexel Hatcher, aka "Superfudge," was born the very same year that the movie *Superman* was released (1978), so it is no great surprise that he believes he may well have been born on Krypton. As far as Fudge's older brother, Peter, is concerned, Fudge can return to Krypton and annoy someone else. In fact, eleven-year-old Peter is primarily concerned that the baby his mother is about to have will turn out to be another version of Fudge. In which case he plans on running away.

However, Tootsie is born and it is Fudge and not Peter who becomes jealous; and the family eventually do run away—to Princeton, New Jersey, where Mrs. Hatcher is going to study and Mr. Hatcher is going to write a book. The story focuses on all the drama that comes with negotiating a new baby and a new city. The climax comes when Peter punishes Fudge for a trick that he played and refuses to let Fudge and his best friend, Daniel, join him and friend, Alex Santo (who also loves Superman) on a picnic. When the boys return from their picnic, they discover that Fudge and Daniel are missing. Peter is wracked with guilt, and just as the family begin to worry, in walks Fudge, having gone out to buy brownies for his mother.

Fudge is based on Judy Blume's son, Larry, and bears all the irresistible hallmarks of a real little boy trying to negotiate the realities of living in a modern family. Issues of sibling rivalry and dealing with a new baby have resonated with eighty million readers in thirty different languages, ensuring that Fudge live on in *Fudge-A-Mania*, *Double-Fudge*, a television series, and countless little imaginations. **JSD**

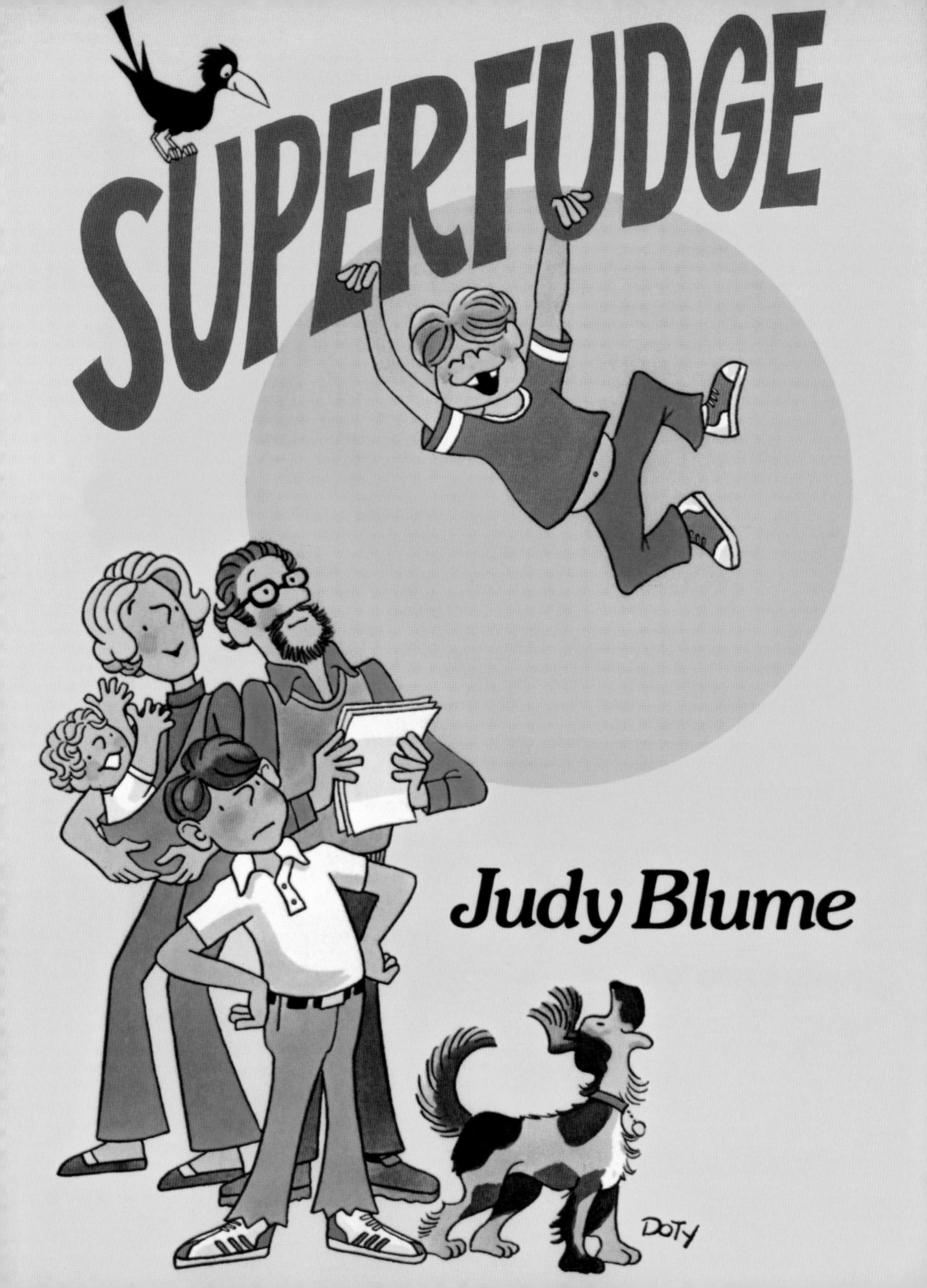
SUPERFUDGE
Judy Blume
DOTY

The Indian in the Cupboard 1980

Lynne Reid Banks  Robin Jacques

Nationality | English, born 1929 (author); English, born 1920 (illustrator)
Publisher | Dent, UK
Theme | Fantasy, Family

Omri, aged nine, receives two presents that will change his life: a plastic miniature North American Indian from his friend, Patrick, and a mysterious old cupboard from his brother. At first he does not like the repainted figure, but his feelings change when he locks it in the cupboard. Turn the key once, and the Indian comes to life. Turn it again and it reverts to being a toy. Problems start when Patrick puts his cowboy Boone into the cupboard too. Although Boone is a crybaby (Boohoo Boone, they call him), the Indian Little Bear is proud, fearless, and defiant. Boone and Little Bear fight and Boone is wounded. All goes dangerously wrong when the key is lost and a hungry pet rat is at large. It ends more than happily, however, with Omri finding a bride for Little Bear and the two swearing blood brotherhood before the Indian returns to his own place (wherever that is: Reid Banks understandably fudges this).

The Indian in the Cupboard is the first of five gripping books featuring savage battles and memorable characters. The clash between Omri and Patrick looms as large as the magic; the cowboy is both comically soft as well as a bigot, and Little Bear not only a hero but also rather a pain. As one might expect from a novelist who also deals with adult themes, Reid Banks is adept at exploring these complexities, which she says she based on her own three sons. Opinion is divided over whether the series favors or stereotypes Native American culture, but it does raise the issue. **VN**

"At last he cautiously turned the key and opened the cupboard. The Indian was gone."

MORE FROM LYNNE REID BANKS

***The Return of the Indian*, 1985**
***Melusine*, 1988**
***The Secret of the Indian*, 1989**
***The Mystery of the Cupboard*, 1993**
***The Key to the Indian*, 1998**

Nothing to Be Afraid Of 1980

Jan Mark / David Parkins

Nationality | English, born 1943 (author); English, born 1955 (illustrator)
Publisher | Kestrel Books, UK
Theme | Family, School

Jan Mark was an acute as well as highly amusing observer of childhood, with a wonderful ear for the type of dialogue the young use when talking to one another when away from the adults in their lives. She also had a strong affinity with children, fascinated by the way that parents and teachers so often misunderstand what their young charges may actually be trying to say or do at any one time. These ten short stories focus on the occasional mismatch between what children want and what their grown-up superiors sometimes insist on choosing for them.

The book opens with a four-year-old boy terrified by the spooky stories an older child tells him, yet still wanting more by the end. There is then an account of a girl pupil who becomes a helpless pawn in the battle between two teachers, both of whom want to use her to get their own way. Another story focuses on what looks like an ideal family, only to show by the end how much children also sometimes want to get away from one another.

A couple of the stories have a creepy edge to them. Does an already sinister-looking piece of furniture actually have the power to move at night? And can two young sisters really cure others with their made-up potions? But for the most part, this is a fun collection of some of the more extraordinary moments in a child's life, not least the tale of how one particular message from a teacher to a pupil becomes so hopelessly garbled as the day goes on. **NT**

Jules's Rat 1981

Peter Hacks / Klaus Ensikat

Nationality | German, born 1928 (author); German, born 1937 (illustrator)
Publisher | Kinderbuchverlag, Germany
Theme | Rhyming stories

In *Jules Ratte*, a little girl called Jules Janke has a major problem: all of her books, bar one, are gone, devoured by sewer rats. One of the rodents, its stomach full of literary wisdom, is still sitting under Jules's bed. What is she to do? Jules decides to part with her last remaining book and put it inside a trap to lure the beast out of its hiding place. And her plan works: she catches the rat and outlines her demands. The animal has to stay with her and help Jules with her homework as well as in class so that the girl can excel.

Thus, the rat becomes Jules's live encyclopedia, helping her to achieve great scholastic success. Alas, when spring arrives, the rat decides to move on and, left to her own devices, Jules realizes that she has not learned anything in the previous months except that she now understands how essential it is for her to do things on her own.

The author, Peter Hacks, was friends with Bertolt Brecht and Erich Koestner, authors whose writings are, at times, laconic and instructive. The language in Hacks's children's books is often deliberately coarse. Instead of waxing lyrically, the four-line stanzas come straight to the point to develop the story. Thus, Hacks creates a modern parable the wit of which is enhanced by the pictures of Klaus Ensikat, one of Germany's most successful illustrators.

Like many German authors living in former East Germany, Hacks used children's literature to covertly voice his criticism of the political system. **CS**

Goodnight Mister Tom 1981

Michelle Magorian

Nationality | English, born 1947
Publisher | Kestrel Books, UK
Theme | War, Family, Friendship, Love, Historical fiction

8+

OTHER GREAT WORLD WAR II READS

Anne Frank: The Diary of a Young Girl by Anne Frank, 1947
The Silver Sword by Ian Serraillier, 1956
When Hitler Stole Pink Rabbit by Judith Kerr, 1971
Carrie's War by Nina Bawden, 1973

The experiences of evacuees during World War II continue to move and fascinate contemporary children. This novel, realistic about the forms that families can take, takes the unconventional view that the war helped some children escape from miserable homes. Eight-year-old Willie, shipped to the country from the East End of London, where his mother beats and starves him, finds safety and a loving home with reclusive widower Tom Oakley and his dog. If life in Tom's village seems a little too idyllic under wartime conditions, it is plausible that it seemed so to Willie.

The plot is minimal: Willie's mother, a deeply disturbed woman whose religious fundamentalism feeds her psychopathic delusions, insists on her son

"The sores will heal. They healed before. It's the wounds inside that will take the longest."

coming home. Tom, sensing that Willie needs help, braves the big city to rescue him and eventually adopts him. With Tom's help and in tiny steps, Willie recovers from his traumatic childhood and later from the death of his friend, fellow evacuee Zach, in an air raid.

The book is a masterpiece of characterization and paints a picture of a supportive village community and the smaller community of evacuees within it. Potentially distressing content is only set out once help has arrived. With conviction and compassion, it charts Willie's feelings as he grows from a cringing, terrified little boy to a confident young teenager who finds room for friendships and later flirtation. Tom, too, is shown to be taking many small but significant steps as Willie's pressing needs divert him from his own unhappiness and lead to his recovery from the loss of his wife and young child many years before. **GB**

Ronia, the Robber's Daughter 1981

Astrid Lindgren

Original Title | Ronja Rövardotter
Nationality | Swedish, born 1907
Publisher | Rabén and Sjögren, Sweden
Theme | Myths and legends, Friendship, Love

Astrid Lindgren wrote with humor and poignancy, weaving myths, legends, and magical creatures into her tales. This is the story of a young girl and boy who grow to love each other deeply and who defy their parents' plans for their futures. Ronia is born in the robbers' lair on Matt's mountain. Her father is chief of the robbers. Ronia is the only baby to have been born there and is destined to be the robbers' "chieftain." As she grows up, the only child on the mountain, Ronia learns about Borka, the leader of a band of rival robbers. She explores the mountain's surrounding forest and river and discovers its animals and strange creatures, such as the sinister gray dwarves that thrive on her fear, and the "beautiful, mad and ferocious" harpies. She also meets, by accident, Birk, son of Borka, who was born the same night she was.

"You're a storm-night child . . . and you're a witch-night child, too."

The two become rivals, fighting over their own small territory, just as their fathers and forefathers have fought over territory for years. However, their rivalry leads them to mutual respect and friendship and the bond between them is cemented when they save each other's lives. Eventually, angry with their parents, they escape to live together in the Bear's Cave, outside both robbers' territories. They are persuaded to return to their homes in winter, by which time the feud between their fathers seems to be mellowing. The two men will never become friends, but the old enmity is slipping away. In the spring, Birk and Ronia return to the cave, with promises to come back when the harsh weather returns, both vowing to each other that they will never become robbers. **LH**

RECOMMENDED WORKS BY LINDGREN

Pippi Longstocking (Pippi Långstrump), 1945
Bill Bergson Lives Dangerously (Mästerdetektiven Blomkvist lever farligt), 1951
Mio, My Son (Mio, min Mio), 1954

8+

The BFG 1982

Roald Dahl Quentin Blake

Nationality | Welsh, born 1916 (author); English, born 1932 (illustrator)
Publisher | Jonathan Cape, UK
Theme | Fantasy, Friendship, Quirky

The Big Friendly Giant, or BFG as he likes to be known, is a vegetarian with a bald head, pointed nose, huge ears, rather odd sandals, and a colorful vocabulary. He lives in Giant Country alongside other giants with blood-curdling, ferocious names, such as Bloodbottler, Fleshlumpeater, Bonecruncher, and Childchewer. Each night, when the other giants gallop off to guzzle human "beans," the BFG takes his trumpet and his suitcase and blows dreams into the windows of boys and girls. One night he is spotted by orphan Sophie, so he kidnaps her, to prevent a great giant hunt that might end up with him shut in a bunkumhouse with squggling hippodumplings and crocodowndillies. Spurred into action by Sophie and with the help of the Queen of England, the BFG captures the child-eating giants and locks them safely out of harm's way, to live, in future, on a diet of repulsant snozzcumbers.

There are some fabulously memorable scenes: Sophie and the BFG in Dream Country, catching golden phizzwizards and frightsome trogglehumpers with a butterfly net; the BFG introducing Sophie to the delights of the glorious drink frobscottle, whose bubbles go downward rather than up, so that the drinkers don't burp but are lifted off their feet with loud whizzpopping; the BFG having breakfast with the Queen, seated on a chest of drawers on top of a piano.

The BFG manages to be as marvelously silly as we expect from Dahl, while at the same time sustaining an exciting and tense plot. The BFG is a charming hero, and the addition of the down-to-earth and sympathetic Queen to the cast is inspired. **CW**

"How wondercrump! . . .
How whoopsey-splunkers!
How absolutely squiffling!
I is all of a stutter."

MORE TO ENJOY FROM ROALD DAHL

***James and the Giant Peach*, 1961**
***Charlie and the Chocolate Factory*, 1964**
***The Magic Finger*, 1966**
***The Enormous Crocodile*, 1978**
***Matilda*, 1988**

The Haunting 1982

Margaret Mahy

Nationality | New Zealander, born 1936
Publisher | J. M. Dent, UK
Award | Carnegie Medal
Theme | Ghost stories, Young adult, Family

Young Barney has a considerable problem. Years ago he was haunted by three different but all moderately friendly ghosts. He is now being followed by the spirit of a boy dressed in blue crushed velvet who is continually repeating "Barnaby's dead!" Helped by his beloved stepmother, Claire, and his sister, Tabitha, plus an assortment of great-uncles, grandparents, and one great-grandmother, Barney slowly unravels the mystery of why he is being haunted. He has additional assistance from his mysteriously unhappy sister, Troy, as well as by his well-meaning father.

Nothing Margaret Mahy writes is ever predictable, and particularly so in this unique ghost story where the entire family takes the existence of a haunting spirit for granted and then works together to put things right. As in all Mahy's novels, though, psychological truth is never far away from physical reality. When Barney, gazing into a mirror, notices that the eyes looking back at him are not his, this is also a metaphor for the way that, during adolescence, young people may indeed become less recognizable to themselves as their body changes kick in at a bewildering speed.

Mahy, a former children's librarian at Christchurch City Libraries, is a witty as well as a wise writer. Who else would describe an evil great-grandmother as "like a wall with furious swear words scribbled all over it"? Always positive, much preferring characters who care for one another, she is truly a genius storyteller, capable of leaving readers gasping with amazement while longing for more of the same. **NT**

The Rattle Bag 1982

Editors Seamus Heaney, Ted Hughes

Nationality | Irish, born 1939 (Heaney); English, born 1930 (Hughes)
Publisher | Faber and Faber, UK
Theme | Poetry

The Rattle Bag offers a selection of the favorite poems of two of the most widely celebrated poets of the late twentieth century. Enjoyed as the ultimate anthology by one generation, it is about to be appreciated by the next.

It is a general collection, in which poems have been selected for their value as poems rather than because they fit into a particular interest, theme, or period. It demands nothing from the reader except to open it at random and read a poem. The poems are left to speak for themselves; they are assembled in alphabetical order by first line rather than by the poet's name or in a chronological sequence. This allows each poem to stand on its own merit. However, the editors have chosen some poems with an eye to achieving unexpected and delightful juxtapositions. There are too many for them all to be happy accidents. "Birches" follows "Binsey Poplars"; "The Properties of a Good Greyhound" follows "Praise of a Collie." Because the editors keep a low profile—there is only a brief introduction—the reader is encouraged to take the credit for these connections, which adds to the enjoyment of the book. It is clearly about poetry for pleasure rather than poetry for self-improvement.

The editors have won friends for oral poetry from various cultures and for poetry in translation, both of which were less widely appreciated at the time of publication than they are today. *The Rattle Bag* contains translations from Czech, German, Greek, Hungarian, Polish, Russian, Serbo-Croat, Spanish, Swedish, and Yoruba. It has completely redefined the way we think about poetry. **GB**

RAYMOND BRIGGS'S

When the Wind Blows

When the Wind Blows 1982

Raymond Briggs

Nationality | English, born 1934
Publisher | Hamish Hamilton, UK
Honor | UK Children's Author of the Year, 1993
Theme | Comics, Humor, Science fiction

This book has unbearably bleak themes: the inadequacy of government preparations for nuclear attack, the pointlessness of official advice, and the inevitability of brutal and painful death. However, young readers who can cope with this material will appreciate the book's power and resonance, which has outlasted the immediacy of the nuclear threat. In this comic-strip treatment of life just before and after the big bang, Raymond Briggs revisits the well-loved characters of Jim the lavatory attendant, created two years earlier in *Gentleman Jim*, and his wife, Hilda.

In *When the Wind Blows*, Briggs's contempt for bureaucrats is taken to logical extremes. In retirement, Jim has retained his unwarranted faith in authority. The text is peppered with phrases that he has picked up from the newspaper but barely understood ("The International Deterrent" and "The Ultimate Situation"). He is dogged in following civil defense instructions, popping out for fourteen loaves and a protractor to measure the angle of the specified refuge. Hilda, in her denial, puts her curlers in and refuses to use the government-specified temporary toilet. The couple survive the blast (represented by a truly terrifying white and pink double-page spread), emerge to a world of withered lettuces and melted buildings, run out of food and water, and die from radiation sickness. Briggs dares to poke fun at them in their desperate moments and gets away with it because he treats them with great compassion and tenderness. **GB**

Me in the Middle 1982

Ana María Machado Regina Yolanda

Nationality | Brazilian, born 1941 (author); Brazilian, birth date unknown (illustrator)
Publisher | Salamandra, Brazil
Theme | Classics, Family

Ten-year-old Bel helps her mother clean out a closet and in the process finds an old photograph of her great-grandmother Beatrice as a girl. Bel is entranced by the uncanny resemblance between herself and "Bisa Bea." Soon Bisa Bea becomes Bel's imaginary friend; she carries the picture close to her heart and her great-grandmother's voice emerges from inside her, telling stories of the old days and what life was like at the turn of the twentieth century in Brazil.

The trouble begins, however, when Bisa Bea advises Bel on what she considers to be proper behavior for young girls, telling her to dress in a certain manner and to be quiet and coy around boys. When her great-grandmother manipulates a situation to test the chivalry of Bel's boyfriend, the girl inevitably loses patience. At this point, another voice emerges, that of Bel's future great-granddaughter, who begins to counsel her as well. Eventually, Bel manages to find a wise balance between the two voices and to control her own life responsibly.

Originally published in Portuguese as *Bisa Bia, Bisa Bel*, this classic story is by one of Brazil's foremost children's writers. Ana María Machado began to write during the military dictatorship, and her fiction mixes social satire with elements of magical realism. Her playful narrative style and reflections on the invisible connections between the generations are skillfully integrated into the concerns of Bel, whose main lesson is that she must be true to herself. **LB**

Schoolboy Jia Li 1982

Qin Wenjun

8+

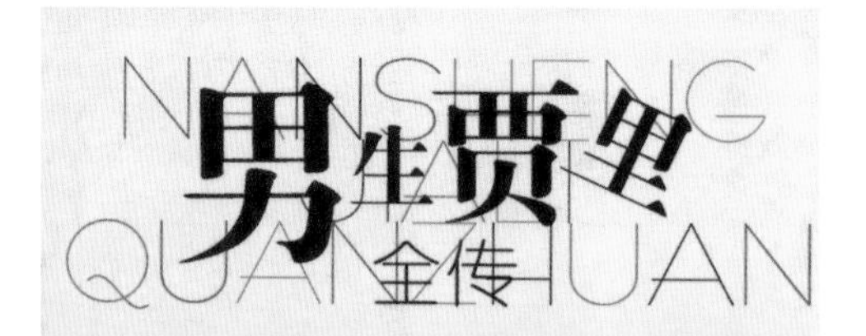

"... One needs to be a boy to understand a boy ..."

NOTABLE WORKS BY QIN WENJUN

School Girl Jia Mei, 2000
The Green Plantation of My Younger Brother, 2000
Curly the Black Goat, Hoopy the White Goat, 2006
Xiao Tou Ji Lai Zhou Yu, 2006

Nationality | Chinese, born 1954
Publisher | Shao Nian Er Tong Chu Ban She, China
Award | Spiritual Civilization Project Award, China
Theme | Young adult, Family, School

Schoolboy Jia Li is a journal recording the daily life of a fourteen-year-old boy, Jia Li, who lives with his parents and twin sister, Jia Mei, in a two-room apartment in the city. He is the elder of the twins and believes that his parents prefer his sister over him. Both his parents work: his father is a children's author and his mother is an actress. A neighbor, Mrs. Ng, helps out in their apartment daily. She proves to be an ally to Jia Li; he feels that she understands him better than his parents do. They both agree that Jia Mei is spoiled because she is a girl.

Jia Li is in his first year of high school, and daily events turn his life into a roller-coaster ride of emotions. Qin vividly describes the frustration that he feels when his deeds are misunderstood by his peers. His attempts to help his sister in the school play, which is attended by a TV producer, also turn into a disaster, causing him to suffer a deep sense of guilt.

Qin has a fundamental understanding of the way teenagers think and feel, and her dialogue is witty and understated. She is one of the top-selling authors of children's books in China and has published more than fifty works of fiction, winning scores of awards in the process, including the China Book Award and the Song Qingling Children's Literature Excellent Novel Award. *Schoolboy Jia Li* sold 1.2 million copies in the first ten years after its publication. Some of Qin's books have been adapted into movies, and she continues to write, ever adding to her base of loyal fans. **HL**

The Demon Headmaster 1982

Gillian Cross

Nationality | English, born 1945
Publisher | Oxford University Press, UK
Theme | School, Science fiction, Family, Friendship

Eleven-year-old Dinah, an orphan since the age of one, goes to live with Mr. and Mrs. Hunter, her new foster parents. She tries to get along with her two initially unfriendly foster brothers, Lloyd and Harvey. However, her experiences at her new school are even worse.

The pupils are always as good as gold: talking like robots and forever doing exactly what they are told. When Dinah also finds herself mindlessly repeating the slogans of the headmaster, even though she does not believe in them, she is determined to find out what is happening to her. Joining a secret society called SPLAT—the Society for the Protection of our Lives Against Them—she discovers that the headmaster is, in fact, using his sea-green eyes to hypnotize his pupils during morning assembly. He also plans eventually to hypnotize the whole country once he finally succeeds in appearing on television.

Although lighthearted in tone, this novel deals with serious issues. The idea of unbridled dictatorial power aided by technology is something of a modern-day nightmare and the theme of outstanding novels, such as George Orwell's *1984*. For children, now required to work harder than ever before at school with ever more government tests to pass, the idea of rebelling against excessive control may have extraspecial appeal, even if only in fantasy. Written by a fine writer who never disappoints and with many sequels to enjoy, this timely novel has proved immensely popular. It was also made into a television series by the BBC. **NT**

Max and Sally 1982

Miloš Macourek Adolf Born

Nationality | Czech, born 1926 (author); Czech, born 1930 (illustrator)
Publisher | Albatros, Czech Republic
Theme | Magical stories

Set in the present day, the story of Max and Sally (originally titled *Mach a Sebestová*) is far from an everyday tale. Neighbors and schoolmates, Max and Sally help a mysterious old gentleman find his glasses in the park, and he gives them a cut-off telephone receiver in return. The two friends soon discover that the somewhat peculiar gift holds tremendous power: it makes their wishes come true. The plot of the book rests upon the humorous situations in which the heroes find themselves, thanks to the magic phone.

A substantial part of the book's charm lies in the low-key attitude Max and Sally adopt when wishing for something. Instead of concocting grand schemes, Max and Sally's wishes are mostly quite humble. They may be bizarre at times (such as visiting prehistoric times or a pirate ship in order to illuminate a boring class in school), but their designs are never malevolent (unlike their rogue classmates, Horáček and Pažout, who get hold of the phone for a while).

Miloš Macourek was a writer whose work focused on children. He was part of the "Everyday generation" of Czech poets in the 1950s, who celebrated everyday reality with all its poetic qualities, while informing their works with an omnipresent sense of the absurd. Adolf Born is a popular and renowned painter. His richly imaginative illustrations are unique and dreamlike while still being attentive to the ordinary things of this world. Their collaboration created one of the most popular Czech children's books of all time. **PO**

War Horse 1982

Michael Morpurgo

Nationality | English, born 1943
Publisher | Kaye and Ward, UK
Award | Whitbread Award (Finalist)
Theme | War, Friendship, Animal stories

"'The world,' said the German officer, shaking his head, 'the world has gone quite mad. . . .'"

MORE ANIMAL FRIENDSHIP STORIES

The Red Pony by John Steinbeck, 1938
Black Stallion by Walter Farley, 1941
Old Yeller by Fred Gipson, 1956
Where the Red Fern Grows by Wilson Rawls, 1961
Pit Pony by Joyce Barkhouse, 1989

One of the first published novels by Michael Morpurgo and runner-up for the Whitbread Award, *War Horse* explores many of the themes that have since characterized the work of the former UK Children's Laureate: the futility of war and the suffering it produces; the ameliorating comfort brought by love and friendship; and the enduring bond between humans and animals. Simply and powerfully written, it offers young readers a shocking indictment of World War I trench warfare as seen through the eyes of Joey, a horse.

Joey is sold from a Devon farm into the army, where he never gives up hope of rediscovering Albert, the young boy with whom he grew up. The horse's narrative reveals the arbitrary and sometimes chaotic nature of war and emphasizes the similarities rather than the differences between the opposing sides. When Joey ends up fighting with the German army, he experiences the same discomfort, debilitating hard work, and mix of good and evil in humanity as he did in the British army.

In one memorable scene, Joey, caught in no-man's-land, watches as a soldier from both sides comes out to claim him, their brief tussle amicably settled with a cheerful conversation and the toss of a coin. "Jerry, boyo," the Welsh soldier comments, "I think if they would let you and me have an hour or two out here together, we could sort out this whole wretched mess." Miraculously, Joey is eventually reunited with Albert but, even as the war ends, there is no guarantee of a happy ending for the horses. A final twist in the tale paves the way for the later book, *Farm Boy*, a story about Albert and his grandson set fifty years later. **KA**

The Sheep-Pig 1983

Dick King-Smith Mary Rayner

Nationality | English, born 1922 (author); English, born 1933 (illustrator)
Publisher | Victor Gollancz, UK
Theme | Animal stories

Farmer Hogget and his wife are principally sheep farmers, although they also own a variety of livestock. This collection includes Babe, an unusually bright piglet recently won by the couple at a country fair. Oblivious to his impending fate, the other farmyard animals eventually let Babe know that he is shortly to be slaughtered for his meat. Briefly adopted by Fly, Farmer Hogget's sheepdog, Babe astonishes everybody by learning from her some of the secrets of herding sheep. But Babe adds an ingredient of his own, talking gently to Ma, the old leading sheep, and winning her willing cooperation rather than trying to bully her sheepdog style. Amazed by Babe's skill, Farmer Hogget spares his life, entering him instead—much to widespread derision—for a major sheep-dog trial. Triumphantly beating all the opposition, Babe's future is now secured.

Written by an author who is also a farmer, this famous tale was made into a successful film, *Babe*, which introduced King-Smith's work to a wider audience. The book was published in the United States in 1985 as *Babe, the Gallant Pig*. Strong on the practical details of everyday farming, its wider message about encouraging individuality even in the most unlikely circumstances has always proved popular with young readers. Although ostensibly a pig, Babe is, in fact, much more like any child setting out to prove themselves, sometimes facing mockery or hostility along the way. Beautifully written, expertly mixing reality with fantasy and never descending into sentimentality, this is a story to cherish. **NT**

Sunday's Child 1983

Gudrun Mebs Rotraut S. Berner

Nationality | German, born 1944 (author); German, born 1948 (illustrator)
Publisher | Sauerländer, Germany
Theme | Family

Sunday's Child (*Sonntagskind*) is an eight-year-old girl who lives in an orphanage and has never met her parents. She has resigned herself to the fact that she does not even have "Sunday parents," that is, people who invite orphans to their homes on a Sunday so the children can experience life in a proper family. The kids who are fortunate enough to have Sunday parents rave about their time away from the orphanage, while our heroine listens sadly to their stories.

One day a mystery woman calls and says she wants to look after a child on a Sunday, be it boy or girl, giving our nameless narrator a chance for some happiness. Alas, right from the start, things go horribly wrong: the girl is terribly nervous and Ulla, the muddle-headed young woman who has requested her presence, does not correspond at all to the girl's mental image of a proper mother. With her short hair and glasses, she looks like a boy and is perennially late, making the girl wait. However, as time goes by, the two of them grow close—until Christian, Ulla's boyfriend, suddenly appears. But any fears of losing her surrogate mother are short-lived, as the girl gets on well with Christian too; so well, in fact, that he decides to marry Ulla so the two of them can adopt her.

On her way to the happy ending the girl reflects on her situation and her experiences inside and outside the orphanage. A good sense of humor helps her through the hard times and endears her to the reader, who is taken by the fact that she generally does not seek to excuse her own little faults and escapades, although she still embellishes them when it suits her. **CS**

Please Mrs. Butler 1983

Allan Ahlberg Fritz Wegner

"Please Mrs. Butler / This boy Derek Drew / Keeps copying my work, Miss / What shall I do?"

MORE POETRY COLLECTIONS TO ENJOY

Mind Your Own Business by Michael Rosen, 1974
Revolting Rhymes by Roald Dahl, 1982
Heard It in the Playground by Allan Ahlberg, 1989
If You're Not Here, Please Raise Your Hand by Kalli Dakos, 1990

Nationality | English, born 1938 (author); British, born 1924 (illustrator)
Publisher | Kestrel Books, UK
Theme | Poetry, School, Friendship

Please Mrs. Butler is representative of a new wave of poetry for children that appeared in the 1980s using children's everyday language. Among the forty-five poems, there are many that simply celebrate school life, friendship, and rapport between children and teachers, but a substantial minority also present ideas about children's fears and worries.

There are deceptively profound poems such as "The Puzzle" about friends who are pretending not to be friends, each for the other's benefit, and "The School Nurse," with its underlying terror of being publicly shamed at having head lice.

There are subtle messages for children to draw from "The Ordeal of Robin Hood," in which a gang who have planned their class play is shaken out of their comfort zone by the new Polish boy Janek, who has not heard of Robin Hood, refuses to die on cue, fights for real, and soon wins his place in the Merrie Men. The poems capture the daily rituals of school life and the heady excitement of any disruption to routine (as in "Dog in the Playground" and "Only Snow"). They show that, while teachers and children are different species, they can coexist happily (as in "The Cane"). It is no surprise that Allan Ahlberg is a former primary school teacher. Fritz Wegner's line drawings perfectly partner the poems in creating a mob of children, with individuals picked out for solo spots. Among the cluster of worn-out and world-weary teachers, also well characterized, there is no doubt about which one is Mrs. Butler. **GB**

Mouth Open, Story Jump Out 1984

Grace Hallworth Art Derry

Nationality | Trinidadian, birth date unknown (author); details unknown (illustrator)
Publisher | Methuen, UK
Theme | Folktales, Traditional

The delightfully explicit title of *Mouth Open, Story Jump Out* sets the tone for this fine collection of narratives set in the West Indies. Grace Hallworth spins a spellbinding web of tales that take place in the Caribbean when friends and strangers meet, exchange news, and tell each other of the unusual happenings in their daily lives.

The well-told stories spring from supernatural events, superstitions and the deep-seated, archetypal fears in Caribbean, and especially Trinidadian, folklore. These are powerful stories, which are at once traditional and splendidly retold with great originality, and have a special hold over young readers.

The mysterious atmosphere they evoke is almost magical. Hallworth is a master at exploiting the French Caribbean setting and making it into an integral part of her breathtaking yarns. Titles such as "Le Diable" and "The Loup Garou" slip intriguingly off the tongue and tease young imaginations even before the stories are begun.

Every culture has its witch stories and the version presented here, woven around the folklore figure of the Soucouyant—a creature that lives by day as an old woman but who strips off her wrinkled skin at night and transforms into a life-sucking, flying monster—is a particularly scary one. This is an enjoyable set of sinister tales, which will have many a young reader insisting on having the light left on at night after reading them. **LB**

The Eye of the Wolf 1984

Daniel Pennac

Original Title | L'oeil du loup
Nationality | French, born Daniel Pennacchioni 1944
Publisher | Éditions Nathan, France
Theme | Animal stories

A solitary wolf and a silent boy regard each other from either side of a cage. Drawn by the challenge of his stare, the wolf allows the boy to look closely into his one good eye. What the boy sees within is the tale of the wolf, Loup Bleu, and of all wolves. The mysterious boy, named Afrique, then reveals his own story and that of the continent that gave him his name. These sometimes unsettling stories, sketched with a traveler's sense for detail, span the ancient and modern world—from the fur hunters of the Alaskan wastes, to the logging companies who mow down the African jungle. Their respective tales and travels come together in the "Other World"—at a European zoo. Although far from naive about the hard realities of the animal world, Pennac's vision is one in which the real beast is man and the only cruelty, his greed.

Pennac (his given name is Daniel Pennacchioni) is an author of diverse talents. In the French presidential elections of 2002 he was a member of the shadow cabinet of Dieudonné, but he originally earned his living as a teacher. Pennac is well-known for writing about the importance of reading. The mirroring image at the heart of *The Eye of the Wolf* brings to life the act of reading: two creatures, separated by bars that force them to look but not touch, find common ground and new insight through storytelling. This poignant fable for modern times will stay with readers long afterward, and zoos will never look the same again. **NA**

8+

Tomb Raiders 1984

Odile Weulersse P. and G. Brizzan

Nationality | French, born 1938 (author); French, birth dates unknown (illustrators)
Publisher | Hachette Jeunesse, France
Theme | Historical fiction

In *Tomb Raiders* (*Les pilleurs de sarcophages*), Tétiki is the son of the governor of the Egyptian province of Eléphantine. His country is divided: the Egyptian pharaoh Ahmosis reigns from Thèbes, while the bellicose Hyksos invaders, worshippers of the god Seth, have installed their own pharaoh, Apopi, in Avaris, on the delta, and intend to extend his power to the whole of Egypt.

One day an emissary of Apopi arrives in Eléphantine and asks for the help of Tétiki's father against Ahmosis, promising gold in return. However, Tétiki finds out that the Hyksos are planning to vandalize and loot the tomb of the last pharaoh, Taa the Brave. He decides to outwit the vandals by warning Pharaoh Ahmosis. Unfortunately, when he arrives in Thèbes it is the feast of the god Amon, which means that he cannot meet the pharaoh for a month. Tétiki goes alone in search of the tomb to try and rescue its treasure.

This suspenseful and well-researched story is told in simple language and is packed with accurate historical detail and fact. Ancient Egypt, with its pyramids and tombs, sarcophagi and mummies, pharaohs and high priests has an enduring fascination for younger and older readers alike, partly because of the extreme age of the civilization and partly, of course, because of the many artifacts to be found in museums that most schoolchildren will have visited at some time. Here, far from being mere backdrop, the historical element is an integral part of the story. Odile Weulersse's narrative brings ancient Egypt to life for young readers. **LB**

Pirate's Heart 1985

Benno Pludra Gerhard Goßmann

Nationality | German, born 1925 (author); German, born 1912 (illustrator)
Publisher | Beltz and Gelberg, Germany
Theme | Family, Friendship

In *Pirate's Heart* (*Das Herz des Piraten*), Jessica lives with her mother Elise near a village by an unspecified northern sea. The eight-year-old girl has never met her father, but she dreams about him frequently. One day she finds a special, reddish pebble that gleams in her hands. And it speaks to her, too. It claims to have previously been the heart of a pirate who died 300 years ago. Jessica's mental image of the long-dead pirate—who was called William—matches the mental image she has of her father: curly, jet-black hair, dark eyes, and a delicate figure like her own.

At this time, the circus, where Jessica's father used to work as a rider, is coming to town. It turns out he is still with the circus. Called Jakko, he looks exactly as Jessica imagined. Jakko is keen for the family to stay together, but Jessica's mother is hesitant because he has let them down in the past. Elise decides to reject Jakko, and Jessica eventually gets over her heartbreak at the decision. Throwing the pirate's heart back into the sea, Jessica abandons fantasy and manages to make new friends of her own age.

Benno Pludras is one of the most important East German children's authors. His books stand out because of their realistic approach to social problems. This work is remarkable because of its lifelike representation of village life and the detailed descriptions of Jessica's transition from childhood to adulthood. This captivating narrative was simultaneously published in East and West Germany, a feat that very few books achieved prior to reunification. It was made into a successful film in Germany. **CS**

Storm 1985

Kevin Crossley-Holland Alan Marks

Nationality | English, born 1941 (author); English, born 1957 (illustrator)
Publisher | Heinemann, UK
Theme | Ghost stories

Storm is a thrilling ghost story for younger readers set on the remote Norfolk, England, coast. Annie lives with her elderly parents and is used to venturing out alone but she is afraid of the dark winter evenings. One night, during a fierce storm, her pregnant sister, Willa, goes into labor. Annie knows that she is the only one who can fetch help. Annie is terrified of the ghost of a man murdered by highwaymen who is reputed to haunt the bleak marshes. As she sets off in the dark, with the wind howling around her, a horseman comes riding by and offers to take her to the doctor in the nearest village. Annie admits: "I'm afraid for my sister and her baby. And I am afraid of meeting the ghost." The stranger sweeps Annie up onto his horse and she feels as if she is flying through the air. When they finally reach the village, the horseman tells her he is called Storm and reveals his true identity before vanishing into the night.

Kevin Crossley-Holland is a poet and an award-winning children's writer. His Arthurian trilogy—*The Seeing Stone, At the Crossing Places,* and *King of the Middle March*—is aimed at older children and has sold more than a million copies. Many of his stories are steeped in myth and legend, and he has produced volumes retelling Norse and Greek myths, as well as the Mabinogion cycle of Welsh tales.

Storm draws on East Anglian folktales and packs a lot of drama into a few short pages. The language is simple but lyrical and Alan Marks's atmospheric illustrations add an almost dreamlike quality to Annie's adventure. Younger readers will be gripped by the pace of the story and thrilled by the scary ending. **HJ**

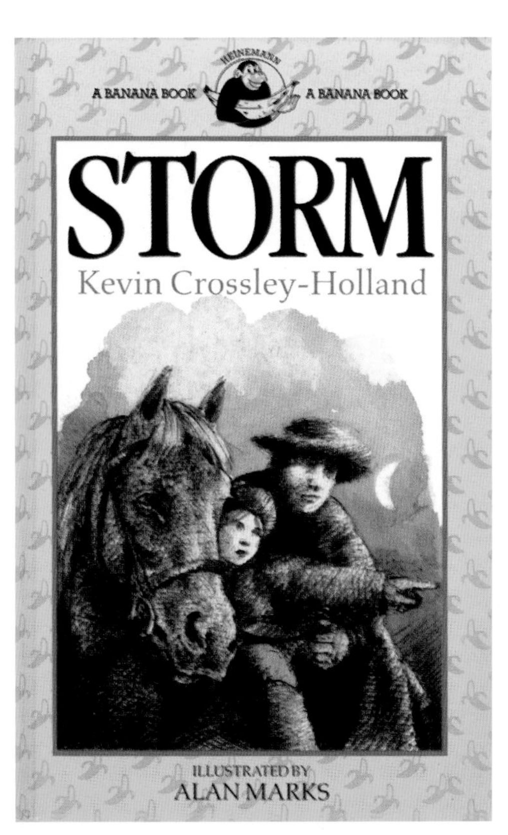

"There are kind ghosts and unkind ghosts, Annie."

OTHER GREAT GHOST STORIES

A Christmas Carol by Charles Dickens, 1843
The Tell-Tale Heart by Edgar Allan Poe, 1843
The Ghost of Thomas Kempe by Penelope Lively, 1973
The Haunting by Margaret Mahy, 1982
The Ghost's Child by Sonya Hartnett, 2007

Sarah, Plain and Tall 1985

Patricia MacLachlan

8+

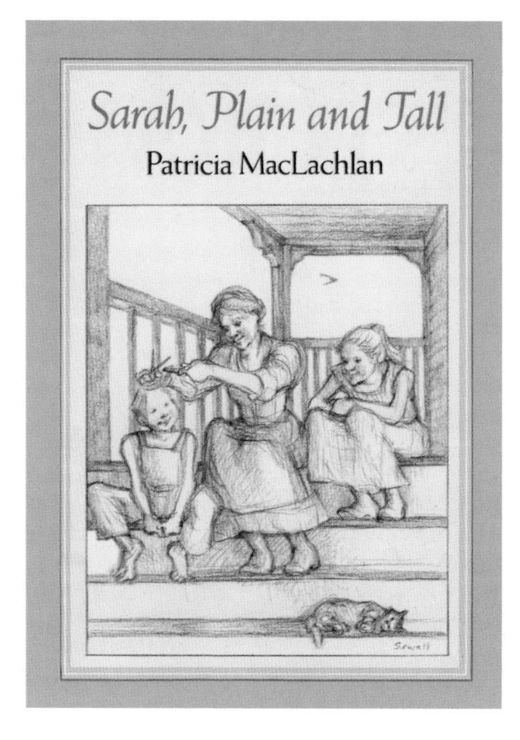

Nationality | American, born 1938
Publisher | HarperCollins, USA
Award | Newbery Medal, 1986
Theme | Family

In deceptively simple prose, Anna tells of the summer on the prairies, when her father advertised for a mail order bride to be a wife to him and a mother to Caleb and herself. Caleb cannot remember their mother because she died when he was born but he knows that she sang beautifully. In her letters Sarah assures them that she can sing, but writes about her love for the sea, and the children worry that Sarah will not be happy far away from the Maine coast.

When she arrives with her cat, Seal, she brings shells from the shores of Maine and tells them about the sea. During the month she stays as a trial, the children seize on her every word to try to find out if she will stay or not. When Sarah insists that Papa teaches her to ride and drive the wagon and then leaves to go into town, the children go about their chores, worrying that she will not return, but at dusk they see the dust of the wagon and Sarah comes home, with colored pencils, blue, gray, and green, to draw the sea.

This is a touching story of the making of a family and of the insecurity of childhood. The reader can sense the growing relationship between Papa and Sarah as the children almost hold their breath waiting for the outcome. Although she has lived in Massachusetts most of her life, author Patricia MacLachlan was born in Wyoming. She says she still feels a strong connection to the wide-open prairie: "I carry around a little bag of prairie dirt with me, like a part of my past." **JF**

"Dear Jacob, I will come by train. I will wear a yellow bonnet. I am plain and tall. Sarah."

MORE FROM PATRICIA MACLACHLAN

***Arthur, For the Very First Time*, 1980**
***What You Know First*, 1998**
***Grandfather's Dance*, 2006**
***Edward's Eyes*, 2007**
***True Gift*, 2009**

Journey to Jo'burg 1985

Beverley Naidoo

Nationality | South African, born 1943
Publisher | Longman, UK
Award | Josette Frank Award, 1986
Theme | Family, Adventure, Historical fiction

In simple prose, the evils of apartheid in South Africa are vividly brought home to the young reader in this story of two children who travel hundreds of miles to find their mother. Mma works as a servant for a white family in Johannesburg while her children remain in their village with their grandmother and aunt. When little sister Dineo becomes very sick, thirteen-year-old Naledi persuades her brother, Tiro, to go with her to find their mother and get her to come home.

The children set off on foot but are given a lift by a truck driver; they then meet Grace who saves them from getting on a "whites-only bus." They see Mma but are not allowed to stay the night with her. Instead they stay with Grace in Soweto where they hear about Grace's brother, Dumi, who was arrested for demonstrating for better education and is now living outside South Africa working for freedom. This awakens in Naledi a sense that there are better things to study for than to be a servant.

The book, banned in South Africa until after Nelson Mandela was released from jail and apartheid was ended, is based on Naidoo's own experiences growing up as a white child with, as she says, two mothers, her own and her black one. She recalls: "When I sent two copies of my first children's book to nephews and nieces in South Africa in 1985, they never received the parcel. Instead, my sister-in-law received a letter telling her that the books had been seized and banned." **JF**

The Valley of the Fireflies 1985

Gloria Cecilia Díaz F. Melendez

Nationality | Colombian, born 1951 (author); Spanish, born 1964 (illustrator)
Publisher | SM Publicación, Spain
Theme | Myths and legends

Ten-year-old Jeronimo, and Anastasia, the wise old woman who raised him, live in the Valley of the Fireflies, a place of incomparable magic and beauty. Jeronimo has only three goals in life: to learn who his parents were; find Dragon, the king of the lizards; and help the bird keeper find a rare bird that he has lost.

In *The Valley of the Fireflies* (*El valle de los Cocuyos)*, readers will enjoy Jeronimo's various, sometimes convoluted but always thrilling adventures as he tries to accomplish his goals—such as rescuing hostages from the Lord of the Shadows. Skillfully interwoven into the narrative of Jeronimo's adventures are Colombian legends, myths, and stories. As in traditional quest narratives, the journey theme is central to the development of the story and connects each story with the others.

Gloria Cecilia Díaz was born and grew up in just such a valley in the foothills of the Andes. She creates a magical atmosphere, vividly describing the Latin American landscapes, with its rich colors and vast, dreamlike expanses. This lovely, poetic tale, set in a timeless world of magic and beauty, teaches the importance of dreams, memories, and love. It is a bedtime story, which is appropriate since Diaz writes at night, spending the day teaching Spanish, reading, and wandering Paris, where she now lives, visiting its museums and monuments. She frequently works on several stories at once. *The Valley of the Fireflies* won the Spanish El Barco de Vapor award in 1985. **LB**

MICHAEL MORPURGO

Why the Whales Came

Why the Whales Came 1985

Michael Morpurgo

Nationality | English, born 1943
Publisher | Heinemann, UK
Honor | UK Children's Laureate, 2003–2005
Theme | Family, Friendship, Adventure

It is 1914 on Bryher, in the Scilly Isles where Gracie and Daniel live. The pivot of the story, however, takes place on the largest uninhabited island, Samson, thought to be cursed and somehow connected to the Birdman, an outsider who the children are forbidden to talk to.

The people of the islands exist by fishing and it is common for the children to help. In their spare time Gracie and Daniel make toy boats. While sailing them in Rushy Bay they make contact with the Birdman and discover that he is deaf and far from sinister. They communicate at first through seashell messages and he gives them a wonderfully carved cormorant. Eventually they visit him in his cottage and he teaches Daniel the craft of carving. One night, the children are accidentally marooned on Samson. They return home to a tragic event, which they believe was caused by the curse. Daniel's brother decides that the Birdman is a German spy and plans to destroy his cottage. Rushing to warn him, the children find him on the beach trying to rescue a beached whale. As the story reaches its climax the history of the curse unravels.

This book deals with our relationship with nature and the demonization of people who are different. There is as much excitement and adventure here as any reader could wish for. Michael Morpurgo discovered his gift when he was a teacher having to read a story every day to his class. The children were uninspired, so he decided to try them with the sort of story he used to tell to his own children. **WO**

Gargling With Jelly 1985

Brian Patten David Mostyn

Nationality | English, born 1946 (author); English, birth date unknown (illustrator)
Publisher | Viking Kestrel, UK
Theme | Poetry

This collection of children's poetry was written for reading aloud and each poem lends itself to being performed. There are eighty-four poems in the book, ranging from four lines in length, including "Teacher's Pet" and "The Venus Take-Away," to "The Saga of the Doomed Cyclist," which roams over five pages (and all over the world).

The poems range from the downright ludicrous, through to the educational, to the serious and sad. "The Trouble with My Sister" (who turns out to be a witch), "The Trouble with My Brother" (a baby cannibal), and "I've Never Heard the Queen Sneeze" appear with serious or historic poems, such as "The Children's Fall-Out Shelter," and contemplative, sad poems like "Looking for Dad" (about a child whose parents separate).

Brian Patten, one of the acclaimed Liverpool Poets from the 1960s, brings children's fears, experiences, and joys alive. Some of his poems are in the tradition of Edward Lear and Hilaire Belloc. He uses a vivid imagination and newly created words to bring weird and wonderful creatures to life, such as the Silly Siposark (who refuses to believe the rains are coming and won't get on Noah's Ark), or to give selfish or stupid people and animals their just desserts. There is Winifred Weasel, who steals into a farmer's barn through a slender crack, but then eats so much she gets too fat to make her escape and stern Miss Frugle, who is so mean to children that none of them cares when she falls through the ice and is never seen again. **LH**

The Hounds of the Morrigan 1985

Pat O'Shea

Nationality | Irish, born 1931
Publisher | Oxford University Press, UK
Theme | Myths and legends, Fantasy, Adventure

8+

Two children, Pidge and his younger sister, Brigit, are asked by the Irish god, the Dagda, to go on a quest to recover a bloodstained pebble before it falls into the clutches of Morrigan, the Celtic goddess of war.

Moving from the human world of Galway to the land of Faery, the children encounter a series of talking insects and animals, all of whom back them in their great adventure. Ranged against them are Morrigan's two sidekicks, Breda Fairfoul and Melodie Moonlight, a brace of motorbike-riding witches in command of a terrifying pack of hounds. Pidge and Brigit have their own army of supernatural allies. In the closing pages, the story builds to a fearful battle that will finally determines which side comes out on top.

"These lovely eyes had the blue of a bluebell wood trapped in them and his gaze held them."

Quirky, shot through with moments of poetic prose, but also brimming with action, this story of more than 400 pages is witty and wise, at times recalling the fantasy novels of John Masefield (*The Midnight Folk*, comes to mind). Drawing on the author's intimate first-hand knowledge of her own countryside and folk customs, *The Hounds of the Morrigan* triumphantly avoids whimsy in favor of tough humor and colloquial speech.

Although a sequel was started, Pat O'Shea unfortunately never progressed beyond writing the first three chapters. However, as a stand-alone first novel, *The Hounds of the Morrigan* remains a fantastic achievement to be enjoyed by each new generation of young readers in search of a truly exciting tale set against a rich background of Celtic mythology. **NT**

OTHER GREAT FANTASY ADVENTURES

The Midnight Folk by John Masefield, 1927
The Box of Delights by John Masefield, 1935
The Thirteen Clocks by James Thurber, 1950
The Moon of Gomrath by Alan Garner, 1963
The Neverending Story by Michael Ende, 1979

Redwall 1986

Brian Jacques

Redwall is the first in a series of fantasy novels that revolve around the peace-loving mice, voles, shrews, and squirrels that inhabit the medieval world of Redwall Abbey. Their tranquil lives are threatened by an evil one-eyed rat warlord, Cluny the Scourge, and his henchmen who are determined to seize Redwall Abbey for themselves. An unlikely hero, in the form of Matthias, a young and bumbling mouse, sets out to find the legendary sword of Martin the Warrior that may save his home and his fellow beings.

Subsequent stories in this saga also feature epic battles between good and evil, and a range of characters who have to undergo a quest or test of courage. For example, in *Mossflower*, the second book in the series, we meet Martin the Warrior who saves a beleaguered community suffering under the tyranny of a wildcat called Verdauga.

"Mice are my heroes because, like children, mice are little and have to learn to be courageous."

Jacques describes his stories as good yarns. They are plot-driven and packed with action, adventure, vengeance, heroic deeds, terrifying villains, and courage and decency in the face of danger.

A truck driver by day, Jacques wrote the first *Redwall* book for children at Liverpool's Royal Wavertree School for the Blind where he was a volunteer reader. He says that the experience made him write in a highly descriptive style. His childhood English teacher showed his writing to a publisher and the rest, as they say, is history. While some critics have described the Redwall series as rather formulaic, they are immensely popular with children and have also attracted a large adult readership. **HJ**

Nationality | English, born 1939
Publisher | Hutchinson, UK
Theme | Animal stories, Fantasy, Favorite characters, Adventure

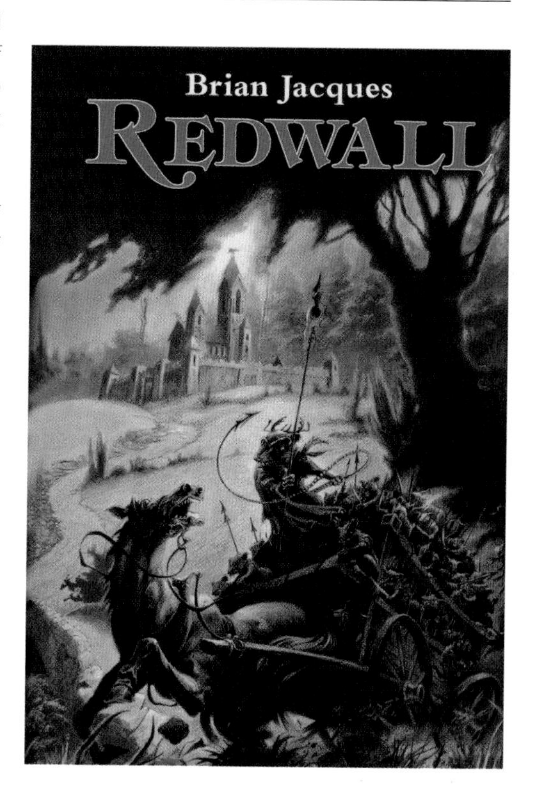

MORE TITLES FROM THE SERIES

Mossflower, 1988
Mattimeo, 1989
Salamandastron, 1992
Martin the Warrior, 1993
Outcast of Redwall, 1995

8+

The Snow Spider 1986

Jenny Nimmo

Nationality | English, born 1944
Publisher | Methuen, UK
Award | Nestlé Children's Book Prize
Theme | Myths and legends

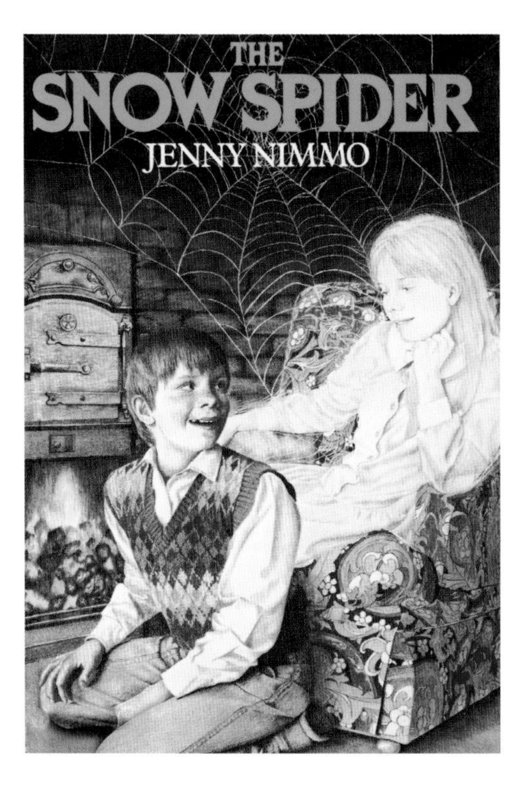

RECOMMENDED READS BY JENNY NIMMO

Emlyn's Moon, 1987
The Chestnut Soldier, 1989
The Stone Mouse, 1993
Griffin's Castle, 1994
Midnight for Charlie Bone, 2002

Gwyn lives on a remote Welsh hillside with his parents who are still mourning the loss of his sister, Bethan, who vanished without a trace some years before. His father is deeply bitter and still blames Gwyn for her disappearance, which causes a deep rift in their relationship. On his tenth birthday Gwyn is given five strange gifts by his eccentric grandmother: a tin whistle, a piece of seaweed, a yellow scarf, a small broken horse, and a metal brooch.

She asks him to find out if he is a magician. She tells him that his ancestors were magicians but warns that the gifts come with great responsibilities and should only be used wisely. When the wind blows the brooch from Gwyn's hand, it is replaced by a tiny silver spider called Arianwen, who spins a magical web allowing Gwyn to see into other mystical worlds. So begins Gwyn's amazing adventures and his quest to find his long-lost sister.

"'Time to find out if you are a magician!' said Gwyn's grandmother."

As he journeys into the unknown, Gwyn becomes isolated and loses his friends at school, who do not believe his stories. He then faces his greatest test as one of his grandmother's gifts threatens him, his family, and the community he lives in.

Nimmo—a former director/editor of the BBC children's program, *Jackanory*—skillfully evokes Welsh myths and the wildness of the Welsh countryside, and her mix of fantasy and the real world is deftly handled. She also writes with great sensitivity about grief, loss, and responsibility. A magical and gripping read, the saga continues in two more books, *Emlyn's Moon* and *The Chestnut Soldier*. **HJ**

Whipping Boy 1987

Sid Fleischman Peter Sís

This is a first-class swashbuckling adventure of the kind often labeled "rollicking." It is a classic prince-and-pauper story with a twist; that twist being a skillful blend of cracking dialogue that sounds simultaneously historical and very modern, mixed in with easy wit and snatches of inventive description.

Our tale is set around the 1700s, when men wore long wigs, pirates and highwaymen roamed abroad, and princes had "whipping boys"—boys who were punished in their places (only kings could punish princes, and kings were busy men). Here, the prince is Prince Brat and the whipping boy is a street-smart orphan called Jemmy, son of a ratcatcher. Prince Brat is lazy, spoiled, and always up to tricks; Jemmy is brave and quick to learn. As a result, Jemmy can read, write, and do math, and gets whipped a great deal, while Prince Brat cannot even write his own name.

"Was it clothes that made a prince, Jemmy wondered, just as rags made a street boy?"

Jemmy longs to escape but, in a surprise turnabout, the prince runs away taking Jemmy with him. When they encounter ruthless villains Cutwater and Hold-Your-Nose Billy (he likes garlic), a fast-moving adventure unfolds. As the characters try to outwit one another, the boys' relationship changes. Pursued by the villains, the boys race through the forest, into city streets filled with jugglers and ballad-sellers, and deep into the sewers, meeting a dancing bear and Captain Nips as they go.

Fleischman's past includes working as a magician and screenwriter. His award-winning adventure stories, filled with ghosts, pirates, magic, derring-do, and a love of historical topics, are the perfect springboard for learning about history in a fresh, fun way. **AK**

Nationality | American, born 1920 (author); Czech/American, born 1949 (illustrator)
Publisher | Greenwillow Books, USA
Theme | Historical fiction

OTHER GREAT SID FLEISCHMAN TITLES

By the Great Horn Spoon!, 1963
The Midnight Horse, 1990
The Giant Rat of Sumatra or Pirates Galore, 2005
Escape! The Story of the Great Houdini, 2006
The Entertainer and the Dybbuk, 2007

8+

I Am Susannah 1987

Libby Gleeson

Nationality | Australian, born 1950
Publisher | Angus and Robertson, Australia
Award | Victorian Premier's Award (shortlist), 1988
Theme | Family, School, Friendship, Young adult

8+

Libby Gleeson is one of Australia's most acclaimed children's authors, with a large and impressive back list of picture books, short novels, and young adult fiction. In 2007 she was awarded membership to the Order of Australia for Services to Literature. Applauded for their realistic protagonists and well-plotted story lines, her books are challenging, imaginative, and socially engaged.

I Am Susannah is written with characteristic integrity although Gleeson refutes descriptions of it as a themed "single parent novel." The schoolgirl heroine, who lives in a quiet Sydney suburb with her mother, is devastated when her best friend and neighbor Kim moves to Melbourne. Susie feels the loss keenly, especially at school, where friendships and alliances between teenage girls are founded on complex and shifting lines. "Who will I sit with? Kim. Always Kim," she reflects. Lonely and bored, Susie develops a fascination with the eccentric lady who has taken up residence in Kim's old house; a mysterious, reclusive figure, often found sketching in the town cemetery. Spying on the "Blue Lady" from her concealed perch high up in a fig tree, Susie wonders what dark secrets her past holds. During a party at a school friend's house, the girls play an intense reckless game of truth and dare. In a heightened, climactic moment, Susie finally discovers the truth about the Blue Lady, but her personal values and courage are tested in the pressure to conform to the rules of the game and the expectations of her schoolmates.

I Am Susannah is a well-loved classic in Australia, where it has been made into a television drama titled *The Blue Lady*. The ending manages to be hopeful and optimistic without being illusory or glib. It is a sensitive and moving exploration of the perennial teenage issues of friendship, loneliness, identity, and peer pressure. **MK**

LIBBY GLEESON
I am Susannah
BY THE AUTHOR OF THE HIGHLY ACCLAIMED
Eleanor, Elizabeth

MORE BOOKS ABOUT FRIENDSHIP

A Little Princess **by Frances Hodgson Burnett, 1905**
Betsy-Tacy **by Maud Hart Lovelace, 1940**
One Hundred Dresses **by Eleanor Estes, 1944**
The Far-Distant Oxus **by Katharine Hull and Pamela Whitlock, 1977**

Quirky Tails 1987

Paul Jennings

Nationality | Australian, born 1943
Publisher | Penguin, Australia
Award | Young Australians' Best Book Award, 1992
Theme | Folktales, Horror, Quirky

Paul Jennings is best known for his short stories for readers with a taste for the bizarre, the blackly comic, the frighteningly hair-raising, and the toe-curlingly embarrassing. Often told in the first person, the directness of the writing and the brevity of each story make his collections accessible to younger readers.

Quirky Tails is one of eleven collections Jennings wrote during the 1980s and 1990s. The titles of some of the stories reflect his love of groan-enducing puns and his gift for turning the ordinary into the sinister. "Santa Claws," for instance, is a Father Christmas with claws rather than hands. The even stranger "Tonsil Eye 'Tis" features a tiny face that takes up residence on a boy's tonsils. Most of the stories in the collection rely on supernatural activity or intervention, while, in a few, the apparently spooky is revealed to have more to do with accident or mere cunning.

"It all started on Christmas Eve. I had to look after my little brat of a brother."

Jennings's stories have some of the flavor of folktales and are often concerned with issues of power, mortality, or love, in which cruelty and greed are punished and virtue is rewarded. For example, "Unhappily Ever After" conjures up a personal hell of role reversal for a teacher too fond of corporal punishment. For Jennings, however, the prospect of surprising, appalling, and disgusting the reader is clearly as important as providing moral lessons.

These collections are immensely popular in Australia and, while the establishment literary prizes have eluded Jennings, the collections have regularly won the Young Australians' Best Book Award, which is chosen by young readers themselves. **CB**

8+

OTHER QUIRKY CHARACTERS

Worzel Gummidge by Barbara Euphan Todd, 1936
Little Onion by Gianni Rodari, 1951
Down with Skool! by Geoffrey Willans, 1953
Gaston by André Franquin et al, 1957
Bill's New Frock by Anne Fine, 1989

Mufaro's Beautiful Daughters: An African Tale 1987

John Steptoe

"When I am queen, everyone will know that your silly kindness is only weakness."

OTHER GREAT TRADITIONAL TALES

The Adventurous Tales of Machu Picchu by Ciro Alegría, 1950
Stradbroke Dreamtime by Noonuccal Oodgeroo, 1972
The Story of Jumping Mouse by John Steptoe, 1984
The Painted House by Monserrat del Amo, 1990

Nationality | American, born 1950
Publisher | Lothrop Lee and Shepard, USA
Award | Caldecott Honor Book, 1988
Theme | Traditional, Folktales

This African tale from Zimbabwe reinvigorates the tradition fable of "pride goes before a fall," or, in more child friendly terms, evokes an African version of the Cinderella fairy tale. Illustrated with breathtaking paintings showing the glory of Africa's beautiful natural world, children will be mesmerized not only by the art, but by the classic story. This is a timeless narrative for all families but, with its positive message and celebration of African heritage, it is one especially treasured by African-Americans.

Mufaro was a happy man, with two beautiful daughters. Nyasha was kind and considerate as well as beautiful, but everyone, except Mufaro, knew that Manyara was selfish, bad-tempered, and spoiled.

One day, word comes that the king has decided to take a wife and invites "The Most Worthy and Beautiful Daughters in the Land" to appear before him. Proud Mufaro, believing that both his daughters are as virtuous as they are beautiful, is sure the king could only choose between Nyasha and Manyara.

Manyara, of course, does not agree. She sets out to make certain that she is chosen. She rushes to the palace in order to be selected first, while Nyasha takes her time, allowing herself to be distracted by the poor and elderly along her way. Of course, inevitably, Manyara's self-interest and haste do not help her cause, and the good and virtuous Nyasha is chosen above her. All-in-all, this is a charming tale with a strong moral lesson. **KD**

A Thief in the Village 1987

James Berry

Nationality | Jamaican/English, born 1925
Publisher | Hamish Hamilton, UK
Award | Nestlé Children's Book Prize
Theme | Traditional, Short stories

Berry brings his childhood to life in this collection of nine short stories, which feature young characters going about their day-to-day lives in their native Jamaica. While all the stories involve children wanting something—money to buy some new shoes, a brand new bike, a mouth organ, or a chance to know their estranged father who has just returned home—they are also stories about children who struggle to seek acceptance from their peers. As a child, Berry had a strong desire to speak English as he read it in books, and it was not until he moved to England and started teaching that he began to appreciate the native speech of his childhood. This compelled him to begin writing books and poems for children, providing a Caribbean voice in the largely white-dominated world of British children's literature.

The title story is about two children, left to guard the family coconut plantation overnight while their parents travel to the market. Armed with shotguns, they hope to catch the mysterious Big-Walk, whose knotted beard, matted hair and habit of keeping to himself make him the village's prime suspect when it comes to missing produce and animals. But the villagers are in for a shock. The thief is in fact one of their respected peers.

This story provides a valuable lesson to children about not judging people without first knowing them, and even then, that they should judge on evidence rather than on prejudice. **CVB**

My Friend the Painter 1987

Lygia Bojunga

Original Title | O meu amigo pintor
Nationality | Brazilian, born 1932
Publisher | José Olimpio, Brazil
Theme | Friendship, Illness and death

The problem, ten-year-old Claudio tells the reader, is that he cannot speak to his friend the painter any more because he is dead. He died three days ago. These shocking words greet the reader in the first few pages of the book. Lygia Bojunga is not afraid of telling young readers about death, guilt, or adultery—the dark parts of human life. Using flashbacks and dreams, Claudio tells us about his strong friendship with a man who lives in his building and whose life is dedicated to art and politics. The artist tells Claudio about the magic of color: everything in life has a color and it is necessary to learn to feel what colors mean.

But the painter is dead, and the neighbors and Claudio's parents say he committed suicide. His death must have something to do with the mysterious Dona Clarice—and with the fact that he has been in prison for political reasons. However, Dona Clarice tells Claudio that the painter did not kill himself: he died the way we all must die some day. But she lied, didn't she? The unhappy boy cannot leave the thought alone and he decides to push Dona Clarice to tell him the truth even though he is a child. At last she tells him the sad story of their love. She had married another man while the painter was away and then he wanted her to leave her family but she could not. The painter felt that he could not paint any more, not the way he wanted to. Claudio is relieved at hearing the truth and feels he can begin to mourn—and develop an understanding of what colors really are. **UL**

The Whale Rider 1987

Witi Ihimaera

Nationality | New Zealander, born 1944
Publisher | Heinemann, New Zealand
Award | Nielsen Bookdata Booksellers' Choice
Theme | Traditional, Family

Witi Ihimaera was the first Maori writer to publish both a book of short stories (1972) and a novel (1973). He went on to become a well-respected novelist and short-story writer, often producing his best work during intensive periods of writing. *The Whale Rider* was written in New York and Cape Cod in the space of three weeks.

The isolated beach setting of *The Whale Rider* on the remote east coast of New Zealand is integral to its success. A magical, mythical story about a young girl whose relationship with a whale ensures the salvation of her village, this novel entwines themes that are both Maori and universal.

When Kahu is born, her great-grandfather is angry because he wanted her to be a boy. By Maori custom, leadership of the tribe is handed down from eldest son to eldest son—in direct descendancy from Paikea, the Whale Rider. As she grows up Kahu develops a special affinity with whales; but her heart is sad because her beloved great-grandfather won't return her love. A mass stranding of whales on the shore is followed by the arrival of an enormous semi-mythical bull whale, representing the tribe's connection to their ancestral life force. To the amazement of her family, Kahu rides the whale to the safety of the open sea, thus saving both her tribe and the whales.

The author believes that of all his work *The Whale Rider* is the story most accepted by the Maori community. It was made into an award-winning movie in 2003, its star being the youngest actress ever nominated for an Academy Award. **LO**

Pit Pony 1989

Joyce Barkhouse

Nationality | Canadian, born 1913
Publisher | Gage, Canada
Theme | Classics, Historical fiction, Animal stories, Young adult

Set in Cape Breton at the turn of the last century, *Pit Pony* is a classic story about a Sable Island pony that is used to navigate through the tight corridors of a Nova Scotia coal mine. Coursing through the narrative are poignant strands of local history, contemporary issues, and timeless coming-of-age dilemmas. As with all exceptional works for children, *Pit Pony* transcends any pigeonholing of its audience, offering great returns for readers of all ages.

"Wee" Willie is forced at the age of eleven to descend the dark and dangerous coal mines that have sustained his entire family for generations. The mine soon becomes his complete world. Poverty pervades, and the lack of opportunities, mixed with a strange self-annihilating pride in staying put in one's place, conspires to maintain a system that requires a steady influx of young labor. Harboring suppressed dreams of a different and better life, Willie befriends Gem, the pit pony he is paired with. Finally, catastrophe releases him into a more promising future.

Pit Pony remains a surprisingly realistic portrait of the indignities faced by the underclass in early rural society. Issues of sheer survival and family honor resonate clearly and affectingly. Joyce Barkhouse's perspective on the exploitation of men, boys, villages, and regions by cynical mining operations is bracing. She blends the child's genuine fascination with the process of mining itself with poignant social realism into a moving message of hope and taking charge of one's destiny. **GTS**

Two Weeks with the Queen 1989

Morris Gleitzman

Nationality | Australian, born 1953
Publisher | Blackie, UK
Theme | Family, Illness and death, Adventure, Friendship

Colin is the sort of determined boy who, once he gets an idea into his head, cannot be distracted by anything or anyone. The story *Two Weeks with the Queen* begins when Colin is really annoyed that his request for a Christmas present has been ignored. Instead of a microscope, he has been given a much more practical pair of shoes. Then his younger brother Luke suddenly becomes very ill with cancer and all the attention is turned on him.

When Luke's condition becomes really serious, Colin is sent from Australia to England to stay with his Aunt Iris and Uncle Bob. Colin fights against this move initially but then realizes that there is someone who can help Luke overcome his illness: that person is the Queen and where better to find her than in England? If you want something done properly, Colin figures, go straight to the top.

Colin's singlemindedness gets him into all sorts of trouble, especially when he coerces his cousin Alistair into joining him in trying to break into Buckingham Palace to see the Queen. Colin's initiative inspires him into making lots of telephone calls, and through one of these he finds the name of the best cancer hospital in England. So, off he goes to find the finest doctor there. As a result of this, he meets a man called Ted and helps him and his partner Griff spend their last few days together. This, in turn, makes Colin realize that what he wants most of all is to be with Luke during his last days. This painful story is told with humor, and there are points where the reader will laugh out loud. **JF**

"... they heard the thump from the lounge. They hurried in. Luke lay on the floor, eyes closed, very pale, very still."

OTHER HEARTRENDING STORIES

Carrot Top by Jules Renard, 1894
A Kid for Two Farthings by Wolf Mankowitz, 1953
Jacob Have I Loved by Katherine Paterson, 1980
The Whale Rider by Witi Ihimaera, 1987
Watch Out for the Cat by Silvana Gandolfi, 1995

8+

Hayflower and Quiltshoe 1989

Sinikka and Tiina Nopola Markus Majaluoma

Nationality | Finnish, born 1953 and 1955 (authors); Finnish, born 1961 (illustrator)
Publisher | Tammi, Finland
Theme | Adventure, Family

8+

Hayflower and Quiltshoe (*Heinähattu ja Vilttitossu* in Finnish) is the first in a series about two sisters who go on an adventure. Hayflower and Quiltshoe are two girls who are not afraid to speak their minds. One morning they decide that they have had enough of their life at home; their busy parents, a father who is a scientist and mother who loves cooking herbs and vegetables—while the girls just want to eat sausages—run the household according to very strict rules, including a complete ban on television.

The sisters are eager to experience new things, such as drinking coffee and eating cakes. Their parents, however, are too busy to hear what they are saying. So the girls leave home and go to stay with their friends, the Alibullen sisters, whom their parents consider two old fools. There the girls are always welcome and there are always delicious things to eat. When they leave the sisters' place, they decide to hitch a ride and the secure a lift from Elvis Star and his parents.

"Do children have to live at home, when there's nothing at home to do?"

After evading the local police, they end up in a bar where they decide they do not like coffee after all. When the thrill of the journey wears off and the girls are tired and want to go home, they are afraid that their parents will not even have noticed that they are gone. And how will they find their way home?

The Nopola sisters' book is guaranteed to entertain. Their writing is descriptive, witty, and full of humor, but still manages to explore some sensitive and relevant themes such as parents being too busy to be with their children. The story was made into a very successful film in 2002. **LKK**

Sinikka Nopola – Tiina Nopola
HEINÄHATTU ja VILTTITOSSU
Kuvitus
Markus Majaluoma
Tammi

MORE GREAT FAMILY ADVENTURES

***The Story of the Treasure Seekers* by E. Nesbit, 1899**
***The Bobbsey Twins* by Laura Lee Hope, 1904**
***The Family from One End Street* by Eve Garnett, 1937**
***The Children of Green Knowe* by Lucy Boston, 1954**
***The Night Swimmers* by Betsy Byars, 1980**

Merryll of the Stones 1989

Brian Caswell

Brian Caswell is a former high school teacher who migrated to Australia at the age of twelve having been born in Wales. The very engaging *Merryll of the Stones*, his lauded first novel, received an Honor Book Award in 1990 (Children's Book Council Awards for Older Readers). Following the success of this book, Caswell gave up teaching altogether and is a popular speaker, sharing his expertise with parents, teachers and aspiring young writers.

As sixteen-year-old Megan recovers from serious injuries sustained in the car accident that killed her parents, she experiences strange and frightening dreams. And, in her sleep, speaks in Welsh, a language she normally doesn't understand.

"A hundred generations, the trust was passed down, and never once lost."

Megan has to return to her native Wales to live with her relatives, and there meets her cousin's friend, the brilliant Emlyn, who has nightmares of his own. The two experience an instant attraction that neither can fully understand—until Megan is transformed by her reading of ancient runes preserved for more than 2,000 years. Magically, she is Meg with her twentieth-century memories and experience—but she is also Merryll, the young shaman-queen of an oppressed Welsh tribe.

Back in Merryll's time, she must understand her role, learn from the Spellmaker who has saved her life, and liberate her people. To defeat the oppressor and his mercenaries without loss of other lives, she must put herself in terrible danger of a very unusual kind.

This is a story powered by poetic imagination and the compelling, ancient stories of the British Isles. **MH**

Nationality | Welsh/Australian, born 1954
Publisher | University of Queensland Press, Australia
Theme | Myths and legends, Family, Friendship

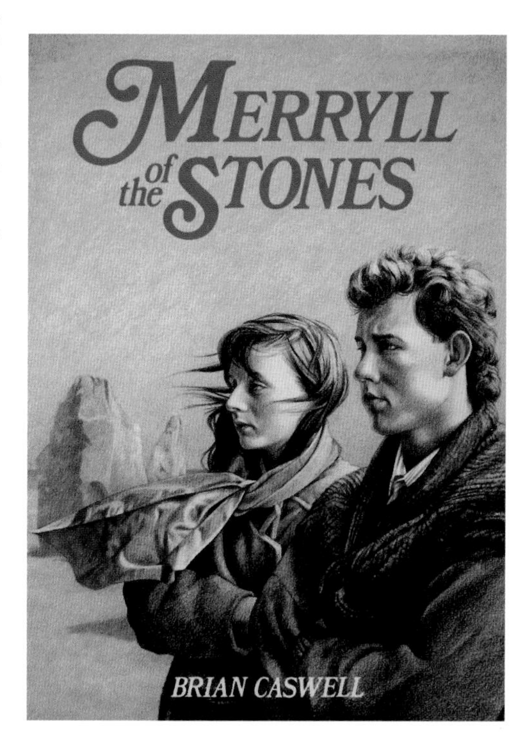

OTHER GREAT BRIAN CASWELL READS

A Cage of Butterflies, 1992
Astarias, 1996
Double Exposure, 2005
Loop, 2006

8+

Bill's New Frock 1989

Anne Fine Philippe Dupasquier

Nationality | English, born 1947 (author); French, born 1955 (illustrator)
Publisher | Methuen, UK
Theme | Fantasy, Friendship, Quirky

MORE BOOKS TO ENJOY BY ANNE FINE

The Chicken Gave It to Me, 1992
The Angel of Nitshill Road, 1993
How to Write Really Badly, 1996
Loudmouth Louis, 1998
Charm School, 1999

8+

Bill is a perfectly normal boy until one morning he discovers he has changed sex overnight. He is promptly dressed for school in a pink frock by his parents, who receive the news very calmly (this is, after all, a satirical fantasy). He hates his loss of useful pockets and the way he is increasingly criticized at school when his clothes start looking the worse for wear. Eventually he is forced to renounce the rougher classroom and playground activities he has previously so much enjoyed.

Bill also resents the way that adults now call him "Dear" and help him do things he can well manage on his own. Even worse, some boys start whistling at him. Soccer games during playtime break up the activities that he and the rest of the girls are trying to follow, with Bill at one stage landing flat on his back as some boys charge past him too intent on their game to care about anyone in their way. There are some compensations—teachers treat him more kindly, and Bill himself finally learns the value of thinking about others. Even so, he is still enormously relieved when by the end of the day he changes back into a boy.

"'This can't be true,' Bill Simpson said to himself. 'This cannot be true!'"

Funny as well as challenging, this brilliantly told story from a former Children's Laureate is bound to make children think while entertaining them richly at the same time. Anne Fine says: "A lot of my work, even for fairly young readers, raises quite serious social issues. . . . Since I write for the reader inside myself, I always end up with the kind of book I would have loved to read (if only someone else had bothered to write for me)." **NT**

Truckers 1989

Terry Pratchett

Nationality | English, born 1948
Publisher | Gollancz, UK
Theme | Fantasy, Favorite characters, Adventure, Quirky

Have you ever thought that we are not alone on this earth? What if there were a race of tiny beings scuttling around under our feet? What would our life look like to them? In the first of the *Bromeliad* trilogy, Terry Pratchett plunges with gusto into this premise, describing a crisis in the chronicles of small beings known as "nomes" (rather than gnomes).

A small band of nomes finds life in the outside tough, so they stow away on a truck and are delivered to a department store, Arnold Bros (est. 1905). Their leader Masklin is quick to make alliances with the different tribes of nomes living in different departments—for instance, the Haberdasheri. But what is the meaning of the notice: Final Sale:

"'Outside! What's it like?' Masklin looked blank. 'Well,' he said, 'it's sort of big.'"

Everything Must Go? And who is the sinister Prices Slashed? In fact, the store is to be demolished in twenty-one days, as Masklin discovers. The nomes in the store refuse to believe this; in any case, they say Arnold Bros (est. 1905) will provide.

Gurder, who can read and has a priestlike role, and Angalo, a scientist, are hard to convince but eventually join Masklin in a daring plan to hijack a truck and drive to freedom. As usual, Pratchett provides hilarious comedy and thought-provoking commentary on (human) flaws and foibles. The nomes literally embody small-mindedness and a "closed shop" on thinking. The second and third in the trilogy continue the story from the point of view of two other nomes. Pratchett has sold more than fifty million books worldwide; children and adults alike enjoy his exhilarating mixture of wordplay, farce, and comedy of character. **VN**

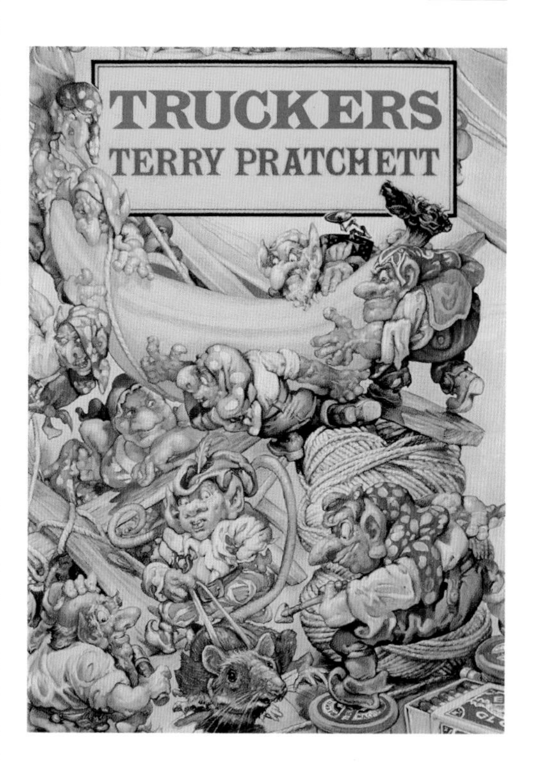

OTHER TALES ABOUT TINY BEINGS

The Hobbit by J. R. R. Tolkein, 1937
Little Grey Men by BB, 1942
The Borrowers by Mary Norton, 1952
The Carpet People by Terry Pratchett, 1971
Diggers by Terry Pratchett, 1990

Haroun and the Sea of Stories 1990

Salman Rushdie

Nationality | Indian/English, born 1947
Publisher | Viking Books, UK
Award | Writer's Guild of Great Britain Award, 1992
Theme | Fantasy, Fairy tales

8+

Rushdie's adult novels are generally categorized as "magical realism," a label rarely applied to children's literature, perhaps because the real and the fantastical are present in so many children's books. This story begins like a fairy tale, but anyone who has been there will recognize at once that this is India: by the road signs ("If you try to rush or zoom / You are sure to meet your doom"), the incomprehensible lines of people waiting for who knows what, and the stunning poverty.

Haroun's father Rashid is a master storyteller—"the Ocean of Notions," "the Shah of Blah"—but, when his wife leaves him, he loses the gift. Haroun discovers a Water Genie turning off Rashid's supply of story water from the Ocean of the Streams of Story, and sets off for the city of Gup on the secret moon, Kahani, on a quest to bring back his father's power. Here he discovers that his father is not the only one with a problem: the story waters are being poisoned by the evil Khattum-Shud, ruler of the dark land of Chup where speech is forbidden. Now Haroun and the entire army of Gup must set off to defeat Khattum-Shud, so that Speech can win over Silence.

"What terrifying eyes they were! Instead of whites, they had blacks."

Like all the best books for reading aloud, this witty and thought-provoking book will amuse and entertain adults as well as children. The book appeared while Salman Rushdie was living in hiding after Ayatollah Khomeini condemned *The Satanic Verses* as blasphemous and issued a fatwa authorizing his assassination. Underpinning this entertaining fantasy is a passionate defense of storytelling and a message about freedom of speech. **CW**

MORE FABULOUS FOLKLORE

Arabian Nights, c. 1400
Uncle Remus Stories by Joel Chandler Harris, 1881
Tales of Uncle Rabbit by Euclides Jaramillo, 1950
Little Bookroom by Eleanor Farjeon, 1955
A Thief in the Village by James Berry, 1987

The Painted House 1990

Montserrat del Amo   Francisco Solé

Today we believe that dreams are not real. But the fact that they are illusory does not make them any less indispensable, especially for a child whose dreams are like the pebbles of a path that has still to be built. This is about Chao, a boy of humble origins, whose dream is that someday he would like to live in a painted house like the emperor of China. It involves the young reader from the beginning and enables him to dream, because he is directly in touch with his feelings, his illusions, and his fears, without any barriers.

Montserrat del Amo devoted more than fifty years of her life to children's literature, driven by her passion for storytelling, which was enriched by her unbounded curiosity about other cultures and every kind of knowledge. *The Painted House* (*La casa pintada*) is a tale with a deep meaning, like an eastern fairy tale, inviting the reader to reflect on aspects that are fundamental to the development of a person, such as the importance of self-sacrifice and of the truth, which can make the difference between success or failure

The author manages to recreate the world of ancient China with vibrant descriptions of the exotic feasts, gardens, and costumes, but she never loses sight of the deeper aspects of this culture: the respect owed to the elders or the solemnity of promises given and of personal challenges. This is why, if he wants to live in a painted house, Chao will have to capture the colors one by one. To do this, he relies on the wisdom of his grandfather, his own intuition, and the invisible help of his friend Li.

Montserrat del Amo is a versatile writer who is able to create books that appeal both to younger and older children. Her work reflects a clear commitment between creativity and humanism, which is why many of her books deal with building bridges of words that shorten the distance between people. **EB**

Nationality | Spanish, born 1927 (author); Spanish, born 1952 (illustrator)
Publisher | Ediciones SM, Spain
Theme | Traditional, Fairy tales

8+

OTHER GREAT FAIRY TALES

Grimm's Fairy Tales (Kinder- und Haus-Märchen) **by Brothers Grimm, 1812**
Morality Tales (Cuentos morales) **by Rafael Pombo, 1854**
The Thirteen Clocks **by James Thurber, 1950**

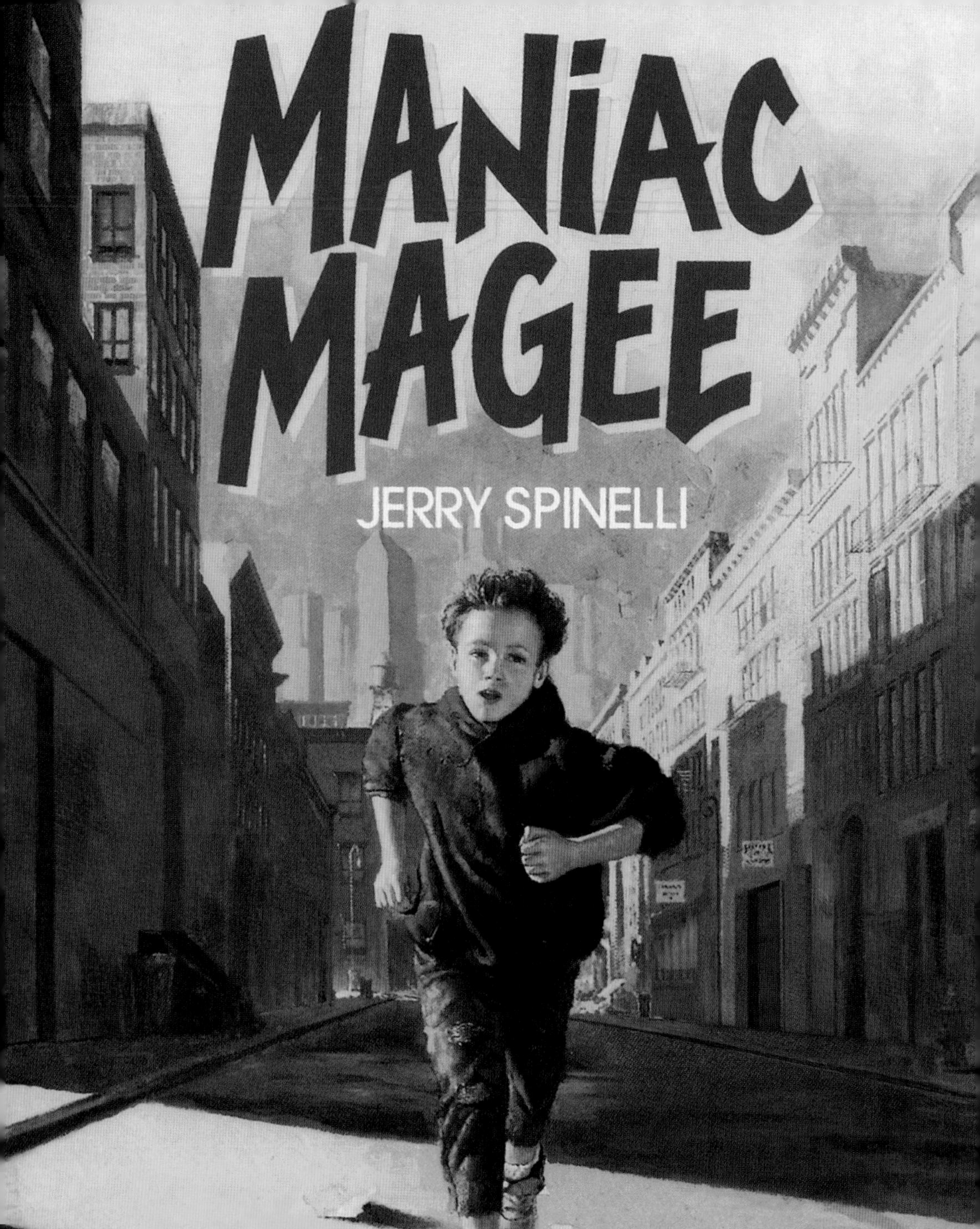
MANIAC
MAGEE
JERRY SPINELLI

Maniac Magee 1990

Jerry Spinelli

Nationality | American, born 1940
Publisher | Little, Brown and Co., USA
Award | Newbery Medal, 1991
Theme | Friendship, Family, Young adult

Orphan Jeffrey runs away from his unhappy home life with his aunt and uncle, and ends up in Two Mills, a town divided along racial lines by a road right down the middle. He befriends those on both sides, and earns the nickname Maniac Magee for his daring athletic ability and fearlessness. With his closest friend, African-American Amanda, he attempts to bring racial unity to the town, but his childish idealism does not always work. Jeffrey spends time with the liberal Beale family on the East side and their opposite, the racist McNabs on the West side, and there are many other setbacks before Maniac Magee can finally find a house where he feels accepted.

The narrative echoes the viewpoint of a rootless child; as an outsider, Maniac can see the town's problems. Yet the book is not just a worthy tale about racism. As Spinelli says, "The history of a kid is one part fact, two parts legend, and three parts snowball," and the opening chapter's assertion that it's "hard to know" truth from fact, is proven by Maniac's tall tales. Spinelli says he had the idea for the book after meeting a girl "who carried her home library to school in a suitcase," and wanted to examine how children can feel both confident and vulnerable at the same time. The book is full of bullying adult characters and accepting younger characters; adults are often shown to be inflexible and uncaring. Although Maniac Magee has suffered the death of both his parents, and the rejection of his foster parents, he remains optimistic. He is an archetypal charming scamp, and it is easy to see why he becomes a small-town legend. **SD**

Shiloh 1991

Phyllis Reynolds Naylor

Nationality | American, born 1933
Publisher | Atheneum, USA
Award | Newbery Medal, 1992
Theme | Animal stories, Friendship

Stories about children and animals often tug at the heartstrings. None more so than this account of Marty Preston, a boy living in poverty in West Virginia, who meets a young beagle hound running away from his cruel master. Marty's father, a mailman, makes Marty return the dog. However, Marty is determined to rescue him. But how? Buying the pup, whom he names Shiloh, is out of the question as he would have to collect an awful lot of bottle tops to meet the original cost.

Shiloh runs away again, and this time Marty decides he will hide him in a pen. He sneaks food out of the house, pretending he is not hungry, but, in the end, an event he could not foresee forces his secret out into the open. Shiloh is attacked by a dog who is out of control and, although after treatment he makes a good recovery, his master discovers his whereabouts and demands his return.

Marty, adamant that he wants to keep the dog, goes to meet the owner, Judd Travers, and discovers that he has shot a doe out of season, an offense punishable by a large fine. Marty finds his ideals compromised by his desire to keep Shiloh, and works for Judd to pay off the cost of the dog.

Shiloh is a deceptively simply story behind which are the strong principles of Marty's poor family, and his gradual understanding that life is not always straightforward and that sometimes compromise is needed. This is the first in the Shiloh trilogy, which is followed by *Shiloh Season* and *Saving Shiloh*, all of which have been made into movie versions. **JF**

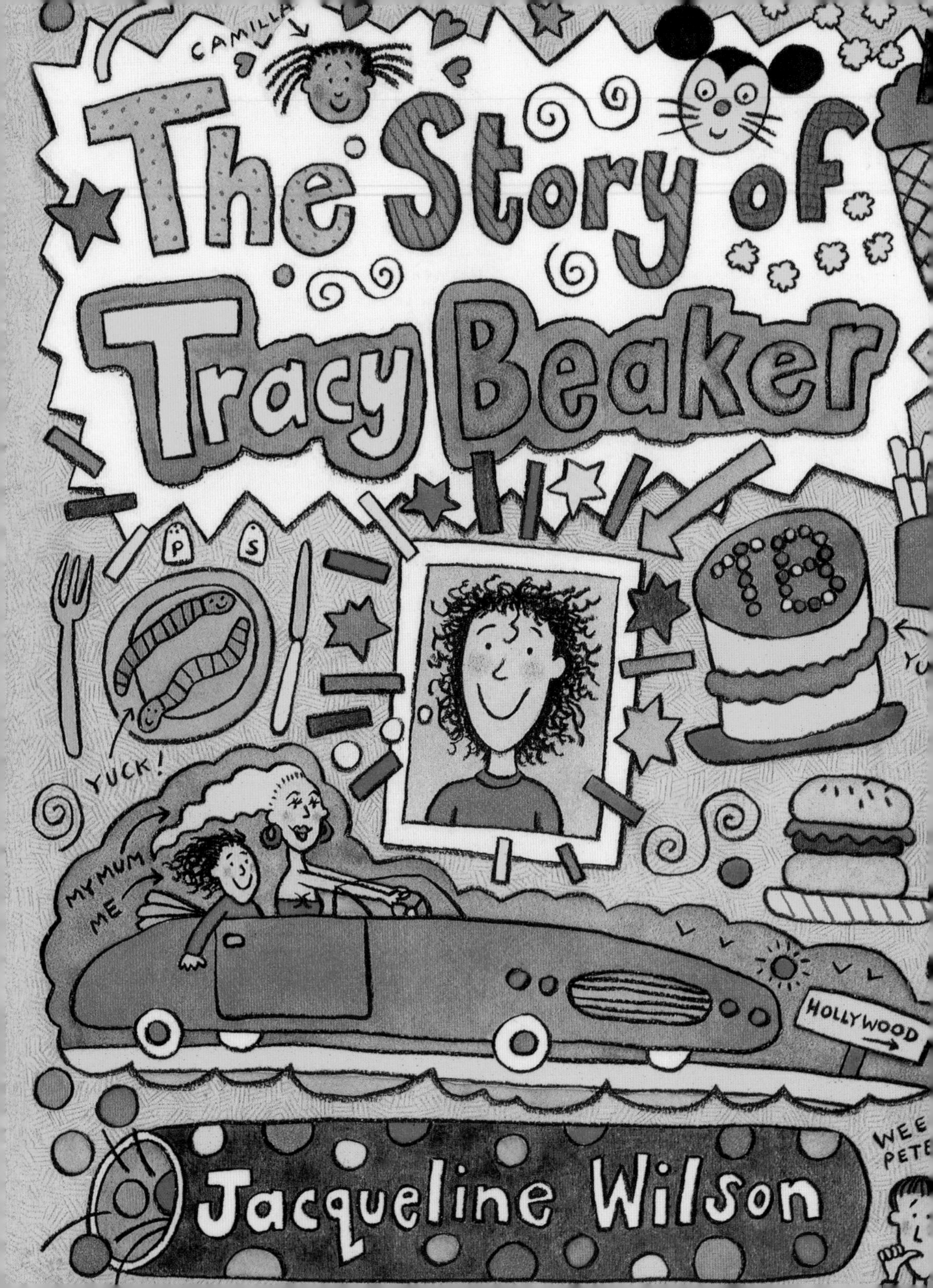
CAMILLA
The Story of Tracy Beaker
P
S
YUCK!
MY MUM
ME
HOLLYWOOD
WEE
Jacqueline Wilson

The Story of Tracy Beaker 1991

Jacqueline Wilson   Nick Sharratt

Nationality | English, born 1945 (author); English, born 1962 (illustrator)
Publisher | Doubleday, UK
Theme | Young adult, Family, Friendship

Pugnacious and moody Tracy Beaker lives in a foster care facility, but craves a real home and family of her own. Described by her social worker as having "behavior problems," the ten-year-old has previously been placed with foster families, but each time sent back to what she terms the "Dumping Ground." Tracy is mistrustful and prickly and passes her time arguing with the other children, being rude to social worker Elaine, and inventing fantasies in which an idealized version of her mother, supposedly a glamorous Hollywood actress, comes to take her away. By the end of the book, thanks to a friendship with a writer who visits the children's home, Tracy has finally learned to get on better with herself and others, but there is no glib conclusion.

Structured like the notebooks in which children in foster care are encouraged to express their feelings, this book provides a heartbreaking insight into the mind of a troubled, volatile girl who puts on a show of tough arrogance, but is actually desperately vulnerable and insecure. Tracy has an uncanny knack for discovering adults' real motives and embarrassing them by honing in on uncomfortable truths. She frustrates those around her by rejecting their help, but her wit and attitude make her as charming as she is exasperating.

Without preaching, Wilson tells a humane, poignant story about the problems of foster care, and, in Tracy, she introduces a lovable, sassy heroine. **MK**

Only You Can Save Mankind 1992

Terry Pratchett

Nationality | English, born 1948
Publisher | Doubleday, UK
Theme | Fantasy, Adventure, Quirky, Favorite characters

Terry Pratchett always begins with an intriguing hypothesis. What if a computer game came alive? What if the little green figures of Space Invaders really lived and really died? And what if all those shoot 'em up, beat 'em up people had feelings too?

Wobbler, a computer genius but social failure, gives twelve-year-old Johnny a pirated edition of a new computer game. But the reptilian Scree-Wee quickly ask to surrender; they are fed up with fighting and want to go home. After this surprising eventuality, Johnny starts dreaming about the Scree-Wee. Having accepted their surrender, it seems that it is his responsibility to get them home, dealing with the suspicious Gunnery Officer, as well as the understanding, motherly Captain. Perhaps it is just a dream, but no one else even remembers having the Scree-Wee in their game. It is only Kirsty, a gender-defying female game player from Johnny's school, who can help.

This is a humorous, humane book in which the grim reality of Johnny's life—plugging his ears when his parents argue and not liking school—is contrasted with the warmth and intelligence of the Scree-Wee. Kirsty, however, cannot see this. For her, they are the enemy, just as unreal as the Iraqi army who appear nightly on their television screens. Johnny is the Chosen One in the game, the Hero with a Thousand Extra Lives, and so he is the one who is finally faced with the age-old decision: if not now, when? **VN**

The Last Giants 1992

François Place

Original Title | Les derniers Géants
Nationality | French, born 1957
Publisher | Casterman, France
Theme | Myths and legends, Science and nature

8+

An extraordinarily large tooth is engraved with a minuscule geographical map. Could it have belonged to a mythical giant that they talk about in legends?

Such is the beginning of *The Last Giants*: an incredible adventure that takes young researcher Archibald Leopold Ruthmore to the far ends of Asia. Ruthmore's tenacity and his limitless curiosity are greatly rewarded, and the land he seeks is revealed.

Thanks to Ruthmore, we enter into the secret and peaceful world of giants Géol and Antala, whose skin, covered in tattoos, tells the history of the world. Taken in by them, the scientist observes, records, and draws a world in which human's relationship with nature is true, simple, and harmonious. On his return to England, Ruthmore strives to convince the scientific community of the truth of his discovery and of the existence of these extraordinary people. On a second expedition, however, the scientist makes an appalling discovery: humankind's pride and greed have led to the annihilation of the population of gentle giants.

The Last Giants is a book inspired by tales of expeditions in former times. Myth and reality are skillfully interwoven. François Place offers us a text that is at once forceful and elegant and that captivates adults as much as children. The watercolors that accompany the narration are like great paintings in which Ruthmore, a tiny human being lost in the immensity of the world, is, in spite of himself, the hero of a tragedy that overwhelms him. **SL**

Almost Everyone Could Topple 1993

Toon Tellegen

Original Title | Bijna iedereen kon omvallen
Nationality | Dutch, born 1941
Publisher | Querido, the Netherlands
Theme | Animal stories

The squirrel is sending a little note to the ant but the bark on which he is writing the invitation is too small, so his message is interrupted in the middle of a word. A poor invitation, but nevertheless the ant still manages to send back a reply. In a different story, the heron does not eat the frog but starts a conversation with him about the art of falling, which the heron would so much like to master. And a beetle does not try to find something to drink but begins to reflect on the various kinds of thirst that there are.

This is a brilliant collection of animal stories in which the animals do unusual things that somehow appear quite normal and logical. The animals do not have wild adventures; rather the stories are thoughts about unexpected, curious events without any particular point, cause, or consequence. Usually the animals have decided to do something specific from which they are easily distracted, often by a conversation about unusual things. Only the squirrel and the ant have a real friendship and often spend time thinking and chatting to each other.

Toon Tellegen's animal stories are unique and they are based on stories that he told his daughter every evening at bedtime. The stories are fantastic, dreamlike, casual, expressive, and full of descriptions of nature and philosophical juggling with language and logic. The first collection was published in 1984 and, unlike traditional animal fables, these stories never have a moralistic tone. **AD**

The Giver 1993

Lois Lowry

Nationality | American, born 1937
Publisher | Bantam Books, USA
Awards | Newbery Medal, 1994
Theme | Science fiction, Controversial

The Giver is set in a future society where poverty, violence, and injustice have been eradicated, but at a price: the loss of free will. The community is controlled by Elders, who assign jobs and partners based on suitability and suppress preferences and emotions with pills. Genetic modification means that everyone looks alike, and most cannot see color or hear music. In each generation one person is selected to bear the collective weight of society's past. As this knowledge is transferred to twelve-year-old Jonas from the incumbent Giver, he becomes aware of the limitations of his world. He and the Giver plan to return the power to feel to their community, but circumstances force Jonas to flee. At the end it is unclear whether he has achieved his aim, or even survived.

Lois Lowry says that there is no "correct" interpretation of the ending. A central precept is that without hatred, pain, and suffering, there can be no love, passion, and diversity of choice. The Giver offers Jonas truth, which can hurt as well as empower. The book has provoked controversy; its dark depiction of a dystopia where undesirables are killed by lethal injection is deemed unsuitable for children by some, whereas others celebrate its thought-provoking message. Lowry is not afraid to tackle somber, serious issues. In this allegory she addresses a very contemporary concern: the vital need of people to recognize their interdependence and respect the shared environment they inhabit. **MK**

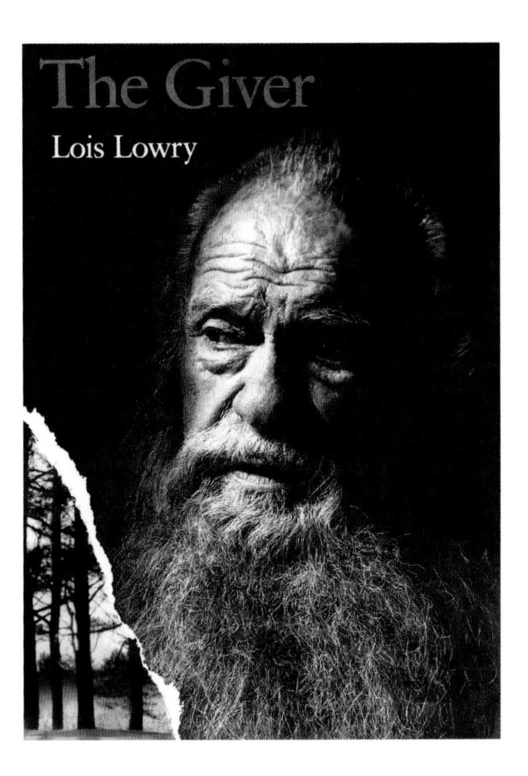

"It was almost December, and Jonas was beginning to be frightened."

OTHER LOIS LOWRY FAVORITES

Later parts of "The Giver" trilogy:
- *Gathering Blue*, 2000
- *Messenger*, 2004

A Summer to Die, 1977
Number the Stars, 1989

Manolito Gafotas 1994

Elvira Lindo   Emilio Urberuaga

Nationality | Spanish, born 1962 (author); Spanish, born 1954 (illustrator)
Publisher | Alfaguara, Spain
Theme | Family, Friendship, Favorite characters

8+

Los trapos sucios (*Clean Cloths*) is the fourth title in Elvira Lindo's entertaining seven-book series about Manolito Gafotas, a ten-year-old boy living in Madrid. If we tell the story of Manolito "from the beginning," as he likes to do, we must go back to the 1980s, when the author was working as a radio presenter and journalist. Manolito was one of the characters she created for radio, and his monologues, read by Lindo and initially written with adults in mind, were broadcast in the early morning. The character later made the transition from radio to children's books.

Manolito recounts tales of his everyday life in the Spanish capital as if they are bizarre adventures, although he rarely leaves Carabanchel, the ordinary district where he lives with his family: "A hero without supernatural power, a hero who is not the smartest, nor the strongest, a hero who is not the leader. What he has is conversation, a sense of humor, and a desire to discover everything about his enormous world, a district called Carabanchel." Taking part in his adventures are his school friends and other characters from the neighborhood, whom we see from our hero's particular viewpoint. Although Manolito has a wild imagination, he remains rooted in the real world, and readers will easily identify with him.

The novels are written in the first person, with lively dialogue, and a sense of humor balanced with a dose of irony that appeals to all ages. The books have become classics of Spanish children's literature. **EB**

A Mole Always Turns Up On Its Own 1994

Hanna Johansen

Original Title | Ein Maulwurf Kommt Immer Allein
Nationality | German/Swiss, born 1939
Publisher | Nagel and Kimche, Switzerland
Theme | Animal stories

Moles need underground tunnels shrouded in pitch-black darkness so that no one can see anything. The smell has to be just right, too—earthworms and soil. It has to be warm and dry, and unwanted visitors must not be able to disturb the calm. Only with these criteria can moles sleep peacefully and dream of delicious things like beetles, grubs, and spiders.

But a mother mole does not enjoy total peace. Baby moles demand to be constantly fed until they open their eyes and their fur begins to grow. And when the mother finally provides them with earthworms, they start fighting. Above all, the little ones have to learn how to distinguish friend from foe.

Soon, the tunnel is too small for growing moles, and they venture out into a world full of hostile beasts. They learn to evade them and to start hunting and digging tunnels, eventually building their own home. For a female mole, a visitor will invariably turn up. Despite her better judgment the female accepts him, and after a while she starts to enjoy the companionship. However, after some fighting and biting, she is alone again. Soon there are five cute little "silkworms" populating the tunnel, and the cycle starts again.

Hanna Johansen uses short sentences, and her observations about the ups and downs of mole life are both detailed and humorous. Young children will relate to her descriptions because the moles' behavior is not so different from their own. This tender book will appeal to young and old alike. **CS**

The Bed and Breakfast Star 1994

Jacqueline Wilson   Nick Sharratt

Nationality | English, born 1945 (author); English, born 1962 (illustrator)
Publisher | Doubleday, UK
Theme | Family

The Bed and Breakfast Star is narrated by Elsa, a likable, loquacious schoolgirl with a mane of unruly hair. After her stepfather loses his job, the family have to move into shabby temporary accommodation.

It is a difficult time: baby Hank and little sister Pippa demand attention, Elsa's mother is constantly on the verge of tears, and her stepfather (nicknamed Mack the Smack by Elsa) gets heavy-handed. Wannabe comedienne Elsa tries to diffuse the tension by cracking a series of bad and ill-timed jokes, but ends up irritating rather than cheering up her unhappy parents. When a television crew turns up at the hotel, she tests her comedy routine, but it falls embarrassingly, crushingly flat. However, after a fire breaks out during the night it is Elsa's strident voice that alerts guests to the danger, resulting in a hero's accolade and a special television appearance. Realizing she does not need to tell endless gags to be amusing, Elsa can finally relax.

The Bed and Breakfast Star's engaging illustrations and divided sections make it an easy read. Elsa's chatty narration and silly jokes do not detract from the more sober issues. Wilson is unafraid of tackling serious themes and authentically depicts a flawed, struggling family. While she aims for "reasonably happy endings" ("I would hate any child to be cast down in gloom and despair"), she avoids sentimentality. It is a bittersweet, touching portrait of a child using humor to get through a challenging time. **MK**

"It wasn't just us and our family. We could hear the people in room 607 having an argument."

FAVORITE JACQUELINE WILSON READS

The Lottie Project, 1997
The Illustrated Mum, 1999
Vicky Angel, 2000
Dustbin Baby, 2001
Cookie, 2008

8+

8+

Way Home 1994

Libby Hathorn Gregory Rogers

Nationality | Australian, born 1943 (author); Australian, born 1957 (illustrator)
Publisher | Random House, Australia
Theme | Adventure

A boy makes his way at night through the shadows of deserted and garbage-strewn alleys and the glaring lights of crowded shopping streets. Along the way he befriends a stray cat, and together they run a gauntlet of dangers: a gang of older boys; screaming lines of traffic; a dog's snarling assault; and a desperate scramble to rescue the frightened cat from a tree.

Libby Hathorn's story contrasts the tenderness of the relationship between the boy and cat with the bleak reality of the neglected parts of the anonymous city in which they find themselves. There are stark contrasts in the look of the book. The text itself is printed white on black and is separated from the illustrations by a white torn edge, an indication of the margins of the throwaway society where the boy and cat survive. Gregory Rogers's naturalistic illustrations are mainly in somber tones of gray, brown, and green, illuminated by occasional striking yellow and white that mark the unattainable promise of warm houses, shops, and restaurants, or the alarm of the oncoming lights of cars and a dog's open jaws. On the final page, the boy and cat crawl into an abandoned wooden crate that the boy has made his home; at last, in the enclosing dark, finding warmth and safety.

This glimpse into the life of a homeless child brings together two major talents in modern Australian children's literature. Hathorn is a prolific writer, many of whose books for older children tackle themes of social justice. Rogers is a versatile illustrator for several authors, who is the only Australian to be awarded the Kate Greenaway Medal for illustration. **CB**

Stories to Fernando 1994

Ema Wolf Jorge Sanzol

Nationality | Argentinian, born 1948 (author); Argentinian, born 1946 (illustrator)
Publisher | Sudamericana, Argentina
Theme | Adventure, Magical stories

The character of Fernando in *Stories to Fernando* (first published in Spanish with the title *Historias a Fernández*) is a reckless cat—although only when he sleeps. He falls asleep on the edge of the roof, especially when the sun warms its tiles in the summer, or on the highest branches of an avocado tree. Can an animal other than a bird rest on electric wires? Well, Fernando does. Fernando's young owner lives in constant fear that her cat will hurt himself one day. "As a kitten, Fernando already showed a prodigious penchant for borders, edges, slopes, and heights from which it was possible to fall."

The fear of Fernando's owner is justified, because one day Fernando falls from the avocado tree. The girl's uncle helps the cat to get better, but warns that to prevent his weak health from deteriorating, Fernando should stay awake for the next three hours. This is a problem for Fernando, who is used to sleeping almost without interruption. To keep him awake, the young girl starts telling him stories and, just like Scheherazade in *Arabian Nights*, the tales become part of the narrative.

These exciting stories include one about a capricious noblewoman whose culinary whims are almost impossible to satisfy ("The Grandduchess and the Potatoes"), a troubled love story with a happy ending ("Confused Hearts"), and an adventure set in eighteenth-century Australia ("Adventures in the Seas of the World or The Fantastic Australian Animal"). The talents of both narrator and writer manage to save Fernando and enchant the reader. **LB**

Halinka 1994

Mirjam Pressler

Nationality | German, born 1940
Publisher | Beltz and Gelberg, Germany
Honor | German Youth Literature Special Prize
Theme | Family, Friendship

Halinka, the heroine of the story of the same name (first published in German as *Wenn das Glück kommt muss man ihm einen Stuhl hinstellen*), is a twelve-year-old Polish girl who has been abandoned by her mother and now lives in a German orphanage. Over the years she has learned how not to despair by blocking out all her feelings. Her only emotional point of reference is her maternal aunt, Lou. In her mind, Halinka thinks about the things Lou says to her, the things they laugh about, and the presents she gets from her.

Her bond with Lou helps Halinka through the constant bullying by her roommates, who call her "gypsy" because of her jet-black hair and dark eyes. In time, Halinka becomes friends with Renate, another outsider, who is slightly younger. The heartfelt descriptions of their friendship are among the most impressive passages in the book. However, the plot centers on a charity collection. Halinka manages to raise more money than anyone else, and she gives in to the temptation to "borrow" some of it to pay for a train ticket to Lou's hometown. But the headmistress of the orphanage notices that the collection box has been opened. Halinka denies any wrongdoing, and the wise headmistress does not pursue the matter further, thus gaining the girl's love and respect. When Aunt Lou sends some money to pay for the train fare, Halinka suddenly has sufficient funds for two tickets, and invites her little friend Renate to come along.

Having grown up as an orphan herself, author Mirjam Pressler understands the predicament of her protagonist only too well. **CS**

"When good fortune comes your way, you should always be sure to offer it a chair."

MORE STORIES ABOUT GROWING UP

Pollyanna by Eleanor H. Porter, 1913
The Boxcar Children by Gertrude C. Warner, 1924
The Good Master by Kate Seredy, 1955
The Night Swimmers by Betsy Byars, 1980
Sunday's Child by Gudrun Mebs, 1983

8+

Watch Out for the Cat 1995

Silvana Gandolfi   Giulia Orecchia

Nationality | Italian, born 1940 (author); Italian, born 1955 (illustrator)
Publisher | Salani Editore, Italy
Theme | Family, Friendship, Illness and death

Silvana Gandolfi loves to mesmerize her readers with meaningful names. In *Watch Out for the Cat* (*Occhio al gatto*), there is a boy called Dante, a cat called Virgilio, and a schoolteacher called Dolente. Historically, the Latin poet Virgil was Dante Alighieri's guide in *The Divine Comedy*. The Dante character in Gandolfi's story, however, feels that his name is too important, especially for a boy who is considered dyslexic.

Dante's world has been turned upside down. His parents are in Hong Kong and he has had to move from Milan to Venice, change schools, and adapt to living with his serious-minded grandmother. But old Dolente (who taught Dante's mother) shows Dante how to journey to the other side of learning by playing and enjoying. When Dolente first pulls out his fake cigarettes made of licorice, making Dante roar with laughter, the reader wonders if he can actually teach. Yet Dante passes his exams. Then old Dolente dies, much to Dante's dismay. When Dante hears the news that his parents are returning, he realizes that he might prefer to stay with his grandmother.

Eyes and seeing are important in this tale, especially to Dante, who sees a girl being kidnapped. Finally, the girl is set free but, when Dante meets her in real life and discovers that she was a neighbor of Dolente's, he has to admit to having "seen" it all in his imagination. The girl shows him how the unconscious gathering of small details can together make the tapestry of a story. **SMT**

Poordog the Starved 1995

Graciela Montes   Oscar Rojas

Nationality | Argentinian, born 1947 (author); Argentinian, birth date unknown (illustrator)
Publisher | Ediciones Colihue, Argentina
Theme | Animal stories

In *Casiperro del Hambre*, Casiperro becomes a stray dog after erroneously eating the family savings that had been hidden in the refrigerator. Long days of hunger and desperation follow, until he joins a circus and becomes an acrobatic dog. Casiperro falls in love with a circus dog, but he soon falls in love with another street dog and leaves. However, both animals are caught and used for cruel scientific experiments.

Casiperro first becomes a model in a toy factory (where he is subjected to electric shock therapy to try and tame him to look and act like a toy). Next he is made a guinea pig in a cosmetic laboratory for animal testing. The laboratory experiments are often brutal. Some cosmetic products have extremely dangerous effects: for example, a particularly strong rejuvenating potion transforms some adult dogs into puppies. However, when Casiperro finally escapes, he is soon plagued by hunger again.

The story has an unexpectedly happy ending: Casiperro and two of his companions make friends with a homeless person, whom they protect in exchange for warmth and food. They finally win their freedom and satisfy their never-ending hunger. Through all of his misadventures, Casiperro remains the outcast, always an external observer of events. Graciela Montes's story, in the tradition of picaresque novels such as *Lazarillo de Tormes*, becomes a powerful social satire using magical realism to refer subtly to the most recent events in Argentine history. **LB**

45 & 47 Stella Street and Everything that Happened 1995

Elizabeth Honey

Nationality | Australian, born 1947
Publisher | Allen and Unwin, Australia
Award | C.B.C.A. Honor Book, 1996
Theme | Family, Friendship

Stella Street is a marvelous place to live; people are friendly and cooperative, and everyone's individual quirks of behavior are accepted. But then a mysterious new couple move in; they want nothing to do with their neighbors and constantly complain about the builders, the landscape gardeners, Briquette (a dog), the garbage cans, the fence, where other people park, and so on. The kids on Stella Street nickname them the "Phonies" and decide to spy on them to see if they can find something to defeat them.

The behavior of the Phonies gives the children plenty of scope for speculation. Where does their money come from? Are they, perhaps, really criminals? Why do they watch soccer matches on TV but show no interest in the games themselves? The story is told by one of the girls, Henni, as the children and Briquette, the ever-greedy dog, use their wits and imaginations to try to discover the truth.

Elizabeth Honey deftly creates a memorable cast of characters, from the boy Zev, whose hair is full of static electricity, to Frank, who is only six ("People underestimate little Frank"). The Stella Street kids even rope in the bad Brown Boys, despite their parents' insisting they have nothing to do with such characters. When the police suspect the kids of trying to set fire to the Phonies' house, trouble ensues. The story gallops along, the sense of community is infectious, and Briquette's passion for anything even remotely edible provides great comic relief. **JG**

"And next door to Mr. Nic is 47. Kids love 47 Stella Street. It is like dreams come true."

MORE BOOKS ABOUT CLOSE COMMUNITIES

The Adventures of Tom Sawyer **by Mark Twain, 1876**
The Family from One End Street **by Eve Garnett, 1937**
The Bonny Pit Laddie **by Frederick Grice, 1960**
Why the Whales Came **by Michael Morpurgo, 1985**
Maniac Magee **by Jerry Spinelli, 1990**

written by
Anna
Fienberg
and
Barbara
Fienberg
illustrated by
Kim Gamble
Tashi

Tashi 1995

Anna & Barbara Fienberg K. Gamble

Nationality | All Australian, born 1956 (Anna); birth date unknown (Barbara); born 1952 (illustrator)
Publisher | Allen and Unwin, Australia
Theme | Fairy tales, Fantasy, Magical stories

Tashi is the first book in a popular series. One evening over dinner, a small boy named Jack announces that he has a new friend, Tashi. This imaginary pal regales Jack with tales of his daring adventures outwitting giants and witches, which Jack recounts to his bemused parents. Tashi is a gnomelike creature from a faraway place who arrived in Australia on the back of a swan, having escaped from the warlord to whom his impoverished parents reluctantly sold him. Exciting action is guaranteed, whether discovering an invisibility ring or cunningly fooling a fearsome dragon.

With the focus firmly on Tashi's extraordinary escapades—or rather, the impressive reaches of Jack's fecund powers of invention—the adults rarely impinge on the narrative, serving mainly as an audience for their son's stories. Pragmatic Dad exasperates Jack by wanting to know irrelevant details, such as the color of the swan. The series arose out of a conversation between Fienberg and her mother, Barbara (who is credited as chief plot devisor). "She was telling me how, when she was a child, she used to tell whoppers. Tall stories," says the author. This was the starting point for an exploration of the thrilling extent of a child's imagination.

Kim Gamble's gray pencil sketches are simple but evocative. They augment the sparse information given in the text, but leave the reader space to dream up the fuller picture. As a recent immigrant in a country of settlers, Tashi's situation may be seen as typically Australian, likewise his sassy attitude. This is a highly original, funny, and unpredictable series. **MK**

Clockwork 1995

Philip Pullman Peter Bailey

Nationality | English, born 1946 (author); English, birth date unknown (illustrator)
Publisher | Doubleday, UK
Theme | Horror

Clockwork, or All Wound Up is set in early nineteenth-century Germany; it will appeal to children who enjoy horror stories and gothic tales. Philip Pullman shows children how to appreciate the structure of stories and how they can draw on other books. This morally complex tale, which itself works like clockwork ticking toward its conclusion, is rich with references to fairy tales and classic horror. The sometimes sour asides from the narrator include great insights into the nature of storytelling as well as the nature of the soul, the basic unfairness of life, and the importance of recognizing that in stories, in clocks, and in life, every action sets consequences in motion.

Clockwork or *All Wound Up* sets many narrative cogs in motion. First, there is the story of two inadequate boys: Karl the apprentice clockmaker, who cannot finish his apprenticeship until he has made a mechanical figure for the Great Clock, and Fritz the writer who cannot finish his latest story about the mysterious Dr. Kalmenius. The doctor himself enters the story to help the boys, offering Karl the figure of a metal knight and Fritz a new chapter, but there is a price to pay.

The narrator/Pullman reinforces the point that neither Fritz nor Karl have worked hard enough for their results. To Fritz's story of Prince Florian, who will only become real if he is given a human heart to replace his clockwork one, Pullman adds a brave innkeeper's daughter who saves him with selfless love, but not before a series of enjoyable cliffhangers, mysteries, and puzzles. **GB**

The View from Saturday 1996

E. L. Konigsburg

8+

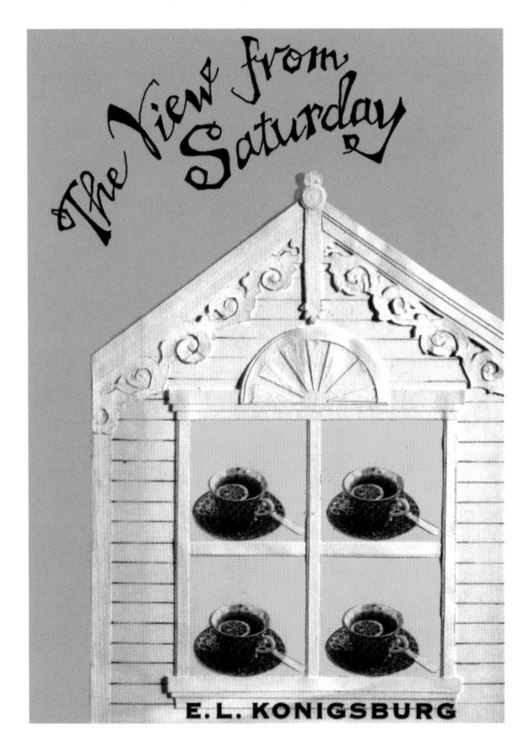

Nationality | American, born 1930
Publisher | Atlantic Books, USA
Award | Newbery Medal, 1997
Theme | School, Friendship

"They told Mrs. Olinski that they were The Souls long before they were a team."

OTHER BOOKS WITH SIMILAR THEMES

What Hearts **by Bruce Brooks, 1992**
The Friends **by Kuzumi Yumoto, 1996**
The Report Card **by Andrew Clements, 2004**
My Most Excellent Year **by Steve Kluger, 2008**

The View from Saturday is the story of a quirky group of twelve-year-olds preparing for a general knowledge contest under the tutelage of their teacher, Mrs. Olinski. Mrs. Olinski, paralyzed from the waist down after a car accident that also left her a widow, has returned to teaching, shattered in both body and spirit. When the team triumphs in the New York State finals, she and the students achieve a huge sense of personal fulfillment. However, the focus of the novel is on the relationships between the sixth-graders, their feelings, ponderings, and ideas.

Calling themselves "The Souls," the four very different children have formed an unusual bond over Saturday morning tea parties instigated by Julian Singh, a British Asian who stands out conspicuously at Epiphany school. An interesting structural device gives the reader the opportunity to learn each child's point of view through a chapter narrated in their unique, individual voice. As we read different accounts of the same events, it becomes clear how intricately connected the students' lives are. Alone, each bright twelve-year-old is a shy misfit, but together they form a brilliant, complementary whole.

The View from Saturday has been criticized for its potentially confusing mixture of narratives and for portraying sixth-graders as unrealistically articulate. Nonetheless, the fans outnumber the detractors, and the end result is a thought-provoking, often amusing, and inspiring read. **MK**

Johnny and the Bomb 1996

Terry Pratchett

Nationality | English, born 1948
Publisher | Doubleday, UK
Theme | Fantasy, Adventure, Quirky, Favorite characters

Poor old Johnny Maxwell. Not only has he already had to rescue space invaders from trigger-happy game-playing kids (in *Only You Can Save Mankind*) and help dead people save their cemetery from the council's bulldozers (in *Johnny and the Dead*), but now he has to deal with all the problems caused by getting lost in "the other trouser leg of time." Fortunately he has his usual crew of misfits (the acerbic Kirsty, the uncool West Indian Yo-less, tough skinhead Bigmac, and computer geek Wobbler) to help him.

Johnny's problems start when he and his friends find an old bag lady, Mrs. Tachyon, lying semi-conscious in the street. She is usually seen pushing an old shopping cart full of black bags around. They take her to the hospital and stow her cart in a garage, only to later discover it works as a time machine. Johnny and his gang accidentally transport themselves back to the moment in 1941 when their hometown was hit by a bomb in World War II. Johnny sees his chance to warn the nineteen residents who were killed by the blast. But, as all science-fiction fans know, trying to change history can be difficult, and even if you succeed, it can cause problems in the future.

Pratchett demonstrates his rare ability to describe fantastical adventures in a thought-provoking and realistic way. The story has laugh-out-loud moments even as he tackles themes such as racism, war, and death. Young and old alike will love Pratchett's highly entertaining imagination and irreverent wit. **JaM**

The Story of a Seagull 1996

Luis Sepúlveda Miles Hyman

Nationality | Chilean, born 1949 (author); American, birth date unknown (illustrator)
Publisher | Tusquets Editores, Spain
Theme | Animal stories, Friendship

Set in the German city of Hamburg, *The Story of a Seagull and the Cat Who Taught Her to Fly* (*Historia de una gaviota y del gato que le enseñó a volar*) is about a seagull called Kengah who, while diving into the sea in search of food, is suddenly hit by the "curse of the sea"—a wave covered in oil coming from an oil tanker in trouble. Expending great effort, the seagull reaches Hamburg where he collapses on the balcony of a house in which a fat black cat called Zorba lives. Before dying, Kengah gives her first and last egg to Zorba, asking her to keep three promises: First, that she does not eat the egg; second, that she takes care of it until the chick is born; and finally, and most surprisingly, that Zorba teaches the chick how to fly.

Zorba promises to take care of the baby seagull and keeps her word. She sits on it until the chick is born, and with the help of her cat friends Colonello, Sabelotodo, and Secretario, she rears the baby seagull with love and protects it from dangers. The little seagull is named Fortunata, the "lucky one." However, the trouble begins when Zorba, having kept the first two promises, must also keep the third one and teach the seagull how to fly. Of course, being a cat, it is not easy. After many failed attempts, Zorba and her friends resort to the help of a human—a sensitive poet—thus breaking an old taboo by speaking to humans in their language. Thanks to their combined help and the intervention of the poet, Fortunata is finally able to fly and return to her own world, the sky. **LB**

Harry Potter and the Philosopher's Stone 1997

J. K. Rowling

Nationality | English, born 1965
Publisher | Bloomsbury, UK
Award | Nestlé Children's Book Prize
Theme | Magical stories, Favorite characters

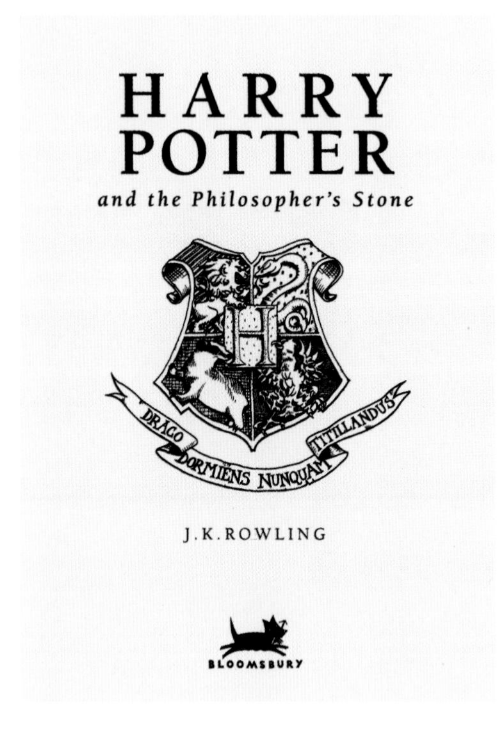

8+

MORE BOOKS ON WITCHES AND WIZARDS

Half Magic by Edward Eager, 1954
The Witches by Roald Dahl, 1983
Winter of the Ice Wizard by Mary Pope Osborne, 2004
The Magic Thief by Sarah Prineas, 2008

There can be few people left on the planet who are unfamiliar with the name Harry Potter. Sadly, some are more familiar with his magical world from viewing the big screen rather than the seven-novel series that made Rowling's characters a global phenomenon.

Rowling's witty prose, rich in classical allusion and ingenious plotting, is captivating. The first book (published as *Harry Potter and the Sorcerer's Stone* in the United States) begins with the young orphan Harry suffering at the hands of his Muggle (nonwizard) aunt and uncle in almost Dickensian fashion. He is transported off to a Blytonesque boarding school for witches and wizards known as Hogwarts, where the mystery behind his own survival and destiny begins to unravel. Rowling's story is strong on morals and the value of friendship and family, and at Hogwarts Harry is befriended by Ron Weasley and Hermione Granger, who help him throughout his numerous adventures.

"This boy will be famous. There won't be a child in our world that won't know his name."

What makes Harry Potter so popular is not just the alternative world Rowling brilliantly creates—populated by enchanted creatures, fast-paced Quidditch matches played on broomsticks, and sympathetic adults, such as the kindly Dumbledore—but the wonderfully drawn interior world of Harry. Readers see an imperfect character come to terms with his fame and notoriety, struggle movingly with the loss of his parents, show courage in the trials he encounters, and display empathy for those on the margins of wizard society, such as Hogwarts's half-giant gardener, Hagrid. The Harry Potter books are a must-read for anyone of any age. **CK**

HARRY POTTER

and the Philosopher's Stone

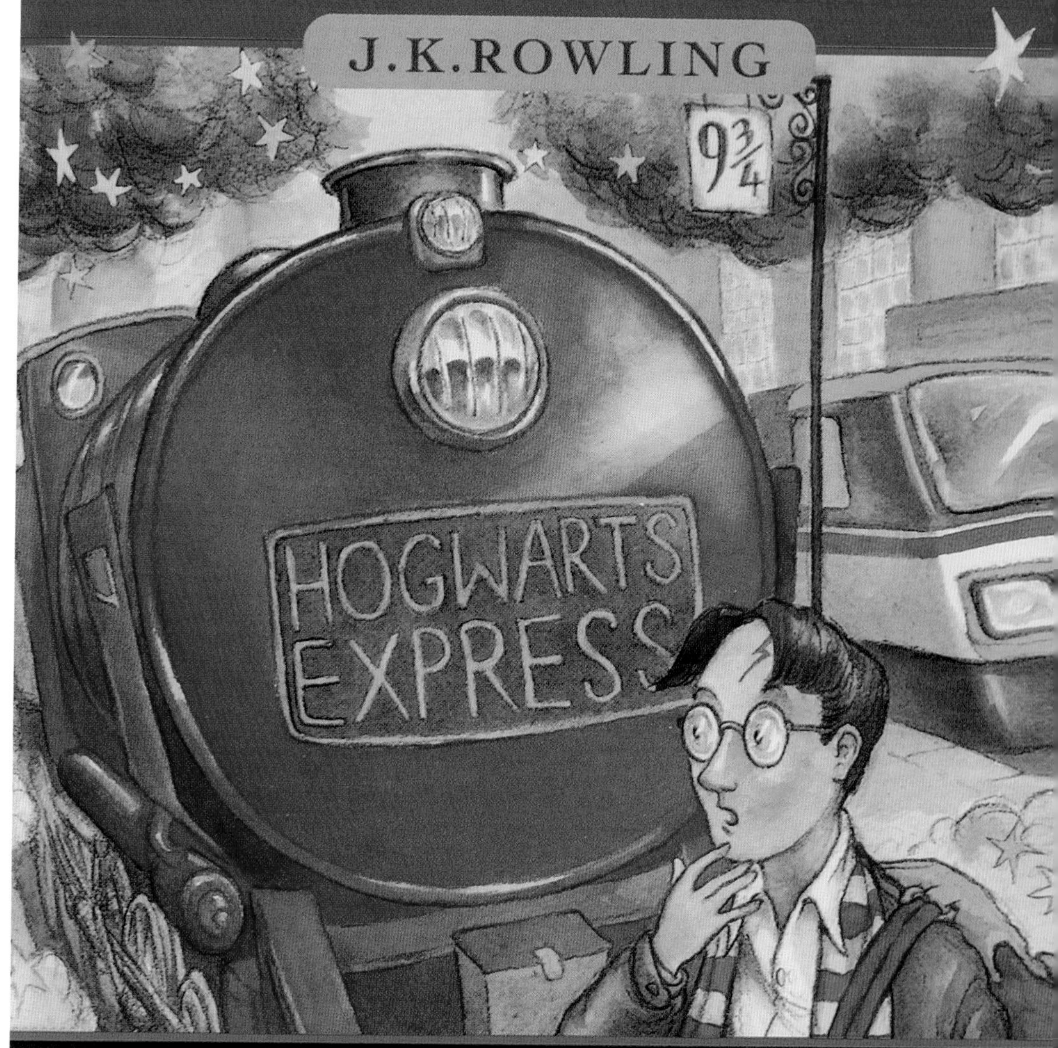

Fire, Bed and Bone 1997

Henrietta Branford

Nationality | English, born 1946
Publisher | Walker Books, UK
Award | *Guardian* Children's Fiction Prize, 1998
Theme | Animal stories, Historical fiction

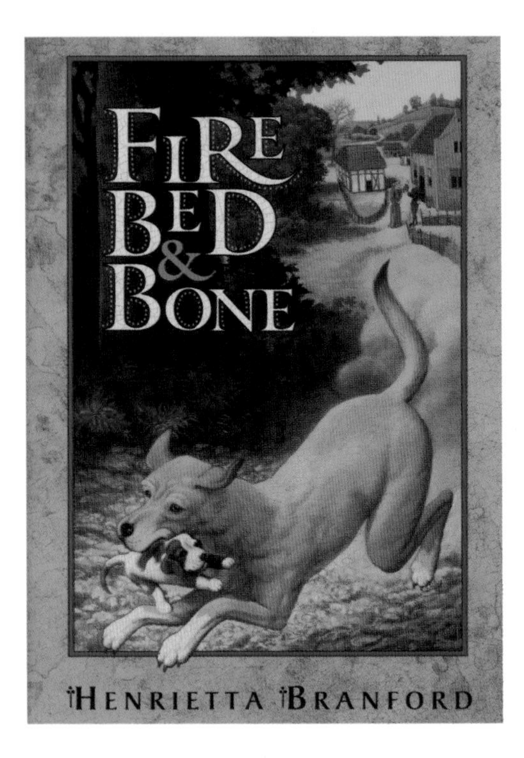

Henrietta Branford drew heavily on her own childhood experiences growing up in a remote part of the New Forest in the writing of this compelling and powerful book about the fourteenth-century Peasants' Revolt.

The year is 1381 and trouble is brewing. England's hardworking peasants, for years oppressed by cruel and unjust landlords, have had enough and decide to rebel. The violence that ensues before the revolt is finally put down is truly terrible. Everyone is affected, even an old hunting hound who is the narrator of this terrific story. Although she is a dog in every other way, she tells this tale with human understanding while never forgetting her own animal needs. Expert in finding her way around the surrounding woods and fields, these skills come in useful after her master is imprisoned and tortured, leaving the old dog—plus some new puppies—to fend for themselves.

"I'd soon begin to see the truth about him, that there'd never been another creature like him."

Animal narrators can act as powerful moral voices in fiction, having the detachment of one species looking in on another. Dogs make particularly good storytellers, since they often see and hear things that humans think are secret. They are used to working hard, and they have no time for self-pity, with survival for themselves and their descendants always their main aim. In this case, the old dog manages to rescue one of her puppies from a cruel master before finally returning home to her former mistress, where she can once again enjoy the *Fire, Bed and Bone* of the title. Readers caught up in her dramatic and turbulent story could hardly wish her less. **NT**

MORE BOOKS BY HENRIETTA BRANFORD

***Royal Blunder*, 1990**
***Dimanche Diller*, 1994**
***The Fated Sky*, 1996**
***White Wolf*, 1998**
***Prosper's Mountain*, 1999**

Matthias and Grandpa 1997

Roberto Piumini Cecco Mariniello

Matthias and Grandpa (first published in Italian as *Mattia e il nonno*) is about a fictional journey that a young boy embarks upon with his dying grandfather. It is a book about the ideas of eternity and transformation. When Matthias is told that his beloved grandpa is leaving on a long journey, his imagination starts to work overtime. But is it the young boy's imagination or that of his Grandpa?

Relatives are pictured crying around a supine figure while Matthias and Grandpa go off on a fantastical journey together. Although they walk through familiar places in the surrounding countryside, the experience is new to them and they have wonderful adventures. They ride a horse, get captured by pirates, and visit a market. At the market, Grandpa has no money and so he exchanges his necktie for a nice juicy apple. The pair are clearly enjoying each other's company: "They continued to walk through the market, listening to the voices, taking in the aromas, looking at the colors." During the outing, the figure of Grandpa gradually becomes smaller and smaller, and eventually Matthias has to carry him. When they return to the house, the grieving relatives are still gathered there. Matthias seems unaware of Grandpa, who is now perched on his head. Although Matthias cannot see Grandpa, he can hear him and understands that he is there all around him, in the places they have visited together and the conversations they have shared. Although his grandfather is dead, he will always be with him, guiding him through life.

Roberto Piumini writes imaginatively and tenderly about death without making it a negative experience or impossible for children to understand. This is a moving and useful book to read together with young children who are experiencing the loss of a friend or relative for the first time. The book was nominated for the Deutscher Jugendliteraturpreis in 1995. **SMT**

Nationality | Italian, born 1947 (author); Italian, birth date unknown (illustrator)
Publisher | Einaudi Ragazzi, Italy
Theme | Family, Illness and death

8+

OTHER GREAT PIUMINI TITLES

***The Six-Wheeled Cart (Il carro a sei ruote)*, 1985**
***The Adventures of Bambilla the Elf (Le avventure del folletto Bambilla)*, 1998**
***The Great Horse (Il grande cavallo)*, 2003**

Toby 1997

Graciela Beatriz Cabal / Alberto Pez

Nationality | Argentinian, born 1939 (author); Argentinian, birth date unknown (illustrator)
Publisher | Grupo Editorial Norma, Colombia
Theme | Family

8+

The protagonist of Graciela Beatriz Cabal's most successful children's story, *Toby* (part of the Torre de Papel collection) is a boy without a mother and with an absent father who works as a sailor. He lives with his grandfather and his unmarried aunt. Toby—who is very different from other children and finds it hard to accept reality—discovers the world around him in his own unique way.

To compensate for his lack of parents, Toby's beloved grandfather tells him imaginative stories and gives him unusual presents. One of these is a beautiful crystal paperweight that changes according to the young boy's moods and in which he visualizes the stories that he hears. Using a tone that is at times colloquial, at times dramatic and intimate, Toby's subjective account incorporates the voices, opinions, and typical expressions of those around him. It is precisely through Toby's eyes that the reader perceives the other characters. This gives Cabal's narrative about the need for tolerance and respect immense power.

The story has no chapters; its structure consists of a series of narrative images—most of which are accompanied by Pez's subtle, profoundly evocative, memorable illustrations—and the short narrative episodes as they are reflected in the paperweight. Far from being a mere literary device, this object also becomes the symbol of Toby's special emotional link with his grandfather. Cabal was a three-times winner of the Quadro de Honor Prize for children's literature (1994, 1995, and 1997). **LB**

The Composition 1998

Antonio Skármeta / Alfonso Ruano

Nationality | Chilean, born 1940 (author); Spanish, born 1949 (illustrator)
Publisher | Editiones Ekaré, Venezuela
Theme | Family, Friendship, Young adult

When a friendly visitor comes to a school classroom in Chile and announces an essay competition entitled "What My Family Does at Night," Pedro, the young protagonist of this story, initially finds the task amusing. However, one day, while playing football on the street, Pedro sees soldiers arrest and take away his friend Daniel's father. After speaking to other classmates, he learns that this has become a regular occurrence. Later, overhearing conversations between adults, he finds out that Daniel's father was arrested for political reasons. Even though his parents have gone to great lengths to avoid exposing him to their political opinions, Pedro knows full well that they are also opposed to the military dictatorship and how dangerous their lives now are. But what can a child do against a military regime? The story ends with Pedro sharing his composition with his parents who realize that Pedro knows more than he has been told, but is aware of the need for secrecy.

The Composition (originally titled *La composición*) is a powerfully tense story that is supported by wonderful illustrations by Alfonso Ruano. Author Antonio Skármeta successfully proves that, with tact and the right touch, even taboo political themes can be convincingly incorporated into children's literature. Skármeta, who is of Croatian descent, was born in Chile and studied philosophy and literature there and at Columbia University, New York. He is one of Latin America's most respected novelists and has won many awards for his fiction. **LB**

Skellig 1998

David Almond

Nationality | English, born 1951
Publisher | Hodder Children's Books, UK
Award | Carnegie Medal
Theme | Fantasy, Illness and death

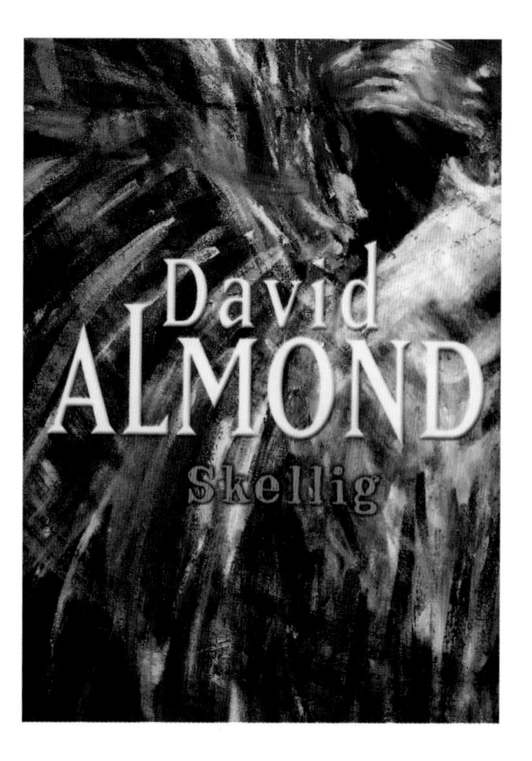

This compelling philosophical novel will please any reader who enjoys mixing reality with adventures in the realm of the imagination. The story is set in a recognizable northeast England but hints at connections with ancient mythical and spiritual worlds, including Greek myths and the poetry of William Blake.

The creature at the center of the story is a mystery: not old or young, not human or bird. Michael, who discovers the frail, malnourished, and arthritic Skellig hiding in the junk-filled garage of his family's new home in Newcastle, gradually comes to believe that Skellig is an angel. Despite the fervency of Michael's belief, David Almond remains deliberately ambiguous about Skellig's true nature.

Caring for Skellig helps Michael through a family crisis (his baby sister seems likely to die). With his neighbor Mina, who is homeschooled, he researches skeletons and explores the myth of Persephone. The children help Skellig to move to an abandoned house, where owls bring him mice to eat. Restored to strength just as Michael's sister's health is at its worst, Skellig visits the baby in the hospital and saves her life.

Michael's terror of death and loss is ever-present throughout the story, but it is held in check by Skellig's benevolent if crotchety presence and baby Mina's zest for living. Skellig can help Michael to resolve his fears when his parents are too preoccupied to help and he feels distant from even his closest friends, but, as in all of Almond's books, there is a strong community waiting to sustain Michael when he is ready to return to everyday life. **GB**

"I wanted to be all alone in an attic like Skellig, with just the owls and the moonlight and an oblivious heart."

MORE EXCITING BOOKS BY ALMOND

Kit's Wilderness, 1999
Heaven Eyes, 2000
Secret Heart, 2001
The Fire Eaters, 2003
Clay, 2005

Just Annoying! 1998

Andy Griffiths Terry Denton

Nationality | Australian, born 1961 (author); Australian, born 1950 (illustrator)
Publisher | Pan Macmillan, Australia
Theme | Quirky

Among Australian children, Andy Griffiths has achieved almost godlike status. Showered with book awards, he has also gained a certain notoriety because some educationalists find elements of his zany humor (although not this book) tasteless. What is undeniable is that Griffiths's work is very funny indeed, as this book clearly shows. The events where he meets his readers are always very well attended because he makes such a good connection with children and never talks down to them.

Part of a popular series, *Just Annoying!* consists of crazy, fictionalized short stories in the unbelievably eventful life of young Andy Griffiths (the idea of the author as central character was inspired by the U.S. sitcom *Seinfeld*). Here Andy displays an impressive talent for annoying just about everyone he comes into contact with. However, this is not "annoying child as underdog"; this is an unashamed celebration of "the annoying child as superhero of annoyingdom." The stories range from Andy attempting to jump back into his father's car at high speed with the aid of a Mad Max–type biker he has befriended, to dressing up as a girl to annoy his sister and receiving some very unwanted attention at a school dance.

"I don't want them to get mad at me—it just happens."

Griffiths has been in rock bands, worked as a schoolteacher, and explored the challenging world of stand-up comedy, and all these elements are clearly influential here. He has a real talent for fast-paced, well-timed slapstick and great comic dialogue. His anarchic brand of humor is illustrated ably by Terry Denton's surreal minicartoons. **AK**

MORE GREAT ANDY GRIFFITHS BOOKS

Just Kidding!, 1997
Just Stupid!, 1999
The Day My Bum Went Psycho, 2001
Just Shocking!, 2007
Just Macbeth!, 2009

My Girragundji 1998

Meme McDonald and Boori Pryor

The *girragundji* first lands shockingly on Gaz's face during a nightmare, but is encouraged to stay to eat the mosquitoes. It gradually assumes a spiritual power for the boy. He believes the little green frog has been sent to him by the old people to protect his spirit. Most of his fears revolve around the bad night spirit: the Hairyman, or Quinkin, whose arm might grab him through the window while he sleeps, or ambush him on trips to the outside toilet. Adults create other anxieties when they drink too much and shout at one another in the night, and at school there are the bullies and more angry adult voices. However, Gaz does not fear crocodiles and snakes, because he has learned to care and respect for the spirits of animals.

"The bullies don't seem so big now my girragundji's with me."

The authors' collaboration (four novels and one nonfiction book based on Pryor's life) is a unique one, and their different cultural backgrounds have contributed greatly to the depiction of Aboriginal experiences in Australian children's literature. The novel elegantly combines photographs and drawings with imaginative variations in typography and layout. Black pages, reverse printing, and underexposed dramatic photographs (by McDonald) graphically represent the darker shades of the boy's fears.

The present-tense narrative balances realistic drama with subtle fantasy. Fears and violence are mediated by gaps in the text and poetic understatement, and Aboriginal words are smoothly integrated. The authors achieve the authenticity of their narrative through honesty and humor in this engrossing book that celebrates universal experiences. **JG**

Nationality | Australian, born 1954 (McDonald); Indigenous Australian, born 1950 (Pryor)
Publisher | Allen and Unwin, Australia
Theme | Folktales

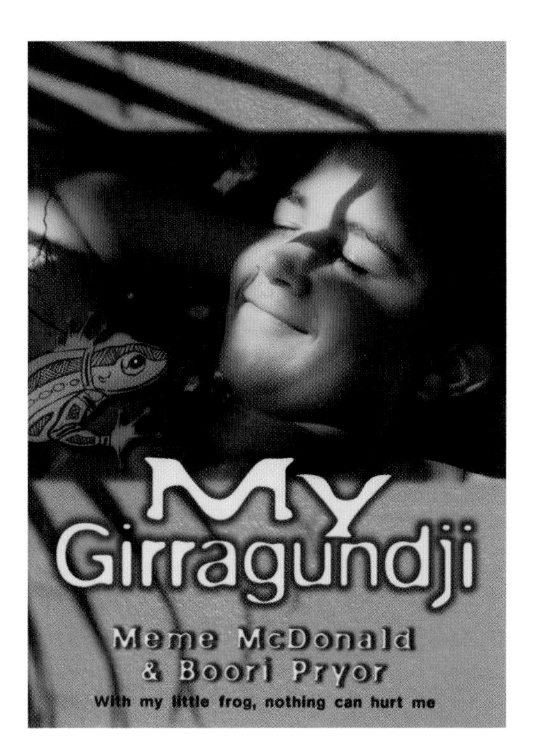

OTHER McDONALD AND PRYOR BOOKS

Maybe Tomorrow, 1998
The Binna Binna Man, 1999
Njunjul the Sun, 2002
Flytrap, 2002

8+

Mary Hoffman reviews:

The Sterkarm Handshake 1998

Susan Price

Nationality | English, born 1955
Publisher | Scholastic, UK
Award | *Guardian* Children's Fiction Prize, 1999
Theme | Historical fiction, Science fiction

8+

MORE GREAT READS BY SUSAN PRICE

Odin's Monster, 1986
The Ghost Drum, 1989
Ghost Song, 1994
Ghost Dance, 1995
A Sterkarm Kiss, 2003

Don't be put off by the strange title—this is one of the most thrilling novels you will ever read. The Sterkarm family is a clan of sixteenth-century reivers—raiders and robbers from the border country between England and Scotland. Technically they are sheep farmers, however, they aren't too fussy about whose sheep they farm and these left-handed men are known for their treachery. So far, so historical novel, but this is a much cleverer book than that.

Scientists in the twenty-first century have discovered time travel and have built a Time Tube that opens at the other end on to the unpolluted border country guarded by the Sterkarms. Corporate greed makes the boss of the company believe he will be able to control these wild border men with cheap aspirins while plundering their unspoiled world for fossil fuels and organizing lucrative safari holidays into the past.

To the sixteenth-century people these creatures from the future are Elves, with powerful magic. A twenty-first-century linguist, Andrea, who has been living with the Sterkarms, is delighted to discover that they regard her as stunningly beautiful. Although in her own time she is considered too big to be attractive, in the past she is admired for her wide child-bearing hips, and healthy skin and hair. In particular by Per, the adored only son of the Sterkarm chieftain. His deceptively beautiful face earns him the nickname of the May (the maiden), but Per is a skilled killer, hunter, and raider, and has sired a couple of children already, even though he is still only twenty.

This is a powerful and often bloody story, as forces that are five hundred years apart clash headlong. But there are tender moments, too, and the love between Per and Andrea is unforgettable. Susan Price brilliantly makes the reader question modern values even as she tells a cracking story.

Ominous detail of the handshake from the cover of the HarperCollins US edition.

The Dog with the Yellow Heart 1998

 Jutta Richter

Original Title | Der Hund mit dem gelben Herzen
Nationality | German, born 1955
Publisher | Hanser, Germany
Theme | Animal stories

Jutta Richter's highly praised novella is the story of an extraordinary stray dog. Simply called Dog, he wears a collar with a yellow heart given to him by a cat as a token of their friendship. He is gifted when it comes to languages—speaking Human, Dove-ish, Cat-ish, and some Rat-ish—and he also knows how to tell a good story. Dog loves crispy chicken skin and is desperate for affection. In order to obtain both from an elderly man called Schulte and his grandchildren, he tells them the story of G. Od and Lobkowitz.

The story is a slightly altered version of the Book of Genesis, where G. Od orders Lobkowitz to leave the paradise that is home to G. Od's dog kennel. The reader also learns about how light and darkness were created, and about how G. Od drew sketches of red wine and human beings before creating them. Yet, Richter does not merely explain or reinvent biblical stories; she also broaches more difficult subjects. Alcoholism is one of them, highlighted in an argument between G. Od and Lobkowitz about the latter's excessive drinking, while Dog's fate is used as an example to illustrate the plight of homeless people. Even though some of the book's topics, such as religion, philosophy, and mythology are not easily intelligible to eight-year-olds, Richter presents them in an engaging way. She describes ways to address social problems and educates her young readership without lecturing them, while encouraging new and intriguing ways of thinking. **GS**

Clarice Bean: That's Me 1999

 Lauren Child

Nationality | English, born 1967
Publisher | Orchard Books, UK
Award | Kate Greenaway Medal (shortlist)
Theme | Family

Poor Clarice, third of four children, can never find a space of her own in her crowded home. First she has to share a room with her brother; there is a line dividing the room which he crosses frequently, resulting in the usual war of words. Her sister Marcie is only into boys, and her brother Kurt suffers from teenage angst. Mom's only time of peace is in the bath, her father has his office to escape to, and Grandfather sleeps through it all. Even in the garden there is the annoying boy next door to invade her space.

Lauren Child's unique style, with ink illustrations mixed with some collage and different type faces, paints a picture of life that will be familiar to most modern families with children at various stages of development. For each family reading this there will be one particular child or incident that strikes a chord. It could be Kurt, in his room that smells of socks, or the youngest Minal Cricket who is at the bottom of the heap, or Mom who is somewhere in the middle of it all. On each spread is a record of the recurring daily annoyances, which can enjoyably be read again and again. The seemingly random placement of the text encourages this exploration of every inch of the pages. The only time when everyone is quiet and getting along is when they watch their favorite tv program. Clarice wins her space by being very naughty but it was worth it! This is a picture book for everyone in the family to enjoy with much on each page to savor together. **JF**

A Series of Unfortunate Events: The Bad Beginning 1999

Lemony Snicket Brett Helquist

Nationality | American, born Daniel Handler 1970 (author); American, details unknown (illustrator)
Publisher | HarperCollins, USA
Theme | Fantasy, Horror, Quirky

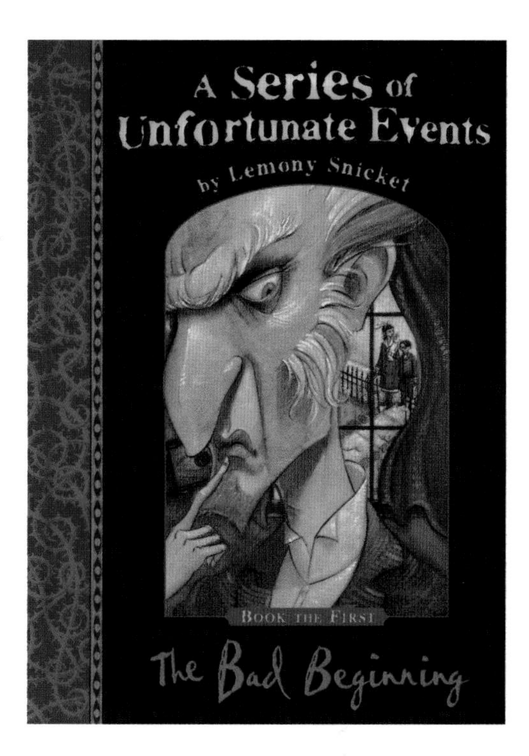

This "Book the First" in Snicket's acclaimed *A Series of Unfortunate Events* establishes the dark, idiosyncratic tone that has made these books rather unlikely bestsellers. In the end it was their cult-style originality that ensured the success of the thirteen-book series. Violence and a cynical, rather sophisticated humor dominate but always stays the right side of a delicate line. The books have even been credited with helping to ease American children through post-9/11 anxieties by offering up the stark, rather adult truth that, no matter what dreadful things life throws at us, we must step up and deal with them. Daniel Handler plays entertaining games by creating a mysterious author—Lemony Snicket, who is also a character in the books—and by turning up at press functions explaining that he is there in Snicket's place.

The Bad Beginning introduces the trio of plucky, resourceful Baudelaire siblings—Violet, Klaus, and Sunny—who will face unbearable tribulations in the books to come. Their ill fortune begins after the death of their parents in a fire, when they are taken in by the dastardly Count Olaf. The count, who performs with a bizarre theatrical troupe, spends his time plotting to seize the children's inheritance. This first book sets the style of the series: self-deprecating Victorian morality tale with a modern, educative twist. The siblings' surname is that of a French nineteenth-century poet, and Handler uses a host of sophisticated phrases that he helpfully explains to readers. **AK**

"Just because you don't understand it, doesn't mean it isn't so."

MORE "UNFORTUNATE EVENTS"

***The Reptile Room*, 1999**
***The Wide Window*, 2000**
***The Miserable Mill*, 2000**
***The Austere Academy*, 2000**
***The Ersatz Elevator*, 2001**

Harry Potter and the Prisoner of Azkaban 1999

J. K. Rowling

Nationality | English, born 1965
Publisher | Bloomsbury, UK
Award | Nestlé Children's Book Prize
Theme | Magical stories, Favorite characters

Harry Potter returns to Hogwarts for a year where not everyone, or everything, is as it first appears. The prisoner of the title is Sirius Black, a former classmate of Harry's late father. Black escapes from the wizard top-security prison of Azkaban and the magical world lives in fear of this convicted murderer.

Author J. K. Rowling excels in the wonderful array of charms and magical instruments she introduces to her series that all prove essential to the plot, from the powerful Patronus spell that can protect its creator to the Marauder's Map that shows where people are in Hogwarts. As ever there are more magical creatures for the gamekeeper Hagrid to fall in love with, this time a flying beaked beast, the Hippogriff, and new characters such as the lovable but hangdog Remus Lupin, the latest victim to take on the most dangerous post at the school, that of teaching Defense Against the Dark Arts. The joy-sucking power of the Dementors is also made evident when these shadowy creatures arrive to protect Hogwarts castle, and their ability to drain happiness from all around them appears to affect Harry more than anyone else.

"When a wizard goes over ter the Dark Side there's nothin' and no one matters to 'em anymore."

The importance of friendship is a strong theme in the Potter books, and in particular here, where Harry learns more about his father's friends, and what happens when a friendship turns sour. He also learns about the power of positive thinking, the benefits of which are to save more than one person's life. Once again Rowling gets her message across about what's important in life in a captivating, fun, and absorbing way that will leave readers burning the midnight oil. **CK**

MORE FUN WITH HARRY POTTER

Harry Potter and the Goblet of Fire, 2000
Harry Potter and the Order of the Phoenix, 2003
Harry Potter and the Half-Blood Prince, 2005
Harry Potter and the Deathly Hallows, 2007
The Tales of Beedle the Bard, 2007

Kensuke's Kingdom 1999

Michael Morpurgo Michael Foreman

Born partly out of his wife's suggestion that he write a story set on a desert island, *Kensuke's Kingdom* has become one of the best known of Michael Morpurgo's novels. It is the story of a boy named Michael (Morpurgo said he named the character after himself so that he could get right inside his story) whose parents are made redundant. They, with their dog Stella Artois, decide to realize their dream of sailing around the world. What begins as an extraordinary, albeit demanding, adventure nearly ends in tragedy when Michael and his dog fall overboard.

Finding themselves on an island, struggling to survive, Michael is conscious of a benevolent "Man Friday" figure, who leaves food and water but never

"The tanker moved inexorably further and further away from me until it began to disappear."

appears to the lonely boy until, desperately trying to attract the attention of a passing ship, Michael incurs the wrath of his helper by lighting a fire. The man, Kensuke, and the boy form an uneasy truce that, over the months that follow, develops falteringly into a warm friendship marred only by their very different desires for the future. Kensuke is a Japanese doctor whose wife and son stayed in Nagasaki when he was conscripted into the navy during World War II. While Michael longs to escape the confines of the island, Kensuke wants only to keep the world at bay.

The twists and turns of the plot that eventually bring a happy ending for Michael are tinged with the regret of the "might-have-beens" that have shadowed Kensuke's life. The skillful portrayal of their nuanced friendship gives emotional depth to a powerful and moving story of isolation and endurance. **KA**

Nationality | English, born 1943 (author); English, born 1938 (illustrator)
Publisher | Heinemann, UK
Theme | Adventure, Friendship

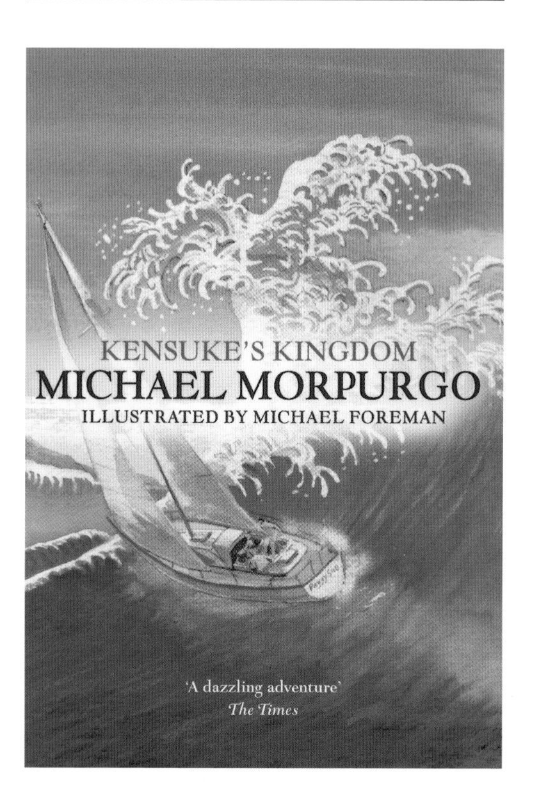

KENSUKE'S KINGDOM
MICHAEL MORPURGO
ILLUSTRATED BY MICHAEL FOREMAN
'A dazzling adventure'
The Times

8+

GREAT BOOKS BY MICHAEL MORPURGO

War Horse, 1982
Why the Whales Came, 1985
The Wreck of the Zanzibar, 1995
The Butterfly Lion, 1996
Private Peaceful, 2003

Hitler's Daughter 1999

Jackie French

Nationality | Australian, born 1953
Publisher | HarperCollins, Australia
Award | C.B.C.A. Book of the Year, 2000
Theme | Historical fiction, War

OTHER GREAT JACKIE FRENCH READS

Rainstones, 1991
The Secret Beach, 1995
Summerland, 1996
Tom Appleby, Convict Boy, 2004
Pete the Sheep, 2005

This powerful, original novel successfully blends contemporary drama with historical fiction. Hitler did not have a daughter, but imagining how such a child might have felt about her notorious father serves as the starting point for a fascinating exploration of notions of good and evil.

A group of Australian children waiting for the school bus amuse themselves by telling stories. Over the course of several rainy days, Anna captivates Mark, Ben, and little Tracey with a vivid description of Heidi—the shy young daughter of Hitler, disfigured by a birthmark—who was never publicly acknowledged but received regular visits from the man she called Duffi. Hidden away in quiet isolation with her governess, Heidi knows little about the shocking realities of Nazi wartime policies, until news of the concentration camps begins to filter through.

Mark is entranced by Anna's evocative descriptions of life in 1940s Germany. The metafictional device acts as a catalyst for the boy to contemplate the thorny issues of complicity, moral responsibility, and guilt. He becomes troubled by difficult questions: How can you tell good from evil? Is the offspring of an evil parent to blame for their actions? Can you love someone universally labeled "evil"?

The lessons of history remain relevant. Mark reflects on how unfairly the land for his family farm was taken from the Aborigines, and whether he is also culpable. After the war, Heidi chooses to forge a new identity and emigrate to Australia, escaping the horrendous burden of her parentage. *Hitler's Daughter* is thought provoking and challenging without being distressing, and it avoids providing easy answers to the moral dilemma presented. Jackie French believes in exposing children to conflicting worldviews, so that they can learn to think for themselves, and as a spark for fresh debate the novel is unrivaled. **MK**

Something's Fishy, Hazel Green! 2000

Odo Hirsch Andrew McLean

Hazel Green is an intelligent and enterprising girl who lives in the bustle of a big city. She is not afraid to stand up to adult authority, although her cleverness frequently gets her into trouble.

When she discovers that a thief has stolen two splendid lobsters from the store of her friend Mr. Petrusca, leaving only a curious note, Hazel decides that it is up to her to crack the code and solve the mystery. With her ability to outwit even the cleverest of adults, Hazel is a formidable heroine. However, even Hazel has things to learn, and she matures and develops throughout the narrative into a more empathetic and understanding character, willing to help those around her achieve their potential.

"Discovering new things was the best fun of all. That was what the world was for."

Hirsch writes in lyrical phrases that whirl off the page at the reader. His entertaining narrative takes off at a breathtaking speed as Hazel negotiates the maze of children's relationships and adult secrecy, eventually discovering her own ability to improve her world through patience and compassion.

With a memorable cast of vibrant youngsters and quirky adults, this is a delightful story that subtly highlights the importance of curiosity in the world around you and empathy for those within it. The narrative is enhanced by the lively and evocative illustrations of Andrew McLean, and Hirsch's great ability to reel off dazzling prose pulls readers into a serious story about hope and compassion.

For fans of the spunky Hazel, there are several other books in the series by Odo Hirsch, the pen name of David Kausman. **CATN**

Nationality | Australian, born 1962 (author); Australian, birth date unknown (illustrator)
Publisher | Allen and Unwin, Australia
Theme | Adventure, Favorite characters

8+

MORE GOOD BOOKS FROM ODO HIRSCH

Antonio S. and the Mystery of Theodore Guzman, 1997
Hazel Green, 1999
Have Courage, Hazel Green!, 2001
Think Smart, Hazel Green!, 2003

Harry Potter and the Goblet of Fire 2000

J. K. Rowling

Nationality | English, born 1965
Publisher | Bloomsbury, UK
Award | Hugo Award (Sci-Fi) for Best Novel
Theme | Magical stories, Favorite characters

The fourth book in the Harry Potter series sees its hero make the shift from boy to teenager. In it, hormones bubble as ferociously as cauldrons, and Harry and his Hogwarts' peers begin to notice the opposite sex—and get jealous. The feeling that love is in the air becomes more acute when some exotic young witches and wizards arrive from abroad to compete at the Triwizard Tournament hosted at the school.

The dusting of young romance provides light relief in a novel much darker than its predecessors. Rowling brilliantly creates a sense of foreboding in what is a departure from previous beginnings set at the home of Harry's adoptive family, the Dursleys. The book opens with a sinister scene depicting the increasingly strong Dark Lord and his slow return to power. Readers are finally made aware of just how dangerous and chilling a presence Voldemort is. One sign of what is to come in the rest of the series is the fact that characters die in this novel, and Rowling does not spare her readership the pain that causes to those around them. New characters—such as the beautiful Fleur Delacour, the handsome Quidditch player Viktor Krum, and the swivel-eyed Alastor Moody—are introduced as Rowling expands her cast.

As the Harry Potter series progresses, the novels become longer, the plots more intricate, and their themes more sophisticated. *The Goblet of Fire* is a roller-coaster ride of fun and excitement as Harry's destiny becomes ever clearer. **CK**

The Day I Learned To Tame Spiders 2000

Jutta Richter

Nationality | German, born 1955
Publisher | Hanser, Germany
Award | German Youth Literature Prize, 2001
Theme | Friendship, Family

The unnamed narrator of this moving story (published in German as *Der Tag, als ich lernte die Spinnen zu zähmen*) is an eight-year-old girl who is scared of many things, including ghosts, the devil, and the pantherlike cat that she believes lives in the basement of her building. Her strict parents do not empathize with her fears, and, instead, punish her for her perceived misdeeds by locking her up or beating her.

Things improve when Rainer moves into the building and joins the girl's group of friends. He may pick his nose and not care about other people's opinions, but he does listen when the narrator tells him about the cat in the basement. In fact, he chases "it" away, so gaining her friendship. Rainer also shows her how to "tame" spiders. First, you have to observe them for a long time. In doing so, you realize how beautiful they really are. After that you let them crawl across your hands, before trapping them inside a match box. Thus, you get rid of them as well as your fear.

One day Rainer fights another boy in the group and knocks him out. At first, the kids fear that he is dead. Rainer runs away and is henceforth shunned by the group, as is his friend, the narrator. She tries to cope, but becomes so desperate to be part of the group again that she ends her friendship with Rainer. Although the girl feels guilty about her betrayal, she is convinced that she could not have acted in any other way. Richter's captivating account of interpersonal conflict is atmospheric and well written. **CS**

Cirque du Freak: A Living Nightmare 2000

Darren Shan

Nationality | Irish, born Darren O'Shaugnessy 1972
Publisher | Collins, UK
Theme | Horror, Fantasy, Favorite characters

8+

Author Darren Shan inserts himself into the story as the central character in *Cirque du Freak*, the first installment of his Vampire Blood trilogy. Darren and his friend Steve visit a traveling freak show, and meet a bizarre cast of performers, including Madame Octa, a goat-eating tarantula who is controlled by a flute played by Larten Crepsley. Steve recognizes Crepsley as a famed vampire in disguise and tries to blackmail him into becoming his helper. The vampire angrily refuses, and the boys steal Madame Octa in revenge. But then the spider bites Steve, and Crepsley will only provide the antidote if Darren becomes his undead assistant. Although he runs away rather than become a vampire's sidekick, Darren is later caught by Crepsley and taken on the road. Just as they are about to leave town, Steve reappears having guessed Darren's secret. He swears he will have revenge on his friend, which leads nicely onto book two, *The Vampire's Assistant*.

Shan's amusingly matter-of-fact tone ("This is a real story, so I have to begin where it really started—the toilet") turns vampires from the dramatic, kitsch figures of legend into a more modern, but no less terrifying, threat. However, the book is dark in places, and may not be suitable for younger readers. Darren is forced to fake his own death so that his family do not discover he is Crepsley's assistant. Despite this, *Cirque du Freak* has a strong sense of morality and a narrative that repeatedly blurs the lines between fact and fiction. A rich and engaging read. **SD**

"I was almost as scared of Steve as I was of Mr. Crepsley. I mean, he WANTED to be a vampire!"

MORE DARREN SHAN VAMPIRE BOOKS

Tunnels of Blood (Vampire Blood Trilogy), 2000
Vampire Mountain (Vampire Rites Trilogy), 2001
Hunters of the Dusk (Vampire War Trilogy), 2002
The Lake of Souls (Vampire Destiny Trilogy), 2003
Sons of Destiny (Vampire Destiny Trilogy), 2004

Because of Winn-Dixie 2000

Kate DiCamillo

Nationality | American, born 1964
Publisher | Walker Books, UK; Candlewick, USA
Award | Newbery Honor Book, 2001
Theme | Family, Friendship

8+

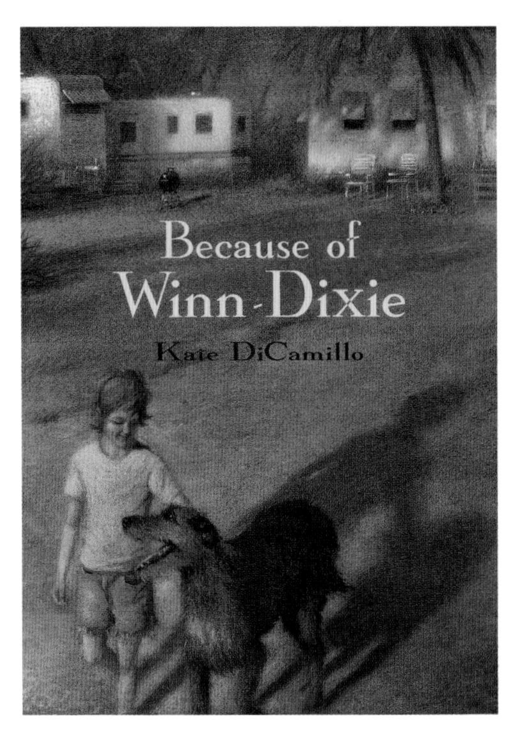

OTHER GREAT KATE DiCAMILLO READS

The Tiger Rising, 2001
The Tale of Despereaux, 2003
The Miraculous Journey of Edward Tulane, 2006
The Magician's Elephant, 2009

Ten-year-old Opal, the daughter of an itinerant preacher, has just moved to a new home in Florida. Still yet to make any friends, she comes across a very large, unkempt but very friendly stray dog causing mayhem in her local supermarket. Pretending to be his owner rather than seeing him taken off to the dog pound, Opal names her new pet Winn-Dixie—the name of the supermarket where he was creating such trouble—and takes him home.

Winn-Dixie soon enables the lonely girl to make new friends, starting with Miss Franny Block, the local librarian—who initially thinks the dog is a bear—and going on to include a five-year-old girl, a blind old lady called Gloria Dump, a shy pet-shop owner Otis,

"My name is India Opal Buloni, and last summer my daddy, the preacher, sent me to the store."

and a couple of boys. These characters finally get together for a big party organized by Opal, and while Winn-Dixie gets temporarily lost, all finishes happily for everyone.

This gentle, feel-good story also has a more serious side; it is only because of Winn-Dixie that Opal feels able to ask her father about why her mother abandoned the family when her daughter was only three. Opening up this previous no-go area between Opal and her father does not bring the mother back, but it does at least answer some important questions and sets their estranged relationship back on track. Spreading love and understanding between the generations, Miss India Opal Buloni is a delightful heroine, narrating this best-selling story in a generally tough-minded way that never for a moment lapses into sentimentality. **NT**

Father Grew Wings in Spring 2000

Tomi Kontio

Original Title	Keväällä isä sai silvet
Nationality	Finnish, born 1966
Publisher	Tammi, Finland
Theme	Fantasy, Family, Friendship

Tomi Kontio's gripping fantasy novel for young readers tells the story of twin boys, Tomi and Timo Kokko. One spring day their normal life comes to an abrupt halt when their father starts to grow feathered wings on his arms. As the boys try to come to terms with this surreal sight, their dad tells them of a faraway place called Austrasia, a magical, almost paradiselike place, where he has to go. The boys are left alone in confusion and fear, not knowing what to do and not really believing what has happened. When the police arrive, asking questions about their dad's disappearance, they do not believe the twins when they recount the bizarre event. In fact, no one believes them, and with no one to take care of them, they are sent to an orphanage.

As the two boys settle in at the orphanage and befriend the other children, Tomi and Timo learn that most of those living there have some kind of supernatural ability or have seen strange and unimaginable things. The institution is run by a tyrannical manageress who uses cruel and torturous methods to control the children. Tomi, Timo, and their young friends soon find out that the orphanage has some kind of connection with Austrasia, but avoiding the watchful eyes of the manageress and finding a way to escape proves to be a difficult task. Will the boys find a way out or do they have to stay in the orphanage for all eternity? Will they ever manage to reach the mysterious Austrasia and see their beloved father again?

Tomi Kontio describes in delicious detail the supernatural events that take place in *Father Grew Wings in Spring*, but this fast-moving and imaginative story also explores some profound themes, such as sorrow, losing one's family, and being taken into care. Readers of all ages will find it difficult to put down this cult favorite. **LKK**

MORE QUIRKY FANTASY TITLES

The Ship That Flew by Hilda Lewis, 1939
Half Magic by Edward Eager, 1954
James and the Giant Peach by Roald Dahl, 1961
A Bad Beginning by Lemony Snicket, 1999
The Wolves in the Walls by Neil Gaiman, 2003

8+

Alex Rider: Stormbreaker 2000

Anthony Horowitz

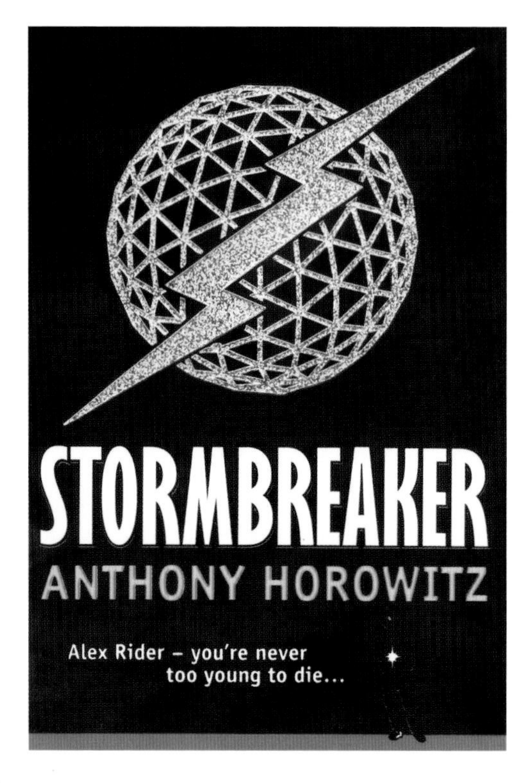

STORMBREAKER
ANTHONY HOROWITZ
Alex Rider – you're never
too young to die...

"When the doorbell rings at 3 am, it's never good news."

MORE THRILLS WITH ALEX RIDER

Point Blanc, 2001
Skeleton Key, 2002
Eagle Strike, 2003
Scorpia, 2004
Ark Angel, 2005

Nationality | English, born 1956
Publisher | Walker Books, UK
Theme | Adventure, Favorite characters, Detective stories

Stormbreaker introduces Alex Rider, the world's first fourteen-year-old superspy. He is an orphan who lives with his mysterious uncle, Ian Rider. After Ian dies, Alex discovers that his uncle was actually a spy. He also discovers that all the exciting skills his uncle made Alex learn—such as karate, skiing, orienteering, mountain-climbing, how to drive, being able to speak several languages—were a cunning way of training Alex to follow in his footsteps. Unwillingly recruited by MI6, Alex is sent to investigate Herod Sayle, the rich inventor of the Stormbreaker computer and software. Almost everyone has been duped into thinking Stormbreaker is the most amazing invention and Sayle a genuine philanthropist, but Ian Rider knew better.

Equipped with an enviable array of gadgets, Alex is sent into the heart of Sayle's domain, posing as an innocent schoolboy who has won a competition to be the first child to try out Stormbreaker. His real mission, however, is to find out what Sayle Enterprises is up to. Herod Sayle is donating computers to schools all over England and there is to be a big ceremony at which the prime minister will start up the first Stormbreaker. Alex discovers that as soon as the first computer is started, it will send out a virus that will wipe out everyone in England. Alex has to prevent the prime minister from pressing the power button.

This is a thrilling, superbly exciting book that began a series of Alex Rider adventures and has been made into a successful film and a graphic novel. **LH**

The Papunya School Book 2000

Nadia Wheatley Mary Malbunka et al.

Nationality | Australian, born 1949 (author); Australian, birth dates unknown (illustrators)
Publisher | Allen and Unwin, Australia
Theme | Family, School

This is a picture storybook about the Papunya School in Australia's central desert. It is also about the history of the Anangu and the country where they have lived for thousands of years. The book was the product of a collaborative project between the staff and students at the school, elders and artists in the community, and children's author Nadia Wheatley and her partner, Ken Searle, who is a painter. Through an engrossing collage of images and text, a multilayered picture of the past 150 years is presented. Illustrations came from Mary Mulbunka and Punata Stockman, as well as the schoolchildren.

We first learn about how Papunya came to be. Through oral accounts, paintings, and photographs, a much bigger history is uncovered of "this mix-up-place." The story is easy to follow, although difficult to swallow, but it is honest, frank, and fascinating. Rich with detail in text and images, it invites rereading.

Papunya School now has a unique way of learning, set out in a Vision Painting. The painting was created in 1994 as a result of community concern that the Anangu children had learned too much white culture and forgotten their own. It showed how community, council, and school could work in partnership. There is a written description of the painting's meaning and directions for how to read it. This book is a generous sharing of an important story about a displaced people whose culture was threatened, as were many indigenous people in Australia. **AJ**

The Vile Village 2001

Lemony Snicket Brett Helquist

Nationality | American, born Daniel Handler 1970 (author); American, birthdate unknown (illustrator)
Publisher | HarperCollins, USA
Theme | Adventure, Fantasy

The seventh novel in Lemony Snicket's *Series of Unfortunate Events* follows the adventures of the three Baudelaire orphans and their ongoing quest for a safe home and a set of parents. This time they take advantage of a new scheme based on the saying, "it takes a village to raise a child," and the trio are entrusted into the care of the Village of Fowl Devotees (VFD). When they arrive, however, Violet, Klaus, and Sunny discover that they are to live with the village handyman and do all of the town's chores. VFD is full of secrets and inequalities, and the noble-minded Baudelaires seek to right the wrongs they discover. The town's initials are known to be related to the evil Count Olaf, who has kidnapped the Quagmire triplets. Hector, the handyman, keeps a secret library and takes the children to the Nevermore Tree, where they find a scrap of poetry written by Isabella Quagmire. The Baudelaires gradually uncover more evidence that will help them find their friends, and discover that Mr. Poe, the banker in whose charge they had been placed, may not have their best interests at heart.

Literary, archaic, and packed full of obscure allusions, Handler's books do not talk down to their readers. His narrator, Lemony Snicket, warns the readers not to pick up the book, and it is left to them to interpret the content, in the same way that the older Baudelaires interpret their baby sister's noises. The series attracts criticism for its dark worldview, archaic vocabulary, and adult nature, but it is phenomenally successful. **SD**

Rupert the Rapper and Aunt Deep Freeze 2001

Sinikka and Tiina Nopola   Aino Havukainen and Sami Toivonen

Nationality | All Finnish, born 1953 (Sinikka); 1955 (Tiina); 1968 (Aino); 1971 (Sami)
Publisher | Tammi, Finland
Theme | Adventure, Family, Favorite characters

OTHER READS BY THE NOPOLA SISTERS

Rupert the Rapper (Hetki lyö, Risto Räppääjä), 1997
Rupert the Rapper and Persistent Spot (Risto Räppääjä ja sitkeä), 2003
Rupert the Rapper and the Last Ice Cream Cone (Risto Räppääjä ja viimeinen tötterö), 2007

Rupert the Rapper (*Risto Räppääjä*) is a popular and entertaining children's series that was created by sisters Sinikka and Tiina Nopola. Rupert the Rapper is an average ten-year-old boy who lives with his Aunt Rauha. He loves to sing songs that he has written himself, and he also likes to play his set of drums all day long.

One day Aunt Rauha has an accident and twists her ankle. For a while she is unable to cook and take care of the everyday needs of the family, so she calls her cousin, Aunt Elvi, to come and help. Aunt Elvi, who loves freezing, is a very strict woman and allows no nonsense. Immediately she enforces her own set of rules and packs most of Rupert's toys away, including his beloved drums—and conflict is unavoidable. Rupert and Aunt Rauha discover that from now on there will be no fun and games in the house and no sweets or treats. Rupert is not at all fond of Aunt Elvi, but as there is no one else to take care of the household, Aunt Elvi has to stay. One night, when Rupert sneaks out of bed, however, he overhears Aunt Elvi talking and realizes that she is not all that she appears to be. Why is she carrying a mysterious jewelry box and a black ski mask in her purse? A little detective work is needed, and with help from a willing team made up of his friend Nelli; Aunt Rauha; Mr. Lindberg, the downstairs neighbor; and Alpo the cat, Rupert sets out to discover Elvi's secret. The ensuing tale includes red herrings, a tape-recording cat, and a surprising proposal.

The sharp writing and sense of humor of the Nopola sisters is guaranteed to make young children laugh out loud. Together the successful duo have penned several popular children's series, including the charming and quirky Hayflower and Quiltshoe (Heinähattu ja Vilttitossu) series, which was made into a film in 2002. **LKK**

Mortal Engines 2001

Philip Reeve

Mortal Engines is the first in a quartet of exciting, fast-paced, science fiction, adventure novels, set many millennia after most of the world has been destroyed in a Sixty Minute War. The seas have dried up or frozen, and most of civilization lives on traction cities that devour smaller towns in a process called Municipal Darwinism, with the traction citizens considering themselves far above those who live in static settlements.

Philip Reeve has created a startling, entirely credible, and highly visual dystopian world that has a flavor of the Victorian industrial age (any technology based on electronics has been destroyed, and fragments of Old Tech such as bits of computer are treasured as antiques), with echoes of ancient Greece in the culture of the hierarchical city-states.

The story centers on the London traction city's attempt to destroy Shan Guo, the world's last free state, using the ultimate weapon, Medusa. Tom Natsworthy, an apprentice historian and Hester Shaw, a disfigured, ruthless, revenge-driven refugee, join forces to foil the Medusa plot after they have both been left for dead in the Out Country. Tom and Hester are complex and engaging characters, whom readers will enjoy meeting in all four novels of the series. The more philosophical readers will appreciate the tension between the Historians, with their reverence for Old Tech, and the Engineers, who believe that they are improving upon the past by reinventing it.

The story is sharp and funny, with clever wordplay, but it is also chilling: good does not triumph completely, and there are tragic deaths. There are many film and science fiction references and added enjoyment for those who have read Dickens or seen *Star Wars*, although this is not essential. The book won the Nestlé Children's Book Prize in 2002 and was shortlisted for the Whitbread Award. **GB**

Alternative Title | The Hungry City Chronicles
Nationality | English, born 1966
Publisher | Scholastic, UK
Theme | Science fiction, Adventure

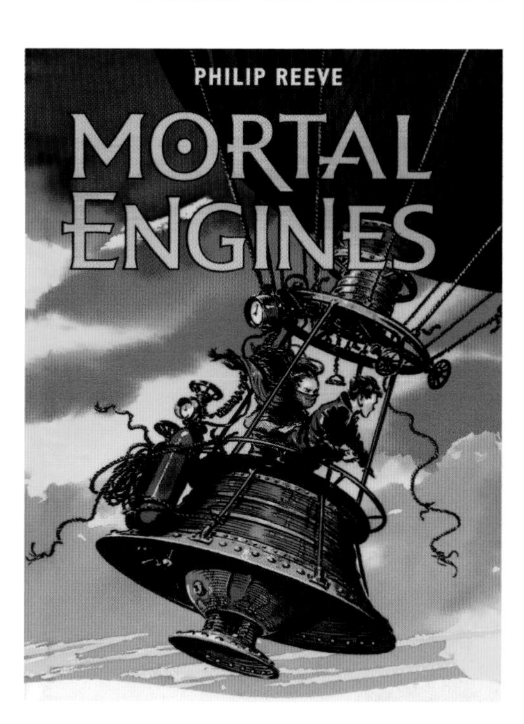

8+

OTHER GREAT SCIENCE FICTION BOOKS

A Wrinkle in Time by Madeleine L'Engle, 1962
Iron Man by Ted Hughes, 1968
Z for Zachariah by Robert O'Brien, 1975
Among the Hidden by Margaret Peterson Haddix, 1998

Artemis Fowl 2001

Eoin Colfer

Nationality | Irish, born 1965
Publisher | Viking Press, UK
Theme | Adventure, Fantasy, Science fiction, Favorite characters

The six Artemis Fowl novels will satisfy any child who has secretly plotted to take over the world. Artemis Fowl II, a teenage megalomaniac crook with a brain the size of a planet, takes on a range of grotesque figures familiar from Irish fairy and folktales (trolls, goblins, and a fairy police force, LEPrecon). Both sides of the conflict have a full range of technology and gadgets at their disposal, and the fairies' powers are made real for a generation who might no longer be drawn to the traditional tales.

In this first book, young Artemis is set on restoring his dynasty's fortunes by dishonest or even foul means. Since Fowl Manor, the family techno-fortress, is in Ireland, Artemis's first scheme involves stealing fairy gold. This pits him against LEPrecon's finest, including Holly Short, a rookie elf policewoman. When Artemis and his sidekick, Butler, kidnap Holly to use as a bargaining tool, war between the humans and fairies seems inevitable.

This first book embodies all the strong points of the series: exciting pace, powerful characters, and the dramatic potential of Artemis's many talents. An intellectual powerhouse, who deciphers ancient languages and develops all-seeing technology, Artemis is a complex character. He seems most vulnerable when he is at the heart of his empire, where the fractures in his family life become obvious. He is also manipulative and cruel to an extent that might be disturbing for some younger readers, but his exploits are delivered with insight and wickedly funny wordplay. **GB**

Aldabra 2001

Silvana Gandolfi Fabian Negrin

Nationality | Italian, born 1940 (author); Italian, birth date unknown (illustrator)
Publisher | Salani Editore, Italy
Theme | Family, Fantasy

Silvana Gandolfi describes herself as a lover of travel and laziness. She has lived in Nepal, Venice, and the Seychelles before settling in Rome. She is a well-loved children's author, having sold 150,000 books in her native country. Her books have been translated into many languages, and this was her first to be translated into English. Aldabra is a World Heritage atoll in the Seychelles Archipelago inhabited by 150-year-old giant tortoises. However, the story of *Aldabra, or The Tortoise Who Loved Shakespeare* is set in Venice, where a grandmother and a granddaughter weave their way through the mysteries of their lives.

In Venice, Elisa walks along cobbled streets and over bridges that link one side of the canal to the other to get to her grandmother's house. Grandmother Eia was once a stage actress, and she and her granddaughter recite Shakespearean lines together, finding much meaning about their lives in Shakespeare's words.

The grandmother, who is approaching her one hundredth birthday, has a secret to pass on to her granddaughter. Eia says that the best thing for her to do at her grand age is to become immortal. How? Elisa asks. Grandmother answers her by turning into a tortoise, much to Elisa's astonishment. But before the transformation is complete, Elisa realizes that the mystery of her mother's relationship with her grandmother needs to be solved. She goes to her grandmother's house alone, taking food that she must say is cooked solely by her and not by her mother, to resolve the unsolved problem. Perhaps the answer lies in the works of Shakespeare. **SMT**

Journey to the River Sea 2001

Eva Ibbotson

Nationality | Austrian/English, born Maria Charlotte Michelle Wiesner 1925
Publisher | Macmillan, UK
Theme | Adventure, Friendship

Maia is an orphan, happy at her boarding school in London but longing for a family. Her guardian discovers that she has relations—Mr. and Mrs. Carter, who have twin girls about her age—who agree to have her come to live with them in Brazil.

Maia is accompanied on the long sea journey to Manaus by the Carters' new governess, Miss Minton. Initially stern, Minty turns out to be kind, intelligent, and a true friend. On the voyage, Maia makes friends with a boy called Clovis, also an orphan, who has been taken in by a troupe of traveling actors. He longs to escape and return to England, but has no money.

When Maia arrives, the Carters are cold and unwelcoming. Unknown to Maia, she has been left a fortune by her parents and the only reason the Carters have taken her in is because of the generous allowance from her guardian. The twins, Gwendolyn and Beatrice, are cruel and bullying. Maia's only friend is Minty, until she makes friends with an orphan boy called Finn, who is half English and half Xanti Indian. Then Clovis turns up, having run away from the theater.

Finn is being sought by two English lawyers who have been instructed to take him to live with his grandfather. Finn is desperate not to go, so he, Maia, and Clovis hatch a plan to have Clovis "caught" and taken to England in his place. The story has some wonderfully macabre touches, such as Mr. Carter's obsession with his collection of glass eyes. Eva Ibbotson writes in a beautifully lyrical style, evoking the wonders of Brazil and Maia's enchantment with her new country. **LH**

"Maia took a deep breath. A home. . . . *Everyone was friendly and kind, but a* home."

OTHER GOOD READS BY EVA IBBOTSON

Which Witch?, 1979
The Secret of Platform 13, 1994
Monster Mission, 1999
The Star of Kazan, 2004
The Beasts of Clawstone Castle, 2005

8+

City of the Beasts 2002

Isabel Allende

Original Title | La Ciudad de las bestias
Nationality | Chilean, born 1942
Publisher | HarperCollins, USA
Theme | Adventure, Fantasy

FABULOUS BOOKS BY ISABEL ALLENDE

Kingdom of the Golden Dragon (El reino del dragón de oro), 2004
Forest of the Pygmies (El bosque de los pigmeos), 2005

Fifteen-year-old Alex Cold finds himself unexpectedly, and a little reluctantly, on a journey down the Amazon as part of an expedition aiming to find a gigantic beast and a previously undiscovered tribe. Among the party are Alex's travel-writer grandmother, an arrogant anthropologist, a beautiful doctor, and a local guide and his teenage daughter, Nadia.

From the start of the journey, the Amazon surrounds the group with threats from which they cannot protect themselves: one member of the party is crushed by a giant anaconda, another is attacked by the mysterious Beast. After the party loses its boats, Alex and Nadia are kidnapped by an Indian tribe, the People of the Mist, and carried off to their secret realm, the Eye of the World. At turns terrified and empowered by their experiences, the two children have to conquer their fears and find the inner strength to embark on individual quests that will save the tribe.

"Everything about this trip was so different from the world Alex had grown up in . . ."

The magic realism for which Isabel Allende is known may be remarkable in the world of adult fiction, but in a children's book it seems completely natural. *City of the Beasts* is rooted in the contemporary world, but shot through with elements of magic and myth. The plot hangs on averting a potential ecological disaster: the destruction of species, environments, and cultures by ruthlessly exploitative people, a topical political theme. The fantastic weaves in and around these realistic elements, as the children experience dreams and visions that give them the power to overcome the obstacles they face and travel into the realm of myth. **CW**

Utterly Me, Clarice Bean 2002

Lauren Child

Readers were first introduced to Clarice Bean in the picture books *Clarice Bean, That's Me!* and *My Uncle Is a Hunkle Says Clarice Bean*, but *Utterly Me, Clarice Bean* was Lauren Child's first children's novel featuring Clarice. The appearance of the novel differs from that of the earlier picture books. Black-and-white drawings replace the collages of watercolor painting, magazine, and photographic images, but the typographical inventiveness remains, scrawled across the page in a pictorial representation of Clarice's emotions.

Clarice is completely fed up with her family and not overly fond of her teacher. Mom nags, Dad complains about work, her brother Minal Cricket is "utterly a nuisance," and Mrs. Wilberton insists on a book project that does not excite Clarice until she realizes that there is a prize to be won. Hooked on the Ruby Redfort mystery books about an eleven-year-old detective, Clarice soon discovers that she has to solve a mystery of her own.

"My family is six people, which is sometimes too many. Not always, just sometimes."

This is an unsentimental view of childhood and tackles head on a child's feelings of restriction, boredom, and frustration with siblings and friends, as well as conveying the breathless excitement of discovering unexpected friendships and one's own power to change things. Clarice Bean is a delight, and irresistible whether you are eight or eighty.

Lauren Child has won many awards for her work, including several Kate Greenaway Medals. *Utterly Me, Clarice Bean* was longlisted for the Carnegie Medal in 2002. A television series based on her Charlie and Lola books began airing in the United States in 2005. **WO**

Nationality | English, born 1967
Publisher | Orchard Books, UK
Theme | Family, Adventure, School, Favorite characters, Friendship

FABULOUS BOOKS BY LAUREN CHILD

***Clarice Bean, That's Me!*, 1999**
***I Will Not Ever Never Eat a Tomato*, 2000**
***My Uncle Is a Hunkle Says Clarice Bean*, 2000**
***Beware the Story Book Wolves*, 2001**
***Hubert Horatio Bartle Bobton-Trent*, 2004**

The Wolves in the Walls 2003

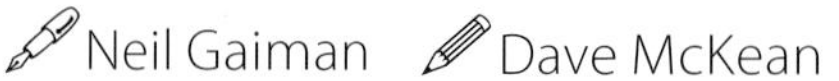

Nationality | English, born 1960 (author); English, born 1963 (illustrator)
Publisher | HarperCollins, USA
Theme | Horror, Fantasy

Lucy is convinced she can hear sinister noises coming from behind the walls of her gothic-looking house. But her brother and parents are unconvinced, until one night they are all chased into the garden by some fearsome wolves who erupt from the walls. Once in charge, the wolves settle down for a long party. After a successful visit to the house to retrieve her beloved pig-puppet, Lucy suggests that the family return to their house in order to do to the wolves what they did to them. So the next evening sees people coming from the walls and the wolves running away in terror, never to come back. But was that an elephant sneezing from behind the walls that Lucy heard on the last page?

Neil Gaiman—who has won numerous awards, including the 2002 Bram Stoker Award for Best Work for Young Readers for his novella *Coraline*—has an extraordinary imagination, and his surreal powers of invention never let up in this picture book. He also has the perfect illustrator in Dave McKean, who is expert in conjuring up domestic scenes that mix the ordinary with the unworldly. Together they show young readers how fearful objects can sometimes have their own areas of cowardice, while those who are afraid can surprise themselves by unexpected acts of bravery. Bursting with energy at one moment, craven at the next, the wolves behave more like naughty boys than evil beasts. Infants initially fearful of these creatures can therefore end up having the last laugh; older readers will find themselves chuckling too. **NT**

The Field Guide 2003

Holly Black Tony DiTerlizzi

Nationality | American, born 1971 (author); American, born 1969 (illustrator)
Publisher | Simon and Schuster, USA
Theme | Fantasy, Adventure, Family

The first book in the Spiderwick Chronicles series, *The Field Guide* draws on writer Holly Black's own experiences of growing up in a "decrepit Victorian house." When their parents' marriage breaks down, Mallory Grace and her twin brothers, Jared and Simon, move into a huge, run-down house in the middle of nowhere that used to belong to their great-uncle. Everyone's hoping that the move will stop Jared from misbehaving, but when items go missing and Mallory's hair is tied to her bed overnight, Jared is blamed and cannot convince his family that he was not responsible.

Jared, a sensitive boy, knows that there is a secret force within the house. After a series of disturbing events, he discovers an ancient book hidden in a secret room. Written by his Great-Uncle Arthur Spiderwick, it is a field guide to all the goblins, boggles, and fairies that surround the house. But after all of his wild behavior, will anyone believe Jared's unlikely tales about a goblin army? The children then meet a strange goblin named Thumbletack, who tells Jared that anyone who reads Spiderwick's field guide is in grave danger, and the family have to fight to save themselves and their house.

This rich, visual book, made into a film in 2007, neatly juxtaposes the modern concerns of a single-parent family with otherworldly descriptions of fantastical creatures. Echoing Lemony Snicket's warnings to readers of his books, the frontispiece of *The Field Guide* also states that danger lies within. **SD**

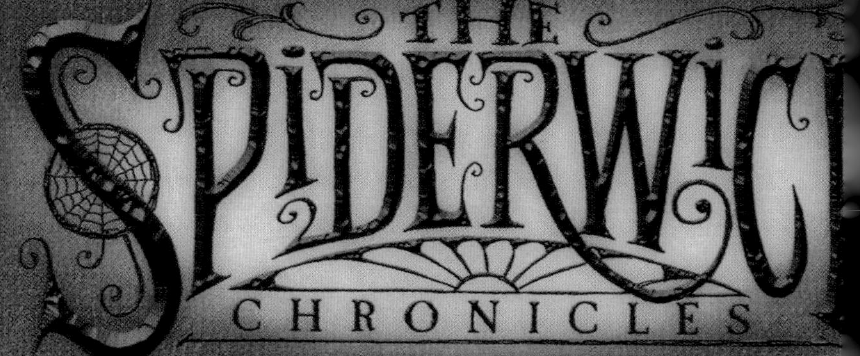

THE FIELD GUIDE

The Naming of Tishkin Silk 2003

Glenda Millard   Caroline Magerl

Nationality | Australian, born 1952 (author); German/Australian, born 1964 (illustrator)
Publisher | ABC Books, Australia
Theme | Fantasy, Illness and death, Family

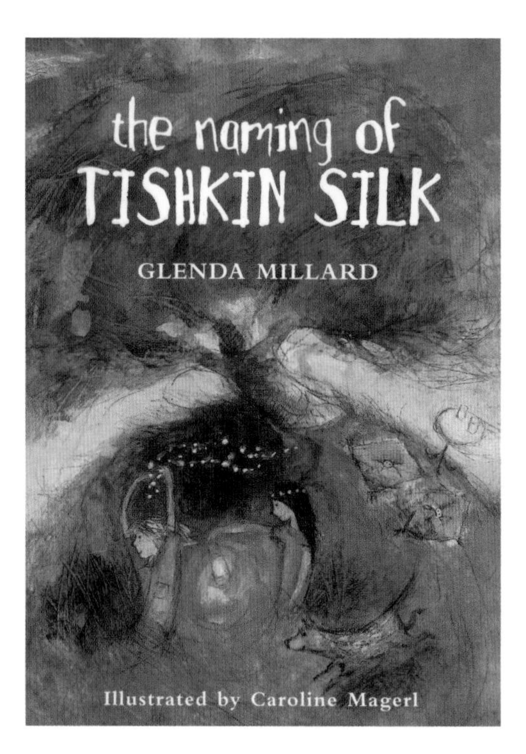

OTHER READS BY GLENDA MILLARD

***When the Angels Came*, 2003**
***Perry Angel's Suitcase*, 2007**
***Kaito's Cloth*, 2008**
***Applesauce and the Christmas Miracle*, 2008**
***Isabella's Garden*, 2009**

8+

Griffin Silk was born on February 29—Leap Day—but that is not the only thing that makes him such an unusual boy. To begin with, his parents named him after a mythical beast, and his grandmother frequently transforms into the Fairy Godmother of Silk Kingdom. Then there is his deaf dog, Blue, and his half-blind crow, Zeus.

Until now, Griffin has been home-schooled, just like his five older sisters—Scarlet, Indigo, Violet, Amber, and Saffron—who are known as "The Rainbow Girls." However, when tragedy strikes the family, everything changes. Attending the local school is something of a challenge for Griffin. He is taunted by the school bully and longs to be normal and ordinary. However,

"The top [part of the sky], where the stars were, was the color of Daddy's Bluey jacket."

then he meets Princess Layla and learns that, with her help, he is able to have the courage to share his secret sorrow and celebrate his uncommonness.

Glenda Millard's heartwarming tale of family, friendship, love, and loss is enhanced by Caroline Magerl's beautiful and atmospheric illustrations. Humor and warmth flood its pages. Invented family rituals, such as "naming days," and frequent flights of imagination highlight the role of spirituality and fantasy in overcoming grief.

In the sequel to *The Naming of Tishkin Silk*—*Layla, Queen of Hearts* (2006)—Layla, who has been such a source of comfort, has become an honorary member of the Silk family. Although Millard did not begin writing until her four children were teenagers, she is fast establishing herself as a full-time, successful writer of children's and young adult fiction. **AH**

Inkheart 2003

Cornelia Funke

Inkheart (*Tintenherz*) is a thrilling and complex fantasy about books and reading. After a mysterious stranger called Dustfinger appears at Meggie's house one night, Meggie, her father Mo, and her great-aunt Elinor are plunged into a threatening world of villains, kidnapping, and arson. It is clear that Mo knows more about what is happening than he is letting on, but it is not until they find themselves locked in a dungeon that his secret is revealed. When Mo reads aloud, characters from the book come out of the pages and enter the real world.

Nine years earlier, Mo "read" Capricorn, his creepy sidekick Basta, and the fire-eater Dustfinger out of a book called *Inkheart*. But there is another side to Mo's power: when something from the book world enters the real world, something from the real world must be exchanged. The night that Capricorn, Basta, and Dustfinger emerged, Meggie's mother disappeared into the book, and Mo has never read aloud since. Now Capricorn wants Mo to use his power to conjure up the deadly monster, the Shadow, from the pages of *Inkheart*. Mo has an idea to set all to rights, which involves *Inkheart*'s author, Fenoglio. But before it can be put into action, Meggie and Fenoglio are captured by Capricorn. Reading out loud to herself for comfort, Meggie discovers she too can read characters out of books. In the nail-biting climax, Meggie must use her newly found power to rescue her mother and destroy Capricorn. All ends happily, leaving just enough loose ends to tease you into reading the next book in the trilogy. **CW**

"The rain cast a kind of pallor on the darkness, and the stranger was little more than a shadow."

Nationality | German, born 1958
Publisher | Cecilie Dressler Verlag, Germany
Award | Book Sense Children's Award, 2004
Theme | Fantasy, Adventure

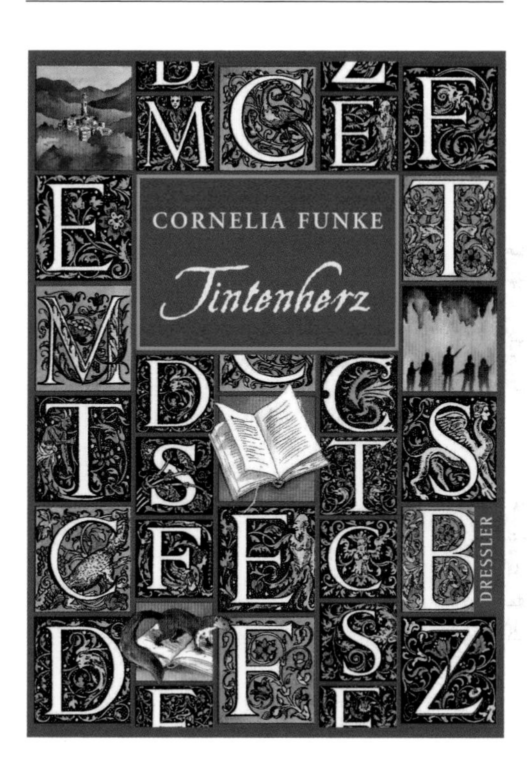

MORE FANTASTIC FUNKE TITLES

***The Thief Lord*, 2000**
***Dragon Rider*, 2004**
***Inkspell*, 2005**
***Igraine the Brave*, 2007**
***Inkdeath*, 2008**

8+

Three Fairy Tales 2003

Gustavo Martín Garzo J. Gabán

Nationality | Spanish, born 1948 (author); Spanish, born 1957 (illustrator)
Publisher | Siruela, Spain
Theme | Fairy tales

Faithful to the tradition of fairy tale literature, these three fairy tales (published as *Tres cuentos de hadas*) open the door to a world in which everything is possible. Only one of the tales actually contains a fairy. She is a capricious fairy, a little frivolous and forgetful, who answers to a new race of fantastic beings who envy the life of children and are driven by alien emotions, mainly sadness. She is quite prepared to inhabit the soul of a dead little girl and impersonate her—to the great surprise of her grieving mother.

One realizes after reading these stories that life in fairy tales may not be easy either, but that it is remarkable. A little girl can talk to the animals and be saved by a nightingale. She can become friends with a dragon who lives in the woods, or she can fall in love with a prince who spreads the illness of dreams. This is because these tales reinvent the sense of wonder that life conceals, inviting the reader to look at reality again, where something surprising and wonderful can happen completely unexpectedly.

This book is an homage to the classics of children's literature and, in particular, to fairy tales that, as the author says, "deal with everything that affects the human condition," and therefore also include sadness and adversity, although in the end the message is always one of hope. Gustavo Martín Garzo's narrative style, although rooted in reality, has the power that is the mark of a true storyteller, capable of making the most unbelievable wonders believable. **EB**

The Tale of Despereaux 2003

Kate DiCamillo Timothy Basil Ering

Nationality | American, born 1964 (author); American, birth date unknown (illustrator)
Publisher | Candlewick Press, USA
Theme | Fairy tales, Friendship

The Tale of Despereaux—subtitled "Being the Story of a Mouse, a Princess, Some Soup, and a Spool of Thread"—is a fairy story in the style of the Brothers Grimm. It is set in a kingdom where soup is banned and treachery lies around every corner.

Despereaux is an unlikely hero: he is a small, sickly mouse with very large ears, who loves music and reading. He defies the rules of the mouse kingdom when he falls hopelessly in love with a beautiful human princess. As punishment he is banished by his fellow mice to a dark, rat-infested dungeon. One of the dungeon's inhabitants, a wily rat called Roscuro, persuades a poor, unloved serving girl called Miggery Sow to kidnap the princess and bring her down into the darkness. However, brave Despereaux, armed only with a spool of red thread, valiantly leads the princess back through the labyrinthine dungeon to the glittering world of her father's castle. Eventually Roscuro and Miggery Sow are forgiven by the princess and her father and, to some degree, the characters live happily ever after.

The central themes of this tale are friendship and forgiveness. It is by turns warm and witty, but it also has a more sinister edge and is at heart a battle between the forces of darkness and light. The voice of the unnamed narrator pulls the story together and provides a wry commentary on the action. This is a book that children will enjoy reading alone, although the witty narrator also makes it a great book to read aloud. **HJ**

KATE DiCAMILLO

author of *Because of Winn-Dixie*

The Tale of Despereaux

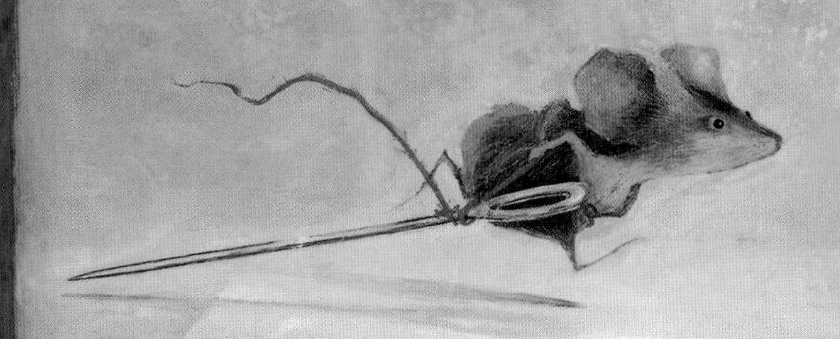

illustrated by Timothy Basil Ering

Millions 2004

Frank Cottrell Boyce

Nationality | English, born 1961
Publisher | Macmillan, UK
Award | Carnegie Medal
Theme | Family, Adventure

8+

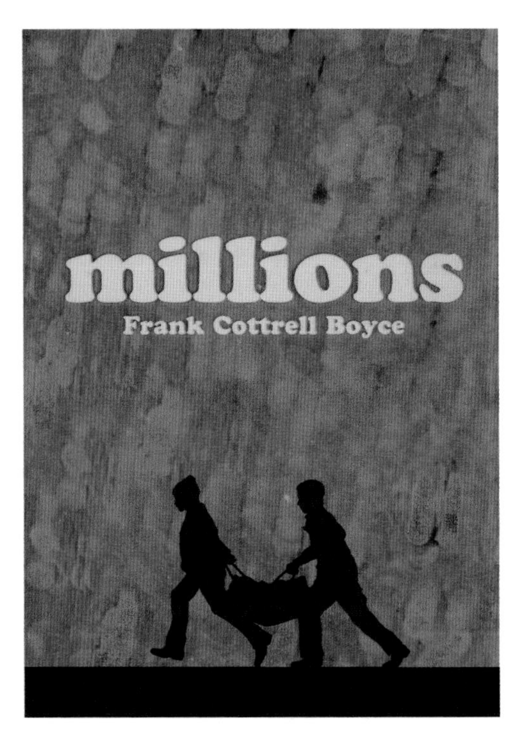

Millions is a rare book: a story told by a seven-year-old that will entertain readers well into adulthood. On one level it is a subversive, well-paced, boy-friendly comedy about children's responses to adult rules and the practical problems of disposing of money you are not supposed to have. It is also, however, touching in its portrayal of a grief-stricken family. It poses big questions about the difficulties of translating principles such as "help the poor" into practice. The moral—that doing good is more complicated than it seems—is delivered through humor and without preaching.

The narrator, Damian, has a busy spiritual life and is inspired by the lives of the saints. They frequently talk to him, as does his late mother, and he tries to mimic them, with hilarious results. When Damian and his older brother, Anthony, find a bag of money that has apparently fallen from the sky, Damian's first instinct is to do good with it, while Anthony, a product of the consumer culture, wants to invest in real estate.

"There is a patron saint of robbers . . . but I'm not an actual robber. I was only trying to be good."

The fictional conversion of the United Kingdom to the euro, making pounds sterling redundant, gives the boys a deadline to spend the money and boosts the already high energy of the action. As Damian struggles to choose the right good cause, there are changes in his home life, and adults begin to take an interest in his windfall. First written as a screenplay, *Millions* has excellent dialogue and a credible child's perspective. Like the author's next two novels, it is completely truthful about how a child's mind works and is respectful of the children it portrays. **GB**

MORE MODERN MORALITY TALES

The Lion, the Witch and the Wardrobe **by C. S. Lewis, 1950**
Holes **by Louis Sachar, 1998**
Skellig **by David Almond, 1998**
Framed **by Frank Cottrell Boyce, 2005**

Wolf Brother 2004

Michelle Paver

Wolf Brother is the first book in the six-part Chronicles of Ancient Darkness series. It is set in the forests of northern Europe thousands of years after the end of the Ice Age. Torak, a twelve-year-old boy, and his father are outcasts from their clan and live alone. When his father is killed by a demon bear, Torak begins a quest to find the mythical Mountain of the World Spirit that will give him the strength to defeat this beast and protect the future of his clan and that of all the creatures of the forest.

Torak, a reluctant hero, is accompanied on his terrifying journey by an orphaned wolf cub with whom he can communicate, and later by Renn, a feisty girl of his own age, who is a skilled archer. The book tells

"Had it come back? Was it out there now watching him with its hot murderous eyes?"

of their struggles and of the dangers they face, both human and supernatural, before a gripping climax where Torak confronts the bear and fulfills his destiny.

Wolf Brother is steeped in atmosphere and powerful natural magic. It conjures up a world that is both fantastical and realistic. Much of this is due to Michelle Paver's intensive research. She traveled through the forests of Lapland and northern Finland, spending time with nomadic people; she learned how to make bows and arrows, slept on reindeer skins, and ate blubber and fish eyes. Paver says of her novel: "Everything in this book had to have happened. Everything is factually possible—it has to be real. I want the reader to believe they are in the ancient forests." Pavel has created a world that is unfamiliar but believable, and Torak's adventures in this and the following five books will enthrall young readers. **HJ**

Nationality | English, born 1960
Publisher | Orion, UK
Theme | Historical fiction, Adventure, Myths and legends, Magical stories

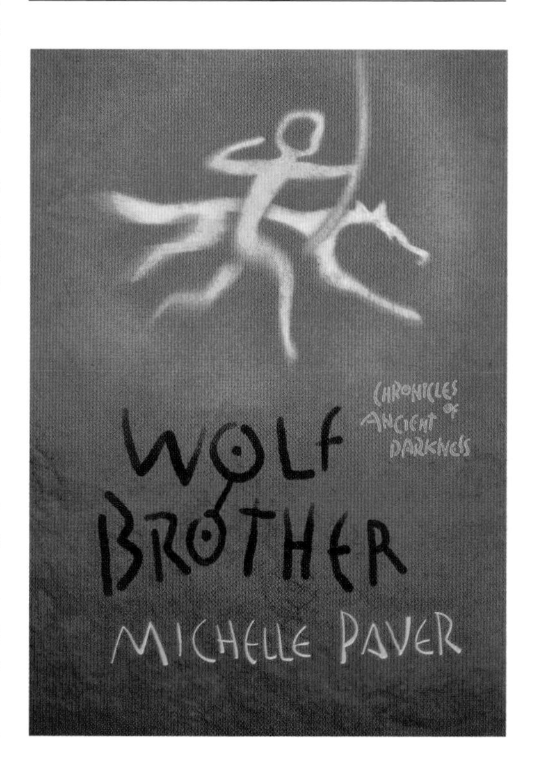

8+

MORE MICHELLE PAVER BOOKS

***Spirit Walker*, 2005**
***Soul Eater*, 2006**
***Outcast*, 2007**
***Oath Breaker*, 2008**
***Ghost Hunter*, 2009**

Ark Angel 2005

Anthony Horowitz

Nationality | English, born 1956
Publisher | Walker Books, UK
Award | Children's Book of the Year Award, 2006
Theme | Adventure, Friendship

Recruited by MI6 after the mysterious death of his uncle, orphan Alex Rider becomes a teenage super-spy and battles the dark forces that assassinated his uncle. In *Ark Angel*—Anthony Horowitz's sixth book in the Alex Rider series—the story begins with Alex in the hospital, still recovering after the attempt on his life at the end of *Scorpia*, the previous book. Alex's near death leaves him determined to give up being a spy and lead a normal life. However, his new friend Paul has a super-rich father, which leads to Alex having to save his friend's life before they have even left the ward, and he is soon lured back into a spy mission fraught with danger and excitement.

Taking in ecoterrorists, unethical billionaires, and the inherent problems of forging new friendships when you are not supposed to trust anyone, Alex Rider books are often dismissed as a junior version of James Bond. That is too simplistic, though this book, like the others, does include spy-story essentials, such as dangerous escapes from moving vehicles, double-crossing agents, evil terrorist groups, and a thrilling climax where Alex is sent into space to defuse a bomb and save the planet.

Despite this and the fast-paced plot, *Ark Angel* never loses sight of Alex's age and his occasional vulnerability. When his new friend Paul turns out to have a reason for seeking Alex's friendship, the spy's disappointment has to take a backseat to his duty to country. One of the PR campaigns used for *Ark Angel* was a competition to design a gadget included in the book. The winner was a fingerprint-sensitive inhaler, which saves Alex's life at a crucial moment. **SD**

Rabbit and Coyote 2005

Beatriz Donnet

Nationality | Mexican, born 1952
Publisher | Selector, Mexico
Theme | Myths and legends, Folktales, Animal stories

The stories in *Rabbit and Coyote* (*Conejo y Coyote* in Spanish) represent a wonderful collection of myths and legends from Mexico. With its broad narrative spectrum, the book offers an alternative, informal introduction to Mexican folklore and its popular culture through a series of simple stories told by one girl. Citlali, a girl from the Mexican region of "Ixtapan de la sal," entertains the reader by narrating the numerous different episodes from old Mexican legends about the two opposing characters: the rabbit and the coyote.

Despite the widely changing settings and plots of the stories, the two protagonists preserve their distinctive, fundamental characteristics. The ferocious coyote always wants to eat the weaker, smaller rabbit, whereas the rabbit always proves to be more intelligent and, without exception, manages to get away, even escaping to the moon on one occasion. Beatriz Donnet's work is highly entertaining, as well as valuable for its retelling of old myths in a new, accessible way. It is a good read for young children (for whom Donnet's simple vocabulary and colorful illustrations are particularly appropriate) and also for adults who want to learn more about the culture of an immensely interesting country.

Beatriz Donnet has produced other similar short story collections drawing, upon Mexican indigenous myths and legends and featuring other creatures, including one on the eagle and the serpent and another on the pheasant and the deer, both of which were published in 2005. **LB**

The Cat: Or, How I Lost Eternity 2006

Jutta Richter   Rotraut Susanne Berner

Nationality | German, born 1955 (author); German, born 1948 (illustrator)
Publisher | Hanser, Germany
Theme | Animal stories

It is the old white cat's fault that Christine is late for school every day. It is summertime, and the cat always sits on the same wall in the mornings and talks to the girl. It seems to Christine that the cat is able to explain the world a lot better than her teacher. But there are some questions that even the cat cannot answer satisfactorily. For example, how can Christine improve her math skills? The cat suggests counting the mice that one catches and eats—not an option for the girl. Christine also has some other doubts about the cat's knowledge. She is worried, for example, about the postman, Buck, who looks lonely in his uniform. The cat argues that pity is peculiar to girls who are bad at math and that uniforms are always lonely. Christine does not want to really believe the cat, because she thinks that we can help people who are lonely.

Eventually, the cat and Christine talk about "original sin"—a topic that Christine has discussed in her religious studies classes. The cat does not believe that God would condemn humankind because of a single apple, even if it had grown on the tree of knowledge: Surely it wouldn't be in his interest for human beings to remain unintelligent, he argues. Christine finally sees the problem with the cat. Although it is capable of understanding eternity, the only other thing it can do is make calculations using mice. Eight-year-old Christine finally realizes that now she has to try to understand the world without the cat's support. Published originally in German as *Die Katze, oder Wie ich die Ewigkeit verloren habe*, this worthwhile book poses philosophical questions for children. **CS**

"'It's his own fault,' she spat. 'He licks the hand that hits him instead of biting it.'"

OTHER PHILOSOPHICAL WORKS

The Little Prince by Antoine de Saint-Exupéry, 1943
The Giving Tree by Shel Silverstein, 1964
Sophie's World by Jostein Gaarder, 1991
Stellaluna by Janell Cannon, 1993
Zen Shorts by Jon Muth, 2005

8+

The Boy in the Striped Pyjamas 2006

John Boyne

Nationality | Irish, born 1971
Publisher | David Fickling Books, UK
Award | Irish Book Award, 2007
Theme | War, Historical fiction, Controversial

8+

Set during World War II, *The Boy in the Striped Pyjamas* focuses on the Holocaust, which some may find a disturbing subject for a children's book. Nevertheless, the book has been widely acclaimed, winning several awards and selling more than four million copies around the world. It was made into a film in 2008.

The book, essentially about friendship, tells the story of two young boys who develop a bond across a fence. But this is no ordinary fence. One of the boys, Shmuel, wears striped pajamas because he is a Jewish inmate of the Auschwitz concentration camp, while the other, nine-year-old Bruno, is the son of the Nazi camp commandant, working for the "Fury" (Fuhrer). Bruno and his family have just moved to Auschwitz and, apart from his sister, Gretel, Bruno finds himself alone and lonely. Bruno's friendship with Shmuel fills the gap in his life, but it has its consequences. Bruno contracts lice and has to have his head shaved, making him look more like the camp inmates. When Shmuel's father goes missing, Bruno wants to help his friend find him, and his ensuing actions have the devastating result of making Bruno's family consider their own behavior.

"All he could say [about his father was] that the Fury had big things in mind for him."

What is challenging and inspiring about the book is its portrayal of intolerance. What is it that causes people to erect barriers based on difference of ethnicity or religion, and what is it in human nature that breaks through those barriers? It will make any reader pause for thought and, although set in an earlier troubled era, it has important messages for today's world, too. **CK**

OTHER HOLOCAUST BOOKS

***I Was There* by Hans Peter Richter, 1987**
***Number the Stars* by Lois Lowry, 1989**
***Once* by Morris Gleitzman, 2005**
***The Book Thief* by Markus Zusak, 2005**
***Then* by Morris Gleitzman, 2008**

The Arrival 2006

Shaun Tan

Using images alone, Shaun Tan's powerful and celebrated work graphically interprets the range of emotions of the migrant experience. Tan believes that illustration is a "quite unique form of story-telling expression," and it allows readers to make sense of a story in their own way and at their own pace.

From an oppressive city of tenements reminiscent of Depression Europe, the immigrant sets out to seek a better life for his family. His journey over the sea is linked with iconic images of twentieth-century European migration. The journey brings him to a surreal metropolis so entirely new and strange that he might be on another planet. The readers share the immigrant's sense of isolation and bewilderment in a place where nothing is familiar and everything is strange. Communication is almost impossible, but a strange yet friendly pet unexpectedly provides help and companionship. Gradually the immigrant meets others, each with their own story of a desperate journey from fear to safety and friendship.

Through a captivating series of marvelously detailed drawings, Tan tells moving stories that emphasize the value of friendship and family. As in Tan's other works, vast buildings and superhuman threats highlight the vulnerability of the comparatively small inhabitants of this world; but there is also a charming sense of whimsicality and humor, and in the end a happy reunion and a welcome new beginning. The wordless book, whose appeal is not restricted to one particular age group, communicates something universal about the experience of the refugee—by escaping from one threat, the immigrant may be faced with another unsettling kind of loss.

Tan, whose Chinese father immigrated to Australia from Malaysia, believes that his childhood experiences growing up in a Perth suburb may have led him to ponder questions of identity. **SM**

Nationality | Australian, born 1974
Publisher | Lothian Books, Australia
Award | C.B.C.A. Picture Book of the Year, 2007
Theme | Family, Friendship

RECOMMENDED READS BY SHAUN TAN

The Playground, 1997
The Lost Thing, 1999
The Red Tree, 2001
Tales from Outer Suburbia, 2008

8+

The Invention of Hugo Cabret 2007

Brian Selznick

Nationality | American, born 1966
Publisher | Scholastic, USA
Award | Caldecott Medal, 2008
Theme | Fantasy, Historical fiction

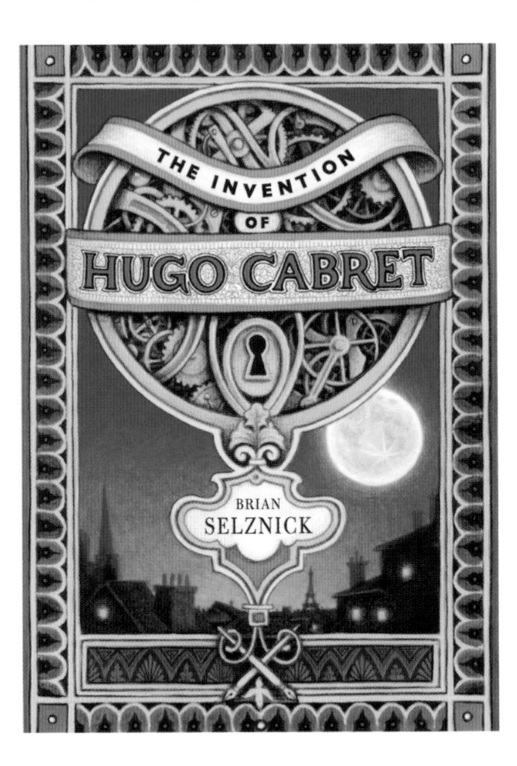

With its 536 pages (divided into 378 of prose and 158 of stunning monochrome cross-hatched illustrations), its luxurious production values, and its eye-catching design, this book immediately demands attention. It defies, however, any straightforward definition of what kind of book it is. Part picture book, part book with illustrations, part graphic novel, part historical fiction—it is at once none of these and all of them.

Some ingredients of the prose narrative seem reasonably standard—a 1930s twelve-year-old Parisian orphan (who happens, initially, to be a thief); clocks and clockmakers; a clockwork robot who can write; a dramatic fire; a toymaker; concealed identities; father-son relationships; separations and reunions—

"Hugo had no choice . . . he had to keep secrets, but he couldn't explain this to the girl."

among many others. There are mysteries to be solved and secrets to be exposed and, although the plot is characterized by complication and coincidence, the charm of the story is such that the reader's occasional disbelief is totally suspended.

Brian Selznick's grainy drawings provide immediate proof of the book's strong cinematic influences. He shows a marked fondness for detailed close-ups in the portrayal of his settings and characters, juxtaposed with numerous telling cutaway shots, and his use of perspective is breathtaking. There is, for example, a marvelous sequence set in a bookshop where the hero, Hugo, finds himself amid "the teetering pile of books"; and another in which Hugo's friend Isabelle grapples with the "decorative panel" on a wardrobe. A book such as *The Invention of Hugo Cabret* gives "reading" a completely new meaning. **RD**

MORE GREAT GRAPHIC NOVELS

The Houdini Box by Brian Selznick, 1991
The Arrival by Shaun Tan, 2006
Coraline by Neil Gaiman and P. Craig Russell, 2008
The Graveyard Book by Neil Gaiman and Chris Riddell, 2008

Darren Shan reviews:

The Graveyard Book 2008

Neil Gaiman Chris Riddell

Nationality | English, born 1960 (author); English, born 1962 (illustrator)
Publisher | Bloomsbury, UK
Theme | Horror, Fantasy

8+

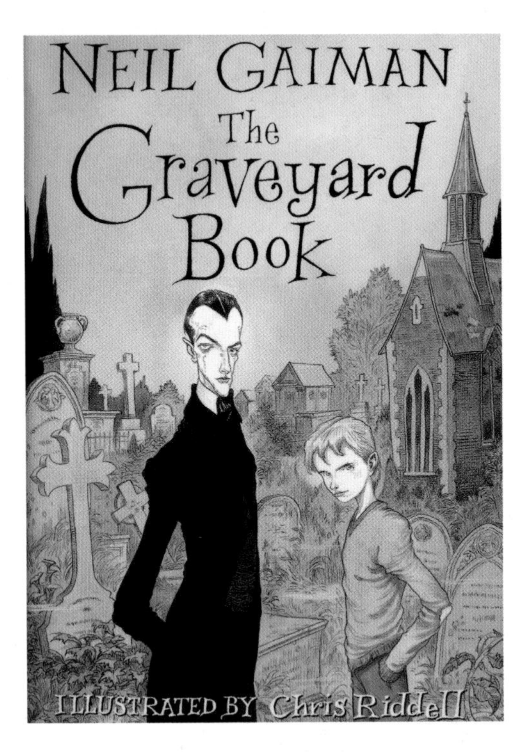

MORE TO ENJOY FROM NEIL GAIMAN

***The Sandman*, 1989–1996**
***Coraline*, 2002**
***The Wolves in the Walls*, 2003**
***Odd and the Frost Giants*, 2008**

One of the books I've enjoyed most in the last few years is *The Graveyard Book* by Neil Gaiman. I've been a huge Gaiman fan since he wrote *The Sandman*, and I've enjoyed all of his work since that series ended—but this is the first of his novels to have as much impact on me as his comics did.

When a baby's parents are murdered, the infant finds sanctuary in a nearby graveyard, where the ghosts agree (after much deliberation) to rear him and protect him from a killer who is hot on his trail and who will never give up. As the boy—named Nobody Owens—comes of age in a world populated by the dead and beings of an even more mysterious nature, he faces a series of adventures that will shape and define him. And, of course, since all great tales revolve around revenge or redemption, ultimately he must toe the line with the sinister, vicious beast who destroyed all that he held dear. The book follows the boy as he grows up, with each chapter telling a story at a different stage of his life.

"... wisps of nighttime mist slithered and twined into the house through the open door."

A magical tale of growing up and learning to stand on your own feet, this is a dark and menacing novel, yet brimming over with warmth and hope. The characters are finely drawn, the plot is packed with clever twists, the gallows humor will delight older readers, and the wonder of Gaiman's imagination will melt all but the iciest and most shriveled of hearts. A book that celebrates youth, but which also stresses the need to mature and move on with your life in order to experience all that the world has to offer. Mesmerizing.

"'I am the master of this place,' . . . 'I guard [it] from all who would harm it.'"

12+

A 1962 illustration for *20,000 Leagues Under the Sea* (1870), written by Jules Verne.

Bertoldo, Bertoldino, and Cacasenno *c.* 1620

Giulio Cesare Croce and A. Banchieri

Nationality | Italian, born 1550 (Croce); Italian, born 1568 (Banchieri)
Publisher | Unknown, Italy
Theme | Folktales, Family, Classics

12+

Giulio Cesare Croce wrote *Bertoldo* in 1606 and *Bertoldino* in 1608. The third part of this work, *Cacasenno*, was written by Adriano Banchieri, a monk and musician, as well as a writer, who put the three novellas together as one collection *c.*1620. The stories originate from the Middle Ages and are a well-known part of the oral heritage of Italian folklore. The novellas tell the stories of Bertoldo, his son Bertoldino, and grandson Cacasenno. Listeners to the stories marvel at the wit, sagacity, and gregariousness of the main character, Bertoldo.

While in conversation with King Albonio, Bertoldo manages to outwit him and prove his superiority. The king asks Bertoldo a series of questions to which he gets no straight answers: "What is the fastest of all things?" "Thought." "Which is the best wine?" That drunk in the home of others." Bertoldo wins the favor of the king, who often consults him for advice. Bertoldo's wife, Marcolfa, is as clever as he is, although she also has to contend with Bertoldino, who is more ingenious even than his father, and Cacasenno. Cacasenno, although a child, has inherited the family magic of wit and ingenuity. When told to mount a horse, Cacasenno sits facing the back of the horse and states that this way he will not have to see the dangers that might lie ahead during the journey.

The antics of Bertoldo, Bertoldino, and Cacasenno recall those of the legendary figure of Giufà, a character from Sicilian folklore, who also has a counterpart in Sufi mythology. **SMT**

Robinson Crusoe 1719

Daniel Defoe

Nationality | English, born *c.*1660
Publisher | William Taylor, UK
Theme | Classics, Adventure, Science and nature, Fantasy

Based on the experiences of Scottish sailor Alexander Selkirk, Daniel Defoe's story, often considered to be the first English-language novel, relates the adventures of Yorkshireman Robinson Crusoe. In the early eighteenth century, Selkirk had spent four years on a desert island off the coast of Chile. While Selkirk did so by choice, Crusoe is shipwrecked and stranded on a Caribbean island for more than twenty-five years.

Ignoring his parents, the young Crusoe embarks on a career as a sailor. After many adventures, his ship sinks, and Crusoe is stranded on an island near the mouth of the River Orinoco. He survives his ordeal and manages to lead a fairly comfortable life, salvaging tools and ammunition from the ship and building a shelter as well as an enclosure for the feral goats that live on the island. To keep his mind stimulated, Crusoe reads from the Bible and, with plenty of time for introspection, he becomes fervently religious. When, after several years, he discovers that his island is occasionally visited by cannibals, it takes him a further two years to build up the courage to rescue a victim. Tremendously grateful for having been rescued, the latter—named Friday by Crusoe—becomes the Englishman's willing servant.

Despite the hero's self-righteousness, a plot that is often driven by implausible coincidences, and racist language (by modern standards), *Robinson Crusoe* is literature's quintessential adventure story and an enduring classic. **DaH**

An 1890 illustration in which Robinson Crusoe meets Man Friday. 

Gulliver's Travels 1726

Jonathan Swift

Nationality | Irish, born 1667
Publisher | Benjamin Motte, UK
Theme | Classics, Adventure, Family, Fantasy, Science and nature

TRAVELS
INTO SEVERAL
Remote NATIONS
OF THE
WORLD.

In FOUR PARTS.

By *LEMUEL GULLIVER*,
Firſt a SURGEON, and then a CAPTAIN of ſeveral SHIPS.

VOL. I.

LONDON:
Printed for BENJ. MOTTE, *at the Middle* Temple-Gate *in* Fleet-ſtreet.
MDCCXXVI.

12+

OTHER GREAT SHIPWRECK STORIES

Robinson Crusoe by Daniel Defoe, 1719
The Swiss Family Robinson by Johann David Wyss, 1812
The Coral Island by Robert Michael Ballantyne, 1858
Kensuke's Kingdom by Michael Morpurgo, 1999

A satire on the political, scientific, and religious absurdities of Stuart and Georgian England, this book has a history of publication for children in abridged forms where the fantastical story is the focus of attention, rather than the satire.

The story was originally published as *Travels Into Several Remote Nations of the World. In Four Parts. By Lemuel Gulliver, First a Surgeon, and Then a Captain of Several Ships*. As this original title suggests, the hero, Lemuel Gulliver, is a ship's doctor. Shipwrecked on Lilliput he awakens to find himself trussed up, a giant at the mercy of the island's tiny inhabitants. Gradually he gains their confidence and his freedom, but internal fighting and a war with a nearby island cause him to leave. His next journey takes him to Brobdingnag, where the inhabitants are giants. He is cared for by a girl called Glumdalclitch but here he has a succession of near fatal accidents, and experiences many indignities. He escapes from Brobdingnag with the intervention of an eagle.

"I could, perhaps, like others, have astonished thee with strange improbable tales."

Next he comes across the flying Island of Laputa, where the people are engaged in obscure philosophical and scientific investigations using mathematics and music. They are totally incapable of creative thinking or expression and are slowly destroying their dominions through science.

In the country of the Houyhnhnms, which is ruled by horses, Gulliver is a Yahoo, a despised human. When he is forced to leave after five years with the civilized Houyhnhnms, he returns home, profoundly disillusioned with the human race. **WO**

A. Coppin's 1850 illustration of Lilliputians building a carriage to move Gulliver.

The Adventures of Baron Münchhausen 1786

Gottfried August Bürger

Original Title | Des freiherrn von Münchhausen
Nationality | German, born 1747
Publisher | Unknown, Germany
Theme | Classics, Adventure, Historical fiction

12+

OTHER FANTASTICAL TALES

Gulliver's Travels by Jonathan Swift, 1726
Journey to the Center of the Earth by Jules Verne, 1864
The Hobbit by J. R. R. Tolkien, 1937
The Neverending Story by Michael Ende, 1983

Baron Karl Friedrich Hieronymus von Münchhausen was a real figure living during the eighteenth century and a contemporary of the author. Famous for embellishing his accounts of his experiences in the Russian war against the Turks, Münchhausen gained widespread fame, and his tales were published in a Berlin-based magazine. The German scholar Rudolf Erich Raspe translated them into English, and they caused a great stir in England. Gottfried August Bürger then translated them back into German, adding some embellishments of his own.

The story begins with the Baron accompanying his father on his travels. They board a ship to Ceylon. Münchhausen describes the voyage as "uneventful," despite the fact that, while stopping on an island, they are caught in a storm that uproots all the trees, throwing them high in the air. The ship's crew is unharmed but the biggest tree hits the island's evil king on the head and kills him.

> *"Münchhausen, Münchhausen, I know you love the truth, but I won't believe that."*

A fortnight after arriving in Ceylon, Münchhausen finds himself cornered by a lion, with a crocodile and a gorge full of poisonous snakes blocking his only escape routes. Defenseless and expecting to be swallowed at any moment, he lies down on the ground, only to witness the lion jumping across him and straight into the crocodile's jaws. Münchhausen immediately jumps up and cuts off the lion's head, which is stuck inside the crocodile's muzzle.

Extravagant and entertaining, Münchhausen's fantastical tales greatly appeal to children with a fascination for fanciful worlds. **DaH**

Géry-Bichard's illustration (1879) captures the Baron's eccentric nature. 

The Three Musketeers 1844

Alexandre Dumas, Sr.

Original Title | Les Trois mousquetaires
Nationality | French, born 1802
Publisher | *Le Siècle*, France
Theme | Adventure, Historical fiction

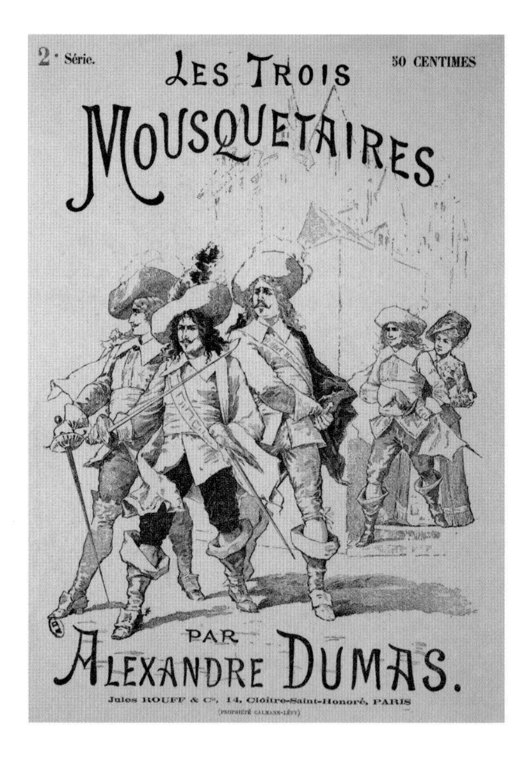

RECOMMENDED READS BY DUMAS, SR.

Twenty Years After (Vingt ans après), 1845
The Count of Monte Cristo (Le Comte de Monte-Cristo), 1845–1846
The Vicomte de Bragelonne (Le Vicomte de Bragelonne), 1847–1850

Everything happens so quickly. The musketeers head toward London in a cloud of dust to save the honor of their queen. And Alexandre Dumas's pen gallops across the page at the same speed. Bent over his table, Dumas wrote serial novels for the newspapers. In a single year, he published two masterpieces—*The Count of Monte Cristo* and *The Three Musketeers*—and several novellas. In the streets of Paris, people fought over the newspapers to find out what happened next.

And in my bed, 150 years later, I can't put the book down. I am thirteen years old. My mother has come in three times to turn the light out, but no, how can I abandon the stampede of Athos, Porthos, Aramis, and the young d'Artagnan?

"D'Artagnan, seeing him approach, drew his sword a foot out of the scabbard."

Dumas can't count! When d'Artagnan joins the musketeers, they become four: four musketeers in the service of King Louis XIII. They love living and eating well, they are funny, they love to swordfight under the moon, and they would gladly die for their friends. Action, romance, politics, and pathos abound, so hold onto your plumed hats for here is the queen of France, Anne of Austria, calling on the musketeers to help her. All four—"one for all, all for one!"—are going to face Cardinal Richelieu and the terrible Milady de Winter, their ravishing enemy. Courage, energy, derision: there is more than enough in this book to inspire the dozens of plays and films that followed, and Dumas knew it. Rumor has it that, not long before his death, someone asked Dumas about another of his books. He replied with the words that I always want to sigh each time I finish a book: "It's no Musketeers."

12+

The front cover of a 1905 serialization, illustrated by Eugene Damblans.

The Children of the New Forest 1847

Captain Frederick Marryat

Nationality | English, born 1792
Publisher | George Routledge and Sons, UK
Theme | Classics, Historical fiction, War, Science and nature, Adventure

Four children living without parental control is a winning formula. Add into the mix Civil War adventure and romance, and you have an enduring story.

Set during the English Civil War, the children, Edward, Humphrey, Alice, and Edith, are the orphans of Royalists. When loyal servant Jacob Armitage discovers a plot to burn down the house with the children inside, he takes them to his cottage in the New Forest. They live as Jacob's grandchildren while he teaches them how to survive in the forest. The children make a great success of their changed situation, even after the death of Jacob. They "adopt" a gypsy boy who becomes a devoted servant and experience adventures with animals, robbers, and cavalrymen, clinging always to their faith and the Royalist cause. Edward, the eldest, learns respect for Mr. Heatherstone, the Puritan in charge of the New Forest, earning his gratitude when he rescues Heatherstone's daughter, Patience, and gradually becoming aware of his Royalist sympathies. Humphrey is content as a farmer, but Edward leaves to fight for the future Charles II after an unfortunate misunderstanding concerning his relationship with Patience. The girls are sent away to be educated as ladies.

After several years, Edward returns with the king to find that his sisters have grown into charming young women and that his beloved Patience still loves him. Her father has, in the meantime, restored the children's family home and returns it to Edward. **WO**

The Scarlet Letter 1850

Nathaniel Hawthorne

Nationality | American, born 1804
Publisher | Ticknor, Reed and Fields, USA
Theme | Classics, Love, Historical fiction, Controversial, Young Adult

Nathaniel Hawthorne's tragedy was, in its time, a call for America to awaken from hypocrisy as much as a heartrending plea for tolerance, pitting sexual love against the moral code of Puritan New England. Although set in seventeenth-century Boston, the story exposes many of the moral dilemmas of the mid-nineteenth century. Using psychological realism, Hawthorne explores the consuming effects of guilt, anger, loyalty, and revenge. The drama of these insights made the novel one of the earliest best sellers.

The story opens with a young woman, Hester Prynne, being led from prison with her baby daughter Pearl in her arms. A scarlet *A* is being pinned to her dress. It stands, so a bystander informs Roger Chillingworth, for "adultery," since Hester's husband had been lost at sea months before the pregnancy. Hester earns her living by sewing, championed by local minister Arthur Dimmesdale, who suffers from a strange illness. It transpires that his chest is branded with a scarlet *A*. Revealed as the husband returned from the dead, Chillingworth determines to hunt down his errant wife's lover. A psychological battle ensues, with Dimmesdale being struck dead on the town gallows just before he and Hester are due to flee the country together. Only a life of good works may provide redemption for Hester, who much later returns to Boston to be buried beside her lover, still wearing the scarlet letter, under a tombstone marked with the letter *A*. **VN**

The Rose and the Ring 1855

William Makepeace Thackeray

Nationality | English, born 1811
Later Illustrated By | Fritz Kredel
Publisher | Smith, Elder, UK
Theme | Magical stories, Fantasy, Quirky

King Valoroso has stolen the crown of Paflagonia from his nephew Giglio. Will he now give the hand of his daughter, Princess Angelica, to Prince Bulbo, son of King Padella of the neighboring kingdom? Poor Giglio loves Angelica, so he gives her his mother's ring, which is imbued by Fairy Blackstick with the power to make the wearer appear beautiful. But when Giglio is jealous of Bulbo, Angelica removes the ring and reveals herself to be plain. Prince Bulbo also has a Blackstick special, a rose with similar powers, and Angelica falls in love with him. There ensues a merry dance with rose and ring being passed around the court and such personages as the governess Countess Gruffanuff and the maid Rosalba in complicated intrigues, before a happy ending pairs off the younger generation. A particularly neat touch is Fairy Blackstick restoring Gruffanuff's husband from the doorknocker into which she had bewitched him years before.

The plot, described by Thackeray as a fireside pantomime, is not the point. The sparkling sentences, in which Thackeray's satire on judging by appearances unfurls, show the reader that Victorian literature was not all moralistic fables and sentimental sighs. Thackeray pounced on feminine vanity and male ineptitude with an equally beady eye, yet with a lightness of touch that has scarcely been equaled. There is much lighthearted fun, with characters called Glumboso and the Marquis del Spinachi, and verses and suggestions for children's games scattered throughout. **VN**

"As long as he had his sport, this monarch cared little how his people paid for it."

OTHER MAGICAL CLASSICS

A Midsummer Night's Dream by William Shakespeare, *c.*1594
The Magic Fishbone by Charles Dickens, 1868
The Weirdstone of Brisingamen by Alan Garner, 1960
The Ghost Drum by Susan Price, 1987

12+

Tom Brown's Schooldays 1857

Thomas Hughes

Nationality | English, born 1822
Later Illustrated By | Edmund J. Sullivan
Publisher | Macmillan, UK
Theme | Classics, School, Friendship

Tom Brown, the easygoing son of the local squire, enjoys himself hugely in the countryside surrounding his home. But after two unsatisfactory years in local schools, he is sent off to Rugby School, an all-male boarding establishment ruled by a strict but kindly headmaster, Dr. Arnold.

Although he makes friends quickly, Tom also has to cope with the school bully, Flashman, at one time getting burned as a result of one of his tormentor's worst acts. Finally defeating his enemy, Tom excels at games but becomes increasingly bored by his lessons. The headmaster puts him in charge of George Arthur, a brilliant but delicate pupil whose goodness eventually wins Tom back to his former cheerful and positive ways, and he is able to prove himself as much a scholar as he is a sportsman. The book ends with his return to Rugby as a man, greatly affected by the news of Dr. Arnold's death.

The most famous boarding school story ever written, this novel, with its detailed descriptions of day-to-day life for pupils living away from home, has fascinated generations of young readers. Some of it may now seem dated, particularly the emphasis on prayer and the importance of living a strictly Christian life, but the descriptions of games on the field and japes in the dormitories are still as fresh as ever, with Tom coming over as a decent boy doing his best to live up to other's expectations while determined to enjoy himself as much as possible at the same time. **NT**

The Coral Island 1857

Nationality | Scottish, born 1825
Publisher | W. and R. Chambers, UK
Theme | Classics, Adventure, Friendship, Young adult

Ralph, Jack, and Peterkin are shipwrecked on an uninhabited coral island in the Pacific. Armed with nothing more than an ax, a length of cord, a broken knife, and a telescope lens, they manage to survive, working out how to hunt, cook, make shelter, and clothes. Their idyllic existence is interrupted when warring cannibals arrive on the island, closely followed by pirates, who carry off Ralph. Eventually Ralph manages to escape and sails the pirate ship single-handedly back to the island. The boys then set out to rescue a native girl who is being forced to marry against her will. They are captured by the cannibals and imprisoned until a missionary converts the cannibals to Christianity and they are released and sail home.

The characters are well-defined: Ralph, the deep-thinking narrator; Jack, the bold leader; and Peterkin, the follower. The action moves along swiftly, and there are some outstanding descriptive scenes, although, since Ballantyne never himself visited the Pacific, we are left to wonder how accurate his descriptions really are.

The Coral Island was one of the most popular nineteenth-century adventure stories. Robert Louis Stevenson was thrilled by it as a boy, and it is easy to see the influence Ballantyne's book had on *Treasure Island*. In the twentieth century, William Golding also took inspiration from the book for his *Lord of the Flies*, where the main characters, Jack, Ralph, and Piggy, find out what might really happen if boys were left to fend for themselves in the wild. **CW**

Twentieth-century watercolor illustration by John Millar Watt. 

Eric, or Little by Little 1858

Frederic W. Farrar

Nationality | English, born 1831
Publisher | A. and C. Black, UK
Theme | School, Friendship, Classics, Young adult

School stories, with their depictions of compulsory sport, bad food, and bullies who get what they deserve, were very popular among children in Victorian England. *Eric, or Little by Little* was one of the most well-loved school books during the period and tells the tale of a schoolboy's tragic downfall. Eric is not a hero but a cautionary figure, and the author makes it clear that his behavior should not be copied.

Eric is the son of British parents stationed in India. As was common at the time, he is sent to Britain to be educated at a boarding school. Eric is full of good intentions, but in a bid to impress his fellow pupils, he succumbs to temptation: he lies, cheats, smokes, and drinks. Despite the dying pleas of his best friend Edwin Russell to change his ways, Eric does not. He runs away to sea, but he hates life aboard ship and returns home before repenting on his deathbed.

Farrar set out to write a moral story that could serve as a warning. He says: "The story of Eric was written with but one single object: the vivid inculcation of inward purity and moral purpose by the history of a boy who, in spite of the inherent nobleness of his disposition, falls into all folly and wickedness, until he has learnt to seek help from above."

Due to its overtly religious tone, the book has fallen out of favor. However, it contains some lively scenes of pillow fights, games, and visits to the pub, which one suspects were the main reasons it was so popular with boys in the nineteenth century. **HJ**

Captain Fracasse 1863

Théophile Gautier

Original Title | Le Capitaine Fracasse
Nationality | French, born 1811
Publisher | Unknown, France
Theme | Adventure, Classics, Historical fiction

Set in the mid-seventeenth century, *Captain Fracasse* is an archetypal cloak-and-dagger classic of children's literature. The Baron of Sigognac is the sole inheritor of a ruined castle in Gascogne—the vestige of a noble family who dedicated their lives to protecting the interests of the kings of France. He hosts an errant theater troupe for one night and decides to accompany them on their journey to Paris, where he intends to appeal to the court of King Louis. The demise of one of the actors spurs him to join the troupe, under the guise of Captain Fracasse, and to protect the honor of Isabelle, fellow actress and love interest, whom he has to protect against the pursuit of the duke of Vallombreuse. Hidden identities are unmasked and duels fought are before the fairy-tale resolution.

The novel is a tribute to baroque literature, with its excessive descriptions, and it borrows from the commedia dell'arte in the comic characters of the captain and Isabella. The boundaries between theater and narrative are consistently blurred in this delightful tale, which only heightens the experience of reading a novel that explores the rich history of France and its medieval tradition of courtship and chivalry. Gautier was a poet, novelist, and critic and was a painter before he turned to writing. He believed the only purpose of a work of art was its intrinsic beauty and that words should be used just as the painter uses his brush and paints. He was among those who inspired the movement against Romanticism. **AR**

Journey to the Center of the Earth 1864

Jules Verne

Original Title | Voyage au centre de la terre
Nationality | French, born 1828
Publisher | Pierre-Jules Hetzel, France
Theme | Classics, Science fiction, Adventure

Along with British author H. G. Wells, French novelist Jules Verne is credited as the inventor of science fiction. Many of his works are concerned with travel by sea, air, land, and space by both conventional and fantastical means. *Journey to the Center of the Earth* tells the story of an underground voyage of a small group of people to find the Earth's core. Verne's depictions of the Earth's interior are speculative and given what scientists know today, they are far from realistic. Nevertheless, the spirit of derring-do and exploration can still be appreciated as a work of fantasy.

The leader of the expedition is German professor Otto Liedenbrock, who lives in Hamburg with his housekeeper, Martha, his seventeen-year-old goddaughter, Grauben, and his nephew, Axel, an orphan who has become his laboratory assistant. The story begins with the professor and Axel unraveling the runic code of an old Icelandic saga. The code reveals that an Icelandic alchemist, Arne Saknussemm, found the entrance to a passage leading to the center of the Earth. The professor sets off for Iceland to locate the passage, said to be the crater of a volcano, and his level-headed nephew reluctantly goes with him. The pair hire a guide when they reach Iceland, Hans Bjelke. The story sees the trio frequently risk life and limb as they encounter many dangers in Verne's subterranean world of strange gases, seas, and magma, as well as prehistoric animals, plants, and humans before eventually coming to the surface in southern Italy. **CK**

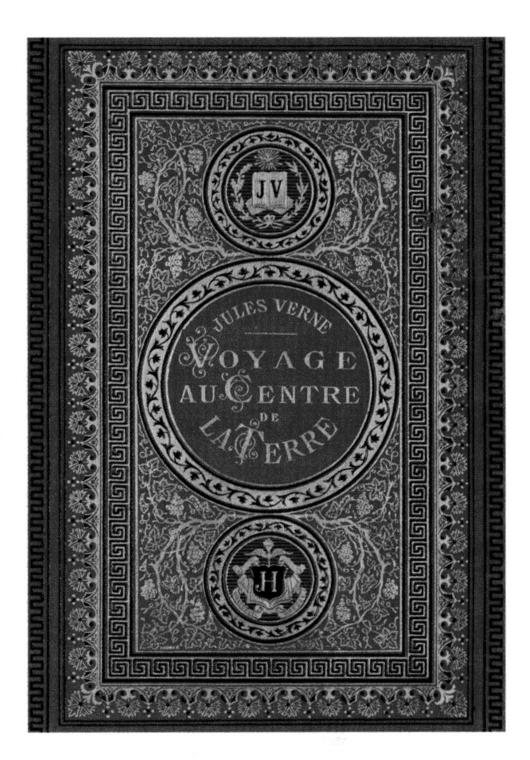

"Was I to believe him in earnest in his intention to penetrate to the center of this massive globe?"

OTHER GREAT READS BY JULES VERNE

20,000 Leagues Under the Sea (20,000 lieues sous les mers), 1869
Around the World in 80 Days (Le Tour du monde en 80 jours), 1873
The Mysterious Island (L'Ile mysterieuse), 1875

The Good Little Devil 1865

Comtesse de Ségur   Horace Castelli

Nationality | French, born Sophie Rostopchine, 1799 (author); French, born 1825 (illustrator)
Publisher | Hachette, France
Theme | Family, Friendship

12+

The story of this good little devil (*Un Bon petit diable*) is set in Scotland in the mid-nineteenth century. Charles, who is twelve years old, is being brought up by his elderly cousin Mac'Miche. She is in charge of the money that his father has left him. But widow Mac'Miche is an extremely miserly woman. Besides her hope of laying her hands on her young cousin's money, she makes his life a misery, refusing to feed him properly and making him wear rags. But her cruelty does not stop there: she locks him up in a storage room and beats him up for the slightest reason. Fortunately the young boy has a strong character and he has more than one trick up his sleeve. With the help of Betty, the maid, and driven by a fertile imagination,

"He goes from one extreme to the other; as sweet as anything or as wicked as a devil."

Charles invents all sorts of ruses involving fairies or the devil to terrify the old lady, who is very superstitious. And when Charles is upset he goes to visit his blind young cousin Juliette who comforts him. She always finds the right words to calm him down when he is angry and thinking of revenge. It is thanks to her that our young hero finds the strength to forgive and gradually learns to be patient and wise.

In *The Good Little Devil*, the Comtesse de Ségur has for the first time chosen a boy as the main character. Like the heroine in *The Misfortunes of Sophie*, he has to put up with constant punishments because he is considered unruly, but he too will be influenced by the example of people around him to grow up and improve himself. The dialogue that punctuates the narrative adds liveliness and cheerfulness to the otherwise sad story of Charles's life. **SL**

OTHER GREAT READS BY THE COMTESSE

***The Misfortunes of Sophie,* 1858**
***The Memoirs of an Ass,* 1860**
***Jean Who Grumbles and Jean Who Laughs,* 1865**
***The Bad Genie,* 1867**
***Diloy the Tramp,* 1868**

"At the sight of the devils and the smoke, Madame Mac'Miche shouted with terror." 

Adèle Geras reviews:

Little Women 1868

Louisa May Alcott May Alcott

Nationality | American, born 1832 (author); American, born Abigail Alcott 1840 (illustrator)
Publisher | Roberts Brothers, USA
Theme | Classics, Family, Historical fiction

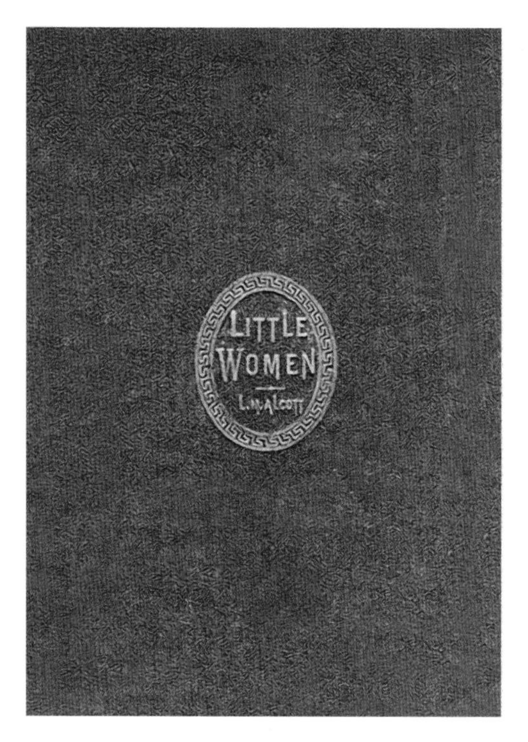

I am an only child, and one of the main reasons I've always loved this book is because it is about four sisters. It seemed to me that there was something deeply glamorous about being part of a big family. My favorite sister is Jo, whose ambition is to be a writer, and who approaches life bravely and acts impulsively but courageously throughout the novel.

The setting of the book appeals to me as well. It begins just before Christmas, with the father of the family away from home and fighting in a war. There is snow outside. There isn't any money for presents, but the girls of the March family have their loving and admirable mother, Marmee, to look after them, and they have one another.

"'Christmas won't be Christmas without any presents,' grumbled Jo, lying on the rug."

Each of the sisters comes alive as we read. We come to know each of them as well as if they were our own real sisters. There's good Meg, who tries to look after the others; clever Jo, who chafes against all the restrictions of a young woman's life in the nineteenth century; dreamy Beth; and pretty Amy, who is spoiled, vain, and silly but still a delight.

On one level, this is a domestic story of winning through in spite of troubles and poverty; a tale of the strength and beauty of the family and of how love can carry you through the worst of times. But there is also humor, high drama, and even tragedy, and through the story the four marvelous March sisters invite us in to share their lives. For those who love it, the story continues in *Good Wives* and *Jo's Boys* but nothing is quite as good as *Little Women*, which is a delicious treat of a book.

MORE CLASSIC FICTIONAL SISTERS

***Pride and Prejudice* by Jane Austen, 1813**
***Ballet Shoes* by Noel Streatfeild, 1936**
***I Capture the Castle* by Dodie Smith, 1956**
***Jacob Have I Loved* by Katherine Paterson, 1980**

The frontispiece from the 1880 Good Tone Library edition.

20,000 Leagues Under the Sea 1869

Jules Verne

Original Title | 20,000 lieues sous les mers
Nationality | French, born 1828
Publisher | Pierre-Jules Hetzel, France
Theme | Science fiction, Adventure, Classics

OTHER SCIENCE FICTION CLASSICS

The Time Machine by H. G. Wells, 1895
Foundation by Isaac Asimov, 1951
The Midwich Cuckoos by John Wyndham, 1957
The Guardians by John Christopher, 1970
Z for Zachariah by Robert C. O'Brien, 1975

20,000 Leagues Under the Sea follows the fortunes of rebellious Captain Nemo and his submarine *Nautilus* as it charts the depths of the world's seas encountering strange marine life, sperm whales, sharks, cannibals, giant squid, and hurricanes. The narrator of the story is French marine biologist Professor Pierre Aronnax, who sets out on an expedition financed by the U.S. government to find a strange sea monster, aided by his Flemish assistant and master of classification, Conseil, and a Canadian harpooner, Ned Land. The sea monster turns out to be Nemo's *Nautilus*, and the trio join the renegade exploring life underwater including the ice shelves of the Antarctic, the Indian Ocean, the Red Sea, the Mediterranean, the Atlantic, and the mythical lost city of Atlantis. Yet the professor and his companions are held prisoner by the mysterious Nemo, who is in self-imposed exile on his submarine. As much as they are fascinated by what they see and experience, they are all keen to escape.

"The deepest parts of the ocean are totally unknown to us. What goes on in those distant depths?"

The book is fascinating for Verne's accounts of natural phenomena from corals to volcanoes, and for his depiction of a large submarine years before such a vessel was built. But above all it is the characters that make the story: the professor, spellbound by what he witnesses but repelled by Nemo's morals, and the intriguing personality of the captain himself, ruthless and anarchic, yet part-genius and not without compassion. The reason the captain has chosen the life of an outcast is not explained, but Verne fleshed out his antihero in a later novel, *The Mysterious Island*. **CK**

What Katy Did 1872

Susan Coolidge

Nationality | American, born Sarah Chauncey Woolsey 1835
Publisher | Roberts Brothers, USA
Theme | Classics, Family, Friendship

Twelve-year-old Katy Carr is a tomboy living with her widowed father and five siblings in a small town. Being a "little mother" to her siblings is hard work, and bright, imaginative Katy is constantly in trouble, particularly with her Aunt Izzie, who looks after the children. Katy dreams of someday doing something "grand" with her life, as well as wanting to be "beautiful, of course, and good if I can." When invalid cousin Helen comes to visit, Katy is so enthralled with her ethereal beauty that she resolves to model herself on her. All too soon, though, Katy suffers a serious accident and becomes bedridden. Bad-tempered and bitter, she alienates her family until a visit from Helen opens her eyes to the "school of pain," in which she learns patience, cheerfulness, hopefulness, and to make the best of things. So Katy grows up; she becomes a better person and finally learns to walk again.

"... Katy tore her dress every day, hated sewing, and didn't care a button about being 'good,'..."

For modern readers, the book splits in two. In the first half, Susan Coolidge's lively, affectionate recounting of the children's plots and plays still captivates. Episodes such as Katy's "adoption" of a poor baby or her befriending of a criminal forger and the monstrously affected girl Imogen are sharply observed social comedy. In the earlier chapters, the children's conversations mingle with their elders' exasperation and the voices of small-town gossip in colloquial gusto. With the arrival of Helen, however, Coolidge brings the social codes of invalidism and genteel womanhood to bear ever more heavily on poor Katy, until the stern Christian abnegation of the "happy" ending is won by suffering. **VN**

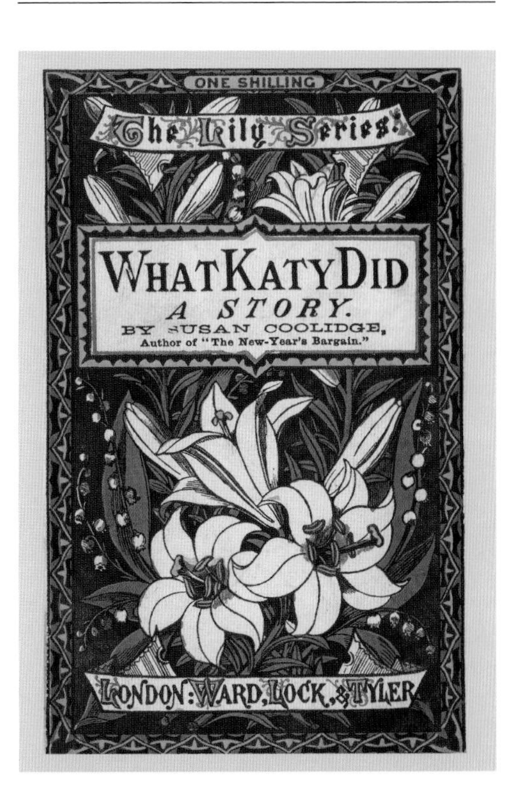

MORE BOOKS WITH STRONG-WILLED GIRLS

Caddie Woodlawn by Carol Ryrie Bank, 1935
I Capture the Castle by Dodie Smith, 1949
Zazie in the Metro by Raymond Queneau, 1959
Hating Alison Ashley by Robin Klein, 1985
Ruby in the Smoke by Philip Pullman, 1985

Around the World in 80 Days 1873

Jules Verne

Original Title | Le Tour du monde en 80 jours
Nationality | French, born 1828
Publisher | Pierre-Jules Hetzel, France
Theme | Classics, Adventure, Love

French author Jules Verne wrote this classic tale when the concept of travel via the new innovations of train and steamer was fresh, exciting, and exotic. The idea of circumnavigating the globe in a set time has been copied and emulated ever since. It captured both the public and the creative imagination and Verne's novel has been adapted for stage, television, and cinema.

Pedantic, wealthy Englishman Phileas Fogg, places a wager of £20,000 among his friends at a gentlemen's club in London that he can make a trip around the world in eighty days. Such a short period of time requires a feat of planning and mathematical precision, and he is aided in his endeavor by his newly hired, blustering French valet, Passepartout.

The pair plan a trip that will take them from London to Suez, Bombay, Calcutta, Hong Kong, Yokohama, San Francisco, New York, and back to London. Inevitably not all goes as planned, and the duo sometimes have to make alternative arrangements, at one point, even traveling by elephant. Their adventure is made more difficult by a case of mistaken identity. A detective from Scotland Yard, Fix, becomes convinced that Fogg is a bank robber on the run, and he decides to doggedly pursue his quarry. Fogg also fails to take into account the effect that the young woman he meets en route, Aouda, will have on his plans. A romance develops between them that humanizes the finicky Fogg and his dull, daily routine. This book is amusing and well plotted, and it has stood the test of time. **CK**

Heidi's Wandering and Learning Years 1880

Johanna Spyri

Original Title | Heidis Lehr- und Wanderjahre
Nationality | Swiss, born 1827
Publisher | Perthes Verlag, Germany
Theme | Family, Friendship, Favorite characters

Although it has been made into many films, there is nothing more rewarding than returning to the original book of *Heidi*. Even though the religious messages can be cloying to contemporary tastes, it is impossible not to be touched by the relationship between the child and the grumpy old grandfather.

After being unceremoniously dumped on the old man by her Aunt Dete, Heidi begins an idyllic life with Grandfather, the goats, and Peter the goatherd. Through her natural goodness she melts Grandfather's heart. He eventually overcomes his hostility to the villagers and gradually renews old friendships, particularly with Peter's grandmother.

One day Aunt Dete unexpectedly takes Heidi to Frankfurt as a companion to the invalid child, Clara. Heidi has lessons with Clara and learns to read with the help of Clara's grandmother but suffers under the rule of the housekeeper Fraulein Rottenmeier. Away from the freedom of the mountains, Heidi becomes ill and is seen sleepwalking. At first the servants and Fraulein Rottenmeier take her for a ghost. Eventually the kindly doctor makes a correct diagnosis, and Heidi returns to Grandfather. Clara visits Heidi, and when Peter pushes her wheelchair over the mountain in a fit of jealousy, Clara learns to walk again to the astonishment of her grandmother and father. With the exception of Fraulein Rottenmeier, everyone who comes into contact with Heidi is transformed in some way in this classic book. **WO**

Geschichten für Kinder und Solche welche Kinder lieb haben

Heidis Lehr- und Wanderjahre

von

Johanna Spyri

Gotha

Friedrich Andreas Perthes.

THE FIFTH FORM AT ST. DOMINIC'S

The Fifth Form at St. Dominic's 1881

Talbot Baines Reed

Nationality | English, born 1852
Publisher | Religious Tract Society, UK
Theme | Classics, School, Friendship, Historical fiction

Rather ironically, Talbot Baines Reed did not go to private school, despite building his career on stories that celebrated an all-male boarding education. *Fifth Form at St. Dominic's* was first published as chapters in *Boy's Own*. The magazine was meant to be improving, but its popularity depended on the stories it serialized, of which *St. Dominic's* was one of the best known.

The book follows shy new pupil Stephen as he starts at his older brother's school. Stephen is forced to fag (be a servant to a senior boy) for the bully Loman, who beats Stephen badly the first time he refuses to obey him. Although his older brother happily fits in at the school, Stephen is angered by the unjust social systems that have been in place for years. Although he hatches plans to defeat his oppressors, ultimately he is powerless to stop them. By the end of the novel he has decided to toughen up to fit in and finally defeats Loman.

The boarding-school atmosphere is depicted as liberating, because there are no parents around, but equally constricting, because the boys have their own suffocating society governed by their rules and secret codes. Boarding-school stories were the subject of all of Baines Reed's work, and *Fifth Form at St. Dominic's* is often credited with keeping the genre alive. Although the number of children who attend boarding school is dwindling, the genre has remained popular, with high-profile examples such as Enid Blyton's Malory Towers series and, of course, the Harry Potter books **SD**

With Clive in India 1884

George Alfred Henty

Nationality | English, born 1832
Publisher | Blackie and Son, UK
Theme | Adventure, Historical fiction, Classics, War

Charlie Maryatt is sent to India to become a clerk in the British East India Company. This is 1751, when the British and French are struggling for control of India. Charlie is a hero in the true sense of the word: a model to aspire to, with no bad qualities or moral doubts: "He was honourable and manly . . . a prime favorite with his masters as well as his schoolfellows." He soon abandons inactive office life in India to volunteer for action under the British military leader Clive. Charlie's adventures take him through battles and sieges, tiger hunts and pirate encounters, quick-witted escapes and daring rescues until, after ten years in India, he returns to England having made his fortune.

Henty was the leading writer of stories for boys in the last two decades of the nineteenth century, producing around eighty novels and books of short stories, mostly involving a young hero at the center of historical events. *With Clive in India* is a tale of derring-do, with all the jingoism and enthusiasm for warfare that were prevalent in Britain during the Victorian era, as well as the race and class stereotypes. To modern readers this may seem more like a history book with an adventure story tacked on, as thirty pages go past at a time with no mention at all of our hero. Henty prided himself on his historical accuracy, and his former career as a war correspondent is evident in the descriptions of the military campaigns, while the sections involving Charlie's adventures are as fast-paced as you would expect from any good adventure story. **CW**

Kidnapped 1886

Robert Louis Stevenson

Nationality | Scottish, born 1850
Publisher | Cassell, UK
Theme | Historical fiction, Classics, Adventure, Friendship

In *Kidnapped*, Robert Louis Stevenson crystallized the legend of noble Highland Jacobites, just as he had shaped sea adventure stories in *Treasure Island*. *Kidnapped* works on two levels—first as a tale of a young man's growing wisdom and second as an exposé of the distortions forced on Scottish society by English rule. David Balfour is kidnapped at the behest of his wicked uncle, who wants to steal his inheritance and sell him into slavery. All seems lost, when David overhears the brutal ship's officers plotting to kill a wealthy Jacobite passenger, Alan Breck. The two band together to defeat the ship's crew. Returning to Scotland, they are shipwrecked and separated, but fight their way back together. David kills the dastardly head of the Campbell clan, Breck's sworn enemy. Thus begins their epic flight through the Highland heather, surviving dragoons, bandit chiefs, and murderous bagpipe players. Finally, David enlists a canny lawyer and regains his inheritance.

Kidnapped played its part in the nineteenth-century revival of pride in the Highland heritage, spearheaded by Sir Walter Scott's popularization of clan tartan. The noblest characters are shown to be those untainted by English commerce, greed, sycophancy, and deceit; inhumanity and cruelty are shown to be inherent in the violence of colonialism. Based on a real-life incident, Stevenson's writing goes deeper; readers empathize with the rebels fleeing persecution through the wild beauty of the Scottish mountains and moorland. The tale is simply told, with a fair mixture of dialect but with clear plot lines. **VN**

Heart 1886

Edmondo De Amicis

Original Title | Cuore
Nationality | Italian, born 1846
Publisher | Treves, Italy
Theme | School, Historical fiction

This is the fictional diary of Enrico Bottini, a ten-year-old boy at a Turin municipal school. The diary includes not only Enrico's thoughts, but also the observations of Enrico's parents and older siblings, who sometimes correspond with him through his diary.

In addition, the diary reports some of the reading homework given to Enrico by his teacher—stories about Italian children acting as role models for Enrico and his classmates. The stories are given in full, as if written by Enrico. Most of them revolve around moral values, the most prominent of which are helping those in need, love for family and friends, and, last but not least, patriotism. The insistence on patriotism is not surprising given the book is set during Italy's newfound national unity. Its author had fought in the siege of Rome in 1870. The book was primarily written to encourage young people to appreciate national unity. Many episodes foster the tolerance of regional differences. At one point a schoolmaster introduces a new pupil with the words: "Remember well what I am going to say. That this fact might come to pass—that a Calabrian boy might find himself at home in Turin, and that a boy of Turin might be in his own home in Calabria, our country has struggled for fifty years, and thirty thousand Italians have died."

The book is often emotional, even sentimental, but gives a vivid picture of urban Italian life at the time, and emphasizes the importance of moral values. Internationally popular, it has been translated into more than twenty-five languages and is part of the UNESCO Collection of Representative Works. **LB**

N. C. Wyeth's illustration of the fleeing murderer from the 1929 American edition.

Seven Little Australians 1894

Ethel Turner

Nationality | English/Australian, born 1872
Publisher | Ward, Lock and Bowden, Australia
Theme | School, Young adult, Family, Friendship, Love

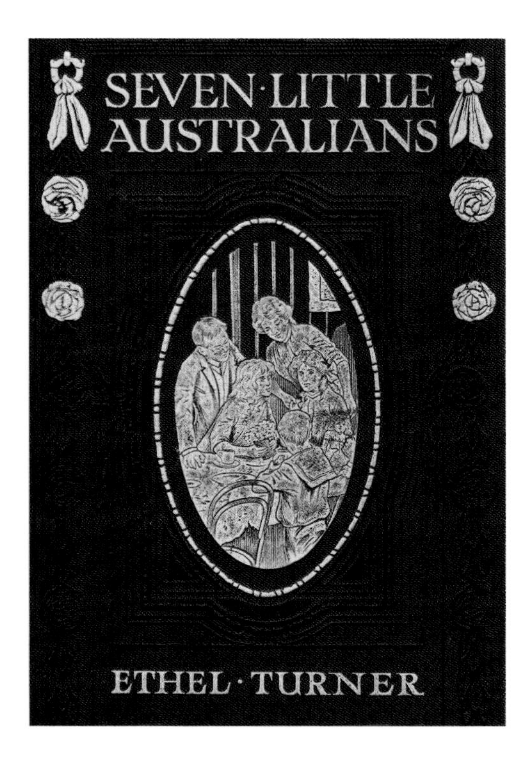

MORE ENJOYABLE FAMILY STORIES

The Family at Misrule by Ethel Turner, 1895
Friday's Tunnel by John Verney, 1959
Nobody's Family Is Going To Change by Louise Fitzhugh, 1974
Sarah Plain and Tall by Patricia MacLachlan, 1985

Beloved by generations of young readers, *Seven Little Australians* has never been out of print since its first publication. Ethel Turner began writing while attending the renowned Sydney Girls High School, and this was the first of her many novels.

The story is about an army officer's brood of unruly children, although the escapades that Turner presents are mild in comparison with the gritty young adult fiction being published a century later. Captain Woolcot, a father of seven who seems bewildered by his children, struggles to do his best to give the children a decent upbringing but fails to appreciate that a family is not an army platoon. Widowed, he has remarried, and his much younger wife, Esther—the mother of his seventh child, a two-year-old nicknamed "The General"—also finds it difficult to discipline her stepchildren.

> *"'Seven of you, and I'm only twenty!' she said pitifully. 'Oh! It's too bad!'"*

Far from being stereotypically naughty children, Turner's characters are engagingly real. Sixteen-year-old Meg wallows in sentimental ideas of romance and learns that this can have a dark side. Greedy Bunty must learn to stop blaming others. Thirteen-year-old Helen, always known as Judy, is the main character and the passionate heart of the family. She is close to her brother Pip and is wild, inventive, and intuitive, with a fierce intelligence and zest for life. As much in love as in anger, her father banishes her to boarding school following an escapade he believes made him look foolish in the eyes of his men. And so begins a chain of circumstances leading to heroism, heartbreak, and changed lives. **MH**

12+

The Prisoner of Zenda 1894

Anthony Hope

Nationality | English, born 1863
Publisher | J. W. Arrowsmith, UK
Theme | Classics, Adventure, Love, Historical fiction

This romantic adventure story will appeal to most age groups. It has all the necessary magic ingredients: a dashing hero, royalty, a fair princess, a swashbuckling villain, and the original Ruritanian setting. Rudolf Rassendyll is an English gentleman who bears an uncanny resemblance to the about-to-be crowned king of Ruritania; he might even be related to the royal owing to a dalliance by an ancestor many years before. Rudolf is looking for a change from his boring and rather dissolute life, and finds it when he decides on a whim to take a holiday to attend the coronation of his Ruritanian double.

His resemblance to the future king helps loyal retainers cover up the king's abduction by his half brother Duke Michael. But what is initially supposed to be an interim arrangement for the coronation ceremony ends up lasting longer than originally planned. Rudolf complicates things by falling in love with the beautiful Princess Flavia, who returns his affection, believing that he is the real king and that he has abandoned his hard-drinking, playboy ways.

"At that moment I believed—I almost believed—that I was in very truth the King . . . "

Despite this turn of events, Rudolf masterminds a plot to rescue the by-then ailing king, and honor is satisfied, although Rupert of Hentzau, the swashbuckling villain, escapes to live again in a sequel *Rupert of Hentzau*. However, Rudolf and Flavia have to go their separate ways because the princess chooses duty over her personal happiness. There is plenty of pace and action—including sword fights, an escape via the moat, and a damsel in distress—in this Dumas-like page-turner. **JF**

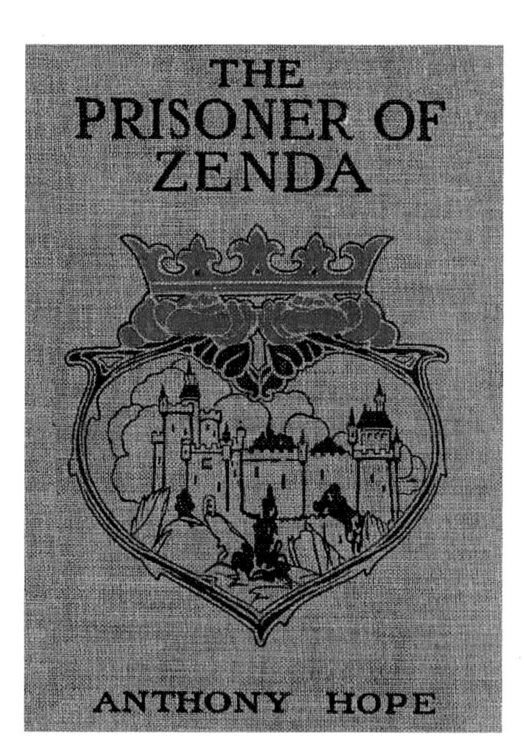

OTHER GREAT TALES OF ADVENTURE

The Three Musketeers by Alexandre Dumas, 1844
Rupert of Hentzau by Anthony Hope, 1898
Captain Blood by Raphael Sabatini, 1922
The Happy Return by C. S. Forester, 1937
The Silver Sword by Ian Serraillier, 1956

12+

The Treasure in Silver Lake 1894

 Karl May

Nationality | German, born 1842
Publisher | Union Deutsche Verlagsgesellschaft, Germany
Theme | Adventure

12+

No other writer has shaped the image of the Wild West for generations of German teenagers better than Karl May. *The Treasure in Silver Lake* (in German *Der Schatz am Silbersee*) is a classic adventure novel in which Old Firehand and the author's alter ego, Old Shatterhand, lead a group of men to Silver Lake in the Rocky Mountains to exploit a silver mine.

The first half of the novel describes how the legendary hunter Old Firehand and his loyal friends fight a group of bandits led by the Red Cornel, Brinkley. Brinkley himself wants to make it to Silver Lake, to recover a hidden treasure using a map he has stolen, and he will stop at nothing to realize his plan. Eventually, however, Old Firehand and his friends manage to foil Brinkley's schemes, and the bandits are defeated. In the second half of the narrative, the brave hunter Old Shatterhand and the Apache chief Winnetou, a "noble savage" in the Romantic tradition, join Old Firehand and his friends, who have to deal with hostile Indian tribes on their way to find their fortunes at Silver Lake.

"Old Firehand is my name because no enemy escapes the fire from my rifle."

Although by today's standards this book is sometimes racist and clichéd, May's vivid narrative conveys the lure the Wild West had when the New World was the favored destination for many European immigrants. Interestingly, the author did not visit North America until long after he wrote the novels that he set there. Although there are a number of extremely violent scenes in the novel, good always prevails over evil, and some of the Native Americans are portrayed as exceptionally virtuous. **FHG**

OTHER GREAT TREASURE HUNTERS

Treasure Island by Robert Louis Stevenson, 1883
Winnetou, The Treasure of Nugget Mountain by Karl May, 1898
The Story of the Treasure Seekers by E. Nesbit, 1899
Gold Dust by Geraldine McCaughrean, 1993

Eclipse of the Crescent Moon 1899

Géza Gárdonyi

Eclipse of the Crescent Moon is a sweeping historical epic full of daring and courage, action and adventure, and heroes and villains. It is a Hungarian classic that is still much loved by children and adults. It was recently voted one of the nation's favorite books.

At the heart of the novel is a fictionalized account of the 1522 Siege of Eger, in which a small castle, commanded by the real-life Hungarian hero Istvan Dobo is besieged by some 200,000 Turkish troops. The central character, however, is Gergely Bornemissza, an orphan boy whose numerous adventures we follow from the age of eight until he is in his mid-thirties.

As a child, Gergely is captured by the Turks along with his childhood friend Eva. They are forced to join a group of other prisoners marching across the countryside but, through a great deal of cunning and bravery, the children manage to escape. Gergely is then educated by a rich aristocrat, and Eva is pledged in marriage to a wealthy older man. Sometime later, Gergely and Eva meet again, fall in love, and elope. After a series of adventures, the couple, now married, arrive in Eger, where Gergely joins Dobo's troops. When Gergely's small son is kidnapped, Eva disguises herself as a man to recover him. After a long and bloody battle, the Turks are defeated and Gergely's family is reunited.

Although *Eclipse of the Crescent Moon* is a long book at more than 500 pages and may appear daunting, there is enough action and excitement to keep young readers entertained, even if they are unaware of Hungarian history and culture. **HJ**

"The following day . . . the tents stood white on the hillsides, but there were no Turks to be seen."

Original Title | Egri csillagok
Nationality | Hungarian, born 1863
Publisher | *Pesti Hirlap*, Hungary
Theme | Historical fiction, Classics

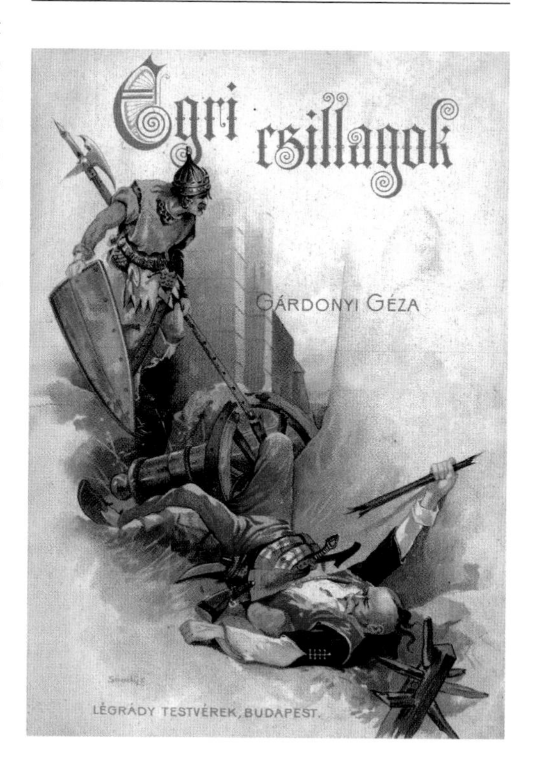

MORE ADVENTURES TO ENJOY

Slave of the Huns by Géza Gárdonyi, 1901
The Cave Children by Alois T. Sonnleitner, 1918
Countdown by Ben Mikaelsen, 1996
The Pirate's Son by Geraldine McCaughrean, 1998
The City of Beasts by Isabel Allende, 2002

12+

The Tigers of Mompracem 1900

Emilio Salgari Pipein Gamba

Nationality | Italian, born 1862 (author); Italian, born G. Garuti birth date unknown (illustrator)
Publisher | Donath, Italy
Theme | Historical fiction, Adventure

OTHER SANDOKAN ADVENTURES

The Pirates of Malaysia (I Pirati della Malesia), 1896
The Two Tigers (Le due Tigri), 1904
King of the Sea (Il Re del Mare), 1906
Sandokan Fights Back (Sandokan alla Riscossa), 1907
The Brahman (Il Bramino dell'Assam), 1911

This work is part of the first series of adventure books that Emilio Salgari wrote. *The Tigers of Mompracem* was originally published in Italian under the title *Le Tigri di Mompracem*. The series is set in Asia, and the hero of the adventures is Sandokan, the famous "Tiger of Malaysia." Together with his Portuguese friend, Yanez de Gomera, Sandokan fights the English to win back his rightful throne, which was taken during the British colonization of India. The narrative is rich in action and dialogue, giving insight into Sandokan's motives and thinking. The exotic setting includes the tropical rain forests of Borneo, the South China Sea, the fictional island of Mompracem, and the Indian Subcontinent.

"Let them try and challenge the pirates in their lair! I shall darken the waters with their blood."

As well as fighting to regain his throne and protect his island home, Sandokan must free the woman known as the Pearl of Labuan. She is Marianna Guillonk, a half-English, half-Italian woman who took the charming Sandokan into her confidence when he secretly stayed in her palace. Above all, however, Sandokan is up against his enemy James Brooke, the White Rajah of Sarawak and Marianna's uncle. Like Salgari's other great romantic hero, the Black Corsair, Sandokan is a pirate who stands against colonialism and seeks to free the oppressed. Both heroes give free reign to their emotions—at times even desperate tears.

The character of Sandokan has captured the imagination of many readers around the world; the books have been translated into several languages, and there have been several movie versions. **SMT**

12+

The Hound of the Baskervilles 1902

Arthur Conan Doyle

This tale of the ancient family of Dartmoor and the apparent persecution into early graves of its heirs by "a gigantic hound" represented Sir Arthur Conan Doyle's first concession to the hungry fans of his most famous character, Sherlock Holmes. The detective had "died" eight years earlier in a standoff with his foe Moriarty at the Reichenbach Falls. Conan Doyle was concerned about becoming trapped as a writer of detective fiction but had not ruled out writing about Holmes again. In fact, he had a successful Holmes play opening in London when the first installment of *The Hound of the Baskervilles* (set before Holmes's "death") appeared in *The Strand* magazine. Such was the acclaim for the story that Holmes was resurrected

"As you value your life, or your reason, keep away from the moor."

in 1903 in "The Empty House"; it emerged that the detective had survived the tussle at the Falls thanks to his Japanese martial arts training.

The Hound of the Baskervilles is both a classic piece of detective fiction and a classic horror story, with deeply atmospheric passages and the exciting cliff-hangers required by the magazine installments. The story opens in the familiar setting of Holmes's study on Baker Street, as the great detective sets up a patronizing test for his sidekick Watson to display his own deductive powers. Holmes is determined that logic and deduction will disprove the myth that the beast of Dartmoor is supernatural. While Watson accompanies the latest Baskerville heir to the scene of the terrors, Holmes appears to take a backseat only to reenter the narrative in a manner that is almost a resurrection in itself. **CK**

Nationality | Scottish, born 1859
Publisher | George Newnes, UK
Theme | Detective stories, Horror, Classics, Favorite characters

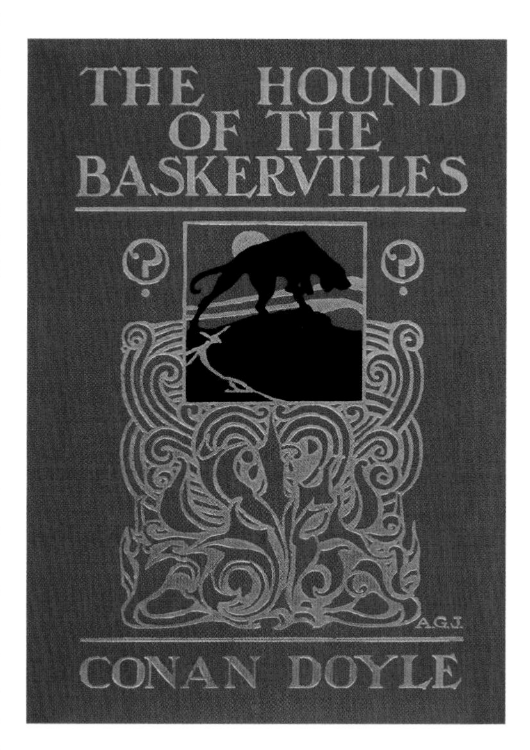

MORE CLASSIC READS BY CONAN DOYLE

A Study in Scarlet, 1887
The Sign of Four, 1890
The Adventures of Sherlock Holmes, 1892
The Memoirs of Sherlock Holmes, 1894
The Return of Sherlock Holmes, 1904

The Call of the Wild 1903

Jack London

Nationality | American, born 1876
Publisher | Macmillan, USA
Theme | Animal stories, Classics, Historical fiction

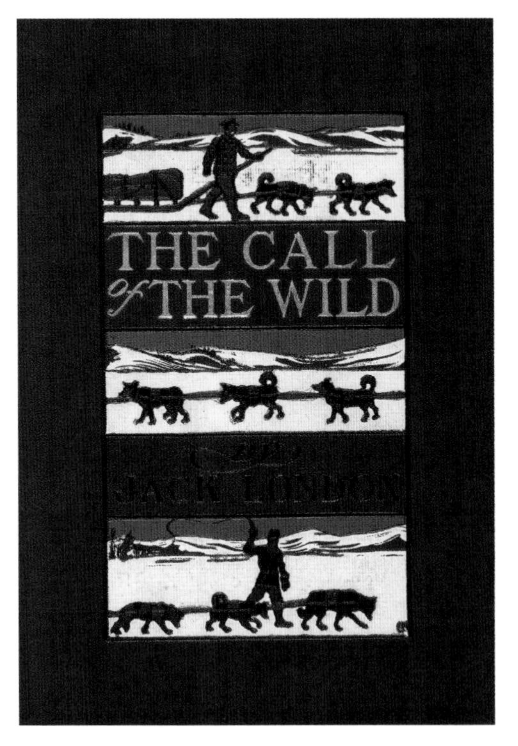

MORE TO ENJOY FROM JACK LONDON

White Fang, 1906
Before Adam, 1907
Martin Eden, 1909
The Scarlet Plague, 1912
The Valley of the Moon, 1913

If there were ever a writer whose vigorous life was truly reflected in his writing, it would have to be Jack London. Born into a poor family that he had left by the age of seventeen to become a sailor in Japan, London's lust for travel and adventure laid the foundation for his stories that were first published by the time he was only twenty-four. His atmospheric, lyrical writing consists of dashing adventures that take place in real settings. *The Call of the Wild* is regarded as one of London's best works.

The story focuses on a sheepdog called Buck, who begins the story as a tame domestic dog but finishes up leading a wolf pack. Buck's journey begins when he is sold to men heading for the Yukon gold rush.

"... he may be seen running at the head of the pack through the pale moonlight."

He is put to work as a sled dog and quickly learns to survive in the wild, regaining his natural instincts as he is passed from one owner to the next. London was fascinated by Darwin's theory of evolution, natural selection, and the survival of the fittest so, in many of the bleak and often violent scenes, he depicts nature at its cruelest in brutal detail, as well as the flimsy line between life and death.

Nearly beaten to death at one point, Buck is saved by a man called John Thorton, whom he befriends and protects until Thorton is killed himself by the Yeehat, a Native American tribe. This sends Buck into an uncontrollable rage, and he kills some of the tribe. With no way back, he returns to the wild and becomes the dominant male of a wolf pack. London delivers one of the most memorable depictions in literature of an animal's life. **NH**

Jolanda, Daughter of the Black Corsair 1905

Emilio Salgari   Alberto della Valle

In *Jolanda la figlia del Corsaro Nero*, the Black Corsair, after finding his lost love Honorata in Florida, returns to Ventimiglia in Piedmont. When the Black Corsair's ship, *La Folgore*, is left badly damaged, it is said that he has died in battle defending Piedmont against French invasion. Meanwhile, the lovely Honorata has died giving birth to Jolanda.

When Jolanda journeys to the Caribbean, the adventure begins anew. Jolanda is captured by a Spanish vessel. Morgan, who had saved the Corsair's ship, hears of her capture and goes to rescue her. In the process he discovers that the governor of Maracaibo, the Count of Medina, is none other than the son of the Black Corsair's old enemy, Van Guld.

"... dressed in black like her father, with a long feather in her hair and a sword on the right."

It is he who captured Jolanda on her arrival in the Caribbean. Morgan, together with Jolanda and his men, pursue the Count of Medina to Gibraltar, where he is in hiding after the attack on Maracaibo. The pirates experience the wildness of the ocean while crossing the Atlantic. Jolanda is once again captured, and an attack on the city of Panama ensues. Finally, Morgan wins a duel with the Count of Medina. The political situation between England and Spain changes, and Morgan, along with the other pirates, can retire. Morgan chooses to settle in Jamaica with Jolanda, where he becomes vice-governor and is knighted by the king of England.

In Salgari's tales, the hero is always in control and morally unquestionable. As the daughter of the Black Corsair, Jolanda follows in this tradition, although she has to rely on Morgan to rescue her. **SMT**

Nationality | Italian, born 1862 (author); Italian, born 1851 (illustrator)
Publisher | Donath, Italy
Theme | Adventure, Historical fiction

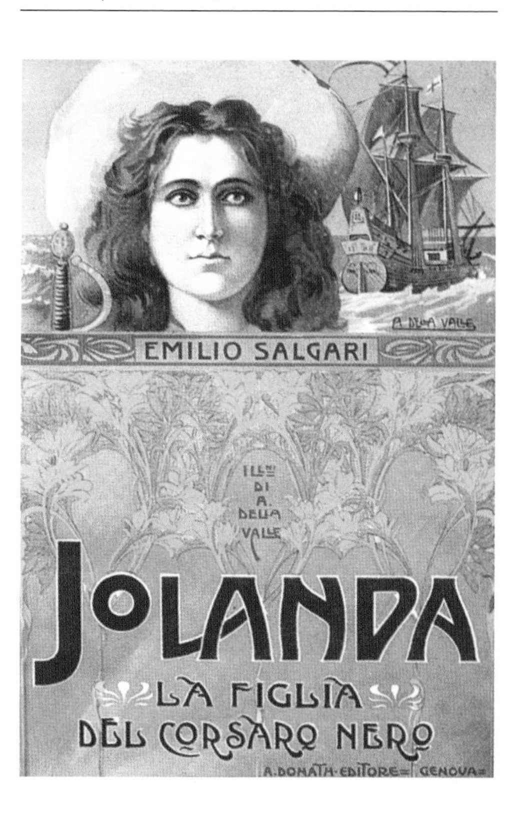

FURTHER EXCITING TALES BY SALGARI

The Black Corsair, 1898
Queen of the Caribbean, 1901
The Son of the Red Corsair, 1908
The Last of the Pirates, 1908

12+

White Fang 1906

Jack London

Nationality | American, born 1876
Publisher | Macmillan, USA
Theme | Animal stories, Classics, Adventure, Historical fiction

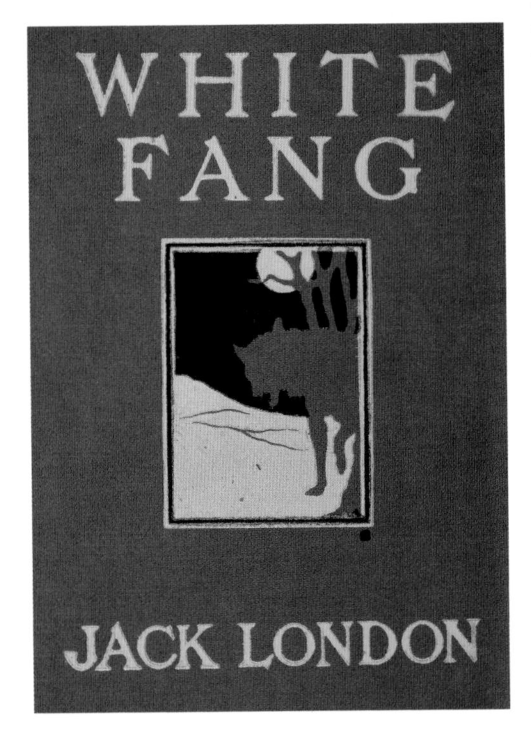

MORE CLASSIC ANIMAL STORIES

Jock of the Bushveld by Percy Fitzpatrick, 1907
Tarka the Otter by Henry Williamson, 1927
The Silver Brumby by Elyne Mitchell, 1958
War Horse by Michael Morpurgo, 1982
The Sight by David Clement-Davies, 2002

Published as a companion but not sequel to *The Call of the Wild*, this tells the opposite story of a wild wolf and his evolution into a domestic dog in the human world. The story opens in the beautiful, wide-open landscapes of the Yukon. Two men, Bill and Henry, are pulling a sled with a coffin strapped to it down a frozen stretch of water, pursued by a pack of wolves. The sled dogs are picked off by the wolves and then later one of the men leaves the fireside to never return. The last man, Henry, is rescued just in time by a search party mysteriously looking for the same coffin.

The second part of the novel switches back to the same story as viewed by the she-wolf of the marauding pack, who later gives birth to White Fang—part wolf, part sheep dog. The young pup passes through various masters, learning to survive and finally ending up in the hands of Beauty Smith, a cruel monster of a man. White Fang fights for his living and comes close to be being mauled to death by a bulldog, but is saved at the last minute.

"Dark spruce forest frowned on either side of the frozen waterway."

His new owner, Scott, tames White Fang and takes him back to California, where he becomes domesticated and even saves a member of Scott's family from an escaped criminal. White Fang has his own litter of pups playing around him in the final pages, a family he has with a Collie dog, and is now answering to the new name of "the blessed wolf."

With its precise style and blend of human and animal insights, *White Fang* portrays the equally violent worlds of animals and humans and how actions within those worlds ultimately seals one's fate. **NH**

12+

The Railway Children 1906

E. Nesbit

Nationality | English, born 1858
Publisher | Wells Gardner, Darton, UK
Theme | Classics, Family, Adventure, Historical fiction

One evening, two men arrive at Bobbie, Peter, and Phyllis's home in London and take their father away. Although clearly very upset, their mother asks the children not to ask where their father has gone, but Ruth the maid hints that something very nasty has happened: "If you don't mend your ways, you'll go straight where your precious Father's gone, so I tell you straight!" Money is now tight, so Mother dismisses the servants and they move to the country, where Mother spends all day writing stories to bring in money (as Nesbit herself did when her family was penniless).

The children become fascinated with the railway line that runs near the house, and make friends with Perks, the porter at the railway station. Each day they wave to a train they name the "Green Dragon," asking it to take their love to Father, and an old gentleman waves back. When Mother falls ill, the children appeal to the old gentleman for help, and he becomes a firm friend. The book is packed with incidents. The children become heroes when they prevent a disaster on the railway line; they rescue a destitute Russian émigré, and an injured boy lying in a tunnel. Then one day, Bobbie learns from an old newspaper that their father has been imprisoned for spying. She asks for the old gentleman's help once again, and he manages to get him released and the real criminal caught.

"They were not railway children to begin with. . . . They were just ordinary suburban children."

The Railway Children was faithfully made into a popular movie in 1970. It can be a little sentimental, but the ending, as Father appears on the railway platform and Bobbie cries: "Oh! my Daddy, my Daddy!" is genuinely moving. **CW**

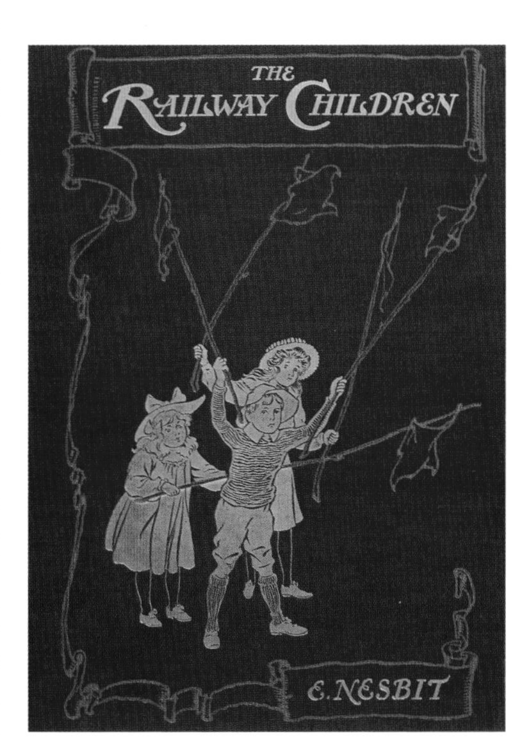

OTHER GREAT BOOKS BY E. NESBIT

The Story of the Treasure Seekers, 1898
The Wouldbegoods, 1899
Five Children and It, 1902
The Phoenix and the Carpet, 1904
The New Treasure Seekers, 1904

12+

The FORTUNES
of PHILIPPA
IES + QVA
by
ANGELA BRAZII

The Fortunes of Philippa 1906

Angela Brazil

Nationality | English, born 1868
Publisher | Blackie and Son, UK
Theme | School, Friendship, War, Historical fiction

Historically, Angela Brazil may have been the first author of girls' books to write her stories from the characters' points of view, although *The Fortunes of Philippa*, her second, is the only one in the first person. Perhaps this is because it fictionalizes her adored mother's childhood, when she came from Rio de Janeiro, only to be plunged straight into the life of a Victorian girls' boarding school. The book is also atypical of the more than forty that followed, in that it paints a gloomy picture of the bullying, oppressive school. Brazil was more concerned about entertaining than preaching. As she once said: "To be able to write for young people depends, I consider, largely upon whether you are able to retain your early attitude of mind while acquiring a certain facility with your pen."

She was perhaps the first author interested in the ups and downs of middle-class schoolgirls, from hockey to midnight feasts, not forgetting the tangle of emotional friendships. She reinvented her characters (with their extraordinary names such as Lesbia, Ethelburga, Morvyth) afresh with each volume. The girls speak in the slang of their time. Their attitudes, particularly in the books written during World War I, are similarly dated. Nonetheless, the pictures painted of teachers who are firm but fair, girls who flock together and apart with petty unkindnesses, girlish glee, and secret intimacies have not really changed all that much, at least in the United Kingdom. Rumors of a gay subtext remain rumors, and Brazil still has many devoted fans. **VN**

Jock of the Bushveld 1907

Percy Fitzpatrick E. Caldwell

Nationality | South African, born 1862 (author); South African, birth date unknown (illustrator)
Publisher | Longmans Green and Co., UK
Theme | Historical fiction, Animal stories

This is the true story of South African author Sir Percy Fitzpatrick who later recounted these stories as bed-time stories to his four children. In the days of the Transvaal gold rush in the 1880s, ox-wagon trains went back and forth to the mines with essential supplies. These journeys were long and hard. The men driving the wagons needed to hunt for meat to eat, which required a dog. The unnamed narrator of this story saves the runt of a litter from being drowned, even though he could have had the best of the litter. He calls him Jock and, despite being thin and ugly, the small puppy grows stronger and survives. Jock, a Staffordshire bull terrier, repays his new master by becoming his devoted companion and warrior.

There are many instances in the story of Jock refusing to give up on the hunt and finishing the quarry. He even chases a crocodile downriver and fights a baboon. When he becomes deaf after being kicked by a kudu antelope, Jock overcomes his disability and makes his other senses work overtime.

Eventually, after the oxen die from being bitten by tsetse flies, the narrator has to find other employment, and he reluctantly finds Jock a new home. There, Jock dies, mistakenly shot while defending his new master's property from another dog. Fitzpatrick recalls a way of life long gone and a tender friendship between man and his best friend in this classic South African story. It is beautifully illustrated in pen and ink by E. Caldwell. **JF**

The Mystery of the Yellow Room 1907

Gaston Leroux

Original Title | La mystère de la chambre jaune
Nationality | French, born 1868
Publisher | *L'Illustration*, France
Theme | Detective stories

12+

This mystery novel of the *huis-clos* or "locked-room" genre, revolves around the attempted murder of Miss Strangerson in the hermetically sealed Yellow Room at the Château du Glandier, which adjoins the scientific laboratory of her well-known father, Professor Strangerson. Joseph Rouletabille, an eighteen-year-old prodigy who works as a reporter for a famous Parisian newspaper, begins to unravel the mysteries surrounding this and subsequent attempts on Miss Strangerson's life—all of which are embroiled in numerous false leads. The mystery seems as impenetrable as the Yellow Room itself, thus shrouding the novel in an atmosphere of the supernatural, but this is itself a ploy to captivate the reader's imagination as well as acting as a distraction from the real crime. The true circumstances can be deduced through a method of pure reasoning that Rouletabille tirelessly extols and perfectly employs, as witnessed by his loyal friend, Mr. Sinclair, who is also the novel's narrator.

Gaston Leroux is most famous for *The Phantom of the Opera*. His Rouletabille seems more a precursor to Hergé's Tintin than a protégé of Sherlock Holmes, and not only because they share a similar round-headedness (the reason for the nickname, Rouletabille). The two intrepid reporters both represent a youthfulness that boldly, if naively, challenges and unravels the tangled adult world of politics and amorous intrigues. **AR**

A Girl of the Limberlost 1909

Gene Stratton-Porter W. T. Benda

Nationality | American, born 1863 (author); Polish, born 1873 (illustrator)
Publisher | Doubleday, Page and Co., USA
Theme | Love, Young adult, School

In the improbably romantic setting of an Indiana swamp, *A Girl of the Limberlost* tells the story of Elnora Comstock, a young impoverished girl living an isolated rural life with her grieving widowed mother.

As a photographer of wildlife with a keen interest in birds and moths, it is easy to see where Gene Stratton-Porter found her inspiration for this book. With both a scientific and romantic interest in wetlands and the creatures living in them, she has created a love story featuring a female role model whose patience and intelligence allow her to decode the world around her.

A coming-of-age story, the plot follows Elnora's progress from starting high school and suffering comparisons with her wealthier classmates, to finding the means to overcome her poverty. Through the help of a neighbor, Elnora realizes that by sourcing and selling moths from the swamp area, she can raise money to help continue her education. The lush, natural backdrop of the swamp inspires and motivates her, and when she discovers her late father's violin, a romantic musical world opens its doors to her.

Quiet, feminine Elnora is a traditional girl, but her strength of character and ability to recognize the important things in life make her an excellent example for young readers. Through hard work and perseverance, Elnora transcends her disadvantaged background, succeeds in coaxing her mother out of her grief, wins the respect of her peers and detractors, and finally, deservedly, begins to fall in love. **LK**

"Elnora ... gathered a few violets and gave them to Philip." 

The War of the Buttons 1912

Louis Pergaud

Original Title | La Guerre des boutons
Nationality | French, born 1882
Publisher | Gallimard, France
Theme | War, Friendship, Family

It is fall and, like every year, great battles are secretly taking place in the woods that border the French villages of Longeverne and Velrans. The great Lebrac, commander in chief of a proud army of soldiers in short pants, has gathered his troops following an insult from one of the "good-for-nothings" from the neighboring Velrans. During the school day, Lebrac and his gang try their hardest to answer Father Simon's formidable questions because they cannot possibly risk being held back at the end of the day.

As the tension mounts between the two sides, each boy in the Longeverne troop is assigned to a key position. Camus is made second lieutenant and Tintin is put in charge of the treasury. The rival bands then begin to wage a war without mercy. For those unlucky enough to be taken prisoner, the punishment is a humiliating one: the individual is spanked, undressed, and sent back with his pants around his ankles, with all of the buttons removed by the enemy as trophies. Lebrac and his army pull off a strategic coup by going into battle naked, but their triumph is short lived..

Some episodes in this philosophical story are truly savage. However, *The War of the Buttons* is also a playful novel, in which the world of childhood, at once tender and unforgiving, is marvelously described. The colorful, authentic words of the time—the book is set in the 1890s—are particularly enjoyable and endow the story with a certain nostalgia. The book inspired a film in 1962 that has also become a classic. **SL**

Tales of the Jungle 1918

Horacio Quiroga

Original Title | Cuentos de la selva
Nationality | Uruguayan, born 1878
Publisher | Sociedad Cooperativa, Argentina
Theme | Animal stories

Horacio Quiroga's *Tales of the Jungle* is a collection of animal stories including "The Giant Turtle," "The Flamingos' Stockings," and "The Peeled Parrot." With extraordinary creativity and imagination—and the splendidly dramatic woodcuts that illustrate the text—Quiroga describes the wild atmosphere of the Argentine province of Misiones, unfolding before his readers the tremendous beauty of an exotic world.

His descriptions of the natural landscape are highly evocative, yet his prose is simple—his language controlled and unadorned by the floweriness that was typical of the time. The vividly portrayed characters are anthropomorphized animals. They display the same emotions as humans; they can talk, laugh, cry, and hate. Above all, they can be jealous and vain. And so, when the snakes invite every animal to the greatest jungle party ever given, the flamingos are both excited and angry because they are tremendously jealous of the stunning red-striped skin of the coral snake. This bittersweet parable about lies and vanity (the flamingos figure out a way to concoct imitation stockings but are punished in the end for cheating) is characteristic of the collection.

Quiroga uses his animals to gently point out the shortcomings and vices of humankind. His vain flamingos, fearsome jaguars, bellicose alligators, and naive little bees are more than just the protagonists of adventures in a remote world; they also represent universal truths about humanity. **LB**

The Cave Children 1918

Alois Theodor Sonnleitner

Original Title | Die höhlenkinder
Nationality | Czech, born Alois Tlučhoř 1869
Publisher | Franckh-Kosmos, Germany
Theme | Adventure, Historical fiction

Alois Theodor Sonnleitner's enthralling story set in the seventeenth century begins shortly after the Thirty Years' War. Orphans Eva and Peter live with Eva's grandmother and her brother Hans in a remote part of the Dolomites until one day when the grandmother is accused of witchcraft and they all have to flee.

During their journey, Hans dies when they are caught in heavy weather. Shortly afterward, the grandmother also dies, of exhaustion, and the children are trapped alone in a valley that is completely isolated from the rest of the world because of a landslide. Unable to escape, they are forced to rediscover the ways of prehistoric man, having to fashion tools out of whatever is available.

Through the three books that make up the adventures of Eva and Peter, Sonnleitner describes the evolution of humankind from Stone Age through Bronze Age to Iron Age. The children have to use whatever nature provides to survive. They move into a cave, light their first fire from a tree trunk that has been struck by lightning, and roam the valley searching for food and defying new threats.

Sonnleitner, a pseudonym for Alois Tlučhoř, came from a Bohemian peasant family. He wrote poems and fairy tales, but it was this series that brought him international fame. His thrilling Cave Children series teaches children about the lives of our prehistoric ancestors in an engaging way and has fascinated and educated generations of readers. **GS**

"... they climbed over screes to a mountain pass leading south."

OTHER WORKS BY SONNLEITNER

The Cave Children in the Stilt House (Die Höhlenkinder im Pfahlbau), 1919
The Cave Children in the Stone House (Die Höhlenkinder im Steinhaus), 1920

12+

The Dark Frigate 1923

Charles B. Hawes A. L. Ripley

Nationality | American, born 1889 (author); American, details unknown (illustrator)
Publisher | Atlantic Monthly Press, USA
Theme | Historical fiction, Adventure, War

Charles Hawes captures the danger, mayhem, and violence of the high seas in this rollicking adventure. English orphan Philip Marsham's story takes a dark turn when he accidentally fires a man's gun, which is the catalyst for the ensuing chaos. He signs on with the *Rose of Devon*, a seventeenth-century dark frigate that is seized by a group of scurrilous men, and Philip is forced to accompany them on their murderous expeditions. Like it or not, Philip becomes a pirate, with only the hangman awaiting him on dry land.

Hawes does not depict a romantic version of adventure at sea. The pirates he describes are evil men—greedy, cruel, and beyond redemption. Philip is forced into the service of these "gentleman of fortune." In almost all elements of the narrative, Hawes deviates from the conventions of the romantic adventure story: Philip never marries the maid to whom he is betrothed, he is never reunited with his grandparents, and his fortune is squandered. In a quest for literary realism, Hawes reveals a true vision of adventure at sea, even to the extent of describing murders in grisly detail. The realism extends to the language. Hawes takes words and phrases from the archaic days at sea and revives them in the speech of the men of the *Rose of Devon*.

The heart of the book recounts a fascinating albeit perilous voyage, and also looks at the very real moral dilemma of the protagonist, a good boy in bad company. However, Hawes is never preachy or moral, and he lets readers make up their own minds about Philip Marsham. **RA**

In Medeleni 1925

Ionel Teodoreanu

Original Title | La Medeleni
Nationality | Romanian, born 1897
Publisher | Details unknown
Theme | Classics, Family, Historical fiction

Ionel Teodoreanu's In Medeleni trilogy—*The Inconstant Border*, *Roads*, and *Amongst Winds*—follows the trajectory of the Romanian upper-middle-class Deleanu family and their countryside estate, Medeleni. The narrative centers on the family's children—Danuţ, Olguţa, and Monica (the latter, an adopted orphan)—tracing their evolution from childhood to maturity.

The first volume, with its portrait of idealized childhood, is the most easily approachable for a young reader. The three children inhabit a fairy-tale land where their ebullience is given free rein. Their childish pranks are encouraged by the family's elderly coach driver, who is for them a timeless benevolent presence of almost mythical proportions. The volume ends with the coach driver's death, which in its unexpected solemnity, represents the end of the joy and innocence of childhood. After this, the tone of the trilogy becomes somber, even disquieting. *Roads* explores teenage restlessness, centering on Danuţ and his progression to maturity. *Amongst Winds* is darker still, bringing the whole world of Medeleni to a close. The protagonists' youthful aspirations are shattered in adulthood: Medeleni has to be sold; Danuţ, instead of becoming a writer, is forced to work as a lawyer, although he does happily marry his sweetheart; and Olguţa, broken by unrequited love and an incurable illness, commits suicide.

Despite its sobriety, *In Medeleni* is a profound exploration of the spirit of youth and its explorations on the road to maturity. It is a thought-provoking read and one of the great Romanian classics. **AWS**

"Holla, o bravest of boatswains! It seems that, if hang I must, I shall not hang alone."

Emily Climbs 1925

Lucy Maud Montgomery

Nationality | Canadian, born 1874
Publisher | Frederick A. Stokes, USA
Theme | Classics, Favorite characters, Family, Friendship, School

EMILY CLIMBS

BY

L. M. MONTGOMERY

Author of "Anne of Green Gables," "Anne's House of Dreams," "Emily of New Moon," etc.

WITH FRONTISPIECE IN COLOUR BY M. L. KIRK

NEW YORK
FREDERICK A. STOKES COMPANY
MCMXXV

MORE FROM LUCY MAUD MONTGOMERY

***Anne of Green Gables*, 1908**
***Anne of Avonlea*, 1909**
***Anne of the Island*, 1915**
***Emily of New Moon*, 1923**
***Emily's Quest*, 1927**

12+

Lucy Maud Montgomery is best known and still loved for her Anne of Green Gables series, and I adored them as a child. But as a young teenager I moved on to her Emily of New Moon books, and it was the second of these, *Emily Climbs*, that I cherished most. I still have the copy I bought when I was fourteen, and in the flyleaf I had written that it was "one of my most treasured possessions." It still is.

Emily's life was very different from my own. She was an orphan and lived on a farm in Canada with her strict aunts, and in many ways her childhood reflects Montgomery's own upbringing, many years before I was born. Yet Emily and I had one thing in common: we both wanted to be writers. In the first paragraph Emily is sitting in her bedroom in front of the fire. Outside it is cold and stormy, but she is engrossed in writing in the black notebook that her cousin has given her. She sees her reflection in the bedroom mirror, and I saw my own reflection there, too. She is acutely aware of the beauty of nature in the world around her, and struggles to draw back the curtain that separates her from it. If only she could find the right words to describe it! Even more frustrating, she is sent to the local school on the condition that she doesn't write another word of fiction while she is there. Instead of creating a fanciful world, she learns to draw on her own life, her adolescent love affairs, her family and her friends, and she pours her thoughts and comments into her diary. To read the book is to know a real girl approaching her future and to take every comical and tragical step with her.

It is also to relish in her love of words. At the back of my copy I filled two pages with the words in it that I loved most, and crossed out the ones I had been able to use. Emily Byrd Starr taught me many things, and—like the best of fictional characters—she has stayed with me all my life.

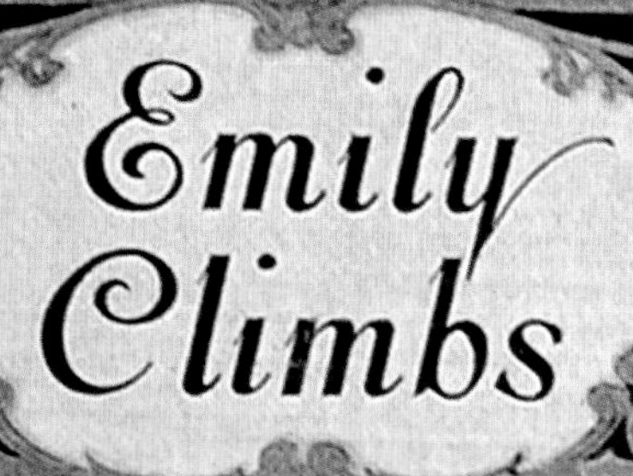

L. M. Montgomery

Tarka the Otter 1927

Henry Williamson C. F. Tunnicliffe

Nationality | English, born 1895 (author); English, born 1901 (illustrator)
Publisher | G. P. Putnam's Sons, UK
Theme | Classics, Animal stories

Tarka of the title is a young male otter who lives in the English county of north Devon. Beautifully written and illustrated, the novel convincingly tells the story of Tarka's life from his point of view. It brings alive the sights, smells, and sounds of the countryside, both on land and as the otter navigates rivers.

But this is also a story of the struggle for survival, as well as a brilliant and loving description of the English pastoral. Tarka is a hunted animal and his most threatening predator is the malevolent hound Deadlock, one of a pack of dogs owned by a local man. Perhaps the dark side to the story is the result of the experiences of its author, Henry Williamson, in World War I. Williamson served in the British army during the war, and was disillusioned by the carnage and waste of human life he witnessed. On his return he began to write novels about the war, and he interspersed those with stories set in nature. The threat undergone by soldiers in the trenches is perhaps reflected by that felt by the young Tarka, who is constantly alert and on the look out for potential enemies.

The illustrations that accompany the narrative are those of notable wildlife artist Charles Frederick Tunnicliffe, and are a delight to look at; they seem to be accurate in their depiction of nature, yet simultaneously breathe life and anthropomorphize the animal characters created by the writer. The book was adapted into a popular movie in 1979. A series of footpaths and cycling paths known as the Tarka Trail have been constructed around north Devon that follow the route taken by Tarka in the novel. **CK**

Ede and Unku 1931

Alex Wedding

Nationality | German, born Margarete Bernheim 1905
Publisher | Malik-Verlag, Germany
Theme | Family, Friendship, Classics

Ede and Unku, set in Berlin during the Weimar Republic, centers on a time of mass unemployment. Ede Sperling is a working-class boy whose father, a toolmaker, is out of work due to a strike. Twelve-year-old Ede wants to help his family survive by working as a paperboy, but his father is against it. However, Ede's big sister lends him the money for the first installment for a bicycle, which he needs for the job.

Ede is friends with Unku, a gypsy girl who lives in a trailer with her parents and attends school infrequently. Unku, whom Ede met at an amusement park, helps him deliver the newspapers. When Mr. Sperling is targeted as a strikebreaker, Ede's friend Max helps resolve the situation. The children also manage to help Max's father, who is also involved in the unlawful strike, to escape from the police. Mr. Sperling finally accepts his son's friends whom he had previously dismissed because of their political convictions and their cultural backgrounds.

The book describes the social conflict of the first half of the twentieth century and is a classic of proletarian children's literature. The main characters are based on people the author actually knew, and in her preface to the 1958 edition she writes about the time she spent with them. Despite its subject, the story has light, humorous moments. In 1933 after the rise of the Nazis, copies of the book were destroyed in the infamous book burnings. The author (born Margarete Bernheim) and her husband, the Czech writer Franz Carl Weiskopf, had to go into exile, but they later returned and lived in East Germany. **CS**

Tarka frolicking underwater in an image by Charles F. Tunnicliffe.

Biggles: The Camels Are Coming 1932

Captain W. E. Johns

Nationality | English, born William Earl Johns 1893
Publisher | John Hamilton, UK
Theme | Favorite characters, War, Adventure

MORE ADVENTURES WITH BIGGLES

The Cruise of the Condor, 1933
Biggles in the Jungle, 1942
Biggles Delivers the Goods, 1946
Biggles, Air Detective, 1952
No Rest for Biggles, 1956

12+

It is World War I and acting Flight-Commander James Bigglesworth, universally known as Biggles, is flying daily sorties in his beloved Sopwith Camel biplane over German enemy lines in France. Still in his teens, he is old beyond his years, having already lost many friends in air battles. His daredevil antics ensure that he regularly runs huge risks of death. For Biggles is an ace pilot, with complete command of his aircraft, a shrewd eye for any weakness in his enemies, and a fearless spirit even when the odds seem stacked against him. He is also magnanimous in victory, respecting German pilots once they are shot down even though a few moments earlier he was doing his best to kill them. Prone to drinking too much and with an eye for female beauty—which, in one story, almost leads him into treason—he is universally respected by his own side but increasingly feared by enemy pilots

"He knew he had to die some time and had long ago ceased to worry about it."

The author himself flew with the Royal Flying Corps in World War I, making a daring escape from a German prison camp in 1918. He continued to write the Biggles books—nearly one hundred in total—until his death in 1968. This book features seventeen self-contained stories about Biggles and his two best pals, Ginger and Algy. Many more titles followed, with Biggles maturing while also becoming a more self-conscious role model for young readers, eventually giving up drinking altogether. Packed with interesting period detail about what it was actually like to fly a light aircraft with virtually no protection, this first story about Biggles is also one of the author's finest. **NT**

The Children from Number 67 1933

Lisa Tetzner and Kurt Held

Nationality | German, born 1894 (Tetzner); German/Swiss, born Kurt Kläber 1897 (Held)
Publisher | D. Gundert, Germany
Theme | War, Family, Friendship

The first volume of Lisa Tetzner and Kurt Held's series *Die kinder aus nummer 67*, set in 1931, introduces a gang of children living in the same tenement complex. The group is led by Erwin and Paul, two friends who are inseparable. Paul's father is unemployed and Paul resorts to stealing the things he craves. Erwin's father, on the other hand, has a job, and Erwin tries to help out his friend. The children from the tenement are always getting into trouble for their pranks, but the admonishments they get only create a stronger feeling of solidarity among them.

The story highlights the difficult financial times Germany was experiencing at the start of the 1930s and describes how people tried to cope with them.

"Often have I wondered how a house may feel in which many people live . . ."

Although some of the boys join a prototype Hitler Youth group and display anti-Semitic attitudes, Tetzner and Held show how friends actually became divided along political lines. When the Nazis come to power, Erwin and his family have to flee to Sweden, whereas Paul's father finally gets a job and Paul becomes a leading member of Hitler Youth. On a more positive note, the children of number 67 meet up in Switzerland after the war where they form an association to promote tolerance and freedom.

This series is a thrilling portrait of one of the most difficult and abhorrent periods in German history. Tetzner—who herself had to flee from the Nazis with her husband and coauthor, fellow children's book author Kurt Held—is not judgmental. Instead, she describes the turbulent events in an evocative and thought-provoking way. **GS**

MORE FROM THE NO. 67 SERIES

When I Came Back (Als ich Wiederkam), 1946
Erwin and Paul (Erwin und Paul), 1947
The Girl of the Front Building (Das Mädchen aus dem Vorderhaus), 1948
The New Alliance (Der neue Bund), 1949

Missing from Saint-Agil 1935

Pierre Véry

Original Title | Les Disparus de Saint-Agil
Nationality | French, born 1900
Publisher | Gallimard, France
Theme | School, Adventure, Friendship

Missing from Saint-Agil (Les Disparus de Saint-Agil) was inspired by the author's time at boarding school. The story takes place at the Saint-Agil school just before World War I. Three school friends are known to one another by their identification numbers: Mathieu Sorgues, number 95; Philippe Macroy, number 22; and André Baume, number 7. They belong to a secret society they founded three years earlier called "Chiche Capon." At night, dodging the supervisor Lemmel on his rounds, they go to their hiding place in the science room cupboard, where they hide a notebook in which all their exploits are written down.

The members of Chiche Capon dream of running away to the United States to live a life of adventure. One evening Mathieu disappears. Has he achieved the dream? Three weeks later, a card arrives from Chicago! André, however, is skeptical. Philippe disappears, too, and then Lemmel dies under suspicious circumstances. André decides to investigate all these mysteries. With the help of Monsieur Raymon, the physical education teacher, who is, in fact, a police officer, and Monsieur Mirambeau, a supervisor, André uncovers a workshop producing counterfeit money on the grounds of the boarding school. Mathieu is rescued from his captors, one of the leaders of whom is Monsieur Boisse, the headmaster. As for Philippe, he really did run away to the United States where he leads the life they had always dreamed of. Although the style is dated, Véry mixes magic and fear in a most delightful manner. **CD**

Caddie Woodlawn 1935

Carol Ryrie Brink Kate Seredy

Nationality | American, born 1895 (author); Hungarian/American, born 1899 (illustrator)
Publisher | Macmillan, USA
Theme | Historical fiction, Family, Classics

Carol Ryrie Brink's tale of pioneer life toward the end of the American Civil War is based on fact. It draws on the life of Brink's grandmother, Caroline Augusta Woodhouse, who moved from Boston with her father John, mother Harriet, and four siblings to the rugged countryside of Dunn County, Wisconsin, in 1857.

Brink's story tells of an eleven-year-old tomboy, Caddie Woodlawn, and the scrapes she gets into with her brothers, Tom and Warren. The trio run free across the prairies, befriending local Native Americans, especially one known as "Indian John." Caddie is the apple of her father's eye and the bane of her mother's life, who longs for Caddie to act like a lady and take up traditional feminine pursuits, such as sewing. But Caddie runs wild, shocking the neighbors and her snobbish Bostonian cousin Annabelle. Caddie's father indulges his daughter's free spirit because he lost another daughter, Mary, to consumption, and he wants Caddie to grow up strong and healthy.

As well as being a story about growing up, this is also a novel that challenges notions of what is important in life: the family has to decide whether to stay in Wisconsin in the pioneer community or go to England when Caddie's father inherits property there. Although the book is of its time and the language sometimes reflects this, unusually it suggests that the Native Americans were as threatened by the white pioneers as the pioneers were of them. Brink advocates tolerance and understanding. **CK**

The Happy Return 1937

C. S. Forester

Nationality | English, born 1899
Publisher | Michael Joseph, UK
Theme | Adventure, Historical fiction, War, Favorite characters

Captain Horatio Hornblower of the British Royal Navy is all any reader can ask of the hero of a sea story: brave, honest, and admired by his men. This is the first Hornblower book that Forester wrote, but the fifth in the series of eleven books, and it set the standard for all naval heroes to follow. The title of this book in the United States, *Beat To Quarters,* refers to the naval signal to prepare for combat. Despite his courage and his seamanship, Hornblower is full of self-doubt and is afflicted with seasickness at the start of his voyages.

Set off the coast of Nicaragua in the early years of the Napoleonic wars, when Britain was at war with both France and Spain, Captain Hornblower has been given sealed orders from the admiralty to offer assistance to the rebellious Nicaraguan, El Supremo, to overthrow Spanish rule and to take the Spanish ship, *Natividad*. This he does, against all odds, only to find that Spain has changed sides and is now an ally of Britain, so now Hornblower has to try and recapture the *Natividad*, which had been taken over by El Supremo's men.

In the middle of a huge storm, the two ships battle, with immense damage to both, but Hornblower wins, sinking the Spanish ship. The story is complicated by the fact that he must take on board Lady Barbara Wellesley, sister of the soon-to-be Duke of Wellington. The entire series of Hornblower books have proved enduringly popular over the years and have been successfully adapted for television. **JF**

"Men who could talk and laugh in that fashion were not likely to be plotting mutiny."

OTHER GREAT HORNBLOWER BOOKS

A Ship of the Line, 1938
Lord Hornblower, 1946
Mr. Midshipman Hornblower, 1950
Lieutenant Hornblower, 1952
Hornblower and the Crisis, 1967

12+

Lois Lowry reviews:

The Yearling 1938

Marjorie Kinnan Rawlings N. C. Wyeth

Nationality | American, born 1896 (author); American, born 1882 (illustrator)
Publisher | Charles Scribner's Sons, USA
Theme | Animal stories, Classics

12+

One spring bedtime in 1945, my mother opened a book and began to read aloud to me the first chapter of *The Yearling*. I was eight years old.

As she read those first few pages, I saw a plume of blue-gray smoke rising from the chimney of a simple cabin, and quietly watching the smoke drift into the sky was a boy named Jody Baxter. I recognized him right away. He was so like me: skinny, blond, solitary. I moved, as my mother read the words, into the clearing in the Florida swampland where the Baxters lived their hardscrabble lives. I could hear the insects buzzing around and the bubbling sound of the little spring, and I could see the glisten of the dark magnolia leaves and smell the thick pines. It was the first time I had slid so effortlessly into the landscape of a novel, and I never wanted to leave.

> *"Ain't he purty, Ma? Lookit them spots all in rows. Lookit them big eyes. Ain't he purty?"*

The Yearling tells of a bleak landscape; desperate poverty on a primitive farm in the swampland of Florida; and a young boy, an only child, with grim, defeated parents. Into his life comes a yearling fawn: an orphaned deer that alleviates the boy's loneliness and gives him something to love. When a tragedy takes Flag, his pet, from him, Jody runs away.

In the concluding paragraphs of *The Yearling*, Jody, who has returned home accepting and more mature, lies awake remembering his childhood and the sound of Flag sleeping on the floor beside his bed. "He did not believe he should ever again love anything, man or woman or his own child, as he had loved the yearling," he muses. "He would be lonely all his life. But a man took it for his share and went on."

OTHER GREAT READS BY RAWLINGS

South Moon Under, 1933
Cross Creek, 1942
The Sojourner, 1953
The Secret River, 1956

THE YEARLING

Marjorie Kinnan Rawlings

AUTHOR OF

SOUTH MOON UNDER

Cue for Treason 1940

Geoffrey Trease, Beatrice Goldsmith

Nationality | English, born 1909 (author); English, born 1895 (illustrator)
Publisher | Blackwell, UK
Theme | Historical fiction, Adventure

In most of Geoffrey Trease's meticulously researched children's historical fiction, there is a journey involving a hero and a heroine who is often disguised as a boy. This story is set in the later years of the reign of Queen Elizabeth I, the Golden Age of Elizabethan England.

The hero, fourteen-year-old Peter Brownrigg, has to leave his home in the Cumberland Fells after being identified as one of a group dismantling a wall erected by the lord of the manor on what was common land for the local community. He escapes by hiding in a clothes chest belonging to a group of actors and after encountering another fugitive, Kit Kirkstone, the two end up working as apprentices to William Shakespeare and appearing in plays at the Globe Theatre in London. Peter soon uncovers Kit's secret; she is fleeing from the lord of the manor, Sir Philip Morton, who wants to marry her for her inheritance. Disguised as a boy actor, Kit plays the female parts in the plays, including Juliet to great acclaim. When Peter's copy of Shakespeare's new play *Henry V* goes missing, Peter and Kit track it down and uncover a plot to kill Elizabeth I at a theatrical performance. An exciting ride north to serve as a spy for Sir Robert Cecil—to try to find out the exact details of the plot—leads to murder, and then a flight for their lives.

This fast-paced adventure story is full of details of life in the Elizabethan theater as well as revealing the political intrigue of the period. Trease also vividly creates the Lake District setting. Other good reads from the same author include *Bows against the Barons* (1934) and *The Hills of Varna* (1948). **JF**

Red Zora 1941

Kurt Held

Original Title | Die rote Zora und ihre Bande
Nationality | German/Swiss, born Kurt Kläber 1897
Publisher | Sauerländer, Switzerland
Theme | Friendship, Adventure

Kurt Kläber's wildly romantic *Red Zora and Her Gang*—published under the pseudonym Kurt Held—is based on characters he met while traveling in Yugoslavia. It is the story of twelve-year-old Branko from the Croatian town of Senj, who is left on his own after his mother suddenly dies. His father, who is a famous fiddler, is constantly away and has no knowledge of his wife's death. Branko has to make ends meet on his own and when he is accused of stealing and put into prison, the redheaded Zora comes to his rescue.

She is the leader of a gang of abandoned children, which Branko joins. The gang is named after a group of opponents to the Ottomans called Uskoci, because the children live a similarly tough and adventurous life. In order to survive they steal, but they also help those in need. They live as outlaws, fight the town's rich children, and play witty tricks on those who insult them. When the citizens of Senj realize they are responsible for the orphans' situation, they offer to accommodate the children in their homes under the condition that the gang dissolves. The children agree, yet continue to meet in secret.

This brilliant and intriguing novel is not merely a thrilling adventure story; it is also a critical appraisal of how society treats those on its periphery. Kläber was forced to leave Germany in 1933 due to an alleged involvement in the Reichstag fire. When he started writing children's books, he continued to criticize social injustice through his stories. *Red Zora and Her Gang* is a highly entertaining book that teaches many valuable lessons to readers of every age. **GS**

Trease's novel is a theatrical romp through Elizabethan England.

We Couldn't Leave Dinah 1941

Mary Treadgold S. Tresilian

Nationality | English, born 1910 (author); English, born 1891 (illustrator)
Publisher | Jonathan Cape, UK
Theme | Adventure, Animal stories

This thrilling adventure and pony story is set during World War II on a fictional Channel Island between France and England. Caroline has no other thought in her head, apart from the Pony Club meetings, but she is stopped in her tracks by the news that the Nazis are about to invade the small island.

In a middle-of-the-night evacuation of the island, she and her brother, Mick, miss the departing boats and have to hide in the cave that acted as the headquarters of the Pony Club and is therefore fortuitously equipped with food, blankets, and water. Caroline and Mick become suspicious of a man who appears to be helping the Nazi invaders, but he in fact turns out to be a double-secret agent. The two children discover that a spy has been leaving notes to be collected and they are drawn into a race against time to prevent the German invasion of England. This book has all the classic ingredients of an adventure story—parents away, camping out in a cave, an enemy to fight, and a bit of spying thrown in. Caroline and Mick are plucky heroes who are missing their absent parents, although not too much.

Mary Treadgold wrote the book in an air-raid shelter in 1940 because she believed that she could write a better pony story than the ones that were submitted to her as an editor. She later became the first children's books editor at Heinemann publishers. She was awarded the Carnegie Medal in 1941 for *We Couldn't Leave Dinah.* **JF**

My Friend Flicka 1941

Mary O'Hara John Steuart Curry

Nationality | American, born 1885 (author); American, born 1897 (illustrator)
Publisher | Lippincott, USA
Theme | Animal stories, Friendship, Classics,

First published as an adult novel, this book draws on Mary O'Hara's experience of life on a remote Wyoming ranch. Ken McLaughlin is the ten-year-old son of a rancher, Rob, who raises horses. Ken, who is a dreamer, is a disappointment to his father, particularly since he failed to write a single word in his English exam and now has to repeat a year at school. Ken desperately wants a horse of his own to break and raise, although Rob denies him this until his wife, Nell, talks him into it.

Flicka, the horse Ken chooses, has a suspect bloodline and he has to fight for her. Flicka does not help matters by showing all the signs of being "loco" or wild because of her mustang blood. Gradually Flicka and Ken build their relationship; he saves her life when she develops a fever and he holds her through a long night in the water, which is the turning point for the filly, but nearly kills Ken.

The strains in the marriage of Rob and Nell, particularly in their very different relationships with their son Ken, are not shied away from, which explains its initial publication for adults. This makes for a deep and satisfying novel, which is so much more than a pony story. The isolation of a Wyoming ranch, the beautiful countryside, and the plight of ranchers and farmers are the backdrop for the story of a boy growing up and the development of his intense bond with the horse Flicka. The Flicka trilogy is among O'Hara's best-remembered works, and all three books were successfully adapted for the big screen. **JF**

"The small boat shot across the bay."

Johnny Tremain 1943

Esther Forbes

Nationality | American, born 1891
Publisher | Houghton Mifflin, USA
Award | Newbery Medal, 1944
Theme | Historical fiction, War, Classics

Esther Forbes was well qualified to write this story, set on the eve of the American Revolution. Already a novelist for adults, she won the Pulitzer Prize in 1942 for her biography *Paul Revere and the World He Lived In*.

Some prominent figures of the Revolution period make an appearance in this novel, Forbes's only work for children, including Revere himself. Yet the most memorable characters are those of her own creation, especially Johnny who—capable, diligent, impulsive, outspoken, and unbearably cocky—leaps off the page. His hopes of becoming a silversmith in Boston are dashed when his hand is burned in a horrendous accident in a workshop. He struggles to survive until he is befriended by Rab, a taciturn young man who works for the printer of one of Boston's newspapers. This friendship not only steadies Johnny's character but also draws him into Revolutionary circles. He takes part in the Boston Tea Party and witnesses, at a distance, the first engagements between the British army and the Revolutionary forces.

Forbes has a sure touch with Boston's social and political life, never allowing it to overwhelm Johnny's story, which is as much about growing up as it is about the fight for freedom. Nor does she tell the story only from the American side. Johnny has acquaintances among the British and, since the book was written during World War II—when the two countries were allies—Forbes stresses the Revolution as a fulfillment of a search for democracy with British roots. Johnny himself perfectly embodies the Yankee virtues of self-reliance and equality of opportunity. **CB**

Woods of Windri 1944

Violet Needham Joyce Bruce

Nationality | English, born 1876 (author); English, birth date unknown (illustrator)
Publisher | Collins, UK
Theme | Historical fiction, Adventure

"The Woods of Windri are strange woods, for they are kind and warm to Windri people, but they appear mysterious and threatening to strangers." So describes the *Woods of Windri*, a tale about the love of Philippa of Windri and Sigismund, Count of Monte Lucio, and the enemies who plot to kill him. It is a tale of the past, combining medieval intrigue, romance, murder, and mystery, populated by proud knights, dangerous outlaws, and faithful friars.

The Lord of Windri has two daughters: Philippa, the elder, who is betrothed to the Count of Monte Lucio, and Magdalen, the tomboy, who takes every chance to slip out from the castle to her beloved Woods of Windri. It is on one of these forbidden expeditions that she meets Theodore Felix Amadeus, a young boy who has run away from the Abbot of Windri and desires to be taken into the Lord of Windri's service. His honest looks and good nature indeed appeal to the sovereign, who resolves to employ him at his castle as a page. As a devout member of the Lord's household, Theodore, helped by a temerarious hermit and the young yet fearless Magdalen, is instrumental in unmasking a plan to murder the Count of Monte Lucio and in thwarting the criminals' designs. The adventurous plot unfolds in the solitude of Windri Castle and in the shire of Monte Lucio, but the most memorable backdrop is the mysterious vast forest, the Woods of Windri. Violet Needham's stirring tales are rich in colorful mystery, danger, and suspense. Her other notable works include *The Black Riders* (1939) and *The Changeling of Monte Lucio* (1946). **LB**

The Otterbury Incident 1948

Cecil Day-Lewis Edward Ardizzone

Nationality | Irish, born 1904 (author); English, born 1900 (illustrator)
Publisher | G. P. Putnam's Sons, UK
Theme | Adventure, School, Friendship, War

Inspired by a French screenplay, *Nous les gosses* (*Us Kids*) filmed in 1941, Cecil Day-Lewis's only successful children's book derives heavily from the French *Nouvelle Vague* (New Wave).

Set in working-class London, it follows what happens after Nick breaks a classroom window with his soccer ball. It happens only because Ted's gang has been fighting Toppy's, so they all join together in Operation Glazier to get the money to replace the window. This is just the beginning of the boys' adventures. They run up against a spiv—one of the shady characters living by their wits in the underworld of postwar London—and the aptly named Johnny Sharp becomes their adversary, along with his henchman, the Wart. This is a ripping yarn in the old-fashioned adventure sense. Although Day-Lewis has been criticized for being out of touch with the society he describes, he is dead on with his depiction of young teenage friendships.

Two strands of the narrative are particularly delightful. George, the narrator, has literary aspirations, so there is a lot of fun in his pretensions to style. And the descriptions of bombed-out London, the otherworldly debris and decay in which the children make their dens and hideouts, form a compelling landscape within which the boys reenact battles and the strategems of war. Nick has not been himself since his house was destroyed during a bombing raid in "the Incident" of the book's title. But have the boys, in righting a wrong, reclaimed that title for the forces of good? **VN**

"The Wart swore a string of absolutely unprintable oaths and made a lunge for his accomplice."

OTHER BOOKS ABOUT WAR

The Silver Sword by Ian Serrallier, 1956
Carrie's War by Nina Bawden, 1973
Fly Away Home (Maikafer flieg) by Christine Nostlinger, 1975
War Horse by Michael Morpurgo, 1982

12+

I Capture the Castle 1949

Dodie Smith

"[Rose said] that she saw nothing romantic about being shut up in a crumbling ruin surrounded by a sea of mud."

BOOKS ABOUT ASPIRING WRITERS

Little Women **by Louisa May Alcott, 1868**
My Brilliant Career **by Miles Franklin, 1901**
Emily Climbs **by Lucy Maud Montgomery, 1925**
A Long Way from Verona **by Jane Gardam, 1971**

Nationality | English, born 1896
Publisher | Little, Brown, USA; Heinemann, UK
Theme | Love, Family, Classics, Young adult

Although she is best known for *The Hundred and One Dalmatians*, Dodie Smith's first career was writing for the stage and screen. She was based in California and was deeply missing England when she began this witty tale of first love and bohemian family fortunes. The story is set in the 1930s in a tumbledown castle that is as enchanting for the reader as it is uncomfortable for the residents.

This is also the story of an emerging writer, as the narrator, Cassandra Mortmain, younger daughter of a penniless and unproductive author, makes up for her father's lack of output by writing copiously in her journal. Seventeen-year-old Cassandra describes the other occupants of the castle, "capturing" their personalities. Her materials reflect the family's shifting circumstances as she graduates to bigger and better notebooks: finally the two-guinea notebook, which represents the wealth and the complications generated by her older sister Rose's engagement to one of the American heirs to the castle.

Cassandra is described as "consciously naïve," yet she declares war on pretension, especially among the metropolitan artistic set. Her stepmother, Topaz, is a professional artists' muse but Cassandra encourages us to admire Topaz as she is most needed: as a valiant homemaker in impossible circumstances. Cassandra wins readers' hearts when she suffers by falling in love with the man who loves her sister, turns down the man who does love her, and finally chooses to put her art first. We are left with a sense of a young woman who can cope with anything life might throw at her. **GB**

12+

Metropolis 1949

Osamu Tezuka

Original Title | Metoroporisu
Nationality | Japanese, born 1928
Publisher | Ikuei Publishing Company, Japan
Theme | Comics, Fantasy

Without manga writer-artist Osamu Tezuka, the Japanese comic book would never have reached the level of commercial success or credibility as a popular art form that it enjoys today. Tezuka expanded the scope of the medium, using manga to create entertaining and visually sophisticated stories that explore such difficult topics as prejudice, the ethical use of technology, environmentalism, and human nature itself. All of these themes are present in *Metropolis*, one of Tezuka's most significant early works.

The title is borrowed from the classic 1927 German film by Fritz Lang. Tezuka had not actually seen the movie when he wrote his *Metropolis,* apart from a single image of its robot in a magazine. The story is set in a future, technologically advanced society in which a secret organization, led by Duke Red, has caused the sun to emit dangerous radiation that mutates living cells. Duke Red forces a scientist to use some of these mutated cells to create Michi, an artificial human child with superpowers. Thinking that he is a normal boy, Michi at first uses his powers for good. However, on learning of his true origins, he instigates a rebellion of robotic workers against human society.

Metropolis prefigures many of the elements that would appear in Tezuka's later work, such as *Astro Boy*, particularly in its portrayal of the unstable, highly politicized relationship between humankind and technology. Tezuka never offers easy answers to the difficult questions he poses, but it is his very willingness to engage with these issues that constitutes his greatest strength as a storyteller. **CR**

The Path 1950

Miguel Delibes

Original Title | El Camino
Nationality | Spanish, born 1920
Publisher | Destino, Spain
Theme | Classics, Family, Friendship

The story of a young boy growing up in rural Spain, *The Path* re-creates that moment in childhood when an individual is on the cusp of great change in his life—about to take the path that will determine his future. The author uses his title to launch the book's central theme: discovering one's path in life and the responsibility of remaining true to oneself.

Eleven-year-old Daniel el Mochuelo is about to be sent away by his father to a reputable boarding school in the city. The night before leaving, Daniel restlessly lies awake reminiscing about his friends and the various characters in the village. He struggles with the idea of being put on a path to a faraway world that he does not understand. Daniel's character epitomizes Miguel Delibes's concerns in the face of progress and his defense of the rural world. The latter—the source of the boy's happiness and wealth—represents the timeless values of integrity and simplicity. Delibes engages a precise, lyrical tone to describe the countryside and to bring the colorful characters of the village to life.

Recollections of childhood and issues of youth figure strongly in Delibes's literary work. He was critical of urban sprawl into the countryside and what he regarded as the dehumanization of society. Despite an indifferent reception from the public at the time, *The Path* established Delibes as a notable author. Filled with humor, charm, and philosophical insight, this simple but powerful novel brilliantly evokes small-town romanticism and has become a classic of postwar literature. **EB**

Big Tiger and Christian 1950

Fritz Mühlenweg Raffaello Busoni

Nationality | German, born 1898 (author); German/American, born 1900 (illustrator)
Publisher | Herder, Germany
Theme | Adventure, Friendship

In the late 1920s, chemist Fritz Mühlenweg joined a Mongolia expedition to explore the possibility of a Lufthansa airline connection between Berlin and Beijing. Taking an unprejudiced view of the local culture, he wrote in a diary, free from the colonial arrogance prevalent among many contemporary travelers. Later he came up with the idea of repackaging his diary as a children's novel, and it was published in 1950 as *In geheimer Mission durch die Wüste Gobi* (*On a Secret Mission Through the Gobi Desert*). An abridged version was later published as *Big Tiger and Christian*.

The eponymous protagonists are two twelve-year-old boys (from China and Germany respectively) who are kidnapped by soldiers just outside Beijing during the political unrest of the late 1920s. Realizing that their lives will be in danger if he allows them to reenter the city he is about to attack, the enemy general sends them to northwestern China to deliver a message to the military authorities. Their trip on the back of an old truck leads them across the Gobi Desert. Along the way, the boys encounter various people, friendly and hostile, and learn how to behave like Mongolians. Mühlenweg paints an authentic picture of the Far East, revealing the modest Mongolian mindset and attitudes toward life. His love of Mongolia shines through in his evocative descriptions as he lovingly re-creates the unforgettable atmosphere of a strange and fascinating way of life and the meeting of two very different cultures. **CS**

The Catcher in the Rye 1951

J. D. Salinger

Nationality | American, born 1919
Publisher | Little, Brown, USA
Theme | Classics, Young adult, Controversial

About to be kicked out of private school for the fourth time, sixteen-year-old Holden Caulfield escapes to New York City to bum around for a few days. He tries to convince his old girlfriend to run away with him, attempts to pick up a prostitute, broods about his dead brother, visits a bar, and goes to the zoo with his little sister, Phoebe, all the while knowing that ultimately he has to deal with his conventional, high-achieving parents. His moods swing from the sweatily sexual to the poignantly wistful. Neither a child nor an adult, he tries to find a way to become a man without losing that contact with the innocence of childhood, as embodied by his brother. Hence, he would like the job of the "catcher in the rye," misunderstanding a song by Robert Burns to evoke the image of a protector who stops children from getting into trouble.

Large numbers of conservative adults have hated the book and tried to have it banned for its sexual content, slang, and disrespect for the hypocrisy of adults. Many more teenagers have devoured it, finding in its laconic, cool prose echoes of their own problems, from zits to the zeitgeist. His does seem an authentic voice, even though Salinger was thirty-two when the book was published. Although the main character does not significantly develop over the forty-eight hours of the story, a certain hopefulness does emerge. Many still point to the novel as an unparalleled window into the vortex of emotion, hormones, and anxiety that afflict adolescence. **VN**

the CATCHER
in the RYE
a novel by J. D. SALINGER

The Wool-Pack: A Tale of Adventure 1951

Cynthia Harnett

Nationality | English, born 1893
Publisher | Methuen, UK
Award | Carnegie Medal, 1951
Theme | Historical fiction, Adventure

Set in the English Cotswolds town of Burford in 1493, this lively historical novel is rooted in the town's wool trade. Nicholas Fetterlock's father is a member of the prestigious fellowship of merchants that controls the wool trade, yet Nicholas doubts his father's assessment of the Florentine businessmen they deal with. He is wary of the Medici agents themselves and of their furtive relationship with his father's wool-packer. His father, however, dismisses his concerns, preoccupied with planning his son's engagement to the daughter of a successful clothmaker.

Despite Nicholas's initial misgivings, Cecily proves both lively and intelligent. Over a summer that sees his father's business increasingly threatened by the distribution of tainted wool and unlicensed sales in Europe, Nicholas, Cecily, and shepherd's son, Hal, pit their wits against the duplicitous Medici agents. Although their ingenuity and perseverance inevitably triumph, the twists and turns of events generate plausible emotional tensions and a sense of intrigue.

Underpinning their adventures are rich details about life in early Tudor England, from Nicholas's mother's gently comic preoccupation with social graces, to the uncomfortable distinction between master and servant that develops between Nicholas and Hal as the two grow older. A useful map showing the route of Nicholas's travels in southern England reminds readers how much of the story is set in towns and villages that are still recognizable today. **KA**

The Sons of the Great Bear 1951

Liselotte Welskopf-Henrich

Original Title | Die Söhne der großen Bärin
Nationality | German, born 1901
Publisher | Altberliner Verlag, Germany
Theme | Adventure, Historical fiction

Set in the Black Hills of Dakota, this charming novel about the life of Harka is a window into the world of Native Americans in the second half of the nineteenth century. Beautifully written, the book authentically portrays tribal life on the Great Plains.

Harka's father Mattotaupa—the former chief of the Bear clan—stands accused of drunkenly revealing the secret location of the Dakota gold, and the two of them are forced into exile. The story follows their journey and describes the many challenges they have to overcome in order to survive as outcasts. When Mattotaupa is killed, Harka returns to his clan, later becoming their new leader. When the Dakota are forced to resettle on a reservation, Harka decides to lead his people out of the territory and into Canada, where they start a new life cultivating the land.

The book, later divided into six novels, is one of many Western stories that have enjoyed great success in Germany since the turn of the twentieth century. Welskopf-Henrich extensively researched her novels, studying, for example, the works of George Catlin and Charles Eastman. Hence, her books have ethnological insights that distinguish them from mere adventure stories. Children are usually very interested in stories that convey the ethics of society and define values such as honor and morality. In this case, the reader also learns about the struggle to adapt to a constantly changing world, a theme the author expanded on in her next novel cycle, *The Blood of the Eagle*. **GS**

"As they sat outside the shepherd's cot, at first the boys' tale amused him."

Adventures of the Ingenious Alfanhuí 1951

Rafael Sánchez Ferlosio

Original Title | Industrias y andanzas de Alfanhuí
Nationality | Spanish, born 1927
Publisher | Destino, Spain
Theme | Adventure, Fantasy

12+

Rafael Sánchez Ferlosio is a fabulist in the tradition of Jorge Borges and Italo Calvino. He belongs to a literary generation that brought together the best novelists to emerge in Spain after the Civil War. Divided into three parts, this rich picaresque fantasy chronicles a young boy's journey from innocence to experience.

Alfanhuí, who is studying under a taxidermist, is so named by his master because he has yellow eyes, like stone curlews. Under his tutelage, Alfanhuí conducts weird and wonderful experiments, such as making trees sprout feathers and creating birds that grow leaves and lizards that turn into gold. He also learns about colors; helped by the rooster weathercock, Alfanhuí captures the bloodred color of the sunset on the horizon and manages to save it in copper pots.

When the taxidermist's house is burned down, our hero goes on a tour of Castile in search of knowledge. Alfanhuí's adventures are filled with vivid imagery; he meets a puppet who thinks he is a man and his aged grandmother, "who incubated chicks in her lap and had a vine trellis of muscatel grapes." As he grows wiser about the world, he also becomes sadder, discovering that life is full of "true lies."

This was Ferlosio's first novel but it was rather unfairly eclipsed by the publication of his next work *El Jarama*, which won the Nadal Prize. The literary quality of the book lies in the striking richness and originality of its language. It is a pleasure for the surreal imagination and a gem in the young adult library. **EB**

The Cloven Viscount 1952

Italo Calvino

Original Title | Il visconte dimezzato
Nationality | Italian, born 1923
Publisher | Einaudi, Italy
Theme | Fairy tales, Fantasy, Classics

The Cloven Viscount (*Il visconte dimezzato*) was the novel that marked Italo Calvino as a fabulist, a teller of fantastical tales rich in allegorical meaning. Set in the seventeenth century, it tells the story of Viscount Medardo of Terralba, who is severed into two halves by a cannonball. The novel can be read simply as a fairy tale, but this work of the highly politicized Calvino has been widely interpreted as reflecting his growing unease about the divisions wrought by the contemporary cold war. It was the first in what has become known as the "heraldic trilogy."

The story relates how the viscount travels across Bohemia with his faithful squire, Kurt, to join the Christian army fighting against the infidel Turks. On the first day, the viscount joins the conflict he is unhorsed by a Turk wielding a scimitar. Although an inexperienced fighter, the courageous Medardo is undeterred, and heads out across the battlefield, sword in hand, but he is struck down when a cannonball hits him in the chest. All is not over for the wounded noble, however; the field doctors perform a miraculous feat of stitching, and are able to save him—albeit as a grotesque half of his former self. He returns triumphant to his home at Terralba with one eye, one nostril, and only half a face, and is compelled by the macabre desire to cut everything in half, from animals to flowers and vegetables. Fortunately the viscount's other, and perhaps better, half returns so that he is once more made whole. **CK**

King Arthur and His Knights of the Round Table 1953

Roger Lancelyn Green Arthur Hall

Nationality | English, born 1918 (author); English, birth date unknown (illustrator)
Publisher | Penguin, UK
Theme | Myths and legends, Folktales, Classics

Drawing on folklore and medieval romances, the legend of King Arthur is one of the Western world's most important myths, with a fantastical setting that appeals to children's imaginations. With his knack for conveying ancient myths in a concise, intelligible way, Oxford academic Lancelyn Green retold Sir Thomas Malory's fifteenth-century stories, making them accessible to a young readership. With *King Arthur and His Knights of the Round Table* he managed to make the previously tangled storylines more coherent, thus creating a highly acclaimed single-volume epic.

The story begins toward the end of the fifth century, when King Uther Pendragon falls in love with Igrayne, the wife of his loyal follower Gorlois. When the two men fight each other for her, Gorlois dies. A son is later born to Uther and Igrayne, but is taken away by the wizard Merlin, who keeps the child's whereabouts secret. When Uther is poisoned by a Saxon traitor, in the absence of leadership, chaos ensues in the land. After several years of instability, Merlin reappears and places a marble stone with a sword stuck in its center in the churchyard of a London abbey. A sign next to it proclaims that whosoever is capable of extracting the sword from the stone is the legitimate king of Britain. The assembled knights all try their luck; none succeeds until Arthur, a sixteen-year-old boy, pulls it out. Arthur becomes king, establishes peace on the island, and sets up a Round Table of prominent knights loyal to him whose aim is to search for the Holy Grail. **DaH**

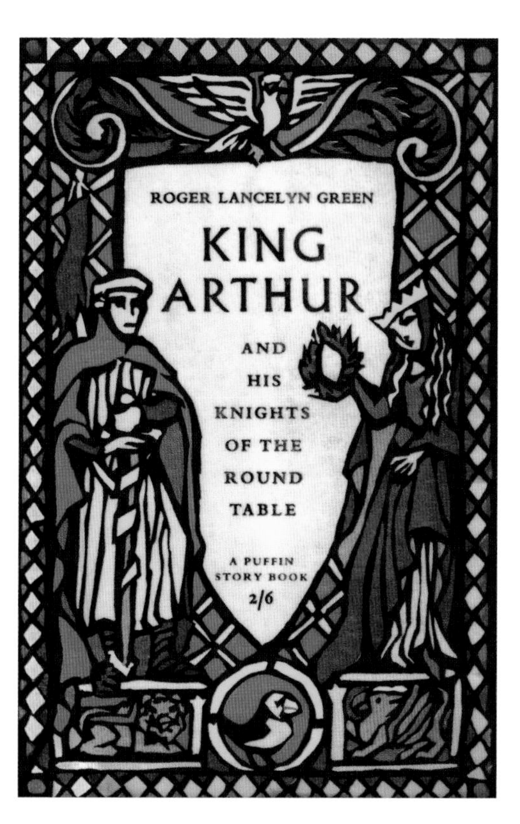

"... and on this night all things shall be accomplished."

OTHER ARTHURIAN TALES

The Once and Future King by T. H. White, 1958
The Dark Is Rising by Susan Cooper, 1973
The Seeing Stone by Kevin Crossley-Holland, 2000
Avalon High by Meg Cabot, 2006
Here Lies Arthur by Philip Reeve, 2007

Wonderful stories
by the author of
THE GOLDEN APPLES
OF THE SUN
RAY
BRADBURY
FIRE
FAHRENHEIT 451
BALLANTINE BOOKS

Fahrenheit 451 1953

Ray Bradbury

Nationality | American, born 1920
Publisher | Ballantine Books, USA
Award | Retro Hugo, 2004
Theme | Science fiction, Classics

Speculative fiction or science fiction? Since its publication at the height of the cold war, readers have disputed the truth or prescience of Ray Bradbury's chilling dystopia. A noted technophobe who still uses a typewriter, Bradbury imagines a future where books are forbidden and the populace lulled into obedience by state-controlled mass media. Bradbury has said that he views with horror such modern inventions as the iPod and computer games, which nullify people's ability to think for themselves. Bradbury's powerful style, with its dark metaphors, expletives, and stunning twists has stamped itself on the popular imagination through his writing.

Fahrenheit 451 is set in the twenty-fourth century, where Guy Montag earns a living by burning illegal books and the homes of their owners. Bradbury claims that 451 degrees Fahrenheit is the temperature at which books burn, and the numbers 451 appear on Montag's helmet. Unhappy in his marriage, Montag begins to question the repressive society in which he lives. He steals a book from a fire in which a woman dies. Although his wife and boss lecture him on the need for conformity, he starts to read in earnest. Soon his empty-headed wife betrays him to the book burners. In a struggle at the bonfire of his own books, he kills his boss and is hunted out of town. Montag joins a secret network of people dedicated to literacy, Each has memorized a book so that one day they can be printed again. When an atomic catastrophe destroys the city and its apparatus of oppression, the literate survivors hope to build a better future. **VN**

Eagle of the Ninth 1954

Rosemary Sutcliff C. W. Hodges

Nationality | English, born 1920 (author); English, born 1909 (illustrator)
Publisher | Oxford University Press, UK
Theme | Historical fiction, Adventure

This is the best known of all Rosemary Sutcliff's acclaimed historical novels. Cold and damp second-century Britain is an uninviting place for a young Roman legionary, but it is where centurion Marcus Flavius Aquila has asked to be posted. For it was here, in the mist beyond Hadrian's Wall, that his father disappeared along with the Ninth Legion.

When injury forces Marcus to leave the army, he turns his attention to finding his father's lost legion and restoring its forfeited honor. Accompanied by Esca, his freed slave and friend, Marcus makes the difficult journey north, traveling from one village to the next disguised as an oculist. Eventually he comes across a former centurion of the Ninth Legion whose description of its ignoble end leaves Marcus sadder, but perhaps wiser. After much perseverance, he discovers its symbolic eagle, now shabby and wingless. The subsequent challenges he encounters in getting the eagle safely back into Roman territory provide him with the opportunity to learn more about his father's valiant conduct, as well as test his own courage and endurance.

Throughout the book the Roman ideals of order and civilization are contrasted with an implicit admiration for the individuals, both human and animal, who resist suppression. With occasional flashes of humor, high adventure, and strong moral values, this story, while dated, remains popular today. Its sequel, *The Silver Branch* (1957), continues Marcus's story; a third book, *The Lantern Bearers* (1959), was awarded the Carnegie Medal. **KA**

The Fellowship of the Ring 1954

J. R. R. Tolkien

Nationality | English, born John Ronald Reuel Tolkien in South Africa 1892
Publisher | Allen and Unwin, UK
Theme | Fantasy, Classics, Adventure

MORE SIMILAR FANTASY TITLES

The Chronicles of Prydain series by Lloyd Alexander, 1964
The Dark Is Rising series by Susan Cooper, 1965
The Wizard of Earthsea series by Ursula K. Le Guin, 1968

Numbering more than 1,000 pages, the Lord of the Rings trilogy (originally conceived as one book) has dominated fantasy fiction since its publication. It was initially published in three volumes because of postwar paper shortages and was anticipated by its publishers to be a literary work that would probably lose money.

Drawing heavily upon the medieval epic literature on which Tolkien lectured at Oxford University, it tells across three separate stories how Frodo, an unwilling hero, eventually saves the fictional universe of Middle-earth. This he achieves by first gaining and then safely returning the magical ring, which makes its bearer all-powerful, to its true home deep in the mountains. Many battles and much suffering ensue in the course of Frodo's quest as he finally beats the evil Sauron, intent on world domination from his base in the dark lands of Mordor.

"In the Land of Mordor where the Shadows lie, One Ring to rule them all . . ."

Frodo himself is a hobbit, a race already described in Tolkien's earlier novel of the same name. He and his trusty band of friends struggle against goblins, beasts, and other malign forces. References to whole spoken languages created by the author (who was a passionate scholar of languages) further intensify the atmosphere of total belief running throughout this trilogy. Moreover, Tolkien's descriptions of an idealized rural countryside, contrasted with dark visions of waste and destruction, have an urgent environmental message for today. This extraordinary epic, eagerly taken up by numerous fans both young and old, is one of the outstanding imaginative feats of the twentieth century. **NT**

Lord of the Flies 1954

William Golding

Nationality | English, born 1911
Publisher | Faber and Faber, 1954
Theme | Classics, Adventure, Young adult, Friendship

Written initially for adults, this famous novel has always had a strong following among younger readers, who often recognize its theme of the universal potential for human violence bubbling below the surface. The book has sold more than twenty-five million copies in the English language alone, and been adapted for radio, screen, and stage.

It starts with a collection of preteenage boys who are stranded on a desert island after a plane crash. But far from making the best of it in the manner of *Robinson Crusoe* and other island narratives, they soon start fighting among themselves. While Ralph and his diminishing number of friends try to maintain order, keeping the bonfire that might lead to their rescue going night and day, his enemy, Jack, finally seizes power by offering his supporters an increasingly dangerous diet of violence and destruction. Finally, on the run from his former companions now turned would-be murderers, Ralph is rescued by the last-minute arrival of a British naval officer.

"With filthy body, matted hair, and unwiped nose, Ralph wept for the end of innocence."

As a former schoolteacher, William Golding understood children well. He wrote the novel shortly after the end of World War II, at a time when many Britons and Americans were blaming the evils of war on their former German and Japanese enemies. Golding believed in the responsibility of the individual to maintain the moral order of society and he often explored spiritual issues in his books. This superb but disturbing novel demonstrates how even ordinary unruly schoolchildren, once unsupervised, can quickly turn into ruthless, cruel tormentors. **NT**

OTHER GREAT ISLAND ADVENTURES

Swiss Family Robinson by Johan D. Wyss, 1812
The Coral Island by R. M. Ballantyne, 1857
The Mysterious Island by Jules Verne, 1874
Kidnapped by Robert Louis Stevenson, 1886
Island of the Blue Dolphins by Scott O'Dell, 1960

12+

Carry On, Mr. Bowditch 1955

Jean Lee Latham

Nationality | American, born 1902
Publisher | Houghton Mifflin, USA
Award | Newbery Medal, 1956
Theme | Historical fiction, Adventure

Jean Lee Latham's forte was writing biographies of historical figures within her children's books. This novel tells the story of Nathaniel Bowditch, a sailor and mathematician, who is regarded as the founder of modern maritime navigation. He wrote *The New American Practical Navigator* (1802), a handbook on oceanography and meteorology that has become a nautical institution.

The story begins in 1779 when six-year-old Nathaniel is growing up in the shipping town of Salem, Massachusetts. He is fascinated by mathematics and dreams of attending Harvard College. However, when his mother and grandmother die, his family fall on hard times, and he is unable to continue his education. Nathaniel is indentured for nine years as an apprentice bookkeeper at a ship chandlery selling nautical equipment. Despite this setback, Nathaniel is determined to continue his education even though he cannot go to school. He teaches himself algebra, calculus, and even French and Latin so that he can read mathematical works, such as Isaac Newton's *Philosophiae Naturalis Principia Mathematica* (1687).

When Nathaniel begins to spot errors in the navigational tables upon which the lives of sailors depend, he resolves to revise the existing tables and command a vessel to prove his theories to the seafaring community. Latham's book vividly describes Nathaniel's adventures at sea and is an inspiring story of one man's determination to achieve his dream. **CK**

Viking's Dawn 1955

Henry Treece Christine Price

Nationality | English, born 1911 (author); English, born 1928 (illustrator)
Publisher | Bodley Head, UK
Theme | Historical fiction, Adventure

No one has written about the Vikings quite as well as Henry Treece. In this, the first of his trilogy about the northern warriors, he tells of the first voyage of Harald Sigurdsson, who sails with Thorkell in the *Nameless*, to bring back riches to their home village. (Sigurdsson's death in 1066 is often regarded as marking the end of the Viking period.)

Harald and his father decide to flee after their home is torched and arrive just in time to join the departing ship. Harald has to leave his own father—who has been hurt in an accident—behind, and Thorkell becomes his substitute father for the voyage. Trouble soon arises when Ragnar, Thorkell's blood brother, goes against the Viking ethos and plunders their hosts' treasure. Thorkell is blinded and not until they are shipwrecked off the coast of Ireland does his sight return in time for his last battle, this time with the sea. Harald is the only survivor, and the tale ends with him and his father planning another voyage.

This is a great heroic story that describes the Viking way of life and the brotherhood of men. As a historian and teacher, Treece was fascinated by the migrations of people through history, and so the Vikings with their wanderlust were a perfect subject for his children's literature. Harald's story continues in *The Road to Miklagard* and *Viking's Sunset*. Treece wrote twenty-five historical novels for children, the last of which, *The Dream-Time*, was about a Stone Age boy who does not want to be a warrior. **JF**

A dramatic linocut of the rough seas by Christine Price.

Captain Thunder 1956

Victor Mora   Ambrós

Nationality | Spanish, born 1931 (author); Spanish, born Miguel Ambrosio Zaragoza 1913 (illustrator)
Publisher | Editorial Bruguera, Spain
Theme | Comics, Adventure

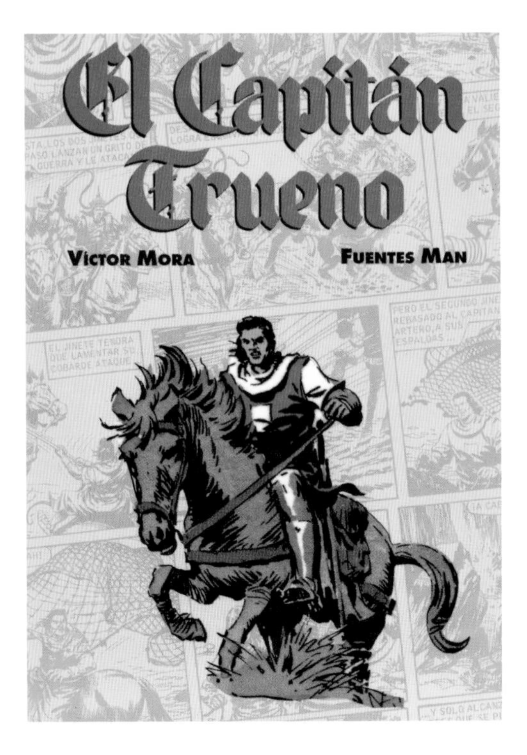

Captain Thunder (*El Capitán Trueno*) is one of the most emblematic characters of Spanish cartoons. Inspired by other famous comic-strip characters such as Prince Valiant and Captain Marvel, he has moved away from the model of the Manichaean hero, imposed by Francoist dictatorship, and also from the North American-style galactic hero. Captain Thunder is a twelfth-century knight-errant with a sword, a shield, and a coat of mail. No one knows his real name or where he comes from.

Some critics believe that the success the Captain Thunder series enjoyed in the 1950s, a period of repression and censorship under the Franco regime, was linked to this role of a liberator, always at the service of women and the oppressed. He is perhaps reminiscent of a saner and more realistic Don Quixote. One of Captain Thunder's main character traits is his humanity, which is reflected in his pleasant, friendly smile. Nonetheless, he is always on his guard. He makes mistakes, he mixes with people, and he solves their problems.

His companions in his numerous adventures are Goliath, a big boy who is always in a good mood, and Crispin, a young boy page who provides a childlike tone to the narratives. Another important character is Sigrid, Captain Thunder's lady, who is later discovered to be the queen of Thule, an island in the north of Europe. Unlike the female stereotypes of the period, Sigrid, while feminine and sweet, is also determined and independent.

Although the series was an immediate success, Ambrós left in 1959 and was succeeded by other cartoon artists, such as Pardo, Buylla, and Oset. However, it is clear that the success of the series depended largely on the quality of Ambrós's groundwork and the chemistry that existed between the two creators, who shared a similar ethos. **EB**

MORE EXCITING TALES OF ADVENTURE

The Three Musketeers by Alexandre Dumas, 1844
Captain Fracasse by Théophile Gautier, 1863
The Prisoner of Zenda by Anthony Hope, 1894
The Tigers of Mompracem by Emilio Salgari, 1900
The Happy Return by C. S. Forester, 1935

Neitah: A Girl in the Far North 1956

Edith Klatt

In this simple yet informative story, a little girl called Neitah is kidnapped by nomadic Sámi people (Laplanders) who, according to their custom, plan to sell her in Norway. Per, a shepherd, is very fond of Neitah and wants her to stay with them, and eventually his relatives relent. Either way, Neitah's situation is difficult because she has been separated from her own family. However, she is allowed to help Per with his work, which is a great responsibility for a young girl. Per is a strong and smart man who is very knowledgeable about nature. As a child, he was also kidnapped, and was brought up with Norwegian farmers. He eventually managed to escape just before he was meant to take over the farm. He returned to his native shores and became a reindeer shepherd. Now he is happy to teach Neitah everything he knows about nature and working with animals. She learns about the ups and downs of a shepherd's life—the cold, harsh winters and the warm, agreeable summers. She mixes with the other children who are part of the extended family, even though she cannot yet speak their language. After years of living with reindeer, the clan suffers various accidents that threaten its existence. The livestock dies, and the family breaks down.

The story's main focus is on the hard life of the nomadic Sámi. People from "southern shores" (that is, from Norway and Sweden) increasingly populate their land, making it difficult for them to preserve their traditional lifestyle. The social constraints and physical demands of the nomadic life force many families to settle down. Eventually, Neitah also finds a new home and starts her own family.

Edith Klatt's characters find themselves in great existential dilemmas. She paints an accurate as well as poetic picture of the Nordic landscapes, describing a people who live happily in harmony with nature. **CS**

Title | Neitah ein Mädchen im hohen Norden
Nationality | German, born 1895
Publisher | Altberliner Verlag, Germany
Theme | Family, Friendship, Science and nature

OTHER GREAT EDITH KLATT BOOKS

The Dog (Der Hund), 1937
Bergit and Andaras (Bergit und Andaras), 1958
Native American Animal Fairy Tales (Indianische Tiermärchen), 1958

12+

The Silver Sword 1956

Ian Serraillier C. Walter Hodges

Nationality | English, born 1912 (author); English, born 1909 (illustrator)
Publisher | Jonathan Cape, UK
Theme | Classics, War, Adventure

This children's classic (*Escape from Warsaw* in the US) is about how war rips people's lives apart and how ordinary people manage to put those lives back together. It is set in Europe from 1945 to 1946, against a landscape of bombed-out towns, bread lines, soup kitchens, displaced-person camps, and occupying armies. The silver sword (a paper knife) is a trinket that symbolizes the hope that is keeping the Balicki family searching, against the odds, for each other. This search changes them, just as the deprivations of the war have changed them, although in the end they are reunited.

In 1940, Joseph, the Nazi-defying father of the family, is arrested and sent to a Polish prison camp. He escapes, but when he returns to Warsaw, his wife has already been taken to a labor camp and his house has been destroyed. His three children—Ruth aged thirteen, Edek aged eleven, and Bronia aged three—are missing, believed dead. Before leaving the city, he gives the talismanic silver sword to Jan, a young orphan, asking him to look out for the children and help them get to Switzerland. Edek has also been imprisoned by the Germans and is malnourished, but as the war ends, he escapes. The four have a difficult journey: Jan is distracted by a chimpanzee escaped from Berlin Zoo; Edek gets tuberculosis and then gets unjustly arrested and tried for looting; and they nearly drown crossing Lake Constance in a boat.

Despite these terrible dangers, the book is a moving affirmation of human decency and loyalty. The children look after one another and try to do the right thing, as represented by the silver sword. **VN**

The Cherry Kids 1956

Constantin Chirita

Original Title | Cireşarii
Nationality | Romanian, born 1925
Publisher | Tineretului, Romania
Theme | Adventure

The Cherry Kids is a fabulous five-volume adventure series named after its heroes, a group of seven children from Cherry Tree Street. They are Victor, Ionel, Dan, Ursu (Bear), Maria, and Lucia, all teenagers, and Maria's younger brother, Tic, who joins them in the first volume together with his dog. In the first book, *Dark Terror*, they embark on an adventure through the Black Forest, intending to retrace the map of a subterranean cave, yet excitingly end up uncovering the illegal activities of a famous spy.

In *The Castle of the Girl in White*, the second installment, while exploring the ruins of an ancient castle, the youngsters find a mysterious girl in white whom they believe to be a prisoner of the castle, but who is eventually revealed as the daughter of an archaeologist working there. In *Wheel of Fortune* the Cherry Kids recover seven ancient Greek statues, previously stolen from the local museum, hidden inside the Wheel of Fortune prizes at a fair. In the fourth book, *White Terror*, the teenagers find themselves trapped in an abandoned mountain lodge in the height of winter, fighting off a group of dangerous enemies in search of a "blue box," an enigmatic war relic. In the final volume, *Goodbye Cherry Kids*, the youngsters uncover Ovid's long lost tomb at the bottom of the Black Sea.

The series, written between 1956 and 1968, includes maps and handwritten notes, so that reading it becomes an adventure in itself. Sensitively and beautifully written, The Cherry Kids won the Romanian Writers' Union prize in 1965. **AWS**

The Balicki children on their perilous journey, by C. Walter Hodges.

Rifles for Watie 1957

Harold Keith

12+

"At the command 'Fire!' Jeff felt a weakness in the pit of his stomach . . ."

OTHER GREAT WAR BOOKS

The Young Carthaginian by G. A. Henty, 1887
Heroes by Robert Cormier, 1998
Tamar by Mal Peet, 2004
An Innocent Soldier by Josef Holub, 2005
Just Henry by Michelle Magorian, 2008

Nationality | American, born 1903
Publisher | Thomas Y. Crowell, USA
Award | Newbery Medal, 1958
Theme | War, Historical fiction

Sixteen-year-old Jefferson Davis Bussey (quite a name for a Kansas farmer's son) joins the Kansas Volunteers at the beginning of the American Civil War in 1861 together with a couple of his friends. Jeff has heard Abraham Lincoln speak and is fired up to fight, but as a result of a falling out with Lieutenant Clardy, he finds himself removed from the battlefront for a time.

When he is sent as an undercover scout among General Watie's troops, he starts to see that there are always two sides to a conflict. This is compounded when he falls in love with Lucy, the daughter of a part-Cherokee Confederate soldier. The complex background of the campaign by the Cherokee Indian fighters and their intermarriage with white settlers is carefully explained along with Jeff's maturing, both as a soldier and a man.

Although the plot is fictitious, it is based on the author's interviews with Civil War veterans and is peopled by real figures, such as General Stand Watie, a Cherokee who fought on the Confederate side and became a hero. Refreshingly, it presents the war from the point of view of an ordinary soldier and in an unusual setting, west of the Mississippi, which is atypical of Civil War novels. The dust, dirt, and hunger of soldiers on the march is not hidden from the reader, nor is the confusion and violence of the battle. The shooting by firing squad of Lucy's brother, caught as a spy, is a particularly poignant moment and brings home to the reader the painful cost of war. **JF**

The Baron in the Trees 1957

Italo Calvino

Original Title | Il barone rampante
Nationality | Italian, born 1923
Publisher | Einaudi, Italy
Theme | Fairy tales

The second novel in Italo Calvino's "heraldic trilogy" Our Ancestors continues his theme of the nature of chivalry, but this time his fantastical tale examines the role of the individual in society and the nature of destiny in a wickedly witty fashion. Calvino had resigned from the Italian Communist Party in 1957, and the story reflects his new role as an outsider.

Set in the eighteenth century, it is the story of a young boy, Cosimo, who can no longer face the future. He is tired of his stubborn father, his unhappy sister, his crazy mother, and their expectations regarding his future as a baron. Cosimo decides to defy parental authority and spurn society, and one day climbs up a tree, swearing never to come back down. At first Cosimo is aided in his arboreal existence by his younger brother, the conformist Biagio, who narrates the story. Eventually Cosimo becomes self-sufficient and watches the progress of the Enlightenment from a distance.

Yet however much the liberated Cosimo attempts to escape society, the more he seems to become involved. His new life is also challenged when his childhood love, Viola, returns to the community. Despite spending his life among the treetops, Cosimo meets a range of colorful characters, from pirates and philosophers to peasants and priests. On one level this is a story of alienation from society, outlining the pros and cons of an intellectual and ascetic existence, yet Calvino's beautiful writing makes this modern fairy tale an uplifting and rewarding read. **CK**

The Witch of Blackbird Pond 1958

Elizabeth George Speare

Nationality | American, born 1908
Publisher | Houghton Miffin, USA
Award | Newbery Medal, 1959
Theme | Historical fiction, Young adult

Most of the early settlers in America came from mainland Europe, but Kit Tyler has come from Barbados, where her grandfather owned a plantation. After his death, Kit has fled to her mother's sister in Connecticut. Kit has not told the family she is coming, so her arrival with seven trunks of beautiful clothes is quite a shock for the Wood family, who are Puritans.

This is 1687, but there are no servants here, so Kit has to work for her keep, resentful and having to mind her tongue. She finds refuge with Hannah Tupper, an old lady who has been outlawed from the colony because she is a Quaker. On the voyage out she meets Nat, son of the ship's captain, and discovers that he too visits Hannah. At church, she meets the rich nineteen-year-old William Ashby who pays court to Kit, seeing in her the beautiful and decorative wife he seeks, and she thinks this might be her way out of the drudgery she is experiencing.

Meanwhile her cousin Judith traps John Holbrook, who is studying with the doctor and preacher in Wethersfield, even though he loves her handicapped sister Mercy. When many children are struck down with a fever, Kit, as the stranger in their midst, is accused of being a witch and is only saved by Nat's intervention. There is no black-and-white version of Puritanism here, just a community working things out with common sense, despite their superstitions, amid the day-to-day hard work needed to survive and against which Kit's story is convincingly told. **JF**

The Silver Brumby 1958

Elyne Mitchell

Nationality | Australian, born 1913
Publisher | HarperCollins, Australia
Theme | Animal stories, Friendship, Classics, Adventure

This lyrical story begins with the wild mare Bel Bel giving birth to a beautiful silver stallion named Thowra. He grows up to be one of the many horses living untamed in the Snowy Mountains of South Australia and known to the locals as "brumbies." His herd is governed by the Brogla, a mighty gray stallion who brooks no opposition.

As Thowra becomes older and stronger, he starts planning how to defeat his hated male rival and take control of the herd himself. After a fearful fight lasting for hours, Thowra finally wins his great battle, claiming the Brogla's two mares, Golden and Boon Boon, as his prize and assumes his place at the head of the herd.

But by now he also knows that he has another serious enemy. This is the solitary figure of the Man, who is determined to capture and tame every wild horse he can find. Can Thowra finally save himself and his herd from a fate he would rather die than suffer?

"Thowra . . . that means wind. *In wind were you born, and fleet as the wind you must be."*

The author was herself devoted to horses, and for many years with her husband and children mustered cattle and handled sheep on a remote farm in the Australian countryside. She made up this story for her daughter, successfully mixing reality with fantasy as her horse characters behave like the animals they are while also addressing one another and any other passing animal with human speech.

Packed with incidents, this evocation of life in the wild produced many sequels featuring Thowra and his descendants, with the author's love and understanding of this remote corner of Australia shining out from every page. **NT**

OTHER BOOKS BY ELYNE MITCHELL

Silver Brumby's Daughter, 1960
Silver Brumbies of the South, 1965
Silver Brumby Kingdom, 1966
Moon Filly, 1968
Silver Brumby Whirlwind, 1973

12+

Marianne Dreams 1958

Catherine Storr   Marjorie-Ann Watts

Nationality | English, born 1913 (author); English, birth date unknown (illustrator)
Publisher | Faber and Faber, UK
Theme | Fantasy, Classics

Marianne's heart sinks when the doctor tells her that she must stay in bed for many weeks. To pass the time, she finds a special pencil and starts to draw pictures that take over her dreams. Her dream house has a boy at the window—a boy called Mark, who Marianne knows of from her tutor, Mrs. Chesterfield. Why has she drawn him in a house without stairs? He has polio and cannot come out. First, Marianne tries to help by drawing presents and luxuries—and stairs. She and Mark become friends and play cards, talk, and look out of the window, to the field, the garden, and the big round boulders surrounding the house. But she becomes jealous, and she draws eyes on the boulders, which make them dangerous. The Watchers start to have a life of their own, which her attempts to correct by adding and crossing out just make worse. These Watchers are the most memorable feature of the novel and give its happy ending the force of liberation.

"'Mother,' Marianne said, 'can you make yourself dream something you want to?'"

Storr, who studied literature and psychoanalysis, was well aware that she wrote frightening stories dealing with children's desire for, and powers of, destruction. She commented: "We should show them that evil is something they already know about or half know. It's not something right outside themselves and this immediately puts it, not only into their comprehension, but it also gives them a degree of power." The book plays with the interface of fantasy and reality, of imagination and agency. Is Mark in Marianne's dream or Marianne in his? Or both? What is the magic pencil? How can a child free him- or herself from a destructive, isolating fantasy? The answers are exhilarating. **VN**

MORE CLASSIC FANTASY BOOKS

The Thirteen Clocks by James Thurber, 1950
A Wrinkle in Time by Madeleine L'Engle, 1962
Tuck Everlasting by Natialie Babbitt, 1975
Artemis Fowl by Eoin Colfer, 2001
Gossamer by Lois Lowry, 2006

The Lion 1958

Joseph Kessel

Original Title | Le Lion
Nationality | French, born 1898
Publisher | Gallimard, France
Theme | Animal stories, Science and nature

When the French journalist-narrator of *The Lion* first discovers the nature reserve on the slopes of Mount Kilimanjaro in Kenya, he is immediately captivated by the wild animals that freely roam the grounds. He also finds himself interested in Patricia, the ten-year-old daughter of the administrator of the nature reserve, John Bullit. Patricia spends her days roaming the African savanna among the buffalo, zebras, gazelles, giraffes, and rhinos. She is gifted with animals and has an extraordinary relationship with a majestic lion called King, whom she has raised from a cub. A fantastical rumor even circulates the region that Patricia is in fact the child of a lion. Winning the trust of the girl, the narrator gradually becomes a privileged witness to the games the two play together.

The narrator also describes the vibrant world of the nature reserve as seen on the excursions led by John Bullit. Through the narrator's words, the reader discovers the smells and colors of the savanna and experiences firsthand the awesome world of the African bush, which is at once moving and cruel. He also describes the traditions of the Masai tribes, who live at the foot of the great mountain.

Ouriounga, a young Masai boy wants to gain Patricia's respect by killing a lion and he chooses King. Patricia's father shoots King to protect Ouriounga from death, and Patricia, her idealism shattered, agrees to go away to boarding school in Nairobi. *The Lion* movingly recounts the end of Patricia's childhood and her loss of innocence, and Kessel pays homage to the complex relationship of humankind with nature. **SL**

Friday's Tunnel 1959

John Verney

Nationality | English, born 1913
Publisher | Collins, UK
Theme | Family, Adventure, Historical fiction, Science and nature

The Callendars are an amusing and bizarre family. The father Gus is a newspaper columnist who is married to January, an American who was once an art student in Paris. They continue the joke with their children, naming the eldest boy Friday for the day he was born. February (the narrator) was born on a Sunday, so they named her after the month instead, and Gus and Jan, tiring of the calendar, named their later children alphabetically: Abigail (Gail), Beryllium (Berry), Chrysogon (Chris), and Desdemona (Des).

February Callendar is an ingenious thirteen-year-old girl: horse-mad, like many girls of that age, a middling scholar, and continually amused by her brother Friday's antics—the latest being an attempt to dig a tunnel through the chalk cliff at the rear of their property, a small holding just north of Chichester, England. As Friday digs deeper into his tunnel, he finds various strange objects. One day Gus brings back some uncannily magnetic and explosive material named caprium. When Friday finds a different tunnel underneath their garden full of caprium, so begins a gripping adventure involving armed thugs, dark tunnels, and crates of explosive.

This skillfully narrated story, written in simple yet powerful language, convincingly mixes adventure and historical setting, providing both a sketch of the political atmosphere of the time, with its technological secrets and untrustworthy officials, and above all a delightful portrait of middle-class English childhood. Verney wrote four other books about the family, each narrated by a Callendar sibling. **LB**

FRIDAY'S TUNNEL

Zazie in the Metro 1959

Raymond Queneau

Original Title | Zazie dans le métro
Nationality | French, born 1903
Publisher | Gallimard, France
Theme | Young adult, Controversial

"'Napoleon my arse,' retorts Zazie. 'I'm not in the least interested in that old windbag.'"

This tells the story of Zazie Lalochère, a girl from a provincial village who goes to Paris to stay with her uncle Gabriel, a female impersonator in a gay night club. Zazie is shipped off to the capital for thirty-six hours so that her mother Jeanne can spend some time with her lover. However, the adventurous, wayward Zazie manages to evade her uncle and sets off to explore Paris on her own. Zazie is desperate to ride on the metro (subway), but is confounded in her efforts because the metro workers are on strike, so she has to navigate Paris by taxi. On route she has some freakish and farcical escapades as she witnesses the adult world, often inhabited by eccentric characters, and in doing so, grows up.

What sets this novel apart from a literary point of view is the author's use of colloquial language rather than the standard French. It was a massive success when first published, selling 50,000 copies in the first month. Raymond Queneau was renowned for his experimental use of language, and attempts to free the French language of its rigid shackles. *Zazie in the Metro* has been compared with James Joyce's *Ulysses* because of its puns, strange spellings, and long, invented words. The book acquired further publicity when it was adapted into a film in 1960 by notable French director, Louis Malle.

This is a humorous coming-of-age tale, sometimes peppered by coarse language and swearing—often from the foul-mouthed heroine. **CK**

OTHER CONTROVERSIAL READS

The Scarlet Letter by Nathaniel Hawthorne, 1850
A Catcher in the Rye by J. D. Salinger, 1951
The Giver by Lois Lowry, 1993
Life is Funny by E.R. Frank, 2000
The Graveyard Book by Neil Gaiman, 2008

My Side of the Mountain 1959

Jean Craighead George

Nationality | American, born 1919
Publisher | Dutton, USA
Award | Newbery Honor Book, 1960
Theme | Adventure, Science and nature

This is pure, unadulterated adventure of a kind that some might feel is outmoded, but it continues to enthrall children, and its ecological bias has a very modern relevance. Sam Gribley is a twelve-year-old boy who finds life in a New York City apartment, with his many siblings, too claustrophobic. Giving a new meaning to the idea of taking matters into his own hands, he heads off to live in the wilderness for a year. He creates his own home inside a tree, endures terrifying blizzards, makes clothes from deerskin, and eats berries and fish he himself has smoked. His companions include Frightful, a falcon he has trained, and Baron the weasel. Sam learns many lessons that build his courage and independence, but also discovers the value of human company.

It is liberating in such urban times to enjoy a tale of unspoiled nature and of someone with the skills to take it on. There is much about plants, animals, and survival here that is fascinating and wonderfully evoked by the author's descriptions and illustrations. George's father was an entomologist who took his family on many wilderness trips. The idea for Sam's mountain home came on such a trip. George herself started training a falcon when she was just thirteen.

George has kept countless animals, many of whom became characters in her books, and she continues to take wilderness trips. She likes writing for children because of their love of nature and the book's narrative perfectly echoes this direct relationship. **AK**

The Nonexistent Knight 1959

Italo Calvino

Original Title | Il cavaliere inesistente
Nationality | Italian, born 1923
Publisher | Einaudi, Italy
Theme | Fantasy

The final novel in Italo Calvino's "heraldic trilogy," Our Ancestors (*I nostri antenati*), this book relates the story of a knight, Agilulfo Emo Bertrandino of Guildiverni, who does not exist but is, in fact, merely a suit of armor. The story is narrated by a nun, Sister Teodora, whose true identity is revealed as the story progresses.

Calvino's wry commentary on the nature of identity and the emptiness of chivalric vows leads to some absurdist moments, such as when Agilulfo is invited to bed by a young woman and, rather than undress to reveal his vacuous nonself, he outlines the erotic advantages of sleeping with a knight still clad in armor.

Despite Agilulfo's shortcomings, Calvino shows him to be the perfect knight and a powerful mental force: he is exacting, pious, a follower of the ninth-century Frankist ruler Charlemagne, and prepared to travel far afield to defend his righteous cause. Agilulfo is admired by a young noble, Rambaldo di Rossiglione, who is seeking his own identity in war and romance; and he is loved by a warrior female knight, Bradamante. Agilulfo is, literally, a cipher, illustrating how humanity creates and participates in history. The author suggests how religious values upheld at one point in time as worth fighting for may be deemed irrelevant at another, so challenging the merits and the nature of those values per se, and commenting on the pointlessness of war. This allegorical fantasy also calls into question and plays with the genre of romantic chivalrous fiction and the nature of fiction itself. **CK**

To Kill a Mockingbird 1960

Harper Lee

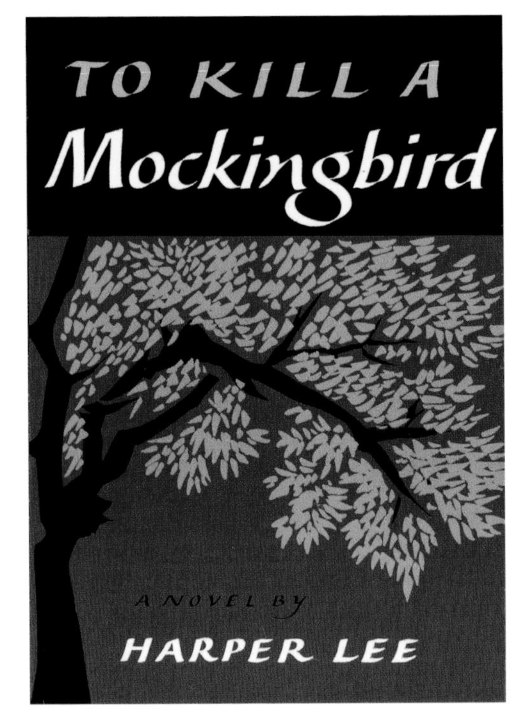

"You never really understand a person until you consider things from his point of view."

OTHER BOOKS ABOUT RACISM

Uncle Tom's Cabin by Harriet Beecher Stowe, 1851
Journey to Jo'burg by Beverley Naidoo, 1985
Roll of Thunder, Hear My Cry by Mildred D. Taylor, 1994
Noughts & Crosses by Malorie Blackman, 2001

Nationality | American, born 1926
Publisher | Lippincott, USA
Award | Pulitzer Prize
Theme | Classics, Young adult, Controversial

Harper Lee's only book deservedly features on lists of classic novels, but it is also controversial. A drama of racism and rape in a small town in the Deep South, it unabashedly uses denigratory epithets (though only in the speech of bigots) and somewhat lurid details.

Based on Lee's childhood memories of life and injustice in rural Alabama, the book melds social realistic comedy with powerful moral rhetoric. At its core is a moving empathy with the dispossessed, be they the black man wrongfully in jail, the white man wrongfully imprisoned in his own house, or the rape victim wrongfully assaulted by her own father.

The story is told through the eyes of Scout, eight-year-old daughter of Atticus Finch, an attorney in the small town of Maycomb. Scout and her older brother, Jem, are fascinated by the reclusive old man Boo Radley, who lives next door. Their lives are fairly mundane: they go to school, play, and get into mischief. Their mother is dead and they are cared for by the black housekeeper Calpurnia and, from time to time, their aunt Alexandra.

Things change when Atticus is picked to defend a black man, Tom Robinson, who is accused of rape. Racism brews into a sinister storm, with lynch mobs and whispering campaigns. Attitudes do not improve when Atticus's skill in the courtroom makes it clear that Robinson has been wrongly accused. And there is danger at the hands of the real villain—danger averted only from an unusual, benign source. **VN**

12+

The Weirdstone of Brisingamen 1960

Alan Garner

Nationality | English, born 1934
Publisher | Collins, UK
Theme | Fantasy, Myths and legends, Fairy tales, Folktales, Magical stories

Alan Garner's first novel is a straightforward, gripping fantasy in the tradition of Tolkien, but it resonates with the author's attachment to place and is rooted in the concept of the past coexisting with the present. It is set around Alderley Edge and Macclesfield in Cheshire, England.

Susan and Colin, staying at their aunt and uncle's farm while their parents are overseas, discover a magical kingdom parallel to their own world and are drawn into an ancient conflict between good and evil forces. Garner borrows from Celtic, Norse, and Arthurian legends to build his plot around a local story he heard as a child from his grandfather, about a farmer who sells his white mare to a wizard on the way home from market. The wizard is Cadellin: he needs the horse for one of his sleeping knights who will one day be called to defend the world from peril when the dark spirit Nastrond returns from banishment.

On his way out of Cadellin's cave, the farmer steals a tear-shaped crystal known as the Weirdstone, in which Cadellin has sealed his magic. When the book opens, the stone has passed through generations of mortals to Susan, who wears it on a bracelet. Once Susan appears on Alderley, the children are pursued not only by Nastrond's evil forces, but also by a shape-shifting sorceress Morrigan and the wizard Grimnir. Their perils unfold at a cracking pace, the sense of terror and claustrophobia is intense, and the writing is tight and energetic enough to draw in young readers. **GB**

Island of the Blue Dolphins 1960

Scott O'Dell

Nationality | American, born 1898
Publisher | Houghton Mifflin, USA
Awards | Newbery Medal, 1961
Theme | Adventure, Young adult

Scott O'Dell's first book for young readers is perhaps one of the most beloved and awarded novels ever written for children. It is a story of survival, based on the true story of a girl who was left on an island near the coast of Southern California. She lived there for eighteen years, alone. While she waited for rescue, she kept herself alive by building shelter, finding food, and fighting her enemies: the wild dogs. She was eventually rescued. However, she died shortly after from an illness to which she had no immunity. This fictional version of that true story of a girl stranded on a Pacific island has a much happier ending. It has been translated into twenty-three languages, and is enjoyed by children the world over.

In the Pacific, off the coast of California there is an island that looks like a big fish sunning itself in the sea. For many years a tribe lived on this island, but when a Russian man comes to prey on the abundant wildlife, the natives' are threatened and they must leave. However, they leave a young girl, Karana, behind.

As the years pass, she watches the seasons change and waits patiently for a ship to come and rescue her. While she waits, she learns how to stay alive. She builds herself a shelter, makes weapons, clothes herself, finds food, and fights off the wild dogs. The story is not only one of survival and of her finding a solitary form of happiness, it is also a tale about natural beauty and personal discovery. Karana's inspirational story will stay with young readers for a lifetime. **KD**

Tangara

Nan Chauncy

Tangara 1961

Nan Chauncy

Original Title | Tangara: Let Us Set Off Again
Nationality | English/Australian, born 1900
Publisher | Oxford University Press, UK
Theme | Fantasy, Friendship

Tangara is a poetic and memorable timeslip fantasy based on a true event: the massacre of an Aboriginal tribe in Tasmania. Lexie is only nine years old when she slips the mysterious shell necklace around her neck. It is a family treasure originally owned by Lexie's great-great-aunt who as a child played with Merrina, an Aboriginal girl, some 130 years earlier. Though Lexie is warned not to go to Blackman's Gully, she is drawn to its mystical beauty and, through her necklace, meets Merrina. The girls play and share lifestyles.

In a deeply moving scene, Lexie witnesses a massacre of the Aborigines. Most horrific of all is that the Aboriginal men believe that it was Lexie who betrayed them. She withdraws in shock, and the memory fades into her subconscious for many years. As a young adolescent, Lexie simultaneously confronts the hazy memory of that event and saves her brother, who lies injured in Blackman's Gully. Merrina reappears, guides Lexie to her brother, and ensures his survival.

Nan Chauncy was born Masterman and immigrated to Australia at age twelve. She returned to England at thirty. She traveled throughout Europe, and it was at this time she began to write. On the voyage home eight years later, she met a German refugee called Helmut Rosenfeld. After they married, they changed their name to Chauncy to avoid the anti-German sentiment at the time. Chauncy was at the forefront of authors writing about Aborigines at the time. She re-creates a terrible moment in history with empathy and understanding. The interaction between Merrina and Lexie is poignant yet natural and believable. **BA**

Friedrich 1961

Hans-Peter Richter

Nationality | German, born 1925
Publisher | Sebaldus-Verlag, Germany
Honor | Mildred L. Batchelder Award, 1972
Theme | Family, Friendship, War

Written to alert young people to the consequences of turning a blind eye to persecution, *Friedrich* traces the development of anti-Semitism into genocide in Nazi Germany. The narrator is an adult German, of about the same age as the writer, looking back on his childhood and his friendship with Friedrich, the Jewish boy who lived upstairs in his apartment house.

The story is told in short chapters, each marked by the date in which they take place. Commonplace joys and sadnesses are mixed with the year-by-year evidence of mounting persecution. It begins with the prejudice voiced by the German boy's grandfather and develops into the unofficial boycotts of Jewish businesses and professionals led by the early Nazi Party. When Hitler comes to power, anti-Semitism is made into law and explodes into vicious assaults on Jews and the looting of their homes and businesses. It ends in the removal of Jews to concentration camps.

This is a tragic indictment of a generation told through two families, in which the unspeakable gradually becomes the unremarkable. The unnamed narrator and his family represent all those Germans who were as well meaning as the family in the book yet who did not protest or resist. They also stand for anyone who, out of complacency, self-interest, or fear, does not challenge injustice and cruelty when it is encountered. Hans-Peter Richter, a psychology and sociology professor who grew up during the Nazi years and served in the German army in World War II, wrote two more novels for young people drawing upon the experiences of his youth. **CB**

Meg Rosoff reviews:

A Wrinkle in Time 1962

Madeleine L'Engle

Nationality | American, born 1918
Publisher | Farrar, Straus and Giroux, USA
Theme | Fantasy, Science fiction, Young adult, Adventure

12+

MADELEINE L'ENGLE

A WRINKLE IN TIME

FARRAR, STRAUS AND GIROUX · NEW YORK

Back in the 1960s, *A Wrinkle in Time* was required reading for every bookish American teenager. The heroine, a geeky intelligent misfit with wild hair and thick glasses, just happened to be named Meg. As a geeky intelligent misfit with wild hair and glasses, I felt a very personal passion for the book.

The story defies categorization. Part fantasy, part sci-fi, part coming-of-age novel, it opens with Meg and Charles (her genius baby brother) musing over the mysterious disappearance of their scientist father. Soon, three strange women, Mrs. Who, Mrs. Which, and Mrs. Whatsit, appear in the back garden and whisk the children off. They travel by tesseract (the actual scientific term for a wrinkle in time) to the planet Camazotz, which has been engulfed in a dark cloud of evil. To prepare the children for their terrifying battle with a disembodied brain, the three strange ladies dole out gifts, whereupon, much to her frustration and disappointment, Meg receives the gift of her own faults. At first appalled, our heroine discovers at last that stubbornness, impatience, and passion may well be the only effective weapons against the powers of evil and mindless conformity.

"A straight line is not the shortest distance between two points."

Unlike *To Kill A Mockingbird* or *The Catcher in the Rye*, *A Wrinkle in Time* was not written for adults. L'Engle wrote specifically for children, and her unapologetic use of challenging moral and scientific concepts gained her enthusiastic fans. "When I have something to say that I think will be too difficult for adults," she wrote, "I write it in a book for children." Nearly half a century later, the book remains a best seller.

OTHER TIME TRAVEL BOOKS

The Time Machine **by H. G. Wells, 1895**
A Traveller in Time **by Alison Uttley, 1939**
A Stitch in Time **by Penelope Lively, 1976**
Cross Stitch **by Diana Gabaldon, 1994**
Johnny and the Bomb **by Terry Pratchett, 1996**

A
WRINKLE
IN
TIME
Madeleine L'Engle

TONKE DRAGT

De brief voor de Koning

The Letter for the King 1962

Tonke Dragt

Original Title | De brief voor de koning
Nationality | Dutch, born 1930
Publisher | Leopold, the Netherlands
Theme | Historical fiction, Adventure

Before the young shield-bearer Tiuri is dubbed a knight, he must keep vigil in silence in a chapel for a whole night. But when he hears a cry of distress, he abandons his watch. He meets an old man who begs him to go in search of the Black Knight with the White Shield and give him a letter for the king of Unauwen. Tiuri finds the knight seriously wounded, and just before he dies he asks Tiuri to continue his mission. The boy accepts the quest, which takes him from one dangerous situation to another. After numerous setbacks he reaches the capital of Unauwen. The country has almost fallen into a trap laid by the neighboring country of Eveillan, which would have led to war.

By not complying with his oath of silence, Tiuri has forfeited his chance of being dubbed a knight. The story shows that you can be a knight by behaving like one and not simply by being knighted. Tiuri keeps his promise to the old man and the Black Knight with the White Shield, and this leads him into dangerous situations that give him a chance to show that he is a true knight. He is often made to face a dilemma and he must make the right decision.

The story is structured like an epic narrative and offers the reader a range of thrilling adventures that take place in the Middle Ages. Tonke Dragt has incorporated a large number of fairy-tale motifs into the story and borrowed elements from Arthurian legend. In 1963 the book was proclaimed the best children's book of the year in the Netherlands. **AD**

The Twelve and the Genii 1962

Pauline Clarke

Nationality | British, born 1921
Publisher | Faber and Faber, UK
Theme | Fantasy, Adventure, Friendship
Magical stories

The Twelve and the Genii weaves a story around the imaginary discovery of the set of twelve soldiers given to Branwell Brontë by his father and subsequently immortalized in the writings of the young Brontë siblings. In the twentieth century, eight-year-old Max, after moving to a new house in Yorkshire, discovers the soldiers in the attic. To his astonishment, the figures he finds are not toys but real miniature people with individual—and fiercely independent—characters who can tell enthralling tales of long ago adventures.

Meanwhile, an American professor is offering an enormous reward for the soldiers, and Max's money-minded older brother, ignorant of their human qualities, has written to the professor, inviting him to see them. Max is resolute that he will never let the soldiers go to America. Conscious of their plight, the soldiers are determined to make their own way home to Haworth. Threatened by the dubious interest taken by bounty-hunting locals, and prey to countryside wildlife, they courageously face their perilous journey, displaying humor, fortitude, and ingenuity. They receive subtle nighttime assistance from Max and his sister, as well as adult "Brontyfan" Mr. Howson, but it takes reconciliation with older brother Phillip before a happy ending is eventually reached.

To a modern reader, both the freedom afforded to Max and the niceties of the social interactions give the book a dated feel, but the central themes and tensions have withstood the test of time. **KA**

Time of Trial 1963

Hester Burton

Nationality | English, born 1913
Publisher | Oxford University Press, UK
Award | Carnegie Medal
Theme | Historical fiction, Family, Young adult

Spurred on by the tragic collapse of a nearby tenement block, gentle bookseller Mr. Pargeter publishes a pamphlet outlining plans for a better future for London's poor. His dream of a world in which houses belong to the parish and where doctors are provided by the state no longer seems misguided or Utopian, but then this is 1801. England is gripped by fear of rebellion and Mr. Pargeter's daughter, Margaret, and godson, Robert, are all too aware that his pamphlet is seditious and that Mr. Pargeter faces prison.

Even they, however, cannot foresee the terrifying hostility of the drunken mob who destroy their home and bookshop. Margaret is left to the mercy of Robert's father, Dr. Kerridge, a coldly ambitious man who clearly wants to destroy any possibility of romance between his son and the poverty-stricken young woman. He removes her to the Suffolk coast.

There, in a bleak windswept town where the social divide between herself and Robert is ever more apparent, Margaret is left wretched, lonely, and in love. Gradually, however, over a bleak winter in which new friends bring some small consolation, she comes to a greater degree of self-knowledge and a fuller understanding of her father's idealistic motives. Margaret and Robert marry, abandoning more worldly ambitions in favor of Mr. Pargeter's latest, more pragmatic scheme: to teach people to read.

The story's pace may be slow and its sentences complex compared to many books in print today, but the preoccupations of its characters and the enduring human dilemmas they face still resonate. **KA**

I Am David 1963

Anne Holm

Nationality | Danish, born Else Annelise Jørgensen 1922
Publisher | Gyldendal, Denmark
Theme | Young adult

At the start of Anne Holm's moving story (published in the United States as *North to Freedom*) is a mystery: just what has happened to David? He has spent all his life in a concentration camp in Eastern Europe. Many teachers and school students have expended energy on puzzling whether David was a victim of Stalinist purges. A better way to understand the book is to compare Holm's intention with Kafka's: by stripping away cultural and personal identifiers, she explores an individual's struggle to overcome an inhumane life. She does so with great tenderness and understanding.

One day, sometime in the 1950s, a guard at the unnamed camp in the unnamed country turns off the perimeter fence just long enough for twelve-year-old David to escape. We never find out why he is there in the first place. He is given bread, water, and a compass by the guard and told to head for Salonika, stow away on a ship to Italy, and then walk north until he reaches a country called Denmark. So David sets off.

He soon realizes that his survival techniques learned in the camp—never thinking past the next meal, being conscious that "they" are after him—are of only limited use to him out in the world. He slowly discovers—along with the taste of oranges and the glory of a bar of soap—that allowing people, like the girl, Maria, whom he saves from the fire, to get close to him is even more rewarding than food. His journey symbolizes the difficult quest of every person coming out of oppression to freedom—the quest to be free inside yourself—and is also perhaps a metaphor for Europe in the years after World War II. **VN**

Pastures of the Blue Crane 1964

H. F. Brinsmead Annette Macarthur-Onslow

Nationality | Australian, born 1922 (author); Australian, born 1933 (illustrator)
Publisher | Oxford University Press, UK
Theme | Family, Friendship, Young adult

Ryl, reserved and self-contained, has been more or less abandoned by her father and spends her life attending boarding school and staying with friends. At the age of sixteen, she suddenly discovers from the family lawyer that her father is dead and that she has a grandfather. Granddaughter and grandfather have inherited a dilapidated farmhouse in New South Wales, and this unlikely pair set up home together. Together Ryl and Dusty set to work to transform and refurbish the rundown farm from top to bottom. Dusty acquires livestock, and Ryl uses her talent for interior design to redecorate the house. Ryl makes real friends for the first time in her life, and learns to love her grandfather.

The first person Ryl meets in New South Wales is a mixed-race boy called Perry. Although the snob in her initially rejects him as a potential friend, she discovers that there is a strong bond between them and she ultimately stands up for him against the racist bullying shown by some of his so-called friends. Gradually Perry comes to help Ryl and Dusty and they, in turn, help him with his elderly grandfather. During this first year Ryl grows to be comfortable in her skin and discovers she has a real family. The beautiful coastline of northern New South Wales, which H. F. Brinsmead knew well, is an integral part of the story, and it also features in some of her other books. Brinsmead was twice the winner of the Children's Book Council of Australia's Book of the Year Award, for *Pastures of the Blue Crane* and *Longtime Passing*. **JF**

"Ryl tossed her head and glared scornfully at Dusty. . . . Dusty returned her look from beneath his ferocious eyebrows."

MORE BOOKS BY H. F. BRINSMEAD

Longtime Passing, 1971
Once There Was a Swagman, 1980
Longtime Dreaming, 1982
Christmas at Longtime, 1983

12+

The Stowaway of the *Ulysses* 1965

Ana María Matute

Original Title | El polizón del Ulises
Nationality | Spanish, born 1926
Publisher | Lumen, Spain
Theme | Friendship, Adventure

This novel has little or nothing to do with the Greek hero Ulysses; it is not even the name of the main character of this story. Our hero is Jujú, a boy of eleven who has been brought up by his three adoptive aunts. Each of them has a different character and tries to make Jujú an educated man: Etelvina is sensitive; Leocadia has good manners but is also strong; and Manuelita is a hard worker. However, when Jujú climbs up to the attic aboard the *Ulysses*, he only dreams of the sea. One day he finds a fugitive hiding there, and together they plan to go in search of adventure. The story captures readers from the very first page and although it begins rather like a fairy tale, it turns into a novel of learning. It focuses on deception and betrayal, but also touches on friendship, solidarity, loyalty, and responsibility for one's actions.

Ana María Matute is one of the Spanish authors who dominated children's literature during the *posguerra*—the period immediately after the Civil War. The child's point of view prevailed in her books, and her characters, like the author herself, are rebellious. They are unique, young people doomed to the loss of innocence, desolate at a frontier between reality and fantasy. A much celebrated author, Matute has several times been a Nobel Prize nominee and is the only female member of the Royal Spanish Academy. She does not write exclusively for children, but the universe of childhood and the experiences and emotions of children inform the core of her work. **EB**

12+

Gentle Ben 1965

Walt Morey John Schoenherr

Nationality | American, born 1907 (author); American, born 1935 (illustrator)
Publisher | Dutton, USA
Theme | Family, Science and nature

The difficult existence of a salmon fisherman, or seiner, off the coast of Alaska is the background for this story of a boy and a brown bear. Ben, the bear, has been held captive for five years, and Mark Wedloe has befriended him. Mark's brother has died of tuberculosis, and his mother sees looking after the bear as a way of getting the benefits of an outdoor life. Mark's father, Karl, is more cautious, aware of the reputation of brown bears as mean and aggressive, but Ben dispels all these notions. All goes well until the previous owner decides to show his cronies in the bar how tame the bear is. This does not go well and, inevitably, Ben attacks him. As a result, the townsfolk decide the bear has to go.

Ben is to be released onto a local island but, during a storm on the way there, is washed overboard. Boy and bear are reunited after some hard times for Karl and the family and the conversion of a big-game hunter to a shooter of photographs instead of animals.

The unlikely friendship between boy and bear is handled without sentimentality, and the tensions aroused about this alliance, coupled with the uncertain financial climate for Karl's family, add depth and background to the story. Also, the excitement of the arrival of the salmon in the few weeks in which the fishermen make their living for the year set against the beautiful landscape of Alaska make this a rewarding read. The story has been the subject of several film and television adaptations. **JF**

Mark leans up against Ben in one of John Schoenherr's scratchboard illustrations. 

The Min-Min 1966

Mavis Thorpe Clark Genevieve Melrose

12+

"You can't hide-out or run away in this kind of country—there's really no place to run to."

MORE FROM MAVIS THORPE CLARK

***The Brown Land Was Green*, 1956**
***Blue Above the Trees*, 1967**
***A Pack-Tracker*, 1968**
***Gully of Gold*, 1969**
***The Sky Is Free*, 1974**

Nationality | Australian, born 1909 (author); Australian, birth date unknown (illustrator)
Publisher | Lansdowne Press, Australia
Theme | Adventure, Family, Young adult

Running away from home can sometimes seem like the only solution, but what if the children involved set out across the Australian desert with only jam sandwiches, two water bottles, and ill-fitting shoes? Sylvie is enjoying school because of a young and inspiring teacher, but everything is ruined when her eleven-year-old brother, Reg, and his friends wreck the schoolroom. After his delinquent behavior in the past, Reg was warned that he would end up in juvenile detention. Their mother is depressed and ill, and leans heavily on Sylvie to raise her three younger brothers and sisters. Meanwhile Sylvie's father flies into drunken rages. His mysterious past brought the family to the isolated settlement.

Desperate, Sylvie and Reg hop on a freight train, then walk for thirty miles to see Mrs. Tucker, who hopefully will advise them. The dust, heat, and danger of their journey across the desert make a powerful impression. The Tucker family has everything that Sylvie and Reg lack: parents who respect and encourage their children; support for education; and drive for achievement. The more Reg sees of the young Tucker boys, the more depressed he becomes about his future. The Tuckers slowly unravel the children's situation, and contact their family and the authorities. An ending that is both realistic, but also has a glimmer of hope for the future, sees Sylvie's family facing their difficulties and making a new start. Clark is renowned for her adolescent novels featuring strong characters and for her historically accurate and evocative settings. **BA**

The Owl Service 1967

Alan Garner

Nationality | English, born 1934
Publisher | Collins, UK
Award | Carnegie Medal
Theme | Myths and legends, Ghost stories

Alan Garner invented an enduring formula for young adult fiction in 1967 with his story about a dysfunctional family papering over the cracks on a holiday from hell. Three teenagers, condemned by their parents to share an uncomfortable summer, are caught up in a tragic conflict rooted in the ancient Welsh legend of Bloudewedd—a woman who was created from flowers but turned into an owl for inciting her lover to kill her husband.

The domestic drama involving Alison; Roger, her stepbrother; and Gwyn, their housekeeper Nancy's son, is interwoven with an unbearably tense ghost story that saves its resolution for the final sentence. The unsettling events are set in motion when Alison finds a strangely patterned dinner set in the attic of the vacation home she has inherited from her late father. In the isolated Welsh valley setting, where the mountains, trees, and river seem like jailers, none of the young people can escape their predestined roles. When Gwyn tries to leave the valley, he is turned back.

The novel reflects a string of cultural and class-related tensions: between the Welsh and the English; between Alison's land-owning family and her new self-made stepfather; between Nancy, who now lives in town, and the rural community; between Gwyn's desire to explore Welsh culture and his mother's retreat from it. The novel has transcended the decades since its publication and was a contender for the public's all-time favorite Carnegie award-winner in 2007, voted one of the ten most important children's books published in the past seventy years. **GB**

The Outsiders 1967

S. E. Hinton

Nationality | American, born 1950
Publisher | Viking Press, USA
Theme | Classics, Young adult, Friendship, Controversial

The Outsiders has been seen as a key book in the growth of gritty realistic writing for young people in the United States since the late 1960s. This fast-moving novel of teenage gang warfare is set in an unnamed American city in the 1960s. Ponyboy is loyal to his fellow greasers, who come from the wrong side of the tracks, but at the same time he sees the stupidity of their habitual rumbles with the upper-class Socs. In one week he witnesses three deaths: one in a drunken assault in a park, another that results from an attempt to rescue children from a burning church, and the last when a desolate friend is gunned down by cops in the street.

Written when Hinton was in high school herself, this is teenage life seen from the inside, without condescension or moralizing, but with some melodrama. There are no important adult characters in the story. Ponyboy's parents have died, and he lives with his older brothers. Although all the main characters have difficult or broken homes, it is the way that they understand and support one another, so often in contrast with how the outside world sees them, that is particularly moving. It is a story in which young people, for better or worse, take responsibility for their own actions.

Although it has the reticence of novels written for the young at the time (there is no explicit cursing and only oblique references to sex), Ponyboy's voice and his account of his life, with its mixture of recklessness, vulnerability, courage, grim comedy, sentimentality, and fatalism, remains entirely convincing. **CB**

Flambards 1967

K. M. Peyton

Nationality | English, born 1929
Publisher | Oxford University Press, UK
Theme | Friendship, Historical fiction, Love, Family

In 1908, twelve-year-old orphan Christina Parsons is sent to live with her uncle Russell at Flambards, a run-down estate in the Essex countryside. Russell has only one end in mind: when Christina comes of age, she is to marry his eldest son, Mark, and use her inheritance to prop up the dilapidated fortunes of the house and, more crucially, its stables.

Christina, however, is an independent, spirited young woman more than capable of standing up for herself in Uncle Russell's misanthropic household. Her cousins provide company: Mark seems almost as backward-looking as his father, but in his intelligent younger brother William, Christina finds true friendship. Injured in a riding accident, William spurns the already dated values of his home and instead spends his time designing and flying airplanes.

Christina, meanwhile, is surprised to find how much she enjoys riding, all the more so since she is taught by Dick, a young servant whose affection for her leads him to jeopardize his own position. Her uncle's harsh treatment of both Dick and his sister, Violet, pregnant with Mark's baby, seems feudal, even by the standards of the time. With romance blossoming between them, it is little wonder that Will and Christina decide to leave in search of a new life.

This is a captivating evocation of England on the brink of war as the old order and its hierarchical class structure give way to new technologies and a more meritocratic way of life. *Flambards* offers a delightfully readable story in which plausible, likable characters establish their identity in a changing world. **KA**

12+

Smith 1967

Leon Garfield Antony Maitland

Nationality | English, born 1921 (author); English, birth date unknown (illustrator)
Publisher | Constable, UK
Theme | Historical fiction, Adventure

Twelve years old but already old beyond his years, Smith lives on the streets and by his wits in eighteenth-century London. After witnessing a cold-blooded murder one morning, he becomes the next intended victim, now that he knows more than is good for him. Arrested on a trumped-up charge, and with his previous life as a pickpocket weighing heavily against him, Smith escapes from prison the night before his planned execution.

He has come into possession of a document that he knows is vitally important, but he must find someone he can trust to read it for him, because he is illiterate. This proves harder than it sounds, with more betrayals and near misses along the way before Smith finally makes it to safety in a good home.

Leon Garfield is a writer who is capable of making the past a living reality, particularly when there is danger afoot. He is also expert in showing that those who initially look truly villainous may sometimes prove superior to those who appear immediately attractive—until readers get to know them better.

Perpetually coining new metaphors while also playing with old ones, Garfield revels in language, creating images in the mind as powerful as any seen in a film or picture. Many of his other fine novels are also set in eighteenth-century London, always for him a city of endless fascination as well as one of danger. This is a recurring plot of Garfield's, where a worthy but lowly character finally finds a good home, and it owes much to Dickens, as much as it does to the London setting and the period. **NT**

"Out of the alley came two men in brown. Curious fellows of a very particular aspect . . ."

The Dolphin Crossing 1967

Jill Paton Walsh

Nationality | English, born 1937
Publisher | Macmillan, UK
Theme | War, Adventure, Friendship, Historical fiction

"Where the lifeboat had been, there was a blazing wall of flame on the water."

OTHER WORLD WAR II BOOKS

Carrie's War by Nina Bawden, 1973
The Machine Gunners by Robert Westall, 1975
Number the Stars by Lois Lowry, 1989
Tug of War by Joan Lingard, 1990
Hitler's Canary by Sandi Toksvig, 2005

The epic rescue of British soldiers from the beaches at Dunkirk during World War II is the theme of this adventure story. Two teenage boys from across the class divide meet after a bullying episode. John, son of a wealthy family, is appalled at the living conditions of Pat, a Cockney from London, and his pregnant stepmother. Together John and Pat fix up the stables where Pat and his stepmother are living.

John is following the progress of the war through the limited information provided by radio and newspapers, and becomes suspicious that something is not being truthfully reported. The desperate plight of the soldiers on the beaches and the realization that many small boats are leaving their moorings make John and Pat determined to be part of this rescue, particularly since Pat's father is somewhere in the region. The subsequent scenes do not spare the readers from the carnage and danger of the Dunkirk evacuation.

John is wounded yet their return home as heroes is blighted by John's collapse and Pat's disappearance. Meanwhile, John's moral fiber shines through when he shames a crooked boatyard manager who is selling fuel on the black market. The slight stiffness of the boys' interactions, stemming from their class differences, comes through, and there is a real sense of the plight of those left at home, who are listening to the radio and desperately waiting for news. A short but thoughtful story about friendship and courage. **JF**

12+

Picnic at Hanging Rock 1967

Joan Lindsay

Nationality | Australian, born 1896
Publisher | Cheshire Publishing, Australia
Theme | School, Friendship, Adventure, Young adult

Part mystery novel, part coming-of-age story dealing with the loss of innocence, this is an emotionally and sexually charged book set in Australia in 1900. It is Valentine's Day and a group of girls at the Appleyard College for Young Ladies go on an outing to Hanging Rock (a real place, not far from Melbourne).

Throughout the day strange events happen. Two of the girls are wearing watches, which stop mysteriously. Some of the party go for a walk and three of the pupils and one of their teachers disappear, never to be seen again. Another girl, Edith, returns terrified and raving, and later claims to have no memory at all about what happened. Two boys, Mike and Albert, who had seen the girls set off on their walk, go to Hanging Rock to search, but cannot find the four missing women. The novel deals with how the disappearance affects the school and the families and friends of those who are missing, as well as the repercussions for the wider community.

The book begins with what is purported to be a genuine document and the novel is often erroneously believed to be based on a true story. Lindsay fed the hype by refusing to answer journalists' questions about whether or not the story was true. In 1987, after the author's death, a "solution" was published. Known as both Chapter 18 and The Secret of Hanging Rock, the publisher claimed Lindsay wrote her supernatural solution as part of the original manuscript, but removed it before publication. **LH**

The Pigman 1968

Paul Zindel

Nationality | American, born 1936
Publisher | Harper Trophy, USA
Award | A.L.A. Notable Children's Book
Theme | School, Friendship

Regarded by many as one of the first American books addressed to a teenage audience, Paul Zindel's novel continues to have considerable appeal and relevance for today's young readers. In essence, it is the story of a friendship between teenagers Lorraine Jensen and John Conlan, students at Franklin High School, and an elderly man called Angelo Pignati. The teens place a prank phone call to Mr. Pignati, allegedly in the name of collecting funds for charity. They subsequently visit his home, accompany him on outings to the zoo to see Bobo, his favorite baboon, and gradually witness many of his eccentricities and learn something of his past, including about his wife's death.

The developing friendship gives a much needed release for the teenagers from the various tensions that characterize their lives at school and at home. John, for example, is on probation from the courts; in helping, as they believe, to assuage an old man's boredom and loneliness, they are simultaneously dealing with their own troubles.

The relationship between Mr. Pignati and the teenagers takes a new turn when the old man suffers a heart attack and is forced to go into the hospital. During his time there, Lorraine and John decide to hold "the party of the year" at his house; the result is chaos and, ultimately, tragedy when Mr. Pignati returns. Narrated in alternate chapters by John and Lorraine, *The Pigman* convincingly and entertainingly manages to blend pathos and humor. **RD**

A Kestrel for a Knave 1968

Barry Hines

"There were no curtains up. The window was a hard-edged block that was the color of the night sky . . ."

BOOKS WITH OTHER FICTIONAL LONERS

Nineteen Eighty-Four by George Orwell, 1949
The Catcher in the Rye by J. D. Salinger, 1951
The Dream Watcher by Barbara Wersba, 1968
The Perks of Being a Wallflower by Stephen Chbosky, 1999

Nationality | English, born 1939
Publisher | Michael Joseph, UK
Theme | Young adult, Animal stories, School, Friendship, Family

Set in Yorkshire in northern England, this is the raw, uncompromising story of Billy, a poor, friendless boy, who is neglected by his mother and bullied by his stepbrother and his physical education teacher at school. The authority figures that should help him, such as the headmaster and employment officer, fail to do so, and resort to corporal punishment and clichés.

Billy climbs into a ruined monastery and takes a kestrel chick from a nest. He teaches himself the art of falconry with a stolen library book and trains the bird, which he names Kes, to return to him.

In a long and very moving passage, a sympathetic teacher, who encourages Billy to articulate his feelings in class, discovers the extraordinary bond between the boy and the kestrel. The same teacher, Mr. Farthing, visits Billy while he exercises and feeds Kes. Having gained the respect of someone in authority—someone who cares—it seems that there is the possibility of a way forward for Billy, out of the poverty and hopelessness of the mining community in which he lives. However, the ending is as savage and bleak as the beginning. There is no escape, either for Billy, his violent brother, or his promiscuous and inadequate mother. Yet, because Billy is capable of an instinctive response to nature, which makes him different, there may be hope for the future.

The book is unusual since most of the story takes place in flashbacks, a plot device more usually associated with film. The book was, however, soon made into a highly acclaimed film, *Kes* (1969), directed by Ken Loach. **WO**

12+

Chocky 1968

John Wyndham

Nationality | English, born John Wyndham Parkes Lucas Beynon Harris 1903
Publisher | Michael Joseph, UK
Theme | Science fiction, Classics

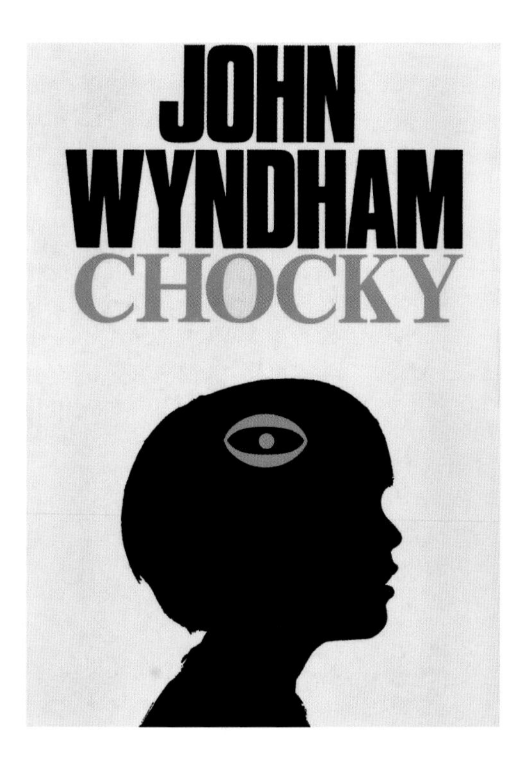

This book by the creator of the classic science fiction novel *The Day of the Triffids* is about a boy called Matthew who starts hearing a voice called Chocky in his head. The story is told through Matthew's father's eyes and begins when he hears his son shouting in the yard. When he investigates, Matthew is having an angry one-sided argument. Initially, Matthew's father assumes that he has created an imaginary friend, but as events become more mysterious and Matthew becomes more distressed by Chocky's constant questions, Matthew's father comes to believe that the voice in his son's head is coming telepathically from another planet.

Chocky does not seem to be a malevolent alien and just wants to learn about Earth, although he is not always impressed by what he regards as its primitive behavior and technology. It is Chocky's mockery that causes the continual arguments with Matthew. The trouble really begins, though, when Matthew starts doing things he couldn't do before. This includes creating realistic, if strange-looking, pieces of art, discussing high-level binary math, and saving his sister from drowning, even though he cannot swim. The media soon start to pay attention and want to know more about the mysterious Chocky.

Chocky is a beautifully written and suspenseful tale, and, like all the best sci-fi mysteries, leaves you guessing right up until the end. It demonstrates John Wyndham's evocative imagination, mastery of describing human behavior, and the author's hopes for the future development of humankind. **JaM**

"... this one-sided conversation aroused my curiosity enough to make me put my head cautiously out of the open window."

OTHER SCIENCE FICTION GREATS

20,000 Leagues Under the Sea by Jules Verne, 1869
The Time Machine by H. G. Wells, 1895
Metropolis by Osama Tezuka, 1949
Dragonsong by Anne McCaffrey, 1976
Taronga by Victor Kelleher, 1986

The Cay 1969

Theodore Taylor

Nationality | American, born 1921
Publisher | Doubleday, USA
Award | Lewis Carroll Shelf Award, 1970
Theme | War, Adventure, Young adult

Theodore Taylor's own story is as exciting as the characters he so carefully brings to life. Raised in North Carolina, the award-winning writer of books, movies, and feature news stories claimed he was never much of a student himself: "My grades in high school were so bad (I never passed freshman math) that no college or university would accept me." And yet he went on to write more than fifty books, the most famous of which is a timeless story of racial prejudice.

This is a classic novel about racism and the realization that skin color does not matter. Phillip, the main character of this novel, knew from a young age that his mother was racially prejudiced. He never thought she was right, but he also never thought he would find out exactly how wrong she was.

Phillip is an eleven-year-old living in the West Indies. As World War II breaks out, he leaves with his mother, who wants to return to Virginia for safety. When their ship is sunk by the Germans, Phillip and his mother are separated, ending up on different life rafts. Phillip, having been hit on the head with a beam from the sinking ship, awakens to find himself blind and alone with Timothy, an old African-American ship hand.

They survive on a raft for several days and eventually come ashore on a small unpopulated island. Phillip must now learn to deal with his blindness and overcome his dislike and preconceived notions about Timothy, who teaches him to survive. After Timothy's death, Phillip continues to live on the island, using the skills Timothy taught him, and is eventually rescued and reunited with his family. **KD**

12+

Sounder 1969

William H. Armstrong

Nationality | American, born 1911
Publisher | Harper, USA
Award | Newbery Medal, 1970
Theme | Animal stories

Sounder is a hunting dog who belongs to an African-American sharecropper in the Deep South of the United States. His master is dragged off to a chain gang for petty theft, and during the arrest the dog is blasted by a deputy's shotgun. He survives, maimed and disfigured, and waits patiently for his master's return. Although this short novel bears the dog's name, it is really the story of the sharecropper's son, who spends his youth working to support the family and wandering from work camp to work camp in search of his father, until, years later, his father is released and returns, also maimed and disfigured.

Written during the rise of Civil Rights and Black Power in the 1960s and 1970s by a white writer, *Sounder* is a tribute to the resilience of generations of poor Southerners and acknowledges a shameful aspect of American history. Although lauded with honors, the novel was criticized by some for its lack of understanding of the African-American community. Yet, written in matter-of-fact language that carries a weight of pain and suffering with restraint and dignity, it has the simplicity and power of universal myth.

Only the dog is named in the story. And what is represented, by implication, is not only the courage and endurance of African-Americans but that of all people who suffer from poverty and injustice. While the portrayal of this oppression, and the frustration and anger it provokes in the boy, is unsparing, the book leaves a final impression of the love, determination, and hope for the future that is represented by the dog and the boy. **CB**

Where the Lilies Bloom 1969

Vera and Bill Cleaver Jim Spanfeller

Nationality | American, born 1919 and 1920 (authors); American, born 1930 (illustrator)
Publisher | Lippincott, USA
Theme | Family

"Once in some near-forgotten time, a traveler, winding his way across the mountains on foot, wandered into our valley which is known as Trial." So begins this award-winning novel set against the harsh realities of life in the Appalachian Mountains. Fourteen-year-old Mary Call Luther is possibly the most cantankerous, stubborn, inspiring heroine in children's literature. She has promised her dying father that she will keep the orphaned family together, and spurns both charity and the help of prying neighbors. With siblings Ima Dean, Romey, and Devola, she starts a business to support the family, harvesting mountain herbs and roots in the wild.

Mary Call tells us her personal thoughts and fears, even though she hides them from her siblings. "You're awful," they tell her. "Don't look so tough, Mary Call. It makes you look ugly." But Mary Call understands her duty. She works herself into illness trying to keep her siblings safe, fed, and sheltered. A series of mishaps eventually leads her to accept the help of neighbor Kiser Pease. Even though she promised never to allow him to marry her older sister Devola, she now realizes that Kiser is not their worst enemy, but in fact a generous friend.

Where the Lilies Bloom, set possibly during the 1950s or 1960s, contrasts old-time, self-sufficient mountain traditions with the need for more openness and trust. While some readers may be surprised at her prayerful reliance on God's provision, Mary Call is an inspirational spirit of self-dependence and persistence in a novel of considerable depth. **CER**

"I have never forgotten what he said—that this land was fair land, the fairest of them all. This is where the lilies bloom."

OTHER STORIES ABOUT SIBLINGS

What Katy Did by Susan Coolidge, 1872
Seven Little Australians by Ethel Turner, 1912
Friday's Tunnel by John Verney, 1959
Jacob Have I Loved by Katherine Paterson, 1980
A Swift Pure Cry by Siobhan Dowd, 2006

12+

The Edge of the Cloud 1969

K. M. Peyton

"She thought that she had never felt so happy, nor so near to tears."

OTHER GREAT READS BY K. M. PEYTON

Flambards, 1967
Fly-by-Night, 1968
Flambards in Summer, 1969
The Team, 1975
Flambards Divided, 1981

Nationality | English, born 1929
Publisher | Oxford University Press, UK
Theme | Historical fiction, Love, Friendship, War, Adventure, Family

The Edge of the Cloud, the sequel to *Flambards*, exhilaratingly depicts the growing freedoms—and associated responsibilities—enjoyed by young people in general and young women in particular in the months immediately preceding World War I. Set largely around an early airfield, it charts the growth of aviation, its allure, and its inherent dangers, allowing readers and characters alike to bask in the social freedom it afforded while shrugging off the cross-generational tensions this created.

The book opens in 1913 where *Flambards* left off: Christina and Will have run away, intending to marry as soon as they come of age. Meanwhile, as practical Aunt Grace makes clear when they land on her doorstep, William must have some way of earning his living. When he eventually finds work in an airfield, Christina, who longs to be near him, finds a job in a local hotel. She is befriended by the dynamic Dorothy who, untrammeled by convention and accustomed to getting her own way, draws Christina and Will into the cheery social life around the airfield, a world apart from the antiquated values of Flambards and Uncle Russell. After a demanding operation to treat his crippled leg, Will and his friend Sandy take on a series of dramatic aeronautical displays, whose tragic outcome is even more shocking in contrast with the earlier gaiety. The story ends in thoughtful, expectant mood, with Will and Christina's wedding taking place just days after the declaration of war. **KA**

12+

Oscar at the South Pole 1970

Carmen Kurtz

Original Title | Oscar en el Polo Sur
Nationality | Spanish, born 1911
Publisher | Juventud, Spain
Theme | Adventure

Oscar is an ordinary boy who enjoys extraordinary adventures in places that most boys his age can only dream of. The stories are reminiscent of the impossible journeys made in the novels of Jules Verne. Oscar accompanies his friend Enrique, who is searching for a stone with special powers, on a trip to the South Pole. Oscar and Enrique embark as stowaways on the *Juliana*, under Captain Dirk, who later lets them join the expedition. They are put under the care of Antón, who has a bad temper but a good heart. In this first book, Oscar does not have his usual companion, Kina the goose. Instead he has a penguin called Pelagio.

Carmen de Rafael Mares lived in exile in France from 1935 to 1943. While there, she met her husband, Peter Kurtz, whose name she used for her literary works. In 1962 she began the Oscar series of books; she had previously considered children's literature a "difficult genre." Her children's books deal with contemporary issues, developed with great imagination and in a style laden with tenderness and humor.

Oscar, an entertaining, intelligent, and generous child, appears in sixteen children's stories, in the first of which he is a cosmonaut. In the stories that follow he is a secret agent, an explorer in Africa, a speleologist, and even an atomic spy. Although Carmen Kurtz wrote many books for adults, her success as an award-winning children's author has eclipsed her career as an adult novelist. **EB**

The Summer of the Swans 1970

Betsy Byars, Ted CoConis

Nationality | American, born 1928 (author); American, born 1927 (illustrator)
Publisher | Viking Press, USA
Theme | Family, Young adult

Set in West Virginia at the end of the long summer vacation, fourteen-year-old Sara is puzzling over why life suddenly appears so different. She feels too tall, skinny, and ugly next to her older sister. She hates the orange sneakers she once loved, and her feelings seem out of control. Her family situation is comfortable, but not ideal. After the death of their mother, Sara, sister Wanda, and younger brother Charlie are looked after by Aunt Willie. Their father has withdrawn into a remote figure, visiting on occasional weekends. Ten-year-old Charlie has brain damage and cannot talk, and Sara has become his close protector.

When the siblings go to see some swans, Charlie is entranced. The next morning, when the family awake, he has disappeared. During the desperate search, Sara learns more about her feelings and the value of friendship from an unexpected quarter. The easy-to-read text is not oversimplistic, and adolescent angst is dealt with in a low-key, genuine way. The story's short timespan (over a couple of days) gives an immediacy and focus. Ted CoConis's black-and-white illustrations are typical of much commercial art of the late 1960s and 1970s, and add to the book's period feel.

Betsy Byars is a prolific, much-loved American author known for addressing the ways young people face up to difficult situations, and this sensitively written classic falls squarely within that mold. Although Sara is fourteen, the book is now more likely to appeal to a younger age group. **AK**

The Lark and the Laurel 1970

Barbara Willard

Nationality | English, born 1909
Publisher | Longmans, UK
Theme | Historical fiction, Young adult, Adventure, Love

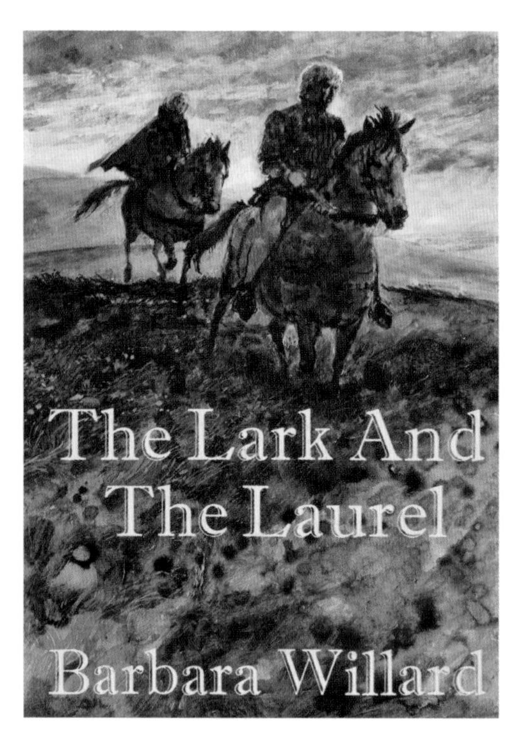

12+

MORE BOOKS BY BARBARA WILLARD

Hetty, 1963
Storm from the West, 1964
Three and One to Carry, 1965
Charity at Home, 1966
A Grove of Green Holly, 1967

The first of Barbara Willard's acclaimed series of Mantlemass novels about the changing lives of two Sussex families over the period from 1485 to the English Civil War, *The Lark and the Laurel* opens shortly after the Battle of Bosworth. With Henry Tudor on the throne, Cecily Jolland's father, a turncoat in the Wars of the Roses, must flee to France, leaving his fifteen-year-old daughter with her aunt at Mantlemass, a manor farm in the Ashdown Forest.

Cecily, who has enjoyed a sheltered upbringing in London, initially despises both the social freedoms and the hard work that constitute forest life, but her aunt Elizabeth is a capable, forthright woman who encourages her to value good sense and integrity over superficial niceties and social aspirations. Elizabeth provides a strong role model, the first in a line of independent, clear-thinking women who feature throughout the Mantlemass novels. In the forest Cecily meets and falls in love with Lewis Mallory, a boy who, like herself, has been left with relatives. Conscious that her own father will insist on choosing a husband for her, their future together seems uncertain, and Cecily is haunted by a distant recollection of a childhood betrothal.

"... remember that God gave you a voice to speak out with, not to coddle under your breath."

An evocative historical novel in which events are seen in terms of the impact they have on ordinary people, this book and its sequels have at their heart powerful themes of change and continuity, of appearance and reality, and—particularly appealing for adolescent readers—of the importance of establishing one's own independent identity. **KA**

Grover 1970

Vera and Bill Cleaver

Nationality | American, born 1919 (Vera); American born 1920 (Bill)
Publisher | Lippincott, USA
Theme | Illness and death, Family, Young adult

With terminal illnesses so common nowadays, few people's lives are likely to remain unaffected. In *Grover*, Vera and Bill Cleaver highlight the harsh circumstances of life, focusing on one boy's efforts to understand the emotions awakened after a personal tragedy.

After a day out with his uncle Ab and friend Ellen Grae, Grover goes home to find his mother unwell and his father anxious. Although he understands that something is wrong, his aunt and uncle refuse to answer his questions. Instead, they choose to shield him by keeping him busy and feeding him half-truths that do nothing to ease his anxiety. Grover becomes even more concerned when his father suddenly provides mother with the things she has long wanted, such as a dishwasher and air-conditioning, leading Grover to suspect that his mother has not long to live. However, despite his suspicions, he is unprepared when she dies by a self-inflicted gunshot wound.

"There was something wrong but it was a secret. He wasn't old enough to be told about it."

Stunned with grief over the suicide, Grover's father withdraws into himself, and Grover has to rely on his friends to support him. With the companionship and understanding of Grover's friends and a few sympathetic adults, he is able to reach a healthy understanding of the misery his father is going through and, thus, a better understanding of himself.

The themes make the book as relevant today as when it was first published. *Grover* delves into the confusion faced by children as they struggle to come to terms with death, and draws attention to the way adults, while grieving, can sometimes ignore the silent pleas for communication children crave. **CVB**

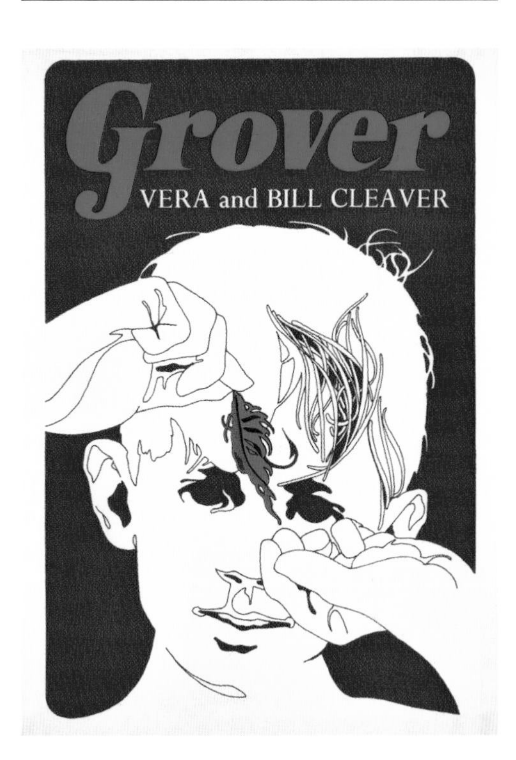

OTHER BOOKS DEALING WITH LOSS

A Summer to Die by Lois Lowry, 1977
Tiger Eyes by Judy Blume, 1981
River Boy by Tim Bowler, 1997
Kit's Wilderness by David Almond, 1999
Before I Die by Jenny Downham, 2007

12+

I'm the King of the Castle 1970

Susan Hill

Nationality | English, born 1942
Publisher | Hamish Hamilton, UK
Award | Somerset Maugham Award, 1971
Theme | Illness and death, Family

Mrs. Kingshaw has moved with her eleven-year-old son, Charles, into a large country house, where she has been hired as a housekeeper. The house is owned by Joseph Hooper, who lives there with his son, Edmund, also aged eleven. Although the adults get on well, Edmund sets out to torment Charles in every way he can. The oversensitive and vulnerable Charles has no answer to this, and to make matters worse, the boys are sent to the same boarding school. At school Charles briefly makes a good friend while Edmund is in the hospital recovering from a fall, but he soon loses his friend to his hated enemy. When Charles hears that his mother is going to marry Edmund's father, the boy gives up all hope and drowns himself.

Susan Hill has written that this is "a novel about cruelty and the power of evil." Few readers would disagree, particularly at the moment when Edmund exults over Charles's death: "When he saw Kingshaw's body, upside down in the water, Hooper thought suddenly, it was because of me, I did that, it was because of me, and a spurt of triumph went through him." Unable to make anyone take his problems seriously, Charles never really has a chance.

Much of the novel is told in dialogue between the two boys. Most children know something about bullying and being bullied, and will sympathize with the accuracy with which this terrifying but compulsive novel describes the dangers that can arise when one person falls so totally under another's power. **NT**

A Long Way from Verona 1971

Jane Gardam

Nationality | English, born 1928
Publisher | Hamish Hamilton, UK
Theme | Historical fiction, School, Friendship, Family

Jessica Vye, a thirteen-year-old would-be writer, tells her own story in this garrulous, self-absorbed, and supremely entertaining first-person narrative. The setting (the northeast coast of England) and family setup (clerical, hard up, and eccentric) are familiar Jane Gardam territory, but this is her first book with an adolescent narrator.

World War II adds dramatic potential as Jessica encounters an Italian prisoner of war and faces the terrors of air raids. In fact, the war is omnipresent in Gardam's portrayal of the expectations and limits that controlled the lives of educated young girls at the time. Despite the period setting, Gardam's ironic humor and avoidance of overwriting means that the story appeals to contemporary readers. The routine of Jessica's school day in a dull spa town, with its cliques and order marks, is soothing as well as stultifying, and Jessica is likable for all her self-indulgence and pretension. There is something compelling about her belief in herself as a writer.

Gardam's stylistic restraint and tight structure contains Jessica's more breathless runaway thoughts, and the reader is firmly on her side when she is put down by starchy teachers or endures the enforced jollity of a house party, surrounded by shallow souls and wearing the wrong kind of dress. When an encounter with a boy at the house party ends with disappointment, we cheer Jessica on as she learns to appreciate her gift of being happy within herself. **GB**

Winter in Wartime 1972

Jan Terlouw   Jan Wesseling

Original Title | Oorlogswinter
Nationality | Dutch, born 1931
Publisher | Lemniscaat, the Netherlands
Theme | War, Adventure

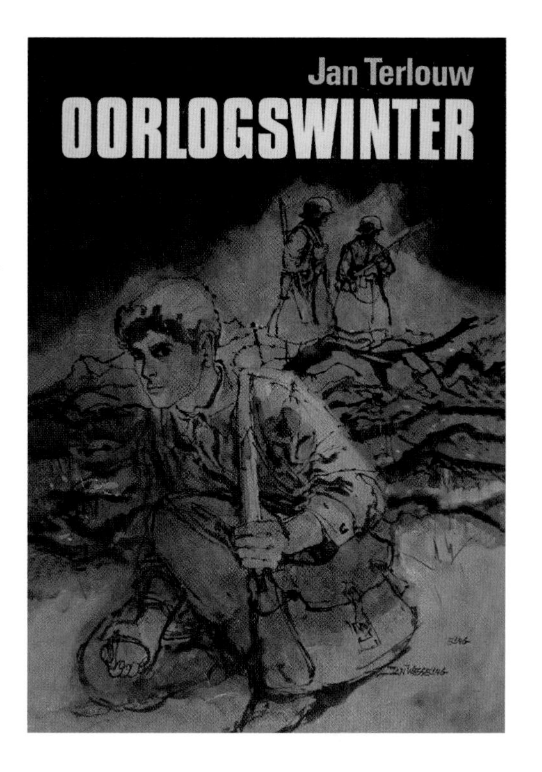

Sixteen-year-old Michiel lives on a road along which countless starving people are traveling in search of food during the infamous "hunger winter" of 1944. The end of World War II is looming but the Germans are still occupying the Netherlands, and Michiel accidentally finds himself fighting with the Dutch resistance. He feels that he cannot trust anyone and that he has to rely entirely on himself.

Jan Terlouw wanted to tell a true-to-life tale about the war without simply just telling a thrilling story. He paints a frank picture of the situation during the harsh winter of starvation and of the real dangers and tensions to which the resistance were exposed. Nor does he shy away from the shocking, gruesome aspects of war. When Michiel's father is executed as a hostage, it fuels the local people's hatred for the Germans. However, Michiel comes to realize that there are also good Germans. A supposed collaborator hides Jews, whereas a good friend of Michiel's turns out to be a traitor. Michiel learns that nothing in life, let alone during war, is black and white, and that you must not be guided by your preconceptions.

Winter in Wartime is based on the author's own experiences. Terlouw gives his readers clear, balanced information wrapped up in a well-structured and exciting narrative. He also injects humor into his tale, preventing it from being overly dark. After working as a physics researcher, Terlouw went into politics and this is often reflected in his writing. **AD**

"It was not serious that he knew these things. He was by nature rather quiet and reserved."

OTHER GREAT READS BY JAN TERLOUW

King of Katoren (Koning van Katoren), 1971
Confidential Mail (Briefgeheim), 1973
Oosterschelde: Wind Force 10 (Oosterschelde: windkracht 10), 1976
The Chasm (De kloof), 1983

12+

No Way of Telling 1972

Emma Smith

Nationality | English, born 1923
Publisher | Bodley Head, UK
Theme | Family, Adventure, Friendship

Amy is a young girl who lives with her grandmother in a picturesque and mountainous area of Wales. The snowflakes falling on the isolated Welsh hill farm seem beautiful until Amy and her grandmother become trapped by the weather. The blizzard is not, however, their only problem, for before long they find themselves confronted by a series of strange visitors. First, a tall, robust man bursts into their kitchen, searches the house, takes food and blankets without saying a word, and then swiftly disappears again. Was the unexpected arrival a criminal or a victim? To quote the book's title, there is no way of telling. . . .

The following day, two men on skis appear, obviously hunting the first man. They claim to be the police, but there is something not quite right about them, and Amy's grandmother treats them with suspicion. The reasons for her behavior gradually become clearer to Amy, and to the reader, as the story unfolds and the band of intruders eventually turns out to be connected with two very dangerous international criminals.

Emma Smith's story, which was nominated for the Carnegie Medal, is a great thriller that will keep readers spellbound. Tense and atmospheric, it also provides a subtle depiction of the relationship between a young girl and her grandmother, a relationship based on the wisdom of the old and the vitality of the young. The book is also highly enjoyable for its beautiful descriptions of the wild Welsh landscape. **LB**

Across the Barricades 1972

Joan Lingard

Nationality | Scottish, born 1932
Publisher | Hamish Hamilton, UK
Award | Buxthuderbulle, 1986
Theme | Friendship, Family, Love

Set in Belfast in the early 1970s, this is the story of Catholic Kevin and Protestant Sadie, two lively, likable figures whose friendship develops against the backdrop of sectarian violence in Northern Ireland.

Three years earlier (in *The Twelfth Day of July*), the pair had been sworn enemies when their childhood gang warfare focused on the Protestant Orange Order marching season. Kevin and Sadie meet again by chance and are drawn to each other by their similarities—both are headstrong, restless, loyal, and passionate. But with the Troubles dividing their communities, their friendship seems to be courting disaster. Willfully defiant, they refuse to be separated, but when Kevin is beaten up and a teacher's house is petrol-bombed, it proves impossible to remain together in the city.

This is a dramatic, thought-provoking story that explores the impact of political and social events on ordinary lives. Scenes take place in both Catholic and Protestant households, which invites readers to consider the similarities as well as the differences between the hostile factions. The two rebellious protagonists are contrasted with their more peaceable siblings, giving readers an insight into the enormously complex issues their relationship generates. Across the strong storyline, there runs also a rich vein of sometimes dark humor that offers lighthearted moments of quick repartee and occasional ironic melodrama. Three subsequent novels follow the couple as they set up home in England. **KA**

The Summer Book 1972

 Tove Jansson

Original Title | Sommarboken
Nationality | Finnish, born 1914
Publisher | Schildts, Finland
Theme | Family, Friendship

An elderly artist and her six-year-old granddaughter, Sophia, arrive on a very small Finnish island for their summer holiday. Sophia's mother has died, and although she is seldom mentioned, her very absence and the palpable loss of her make the mother's personality seem ever present.

During this summer, the granddaughter and grandmother have adventures, arguments, and long, far-reaching conversations. They learn to adjust to one another's foibles and to share in each other's fears and desires. By the end of the book, their love for each other has grown much stronger and there is greater understanding between them. Their adventures include breaking into a newly built house on a neighboring island. They are incensed to discover that it has been built only as a summer house by a rich businessman, who does not visit, leaving it lonely and locked. They hatch a plan to break in and give it life.

During the summer, Sophia overcomes her fear of deep water, signifying her growth from child to more independent being. Despite the chasm of age between them, the pair find common ground, discussing everything from trivialities to grand questions, from insects and boats to love, religion, and death. Many simple but striking observations emerge on the way—"It was just the same long summer as always, and everything lived and grew at its own pace." Funny, wise, and unsentimental, *The Summer Book* is a modern classic of Scandinavian literature. **LH**

"All the suitcases were open and full of darkness and moss."

MORE STORIES OF GRANDPARENTS

Love, Ruby Lavender by Deborah Wiles, 1970
Song and Dance Man by Karen Ackerman, 1988
Walk Two Moons by Sharon Creech, 1994
In My Grandmother's House edited by Bonnie Christensen, 2003

Julie of the Wolves 1972

J. Craighead George J. Schoenherr

Nationality | American, born 1919 (author); American, born 1935 (illustrator)
Publisher | Harper and Row, USA
Theme | Adventure, Animal stories, Friendship

With her mother long dead and her father, a great hunter, presumed dead after not returning from a hunting trip, thirteen-year-old Julie decides to escape. Her only friend in the world is pen pal Amy, who lives in San Francisco, so Julie decides to cross the Arctic tundra to the ocean, where she plans on finding a job aboard an ocean liner that will take her to California.

She is lost before she even sets foot outside her home, though. It is while she is fighting to survive in the Arctic landscape that she begins to find herself. Drawing on the hours she spent watching wolves with her father, she learns to communicate with, and later joins, a wolf pack. The onset of the hunting season brings danger; Julie must decide how to preserve herself—but not at the expense of her lupine friends.

This conflict is mirrored in the turmoil that she faces over her heritage: After the death of her mother, she had been raised in the Eskimo tradition, where she was known as Miyax; however, following her father's disappearance, Julie's guardian aunt enrolled her in an American school away from her Eskimo community. It is here that she is renamed Julie. In contemplating the threat of extinction of the wolves, Julie comes face-to-face with the possible extinction of her own Eskimo culture; and in considering the unique choice she has between pursuing a future as "Julie" or as "Miyax," her story reminds us that communication between species—or cultures—is as vital to survival as understanding those outside our own tribe. **JSD**

Stories from the Year One Thousand 1972

Tonino Guerra Adriano Zannino

Nationality | Italian, born 1920 (author); Italian, birth date unknown (illustrator)
Publisher | Bompiani, Italy
Theme | Adventure, Friendship, War

Although Tonino Guerra is best known as a poet, he is also a playwright, screenwriter, writer, and artist. The visual and the extravagant is foremost in his writing.

In *Stories from the Year One Thousand (Storie dell'anno mille)* the hero, Millemosche (Thousand Flies), is a mercenary who rides through the war-torn countryside of the Middle Ages with his friends Pannocchia (Corncob) and Carestia (Famine). He has deserted from the army on principle against the fighting that dominates the country. With war raging, food is scarce, and so the top priority for the three vagabonds, who often go without eating, is the search for food. They scour the inhospitable countryside for any morsel that will calm their growling stomachs. Their attempts are often in vain, but are frequently hilarious, too. Who will have the courage to kill the kidnapped pig once they have him in their clutches? The three friends constantly have to deal with the unexpected and with people who are not amused by them, as well as with their own hunger pangs.

The adventures of Millemosche demonstrate that only with astuteness can disadvantaged characters save themselves. He and his two companions are constantly having to find an escape route out of trouble. In a similar vein to the Bertoldo tales, these wonderfully funny stories were based on earlier ones and are written in collaboration with Luigi Malerba. Throughout, Adriano Zannino's drawings display a fine comic style. **SMT**

12+

A portrait of Miyax by John Schoenherr.

The Spirit Wind 1973

Max Fatchen / Trevor Stubley

Nationality| Australian, born 1920 (author); English, born 1932 (illustrator)
Publisher | Hicks Smith, Australia; Methuen, UK
Theme | Adventure

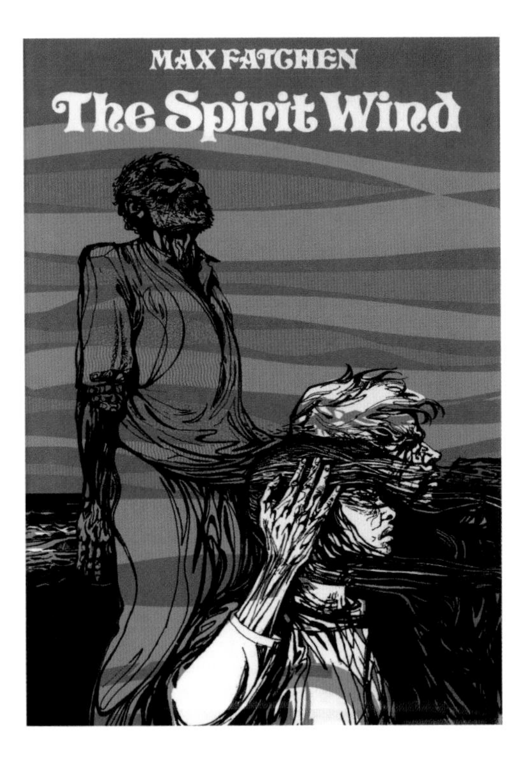

12+

The Spirit Wind is a rollicking adventure story. Jarl Hansen is a young cabin boy and the target of the ire of the first mate, Heinrich the Bull, aboard the Norwegian square-rigger, the *Hootzen*. The ship is bound for South Australia, where it is to collect a cargo of golden wheat.

Jarl plans to jump ship once they reach their destination, but he does not bargain on what happens as soon as he is off the ship. As he is paddling, he saves the old Aboriginal man Nunagee from being drowned by a stingray caught up in his fishing net. Nunagee takes Jarl to his remote hut where he hides him, knowing that the Trooper and the first mate will be out looking for the boy.

"Law or no law, Harry Horson, that boy can't go back to that awful ship."

Jarl is a wanted boy being hunted and he draws others into his dangerous situation when he befriends a supportive local family. A court hearing determines that the Norwegian Consul will be asked to let the boy stay. Furious at the decision, the first mate teams up with Ned Ganger, an escaped prisoner, who also has a grudge against the boy, because Jarl helped in his recapture. Together they set out to find the boy.

The final chapters of the book bring in the Spirit Wind of the title, a storm wind called up by Nunagee to save Jarl and to sink the *Hootzen*. The climax sees the cooperation of Jarl's friends as they rescue the sailors from the stricken ship. *The Spirit Wind* is a tale of early Australia, a time in which many peoples from around the globe came together and old customs mingled with the new as they attempted to live successfully in the harsh environment. **BH**

OTHER MAX FATCHEN FAVORITES

The River Kings, 1966
Conquest of the River, 1970
A Country Christmas, 1990
The Country Mail Is Coming: Poems from Down Under, 1990

Fly Away Home! 1973

Christine Nöstlinger

Original Title | Maikäfer, flieg!
Nationality | Austrian, born 1936
Publisher | Beltz and Gelberg, Germany
Theme | Adventure, Family, War

Christel Göth is a fiercely independent young girl living in Vienna at the end of World War II, during the Russian occupation. After her building is bombed, her family is lucky enough to be offered refuge in a spacious villa in Neuwaldegg, a wealthy area that was previously inhabited by Nazi supporters, most of whom have already fled to the West. Christel's father, a deserter from the German army, comes with them but is forced to stay in hiding to avoid soldiers from the German and Russian camps, both of whom now consider him the enemy.

While in Neuwaldegg, Christel befriends the grandchildren of the villa's owner, and together with her older sister, they get up to all kinds of mischief—

"I could not even remember a time when the war had not been on."

from teasing the next-door neighbors to stealing pickled food from an abandoned house. When a group of Russians come to take over the villa, Christel and her family strike up an uneasy camaraderie with them, which is interspersed with moments both of mirth and hostility.

Based on Nöstlinger's childhood experiences, *Fly Away Home!* is the story of one girl's emotional and physical growth during a time when most people are reduced to mere tatters of their former selves. Although the mood of the story is understandably solemn, Christel's crazy antics mean that Nöstlinger is occasionally able to provide humorous relief. But more importantly, with the war remaining a constant backdrop, the efforts of Christel and her family to survive provide a poignant reminder of the horrors and inhumanities of war. **CVB**

Christine Nöstlinger
Maikäfer, flieg!
Diese Geschichte ist wirklich passiert. Ich habe sie erlebt. Sie handelt von der Zeit, als mein Vater im Krieg war und als einmal der Frühling sehr früh kam. Mit ihm kam auch Cohn, mein russischer Freund. Es ist lange her.
BELTZ
& Gelberg

BOOKS BY CHRISTINE NÖSTLINGER

Fiery Frederica (Die feuerrote Friederike), 1970
Mr. Bat's Great Invention (Mr. Bats Meisterstück; oder, Die total verjüngte Oma), 1971
The Disappearing Cellar (Die Kinder aus dem Kinderkeller), 1971

12+

The Nargun and the Stars 1973

Patricia Wrightson Robert Ingpen

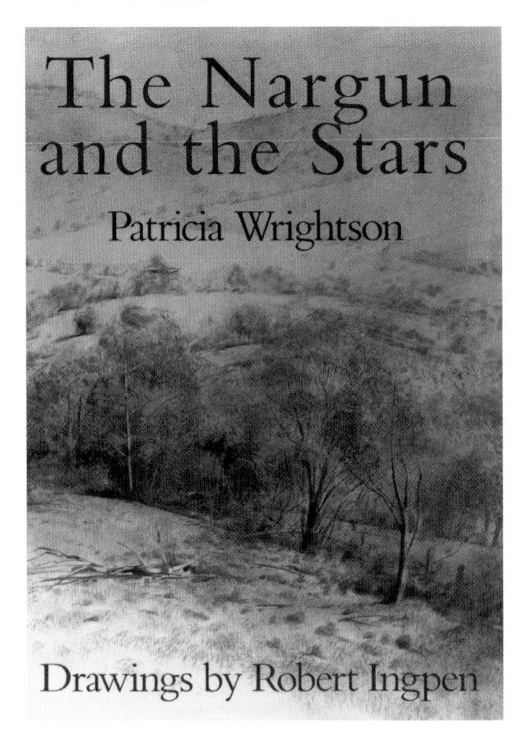

"He wanted to put out a hand to discover what moved close by—but the dark places in his mind told his hand to be still. . . ."

MORE BOOKS BY PATRICIA WRIGHTSON

The Crooked Snake, 1955
The Ice Is Coming, 1977
The Dark Bright Water, 1978
Behind the Wind, 1981
A Little Fear, 1983

Nationality | Australian, born 1921 (author); Australian, born 1936 (illustrator)
Publisher | Hutchinson, Australia
Theme | Folktales, Fantasy

The Nargun is an immensely interesting and unique character: ancient, born of rock and fire, alternately peaceful or deeply enraged, neither good nor evil. It represents the Australian landscape in its many moods. Now the Nargun's relentless journey across Australia has brought it to Wongadilla, a sheep property owned by Charlie and Edie. After Simon Brent's parents are killed in a car crash, he comes to live with these cousins. There he discovers the wrath of the Nargun; the fun-loving Potkoorok, trickster of the swamp; the wispy-shaped and teasing Turongs who live in the trees; and the stern Nyols hidden deep in the mountain caves. All are depicted, by the author, true to their nature as revealed in Aboriginal lore.

The Nargun, though, does not belong in this region, and its menacing presence is not wanted. Threatening and unpredictable, it slowly moves toward the house where Simon and his cousins live. Those who live at Wongadilla concoct a clever ruse to waylay the Nargun and return the land to peace. The plan is inventive but very dangerous. Gentle humor lightens the novel, as humans and the mythological creatures play tricks upon each other. The ending is ferocious and immensely satisfying.

Wrightson writes with such power and elegant simplicity that her fantasy world seems very real. A later edition (1988) includes haunting illustrations by Robert Ingpen, winner of the Hans Christian Andersen Award. These add immeasurably to the atmosphere and accurately reflect the majestic Australian landscape. **BA**

12+

The Slave Dancer 1973

Paula Fox Eros Keith

Nationality | American, born 1923
Publisher | Bradbury Press, USA
Award | Newbery Medal, 1974
Theme | Adventure, Historical fiction

In this harrowing novel, Jessie Bollier is kidnapped and taken aboard a slave ship. From the moment the canvas is thrown over his head in a back alley in New Orleans to the moment he emerges on the shore of Cuba after the wreck of the *Moonlight*, Jessie struggles to survive from the dark and dangerous trade to which he has become unwittingly apprenticed. The story is set during a time when the British had outlawed the slave trade, and though slavery remained legal in the United States, America too had banned the importation of slaves. The *Moonlight* therefore sails outside every law and under any flag that affords it temporary protection.

Wrenched from his home and family, Jessie seeks to keep his self-respect and find someone he can trust among the crew. But these are men who have been degraded by their work, and whose brutality to one another is surpassed only by their treatment of the slaves. Jessie plays a fife for the slaves to dance when they are hauled on deck in chains, and, at this worst moment in his helpless complicity in their fate, discovers to his horror and disgust that he, too, hates them: "I wished them all dead! Not to hear them! Not to smell them! Not to know of their existence!"

Jessie redeems himself from the curse of slavery by helping a slave boy, Ras, escape from the wreck of the *Moonlight*. However, his experience of the trade haunts the rest of his life. The novel contributed to Paula Fox's reputation for looking honestly at how people endure in desperate circumstances, whether she was writing for young people or adults. **CB**

The Friends 1973

Rosa Guy

Nationality | American, born 1925
Publisher | Holt, Rinehart and Winston, USA
Award | A.L.A. Best Book for Young Adults
Theme | Family, Friendship, School

Rosa Guy's first novel for young people draws on her own experience as a young woman from the Caribbean growing up poor in Harlem, New York. Fourteen-year-old Phyllisia and her family have been brought to the city by their ambitious father, Calvin. The book tells the disturbing, claustrophobic story of her coming of age, in which the poverty and social conflicts of the city's African-American community are played out tragically in friendships and family life.

The novel begins in an airless summer classroom in which the frustrations and tensions of the white teacher and her black students crackle like a gathering storm. It moves on into autumn and winter in the closeted family apartment, where Phyllisia's mother dies of cancer. Through these trials, and Phyllisia's growing awareness of herself as a young woman, the story follows her friendship with tough and generous Edith, who struggles to keep her own family together by poorly paid domestic work, after her father disappears and her brother is shot by the police.

Guy writes with an unflinching eloquence that acknowledges the cadences of the Caribbean, the rough poetry of the Harlem streets, and the language of the Bible. Phyllisia painfully gains understanding of herself and others. It is her relationships with her father and Edith that matter most. Gradually she sees that Calvin, although boastful and sometimes violent, is neither the great man of his pretensions nor entirely thoughtless and cruel. She also realizes, through her friendship with Edith, how much of her father's view of people she has herself unthinkingly absorbed. **CB**

The Dark Is Rising 1973

Susan Cooper Alan E. Cober

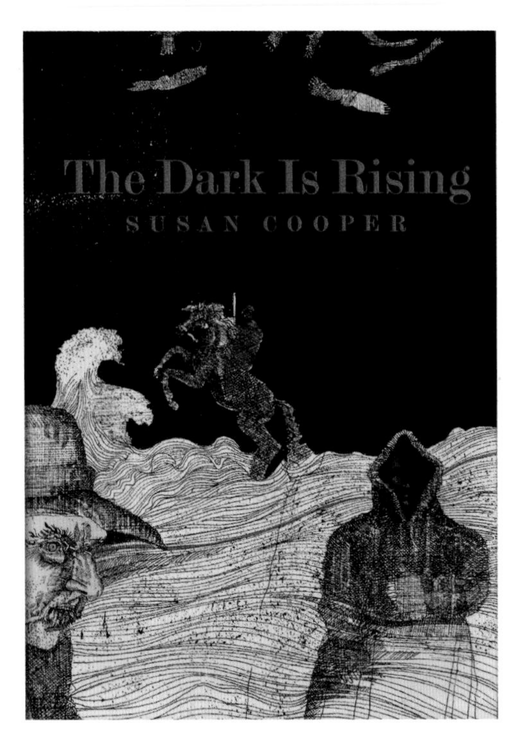

Nationality | English, born 1935
Publisher | Chatto and Windus, UK
Award | Newbery Honor Book, 1974
Theme | Fantasy, Myths and legends

The second of the five novels known as The Dark Is Rising series, this story is resonant with the magic and myth of Celtic and Arthurian legends. It cries out to be read at Christmastime, with its opening set in a gray-skied midwinter as a young boy wishes for snow, worries about his frightened rabbits, and wonders about the strange hunched figure he has seen hiding behind a tree. There is precious little festive cheer about the tale, however.

On his eleventh birthday, Will gets his snow, but finds himself in an ancient world where he is surrounded by evil. Will is the seventh son of a seventh son and lives a parallel life as one of the Old Ones who must help the forces of Light to overcome Dark. He has to follow his instinct, learn who to trust, work out how to use his powerful gifts, and evade those who want to control him.

The first book in the sequence, *Over Sea, Under Stone*, introduced the characters of Simon, Jane, and Barney, who are engaged in the same struggle as Will, and are guided by their mysterious Great-Uncle Merriam, a Merlinlike figure who is also Will's mentor. There is no disadvantage to reading *The Dark Is Rising* first. As well as exploring the mythic world of ancient Britain, it offers insights into human nature and into the ambiguities of people's motivations.

Will's story makes it easy for today's children to believe in the existence of myth and to understand the source of the Dark. It comes not only from prejudice and hatred, but also from people's failure to take responsibility and act against them. **GB**

"All the broad sky was gray, full of more snow that refused to fall. There was no color anywhere."

OTHERS IN THE DARK IS RISING SERIES

Over Sea, Under Stone, 1965
Greenwitch, 1974
The Grey King, 1975
Silver on the Tree, 1977

12+

Carrie's War 1973

Nina Bawden

Nationality | English, born 1925
Publisher | Gollancz, UK; Lippincott, USA
Award | Phoenix Award, 1993
Theme | Family, War, Classics

Carrie Willow and her brother, Nick, make the experience of evacuees during World War II real and immediate to contemporary readers, who share in their bemusement and sense of disconnection when they have to leave their familiar Welsh village. The children's homesickness and difficulty in adjusting to the exacting expectations of their host, the strict and bullying shopkeeper Mr. Evans, is only bearable because they are together and Mr. Evans's downtrodden sister Lou is kind to them. They soon find more friends in Hepzibah, the housekeeper of Mr. Evans's estranged older sister, Mrs. Gotobed, and another evacuee child, Albert Sandwich. When Carrie's vivid imagination is fired by Hepzibah's stories of the past, she starts to piece together the half-understood truth behind the Evans's family feud. As Carrie and Nick become part of the fabric of village life, the reader watches the story of the entire community unfold through the children's eyes.

In the course of this subtle, sensitive, and affectionate book, Carrie matures and learns not to leap to conclusions about the feelings and motives of others. She even begins to see some of Mr. Evans's points of view and sympathizes with his exhaustion and despair, while feeling irritated at Lou's passivity. However, she leaves the village convinced that she has been led into doing a great wrong in her urge to support Hepzibah after Mrs. Gotobed's death. It takes the adult Carrie, who visits the village with her own children thirty years later in a framing narrative, to complete the picture. **GB**

M. C. Higgins 1974

Virginia Hamilton

Nationality | American, born 1936
Publisher | Macmillan, USA
Award | Newbery Medal, 1975
Theme | Family, Friendship

Virginia Hamilton was the most celebrated American writer for young people of her generation. This early novel began the landslide of awards and accolades that she was to receive over the next thirty years.

M. C. Higgins, the Great is the story of a boy who lives with his family on the side of Sarah's Mountain in Ohio. While his parents work in nearby cities, M. C. and his younger brothers and sister roam freely, hunting, swimming, and spending time with his "witchy" six-fingered friend, Ben Killburn. Perched on a bicycle seat on top of a forty-foot-high steel pole next to his house, he surveys his family's kingdom, which has been theirs since his great-grandmother Sarah arrived there with her child escaping from slavery. The Higgins household is now under threat from strip mining on the mountain's summit, which has produced a waste heap that hangs ominously over their home.

The story centers on M. C.'s friendship with two newcomers. The first is a collector of folk songs and singers, whom M. C. imagines will make his mother famous and take them away from the mountain and its dangers. The other is a girl whose openness to new experiences contrasts with M. C.'s settled ways. The novel conveys a feeling for unique places, people, and their history, drawing upon a vein of American, and particularly African-American, folk culture. It is written in a style that has the rhythm and syntax of heightened conversation. Its characters live and breathe in a space that is recognizably the real world but has been stretched and shaped by Hamilton to become seductively surprising and brilliant. **CB**

12+

Nobody's Family Is Going to Change 1974

Louise Fitzhugh

Nationality | American, born 1928
Publisher | Farrar, Straus and Giroux, USA
Award | Children's Book Bulletin, 1976
Theme | Family, Friendship

Louise Fitzhugh's first book, *Harriet the Spy* (1964), has a heroine who spends her time making observations about other people in a notebook, some of which are less than flattering. It caused controversy among reviewers, some praising its shrewd characterization and satiric wit, others finding its outlook jaundiced.

Nobody's Family Is Going to Change enters the mind of Emancipation (Emma for short) Sheridan and recounts, in her own words, her struggles with her overbearing father and her unassertive mother. Emma is a bright girl with a sense of injustice that is provoked by her father's refusal to allow her talented brother, Willie, to pursue a career as a dancer. Frustrated, too, by her parents' assumption that she will be content as a wife and mother, even though she wants to be a lawyer, she becomes Willie's defense attorney in family arguments and joins a secret organization of children bent on fighting parental abuse.

The novel explores issues of children's rights and gender stereotyping with dialogue as sharp and witty as the best American situation comedy. The children's confrontations with their parents move between desperation and farce as, however inappropriately, Emma turns them into courtroom drama. She is fascinating: a loner, perceptive, critical of herself and others, as insecure as she is resourceful, and determined to be her own person. Ultimately, she finds friends among girls of her own age, even as she realizes her parents will never understand her. **CB**

The Trouble with Donovan Croft 1974

Bernard Ashley Fermin Rocker

Nationality | English, born 1935
Publisher | Oxford University Press, UK
Theme | Family, Friendship, School, Adventure

Young Keith Chapman's cozy domestic world is turned on its head when his parents decide to foster Donovan, a Jamaican boy whose mother has returned home and whose father cannot cope both with work and child care. But Donovan has been missing his mother for so long now, he is too unhappy even to speak. The presence of an elective mute in the house is hard enough, but things get worse when Donovan is picked on at school by Keith's friends and also by his racist teacher. Things improve with the arrival of Donovan's father, who sees his son save Keith from a speeding car by shouting out a warning just in time—the first words he has uttered in a long time. After that, Donovan slowly starts talking again, and everything appears much more hopeful.

Bernard Ashley is a teacher as well as an author, who is familiar both with children at school and at home. He knows from experience that young readers do not like being preached at, which never happens in this engrossing story. Rather, the characters tell the story themselves through their own actions and dialogue. Soccer-mad Keith is a nice boy but no saint; he hates feeling excluded by his friends when they initially take against Donovan, but also feels honor bound to protect this unhappy boy whom he gets to know despite their lack of communication. As an argument for tolerance and understanding cleverly dressed up in a story whose interest never flags, this novel is a triumph. **NT**

Who Does This Kid Take After? 1974

Éva Janikovszky   László Réber

Original Title | Kire ütött ez a gyerek?
Nationality | Hungarians, born 1926 and 1920
Publisher | Móra Könyvkiadó, Hungary
Theme | Family, Young adult

The hero of *Who Does This Kid Take After?* is a moody teenager who was once considered "little and sweet," but is now gawky and a mystery to his parents. This charming book tells teenagers that they are not alone and reminds adults what it is like to be young.

Éva Janikovszky is one of Hungary's best-loved children's writers. She received the Deutscher Jugendliteraturpreis in 1983 and her books have been translated into thirty-five languages. One of Janikovszky's best-known books outside her native country is *If I Were a Grown-up* in which the child protagonist believes it is preferable to be grown-up and in charge rather than constantly being told what to do. Another of her novels, *Happiness*, explores how a child comes to realize that other people do not exist purely to satisfy him and that making other people happy is a real pleasure in itself.

Janikovszky's work often revolves around the sometimes complicated relationships that develop between children and parents, aunts, uncles, and grandparents. She creates a unique fictional world in which she takes a child's-eye view of everyday events and often undermines the authority of grown-ups. Part of the charm of Janikovszky's books is down to the illustrations provided by her long-time collaborator, Lázsló Réber. His simple drawings are full of humor and the lanky teenager on the cover of *Who Does This Kid Take After?* deftly conveys all the awkwardness of being on the cusp of adulthood. **HJ**

"I am big and loopy, and flippant and unsightly."

OTHER BOOKS BY ÉVA JANIKOVSZKY

If I Were a Grown-up (*Ha én felnött volnék*), 1965
Happiness (*Jó nekem*), 1967
The Thing is . . . (*Az úgy volt . . .*), 1979
Written to Adults (*Felnötteknek irtam*), 1997

12+

The Chocolate War 1974

Robert Cormier

Nationality | American, born 1925
Publisher | Pantheon, USA
Award | A.L.A. Best Book for Young Adults
Theme | School, Young adult

There is a poster hanging in a locker at Trinity Catholic High School illustrating a well-known quotation from T. S. Eliot: "Do I dare disturb the universe?" The poster belongs to a teenage boy called Jerry Renault and it is the dilemma that this quotation poses for him that is searingly explored in Cormier's controversial novel. The school he attends is repressive and authoritarian, being nominally run in the principal's absence by the sadistic Brother Leon but in reality it is more under the control of the school's "secret" society, the Vigils. It soon becomes clear that the most disturbing element of the novel is the way it highlights the extent to which children and adults collude in the exploitation. The Vigils are led by Archie Costello whose corruption and addiction to cruelty easily match those of Brother Leon.

Singled out by Archie and his fellow Vigils as a potential victim, Jerry refuses to participate in the school's annual fund-raising chocolate sale. When he continues to do so, in spite of the Vigils' instruction to the contrary, his temporary status as hero is shattered in an onslaught of physical and psychological abuse. The final humiliation comes in the form of a boxing bout with Emile Janza, the school's most notorious bully. As readers ponder the final outcome they are forced to rethink the very considerable price to be paid by Jerry for "daring to disturb" his particular universe and, by extension, to think about the uses and abuses of power in a universe well beyond the confines of an American school. This is a very dark story, set in a very dark world. **RD**

Twopence a Tub 1975

Susan Price

Nationality | English, born 1955
Publisher | Faber and Faber, UK
Theme | Historical fiction, Family, Friendship

Susan Price's second novel is one of the few accounts of an industrial dispute in British children's literature. Partly based on the folk memory of the community in which Price grew up, it is the story of a nineteenth-century miners' strike in England's Black Country.

Told sympathetically from the miners' points of view, it is unsparing both in its description of their poverty and squalid living conditions and of a family and community life that, facing this hardship, could be demoralized and brutal. The strike is seen through the eyes of Jek, a young miner, who, while committed to the strike, is also appalled at the way it sets neighbor against neighbor as the mine owners refuse to compromise and men are driven back to work.

Price re-creates a convincing working-class world in which kindness, friendship, dignity, and a sense of natural right and common cause sit alongside ignorance, fear, clannishness, aggression, and deference bred of poverty and the callous indifference of the employing class—"the Gaffers." The strike fails, and the final chapter is full of the bitterness that Jek feels, yet he has also begun a relationship with Rachel, the daughter of a nailer in the nearby town. This courtship promises hope for the future, for Rachel can read and brings intelligence and quiet determination to match Jek's courage and impetuousness.

Price went on to produce work of a consistently high standard for a wide age range, mixing fantasy, the supernatural, and historical settings with the strong sense of emotional and social realism that is apparent in this book. **CB**

Tuck Everlasting 1975

Natalie Babbitt

Nationality | American, born 1932
Publisher | Farrar, Straus and Giroux, USA
Award | A.L.A. Notable Children's Book
Theme | Fantasy, Family, Classics

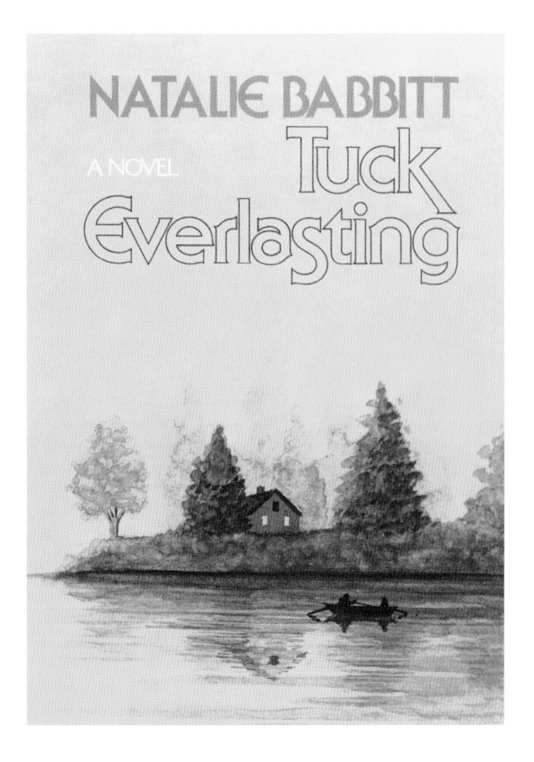

Does the spring in the wood really hold the secret of everlasting life? The Tuck family have certainly found it to be so. When runaway Winnie finds the spring—purely by chance—she is dazzled by the sight of Jesse Tuck nearby. Winnie goes willingly with the Tucks on their everlasting horse, but then doubts begin to creep in and she decides that she wants to go home. One evening Jesse takes Winnie out on the lake and there he makes her understand what it has been like to be eternally seventeen and not grow older.

Unbeknown to them all, however, a man in a yellow suit has been watching and overhears the Tucks telling Winnie about the secret of the spring. Eager to acquire it for himself, the man tries to abduct Mae and con her family into selling him the wood in return for her. The plan goes wrong, though, when Mae kills this mysterious interloper rather than run the risk of having him exploit the spring's secret and use her family as if they were part of a sideshow.

Mae is taken off to jail to await trial—and most probably to be hanged on the gallows—but the resourceful Tucks and Winnie hatch a plan to help her escape. Before they do, however, Jesse gives Winnie a bottle of the water so that when she is seventeen she can drink from it and they can be together. In the end, however, Winnie chooses not to drink the water because as Mae's husband tells her "all living things change" and the Tucks just "are."

This is a deep and, at times, dark fantasy, that contains a great deal of material for the reader to think about and discuss. **JF**

"For Mae Tuck, and her husband, and Miles and Jesse, too, had all looked exactly the same for eighty-seven years."

GREAT READS BY NATALIE BABBITT

The Search for Delicious, 1969
Knee-Knock Rise, 1970
The Eyes of the Amaryllis, 1977
Elsie Times Eight, 2001
Jack Plank Tells Tales, 2007

12+

The Machine Gunners 1975

Robert Westall John Williamson

12+

"Chas gulped. The machine gun was still there, hanging from the turret, shiny and black."

CLASSIC FICTION BY ROBERT WESTALL

Fathom Five, 1975
The Scarecrows, 1981
Futuretrack Five, 1983
Blitzcat, 1989
The Kingdom by the Sea, 1990

Nationality | English, born 1929
Publisher | Macmillan, UK
Award | Carnegie Medal, 1975
Theme | Historical fiction, School, War

Schoolboy Chas McGill, an avid collector of war souvenirs, finds a machine gun in the wreckage of a German plane. While the adults are preoccupied by the nightly bombings, Chas and his gang steal the gun and build it an emplacement and a camp for themselves in the garden of a bombed-out house.

With invasion apparently imminent, Chas's outmaneuvering of the adults and their questions lends a sense of plausibility to their exploits. Even when the gang captures and imprisons a Luftwaffe sergeant, the narrative creates credible emotional and logical explanations for his failure to escape. While outside all the usual hierarchies and domestic comforts have been destroyed by the war, inside their comfortable encampment the children provide a family of sorts for one another, offering understanding and support that, for many of them, is now lacking at home. Discovery inevitably looms, however, and with it the possibility of a reform school for some and the certainty of a children's home for others.

When it happens, Westall offers no compromising happy ending. The only consolation comes from the angry parents' approval of their children's "guts" and the Home Guard's admiration for their skilled building work. The book's strength lies partly in its detailed realism but also in the power of its narrative which, with its accomplished shifts between settings and voices, demonstrates the command of structure, tension, and character that typifies Westall's work. **KA**

The Peppermint Pig 1975

Nina Bawden Charles Lilly

Nationality | English, born 1925
Publisher | Gollancz, UK; Lippincott, USA
Award | *Guardian* Children's Fiction Prize, 1976
Theme | Family, Historical fiction, Friendship

This enchanting story, set in late-Victorian England, follows the fortunes of Poll and her family. Her father loses his job after confessing to a crime that he did not commit in order to save his employer from finding out that the criminal was his own son. Poll's mother and the children are forced to leave their home and live with Poll's aunts in rural Norfolk, while her father joins his brother to seek fortune in America.

Poll looks out for her brother Theo who, although older than Poll, is small for his age. Theo shows courage and ingenuity, however, as he strikes out on his own against the village bully. Poll herself makes what her mother thinks is an "unsuitable friend" in Annie, and nearly dies from the consequences of a visit to her house.

The pig of the title is the runt of the litter. He is house-trained until he becomes too big for comfort and meets his end—a fate hidden from Poll and one that she finds hard to accept. Her father's sisters, both whom are teachers, help the family out in many ways, and her mother swallows her pride and attempts to find dressmaking work. Intriguingly, the poverty of the fatherless family is partly hidden from the reader as it is from Poll.

It is the small details of everyday life that make this family story so convincing, but underlying it all is the strength of the family unit, even without Poll's father. Poll grows up a great deal during this year but she is always sheltered by her family's love. **JF**

Crisis on Conshelf Ten 1975

Monica Hughes G. Humpreys

Nationality | English/Canadian, born 1925
Publisher | Copp Clark, Canada
Theme | Adventure, Fantasy, Science fiction

The year is 2005 and humans, naturally, live on the moon (or, rather, "Moon," as it is properly called). As the colony has developed from frontier backwater to a self-defining society with dreams of its own, a diplomatic push is underway to convince the United Nations to grant the colony the right to self-determination. Fifteen-year-old Kepler Masterman, Moon's first natural-born citizen, accompanies his father, Moon's leader, to Earth to deliver the message. But quite early in his stay he reacts poorly to the planet's gravity and is sent to spend the balance of his trip with relatives in an underwater colony. This is when the real adventure begins.

Crisis on Conshelf Ten, set mostly in an underwater world of dissidence and intrigue, sees our young narrator implicated in not one but three independence struggles, with a prescient eye to acts of political terrorism and disaffected minorities. Loyalties are tested, lines are blurred, morality is made to seem relative, and the whole heady rush of cold war–era confusion sets in.

This timely look at international relations via the lens of outer space is essentially an adventure story—an updated Hardy Boys—reflecting Hughes's ardent admiration for the genre. Although its resolution might seem rather innocent in light of subsequent political upheavals, it remains a richly satisfying book with enough twists, turns, and timeliness to cement its place in the canon of children's literature. **GTS**

The October Child 1976

Eleanor Spence   Malcolm Green

"'You're not my brother!' Douglas whispered. 'You never were my brother!'"

MORE BOOKS BY ELEANOR SPENCE

Lillipilly Hill, 1960
A Candle for Saint Antony, 1977
The Left Overs, 1982
Deezle Boy, 1987

Nationality | Australian, born 1928
Publisher | Oxford University Press, UK
Award | C.B.C.A. Book of the Year, 1977
Theme | Family

Few stories reveal the impact that an autistic child can have on family interactions as well as this book. As one critic put it, Spence was known for her "fearless examination of difficult social questions." She is well placed to fictionalize the situation—she taught autistic children and adolescents for several years. Yet this is not a case study; Spence convincingly and vividly portrays each of the Mariner family, especially Douglas, who is the closest to his autistic brother, Carl.

Carl's autism is the reason the Mariner family reluctantly leave their business at a coastal resort and move to Sydney. The contrast in lifestyles is an extended metaphor for the change in the family's circumstances. Typically, in novels for young people the parents are not presented in great depth, but here they are sufficiently drawn to reveal how adults might react under these circumstances. Family pressures overwhelm the mother and keeping the family peace depresses the father. Neither parent copes well, and it is Douglas who becomes the major support for Carl. The elder teenager, Kenneth, plans to leave home, while the younger Adrienne is glued to the television. The most evocative scenes are those featuring Carl, who is unable to speak and alternately has unpredictable rages or short periods of calm and contentment. Douglas is finely drawn as the central character, and experiencing Carl through his eyes gives readers an understanding of autism and an empathy for the Mariner family. By the novel's realistic end, Douglas has found ways to support Carl while still pursuing his own interest in music. **BA**

12+

Dragonsong 1976

Anne McCaffrey

Nationality | American, born 1926
Publisher | Atheneum Books, USA
Theme | Adventure, Fantasy, Science fiction, Young adult

Best-selling science fiction and fantasy writer Anne McCaffrey is famed for her "Pern" books, which have entertained a wide range of readers for decades. *Dragonsong* is the first of the Harper Hall trilogy, the other two being *Dragonsinger* and *Dragondrums*. Planet Pern forms the backbone of *Dragonsong* and its related books. Times have been tough on Pern since Thread began raining down deadly spores. Only the dragons of Pern, aided and abetted by their brave human riders (with whom they have telepathic links), are able to fight back by breathing fire at the Threads.

The Harper Hall trilogy focuses less on the dragonriders and more on the musical activities of Harper Hall—a place of learning that was devoted to scientific pursuit before Thread brought destruction and took the planet back to less technologically savvy times. Teenager Menolly is the central character; her talent is for music, but those around her, including her own parents, feel that this is not woman's work and cruelly stifle her interest. Menolly runs away from home and lives off her own resources, encountering fire lizards and deadly Threadfall along the way, but also indulging her passion for music. Finally, she can be herself when the Masterharper of Pern discovers her gift and makes her his apprentice.

This is a coming-of-age tale with a twist. While exploring gender roles and echoing the author's own interest in music, it also provides plenty of excitement and suspense, plus an escape into the kind of entirely "other" world that appeals so much to children and young adults. **AK**

Bilgewater 1976

Jane Gardam

Nationality | English, born 1928
Publisher | Hamish Hamilton, UK
Theme | School, Young adult, Love, Friendship

Seventeen-year-old Marigold is ill-equipped for the rocky path to first love and beyond. Brought up in the boys' boarding school where her widowed father is housemaster, she is treated by the world as part of the institution. ("Bilgewater" is the boys' nickname for her, based on "Bill's daughter.") She has been cherished by her distracted father and the kind school matron, but cannot compete with the headmaster's beautiful, worldly, and notorious daughter.

At her own school, Marigold's introversion has led to her being overlooked until she passes her school exams early and is allowed to apply to Cambridge University. Her vision of romantic love, straight from John Keats and Thomas Hardy, fits badly with the reality of boys' duplicities. Makeovers and new clothes cannot take the edge off her gawky shyness and, of course, there is no Internet to help her find soulmates. Readers a little younger than Marigold will relate well to her dilemmas.

It takes two transforming journeys for Marigold to find a place for herself in the world: a miserable and humiliating visit to the brassy family of her first love and an idyllic day trip with the like-minded souls who have been close to home all along. The many coincidences and tied-up loose ends make the story itself a safety net as Marigold leaps into the unknown. The message of not judging by appearances, not being led by assumptions, and valuing old acquaintances unifies the various story strands in the eccentric but supportive school community; a framing narrative delivers a satisfactory resolution. **GB**

Roll of Thunder, Hear My Cry 1976

Mildred D. Taylor Jerry Pinkney

"Ole man coming down the line . . . to beat me down. But I ain't gonna let him turn me 'round."

GREAT READS BY MILDRED TAYLOR

Song of the Trees, 1975
Let the Circle Be Unbroken, 1981
The Gold Cadillac, 1987
The Road to Memphis, 1990
The Land, 2001

Nationality | American, born 1943
Publisher | Dial Books, USA
Award | Newbery Medal, 1977
Theme | Family, Historical fiction

This important historical novel about segregation is based on the author's own African-American family history. It is set during the 1930s Depression, in rural Mississippi, where Cassie Logan and her family experience firsthand prejudice and discrimination on a daily basis. Despite the hardship they suffer, however, they ultimately emerge wiser and happier, having learned that no matter what happens, no one can ever take away a family's courage and pride.

Land is the lifeblood of the Logan family—owning it (although many in their community were nonowning sharecroppers), working it, and living off it—because it gives them a sense of place. As her papa explains, "Look out there, Cassie girl. All that belongs to you. You ain't never had to live on nobody's place but your own and long as I live and the family survives, you'll never have to. That's important. You may not understand that now but one day you will."

Told over the course of twelve very confusing and turbulent months, the narrative describes how Cassie and her family face brutal attacks, illness, financial hardship, lynchings, and betrayal. Life teaches Cassie some tough lessons—not least of which is her discovery of racism, specifically through the activities of the frightening night riders—but she survives them to become a wiser and stronger individual.

The Logan family saga continues in Mildred D. Taylor's books *Let the Circle Be Unbroken* and *The Road to Memphis*, and a prequel, *The Land*. **KD**

12+

Thunder and Lightnings 1976

Jan Mark

Nationality | English, born 1943
Publisher | Kestrel Books, UK
Award | Carnegie Medal
Theme | Adventure, Fantasy

Moving to Norfolk, England, far away from his detested former school, Andrew is understandably nervous about starting out in another one. But his new friend Victor helps ease Andrew in while also sharing with him his consuming love of the Royal Air Force planes so frequently flying overhead. Unhappy at home with his strict and unloving parents, Victor lives for these planes and in particular for his beloved Lightnings. Victor dreads the moment when these graceful machines will be replaced by Jaguars, but, helped by Andrew, he begins to accept the inevitability of change while also discovering some equally engrossing new interests.

Jan Mark's first novel is already packed with all the trademark tricks of style soon to become familiar in her other published work. Characters are largely defined by what they say, with plenty of throwaway comic lines to keep readers happy. But the central plot is as always a serious one, involving Victor's attempt to become and then stay his own person, despite discouragement and sometimes cruelty from those who should be supporting him. Every reader will be glad when he finally comes good, still able to enjoy memories of the past but now looking forward to new experiences as well. Moving as well as funny and always sharply observed, this novel offers plenty for those also in the process of having to accept change in themselves and others while still trying to hold on to favorite moments and memories. **NT**

First of Midnight 1977

Marjorie Darke Anthony Morris

Nationality | English, born 1929 (author); English, birth date unknown (illustrator)
Publisher | Kestrel Books, UK
Theme | Adventure, Historical fiction

This is the thought-provoking story of two slaves, one white and one black, set in 1797. African slave Midnight has been sold from a sugar plantation, where he learned to read and write, to Captain Meredith, a slave trader from Bristol, England. The slave trade is booming although slavery itself is illegal in England. Seventeen-year-old Jess, an orphan brought up in the workhouse, has been sold several times during her short life. After running away disguised as a boy, Jess meets Midnight when they are shackled together onboard ship. Coincidentally, both of them know something of Captain Meredith's illegal business ventures, one having served on his ship and one by overhearing a conversation.

After a meeting of the shareholders and the insurance company representative at the Jarman's house where Jess is working, Midnight is savagely beaten and Jess nurses him back to health. Ironically he is hidden in Harriet Jarman's stables and she is a member of the board that owns Captain Meredith's ship and trade. After Midnight is freed, he earns enough through bare-knuckle boxing to buy his passage back to Africa, but he and Jess realize that it simply would not work for her to accompany him.

The savagery of the slave trade and the mendacity of those who run it are set against the lowlifes of the Bristol docks, where a girl can be bought and sold. There is much dialect here, but once the reader has its rhythm the place and time come vividly to life. **JF**

Underground to Canada 1977

Barbara Smucker · Imre Hofbauer

Nationality | Canadian, born 1915 (author); Hungarian, born 1905 (illustrator)
Publisher | Clark, Irwin and Company, Canada
Theme | Adventure, Family, Historical fiction

The Underground Railway to Canada was a way for escaping slaves to get to freedom from the southern states of America. Twelve-year-old Julilly is sold and sent away from her mother and the plantation where she grew up. She ends up on a plantation run by a cruel and vicious slave master called Sims, and here she meets Liza, who has been whipped and beaten, and is crippled by her wounds.

Before Julilly left, Mammy Sally, her mother, told her of a possible haven: "There's a place the slaves been whisperin' around called Canada. The law don't allow no slavery there." So, when Canadian Alexander Ross (a real figure) appears at the plantation masquerading as a bird collector, Julilly is determined to escape. Despite her injuries, Liza decides to join her and the two girls hide food and creep away to meet Mr. Ross.

Escaping is easier said than done, of course, and the sound of the dogs tracking them echoes throughout the pages. Two adult slaves, Lester and Adam, are recaptured but the two girls, who disguise themselves as boys, manage to escape to Canada with the help of brave Quakers and Mr. Ross. By following the route on the map provided with this novel, the reader comes to a dramatic understanding of the magnitude of the journey the girls are attempting.

Julilly and Liza finally reach St. Catherine's, Ontario, only to discover that there is prejudice there, too. The two girls are free at last, though—and best of all for Julilly, Mammy Sally is there to greet her. **JF**

The Westing Game 1978

Ellen Raskin

Nationality | American, born 1928
Publisher | E. P. Dutton, USA
Award | Newbery Medal, 1979
Theme | Adventure, Detective story

After the sudden death of Samuel W. Westing—chess enthusiast and founder of Westingtown, Wisconsin, and Westing Paper Products Corporation—sixteen tenants of the Sunset Towers apartment building are summoned for the reading of his will. The will sets up the rules of the "game." The sixteen are divided into pairs, and each is given one of eight clues to the mystery of who killed Mr. Westing. As the participants follow the clues down an increasingly convoluted path and develop increasingly outlandish theories, one of them puts the pieces together to figure out what has been right under their noses the entire time.

Like a *Gosford Park* for preteens, the central puzzle is partially just an excuse to watch the interactions of a group of fascinating characters from all walks of life. The inhabitants of Sunset Towers are a multiethnic group of doctors, judges, restaurant owners, and children, but as they try to solve the crime together, they are able to rise above petty differences and learn to respect each other on their own terms. The fact that Westing's first name is Sam, and he calls the heirs his "nephews and nieces," shows that this cooperation is all part of the point: Not just a screwball mystery, this is a novel about the American dream, and how the best way for the characters to inherit what "Uncle Sam" has promised them is to work together.

A quirky, hilarious page-turner, *The Westing Game* is sheer pleasure and a must-read for any budding whodunnit enthusiast. **SY**

A caricature of Uncle Sam's Sunset Towers. 

1000
UNITED STATES OF AMERICA
1000
AMERICA
1000
1000
1000
OF AMERICA
1000
1000
DOLLARS
1000
1000
1000
AMERICA
1000
1000
DOLLARS
1000

Hey, Dollface 1978

Deborah Hautzig

Nationality | American, born 1957
Publisher | Greenwillow Books, USA
Theme | Friendship, Young adult, Love, Illness and death, Controversial

A female rite-of-passage novel dealing with death, lesbian curiosity, and sexual awakening, *Hey, Dollface* is the diary-style narrative of Valerie Hoffman, the new girl at an elite New York private school. Valerie's only ally against her arrogant cohorts is fellow freshman, Chloe Fox, with whom she develops a strong camaraderie, verging on infatuation. Valerie and Chloe embark on a wild and passionate friendship, cutting class to idle away the day in Manhattan clothes stores and coffee shops, gossiping about their hated classmates, and discussing common topics of adolescent fixation—love, lust, and sex.

Following the sudden death of Chloe's father, the girls are drawn closer together and Valerie begins to realize that what she feels for Chloe is moving beyond friendship to desire. Terrified that by admitting her feelings to Chloe she will lose the friendship, Valerie descends into depression. At the rather anticlimactic conclusion, Chloe and Valerie mutually acknowledge their sexual attraction but resolve instead to simply remain best friends.

"I don't think I ever said how beautiful Chloe was. But beautiful like no one else."

The novel successfully addresses many of the bewildering elements of adolescence and emphasizes the importance of companionship and accepting advice from parents and elders. The story's authenticity is no doubt due in part to its being Hautzig's first novel that was published while she herself was still a student at Sarah Lawrence College. Since then she has written other novels, including *Second Star to the Right* (1981) and published a number of acclaimed retellings of fairy tales. **ML**

OTHER COMING-OF-AGE NOVELS

Who Does This Kid Take After? by Éva Janikovszky, 1974
What I Was by Meg Rosoff, 2007
Alice, I Think by Susan Juby, 2008
What I Saw and How I Lied by Judy Blundell, 2008

After the First Death 1979

Robert Cormier

Nationality | American, born 1925
Publisher | Pantheon Books, USA
Theme | Adventure, Young adult, Friendship, Love

Seventeen-year-old high school student Kate Forrester is driving a group of preschool children to their summer camp in Massachusetts when her bus is hijacked by four armed terrorists. The kidnappers demand huge sums of money and the release of jailed comrades as ransom for the hostages. Things deteriorate when one of the children dies from an allergic reaction. After Kate makes a failed attempt at driving off, she is closely shadowed by Miro, who is, at sixteen, the youngest of the kidnappers. Despite their growing relationship, Miro proves ruthless when the time comes. Another subplot involves the arrival of Ben, a courier with ransom money supplied by General Briggs, the head of a top-secret antiterrorism unit that the kidnappers have demanded be closed down. This plan also ends in tragedy. Injured, Miro prepares himself for his next atrocity.

"I will shoot you if I have to, Kate. My orders from the beginning were to shoot you."

Cormier is an unflinching writer, never afraid to tackle disturbing and challenging themes, as seen in other works such as *The Chocolate War* (1974) and *We All Fall Down* (1991). While not sympathizing with the hijackers in this novel, he does present their case, showing particular understanding of the troubled Miro. Miro is clearly attracted to Kate, who is beautiful, brave, and good, and battles within himself between what he sees as his duty to his cause and his growing understanding that there must be better ways of winning political objectives than acts of terrorism. Written years before the 9/11 attacks of 2001, this fine novel offers insights into the minds and feelings of terrorists that are now more relevant than ever. **NT**

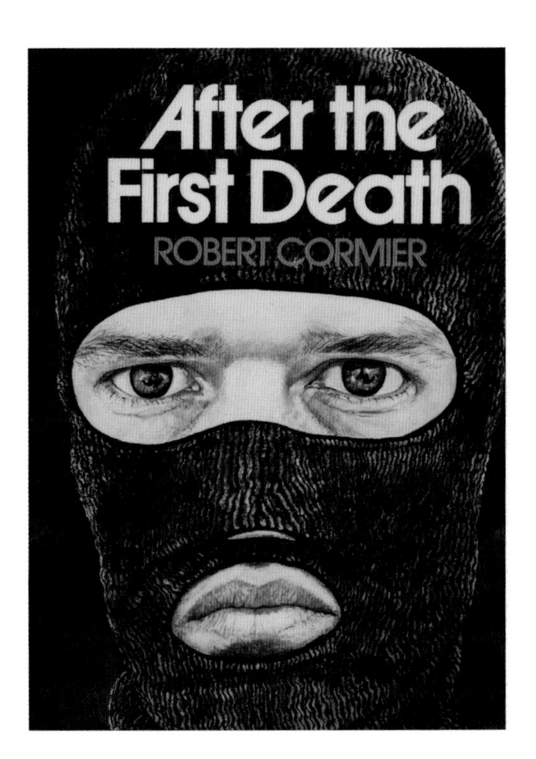

OTHER EXCITING THRILLERS

The Arm in the Starfish by Madeleine L'Engle, 1965
The Ruby in the Smoke by Philip Pullman, 1985
Neverwhere by Neil Gaiman, 1996
Scorpia by Anthony Horowitz, 2004
The Sleepwalker by Robert Muchamore, 2008

Tulku 1979

Peter Dickinson

Nationality | English, born 1927
Publisher | Gollancz, UK; Dutton, USA
Award | Carnegie Medal, 1979
Theme | Adventure

Thirteen-year-old Theodore lives with his missionary father in a remote part of nineteenth-century China. One dreadful night, an attack in the dark from a section of a rebel Chinese army leaves Theodore's father dead and his life's work destroyed.

On the run, Theodore falls in with Mrs. Jones, an eccentric Cockney botanist on her way to Tibet with her own band of travelers. No longer young and with a not entirely respectable past, this feisty character successfully avoids nests of dangerous bandits as she finally leads her group across the Chinese border.

Shortly after this, they meet the old Lama ruling in the gold-domed monastery of Dong Pe, high in the Tibetan mountains. Theodore decides that together they hold the clue to the birth of the next, long-awaited Tulku, the name given to the reincarnated spiritual master destined to rule over the whole of Tibet. But Theodore's intentions are now on returning to Britain and starting a new life there.

Peter Dickinson was born in Africa but tutored in England. He worked as a journalist and spent seventeen years on the satirical magazine *Punch* in London, England. He has one of the most remarkable imaginations among anyone writing for children, and this extraordinary novel sees him at his best. His descriptions of life at the Lama's court are so close and detailed it is as if he has been there himself. Equally at home with nineteenth-century theories of botany and Tibetan religious beliefs, he also has a gift for telling a good but never predictable story, keeping one of his chief surprises until almost the end. **NT**

Neverending Story 1979

Michael Ende Roswitha Quadflieg

Nationality | German, born 1929 (author); German, born 1949 (illustrator)
Publisher | Thienemann, Germany
Theme | Classics, Fantasy

Bastian Balthazar Bux is a name that can only belong to an extraordinary boy. However, he thinks of himself as a loser, as do his fellow students, who bully him because of the way he looks—small, fat, geeky, scared, and terribly lonely since the death of his mother.

One day at a bookshop, he finds a book bound in red satin (just like the actual book written by Ende) and steals it. Later on it turns out that the book was supposed to find him, so that he, the human child, could enter the magical land of Fantastica and save its ruler, the Childlike Empress, from a recurring unknown disease. But in the meantime, long before he realizes that he is the protagonist of the book he is devouring, Bastian becomes more and more absorbed in the adventures he is reading about. At times, the task at hand seems too big for him, but eventually he manages to reach the Childlike Empress and give her a new name (Moon Child), thereby defeating the Nothing that is threatening to destroy Fantastica.

The empathy Bastian and the Childlike Empress feel for the inhabitants of this fantastical land becomes a lifesaving quality in the two parallel societies. In the "real" world, the whole experience works as a cathartic event for the boy: he becomes more self-confident and restores a good rapport with his father, who had sought solace in work after the death of Bastian's mother. Ende writes captivatingly about a land that transcends time and space while also trying to convey a philosophical message: a society—whether fictional or real—that is devoid of imagination and creative thought is not sustainable and is therefore destined to disappear. **CS**

Roswitha Quadflieg's illustrations resemble illuminated manuscripts. 

My One-legged Friend and Me 1980

Anna-Liisa Haakana

Original Title | Ykä Yksinäinen
Nationality | Finnish, born 1937
Publisher | WSOY, Finland
Theme | Illness and death, Young adult

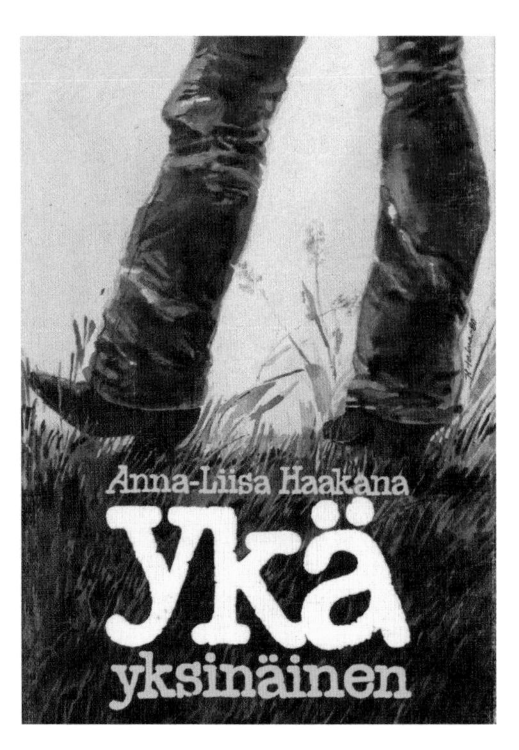

Heavy themes—such as loneliness, disability, and death—color this celebrated novel. It is set in Finnish Lapland, where the beauty of nature is ever present, but friends are extremely difficult to find and keep because of the long distances between houses, and between home and school.

My One-legged Friend and Me tells the story of Ykä, a fifteen-year-old boy who is very lonely and who feels disconnected from the few friends he has. He struggles frequently with peer pressure and with inner conflicts about what he wants for himself and his future. This all changes when he crosses paths with a boy who has lost his leg and is terminally ill. In this boy, Ykä finds the close friend that he has longed for without even knowing it. The two boys think alike, but what the friends really have in common is that they both feel extremely lonely. They establish a real connection, and, throughout a year, Ykä gets to know, not only his new friend but also himself and what he really desires in life. Unfortunately Ykä does not realize how much his new companion means to him until his one-legged friend is gone. However, instead of being just sad and withdrawing into himself, as many would do, he subsequently discovers an inner strength and a lust for life that he did not have before.

This is a simple yet beautiful portrayal of a boy's life as he approaches adulthood. Anna-Liisa Haakana explores her raw themes with delicate but realistic language, and with a sincerity that speaks to young readers. Although loneliness is a recurring theme in her books for young adults, she tries to instill hope into all her stories. She says: "I refuse to write a book for young people that just ends in despair. I want to point out that, even after a bad day, comes a good one, and that after sorrow comes joy." *My One-legged Friend and Me* touches people on many levels, whatever their age. **LKK**

OTHER READS WITH SIMILAR THEMES

Peeling the Onion by Wendy Orr, 1996
Pig-Heart Boy by Malorie Blackman, 1997
Postcards to Father Abraham by Catherine Lewis, 2000
Both Sides Now by Ruth Pennebaker, 2000

12+

Playing Beatie Bow 1980

Ruth Park

Fourteen-year-old Abigail Kirk feels restless and rebellious at home in Sydney, Australia, after her father leaves the family for another woman. One day, following a mysterious girl with an old-fashioned look, she finds herself transported to the same place one hundred years earlier, in 1873. She is now forced to live the life of a poor recent immigrant, staying with a family originally from Orkney, who seem to have been expecting her. Appalled by the poverty surrounding her at a time when proper sanitation barely existed, she sees many strange sights, including convicts shuffling past her wearing manacles.

Yet she slowly begins to respect the family who take her in; she also falls seriously in love with Judah,

"... [It] wasn't the absence of her father that caused the empty place inside. It was a part of her."

the nineteen-year-old son. Finally returning to the present, Abigail has now become a much calmer and more reflective person. She also realizes exactly why she was chosen to make the trip in the first place.

Time travel is a popular theme in children's books, and Ruth Park is certainly one of the best in the genre. While never playing down the worst horrors of the past, she does suggest some advantages as well—most notably the absence of the arms technology that was later going to plunge the twentieth century into two savage and bloody world wars. Most of *Playing Beatie Bow* is set around the historical Rocks district of Sydney. Park's vivid portrayal of the warmth of Abigail's adoptive family also reminds readers that while physical conditions continually change, the human need for love and security endures. **NT**

Nationality | New Zealander, born 1923
Publisher | Thomas Nelson, Australia
Award | C.B.C.A. Book of the Year, 1981
Theme | Historical fiction, Fantasy, Adventure

OTHER GREAT BOOKS BY RUTH PARK

The Hole in the Hill, 1961
Callie's Castle, 1974
Come Danger, Come Darkness, 1978
When the Wind Changed, 1980
Callie's Family, 1988

12+

The Sentinels 1980

Peter Carter

Nationality | British, born 1929
Publisher | Oxford University Press, UK
Award | *Guardian* Children's Fiction Prize, 1981
Theme | Historical fiction

At the age of fifteen, orphaned John Spencer finds that his uncle has taken charge of his future and decided to send him off to join a ship in the West Africa Squadron of the British Royal Navy, the antislavery patrol. Alongside John's adventures are told the experiences of Lyapo, an African captured as a slave; John's captain; and the crew of HMS *Sentinel*.

The difficulties of command for Captain Murray and the graphic descriptions of life belowdecks, including the deterioration of the food supplies, make this book more than just a story of sea adventure. The sickening stench when the holds are opened, the swarming insects, the constant fear of disease, and being at the mercy of the sea and marauders all make for a vivid picture of life at sea in the 1840s. The appalling trade in human life, including Africans imprisoning Africans, is depicted in all its cruelty and squalor amid the heat and humidity of the West African coast. John experiences a Robinson Crusoe adventure when he is marooned on an island with Lyapo, and the two begin to speak each other's languages and play ferocious games of checkers. Part of the story is based on real historical events.

Author Peter Carter, himself, came from a humble background, starting his working life as a builder's laborer before becoming a mature student at Oxford University and writing historical fiction. He traveled extensively throughout Europe, Japan, North America, the Middle East, and across the Sahara. He has also written about William Blake in *The Gates of Paradise* and of cowboys in *Leaving Cheyenne*. **JF**

Homecoming 1981

Cynthia Voight Sharon Scotland

Nationality | American, born 1942
Publisher | Atheneum Books, USA
Theme | Family, Young adult, Adventure

Dicey Tillerman is one of the great characters of American children's literature. She first appears in *Homecoming*, the first of seven related novels about the Tillerman family. She finds herself, at thirteen, in charge of her siblings, James, Sammy, and Maybeth, after their mother abandons them in the parking lot of a shopping mall. Led by Dicey, they walk from Connecticut to find an aunt they have never met.

They have very little money, so buy food on sale, catch fish, and sleep outside wherever they can. When they do find the address, they discover that the letters this aunt wrote were fiction and that she is dead. Her daughter, their cousin Eunice, offers to take them in as she feels it is her duty, but there is the strong possibility that the small family will be split up.

So they travel on again to find their estranged grandmother in Crisfield, Maryland. Upon their arrival at the old ramshackle farmhouse near the Chesapeake shore, Eunice and Dicey engage in an unspoken battle of wills. Dicey finds tasks to do that will prolong their stay. Dicey's fight to keep her small family together and keep alive their belief that their mother did love them makes for a heartwarming and, at times, heartrending story that is also full of suspense and humor.

Cynthia Voigt was born in Boston, Massachusetts, and worked as a secretary and as a teacher. She began her writing career when her son, Peter, was born and she found she had time for it. She says: "I enjoy almost everything I do, perhaps because when I don't enjoy something, I don't do it." **JF**

The Scarecrows 1981

Robert Westall

Nationality | English, born 1929
Publisher | Chatto and Windus, UK
Award | Carnegie Medal, 1981
Theme | Family, Young adult, Ghost stories

Three scarecrows loom threateningly over a turnip field near to where Simon has moved with his mother, little sister, and the new man in his mother's life. Simon is thirteen and deeply connected to his deceased father, who is forever preserved in his memory as a fearless military hero and his only soul mate. A dangerously bitter anger emerges in Simon, both at his boarding school and at home, and boils over during the series of disturbing incidents in the story.

When Simon's mother takes up with successful artist, Joe, Simon feels betrayed and profoundly jealous. Near Joe's house, Simon discovers a derelict and hauntingly unnerving mill. As the mill and Joe's house give up their chilling secrets, Simon becomes possessed by devils from his own, and others', past and the three scarecrows embody darkly supernatural forces.

Westall is a major writer, whose work stretched the parameters of teenage fiction. Along with his groundbreaking first book *The Machine Gunners*, *The Scarecrows* shocked some. It is an extremely well written and powerful book that is frank and brutally unsettling. It deals with familiar Westall themes: war (Westall was a boy during World War II), facing unknown forces, the supernatural, and buildings with human qualities. It examines the intense feelings of anger and confusion often felt by people, especially teenagers, some of which must have been informed by the death of Westall's only son in a motorcycle accident. The book is also an evocative slice of British life in 1975, but one whose underlying ideas will connect easily with a contemporary audience. **AK**

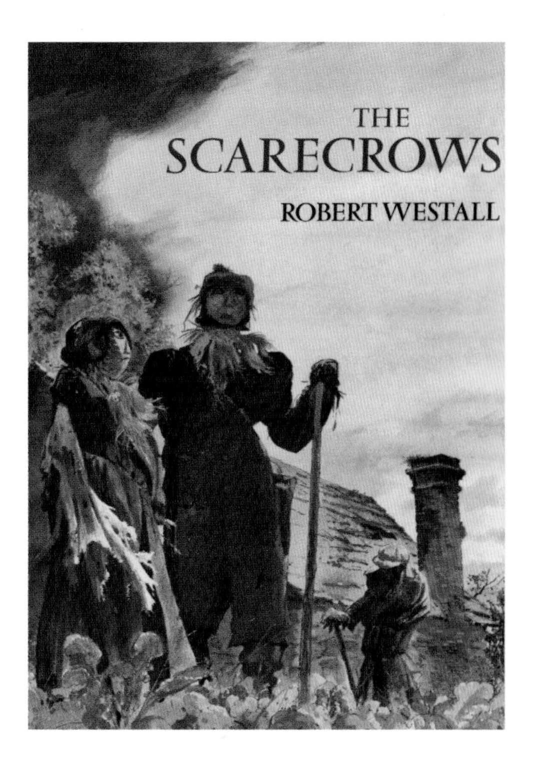

"He lay inside a green tunnel of turnip leaves. He sat up with an ouch, and broke surface into a golden mist of sunrise."

MORE GREAT SPOOKY STORIES

The Owl Service by Alan Garner, 1967
The Time of the Ghost by Diana Wynne Jones, 1981
The Changeover by Margaret Mahy, 1984
Agnes Cecilia by Maria Gripe, 1990
Breathe: A Ghost Story by Cliff McNish, 2006

Agnes Cecilia 1981

Maria Gripe

Nationality | Swedish, born 1923
Publisher | Albert Bonniers, Sweden
Theme | Ghost stories, Young adult, Family, Friendship

OTHER UNSETTLING TALES OF INTRIGUE

The Canterville Ghost by Oscar Wilde, 1887
The Glassblower's Children by Maria Gripe, 1973
The Killer's Cousin by Nancy Werlin, 1978
Mokee Joe Is Coming by Peter J. Murray, 2003
The Graveyard Book by Neil Gaiman, 2008

Essentially a ghost story, what lingers after reading *Agnes Cecilia* is not so much an appreciation of the tense, suspenseful plot but a feeling for the emotion of the characters. Maria Gripe links the supernatural events with an emotional journey that is heartfelt and honest. Even melodramatic events are anchored in reality by Gripe's psychological insight.

Strange things have been happening to Nora since she moved with her foster family into a new apartment. Her life has been inexplicably saved twice, she hears footsteps and feels a presence in her room, and she is given a beautiful doll—the Agnes Cecilia of the title—in a series of unexplainable events. She must solve the mystery of the strange presence in her room—a presence that is linked to the loss of her parents in her own life. By solving the supernatural mystery, Nora finds a new sense of peace and also gains a new friend, who is connected to both her parents and the ghost who haunts her room.

"She could feel it in the air—an unreal atmosphere that could not be described."

There is a dreamy sense of time and place in *Agnes Cecilia*. The world that the characters inhabit is imbued with supernatural possibilities. At the heart of the story is an orphan child's desire to be loved and wanted. Nora struggles with feelings of estrangement from her foster family. It is clear that she is well loved, but Gripe alludes to the fact that many children are not as fortunate. What is powerful in this story is the psychology of the characters, and Gripe draws them with startling humanity. She makes you believe both in the reality of them, and in the possibility of all things supernatural. **RA**

The Island on Bird Street 1981

 Uri Orlev

This captivating novel—set in Warsaw, Poland, in 1943—tells the story of eleven-year-old Jewish boy Alex. The world is at war, Alex's mother has mysteriously vanished, and his father has been taken away by the Germans. Alex is left alone in the ghetto with only a small, white mouse called Snow for company. He does not really understand what is going on around him, but he builds a small hideout in a derelict building at 78 Bird Street.

Like his hero Robinson Crusoe, Alex explores his surroundings and manages to collect enough food and clothing to survive. He learns to fend for himself, and is also brave enough to help others, even if it means risking his own life. From the abandoned

"I threw down a rope and hauled up the package that he tied to it. It was full of goodies."

house—his "island"—he can survey both the ghetto and the city that lies beyond the ghetto wall, a world with shops and food and a world where children can play freely. Sometimes Alex ventures out into this world and there he meets all kinds of different people. To do this he must use underground tunnels and secret passageways so that he is not caught. He refuses to escape because he wants to wait for his father's return, even if it takes a week, or even a year.

Based on Uri Orlev's own childhood experiences, this novel is alive with vivid sounds and imagery: the silence of the city at nighttime, the crunch of footprints in the snow, the unexpected shot of gunfire, the thrill of finding hidden bunkers, and the taste of a hearty stew after weeks of crackers and water. It is a wonderful and engaging adventure full of heart-stopping bravery and suspense. **GFM**

Original Title | Ha-I bi-Rehov ha-Zipporim
Nationality | Polish/Israeli, born 1931
Publisher | Keter Publishing House, Israel
Theme | War, Historical fiction

OTHER GREAT BOOKS BY URI ORLEV

The Thing in the Dark, 1976
The Dragon's Crown, 1986
The Man from the Other Side, 1988
The Lady with the Hat, 1990
Run, Boy, Run, 2001

12+

The Secret Diary of Adrian Mole 1982

Sue Townsend   Caroline Holden

Nationality | English, born 1946 (author); English, born 1954 (illustrator)
Publisher | Methuen, UK
Theme | Young adult, Family, School, Humor

Since its first publication, Adrian Mole has been a phenomenon. The first book in the series was an immediate favorite with teens, preteens, and their parents. It records, in unwittingly hilarious detail, the trials and tribulations of Adrian's adolescence.

Poignantly written, *The Secret Diary of Adrian Mole* chronicles fifteen angst-ridden months in the young diarist's life. It begins with Adrian recording his New Year's resolutions for 1981, which include "I will not start smoking. . . . I will stop squeezing my spots. . . . After hearing the disgusting noises from downstairs last night, I have also vowed never to drink alcohol." The diary records his most candid thoughts about his parents' extramarital affairs; his frustration at being an unrecognized intellectual; his poetry (which he sends relentlessly to the BBC); his adoration for Pandora Braithwaite; and his agony when his best friend, Nigel, not only gets a racing bike, but also starts going out with Pandora. The diary also records Adrian's triumph after Pandora and Nigel break up and when she tells her best friend, who tells Nigel, who tells Adrian that Pandora is in love with him: "I told Nigel to tell Claire to tell Pandora that I return her love."

"Pandora smiled at me today, but I was choking on a piece of gristle so I couldn't smile back."

This is a book that will be read and reread for its classic moments, including Adrian's minutely detailed account of the school bus trip to the British Museum and the chaos that ensues after he wears red socks to school. Memorable characters include Bert Baxter, a foul-mannered, beet-obsessed old man; Bert's fearsome Alsatian dog, Sabre; and the Singh family, who live down the road. **LH**

MORE BOOKS ABOUT ADRIAN MOLE

The Growing Pains of Adrian Mole, 1984
The True Confessions of Adrian Albert Mole, 1989
Adrian Mole: The Wilderness Years, 1993
Adrian Mole: The Cappuccino Years, 1999

"I can't live a moment longer with Noddy wallpaper." 

The Village by the Sea 1982

Anita Desai

"The sun lifted up over the coconut palms in a line along the beach and sent slanting long rays over the silvery sand. . . ."

OTHER MOVING FAMILY SAGAS

Seven Little Australians by Ethel Turner, 1894
Ede and Unku by Alex Wedding, 1931
Where the Lilies Bloom by Vera and Bill Cleaver, 1969
Out of the Dust by Karen Hesse, 1997
Refugee Boy by Benjamin Zephaniah, 2001

Nationality | Indian, born 1937
Publisher | Heinemann, UK
Award | *Guardian* Children's Fiction Prize, 1983
Theme | Family

Hari and his sister Lila are the two oldest children in a family living in Thul on the west coast of India. Their mother is seriously ill, and their father, a former fisherman, is nearly always drunk. With no work available locally, Hari moves to Bombay, since renamed Mumbai, to earn some money, leaving Lila to cope with their two younger sisters.

He gets a job as a dishwasher in a restaurant kitchen and is able to help pay for the children's mother to go to the hospital, where she slowly recovers her health. However, Hari is pleased to return to his village when he hears that a new fertilizer factory will be opening shortly. Although much of the area's natural beauty will be spoiled by the new industry, with the wildlife suffering in particular, there is renewed hope for the future as the village's way of life seems set to change irreparably.

Thul is a real place, where Anita Desai often stayed for her holidays. She writes about it from a neutral position, regretting the type of changes that will inevitably cause more pollution but also recognizing how desperately local people need the wages that come as a result. Desai is always on the side of Hari and Lila, admiring the way that they take on such heavy family responsibilities without ever complaining and telling their engrossing story with all the skill of a natural born novelist.

Desai, born of a German mother and Bengali father, is Emeritus Professor of Humanities at the Massachusetts Institute of Technology. She has been shortlisted for the Booker Prize three times. **NT**

Nausicaä 1982

Hayao Miyazaki

Original Title | Kaze no Tani no Naushika
Nationality | Japanese, born 1941
Publisher | *Animage* magazine
Theme | Fantasy

It is not surprising, perhaps, that so many science fiction manga (Japanese comics) are set in postapocalyptic futures, the characters struggling for survival after human civilization has been decimated by a great disaster. Hayao Miyazaki's *Nausicaä* is a particularly poignant and complex rendering of this scenario and he uses it to tackle issues such as warfare, political oppression, and environmental destruction.

A dwindling human population lives in feudal societies on the outskirts of dense forests inhabited by giant insects. This uninhabitable "sea of Corruption" contains plants and fungi that release a deadly miasma. When war breaks out between two powerful empires, Nausicaä, a highly skilled but reluctant warrior, must leave and fight to protect her homeland. Her journey leads her to an understanding of the true purpose of the forest and its guardian insects, with whom she shares a special bond, and finally to a confrontation with the godlike beings who engineered this new world. She embodies in this quest the dual roles of savior and destroyer, creating a path toward a new future wherein respect for life and nature may become humanity's guiding principle.

Miyazaki is best known as the writer and director of animated films such as *Spirited Away*, which feature strong female protagonists. Indeed, he made the first section of *Nausicaä* into a popular animated motion picture in 1984. Although he modestly professes to be unskilled as a manga author, *Nausicaä* remains one of the most profoundly meaningful and beautifully drawn examples of the genre ever produced. **CR**

Handles 1983

Jan Mark David Parkins

Nationality | English, born 1943 (author); English, born 1955 (illustrator)
Publisher | Kestrel Books, UK
Theme | Family, Humor

Strictly urban, Erica Timperley is not enjoying her stay in the country with her graceless cousin Robert and her equally unattractive aunt and uncle, who grow vegetables. There seems little to do other than vandalize beds of summer squash, which gets her into lots of trouble. But one day she sees a cat with false teeth and discovers a ramshackle workshop in a nearby town run by an odd bunch of characters, each with their own nickname—or "handle"—and all sharing Erica's love of motorbikes.

Gradually Erica is accepted by this unpredictable but kindly group at Mercury Motor Cycles and allowed to help out with odd tasks. She is finally granted her own handle and told there would always be a job for her there if she wanted. Eventually sent home in disgrace by her mean relations, this has still been the best vacation experience of her life.

Jan Mark is a brilliantly impressionistic writer, making every word count by cutting down her prose to the bare minimum. Readers are often left to work out for themselves the exact significance of long passages of dialogue, almost as if they were overhearing real conversations. But with a writer as witty and perceptive as Mark this is no hardship, with her characters endlessly cracking jokes as one mini-drama follows another all the way to the last page. She said: "I like to make my readers work very hard all the way through. It seems a pity to waste it, if they're going to stop thinking." *Handles* was Jan Mark's second book to win the Carnegie Medal. Its realism has been particularly commended. **NT**

A Parcel of Patterns 1983

Jill Paton Walsh

". . . [For] this task of writing I have undertaken, I lack wit and skill, and set things down awry."

OTHER SIMILAR HISTORICAL READS

Captives of Time by Malcolm Bosse, 1987
A Time of Angels by Karen Hesse, 1995
Fever, 1793 by Laurie Halse Anderson, 2000
Nory Ryan's Song by Patricia Reilly Giff, 2000
At the Sign of the Sugared Plum by Mary Hooper, 2003

Nationality | English, born 1937
Publisher | Viking Kestrel, UK
Award | Universe Literary Prize
Theme | Historical fiction

Based on fact, this heartrending story is set in the 1660s in the English village of Eyam, Derbyshire, during the devastation of the bubonic plague. It is the time of the Restoration, when King Charles II is back on the throne and Oliver Cromwell's Puritanism is being stamped out by the Church of England. Consequently, Eyam has two warring ministers who pull together and place the village under quarantine in an attempt to prevent the spread of the disease.

The story is touchingly told by sixteen-year-old villager Mall Percival, who is in love with Thomas, a young man from a neighboring village. At great personal sacrifice, the resolute Mall keeps her sheep out of the hills and stops herself from seeing Thomas. But he disregards her wishes and comes to find her in the quarantined village, knowing he will not be able to leave. They marry and find a brief period of happiness together, but when the plague-bearing parcel of the title arrives, there is nothing that can be done to save the villagers. When the plague eventually leaves, 267 of the 350 villagers are dead, among them Thomas. Grief-stricken, Mall decides to write a chronicle of all she has witnessed.

She conveys all the conflicting emotions that are stirred up by the tragedy, which Jill Paton Walsh tells in the language of eighteenth-century England, an entertainment and education in itself. The reader becomes immersed in the difficulties of religious tension and the horrors of the plague. **JF**

12+

Talking in Whispers 1983

James Watson

Nationality | English, born 1936
Publisher | Gollancz, UK
Award | Shortlisted for the Carnegie Medal
Theme | Young adult

This coming-of-age tale has a much more searing storyline than most. The setting is Chile; the time frame is "somewhere between the present and the future." The theme is nationwide political oppression by the ruthless Junta, and so the novel's origin in recent Chilean history is blatant. That said, James Watson is at pains in his introductory note to say that such events happen not just in Chile but also in "many countries where the force of arms rules the people instead of democracy and the rule of justice."

The story opens as Andres watches his father—a political activist—being taken away by the security forces of Chile's military government. Andres's life becomes a nightmare on the run as he discovers his family home has been looted, witnesses violence and oppression wherever he goes, and finds that he can trust no one. He almost eludes the security forces, but not quite, and finds himself in the chillingly named "House of Laughter," a notorious detention and torture center. Ultimately, armed with some crucial and incriminating photographs, Andres and his friends are able to continue the fight for civil liberty and justice.

Watson writes mostly for young people on history and human rights issues in different parts of the world. His style here is fittingly spare, direct, and detached, apart from the more personalized writing of Andres's torture scene. This passage, and his effectively urgent dialogue, betrays his work as a journalist and writer of radio plays. **AK**

Hating Alison Ashley 1984

Robin Klein

Nationality | Australian, born 1936
Publisher | Penguin, Australia
Theme | School, Friendship, Young adult, Humor

Erica Yurken is planning a fabulous life. Once she is old enough to change her name to something much more elegant, her real life will begin. In the meantime, she contents herself by feeling superior to everyone around her. But then Alison Ashley turns up. Competing with this beautiful, poised new arrival becomes Erica's new obsession. School camp is coming, and Erica is determined to prove to Alison—and the world—that she is destined for big things.

Erica, the narrator and heroine, is amusing and entertaining. She has an extremely well-developed imagination, using hypochondria and desperation to escape the perceived shortcomings of her own life. She paints vivid pictures of her "socially disadvantaged" school, embarrassing family, and innermost fantasies. Yet Erica is finding out that many things are not as she thought them to be. Her pursuit of perfection may just lead her on an unexpected journey and it seems likely to be a most amusing one.

Klein's comedy shows a keen understanding of teenagers and of the highs and lows of fitting in, growing up, and finding your place in the world. This popular book has been made into a play and a film. Any girl will relate to the angst and will enjoy the adventures of Erica as she keeps herself busy hating Alison Ashley. The book has a strong moral undercurrent about the pursuit of happiness and perfection, the pressures of growing up and the power of friendship. **KW**

Brother in the Land 1984

Robert Swindells

Nationality | English, born 1939
Publisher | Oxford University Press, UK
Theme | Family, Friendship, Science fiction

Robert Swindells was a supporter of the Campaign for Nuclear Disarmament. His staunch opposition to the use of nuclear weapons inspired the postapocalyptic vision of *Brother in the Land*. This troubling tale has been a feature on the school curriculum for many British children, its antiwar sentiments warning younger generations of the impact a nuclear war would have.

Danny Lodge is the chief protagonist, one of the few survivors of a sudden and devastating nuclear bomb that all but destroys the Yorkshire town in which he lives. Conflict is a key element of the story, especially in terms of how humans can behave in times of desperate need. In the aftermath of the bomb, Danny's father's shop, with its basement full of food, becomes an immediate target for the newly formed local government, led by the commissioner. Having already lost his mother in the initial attack, Danny is faced with the loss of his father when survivors stage a violent riposte against the commissioner and his forces. Danny is left to take on the parent role for his brother and teams up with new friend, Kim, whose friendship is one of the few positive outcomes of the nuclear attack.

> *"Then I saw the flash. It was terrifically bright. I screwed up my eyes and jerked my head away."*

Swindells is quoted as saying the work "came out of my own anger and frustration . . . you can't kill selectively with nuclear weapons, you wipe out millions of people." *Brother in the Land* deals with the serious themes of war and death, making it a sober and often sad read, but as Danny Lodge grows up in the face of his changing universe, so does the reader, who is shown that hope and friendship can overcome all. **LK**

MORE GREAT ROBERT SWINDELL READS

When Darkness Comes, 1973
A Candle in the Night, 1974
The Ice Palace, 1977
Room 13, 1990
Abomination, 1998

Badger on the Barge 1984

Janni Howker

Nationality | English, born 1957
Publisher | Julia MacRae Books, UK
Theme | Friendship, Quirky, Short stories
Illness and death

"'What's it like, being old?' asked Steven, staring into the red flames. 'Wait and see, lad,' Jakey said. 'Wait and see.'" In many respects this exchange from "Jakey," one of the five short stories in this superb collection, typifies the themes and concerns of the book. These center on the relationships between the young and the elderly, which are given expression in a sequence of narratives with excellently described settings and equally well-observed characters.

Totally free of sentimentality and condescension, the stories also have a delightful quirkiness and sense of humor, neither of which ever threaten their underlying seriousness. The opening title story of the collection describes the developing friendship between a young girl called Helen and an old woman called Miss Brady. For Helen, who is coping with the sadness of a brother's death in a road accident, the friendship comes at precisely the right moment. But for Miss Brady, "cunning old rascal" that she is, the friendship also has its timely benefits.

"Jane had always thought there were some things you had to keep from adults."

"The Egg-Man," perhaps the most poignant of the stories, reveals how two young girls, Jane and Bridget, are drawn into the tragically sad life of Isaiah Black, a recluse who continues to live among the memories of his late wife; his loneliness, for Jane, is "like an ache in her throat." The final story, "The Topiary Garden," is a highly atmospheric tale of an encounter between a twelve-year-old girl and a ninety-one-year-old woman, the latter of whom has an amazing revelation to make about the years she disguised herself as a boy. **RD**

MORE COLLECTIONS OF SHORT STORIES

Every Living Thing by Cynthia Rylant, 1985
Not So Stupid by Malorie Blackman, 1990
Thicker Than Water edited by Gordon Snell, 2001
Friendships by Budge Wilson, 2006
Shining On edited by Lois Lowry, 2006

12+

The Changeover 1984

Margaret Mahy

Nationality | New Zealander, born 1936
Publisher | Dent, UK
Award | Carnegie Medal, 1984
Theme | Ghost stories, Young adult, Love

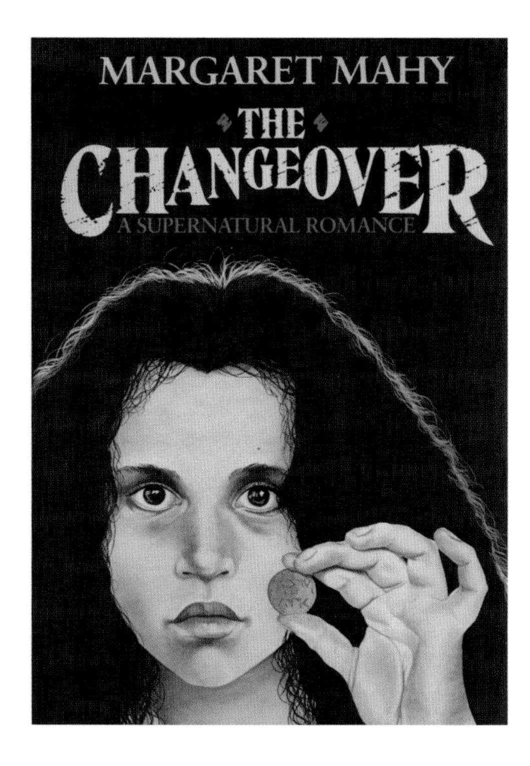

12+

The Changeover, subtitled "A Supernatural Romance," is a fascinating and at times terrifying story and is undoubtably one of Margaret Mahy's finest. It describes how fourteen-year-old Laura Chant, living an uneventful life in Christchurch, New Zealand with her divorced mother, becomes involved in a life-and-death struggle to save her three-year-old brother Jacko. He has become the victim of Carmody Braque, an evil spirit in need of rejuvenation, who is currently passing himself off as a bric-a-brac shop owner.

The vampiric Braque thrives as Jacko visibly wastes away, leading Laura to call on the skills of Sorensen "Sorry" Carlisle, an older boy at her school who has special powers. He, his mother, and grandmother tell

"You'll make a hole in him through which he'll drip away until he runs dry."

Laura she has to become a witch in order to save Jacko, and after completing a sometimes harrowing spiritual trial in which she becomes "a woman of the moon," Laura eventually wins the day. She has also entered adolescence, with Sorry now her acknowledged boyfriend.

Mahy describes the emotional journey involved in changing from child to teenager in terms of a magical process, beset by danger but with great rewards. The blood Laura spills can be seen as symbolizing her first experience of menstruation, while her first kiss with Sorry is the start of a new range of emotional possibilities. Mahy reminds her readers that real changes in life can seem just as amazing as anything found in a supernatural story. Beautifully written and constantly engrossing, this is a novel never to be forgotten. **NT**

OTHER SUPERNATURAL STORIES

The Chrysalids by John Wyndham, 1955
The Haunting by Margaret Mahy, 1982
Tithe by Holly Black, 2002
The Supernaturalist by Eoin Colfer, 2004
Breaking Dawn by Stephenie Meyer, 2008

The Ruby in the Smoke 1985

Philip Pullman

Nationality | English, born 1946
Publisher | Oxford University Press, UK
Honor | Astrid Lindgren Memorial Award, 2005
Theme | Historical fiction, Adventure

The first of the Sally Lockhart quartet introduces us to Sally at the age of sixteen, arriving at her drowned father's offices where, within fifteen minutes, she is "going to kill a man." This irresistible hook leads into a compelling historical thriller and a real page turner, not least because of the clear, direct language and the meticulously researched setting of Victorian London.

It is nineteenth-century England, and Sally has received a letter warning her against the "seven blessings." As she investigates, she learns that she is in danger. When her father's secretary hears the words "seven blessings," he drops dead. The office boy, Jim Taylor, decides to help Sally solve the mystery. She is given a book about her father by Mr. Marchbanks who warns her of an enemy, a Mrs. Holland. The book tells of her father's experiences in India and of a ruby. While escaping from Mrs. Holland, Sally becomes friends with Frederick Garland, a photographer.

"It's the girl . . . I'll have her and I'll tear her open, I will. I'm angry now, and I'll have her life."

The book is stolen—except for one page—and Mr. Marchbanks is murdered by Mrs. Holland, who also blackmail's the partner of Sally's father and arranges to have the missing page recovered and Sally killed. Sally escapes and moves in with Frederick and his sister, helping them with their bookkeeping in return. The story quickly becomes complicated and more deadly, involving the opium trade, pirates, kidnapping, murder and betrayal, before its surprising ending.

In the spirit of such books as *The Moonstone* by Wilkie Collins, this is a first-class adventure from a master storyteller. It was adapted for BBC television starring Billy Piper as Sally. **WO**

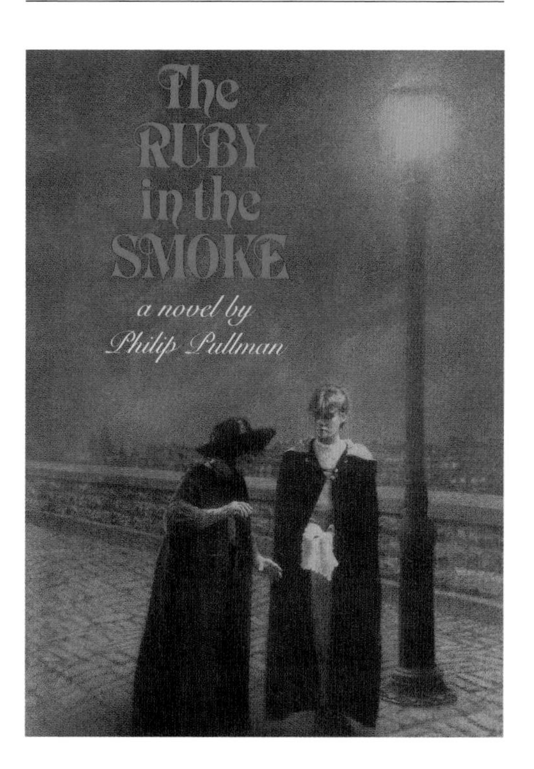

MORE FIRST-CLASS PHILIP PULLMAN

The Shadow in the North, 1986
The Tiger in the Well, 1991
The Tin Princess, 1994
The Firework-Maker's Daughter, 1995
The Amber Spyglass, 2000

12+

Johnny, My Friend 1985

Peter Pohl

Original Title | Janne, min vän
Nationality | Swedish, born 1940
Publisher | AWE Gebers, Sweden
Theme | Young adult

Johnny, My Friend is written as if straight from the mind of Chris the narrator, and the reader is sucked right into this hard-hitting novel from the outset. At the core of Peter Pohl's text is the mystery of Johnny: a red-haired, freckle-faced boy who dazzles Chris and his mates with his bicycle skills and his ability to fix mechanical problems: "The slightest squeaking or scraping or rattling and Johnny would be on to the culprit, tightening screws, adjusting nuts, oiling, testing, muttering magic formulae." Even though he is small and looks like a girl, Johnny can deal with anyone, however big, with his ferocious fists. Johnny appears as if from thin air, and Chris spends the novel piecing together the mystery that is his friend Johnny.

The story begins with Chris being interrogated by the police, who have Johnny's bicycle and his tangerine pants, two things he would never let out of his sight. They want to know everything about Johnny, but Chris does not have all the answers. The story unfolds in flashback as the cops question Chris. Even at the story's end, not all the answers are revealed. The mystery at the center of *Johnny, My Friend* remains tantalizingly just out of reach.

Set in and around a real Stockholm inner-city school, the story is vividly true to life. Many of Pohl's books have autobiographical elements, and he writes teenager characters with honesty and understanding. *Johnny, My Friend* like Pohl's other books, defies categorization. It goes beyond young adult fiction as a genre, to reveal universal themes of loneliness and the mystery of life. **RA**

Hatchet 1986

Gary Paulson

Nationality | American, born 1939
Publisher | Bradbury Press, USA
Award | Newbery Honor Book, 1988
Theme | Adventure

Award-winning author Gary Paulson has written more than one hundred books for children and young adults. An outdoors adventurer himself, Paulson has twice completed the grueling Alaskan Iditarod dog sled race and his own experiences surviving in the brutal cold of the raw Alaskan landscape informs the novel. He is known for his books featuring teenage male characters who must draw on their courage, wits, self-reliance, and reserves of strength to beat the odds and survive harrowing situations. *Hatchet* is a novel that is hard to put down.

While traveling in a single-engine plane on his way to see his father, the pilot has a heart attack and dies, forcing Brian to crash-land the plane in a lake in the Canadian wilderness. Not knowing how long he might be stranded, Brian has to figure out how to survive, how to make fire, what he can eat, as well as deal with wild animals. With the hatchet his father gave him as his only tool, he becomes a craftsman, eventually making a bow, arrows, and a spear. During his fifty-four days alone in the woods, Brian also has to come to terms with his parents' divorce and the not-so-secret affair his mother had that was at the root of the family's break-up.

After a near-death experience when he comes close to losing his hatchet forever, Brian is eventually rescued and reunited with his father, although he is still unable to tell him about his mother's affair. For readers with an adventurous spirit, this book by a master storyteller—so realistic in its details and so lyrical in its language—will make compelling reading. **KD**

Taronga 1986

Victor Kelleher

Nationality | English/Australian, born 1939
Publisher | Viking Kestrel, Australia
Theme | Science fiction, Animal stories, Adventure, Young adult

In a postapocalyptic Australia, fourteen-year-old Ben lives rough in the bush, under the control of an older boy. Ben is valuable because he has a strange ability to control the animals his companion hunts, but to Ben this feels like a betrayal. However, when Ben runs away to Sydney, he finds the city an even worse nightmare, until he reaches Taronga Zoo: a green fortress of lawfulness. Here he meets Ellie, his first friend since Last Days. Protecting the zoo's animals seems like Ben's chance to atone for past betrayals, but Ben and Ellie soon realize that this is not a place of safety at all, for the animals or anybody else. They concoct a desperate plan to break the animals out of the zoo. As the book ends, Taronga lies in ruins while Ben and Ellie, along with the animals, slowly trace their way out of the city, to find a place in this new Australia where they can wait out the madness.

Victor Kelleher was born in London, but traveled to Africa when he was a teenager. He lived in various parts of the African continent for two decades, before moving to New Zealand and finally Australia. *Taronga* shows the influence of both Africa and Australia, with its imagery of tigers and leopards prowling the ruins of Sydney, and the central theme of Ben's struggle against and alliance with wild animals, especially the ferocious and unforgiving tiger Raja. He concocts a powerful image of a possible future—dark, exhilarating, and, in the end, hopeful—but the story is also an exciting, tense adventure. Younger readers, who might not pick up on some of the philosophy, will enjoy the danger, the savagely menacing tigers, and the desperate plans. **JM**

"[Taronga's] just a great big cage, and what went wrong in Sydney is already locked in here, waiting to go wrong again."

OTHER SCIENCE FICTION GREATS

Fahrenheit 451 by Ray Bradbury, 1953
Chocky by John Wyndham, 1968
Crisis on Conshelf Ten by Monica Hughes, 1975
Memories of Idhún: The Resistance by Laura Gallego, 2004

12+

The Ghost Drum 1987

Susan Price

Nationality | English, born 1955
Publisher | Faber and Faber, UK
Award | Carnegie Medal, 1987
Theme | Magical stories

Price wrote and published her first novel at sixteen, and has since stuck to teen and young adult fiction and fantasy. First in the *Ghost World* trilogy, *The Ghost Drum* is set in imperial Russia. A scholar-cat narrates the story of a power struggle between royalty and magic. When cruel Czar Guidon has a son, Safa, he becomes paranoid and imprisons him in a tall tower.

Safa's only companion, his maid Marien, is murdered when she complains about the prince's imprisonment. Far away in the forest, the almost feral witch-girl Chingis is taught magic by her mother, and discovers she has a particular skill on a drum that can carry messages across the land. Marien's message about Safa reaches her, and she decides to rescue him and teach him about a world he has never experienced. But when the czar dies, and his sister Margaretta succeeds him, the new czarina decides to protect her reign by killing her nephew and sends soldiers into the wood to destroy him. Chingis tries to teach magic skills to the defenseless Safa, and then discovers that court advisor and powerful shaman Kuzma has become jealous of her powers and wants to jail her. Ultimately, Chingis has to battle against evil to defend herself, Safa, and the whole land.

Full of dark magic, rich language, and ancient legend, *The Ghost Drum* is enthralling and unusual. Every character has complex motives, and the storyline is similarly complicated. This, combined with the lengthy and beautiful descriptive passages, may put off younger children, but there's plenty of depth and detail for the discerning reader. **SD**

Madame Doubtfire 1987

Anne Fine

Nationality | English, born 1947
Publisher | Hamish Hamilton, UK
Award | *Guardian* Children's Fiction Prize (shortlist)
Theme | Family, Humor

This is the bitingly funny story of a family caught up in the painful aftermath of an acrimonious divorce. Father Daniel, a disorganized, out-of-work actor turned life-model, incurs mother Miranda's wrath with his repeatedly tardy maintenance payments and provokes her disapproval with his grubby, cluttered apartment. Meanwhile her regular interruptions to his time with the children leave Daniel threatening that he will "cheerfully slit her throat."

Caught in the crossfire, Lydia, Christopher, and Natalie each have their own strategies for dealing with the barrage of sarcastic observations that characterize parental interactions. When Mom decides she needs a housekeeper, Daniel disguises himself as a flamboyant older woman and gets the job. Although the children quickly see through the deception, their mother remains comically ignorant of the subterfuge, even as she gossips with the new housekeeper about the many shortcomings of her ex-husband. The arrangement works to everyone's benefit, and all runs more or less smoothly for a time with Daniel, although struggling to control his anger, gaining a greater understanding of the problems faced by his ex-wife.

Eventually the children grow tired of the pretense and—with delightful inevitability—the game is finally up. Characterized by its sparkling dialogue between articulate and flawed characters, this wickedly funny and brutally honest depiction of contemporary family life by former Children's Laureate Anne Fine was filmed in 1993 as *Mrs. Doubtfire*, starring Robin Williams in the title role. **KA**

Madame Doubtfire

ANNE FINE

Strollers 1987

Lesley Beake

Nationality | South African, born 1949
Publisher | Maskew Miller Longman, South Africa
Award | Young Africa Award
Theme | Adventure, Family

Strollers are runaway children who live on their own, but do not join gangs. They can subsist as long as they can successfully beg, scavenge, steal, or devise scams such as collecting for nonexistent church charities. Lesley Beake's stroller hero is Johnny, the eighth runaway in a township family of eight children. His seven brothers have been "swallowed up in the welter of people who no longer live at their home address."

With the exception of brother Abraham, nothing is said about Johnny's vanishing brethren. Abraham enters the tale because, as the leader of a criminally active gang, he has recruited some strollers for drug trafficking, and Johnny's group leader, Koosie, has informed on the gang when he is picked up by the police. Thus, Koosie is banished to Johannesburg and Johnny takes charge.

The plot line moves Johnny around Cape Town: to a squatter community on Table Mountain, to the Saturday market stalls and the musicians who entertain customers, and finally to prison. This pilgrimage convinces him to return home and revise his notion that a vagabond's life is a life of freedom. It has included only the freedom to get high, to get sick, and to die (as is the fate of one TB-infected stroller in Johnny's group).

The novel is absorbing and exceptionally well written, with a genuine concern for social injustice and the dysfunctional aspects of urban life. Beake manages to inject warmth and even humor into Johnny's story, which deserves the international acclaim it has received. **LB**

The Cloud 1987

Gudrun Pausewang

Original Title | Die Wolke
Nationality | German, born 1928
Publisher | Ravensburger, Germany
Theme | Young adult

Published only a year after the Chernobyl disaster, Gudrun Pausewang's gripping novel paints a similar doomsday scenario in Germany. The central character is fourteen-year-old Jana-Berta, who—in the aftermath of an explosion at a nuclear reactor in a nearby village—has to take care of her younger brother, Uli, and flee from the spreading toxic cloud. Their parents die as a result of the nuclear fallout, and Uli is killed in an accident during their escape. As a result of this trauma, Jana-Berta becomes detached from the world. Not caring about where she is heading, she is caught in toxic rain and subsequently ends up in an infirmary. There, the extent of the catastrophe becomes apparent: more than 18,000 people have died, and many more have been exposed to radiation.

The victims—such as Jana-Berta—are conspicuous because of their bald heads, and those unaffected by the catastrophe try to avoid them. The world wants to move on and forget about the disaster, but Jana-Berta refuses to comply. She goes to live with relatives, who assist victims, and this helps her to finally move on.

Pausewang's engrossing story is clearly intended as a warning against the dangers of nuclear energy. The nuclear power plants in this story continue to be used after the accident. Pausewang illustrates that the victims of disasters are often blamed for reminding others of what has happened. She stresses that no one ever chooses to become a victim or a refugee, and she criticizes society for preferring to forget instead of taking responsibility. **GS**

Alex 1987

Tessa Duder

Nationality | New Zealander, born 1940
Publisher | Oxford University Press, New Zealand
Theme | Young adult, School,
Family, Friendship

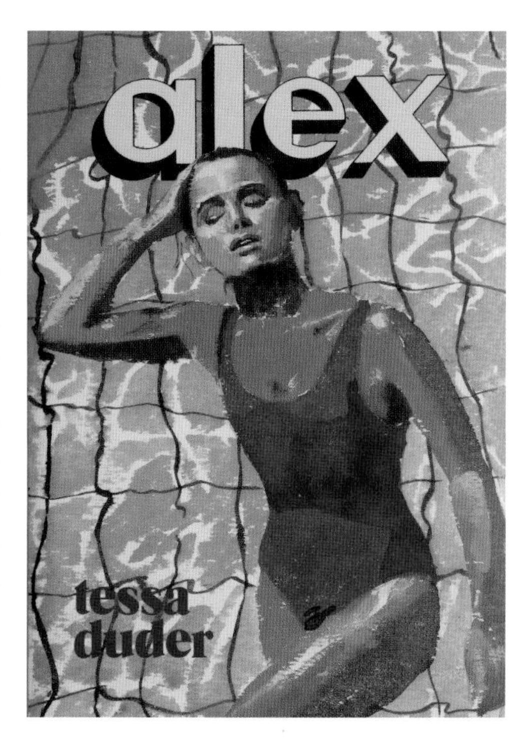

Fifteen-year-old Alexandra Archer stands out from other girls her age—tall, with Juno-esque proportions, she is a little bit awkward and always seems to invite attention for the wrong reasons. She focuses on her training because she wants to qualify for the 1960 New Zealand Olympic swimming team. However, her sporting rival, Maggie, also wants a place on the team, and her mother, the indomitable Mrs. Benton, is determined to see her daughter win gold in Rome. The story follows Alex's struggles as she deals with falling in love, a tragic loss, and everything else that teenagers go through, while trying to maintain the mature and focussed attitude required in order to achieve her dreams.

Author Tessa Duder swam for New Zealand in the Commonwealth Games when she was only eighteen years old. Although the book is not autobiographical, Duder's experience of becoming a swimming champion while also grappling with the more everyday challenges experienced by all teenagers lend authenticity to the portrayal of the trials and tribulations faced by her character, Alex, as she strives to excel both in and out of the water.

While *Alex* addresses a wide range of adolescent issues, it also looks at the psychological and physical stresses that are placed on young achievers. Although she is only fifteen, Alex faces intense scrutiny from the media, and Duder raises questions about the pressures of competing at an elite level in sport. Still, *Alex* is an inspiring story for any young readers who aim to reach the highest level in their chosen field. **CVB**

"[Maggie's] stroke has disintegrated a bit. Her mother is frozen, still as stone, white-faced. She thinks it's all over."

OTHER STORIES SET IN SCHOOL

Missing from Saint-Agil by Pierre Véry, 1953
The Chocolate War by Robert Cormier, 1974
Hating Alison Ashley by Robin Klein, 1984
Stargirl by Jerry Spinelli, 2000
Whale Talk by Chris Crutcher, 2001

12+

The Devil's Arithmetic 1988

Jane Yolen

"Gitl shook her head, 'There is nowhere to run Fayge. We are where we are. Hush.'"

MORE MOVING STORIES ABOUT WAR

Journey to America by Sonia Levitin, 1970
When Hitler Stole Pink Rabbit by Judith Kerr, 1971
The Upstairs Room by Johanna Reiss, 1972
After the War by Carol Matas, 1997
The Boy in the Striped Pyjamas by John Boyne, 2006

Nationality | American, born 1939
Publisher | Viking Penguin, USA
Award | National Jewish Book Award
Theme | Historical fiction

Award-winning author Jane Yolen has been called the Hans Christian Andersen of America and the Aesop of the twentieth century, and this beautifully written story is truly unputdownable. One warning to parents, though: the book deals frankly with the Holocaust and may be too much for some younger readers.

Hannah is a young girl who, at the start of the book, is celebrating Passover with her family. She is bored and tired of hearing about her grandparents survival of the Holocaust day after day, year after year. She just does not care about the numbers tattooed on their arms and the stories they push on her about remembrance. How can you remember something that happened before you were born? Part of the Passover Seder involves opening the door of the home for the prophet Elijah. When Hannah is asked to do this, she is magically transported back in time. Now she is the orphaned Chana, about to be shipped off to Auschwitz with the rest of her extended family. What she experiences there, and her eventual willingness to make ultimate sacrifice for those she loves, will change her views on remembrance forever.

Chana/Hannah does survive. At the last moment she is transported back to her family living room, only to discover that she has just relived her own grandmother's concentration camp story. Hannah starts to really listen to her grandparents and to understand what their suffering has meant to her, her family, and people everywhere. **KD**

12+

A Pack of Lies 1988

Geraldine McCaughrean

Nationality | English, born 1951
Publisher | Oxford University Press, UK
Award | Carnegie Medal, 1988
Theme | Quirky

Ailsa works with her mother in the family antique shop. One day she meets an eccentric, jobless young man who tells her his name is MCC Berkshire. Disbelieving him, she still finds herself offering him some work in the shop, which he is willing to do for nothing. From then on, whenever the customers hesitate about buying a particular piece, MCC Berkshire tells them a story that is so compelling that they end up purchasing the item after all. Ailsa worries that these stories are simply untrue. And who is MCC Berkshire anyway?

There are many more surprises to come before this ingenious novel comes to its teasing end. McCaughrean is an endlessly inventive writer. Like MCC Berkshire, her head is teeming with stories, each one more fantastic than the last, but all with enough truth to carry conviction. Whether the mysterious young man is talking about horseracing, missing jewels, Chinese pottery, stowaways, or magic umbrellas, he always manages to engage his audience. Each of the stories could well have made a novel on their own, but the author is happy simply to present one tale after another with the certain knowledge that there will always be more to draw upon when the time comes.

In 2005, Geraldine McCaughrean had the honor to be selected by Great Ormond Street Hospital for Children to write an official sequel to J. M. Barrie's *Peter Pan*, titled *Peter Pan in Scarlet*. **NT**

Caperucita in Manhattan 1989

Carmen Martín Gaite

Original Title | Caperucita en Manhattan
Nationality | Spanish, born 1925
Publisher | Siruela, Spain
Theme | Myths and legends

There have been many modern versions of Perrault's "Red Riding Hood" tale, some of the most interesting being those that subvert the myth of the helpless girl who allows herself to be charmed by the wolf.

In this novel, Sara Allen, a ten-year-old New York girl, is the new Little Red Riding Hood, and the forest she must traverse is the route between Brooklyn and Manhattan, where her grandmother lives. For Sara Allen, these visits are purely routine, and she makes the journey every Saturday with her apprehensive mother. One day her parents are absent, and Sara, defying her mother's warnings, goes to Manhattan alone to take a strawberry tart to her grandma. This episode concludes the first part of the book, "Dreams of Freedom," in which we are presented with the characters and the setting of the story. From that moment onward "the Adventure" unfolds: Sara meets Miss Lunatic, a sort of fairy godmother who helps her to face her fears and guides her through the city; later in Central Park she meets Mr. Wolf, a baker millionaire who tries to deceive the girl by appropriating the secret of the family recipe for the strawberry tart.

But Sara Allen and Martín Gaite are both defenders of the imagination and they ensure that the fantasy adventure has no end. The novel finishes just where another story, *Alice in Wonderland*, begins; and like Alice, Sara enters an underground passageway that leads to a wonderful place: the Statue of Liberty. **EB**

Number the Stars 1989

Lois Lowry

Nationality | American, born 1937
Publisher | Houghton Mifflin, USA
Award | Newbery Medal, 1990
Theme | War, Friendship

Number the Stars is a classic tale about the evacuation of the Jews from Nazi-occupied Denmark during World War II. On September 29, 1943, word got out in Denmark that Jews were to be detained and then sent to the death camps. Within hours the Danish resistance, population, and police arranged a small flotilla to herd 7,000 Jews to Sweden. Lois Lowry creates a fictionalized version of this event and tells her story through the voices of Annemarie Johansen and her best friend, Ellen Rosen.

On the eve of the roundup, Annemarie's family, along with their friend Peter, a member of the Danish resistance (and formerly fiancé of Annemarie's older sister, who died), smuggle the Rosen family out of the country. The story of one family's bravery in the face of certain death had they been caught—and the plight of the Rosen's as they make their way out of the country—along with all the scares, close calls, and challenges make for compelling reading.

"'When will there be cupcakes again?' 'When the war ends,' Mrs. Johansen said."

In the end we discover that Annemarie's sister died serving the resistance and that the Rosens, along with many other Jewish families, were welcomed back into Denmark after the war. Unlike many Holocaust stories for children, this one ends happily, but the brutality of war is clearly and poignantly portrayed.

Lois Lowry says: "My books have varied in content and style. Yet it seems that all of them deal, essentially, with the same general theme: the importance of human connections. *Number the Stars*, set in a different culture and era, tells . . . of the role that we humans play in the lives of our fellow beings." **KD**

RECOMMENDED LOIS LOWRY WORKS

A Summer to Die, 1977
Anastasia Krupnick, 1979
The One Hundredth Thing About Caroline, 1983
The Giver, 1993
Gossamer, 2006

Thunderwith 1989

Libby Hathorn

This tells the story of Lara, sent to live with her father, who she barely remembers, after her mother dies of cancer. Stranded in the remote Australian outback, the fourteen-year-old struggles to deal with her painful loss, a process made more difficult by the open hostility of her new family. Critical stepmother Gladwyn resents having another dependent on the impoverished farm, and matters worsen when Lara's father, the girl's only ally, goes away on business.

To add to these domestic tensions, Lara endures cruel taunts from a delinquent neighbor on the school bus. In a highly charged episode, a mysterious dog appears out of the darkness of a stormy night, as if in answer to a hysterical prayer. Lara names him Thunderwith, and the dog's affectionate company becomes a substitute for the physical loss of her mother. In a dramatic climax, Thunderwith is shot, and it is revealed that the dog, answering to the more prosaic name of Rover, belonged to the bully. Lara realizes that her bond with the dog helped her come to terms with her mother's absence, and is reconciled with her stepmother when Gladwyn realizes that she has been too hard on the grieving teenager.

"With thunder, with thunder, come to me with thunder."

The novel's success lies in the commanding prose, incisive dialogue, and sharply defined characters, as well as the deft way Hathorn weaves elements of Aboriginal legends with Lara's emotional journey. The tale is firmly rooted in the eerie beauty of the New South Wales landscape, Lara's memories of her mother, the folktales she hears from a Koori storyteller, and her own experience of life. **MK**

Nationality | Australian, born 1943
Publisher | Reed Heinemann, Australia
Theme | Young adult, Family, Folktales, Friendship, Animal stories

OTHER GREAT ANIMAL STORIES

The Yearling by Marjorie Rawlings, 1938
Where the Red Fern Grows by Wilson Rawls, 1961
The Cry of the Crow by Jean Craighead George, 1980
Taming the Star Runner by S. E. Hinton, 1988
Crowstarver by Dick King-Smith, 1998

12+

Strange Objects 1990

Gary Crew

Nationality | Australian, born 1947
Publisher | Heinemann, Australia
Award | C.B.C.A. Book of the Year, 1991
Theme | Adventure, Historical fiction

MORE GREAT READS BY GARY CREW

First Light, 1993
The Watertower, 1994
Angel's Gate, 1994
Mama's Babies, 1998
Memorial, 1999

In this complex novel, a number of strands are woven together. The first is the discovery by a schoolboy, Steven Messenger, of an old diary and a mummified hand in an iron pot. Steven chooses not to reveal another object from the pot: a ring. When the diary is authenticated and the Old Dutch translated, its author becomes known as Wouter Loos.

Another strand of the story involves the 1629 shipwreck of the *Batavia*. About 260 people survived the wreck and the captain set off for help; when he returned fourteen weeks later, more than 120 survivors had been brutally murdered. Those guilty were executed, except for Jan Pelgrom and Wouter Loos who were cast away in a boat and never heard of again.

"But if someone took the ring and put it in a glass case what would that prove?"

The ring Steven found exerts a strange power over him; he experiences mystical dreams and visions and is desperate to find out more about it. The only person who can help is Charlie, a very old Aborigine. The mummified hand belonged to Eli, a young European girl—the victim of another shipwreck—whom the castaways Pelgrom and Loos found living with the Aborigines.

The book is presented as a collection of diary entries, newspaper reports, personal accounts, psychological reports, and letters. It mixes historical fact with fiction to create a complex psychological thriller that is frightening in its intensity. The realization of landscape is an integral part of the novel—it is set in western Australia—and the dryness and unremitting heat pervade every page. The novel's open ending adds to the sense of mystery. **JG**

Redwork 1990

Michael Bedard

Bedard is known for novels that blend convincing realism, eerie fantasy, and multilayered mystery, as well as elements of psychological thrillers. *Redwork* tells the story of fifteen-year-old Cass after he moves into an apartment in a ramshackle old house in Toronto. While his distracted mother writes a thesis on William Blake, the teenager is left largely to his own devices. He finds part-time work as an usher in a rundown cinema, under the supervision of a vindictive boss. Cass is increasingly intrigued by the sinister behavior of his landlord. Reclusive Mr. Magnus, who is rumored to be insane, carries out nocturnal experiments in his dingy garage. Cass and his new friend Maddy decide to investigate, but when Mr. Magnus catches them he threatens Cass with eviction.

Gradually, the elderly man relaxes his hostile guard, allowing the teenagers to participate in his secret nocturnal work. Mr. Magnus, a veteran of World War I who was left permanently traumatized by his experiences in the trenches, is obsessed with "redwork" —an alchemical process with reputed transformative powers. He is trying to recover his lost youth—or, more specifically, his pure spiritual state prior to the terrible emotional damage sustained during the war. As Cass becomes ever more involved in the experiments, a sinister psychic connection develops between the boy and the former soldier—Cass becomes haunted by nightmares of gas attacks, blood, pain, and fear—with potentially disastrous consequences.

Michael Bedard is concerned with exploring the unknown and lifting the constrictions imposed on the imagination by the hectic pace and noise of modern urban living. "You need solitude to face the dark," he says, advocating calm, isolated reflection as a means of confronting the dark mysteries of our world. Graceful and poetic, *Redwork* is a mesmerizing philosophical fable. **MK**

Nationality | Canadian, born 1949
Publisher | Atheneum Books, USA
Award | C.L.A. Book of the Year, 1991
Theme | Fantasy, War

OTHER GREAT FANTASY WORKS

A Swiftly Tilting Planet by Madeleine L'Engle, 1978
Eragon by Christopher Paolini, 2003
Dragon Rider by Cornelia Funke, 2005
Who is Charlie Keeper? by Marcus Alexander, 2008
Nation by Terry Pratchett, 2008

12+

Rocco 1990

Sherryl Jordan

Nationality | New Zealander, born 1949
Publisher | Ashton Scholastic, New Zealand
Award | AIM Book of the Year, 1991
Theme | Fantasy

Sherryl Jordan freely admits that she wrote twelve unpublished novels before she produced her futuristic fantasy *Rocco* (known as *A Time of Darkness* in the United States). Thus began a stellar career as an author. To date she has published seventeen books for young readers, many of which have won awards.

Rocco is an ordinary teenage lad who is troubled by a strange dream involving a cave and a wolf. One day he is transported to an isolated valley inhabited by a primitive tribe. Initially he is not welcomed, but the leader of the tribe, a wise old woman named Ayoshe, commands them to accept Rocco as one of their own. Rocco is trained in basic survival skills and learns a great deal about life, death, trust, and family values. He struggles to work out why he has been transported there, and is angry with Ayoshe when she won't tell him. His switch back to twentieth-century life is equally abrupt. He suddenly wakes to find himself in a hospital bed. He undergoes more soul-searching as he realizes that his travel was to a possible time in the future, not to the past as he had previously assumed. He eventually discovers that he is connected to Ayoshe in a more intimate way than he ever imagined.

Sherryl Jordan is an intensely spiritual writer who explores the boundless margins between fact and fantasy, the real truth and the truth we imagine. She believes that the truth of the imagination is the foundation of good fantasy, and that fantasy is a training ground for lateral thinkers, inventors, and philosophers of the future. **LO**

The Visits 1991

Silvia Schujer

Nationality | Argentinian, born 1956
Publisher | Editorial Alfaguara, Argentina
Theme | Fantasy, Young adult, Family, Friendship

This story about a seemingly normal Argentine family is told by twelve-year-old Fernando. However, Fernando suddenly discovers that he has been lied to throughout his childhood. When his father disappeared, Fernando, then a four-year-old child, was told that he had gone on a long journey. Although little Fernando sensed that it was not the truth, he went along with the story. When he turned five, he was shocked by his mother's confession that his father was actually in jail. Fernando and his mother start to visit him on Sundays, and the boy soon develops a good relationship with his father. Ashamed of his secret, Fernando has to lie about his father at school, and he tells the truth only to his friend Tolle.

The situation at home deteriorates when Fernando's mother meets another man and the precarious relationship between Fernando's parents crumbles. Fernando takes refuge in a fantasy world. It is not until, at the age of twelve, he falls in love with a girl that he finds the courage to tell her the true story of his family. The story is told piece by piece, in a long, nonlinear monologue that reflects the association of Fernando's memory and its oscillation between confession and repression. It is written in the colloquial language of an Argentine adolescent (peppered with the recurring phrase "what do I know?"), which gives this memorable book great authenticity. However, Schujer's greatest achievement with the novel (published in Spanish as *Las Visitas*) is in showing that every person, no matter how difficult their childhood may have been, can find happiness. **LB**

Dear Nobody 1991

Berlie Doherty

Nationality | English, born 1943
Publisher | Hamish Hamilton, UK
Award | Carnegie Medal, 1991
Theme | Young adult, Love, Family, Controversial

Dear Nobody is about the intensity of first love, the turbulence caused by an unwanted teenage pregnancy, and the ripple effects across two families. It is about the journey that the bright and likable high school lovers, Helen and Chris, make out of their childhood, and the journey they make toward understanding their parents. They are prompted in both cases by the news that they are themselves staring parenthood in the face. Helen at first has nobody to confide in about her pregnancy, and her perspective is revealed in letters to her unborn child. This leaves Chris to tell the couple's story, exploring his shock and terror at Helen's news in a way that adds relevance for young male readers.

Once their secret is out, Helen and Chris move from being isolated to becoming aware of themselves as part of a family network at a stage in life when many of their peers are thinking only of their individual futures. The experiences and outlook of previous generations are explored with insight, winning the sympathy of readers for the reactions of the couple's parents.

In Helen, Berlie Doherty has created a character strong-willed and clear-sighted enough to make tough unilateral decisions and face up to the challenges that these involve. Ultimately, this is a story about accepting responsibility for one's actions and realizing that everything we do affects others. Doherty has never written the sequel that readers have asked for, but *The Snake-Stone* explores similar events from the perspective of an adopted child who decides to trace his birth mother. **GB**

"She knew I was watching her, just as I knew that she was holding me snug in the middle of her thoughts."

GREAT READS BY BERLIE DOHERTY

Granny Was a Buffer Girl, 1986
Spellhorn, 1989
The Snake-Stone, 1995
Daughter of the Sea, 1996
Deep Secret, 2003

Listen to My Heart 1991

Bianca Pitzorno

Original Title | Ascolta il mio cuore
Nationality | Italian, born 1942
Publisher | Mondadori, Italy
Theme | School, Friendship, Family

In *Listen to My Heart* (published in Italian as *Ascolta il mio cuore*), Bianca Pitzorno guides her readers through a maze of childhood experiences. This story, set in Sardinia in the 1950s, takes readers into the lives of Italian schoolchildren for an entire year. It is a trying time for Prisca, Elisa, and Rosalba, three of the classmates, because they have a new teacher who is a tyrant. The story shows how they adapt and manage to make their unlikable new teacher—Miss Argia Sforza (nicknamed "Arpia Sferza," meaning "Harpy Whip")—more tolerant toward them and their classmates.

Pitzorno writes convincingly of the interactions, emotions, and interests of schoolchildren. *Listen to My Heart,* one of her most autobiographical books, is written as if it were a letter to the children of today, telling them how it was when she was a child at school. The harshness of the teaching ethos of the time is very powerfully described. Argia Sforza is a severe woman who uses harsh methods of discipline. She also discriminates against Prisca, the heroine of the story, whose sense of injustice grows throughout the year until she finds the courage to stand up to the tyrannical teacher.

Pitzorno conveys the joys and challenges of young girls growing up and highlights the relationships that are important to them—with friends, teachers, and parents. Young girls will delight in the intimacy of this feminine world. **SMT**

Memoirs of a Basque Cow 1991

Bernardo Atxaga

Original Title | Memorias de una vaca
Nationality | Spanish, born Joseba Irazu 1951
Publisher | Pamiela, Spain
Theme | Friendship, Animal stories

What could a cow say that might be of interest? That, as this book demonstrates, depends on the cow. These memoirs of Mo, a Basque cow, tell of her life in Balanzategui, and her adventures with her best friend, Laughing Cow, at the end of the Spanish Civil War.

Now old and lovingly looked after by a nun, Bernadette, and at the insistence of the "Pesado"—an inner voice that Mo began to hear as soon as she was born—Mo decided to write her memoirs with the aim of recalling her life and replying to the "many questions, too many questions" that arise out of life. Although Mo realized, with horror, at the beginning of her life that she was no more than an ordinary cow, she did her best to get away from her daily routine, marked by boredom and confusion. Thanks to her efforts she has succeeded in reflecting and thinking more logically.

The novel also explores friendship, respect for others, loneliness, and the relationship between animals and humans. Atxaga achieves all this using simple language, enlivened by linguistic games and plentiful dialogue that enrich the plot and make it more approachable for younger readers.

Bernardo Atxaga, the pseudonym of Joseba Irazu, had been a professor of Basque, a scriptwriter, a bookseller, and even an economist before he decided to devote himself entirely to literature in the early 1980s. In 1989 he won the Premio Nacional de Literatura with *Obabakoak*. **EB**

Looking for Alibrandi 1992

Melina Marchetta

Nationality | Australian, born 1965
Publisher | Penguin, Australia
Award | C.B.C.A. Book of the Year, 1993
Theme | Young adult, Illness and death, Family

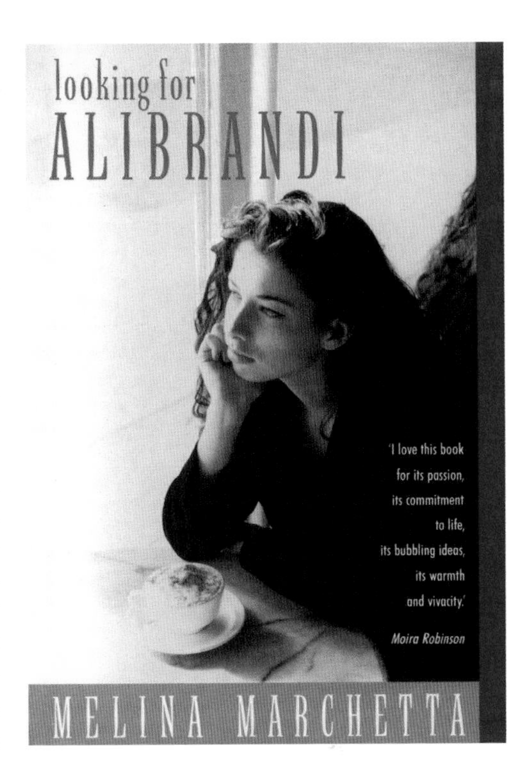

looking for
ALIBRANDI
'I love this book for its passion, its commitment to life, its bubbling ideas, its warmth and vivacity.'
Moira Robinson
MELINA MARCHETTA

Looking for Alibrandi is an intelligently written coming-of-age novel charting the experiences of seventeen-year-old Josephine Alibrandi. A sensitive but sassy second-generation Italian-Australian girl, Josie feels herself caught between old-world values and the struggle for acceptance by the wealthy Sydney elite she tries to emulate.

The story is set during Josie's final year of school, as she faces the dual stresses of important exams and the reappearance of her father after a sixteen-year absence. Further tensions stem from regular fights with her nagging grandmother and a deep-seated anxiety over her illegitimacy. When an admirer with an unrequited crush commits suicide, and she is cracking under the pressure to score top grades, Josie finds solace in the arms of bad boy Jacob, who hides an unpretentious heart beneath his tough facade.

The novel is a convincing portrayal of teenage preoccupations. Marchetta's snappy dialogue lends it authenticity, and the fully drawn characters are an amalgam of real people, including the author's own family. Much of the comedy comes from the hilarious diatribes of the uncomprehending grandmother.

Looking for Alibrandi has been applauded for its insights into the issues facing second-generation immigrants. By the end of the novel Josie has learned to define herself as both Italian and Australian. More responsible, open-minded, and self-accepting, she is able to take control over her own life choices. **MK**

"I'm not sure if anyone has ever died of the fact that their granddaughter looks untidy."

MORE BOOKS BY MELINA MARCHETTA

Saving Francesca, 2003
On the Jellicoe Road, 2006
Finnikin of the Rock, 2008

There Will Be Wolves 1992

Karleen Bradford

Nationality | Canadian, born 1936
Publisher | HarperCollins, Canada
Theme | Historical fiction, Adventure, Love, Family, War

GREAT READS BY KARLEEN BRADFORD

***Thirteenth Child*, 1994**
***Shadows on a Sword*, 1996**
***Lionheart's Scribe*, 1999**
***Angeline*, 2004**
***The Scarlet Cross*, 2006**

There Will Be Wolves is the first in a trilogy of historical novels set during the medieval Crusades. In Cologne sixteen-year-old Ursula has learned about the healing powers of herbs and roots from her apothecary father. She has also taught herself "radical" new methods of curing ailments, such as setting broken bones in splints. In a city where raw sewage fouls the streets (pestilence has killed her mother and brothers), superstition is rife. Ursula's outspokenness, coupled with habits, such as her penchant for learning and bathing, mark her out as "different." When a malicious neighbor accuses her of witchcraft, Ursula pledges to march with the People's Crusade to the Holy City of Jerusalem as proof of her true faith.

"The stench of the street was overshadowed here by pungent, even mysterious scents."

Examining the moral contradictions of the 1096 Crusade provides an interesting background to the tale of a young girl becoming a woman. Bradford describes the slaughter of the Rhineland Jews by the ransacking Christians. Although Ursula has escaped a witch's pyre, she finds traveling with the militant Crusaders equally perilous. She survives, partly thanks to the support of her best friend (and future husband) Bruno, and partly to her own inner resources.

Despite the historic setting, *There Will Be Wolves* remains relevant to contemporary readers, due to its critique of the dangers of prejudice, intolerance, and discrimination. In Ursula, Karleen Bradford has created an independent heroine with thoroughly modern sensibilities, characterized by a passionate belief in helping the weak and vulnerable. A fast-paced and gripping adventure story. **MK**

Pagan's Crusade 1992

Catherine Jinks

Nationality | Australian, born 1963
Publisher | Oxford University Press, Australia
Theme | Historical fiction, Adventure, War, Friendship

Pagan is a street urchin in Jerusalem at the time of the Crusades. He is desperate to pay back a debt, and seeks work with the Templars; he is assigned to Lord Roland as his squire. The two are very different: Pagan is quick-witted, bent on survival, and not too fussed about obeying rules, whereas Roland is idealistic and bound by the strict code of the Templars. Lying comes easily to Pagan while to Roland the very idea is anathema. Jinks depicts their growing understanding of each other with a delicate and convincing subtlety. Roland sets out to teach Pagan how to survive warfare and tries to inculcate his own code of behavior. But Saladin's army is getting ever closer, and in time Roland learns that

"If a Templar wants a bath he can go and stand in the rain. That's what God put it there for."

idealistic behavior is not necessarily the way to achieve one's aims.

Jinks is passionate about history and the Crusades. She discovered a kind of pilgrims' handbook about religious sites, which set her wondering if they behaved like modern groups on guided tours. One of the funniest episodes in the novel occurs when Pagan and Roland escort just such a group to the River Jordan. There are many complaints, a threat of brigands, and the strict limit of twelve bottles of "holy" river water per pilgrim has to be enforced. This vivid recreation of an exciting period in history has an immediacy that is instantly engaging. Pagan is a convincing blend of a medieval boy and a tough, modern streetwise survivor. This is the first of three novels about the changing relationship between Pagan and Roland. **JG**

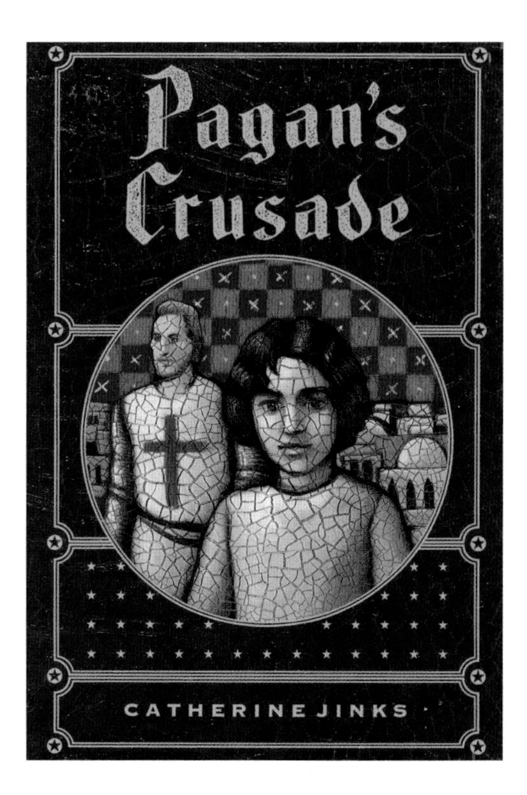

GOOD BOOKS BY CATHERINE JINKS

Pagan in Exile, 1994
Pagan Vows, 1995
Pagan's Scribe, 1995
Pagan's Daughter, 2006
The Reformed Vampire Support Group, 2009

Flour Babies 1992

Anne Fine

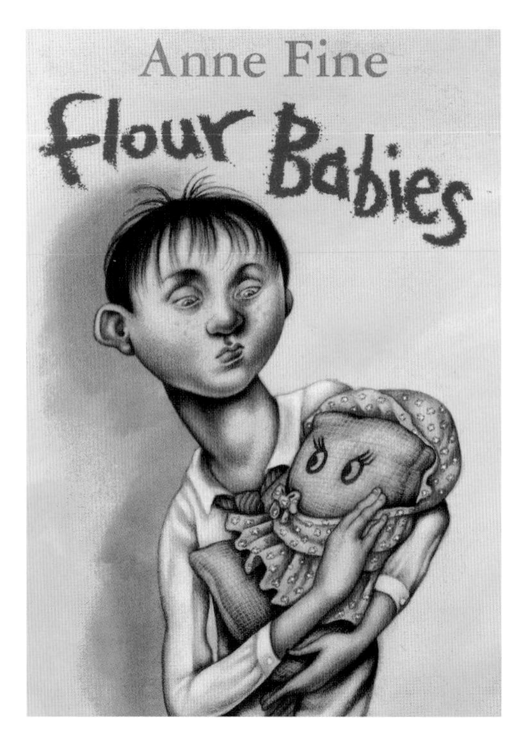

"Half of them looked as if they'd left their brains at home. The other half looked as if they didn't have any."

MORE ENTERTAINING SCHOOL READS

The School for Cats by Esther Averill, 1947
Down with Skool! by Geoffrey Willans, 1953
The Demon Headmaster by Gillian Cross, 1982
Please Mrs. Butler by Allan Ahlberg, 1983

Nationality | English, born 1947
Publisher | Hamish Hamilton, UK
Award | Whitbread Children's Book Award, 1993
Theme | School, Family

Simon Martin does not greatly relish schoolwork, and particularly so when he, along with the rest of his class, is required to take home and look after a very large bag of flour. The idea is to give adolescent pupils some idea of what it might be like to be totally responsible for something. The hope, of course, is that this experience will make them think twice before embarking on parenthood while they are still naive and uninformed about what this type of commitment really means.

Simon is asked to keep a diary of his feelings on this topic and passes from initial disgust to beginning to understand, for the very first time, why his mother often seems irritated and the probable reason why years ago his father walked out on the family when his son was only a few weeks old. Simon finishes his story wiser, although still something of a handful. In the long run he does much better with his flour baby than any of his other friends.

Anne Fine is one of the funniest authors writing for children. A former UK Children's Laureate, she has written more than fifty children's books, which often have serious issues running through them, despite the comedy. Beneath her wonderful command of dialogue and her genius in producing unexpected moments of comedy there is also a serious purpose. She has a remarkable insight into the feelings both of children and of the adults who care for them. She also never loses sight of a child's ultimate need for love and security from those they also often quarrel with, sometimes on a daily basis. **NT**

12+

Titeuf 1992

Zep

Nationality | Swiss, born 1967
Publisher | Glénat, France
Theme | Comics, Young adult, Friendship, School

Since his first appearance in 1992, the comic-strip character Titeuf has taken schoolyards by storm, far outstripping older characters such as Astérix or Spirou in popularity. With his trendy white trousers, red T-shirt, plume of blond hair, and street-wise language, Titeuf resonates with today's urban children, caught between childish games and the adolescent attractions of computer games, TV, and the Internet.

The concept behind this best-selling series is simple. Each album is about fifty pages long, with a comic strip per page, showing one of Titeuf's adventures (or more often misadventures), as he attempts to play some new prank on the school caretaker, dodge an impending math test, or invite the pretty Nadia around to his house. Most of the strips are set in Titeuf's schoolyard, and they feature several recurring characters, such as the timid, bespectacled Manu, Titeuf's sidekick and best friend; the overweight but savvy Hugo, who knows all about girls and lovemaking; and poor Vomito, so-named because he throws up at the slightest emotion.

As can be gathered from the name of this last character, there is some amount of scatological humor in Titeuf. However, even the crudest pranks are described with wit and there is something very true-to-life about them all. The greatest draw of this series may in fact lie in the way Zep mixes this light humor with larger issues—such as love, disability, war, divorce, joblessness, sexuality—providing a serious, and at times very moving, undercurrent to the happy anarchy of Titeuf's world. **CFR**

See Ya, Simon 1992

David Hill

Nationality | New Zealander, born 1942
Publisher | Mallinson Rendel, New Zealand
Theme | Illness and death, Friendship, School, Young adult

Simon Shaw is a typical teenage boy in every respect apart from the fact that he has muscular dystrophy and is confined to a wheelchair. He arrives at high school each day in a van equipped with a hydraulic hoist for lowering his wheelchair to the ground. His debilitating disease is progressively worsening and, despite physiotherapy and the best of drugs, Simon is aware that his death is imminent, since most sufferers die in their teens.

Simon's classmates and his teacher, the talented Ms. Kidman, feel admiration for his willingness to live life to the full, despite his limitations. His irrepressible sense of humor, although caustic at times, touches everyone in the class. His forthright, candid nature and acceptance of the inevitable make everyone—and in particular his best friend, Nathan—reassess their own lives.

Simon and Nathan spend most of their time together, role-playing and talking about girls. The two boys experience many humorous moments, such as when Simon applies his wheelchair brakes while being pushed uphill. When Simon inevitably dies, Nathan is bereft, although in time he comes to accept that his life must go on.

This moving debut teenage novel was shortlisted for the New Zealand Children's Book Awards, but it deservedly won recognition ten years later when it won the Storylines Gaelyn Gordon Award for a Much-Loved Book in 2002. David Hill's thought-provoking story was based on a real-life friend of his daughter. **WM**

Heart's Delight 1992

 Per Nilsson

Original Title | Hjärtans fröjd
Nationality | Swedish, born 1954
Publisher | Rabén and Sjögren, Sweden
Theme | Young adult, Love

In *Heart's Delight* Per Nilsson captures the intensity and pain of first love and teenage heartbreak. The novel reads honestly and straight from the heart and brings a unique Swedish viewpoint to a universal theme of lost love.

A sixteen-year-old boy sits alone in his room with all the objects collected from his short-lived relationship with Ann-Katrin, the girl from his bus, the girl with red hair, the girl who mesmerized him—his heart's delight. He tears the bus pass from their first meeting into tiny pieces. He throws the pot of lemon balm she gave him over the balcony. He tosses a record they listened to together, like a Frisbee, out into the parking lot. He burns a postcard she gave him. As each item is disposed of, readers learn a little more about the events that have been playing over and over in the boy's head. Attached to each item are memories that tell his story—a story that is sweet, awkward, and ultimately heartbreaking. This is no gushing sentimental love story, however. It does not have a traditional happy ending, and is true to life, expressing the anguish and angst that teenagers feel.

The book has an unusual structure; the chapters are broken up into each collected object, as Nilsson shifts his narration from the first person to the third person perspective. This original viewpoint, combined with Nilsson's taut prose, builds suspense. A master of young adult fiction, Nilsson conveys the truth of what it means to be young and in love for the first time. **RA**

Tomorrow, When the War Began 1993

 John Marsden

Nationality | Australian, born 1950
Publisher | Pan Macmillan, Australia
Theme | Adventure, War, Friendship, Family, Young adult

Survival against all the odds is the theme of this, the first of seven books in the best-selling, Australian Tomorrow series. In it, Ellie tells the story of how a group of friends go off into the Australian bush, to a place called Hell, for a Christmas holiday camping trip. When they return they find that their homeland has been invaded by an unknown enemy. Ellie's home is deserted, the animals dead, and her parents are being held prisoner. The group retreat to Hell, but once they face up to their options—hide, surrender, or fight—they choose the latter and begin a two-pronged strategy: to scavenge and to attack.

In the first of their forays into the town to find out exactly what has happened, Ellie has to confront the reality of what they have to do to in order to survive. When one of the group, Lee, is wounded, Ellie rescues him in the shovel of a backhoe, running over a jeep in the process. The young people all have to confront their fears in different ways, and the dynamics of the previously light-hearted group of friends changes. Four of the group determine to fight back against the enemy and, in an exciting scene, they ignite a gas tanker to destroy a bridge used by the invading forces to move troops and supplies. This success is tempered by the shooting of Ellie's best friend.

As Ellie narrates the story, we witness her transformation and that of her friends, as each discovers the depths of their courage and loyalty to one another, their families, and their country. **KW/JF**

Some of the Kinder Planets 1993

Tim Wynne-Jones

Nationality | English/Canadian, born 1948
Publisher | Groundwood Books, Canada
Theme | Magical stories, Adventure, Science and nature

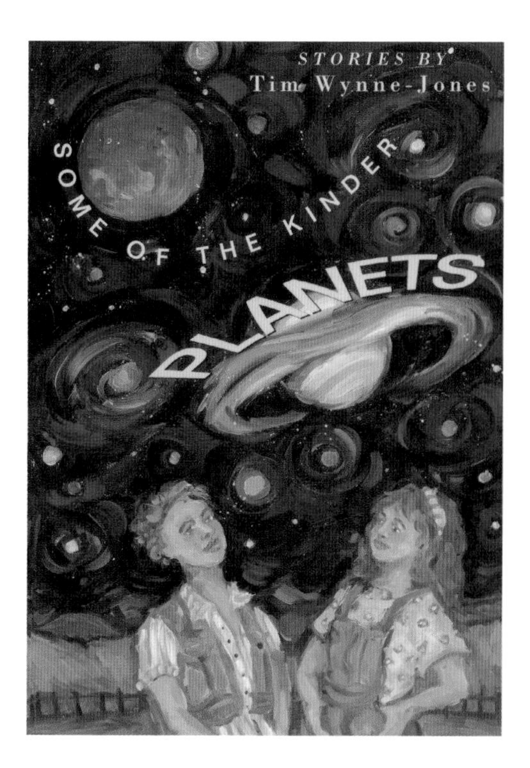

STORIES BY
Tim Wynne-Jones
SOME OF THE KINDER
PLANETS

The nine short stories in this anthology are united by their whimsical insight into the individual, esoteric preoccupations of ordinary Canadian teenagers. In "The Night of the Pomegranate," schoolgirl protagonist Harriet is enchanted by two novel sights: a little-seen view of Mars and the strange interior of a pomegranate, its glutinous red seeds encased in soft, white cushioning. Her nighttime stargazing crashes to Earth when her science project model of the galaxy, hastily cobbled together from scrunched up newspaper, masking tape, and chewing gum, begins to disintegrate. Yet though her model lacks finesse, Harriet's evident fascination for the mysterious red planet entrances the whole class.

The other stories in the collection are similarly original and of a slightly philosophical bent. In "Save the Moon for Kerdy Dickus," a girl attempts to publish a magazine dedicated to people with unusual names. Another tale describes the experiences of a lost traveler who ends up believing that he has had a "close encounter of the third kind." A different story introduces a bedridden invalid who fantasizes about traveling to exotic destinations, pasting their names onto his chest and stomach.

The charm of this offbeat anthology lies in the small details and evocative descriptions. Tim Wynne-Jones studied art and is concerned with creating a strong visual impact through words. This intelligent, sensitive portrait of "the wonder years" is sure to enchant. **MK**

"Until last night, Harriet had never seen the inside of a pomegranate before."

OTHER FICTION BY TIM WYNNE-JONES

The Dead of Night, 1994
Darkness Be My Friend, 1996
Burning for Revenge, 1997
The Night Is for Hunting, 1998
The Other Side of Dawn, 1999

Rowan of Rin 1993

Emily Rodda

"He never gave up. He would not give up. The smallest and the weakest among us proved the strongest and bravest."

FANTASTIC READS BY EMILY RODDA

Something Special, 1984
Finders Keepers, 1990
The Timekeeper, 1992
Deltora Quest series, 2000–2005
The Key to Rondo, 2007

Nationality | Australian, born Jennifer Rowe 1948
Publisher | Omnibus Books, Australia
Award | C.B.C.A. Book of the Year, 1994
Theme | Fantasy, Adventure, Family

In *Rowan of Rin*, Emily Rodda—the pen name of one of Australia's most prolific and successful authors, Jennifer Rowe—has produced a fine story for teenage readers about facing one's fears, speaking out, and finding the courage to take action for what one believes is right. Rowan lives with his mother, Jiller, and sister, Annad, in a small village named Rin, which sits in the shadow of a mountain from which the villagers constantly hear the roar of a dragon.

Rowan is known to be timid, and looks after the town's bukshah animal herd, a job considered suitable for a much younger child. His brave father, Sefton, died when his son was young, saving the family from their burning house. Rowan takes his work seriously, and he and his favorite animal Star share a special bond. When the water in the bukshah pool dries up, he is as concerned as the rest of the village. The wise woman, Sheba, who speaks in riddles, gives Rowan a magical map that only he can decipher. He joins the party of villagers that sets out to climb the forbidden mountain and find the source of the stream. As they encounter one frightening trial after another, it is Rowan who finds the determination and courage to persevere.

Rowan of Rin (along with the rest of the five-book series, published together as *The Journey*) is written in the tradition of a quest and Rodda cleverly includes riddles for readers to decipher along the way. Rowan is the reluctant hero who saves first his village, then his people, and ultimately the bukshah on whom the entire community depend. **BH**

12+

The Gathering 1993

Isobelle Carmody

Nationality | Australian, born 1958
Publisher | Penguin, Australia
Award | C.B.C.A. Book of the Year, 1994
Theme | Fantasy, Young adult

Isobelle Carmody is a popular and prolific author of science fiction, fantasy, and horror stories. She is perhaps best-known for the Obernewtyn Chronicles, the first book of which—*Obernewtyn* (1987)—she actually wrote while still a schoolgirl.

Nathaniel Delaney and his mother have moved yet again. Nathaniel had been happy and settled at his last school, where he'd achieved good grades, but he is not happy with the seaside town of Cheshunt, nor with his new school, Three North. He senses an evil darkness about the place that is as pervasive as the sickening stench from the nearby abattoir. A palpable malevolence seems to descend over Cheshunt at nightfall, when dangerous, feral dogs roam the streets.

Nathaniel's new school is dominated by bullies, such as Buddha, who are members of the youth group known as "The Gathering." Nathaniel refuses the invitation to join the group, but when he is beaten into a concussion during a basketball game supervised by Mr. Karle, the sinister, intimidating deputy principal of the school, Nathaniel glimpses the price to be paid for individualism. There is worse to come.

When Nathaniel comes across another group, known as "The Chain," who claim to have been brought together to fight the evil in Cheshunt, he learns that his presence there is no accident. The fragile mystic, Lallie, identifies him as the fifth and vital link in the chain that can defeat the dark forces. But what ritual must they perform to banish this evil and heal the wounded Earth? **MH**

Gold Dust 1993

Geraldine McCaughrean

Nationality | English, born 1951
Publisher | Oxford University Press, UK
Award | Whitbread Children's Book Award, 1994
Theme | Adventure

One day Maro and his sister, Inez, find that a large hole has been dug outside their father's shop in the Brazilian town where they live. Other holes start appearing too, until the main street is almost impassable. The two children realize that they are in the middle of a modern-day gold rush, with adults caught up in the fever, behaving in ridiculous ways as ever more rumors fan their frantic greed.

Maro and Inez remain unconvinced, showing far more maturity than those older speculators who are willing to bring the whole town to a standstill in their rush for something that may not even be there. By the end of the story, Maro and his sister are more than happy to resume their education, realizing that hard work is always going to prove more fruitful in the long run than unreal dreams of instant wealth.

This story is totally compelling from first word to last. Its main characters are so well delineated that readers feel that they have known them all their lives. The sensation of living in a very different place and climate is conveyed just as cleverly. The author is not out to condemn poor people who believe they may suddenly become rich, but she does show the consequences of such actions. There are also other local characters who still manage to keep their heads, not least the two children who play such a central part in this superb story.

McCaughrean won the Whitbread Children's Book Award for *Gold Dust*, *A Little Lower Than the Angels*, and *Not the End of the World*—the only writer to have won the prize three times. **NT**

Dougy 1993

James Moloney

Nationality | Australian, born 1954
Publisher | University of Queensland Press, Australia
Theme | Young adult, Family, School

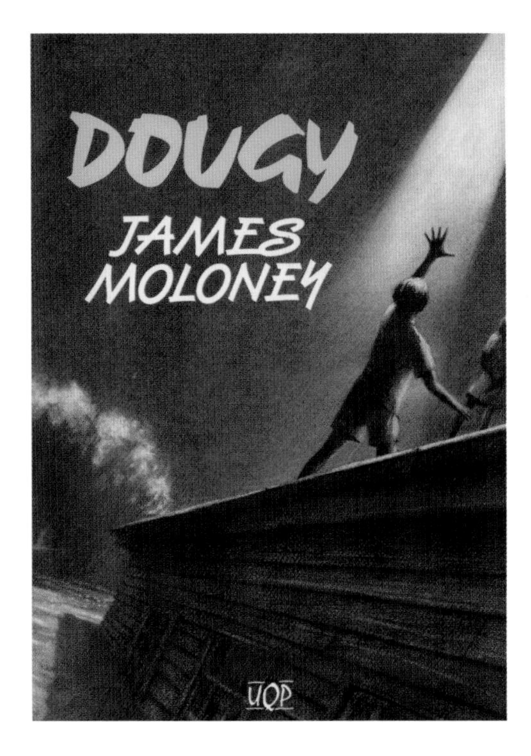

EXCELLENT READS BY JAMES MOLONEY

Gracey, 1994
The House on River Terrace, 1995
Swashbuckler, 1996
Angela, 1999
Black Taxi, 2005

Brisbane-based James Moloney is a prolific writer of award-winning books for children and young adults. In his former career as a teacher-librarian, he taught in towns not unlike the one depicted in *Dougy*, and has said that these experiences influenced his writing.

This is the first book in Moloney's trilogy about a young Aboriginal athlete; it is followed by *Gracey* (1994) and *Angela* (1999). Dougy is Gracey's younger brother, a shy thirteen-year-old who sees himself as a terrible failure. Despite his age, he is still in elementary school and he feels awkward being the tallest boy. He is, however, one of the few Aborigines left in his town who is still attuned to the old Dreaming tales, and yearns for their telling.

"I don't know what people think when they feel the weight of a gun in their hands."

In a town where racial tensions simmer never far from the surface, all share delight when Gracey wins a state athletics championship. However, when an exclusive Brisbane boarding school offers Gracey a scholarship, "whitefella" resentment blatantly bubbles over. Then a teenage girl is discovered, unconscious, in the sandhills, and an Aboriginal youth is blamed on the basis of circumstantial reports. The hostility between the two communities erupts into violence. While this is happening, rain from many miles upstream causes the river to flood. In the resulting crisis, young Dougy discovers a courage and resourcefulness that he did not know he possessed.

James Moloney dedicated this book to a student he had taught, named Douglas, who had collapsed and died during a rugby match. **MH**

Stone Cold 1993

Robert Swindells

The author slept on the rough streets of London as research for this book, and authenticity runs through his raw tale of homelessness. Controversy raged over the fact that *Stone Cold* won the Carnegie Medal, with some judging it too unsavory for the young. Others, however, were delighted to see real issues being tackled in a way that teenagers could relate to. The book's main protagonist is Link—a street nickname he has given himself, taken from a London train service. Link is a teenager from the north of England, who, in a depressingly familiar cycle, escapes a life tainted by abuse and stunted opportunity to slide into one where he lives huddled in London's doorways.

The story has a brutally direct approach, dominated by convincing dialogue and Link's own narrative. In parallel to the main story is another chilling narrative: the words of a serial killer, an ex-military man whose mission is to clear the streets of "dossers and junkies and drunks." His strategy is to murder them and lay them out under the floorboards of his Camden flat—members of his battalion of "Camden Horizontals." When Link's close streetmate, Ginger, disappears, danger draws nearer. Link's situation is made more complex when he falls in love with Gail, who is new to homelessness and clings to Link. But she has a secret that he cannot quite fathom.

Robert Swindells's trademark is young adult fiction that convincingly explores gritty social issues and that reflects his personal experiences and beliefs. He has been in the armed forces, was imprisoned for taking part in antinuclear protests, and Link's birth date and hometown are the same as his own (March 20, Bradford, England). Although he left school at fifteen, he eventually qualified as a teacher. Swindells's empathy with those who have to make their own way in life is the shining point of this powerful story. **AK**

Nationality | English, born 1939
Publisher | Hamish Hamilton, UK
Award | Carnegie Medal, 1993
Theme | Young adult, Controversial

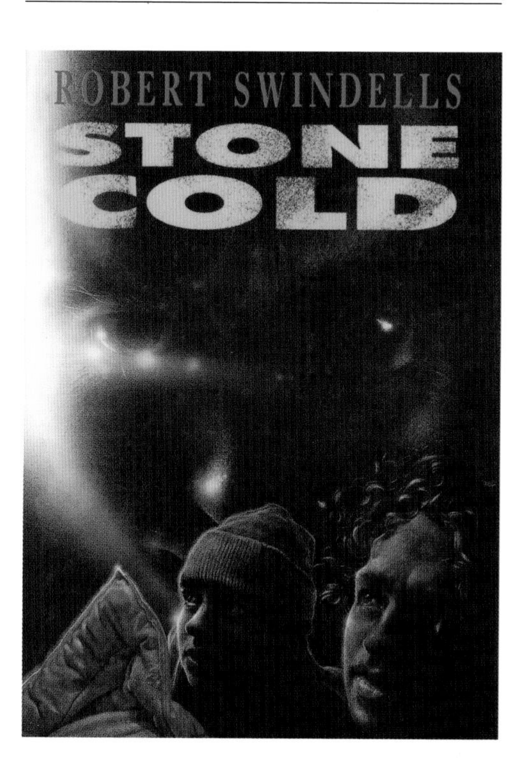

12+

MORE FROM ROBERT SWINDELLS

Brother in the Land, 1984
Room 13, 1990
Daz 4 Zoe, 1990
Nightmare Stairs, 1998
Blitzed, 2003

Foxspell 1994

Gillian Rubinstein

"Tod stood frozen. . . . He felt as if something wild leaped from the animal's eyes and planted itself deep inside him."

GREAT BOOKS BY GILLIAN RUBINSTEIN

***Space Demons*, 1986**
***Beyond the Labyrinth*, 1988**
***At Ardilla*, 1991**
***Galax-Arena*, 1992**
***Under the Cat's Eye*, 1997**

Nationality | English/Australian, born 1942
Publisher | Hyland House, Australia
Award | C.B.C.A. Book of the Year, 1995
Theme | Young adult, Fantasy, Family

12+

In *Foxspell,* Gillian Rubinstein cemented her reputation for complex young adult fiction with an edgy novel about displacement, exile, and alienation. After his father's abandonment, preteen Tod Mahoney, his mother, and sisters are forced to leave their beloved inner-city Sydney home and move to his maternal grandmother's suburban Adelaide residence. The slaughtered fox Tod discovers en route to his new school symbolizes what relocation to this alien environment has cost him—his past and, with it, his sense of place and belonging.

Tod's burgeoning identification with foxes enables him to access a spirit world where the fox spirit initiates his magical transformation into a "human-cub" and offers Tod immortality if he remains a fox. Tod's relationship with his vivid imagination reflects Rubinstein's belief as stated in a 1994 interview that fiction's role is to help humans "work out their problems." After reattaching connections eliminated from the landscape, such as lore and rock art, Tod learns to appreciate the value of his home, ancestors, and community. Yet the book's ending is ambiguous. Does Tod resolve the problem of his father's absence through fantasy, or does he retreat from reality into the fantasy world of a wild fox?

Gillian Rubinstein was born in England but has been a resident of Australia since 1973. She is a prolific, children's author who also writes under the names G. M. Hanson (her maiden name) and Lian Hearn. The first of her Tales of the Otori series, under the latter pseudonym, was published in 2001. **RC**

Walk Two Moons 1994

Sharon Creech

Nationality | American, born 1945
Publisher | HarperCollins, USA
Award | Newbery Medal, 1995
Theme | Young adult, Friendship, Family

Salamanca "Sal" Hiddle is a thirteen-year-old girl proud of the "Indian-ness in her blood." Her world changes, however, following the sudden departure of her mother. Taken away by her father to live in unfamiliar Ohio, Sal soon makes friends with Phoebe Winterbottom, a girl her own age whose mother has also recently disappeared. Worried about strange messages left at her door and what she thinks is a "lunatic" lurking in the house, Phoebe confides her fears to Sal who, in turn, tells her grandparents about her strange new friend during a 3,000-mile trip they take to Idaho. They are making this journey in order to visit Sal's mother on her birthday, in the hope that they can persuade her to return home. Although Phoebe's mother does eventually come back, Sal has to accept that this will never happen in her own case.

This richly textured novel combines a girl's search for her own identity with her coming to terms with separation and grief. Funny on occasions, sad on others, it is full of memorable characters, not least Sal's feisty grandparents, who are always up for a new adventure on behalf of their beloved granddaughter. The parallel stories of Sal and Phoebe finally converge, with each girl learning from the other. Readers will be thrilled by this cunning and poignant story, where nothing is ever quite what it seems and whose ending is never certain until the last page.

Sharon Creech is an award-winning American author of children's fiction. Born in Ohio, she lived in Switzerland and in England for many years before returning to the United States. **NT**

Switchers 1994

Kate Thompson

Nationality | English, born 1956
Publisher | Aran Press, Ireland
Theme | Fantasy, Myths and legends, Friendship, Adventure

Although born in England, Kate Thompson has lived for many years in Ireland, a country that has influenced the themes of many of her children's novels. She has drawn on various areas of the country for her settings and, in more general terms, on Irish mythology, legend, and folklore. In *Switchers*, her first novel, she is particularly interested in the phenomenon of shape-shifting, combining this with a strong awareness of twentieth- and twenty-first century concerns with climate crisis and eco-politics.

The novel's thirteen-year-old heroine, Tess, lives in Dublin, where she meets Kevin, who is nearly fifteen. She soon discovers that, like her, Kevin also possesses the ability to "switch"—that is, to assume the form of any animal they choose. He asks her to accompany him on a visit to Lizzie, a former "switcher" who is now an old woman. Lizzie tells them that sluglike creatures known as "Grokes" (or "Krools" as they become known in later editions of the novel), found in Arctic regions, are determined to bring about a new Ice Age. Tess and Kevin embark on a hazardous journey to the North Pole, where their protean abilities to transform themselves stand them in good stead. As circumstances demand, they become rats, whales, mammoths, or dragons and, as if the Grokes were not sufficient opposition, they also have to contend with U.S. military forces. Tragedy befalls Kevin, but some time after Tess's return home she is visited by her former companion, who is now a phoenix. *Switchers* is an engrossing fantasy celebrating the richness of the human imagination. **RD**

Whispers in the Graveyard 1994

Theresa Breslin

Nationality | Scottish, birth date unknown
Publisher | Methuen, UK
Award | Carnegie Medal, 1994
Theme | Myths and legends, Young adult

MORE FICTION BY THERESA BRESLIN

***Simon's Challenge*, 1988**
***The Dream Master*, 1999**
***Remembrance*, 2002**
***Divided City*, 2005**
***The Medici Seal*, 2006**

12+

Solomon is a troubled boy. He struggles with severe dyslexia, and he hates school, where he is bullied by his teachers. His home life is no better—his mother has left and his father is an alcoholic. He is angry and confused. His only escape is an ancient, Scottish churchyard, but when workmen open an old grave, he hears whispers and strange powers are unleashed. Solomon discovers that the churchyard is cursed and that he must battle against forces of evil to save Amy, the daughter of a professor who is studying the church.

Steeped in atmosphere, the Scottish landscape, and its myths and legends, *Whispers in the Graveyard* is a gripping and powerful novel for young adults. The author says that it is not only a fantasy but also a quest and a voyage of self-discovery. Solomon is put to the test and has to choose between good and evil; his challenge in the graveyard is a metaphor for his struggle with the world around him. In the process, he discovers things about himself and finally succeeds. Ultimately he battles to save Amy and confronts his father about his alcoholism. At the end of the novel he is a stronger character and begins to deal with his dyslexia.

"Now I have to cross my bridge. I make the letters. Carefully and complete. Solomon, my name."

Theresa Breslin is the award-winning author of more than thirty books. She started writing as a teenager. When a nearby steel mill closed, she was compelled to write about it. She has an enormous range, from science fiction to school stories, and writes for early readers as well as young adults. Her work is used extensively in schools, and Breslin often gives "challenged children" a major role in her books. **HJ**

See How They Run 1994

David McRobbie

See How They Run is a gripping thriller that keeps the reader turning the pages as fifteen-year-old narrator Emma Cassidy and her family grapple with having their world turned upside down. Emma's father, Don, is an accountant, who agrees to testify as a witness against one of his clients who is charged with serious criminal offenses. What follows is a nail-biting suspense story.

Emma, her younger sister Nicola, their mother Lil, and Don live a comfortable life in Manchester, England, until they are forced to go into hiding one afternoon after school, forsaking their dog, Barney, the family photos, and their beloved Daimler for an unpredictable and frightening life on the run.

"'Turn the other cheek? . . . Wouldn't we like to get back at the Gorgon?'"

The Cassidy family settle into a new neighborhood in a new town; then their old house is burned down. Don goes to look at the damage, but he has fallen for a trap. He is followed back to their safe house, and the family must flee to Don's native Australia. Even on the other side of the world, the family still has to be vigilant, which is not always easy, and the tensions of living with lies and secrecy, despite trying to maintain integrity in the face of criminality, takes its toll on the whole family.

As the trial date approaches, the criminal's henchmen come too close in a bid to keep Don away from court. Don falters but then, remembering his daughter's words, resolves to appear. Once back in Manchester, he goes public. His courage helps other witnesses to come out in support so that truth wins in the end. **BH**

Nationality | Scottish/Australian, born 1934
Publisher | Penguin, Australia
Theme | Adventure, Family, Thriller
Young adult

David McRobbie
See how they run
Is the price of truth too high?

FANTASTIC READS BY DAVID McROBBIE

Tyro, 2000
Fegus McPhail, 2003
Mad Arm of the Y, 2005
A Good Arriving, 2008

12+

A Jump into the Other World 1994

Bruno Tognolini / Roberto Luciani

Nationality | Italian, born 1951 (author); Italian, born 1954 (illustrator)
Publisher | Giunti, Italy
Theme | Fantasy, School, Friendship

Teenagers Ernesto (Ce), Andrea (Dos), Alessia (Ale magna), Martino, and Francesca are all in the same class at school. Their classmate Angelo Buioli (Buio) has gone into the "Other World," and together, his loyal friends plan to get him back from this parallel world. In turn, the classmates lower themselves with a security rope into the Other World, which their teacher suggests is simply a product of their vivid imaginations. "Each one of us at certain moments uses a kind of invisible screen to isolate oneself from their surroundings," he tells them. "At these times dreams, desires, daydreams, fantasy are evoked. One speaks with people who do not exist, with imaginary friends, imaginary animals; with one's imagination one visits marvelous and legendary places; one becomes a hero, a champion, a warrior. But do you think this world really exists?"

In the process of looking for Angelo, who has become stuck in his daydreams in the Other World, each teenager discovers something "real" about their individual daydreams and about their own identity. Using the language, expressions, and reasoning of his teenage audience, Tognolini raises important questions for young people about their place and meaning in the world.

As well as producing books and poetry for children, Tognolini has also written for children's television. In 1994 he won the Premio Andersen: Best Author of the Year Award for *Salto nell'Ultramondo*. **SMT**

When the World Was Still Young 1995

Jürg Schubiger / Susanne Rotraut

Original Title | Als die Welt noch jung war
Nationality | Swiss, born 1936
Publisher | Beltz and Gelberg, Switzerland
Theme | Fantasy, Quirky

This collection of forty-three engaging and thought-provoking stories by Jürg Schubiger draws the reader into a fantastical world of wandering cities and girls who can cheat death by posing the Grim Reaper difficult math riddles. The stories encompass six topics: Heaven and Earth; animals; names; mysteries and magic; different lives; and simply "stuff." Some of the stories deal with everyday life. In the "stuff" section, for example, there is a story about an ordinary chair that is overlooked until people realize its usefulness. The title story, on the other hand, is one of many religiously themed stories.

The common denominator of the stories, however, is that they all confound the reader's expectations. The narratives defy logic, and yet Schubiger presents them as rational and unavoidable. Dreamlike images turn into reality, with spaced-out imagery reminiscent of a kaleidoscopic, drug-fueled dream. Highly philosophical notions become mere sources of entertainment. Nothing in this collection is quite the way one would normally expect.

In this sense the work is similar to Schubiger's life. There seems to be hardly any job that he has not done. He has worked as a gardener, lumberjack, copywriter, publisher, and as a psychotherapist. These eclectic experiences and the various outlooks of people employed in those fields inform Shubiger's writing. This collection is not only highly instructive for children, but also incredibly intriguing for adults. **GS**

Northern Lights 1995

Philip Pullman

Nationality | English, born 1946
Publisher | Scholastic, UK
Award | Carnegie Medal, 1995
Theme | Fantasy, Adventure, Classics

This is the first novel in Pullman's His Dark Materials trilogy, which is arguably one of the most significant works for children of all time. Shifting between universes that are subtly different from our own world and from each other, yet similar enough to make the novels' conclusions about good, evil, and human potential profoundly relevant to us, the trilogy was soon recognized as a classic.

It is important when introducing a child to His Dark Materials not to allow an adult reader's concept of the work's overall significance to override the child's appreciation of a great story. *Northern Lights* opens by presenting Lyra, the lynchpin of the three books, as a wild tomboy who does not let her Oxford college guardians stop her from throwing herself into local gang warfare. Her natural appetite for adventure and questioning spirit lead her into more dangerous pursuits after she foils the attempted murder of her powerful uncle, Lord Asriel. As connections emerge between the disappearance of children, including Lyra's friends Roger and Billy; Lord Asriel's business in the far north; and the preoccupation of her new guardian, Mrs. Coulter, with a mysterious substance called Dust, Lyra needs to draw on all her reserves of courage. Add the world Pullman has created, in which talking animal spirits, armor-plated bears, and sinister experiment centers are only the tip of the fictional iceberg, and the reader will be swept away by the story, at the mercy of a greater force, just as Lyra is. **GB**

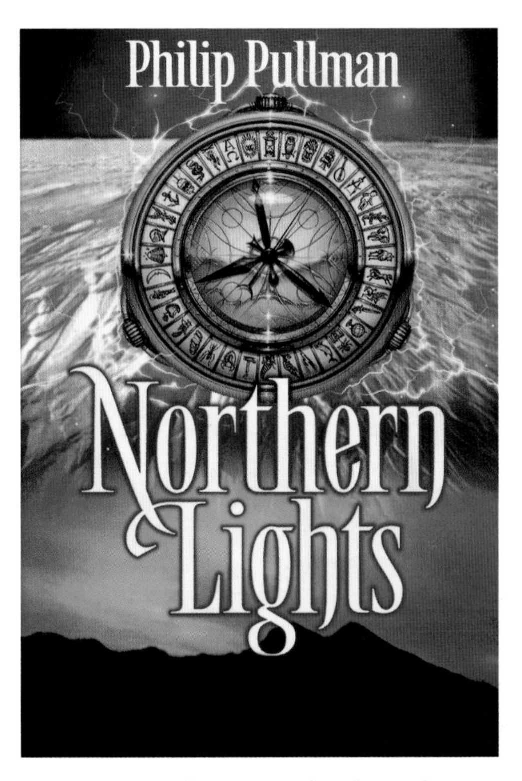

". . . Something in the bear's presence made her feel close to coldness, danger, brutal power."

OTHER GREAT PHILIP PULLMAN BOOKS

Galatea, 1976
The Subtle Knife, 1997
The Amber Spyglass, 2000
Lyra's Oxford, 2003
Once Upon a Time in the North, 2008

When the Snow Fell 1996

Henning Mankell

Original Title | Pojken som sov med snö i sin säng
Nationality | Swedish, born 1948
Publisher | Rabén and Sjögren, Sweden
Theme | Young adult, Love

12+

Henning Mankell is perhaps better known for his prolific adult fiction and best-selling titles about his police inspector Kurt Wallander. When Mankell writes for young people, he weaves existential and universal problems into a dense, exciting plot. His characters are believable people in real-life situations.

When the Snow Fell is the third book in Mankell's Joel Gustafson series. Here, thirteen-year-old Joel is about to leave his childhood behind. The little village in the north of Sweden where he has grown up is starting to feel too small, and he is beginning to experience the strange and wonderful feelings of love for the first time. The only problem is that the girl of his dreams is ten years his senior. To get out of his troublesome situation, Joel decides to become a rock star. He reasons that as a rock star, he would have the chance to leave the village behind and travel the world beyond the river and the deep forest.

"Snow was like an Indian. It moved silently and came when you least expected it."

The characteristic compassion, strong pathos, and engagement found in Mankell's work is also present in his books about Joel. They are poetic, wise, full of insight, and deeply touching. This rich story talks to youth and adults alike.

As well as his Joel Gustafson series, Henning Mankell has written a series about a girl called Sofia, also for children. In addition to these, he has produced numerous adult novels, plays, and television adaptations, which have garnered many awards. The author has established his own publishing house, Leopold Förlag, and is committed to supporting young talent from Sweden and Africa. **CC**

POJKEN SOM SOV MED SNÖ I SIN SÄNG
Henning Mankell

MORE IN THE JOEL GUSTAFSON SERIES

A Bridge to the Stars (Hunden som sprang mot en stjärna), 1990
Shadows in Twilight (Skuggorna växer i skymningen), 1991
Journey to World's End (Resan till världens ände), 1998

Peeling the Onion 1996

Wendy Orr

Nationality	Canadian, born 1953
Publisher	Allen and Unwin, Australia
Award	C.B.C.A. Honor Book, 1997
Theme	Young adult, Family, Friendship

Seventeen-year-old karate champion Anna Duncan is on top of the world when another car hits hers and she wakes up with a broken neck. People say she is lucky to be alive, but being told she'll never walk without a cane and seeing her boyfriend and a best friend slip away because they can't cope with her accident, she finds it hard to share that sentiment.

In the year following the accident, Anna struggles with a body that will not do what she wants anymore, and she comes close to giving up on everything. Yet, she also falls in love, and eventually works out that sometimes you need to face everything you have lost before you can recognize the things that you've gained. Although Anna is never going to be grateful for her accident, in the end she is fiercely glad to be alive and still standing.

"I'm so scared that if I peel everything away there'll just be a big . . . hole with nothing inside."

Peeling the Onion is partly based on Orr's involvement in a serious car accident in 1991 and her recovery from it, and is an immensely appealing example of the accident-recovery genre. This book is written in a lightly sketched style and moves from one fragmented scene to the next in a way that is never confusing. It is about serious events written with a sense of humor and a strong message of hope. It is also a coming-of-age story intertwined with a love story that is bound to continue picking up fans.

Wendy Orr was born in Canada. After finishing high school she spent three years in England studying occupational therapy. She later moved to Australia after marrying an Australian farmer. She has written many books for children and one adult novel. **JM**

OTHER GREAT READS BY WENDY ORR

Leaving it to You, 1992
A Light in Space, 1995
Dirtbikes, 1995
Nim's Island, 1999
Nim at Sea, 2007

12+

The Gifting 1996

Sophie Masson

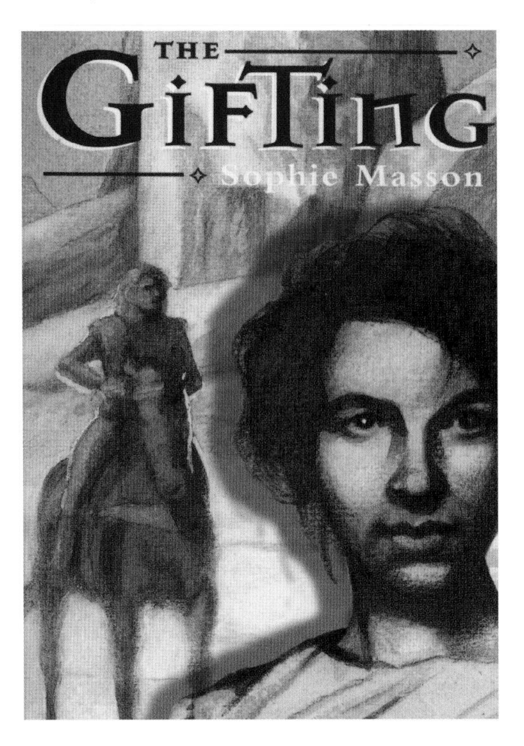

"The Empire is dying. . . . Its dying throes infect all who live within it. But there is another place, undying, true, real."

GREAT FANTASY BY SOPHIE MASSON

Red City, 1998
The Green Prince, 2000
The Firebird, 2001
The Hand of Glory, 2002
In Hollow Lands, 2004

Nationality | Australian, born 1959
Publisher | HarperCollins, Australia
Theme | Fantasy, Adventure, Family, Friendship

Born in Indonesia of French parents, Sophie Masson went to Australia when she was five. In her autobiography, she explains: "I don't just dream fantasy and legend; I live it." In her brilliant fantasy novel *The Gifting*, Masson dramatizes the importance of the past in relation both to the present and the future. She also examines the role of the past in determining historical and cultural truth, through an allegory of a civilization in decay.

After the death of her father, Sulia leaves her third-century Roman city in search of the mother she never knew. Her longing to restore a lost ancestral bond is shared by fellow traveler, Rufus, who is looking for his absent father. Their journey across the sea into Alainan and its interior, Gealan, is a quest to remedy the sense of rootlessness and uncertainty generated by Sulia's and Rufus's disconnection from their past and lineage.

The supernatural competition that decides which version of the past is true is contested by Sulia, who traverses the spirit and life worlds. As "the gifting" appropriates objects and people, it controls which aspects of the past survive as heritage. To succeed in the gifting and resist amnesia, identity loss, and oblivion, Sulia must join the voices of the dead and other echoes of the past to her present. Sulia therefore embodies the idea expressed in Masson's 1997 essay, "Times Past, Times to Come," that "a study of the past is essential to a presentiment of the future; and an appreciation of the present." **RC**

12+

Out of the Dust 1997

Karen Hesse

Nationality | American, born 1952
Publisher | Scholastic, USA
Award | Newbery Medal, 1998
Theme | Young adult, Family

Billie Jo's story, which spans two years of her life as a farmer's daughter in Oklahoma, starts in the winter of 1934; the period known as the Dust Bowl years. Told in episodes in free verse, which reads like very personal letters to the reader, Billie Jo's story is poignant and raw. "Daddy named me Billie Jo. / He wanted a boy. / Instead, / he got a long-legged girl / with a wide mouth / and cheekbones like bicycle handles. / He got a redheaded, freckle-faced, narrow-hipped girl / with a fondness for apples / and a hunger for playing fierce piano."

Billie Jo is an only child and has inherited her mother's musical ability. She persuades Ma to let her play the piano on the stage, even though it is not the sort of music Ma likes to play and she fears it might interfere with her daughter's school work. Ma becomes pregnant and life is full of hope, although hanging over all their lives is the ever-present dust and lack of rainfall.

Then there is a terrible accident, in which a pail of kerosene left by the stove catches fire and both Ma and Billie Jo are badly burned. Ma dies a few days later while giving birth to the baby, who dies soon afterward. Billie Jo and her father grow distant in their grief, and the burns to Billie Jo's hands mean that she does not even have the solace of playing the piano. When she tries to leave, however, the pull of home proves too great, and the story ends on a note of hope as Billie Jo's father decides to diversify on the farm and also takes a new wife, whom Billie Jo grows to like. **JF**

Deadly, Unna? 1997

Phillip Gwynne

Nationality | Australian, born 1958
Publisher | Penguin, Australia
Award | C.B.C.A. Book of the Year, 1999
Theme | Young adult, Friendship

Before he became an award-winning writer, Phillip Gwynne had a diverse range of occupations, including as an "Australian Rules" footballer. Not surprisingly, his semiautobiographical debut novel, set in a small, coastal town in South Australia, centers on football. It has a complex, involving plot and memorable characters, such as Arks, the despairing football coach, and old Darcy, who augments his pension by breeding maggots he sells as fish bait.

The narrator is Blacky (Gary Black), a football-mad teenager considered a "gutless wonder" by his violent, alcoholic father. Blacky, who is white, is proud to be friends with Dumby Red, who lives on the Aboriginal mission a few miles away. Dumby is the most talented player on the team and can kick a goal from anywhere in the field. He also has a feisty younger sister to whom Blacky is attracted. When Dumby is tragically killed during a break-in, Blacky has to stand up for what he really believes in.

Dealing with the tensions and tragedy associated with racism, this is a hard-hitting and honest rites-of-passage novel that doesn't push its political messages too overtly. The hard-won victory Blacky and his siblings achieve in *Deadly, Unna?* might be a small one in the scheme of things, but it stands as a metaphor for wiping out the vocabulary of racism.

Blacky's story continues in the sequel novel *Nukkin Ya*, in which the prejudices of small-town life remain a theme, especially when the young protagonist falls in love with an Aborigine girl. The two novels were adapted for the 2002 movie *Australian Rules*. **MH**

River Boy 1997

Tim Bowler

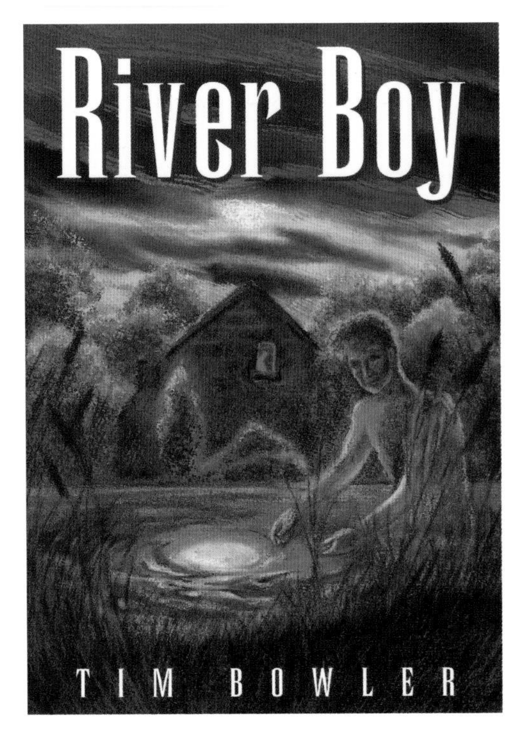

"... in a strange way the river boy had been part of her all along, like the figment of a dream."

MORE BOOKS THAT DEAL WITH LOSS

Grover by Vera and Bill Cleaver, 1970
Looking for Alibrandi by Melina Marchetta, 1992
See Ya, Simon by David Hill, 1992
Out of the Dust by Karen Hesse, 1997
I Am Polleke by Guus Kuijer, 2001

Nationality | English, born 1953
Publisher | Oxford University Press, UK
Award | Carnegie Medal, 1997
Theme | Illness and death, Family, Friendship

At the heart of this beautifully written novel is the relationship between Jess, a fifteen-year-old girl, and her dying grandfather, a cantankerous amateur artist. Although he is dying, he is determined to revisit the isolated valley where he grew up. Jess and her parents go with him and they all, for different but related reasons, come to be fascinated by a river that dominates the landscape. For the grandfather, it is the subject for a haunting painting to be entitled "River Boy," even though there is no boy in it. For Jess, the river is initially the spot where she can indulge her passion for swimming and develop her already considerable expertise in the water.

In the course of her early visits to the river, Jess becomes gradually aware of the presence of a mysterious teenage boy who is also a gifted swimmer. When he suggests that she should accompany him on a forty-mile swim following the river from its source to the sea, she accepts the challenge, an undertaking that will have significance when she experiences the death of her much-loved grandfather. That death coincides with the disappearance of the boy, but not before he has suggested that Jess help complete her grandfather's painting.

This novel has a haunting and powerful appeal: the story itself is moving and engaging, cleverly linking realistic and unworldly elements; and the lyrical prose skillfully reflects the fluidity of the river and its many changing moods. Rarely in the area of young adult fiction have the themes of death and loss and familial love been treated with such sensitivity. **RD**

Pig-heart Boy 1997

Malorie Blackman

Nationality | English, born 1962
Publisher | Doubleday, UK
Theme | Young adult, Family, Illness and death

Sporty thirteen-year-old Cameron's heart is badly damaged by a viral infection. He must have a transplant in order to survive, but since no human replacement is available the only choice left for him is a pig's heart. Such an operation has never succeeded before, but after much discussion, Cameron and his family begin to warm to the idea. Others outside the family, however, remain critical and Cameron finds himself the unwilling center of media interest. Some of his friends are unsympathetic, making wounding jokes at his expense. To cap it all off, the operation, when it happens, is not a success. On the point of giving up altogether, Cameron is inspired by his beloved grandmother and opts for another operation that is more successful.

Written with understanding, this moving and intelligent novel is set in a close-knit African-British family. While trying to remain united, Cameron's parents cannot agree with each other about the ethics of their son's impending operation, and readers are bound to get caught up themselves in the arguments and counter-arguments of the topic rumbling through these pages. What is never in doubt is Cameron's own courage and sensitivity as he strives to do what is best—not just for himself but for everyone else he cares for and who cares for him.

Pig-heart Boy simply demands to be read. It is a deeply engrossing novel with an unusual theme and it keeps readers guessing until the last page. Malorie Blackman is a prolific writer for children and young adults who has won numerous awards. **NT**

"So we have a simple choice. We can allow our son to have a pig's heart or we can watch our son die."

MORE FICTION BY MALORIE BLACKMAN

Hacker, 1992
Words Last Forever, 1998
Noughts & Crosses, 2001
An Eye for an Eye, 2003
The Stuff of Nightmares, 2007

12+

Holes 1998

Louis Sachar

Nationality | American, born 1954
Publisher | Frances Foster Books, USA
Award | Newbery Medal, 1999
Theme | Adventure, Young adult

Obese teenager Stanley Yelnats has never had much luck, a trait that runs in his family, so he is not that surprised when, after a ridiculous miscarriage of justice, he finds himself at Camp Green Lake, a juvenile detention center for boys set in the middle of a Texan desert. Presided over by a ruthless female head warden, the luckless inmates are required to dig a large hole every day out in the blazing sun as part of their punishment. It later transpires that the warden is searching for treasure that was buried long ago and is using the boys as cheap labor. Backed up by her two sidekicks—Mr. Sir and Mr. Pendanski—she institutes a reign of terror based on the ultimate threat of a scratch from her fingernails, which are perpetually bathed in rattlesnake venom. Stanley, however, proves tougher than he looks, and in the company of Zero, his new best friend, escapes the dreaded camp, finds the buried treasure, and sees the evil warden brought to justice.

This startlingly original novel has sold more than five million copies throughout the world, with readers drawn to the author's impressionistic, laid-back writing style. Sometimes satirical, at other times exciting and dramatic, this is truly a story without a dull moment. It also has something important to say about the resilience of the human spirit under even the most dreadful conditions. Stanley Yelnats is not a natural hero, but his intelligence and strong sense of right and wrong finally see him through to a much-deserved happy ending, although not without plenty of adventures and some suffering along the way. **NT**

The Crowstarver 1998

Dick King-Smith

Nationality | English, born 1922
Publisher | Doubleday, UK
Award | Nestlé Children's Book Prize, 1998
Theme | Animal stories, Illness and death

Young Spider Sparrow, although clumsy and poor at speech, develops a remarkable affinity with animals. He lives deep in the English countryside with his adoptive parents, Tom and Kathie Sparrow, who found him as a baby after he had been abandoned. On leaving school, which he never enjoyed, Spider is given the job of crow-scaring, which he does happily enough, shouting and banging on a tin can, because it also leaves him time for himself to make more animal friends. The novel follows Spider's life from his first year to his premature death from a serious heart problem when he is only sixteen. Fortunately, his grieving parents can console themselves with the knowledge that during his short life Spider had always been happy, surrounded by the animal friends that had meant so much to him.

Dick King-Smith is himself a farmer, and in this beautiful and moving story he describes the working countryside as he knew it himself many years ago. Kindly Tom is a shepherd, while other local characters repair fences, cut thistles, plow fields with horses, and help with the harvest. Odd adventures happen every now and again, such as a German plane crashing during the war, but otherwise little disturbs the harmony of a way of life that now seems very remote. Spider himself fits in well to this ancient pattern, but he would certainly have had problems had he lived to see the end of traditional farming practices. While his life was short, he always enjoyed it to the fullest. Readers too can enjoy his story, written by someone so close to the countryside he experienced himself. **NT**

I Am Not Esther 1998

Fleur Beale

Nationality | New Zealander, born 1945
Publisher | Longacre Press, New Zealand
Award | *New Zealand Post* Honor Book, 1999
Theme | Young adult, Family

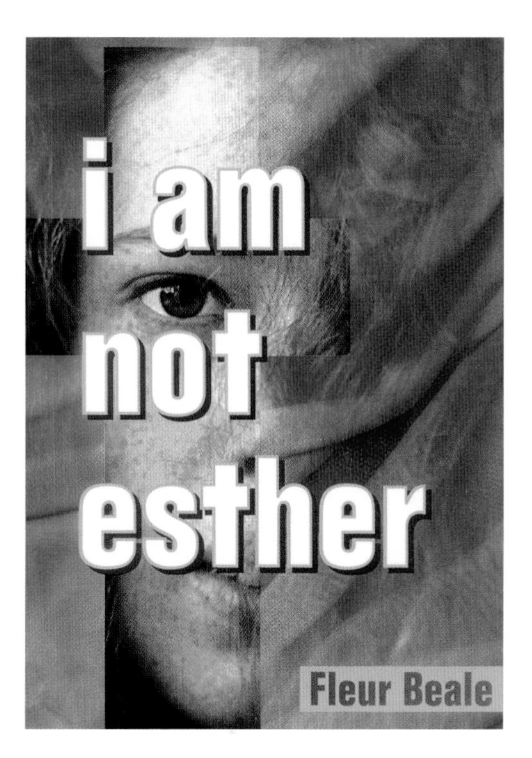

Fleur Beale was originally a teacher and was inspired to write this gripping psychological thriller when one of her students was beaten and thrown out by his family for going against their religious beliefs.

Kirby's mother disappears, supposedly to look after refugees, after leaving her with a previously unknown uncle, Caleb, who belongs to a religious sect called the Children of the Faith. The sect shuns all the conveniences of modern life, including television, radio, newspapers, books, and mirrors. Instead, the members devote themselves to industry and bible study. Kirby is renamed Esther; she gains some relief by interacting with her young cousins who are not yet completely brainwashed, but the shocks keep coming. She discovers the existence of an older cousin, a girl, who was expelled from the family for drawing a picture, while another older cousin, Daniel, is denied his ambition to go to college to become a doctor. Meanwhile, Kirby puzzles endlessly over her mother's hasty and unexplained disappearance. A series of tense scenes describe Daniel's beating and expulsion from the sect, Kirby's discovery of a previously unknown half-brother, and the revelation of what has really happened to her mother.

On the surface this novel is about a girl battling bigotry and cruelty, but its wider theme takes in the need for modern adolescents to define their own identities. Fleur Beale is a prolific and versatile writer whose teen novels tackle gritty themes, such as parental conflict, family origins, relationships with friends, and family responsibility. **LO**

"I knelt down on the hard floor and clamped my mouth and my eyes shut so that I wouldn't yell and I couldn't cry."

GREAT TEEN BOOKS BY FLEUR BEALE

***Slide the Corner*, 1993**
***A Respectable Girl*, 2006**
***The Transformation of Minna Hargreaves*, 2007**
***Juno of Taris*, 2008**
***End of the Alphabet*, 2009**

Bud, Not Buddy 1999

Christopher Paul Curtis

Nationality | American, born 1953
Publisher | Delacorte, USA
Award | Newbery Medal, 2000
Theme | Family, Young adult

Multiple award-winning author Christopher Paul Curtis takes on the plight of an orphaned African-American boy trying to find the father he has never known during the middle of the Great Depression in the 1930s. Bud's search, filled with humor and adventure, begins with a flyer his mother had left in his suitcase before her death when he was six, advertising the jazz band Herman E. Calloway and the Dusky Devastators of the Depression. Bud is convinced that Calloway is his father and that he must travel to Grand Rapids, Michigan, to find him.

After leaving the orphanage and running away from an abusive foster home, where he was treated cruelly, ten-year-old Bud sets off on his own to find his father. He carries only his suitcase, which holds a few meager possessions (including his self-penned book *Bud Caldwell's Rules and Things for Having a Funner Life and Making a Better Liar Out of Yourself*). Bud is determined to succeed. Along the way, he encounters racism, the dehumanizing effects of the Depression, fear, and hunger. But he also discovers several good Samaritans who demonstrate the amazing resilience of people, especially within the African-American community, and learns how jazz can provide the community and self-respect he so desperately seeks.

This truly inspirational tale is historically accurate, and at times both sorrowful and very funny. It is a must-read for all readers, both young and old, and particularly those of African-American descent. **KD**

Stony Heart Country 1999

David Metzenthen

Nationality | Australian, born 1958
Publisher | Penguin, Australia
Award | C.B.C.A. Book of the Year (shortlist), 2000
Theme | Young adult

Stony Heart Country is the compelling story of young Aaron Knott who is moved from an affluent life in the city with his parents to a country town while his father works to downsize the local factory, Walkers.

Aaron has been moved around a lot in his life, to the United States and back, but he has never been quite so confronted as in the small town. From the beginning he is an outsider; the family move into a sleek modern house, "the fish bowl," on the outskirts of town. Everyone knows who he is and what his father is in town to do, and he is made to feel very unwelcome. The other kids at school are hearing at home how their parents face being fired from the factory and Aaron has to deal with the hostility on his own.

The Knott's neighbors, the Tollivers, are at the opposite end of the social spectrum. Mick Tolliver works at Walkers; his wife, Brigid, never leaves the house; their son, Bernie, is an up-and-coming soccer player; and daughter, Rose, has recently had a breakdown. It is the teenagers who befriend Aaron from a distance. When it is time to go back to the city, and despite having to walk through fire to get there, Aaron emerges stronger and more focused.

Metzenthen, known for writing stories with a moral at their center, has crafted a fine story with many thematic layers. *Stony Heart Country* is primarily about tolerance, acceptance, hope, and the possibility of peace if people learn to accept difference and work together for positive change. **BH**

The Illustrated Mum 1999

Jacqueline Wilson Nick Sharratt

Nationality | English, born 1945 (author); English, born 1962 (illustrator)
Publisher | Doubleday, UK
Theme | Young adult, Family

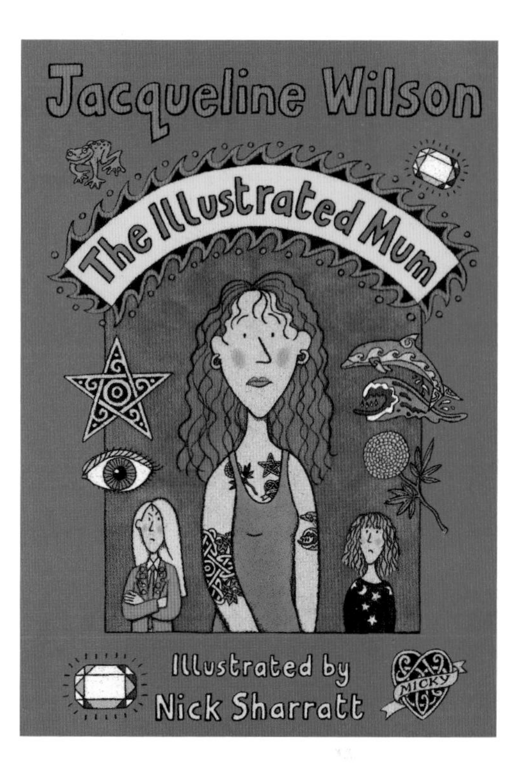

Jacqueline Wilson is adept at presenting the worst difficulties that families face in a way that can be understood and absorbed by children who may be facing something similar. She achieves this without compromising on story quality.

The situation of Marigold, an alcoholic with manic depression, and her daughters, Dolphin and Star, is particularly challenging. On her good days, Marigold is a committed mother who loves dressing up, inventing games, and telling stories. On her bad days, she has to be parented by the girls. For thirteen-year-old Star, love has become mixed with cynicism, shame, and contempt. It is left to Dolphin, the narrator, to acknowledge her charismatic mother's good days as she tells the fragile family's story. Dolphin is fascinated by the tattoos that cover Marigold's body and which illustrator Nick Sharratt integrates into the text. The reader is left to imagine Star's childhood and speculate that she might once have loved Marigold in the less complicated way that Dolphin does.

Wilson makes it clear that Marigold does not frighten her daughters; it is the situations she leads them into that are frightening. Other adults are scared of Marigold's "crazy" side, and the girls suffer when their respective fathers cannot cope with the troubled times. There is hope as Dolphin finds support through a friend at school and a kind librarian. Unsentimental compassion makes what can be a harrowing story palatable for young teenage readers. **GB**

"One mother had a tiny butterfly on her shoulder blade. But no one had tattoos like Marigold."

MORE BOOKS ABOUT FAMILY DYNAMICS

The Min-Min by Mavis Thorpe Clark, 1966
A Kestrel for a Knave by Barry Hines, 1968
The Secret Diary of Adrian Mole by Sue Townsend, 1982
The Visits by Silvia Schujer, 1991

Not Chicago. Not Here. 1999

Kirsten Boie

Original Title | Nicht Chicago. Nicht hier.
Nationality | German, born 1950
Publisher | Friedrich Oetinger, Germany
Theme | School, Young adult

12+

This gripping novel by one of Germany's most renowned children's authors deals with a topic that is, unfortunately, part of many people's everyday life: bullying. The protagonist of Boie's story is thirteen-year-old Niklas, who has to collaborate on a school assignment with Karl, the new boy in class. Karl is very cool and not friendly at all. Soon a CD owned by Niklas's sister disappears, and then Karl borrows Niklas's dad's CD-ROM drive but never returns it. Even when Karl becomes physically violent toward Niklas, the latter does not dare to tell anyone because he is afraid that he will be branded a "snitcher."

However, when Niklas cannot take it anymore he realizes that he has put up with Karl's behavior for too long. Yet when he informs his parents of what has been happening, they refuse to believe that Karl has been cruel. When they do finally start to believe him, they are flabbergasted that no one believes them either. Karl's parents protect their child, and even the police deem the incidents trifling.

This tragic story about a boy who loses his self-esteem because of bullying is not an easy read but it keeps readers spellbound. Boie, who probably witnessed bullying as a teacher, acutely describes Niklas's emotional turmoil and his fears. Her detailed descriptions of the effects of bullying and the desperation experienced by those who are bullied are a real eye-opener. The book raises awareness about bullying and is often read in German schools. **GS**

"Niklas feels shaken: of all the kids in his class he has to work with Karl."

MORE FICTION ABOUT BULLYING

The Chocolate War by Robert Cormier, 1974
Stepping on the Cracks by Mary Downing Hahn, 1993
Bad Girls by Jacqueline Wilson, 1996
Alabama Moon, by Watt Key, 2006

Postcards from No Man's Land 1999

Aidan Chambers

Nationality | English, born 1934
Publisher | Bodley Head, UK
Award | Carnegie Medal, 1999
Theme | Young adult, Family, Controversial

Before Aidan Chambers became an author, he was a teacher and then a monk. He is vocal about the need for children's books to deal with important issues. This book has two narratives. One, set in the 1990s, follows Jacob, a typically intense and self-conscious teenager, as he travels to the Netherlands to retrace the journey his soldier grandfather took during the war. There, he plans to meet up with Geertrui, an elderly nurse who cared for Jacob's grandfather fifty years ago when he was wounded in battle. Unfortunately, Jacob is mugged before he can meet her and is forced to stay with her flamboyant grandson, Daan. In the second narrative, Geertrui recalls her love affair with Jacob's grandfather, and the two stories finally intersect.

Both narratives are about the difficulty of being an individual in a society that demands conformity. Chambers's novel celebrates ambiguity, especially in his refusal to provide the reader with any easy resolutions. Geertrui's terminal illness is presented without sentiment. Jacob accepts his bisexuality, just as he accepts that his memories of his grandfather are vastly different to those of Geertrui's. The book is full of large and complex issues, such as bisexuality, adultery, and euthanasia, but these are used to explore the life choices that people make, rather than to present ethical lessons. Geertrui's journeys of discovery are intellectually challenging, emotionally rich, and beautifully written. *Postcards from No Man's Land* is a big, rewarding story. **SD**

Thursday's Child 2000

Sonya Hartnett

Nationality | Australian, born 1968
Publisher | Penguin, Australia
Award | *Guardian* Children's Fiction Prize, 2002
Theme | Historical fiction, Family

This haunting coming-of-age tale is told by Harper Flute, who at the story's starts is the seven-year-old daughter of a large and poor rural family only just surviving during Australia's Great Depression in the 1930s. Requested one day to look after her four-year-old brother Tin (the Thursday-born child of the title), Harper is horrified when he is swallowed up by a mudslide in a nearby creek. Tin is rescued only at the last moment and becomes obsessed with living underground, digging tunnels under the shanty house where the family lives. A series of calamities follows, with the family's chickens and cows stolen and then their house collapsing due to Tin's incessant digging. With his father taking to drinking, Tin finally disappears for good into the labyrinth of tunnels he has created, and meets Harper only one more time, when she is twelve.

Sonya Hartnett is one of the most original of contemporary Australian writers. She has won many awards, including the Astrid Lindgren Memorial Award in 2008. In this novel she creates a haunting, dreamlike atmosphere laced with sharp recall of the rural poverty she experienced herself as a child. The heartrending story mixes a poetic vision along with salty dialogue and an eagle eye for character, particularly the villainous neighbor Mr. Cable, with his designs on Harper's older sister, Audrey. This book is beautifully written, with each sentence perfectly framed, and is writing for young people at its very best. **NT**

The Wind Singer 2000

William Nicholson

Nationality | English, born 1948
Publisher | Mammoth, UK
Award | Nestlé Children's Book Prize, 2000
Theme | Fantasy, Adventure

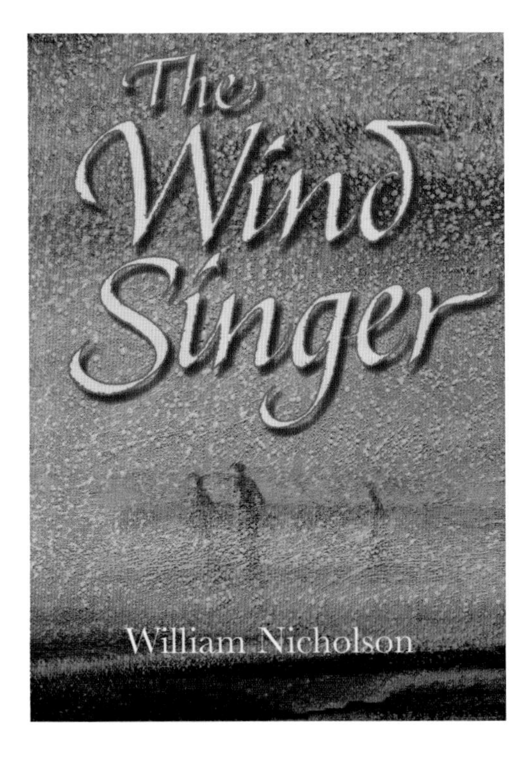

12+

Legend has it that long ago when the strange Wind Singer, which stands in the center of the walled city of Aramanth, sang, everyone was happy. Their happiness angered the spirit-lord, the Morah, who sent an army of Zars to destroy the city. The people gave the Morah the voice of the Wind Singer, and the Zars turned back.

When Kestrel (Kess) Hath, dares to rebel against the city's strict hierarchy, which is dictated by a system of tests, she brings severe punishment upon her family. Armed with a map given to her by the childlike emperor, Kess leaves the city with her brother, Bowman, and Mumpo, the class fool, on a quest to find the Wind Singer's voice and set the city free.

"We are the Morah, said the million eyes to him. We are legion. We are all."

Their quest takes them into the domain of the mud people, who live under the city, and among the warlike Chakas and Barakas, who live in a town that moves across the desert using great sails. When they reach the Morah's palace, the children accidentally wake the Morah, and the army of Zars marches toward Aramanth, joyously singing their terrifying song: "Kill, kill, kill, kill!" The children reach the city with the army of Zars close behind them. In the middle of the Great Examination, when the heads of families are tested, they return the Wind Singer's voice and it begins to sing. The Zars crumble to dust and everyone wakes up from the trance they have been in for generations.

Nicholson invents his world on an immense and satisfying scale. This gripping fantasy adventure has a conclusion with just enough tantalizing loose ends to lead the reader to the next book in the trilogy. **CW**

GOOD READS BY WILLIAM NICHOLSON

Wind on Fire trilogy:
- *Slaves of the Mastery*, 2001
- *Firesong*, 2002

The Society of Others, 2004
The Trial of True Love, 2005

Troy 2000

 Adèle Geras

Nationality | English, born 1944
Publisher | Scholastic, UK
Award | Whitbread Book of the Year (shortlist)
Theme | Historical fiction, War, Love

Adèle Geras has taken the story of the siege of Troy and has written a multilayered novel about the main protagonists involved—Helen, Paris, Achilles, and Hector. Interwoven into this is the story of two sisters, Xanthe and Marpessa. Xanthe works in the Blood Room, where the wounded soldiers are taken and treated, and falls in love with Alastor when he is brought in injured. However, with the intervention of the god Aphrodite, her sister, Marpessa, also falls in love with him and that love is returned.

Meanwhile the ten-year siege of Troy drags on with the inhabitants becoming increasingly short of food and wondering when it will all end. This, of course, is all in the lap of the gods, who appear to the various characters, guiding and warning them. Hector is killed by Achilles and his body dragged around the city walls against all the conventions, and his wife Andromache is inconsolable. This death is avenged as foretold by Paris, who finds Achilles's heel, but who is then killed in his turn. Then the Greeks play their trump card and build the Trojan horse—a statue built as an offering to the gods—and wreak their awful vengeance on the Trojans, taking the women away, killing all the men, and throwing Hector's son from the battlements.

"The poor little baby was smashed against the stones that were sharp and jagged."

The huge sweep of the story does not let the reader lose sight of the individual human beings within it, creating for the reader the Troy of the time with all its heroes and gods. Geras, who has written more than ninety books for children, excels in this glorious yet moving love story set against the tumultuous background of the Trojan War. **JF**

FANTASTIC FICTION BY ADÈLE GERAS

Voyage, 1983
Silent Snow, Secret Snow, 1998
Ithaka, 2005
Happy Ever After, 2005
Cleopatra, 2007

Witch Child

Celia Rees

Witch Child 2000

Celia Rees

Nationality | English, born 1949
Publisher | Bloomsbury, UK
Theme | Historical fiction, Young adult, Adventure

The arresting title leads to a tale of bigotry and hatred in the name of religion, set partly in Puritan England and partly in Salem and Beulah, in the new colonies of seventeenth-century America. Mary's grandmother is hanged as a witch, persecuted by the very people who relied on her for help with ailments, and Mary, in fear of her life, is spirited away to join a group of Protestants bound for the New World. She has been warned to keep her gift of second sight to herself and treads a dangerous path among the small community. The community live together on one deck and the difficult living conditions are clearly described in Mary's journal, as are all the events that take place. The ship docks at Salem and after a few weeks' recovery the small band set off to join friends and family inland at Beulah. The small community there is dominated by the bigoted religion of Reverend Johnson and his superstitious henchmen.

Martha takes Mary under her wing, together with Jonah and Tobias who are also outsiders in the community. They set up a home together and start building a physic garden. To assist in this, Mary goes into the forest to search for plants and herbs, and encounters Jaybird, a native Indian who helps her. Soon there is talk among the gossips about her solitary wanderings and hysteria grabs the insular community who, in a cruel twist of fate, end up accusing Mary of witchcraft. This gripping story is told in the form of fragments from Mary's journal, found sewn into an old quilt, and is concluded by Martha telling of Mary's flight into the forest. **JF**

Oh, Boy! 2000

Marie-Aude Murail

Nationality | French, born 1954
Publisher | L'École des Loisirs, France
Theme | Family, Young adult, Controversial, Friendship

"Oh, boy!" is what Barthélémy Morlevent exclaims when his previously unknown three half-siblings suddenly become his own children. After their father's sudden departure and their mother's tragic suicide, the three children make a pact never to leave one another. Extremely intelligent, fourteen-year-old Siméon is studying for his baccalaureate. Morgane is eight and very talented, but suffers from the eternal problem of the middle child: adults always tend to forget that she exists. The youngest of the family, five-year-old Venise has blue eyes and blond hair, and likes to enact passionate love stories with her Barbie dolls. After proper consultation, the three siblings decide to look for a family that will adopt all three of them, which proves, of course, to be a problem.

Meanwhile, two close relatives turn up who might be interested in adopting the children: their half-brother, twenty-five-year-old Barthélémy, also known as Bart, who is clearly irresponsible and openly gay; and their half-sister Josiane, a young female optician in a childless marriage, whom the children do not warm to on their first encounter.

Marie-Aude Murail has written more than eighty novels for children in which she exploits all the comic and dramatic resources of the contemporary family. In *Oh, Boy!* the language used is simple, yet her story has sensitivity and psychological depth. The narrative touches on important topics, such as friendship and love, family losses, and homosexuality (a very rare theme in children's literature) with great subtleness, emotion, and a good deal of humor. **LB**

Arthur 2000

Kevin Crossley-Holland

Original Title | Arthur: The Seeing Stone
Nationality | English, born 1941
Publisher | Orion, UK
Theme | Historical fiction

This is the first book in a deeply satisfying and compelling trilogy that interweaves the legends of King Arthur with the fortunes of another Arthur growing to manhood in the era of the Crusades. .

In the Welsh Marches, on the eve of the thirteenth century, Arthur de Caldicot is frustrated by life at the family manor and longs to leave home to enter a knight's service. He is a privileged but apparently powerless younger son, and is often in trouble for helping his father's steward's daughter, Gatty, in the fields rather than perfecting his tournament skills. When his mentor, Merlin, a mysterious family friend, gives him the polished piece of obsidian in which he can glimpse the world of his namesake and would-be king, Arthur de Caldicot finds that "Arthur-in-the-stone" is also questioning his place in the world and being guided by a man called Merlin.

Arthur de Caldicot loves writing, and Kevin Crossley-Holland has given him a convincing voice that replicates the medieval imagination without being contrived. The plain language of the book and its short chapters illuminating the lives of the de Caldicots enhance this effect.

Crossley-Holland has a historian's sense of this turbulent period and the tensions between rich and poor, Christianity and ancient folk wisdom, and the supporters of Richard the Lionheart and the harsh directives from his successor, King John. This profound and imaginative story leaves readers hungry for the following books in the trilogy, especially for more of the bright and courageous Gatty. **GB**

Coram Boy 2000

Jamila Gavin

Nationality | Indian/English, born 1941
Publisher | Mammoth, UK
Award | Whitbread Book of the Year
Theme | Historical fiction, Adventure

This story of the underbelly of eighteenth-century society falls into two halves. Two friends are at the center of each half-section. As well as sharing initials—Alexander and Thomas, fellow choirboys in Gloucester Cathedral, and Aaron and Toby, Coram foundlings in London—the matching pairs of boys have a parallel role in embodying the key themes of the book: the power of friendship and courage to overcome evil, the importance of pursuing dreams, and the healing effect of music. The common enemy in both sections is Otis Gardiner, the child-stealer of Gloucestershire, reinvented in the London chapters as a lynchpin of the slave trade, with his abused and all-seeing son Meshak as an unwitting force for good throughout. Meshak's reflections on his condition, his longing for death, and his visions of angels are very moving.

The wide scope of *Coram Boy* seems to belong to a much longer book, and the engaging story is delivered at a measured pace. Readers will need emotional maturity to be drawn into the sometimes harrowing account of the perils facing children in times past, as the wiles of Otis and his accomplices are pitted against the not-always-effective goodwill of a few kind gentlefolk. The fate of unwanted children is a dirty secret of the countryside's dark drovers' roads and silent ditches. Alexander, forced by his landowner father to give up his music, is a reminder that in this world the children of the rich are as powerless as the children of the poor. This story reinforces the importance of standing up for your beliefs. **GB**

Refugee Boy 2001

Benjamin Zephaniah

Nationality | English, born 1958
Publisher | Bloomsbury, UK
Award | Portsmouth Book Award, 2002
Theme | Family, War, Young adult

Benjamin Zephaniah is best known for his poetry, and this text is lyrical, beautifully composed, and easy to read. The story begins in Ethiopia, where Alem lives with his Eritrean mother and Ethiopian father, who work for a charity trying to promote peace in East Africa. One day soldiers kick down the door of their home and threaten them at gunpoint. The family moves to Eritrea, where the same thing happens. The two countries are at war, and Alem is despised for his mixed parentage.

One day Alem's father takes him on vacation to England and leaves him there, sneaking away while Alem sleeps, trusting the English government to look after him. He knows that if Alem stays in either Eritrea or Ethiopia he will be killed. Alem is helped by Pamela, an Ethiopian who works with the Refugee Council, and several social workers, teachers, and caregivers. The story follows Alem through time spent in a violent children's home to the comfort of kind foster parents, a white couple who Alem grows to love. Their daughter, Ruth, is initially very unwelcoming, but by the end of the book they have become firm friends.

Alem learns through his experiences that people cannot be judged by their color, their nationality, or their parents. He grows to love London, although he misses his parents and Africa. His father writes to him, but the letters grow more and more sad. Alem ends up having to fight a court battle to stay in England, as well as having to cope with the loss of his parents. This book, already hailed as a modern classic, should be read by every teen and preteen. **LH**

"Alem tried to practice his English by reading the notices in the cab, whispering the words as he read them: No smok-ing."

MORE PROVOCATIVE REFUGEE TALES

Kiss the Dust by Elizabeth Laird, 1991
The Other Side of Truth by Beverley Naidoo, 2000
Home of the Brave by Katherine Applegate, 2007
Diamonds in the Shadow by Caroline B. Cooney, 2007

12+

Noughts & Crosses 2001

Malorie Blackman

12+

"As long as the schools are run by Crosses, we'll always be treated as second-class, second-best nothings."

MORE BOOKS THAT DEAL WITH RACISM

Adventures of Huckleberry Finn by Mark Twain, 1884
To Kill a Mockingbird by Harper Lee, 1960
Roll of Thunder, Hear My Cry by Mildred Taylor, 1976
Smash by Robert Swindells, 1997
Gabriel's Story by David Anthony Durham, 2001

Nationality | English, born 1962
Publisher | Doubleday, UK
Theme | Young adult, Family, Friendship, Controversial

Noughts & Crosses was the only book by a black author on the BBC's list of 100 Big Reads in 2003. It is the first in a quartet of novels by Blackman that explore racism, including hatred and violence, through the setting of a dystopia in which a white underclass is controlled by a black ruling elite. The revelation of this role reversal is delayed, so the reader is forced to question any preconceptions. Both a fast-paced political thriller and a tale of doomed teenage love, it encourages reflection on contemporary society.

Sephy is the privileged daughter of a prominent corrupt "Cross" politician; her childhood playmate Callum, son of her mother's cleaner, is one of the token "Noughts" who are allowed to attend her high-achieving school. Their friendship leads to pressure from their families and friends as it develops into a love relationship. They are both perceived as betraying their roots, especially when Callum's family becomes involved with a terrorist group intent on reversing the balance of power through violence. Unfolding events prompt connections with sectarian Northern Ireland, apartheid South Africa, and with more recent incidents of terrorism in the United Kingdom.

Blackman has created a bleak world, in which both sides of the racial divide suffer, either directly or through the opportunities they have lost to connect with each other as human beings. The book is full of profound messages for young people as they observe racism operating in their everyday lives. The novel has a distressing resolution but Callum and Sephy's daughter is a symbol of hope. **GB**

I Am Polleke 2001

Guus Kuijer Alice Hoogstat

Original Title | Ik ben Polleke hoor!
Nationality | Dutch, born 1942
Publisher | Querido, the Netherlands
Theme | Young adult, Illness and death

Polleke, an almost thirteen-year-old girl, is very good at coping with life, despite what comes her way. She has a matter-of-fact way of looking at the world and at the grown-ups around her, some of whom are rather strange to say the least. Her grandfather has just died, and she is trying to deal with this loss, which is made harder by the fact that it is the summer vacation and there are fewer distractions. Although her friend Mimoen is in Morocco, her friend Consuela is fortunately around and, being Mexican, she has her own rituals concerning death.

Polleke is the cheeky, pig-headed, but highly likable heroine of a five-book series. She takes life very seriously, looks at things in a critical manner, and deals with what is most difficult in life: learning to live. She is about to leave childhood behind and leap into the throes of adolescence. The final chapter consists only of the chapter title: "Chapter eleven. About the fact that I am now thirteen" and one sentence: "I am now thirteen.'"

Guus Kuijer is always openly on the side of his heroine. The simplicity and clarity of his narrative strikes the perfect balance between describing actual problems and the seemingly childish simplicity with which Polleke copes with them. Readers quickly identify with Polleke's way of thinking and behaving. Kuijer wrote another popular series about a younger but equally headstrong, inquisitive girl, Madelief. The Dutch writer has won numerous awards for his work and is one of the most celebrated authors of children's books in the Netherlands. **AD**

Walking Naked 2002

Alyssa Brugman

Nationality | Australian, born 1974
Publisher | Allen and Unwin, Australia
Award | C.B.C.A. Honor Book, 2003
Theme | Young adult, Friendship, School

A Perdita Wiguiggan exists in every school. Labeled as being "different"—because of a physical defect or odd behavior—such students are despised by their peers. In this portrait of friendships between teenage girls, Burgman demonstrates that joining the malicious chorus of bullies stems from the fear of becoming the outcast. Perdita is seen as a weirdo because of her refusal to conform, a persona she deliberately cultivates by hissing poetry at pupils.

Her solitary existence is worlds apart from the busy social sphere of narrator Megan Tuw, a popular founding member of "the group," a highly selective clique. However, their paths cross in detention. Although initially repelled by Perdita's notorious reputation and imperfect oral hygiene, Megan is gradually impressed and intrigued by her witty, ironic compositions. An unlikely acquaintance begins, whereby the well-read and intelligent Perdita introduces Megan to poetry, and the girls begin a journey of self-discovery. When the group finds out about this unconventional association, however, Megan is forced to choose: them or "the freak."

Megan's circle of so-called friends is a complicated hierarchy, riddled with emotional manipulation. A system of "interventions" invokes intense peer pressure to control everything from hairstyle to choice of boyfriend and academic performance. Megan is also prey to typical teenage insecurities and jealousies. In a refreshing style, Brugman accurately depicts the adolescent agony of desiring both the security of a group and wanting to stand out as an individual. **MK**

The Slightly True Story of Cedar B. Hartley 2002

Martine Murray

"It's the way girls talk that's different . . . you chomp right through the facts."

OTHER QUIRKY BOOKS FOR TEENS

Zazie in the Metro by Raymond Queneau, 1959
The Perks of Being a Wallflower by Stephen Chobsky, 1999
Not as Crazy as I Seem by George Harrar, 2003
Finding Violet Park by Jenny Valentine, 2007

Nationality | Australian, born 1965
Publisher | Allen and Unwin, Australia
Theme | Family, Friendship, Quirky, Young adult

Martine Murray studied art, acrobatics, and dance, and all these subjects appear in her humorous and quirky stories for children. This novel features the bubbly, idiosyncratic voice of Cedar (who would prefer to be called Lana Munroe), an outgoing, perceptive young person, wise beyond her thirteen years.

The novel focuses on the small, everyday moments of life and has a cast of characters worth caring about. Handling serious themes with a light touch, Murray presents her cast of marginalized young people: chubby Caramella; brain-damaged and poetic Oscar; Kite, wounded by his parents' estrangement; and Cedar herself, who is troubled by an absent brother and the mysterious death of her father. Kite is Cedar's first crush, and she is alternately confused, exhilarated, and irritated by this talented young man. This large cast of improbable characters form the Acrobrats, who, after a dedicated stint of group practice, put on a tumbling and balancing show to fund the medical care of a neighbor's dog.

On the verge of adolescence, Cedar is always questioning and doubting her own emotions and feelings, family relationships, and friendships. Murray touches on the thoughts and emotions universally experienced by children in this effortlessly told tale of people from different backgrounds, working together to solve problems. Her tiny, captivating line illustrations that appear throughout the novel also capture the story's essence. **BA**

Across the Nightingale Floor 2002

 Lian Hearn

Nationality | English/Australian, born Gillian Rubinstein 1942
Publisher | Macmillan, UK
Theme | Fantasy, Adventure, Young adult

To protect himself from would-be assassins, Iida Sadumu, a fearsome warlord, installs a nightingale floor in his bedroom that "sings" when someone tries to sneak across it. Into his dark and threatening fortress comes the sixteen-year-old hero, Takeo, who must use his supernatural powers to traverse the floor, overcome his enemy, and fulfill his destiny.

Across the Nightingale Floor is the first in the epic series Tales of the Otori. Set in a mythical, ancient Japanese feudal society, it is a story of feuding clans, betrayal, revenge, and honor. Takeo is torn between loyalty to his own persecuted religious community, called "the Hidden," and the Otori clan to whom he is indebted for having saved his life earlier. It is also a tale of impossible love between Takeo and Kaede Shirakawa, a strong and impetuous woman who is said to be cursed.

Lian Hearn is the pseudonym of award-winning children's writer Gillian Rubinstein, who has enjoyed great success with books for younger readers, such as *Space Demons* and *Galax Arena*, but she adopted a new name to differentiate this series and to attract an older readership. Hearn learned the Japanese language and immersed herself in the history and culture of Japan to create a real sense of authenticity and atmosphere in her writing. The result is a vivid and sweeping series that will plunge readers into a completely new fantasy world with complex codes of honor and unforgettable characters. **HJ**

Parvana's Journey 2002

 Deborah Ellis

Nationality | Canadian, born 1960
Publisher | Groundwood Books, Canada
Theme | Adventure, War, Family, Friendship, Young adult

This book, set in Afghanistan, is an award-winning and thought-provoking tale of female empowerment against terrible odds. Parvana is just eleven years old when the Taliban rise to power. Parvana's future is further complicated when her beloved father, a history teacher educated in England, is imprisoned. Into this bleak situation enters the delightful agitator Mrs. Weera, who comes up with a cunning plan to help the family survive: Parvana is to be disguised as a boy. This daring transformation forms the core of the book, and Parvana's journey from a frustrated and hidden girl into a proud young boy, confidently dealing with the Taliban and earning money, is beautifully handled.

A key feature of this engaging work is the way it sensitively deals with issues to which all girls can relate. For example, Parvana's friend is anxious by the onset of puberty and uncertain about what the future will hold for her during this transition. Parvana's world is dominated by the decisions of adults, which contribute to the problems surrounding her, making this as much a narrative of a young person finding her own voice as anything else.

Deborah Ellis is a strong and compassionate voice who dares to portray honestly the brutality and arbitrariness of war to her young readers. This is an important book about the necessity of hope coupled with the courage of action that can change lives even in the most terrible conditions. **CATN**

The Messenger 2002

Markus Zusak

Nationality | Australia, born 1975
Publisher | Pan Macmillan, Australia
Award | C.B.C.A. Book of the Year, 2003
Theme | Young adult

Ed Kennedy, a twenty-year-old taxi driver, lives with his dog, the Doorman. He plays cards with his friends Ritchie, Marv, and Audrey, and he is in love with Audrey, although she is not in love with him. One day, Ed mysteriously receives an ace of diamonds in the mail; on it, three times and addresses are written. Eventually his curiosity is piqued and he finds himself standing outside the first address at midnight. The domestic violence he witnesses makes him sick, and it slowly dawns on him that it is up to him to do something about it.

At each of the next two addresses, there is someone who needs his help in some way. Then more playing cards arrive. With each card he must decipher the clues and deliver three messages. The messages are not always seemingly vital, but they mean a lot to the recipient. Ed becomes a directed angel; a messenger who changes lives.

The Messenger (published as *I Am the Messenger* in the United States) is a redemptive story about healing. It is about hope and the possibilities of forging connections with small acts of human kindness. Using themes of identity, faith, friendship, and ultimately love, Markus Zusak has woven a compelling yet humorous story. Ed is constantly challenged, yet each time he works through his fear and rises to the task at hand, whether it be kissing Audrey or standing up to a bully. It is through these challenges that Ed matures into a manhood in which he does not end up like his father. Instead, Ed will shrug off his fears and walk tall his whole life. **BH**

Dragonkeeper 2003

Carole Wilkinson

Nationality | English/Australian, born 1950
Publisher | Black Dog Books, Australia
Award | C.B.C.A. Book of the Year, 2004
Theme | Fantasy, Historical fiction

Ping, the plucky but believable young heroine of *Dragonkeeper*, has been dealt a poor hand but pits herself bravely against incredibly tricky situations, gains awareness of her special skills, grows in confidence, and emerges triumphant. In other words, this is a tale that is especially inspiring and appealing for children and young adults.

The setting is China's Han dynasty, in 141 B.C.E. Ping is a girl of ten or eleven (inability to count past ten makes her uncertain of her age), sold into slavery by her parents when she is very young. Her home is a far-flung imperial palace compound that the emperor hardly ever visits and her cruel master, Lan, is the keeper of the last two imperial dragons. One dragon perishes and Ping audaciously escapes with the survivor, a laconic dragon called Danzi that can morph into other forms and is given to philosophical statements such as: "Recognizing one's limitations is wisdom." Ping's pet rat, Hua, joins the duo on an epic, perilous journey in search of Ocean, pursued by an evil dragon-hunter. Ping's task is to hang onto the beautiful "dragon stone" at any cost as part of her growing role as the true imperial dragonkeeper, despite having no idea of the stone's true nature.

Wilkinson's adventure is riveting; her language fluent, and often poetic. She is famed for her love of history and meticulously researched detail, and the book's mixture of fact and fiction offers both the magical backdrop of imperial China and room for discussion about history and the rigors of growing up. This book is the first of her Dragonkeeper series. **AK**

Dragonkeeper
by Carole Wilkinson

Crispin 2002

 Avi

Nationality | American, born Edward Irving Wortis 1937
Publisher | Hyperion Books, USA
Theme | Historical fiction

Crispin: The Cross of Lead is a novel set in England during the time when Edward III rules the country and noblemen control the lives of ordinary people. Hunger, poverty, filth, heavy taxes, and hard work are everyday realities for the population. The orphaned Crispin has nothing: no family, no name, and no future. He faces the relentless enmity of the estate steward, who falsely declares him a thief and murderer, and has him outlawed. His only chance of survival is to escape from the village. His true identity is written on his mother's lead cross, but Crispin cannot read and sets off to uncover the secret behind the cross. Alone and on the run, Crispin's life is turned upside down when he meets Bear.

Bear, a gigantic, puzzling man, at first seems harsh, but he takes Crispin under his protection and teaches him many useful skills, as well as the rudiments of music. Bear is a wandering juggler and jester, but he dreams of a better life, where every man is free of the slavery of serfdom. Although they do not realize it, the combination of Bear's dangerous dreams and Crispin's hidden heritage put them both in deadly peril.

Avi (the pet name his twin sister gave the author) writes with real understanding of his audience. His many books—*Crispin: The Cross of Lead* is his fiftieth—affirm the actions of his young characters as they navigate the world—whether historical, fantastic, or modern—that they inhabit. Crispin, for example, desperately wants to find someone he can trust and love on his lonely journey, and we can see why a bond grows between him and Bear. **CER**

Four Sisters 2003

 Malika Ferdjoukh

Original Title | Quatre soeurs
Nationality | French, born 1957
Publisher | L'École des Loisirs, France
Theme | Family, Friendship, Love

Four stories, four protagonists, and four seasons. Nine-year-old Enid, the heroine of the first book, is the youngest of the Verdelaine sisters (who are actually five: Charlotte, the oldest, and the four protagonists Enid, Hortense, Bettina, and Geneviève). Enid sleeps with her cats, Ingrid and Roberto, and has one dream: to discover the ghost that haunts their home. Unfortunately, none of her sisters believe her. Their parents might have believed her, but they died almost a year ago. Swift, her little bat, might also have believed her, but it recently disappeared in a storm. The second more reserved sister, eleven-year-old Hortense, spends her life reading and keeping a secret diary about her difficult life as one of five sisters, and whether she should become a surgeon, a comedienne, or an architect.

The third story is about thirteen-year-old Bettina, who is always surrounded by her inseparable friends Denise and Béhotéguy. She falls in love with the twenty-eight-year-old Tancrède—who rents a room in their house—and the focus shifts to the problems that such an infatuation causes among her sisters. The last story centers on Geneviève who, under the cover of babysitting, does very different things. She meets the mysterious Vigo during the summer, when she sells ice cream on the beach near their house.

Dialogue and action are woven with spellbinding rhythm in this intriguing collection of stories. *Four Sisters* is a well-told story that successfully mixes serious issues, such as mourning, with the lighter themes of boyfriends, lying, and love with humor. **LB**

Slaves of Quentaris 2003

Paul Collins

Nationality | Australian, born 1954
Publisher | Lothian Books, Australia
Theme | Fantasy, Adventure, Magical stories, Young adult

The Quentaris Chronicles are the brainchild of prolific, Australia-based authors Paul Collins and Michael Pryor. In 2003 the pair invented a magical city, Quentaris, with its own history, cartography, climate, and customs. As well as both writing novels set in this shared fantasy world, they invited other authors to contribute, and more than fourteen different storytellers have published Quentaris-based titles. In the first series, each book can be read independently in any order; the second series builds sequentially. Connecting the tales is a familiar landscape, some recurring characters, and an enthralling adventure.

Slaves of Quentaris, the fourth title in the first series by Collins, follows the fortunes of the valiant Yukin and his partner, Yulen, after they are abducted from their peaceful nomadic tribe by Akcarum slave traders, in the talons of monstrous hunting birds. They are forcibly transported to the foreign world of Quentaris through the mysterious rift caves, a labyrinthine network of rock formations in the cliffs flanking the city. In this continuously shifting zone, temporary tears appear in the fabric of the universe, allowing access to other worlds. After accidentally attuning to the dynamic energies of this site, Yukin succeeds in unmasking a fearsome source of power, which, when he can harness it, will result in the slaves' liberation.

A tense, dramatic story in its own right, *Slaves of Quentaris* also perfectly complements the other titles in the chronicles. The success of the series lies in its consistency; by paying attention to continuity, the authors have created a convincing fantasy world. **MK**

"The leather-sheathed talons of a hunter bird clamped down on his shoulders and he was lifted into the air."

MORE OF THE QUENTARIS CHRONICLES

Swords of Quentaris, 2003
Dragonlords of Quentaris, 2004
Princess of Shadows, 2005
The Forgotten Prince, 2006
Vampires of Quentaris, 2008

12+

The Keys to the Kingdom: Mister Monday 2003

 Garth Nix

Nationality | Australian, born 1963
Publisher | Allen and Unwin, Australia
Theme | Fantasy, Young adult, Adventure, Friendship

12+

Mister Monday, the first in the seven-volume Keys to the Kingdom fantasy series, introduces reluctant hero Arthur Penhaligon, who, through no fault of his own has been chosen as the Rightful Heir and the person who will restore the seven parts of the Will.

Arthur has just moved to a new school again. He collapses due to an asthma attack on his first day there and sees some strange people: Mister Monday and his dog-faced lackeys, the Nithlings. Only Arthur, a couple of other students, and the librarian can see them. Mister Monday hands Arthur a "key," which looks very much like the hand of a clock, and a small atlas. Holding the key in his hand miraculously stops his asthma, but in the process the school library burns down and a quarantine is declared, as people begin succumbing to a deadly virus.

Arthur realizes it must have something to do with the mysterious House that only he can see, and with the help of the Lesser minute hand key and the atlas, eventually finds his way inside, hoping that he can stop the viral outbreak. However, life and fantasy adventure are never that simple. Arthur must first face many challenges and claim the Greater hour hand key from Mister Monday, who incidentally would like his minute hand key back, before being allowed to go home to resume his life as a normal boy. Or so he thinks. Little does Arthur know that the quest has only just begun. Arthur embarks on a journey with the help of the Will, to defeat the seven Trustees and claim the seven keys. He is accompanied during most of his travels by a Cockney girl called Suzy Turquoise Blue, who was brought to the House with other children. The story embraces seven books, many magical creatures, and compelling adventures in the House, all from the vivid imagination of Garth Nix. **BH**

MORE KEYS TO THE KINGDOM BOOKS

Grim Tuesday, 2004
Drowned Wednesday, 2005
Sir Thursday, 2006
Lady Friday, 2007
Superior Saturday, 2008

The Curious Incident of the Dog in the Night-time 2003

Mark Haddon

Fifteen-year-old Christopher, the narrator of this extraordinary novel, has Asperger's syndrome. This means that while he is incredibly good at some school subjects, he finds communicating with others extremely hard. He is also liable to panic in social situations he is unused to, experiencing anything outside his own set routines as a considerable threat. He attends a special school and lives with his affectionate but often hard-pressed father (his mother having previously left the family home). When Wellington, the pet poodle who lives across the street, is found speared by a garden fork, Christopher decides to investigate, although he is limited by his fears and difficulties when interpreting the world around him. He records his experiences in a book, *The Curious Incident of the Dog in the Night-time*.

Told with warmth and humor, the story ingeniously explains both how Christopher views the world and how the other people in his life see him. Seeking to order his life by the number of cars he sees of the same color each day (four red cars in a row means a wonderful day; four yellow ones means he has to go straight to bed), Christopher battles his way through to making some genuine discoveries—both about himself and his long-suffering family. The courage he needs to fulfill this task and the near-misses he experiences while doing so render the novel both enthralling and exhilarating.

As for the dead poodle, Christopher does, indeed, solve the mystery that has foiled everyone else, although in doing so he comes perilously close to family secrets involving both of his parents and with an explosive kick all of their own. The book closes, however, with an optimistic outlook for the future for both Christopher and his family. **NT**

Nationality | English, born 1962
Publisher | David Fickling Books, UK
Award | Whitbread Book of the Year
Theme | Detective stories, Quirky, Young adult

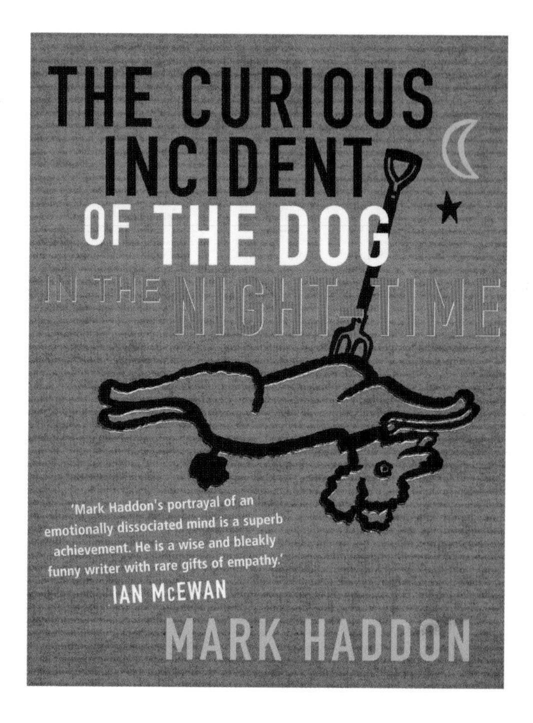

THE CURIOUS INCIDENT OF THE DOG IN THE NIGHT-TIME
'Mark Haddon's portrayal of an emotionally dissociated mind is a superb achievement. He is a wise and bleakly funny writer with rare gifts of empathy.'
IAN McEWAN
MARK HADDON

MORE GREAT READS BY MARK HADDON

Agent Z and the Penguin from Mars, 1995
Agent Z and the Killer Bananas, 2001
The Talking Horse, the Sad Girl and the Village Under the Sea, 2005
A Spot of Bother, 2006

12+

The Fire-Eaters 2003

David Almond

Nationality | English, born 1951
Publisher | Hodder Children's Books, UK
Award | Nestlé Children's Book Prize, 2003
Theme | School, Young adult

Eleven-year-old Bobby Burns seems to have everything. Living by the sea in Northumberland, England, with his close family and lots of good friends, he has until now enjoyed life to the fullest. But things start to change in the autumn of 1962. From what he can understand about the ongoing Cuban Missile Crisis, it could well be that the world is on the verge of a disastrous nuclear war. His father's health has also started to give way, and Bobby—cut off from his friends for the first time—has just started at a new and exclusive school that he finds cold and brutal. He is also haunted by the strange figure of McNulty, a wild-eyed, bare-chested, former circus fire-eater, whose skin is covered in scars, bruises, and tattoos. Fearful that his father might die, Bobby has to learn how to overcome his uncertainties in order to survive as an individual himself.

Almond is a visionary writer with superb recall of his own childhood. He is an expert storyteller and has written several award-winning children's novels, including *Skellig* and *Kit's Wilderness*. He is adept at teasing out the wider meanings of what he is writing about, often about those who are left out—the ill, the damaged, and the lost. All his characters have an unmistakable stamp of reality, even the mysterious McNulty, who is based on memories of a strongman/escapologist that Almond once saw performing at a quayside market. *The Fire-Eaters* explores the nature of class and speaks sensitively of a young boy's fears. Poetic at times, down to earth at others, this beautifully written novel is an extraordinary achievement. **NT**

Private Peaceful 2003

Michael Morpurgo

Nationality | English, born 1943
Publisher | Collins, UK
Award | Whitbread Book of the Year (shortlist)
Theme | War, Historical fiction, Young adult

Set prior to and during World War I, *Private Peaceful* provides an accurate description of the brutal hierarchies then existing within British society and the military. Contrasted with this is the unspoiled rural landscape of Britain, abundant with wildlife and its endless opportunities for poaching rabbits, trout, and salmon, an idyll for Tommo and his brothers.

Each chapter of Michael Morpurgo's book begins with a short passage in the present tense before it turns to a reminiscence of childhood and later, the more immediate past. As the novel progresses, the reader slowly becomes aware of Tommo's appalling situation as he waits during one long night, and is gripped as it drives toward the terrible conclusion.

The connecting force that runs throughout the narrative is Tommo's love for his brothers (the fearless Charlie and the brain-damaged Joe), his wonderfully resilient mother, and Molly, the girl who marries Charlie. Although Tommo is in some ways seemingly weaker than the other characters, by the end of the book he has grown from a boy into a man who will fulfill his promises.

As with all Morpurgo's work, there is a basic assumption that children deserve honesty and so the horrors of trench warfare are not diluted, nor are the hideous injustices that occurred during the war. This is a life-changing book for older children that adults can also enjoy. The style of *Private Peaceful* is simple but powerful, and the pace is gentle yet ominous as the chapters unfold. Although the tragedy of war is never overplayed, the story is profoundly moving. **WO**

Keeper 2003

 Mal Peet

Nationality | English, birth date unknown
Publisher | Walker Books, UK
Award | Branford Boase Award, 2004
Theme | Adventure, Ghost stories

This novel is more than just a soccer story. Laden with mystery and suspense, it weaves South American myths and concerns about the jungle environment into a ghost story. It also poses philosophical questions about how to nurture talent and the symbolism of the goalkeeper's role, all in clear prose. There is plenty of soccer to draw in readers who love the sport, and those who could not care less about soccer could have their interest sparked by Peet's passionate descriptions of the craft of the goalkeeper, and the joy of playing.

The narrative is driven by Paul Faustino, a world-weary South American sportswriter. Peet sets his novel in a fictional South American country that he, through Faustino's caustic gaze, has endowed with a bloody history and a turbulent present. *Keeper* explores one aspect of the troubled country: the destruction of the jungle and along with it, the way of life of the indigenous people. There are also signs that this is a deeply divided, corrupt, and racist society, although soccer is a unifying force for good and a way out of poverty for some skilled players.

Faustino asks the questions that are in the reader's mind when he is assigned to interview the World Cup–winning goalkeeper, who is known as El Gato (the Cat), born into a jungle logging community. The journalist is initially skeptical and uncertain about the star player's tale of the ghostly Keeper who taught him his skills in a jungle clearing. Slowly the interviewer, and the reader, begin to understand that the goalkeeper is defending more than just the net. **GB**

"Standing there, with its back to the trees, was a goal. A soccer goal. Two uprights and a crossbar. With a net."

MORE GREAT FICTION FROM MAL PEET

Tamar, 2005
The Penalty, 2006
Exposure, 2008

12+

The Amulet of Samarkand 2003

Jonathan Stroud

Nationality | English, born 1970
Publisher | Hyperion, USA
Award | A.L.A. Notable Book, 2004
Theme | Adventure, Magical stories

This is the first volume of Jonathan Stroud's tirelessly inventive, compulsively readable Bartimaeus Trilogy. Nathaniel, a young magician's apprentice in London, secretly summons a djinni to work vengeance upon the powerful and sinister Simon Lovelace, through the theft of the eponymous amulet. The djinni is Bartimaeus, a cynical, wise-cracking shape-shifter who serves as our sardonic guide to Stroud's parallel universe. It is a world that bears a deftly distorted relationship to our own in its history and topography. For example, Gladstone is a famous dead British prime minister, but also a great magician and victor in a war against the magical forces of Prague. Magicians form a ruling class, dominating commoners through their ability to summon and enslave spirits. A multiplicity of detail about the workings of this world is woven effortlessly into the text.

None of this subtlety and complexity is ever allowed to dull the verve and wit of the storytelling. The relationship between the insecure but courageous Nathaniel and the rebellious Bartimaeus is superbly drawn and the action moves at a cracking pace, with thrills and mysteries aplenty. The introduction of the Resistance, a shadowy terrorist movement dedicated to the overthrow of the government of magicians, also brings Kitty Jones into play, an engaging heroine destined to flourish in the later volumes. Stroud's trilogy manages to be utterly distinctive with an irresistible humor and a fertility of imagination. **RG**

The Running Man 2004

Michael Gerard Bauer

Nationality | Australian, born 1955
Publisher | Omnibus Books, Australia
Award | C.B.C.A. Book of the Year, 2005
Theme | Young adult

This debut novel follows the interlinked lives of various residents of an ordinary Brisbane suburb as they attempt to escape their personal demons. The action centers on fourteen-year-old Joseph. Invited to draw the portrait of reclusive neighbor, Tom Leyton, Joseph's initial impulse is to decline, repelled by the rumors that cling to the surly stranger. However, he is goaded into accepting the offer in an effort to prove narrow-minded Mrs. Mossop wrong about his own shyness. In trying to capture the identity of irascible Tom on canvas, Joseph must unlock the "tantalizing riddle" of the man's past. Tom is a war veteran who has taken refuge from the world and devoted himself to raising silkworms. Another local eccentric whose story Joseph begins to unravel is that of the "Running Man," a disheveled, manic figure who lurches around the neighborhood as if fleeing from a pursuer. The story is also a journey of self-discovery for Joseph, forced to confront his own relationship with his scornful father. The lives of three men who have never met become inextricably bound up with the teenager's.

The Running Man has won praise for its insightful depiction of an adolescent gaining wisdom beyond his years, in his struggle to overcome deep-seated fears. The silkworm, safely cocooned from harm, acts as an effective metaphor for the insular existences of the main characters, all shunning reality and hiding from uncomfortable truths. This seemingly simple tale has profoundly moving depths. **MK**

By the River 2004

Steven Herrick

Nationality | Australian, born 1958
Publisher | Allen and Unwin, Australia
Award | C.B.C.A. Honor Book, 2005
Theme | Young adult

In *By the River,* Steven Herrick has crafted a fine verse novel consisting of seven chapters filled with simple poems, most of them only one page in length. They recount a delicate coming-of-age story, and it is in the detail that Herrick has triumphed.

Harry Hodby lives with his brother Keith and their father in a small country town, their mother having died. Harry describes the small and not-so-small events that make up his life and the people who populate it: his nemesis-turned-friend Johnny Barlow; the girl Linda Mahony, who they both liked and who was washed away in last year's flood; the school secretary, Miss Spencer, who has to leave town in disgrace, a fallen woman. Harry muses about getting out of the town, as all these others have.

It is in the rendering of the relationship with his brother and father that Harry's character is mostly revealed. The images of the boys cooking, cleaning, and caring for their father when he's in a mood, and of their father kissing them when he comes home after losing a finger at work that day. The last time he had kissed them was the day after their mother had died. *By the River* is also a story about hope. Harry has the directions for getting out of town, and sometime soon he will have to choose to stay or to go.

Herrick is an Australian author who specializes in writing verse novels for children and adults. His books have been shortlisted by the Children's Book Council of Australia many times. **BH**

"[My dad's] legs were muscle brown from riding his old pushbike three miles to work…"

OTHER GREAT VERSE NOVELS

Make Lemonade by Virginia Wolff, 1993
Frenchtown Summer by Robert Cormier, 1999
Keesha's House by Helen Frost, 2003
Birdland by Tracy Mack, 2003
Wolf by Steven Herrick, 2007

A Boat in the Forest 2004

Paola Mastrocola

Original Title | Una barca nel bosco
Nationality | Italian, born 1956
Publisher | Guanda, Italy
Theme | School, Friendship

What happens when a teenager who reads Latin is displaced from his hometown and catapulted into another world? Our protagonist finds himself in the city of Turin in northern Italy, and because he comes from an island in the south of Italy, this presents enough of a difference for him to experience "culture shock." The book follows Gasparre's transformation from amiable teenager with an interest in studying into a culturally overwhelmed young man who feels out of place in his new surroundings. When he has to suppress his true interests, Gasparre fills the void that is left with another identity—one that is attempting to catch up with the "others."

The title points to the incongruity that comes with displacement, and the book raises questions about integrity, identity, and adjusting to an unfamiliar world. Nevertheless it is a fun read. Gasparre is constantly up against disorienting experiences: unfamiliar technology, the language used by his classmates, and the intrigue of an urban map. Armed with a healthy sense of irony, Gasparre manages to survive. His love of Latin remains an important part of him, and, once he is enrolled at the university, he no longer has to hide his unusual interest. By the novel's end, his life has changed dramatically, and he must choose whether to remain in Turin or return to his Mediterranean island. *A Boat in the Forest* was published to critical acclaim and continues to move readers with its thought-provoking themes. **SMT**

How I Live Now 2004

Meg Rosoff

Nationality | American, born 1956
Publisher | Penguin, UK
Award | *Guardian* Children's Fiction Prize, 2005
Themes | Family, War, Young adult

How I Live Now is a novel about trying to make sense of a world that is ruled (badly) by adults; about having to learn to be resourceful and brave; and about seizing control of one's life in a world that is falling apart. It is set in a contemporary or near-future England that is occupied by an enemy power.

Daisy is an angry and cynical teenager who has been sent from New York to spend the summer with her English cousins. She is furious at her father's remarriage and has developed an eating disorder because of it. Her addictive narrative voice is insistent, forcing the reader to consider a twenty-first-century war that returns society to primitive living conditions and brings out the best and worst in outwardly respectable people. Daisy's wounds seem to heal, especially when she falls in love with her cousin Edmond. Yet food runs short, health care collapses, the children are evacuated, and Daisy and Piper, Edmond's young sister, are separated from the boys.

As long as Daisy's aim to reunite the family seems achievable, the tale reads like an adventure story with the hope of a positive resolution. However, once the girls witness their first outbreak of violence, the stakes become higher. On the run, Daisy finds her eating disorder has been eclipsed by the threat of starvation. Her account shows the reader how war operates, how fragile our social fabric is, how the first to suffer are those who are already weak, and how anyone who has found a true home will fight to get back to it. **GB**

Memories of Idhún: The Resistance 2004

Laura Gallego

Nationality | Spanish, born 1977
Publisher | Ediciones SM, Spain
Theme | Science fiction, Adventure, Magical stories

The complex plot of the Memories of Idhún *(Memorias de Idhún)* trilogy unrolls between Earth and Idhún, a magical world where different races live together, their survival threatened by the necromancer Ashran. In the first installment *The Resistance (La Resistencia)*, a warrior and a wizard who have been exiled from Idhún are joined by Jack and Victoria, two teenagers from Earth. Together they fight to end the reign of the serpents and find the last winged unicorn and the last dragon.

Fairies, wizards, dragons, and unicorns all feature prominently throughout the story—a combination that is apparently synonymous with literary success. However, there is much more to this science fiction trilogy than a parade of magical creatures: mythology, poignant epic fragments, evocative descriptions, abundant resources to explain the magic, and a developing love story.

Award-winning author Laura Gallego began to write *Memories of Idhún* at the age of fifteen. She studied Hispanic Philology in college and is a specialist in books of chivalry of the sixteenth century. So far she has published more than twenty books, including novels and short stories, mostly science fiction, a genre for which she feels a predilection. But her stories, despite being part of the escapist genre, invite reflection. The result, as with this book, is young adult fiction that tempts teenagers to engage in reading. *Triad* and *Pantheon* are the second and third books in the trilogy. **EB**

"But there was no doubt. The gaze of his mother was empty, inexpressive. Her eyes were dead."

MORE TO ENJOY BY LAURA GALLEGO

The End of the World (Finis Mundi), 1999
The Valley of the Wolves (El valle de los lobos), 2001
Tara's Daughters (Las hijas de Tara), 2002
The Empress of the Ethereal (La emperatriz de los etéreos), 2007

12+

Twilight 2005

Stephenie Meyer

Nationality | American, born 1973
Publisher | Little, Brown, USA
Theme | Love, Horror, Controversial, Fantasy, Young Adult

Twilight is the first in a series of novels about Bella Swan, who becomes involved with a family of vampires. It is a teenage love story with several huge twists.

The story begins when Bella moves from the hot, dusty town of Phoenix, Arizona, to live with her father in Forks, Washington, a town where the sun seldom shines. At high school, Bella makes friends quickly, but becomes fascinated by the five Cullen siblings. The Cullens are very beautiful and highly mysterious. They keep to themselves, and most of the students find them standoffish and weird. From the start Bella has a strange fascination for Edward. He continually warns her to stay away from him, but she perseveres and, as their relationship grows, she uncovers the truth about him and his "family." Edward, who will always remain seventeen years old, has been alive since 1901. As he and Bella fall in love, there are grave repercussions for Bella, a tasty human in a vampire world, as well as constant fears for Edward, whose superhuman powers allow him a greater awareness of the terrible trouble Bella has unwittingly attracted, as well as his desperate need to keep her safe.

Edward and his family call themselves "vegetarian vampires," meaning that they do not prey on humans, only animals. Over many years they have suppressed their need for human blood by hunting wild beasts, rationalizing that if they ate venison when they were in human form, what could be wrong with hunting wild deer now they are blood-drinking immortals? Yet, as Bella discovers, the Cullens are not the only vampires to dwell in this strange twilight world. **LH**

Grimpow 2005

Rafael Ábalos

Nationality | Spanish, 1956
Publisher | Montena, Spain
Theme | Historical fiction, Adventure, Friendship

Grimpow is a fourteenth-century petty thief who one day finds the corpse of a man slumped in the snow. Following this discovery, which a little later mysteriously disappears before his very eyes, Grimpow begins a journey that will change his fate. He becomes caught up in the mystery of the Knights Templar and meets Salietti and the beautiful Weinell, with whom he shares an extraordinary adventure that is full of riddles, mysteries, and challenges to his courage, his wit, and his friendship.

This children's novel, which takes place in the late Middle Ages and whose protagonist is a teenager with a thirst for knowledge, successfully combines the best of a historical novel, a thriller, and an adventure story. At the same time it is one of those texts that one consumes as an antidote to bad prose. Its success was immediate.

At a time when it is hard to mark the boundary between children's and adult literature, if, indeed, it ever existed, the third novel by Rafael Ábalos came out; the rights to this book by a virtually unknown author were sold in nine countries before it was published in Spain. It is a novel of universal values, full of secrets, original and intelligent, and it will bring pleasure to readers of any age.

Rafael Ábalos, a lawyer by profession, began to be published at the turn of the century. In less than a decade, and with only four books, he has managed to devote himself entirely to writing: the child "ended up throwing out the lawyer," he says, referring to his new job of creating imaginary worlds. **EB**

GRIMPOW

RAFAEL ÁBALOS

El camino invisible

New Policeman 2005

Kate Thompson

Nationality | English, born 1956
Publisher | Bodley Head, UK
Award | *Guardian* Children's Book Prize, 2005
Theme | Fantasy

For generations the Liddys of Kinvara have been Irish folk musicians, and fifteen-year-old JJ is continuing the family tradition. He gets a shock one day when a school friend tells him that his great-grandfather had murdered the village priest years ago. There is also another worry: for everyone, time is flying by much too fast, with JJ's mother begging her son simply to give her more of it as a birthday present. Although JJ dismisses this as mere wishful thinking, he is anxious to find out what is really going on, so he starts on a journey of discovery that finally lands him in Tír na n'Óg—the land of eternal youth that runs parallel to human existence. Once there, he discovers the truth both about his great-grandfather and why time is rushing by at such an alarming rate. It is now up to him to save both his own world and his new fairy friends before it is too late.

The author is a fiddle player herself, and each chapter of this enthralling story is introduced with a stave of traditional Irish music. Music is also the way that the fairy and human worlds communicate with each other, with even Larry O'Dwyer, the new policeman of the title, proving to be an expert violinist. But like everything else in this story, he is not quite what he seems. He has a significant bearing on the plot, but his identity is kept secret until the end. No plot summary can do justice to this rich, haunting, and utterly original story, told by an author very much at home with the realities of modern-day Ireland yet also able with equal conviction to take readers into a different realm of the imagination. **NT**

My Big Birkett 2006

Lisa Shanahan

Nationality | Australian, birth date unknown
Publisher | Allen and Unwin, Australia
Award | C.B.C.A. Book of the Year (shortlist), 2007
Theme | Friendship, Young adult

My Big Birkett: The Sweet, Terrible, Glorious Year I Truly, Completely Lost It is a wonderful novel about the unexpected nature of growing up. Gemma enjoys her ordinary life and copes very well with being the only sane member of her family, until her sister, Donna, suddenly announces her engagement to Brian. Her previous disastrous boyfriend is remembered by the family's use of his name, Birkett, to describe any big emotional outburst—to "chuck a birkett." The engagement brings unexpected consequences. Donna has very definite ideas about her wedding. She selects a theme of "animals that mate for life" and proclaims that Gemma and Brian's sister will be flower girls dressed as swans. To make matters worse, Brian's family turns out to be obsessed with war; his sister usually wears army fatigues and is combat ready.

At school Gemma, who is so shy that she regularly throws up in front of an audience, auditions for the school play, *The Tempest*, to get close to her heartthrob Nick. But Raven De Head, a member of the infamous family that lives by the town's tip, also auditions and wants to practice his lines with Gemma. She is quick to make assumptions about the De Heads, especially when she visits their run-down house, but as rehearsals begin and she plays Miranda to Raven's Caliban, the events of the play resonate with the choices facing her, and she is forced to reassess her views.

Lisa Shanahan cleverly uses humor to examine deeper issues of prejudice in *My Big Birkett*, and the resulting book is both thoughtful and engaging. **JG**

The Red Shoe 2006

Ursula Dubosarsky

Nationality | Australian, birth date unknown
Publisher | Allen and Unwin, Australia
Award | C.B.C.A. Honor Book, 2007
Theme | Family, Young adult

This story depicts family life in suburban Australia in the 1950s as seen through the eyes of three sisters. Elizabeth is fifteen and suffering from a nervous breakdown. She sits at home with the *Sydney Morning Herald,* extracts of which are interspersed throughout the novel. Eleven-year-old Frances is quiet and self-possessed. Mostly, however, we see into the skewed world of six-year-old Matilda, in whose mind the boundaries of the probable, the possible, and the fantastic have not yet formulated. She is told not to make friends with strangers, but is adamant that she will be friends "even with stones and houses and big blocks of wood and glass." She has an invisible friend, Floreal, who whispers things she would rather not hear.

The girls' lives are apparently ordinary and orderly, distinguished only by the long absences of their father, a merchant seaman. The highlights are the pet competition at school, a visit to the cinema, a picnic at the beach, and the visits of Uncle Paul in their father's absence. Through Matilda's eyes even these mundane events appear vivid and strange. As the novel develops, it is clear that there are disturbing aspects to the girls' lives. The peculiar turmoil of adult life, which they glimpse through the media and sometimes nearer home, is too close for comfort, and each has found a means of keeping anxiety at bay.

This mesmerizing novel sets the fears and joys of childhood against a particular social reality in prose that is intriguing, amusing, and disconcerting to the reader. Dubosarsky is a writer who ought to be better known outside her native country. **CB**

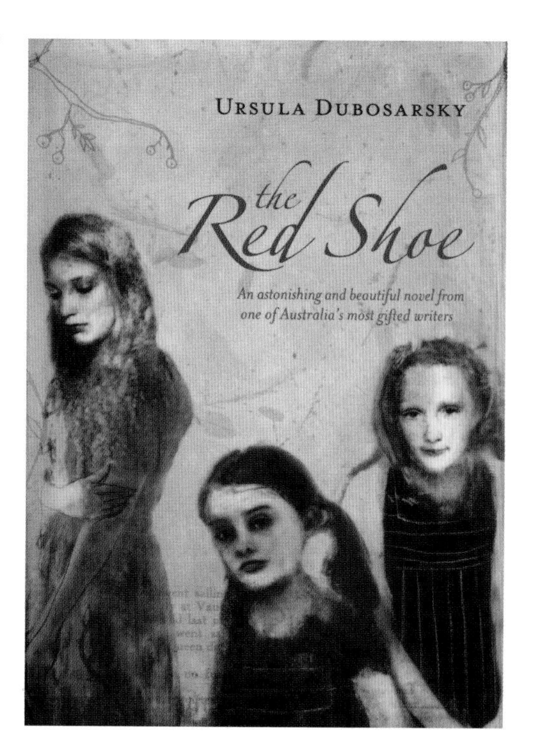

URSULA DUBOSARSKY
the Red Shoe
An astonishing and beautiful novel from one of Australia's most gifted writers

"Karen wore the shiny red shoes to her confirmation and everyone thought she was very wicked to wear red shoes to church."

MORE STORIES ABOUT SISTERS

I Capture the Castle by Dodie Smith, 1949
Homecoming by Cynthia Voigt, 1981
The Illustrated Mum by Jacqueline Wilson, 1999
Wasted by Mikki Goffin, 2001
Caddy Ever After by Hilary McKay, 2006

12+

Toby Alone 2006

Timothée de Fombelle François Place

Nationality | French, born 1973 (author); French, born 1957 (illustrator)
Publisher | Gallimard, France
Theme | Adventure

12+

OTHER ECO-FRIENDLY TALES

The Baron in the Trees by Italo Calvino, 1957
A Serpent's Tooth by Robert Swindells, 1988
The People Who Hugged the Trees by Deborah Rose, 1990
Ryland Footsteps by Sally Prue, 2003

The protagonist of Timothée de Fombelle's fast-paced story, *Toby Alone (Tobie Lolness)* is a very peculiar child: Toby is only "one and a half millimeters tall" and he lives with his family in an oak tree. His life in the tree's majestic foliage is quiet and pleasant until one day when Toby's father, who is a talented scientist and philosopher, refuses to disclose the secret of a revolutionary energy source for fear that the tree might be exploited and damaged. As a consequence, he falls out of favor with the Great Tree Council, and the family is banished to the "Lower Branches," a wild and dark territory. Here Toby meets Elisha, who becomes his best friend. The family are then sentenced to death. Only Toby manages to escape and attempts to save his parents, pursued by the merciless snout beetle breeder and his ruthless army.

"His leg was injured, he had cuts on both shoulders and his hair was matted with blood."

By means of skillfully calculated flashbacks, the author unfolds a multilayered plot that chronicles the adventures of the minute protagonists, alongside themes of betrayal, friendship, and love. With poetic force he creates a self-sufficient microcosm of tame aphids, endearing slugs, and horrific fighting ants. Timothée de Fombelle presents the tree with its labyrinths of branches, moss forests, and foliage as a habitat worthy of protection. His fabled tree-world also deals with controversial themes, including shortages of natural resources and climatic change as well as xenophobia and the emergence of dictatorships through intimidation and manipulation. *Toby Alone* is a fascinating novel, full of exciting twists and turns with unforgettable and lovable characters. **LB**

Monster Blood Tattoo: Foundling 2006

David Cornish

For thirteen years Cornish used little black notebooks to record, in words and drawings, the incredible alternative world that he was creating in his imagination. When notebook number twenty-three literally fell at a publisher's feet, she was amazed at the intricate detail and talked him into writing a story about it. The result is this first volume in the Monster Blood Tattoo series.

Rossamünd has been waiting at Madam Opera's Estimable Marine Society for Foundling Boys and Girls to go into the navy. To his surprise, he becomes a lamplighter instead. He is not sorry to leave the orphanage, where he was bullied because of his girlish name, and so he sets off on his journey. The

"Rossamünd had expected . . . taunts or threats, but there was just this dreadful . . . hesitation."

Half-Continent is a dangerous place, with villains and monsters everywhere, as well as the even more dangerous people who have been surgically altered to fight them. The challenges begin immediately when he embarks on the wrong ship. Knowing who to trust is tricky, and it seems at times unlikely that he will ever reach the Lamplighters' Guild.

This is an intricately plotted world, with detailed maps and illustrations by the author that aid readers' understanding. It also contains an expanded glossary, or "Explicarium," to the world. There are also appendices that include the Half-Continent's calendar, costumes, and weapons, and the various naval ships. These features allow readers to choose whether to concentrate on the exciting story or to pause to find out more. The first limited edition is a sumptuous production, worth seeking out. **JG**

Nationality | Australian, born 1972
Publisher | Omnibus Books, Australia
Award | C.B.C.A. Honor Book, 2007
Theme | Fantasy

OTHER SIMILAR BOOKS TO ENJOY

Sabriel by Garth Nix, 1995
Feral by Kerry Greenwood, 1998
Wildwood Dancing by Julie Marrillier, 2006
Monster Blood Tattoo: Lamplighter by David Cornish, 2008

12+

Winter Song 2006

Jean-Claude Mourlevat

Original Title | Le Combat d'hiver
Nationality | French, born 1952
Publisher | Gallimard, France
Theme | Adventure, Friendship, Fantasy

In an imaginary country governed by the Phalanx, a tyrannical and cruel regime, four adolescents on the run take up the struggle against barbarism previously led by their parents. Hunted by a group of terrifying dog-humans, the young people show immense courage before finding, little by little, numerous allies. They come to rely on the help of the horse-people, welcoming and committed creatures, and become part of a secret organization for all those who have chosen to fight for their freedom. It is the marvelous and captivating voice of Milena, loved by all, that will be able to rekindle hope in everyone and allow the necessary rebel forces to unite.

Winter Song is a somber and disquieting novel, but one in which emotions are deep and human warmth is attainable and comforting. The characters of the consolers are perfect examples of this: maternal figures full of love, they offer true moments of respite in the midst of a riveting adventure that will leave you holding your breath in suspense. The four young protagonists leave the sad world of their childhood and must grow up and rediscover the values of humanity, love, and friendship. Tough and courageous, they want to fight with all of their spirit, never ceasing to hope of one day glimpsing the patch of blue sky painted at the back of the dungeon, or the bright colors of a large, luck-bringing bird.

It is a thrilling story where fantasy and reality coexist harmoniously, a strong plot with numerous twists, and engaging characters who will be liked by readers of all ages. **SL**

12+

The Silver Jaguar 2007

Hermann Schulz

Original Title | Der silberne Jaguar
Nationality | German, born 1938
Publisher | Carlsen, Germany
Theme | Friendship, Young adult

Teenager Rufus is staying with his aunt, Josephine, while his parents are away. She is a teacher who is very involved with the plight of the Belarussian victims of the Chernobyl disaster. She is about to go to Belarus to deliver a donated wheelchair to a young woman. Rufus has helped her repair the precious apparatus, installing a new seat, new spokes, and new wheels.

Arriving in Belarus after a long train journey, Rufus is intrigued as well as confused by the differences in Belarussian life. His peers there have very strong friendships forged as a result of the government's attempts to restrict their freedom. Rufus doesn't know the significant role that wheelchairs play in the lives of these boys. The former leader of their group—a bright student who suffered disabilities as a result of the nuclear reactor accident—had instigated wheelchair races before he died of cancer. Now, the boys hold races in his honor, taking old wheelchairs from the hospital basement to enjoy some excitement.

One of the boys steals the wheelchair donated by Josephine because he wants to impress his friends. Due to the wheelchair's perfect western European design, they call it "the Silver Jaguar." While the search for the valuable item is under way, Rufus establishes a rapport with the Belarussian boys. Eventually the wheelchair reaches its intended recipient.

Schulz's stories often focus on the plight of people who exist on the fringes of society, and in this captivating book readers will learn about the living conditions of people who have little social security and freedom of expression. **CS**

Finding Violet Park 2007

Jenny Valentine

Nationality | English, born 1970
Publisher | HarperCollins, UK
Award | *Guardian* Children's Fiction Prize
Theme | Young adult

Jenny Valentine
FINDING VIOLET PARK
I met Violet after she died. But it didn't stop me from getting to know her.

Fifteen-year-old Lucas Swain finds himself strangely drawn toward a lost urn left on the shelf of a taxi-cab office for more than four years after it was found in the backseat of one of the cars. It contains the ashes of a former concert pianist named Violet Park, and Lucas is convinced that she is trying to communicate with him. Seizing the urn when no one is looking, he sets out on a journey of discovery, during which he also finds out a great deal about himself and his family. It turns out that his journalist father, who abandoned the family home years ago, had actually interviewed Violet Park shortly before he himself disappeared. So what is the connection between the two, and what is the dead woman still trying to tell Lucas?

This first novel, written with great clarity of style, perfectly captures that moment during adolescence when teenagers start understanding much more about themselves and their families. During this process, Lucas has to put away his former idealization of his missing father, and no longer wears his discarded clothes as a way of feeling closer to him. He also begins to understand his mother much better than before, although he still finds her irritating. Best of all, he discovers new strengths within himself, particularly his capacity for the brilliant detective work that finally manages to unravel secrets from the past. Lucas is an immensely engaging character, often extremely witty and never in the least self-pitying. His presence in this expertly plotted novel is a constant pleasure, and never more so when everything finally falls into place in its concluding pages. **NT**

"When Dad went, the thing that bound us was the lack of Dad. . . . In a weird way, the hole he left was the glue."

OTHER WITTY BOOKS FOR OLDER KIDS

Secret Diary of Adrian Mole by Sue Townsend, 1982
Holes by Louis Sachar, 1998
Oh, Boy! by Marie-Aude Murail , 2000
Four Sisters by Malika Ferdjoukh, 2003
The Schwas Was Here by Neal Shusterman, 2004

Index by Author/ Illustrator

Featured Reviewers

Isabel Allende (page 430) is a renowned Chilean writer best known for her vivid literary style and use of magical realism. In addition to her novels, short stories, and memoirs, she has written many books for children.

David Almond (page 358) won the Carnegie Medal and the Whitbread Children's Book Award for his first novel for children, *Skellig* (1998). He has gone on to write many more award-winning novels. He lives with his family in Northumberland, England.

Margaret Atwood (page 452) is a Booker Prize-winning author who is probably best known for her novels for adults. As a child she loved reading fairy tales and stories about animals, a passion that went on to inspire her poetry and children's fiction.

Gavin Bishop (page 200), a New Zealand writer and illustrator, has published forty picture books. His awards include the Noma Concours Grand Prix (Japan,1984), the Margaret Mahy Medal 2000, and the New Zealand Children's Book of the Year 2000, 2003, and 2008. He has also written for television and the Royal New Zealand Ballet.

Judy Blume (page 78) is a best-selling and award-winning U.S. novelist whose work has caused much controversy. She writes gently humorous books, mainly for children and teenagers, that tackle uncomfortable subjects such as bullying, racism, and menstruation. More than 80 million copies of her books have been sold worldwide.

John Burningham (page 496) studied at the Central School of Arts in London. He has written and illustrated more than thirty picture books and has compiled books for adults. He has twice been awarded the Kate Greenaway Medal, along with numerous other awards.

Nick Butterworth (page 424) is an author and illustrator whose avowed aim is to produce books that children will love. He enjoys meeting the children who inspire his books in live storytelling and drawing sessions. His most successful work, the "Percy the Park Keeper" series of picture books, has been made into an animated television series.

Eric Carle (page 406) was brought up in Germany and was conscripted into the army at the age of fifteen. He has produced more than fifty books, mostly for very young children. Many of his books are illustrated in his unique style of collage, made from layers of brightly colored paper. He published his best-selling book, *The Very Hungry Caterpillar*, in 1969.

Lauren Child (page 586) shot to fame in 1999 with the publication of *Clarice Bean, That's Me*, her first book as author and illustrator. She is the winner of a Kate Greenaway medal and two Nestlé Children's Book Prizes, as well as numerous other awards. Her work includes collage, photography, and watercolor, but she always draws her figures in pencil.

Timothée de Fombelle (page 714) began his career as a teacher and lecturer but is now well known in France as a playwright. In 2006 he published the first book of his "Tobie Lolness" children's series; *Toby Alone* has since been translated into 23 languages. The series' second book, *Elisha's Eyes*, followed in 2007.

Berlie Doherty (page 752) was employed as a social worker and teacher before she became a full-time writer. She is famous for her children's literature and has won two Carnegie Medals, for *Granny Was a Buffer Girl* (1986) and *Dear Nobody* (1991). She also writes poetry, plays, libretti, and books for adults.

Tessa Duder (page 202) has published nearly forty books, including novels, short stories, plays, and a number of anthologies. Her nonfiction includes histories and the first full-length portrait of Margaret Mahy. She is also a trustee for New Zealand's Storylines Children's Literature Trust.

Anne Fine (page 502) is a prolific author of both adult and children's fiction. Many of her books deal with vexing and problematic social issues yet they still have readers laughing out loud. Anne continues to write new books, always in complete silence. She lives with her partner by a river in County Durham, England.

Gustavo Martín Garzo (page 444) is a Spanish writer who trained as a psychologist before becoming a full-time writer and contributor to literary journals in the 1990s. In addition to more than twenty books written for adults, his children's books include *Breadcrumbs* (2000) and *Three Fairy Tales* (2003), for which he won Spain's National Children's Book Prize in 2004.

Jamila Gavin (page 192) was born in India and moved to England when she was twelve. She worked on music and arts programs for BBC radio and television before becoming a writer at the age of thirty-eight. Her novel *Coram Boy* won the Whitbread Children's Book of the Year in 2000 and was adapted for the stage in London and New York.

Jean Craighead George (page 426) is a U.S. author who was born into a family of naturalists. She has written more than 100 books for children and teenagers, and her love of animals and the natural world is often reflected in her work. Her *Julie of the Wolves* (1972) was awarded the Newbery Medal; another work, *My Side of the Mountain* (1959), is a Newbery Honor Book.

Adèle Geras (page 724) has written more than ninety books, many of them inspired by the places she has visited. Born in Jerusalem, she lived in different countries while growing up because her father was in the French Colonial Service. She worked as an actress, singer, and French teacher before settling down to full-time writing in 1976. *Troy* (2000) was shortlisted for the Whitbread Prize and commended for the Carnegie Medal.

Mary Hoffman (page 670) is a British author, critic, and journalist who produces *Armadillo*, the children's book-review magazine. When she was at elementary school in London she wrote plays that were performed by friends. She loves Italy and spends a lot of time there, a fact reflected in her popular "Stravaganza" series of novels.

Lois Lowry (page 760) dreamed of being a writer from childhood but worked as a photographer and journalist before her first book was published, in 1977. She has won the Newbery Medal twice, for *Number the Stars* (1989) and *The Giver* (1993). Although her books are varied, their central theme is always the importance of human connections.

Michael Morpurgo (page 208) discovered his vocation while working as a teacher. When he read the students one of his own stories, he "realized there was magic in it." He was the British Children's Laureate (2003–05) and has won numerous awards including the Nestlé Children's Book Prize for *The Butterfly Lion* (1996).

Marie-Aude Murail (page 416) is a best-selling French children's author who has been writing since the age of twelve. She has written more than eighty books including the "Emilien" and "L'Espionne" series of novels. Her most popular young adult book, *Oh, Boy!* (2000), was awarded the Deutscher Jugendliteraturpreis by a jury of German teenagers at the Frankfurt Book Fair.

Jenny Nimmo (page 204) grew up on a poultry farm in Surrey, England, and worked in repertory theater after leaving school. She is convinced that reading to her own children made her a better writer. The landscape and mythology of Wales, where she now lives, have inspired her fantasy and adventure novels, particularly the award-winning "Snow Spider" trilogy.

Helen Oxenbury (page 476) specialized in theater design at the Central School of Art, London. She worked in theater and television before becoming a freelance children's book illustrator. She has twice won the Kate Greenaway Medal and has won two Kurt Maschler Awards.

François Place (page 236) is one of the leading artist-illustrators in France and has also written fiction, including *Le Derniers Géants* (The Last Giants) and *Le Vieux Fou de Dessin* (The Old Man Mad About Drawings). Among the well-known children's books he has illustrated are *War Horse* by Michael Morpurgo and *Toby Alone* by Timothée de Fombelle.

Philip Pullman (page 524) is best known for the trilogy "His Dark Materials," which began with *Northern Lights* (*The Golden Compass* in the United States) in 1995, continued with *The Subtle Knife* in 1997, and concluded with *The Amber Spyglass* in 2000. These books have been honored by several prizes, including the Carnegie Medal, the Guardian Children's Book Award, and (for *The Amber Spyglass*) the Whitbread Book of the Year Award —the first time in the prize's history that it was given to a children's book. He was the 2002 recipient of the Eleanor Farjeon Award for children's literature.

Michael Rosen (page 98) is an award-winning British poet, children's novelist, and broadcaster. His humorous verse—published in books such as *Mind Your Own Business* and *Quick, Let's Get Out of Here*—draws closely on his own childhood experiences. He has played a significant role in engaging children with poetry. He was British Children's Laureate from 2007 to 2009 and was made Chevalier of the Order of Arts and Literature by the French government in 2008.

Meg Rosoff (page 798) won several prizes including the Michael L. Printz Award for her debut novel, *How I Live Now* (2004). She worked in publishing and advertising in New York for nine years before writing her first book, which followed the death of her younger sister from breast cancer. Her second novel, *Just in Case* (2006), won her the Carnegie Medal. Rosoff now lives in London.

Darren Shan (page 704) is the pen name of Darren O'Shaughnessy, an internationally best-selling Irish author of fantasy books. Although he gained fame as a children's writer—with his first vampire book *Cirque du Freak* (2000)—he originally wrote for adults, which he continues to do under the pen name D. B. Shan.

Grégoire Solotareff (page 260) was born in Alexandria, Egypt, the son of a Lebanese doctor and a Russian painter, Olga Lecaye, herself also an author of children's books. He practiced medicine for several years, and since 1985 has written approximately 150 books, many of which have been translated into multiple languages, mainly in Europe and Asia. He lives and works in Paris.

Jacqueline Wilson (page 28) had written around forty books before she rose to fame with *The Story of Tracy Beaker* in 1991. Her books often tackle controversial themes, such as adoption and divorce, and are usually illustrated with distinctive, colorful artwork by Nick Sharratt. The multi-award-winning author is a former British Children's Laureate and her books have sold more than 25 million copies in the United Kingdom alone.

Contributors

Kate Agnew (KA) works part-time as a children's bookseller, in addition to which she is a reviewer of children's books and a consultant to publishers and schools. She has been chair of the Booksellers Association Children's Group, a judge for the Nestlé and Whitbread awards, and a contributor to various books and other publications about children's books.

Dr. Belle Alderman (BA) is Emeritus Professor of Children's Literature at the University of Canberra. She was made a Member of the Order of Australia in recognition of "service to Australian children's literature as an academic, researcher, and mentor to emerging writers and illustrators, to the development and management of the Lu Rees Archives of Australian Children's Literature, and to professional associations."

Neil Archer (NA) is a teacher and writer. He is currently working on a book about travel as it features in recent French movies.

Romy Ash (RA) is a freelance writer. She writes for *frankie* magazine and *Big Issue Australia*. Her fiction has been published in literary journals. She teaches Creative Writing at the University of Melbourne.

Clive Barnes (CB) recently retired as a children's librarian and is a freelance researcher and writer. He reviews and writes for the London-based children's book magazine, *Books for Keeps*. He received a Master's degree in Children's Literature from the University of Surrey, England. He is the author of scholarly articles on twentieth-century children's literature, and he has served on the judging panels for the Branford Boase Book Award and the Booktrust Early Years Award.

Lorenzo Bellettini (LB) holds an MPhil and a PhD in Modern Languages from Cambridge University, England.

Estrella Borrego del Castillo (EB) is qualified in the publishing of children's and youth literature. She works as a project coordinator at the publishing house Random House Mondadori and is an editor of children's and youth literature.

Geraldine Brennan (GB) is Books Editor of *The Times Educational Supplement*, which has approximately half a million readers working in education. She has worked in print journalism since 1978. Her areas of interest and expertise include educational and children's publishing, creating reading cultures in schools and communities, tackling social exclusion through reading, and innovative work with writers in education. A Fellow of the Royal Society of Arts, she has been a judge for the Booktrust Teenage Prize (2005) and the Nestlé Smarties Award for children's books (2004). She was also a contributor to *Frightening Fiction* (2001), a critical work on popular fiction for young adults in the series "Contemporary Classics in Children's Literature," which is published by Continuum in the United Kingdom.

Rachael Cameron (RC) is an Australian writer specializing in children's literature and memory studies. She holds an honors degree from Monash University, Melbourne, where she was awarded the Henry Handel Richardson Prize, Arthur Brown Memorial Prize, Cecile Parrish Scholarship, and an Australian Postgraduate Award.

Charlotte Celsing (CC) is a Swedish freelance journalist and author of a children's book, *The Adventure of Alexander the Great* (2005). She was also a contributing author to the cooking ingredients guide *1001 Foods* (2008). She has a Master's degree in Literature, Arts, and Cultural Anthropology.

Philip Contos (PC) studied English and Italian literature at Columbia and Oxford universities. He currently works as an editor in London.

Kaylee Davis (KD) was Editor-In-Chief of the Children's Book-Of-The-Month Club in the United States.

Catherine Despinoy (CD) is a newspaper and radio journalist in Paris, France. She has also led master classes in journalism. Recently she became the artistic programmer for La Guinguette Pirate, a concert hall and restaurant in Paris.

Jenny Doubt (JSD) completed her Master's degree from the University of Sussex, England, and has since worked as a senior editor in illustrated book publishing in London. Originally from Canada, Jenny also works as a freelance writer, usually with a focus on postcolonial literature.

Sarah Drinkwater (SD) is a freelance writer and journalist. She writes for magazines and newspapers and was awarded a Master's degree in Renaissance Literature from University College London.

Robert Dunbar (RD) has taught children's literature at primary, secondary, and tertiary level in Ireland. He has edited or co-edited five anthologies for children and is a regular reviewer of children's books, contributing to a wide range of publications as well as a variety of radio programs.

Toin (Antonius) Duijx (AD) was for years Associate Professor for Children's Literature at Leiden University, The

Netherlands. He is currently a reviewer; freelance publicist; secretary of the Dutch IBBY (International Board on Books for Young People) Section; editor of *Literature Without Age*, the only Dutch magazine about children's literature; and a visiting lecturer at the International Youth Library in Munich. He has written several books about children's literature and compiled with Joke Linders a very successful and many times reprinted anthology of Dutch children's songs: *Liedjes met een hoepeltje erom*.

Cécilia Falgas-Ravry (CFR) was born in 1985 of a French father and a Swedish mother. She is completing a doctorate in French Literature at the University of Cambridge, England.

Janet Fisher (JF) is a children's and school librarian, having worked in the United Kingdom, Saudi Arabia, and Canada. She also reviews children's books for several journals, and serves as a children's literature consultant.

Marine Ganofsky (MGR) was born in 1985 in Marseille, France. She completed her Bachelor and Master degrees in English Literature at the Université de Provence in France and is studying for a PhD in French Literature at the University of Cambridge, England. Among the academic dissertations she has written is "Transgression in John Updike's *Rabbit at Rest*" and she is writing a thesis on evil lovers and wicked seducers in eighteenth-century French novels.

Jo Goodman (JG) lives in Melbourne, Australia, where she was a teacher-librarian for many years. She has edited collections of poetry and short stories, and regularly reviews, lectures, and writes articles about children's books. She has also judged for the Children's Book Council of Australia.

Reg Grant (RG) is an author who has written more than twenty books for schools, on subjects ranging from the slave trade to the poetry of World War II. He has enjoyed nothing more than reading stories to his own children most evenings for the last 10 years.

Frederik H. Green (FHG) is Assistant Professor in Asian Studies at Macalester College in Saint Paul, Minnesota. He was educated at St. John's College, Cambridge, England, and at Yale University, Connecticut. Green has researched twentieth-century Chinese and Japanese literature, as well as the reception of European Modernism in East Asia.

Margaret Hargrave (MH) is a retired English teacher who now serves as an elected local councillor. Her second novel, *A Woman of Air*, was awarded the Elle/Random House Fiction Prize in 1996. She currently has several works of fiction in progress.

Lucinda Hawksley (LH) is an art historian, biographer, and freelance writer, with a specialism in the nineteenth and early twentieth centuries. Her books for adult readers include *Katey: The Life and Loves of Dickens's Artist Daughter*, *Lizzie Siddal: The Tragedy of a Pre-Raphaelite Supermodel*, and *Essential Pre-Raphaelites*.

Bridget Haylock (BH) lives in rural Victoria, Australia, where she currently teaches literacy, regularly reviews plays and educational material for *Screen Education* magazine, and has various writing projects underway including poetry, plays, screenplays, and fiction and nonfiction books.

Neal Hoskins (NH) is the owner of Wingedchariot Press, which was set up to bring the best of children's picture books from Europe to the United Kingdom.

Alina Hoyne (AH) is not at all grown up. She loves going on midnight walks, visiting bizarre museums, and taking baths with all her clothes on. She is writing a PhD, and when finished will insist people call her "The Doctor."

David Hutter (DaH) was born in Germany and briefly lived in both England and France during his teens. After finishing high school he moved to Italy for a lackluster and ultimately futile attempt at studying economics. Two years later, he moved to England to study creative writing and religious studies at Middlesex University. Having graduated with flying colors, he now works as a freelance writer and editor and is based in London.

Ann James (AJ) is a children's illustrator and author, with over sixty books published. With partner Ann Haddon she runs Books Illustrated, a gallery specializing in exhibitions of book illustration in Australia and overseas. James was awarded the Dromkeen Medal in 2002 for services to children's literature in Australia.

Helen Jones (HJ) is a freelance

Ann Kay (AK) has many years' experience as a writer and editor for the family market. Words have been her passion from a very early age, so she is delighted by the opportunity of this book to promote the great writing available to children today.

Carol King (CK) is a freelance journalist. She studied English Literature at the University of Sussex, England, and Fine Art at St. Martin's art school in London.

Melanie Kramers (MK) is a freelance writer and editor from London currently living in Buenos Aires, Argentina. She has worked for BBC Worldwide, Pearson, and *Time Out* magazine, and contributes regular fashion and travel blogs to orangelifemagazine.com. Her favorite children's author is Diana Wynne Jones.

Laura Kyllönen (LKK) studied creative writing at Middlesex University in London before returning to her native Finland to pursue a Master's degree in the same field at the University of Jyväskylä.

Helena Lam (HL) studied in England before going to Hornsey School of Art in North London; she then studied fashion design at the London College of Fashion. She worked as a fashion designer and then switched to investment properties management. She is currently studying jewelry design.

Signe Mellergaard Larsen (SML) is a Danish writer and researcher who earned a Bachelor's degree in Art History at Plymouth University, England, and a Master's degree in Art History at the Courtauld Institute of Art, London. She is now a freelance writer and translator based in Copenhagen. Her research areas include Nordic art, architecture, and cultural studies between the nineteenth and the twenty-first century.

Maya Linden (ML) is a writer, researcher, freelance food critic, literature reviewer, and tutor at the University of Melbourne, Australia, where she is completing her PhD. Her creative and critical writing has been published in many journals and magazines including *Australian Book Review* and several anthologies.

Sophie Lucas (SL) was born in 1973 in Amiens, France, and studied Philosophy at the University of Bordeaux. Based in Paris, she now teaches French as a foreign language and enjoys taking part in children's illustration projects.

Ulla Lundqvist (UL) is a lecturer, critic, and writer of facts and fiction, especially for the young. She has been a member of the Astrid Lindgren Memorial Award jury since 2003.

Jamie Middleton (JaM) is a freelance writer and editor for various lifestyle magazines and books. With a keen interest in literature he is enjoying the chance to revisit the books of his youth by reading them to his son.

Giulia F. Miller (GFM) holds a doctorate in Modern Hebrew literature from the University of Cambridge, England. She is currently a Postdoctoral Fellow in Jewish Studies at Pennsylvania State University.

Wayne Mills (WM) is a Senior Lecturer in the Faculty of Education at the University of Auckland, New Zealand, and is the creator of the international Kids' Lit Quiz.

Sue Mooney (SM) studied graphic art before gaining a Bachelor's degree in English Literature at the University of Melbourne, Australia. She has illustrated several books, and has also published works on the nineteenth-century designer William Morris. She currently works in a library and lives with her family in central Victoria.

Jarrah Moore (JM) is a writer of short speculative fiction for the young-adult market. She is based in Melbourne, Australia. She once wrote an Honours thesis on fairy tales, and was delighted to return to the subject for one of her entries in this book.

Carina Nandlal (CATN) is a PhD student in Art History at Melbourne University, Australia.

Victoria Neumark (VN) began her love affair with children's books at the age of four with Beatrix Potter's *Peter Rabbit*. The affair continued during the upbringing of three sons, when she also ran many children's drama classes. An experienced education journalist, she currently leads the degree course in Journalism at London Metropolitan University. She also contributes to the national press and writes short stories.

Petr Onufer (PO) is a translator and critic from the Czech Republic. He studied Czech and English at Charles University in Prague and at the University of Texas, located in Austin. He currently works as a senior editor at Albatros Publishing in Prague, and contributes to *Revolver Revue*, a leading Czech literary journal.

Lorraine Orman (LO) was formerly a book reviewer and a librarian specializing in children's literature. She is now the author of nine books for children and young adults, and she also co-edited an anthology of children's short stories with Tessa Duder.

Wendy Osgerby (WO) is a freelance art historian, curator, and writer.

Cynthia Quarry (CQ) is currently engaged in writing her doctoral dissertation on the contemporary British novel at the University of Toronto, Canada.

Dr. Stephanie Owen Reeder (SOR) has been involved in children's literature in Australia for over twenty years as both an editor and author. Stephanie is also an award-winning reviewer who contributes reviews of children's books to *The Canberra Times* and *Australian Book Review*.

Ulla Rhedin (UR) was for thirty years senior lecturer at Karlstad University in Sweden. She has written books and articles about picture books since 1977. Since 1980 she has been a critic in the daily newspaper *Dagens Nyheter*, and a member of the Astrid Lindgren Memorial Award jury.

Clare Rhoden (CER) is a speech pathologist who has worked extensively with children from preschool to college age. She is the author of three books on study skills for first-year university students in law, science, and engineering disciplines.

Simon Robertson (SR)

Astarte Rowe (AR) moved to Australia having previously lived in numerous countries. She is a PhD candidate in Aboriginal Art and Culture at the University of Melbourne.

Christopher Rowe (CR) is from St. John's, Newfoundland, Canada. He obtained his Master's degree in Comparative Literature from the University of Western Ontario, and his PhD in Cinema Studies from the University of Melbourne, Australia.

Jana Rumannová (JR) studied children's literature at the University of Trnava, Slovakia. She currently works for an educational publisher in London.

Glen T. Sheppard (GTS) was born in London, Canada, currently based in London, England. After finishing theater school in Toronto he worked as an actor and theater artist for some years before turning his attention almost exclusively to writing. Since then he has completed several manuscripts and contributed to a number of publications, while also occasionally returning to the stage as a performer and musician.

Georg Sponholz (GS) is a German graduate and translator who was brought up on German children's books and youth literature. He works as a freelance translator and writer in Germany and the United Kingdom. He contributed as editorial assistant to *1001 Historic Sites*, a compendium of the world's foremost historical locations.

Christa Stegemann (CS) has worked since 1981 as Editorial Director for German-speaking Countries in the International Youth Library in Munich, Germany, the largest library for international children's and youth literature in the world.

Robert Stroud (RS) was born in Worcestershire, England, in 1983. He moved to Weston-Super-Mare as a young boy. Pursuing a career in music, he found his way to London where he now resides. Halfway through his first novel, Stroud now works as a freelance writer.

Silvana Tuccio (SMT) is currently completing a PhD at the University of Melbourne, Australia, on the cinema of Giorgio Mangiamele. She has published several articles on Australian contemporary cinema, including *Studies in Australasian Cinema* (2008). She also edited the 2005 book *Sguardi australiani: idee, immaginari e cinema degli antipodi* (Australian Views: the ideas, imagination, and cinema of the Antipodes).

Nicholas Tucker (NT) is Honorary Senior Lecturer in Cultural Studies at the University of Sussex, England. Formerly a teacher and then an educational psychologist, he is the author of nine books about children, childhood, and reading, including *The Child and the Book* (1981). He has also written six books for children, broadcasts frequently, and contributes reviews to the *Independent* and *The Times*. Recent publications include *Family Fictions: Contemporary Classics of Children's Literature* (with Nikki Gamble, 2001); *The Rough Guide to Children's Books 0–5 and 5–11* (2002); and *The Rough Guide to Teenage Books* (with Julia Eccleshare, 2003).

Catherine Van Bergen (CVB) has recently finished her final year at Deakin University in Geelong, Australia, majoring in journalism and literature. She lives with her parents, three younger brothers, and an unusual assortment of pets, and enjoys reading, watching movies, spending time with friends, and listening to alternative and independent music.

Claire Watts (CW) has a degree in French from King's College London. She has been a freelance writer and editor for the last twenty years.

Andreea Weisl-Shaw (AWS) is originally from Romania. She studied French and Spanish at Trinity College Cambridge, England, where she is now completing a PhD in Medieval French and Spanish Literature. She has recently been appointed Fellow and College Lecturer in Spanish at Corpus Christi College, Cambridge

Ilana Wistinetzki (IW) holds a M.Phil degree in Chinese Language and Literature from Yale University, Connecticut. She is currently teaching Chinese and French at Pierrepont School in Westport, Connecticut.

Katie Wyatt (KW) is an Australian writer with a specific interest in children's book publishing.

Stephen Yeager (SY) has a PhD in English Literature. He lives in Toronto, Canada.

Picture Credits

Every effort has been made to credit the copyright holders of the images used in this book. We apologize for any unintentional omissions or errors and will insert the appropriate acknowledgment to any companies or individuals in subsequent editions of the work.

Preface, Bookplates, Endpapers © Quentin Blake 2009 **18–19** From Rosie's Walk, text and illustrations ©1968 Pat Hutchins. Reproduced by permission of Random House **20** Christie's Images **22** Penguin ©1941 Robert McCloskey **23** HarperCollins ©1942 Margaret Wise Brown **24–25** © Britt Allcroft Productions LLC **26** Goodnight Moon ©1947 by Harper & Row. Text © renewed 1975 by Roberta Brown Rauch. Illustrations © renewed 1975 by Edith Hurd, Clement Hurd, John Thacher Hurd and George Hellyer, as Trustees of the Edith & Clement Hurd 1982 Trust **27** Goodnight Moon ©1947 by Harper & Row. Text ©renewed 1975 by Roberta Brown Rauch. Illustrations © renewed 1975 by Edith Hurd, Clement Hurd, John Thacher Hurd and George Hellyer, as Trustees of the Edith & Clement Hurd 1982 Trust **28** Oxford University Press ©1954 Harold Jones **29** Oxford University Press ©1954 Harold Jones **30** Courtesy of the Bodleian Library. Used by permission of HarperCollins Publishers **31** Illustration Dick Bruna © Mercis bv, 1963 **32** Courtesy of the Bodleian Library. Random House ©1968 Pat Hutchins **33** © Elfrida Vipont Foulds, 1969 **34** ©1969 Eric Carle **35** Courtesy of the Bodleian Library. Random House ©1970 John Burningham **36** Egmont ©1972 Helen Nicoll/Jan Pieńkowski **37** Egmont ©1972 Helen Nicoll/Jan Pieńkowski **38** The Swedish Institute for Children's Books/Rabén & Sjögren ©1972 Gunilla Bergström **39** Bayard Jeunesse ©1975 Claude Lebrun **40** The Swedish Institute for Children's Books/Rabén & Sjögren ©1977 Inger and Lasse Sandberg **42** Copyright ©Eric Hill, 1980/Reproduced by permission of Ventura Publishing Ltd **43** © Janet and Allan Ahlberg, 1982 **44** Penguin ©1982 Rod Campbell **45** Simon and Schuster ©1985 Alexandra Day **46** Cover illustration ©1985 Shirley Hughes. Reproduced by permission of Walker Books Ltd, London SE11 5HJ **47** Cover illustration ©1987 Helen Oxenbury. Reproduced by permission of Walker Books Ltd, London SE11 5HJ **48** Courtesy of the Bodleian Library. Penguin ©1989 David McKee **49** Penguin ©1989 David McKee **50** Cover illustration ©1989 Helen Oxenbury. Reproduced by permission of Walker Books Ltd, London SE11 5HJ **51** Rabén & Sjögren ©1990 Lena Andersson **52** Hachette ©1991 Mick Inkpen **53** Hachette ©1991 Mick Inkpen **54** Cover illustration ©1992 Lucy Cousins. Reproduced by permission of Walker Books Ltd, London SE11 5HJ **55** Cover illustration ©1992 Barbara Firth. Reproduced by permission of Walker Books Ltd, London SE11 5HJ **57** Random House ©1999 John Prater **58** © Sally Hunter, 1999 **60–61** Illustration ©1983 Anthony Browne. From Gorilla. Reproduced by permission of Walker Books Ltd. London SE11 5HJ. **63** Courtesy of the British Library **64** Private collection **66** Copyright © Frederick Warne & Co. 1902, 2002/Reproduced by permission of Frederick Warne & Co. **67** Copyright © Frederick Warne & Co. 1902, 2002/Reproduced by permission of Frederick Warne & Co. **68** Private collection **69** Copyright © Frederick Warne & Co. 1908, 2002/Reproduced by permission of Frederick Warne & Co. **71** © E.H. Shepard, colouring © 1970, 1973 by E.H. Shepard and Egmont Books Ltd. Reproduced with permission of Curtis Brown Group Ltd./From WINNIE-THE-POOH by A.A.Milne, illustrated by E.H.Shepard, copyright 1926 by E.P.Dutton, renewed 1954 by A.A.Milne. Used by permission of Dutton Children's Books, A Division of Penguin Young Readers Group, A Member of Penguin Group (USA) Inc., 345 Hudson Street, New York, NY 10014. All rights reserved. **72** Librarie Hachette ©1931 Jean de Brunhof **73** Librarie Hachette ©1931 Jean de Brunhof **74** Penguin ©1933 Marjorie Flack **77** Penguin ©1939 Hardie Gramatky **78** Simon and Schuster ©1939 Ludwig Bemelmans **79** Simon and Schuster ©1939 Ludwig Bemelmans **81** Houghton Mifflin ©1941 HA and Margret Rey **82** Houghton Mifflin ©1942 Virginia Lee Burton **83** Houghton Mifflin ©1942 Hildegarde Burton **84** Schildts Förlags Ab ©1952 Tove Jansson **87** Christie's Images **88** Courtesy of the Bodleian Library. Used by permission of HarperCollins Publishers **89** "Book cover" copyright ©1957, 1985 by Random House, Inc., from The Cat in the Hat by Dr. Seuss, ™ and copyright © by Dr. Seuss Enterprises, L.P. 1957, renewed 1985. Used by permission of Random House Children's Books, a division of Random House, Inc. **90–91** Random House ©1957 Peter Spier **93** "Book cover", copyright ©1960, 1988 by Random House, Inc., from Green Eggs and Ham by Dr. Seuss, ™ and copyright © by Dr. Seuss Enterprises, L.P. 1960, renewed 1988. Used by permission of Random House Children's Books, a division of Random House, Inc. **94** "Book cover", copyright ©1961, 1989, from Go, Dog. Go! by P.D. Eastman, copyright ©1961 by P.D. Eastman. Copyright renewed 1989 by Mary L. Easatman. Used by permission of Random House Children's Books, a division of Random House, Inc. **95** "Book cover", copyright ©1962 by Random House, Inc., from The Big Honey Hunt by Stan and Jan Berenstain, copyright © 1962, renewed 1990 by Stanley and Janice Berenstain. Used by permission of Random House Children's Books, a division of Random House, Inc. **96** ©1962 Oliver Postgate **98** Used by permission of HarperCollins Publishers ©1963 Maurice Sendak **99** Used by permission of HarperCollins Publishers ©1963 Maurice Sendak **100** Houghton Mifflin ©1965 Bernard Waber **101** Courtesy of the Bodleian Library. Houghton Mifflin ©1967 Bill Martin Jr. **102** Beltz & Gelberg ©1967 Josef Guggenmos **103** Random House ©1968 Richard Scarry **104** Viking Children's Books. Courtesy Roy Freeman ©1968 Don Freeman **105** The Swedish Institute for Children's Books ©1969 Ulf Lögren **106** Used by permission of HarperCollins Publishers ©1970 Maurice Sendak **108** The Swedish Institute for Children's Books/Rabén & Sjögren ©1971 Astrid Lindgren **110** Simon and Schuster ©1972 Graham Oakley **111** HarperCollins ©1972 Russell Hoban **112** © Raymond Briggs, 1973 **113** © Eve Sutton, 1973. Illustrations © Lynley Dodd, 1973 **115** The Finnish Institute for Children's Literature **116** Text and illustrations ©Janet and Allan Ahlberg, 1977 **117** Text and illustrations ©Janet and Allan Ahlberg, 1977 **118** Random House ©1977 Shirley Hughes **119** Canadian Children's Book Centre ©1978 by Margaret Atwood, O.W. Toad Ltd. Reprinted by permission of Groundwood Books Ltd. **120** ©Raymond Briggs, 1978 **121** ©Raymond Briggs, 1978 **122–123** HarperCollins ©1978 Donald Crews **125** HarperCollins ©1980 Jill Murphy **126** HarperCollins ©1980 Pamela Allen **127** Bauard Jeunesse ©1980 Marie-Agnes Gaudrat **128** Courtesy of the Bodleian Library. Carlton ©1981 John Cunliffe **129** Editions Casterman ©1981 Gabrielle Vincent **131** Random House ©1982 John Burningham **132** Cover illustration ©1983 Anthony Browne. Reproduced by permission of Walker Books Ltd, London SE11 5HJ **133** Penguin ©1983 Katharine Holabird **134** Rabén & Sjögren ©1983 Inger and Lasse Sandberg **135** Arin ©1983 Roser Capdevila **136** Mallinson Rendel ©1983 Lynley Dodd **137** From Possum Magic by Mem Fox and Julie Vivas. Text © Mem Fox, 1983; illustrations © Julie Vivas, 1983. First published by Omnibus Books, a division of Scholastic Australia Pty Ltd, 1993. Reproduced by permission of Scholastic Australia Pty Ltd. **138** Oxford University Press ©1985 Terry Denton **141** Random House ©1986 Jane Hissey **142** Penguin ©1987 Jane Yolen **143** Oxford University Press ©1987 Valerie Thomas **144** Cover illustration ©1988 Patrick Benson. Reproduced by permission of Walker Books Ltd, London SE11 5HJ **146** The Swedish Institute for Children's Books ©1989 Lena Andersson **147** Allen and Unwin ©1989 Janet McLean **148** HarperCollins Publishers Ltd ©1989 Nick Butterworth **149** Cover illustration ©1990 Nicola Bayley. Reproduced by permission of Walker Books Ltd, London SE11 5HJ **150** Frances Lincoln ©1991 Mary Hoffman **153** National Library of the Netherlands ©1992 Max Velthuijs **154** Cover illustration ©1992 Jez Alborough. Reproduced by permission of Walker Books Ltd, London SE11 5HJ **156** Sauerländer ©1993 Quint and Quinn Buchholz **157** Sauerländer ©1993 Quint and Quinn Buchholz **158** Pan Macmillan ©1993 Michael Rosen **159** Cover illustration ©1994 Anita Jeram. Reproduced by permission of Walker Books Ltd, London SE11 5HJ **160** Holzwarth/Erlbruch, Vom kleinen Maulwurf, der wissen wollte, wer ihm auf den Kopf gemacht hat Peter Hammer Verlag Wuppertal, 1989 **161** Gallimard Jeunesse, Giboulées © Antoon Krings, 1994 **162** Random House ©1995 Quentin Blake **164** © Babette Cole, 1998 **165** Random House ©1998 Helen Cooper **166** The Swedish Institute for Children's Books ©1998 Eva Eriksson **168** Frances Lincoln ©1999 Niki Daly **169** Text ©Ian Whybrow, 1999/Illustrations ©Adrian Reynolds, 1999 **170** Pan Macmillan ©1999 Julia Donaldson **172** Cover illustration ©2000 Blackbird Design Pty Ltd. Reproduced by permission of Walker Books Ltd, London SE11 5HJ **173** Simon and Schuster ©2000 Ian Falconer **174** Used by permission of Farrar, Straus and Giroux, LLC. Jacket design by Peter Sis from MADLENKA by Peter Sis. Jacket design copyright © 2000 by Peter Sis **175** Editorial Kokinos ©2001 Gabriela Kesselman **176** Didier Jeunesse ©2001 Francine Vidal **177** The Finnish Institute for Children's Literature ©2003 Aino Havukainen **178** Hyperion ©2003 Mo Willems **179** Hyperion ©2004 Mo Willems **180** Hachette Livre ©2004 Philippe Lechermeier **181** HarperCollins Publishers Ltd ©2005 Oliver Jeffers **182–183** Houghton Mifflin ©2006 David Wiesner **184** © Shanghai People's Art Publisher **185** Private collection **186** Mary Evans Picture Library **189** Getty Images **190** Private collection **192** Courtesy of Henry Sotheran Ltd **193** akg-images/Ullstein **195** Courtesy of the Bodleian Library **196** akg-images **197** akg-images **198** Courtesy of the Bodleian Library **199** Bodleian Library, Oxford, UK **200** National Library of Australia **201** National Library of Australia **202** Lebrecht Photo Library **203** Lebrecht Photo Library **204** Courtesy Peter Harrington Antiquarian Bookseller. **205** Courtesy Peter Harrington Antiquarian Bookseller. **206** Mary Evans Picture Library **208** Courtesy Peter Harrington Antiquarian Bookseller **209** The Granger Collection, NYC/TopFoto **210** Courtesy of the Bodleian Library. Private collection **212** Courtesy of the Bodleian Library. HarperCollins ©1918 Norman Lindsay **213** HarperCollins ©1933 May Gibbs **214** Hachette ©1920 Constance Heward **216** Courtesy Peter Harrington Antiquarian Bookseller. © Elizabeth Banks **218** © E.H. Shepard, colouring 1989 by Mark Burgess and Egmont Books Ltd. reproduced with permission of Curtis Brown Group Ltd./From WHEN WE WERE VERY YOUNG by A.A.Milne, illustrations by E.H.Shepard, copyright 1924 by E.P.Dutton, renewed 1952 by A.A.Milne. Used by permission of Dutton Children's Books, A Division of Penguin Young Readers Group, A Member of Penguin Group (USA) Inc., 345 Hudson Street, New York, NY 10014. All rights reserved. **221** Courtesy of the Bodleian Library. Egmont ©1929 Alison Uttley **222** ©1929 Josef Capek **224** © Edward Ardizzone, 1936 from Little Tim and the Brave Sea Captain (published by Frances Lincoln) **227** HarperCollins ©1940 & 1947 Esphyr Slobodkina. Copyright renewed 1968 by Esphyr Slobodkina **228** Editions Flammarion ©1941 Marie Colmont **229** Courtesy of the Bodleian Library. Faber & Faber ©1942 Diana Ross **231** Rabén & Sjögren/SALTKRÅKAN AB ©1945 Astrid Lindgren **232** Simon and Schuster ©1947 Marcia Brown **233** © Rumer Godden, 1971 **234** "Book cover", copyright ©1948 by Random House, Inc., from My Father's Dragon by Ruth Stiles Gannett. Used by permission of Random House Children's Books, a division of Random House, Inc. **236** Edition Flammarion ©1948 Paul Emile Victor **237** Edition Flammarion ©1948 Paul Emile Victor **238** Jacket cover from Foxie, the Singing Dog by D'Auliare. Used by permission of Yearling, an imprint of Random House Children's Books, a division of Random House, Inc. **239** Peanuts © United Feature Syndicate, Inc. **240** Edition Flammarion ©1950 Natha Caputo **241** Edition Flammarion ©1950 Natha Caputo **242** Penguin ©1952 Robert McCloskey **243** Simon and Schuster ©1952 Alice Dalgliesh **244** Houghton Mifflin ©1952 Lynd Ward **245** Courtesy Peter Harrington Antiquarian Bookseller. © Graham Greene, 1952 **246** HarperCollins US/cover art ©renewed by the Estate of Garth Williams **249** HarperCollins US/text ©1955 by Crockett Johnson, © renewed by Ruth Krauss **250** Faber and Faber ©1955 Catherine Storr **253** From Captain Pugwash by John Ryan published by France Lincoln Ltd, © John Ryan 1957. Reproduced by permission of Frances Lincoln Ltd. **254** Used by permission of HarperCollins Publishers. Courtesy of the Bodleian Library. **255** Used by permission of HarperCollins Publishers **256** Used by permission of HarperCollins Publishers **259** Edition Flammarion ©1961 Nathan Hale **260** Tomi Ungerer Die Drei Räuber ©1967 Diogenes Verlag AG Zürich. All rights reserved **261** Tomi Ungerer Die Drei Räuber ©1967 Diogenes Verlag AG Zürich. All rights reserved **263** Otfried Preußler, Der Räuber Hotzenplotz, mit Illustrationen von F.J.Tripp ©1962 by Thienemann Verlag (Thienemann Verlag GmbH), Stuttgart - Wien **264** Courtesy of the Bodleian Library. Penguin ©1962 Ezra Jack Keats **265** Used by permission of HarperCollins Publishers ©1962 Charlotte Zolotow **266** Courtesy of the Bodleian Library. Random House ©1963 John Burningham **267** "Book cover", copyright ©1963, 1991 by Knopf Children, from Swimmy by Leo Lionni. Used by permission of Alfred A. Knopf, an imprint of Random House Children's Books, a division of Random House, Inc. **268** Courtesy of the Bodleian Library. Used by permission of HarperCollins Publishers **271** ©1964 Evil Eye Music, LLC. **273** Hachette ©1966 Val Biro **275** HarperCollins Publishers Ltd ©1968 Judith Kerr **276** "Book cover", copyright ©1968, 1996 by Random House, Inc., from The Best Nest by P.D. Eastman. Used by permission of Random House Children's Books, a division of Random House, Inc. **278** Courtesy of the Bodleian Library. From A Necklace of Raindrops, text ©1968 Joan Aiken, illustration ©1968 Jan Pieńkowski. Reproduced by permission of Random House **281** Courtesy of the Bodleian Library. Oxford University Press ©1969 Charles Keeping **282** Cover art ©1970 Arnold Lobel **283** HarperCollins Publishers Ltd ©1970 Judith Kerr **284** Pan Macmillan ©1970 Charles Causley. Courtesy of Launceston Bookshop **285** Gyldendal ©1970 Ole Lund Kirkegaard. Courtesy of Center for Børnelitteratur, Danmarks Pædagogiske Universitetsskole/Centre for Children's Literature, Danish School of Education **286** Pluk van de Petteflet by Annie MG Schmidt and

Fiep Westendorp, Amsterdam, 1971, Em. Querido's Uitgeverij B.V. **287** "Book cover", copyright ©1968, 1996 by Random House, Inc., from What Do People Do All Day? by Richard Scarry, copyright ©1968 by Richard Scarry, copyright renewed 1996 by Richard Scarry II. Used by permission of Random House Children's Books, a division of Random House, Inc. **288** Used by permission of Farrar, Straus and Giroux, LLC. Jacket design by William Steig from AMOS & BORIS by William Steig. Jacket design copyright © 1971 by William Steig **289** Lebrecht Photo Library **290** Simon and Schuster ©1972 Judith Viorst **291** Courtesy of the Bodleian Library. Random House ©1972 John Vernon Lord **292** Courtesy of the Bodleian Library. © Michael Foreman, 1974 **295** ©1974, renewed 2002 Evil Eye, LLC. Reprinted with permission from the estate of Shel Silverstein and HarperCollins Children's Books. **297** Simon and Schuster ©1975 Tomie DePaola **299** Courtesy of the Bodleian Library. Pan Macmillan ©1976 Mary Rayner **300** Penguin Books (Australia) ©1977 Jenny Wagner **301** Random House ©1977 John Burningham **302** Carlton ©1977 Rhonda Armitage **305** © Raymond Briggs, 1977 **307** Houghton Mifflin ©1977 Harry Allard **308** Lebrecht Photo Library **309** Lebrecht Photo Library **311** Simon and Schuster ©1978 Paul Goble **312** Courtesy Roy Freeman ©1968 Don Freeman **313** HarperCollins ©1978 Percy Trezise and Dick Roughsey **314** Random House ©1978 Roald Dahl **315** Egmont ©1979 Jan Pieńkowski **316** Gallimard Jeunesse, Albums Gallimard Jeunesse © Pef, 1980 **317** Courtesy of the Bodleian Library. Random House ©1980 David McKee **318** Courtesy of the Bodleian Library. Cover illustration by Michael Martchenko. From The Paper Bag Princess, written by Robert Munsch, and published by Annick Press, Toronto, Canada © 1980 **319** Houghton Mifflin ©1981 Chris Van Allsburg **320** ©1982 Gavin Bishop **321** Courtesy of the Bodleian Library. HarperCollins Publishers/©1982 by Vera B. Williams **322** Used by permission of Farrar, Straus and Giroux, LLC. Illustration by William Steig from DOCTOR DE SOTO by William Steig. Illustrations copyright © 1982 by William Steig **325** ©Humphrey Carpenter, 1984/Illustrations © Frank Rodgers, 1984 **326** Used by permission of HarperCollins Publishers **329** Illustrations ©1985 by Felicia Bond **330** Courtesy of the Bodleian Library. Hachette ©1985 Niki Daly **331** Rabén & Sjögren ©1985 Christina Björk **332** Houghton Mifflin ©1985 Chris Van Allsburg **333** Egmont ©1986 Allan Ahlberg **335** Used by permission of Farrar, Straus and Giroux, LLC. Illustration by Richard Egielski from HEY, AL by Arthur Yorinks. Illustrations copyright © 1986 by Arthur Yorinks **336** Ediciones Ekaré ©1986 Ana Maria Machado **337** Hachette ©1988 John Agard **338** Simon and Schuster ©1987 Cynthia Rylant **340** Hachette ©1988 Nigel Gray **342** Random House ©1988 Roald Dahl **344** L'École des Loisirs ©1989 Grégoire Solotareff **345** Penguin ©1989 John Scieszka **346** "Book cover", copyright ©1990 by Random House, Inc., from Oh, The Places You'll Go ™ & © 1990 Dr. Seuss Enterprises, L.P. Used by permission of Random House Children's Books, a division of Random House, Inc. **347** Oh, The Places You'll Go ™ & © 1990 Dr. Seuss Enterprises, L.P. All rights reserved. Used by permission. **348** The Swedish Institute for Children's Books/Bonnier ©1990 Pija Lindenbaum **349** The Swedish Institute for Children's Books/Bonnier ©1991 Ulf Stark **350** "Book cover", copyright ©1991 by Crown Children, from Tar Beach by Faith Ringgold. Used by permission of Crown Publishers, an imprint of Random House Children's Books, a division of Random House, Inc. **351** Penguin ©1992 John Scieszka **352** HarperCollins India ©1993 Paro Anand **353** Verlagsgruppe Oetinger ©1997 Gloria Anzaldúa **355** Penguin Books (Australia) ©1994 Leigh Hobbs **356** HarperCollins Canada ©1995 Frieda Wishinsky **358** HarperCollins Publishers/Art ©1996 by Kevin Henkes **359** HarperCollins Publishers/Art ©1996 by Kevin Henkes **361** HarperCollins ©1997 Tohby Riddle **362** From Henry and Amy by Stephen Michael King. Text and illustrations © Stephen Michael King, 1998. First published by Scholastic Press, a division of Scholastic Australia Pty Ltd, 1998. Reproduced by permission of Scholastic Australia Pty Ltd. **363** From A Bad Case of Stripes by David Shannon. Scholastic Inc./The Blue Sky Press. ©1998 David Shannon. Reprinted by permission. **364** Faber and Faber ©1999 Carol Ann Duffy **365** The Swedish Institute for Children's Books/Rabén & Sjögren ©1999 Pernilla Stalfelt **366** Cover art from I Will Not Ever Never Eat a Tomato. Hachette ©2000 Lauren Child **367** Allen and Unwin ©2000 Margaret Wild **368** Houghton Mifflin ©2001 David Wiesner **369** Simon and Schuster ©2001 Petra Mathers **370** Random House ©2001 Raymond Briggs **371** The Swedish Institute for Children's Books/Rabén & Sjögren ©2001 Pernilla Stalfelt **372** Cover art from That Pesky Rat. Hachette ©2002 Lauren Child **373** Random House ©2003 Alexis Deacon **374** The Swedish Institute for Children's Books/Rabén & Sjögren ©2004 Pija Lindenbaum **376** Random House ©2003 Jeanne Willis **377** Penguin ©2003 Judith Byron Schachner **379** The Finnish Institute for Children's Literature/Bonnier ©2004 Riitta Jalonen **380** Candlewick Press ©2004 Sam McBratney **381** Penguin Books (Australia) ©2004 Alison Lester **382** Random House ©2005 Christopher Wormell **383** From Zen Shorts by Jon J Muth. Scholastic Inc./Scholastic Press. ©2005 Jon J Muth. Reprinted by permission **385** From LLAMA, LLAMA RED PAJAMA by Anna Dewdney, copyright © by 2005 Anna Dewdney. Used by permission of Viking Children's Books, A Division of Penguin Young Readers Group, A Member of Penguin Group (USA) Inc., 345 Hudson Street, New York, NY 10014. All rihgts reserved. **386** Pan Macmillan ©2005 Emily Gravett **387** Text ©2005 by Jen Wojtowicz/Illustrations ©2005 by Steve Adams/permission granted by Barefoot Books, Inc., 2067 Massachusetts Avenue, Cambridge, MA 02140 **388** Hachette ©2005 Mara Bergman **389** Egmont ©2005 Pete Harris **390–391** Houghton Mifflin ©2006 David Wiesner **392** Random House ©2006 Mini Grey **393** From The Dish and the Spoon, text and illustrations ©2006 Mini Grey. Reproduced by permission of Random House **394–395** Private Collection © Chris Beetles, London, UK/Bridgeman Art Library **397** Private Collection/Roger Perrin/Bridgeman Art Library **399** akg-images **400** Private Collection © Chris Beetles, London, UK/Bridgeman Art Library **402** akg-images/Ehrt **404** Courtesy Peter Harrington Antiquarian Bookseller **405** Art Archive **406** akg-images **407** akg-images **409** Lebrecht Photo Library **410** Private Collection/Bridgeman Art Library **412** Private collection **414** Mary Evans Picture Library **416** Private Collection/Archives Charmet/Bridgeman Art Library **417** The Art Archive **418** Private collection **419** Private collection **420** Courtesy Peter Harrington Antiquarian Bookseller **421** Courtesy Peter Harrington Antiquarian Bookseller **423** Private Collection/Archives Charmet/Bridgeman Art Library **424** Mary Evans Picture Library **425** Private Collection/Bridgeman Art Library **426** Courtesy Peter Harrington Antiquarian Bookseller and Random House **427** Courtesy Peter Harrington Antiquarian Bookseller and Random House **428** Courtesy of the Bodleian Library and Simon and Schuster **429** Courtesy of the Bodleian Library. Courtesy of Simon and Schuster **430** Courtesy of the Bodleian Library **431** Courtesy of the Bodleian Library **432** Courtesy Peter Harrington Antiquarian Bookseller **434** Courtesy of Dr. Corinne D'Angelo **435** Courtesy of the Bodleian Library and HarperCollins UK **436** Courtesy Peter Harrington Antiquarian Bookseller **437** Courtesy Peter Harrington Antiquarian Bookseller **438** Courtesy of Dr. Corinne D'Angelo **440** Courtesy of the Bodleian Library and HarperCollins UK **441** Courtesy of the Bodleian Library and Houghton Mifflin **443** Courtesy of the Bodleian Library and Penguin UK **444** Courtesy of Dr. Corinne D'Angelo **445** Courtesy of Dr. Corinne D'Angelo **447** Courtesy Peter Harrington Antiquarian Bookseller **448** Private collection **449** Bibliotheque Nationale, Paris, France/Lauros/Giraudon/Bridgeman Art Library **450** ©1907 Selma Lagerlöf **451** Courtesy Peter Harrington Antiquarian Bookseller. Methuen ©1908 Kenneth Grahame and Arthur Rackham **452** Courtesy Peter Harrington Antiquarian Bookseller. Penguin Canada ©1908 LM Montgomery **453** Courtesy Peter Harrington Antiquarian Bookseller. Penguin Canada ©1908 LM Montgomery **454** Editorial Casals ©1910 Josep Maria Folch i Camarasa **456** akg-images **459** Courtesy Peter Harrington Antiquarian Bookseller. ©1920 Hugh Lofting **460** Pan Macmillan ©1922 Richmal Crompton **462** Courtesy of the Bodleian Library. Hachette ©1925 Elinor M. Brent-Dyer **463** Penguin ©1927 Franklin W. Dixon **464** © Hergé/Moulinsart 2009 **465** akg-images **467** Courtesy Peter Harrington Antiquarian Bookseller. Random House ©1930 Arthur Ransome **468** Thanks to Jennifer Fisher, www.nancydrewsleuth.com **471** Courtesy of the Bodleian Library. HarperCollins Publishers/Illustrations ©1953, 1981 by Garth Williams **473** Bunpodo ©1934 Kenji Miyazawa **474** Courtesy of the Bodleian Library. Houghton Mifflin ©1934 PL Travers **476** Penguin ©1935 Kate Seredy **477** From THE GOOD MASTER by Kate Seredy, copyright 1935 by Kate Seredy, renewed © 1963 by Kate Seredy. Used by permission of Viking Penguin, A Division of Penguin Young Readers Group, A Member of Penguin Group (USA) Inc., 345 Hudson Street, New York, NY 10014. All rights reserved. **479** Harriet Jordan, http://www.whitegauntlet.com.au **480** Oxford University Press ©1936 Barbara Euphan Todd **483** Lebrecht Photo Library **484** Courtesy Peter Harrington Antiquarian Bookseller. HarperCollins Publishers Ltd ©1937 JRR Tolkien **487** Courtesy Peter Harrington Antiquarian Bookseller. HarperCollins Publishers Ltd ©1938 TH White **488** Courtesy Peter Harrington Antiquarian Bookseller. Faber and Faber ©1939 TS Eliot **491** "Book cover", copyright ©1941, 1969 by Random House, Inc., from The Black Stallion by Walter Farley, copyright © 1941, 1969 by Walter Farley. Used by permission of Random House Children's Books, a division of Random House, Inc. **493** Courtesy of Tony Summerfield of the Enid Blyton Society, http://www.enidblytonsociety.co.uk **494** Courtesy Peter Harrington Antiquarian Bookseller. Editions Gallimard, Collection Folio © Antoine de Saint-Exupéry, 1943 **496** Jane Nissen Books/© BB/DJ Watkins-Pitchford **497** Courtesy of the Bodleian Library. Jane Nissen Books/© BB/DJ Watkins-Pitchford **499** Courtesy Peter Harrington Antiquarian Bookseller. HarperCollins/Cover art renewed ©1973 by Garth Williams **501** Deborah Gaudin, www.elizabethgoudge.org/ **502** Courtesy of Henry Sotheran Ltd/©TH White, 1963 **503** © TH White, 1963 **504** Schildts Förlags Ab ©1946 Tove Jansson **506** Simon and Schuster ©1947 Marguerite Henry **508** Courtesy of the Bodleian Library. Hurray for St. Trinians © Ronald Searle, 1948. Reproduced with kind permission of the Artist and The Sayle Literary Agency **510** Sue Sims/Faber and Faber ©1948 Antonia Forest **512** The National Library of the Netherlands/Ploegsma ©1949 Anna Rutgers van der Loeff **514** Courtesy Peter Harrington Antiquarian Bookseller. Illustration by Pauline Bryant from The Lion, the Witch and the Wardrobe by CS Lewis ©CS Lewis Pte. Ltd. 1950 **515** Courtesy Peter Harrington Antiquarian Bookseller. Illustration by Pauline Bryant from The Lion, the Witch and the Wardrobe by CS Lewis © CS Lewis Pte. Ltd. 1950 **516** Editorial Iquiema ©1950 Maria Luisa Gefaell **519** ©1951 Gianna Rodari **520** Courtesy Peter Harrington Antiquarian Bookseller. Illustration by Pauline Bryant from The Voyage of the Dawn Treader by CS Lewis © CS Lewis Pte. Ltd. 1952 **521** Courtesy Peter Harrington Antiquarian Bookseller. Hachette ©1952 Mary Norton **523** HarperCollins Publishers Ltd ©1952 Anthony Buckeridge **524** Courtesy of the Bodleian Library. ©1953 Geoffrey Willans **525** Courtesy of the Bodleian Library. Down With Skool! © Ronald Searle, 1953. Reproduced with kind permission of the Artist and The Sayle Literary Agency **526** Lebrecht Photo Library **527** Houghton Mifflin ©1954 Edward Eager **528** Courtesy of the Bodleian Library. Diana Boston, owner of Green Knowe **530** Courtesy of Henry Sotheran Ltd. ©1955 KM Briggs **532** Bibliotheque Rouge et Or ©1955 Paul Berna **533** Courtesy of the Bodleian Library. HarperCollins ©1956 Fred Gipson **534** Courtesy Peter Harrington Antiquarian Bookseller. Egmont ©1956 Dodie Smith **535** ©1957 Gillian Avery **537** Oxford University Press ©1958 Philippa Pearce **538** Oxford University Press ©1958 Rosemary Sutcliff **540** Doncel ©1959 Miguel Buñuel **541** Doncel ©1959 Miguel Buñuel **542** Institut für Jugendliteratur, Vienna/Verlagsgruppe Oetinger ©1959 James Krüss **544** Oxford University Press ©1960 Rosemary Sutcliff **545** Institut für Jugendliteratur, Vienna/Michael Ende, Jim Knopf und Lukas der Lokomotivführer, mit Illustrationen von FJ Tripp ©1960 by Thienemann Verlag (Thienemann Verlag GmbH), Stuttgart - Wien **546** www.asterix.com ©2009 Les Éditions Albert René/Goscinny-Uderzo **548** Courtesy Peter Harrington Antiquarian Bookseller. Random House ©1961 Roald Dahl **550** "Book cover", copyright ©1961, 1989, from The Phantom Tollbooth by Norton Juster, illustrated by Jules Feiffer. Used by permission of Random House Children's Books, a division of Random House, Inc. **553** Used by permission of Farrar, Straus and Giroux, LLC. Jacket design by Hilda Van Stockum from THE WINGED WATCHMAN by Hilda Van Stockum. Jacketdesign copyright © 1962 by Hilda Van Stockum **555** Random House ©1962 Joan Aiken **556** Courtesy Peter Harrington Antiquarian Bookseller. Dobson Books ©1963 Spike Milligan **558** © Edward Ardizzone from Stig of the Dump, published by Penguin 1963/Permission granted by the Artist's Estate **559** Courtesy Peter Harrington Antiquarian Bookseller. Random House ©1963 JP Martin **560** Courtesy Peter Harrington Antiquarian Bookseller. Random House ©1964 Ian Fleming/Reproduced with permission of the Fleming estate **561** Random House ©1964 John Burningham **562** The Swedish Institute for Children's Books/Bonnier ©1964 Gunnel Linde **563** Courtesy of the Bodleian Library. HarperCollins ©1964 Louise Fitzhugh **565** Courtesy Peter Harrington Antiquarian Bookseller. Random House ©1964 Roald Dahl **567** Courtesy of the Bodleian Library. Bloomsbury ©1964 Christianna Brand **569** National Széchényi Library (Országos Széchényi Könyvtár) ©1965 István Fekete **570** HarperCollins ©1965 Beverley Cleary **573** Penguin ©1966 Roald Dahl **575** Courtesy of Henry Sotheran Ltd/Reprinted by arrangement with the author and Writers House LLC, acting as agent for the author **576** Simon and Schuster ©1967 EL Kongisburg **579** Courtesy of the Bodleian Library. Faber and Faber ©1968 Ted Hughes **581** Random House ©1969 Sylvia Sherry **582** Random House ©1968 Penelope Farmer **583** The National Library of the Netherlands/Uitgeverij Holland ©1970 Paul Biegel **584** Jacket cover from Are You There God? It's Me, Margaret by Judy Blume. Used by permission of Yearling, an imprint of Random House Children's Books, a division of Random House, Inc. **586** Illustrations published by arrangement with The Edward Gorey Charitable Trust **587** Illustrations published by arrangement with The Edward Gorey Charitable Trust **589** Institut für Jugendliteratur, Vienna/Beltz and Gelberg ©1970 Christine Nöstlinger **590** Courtesy Peter Harrington Antiquarian Bookseller. © Richard Adams, 1972 **592** HarperCollins Aus ©1972 Noonuccal Oodgeroo **595** Rabén & Sjögren ©1973 Astrid Lindgren **596** The National Library of the Netherlands/Lemniscaat ©1973 Thea Beckman **598** Institut für Jugendliteratur, Vienna/Verlagsgruppe Oetinger ©1975 Christine Nöstlinger **600** Faber and Faber ©1977 Helen Cresswell **601** HarperCollins ©1977 Katherine Paterson **602** Faber and Faber ©1977 Gene Kemp **605** ©1979 Maurice Gee **607** Penguin ©1980 Katherine Paterson **609** Penguin ©1980 Judy Blume **610** Hachette ©1980 Lynne Reid Banks

612 Courtesy of Henry Sotheran Ltd/© Michelle Magorian, 1981 **613** The Swedish Institute for Children's Books/Rabén & Sjögren ©1981 Astrid Lindgren **614** Random House ©1982 Roald Dahl **616** © Raymond Briggs, 1982 **618** © Shanghai People's Art Publisher **620** Courtesy of the Bodleian Library. Egmont ©1982 Michael Morpurgo **622** © Allan Ahlberg, 1983 **625** Egmont ©1985 Kevin Crossley-Holland **626** HarperCollins Publishers/Jacket art ©1985 by Marcia Sewall **628** Egmont ©1985 Michael Morpurgo **630** Oxford University Press ©1985 Pat O'Shea **631** Random House ©1986 Brian Jacques **632** Methuen ©1986 Jenny Nimmo **633** HarperCollins ©1986 Sid Fleischman **634** HarperCollins ©1987 Libby Gleeson **635** Penguin Books (Australia) ©1987 Paul Jennings **636** Penguin ©1987 John Steptoe **639** Penguin © Morris Gleitzman, 1989 **640** The Finnish Institute for Children's Literature. Bonnier ©1989 Sinikka and Tiina Nopola **641** University of Queensland Press ©1989 Brian Caswell **642** Methuen ©1989 Anne Fine **643** Courtesy Peter Harrington Antiquarian Bookseller. Hachette ©1989 Terry Pratchett **644** Courtesy Peter Harrington Antiquarian Bookseller. ©Salman Rushdie, 1990 **645** The Barahona Center, California State University San Marcos/ Ediciones S.M. ©1990 Montserrat del Amo **646** Hachette ©1990 Jerry Spinelli **648** Random House ©1991 Jacqueline Wilson **651** Random House ©1993 Lois Lowry **653** Random House ©1994 Jacqueline Wilson **655** Staatsbibliothek zu Berlin ©1994 Mirjam Pressler **657** Allen and Unwin ©1995 Elizabeth Honey **658** Allen and Unwin ©1995 Anna Fienberg **660** ©1996 EL Konigsburg. Reproduced by permission of Walker Books Ltd, London SE11 5HJ **662** Bloomsbury ©1997 JK Rowling **663** Bloomsbury ©1997 JK Rowling **664** ©1997 Henrietta Branford. Reproduced by permission of Walker Books Ltd, London SE11 5HJ **665** Courtesy of Michele Piumini/Einaudi Ragazzi ©1997 Roberto Piumini **667** Hachette ©1998 David Almond **668** Pan Macmillan ©1998 Andy Griffiths **669** Allen and Unwin ©1998 Meme and Boori Macdonald **670** Scholastic ©1998 Susan Price **671** HarperCollins Children's Books ©Peter Bollinger **673** HarperCollins ©1998 Lemony Snicket **674** Bloomsbury ©1999 JK Rowling **675** Egmont ©1999 Michael Morpurgo **676** HarperCollins ©1999 Jackie French **677** Allen and Unwin ©2000 Hirsh Odo **679** HarperCollins Publishers Ltd ©2000 Darren Shan **680** Candlewick Press ©2000 Kate DiCamillo **681** The Finnish Institute for Children's Literature/Bonnier ©2000 Tomi Kontio **682** ©2001 Anthony Horowitz. Boy with torch logo™ & Alex Rider™ © 2005 Stormbreaker Productions, Ltd. Reproduced by permission of Walker Books Ltd, London SE11 5HJ **684** The Finnish Institute for Children's Literature/Bonnier ©2001 Sinikka and Tiina Nopola **685** Scholastic ©2001 Philip Reeve **687** Pan Macmillan ©2001 Eva Ibbotson **688** Random House Mondadori 2002 **689** Cover art from Utterly Me Clarice Bean. Hachette ©2002 Lauren Child **691** Simon and Schuster ©2003 Holly Black **692** ABC Books, a division of HarperCollins Publishers, Australia ©2003 Glenda Millard **693** © Cecilie Dressler Verlag **695** Candlewick Press ©2003 Kate DiCamillo **696** Pan Macmillan ©2004 Frank Cotrell Boyce **697** Hachette ©2004 Michelle Paver **699** Carl Hanser Verlag GmbH & Co. ©2006 Jutta Richter **700** Random House ©2006 John Boyne **701** Lothian Children's Book, an imprint of Hachette Australia ©2006 Shaun Tan **702** From The Invention of Hugo Cabret by Brian Selznick. Scholastic Inc./Scholastic Press. ©2007 Brian Selznick. Reprinted by permission **703** From The Invention of Hugo Cabret by Brian Selznick. Scholastic Inc./Scholastic Press. ©2007 Brian Selznick. Reprinted by permission **704** Bloomsbury © Neil Gaiman/Chris Riddell 2008 **705** © Chris Riddell 2008 **706–707** Leemage/Lebrecht Photo Library **709** Courtesy of Henry Sotheran Ltd **710** Courtesy Peter Harrington Antiquarian Bookseller. **711** The Art Archive/Kharbine-Tapabor **712** akg-images **713** akg-images **714** Bibliotheque des Arts Decoratifs, Paris, France/Archives Charmet/Bridgeman Art Library **715** Leemage/Lebrecht Photo Library **717** Courtesy of the Bodleian Library. **719** Private Collection/© Look and Learn/Bridgeman Art Library **721** akg-images/Bibl. Amiens Métropole **722** Private Collection/ Archives Charmet/Bridgeman Art Library **723** Private Collection/Archives Charmet/Bridgeman Art Library **724** Private collection **725** Courtesy of the Bodleian Library. **726** akg-images **727** Courtesy of the Bodleian Library. **729** akg-images **730** Courtesy of the Bodleian Library **732** Mary Evans Picture Library **734** Penguin Books (Australia) ©1912 Ethel Turner **735** Private collection **736** akg-images **737** National Széchényi Library (Országos Széchényi Könyvtár) **738** Courtesy of Dr. Corinne D'Angelo **739** Courtesy Peter Harrington Antiquarian Bookseller **740** Courtesy of the Bodleian Library **741** Courtesy of Dr. Corinne D'Angelo **742** Courtesy of the Bodleian Library **743** Courtesy Peter Harrington Antiquarian Bookseller **744** Courtesy of the Bodleian Library. ©1906 Angela Brazil **747** Courtesy of the Bodleian Library. Random House ©1909 Gene Stratton-Porter **749** Die Bildagentur für Kunst, Kultur und Geschichte. Staatsbibliothek zu Berlin PK/Kinder- und Jugendbuchabteilung. Fotografin: Carola Seifert/© BPK, Berlin **750** Courtesy of the Bodleian Library **752** Courtesy of Cameron at Aquilla Books. ©1925 LM Montgomery **753** Courtesy of Cameron at Aquilla Books. ©1925 LM Montgomery **754** Courtesy of the Bodleian Library. Reproduced by permission of the Estate of CF Tunnicliffe OBE RA **756** ©1932 WE Johns **757** Die Bildagentur für Kunst, Kultur und Geschichte ©1933 Lisa Tetzner. Staatsbibliothek zu Berlin PK/Kinder- und Jugendbuchabteilung. Fotografin: Carola Seifert/© BPK, Berlin **759** © CS Forester, 1951 **760** Courtesy Peter Harrington Antiquarian Bookseller. Simon and Schuster ©1938 Marjorie Kinnan Rawlings **761** Courtesy Peter Harrington Antiquarian Bookseller. Simon and Schuster ©1938 Marjorie Kinnan Rawlings **762** Courtesy of the Bodleian Library. Wiley ©1940 Geoffrey Trease **764** Courtesy of the Bodleian Library. Random House ©1941 Mary Treadgold **767** Text © Cecil Day-Lewis, 1961/Illustrations © Edward Ardizzone from The Otterbury Incident, published by Putnam & Company 1948/Permission granted by the Artist's Estate **768** Courtesy Peter Harrington Antiquarian Bookseller. Hachette ©1949 Dodie Smith **771** Hachette ©1951 JD Salinger **772** Courtesy of the Bodleian Library. Methuen ©1951 Cynthia Harnett **775** courtesy of Tony Henderson Books **776** "Book cover", copyright ©1953, 1981, from Fahrenheit 451 by Ray Bradbury, copyright © 1953, 1981 by Ray Bradbury. Used by permission of Ballantine Books, a division of Random House, Inc. Courtesy Phantom Bookshop and John Anthony Miller, artist **778** Courtesy Peter Harrington Antiquarian Bookseller. HarperCollins Publishers Ltd ©1954 JRR Tolkien **779** Courtesy Peter Harrington Antiquarian Bookseller. Faber and Faber ©1954 William Golding **781** Courtesy of the Bodleian Library. Random House ©1955 Henry Treece **782** The Barahona Center, California State University San Marcos ©1956 Victor Mora **783** Altberliner Verlag ©1956 Edith Klatt **784** Courtesy of the Bodleian Library. By permission of C Walter Hodges' Estate **786** HarperCollins ©1957 Harold Keith **788** HarperCollins ©1958 Elyne Mitchell **789** www.booksfoundfast.co.uk ©1956 Catherine Storr **791** HarperCollins Publishers Ltd ©1959 John Verney **792** Courtesy of Brickbat Books. Gallimard Jeunesse, Collection Folio Junior, text © Raymond Queneau, 1959; illustration © Catherine Meurisse, 1959 **794** HarperCollins ©1960 Harper Lee **796** ©1961 Nan Chauncy **798** Used by permission of Farrar, Straus and Giroux, LLC. Jacket design by Ellen Raskin from A WRINKLE IN TIME by Madeleine L'Engle. Jacket design copyright © 1962 by Ellen Raskin **799** Used by permission of Farrar, Straus and Giroux, LLC. Title page from A WRINKLE IN TIME (1979 Edition) by Madeleine L'Engle. Copyright © 1979 by Farrar, Strauss and Giroux **800** The National Library of the Netherlands/Brief voor de Koning–Leopold Amsterdam **803** ©1964 HF Brinsmead **805** From GENTLE BEN by Walt Morey, illustrated by John Schoenherr, copyright © 1965 by Walt Morey. Used by permission of Dutton Children's Books, A Division of Penguin Young Readers Group, A Member of Penguin Group (USA) Inc., 345 Hudson Street, New York, NY 10014. All rights reserved. **806** ©1966 Mavis Thorpe Clark **809** Courtesy of the Bodleian Library. ©1967 Anthony Maitland **810** Pan Macmillan ©1967 Jill Paton Walsh **812** www.jamesmpickard.com/©Barry Hines, 1968 **813** © John Wyndham, 1970 **815** ©1969 Vera and Bill Cleaver **816** Oxford University Press ©1969 KM Peyton **818** ©1970 Gareth Floyd **819** ©1970 Vera and Bill Cleaver **821** The National Library of the Netherlands/Lemniscaat ©1972 Jan Terlouv **823** The Finnish Institute for Children's Literature/Schildts ©1972 Tove Jansson **824** Courtesy of the Bodleian Library. HarperCollins Publishers/illustrations ©1972 by John Schoenherr **826** Methuen ©1973 Max Fatchen **827** Institut für Jugendliteratur, Vienna/Beltz and Gelberg ©1973 Christine Nöstlinger **828** Random House ©1973 Patricia Wrightson **830** Random House ©1973 Susan Cooper **833** National Széchényi Library (Országos Széchényi Könyvtár)/Mora Konyvkiado ©1974 Éva Janikovsky **835** Used by permission of Farrar, Straus and Giroux, LLC. Jacket design by Natalie Babbitt from TUCK EVERLASTING. Jacket design copyright © 1975, renewed 2003 by Natalie Babbitt **836** Pan Macmillan ©1975 Robert Westall **838** ©1976 Eleanor Spence **840** Jacket cover from Roll of Thunder, Hear My Cry by Mildred Taylor. Used by permission of Bantam Books, a division of Random House Inc. **843** Courtesy of the Bodleian Library. From THE WESTING GAME by Ellen Raskin, copyright © 1978 by Ellen Raskin. Used by permission of Dutton Children's Books, A Division of Penguin Young Readers Group, A Member of Penguin Group (USA) Inc., 345 Hudson Street, New York, NY 10014. All rights reserved. **844** Used by permission of HarperCollins Publishers **845** "Book cover", copyright ©1979 by Random House, Inc., from After the First Death by Robert Cormier. Used by permission of Alfred A. Knopf, an imprint of Random House Children's Books, a division of Random House, Inc. **847** Michael Ende, Die unendliche Geschichte, mit Illustrationen von Roswitha Quadflieg ©1979 by Thienemann Verlag (Thienemann Verlag GmbH), Stuttgart - Wien **848** The Finnish Institute for Children's Literature/ WSOY ©1980 Anna-Liisa Haakana **849** Penguin Books (Australia) ©1980 Ruth Park **851** Random House ©1981 Robert Westall **852** Bonnier ©1981 Maria Gripe **853** Houghton Mifflin ©1981 Uri Orlev **854** Methuen ©1982 Sue Townsend **855** Methuen ©1982 Sue Townsend **856** Egmont ©1982 Anita Desai **858** © Jill Paton Walsh, 1983 **860** Oxford University Press ©1984 Robert Swindells **861** ©1984 Janni Howker. Reproduced by permission of Walker Books Ltd, London SE11 5HJ **862** Storylines, New Zealand/Hachette ©1984 Margaret Mahy **863** Oxford University Press ©1985 Philip Pullman **865** Penguin Books (Australia) ©1986 Victor Kelleher **867** © Anne Fine, 1987 **869** ©1987 Tessa Duder **870** Penguin US ©1988 Jane Yolen **872** Houghton Mifflin ©1989 Lois Lowry **873** ©1989 Libby Hathorn **874** Mammoth Australia, an imprint of Hachette Australia ©1990 Gary Crew **875** Canadian Children's Book Centre/Simon and Schuster ©1990 Michael Bedard **877** © Berlie Doherty, 1991 **879** Penguin Books (Australia) ©1992 Melina Marchetta **880** HarperCollins Canada ©1992 Karleen Bradford **881** ©1992 Catherine Jinks **882** © Anne Fine, 1992 **885** ©1993 by Tim Wynne-Jones. First published in Canada by Groundwood Books Ltd. Reprinted by permission of the publisher. **886** From Rowan of Rin by Emily Rodda. Text © Emily Rodda, 1993; cover © Jane Tanner, 1993. First published by Omnibus Books, a division of Scholastic Australia Pty Ltd, 1993. Reproduced by permission of Scholastic Australia Pty Ltd. **888** University of Queensland Press ©1993 James Moloney **889** © Robert Swindells, 1993 **890** Hyland House ©1994 Gillian Rubinstein **892** Methuen ©1994 Theresa Breslin **893** Penguin Books (Australia) ©1996 David McRobbie **895** Scholastic ©1995 Philip Pullman **896** The Swedish Institute for Children's Books/Rabén & Sjögren ©1996 Henning Mankell **897** Allen and Unwin ©1996 Wendy Orr **898** HarperCollins ©1996 Sophie Masson **900** Oxford University Press ©1997 Tim Bowler **901** Random House ©1997 Malorie Blackman **903** Longacre Press ©1998 Fleur Beale **905** Random House ©1999 Jacqueline Wilson **906** Verlagsgruppe Oetinger ©1999 Kirsten Boie **908** Courtesy of Henry Sotheran Ltd. Egmont ©2000 William Nicholson **909** Scholastic ©2000 Adéle Geras **910** Bloomsbury ©2000 Celia Rees **913** Bloomsbury ©2001 Benjamin Zephaniah **914** Random House ©2001 Malorie Blackman **916** Allen and Unwin ©2002 Martine Murray **919** Hyperion ©2003 Carole Wilkinson **921** Lothian Children's Book, an imprint of Hachette Australia ©2003 Paul Collins **922** Allen and Unwin ©2003 Garth Nix **923** Random House ©2003 Mark Haddon **924** HarperCollins Publishers Ltd ©2003 Michael Morpurgo **925** ©2003 Mal Peet. Reproduced by permission of Walker Books Ltd, London SE11 5HJ **927** Allen and Unwin ©2004 Steven Herrick **929** The Barahona Center, California State University San Marcos/Ediciones SM ©2004 Laura Gallego **931** Montena ©2005 Rafael Ábalos **933** Allen and Unwin ©2006 Ursula Dubosarsky **934** Gallimard Jeunesse, Hors-Série Littérature, text © Timothée de Fombelle, 2006; illustration © François Place, 2006 **935** From Monster Blood Tattoo: No. 1 by DM Cornish. Text © DM Cornish, 2006; Cover and text © DM Cornish, 2006; Maps © DM Cornish, 2006. First published by Omnibus Press, a division of Scholastic Australia Pty Ltd, 2006. Reproduced by permission of Scholastic Australia Pty Ltd. **937** HarperCollins ©2007 Jenny Valentine.

Quintessence would like to thank the following individuals and organizations for their assistance in the creation of this book:

Dr. Belle Alderman, University of Canberra, Lu Rees Archive • Brian Aldersen, Bodleian Library • James Allen, Bodleian Library • Rex Anderson • Mathew Andrews, Bodleian Library • Aquilla Books • Helena Baser • Ghislaine Bavoillot, Flammarion Andrew Berkhut, Scholastic Australia • Maxime Boucknooghe • Corinne D'Angelo, www.emiliosalgari.it • Dr. Samuel Fanous, Bodleian Library • Jennifer Fisher, www.nancydrewsleuth.com • Sue Grabham • Pom Harrington, Peter Harrington Antiquarian Booksellers • Lucinda Hawksley • Heather Haynes • Clive Hurst, Bodleian Library • Joe Jameson, Peter Harrington Antiquarian Booksellers • Aubrey Lawrence, Rosetta Translations • Josie Lister, Bodleian Library • Irene Lyford • Camille Mandron Ann Marangos • Hélène Millot, L'Ecole des Loisirs • Hannah O'Connell, British Library Agnès Rigou • Christelle Roucheray, L'Ecole des Loisirs • Jacqueline Sanson, Bibliotheque National de France • Ruth Segarra, Peter Harrington Antiquarian Booksellers • Rosie Shannon, Save the Children • Southerans Antique Books, www.southerans.co.uk • Erik Titusson, Astrid Lindgren Memorial Fund • Hélène Wadowski, Père Castor • www.jamespicard.com • Christine Young, Storylines Children's Literature Trust (NZ)